College & University Curriculum

Placing Learning at the Epicenter of Courses, Programs and Institutions

Second Edition

Lenoar Foster, Series Editor

Edited by

Clifton F. Conrad
Jason Johnson

PEARSON

Custom
Publishing

Printed in the United States of America

2 3 4 5 6 7 8 9 10 V0CR 16 15 14 13 12

ISBN 0-536-09023-8

2007220209

SB/MR

Please visit our web site at *www.pearsoncustom.com*

PEARSON CUSTOM PUBLISHING
501 Boylston Street, Suite 900, Boston, MA 02116
A Pearson Education Company

CONTENTS

College and University Curriculum: Placing Learning at the Epicenter of Courses, Programs, and Institutions

Editors' Introduction

Following a trend that doubtless will continue throughout the foreseeable future, major higher education stakeholders are holding American colleges and universities increasingly accountable for student learning at the undergraduate level. From governmental bodies to private funding agencies to scholarly critics and other commentators to students and their families, the voices calling for answers are as diverse as are their demands. Nested in this context of accountability, colleges and universities have engaged in curriculum enhancement and transformation initiatives of every sort, and scores of scholars have dutifully documented and analyzed the aims and structures of undergraduate education. Animated by an abundance of ideas for refiguring undergraduate curricula, the purpose of this volume is to advance a representative and provocative set of readings which invite you, the reader, to engage in ongoing and vibrant discussions about college and university curricula. These dialogues are important because, while we would be hard-pressed to find a person who disagrees with the proposition that learning ought to be placed at the epicenter of courses, programs, and institutions, precisely how that can and should be done are unresolved and are often highly contentious matters.

More specifically, our intention with this book is to promote critical reflection and dialogue about the major challenges and opportunities in conceptualizing, designing, implementing, and assessing curriculum, teaching, and learning. Toward this end, we envision three overlapping audiences: (1) students and faculty studying undergraduate curriculum in higher education graduate programs and related fields; (2) individuals at colleges and universities who are responsible for planning, designing, and improving general education, concentrations, and other undergraduate programs; and (3) college and university faculty, as well as those responsible for instructional training and support of current and future faculty, who are working on the curricula of their courses. Given our broad focus on undergraduate education, we anticipate that these readings will be helpful for individuals whose institutional affiliations and interests reside within or across two-year colleges, four-year colleges and universities, and public and private institutions.

Consonant with the intended aims and audiences for the volume, we worked closely with an advisory board of prominent scholars and practitioners to assemble a set of readings that span a number of continua: readings that represent a wide range of theoretical and philosophical approaches and perspectives, from rationalist and constructivist to postmodern; readings that are drawn from primary documents as well as miscellaneous sources that address a wide range of theoretical and applied concerns, both within and across disciplines and fields of study; and readings that challenge readers to reflect on the intersections between theory and practice. In so doing, we trust that the readings can help cultivate a broader and deeper understanding of curriculum in higher education as we are challenged us to move beyond surface-level conceptualizations of curriculum as only content and structure to other major considerations such as historical, social, and political contexts of curriculum, pedagogy and the "black-box" of teaching and learning, and formative and summative assessment as curricular lenses.

We have organized the readings selected for this volume into six sections, each of which brings into focus critical domains of scholarship and practice vis-à-vis college and university curricula:

    I. Points of Departure
    II. Curricular Conversations
    III. Curricular Design
    IV. Curricular Change
    V. Teaching, Learning, and the Curriculum
    VI. Evaluation, Assessment, and the Curriculum

Comprised of philosophical and normative statements regarding the aims of higher education as well as historical accounts and contemporary appraisals of the curriculum, the first section invites you to consider the foundations of curriculum purposes and structures as a foundation for further reading. The second section provides a glimpse at the rigorous and creative discourse regarding college and university curriculum by presenting a series of ongoing debates and related analyses. The volume then takes a pragmatic turn in the third section by focusing on a range of models and approaches for planning and building programs and courses. Closely related in the fourth section, our attention is drawn to two of the most formidable challenges in enacting new curricular designs—namely, identifying and overcoming barriers to change and reflecting on the implications of change, not least of which is its unintended consequences. In the fifth section, the importance of mutually reinforcing teaching and learning is emphasized, a critical yet often overlooked corollary to thoughtful and meaningful curricular design and change. Finally, the diverse perspectives on the foundations and practices of meaningful evaluation and assessment of curriculum in the sixth section prompt us to question how we know what we know—and how we might know better—about the educational experiences of students in courses, programs, and institutions writ large.

For each section, we have composed an introductory essay in an effort to share some thoughts we've developed in the construction of this volume. In each essay, we offer a narrative description of the section's readings to provide a brief summary of each piece as well as a sense of the connections among the readings.

PART I

POINTS OF DEPARTURE

Part I: Points of Departure

From philosophical arguments regarding the purposes of higher education to historical analyses of curriculum to critical interpretations of trends and issues which color the contemporary landscape of the higher learning, each reading in this section invites you to think about college and university curriculum in the broadest of strokes. In so doing, these readings provide "points of departure" for further inquiry and reflection when reading through subsequent sections of this volume. Indeed, the curricular ideas and structures advanced here—through provocation and persuasion—encourage you to raise questions rather than search for steadfast answers.

Since the days of the colonial colleges, scholars and critics alike have customarily celebrated—and confounded—connections between American higher education and democracy. Among the most highly regarded contributors to contemporary thinking on the subject is Amy Gutmann, the author of this volume's first reading. In "The Purposes of Higher Education," an article from her widely read book entitled *Democratic Education*, she outlines characteristics of a higher education system that contribute to and militate against a thriving democracy. She begins by locating colleges and universities within a systematic educative continuum and arguing that higher education serves democracy well only if pre-collegiate education instills "basic democratic virtues, such as toleration, truth-telling, and a predisposition to nonviolence." Such an education characterizes a compulsory "democratic threshold" and, as such, it ought to be the product of compulsory education—namely, primary and secondary schooling. According to Gutmann, postsecondary schooling ought to be concerned with building on and extending democratic values by helping students learn "how to think carefully and critically about political problems, to articulate one's views and defend them before people with whom one disagrees." Stopping short of making a full indictment, she implies that higher education institutions are too often compelled to make up for high schools' deficiencies with respect to democratic education. Assuming that the full force of pre-collegiate education is cultivated and maintained—matters she details in other article of her book—she provides an account of why and how higher education serves democracy by preserving academic freedom, educating officeholders, and fostering associational freedom. In short, she contends that colleges and universities play roles vital to a democracy by ensuring freedom of thought without repression or discrimination—for faculty who build lives within the academy and for students who pass through it en route to public and private life roles. She addresses college and university curricula in light of this systematic, moral context: "Universities serve democracies best when they try to establish an environment conducive to creating knowledge that is not immediately useful, appreciating ideas that are not presently popular, and rewarding people who are—and are likely to continue to be—intellectually but not necessarily economically productive." In so doing, she argues, higher learning institutions' function as educators of officeholders ought to supersede their role as "gatekeepers" to vocational posts.

In "Citizens of the World," an article from *Cultivating Humanity*, Martha Nussbaum builds on and extends Gutmann's concerns regarding higher education's contributions to democracy. According to Nussbaum, "the future of democracy in this nation and in the world is bleak" if colleges and universities do not tend to ensuring that their graduates become "world citizens," a concept she develops for the contemporary landscape of higher education in light of perspectives derived from ancient Greek and Roman philosophers. "The task of world citizenship requires the would-be world citizen to become a sensitive and empathic interpreter. . . . What this means in higher education is that an attitude of mutual respect should be nourished both in the classroom itself and in its reading material." Lest it be assumed that such means and ends are already centerpieces of undergraduate curricula—one would no doubt be hard-pressed to find an institution that would not assert that it works toward these objectives—she observes that many popular curricular reforms of recent years run counter to educating

3

for world citizenship. Specifically, she critiques curricula that aim to affirm local cultural or racial identities, arguing that such efforts are "divisive and subversive of the aims of world community" because they tend to "neglect commonalities and portray people as above all members of identity groups." From our perspective, Nussbaum's incisive analysis of this matter is destabilizing and, in our estimation, as relevant today as it was when she introduced it nearly a decade ago.

Derek Bok's work, "Purposes," an article from his book entitled *Our Underachieving Colleges*, explores avenues opened by Gutmann and Nussbaum, including how higher education stands in relation to democracy and globalization. He argues against prescribing "a single overriding aim or to limit the purposes of college to the realm of intellectual development" in favor of advocating for a medley of aims that institutions of higher learning ought to pursue through their undergraduate curricula. Specifically, he puts forward eight aims: the ability to communicate, critical thinking, moral reasoning, preparing citizens, living with diversity, living in a more global society, a breadth of interests, and preparing for work. In the aggregate, he argues that all of these aims fit within an overarching "mandate"—namely, that "colleges should pursue a variety of purposes, including a carefully circumscribed effort to foster generally accepted values and behaviors, such as honesty and racial tolerance." The position he formulates in his article is clearly a reaction to both higher education outsiders and insiders, such as Stanley Fish, who believe that colleges and universities shouldn't be in the business of anything but teaching students knowledge and skills of the intellectual variety. Further, he maintains that "it is perfectly possible to teach moral reasoning or prepare students to be enlightened citizens without having instructors impose their personal ideologies or policy views on their students."

The next reading is a section excerpted from the "College Learning for the New Century" report issued by the National Leadership Council for Liberal Education and America's Promise (LEAP), one of a host of curriculum-related initiatives led by the Association of American Colleges and Universities (AAC&U). The report's authors openly advance the following contentious observation in the report's introduction (not included here): "Stunningly, however, American society has yet to confront the most basic and far-reaching question of all. Across all the work on access, readiness, costs, and even accountability, there has been a near-total public silence about what contemporary college graduates need to know and be able to do." The veracity of the "near-total public silence" claim notwithstanding—to wit, public discourse about access, readiness, costs, and accountability surely includes presuppositions about what graduates need to know and be able to do—the report's assertions regarding the purposes of undergraduate education are concise and nested firmly in political and ethical contexts. In the selection included here—"Part 2: From the American Century to the Global Century"—the report explains how the learning outcomes pursued by colleges and universities—specifically, those outcomes that are at the crux of a liberal education—must shift as the American higher education landscape morphs from a national scene to a global scene.

Whereas the readings by Gutmann, Nussbaum, Bok, and the AAC&U may be considered to be prescriptive with respect to the purposes of undergraduate curricula, the three readings that follow shift to more descriptive in form—that is, they address "what?" questions more than "ought?" questions. In "Mutual Subversion: A Short History of the Liberal and the Professional in American Higher Education," a version of his History of Education Society presidential address published in *History of Education Quarterly*, David Labaree offers contrasting definitions of "liberal" and "professional" education and analyzes two historical arguments: that professional education has gradually overtaken liberal education, and vice versa. He conjoins these two ostensibly mutually exclusive perspectives by arguing that "the professional has come to dominate the goals of higher education while the liberal has come to dominate its content." He ultimately concludes that this is far from an elegant fusion of evolving interests, noting sharply that the liberal and the professional have become a "fugue" that is "educationally dysfunctional."

In the article "From the Liberal to the Practical Arts in American Colleges and Universities: Organizational Analysis and Curricular Change," Steven Brint and associates identify a unit of analysis that adds a wrinkle to Labaree's "goals" and "content" distinction by bringing into focus numbers of degrees awarded in programs of study. Reporting on a quantitative study they conducted to understand the implications of the fact that the proportion of degrees awarded in "occupational-professional" fields has increasingly outpaced the proportion of degrees awarded in "the old arts and sciences core," Brint et al. argue that we may well be experiencing a proverbial swinging of a pendulum but the changes we are experiencing are not without consequence. Specifically, they offer evidence that the increase in occupational-professional degrees has occurred primarily at non-elite institutions, while arts and sciences degrees have become more concentrated at elite institutions, thus creating a "status divide" in educational pipelines. Their concluding discussion of the future prospects of the arts and sciences illuminates the importance of paying attention to tectonic shifts in degree attainment in disaggregative terms—as they imply, curriculum does not simply evolve unaffected by educators' choices.

W. Norton Grubb and Marvin Lazerson also examine professional and liberal influences in curriculum change in their article, "Vocationalism in Higher Education: The Triumph of the Education Gospel." Invoking the religious metaphor "gospel" in describing the language commonly used to communicate the ways in which education must respond to the emergence of the "knowledge revolution" and other such sweeping changes in the world of work, Grubb and Lazerson argue that colleges and universities have already undergone a "conversion" and those who would prefer to "wish away" occupational/vocational/professional education ought to "focus on ways to integrate vocational purposes with broader civic, intellectual, and moral goals." After providing an account of how higher education has moved away from these latter goals, they urge their readers to avoid engaging in "stale debates" by thinking about how to "integrate non-vocational ideals with vocational realities." They suggest that doing so would involve a serious rethinking of all aspects of higher education, including but not limited to finding ways to appreciate the value of occupational training, addressing the static segmentation of colleges and universities, and reflecting on what our ideas of what "college" is.

In "History, Rationale, and the Community College Baccalaureate Association," Kenneth Walker summarizes a recent development—bachelor's degrees being offered at community colleges—that reflects a significant rethinking about how we categorize higher education institutions and degrees. Walker briefly sketches the origins of the community college (i.e., the early 20th century "junior college"), how they came to offer four-year degrees, and the formation of the Community College Baccalaureate Association (CCBA), an "international organization dedicated to advocacy for access to the baccalaureate." He cannily credits the "three Cs—competition, cooperation, and collaboration" as influential forces behind the community college baccalaureate movement, noting how the American system of higher education is strengthened by this blurring of boundaries (e.g., increased access, cost efficiencies, economic and workforce development), addressing critics of the CCBA and its related efforts (e.g., the community college baccalaureate expands—not abandons—the community college mission), and identifying future directions based on maintaining community colleges' historical strengths (e.g., lower tuition prices, learner-centeredness). In Walker's words: "The time has come to stop defining the community college as a two-year institution."

Like Walker, David Ayers communicates unapologetic scholarly advocacy for community colleges in "Neoliberal Ideology in Community College Mission Statements: A Critical Discourse Analysis." Reporting on a study in which he analyzed 144 mission statements in light of neoliberal ideology and human capital theory, he argues that the democratic purposes of community colleges have been supplanted by "the interests of those in the upper social strata." Specifically, he advances two key interpretations of how ideology is revealed in mission statements. One, he demonstrates how language in mission statements reduces students to human capital or "economic entities"—that is, the ways in which learning benefits anything but the economy are either distant background material or are altogether absent. Two, he reveals how business and industry are given primacy in the language of mission statements as references to curricula are commonly circumscribed by claims of the contributions they make to specific labor markets or the workforce writ large. These are troubling developments, according to Ayers, not least because "the community college mission is much more extensive than that represented in neoliberal discourse." He closes by entertaining the degree to which neoliberal ideology in community college mission statements is pervasive and what room there is for crafting alternative "discursive formations" through the re-writing of mission statements and otherwise.

There has arguably been no contributor to counter-hegemonic discourse in higher education more influential than Henry Giroux, who co-authors with Susan Giroux, "Race, Rhetoric, and the Contest over Civic Education." By examining the contours of a complex web spun by the threads of capitalism, immigration, scientific discourse, and racial segregation from the 18th to the 20th centuries, Giroux and Giroux chronicle how curricula grounded in classical rhetoric have given way to curricula centered on literary interests. In turn, they detail how higher education's commitment to producing "good citizens" has endured while undergoing a shift from conceptualizing citizenship as "participatory and public" to "nationalistic and privatized." Maintaining that "citizenship and civic education are highly and historically contested terms" and that "there is nothing self-evident about [the] concept of an appropriate college curriculum for producing good citizens," they invite others to embrace their political agency (not their passive consumerism, as often cultivated by contemporary curricula) and engage in ameliorative acts that subvert the "racist invention" of transmitting and preserving national *qua* cultural traditions through literary studies.

A reading by Timothy Caboni and Mitiku Adisu, "*A Nation at Risk* After 20 Years: Continuing Implications for Higher Education," closes this section in a manner similar to its opening by Gutmann—namely, by situating higher education in a K-16 continuum. In contrast to Gutmann's philosophical analysis, Caboni and Adisu offer a policy analysis—specifically, an assessment of the current state of affairs of postsecondary education in light of the two decades that have transpired since the publication of *A Nation at Risk: The Imperative for Educational Reform (NAR)*, one of the most influential education reports ever issued by the federal government. Following a summary of the initial recommendations put forth in *NAR*, they discuss matters from the report that remain relevant for higher education (e.g., K-16 curricular alignment, remedial education, teacher preparation, accountability) and identify future directions that researchers, practitioners, and policymakers may pursue (e.g., K-16 enrollment and information systems partnerships, revising admission standards for colleges and universities).

The readings in this section may be used as points of departure in many ways. Most obvious, each selection contains references to other readings that may be read to expand breadth or depth of knowledge and perspective. Further, the readings can be used to interpret and critique one another as the questions that follow illustrate. The AAC&U report expresses links between higher education and democracy and higher education and globalization—for example, how might Gutmann or Nussbaum evaluate efforts toward these ends? What points of convergence and divergence are there between being a democratic citizen (Gutmann) and a world citizen (Nussbaum)? Inasmuch as Bok critiques the concept of there being "one dominant purpose for undergraduate education," would he thus criticize Gutmann or Nussbaum for being too narrow in their prescriptions for the future of higher education? Binaries abound in college and university curriculum scholarship (e.g., professional and liberal, vocational and traditional), where do these come from, how are they (not) helpful, and whom do they (not) benefit? Is the community college baccalaureate a movement to celebrate or does it only exacerbate the concern expressed by Brint et al. regarding the stratification of degrees along socio-economic lines? Such questions give rise to more practical and personal considerations, too. The readings by Walker, Ayers, Giroux and Giroux, and Caboni and Adisu each, in their own way, compel us to think about what room for influence there is in curriculum development and change—and to what extent we are simply subject to forces beyond our individual or collective control.

THE PURPOSES
OF HIGHER EDUCATION

A. GUTMANN

Higher education cannot succeed unless lower education does. If high schools are not educating most students up to the democratic threshold, then many colleges and universities will continue the primary education of their students. Many American colleges have already assumed this role: most community colleges offer high-school graduates a second chance at achieving basic literacy, often for the explicit sake of helping them get a job. The fact that most American colleges compete for students rather than vice versa reinforces this market perspective on higher education. The perspective is both pedagogically and morally uncomfortable. Most professors are neither trained nor motivated to teach either basic literacy or job skills. Many students who could benefit from an extended high-school education are effectively excluded from receiving one, because even community colleges are costly, if only by virtue of the income that students from poor families must forego to attend them.

If college education is to be part of primary education, it should be made free and compulsory. One might argue that the time has come in the United States for an extension of compulsory schooling, since every increase in compulsory schooling so far has been a step towards equalizing democratic citizenship by excluding fewer children from a more adequate primary education. Twelve years of schooling may not be enough time to cultivate the character and teach the basic skills of democratic citizenship.[1] Then why not require a college education in the name of nonexclusion?

There are at least two reasons to look for a better alternative. First, colleges are unlikely to succeed for students after high school has failed them. Most poorly educated students needed better, not more, schooling. Second, even if college could succeed in adequately educating all students, its success would come at a very high price, and not just in dollars. "For some children, beyond a certain age, school is a kind of prison (but they have done nothing to deserve imprisonment). . . ."[2] Making college part of primary education would extend the prison sentence of many young people after they have ceased to be children. Were a college education necessary for the sake of citizenship, the extended sentence could be justified. But until we do more—much more—to improve the first twelve years of schooling, we cannot conclude that a college education is necessary.

A far better option than to extend compulsory schooling into college is to improve earlier education and, if necessary, to begin compulsory schooling at an earlier age (when it also can serve as childcare for working parents). The alternative of making college compulsory is morally worse and politically no more feasible—it would be a victory not for citizenship but for schooling, and a further imposition on adolescents of an unnecessary tendency to make a college degree necessary for living a good life in our society.

Schooling does not stop serving democracy, however, when it ceases to be compulsory—or when all educable citizens reach the democratic threshold. Its purposes change. Higher education should not be necessary for inculcating basic democratic virtues, such as toleration, truth-telling, and a predisposition to nonviolence. I doubt whether it can be. If adolescents have not developed these character

Reprinted from *Democratic Education*, by Amy Gutmann (1999), Princeton University Press.

traits by the time they reach college, it is probably too late for professors to inculcate them by "preaching, witnessing, [and] setting a good example" for their students. If, as Mark Lilla argues, "this is the only way students can understand, in a complex way, what their roles will be in a democracy and what virtue is in those roles," then that understanding had better precede their college education.[3]

There is, I have already argued, another, equally complex and intellectually more challenging way in which students can be taught to understand the moral demands of democratic life. While not a substitute for character training, learning how to think carefully and critically about political problems, to articulate one's views and defend them before people with whom one disagrees is a form of moral education to which young adults are more receptive and for which universities are well suited. Many of the same arguments for teaching primary-school students to deliberate hold for college students, for whom engaging in a "bit of 'indoctrination' in the virtues of democracy" is less likely to be effective.[4] Not only is this reason for democratic control (the inculcation of common values) missing, but there are other reasons—rooted in the democratic purposes of universities—that support a case for the relative autonomy of universities from democratic control.[5]

The relative autonomy of a university is rooted in its primary democratic purpose: protection against the threat of democratic tyranny. The threat of democratic tyranny was most eloquently characterized by Tocqueville:

> [I]n democratic republics . . . tyranny . . . leaves the body alone and goes straight for the soul. The master no longer says: "Think like me or you die." He does say: "You are free not to think as I do; you can keep your life and property and all; but from this day you are a stranger among us. . . . You will remain among men, but you will lose your rights to count as one. When you approach your fellows, they will shun you as an impure being, and even those who believe in your innocence will abandon you too, lest they in turn be shunned. Go in peace. I have given you your life, but it is a life worse than death.[6]

Control of the creation of ideas—whether by a majority or a minority—subverts the ideal of *conscious* social reproduction at the heart of democratic education and democratic politics. As institutional sanctuaries for free scholarly inquiry, universities can help prevent such subversion. They can provide a realm where new and unorthodox ideas are judged on their intellectual merits; where the men and women who defend such ideas, provided they defend them well, are not strangers but valuable members, of a community. Universities thereby serve democracy as sanctuaries of nonrepression. In addition to creating and funding universities, democratic governments can further this primary purpose of higher education in two ways: by respecting what is commonly called the "academic freedom" of scholars, and by respecting what might be called the "freedom of the academy."

Academic Freedom and Freedom of the Academy

What is academic freedom, and what does it demand of democracies? As derived from the German concept of *Lehrfreiheit*, academic freedom is neither a universal right of citizenship nor a contractual right of university employees. It is perhaps best understood as a special right tied to the particular office of scholar, similar in form (but different in content) to the particular rights of priests, doctors, lawyers, and journalists. The core of academic freedom is the freedom of scholars to assess existing theories, established institutions, and widely held beliefs according to the canons of truth adopted by their academic disciplines, without fear of sanction by anyone if they arrive at unpopular conclusions. Academic freedom allows scholars to follow their autonomous judgment wherever it leads them, provided that they remain within the bounds of scholarly standards of inquiry.

The proviso of remaining within the bounds of scholarly standards is sometimes overlooked,[7] but it is necessary to justify the social office that scholars occupy, and to distinguish academic freedom from the more general freedoms of citizens to think, speak, and publish their ideas. If academic freedom knew no scholarly bounds, the freedom of scholars would be indistinguishable from these more general freedoms. These general freedoms also apply to scholars in their role as citizens, but academic freedom is more demanding—of scholars and therefore of their society. Scholars must recognize a duty to observe scholarly standards of inquiry as a condition of their social office.[8] (I return to examine the contextual conditions of this duty below.) Democratic citizens must observe an obligation not to restrict the intellectual freedoms of individual scholars or those freedoms of liberal universities that secure an institutional environment conducive to the exercise of scholarly autonomy.

Control of the educational environment within which scholarship and teaching take place is the form of academic freedom most often neglected by its democratic defenders. The historical reason for this neglect is not difficult to discern. Whereas German universities were generally self-governing bodies of scholars who made administrative decisions either collegially or through democratically elected administrators, American universities (with few exceptions) are administered by lay governing boards and administrators chosen by those boards.[9] Therefore, while the scholar's right of academic freedom in the German context could readily be extended to a right collectively to control the academic environment of the university, the academic freedom of faculty in the American context had to be used as a defense *against* the university's legally constituted (lay) administrative authority. Recurrent threats by universities' trustees and administrators to the academic freedom of faculty members made it easy for faculty to overlook their stake in defending their universities against state regulation of educational policies.[10]

Despite this historical neglect, the stake of scholars and citizens in the autonomy of the academy is great—not only because public officials have directly threatened the academic freedom of individual scholars, but also because governmental regulations can indirectly threaten academic freedom by making universities unconducive to good scholarship and teaching. When HUAC and state legislative committees pressured universities in the 1950s to dismiss faculty members for their alleged Communist loyalties or for their failure to testify concerning their political beliefs, universities could legitimately assert their autonomy as a means of protecting the academic freedom of their faculty.[11]

Even when the academic freedom of individual faculty members is not directly at stake, the academic freedom of universities may be. Constraints upon a university's hiring and admissions standards are likely to affect the future academic standards within disciplines and the environment within which scholarship and teaching take place. Administrative time and money spent complying with state regulations may be time and money not spent on improving academic departments or responding to the concerns of faculty and students. Like other large institutions, universities have responsibilities that extend beyond their specific social function. They therefore cannot claim a "right" to be free from all external regulations that make it more costly or administratively difficult to pursue their academic goals. But they may claim a right to be free from those regulations that threaten the very pursuit of those goals. When governmental regulations threaten to destroy the environment for scholarship and teaching, either by substantially lowering the intellectual quality of faculty and students or by draining essential resources from academic to nonacademic areas, universities dedicated to free scholarly inquiry can legitimately assert an institutional right to academic freedom, consistent with (indeed, derived from) the right of their faculty to academic freedom.

Taken together, the academic freedoms of scholars and of liberal universities serve as safeguards against political repression, not just for scholars but also for citizens. They help prevent a subtle but invidious form of majority tyranny without substituting a less subtle and worse form of tyranny—that of the minority—in its place. Democracies can foster the general freedom of conscious social reproduction within politics by fostering the particular freedom of defending unpopular ideas within universities, regardless of the political popularity of those conceptions (but not regardless of their scholarly merits).

Scholars and universities that claim academic freedom against interference with their intellectual and institutional pursuits also must acknowledge duties that accompany the right. What duties does devotion to free scholarly inquiry entail for the individual scholar? Consider Abraham Flexner's description of the career of Louis Pasteur:

> When the prosperity and well-being of France were threatened by silk-worm disease, by difficulties in the making of wines, in the brewing of beer, by chicken cholera, hydrophobia, etc., Pasteur permitted himself to be diverted from his work in order to solve these problems, one after another; having done so, he published his results and returned to his laboratory. His approach was intellectual, no matter whether the subject was poultry, brewing, or chemistry. He did not become consultant to silk-worm growers, wine makers, brewers, or poultry men. . . . The problem solved, his interest and activity ceased. He had indeed served, but he had served like a scientist, and there his service ended.[12]

Flexner does not say precisely what serving "like a scientist"—or, more generally, like a scholar—entails, but his description of Pasteur provides some clues. Although Pasteur pursued knowledge for the sake of serving society, he was sufficiently independent to decide when to leave pressing social problems behind to work on problems that would take longer to solve. Pasteur directed some of his work towards helping particular groups in society, but he did not serve only those groups that could afford to pay for his services. Pasteur did not isolate himself in an "ivory tower," to avoid all influences of the "real world," but he did shield himself from improper influences, those that would impede the exercise of his scholarly judgment.

The duty of a scholar, one might say, is to avoid those influences that are likely to impede—or to give the appearance of impeding—scholarly judgment.[13] What influences constitute impediments to free scholarly judgment? Financial influences are the most obvious, but not all financial influences are improper. It clearly would have been wrong for Pasteur to accept money from the wine-makers had they restricted the methods or results of his research in exchange for payment—in an attempt to use his intellectual authority to persuade the public, say, that wine was good for their health (not that the French needed to be convinced). Such a contract would be tantamount to bribery ("we'll pay you not to exercise your best intellectual judgment") and would clearly violate scholarly autonomy in a way that drawing salary directly from a university does not. Most consulting contracts today are not restricted in this invidious fashion. The more common and complex problem lies not in the influence that a particular consulting contract has on the integrity of one scholar's work but in the way in which the widespread acceptance of consulting contracts can skew the types of problems that scholars pursue—drawing them away from investigating more serious social problems that have fewer immediate pay-offs or away from equally serious problems that afflict people who cannot afford to hire consultants. Not all types of research contracts interfere with the collective autonomy of scholarship, but many do. The more freedom that contracts give scholars to define their own research problems, the less they interfere with the collective autonomy of scholarship, which provides an intellectual sanctuary against political control of the creation of ideas. The less freedom contracts give scholars, the more suspect they are on these grounds and the greater the need for scholars collectively to limit their right to accept such contracts.

Just as the academic freedom of scholars carries with it an individual duty to resist improper influences, so the freedom of the academy carries with it an institutional duty not to exert improper influences on scholars, for example, by making promotions depend on popularity rather than on the intellectual merits of research and teaching, by failing to defend faculty against political attacks by alumni or trustees, or simply by burdening scholars with too many nonacademic duties. By virtue of their democratic purpose, universities have not only a right to relative autonomy from external political control but also an obligation to create an environment that is conducive to the exercise of scholarly autonomy. When they live up to that obligation (by securing for scholars an intellectual realm free from improper pressures), universities provide an institutional sanctuary against repression, which prevents majorities or coalitions of minorities from controlling the creation of politically relevant ideas. The sanctuary protects democracy not only against its own excesses but also against nondemocratic tyranny.

Because the institutional right of academic freedom ("freedom of the academy") is derived from the democratic value of scholarly autonomy and not from a private property right, the right may be claimed with equal force by public and private universities that are dedicated to defending the scholarly autonomy of their faculty. A state-enforced loyalty oath requirement, for example, does not cease to be problematic when it is applied only within state-owned universities. Nor may private universities invoke their "academic freedom" to defend racially and sexually discriminatory promotion practices. The democratic purpose of a university, not the contractual arrangements between owners and employees, grounds the academic freedom of faculty, as well as the freedom of the academy.

Academic freedom is not a legitimate defense against governmental regulations that are compatible with preserving, or instrumental to achieving, an environment conducive to scholarly autonomy. Some of the most controversial legislation of the past twenty-five years—the Equal Pay Act of 1963, Executive Order 11246 defining affirmative action guidelines for universities, and Title IX forbidding sex discrimination in student athletic programs—limit the authority of universities with regard to important internal practices, but in ways that are compatible with (perhaps even instrumental to) their professed educational purposes. One can therefore agree with the general claim that "an institution which lacks freedom from government interference in the management of its educational functions cannot protect its faculty from government interference with theirs"[14] and yet refuse to shout "Academic Freedom!" whenever a university defends itself against governmental regulation.

In some cases, a conflict arises from the fact that a (so-called) university is committed to certain sectarian religious purposes that are incompatible with both nondiscrimination in the distribution of offices and freedom of scholarly inquiry. The associational purposes of fundamentalist Christian universities whose members "genuinely believe that the Bible forbids interracial dating and marriage"[15] are incompatible with a requirement that tax-exempt institutions not discriminate on the basis of race. The proper defense against governmental regulation by such institutions is not academic freedom, but freedom of association. In these cases, democracies must decide whether the associational freedom of a sectarian academy should be honored against the competing rights of nondiscrimination and free scholarly inquiry. One way of honoring associational freedom without dishonoring nondiscrimination is for governments to allow sectarian academies to discriminate but deprive them of the tax-exempt and the credentialing statuses of universities, statuses rightly reserved for academies of higher learning that respect the academic freedom of their faculty and the principle of nondiscrimination in distributing opportunities to social office.

The autonomy of universities, like that of social institutions more generally, is relative to their democratic purposes. A defense of university autonomy on grounds of free association cannot be conclusive because the democratic purposes of universities include far more than supporting membership in consensual communities. Universities also serve as gatekeepers, to many social offices; they have a virtual monopoly on the education necessary for many of the most valued jobs in our society. As gatekeepers, they share responsibility for upholding the democratic principle of nondiscrimination in the distribution of office. Democratic governments therefore properly concern themselves with safeguarding the interests not only of current members of universities but also of students seeking admission to, and academics seeking jobs within, universities. When the interests of members conflict with those of nonmembers, as they do in the case of sectarian academies that discriminate against blacks, then a democratic state should uphold the more important democratic interest at stake. Because the claim to autonomy is derived from the democratic purposes served by universities, a democratic state does not violate an absolute right of universities when it regulates them for the sake of making the system of universities function more democratically.

The question that must be asked in every case is whether a proposed restriction on their decisionmaking authority will bring universities closer to serving their democratic purposes. In answering this question, the interests both of members and of nonmembers who seek membership in a university must be considered. By virtue of recognizing both sets of interests, legislatures will sometimes be forced to make hard choices in deciding whether and how to regulate universities, and courts may then face equally hard choices in deciding whether regulations that are challenged violate associational freedom or are necessary to protect citizens against unjustified discrimination. Defenders of state regulation point out that universities often invoke academic freedom to rationalize what would otherwise be blatantly discriminatory practices, such as not admitting or hiring blacks. Those who defend universities against state regulation respond that the standard of nondiscrimination taken to its logical extreme leaves little or no room for associational freedom. One need not disagree with either of these claims to defend the relative autonomy of universities based on their democratic purposes. The alternatives of granting universities full autonomy from democratic control or none at all are worse than facing up to the hard choices entailed in establishing a principled middle ground.

Educating Officeholders

In addition to serving as sanctuaries of nonrepression, universities also serve as gatekeepers to many of the most valuable social offices, particularly in the professions. Economists often view the university's gate-keeping function as a piece of its primary purpose: maximizing social value, welfare, or utility (the terms are used interchangeably). The view is apparently attractive. Why, one might ask, should universities not try to maximize social value? The rhetorical force of the question can best be countered by considering how a self-consciously utility-maximizing university would behave with regard to selecting and then educating future officeholders.

The aim of the utilitarian university is most fully elaborated with regard to its function in "screening" students and then "signaling" employers of their relative value by grading, recommending, and certifying them.[16] To maximize social productivity, a utilitarian university does more than educate students. A university education, as Joseph Stiglitz suggests, "provides information as well as skills. . . ." It supplies society with "a 'commodity' for which it is well known that the market 'fails'. . . ."[17]

But how successful are universities in making up for market failure? The best studies tend to agree that although "there is no more consistent social science finding than that of the correlation between educational attainment and higher personal income,"[18] there are few less well understood relationships than that between educational attainment and success in later life, measured by income, occupational status, or any other (more or less meaningful) measure of social contribution.[19] "The voluminous literature on academic variables and later-life success is not worthless. . . ," Robert Klitgaard comments. It teaches us that "[d]efining them as we will, 'later life contributions' are very difficult to forecast."[20] Differences in academic success explain a very small portion of the differences in income, occupational status, or any other (more or less) meaningful measure of social contribution. To the extent that a university education is associated with future success, the data do not indicate whether it is the education, the information, or the mere credential supplied by a university that accounts for the association.

In face of this evidence that universities do not maximize social welfare, economists look for means by which they might. The descriptive model—which measures how well universities screen students according to their future social contribution—is easily translated into a prescriptive model— which recommends ways in which universities can do a better job in predicting future social success. "The problem," Klitgaard concludes, "is not with our objectives [to predict future success] but with what at present can be measured and predicted."[21] But *is* this the problem? Before we advise universities to get on with the task of trying to develop better measurements and make more accurate predictions, we should question the "framework that suggests that . . . the institution [of the university is] . . . a production process whose value added is to be maximized."[22]

Utilitarianism *can* translate all the purposes of universities into positive and negative utilities or into values added or subtracted, but "can" does not imply "ought." As long as they must look for measurable and commensurable values, universities that try to maximize the social value added of their students must take their signals from the job market. If employers are racist or anti-semitic, so will universities be in the guise of maximizing social utility.[23] If the demand for engineers far exceeds the supply while humanities majors are having difficulty finding jobs, then utility-maximizing universities will admit more potential engineers and fewer potential humanists until the job market reaches an equilibrium (or some universities discover that they have a "comparative advantage" in admitting and educating humanists). It is a simplification to describe utility-maximizing universities as being signaled by the market and then signaling it back, but an informative simplification. More complicated utility-maximizing models conceal their fundamental tendency by translating into utilitarian language every purpose a university can serve,[24] except the purpose of *not* maximizing social utility.

There is good reason, however, for making the utilitarian exception the democratic rule. Universities are more likely to serve society well not by adopting the quantified values of the market but by preserving a realm where the nonquantifiable values of intellectual excellence and integrity, and the supporting moral principles of nonrepression and nondiscrimination, flourish. In serving society well by preserving such a realm, a university acts as an educator of officeholders rather than simply a gatekeeper of office. Acting as an educator entails appreciating rather than abolishing the discrepancies between intellectual standards and market practices, since such discrepancies often signal a moral failure of the market rather than an intellectual failure of the university. To serve as an educator of officeholders and not just a gatekeeper for the market, a university must distinguish between these two very different kinds of failure.

Far from appearing to maximize social utility, universities that uphold intellectual standards in the face of conflicting social practices may seem to be a source of considerable social disutility. By democratic standards, universities should be a source of social tension as long as a conflict exists between social standards and social practices. Consider the tension as it applies to professional practices. Doctors, lawyers, and politicians are often tempted to deceive the rest of us, more tempted than they would be in a society where the democratic norms of professionalism were better understood and more effectively enforced, although surely they would be tempted even in such a society. Many professionals and politicians in our society not only succumb to temptation when they should not, but profit handsomely by succumbing. Universities can do little to prevent professionals and politicians from profiting by their transgressions, but they can do a great deal to articulate the moral standards of professional and political life that would support public criticism of such transgressions. Universities serve an essential democratic purpose by preserving the tension between social standards and practices and thereby helping citizens contain professional authority within its proper realm. But they can serve that purpose only if they do not take their cues from the market in an effort to maximize social utility.

Utilitarians can accommodate this view of the university by integrating long-range, nonquantifiable considerations into their conception of social utility. But in making their analysis more sophisticated, they often obscure a crucial point about the democratic value of universities: universities do not serve democracy best when they *try* to maximize existing social preferences or to predict (rather than shape) future ones. Universities serve democracies best when they try to establish an environment conducive to creating knowledge that is not immediately useful, appreciating ideas that are not presently popular, and rewarding people who are—and are likely to continue to be—intellectually but not necessarily economically productive.

If this is what "maximizing the social good" requires of universities in a democratic society, then the most sophisticated utilitarians must agree with nonutilitarians that universities should not think in utilitarian terms. Universities that try to maximize social utility are less likely to succeed in doing so than universities that try to serve as sanctuaries of nonrepression and as educators of officeholders, even when they do not appear to be maximizing social utility. If universities serve society best when they resist the temptations to repress unpopular ideas and to discriminate against less marketable but more intellectual students, then utilitarians should recommend that universities not think like utilitarians. Universities are likely to serve democracies better, even by utilitarian standards, when they think like democrats about their social purposes, and act as educators of officeholders rather than mere gatekeepers of office.

Fostering Associational Freedom

Safeguarding academic freedom and educating officeholders are the primary purposes of universities, but not their only socially significant purposes. Universities are also communities of scholars, students, and administrators who share intellectual, educational, and (in some cases) also religious values. Although they are not truly voluntary communities (since so many careers today require a college degree), many students and faculty choose where they want to study or to teach. The relative intellectual worth of various institutions is only one factor in their decisions. Universities are also chosen for the kinds of academic communities they are. In the case of many private universities, trustees first determined the nature of their community, but they rarely remain the sole force behind perpetuating or redefining communal standards. Faculty and students as well as administrators also influence the communal life of their university. They generally have more of an interest in defining communal standards than do nonmembers, at least as long as a university is not threatening the principles of nonrepression and nondiscrimination.

Is there an ideal academic *community* by democratic standards? The most commonly invoked ideal—the ivory tower, all of whose members are dedicated to the pursuit of knowledge for its own sake—is not the most democratic one. The ideal is based on an interpretation of the classical Greek understanding of knowledge and its relation to the good life and the good society: the pursuit of knowledge is the good of the mind, and the good of the mind is the highest good to which humans can aspire and that societies can support. All members of a genuine academic community must be dedicated to the pursuit of knowledge for its own sake, according to this view, not only because no higher purpose exists but also because all other purposes (such as professional education) prevent scholars and students from searching for the most fundamental form of knowledge, which is metaphysical rather than practical.[25]

The ideal of a community united solely by the pursuit of knowledge for its own sake may have made more sense where it first flourished: within the Athenian *polis*, where much work was reserved for resident aliens (metics), slaves, and women, who were excluded from citizenship.[26] Even with regard to Athens, however, the ideal is not beyond criticism, since many Athenian citizens were artisans who had to work for their living (to what degree they actually shared in ruling is difficult to determine).[27] But whatever one thinks of Athens, consider what it would mean today for a society of citizens who both rule and work to claim that "the only kind of university worth having" is one dedicated solely to the pursuit of knowledge for its own sake.[28] It would mean that most citizens are not worthy of membership in such a community, not because they lack sufficient intellect or motivation to learn but because they lack independent income or they are dedicated to learning for the sake of being socially useful.

Nonexclusive democracies cannot support the claim that genuine academic communities consist only of ivory towers, but they can support the pursuit of knowledge for its own sake within universities, as within individual lives. Many people value lives that depend at least partly on the pursuit of knowledge for its own sake. Many others value being part of a society in which other people live such lives. We therefore need not return to Athens nor await discovery of a deep metaphysical defense of the pursuit of knowledge for its own sake to support communities that are "liberal" in this classical sense of being dedicated to studies that liberate students from the more immediate and material concerns of their daily lives. On a democratic view, ivory towers are desirable rather than necessary features of a community of higher learning.

If there is an ideal university community by democratic standards, one might expect it to be democratic. Paul Goodman and Robert Paul Wolff have argued that a genuine "community of learning" must be democratically self-governing.[29] An ideal university community, on their understanding, would consist of a small group of faculty and students who are self-governing and fully autonomous from all external authorities. On this view, self-government within a university is necessary to create commitments that are morally binding on scholars and students just as self-government in a society is necessary to create binding commitments on citizens. Autonomy from external authority is essential because the intellectual commitments of scholars and students are foreign to the loyalties of citizens and public officials. "It is finally this foreignness," Goodman comments, "that makes a university; it is not the level of the studies, the higher learning, the emphasis on theory, or anything like that."[30]

In a society that increasingly renders self-governing communities anachronistic, the "community of learning" is an appealing vision of a university that by virtue of its absolute autonomy from external authority furthers both knowledge and self-government. Given the legal authority of lay trustees and the growth of administration within American universities, it is also a radical vision, summarized by the slogan, "All Power to the Faculty and Students."[31]

The democratic appeal of the autonomous community of learning is limited, however, by the very principles that Goodman and Wolff invoke in its defense. The foreignness of a university and its claim to absolute autonomy from external control are ultimately justified on the grounds that intellectual standards of truth and value inevitably conflict with social standards. The conflict enters the university—only to corrupt it—whenever scholars or students pursue knowledge other than for its own sake. Students must not be graded and certified for entry into the professions. Faculty and students must not be governed by lay trustees and administrators whose commitments extend beyond the university community. Yet these practices could be sanctioned by democratic deliberations within a community of learning: students and faculty might recommend grading and a substantial degree of hierarchical administration for reasons that are not reducible to the corrupting pressures of the external world. The argument that democratic communities of learning must be prevented from grading and certifying students depends on a version of the view from the ivory tower: that the highest—or only "pure"—form of knowledge must be pursued for its own sake. The argument that genuine academic communities must eschew any administration collapses with the claim that the commitments of administrators necessarily conflict with those of faculty and students, who pursue knowledge only for its own sake.

The conflict between university and society lies elsewhere, I have argued, not between intellectual and social standards of judgment, but between social *standards* and social *practices*. This tension enters a university in many ways, perhaps the most obvious being when it admits and educates future professionals. A genuine "community of learning," on Goodman's and Wolff's understanding, excludes this tension by refusing to admit students who want to become professionals, or by refusing to grade and certify students. A university that admits the tension must complicate rather than compromise its task of scholarship and teaching. Its scholars are called upon to articulate standards of judgment that apply not just to an ideal world but also to *their* world, and its students are encouraged to pursue knowledge not just for its own sake but for the sake of better serving their society. Public attacks on universities for being sanctuaries for social critics are evidence not of the foreignness of universities, but of one of the ways in which they belong to democracies. As communities of critics, universities make it more difficult for public officials, professionals, and ordinary citizens to disregard their own standards when it happens to be convenient. Universities make it more difficult to the extent that scholars base their judgments on widely shared (although frequently violated) social standards. In excluding scholars and students who are interested in socially useful knowledge, a community of learning therefore misses a democratic opportunity: to cultivate a sense of social responsibility among future professionals and to criticize society on the basis of shared rather than "foreign" standards.

Seizing the opportunity, however, also entails running a risk, which the community of learning avoids. A university that admits the tension between social standards and social practices risks elevating social practices into social standards, thereby serving as apologists for the status quo. Pre-professional students tempt faculty to teach more "practical" courses; government agencies and private businesses seek the services of faculty in search of "practical" answers to their problems. The distinction between seeking knowledge for the sake of serving society and seeking it for the sake of satisfying a social demand is lost by a university that defines itself as a service station for the rest of society. Communities that pursue knowledge solely for its own sake and those that supply all social demands for knowledge are both unlikely to be sanctuaries of nonrepression. Radical separation from society and radical submersion in it tend to create disinterest in social problems and indifference to critical standards. Ivory towers and communities of learning foster too much intellectual distance, service stations too little.

Many of the most prominent American universities claim to strike a balance between the tendencies of the ivory tower, the community of learning, and the service station: to preserve a place for the pursuit of knowledge for its own sake, to accommodate subcommunities united by common academic and social purposes, and also to open their gates to the pursuit of some but not all socially useful knowledge. Clark Kerr popularized the term "multiversity" to describe this "remarkably effective educational institution. A university anywhere can aim no higher than to be as British as possible for the sake of the undergraduates, as German as possible for the sake of the graduates and the research personnel, as American as possible for the sake of the public at large—and as confused as possible for the sake of the preservation of the whole uneasy balance."[32] If Kerr's defense of the multiversity is correct, even its confusion serves a cause: securing a diversity of educational purposes and of intellectual communities within one institution of higher learning.[33]

Although such diversity is appealing, a multiversity has other, less attractive features. The mark of a multiversity "on the make," Kerr noted, "is a mad scramble for football stars and professional luminaries. The former do little studying and the latter little teaching, and so they form a neat combination of muscle and intellect."[34] Kerr therefore questioned whether the multiversity "has a brain as well as a body."[35]

Derek Bok's more recent discussion of the social responsibilities of a university offers a set of moral standards that would enable a multiversity to secure a brain to its body. The ideal multiversity would "avoid undertaking tasks that other organizations can discharge equally well" and commit itself to supplying only those demands for knowledge that are consistent with "the preservation of academic freedom, the maintenance of high intellectual standards, the protection of academic pursuits from outside interference, the rights of individuals affected by the university not to be harmed in their legitimate interests, [and] the needs of those who stand to benefit from the intellectual services that a vigorous university can perform."[36] Bok's conception of the multiversity is probably the dominant American ideal of a university community. As an ideal, the multiversity combines a variety of intellectual communities within one institution without being unprincipled in its pursuit of knowledge. Multiversities combine liberal arts with career education, and by virtue of their intellectual diversity, tend to be socially diverse as well.

Although multiversities pursue more democratic purposes and include more communities than other universities, more is less for some students and faculty. More choice among undergraduate courses, for example, may reflect the unwillingness of many faculty to teach anything other than specialized courses directly related to their research. Smaller liberal arts colleges with faculties less involved in research and consulting are often better for students primarily interested in getting a good general education and close faculty attention. The faculties of smaller liberal arts colleges are also more likely to reach agreement on basic scholarly standards, such as not sponsoring classified research.

The willingness of major American universities to support classified research is one important piece of evidence against elevating the multiversity into the ideal community of higher learning. Classified research cannot by its very nature satisfy a basic standard of scholarly inquiry: it cannot be placed before other scholars—or the public—for their scrutiny. The demand for classified research, moreover, defies a university to judge the social value of its undertaking. The government agency is, in effect, saying to scholars and universities: "Trust us." Scholars and universities should say in response: "If we trust you, then democratic citizens should not trust us, either for living up to our scholarly standards or for serving the public welfare instead of whomever happens to demand our services." Despite the apparent and irreconcilable conflict between scholarly standards and secretive research, many multiversities cannot reach an internal agreement to restrict classified research. Some even support classified research in the name of academic freedom, thereby reducing academic freedom to an unrestricted license of scholars and universities to pursue knowledge for the sake of politics or profit, without any responsibility to account to a scholarly community for their findings. More diversity within a university is less democratically desirable to the extent that it undermines support for the scholarly standards that justify the rights of academic freedom and the freedom of the academy.[37]

Multiversities also fall short of an ideal academic association insofar as their members are excluded from decisionmaking on matters central to their interests and expertise. Some of the same divisions that prevent members of the multiversity from agreeing on substantive issues also lead them to disagree on deliberative procedures by which such issues might be resolved. Quite apart from the level of internal disagreement, the sheer size of multiversities makes it difficult for faculty and students in multiversities to share in policymaking or even to be consulted before others make policy. The "pluralism" of multiversities is therefore a partial rather than an inclusive value: favoring choice among educational offerings over a more intensive, general education; cultivating a faculty that is more involved in research and graduate teaching instead of one that is more involved in undergraduate teaching; offering a more hospitable environment to students and faculty who prefer diversity than to those who prefer to participate in a more democratic community.

One need not think that an ideal university community would be thoroughly democratic to recognize the benefits of more democratization than now exists within most American universities: participation can improve the quality of decisions made by universities on many significant issues, it can be educationally valuable for students, it can make both faculty and students more committed to the university's educational purposes and more united in their understanding of what those purposes are.[38] The community of learning contains an important but inverted insight: participation within universities is desirable not because students and faculty enter with the same intellectual commitments, but because self-government tends to create mutual, and mutually recognized, commitments to scholarly standards.

If participation tends to be the cause rather than the effect of agreement on purpose, then university trustees and administrators need not, and probably should not, be excluded from participating in university governance. The educative effects of participation on trustees and administrators is not an insignificant consideration, although the primary purpose of participation by trustees and administrators is to guard the university's long-term interests, especially its financial interests.[39] On most academic matters, however, faculty have considerably greater competence than trustees and administrators, although on some academic matters—such as assessing the results of teaching that they have experienced—students may be the best judges. Even this very rough and incomplete sketch suggests the need for a wider distribution of authority than typically exists in American universities.

The tendency among many American universities has been to elevate financial guardianship into the controlling consideration of university governance, and therefore to concentrate authority in the hands of trustees and administrators, who govern largely to the exclusion of faculty and students. When students revolted at Columbia in 1969, "there existed no faculty body that could debate important academic issues, generate a consensus about them, and make sure that that consensus took effect. (There was a University Council, but it was dominated by administrators and traditionally had concerned itself with bagatelles.)"[40] A similar problem existed at Berkeley, leading critics along with supporters of the Free Speech Movement to criticize the concentration of authority in administrative hands.[41]

Insofar as fostering free scholarly inquiry is the primary purpose of universities, neither their social value nor their autonomy from external political control varies directly with the degree to which they are internally democratized. But insofar as universities are also valued—and valuable—as communities, whose associational purposes are advanced by faculty and student participation, democratic societies have an interest in supporting a greater degree of self-governance within universities. Many American universities are not self-governing communities in any meaningful sense, but rather are autocratically governed institutions even on issues central to the interests and expertise of their faculty and their students. The two major reasons to respect the autonomy of universities—as a means of securing the academic freedom of their faculty and the associational freedom of their members—both point in the direction of securing a broader distribution of power within universities.

Is there, then, an ideal university community by democratic standards? Yes and no. To the extent that there is an ideal community, it is one whose members are dedicated to free scholarly inquiry and who share authority in a complex pattern that draws on the particular interests and competencies of administrators, faculty, students, and trustees. This ideal serves as a critique of autocratically governed universities that do not secure the academic freedom of their faculty, but it also leaves room for a variety of university communities to flourish, all of which are dedicated to academic freedom but each of which support a different set of intellectual and social commitments.

Consider how the educational commitments of larger and smaller universities typically vary. Larger universities generally offer undergraduates a broader curriculum, smaller liberal arts colleges a more intensive, general education. The faculty of the former may be more involved in research and graduate teaching; those of the latter in undergraduate teaching. Larger universities offer a hospitable environment to students who prefer more social diversity, liberal arts colleges to those who prefer to participate in more face-to-face communities.

In combining secular with religious education, church-run universities add even more diversity among communities of higher learning, a diversity that furthers the primary purpose of higher education insofar as these universities also respect the academic freedom of their faculty (as do many church-run universities in the United States). Because no single kind of university community can offer everything that is democratically valuable in higher education to everyone, the democratic ideal of a university community is best conceived as a "principled pluralism" of universities, each of which is dedicated to nonrepression and nondiscrimination, and all of which together foster freedom of academic association.

Notes

1. Most school-leaving age laws today stop just short of the normal age of completing high school. A further extension of compulsory education to coincide with the normal age of high-school graduation might be yet another victory for democratic citizenship. Although a much larger proportion of citizens in the 1980s than in the 1970s completed four years of high school, a substantial minority (13.8 percent of citizens between the ages of 25 and 29 in 1982) still lack a high-school education. See *Digest of Educational Statistics 1983–84* (Washington, D.C.: U.S. Government Printing Office, 1984), p. 13.
2. Walzer, *Spheres of Justice*, pp. 207–208.
3. Lilla, "Ethos, 'Ethics,' and Public Service," *The Public Interest*, no. 63 (Spring 1981): 17.
4. Ibid. For extended analyses of the reasons for teaching applied ethics at the university level, see Derek Bok, *Beyond the Ivory Tower: Social Responsibilities of the Modern University* (Cambridge, Mass.: Harvard University Press, 1982), pp. 116–35; Daniel Callahan and Sissela Bok, eds., *Ethics Teaching in Higher Education* (New York: Plenum Press, 1980); and Dennis Thompson, "Political Theory and Political Judgment," *PS*, vol. 17, no. 2 (Spring 1984): 193–97.
5. A case can also be made (although I do not make it here) for the relative autonomy of professional schools. To determine precisely what the relative autonomy of professional schools—as distinct from that of universities—entails, one would consider the partly distinct democratic purposes of professional education. Because law schools, for example, serve as educators of both technically competent lawyers and critical legal scholars, one might conclude that the standard of relative autonomy justifies state licensing of lawyers but not control of the content of legal education.
6. Alexis de Tocqueville, *Democracy in America* (1848), trans. George Lawrence, ed. J. P. Mayer (Garden City, N.Y.: Doubleday and Co., 1969), vol. 1, pt. 2, ch. 7, pp. 255–56.
7. Clark Kerr, for example, confuses academic freedom with the freedom of a professor to do as he pleases, and therefore mistakenly concludes that a professor has more academic freedom in a multiversity than in any other university because "he has a choice of roles and mixtures of roles to suit his taste as never before. He need not leave the Groves for the Acropolis unless he wishes; but he can, if he wishes. He may even become, as some have, essentially a professional man with his home office and basic retainer on the campus of the multiversity but with his clients scattered from coast to coast. He can also even remain the professor of old, as many do. There are several patterns of life from which to choose. So the professor . . . has greater freedom, *Lehrfreiheit*, in the old German sense of the freedom of the professor to do as he pleases, also is triumphant." Were academic freedom "the freedom of the professor to do as he pleases," neither academic freedom nor universities that fostered such freedom would have any special democratic value. Kerr, *The Uses of the University* (Cambridge, Mass.: Harvard University Press, 1982), p. 44.
8. For an explanation of the (common) understanding of social office on which I rely, see Walzer, *Spheres of Justice*, pp. 129–35: "[A]n office is any position in which the political community as a whole takes an interest, choosing the person who holds it or regulating the procedures by which he is chosen"(p. 129).
9. See Ralph F. Fuchs, "Academic Freedom—Its Basic Philosophy Function, and History," in Hans W. Baade and Robinson O. Everett, eds., *Academic Freedom: The Scholar's Place in Modern Society* (Dobbs Ferry, N.Y.: Oceana Publications, 1964), pp. 5–6; and Richard Hofstadter and Walter Metzger, eds., *The Development of Academic Freedom in the United States* (New York: Columbia University Press, 1955), pp. 383–98. The first systematic formulation of this understanding of academic freedom seems to have been Frederich Paulsen's in *The German Universities and University Study* (1902), trans. F. Thilly and W. W. Elwang (New York: C. Scribner's Sons, 1906), pp. 228–31.
10. For evidence of such threats, see the AAUP's list of "Censured Administrations, 1930–1968," in Louis Joughin, ed., *Academic Freedom and Tenure: A Handbook of the American Association of University Professors* (Madison: University of Wisconsin Press, 1969), pp. 143–47.

11. For an account of governmental attacks in the 1950s, see Robert M. MacIver, *Academic Freedom in Our Time* (New York: Columbia University Press, 1955), pp. 46–55, 158–87. For the failure of universities under attack to defend academic freedom, see Ellen Schrecker, *No Ivory Tower* (New York: Oxford University Press, 1986).

12. Abraham Flexner, *Universities: American, English, German* (New York and London: Oxford University Press, 1930), pp. 131–32.

13. Avoiding the appearance of improper influence is important because scholarship must be taken seriously to serve its social purpose.

14. Dallin Oaks, "A Private University Looks at Government Regulation," *Journal of College and University Law*, vol. 4, no. 1 (February 1976): 3.

15. *Bob Jones University v. United States*, 461 U.S. 574 (1982) at 580.

16. On screening and signaling, see A. Michael Spence, *Market Signaling* (Cambridge, Mass.: Harvard University Press, 1974); Joseph E. Stiglitz, "The Theory of 'Screening,' Education, and the Distribution of Income," *American Economic Review*, vol. 65, no. 3 (June 1975): 283–300; Kenneth Wolpin, "Education and Screening," *American Economic Review*, vol. 67, no. 5 (December 1977): 949–58; and John G. Riley, "Testing the Educational Screening Hypothesis," *Journal of Political Economy*, vol. 87, no. 5 (October 1979): 227–52.

17. Stiglitz, "The Theory of 'Screening,' Education, and the Distribution of Income," p. 298.

18. Douglas M. Windham, "The Benefits and Financing of American Higher Education: Theory, Research, and Policy," no. 80-A19 (Stanford, Calif.: Institute for Research on Educational Finance and Governance, Stanford University, November 1980), p. 5. Quoted in Robert Klitgaard, *Choosing Elites* (New York: Basic Books, 1985), p. 118.

19. For an excellent summary and analysis of the relevant literature, see Klitgaard, *Choosing Elites*, pp. 116–31.

20. Ibid., p. 119.

21. Ibid., p. 184: "I have cited Raymond Cattell's view that the ultimate object is not to select those who will do well in school. In theory, we should also look for those other attributes that go along with success after school. But how might we do that in practice?"

22. Ibid., pp. 60–61.

23. For evidence that universities have actually used the market rationale to justify not admitting Jews, see Seymour Martin Lipset, "Political Controversies at Harvard, 1936–1974," in S. M. Lipset and David Riesman, eds., *Education and Politics at Harvard* (New York: McGraw-Hill, 1975), p. 150.

24. For a sophisticated utilitarian model for admissions policies at elite universities, see Klitgaard, *Choosing Elites*, pp. 61–84.

25. "The aim of higher education is wisdom. Wisdom is knowledge of principles and causes. Metaphysics deals with the highest principles and causes. Therefore metaphysics is the highest wisdom." Robert Maynard Hutchins, *The Higher Learning in America* (New Haven, Conn.: Yale University Press, 1936), p. 98.

26. "The freemen were trained in the reflective pursuit of the good life: their education was unspecialized as well as unvocational; its aim was to produce a rounded person with a full understanding of himself and of his place in society and in the cosmos." *General Education in a Free Society: Report of the Harvard Committee* (Cambridge, Mass.: Harvard University Press, 1945), pp. 52–53. The purpose of higher learning in Athenian democracy was not wholly noninstrumental, even if it was wholly unspecialized and unvocational. Knowledge was useful for the *polis*, or at least for a well-governed *polis*. Socrates and the Sophists agreed on this much, although they disagreed on what kind of knowledge was useful, and who was capable of learning it.

27. For accounts of citizenship and political participation in Athens, see A.H.M. Jones, *Athenian Democracy* (Oxford: Basil Blackwell, 1957), esp. pp. 4–11; and M. I. Finley, *Politics in the Ancient World* (Cambridge: Cambridge University Press, 1983), pp. 70–75.

28. Hutchins, *The Higher Learning in America*, p. 118.

29. A true university, according to Wolff, is "a *community of persons* united by collective understandings, by common *and communal* goals, by bonds of reciprocal obligation, and by a flow of sentiment which makes the preservation of the community an object of desire, not merely a matter of prudence or a command of duty." Robert Paul Wolff, *The Ideal of the University* (Boston: Beacon Press, 1969), p. 127. See also Paul Goodman, *The Community of Scholars* (New York: Random House, 1962).

30. Goodman, *The Community of Scholars*, pp. 5–6.

31. Wolff, *The Ideal of the University*, p. 133.

32. Kerr, *The Uses of the University*, p. 18.
33. Ibid., p. 118.
34. Ibid., p. 90.
35. Ibid., p. 123. For Kerr's analysis of the problems facing multiversities, see pp. 118–23.
36. Bok, *Beyond the Ivory Tower*, pp. 76–77, 88. This is only a partial list of Bok's criteria.
37. "The intellectual world has been fractionalized as interests have become more diverse; and there are fewer common topics of conversation at the faculty clubs. Faculty government has become more cumbersome, more the avocation of active minorities; and there are real questions whether it can work effectively on a large scale, whether it can agree on more than the preservation of the status quo," Kerr, *The Uses of the University*, p. 43.
38. For a more complete argument to this effect, see Dennis F. Thompson, "Democracy and the Governing of the University," *Annals of the American Academy of Political and Social Science*, vol. 404 (November 1972): 160–62.
39. For a case for giving nonresident trustees decisionmaking authority over many fiscal matters, see Special Committee on the Structure of the University, *The Governing of Princeton University* (Princeton, N.J.: Princeton University, 1970), pp. 53–57. See esp. p. 54: "The interests of faculty, staff, and students are likely to bias them toward expenditures for present, as opposed to future, needs, and they have direct, personal interests in the outcome of decisions regarding tuition, scholarships, and fellowships, rent subsidies, fringe benefits, and the many services provided by the university, as well as in those regarding salaries. While decisions on all of these matters are likely to be better made if the views of faculty, staff, and students are taken into account, no one should want the making of such decisions to become either an exercise in logrolling or a contest of power among interested parties. The involvement of non-residents in the governing of the university can help to insure that decisions do not become either of these things."
40. Walter Metzger, "Authority at Columbia," in Immanuel Wallerstein and Paul Starr, eds., *The University Crisis Reader: Confrontation and Counterattack*, vol. 2 (New York: Random House, 1971), pp. 333–34.
41. "The constitution of the university—the distribution of powers among its various elements—may well be out of joint," Nathan Glazer commented in the context of a critique of the Berkeley student movement. "What Happened at Berkeley," in Seymour Martin Lipset and Sheldon S. Wolin, eds., *The Berkeley Student Revolt: Facts and Interpretations* (Garden City, N.Y.: Doubleday and Co., 1965), p. 301.

CITIZENS OF THE WORLD

M.C. NUSSBAUM

When anyone asked him where he came from, he said, "I am a citizen of the world."
—Diogenes Laertius, *Life of Diogenes the Cynic*

Anna was a political science major at a large state university in the Midwest. Upon graduation she went into business, getting a promising job with a large firm. After twelve years she had risen to a middle-management position. One day, her firm assigned her to the newly opened Beijing office. What did she need to know, and how well did her education prepare her for success in her new role? In a middle-management position, Anna is working with both Chinese and American employees, both male and female. She needs to know how Chinese people think about work (and not to assume there is just one way); she needs to know how cooperative networks are formed, and what misunderstandings might arise in interactions between Chinese and American workers. Knowledge of recent Chinese history is important, since the disruptions of the Cultural Revolution still shape workers' attitudes. Anna also needs to consider her response to the recent policy of urging women to return to the home, and to associated practices of laying off women first. This means she should know something about Chinese gender relations, both in the Confucian tradition and more recently. She should probably know something about academic women's studies in the United States, which have influenced the women's studies movement in Chinese universities. She certainly needs a more general view about human rights, and about to what extent it is either legitimate or wise to criticize another nation's ways of life. In the future, Anna may find herself dealing with problems of anti-African racism, and with recent government attempts to exclude immigrants who test positive for the human immunodeficiency virus. Doing this well will require her to know something about the history of Chinese attitudes about race and sexuality. It will also mean being able to keep her moral bearings even when she knows that the society around her will not accept her view.

The real-life Anna had only a small part of this preparation—some courses in world history, but none that dealt with the general issue of cultural variety and how to justify moral judgments in a context of diversity; none that dealt with the variety of understandings of gender roles or family structures; none that dealt with sexual diversity and its relationship to human rights. More important, she had no courses that prepared her for the shock of discovering that other places treated as natural what she found strange, and as strange what she found natural. Her imaginative capacity to enter into the lives of people of other nations had been blunted by lack of practice. The real-life Anna had a rough time getting settled in China, and the firm's dealings with its new context were not always very successful. A persistent and curious person, however, she stayed on and has made herself a good interpreter of cultural difference. She now plans to spend her life in Beijing, and she feels is making a valuable contribution to the firm.

Two years ago, after several years in China, already in her late thirties, Anna decided to adopt a baby. Through her by then extensive knowledge of the Chinese bureaucracy, she bypassed a number of obstacles and quickly found an infant girl in an orphanage in Beijing. She then faced challenges

Reprinted from *Cultivating Humanity: A Classical Defense of Reform in Liberal Educations,* by Martha C. Nussbaum (1997), by permission of Harvard University Press.

of a very different kind. Even in the most apparently universal activities of daily life, cultural difference colors her day. Her Chinese nurse follows the common Chinese practice of wrapping the baby's limbs in swaddling bands to immobilize it. As is customary, the nurse interacts little with the child, either facially or vocally, and brings the child immediately anything it appears to want, without encouraging its own efforts. Anna's instincts are entirely different: she smiles at the baby, encourages her to wave her hands about, talks to her constantly, wants her to act for herself. The nurse thinks Anna is encouraging nervous tension by this hyperactive American behavior; Anna thinks the nurse is stunting the baby's cognitive development. Anna's mother, visiting, is appalled by the nurse and wants to move in, but Anna, by now a sensitive cross-cultural interpreter, is able to negotiate between mother and nurse and devise some plan for the baby's development that is agreeable to all. To do this she has had to think hard about the nonuniversality and nonnaturalness of such small matters as playing with a baby. But she has also had to think of the common needs and aims that link her with the nurse, and the nurse with her own mother. Her university education gave her no preparation at all for these challenges.

Had Anna been a student at today's St. Lawrence University, or at many other colleges and universities around the United States, she would have had a better basis for her international role, a role U.S. citizens must increasingly play (whether at home or abroad) if our efforts in business are to be successful, if international debates about human rights, medical and agricultural problems, ethnic and gender relations, are to make progress as we enter the new century. As Connie Ellis, a forty-three-year-old waitress at Marion's Restaurant in Sycamore, Illinois, put it on the Fourth of July, 1996, "You can't narrow it down to just our country anymore—it's the whole planet." We must educate people who can operate as world citizens with sensitivity and understanding.

Asked where he came from, the ancient Greek Cynic philosopher Diogenes replied, "I am a citizen of the world." He meant by this that he refused to be defined simply by his local origins and group memberships, associations central to the self-image of a conventional Greek male; he insisted on defining himself in terms of more universal aspirations and concerns. The Stoics who followed his lead developed his image of the *kosmopolitēs*, or world citizen, more fully, arguing that each of us dwells, in effect, in two communities—the local community of our birth, and the community of human argument and aspiration that "is truly great and truly common." It is the latter community that is, most fundamentally, the source of our moral and social obligations. With respect to fundamental moral values such as justice, "we should regard all human beings as our fellow citizens and local residents." This attitude deeply influenced the subsequent philosophical and political tradition, especially as mediated through the writings of Cicero, who reworked it so as to allow a special degree of loyalty to one's own local region or group. Stoic ideas influenced the American republic through the writings of Thomas Paine, and also through Adam Smith and Immanuel Kant, who themselves influenced the Founders. Later on, Stoic thought was a major formative influence on both Emerson and Thoreau.

This form of cosmopolitanism is not peculiar to Western traditions. It is, for example, the view that animates the work of the influential Indian philosopher, poet, and educational leader Rabindranath Tagore. Tagore drew his own cosmopolitan views from older Bengali traditions, although he self-consciously melded them with Western cosmopolitanism. It is also the view recommended by Ghanaian philosopher Kwame Anthony Appiah, when he writes, concerning African identity: "We will only solve our problems if we see them as human problems arising out of a special situation, and we shall not solve them if we see them as African problems generated by our being somehow unlike others." But for people who have grown up in the Western tradition it is useful to understand the roots of this cosmopolitanism in ancient Greek and Roman thought. These ideas are an essential resource for democratic citizenship. Like Socrates' ideal of critical inquiry, they should be at the core of today's higher education.

The Idea of World Citizenship in Greek and Roman Antiquity

Contemporary debates about the curriculum frequently imply that the idea of a "multicultural" education is a new fad, with no antecedents in longstanding educational traditions. In fact, Socrates grew up in an Athens already influenced by such ideas in the fifth century B.C. Ethnographic writers such as the historian Herodotus examined the customs of distant countries, both in order to understand their ways of life and in order to attain a critical perspective on their own society. Herodotus took seriously the possibility that Egypt and Persia might have something to teach Athens about social values. A cross-cultural inquiry, he realized, may reveal that what we take to be natural and normal is merely parochial and habitual. One cultural group thinks that corpses must be buried; another, that they must be burnt; another, that they must be left in the air to be plucked clean by the birds. Each is shocked by the practices of the other, and each, in the process, starts to realize that its habitual ways may not be the ways designed by nature for all times and persons.

Awareness of cultural difference gave rise to a rich and complex debate about whether our central moral and political values exist in the nature of things (by *phusis*), or merely by convention (*nomos*). That Greek debate illustrates most of the positions now familiar in debates about cultural relativism and the source of moral norms. It also contains a crucial insight: if we should conclude that our norms are human and historical rather than immutable and eternal, it does not follow that the search for a rational justification of moral norms is futile.

In the conventional culture of fifth-century B.C. Athens, recognition that Athenian customs were not universal became a crucial precondition of Socratic searching. So long as young men were educated in the manner of Aristophanes' Old Education, an education stressing uncritical assimilation of traditional values, so long as they marched to school in rows and sang the old songs without discussion of alternatives, ethical questioning could not get going. Ethical inquiry requires a climate in which the young are encouraged to be critical of their habits and conventions; and such critical inquiry, in turn, requires awareness that life contains other possibilities.

Pursuing these comparisons, fifth-century Athenians were especially fascinated by the example of Sparta, Athens' primary rival, a hierarchical and nondemocratic culture that understood the goal of civic education in a very un-Athenian way. As the historian Thucydides depicts them, Spartan educators carried to an extreme the preference for uniformity and rule-following that characterized the Old Education of Athens in Aristophanes' nostalgic portrait. Conceiving the good citizen as an obedient follower of traditions, they preferred uncritical subservience to Athenian public argument and debate. Denying the importance of free speech and thought, they preferred authoritarian to democratic politics.

Athenians, looking at this example, saw new reasons to praise the freedom of inquiry and debate that by this time flourished in their political life. They saw Spartan citizens as people who did not choose to serve their city, and whose loyalty was therefore in a crucial way unreliable, since they had never really thought about what they were doing. They noted that once Spartans were abroad and free from the narrow constraint of law and rule, they often acted badly, since they had never learned to choose for themselves. The best education, they held, was one that equips a citizen for genuine choice of a way of life; this form of education requires active inquiry and the ability to contrast alternatives. Athenians denied the Spartan charge that their own concern with critical inquiry and free expression would give rise to decadence. "We cultivate the arts without extravagance," they proudly proclaimed, "and we devote ourselves to inquiry without becoming soft." Indeed, they insisted that Sparta's high reputation for courage was ill based: for citizens could not be truly courageous if they never chose from among alternatives. True courage, they held, requires freedom, and freedom is best cultivated by an education that awakens critical thinking. Cross-cultural inquiry thus proved not only illuminating but also self-reinforcing to Athenians: by showing them regimes that did not practice such inquiry and what those regimes lacked in consequence, it gave Athenians reasons why they should continue to criticize and to compare cultures.

Plato, writing in the early to mid-fourth century B.C., alludes frequently to the study of other cultures, especially those of Sparta, Crete, and Egypt. In his *Republic*, which alludes often to Spartan practices, the plan for an ideal city is plainly influenced by reflection about customs elsewhere. One particularly fascinating example of the way in which reflection about history and other cultures awakens critical reflection occurs in the fifth book of that work, where Plato's character Socrates produces the first serious argument known to us in the Western tradition for the equal education of women. Here Socrates begins by acknowledging that the idea of women's receiving both physical and intellectual education equal to that of men will strike most Athenians as very weird and laughable.

(Athenians who were interested in cultural comparison would know, however, that such ideas were not peculiar in Sparta, where women, less confined than at Athens, did receive extensive athletic training.) But he then reminds Glaucon that many good things once seemed weird in just this way. For example, the unclothed public exercise that Athenians now prize as a norm of manliness once seemed foreign, and the heavy clothing that they think barbaric once seemed natural. However, he continues, when the practice of stripping for athletic contests had been in effect for some time, its advantages were clearly seen—and then "the appearance of absurdity ebbed away under the influence of reason's judgment about the best." So it is with women's education, Socrates argues. Right now it seems absurd, but once we realize that our conventions don't by themselves supply reasons for what we ought to do, we will be forced to ask ourselves whether we really do have good reasons for denying women the chance to develop their intellectual and physical capacities. Socrates argues that we find no such good reasons, and many good reasons why those capacities should be developed. Therefore, a comparative cultural study, by removing the false air of naturalness and inevitability that surrounds our practices, can make our society a more truly reasonable one.

Cross-cultural inquiry up until this time had been relatively unsystematic, using examples that the philosopher or historian in question happened to know through personal travel or local familiarity. Later in the fourth century, however, the practice was rendered systematic and made a staple of the curriculum, as Aristotle apparently instructed his students to gather information about 153 forms of political organization, encompassing the entire known world, and to write up historical and constitutional descriptions of these regimes. The *Athenian Constitution*, which was written either by Aristotle or by one of his students, is our only surviving example of the project; it shows an intention to record everything relevant to critical reflection about that constitution and its suitability. When Aristotle himself writes political philosophy, his project is extensively cross-cultural. In his *Politics*, before describing his own views about the best form of government, he works through and criticizes many known historical examples, prominently including Crete and Sparta, and also a number of theoretical proposals, including those of Plato. As a result of this inquiry, Aristotle develops a model of good government that is in many respects critical of Athenian traditions, though he follows no single model.

By the beginning of the so-called Hellenistic era in Greek philosophy, then, cross-cultural inquiry was firmly established, both in Athenian public discourse and in the writings of the philosophers, as a necessary part of good deliberation about citizenship and political order.

But it was neither Plato nor Aristotle who coined the term "citizen of the world." It was Diogenes the Cynic. Diogenes (404–323 B.C.) led a life stripped of the usual protections that habit and status supply. Choosing exile from his own native city, he defiantly refused protection from the rich and powerful for fear of losing his freedom, and lived in poverty, famously choosing a tub set up in the marketplace as his "home" in order to indicate his disdain for convention and comfort. He connected poverty with independence of mind and speech, calling freedom of speech "the finest thing in human life." Once, they say, Plato saw him washing some lettuce and said, "If you had paid court to Dionysius, you would not be washing lettuce." Diogenes replied, "If you had washed lettuce, you would not have paid court to Dionysius." This freedom from subservience, he held, was essential to a philosophical life. "When someone reproached him for being an exile, he said that it was on that account that he came to be a philosopher."

Diogenes left no written work behind, and it is difficult to know how to classify him. "A Socrates gone mad" was allegedly Plato's description—and a good one, it seems. For Diogenes clearly followed the lead of Socrates in disdaining external markers of status and focusing on the inner life of virtue and thought. His search for a genuinely honest and virtuous person, and his use of philosophical arguments to promote that search, are recognizably Socratic. What was "mad" about him was the public assault on convention that accompanied his quest. Socrates provoked people only by his questions. He lived a conventional life. But Diogenes provoked people by his behavior as well, spitting in a rich man's face, even masturbating in public. What was the meaning of this shocking behavior?

It appears likely that the point of his unseemly behavior was itself Socratic—to get people to question their prejudices by making them consider how difficult it is to give good reasons for many of our deeply held feelings. Feelings about the respect due to status and rank and feelings of shame associated with sexual practices are assailed by this behavior—as Herodotus' feelings about burial were assailed by his contact with Persian and Egyptian customs. The question is whether one can then go on to find a good argument for one's own conventions and against the behavior of the Cynic.

As readers of the *Life* of Diogenes, we ourselves quickly become aware of the cultural relativity of what is thought shocking. For one of the most shocking things about Diogenes, to his Athenian contemporaries, was his habit of eating in the public marketplace. It was this habit that gave him the name "dog," *kuōn*, from which our English label Cynic derives. Only dogs, in this culture, tore away at their food in the full view of all. Athenians evidently found this just about as outrageous as public masturbation; in fact his biographer joins the two offenses together, saying, "He used to do everything in public, both the deeds of Demeter and those of Aphrodite." Crowds, they say, gathered around to taunt him as he munched on his breakfast of beets, behaving in what the American reader feels to be an unremarkable fashion. On the other hand, there is no mention in the *Life* of shock occasioned by public urination or even defecation. The reason for this, it may be conjectured, is that Athenians, like people in many parts of the world today, did not in fact find public excretion shocking. We are amazed by a culture that condemns public snacking while permitting such practices. Diogenes asks us to look hard at the conventional origins of these judgments and to ask which ones can be connected by a sound argument to important moral goals. (So far as we can tell, Cynics supplied no answers to this question.)

Set in this context, the invitation to consider ourselves citizens of the world is the invitation to become, to a certain extent, philosophical exiles from our own ways of life, seeing them from the vantage point of the outsider and asking the questions an outsider is likely to ask about their meaning and function. Only this critical distance, Diogenes argued, makes one a philosopher. In other words, a stance of detachment from uncritical loyalty to one's own ways promotes the kind of evaluation that is truly reason based. When we see in how many different ways people can organize their lives we will recognize, he seems to think, what is deep and what is shallow in our own ways, and will consider that "the only real community is one that embraces the entire world." In other words, the true basis for human association is not the arbitrary or the merely habitual; it is that which we can defend as good for human beings—and Diogenes believes that these evaluations know no national boundaries.

The confrontational tactics Diogenes chose unsettle and awaken. They do not contain good argument, however, and they can even get in the way of thought. Diogenes' disdain for more low-key and academic methods of scrutinizing customs, for example the study of literature and history, seems most unwise. It is hard to know whether to grant Diogenes the title "philosopher" at all, given his apparent preference for a kind of street theater over Socratic questioning. But his example, flawed as it was, had importance for the Greek philosophical tradition. Behind the theater lay an important idea: that the life of reason must take a hard look at local conventions and assumptions, in the light of more general human needs and aspirations.

The Stoic philosophers, over the next few centuries, made Diogenes' insight respectable and culturally fruitful. They developed the idea of cross-cultural study and world citizenship much further in their own morally and philosophically rigorous way, making the concept of the "world citizen," *kosmou politēs*, a centerpiece of their educational program. As Seneca writes, summarizing older Greek Stoic views, education should make us aware that each of us is a member of "two communities: one that is truly great and truly common . . . in which we look neither to this corner nor to that, but measure the boundaries of our nation by the sun; the other, the one to which we have been assigned by birth." The accident of where one is born is just that, an accident; any human being might have been born in any nation. Recognizing this, we should not allow differences of nationality or class or ethnic membership or even gender to erect barriers between us and our fellow human beings. We should recognize humanity—and its fundamental ingredients, reason and moral capacity—wherever it occurs, and give that community of humanity our first allegiance.

This does not mean that the Stoics proposed the abolition of local and national forms of political organization and the creation of a world state. The Greek Stoics did propose an ideal city, and the Roman Stoics did put ideas of world citizenship into practice in some ways in the governance of the empire. But the Stoics' basic point is more radical still: that we should give our first allegiance to *no* mere form of government, no temporal power, but to the moral community made up by the humanity of all human beings. The idea of the world citizen is in this way the ancestor and source of Kant's idea of the "kingdom of ends," and has a similar function in inspiring and regulating a certain mode of political and personal conduct. One should always behave so as to treat with respect the dignity of reason and moral choice in every human being, no matter where that person was born, no matter what that person's rank or gender or status may be. It is less a political idea than a moral idea that constrains and regulates political life.

The meaning of the idea for political life is made especially clear in Cicero's work *On Duties* (*De Officiis*), written in 44 B.C. and based in part on the writings of the slightly earlier Greek Stoic thinker Panaetius. Cicero argues that the duty to treat humanity with respect requires us to treat aliens on our soil with honor and hospitality. It requires us never to engage in wars of aggression, and to view wars based on group hatred and wars of extermination as especially pernicious. It requires us to behave honorably in the conduct of war, shunning treachery even toward the enemy. In general, it requires us to place justice above political expediency, and to understand that we form part of a universal community of humanity whose ends are the moral ends of justice and human well-being. Cicero's book has been among the most influential in the entire Western philosophical tradition. In particular, it influenced the just-war doctrine of Grotius and the political thought of Immanuel Kant; their views about world understanding and the containment of global aggression are crucial for the formation of modern international law.

Stoics hold, then, that the good citizen is a "citizen of the world." They hold that thinking about humanity as it is realized in the whole world is valuable for self-knowledge: we see ourselves and our customs more clearly when we see our own ways in relation to those of other reasonable people. They insist, furthermore, that we really will be better able to solve our problems if we face them in this broader context, our imaginations unconstrained by narrow partisanship. No theme is deeper in Stoicism than the damage done by faction and local allegiances to the political life of a group. Stoic texts show repeatedly how easy it is for local or national identities and their associated hatreds to be manipulated by self-seeking individuals for their own gain—whereas reason is hard to fake, and its language is open to the critical scrutiny of all. Roman political life in Seneca's day was dominated by divisions of many kinds, from those of class and rank and ethnic origin to the division between parties at the public games and gladiatorial shows. Part of the self-education of the Stoic Roman emperor Marcus Aurelius, as he tells the reader of his *Meditations*, was "not to be a Green or Blue partisan at the races, or a supporter of the lightly armed or heavily armed gladiators at the Circus." Politics is sabotaged again and again by these partisan loyalties, and by the search for honor and fame that accompanies them. Stoics argue that a style of citizenship that recognizes the moral/rational community as fundamental promises a more reasonable style of political deliberation and problem-solving.

But Stoics do not recommend world citizenship only for reasons of expediency. They insist that the stance of the *kosmou politēs* is intrinsically valuable: for it recognizes in people what is especially fundamental about them, most worthy of reverence and acknowledgment, namely their aspirations to justice and goodness and their capacities for reasoning in this connection. This essential aspect may be less colorful than local tradition and local identity, but it is, the Stoics argue, both lasting and deep.

To be a citizen of the world, one does not, the Stoics stress, need to give up local affiliations, which can frequently be a source of great richness in life. They suggest instead that we think of ourselves as surrounded by a series of concentric circles. The first one is drawn around the self; the next takes in one's immediate family; then follows the extended family; then, in order, one's neighbors or local group, one's fellow city-dwellers, one's fellow countrymen—and we can easily add to this list groups formed on the basis of ethnic, religious, linguistic, historical, professional, and gender identities. Beyond all these circles is the largest one, that of humanity as a whole. Our task as citizens of the world, and as educators who prepare people to be citizens of the world, will be to "draw the circles somehow toward the center," making all human beings like our fellow city-dwellers. In other words, we need not give up our special affections and identifications, whether national or ethnic or religious; but we should work to make all human beings part of our community of dialogue and concern, showing respect for the human wherever it occurs, and allowing that respect to constrain our national or local politics.

This Stoic attitude, then, does not require that we disregard the importance of local loves and loyalties or their salience in education. Adam Smith made a serious error when he objected to Stoicism on those grounds, and modern critics of related Kantian and Enlightenment conceptions make a similar error when they charge them with neglect of group differences. The Stoic, in fact, must be conversant with local differences, since knowledge of these is inextricably linked to our ability to discern and respect the dignity of humanity in each person. Stoics recognize love for what is near as a fundamental human trait, and a highly rational way to comport oneself as a citizen. If each parent has a special love for his or her own children, society will do better than if all parents try to have an equal love for all children. Much the same is true for citizenship of town or city or nation: each of us should take our stand where life has placed us, and devote to our immediate surroundings a special affection and attention. Stoics, then, do not want us to behave as if differences between male and female, or between African and Roman, are morally insignificant. These differences can and do enjoin special obligations that all of us should execute, since we should all do our duties in the life we happen to have, rather than imagining that we are beings without location or memory.

Stoics vary in the degree of concession they make to these special obligations. Cicero, for example, takes a wise course when he urges the Roman citizen to favor the near and dear on many occasions, though always in ways that manifest respect for human dignity. These special local obligations have educational consequences: the world citizen will legitimately spend a disproportionate amount of time learning about the history and problems of her or his own part of the world. But at the same time we recognize that there is something more fundamental about us than the place where we happen to find ourselves, and that this more fundamental basis of citizenship is shared across all divisions.

This general point emerges clearly if we consider the relationship each of us has to a native language. We each have a language (in some cases more than one) in which we are at home, which we have usually known from infancy. We naturally feel a special affection for this language. It defines our possibilities of communication and expression. The works of literature that move us most deeply are those that exploit well the resources of that language. On the other hand, we should not suppose—and most of us do not suppose—that English is best just because it is our own, that works of literature written in English are superior to those written in other languages, and so forth. We know that it is more or less by chance that we are English speakers rather than speakers of Chinese or German or Bengali. We know that any infant might have learned any language, because there is a fundamental language-learning capacity that is shared by all humans. Nothing in our innate equipment disposes us to speak Hindi rather than Norwegian.

In school, then, it will be proper for us to spend a disproportionate amount of time mastering our native language and its literature. A human being who tried to learn all the world's languages would master none, and it seems reasonable for children to focus on one, or in some cases two, languages when they are small. On the other hand, it is also very important for students to understand what it is like to see the world through the perspective of another language, an experience that quickly shows that human complexity and rationality are not the monopoly of a single linguistic community.

This same point can be made about other aspects of culture that should figure in a higher education. In ethics, in historical knowledge, in knowledge of politics, in literary, artistic, and musical learning, we are all inclined to be parochial, taking our own habits for that which defines humanity. In these areas as in the case of language, it is reasonable to immerse oneself in a single tradition at an early age. But even then it is well to become acquainted with the facts of cultural variety, and this can be done very easily, for example through myths and stories that invite identification with people whose form of life is different from one's own. As education progresses, a more sophisticated grasp of human variety can show students that what is theirs is not better simply because it is familiar.

The education of the *kosmou politēs* is thus closely connected to Socratic inquiry and the goal of an examined life. For attaining membership in the world community entails a willingness to doubt the goodness of one's own way and to enter into the give-and-take of critical argument about ethical and political choices. By an increasingly refined exchange of both experience and argument, participants in such arguments should gradually take on the ability to distinguish, within their own traditions, what is parochial from what may be commended as a norm for others, what is arbitrary and unjustified from that which may be justified by reasoned argument.

Since any living tradition is already a plurality and contains within itself aspects of resistance, criticism, and contestation, the appeal to reason frequently does not require us to take a stand outside the culture from which we begin. The Stoics are correct to find in all human beings the world over a capacity for critical searching and a love of truth. "Any soul is deprived of truth against its will," says Marcus Aurelius, quoting Plato. In this sense, any and every human tradition is a tradition of reason, and the transition from these more ordinary and intracultural exercises to a more global exercise of critical argument need not be an abrupt transition. Indeed, in the world today it is clear that internal critique very frequently takes the form of invoking what is found to be fine and just in other traditions.

People from diverse backgrounds sometimes have difficulty recognizing one another as fellow citizens in the community of reason. This is so, frequently, because actions and motives require, and do not always receive, a patient effort of interpretation. The task of world citizenship requires the would-be world citizen to become a sensitive and empathic interpreter. Education at all ages should cultivate the capacity for such interpreting. This aspect of the Stoic idea is developed most fully by Marcus Aurelius, who dealt with many different cultures in his role as emperor; he presents, in his *Meditations*, a poignantly personal account of his own efforts to be a good world citizen. "Accustom yourself not to be inattentive to what another person says, and as far as possible enter into his mind," he writes (6.53); and again, "When things are being said, one should follow every word, when things are being done, every impulse; in the latter case, to see straightway to what object the impulse is directed, in the former, to watch what meaning is expressed" (7.4). Given that Marcus routinely associated with people from every part of the Roman Empire, this idea imposes a daunting task of learning and understanding, which he confronts by reading a great deal of history and literature, and by studying closely the individual characters of those around him in the manner of a literary narrator. "Generally," he concludes, "one must first learn many things before one can judge another's action with understanding" (11.18).

Above all, Marcus finds that he has to struggle not to allow his privileged station (an obstacle to real thought, as he continually points out) to sever him, in thought, from his fellow human beings. "See to it that you do not become Caesarized," he tells himself, "or dyed with that coloring" (6.30). A favorite exercise toward keeping such accidents of station in their proper place is to imagine that all human beings are limbs of a single body, cooperating for the sake of common purposes. Referring to the fact that it takes only the change of a single letter in Greek to convert the word "limb" *(melos)* into the word "(detached) part" *(meros)*, he concludes: "if, changing the word, you call yourself merely a (detached) part instead of a limb, you do not yet love your fellow men from the heart, nor derive complete joy from doing good; you will do it merely as a duty, not as doing good to yourself" (7.13). The organic imagery underscores the Stoic ideal of cooperation.

Can anyone really think like a world citizen in a life so full of factionalism and political conflict? Marcus gives himself the following syllogism: "Wherever it is possible to live, it is also possible to live a virtuous life; it is possible to live in a palace; therefore it is also possible to live a virtuous life in a palace" (5.16). And, recognizing that he himself has sometimes failed in citizenship because of impatience and the desire for solitude: "Let no one, not even yourself, any longer hear you placing the blame on palace life" (8.9). In fact, his account of his own difficulties being a world citizen in the turmoil of Roman politics yields some important advice for anyone who attempts to reconcile this high ideal with the realities of political involvement:

> Say to yourself in the morning: I shall meet people who are interfering, ungracious, insolent, full of guile, deceitful and antisocial; they have all become like that because they have no understanding of good and evil. But I who have contemplated the essential beauty of good and the essential ugliness of evil, who know that the nature of the wrong-doer is of one kin with mine—not indeed of the same blood or seed but sharing the same kind, the same portion of the divine—I cannot be harmed by any one of them, and no one can involve me in shame. I cannot feel anger against him who is of my kin, nor hate him. We were born to labor together, like the feet, the hands, the eyes, and the rows of upper and lower teeth. To work against one another is therefore contrary to nature, and to be angry against a man or turn one's back on him is to work against him. (2.1)

One who becomes involved in politics in our time might find this paragraph comforting. It shows a way in which the attitude of world citizenship gets to the root of one of the deepest political problems in all times and places, the problem of anger. Marcus is inclined to intense anger at his political adversaries. Sometimes the anger is personal, and sometimes it is directed against a group. His claim, however, is that such anger can be mitigated, or even removed, by the attitude of empathy that the ideal of the *kosmou politēs* promotes. If one comes to see one's adversaries as not impossibly alien and other, but as sharing certain general human goals and purposes, if one understands that they are not monsters but people who share with us certain general goals and purposes, this understanding will lead toward a diminution of anger and the beginning of rational exchange.

World citizenship does not, and should not, require that we suspend criticism toward other individuals and cultures. Marcus continues to refer to his enemies as "deceitful and antisocial," expressing strong criticism of their conduct. The world citizen may be very critical of unjust actions or policies, and of the character of people who promote them. But at the same time Marcus refuses to think of the opponents as simply alien, as members of a different and inferior species. He refuses to criticize until he respects and understands. He carefully chooses images that reflect his desire to see them as close to him and similarly human. This careful scrutiny of the imagery and speech one uses when speaking about people who are different is one of the Stoic's central recommendations for the undoing of political hatred.

Stoics write extensively on the nature of anger and hatred. It is their well-supported view that these destructive emotions are not innate, but learned by children from their society. In part, they hold, people directly absorb negative evaluations of individuals and groups from their culture, in part they absorb excessively high evaluations of their own honor and status. These high evaluations give rise to hostility when another person or group appears to threaten their honor or status. Anger and hatred are not unreasoning instincts; they have to do with the way we think and imagine, the images we use, the language we find it habitual to employ. They can therefore be opposed by the patient critical scrutiny of the imagery and speech we employ when we confront those our tradition has depicted as unequal.

It is fashionable by now to be very skeptical of "political correctness," by which the critic usually means a careful attention to the speech we use in talking about minorities, or foreigners, or women. Such scrutiny might in some forms pose dangers to free speech, and of course these freedoms should be carefully defended. But the scrutiny of speech and imagery need not be inspired by totalitarian motives, and it need not lead to the creation of an antidemocratic "thought police." The Stoic demand for such scrutiny is based on the plausible view that hatred of individuals and groups is personally and politically pernicious, that it ought to be resisted by educators, and that the inner world of thought and speech is the place where, ultimately, hatred must be resisted. These ideas about the scrutiny of the inner world are familiar to Christians also, and the biblical injunction against sinning in one's heart has close historical links to Stoicism. All parents know that it is possible to shape a child's attitudes toward other races and nationalities by the selection of stories one tells and by the way one speaks about other people in the home. There are few parents who do not seek to influence their children's views in these ways. Stoics propose, however, that the process of coming to recognize the humanity of all people should be a lifelong process, encompassing all levels of education—especially since, in a culture suffused with group hatred, one cannot rely on parents to perform this task.

What this means in higher education is that an attitude of mutual respect should be nourished both in the classroom itself and in its reading material. Although in America we should have no sympathy with the outright censoring of reading material, we also make many selections as educators, both in assigning material and in presenting it for our students. Few of us, for example, would present anti-Semitic propaganda in a university classroom in a way that conveyed sympathy with the point of view expressed. The Stoic proposal is that we should seek out curricula that foster respect and mutual solidarity and correct the ignorance that is often an essential prop of hatred. This effort is perfectly compatible with maintaining freedom of speech and the openness of a genuinely critical and deliberative culture.

In our own time, few countries have been more rigidly divided, more corroded by group hatred, than South Africa. In spelling out its goals for society in its draft for the new Constitution, the African

National Congress (ANC) recognized the need to address hatred through education, and specified the goal of education as the overcoming of these differences:

> Education shall be directed towards the development of the human personality and a sense of personal dignity, and shall aim at strengthening respect for human rights and fundamental freedoms and promoting understanding, tolerance and friendship amongst South Africans and between nations.

Some of this language would have been new to Marcus Aurelius—and it would have been a good thing for Roman Stoics to have reflected more about the connections between the human dignity they prized and the political rights they frequently neglected. But the language of dignity, humanity, freedom, understanding, tolerance, and friendship would not have been strange to Marcus. (He speaks of his goal as "the idea of a Commonwealth with the same laws for all, governed on the basis of equality and free speech"; this goal is to be pursued with "beneficence, eager generosity, and optimism".) The ANC draft, like the Stoic norm of world citizenship, insists that understanding of various nations and groups is a goal for every citizen, not only for those who wish to affirm a minority identity. It insists that the goal of education should not be separation of one group from another, but respect, tolerance, and friendship—both within a nation and among nations. It insists that this goal should be fostered in a way that respects the dignity of humanity in each person and citizen.

Above all, education for world citizenship requires transcending the inclination of both students and educators to define themselves primarily in terms of local group loyalties and identities. World citizens will therefore not argue for the inclusion of cross-cultural study in a curriculum primarily on the grounds that it is a way in which members of minority groups can affirm such an identity. This approach, common though it is, is divisive and subversive of the aims of world community. This problem vexes many curricular debates. Frequently, groups who press for the recognition of their group think of their struggle as connected with goals of human respect and social justice. And yet their way of focusing their demands, because it neglects commonalities and portrays people as above all members of identity groups, tends to subvert the demand for equal respect and love, and even the demand for attention to diversity itself. As David Glidden, philosopher at the University of California at Riverside, expressed the point, "the ability to admire and love the diversity of human beings gets lost" when one bases the demand for inclusion on notions of local group identity. Why should one love or attend to a Hispanic fellow citizen, on this view, if one is oneself most fundamentally an Irish-American? Why should one care about India, if one defines oneself as above all an American? Only a human identity that transcends these divisions shows us why we should look at one another with respect across them.

World Citizenship in Contemporary Education

What would an education for world citizenship look like in a modern university curriculum? What should Anna, the future businesswoman in Beijing, learn as an undergraduate if she is to be prepared for her role? What should all students learn—since we all interact as citizens with issues and people from a wide variety of traditions?

This education must be a multicultural education, by which I mean one that acquaints students with some fundamentals about the histories and cultures of many different groups. These should include the major religious and cultural groups of each part of the world, and also ethnic and racial, social and sexual minorities within their own nation. Language learning, history, religious studies, and philosophy all play a role in pursuing these ideas. Awareness of cultural difference is essential in order to promote the respect for another that is the essential underpinning for dialogue. There are no surer sources of disdain than ignorance and the sense of the inevitable naturalness of one's own way. No liberal education can offer students adequate understanding of all they should know about the world; but a detailed understanding of one unfamiliar tradition and some rudiments about others will suffice to engender Socratic knowledge of one's own limitations. It would have helped Anna to have learned a great deal about China; but to have studied the culture of India would have been almost as valuable, since it would have showed her how to inquire and the limitations of her experience.

World citizens will legitimately devote more attention and time to their own region and its history, since it is above all in that sphere that they must operate. This need for local knowledge has important educational consequences. We would be absurdly misguided if we aimed at giving our students an equal knowledge of all histories and cultures, just as we would be if we attempted to provide a bit of knowledge of all languages. Besides the fact that this would produce a ridiculously superficial result, it would also fail in the task of giving students a detailed acquaintance with the local sphere in which most of their actions will be undertaken. Education at all levels, including higher education, should therefore strongly emphasize the history of American constitutional traditions and their background in the tradition of Western political philosophy. In a similar way, literary education should focus disproportionately on the literature of Anglo-American traditions—which, however, are themselves highly complex and include the contributions of many different groups.

On the other hand, it is also extremely important that this material be presented in a way that reminds the student of the broader world of which the Western traditions are a part. This may be done with good educational results in the Western tradition courses themselves, where one can emphasize what is distinctive about this tradition through judicious and illuminating contrasts with developments elsewhere. But it must above all be done by the design of the curriculum as a whole, which should offer students the rudiments of knowledge about the major world traditions of thought and art, and the history that surrounds them, and, even more important, make them aware how much important material they do not know.

Education for world citizenship needs to begin early. As soon as children engage in storytelling, they can tell stories about other lands and other peoples. A curriculum for world citizenship would do well to begin with the first grade, where children can learn in an entertaining and painless way that religions other than Judaism and Christianity exist, that people have many traditions and ways of thinking. (One such curriculum has been developed by E. D. Hirsch Jr. and is being used in a number of elementary-school districts around the country: first-graders tell stories of Buddha under the *boddhi* tree; they think about Hindu myths of the gods, about African folktales, about the life of Confucius.) By the time students reach college or university, they should be well equipped to face demanding courses in areas of human diversity outside the dominant Western traditions.

This exposure to foreign and minority cultures is not only, and not primarily, a source of confirmation for the foreign or minority student's personal sense of dignity—though of course this will be one important function such exposure can often serve. It is an education for all students, so that as judges, as legislators, as citizens in whatever role, they will learn to deal with one another with respect and understanding. And this understanding and respect entail recognizing not only difference but also, at the same time, commonality, not only a unique history but also common rights and aspirations and problems.

The world citizen must develop sympathetic understanding of distant cultures and of ethnic, racial, and religious minorities within her own. She must also develop an understanding of the history and variety of human ideas of gender and sexuality. As a citizen one is called upon frequently to make judgments in controversial matters relating to sex and gender—whether as a judge, deciding a case that affects the civil rights of millions, or simply as a democratic voter, deciding, for example, whether to support a referendum like Colorado's Amendment 2, declared unconstitutional by the U.S. Supreme Court in 1996, which restricted the abilities of local communities to pass laws protecting the civil rights of gays and lesbians. To function well as a citizen today, one needs to be able to assess the arguments put forward on both sides; and to do so one needs an education that studies these issues. There are complex connections between cross-cultural study and the study of gender and sexuality. Cross-cultural study reveals many ways of organizing concepts of gender and sexuality; and thinking about gender and sex is essential to thinking critically about a culture. A good undergraduate education should prepare students to be informed and sensitive interpreters of these questions.

Building a curriculum for world citizenship has multiple aspects: the construction of basic required courses of a "multicultural" nature; the infusion of diverse perspectives throughout the curriculum; support for the development of more specialized elective courses in areas connected with human diversity; and, finally, attention to the teaching of foreign languages, a part of the multicultural story that has received too little emphasis.

Basic "diversity" requirements come in two varieties. There are elective requirements that allow the student to choose one or two courses from among a wide range of offerings. Such, for example, is the requirement at the University of Nevada at Reno, where students, in addition to completing a "World Civilizations" core course, must elect a course focusing on at least one area of human diversity outside the dominant culture of her own society. Areas included are the history and culture of non-Western peoples, the history and culture of minorities in the United States, women's studies, and the study of the varieties of human sexuality. Reno, like many institutions, cannot afford to hire new faculty to create integrative courses or to free existing faculty from many of their other commitments. Making a menu of what is on hand, and then giving students a choice from that menu, is these institutions' only option if they wish to diversify their curricula.

Such requirements can fulfill basic Socratic functions, showing students the possible narrowness and limitedness of their own perspective and inviting them to engage in critical reflection. And they can frequently impart methodological tools that will prove valuable in approaching another area of diversity. But this is not always the case: a student who has taken a course on American women writers of the nineteenth century is still likely to be in a weak position with respect to the sort of cultural diversity she will encounter if she finds herself in dialogue with people from China and the Middle East. Even a course in non-Western literature may leave the student blankly ignorant of non-Western history and religion. A student who has studied the history and literature of China may remain unaware of the variety and diversity of minorities within her own nation. It is odd and arbitrary to put all these different topics together in an area called "diversity," as if the grasp of any part of any one of them would somehow yield a person the breadth of learning that could be yielded only by some grasp of each area. This problem will be especially grave if, as at Reno, the courses listed as satisfying the "diversity" requirement are unrelated to one another by any common discussion about methodology, beyond the deliberations of the faculty group that put the requirement together in the first place. Such courses may not even produce a student who knows how to inquire about diversity in a new context.

One can make a still stronger criticism of the amorphous elective requirement: that the failure to confront all the areas of diversity undercuts the encounter with each of them. A student of Chinese history who does not have some awareness of the history of women and the family, and of the different ways of understanding gender roles, will be likely to miss a good deal that is of urgent importance to the person who gets involved with China today, whether through politics or through business. If Anna hears the political rhetoric in today's China about the "natural" suitability of a situation in which women leave the workplace to return home, she will need to evaluate these statements and policies. It would be best to evaluate them against the background not only of the Confucian tradition but also of a critical awareness of gender roles and their variety. Successful and fair business dealings with China require such an awareness, which will not be provided by courses on Chinese history alone.

For these many reasons, an amorphous elective diversity requirement does not adequately prepare students for the complex world they will confront. It is better than no diversity program at all, and it may well be the best that many institutions can do. But it does not provide sufficient direction to fulfill completely the goals of world citizenship.

Despite these drawbacks, the particular version of an elective diversity requirement that was designed at Reno has some strong virtues. Particularly admirable is the reasoning that justified the requirement when it was publicly presented to faculty, students, and the community. The argument crafted by the faculty committee focuses on goals of world citizenship rather than on identity politics. Deborah Achtenberg, professor of philosophy, expert on Aristotle's ethics, and chair of the Diversity Committee, reflects that her approach to curricular politics was colored by her own particular history, as "a woman, a Jew, a former sixties activist, a St. John's College alumna, a philosopher." From St. John's, she says, she learned respect for the intrinsic value of great texts; the diversity requirement strongly emphasizes these values. From the civil-rights movement she learned "how exclusion of groups leaves the dominant culture unable to benefit from the perspectives and contributions of those groups"; this experience gave her a strong motivation to work for inclusion of those perspectives in the curriculum. As a woman, she knows how difficult it is to speak when one wonders whether the terms of the debate have been set by someone else; the courses in which she is involved focus on these issues of voice and methodology. As a Jew, she knows how easy it is for excluded groups to internalize demeaning stereotypes of themselves; she therefore urges questioning of all stereotypes, including those fostered by identity politics. Finally, as a philosopher, she is committed to making the continual attempt to "transcend all this particularity towards commonality," communicating what she perceives to others whose perspectives and experiences are different from her own. The curriculum she helped design draws inspiration both from Greek ideas of world citizenship and from biblical demands for equality of attention and love.

For a university that is skeptical of the elective approach and can support a more ambitious undertaking, a more arduous, but potentially more satisfying, approach is to design a single basic "multicultural" course, or a small number of such courses, to acquaint all students with some basic conceptions and methods. A very successful example of such a course, in a nonelite institution with a mixed student body, is "American Pluralism and the Search for Equality," developed at the State University of New York at Buffalo in 1992. This course is required in addition to a two-semester world civilization sequence that provides basic instruction in non-Western religions and cultures. The pluralism course complements the primarily historical world civilization course by enhancing students' awareness of the many groups that make up their own nation, and of the struggle of each for respect and equality. Since these moral issues arise in the international context as well, reflection about them retrospectively enriches the other course.

The outstanding feature of the pluralism course is its careful design. In striking contrast to the catch-as-catch-can approach to diversity that one often finds, the faculty designing this course met for months to work out a coherent set of goals and methodologies. They justified their plan in documents available not only to the university community but also to the general public. The statement of goals and purposes shows the relation of the course to the goals of citizenship:

> A goal of the course is to develop within students a sense of informed, active citizenship as they enter an American society of increasing diversity by focusing on contemporary and historical issues of race, ethnicity, gender, social class, and religious sectarianism in American life. A goal of the course is to provide students with an intellectual awareness of the causes and effects of structured inequalities and prejudicial exclusion in American society. A goal of the course is to provide students with increased self-awareness of what it means in our culture to be a person of their own gender, race, class, ethnicity, and religion as well as an understanding of how these categories affect those who are different from themselves . . . A goal of the course is to expand students' ability to think critically, and with an open mind, about controversial contemporary issues that stem from the gender, race, class, ethnic, and religious differences that pervade American society.

John Meacham, a professor of psychology who is among its architects, enunciates several principles that contributed to the success of the Buffalo course and that should, in his view, guide the development of other such courses.

1. *"Design multicultural courses with broad content."* The Buffalo course is designed to acquaint students with five categories of diversity: race, gender, ethnicity, social class, and religious sectarianism. Each section of the course must cover all five and must focus in depth on three. This approach gives the advantage of breadth and also ensures that students see one category in its relation to the others. Meacham argues persuasively that such a course contributes a deeper understanding of each of its topics than would a narrower course focusing on a single topic.

2. *"Base multicultural courses on faculty disciplinary expertise."* Faculty staffing the course are drawn from ten different disciplines. Meacham comments: "For example, an intelligent discussion of affirmative action should be grounded at least in history, biology, law, economics, political science,

psychology, and sociology." Nothing was included in the course that faculty were not equipped to teach expertly; and different faculty groups in different years approached the basic course plan differently, in accordance with their preparation and training. This allowance for flexibility is very important. Interdisciplinary courses frequently falter if they lack a strong disciplinary base, and faculty cannot do a good job if they are asked to stretch far beyond their training.

The difficulty of finding enough faculty with the relevant expertise is frequently cited as a point against such multicultural courses, as if they were bound to be specially problematic from this point of view. But "great books" courses, for example the countless courses focusing on ancient Greece and Rome, are hardly free of similar problems. The classics department of any university is small, comprising only a few of the faculty who will be teaching such courses. A large proportion of those who routinely teach Euripides and Sophocles and Plato lack disciplinary expertise in classics and never learn either Greek or Latin. They often do a remarkable job within these limits, and sometimes can bring new life to the material in a way that specialists may not. But they do have limits, and need to rely for guidance on secondary literature prepared by specialists. It would therefore be entirely unfair to mention these problems when criticizing new multicultural courses and not to bring the same objections against standard Western civilization courses.

There are, of course, special problems involved in teaching any area in which the relevant scholarly literature is small and still evolving. The non-specialist teaching Plato can choose from among a wide range of translations and annotated editions of the dialogues, and can prepare by using the many helpful and rigorous books and articles that are easily available. The non-specialist who wishes to teach the history of women in antiquity, or the history of slavery, would have had a much more difficult time twenty years ago, since the materials for such a study were available only to specialists who knew Greek and Latin—and not easily to these, since many documents had not been edited. But by now this is far less a problem in all the areas of human diversity. In most areas, outstanding volumes responsibly present the results of specialist research to nonspecialist academics. In the areas covered by Meacham's course there is no problem at all, since there is no language barrier, and the topics of the course have by now generated an enormous, excellent, and easily available literature.

3. *"Design programs for faculty development."* Faculty should not be asked to teach material that lies to some extent outside their prior expertise without being given financial support for the time spent in retraining. Retraining involves time taken away from their course preparation in their own original areas, and also from the research that is an integral part of an active scholar's life. First-rate faculty will not choose to get involved in such new courses unless they are compensated for these sacrifices. It is standard practice to pay faculty summer salary for undertaking new course development projects. Where, in addition to retraining, the course will require extensive cooperation among faculty in different fields, such compensation is particularly important. SUNY Buffalo was able to provide funds for four-week faculty development seminars during two consecutive summers. These seminars were absolutely crucial to the program's success, since even faculty who bring a disciplinary expertise to the course are ill prepared for a complex interdisciplinary exchange without concerted preparation, reading, and dialogue. In the seminars the faculty learned about one another's approaches and methods, discussed common readings, and designed readings and methods that were appropriate for the students in their institution.

4. *Spend time reflecting about methodological and pedagogical issues.* Faculty drawn from literature, economics, political science, and philosophy will not intuitively approach a problem such as voting rights or affirmative action with the same set of questions in mind or the same standards of argument and inquiry. This heterogeneity is basically a good thing, since they can complement one another. But careful thought needs to be given to the methods and concerns that will be built into the course. How much, for example, will the course focus on general philosophical questions, such as the nature of rights and the contrast between relativism and universalism? How much empirical information about the history of the relevant issues will

students be expected to master? How will quantitative analyses deriving from economics be presented, if at all? If these questions are not settled beforehand, the course will be a grab-bag of issues, with no intellectual cohesion.

Faculty need to devote extra consideration to problems that arise when we approach issues on which people in our society have conflicting and strongly held views. Such issues—and these constitute most of the course—raise particular problems for classroom methodology. Here there is a particular need to be aware of the background and character of one's students and to design classroom methods to elicit the best sort of active critical participation. Buffalo students, Meacham argues, tend to be submissive and deferential. Faculty need to discourage them from simply following authority if the benefits of the course for citizenship are to be gained. In this course more than in others, then, instructors carefully withhold their own personal views, designing strategies for evenhanded classroom debate and not seeking to bring debate to a conclusion prematurely. As one instructor in the course said, it is important "to give students permission to be confused."

The Buffalo course is a success because of the careful thought that went into its design and the availability of funding to support faculty development. One should also commend the determination of faculty to criticize themselves and to monitor carefully the development of the course, insisting on high standards of both expertise and teaching. SUNY Buffalo faculty are under substantial public pressure to justify the development of a multicultural course, since their constituency is aware of many criticisms of such courses. Part of their success is explained by the fact that they have devoted a good deal of thought to public relations both in the university and in the community. They publicize the course and discuss it in a variety of public media, focusing in particular on answering the criticism that such courses are "ideological." They articulate the relation of the course to the goals of democratic citizenship in a convincing way, satisfying the public that the effort contributes to public reasoning, not simply to the affirmation of various groups' identity. This is a legitimate area of public concern, and Buffalo has done more to address it than have many comparable institutions.

A different but equally promising basic core course is the newly designed humanities core course at Scripps College, in Pomona, California. The college enrolls around 700 students, all female; although it shares courses with the other Claremont Colleges, the freshman core course is designed for the entire Scripps entering class, and for them alone. It replaces an earlier Western civilization sequence, which was thought to be too amorphous and unfocused. Called "Culture, Knowledge, and Representation," the course studies the central ideas of the European Enlightenment—in political thought, history, and philosophy, in literature, in religion, to some extent in art and music. Sixteen instructors from all departments in the humanities take turns giving lectures, and each leads a small discussion section. The study of the Enlightenment is followed by a study of critical responses to it—by formerly colonized populations, by feminists, by non-Western philosophy, by Western postmodernist thought. The course ends with an examination of Enlightenment responses to these criticisms. (I was invited to lecture to the group on the ways in which feminists could defend liberalism against the criticisms made by other feminists, and on the responses of the international human rights movement to postcolonial critiques of universal categories.)

This course has produced excitement and lively debate among students. Its clear focus, its emphasis on cross-cultural argument rather than simply on a collection of facts, and its introduction of non-Western materials via a structured focus on a central group of issues all make it a good paradigm of the introductory course. Its ambitious interdisciplinary character has been successful in lecture, less so in sections—where students report that some faculty sections deal far more helpfully with the philosophical texts and issues than do others. This unevenness is to be expected in the first year of such a cooperative venture (the course was instituted in 1995–96) and should not be taken to negate the worth of the experiment. Above all, the course has merit because it plunges students right into the most urgent questions they need to ask today as world citizens, questions about the universal validity of the language of rights, the appropriate ways to respond to the just claims of the oppressed. The college community becomes from the very beginning a community of argument focused on these issues of urgent relevance. (It seemed especially commendable that postmodernism was not given the last word, as though it had eclipsed Enlightenment thinking: students were left with a vigorous debate, as instructors sympathetic to postmodernism welcomed my highly critical challenge to those views.)

Infusing world citizenship into the curriculum is a much larger project than the designing of one or two required courses. Its goals can and should pervade the curriculum as a whole, as multinational, minority, and gender perspectives can illuminate the teaching of many standard parts of the curriculum, from American history to economics to art history to ancient Greek literature. There are countless examples of the successful transformation of familiar courses to incorporate those perspectives. Some involve the redesigning of a basic introductory course. At the University of New Hampshire, a grant from the National Endowment for the Humanities produced a new Western civilization course, team-taught in an interdisciplinary manner by four excellent young faculty hired primarily for this course, from philosophy, the history of science, art history, and comparative literature. The four were given time and support to work together designing a course that integrated all these disciplinary perspectives with a focus on ancient Greece and Rome, at the same time incorporating a comparative dimension that correlated Greek achievements in art, literature, science, and politics with those in China at the same period. (The historian of science specialized in Chinese science; the others were supported in doing research into the comparative dimension of their own discipline.) From the beginning, then, students learned to see familiar landmarks of the Western tradition in a broader world context, understanding what was distinctive about Greek science, for example, in part through the Chinese contrast. As a result of the support and stimulation provided by the program, one of the original four teachers, Charlotte Witt, has gone on to produce not only outstanding scholarship on Aristotle's metaphysics but also admirable discussions of the role of rational argument in feminist criticism.

Some transformations involve the redesigning of a standard departmental course offering. At Brown University, a standard moral problems course has recently taken as its focus the feminist critique of pornography and related issues of free speech. In this way students learn to confront these divisive issues and learn basic facts about them while learning the techniques of philosophical analysis and debate. At Bentley College, Krishna Mallick offers a non-Western philosophy class, focusing on the philosophy of nonviolent resistance. At Harvard University, Amartya Sen offers a course called "Hunger and Famine." Standard topics in development economics are given a new twist, as students learn to think about the relationship of hunger to gender and also to democratic political institutions in areas of the world ranging from Africa to China to India. At the University of Chicago, historian David Cohen has developed a comparative course on war crimes that brings current events in Bosnia and Rwanda together with historical examples from many cultures. Other topics that invite a global perspective, such as environmental studies and climatology, world population, and religious and ethnic violence, are increasingly taking center stage in the social sciences and are an increasing focus of student interest.

Such integrative courses acknowledge that we are citizens of a world that is diverse through and through—whose moral problems do prominently include the problems of women seeking to avoid violence, whose history does include a complex international history of both nonviolence and war, whose thought about hunger and agriculture must take cognizance of the unequal hunger of women and of the special circumstances of developing nations. This way of incorporating diversity has the advantage of relying on the disciplinary expertise of the instructor. Students who study Indian famines with Sen probably learn more that is important about India than will those who take a broad and general introduction to world civilization, although they will profit more from Sen's course if they have already had such an introduction. They will learn about religious and economic diversity in the process of thinking about hunger, but in a way that will be focused and made more vivid by being connected to a specific problem analyzed with rigor and detail. Such focused courses, taught by expert faculty, should be strongly encouraged, whatever else we also encourage.

In many institutions, however, there are few faculty available to teach such international courses, at least beyond the introductory level. If even the introductory level requires combining existing expertise with new interdisciplinary training, as the Buffalo course shows, the generation of more advanced elective courses integrating the perspective of world citizenship requires even more planning and institutional support. One particularly imaginative and successful example of a program for faculty development has recently been designed at St. Lawrence University. Called "Cultural Encounters: An Intercultural General Education," the program exemplifies the values of world citizenship both in its plan and in its execution. Cultural Encounters is a program containing courses at both the introductory and the more advanced levels. But its focus has been on redesigning disciplinary courses toward an emphasis on the student's encounter with a non-Western culture.

St. Lawrence is a small liberal arts college. It is a relatively wealthy institution, able to attract a high-quality young faculty. It is well known for the high quality of its study-abroad programs, and 33 percent of its students do study in a foreign country at some point. Its students are a mixed group. The 70 percent who receive financial aid tend to be stronger academically than the other 30 percent, many of whom are intellectually unaggressive. This circumstance required careful thought by the faculty as they tried to design a program that would awaken critical and independent thinking about cultural diversity, and about the more general question whether values are universal or culturally relative. Since 1987 the college has had a requirement that all students take one course on a non-Western or Third World culture; the Cultural Encounters program is intended to supplement the strong offerings in these areas by promoting rigorous foundational questioning.

The program began when St. Lawrence received faculty and curriculum development grants from the Andrew Mellon Foundation and the Fund for the Improvement of Post-Secondary Education. In its initial phase, grants were given to a group of seventeen humanities faculty from different departments, enabling them to meet in a weekly seminar throughout the year, discussing common readings and eventually generating new courses, each in their separate disciplines. The course was informed from the beginning by three decisions. The first was to put philosophy at the heart of the matter, in the sense that all participants did a lot of serious discussing of issues of cultural relativism, along with whatever cross-cultural readings they also did. Grant Cornwell of Philosophy and Eve Stoddard of English, the two directors of the program, shared an orientation to the material that stressed the universal aspect of human needs and strivings and was critical of cultural relativism. They did not wish, however, to impose this perspective on the program as a whole; they wished to use the issue as a basis for faculty dialogue.

Cornwell and Stoddard's second decision was to focus on just two areas of diversity, by selecting two non-Western cultures, the cultures of India and Kenya. They decided to start from these two concrete areas in raising issues about ethnic and religious diversity, gender, race, and sexuality. They decided that they had a reasonable shot at understanding something of the history and traditions of these two places if they used the grant-supported faculty seminar to spend an entire year doing common research on each, but that they would have no chance at all of achieving responsible coverage if they cast their net more widely. Faculty in the group were drawn from philosophy, art history, anthropology, English, religious studies, biology, government, geology, economics, and Spanish.

The group's third decision was its most surprising. This was that all ten faculty involved should live for a month in the regions they studied, after a year of intensive seminar preparation, so that their teaching would be informed by a firsthand sense of what it was like to live to live the life of ordinary women and men in these countries. This undertaking was made financially possible because of the grant, and it proved to be the crucial point in the program. During each of the two visits, the group kept a public diary to exchange and refine views. It is clear that this experience permitted a level of insight into controversial issues such as female circumcision and population control that would not easily have been available from reading alone. It also infused the abstract readings with vividness and made the instructors feel that, for a brief time at least, they had been actual participants in the foreign culture.

Returning to St. Lawrence, the group designed courses reflecting their own disciplinary expertise. David Hornung of Biology and Catherine Shrady of Geology teach a seminar called "Cross-Cultural Perspectives of Healing," comparing the Western medical tradition with Islamic, Hindu, and traditional African approaches. Economics professor Robert Blewett teaches "African Economies," comparing several African economic institutions with their North American counterparts, and focusing on the impact of cultural difference on economic structure. "Students," Blewett writes, "will learn not only of the diversity and complexity of economic relationships in African societies but will increase their understanding of economics in their own society." Codirector Eve Stoddard teaches a comparative course on the discipline and management of the female body, studying practices ranging from female circumcision to veiling to plastic surgery, dieting, and exercise. There is no naive assumption that all these practices are on a par—indeed, one of the aims of the course is to get students to make increasingly refined evaluations. Stoddard's teaching was informed by lengthy, complicated discussions with women in the regions she visited; she is therefore able to give an informed account of the societies' internal debates about these practices. Student writing is encouraged to analyze issues of cultural relativism in a rigorous way.

At the same time, the group required that students who chose the Cultural Encounters "track," taking both introductory and advanced courses within the program, should have a foreign language requirement. If at all possible, they must live and study abroad for their junior year. Two-thirds of the students who go abroad go to Europe, the other third to Costa Rica, Kenya, India, and Japan. Not all the programs, then, directly support the intellectual aims of the Cultural Encounters course material. But even the apparently unrelated exposure to a European culture and its language indirectly serves the program's goals, since mastery of a foreign language and the ability to make oneself at home in a foreign culture are essential abilities of the world citizen, and build an understanding that can be used to approach a further and even more remote culture.

The Cultural Encounters program is a model of responsible teaching in several areas of human diversity. By design, it encompasses not only the encounter with a foreign culture but also related issues of gender, ethnic and religious pluralism, and sexuality, presenting issues of American pluralism in relation to those of global cultural diversity. Its interdisciplinary character ensures that these issues will be faced from many interlocking perspectives, including those of literary study and anthropology, long prominent in multicultural teaching, but also those of economics, biology, philosophy, and foreign language teaching. Where faculty are concerned, the program's focus on intensive training and dialogue and its demand for actual immersion in the culture sets it apart from many programs of this sort, as does its focus on foundational philosophical questions of relativism and universality. On the side of the student, the requirement to learn a foreign language and, where possible, to visit a foreign culture makes the "encounter" serious and prolonged, while critical discussion of basic issues about culture and values in the classroom ensures that the encounter will be conducted in the spirit of Socratic searching rather than of mere tourism, and will prompt dialectical reflection on the beliefs and practices of the student's own culture while the student explores a foreign culture.

Cornwell and Stoddard write that they prefer the term *interculturalism* to the terms *multiculturalism* and *diversity*, since the latter are associated with relativism and identity politics, suggesting a pedagogy "limited to an uncritical recognition or celebration of difference, as if all cultural practices were morally neutral or legitimate." *Interculturalism*, by contrast, connotes the sort of comparative searching that they have in mind, which, they argue, should prominently include the recognition of common human needs across cultures and of dissonance and critical dialogue within cultures. The interculturalist, they argue, has reason to reject the claim of identity politics that only members of a particular group have the ability to understand the perspective of that group. In fact, understanding is achieved in many different ways, and being born a member of a certain group is neither sufficient nor necessary. Knowledge is frequently enhanced by an awareness of difference.

The Cultural Encounters program has had an influence beyond St. Lawrence. Its success has spawned imitations in a wide range of colleges and universities, including Northern Arizona University, the University of Tulsa, Towson State University, Colgate University, Mount St. Mary's College, and Bowling Green State University. In 1995 a national conference brought the many participants in this movement together for an institute to discuss experiences and methodology. Much thought needs to be given to how such a program, designed for a small, prosperous college, can be adapted to colleges with larger student populations and fewer resources.

Meanwhile, at St. Lawrence itself, the program received a major grant from the Christian Johnson Endeavor Foundation in 1995 to support further curricular development of "intercultural studies." Over four years, the faculty group will focus on interdisciplinary study of four themes: transmission of culture across boundaries; gender and culture; questioning development: equity and the environment; and health across cultures. Expanding its focus to include Latin America, the faculty group spent the summer of 1996 doing research in the Caribbean. Cheerfully describing the group's members as "pathological workaholics," Stoddard expresses keen excitement about their new task.

The Cultural Encounters program brings us back to the issues raised by the Stoics. Its designers firmly reject an approach to "multiculturalism" that conceives of it as a type of identity politics, in which the student receives the impression of a marketplace of cultures, each asserting its own claim. They insist on the importance of teaching that the imagination can cross cultural boundaries, and that cross-cultural understanding rests on the acknowledgement of certain common human needs and goals amid the many local differences that divide us. Like much of the ancient Greek tradition, beginning with Herodotus, Stoics suggest that the encounter with other cultures is an essential part of an examined life. Like that tradition, they believe that education must promote the ability to doubt the unqualified goodness of one's own ways, as we search for what is good in human life the world over.

Becoming a citizen of the world is often a lonely business. It is, in effect, a kind of exile—from the comfort of assured truths, from the warm nestling feeling of being surrounded by people who share one's convictions and passions. In the writings of Marcus Aurelius (as in those of his American followers Emerson and Thoreau) one sometimes feels a boundless loneliness, as if the removal of the props of habit and convention, the decision to trust no authority but moral reasoning, had left life bereft of a certain sort of warmth and security. If one begins life as a child who loves and trusts its parents, it is tempting to want to reconstruct citizenship along the same lines, finding in an idealized image of nation or leader a surrogate parent who will do our thinking for us. It is up to us, as educators, to show our students the beauty and interest of a life that is open to the whole world, to show them that there is after all more joy in the kind of citizenship that questions than in the kind that simply applauds, more fascination in the study of human beings in all their real variety and complexity than in the zealous pursuit of superficial stereotypes, more genuine love and friendship in the life of questioning and self-government than in submission to authority. We had better show them this, or the future of democracy in this nation and in the world is bleak.

PURPOSES

D.C. BOK

Any useful discussion of undergraduate education must begin by making clear what it is that colleges are trying to achieve. As W. B. Carnochan has observed, "Lacking adequate criteria of purpose, we do not know how well our higher education works in practice or even what working well would mean." What, then, should colleges try to have their students take away after four years? How should they help young people to grow and develop during this formative period in their lives?

In pondering these questions, several critics of undergraduate education assume that there must be a *single* overarching purpose to college that faculties have somehow forgotten or willfully ignored. For Bruce Wilshire in *The Moral Collapse of the University*, it is to help students integrate fragmented, specialized fields of knowledge in order to address larger questions "about what we are and what we ought to be." For Charles Anderson in *Prescribing the Life of the Mind*, it is "the cultivation of the skills of practical reason." For Bill Readings in *The University in Ruins*, the unifying aim of a college education used to be the interpretation, advancement, and transmission of the "national culture," and it is the demise of this traditional purpose that has left the contemporary university "in ruins," bereft of any animating goal save the vapid claim of "excellence" in all it tries to do.

Nowhere in their writings do the authors make clear why there should be only one dominant purpose for undergraduate education. The very idea seems instantly suspect, since human beings develop intellectually in a number of different ways during their undergraduate years. It is especially implausible in the United States, for American colleges, at least those of the residential variety, to not merely offer courses but also undertake to organize the living arrangements, the recreational and extracurricular activities—indeed, virtually the whole environment in which their students spend four years of their lives. If colleges exercise such a pervasive influence, they should presumably try to help undergraduates develop in even more ways than those fostered by the curriculum alone. Anyone who tries to conflate these forms of growth into a single comprehensive goal is bound to suggest a purpose that is either far too narrow to capture all that colleges should accomplish or far too broad to convey much useful meaning.

Once college faculties look for a series of goals, they will quickly encounter an important threshold problem. According to a school of thought recently expressed by Stanley Fish, the only proper ends of the university are those that involve "the mastery of intellectual and scholarly skills." Fish is not the only professor to hold this view, but his opinion is clearly at odds with the official position of many institutions. College catalogues regularly announce an intention to go beyond intellectual pursuits to nurture such behavioral traits as good moral character, racial tolerance, and a commitment to active citizenship.

Fish's principal argument against trying to develop character or prepare active citizens is that such goals are simply "unworkable." In his words, "There are just too many intervening variables, too many uncontrolled factors that mediate the relationship between what goes on in a classroom and the shape of what is finally a life." Fish believes that universities should confine themselves to what they know how to do. He urges faculty members "to put your students in possession of a set

Reprinted from *Our Underachieving Colleges: A Candid Look at How Much Students Learn and Why They Should Be Learning More*, by Derek Bok (2006), Princeton University Press.

of materials and equip them with a set of skills (interpretive, computational, laboratory, archival) and even perhaps (although this one is really iffy) instill in them the same love of the subject that inspires your pedagogical efforts."

In making his argument, Fish commits one of the basic errors identified in the preceding article: he equates what an undergraduate education should accomplish with what professors can achieve in their classrooms. This is a cramped and excessively faculty-centered point of view. Colleges can hardly undertake to shape the environment in which their students live, in and out of the classroom, throughout four formative years and then insist that their aims are limited to the things their professors know how to do. By tailoring the role of the college to fit the capabilities and interests of its faculty rather than the needs of its students, Fish overlooks all that admissions policies, residential living arrangements, and extracurricular life can contribute to an undergraduate's development. There is much evidence that these aspects of college do have significant, reasonably foreseeable effects on the attitudes, the values, and even the behavior of students (including their moral and civic behavior). Rather than deal with these findings, Fish commits another error common to faculty debates about undergraduate education. He is content to rest his case on his own personal observations during 14 years on the Duke University faculty, pointing out that "While Duke is a first-rate institution with many virtues, I saw no evidence whatsoever that its graduates emerged with a highly developed sense of civic responsibility as they rushed off to enter top-10 law schools, medical schools, and business schools."

In fact, researchers have shown that college graduates are much more active civically and politically than those who have not attended college (even after controlling for differences in intelligence, parental education, and socioeconomic background). In fact, political scientists find that formal education is the *most* important factor in explaining who does or does not go to the polls. Several studies also suggest that certain courses and concentrations, notably in the social sciences, and certain outside activities, such as community service programs, have a positive effect on students' willingness to vote or to work to improve their communities following graduation. Other large-scale studies have found that a variety of extracurricular experiences affect student values in consistent ways. For example, several researchers have concluded that efforts to admit a racially diverse student body and to promote interracial contact through policies on such matters as student living arrangements and racial awareness programs can build greater tolerance. One can surely question such findings or disagree with the methods used in the studies. By ignoring the evidence entirely, however, and relying instead on casual, personal observations, Fish ultimately renders his arguments unconvincing.

Of course, one can accept the possibility of shaping student values and still balk at deliberate efforts to prepare active citizens, build stronger moral character, or promote greater racial tolerance. When colleges seek not merely to sharpen students' minds but also to improve their behavior, thoughtful faculty members may worry that such intentions smack of human engineering and raise the specter of indoctrination.

Anyone harboring such concerns would only be more troubled after reading essays from faculty members of the left, such as Henry Giroux, Frederic Jameson, or Frank Lentricchia. These authors are explicit about their desire to transform undergraduates into citizens committed to fighting social injustice. Lentricchia plainly acknowledges that "I come down on the side of those who believe that our society is mainly unreasonable and that education should be one of the places where we can get involved in the process of changing it." Literature professor Jameson announces that his purpose is to "make converts" and "form Marxists." According to Giroux, professors should try to change society for the better by engaging their students with "critical pedagogy," that is, "pedagogical practices informed by an ethical stance that contests racism, sexism, class exploitation, and other dehumanizing and exploitative social relations . . . [and that] seeks to celebrate responsible action and strategic risk taking as part of an ongoing struggle to link citizenship to the notion of a democratic public community, civic courage to a shared conception of social justice."

Many people would agree with Giroux's objectives, couched in these terms. Who could be against encouraging students to promote social justice and to oppose "dehumanizing and exploitative social relations"? Who is in favor of "racism, sexism, [and] class exploitation"? But problems start to emerge as one reads further. Behind the protective covering of "social justice" lies a distinct political view of society and a specific program of reform. There are official villains: "corporations have been given too much power in this society, and hence the need for educators and others to address the threat this poses to all facets of public life." Giroux likewise has a specific political agenda: "progressive academics must take seriously the symbolic and pedagogic dimensions of struggle and be able to fight for public services and rights, especially the right to decent health care, education, housing, and work." Apparently, then, faculty members must oppose corporations and promote a progressive welfare state agenda not only as private citizens but through their teaching as well.

Since these political goals are matters of legitimate debate, the vision of a university committed to promoting Giroux's agenda is deeply unsettling.[1] Could students who disagree with the agenda feel entirely free to express opposing views? Would appointments and promotions committees in Giroux's university evaluate faculty candidates on their intellectual merits or be swayed by how closely the candidates' teaching and writing conformed to his political vision? As Giroux has clearly stated, educators must regard "all calls to depoliticize pedagogy [and presumably scholarship as well] as simply a mask for domination." What he seems to argue is that everything that goes on in a university is inescapably political, that all efforts at neutrality and objectivity are impossible and disingenuous, and that universities should therefore consciously adopt a political agenda and promote it through their teaching and writing.

To be sure, Giroux and others like him often add that students should be free to disagree with their professors. Still, in Giroux's university, one wonders whether undergraduates concerned about their grade point averages will dare to differ with their instructors when they write their papers and take their exams. One also suspects that junior professors of different political persuasions will feel inclined to follow the prevailing party line in their teaching and writing, lest they be deemed expendable when they are considered for tenure. Since Giroux is not alone in his views, one can understand why some professors (and some others as well) might worry about proposals to shape the character and values of students.

Is there any way of promoting certain values and behaviors that does not amount to unacceptable indoctrination? Yes, but the limits need to be clearly defined and carefully circumscribed. Institutional efforts to build character or change behavior should include only goals with which no reasonable person is likely to disagree.[2] For example, virtually no one would quarrel with attempts to encourage students to be more honest, more scrupulous about keeping promises, more understanding of those of different races, backgrounds, and religions. Nor would anyone in a democracy oppose efforts encouraging undergraduates to vote, inform themselves about public issues, and participate in their communities. It is only when professors use their classrooms to influence *which* promises students keep, *how* they vote, or *what* kind of community programs they support that their teaching is open to criticism.

Even seemingly unexceptionable goals, of course, raise serious questions at the margin. There are surely *some* cases in which principled people can be excused for not telling the truth or for refusing to vote. That being so, a student should always be free to question principles of behavior both in and out of class, no matter how correct they may seem. Although professors may disagree with students about their views on moral or civic questions, they must never use their power to suppress opposing opinions. Nor should the university use coercive authority to impose its moral or civic principles on its students except where necessary to maintain order, protect persons and property, or uphold the integrity of the academic process (e.g., by punishing cheating or plagiarism). In other words, attempts to shape behavior and character, even for widely accepted ends, should be carried out, insofar as possible, through argument, persuasion, and example, not by force or coercive authority.

Notwithstanding Professor Fish, it is perfectly possible to teach moral reasoning or prepare students to be enlightened citizens without having instructors impose their personal ideologies or policy views on their students. Of course, it is conceivable that instructors will abuse their authority in these ways. All manner of familiar subjects can and occasionally do degenerate into indoctrination in the hands of instructors intent on forcing their own beliefs on students.[3] Courses on American politics or political philosophy or international economics are obvious examples. Even required courses in English composition are sometimes used to promote a radical political agenda. It would be folly to abolish all courses susceptible to such instruction. Such a response would decimate the curriculum. Rather, the proper course is surely to rally the entire faculty to consider their responsibilities as teachers and to discourage efforts by particular instructors to misuse their positions by trying to indoctrinate students.

To sum up, attempts to prescribe a single overriding aim or to limit the purposes of college to the realm of intellectual development take too narrow a view of the undergraduate experience and threaten to impose a moratorium on efforts to nurture some extremely important human qualities during four formative years of students' lives. Instead, colleges should pursue a variety of purposes, including a carefully circumscribed effort to foster generally accepted values and behaviors, such as honesty and racial tolerance. Within this ample mandate, several aims seem especially important.[4]

The Ability to Communicate

All undergraduates need to develop the capacity to communicate well with various audiences. The ability to write with precision and grace is the most familiar of these competencies, followed by an ability to speak clearly and persuasively. These skills are widely used by students both during college and after. They are essential in civic life and in almost all the careers that students are likely to enter. When asked what they look for in the college graduates they hire, employers repeatedly emphasize the importance of good writing and effective speaking.

Professors have long entertained the hope that students would acquire these skills *before* coming to college. Efforts were even made more than a century ago to force high schools to do a better job of teaching composition by introducing writing exams for students seeking admission to college. Unfortunately, the wish has never been fulfilled. Freshmen have always arrived on campus deficient in their ability to communicate. They are especially likely to do so now that such a high proportion of young people come to college, often from mediocre schools and from families in which English is not commonly spoken. However welcome or unwelcome the task may be, colleges cannot escape the responsibility of preparing all their undergraduates to speak and write with reasonable precision, clarity, and style.

Critical Thinking

Another aim basic to every college is to enhance the ability of students to think clearly and critically. The importance of this goal is so widely acknowledged that nationwide polls have found that more than 90 percent of faculty members in the United States consider it *the most* important purpose of undergraduate education. In view of the wide variety of interests and backgrounds represented in a typical college faculty, such a strong consensus is impressive.

Defining what critical thinking actually entails, however, is more complicated than many people realize. Some psychologists have invoked a line of thought stretching back to Edward Thorndike's experiments at the beginning of the twentieth century and insisted that there is no such thing as "critical thinking," only an endless series of particular ways to reason about different kinds of problems. There is clearly some truth to this observation. Many subjects are sufficiently complex and unique that no student can think about them productively without first mastering a body of specialized analytic methods and technical knowledge. If all thinking involved such methods, the scope for developing rigorous habits of thought in college would be severely limited, since few undergraduates could acquire enough of the necessary skills and knowledge to address more than a few of these subjects.

Fortunately, many problems arising in everyday life and experience do not require such highly specialized knowledge. Recent research suggests that certain familiar qualities of mind and habits of thought may help resolve such a wide range of problems that every student would benefit from acquiring them. Among these qualities are an ability to recognize and define problems clearly, to identify the arguments and interests on all sides of an issue, to gather relevant facts and appreciate their relevance, to perceive as many plausible solutions as possible, and to exercise good judgment in choosing the best of these alternatives after considering the evidence and using inference, analogy, and other forms of ordinary reasoning to test the cogency of the arguments. These methods will not solve all problems; far from it. But they will solve many and clarify many more, enough to make proficiency in their use well worth the effort.

In addition to these habits of disciplined common sense, certain basic quantitative methods seem applicable to a wide enough range of situations to be valuable for almost all students. For example, a reasonable grasp of statistics and probability may prove useful in thinking about a host of familiar problems, from understanding newspaper articles about risks to personal safety and health to calculating the odds of getting into graduate school or understanding the reliability of opinion polls. A knowledge of mathematics accompanied by practice applying such knowledge to everyday problems and situations can likewise be helpful to students in completing their income tax forms, balancing their budgets, and thinking more rigorously about a variety of complicated subjects. A facility with computers can serve a wide and growing range of purposes in acquiring information and using it to solve problems.

Beyond these few examples, it is hard to think of general problem-solving skills that can be profitably used in enough situations to justify making their study mandatory. Formal logic and advanced calculus, for example, have not proved especially helpful except for solving a limited set of abstract problems. As a result, courses on methods such as these should be available for those who need to learn them, but there is no compelling reason to force every student to master this material.

Moral Reasoning

A related but more controversial aim of college is to help students develop a clearer, stronger set of ethical principles. After decades of neglect, spurred by heated controversies in the 1960s over moral values in public and private life, universities began to offer courses challenging students to think about a variety of practical ethical problems. The growth of these new courses, however, has not persuaded all the skeptics in the faculty. "As for ethics," one sometimes hears, "by the time students begin college, they either have 'em or they don't." According to this line of thought, moral development is the responsibility of parents and schoolteachers, and universities that try to assume the task are destined not to succeed.

Comments of this kind reveal a failure to distinguish between two aspects of ethical behavior. One is the ability to think carefully about moral dilemmas, evaluate the arguments on all sides, and decide on the right thing to do. The other is the desire and self-discipline to put one's conclusions into practice. Parents may have the preeminent role in developing the desire and determination to act responsibly toward others, although, even here, experience teaches that other influences later in life can have an effect. However, when it comes to helping young people to identify ethical problems and to ponder them with care, colleges can certainly make a significant contribution, especially today, when so many students come to college with an easy relativism that clouds their ability to reason about many complex questions, ethical and otherwise.[5]

Analyzing ethical issues, then, is a form of critical thinking much like other forms that faculties regularly teach. Learning to act on one's beliefs, on the other hand, presents a more formidable challenge. For now, the chance to help students learn to identify ethical issues and think about them rigorously is reason enough to include moral education among the aims of college, even if it is not clear whether students will act more ethically as a result. After all, business schools teach students to analyze issues confronting corporations, although one cannot be sure that graduates will have the resolve to act on what they have learned instead of using their powers of rationalization to justify a more expedient course of action. Law schools continue teaching how to reason about legal questions, although they know that students will sometimes ignore the proper answer in order to tell important clients what they want to hear. Much of what faculties teach their undergraduates is conveyed in the faith that most students will use their knowledge and skills for proper ends. There is no reason why colleges should not make the same assumption when they teach students how to think carefully about moral issues.

Preparing Citizens

Another widely neglected aim of liberal education is to prepare students to be informed and active participants in the process of democratic self-government.[6] Until the mid-twentieth century in America, educators believed that a sound liberal education would suffice to serve this purpose adequately. During the intervening decades, however, circumstances have changed in important ways that cast serious doubt on this assumption. For one thing, the amount of information citizens need to fulfill their civic duties has become far larger. To understand the broad array of important policy issues and make informed choices among rival candidates, today's voters would need a working knowledge of a vast agenda of complicated subjects, such as healthcare, social security, international relations, and global warming. It is impossible to familiarize students with all these issues, let alone prepare them for the many new questions that will arise during their lifetimes. How to respond to this problem poses an extremely difficult challenge, but one cannot assume that it will be enough merely to offer a traditional liberal education.

In addition, prior to World War II, college students were a small elite, and educators could safely assume that they would take an active part in political and civic life. Now undergraduates in America make up a large share of a generation in which civic apathy is the norm. Young people vote less than any other age group and less than people of their age voted in generations past. For the first time in modern memory, a majority of young Americans turning 18 will have grown up in a home in which no parent *has ever voted*. In such an environment, one cannot assume that graduates will even bother to go to the polls, let alone play an active part in their communities. Civic education is arguably no longer simply a matter of conveying the knowledge and skills to help students make enlightened judgments about politics and public affairs; colleges must consider whether there is anything they can do to imbue undergraduates with a stronger commitment to fulfill their civic responsibilities.

Living with Diversity

Along with acquiring civic and moral responsibility, undergraduates need to learn to live and work effectively with other people and enter into fulfilling personal relationships. For generations, this part of growing up was taken for granted as a fact of life; it did not entail significant responsibilities for American colleges beyond enacting prohibitions against violence and theft and establishing parietal rules to limit contact between the sexes. In the aftermath of the civil rights revolution, however, blacks, Hispanics, and other minority groups began to enroll in growing numbers on predominantly white campuses, forcing universities to deal with a series of problems and controversies growing out of the troubled history of race in America. The feminist movement and the heightened awareness of subtle and not-so-subtle discriminations against women infused relationships between the sexes with new and urgently felt tensions. Gay rights activists began to assert themselves and urge college administrators to meet the needs of those with different sexual preferences.

Universities have not been the only institutions to experience these changes. All sorts of organizations find themselves employing a more diverse workforce and offering goods and services to a more heterogeneous set of publics. In this environment, with a population growing steadily more multiracial and a legal system bristling with safeguards for ethnic and religious groups, institutions of every kind expect colleges to prepare their students to work effectively with many different kinds of people. Meanwhile, some intellectuals worry whether a nation divided among so many ethnic and religious groups can hold together as a society, and they look to universities to do their part in fostering tolerance and understanding.

No college can sensibly refrain from doing what it can to help students learn to function successfully in this self-consciously diverse population. Failure to do so would not only seem insensitive to evident needs in the society and workforce; it would ignore deeply felt concerns that exist on every campus. When racial tensions flare, or women angrily protest against sexual violence, or gay students are openly persecuted, campus authorities must respond. They quickly find that merely enacting rules and meting out punishment will not suffice. In one way or another, every college must seek to apply the words of Martin Luther King Jr.: "We have inherited a large house, a great world house, in which we have to live together, black and white, Gentile and Jew, Catholic and Protestant, Moslem and Hindu, a family unduly separated in ideas, culture, and interest, who, because we can never again live apart, must learn somehow to live with each other in peace." The challenge is to determine how to help students learn to live together with understanding and mutual respect while not appearing insensitive to the aggrieved, unfairly accusatory to the majority, or rigidly doctrinaire to the larger society.

Living in a More Global Society

Americans increasingly find themselves affected by circumstances beyond our borders—by other governments, distant cultures, foreign nationals, international crises. Freer trade exposes American workers to overseas economies that can create new jobs or take them away. The lives of ordinary citizens are touched by distant wars, terrorist threats, Middle East oil shortages. Changing methods of communication and travel multiply opportunities for contact across national boundaries. Problems ranging from environmental dangers and narcotics trafficking to trade wars and nuclear weapons draw our government into new collaborative relationships with other nations. All these developments suggest that students today will need to know more than earlier generations of undergraduates about international affairs and about other countries and cultures.

Colleges must respond to these challenges, since their graduates are so likely to be involved with other nations and foreign nationals as business executives, public officials, lawyers, or simply citizens. Exactly how to prepare students for such a future, however, poses great difficulties. No one can hope to gain even a rudimentary knowledge of the many nations of the world, each with its own language and culture. Nor can undergraduates foresee in college just which cultures and languages will prove important to them after they graduate. No one can predict future events in the international arena with any certainty. Thus the peculiar challenge colleges face is how to construct a foundation of knowledge and understanding that will help their students adapt and respond effectively to whatever international problems and opportunities may confront them in their later lives. More than most of the aims that colleges pursue, this task is novel and remains clouded by uncertainty and confusion.

A Breadth of Interests

Another, more traditional, aim of a college education is to give students the capabilities, knowledge, and breadth of interests to enable them to enjoy full and varied lives. Some of these interests may be intellectual—for example, in history or philosophy. Others may be artistic—understanding and enjoying music, poetry, and painting or actually practicing some form of art as an avocation. Still others may involve engaging in a lifetime sport, such as tennis, swimming, or running.

Such a variety of interests brings many blessings. It can help to avoid the dangers of excessive specialization by providing wider perspectives to enlighten judgment. It offers escape from a life too preoccupied with vocational concerns. It supplies the knowledge to understand more of what is occurring in the world, from global warming to presidential campaigns to chronic trade deficits. It furnishes the mind to contemplate the perennial human problems of good and evil, justice and injustice, war and peace. It affords a means for escaping boredom through all manner of absorbing private pursuits.

Although the case for acquiring a breadth of interests and knowledge seems compelling, it is hard to know exactly how colleges should respond. The task may seem manageable on first impression, but only so long as one assumes that students will remember most of what they are taught, especially in their general education classes. Unfortunately, this assumption is patently unrealistic. Most students retain only fragments, and even these will steadily disappear beyond recall if there is no occasion to use them. The limitations of memory are an important reason why attempting to compile lists of essential facts and ideas that every student should know is likely to prove a fruitless enterprise. They also cast doubt on ambitious schemes to expose all students to a grand array of courses covering vast areas of human experience.

How, then, should colleges proceed? By trying to awaken interests that will inspire students to continue learning in a variety of fields throughout their lifetimes? By teaching undergraduates basic methods of inquiry that will enable them to explore subjects that might otherwise seem remote and impenetrable? By concentrating on a few fundamental ideas and texts in enough detail that students will conceivably remember much of what they have learned?

There are no easy answers to these questions. That is doubtless one reason why the subject of general education has attracted so much interest since its inception more than a century ago, and why it continues to provoke such heated debates.

Preparing for Work

A last, but still contested, aim of undergraduate education is to prepare students for a career. In his *Politics*, Aristotle asks, "should the useful in life, or should virtue, or should the higher knowledge be the aim of our training?" Disagreement on this point persists to this day. Humanists have expressed special hostility toward attempts to dilute the liberal arts with courses that prepare students for work. To William Schaefer, former chair of the English department and an academic vice chancellor at the University of California, Los Angeles, "the most critical issue [is] purging the undergraduate curriculum of vocational training." More than 30 years ago, philosopher Robert Paul Wolff also urged that all vocational courses be banished from the curriculum, arguing that such instruction inevitably diverted students from a pure desire to master a subject. Only through an effort to achieve such mastery, he believed, "sharply different from both the dilettante's superficiality and the professional's career commitment, can a young man discover who he is and whom he wants to be."

These opinions seem strangely out of touch with the realities of contemporary American life. For the vast majority of college students, regardless of the college they attend, the undergraduate years are a time when they must choose a vocation. This decision will have a profound effect on their lives, and it is only natural that they should take it seriously and seek whatever help their college can give them. Indeed it is hard to know how any student could truly understand "whom [he wants] to be" *without* thinking carefully about what career to pursue. To make such choices wisely, students need to learn more about the role different professions play in society; the moral dilemmas their members commonly face; the social, psychological, and material rewards they can bring; and the mental, physical, and temporal demands they impose. Surely colleges should do something to help students acquire such knowledge so that they can make informed decisions about a question so vital to their future lives.

In most American colleges, a majority of undergraduates will not merely have to choose a vocation; they will move directly into the workforce and look for a job. For them, college is the last chance to prepare themselves for work by acquiring skills and knowledge of the kind best learned through formal education. Institutions with large numbers of such students can hardly deny them the opportunity. Colleges that did so would soon have to close their doors for lack of enough applicants, and deservedly so, since they might leave their students ill equipped to enter their chosen callings.

Preparing students for a career, of course, does not merely mean giving them the essential skills for their first or second jobs. Such a curriculum might have only temporary value and could easily crowd out other important purposes of undergraduate education. Devising a more appropriate preparation, however, presents a number of problems. How much time should faculties allot to the purpose in view of the other aims of a college education? How can vocational and liberal arts courses reinforce each other instead of existing in isolation, or even at cross-purposes with one another? Will vocational courses of the traditional kind actually help undergraduates to have a successful career, or will a solid grounding in the liberal arts accomplish more over the long run? These are questions that call for answers from any college with substantial numbers of students moving directly into the workforce. What is not justifiable—nor even practical—is to reject out of hand the very possibility of vocational courses or the legitimacy of preparing students for productive, satisfying careers.

This completes my list of the basic goals of undergraduate education. Although these aims have been treated separately for purposes of clarity, they interact and overlap in many important ways. Courses on moral reasoning help to develop skills in critical thinking and do so using problems that are especially interesting and provocative for many students. Classes in writing can also teach students to think critically and carefully. Courses that prepare students for enlightened citizenship can add breadth to their studies. Conversely, studying moral issues, or living with classmates of different races, or learning about globalization can all help develop more enlightened citizens. These reinforcing qualities do not constitute a problem but an advantage. If particular courses and activities can serve several purposes simultaneously, colleges are more likely to succeed in embracing a number of separate goals within a single four-year curriculum.

Despite the great variety of American four-year colleges, the aims described here seem suitable not only for all students but for all institutions as well. It is hard to imagine a college that would not want to improve the critical thinking of its undergraduates, enhance their communication skills, broaden their interests, and address in some manner their vocational needs. It is equally hard to understand why every college should not try to improve students' capacity to think carefully about moral questions and to fulfill their responsibilities as citizens. Naturally institutions will differ about how best to pursue these goals. Variations in student bodies, resources, and educational philosophy will dictate different choices. Yet the basic ends to which colleges should direct their efforts seem likely to be and to remain more or less the same.

After reflecting on the purposes just listed, some readers are bound to object that worthy goals have been omitted. How about nurturing powers of imagination and creativity? Fostering leadership ability? Developing judgment and wisdom? These are all valuable aims for any college that is able to pursue them. As the preceding article pointed out, however, many faculties have adopted impressive goals without knowing how to achieve them. Such quixotic efforts waste students' time and often leave them disappointed and disillusioned. These are consequences every college should try to avoid. With that cautionary note, the purposes described in this article are included not because they are the only important goals that human ingenuity can conceive, but because they are the only worthwhile aims for colleges to pursue that this author is able to recommend with enough confidence and understanding to warrant their inclusion.

Notes

1. The problem of indoctrination is not limited to left-wing professors. Well-meaning programs sponsored by a university to improve race or gender relations can easily fall into the hands of officials who announce as fact to incoming freshmen such debatable propositions as "all institutions in America are deeply sexist" or "racism involves only acts of discrimination by whites against minorities." See, for example, Charles Alan Kors, "Bad Faith: The Politicization of the University *In Loco Parentis*," in Howard Dickman (ed.), *The Imperiled Academy* (1993), p. 153. Race and gender programs can be helpful when they allow open discussion of differences of opinion, potentially unfair practices, misunderstandings, and the like, but dogmatic assertions and indoctrination by persons in authority can be just as wrong in the context of promoting understanding among the races or between the sexes as in other academic settings.
2. Exceptions may be made for private colleges, such as religiously affiliated institutions, that actively promote a set of special beliefs or behaviors, provided they make this clear to prospective students and their families.
3. The meaning of indoctrination is not as obvious as it may seem. For example, teachers of "the dismal science" are sometimes accused of indoctrination because they accept the basic assumptions of neo-classical economics and do not devote class time to an in-depth discussion of possible alternatives. Similarly, professors of Constitutional law can be said to indoctrinate by refusing to entertain challenges to the legitimacy of the Constitution and the form of government it embodies. Nevertheless, there is a difference between these examples and, say, using a basic writing course to teach students how language is employed to oppress women, minorities, and the poor. In providing instruction on economics or Constitutional law, a college may well decide to offer elective courses in which to consider alternative systems, but it is perfectly legitimate to refuse to use basic courses in these fields for this purpose. In such classes, as currently taught, instructors are not seeking to use the classroom to spread their own private set of controversial beliefs; they are making a commonsense judgment about how best to use scarce class time in a basic course to be of greatest use to the largest number of students. In the writing class, instructors cannot make this claim. Rather, they are taking a required course established for other purposes and deliberately using it to promote their personal political agendas.

4. The list that follows does not attempt to include the multitude of purposes that might be appropriate for particular groups of students—learning Russian, for example, or writing poetry, playing football, or acquiring a knowledge of chemistry. The aims described here are those of broad enough applicability to be appropriate for virtually all undergraduates.

5. Even those who understand the difference between moral reasoning and the will to act on one's beliefs sometimes dismiss the former as relatively unimportant. Gordon Marino, philosophy professor at Saint Olaf College, illustrates this tendency in a recent article in the *Chronicle of Higher Education*. "The fantasy," he declares, "seems to be that if up-and-coming accountants just knew a little more about ethics, then they would know better than to falsify their reports so as to drive up the value of company stock. But sheer ignorance is seldom the moral problem. More knowledge is not what is needed. Take it from Kierkegaard: The moral challenge is simply to abide by the knowledge we already have." Gordon Marino, "Before Teaching Ethics, Stop Kidding Yourself," *The Chronicle Review*, 50 *Chronicle of Higher Education* (Feb. 20, 2004), p. B5.

   If Professor Marino were correct, one wonders why philosophers spent so much time in years past on practical moral issues. In fact, such questions are often not as simple as he suggests, and the problems have only grown more complicated in recent decades. Today, more than ever before, there is good reason for college graduates to know "a little more about ethics." Modern medicine has created a host of ethical problems that demand the most careful analysis: stem cell research and cloning, for example, not to mention the dilemmas doctors face in deciding whether to withhold the truth from patients or to test new drugs made by companies to which they have financial ties. Lawyers face vexing questions in reconciling their duties to a client with their obligations to court and society. Even accountants will often encounter difficult choices when they discover practices that seem to meet the letter of the accounting rules but arguably raise broader issues of public policy. In all these cases, students need to develop habits of thought that will help them to recognize moral problems when they arise and to reason about them carefully enough to arrive at thoughtful decisions on how to respond.

6. Colleges do devote much attention to developing qualities of mind and spirit that can contribute to enlightened citizenship. Critical thinking, racial tolerance, general knowledge—indeed, almost everything a college tries to do—can be described as civic education in the broadest possible sense. For present purposes, however, the term *civic education* is used more narrowly to refer to efforts to give all students the essential knowledge that every citizen needs and to strengthen their commitment to participate effectively in the process of democratic self-government—as, for example, voters, candidates, public servants, commentators, campaign workers, or simply concerned citizens.

FROM THE AMERICAN CENTURY TO THE GLOBAL CENTURY

ASSOCIATION OF AMERICAN COLLEGES AND UNIVERSITIES

In recent years, the ground has shifted for Americans in virtually every important sphere of life—economic, global, cross-cultural, environmental, civic. The world around us is being dramatically reshaped by scientific and technological innovations, global interdependence, cross-cultural encounters, and changes in the balance of economic and political power. Only a few years ago, Americans envisioned a future in which this nation would be the world's only superpower. Today it is clear that the United States—and individual Americans—will be challenged to engage in unprecedented ways with the global community, collaboratively and competitively.

These seismic waves of dislocating change will only intensify. The world in which today's students will make choices and compose lives is one of disruption rather than certainty, and of interdependence rather than insularity. To succeed in a chaotic environment, graduates will need to be intellectually resilient, cross-culturally and scientifically literate, technologically adept, ethically anchored, and fully prepared for a future of continuous and cross-disciplinary learning. Learning about cultures and social structures dramatically different from one's own is no longer a matter just for specialists. Intercultural learning is already one of the new basics in a contemporary liberal education, because it is essential for work, civil society, and social life. Scientific and technological learning are equally fundamental and may well determine the difference between those who are prepared to deal with change and those who are buffeted by it.

Narrow Learning Is Not Enough

The general public—and many college students—continue to believe that choosing a "marketable" college major is the key to future economic opportunity. Guided by this conviction, many students see study in their major field as the main point of college, and actively resist academic requirements that push them toward a broader education. Many policy makers hold a similar view of career preparation, evidenced by their support for occupational colleges and programs that promise initial job readiness but not much else.

Those who endorse narrow learning are blind to the realities of the new global economy. Careers themselves have become volatile. Studies already show that Americans change jobs ten times in the two decades following college, with such changes even more frequent for younger workers. Moreover, employers are calling with new urgency for graduates who are broadly prepared and who also possess the analytical and practical skills that are essential both for innovation and for organizational effectiveness:

- "Employers do not want, and have not advocated for, students prepared for narrow workforce specialties. . . . Virtually all occupational endeavors require a working appreciation of the historical, cultural, ethical, and global environments that surround the application of skilled work." (Roberts T. Jones, president, Education Workforce Policy, LLC)

Reprinted from *College Learning for the New Global Century* (2007), Association of American Colleges & Universities.

Employers' Views

"At State Farm, only 50 percent of high school and college graduates who apply for a job pass the employment exam. . . . Our exam does not test applicants on their knowledge of finance or the insurance business but it does require them to demonstrate critical thinking skills and the ability to calculate and think logically. These skills plus the ability to read for information, to communicate and write effectively, and to have an understanding of global integration need to be demonstrated. This isn't just what employers want; it's also what employees need if they are to be successful in navigating the workplace."

—Edward B. Rust Jr., Chairman and CEO, State Farm Insurance Companies

"To be successful in global companies like Siemens, business managers must be able to navigate local market differences, seek opportunities for collaboration between businesses, and promote cooperation across functions. A solid foundation in the liberal arts and sciences is necessary for those who want to be corporate leaders."

—George C. Nolen, President and CEO, Siemens Corporation, New York

---

- "Intel Corp. Chairman Craig Barrett has said that 90 percent of the products his company delivers on the final day of each year did not exist on the first day of the same year. To succeed in that kind of marketplace, U.S. firms need employees who are flexible, knowledgeable, and scientifically and mathematically literate." (Norman R. Augustine, retired chairman and chief executive of Lockheed Martin Corporation)

- "[The] curriculum needs to help students develop. . .leadership, teamwork, problem solving, time management, communication and analytical thinking." (Business-Higher Education Forum)

- "[Business leaders are] frustrated with their inability to find '360 degree people'. . . . " (Findings from 2006 focus groups among business executives)

- "Integrated capabilities are the key to this industry's future." (Keith Peden, senior vice president of human resources, Raytheon Company, 2006)

Using a business rather than an academic vocabulary, employers are urging more—and better—liberal education, not less. Because employers view innovation as their most important comparative advantage, they seek to hire graduates who can think beyond the routine, and who have the ability not just to adapt to change, but to help create it.

Responding to employer concerns, the engineering community is already pioneering the approach to a twenty-first-century liberal education recommended in this report. The engineers' goal is to graduate what some are calling "T-shaped students," with the vertical part of the "T" representing the traditional parts of an engineering degree, and the crossbar pointing to competencies traditionally identified with the "liberal arts"—including ethics, global knowledge, intercultural literacy, and strong communication and collaborative skills (see fig. 1). The "T" itself shows that these different capabilities need to be *integrated* so that students can apply them in work and community settings.

Humanists may see similar potential in the letter "H," where the crossbar represents field-specific knowledge and skills and the vertical bars represent capacities related to context and community. Whatever the model, the message to students is the same. Employers do not want "toothpick" graduates who have learned only the technical skills and who arrive in the workplace deep but narrow. These workers are sidelined early on, employers report, because they cannot break out of their mental cubicles.

Broad capabilities and perspectives are now important in all fields, from the sciences to business to the humanities. The new economic reality is that narrow preparation in a single area—whether that field is chemistry or information technology or history—is exactly the opposite of what graduates need from college. Study-in-depth remains an important part of the overall pattern for college learning. But students deserve to know that focusing only on one specialty is far from enough.

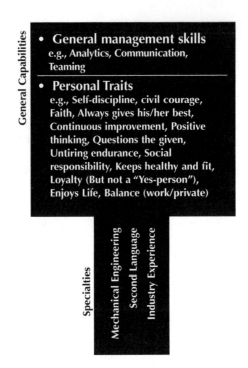

Figure 1 What Siemens Advises for Success: Build a T-shaped Profile

By now, readers who value liberal education may be actively protesting: it's not just about the economy! And we agree. The aims and benefits of liberal education go far beyond work to enrich every sphere of life—environmental, civic, cultural, imaginative, ethical. These important topics are addressed in later pages.

But this report places special emphasis on liberal education as the portal to economic opportunity because so much of the public—and so many students—have been told just the opposite. Today, powerful social forces, reinforced by public policies, pull students—especially first-generation and adult students—toward a narrowly instrumental approach to college. This report urges educators to resist and reverse that downward course. It is time to guide students away from limiting choices and toward a contemporary understanding of what matters in college.

The way forward is to make a new commitment to provide a horizon-expanding liberal education for all college students, not just for some. Through much of the twentieth century, liberal education was identified only with selected academic fields—the arts and sciences—and, more recently, with the most selective colleges and universities. The net effect has been to position liberal education as an elite option, the expected form of learning at The University of Chicago, Pomona College, or the University of Virginia—and in all campus honors programs—but hardly necessary for everyone.

In this new global century, these older views stand in the way of needed change. Liberal education has been America's premier educational tradition since the founding, and the recommendations in this report build on its core strengths: broad knowledge, strong intellectual skills, personal and social responsibility. But in a democratic society, the goal must be to extend opportunity and excellence to everyone, and not just to a fortunate minority.

The way to achieve this goal is to make the essential learning outcomes a shared priority for all students, whatever their chosen areas of study, and wherever they enroll in college.

The World Is Changing and Liberal Education Must Change Too

This report recommends, in sum, a challenging and liberating education that develops essential capacities, engages significant questions—both contemporary and enduring—in science and society, and connects analytical skills with practical experience in putting knowledge to use.

In doing so, this report also calls on educators to adapt liberal education to the needs of our time. Certain aims of liberal education are enduring through every era, to be sure. Helping students master the arts of inquiry, analysis, and communication is the signature strength of a liberal education and a core reason why it is the best and most powerful preparation both for the economy and for democracy.

But the key to continued national vitality is the ability of citizens to adapt creatively to new challenges. Liberal education in the United States did transform its practices, dramatically, just a century ago. Starting about 1870 and continuing into the next century, the rise of new disciplines and a new role for the United States in the world led to revolutionary change in the organization of the undergraduate curriculum. A comparably dramatic change in the approach to liberal education is needed today to better prepare college graduates for the complex realities of this new global century (see fig. 2).

The first step toward a contemporary approach to liberal education is to remap the educational landscape so that all parts of the academy and all fields of study address—in ways appropriate to their subjects—the essential learning outcomes.

To take this step, higher education will also need to break out of the academic categories and silos that were established in the last curriculum revolution, and that still organize the division of labor across most campuses, from community colleges to research universities.

As a result of the last curricular revolution, liberal or liberal arts education is conventionally defined as study in selected academic fields: the humanities, the social sciences, the sciences, and, by the last quarter of the twentieth century, the arts as well. The many professional and applied fields—including engineering, business, education, and health—have not traditionally been seen as part of a liberal education.

The resulting lines of demarcation guide students' educational choices to this day on thousands of campuses. Because of these inherited dividing lines, millions of college students are routinely compelled to choose *either* a liberal arts and sciences pathway *or* a professional pathway just to fill out their college applications. The message sent by this forced choice is exactly the opposite of what students need to know.

The traditional boundaries between the liberal arts and the professional fields are not just a bureaucratic inconvenience. In practice, they have created academic silos that impede faculty and staff efforts to foster a more holistic and integrative approach to college learning. It is in everyone's interest to create new crosswalks and communal spaces that support educational collaboration across the traditional academic dividing lines between the liberal arts and sciences and the professional

	Liberal Education in the Twentieth Century	Liberal Education in the Twenty-First
What	• an elite curriculum • nonvocational • an option for the fortunate	• a necessity for all students • essential for success in a global economy and for informed citizenship
Where	• liberal arts colleges or colleges of arts and sciences in larger institutions	• all schools, community colleges, colleges, and universities; across all fields of study (recommended)
How	• through studies in arts and sciences fields ("the major") and/or through general education in the initial years of college	• through studies across the entire educational continuum: school through college (recommended)

Figure 2 Remapping Liberal Education

fields. But if collaborations are to succeed, they need to be based in shared goals. The essential learning outcomes, which place strong emphasis on teaching students to integrate and apply their learning, provide this larger sense of shared interests.

Within this altered educational landscape, many different pathways to a liberal education are possible. Students will continue to be able to choose among a variety of educational settings: universities, colleges, community colleges, faith-based institutions, technical institutes. Students will still concentrate in selected fields because, while not sufficient, studies in depth are important. They will certainly need a rich mix of arts and sciences courses in order to learn about the wider world. **The key change is that, whatever and wherever they elect to study, each college student will be helped to achieve, in ways appropriate to his or her educational interests, a high level of integrative learning and demonstrated accomplishment across the full range of essential learning outcomes.**

Movement toward this needed remapping has already begun. The long-standing boundaries between the professional fields and the arts and sciences have started to blur. Engineering and technology fields have forged the way. The Accrediting Board for Engineering and Technology now looks for evidence that programs are teaching students to integrate their liberal arts competencies with their technical studies. Similar developments are emerging across many professional fields, and on many campuses.

Simultaneously, many arts and sciences departments are placing new emphasis on "practical experience" and "applied learning" through internships, service learning, student projects, and community-based research. Many campuses also are inventing a "vertical" or four-year framework for general education, with the explicit goal of fostering new connections between students' specialized studies and their broader learning about science, cultures, and society.

Students themselves are adding to this remapping by choosing double majors or majors and minors that freely span the "liberal arts/professional" divide.

These forward steps notwithstanding, many of the most imaginative efforts to forge new connections between the liberal arts and sciences and professional studies still hover on the margins. Higher education needs new leadership and new determination to move these promising developments from the margins to the center.

Engaging Twenty-First-Century Realities

Breaking out of the academic silos is a good beginning, but much more needs to be done in order to align teaching and learning practices with the realities of the new global century. In the twentieth century, both school and college studies were organized, reflecting the sensibilities of the industrial age, in terms of modular parts: disciplines, subjects, courses, credit hours. But this modular curriculum, organized a century ago and still largely intact, has become increasingly dysfunctional. The disciplines are taught as ends in themselves, and so too are most courses. Yet students are taking courses in many different disciplines, and often at two or more institutions. For many, the result is a fragmented and incoherent educational experience rather than steady progress toward deeper and more integrated understandings and capacities.

The expected curriculum is usually defined, often with enabling state regulation, in terms of specific "core" subjects in school and specific general education categories in college (see fig. 3). State "distribution" requirements for students' general education courses are the far-reaching legacy of the mid-twentieth-century view that equated liberal education with general education, and assigned it to the first two years of college.

But the frontiers of knowledge, both in scholarship and the world of work, now call for cross-disciplinary inquiry, analysis, and application. The major issues and problems of our time—from ensuring global sustainability to negotiating international markets to expanding human freedom—transcend individual disciplines. The core subjects provide a necessary foundation, but they should not be taught as ends in themselves. From school through college, students also need rich opportunities to explore "big questions" through multifaceted perspectives drawn from multiple disciplines.

Even in terms of the old modular curriculum, where each subject has been implicitly defined as a self-contained area of learning, the curricular pathways from school to college have become chaotic and redundant. Thanks to the vigorous promotion of Advanced Placement courses and dual enrollment

Core Subjects in the Schools

The National Commission on Excellence in Education (1983) made influential recommendations for the four years of high school. Most states are still working to meet these goals for all students.

4 years	English
3 years	Social studies
3 years	Science
3 years	Mathematics
½ year	Computer science
2 years	Foreign language (for college-bound students)

Statewide Guidelines for General Education Distribution Requirements at the Collage level

Forty States provide guidelines for general education for all public institutions in the state, for a system within the state, and/or to guide student transfer. Almost all conform to the following general pattern:

1-2 courses	Writing
3-4 courses	Arts and Humanities
2-3 courses	Social Sciences
2 courses	Science
1 course	Mathematics

Five states have made global and/or intercultural studies a requirement, and several others specify particular disciplines.

Figure 3 A Fragmented Curriculum: Many Courses, Few Connections

SOURCES: The National Commission on Excellence in Education, A Nation at Risk: The Imperative for Educational Reform: A Report to the Nation and the Secretary of Education (Washington, DC: U.S. Department of Education, 1983); Robert Shoenberg, ed., General Education and Student Transfer: Fostering Intentionality and Coherence in State Systems (Washington, DC: Association of American Colleges and Universities, 2005).

(college courses for high school students), as many as three million students are already taking "college-level" courses before finishing the twelfth grade. At the same time, because of the shortcomings of school preparation, at least 40 percent of all college students have to take at least one remedial course in college, essentially revisiting material that they should have learned in high school.

Calls for aligning high school outcomes with college-level skills abound. But the learning students need for this new global era cannot be achieved simply by rearranging the existing patchwork of "core courses" at the school level and "general education requirements" at the college level. To help students achieve the essential learning outcomes, it will be necessary to spend time, across all levels of school and college education, revisiting the larger purposes of education and rethinking the kinds of connections across disciplines and levels of learning that will best prepare graduates for a complex and fast-paced world.

Key Questions to Guide School-College Planning

The following questions, keyed to twenty-first-century challenges, are intended to spark the needed school-college dialogues—among educators, across disciplines, with employers and policy leaders, and with the wider public. Ultimately, these questions call for the mapping of more purposeful curricular pathways, from school through college and across the disciplines.

How can we ensure that graduates are well prepared to participate in an interdependent global community?
"The Global Situation: The benefits of development are not shared equitably. . . . Injustice, poverty, ignorance, and violent conflict are widespread and the cause of great suffering. . . . The foundations of global security are threatened. These trends are perilous—but not inevitable."
—The Earth Charter

Global integration is now our shared context. The potential benefits of global interdependence are extraordinary, but so too are the challenges. Wealth, income, and social power are dramatically unequal within and across international boundaries. We are reminded daily of the clash of cultures, histories, and worldviews. The globe itself is fragile and vulnerable as are our shared civic spaces. These global challenges will be with us for the foreseeable future. Yet today, less than 10 percent of four-year graduates are leaving college globally prepared. The United States is a world power. But it provides most of its students with a parochial education.

In this new era of interdependence, how should Americans prepare to contribute to a shared and sustainable future? What should Americans learn about the global economy and its changing dynamics? About world ecosystems and our capacity to sustain them? About the United States as a world power? About the realms of human heritage, cultures, religions, and laws, as well as the continuing quests to advance human dignity and justice? And, in this era of fundamentalisms and competing certainties, how will students engage and learn with people whose worldviews, histories, beliefs, and aspirations may be different in crucial ways from their own?

How can we prepare graduates for a global economy in which change and innovation are constants?
"The way forward is to become more open, more experimental, and to embrace the unknown. . . . The bar for innovation is rising. And simply running in place will not be enough."
—The Council on Competitiveness

Innovation is widely touted as America's most important competitive advantage and the key to continued prosperity. But the currently dominant educational practices in American education were forged over a century ago, in an era that placed high value on broad understanding, reasoning, and abstract analysis and that gave only passing educational attention to collaboration, problem solving with external communities, and learning from experience.

In the context of a global economy that demands innovation, technological savvy, entrepreneurship, and risk taking, what kinds of educational practices will prepare graduates to get things done in the world? How do we teach them to critically evaluate the quality of information and convert this information into knowledge and action? How will students learn to solve problems effectively in collaboration with people from very different backgrounds and cultures? How will we teach students to combine entrepreneurial creativity and technological know-how with humanistic values and vision?

How can we prepare all graduates for a world shaped by scientific and technological advances and challenges?
"Together, we must ensure that U.S. students and workers have the grounding in math and science that they need to succeed and that mathematicians, scientists and engineers do not become an endangered species in the United States."
—The Business Roundtable

Americans have grown accustomed to world leadership in science, technology, engineering, and mathematics (the STEM fields). As a society, we take for granted the unprecedented prosperity that this world leadership provides. But the majority of Americans are scientifically illiterate.

What progression of studies, beginning in school and continuing in college, will dramatically raise the level of STEM preparation and literacy for all students? How do we reverse the alarming trends that show Americans falling steadily behind *both* in the percentage of college graduates who prepare in STEM fields *and* in the actual numbers of Americans who go on to successful careers in science and technology? How can we persuade all Americans that STEM literacies are essential rather than a special option reserved for the gifted? What will be required to dramatically change the way STEM fields are taught so that the majority of Americans will no longer be left behind?

What kinds of learning are needed for knowledgeable and responsible citizenship?
"The death of democracy is not likely to be an assassination from ambush. It will be a slow extinction from apathy, indifference, and undernourishment."

—Robert Maynard Hutchins

Americans live in the world's most powerful democracy. But democracy, as the founders recognized, is much more than a design for government and lawmaking. Rather, it is a framework for a special kind of society in which citizens must take mutual responsibility for the quality of their own communities and their shared lives. Democracies are founded on a distinctive web of values: human dignity, equality, justice, responsibility, and freedom. The meanings and applications of these values are rarely self-evident and frequently contested. Moreover, most students never actually study such issues in any formal way, either in school or in college. Many students, the research shows, do not think that civic engagement is even a goal for their college studies.

What are the complementary roles of school and postsecondary education in educating citizens? What is the particular role of college in preparing graduates to contribute to the greater good, both at home and abroad? What should Americans learn about the history and prospects for democracy, in our own society and in other parts of the world? How do we cultivate what Martha Nussbaum has called the "narrative imagination" so that graduates are better able to engage diverse communities and other societies? How do we prepare citizens to address the growing and destabilizing divisions between those with hope and those who still live on the margins of our own and other societies?

How do we help graduates compose lives of meaning and integrity?
"It is difficult/to get the news from poems/yet men die miserably every day/for lack/of what is found there"

—William Carlos Williams

Throughout history, liberal education—and especially the arts and humanities—have been a constant resource, not just for civic life but for the inner life of self-discovery, values, moral inspiration, spiritual quests and solace, and the deep pleasures of encountering beauty, insight, and expressive power. Ultimately, it is this dimension—serious engagement with questions of values, principles, and larger meanings—that marks the essential difference between instrumental learning and liberal learning. For communities and individuals that are denied social power and voice, the arts and humanities make possible what Azar Nafisi calls "the Republic of the Imagination," a space where those who have been marginalized and persecuted can draw courage and hope from stories, language, culture, and example. For all human beings, the arts and humanities invite exploration of the big and enduring questions about what it means to be human. They also foster the crucial human and civic capacity of empathy, the ability to care about and even identify with perspectives and circumstances other than one's own. The moral power of the arts and humanities has been one of the secrets of their lasting influence; those who experience these sources of inspiration readily see their importance, both for the human spirit and for community.

In this new century, the dizzying pace of change and the unabated prospects for social and environmental disruption will continue to place enormous strains on individuals as well as communities. Each individual will need sources of inner fortitude, self-knowledge, and personal renewal.

Liberal Education and Values

"Liberally educated students are curious about new intellectual questions, open to alternative ways of viewing a situation or problem, disciplined to follow intellectual methods to conclusions, capable of accepting criticism from others, tolerant of ambiguity, and respectful of others with different views. They understand and accept the imperative of academic honesty. Personal development is a very real part of intellectual development."

—AAC&U Board of Directors' Statement on Academic Freedom
and Educational Responsibility

Taking time for reflection on one's own values will be crucial. Everyone will need to consider not just how to pursue a course of action, but the value and integrity of alternative courses of action.

How, in this kind of environment, do we prepare students to cultivate their own inner resources of spirit and moral courage? How do we enable them to engage moral and social dilemmas with clarity about their own values as well as the capacity to hear and respond to others' deeply held commitments? How do we prepare graduates to make difficult ethical choices in the face of competing pressures? And how, without proselytizing, do we foster students' own development of character, conscience, and examined values?

Fulfilling the Promise of College in the Twenty-first Century

In college and university classrooms, in think tanks, in business organizations, and in government and corporate offices across the country, thoughtful people have begun to discuss the key questions with a new sense of urgency. Commissions have formed; reports are starting to multiply; resolve is growing. And, on many college campuses, one can find substantial centers of innovation where dedicated groups of faculty and staff already are responding creatively to just these kinds of questions. Many have invented impressive interdisciplinary curricula that engage learners brilliantly with every one of the questions outlined above. There are dozens of active reform movements across every facet of collegiate learning—from the first to the final year, and between the curriculum and student life.

To date, however, both these emerging discussions and the educational changes inspired by them are too preliminary, too fragmented, and far too limited. New approaches are emerging. (For a list of effective educational practices, see appendix A.) But these are too often relegated to the margins of institutional life. Many of the most significant reforms advance without reference to one another, and there is no shared sense of the whole. As a result, the impact on student learning is fragmented and diluted.

These discussions do not yet include the public, nor have they had much impact on education policy at the state and national levels. In fact, for the public universities and community colleges that educate over 75 percent of college students, state requirements concerning "general education" are locked into an old system of required credits in specific areas of study (a few courses each in the arts and humanities, social sciences, and sciences) that functions today as a resistant barrier to the innovative curricula many faculty members want to create (see fig. 3 on p. 55).

The twentieth-century legacy of relegating liberal/general education to the first two years of college alone was codified across the nation. But that code has become a stranglehold on educational creativity and needs revision.

Students, for the most part, have been left entirely out of the debates about their own long-term educational interests. It is the nation's first-generation and less advantaged students—young and old alike—who are the most likely to enroll in institutions and programs that provide narrow training. First-generation students also are less likely than others to take courses in mathematics, science, social studies, humanities, history, foreign languages, or even computer science. First-generation students are flocking to college. But many are missing out on a twenty-first-century education.

Because the prospects for American society are dependent on the quality of learning, insider discussions and educational reforms that mainly serve the most fortunate are inadequate. It is time to create a genuinely inclusive national dialogue about higher learning in the twenty-first century, and to embrace a vision for the future that is worthy of a great democracy.

And it is time to mobilize new determination and new leadership commitments—on the part of educators, policy makers, and the public as a whole—to advance substantially our national investment in educationally effective practices that can help all students understand, prepare for, and achieve the important outcomes of a twenty-first-century liberal education.

MUTUAL SUBVERSION: A SHORT HISTORY OF THE LIBERAL AND THE PROFESSIONAL IN AMERICAN HIGHER EDUCATION

DAVID F. LABAREE

I want to tell a story about American higher education. Like many historical accounts, this story has a contrapuntal quality. As we know, historians frequently find themselves trying to weave discordant themes into complex patterns in the hope of making harmony. The reason for this is that simple themes are hard to find in the account of any complex social institution, especially one like education, which is composed of a motley accumulation of historical residues and social functions. We often come across one point about education that makes sense and then find a counterpoint that also makes sense. If we cannot eliminate one in favor of the other, then we try to put them together in a way that does not violate the rules of harmony and historical logic. In the effort to do so we, therefore, find ourselves in the business of writing fugues.

In this case I will be making two alternative arguments about long-term trends in the history of American colleges and universities. The initial argument is that over the years professional education has gradually subverted liberal education. The counterpoint is that, over the same period of time, liberal education has gradually subverted professional education. My aim is to show how these two views can be woven together by arguing that the professional has come to dominate the goals of higher education while the liberal has come to dominate its content. I will let you be the judge of whether this attempt produces more noise than music.

Point: The Shift from the Liberal to the Professional

One recurring theme in the history of American higher education is that the professional has been displacing the liberal. In a recent book, Norton Grubb and Marvin Lazerson develop this theme with great effectiveness, arguing that American education, especially at the tertiary level, has become increasingly vocationalized and professionalized over the years.[1] At the root of this change is what they call "the education gospel," the firmly held belief that education exists in order to provide society with the job skills it needs and to provide individuals with the job opportunities they want. The authors acknowledge that this belief has yielded some real social and educational benefits. It has made higher education more attractive, both to students seeking jobs and employers seeking workers, and it has provided a strong basis for public support of higher education by demonstrating that the university is not simply a stronghold protecting the privileges of the elite but a people's college promoting the public welfare. But they also point out the downside of this shift toward the professional. From that angle, the change has replaced broad liberal curriculum with narrow vocational curriculum, undercut the quality of learning by focusing on winning jobs rather than gaining knowledge, and stratified educational programs and institutions according to the status of students' future jobs.

Reprinted from *History of Education Quarterly* 46, no. 1 (spring 2006), Blackwell Publishing, Ltd.

What is new about Grubb and Lazerson's book is their view that this trend toward the vocational has a plus side, whereas the scholarly literature, in general, has portrayed the change as overwhelmingly negative. But the argument that this change has been taking place is commonplace in the historical scholarship on American higher education. In Laurence Veysey's classic account, the rise of the American university in the late nineteenth century was characterized by the emergence of utility and research as dominant orientations, only partially offset by a lingering attachment to liberal culture.[2] Clark Kerr argued that the American university drew on two European precursors—the British college, with its emphasis on undergraduate liberal education, and the German graduate school, with its emphasis on research and graduate education—but then added a third distinctively American element, the land-grant college, with its emphasis on vocational education and providing practical solutions to public problems.[3]

Most historical accounts have emphasized this third element, which, in combination with the second, is seen pushing the university from a focus on providing students with a liberal education to a focus on preparing them for work and producing economically useful research. The evidence supporting this position is strong. The United States did not invent the university, but it did invent three distinctive forms of higher education, all of which had a strong vocational mission: The land-grant college was designed to prepare graduates in the practical arts and to enhance industry, as reflected in the use of the words "agricultural" and "mechanical" in the titles of so many of these institutions; the normal school was targeted solely at the preparation of school teachers; and the junior college and its heir, the community college, were invented primarily to provide vocational education for what some founders called the "semi-professions."[4] The large majority of college students in the United States today are enrolled in colleges and universities that had their origins in one of these three types of vocational institutions.

The main explanation for the growing vocational orientation of the American university is its vulnerability to the market. As Martin Trow and others have pointed out, in the absence of strong state funding and state control, institutions of higher education in the United States have always been subject to strong market pressures.[5] They depend heavily on student enrollments to generate income, in the form of both student-paid tuition and per-capita state appropriations, which means they have to cater to the demands of the consumer. They also rely on income from alumni donors and research grants. Their partial autonomy from state control gives them the freedom to maneuver effectively in the educational market in order to adapt to changing consumer preferences, donor demands, and research opportunities. Over the years, student consumers have increasingly expressed a preference for getting a good job over getting a liberal education, and donors and research funding agencies have demonstrated their own preferences for useful education and usable knowledge.

A broad literature has emerged that explores this market-based shift from the liberal to professional in American higher education. For example, there is: David Brown on the role of credentialism in generating the expansion of higher education in the late nineteenth century;[6] Donald Levine on the rise of vocationally oriented programs, schools, and colleges in the 1920s and 30s;[7] Alden Dunham on the emergence of practically oriented regional state universities in the 50s and 60s;[8] Steven Brint and Jerome Karabel on vocationalization in community colleges over the twentieth century;[9] Steven Brint on the shift in the numbers of students, degrees, and faculty members within universities from liberal arts to professional schools in the late twentieth century;[10] and Roger Geiger on the rise of consumerism and market-oriented research in the research university at the end of the century.[11] Also there is my own work, which has explored the consequences of the historical shift in educational goals, especially at the higher levels, away from democratic equality and toward social efficiency and social mobility.[12]

Counterpoint: The Shift from the Professional to the Liberal

The evidence strongly supports the thesis that American higher education has seen the expansion of the professional at the expense of the liberal. However, in many ways this argument may be dead wrong. Instead of professionalizing liberal education, maybe we have really been liberalizing professional education.

There is also a lot of historical evidence to support this counter thesis—especially when you look at the *content* of the expanding professional sector of higher education. Although most of the growth in higher education has been in the professional schools rather than the core disciplinary departments, Brint points out that the curriculum of the professional schools has become increasingly disciplinary. As he puts it: "Occupational and professional programs have moved closer to the center of academic life partly because they have modeled themselves on the arts and sciences—developing similarly abstract vocabularies, similarly illuminating theoretical perspectives, and similarly rigorous conceptual schemes."[13]

Professional education has only recently taken this academic turn. Before the twentieth century, most professional training took place through an apprenticeship to an experienced practitioner, with the academic component of this preparation largely consisting of reading the books in the practitioner's library.[14] The shift toward the academic occurred as a result of the gradual incorporation of professional education into the university beginning in the late nineteenth century. Since World War II, the academic content of professional education in a wide range of fields has steadily increased, only recently provoking a reaction demanding more attention to practice-based preparation.

Consider how academic the content of professional education has become in most professional schools, starting with the two most extreme cases—divinity and law. Practicing clergy have long derided their seminary training as largely useless in developing the skills they need to practice their profession effectively. Divinity schools are notorious for focusing primarily on the academic study of theology, not on preaching, pastoral care, finance, leadership, and the other central practices in the profession.[15] Likewise law schools (especially at elite universities) have long focused on the study of jurisprudence, logic, and argumentation, all central elements in a liberal education. Little time is spent on developing skills at doing things that form the core of professional legal practice, like writing briefs, arguing cases in court, negotiating deals, and handling clients.[16] In recent years both fields have developed movements to introduce clinical professional studies within the almost entirely academic programs in their fields, and these movements have encountered considerable resistance.

But what about other professional fields which have reputations for being less academic? Teacher education, for example, is considered a baldly vocational program by the arts and sciences faculty on campus. But the graduates of these programs have long complained that their professional education was relentlessly theoretical, focused on the psychology of learning and curriculum, the sociology of the teacher and the school, the history and philosophy of education, while offering little guidance about how to carry out the role of classroom teacher—that is, teaching a set curriculum to a particular group of students.[17] Business schools have the same reputation. The master's degree in business administration in most business schools is remarkably abstract and academic, largely cut off from practices in the real world of business. Whereas the dominant discipline in education schools is psychology, the dominant discipline in business schools is economics. An M.B.A. provides a grounding in the theory of economics, enhanced by studies in the sociology of organizations, the psychology of effective leadership, and other disciplinary explorations of the business environment; business practice is something students are expected to learn on the job. Business education used to be more practical in orientation, but reforms initiated by the Ford Foundation and Carnegie Corporation in the 1950s promoted a model of business education that was academic, research based, disciplinary, and graduate level.[18] Medical education has a much stronger component of preparation for clinical practice than most other professional programs, but even here most clinical training takes place after completion of the four-year medical degree program, which is dominated by academic study of the human sciences.

If the content of professional education has been growing more academic, then how can we understand the growth of professional schools relative to the arts and sciences? The traditional interpretation of the latter development is that the disciplines have been losing out to the professions within the university, thus demonstrating the growing triumph of the vocational over the liberal. Instead, however, the growth of professional schools may be a sign of the expanding power of the disciplines. Maybe the university is not becoming more professional; professional schools are becoming more academic. From this view, the theoretical is actually displacing the practical in higher education. The disciplines are in effect colonizing the professional schools, transforming professional education into liberal education in professional garb.

Our own field in the history of education is an interesting case in point. Only about a third of the members of the History of Education Society are found in history departments, whereas two-thirds are in schools of education. One interpretation is that this represents a decline in the field, showing a loss of our identity as historians and the subordination of the discipline to the professional mission of the education school. But the interpretation I favor is the reverse; that we are a strong field expanding its influence into the realm of professional education. We have a greater impact this way than if we remained within history departments. I have been teaching in education schools for twenty years, but my job is to provide students with a liberal education. I teach critical reading and analytical writing, and the material I use for this is the history of education. This is what education schools want me to teach; this is what the students need me to teach. I think large numbers of us are in the same situation. In many ways, students in professional schools need us more than students in history departments. Unlike the latter, education students are not in college to get a liberal education, but being there offers us an opportunity to give them a liberal education anyway. In this way the growth of professional education in the university provides rich opportunities for the growth of the disciplines. The latter is unintended, even unwanted, but it is nonetheless real.

From this perspective, then, the shift toward the professional and the vocational in the history of American higher education has been more rhetorical than substantive.[19] Maybe it is best understood as largely a marketing tool, which makes a university education seem more useful and relevant than it really is. David O. Levine showed how liberal arts colleges after World War I marketed their traditional liberal programs as places to learn the practical skills needed for success in the white-collar workplace.[20] We see colleges and universities doing the same today. Liberal learning has come to be represented as training in business-relevant skills in communications, problem solving, and entrepreneurship. Over the past century, higher education in general may have simply been relabeling old curricula as new professional programs—more spin than substance. This is an old story in higher education, where the medieval curriculum and medieval structure of degrees have persisted in the face of enormous changes in economy and society in the last thousand years.[21]

If the disciplines have indeed subverted the professional schools in higher education, one explanation is academic inertia. Old curriculum content keeps colonizing new institutional forms and gaining new rationales for its relevance: a case of old wine in new bottles. Another explanation comes from Ralph Turner's characterization of American education as a system of contest mobility.[22] From this perspective, the aim of education is to prepare students to compete effectively in the contest for social positions, and that means a system that maintains maximum flexibility for students by providing an education that allows access to the broadest array of occupational possibilities. In practical terms this leads us to defer specialization until the last possible moment in order to keep options open. Thus American education emphasizes general education over specialized education, and this is true even in the most advanced studies and in professional training programs. So, unlike most of the rest of the world, doctoral programs in the United States require extensive coursework before launching students into a dissertation, and most of these courses are aimed at providing a general background in the field. At the same time professional programs of study include a hefty component of liberal arts content. Both Ph.D. and M.B.A. students want to be prepared for a variety of possible positions and not just one, and our consumer-responsive system of higher education gladly accommodates them.

Trying to Resolve the Paradox

So we have two opposing theses about the history of American higher education. One says that this has been a story of growing market influence, which has elevated professional education over liberal education. The other says that this is a story of curriculum inertia and consumer ambition, in which liberal education has perpetuated itself by colonizing professional education and in general has displaced specialized education. Both arguments have a lot of evidence to support them, and I do not want to abandon either. But how can we resolve these differences? I argue that these two themes can be brought together in harmony if we understand how they both resonate with several fundamental characteristics of American education. One such characteristic is *stratification*: the peculiar dynamic that organizes American education into an extended hierarchy. The other is *formalism*: the peculiar dynamic in American education that creates a gap between form and substance, between the purpose of education and its content.

Position in the Educational Pecking Order

Stratification is at the heart of American education. It is the price we pay for the system's broad accessibility. We let everyone in; but they all get a different experience, and they all win different social benefits from these experiences. In this way the system is both strongly populist and strongly elitist, allowing ordinary people a high possibility of getting ahead through education and a low probability of getting ahead very far.

If stratification is a central element in both elementary and secondary education, it is the dominant element in higher education. In this way, as in others, American universities are schools on steroids. A college or university's position in the academic pecking order is a fact of life that shapes everything else in that institution. And one of the key ways that institutions differ according to academic rank is in their location on the spectrum between the vocational and the liberal. At the bottom of the hierarchy are community colleges, which have a strong identity as places that provide practical vocational preparation for a wide variety of occupational positions. At the top are the leading research universities, which have an equally strong identity as places that provide theoretical and liberal education, even in programs designed to prepare professionals. In between is an array of colleges and universities that are more practical than the schools at the top and more theoretical than the schools at the bottom. In the public sector of higher education in my own state of California, the community college system is at the bottom, the University of California system is at the top, and the California State University system is in the middle. Every state has its own equivalent distribution. It is just the way things are.

What this system of stratification suggests is that the changing historical balance between the liberal and professional, like so much else about American higher education, has varied according to the institution's position on the status ladder. So the expansion of community colleges and regional state universities have represented a shift toward the vocational, while the liberal disciplines have been holding their own at research universities and even expanding into professional programs. That is what observers like Steven Brint, Richard Chait, and Andrew Abbott have concluded.[23] If so, then what we are observing is just a simple bifurcation of change processes, where the professional is subverting the liberal at the bottom of the system while the liberal is subverting the professional at the top. From this perspective, the resulting dualism is just another case of stratified access to knowledge, which is an old story in American education at all levels.

Dynamics of the System

This characterization is true, as far as it goes. But I want to suggest that what is really going on is both more complicated and more interesting than this. There is a fascinating double dynamic that runs through the history of American higher education, pushing the system simultaneously to become more professional and more liberal. Like so much else about the system, this process has operated through market mechanisms rather than conscious planning. It is a story of how individual institutions have struggled to establish and enhance their positions in the highly competitive higher education market. The result is a set of institutional trajectories that are rational from the perspective of each institution's interests; but these trajectories accumulate into a dynamic structure of higher education that is both pathological (in the way it is at odds with itself) and dysfunctional (in its impact on society).

The general pattern is this: The system expands by adding a new lower tier of institutions that are more vocational in orientation than those already in existence. Over time these new institutions zealously imitate their higher status predecessors by shifting toward producing a more liberal form of education. Then another tier of institutions comes forward to fill the vacated vocational role. Thus the system as a whole is continually expanding the realm of vocational education while individual institutions are relentlessly turning away from the vocational and aspiring to the liberal.

There are three core dynamics that fuel these processes. One is that existing institutions of higher education enjoy enormous advantages over newcomers: they have more social capital (since they have educated society's leaders), more cultural capital (since they have already enlisted the best academic talent), and more economic capital (since they have established access to wealthy alumni and accumulated substantial endowments).

The second core dynamic is that institutions at all levels of the status order in higher education have a strong incentive to seek a higher level: moving up promises to increase an institution's enrollments, grants, contributions, faculty recruitment, public influence, and overall prestige. And in order to move up the ladder, institutions need to imitate their betters, adopting the educational forms and functions that worked so well for those above them. Of course, since the older schools have a huge advantage in the status race, odds are that the aspirations of the newcomers will not be met. But this does not eliminate continuing hopes for future glory. As is true with the aspirations that individual citizens harbor for personal social mobility, a few successes are enough to keep hope alive for the many. High possibilities can trump low probabilities in the mind of the aspirant. Every up and coming college president looks at the great historical success stories of institutional mobility for their inspiration: Berkeley, Hopkins, Chicago, and Stanford were all relative latecomers who made it to the top. We could be next.

The third dynamic in the system is that expansion comes by introducing new institutions rather than by expanding the old ones. Existing colleges have every reason for letting others handle the influx. To increase enrollments would be to dilute the college's social exclusiveness, its academic reputation, and its distinctive identity. Better to segment the market by holding the high ground for yourself and letting newcomers establish positions in the less valuable ground below you. That way, the system grows by maintaining the classic dual principles of American education—accessibility and exclusivity.

Four Tiers of American Higher Education

Let us look at how this process has played out over time. In the beginning, there were the colonial colleges. Through the luck of being first more than through intellectual eminence, these colleges established a dominant position that proved largely unshakable over the next two centuries. They were followed in the nineteenth century by a series of public colleges that eventually developed into flagship state universities. Most of the first group and many of the second came together to form what is now the top tier of American higher education: research universities. The institutions in this tier are the most prestigious, selective, and academically credible in the country; they have the greatest wealth, offer the most liberal curriculum, and educate the smallest proportion of students.

Next up was an American invention, the land-grant college. These institutions were funded by an array of public land distributions, starting in the 1830s and continuing through the end of the century (most particularly the Morrill Acts of 1862 and 1890). They were explicitly (though not exclusively) given a vocational mission. In the words of the original Morrill Act, these colleges were intended "to teach such branches of learning as are related to agriculture and the mechanic arts . . . in order to promote the liberal and practical education of the industrial classes in the several pursuits and professions of life. . . ."[24] These institutions became the core of the second tier of American higher education, made up of public universities below the top level, often identified by the label "A & M" or the word "State" in the title, to distinguish them from the flagship state university.[25]

The next arrival was another institutional invention, the normal school, which began before the Civil War and flourished in the second half of the nineteenth century. These schools were founded for an explicitly vocational purpose, to train schoolteachers. They formed the core of what evolved into the third tier of American higher education, the regional state universities that educate the lion's share of this country's university students.

Last up was the junior college, which first emerged in the 1920s and later evolved into the community college. This became the fourth and final tier in the system. Like the land-grant college and the normal school, its mission was vocational—in this case to prepare people for semi-professional job roles (that is, jobs below the level sought by graduates of four-year colleges).

Running Away from Vocationalism

These are the four tiers of American higher education. As you go down the hierarchy, these institutions progressively show the following characteristics. They have: arisen more recently, adopted a more vocational mission, opened themselves to a broader range of students, and channeled graduates to lower-level occupations. And each of the lower three tiers continues to show more vocational tendencies than the tier above it. However, and this is the crucial point, these institutions all tried very hard to run away from their original vocational mission in order to imitate the high-status liberal model offered by the top tier. The result, of course, was not a replication of the latter model so much as a pale imitation. For each tier as a whole and for most of the institutions within it, attaining the next level up the scale was simply not possible. The incumbents retained too many advantages, and the newcomers did not have any of the three forms of institutional capital (social, cultural, or economic) in sufficient quantities to compete effectively with their betters. But this did not keep them from trying.

The pattern over time is clear. Students wanted the most socially advantageous form of college education they could get, and this meant one that looked as much as possible like the Ivies and that opened up the maximum number of job opportunities. So each new tier of institutions expanded liberal studies at the expense of vocational training. As the research university became the hegemonic model for American higher education in the early twentieth century, the lower-tier institutions evolved into places that called themselves, and looked like, universities. Land-grant colleges led the way in this development. Normal schools had farther to go and their evolution took longer, but they got there as well. Starting as the equivalent of high schools in the mid nineteenth century, they evolved into teacher colleges at the turn of the twentieth century, became state liberal arts colleges in the 1930s and 40s, and finally turned into full service state universities in the 1950s, 60s, and 70s.

The exception in this evolutionary process was the community college, but not for lack of trying. Large numbers of students in junior colleges and community colleges have long been voting with their feet for transfer programs that allow them access to liberal education at four-year colleges and universities. If past practice had persisted, this consumer pressure would have forced these institutions to develop into universities, just like their predecessors in land-grant colleges and normal schools. But state legislators and policymakers finally drew the line. After all, it is an enormously expensive proposition to transform a narrowly focused vocational institution into a university, and the social benefits of this transformation are questionable. The university allows more consumers access to the high status model of higher education. But this model is much more costly than vocational education, and it produces a glut of graduates who compete for the top occupational positions, leaving middle-level jobs to be filled by the also-rans from the elite competition, who lack the required vocational skills. Social mobility goals have generally trumped social efficiency goals in the history of American education, but there are fiscal and occupational limits to America's willingness to subsidize individual ambition. Social efficiency calls for a more rational process of allocating people to positions and for an educational system that provides vocational as well as general education. So state governments in the twentieth century overwhelmingly refused to allow junior colleges to grant four-year degrees. Instead, they were encouraged to develop into the enormous community college system we see today. The process of institutional evolution finally came to a halt with the fourth tier.

Consider where this leaves me in my analysis. I began with the argument that American higher education has been shifting toward the professional, and then I tried to show how the system has actually been moving toward the liberal. But in light of the dual dynamic that mobilizes the history of American higher education, one answer to this paradox is that the system has been going both ways. It has recurrently moved from the liberal to the professional and then quickly returned toward the liberal over time. Each tier began as an exercise in vocational education and then regressed to the liberal mean under the influence of market pressure and status emulation. This then prompted the development of another vocational tier, which also soon remodeled itself in imitation of the top institutions.

All of this finally ended with the community college, which was not allowed to pursue the path of its predecessors. But is the process still going on in the second and third tiers of the system? I think so. Many of the land-grant schools in the second tier have made it into the inner circle of the research university, as signaled by membership in the American Association of Universities, and others are trying. Regional state universities in the third tier run into structural problems: for example, the reluctance by state educational leaders to allow California State University campuses to offer doctoral degrees, which are generally reserved for the research universities in the University of California system. But this does not keep students at San Jose State from demanding an education that is as much like Berkeley as they can get. Given the vulnerability of universities to consumer pressure and the ingenuity of university presidents in pursuing institutional mobility, it would be risky to bet that these institutions will not continue to evolve toward the research university model. Faculty members are another important factor pushing hard in this direction. A hefty proportion of the faculty in third-tier universities are graduates of doctoral programs from first-tier universities. This is a simple consequence of the status order of higher education, where advanced graduate education is concentrated at the top while undergraduate education is concentrated at the bottom. Thus most professors experience severe downward mobility when they graduate and take their first academic positions. Their preference in resolving this status loss is generally to move up the ladder and return to a position at a research university; but since the math clearly shows that this is unlikely, a second best option is to increase the liberal content and graduate orientation of their institution. Thus the ambitions of students, faculty, and administrators in third-tier institutions all converge in a conspiracy to drive these universities to pursue the brass ring.[26]

Vocational Purpose, Liberal Content

In my analysis of the relation between the professional and the liberal in higher education, the central message is this: *Professional education may be the biggest recurring loser in the history of American higher education.* Responding to the rhythms of the educational status order, the professional keeps surging forward as the central thrust of new colleges and then retreating, as new institutions revert to the liberal norm.

Yet there is one way in which vocationalism has emerged as an increasingly dominant factor in American education at all levels: in shaping the system's purpose. In elementary, secondary, and higher education in the United States, practical education has indeed come to be dominant, but primarily in the broad realm of purpose rather than the contained realm of curriculum. The process of shifting educational purposes toward the practical has been going on in American education at all levels over the last 150 years. If you examine closely the sources I cited earlier in support of the proposition that higher education has become more professional, they are actually making a case for the dominance of professional purpose rather than practice.[27] Taxpayers and government officials have increasingly approached education as an investment in human capital, by providing the economy with the skilled workers it needs—a purpose I have called social efficiency. At the same time, students and their parents have increasingly approached education as a way to get ahead in society, by helping graduates to get a good job, a nice spouse, and a boost up the social ladder; I have called this goal social mobility. In my own work, I have argued that the social mobility goal in particular has come to the fore in the last century, pushing democratic equality and even social efficiency into the background. Since this is an argument I have made at great length elsewhere, I will not belabor it here.[28] Suffice it to say that the growing power of the social mobility goal has dramatically distorted the teaching and learning process by focusing students' attention on the extrinsic rewards that come from acquiring an academic credential and thus undermining the incentive to learn. The result is a rising culture of credentialism and consumerism in both lower and higher education in the United States, where the emphasis is on the exchange value of education rather than its use value.

However, just because practical purposes have come to infuse and disfigure American education at all levels does not mean that the content of higher education is also becoming more practical. On the contrary, as I have shown earlier, higher education is liberalizing professional schools and colonizing them with disciplinary theorists. At the same time that the purpose of education is becoming more practical, the content of education is becoming more liberal. This pattern is not as contradictory as it seems. As Ralph Turner points out, the same consumer pressure that promotes credential accumulation over learning also promotes general over specialized education, since general education is what opens up the most possibilities and defers the longest the need to put all your eggs in one vocational basket. Vocational education has always carried with it a degree of specialization that can easily turn into a dead end, as we have seen with high school vocational education programs, which too often have prepared people for jobs that no longer exist. The liberalization of professional education is in part driven by the contest mobility system of keeping your options open. But in part it is also driven by the realization that too much specialization is dangerous; that the best preparation for work is a liberal education; and that specialized training is more efficiently provided on the job than in the university.

In fact, the process of liberalization would be a great thing if it were not for the fact that credentialism manages to empty the quest for liberal learning of much of its learning. What we end up with, then, is an increasingly liberal form of education even in professional schools and doctoral programs—the opposite of what much of the literature has been telling us. But this expanded sphere of liberal education has been emptied of content by the same vocational purposes that brought about this expansion in the first place.

Therefore, maybe what we have is a case of *formalism* playing itself out at two levels in higher education. At one level, we have liberal content masquerading as professional education, where the practicality of the education rides on its ability to land you a job rather than to teach you vocational skills. But at another level, we have a system that offers students little inducement to learn this liberal content because their attention is focused on what they can buy with their educational credentials rather than how they can apply their knowledge. So liberal education has succeeded in colonizing professional education, but credentialism has turned this liberal education back toward vocational goals. The content is liberal, but credentialism means that the content does not really matter.

One thing is clear: This process is educationally dysfunctional. But colleges and universities still provide the degrees students need in order to quality for the jobs they want, and employers still hire people based on these degrees; so for practical purposes, the system works. As a result, American higher education is both increasingly vocational in purpose and increasingly liberal in content. In light of the shaping power that vocational purposes have had over the years on American education at all levels, however, the victory of the liberal in the realm of curriculum seems largely Pyrrhic. So in the end, the two themes we started out with—the liberal and the professional—ultimately weave together into a fugue, but this fugue may not be music to our ears.

Notes

1. W. Norton Grubb and Marvin Lazerson, *The Education Gospel: The Economic Power of Schooling* (Cambridge: Harvard University Press, 2004).
2. Laurence R. Veysey, *The Emergence of the American University* (Chicago: University of Chicago Press, 1965).
3. Clark Kerr, *The Uses of the University*, 5th ed. (Cambridge: Harvard University Press, 2001), 7–14.
4. Gregory L. Goodwin, "A Social Panacea: A History of the Community-Junior College Ideology" (ERIC document ED 093–427), 157.
5. Martin Trow, "American Higher Education: Past, Present, and Future," *Educational Researcher* 7:3 (March 1988): 13–23; Dominic J. Brewer, Susan M. Gates, and Charles A. Goldman, *In Pursuit of Prestige: Strategy and Competition in U.S. Higher Education* (New Brunswick: Transaction Publishers, 2002).
6. David K. Brown, *Degrees of Control: A Sociology of Educational Expansion and Occupational Credentialism* (New York: Teachers College Press, 1995).
7. David O. Levine, *The American College and the Culture of Aspiration, 1915–1940* (Ithaca: Cornell University Press, 1986).
8. Edgar Alden Dunham, *Colleges of the Forgotten Americans: A Profile of State Colleges and Universities* (New York: McGraw Hill, 1969).
9. Steven Brint and Jerome Karabel, *The Diverted Dream: Community Colleges and the Promise of Educational Opportunity in America, 1900–1985* (New York: Oxford University Press, 1989).
10. Steven Brint, "The Rise of the 'Practical Arts,'" in *The Future of the City of Intellect: The Changing American University* ed. Steven Brint (Stanford: Stanford University Press, 2002), 231–259.
11. Roger L. Geiger, *Knowledge and Money: Research Universities and the Paradox of the Marketplace* (Stanford: Stanford University Press, 2004).

12. David F. Labaree, *How to Succeed in School Without Really Learning: The Credentials Race in American Education* (New Haven: Yale University Press, 1997).
13. Brint, "The Rise of the 'Practical Arts,'" 238.
14. John S. Brubacher and Willis Rudy, "Professional Education," in *ASHE Reader on the History of Higher Education* ed. Lester F. Goodchild and Harold S. Wechsler (2nd ed.) (Boston: Pearson Custom Publishing, 1997), 379–393.
15. Everett C. Hughes and Agostino M. DeBaggis, "Systems of Theological Education in the United States," in *Education for the Professions of Medicine, Law, Theology, and Social Welfare* eds. Everett C. Hughes, Barrie Thorne, Agostino M. DeBaggis, Arnold Gurin, and David Williams (New York: McGraw-Hill, 1973), 169–200.
16. Barrie Thorne, "Professional Education in Law," in *Education for the Professions of Medicine, Law, Theology, and Social Welfare* Hughes et al. (eds.). 101–168.
17. John I. Goodlad, *Teachers for Our Nation's Schools* (San Francisco: Jossey-Bass, 1990), 247.
18. Steven Schlossman, Michael Sedlak, and Harold Wechsler, *The "New Look:" The Ford Foundation and the Revolution in Business Education* (Santa Monica, CA: Graduate Management Admission Council, 1987); Steven Schlossman and Michael Sedlak, *The Age of Reform in American Management Education* (Santa Monica, CA: Graduate Management Admission Council, 1988); Steven Schlossman, Robert E. Gleeson, Michael Sedlak, and David Grayson Allen, *The Beginnings of Graduate Management Education in the United States* (Santa Monica, CA: Graduate Management Admission Council, 1994).
19. There is a parallel in secondary education as well. As Angus and Mirel have shown, vocational courses in the high school never constituted more than 10 percent of course-taking, and a lot of those courses were general education under vocational labels (business English, business math). David Angus and Jeffrey Mirel, *The Failed Promise of the American High School, 1890–1995* (New York: Teachers College Press, 1999).
20. Levine, *The American College and the Culture of Aspiration*, 60.
21. Emile Durkheim, *The Evolution of Educational Thought: Lectures on the Formation and Development of Secondary Education in France* [1938] (Boston: Routledge and Kegan Paul, 1969).
22. Ralph Turner, "Sponsored and Contest Mobility and the School System," *American Sociological Review* 25 (October 1960): 855–867.
23. Brint, "The Rise of the 'Practical Arts;'" Richard Chait, "The 'Academic Revolution' Revisited," in Brint (ed.), *The Future of the City of Intellect*: 293–321; Andrew Abbott, "The Disciplines and the Future," in Bring (ed.), *The Future of the City of Intellect*: 2002, 205–230.
24. The Morrill Act, 1862 (12 United States Statutes at Large, 503–505), section 4.
25. For example, there are Michigan and Michigan State, Texas and Texas A & M. An exception that proves the rule is Ohio State, whose official name is The Ohio State University, in order to distinguish itself from the older private institution named Ohio University and also show that the "State" label should not lead anyone to assume it is not the flagship institution.
26. As Jeff Mirel has pointed out to me, even community colleges have made moves in this direction. They are prevented from evolving into universities, but educational compacts in many states offer community college graduates with AA degrees junior standing at public universities. This makes community colleges major providers of general liberal education in those states.
27. *Veysey, The Emergence of the American University*; Kerr; *The Uses of the University*; Brown, *Degrees of Control*; Levine, *The American College and the Culture of Aspiration*; Dunham, *Colleges of the Forgotten Americans*; Brint and Karabel, *The Diverted Dream*; Brint, "The Rise of the 'Practical Arts;'" and Geiger, *Knowledge and Money*.
28. Labaree, *How to Succeed in School Without Really Learning*; see also Randall Collins, *The Credential Society: An Historical Sociology of Education and Stratification* (New York: Academic Press, 1979).

From the Liberal to the Practical Arts in American Colleges and Universities: Organizational Analysis and Curricular Change

Steven Brint, Mark Riddle, Lori Turk-Bicakci
and Charles S. Levy

One of the most important changes in American higher education over the last 30 years has been the gradual shrinking of the old arts and sciences core of undergraduate education and the expansion of occupational and professional programs. Occupational fields have accounted for approximately 60% of bachelors' degrees in recent years, up from 45% in the 1960s, and hundreds of institutions now award 80% or more of their degrees in these fields (Brint, 2001)

The arts and sciences originated historically for the pursuit of knowledge "for its own sake" and, simultaneously, as the educational foundation for youths preparing to occupy positions of power and influence in society. They include the basic fields of science and scholarship, such as chemistry, economics, history, literature, mathematics, philosophy, and political science. By contrast, programs in occupational fields are designed to educate students for jobs—in business, education, engineering, nursing, public administration, and many others. These applied programs are often housed in their own professional schools or colleges distinct from colleges of arts and sciences. In this paper, we will sometimes refer to these programs collectively as the "practical arts," a term we consider an apposite contrast to the familiar term "liberal arts." For the most part, however, we will use the more conventional term "occupational-professional" programs.

This paper is not intended as a critique of occupational-professional education in American colleges and universities. Indeed, many writers, including Jencks and Riesman (1968) and Clark (1983), have argued that a key strength of American higher education has been its receptivity to practical training, beginning well before the original Morrill Act (Geiger, 1998), but of course stimulated greatly by the land grant commitments of the federal government. It is worth noting in this context that most educational systems in the industrialized world are much less focused on the arts and sciences than the American system. The French and Swedish, for example, extend vocational tracks from secondary to higher education. Countries like Germany in which arts and sciences predominate are able to maintain this focus primarily because of the early differentiation of primary and secondary schooling into vocational and academic tracks (Allmendinger, 1986). Nor do most European countries have general education requirements at all in the undergraduate curriculum. The Continental pattern is to channel students directly into specialized study in a discipline.[2]

Reprinted by permission from the *Journal of Higher Education* 76, no. 2 (March/April 2005).

At the same time, there can be little doubt that the conflict between market-based utilitarianism and the liberal arts tradition of education for understanding and democratic citizenship has been an important touchstone in the American context. Decisive shifts in one direction or the other have often been interpreted as indicators of the state of relations between the great forces of the market and cultural idealism among American elites. Even today, advocates of the arts and sciences frequently argue that the basic disciplines are superior sources of study for broadening the horizons of undergraduates (Geiger, 1980; Shapiro, 1997) and for developing skills in analysis, written and oral communication, and critical thinking (Bowen & Bok, 1998: 209–216). These views are supported by findings of sharp declines in self-reported gains among American college students in the 1990s as compared to college students in the late 1960s in awareness of different philosophies and cultures; in understanding and appreciation of science, literature and the arts; and in personal development when compared to American college students from the late 1960s (Kuh, 1999). A significant portion of these declines can be attributed to lower levels of course taking in arts and sciences fields (Adelman, 1995).

In this paper, we will try to answer two key questions about this rise of the practical arts in American four-year colleges and universities. First, is this shift a historical departure, or is it instead a continuation of the dominant tendency in American higher education in the twentieth century, a tendency which was interrupted briefly in the 1960s by an unusual conjunction of forces favorable to the arts and sciences? Second, what institutional characteristics are most strongly associated with the production of a large number of degrees in occupational-professional fields as opposed to the arts and sciences?

These questions are important; scholars do not know whether the situation today is anomalous from a historical perspective. If American higher education has been predominantly concerned with occupational education for most of the last century, perhaps concerns about the "endangered" liberal arts are overstated, or at least should be evaluated in this larger context. Scholars also do not have a confident sense of where change since 1970 has been greatest. Are institutions focusing on applied fields central or marginal in the American system of higher education? Are they mainly public or not? Are they spread throughout the system or located mainly in particular regions and market segments? Because answers to these questions allow us to identify the locations in which the arts and sciences are weakest, they have potentially significant implications for higher education policy, particularly for efforts to revive or "reinvent" the arts and sciences in the context of predominantly occupationally oriented curricula (see, e.g., Shulman, 1997), and for efforts to reverse declines in the personal, civic, and cultural development of American college students.

The paper is divided into two major sections, reflecting the two key questions under consideration and the different methodological approaches that we bring to bear on each. We will first address the debate about historical trends in occupational-professional versus arts and sciences degrees. This analysis is based on a historical time series showing how the proportion of graduates in these two areas has changed from the 1910s to today. We will then discuss theories of the social bases of occupational-professional versus liberal arts organization among four-year colleges and universities. These theories focus, respectively, on (1) organizational functions, (2) status and selectivity, (3) historical traditions, and (4) socioeconomic and political contexts. We will present multiple-regression analyses to examine these theories and to locate the centers of occupational-professional and arts and sciences education among American four-year colleges and universities. We will conclude by considering what the findings imply about the future of American higher education.

Undergraduate Degree Trends, 1915–2000

Has the American undergraduate experience been primarily utilitarian in emphasis over the past century or has it been devoted primarily to education in the arts and sciences? Oddly, no one, so far as we know, has attempted to answer this question through the development of a historical time series.[3] There are reasons to believe, as many do, that the 1960s and early 1970s represent a historically unusual period favoring the arts and sciences in the context of an otherwise longstanding historical commitment of most students and institutions to occupational majors. The land grant universities, after all, were strongly oriented to occupational-professional education from the beginning, and public institutions have long educated a large proportion of American college students. Yet there are also good reasons to believe that the practical arts have become dominant at the undergraduate level only recently. Before World War II, college going was more completely the preserve of the middle and upper-middle classes. Goyette and Mullen (2002) show that social class is strongly associated with majoring in the arts and sciences today, and it is likely that it was also associated with this preference in the past.

The vagaries of official statistics make it difficult to know with certainty whether the recent shift toward occupational-professional fields represents a long-term continuity in the organization of American higher education or a relatively new departure. Before the mid-1960s, government statistics do not separate first professional degrees from bachelors' degrees. In addition, the fields used for classification in the 1920s and 1930s vary greatly from those used in the 1950s and 1960s, and still more so from those in use today. To develop a time series for the percentage of bachelors' degrees awarded in occupational-professional fields, we have had to make two adjustments to government statistics: first, eliminating first professional degree fields (concentrated in law, medicine, and theology), because they are not truly bachelors'-level degrees, and, second, creating tables of correspondence for degree fields used in earlier years and those used by the National Center for Education Statistics (NCES) today.[4]

The time series also includes a solution to one other major problem in estimation. Before 1930–31, two major categories are used in government statistics: degrees awarded in Arts and Sciences (A&S) and degrees awarded in Professional Schools. Only aggregate degrees are given for A&S, while degrees awarded in professional schools are disaggregated by field. Between 1930–31 and 1943–44, by contrast, degrees in A&S are divided between traditional A&S fields and occupational programs within arts and sciences colleges. We know from this data that A&S degrees before 1930–31 must include significant numbers of degrees that we would today classify as occupational-professional. These include degrees in such fields as agriculture, commerce, engineering, and journalism. (During this period, colleges and universities did not consistently locate their occupational programs in separate professional schools; some located them within colleges of arts and sciences.) Fortunately, for the period 1915–15 through 1929–30, it is possible to estimate the percentage of occupational-professional degrees within A&S by fitting a polynomial spline through data points associated with occupational degrees bestowed within arts and sciences colleges during the period 1930–31 through 1943–44.[5] Our estimates for these early years in the time series are corrected in this way. An extrapolation of the rate of error across the relatively short length of the estimated section suggests that deviations from the prediction line will be within the range of plus or minus two percentage points.

Because detailed data by subfields is not available before the 1960s, we have allocated fields to the category in which a majority of graduates belong. We do not believe the accuracy of the time series is greatly affected by this allocation rule, because the great majority of fields clearly belong either to the arts and sciences or the occupational-professional category. Even in the few divided fields (notably, communications, legal studies, psychology, and visual and performing arts), the great majority of graduates clearly belong either to one category or the other. Communications, for example, is and has been predominantly applied. For most of the period, it was mainly journalism. Similarly, psychology is and has been predominantly arts and sciences. We therefore believe the data presented in Figure 1 to be accurate within 1–2% of the true proportion for each of the years reported.

The time series includes all available years from 1915–16 to 2000–01. For years before 1949–50, data are available biennially through the *Biennial Survey of Education*. For years since 1949–50, data are available annually. Due to wartime exigencies and postwar reorganizations, data on degrees awarded for 1945–46 and 1947–48 were not collected.

Figure 1 shows that the arts and sciences dominated in the 1910s and 1920s, at a time when higher education was a preserve of the middle and upper-middle classes, and the English model of liberal arts education at the collegiate level remained strong. This dominance began to slip just

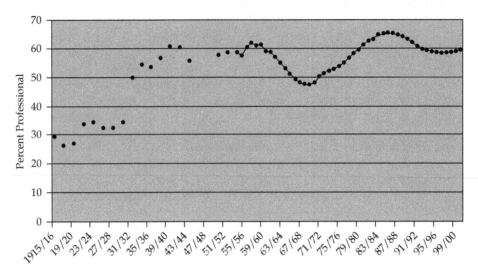

Figure 1 Percent Occupational-Professional Degrees, 1915–2000

SOURCES: U.S. Department of the Interior (1917), pp. 298, 300; U.S. Department of the Interior (1919), pp. 732, 734; U.S. Department of the Interior (1922), pp. 19, 21; U.S. Department of the Interior (1925), pp. 589, 591; U.S. Department of the Interior (1927), pp. 14, 16; U.S. Department of the Interior (1929), pp. 19–20, 22; U.S. Department of the Interior (1931), pp. 355–57, 360–61; U.S. Department of the Interior (1933), pp. 91–101; U.S. Department of the Interior (1935), pp. 88–97; U.S. Department of the Interior (1937), pp. 78–87; U.S. Department of the Interior (1939), pp. 104–109; U.S. Department of the Interior (1943), pp. 55–56; Federal Security Administration (1945), pp. 62–63; Federal Security Agency (1950); Federal Security Agency (1951); Federal Security Agency (1952); U.S. Department of Health, Education, and Welfare (1953); U.S. Department of Health, Education, and Welfare (1954); U.S. Department of Health, Education, and Welfare (1956), p. 72–74; National Center for Educational Statistics (1958), pp. 18–19; U.S. Department of Health, Education, and Welfare (1960), pp. 83–85; National Center for Educational Statistics (1966), p. 8; National Center for Educational Statistics (1967), pp. 258–64; National Center for Education Statistics (1968), p. 8; National Center for Educational Statistics (1969), p. 9; National Center for Educational Statistics (1970), p. 8; National Center for Educational Statistics (1971), pp. 8–9; National Center for Educational Statistics (1988), pp. 79–83; National Center for Educational Statistics (2001), p. 295.

before the Great Depression. By the mid-1930s, occupational-professional programs were significantly stronger. Data from the World War II period are potentially somewhat misleading because of the large numbers of men fighting in the war. However, following World War II and through the 1950s, occupational-professional programs were once again decisively stronger than the arts and sciences, encouraged no doubt at first by the returning G.I.s who were older than traditional students and inclined toward degrees that would give them a leg up on their careers. In the early and mid-1960s, the arts and sciences regained control, with nearly 55% of graduates. In terms of absolute numbers of students and professors, this was a high watermark for many arts and sciences fields. The conjunction of a continuing national commitment to basic science following World War II and Sputnik, combined with promising developments in the arts and humanities, and the sophisticated social criticism found in some social science disciplines created unusually favorable grounds for the advance of the arts and sciences, even at a time of great expansion in enrollments. If we restrict our focus to the post-World War II period, the term "resurgence" is accurate; patterns in degrees awarded after 1971 are reminiscent of the patterns found in the late 1940s and throughout the 1950s.

Thus, a long-term historical view suggests an underlying trend toward occupational-professional programs combined with shorter-term cyclical movements. Within these cyclical movements, periods of change coincide with economic declines (the Great Depression of the 1930s and the tightening of the college labor market at the end of the 1960s). By contrast, periods of prosperity are sometimes (but not always) associated with stronger preferences for the arts and sciences. Economic declines are not, however, the only force involved in the two marked shifts toward occupational-professional degrees during the period covered by our times series. The development of college-level credential requirements in newly professionalizing occupations is clearly another important factor. For example, the proportion of all bachelors' degrees awarded in education increased by more than 7% between 1915 and 1929, as many normal schools were transformed into teachers' colleges.

The Resurgence of the Practical Arts, 1970–2000

The most recent turn toward the practical arts dates from the depressed college labor market of the early 1970s (Freeman, 1976), and it continues to be encouraged by demographic and economic forces: an ever-growing number of students vying for a less rapidly growing number of good careers. In addition, a shift in federal financial aid policy from grants to loans may have encouraged lower-income students to choose curricula linked to jobs that could allow rapid loan repayment (Slaughter, 1998).

In the fifteen years between 1970–71 and 1985–86, occupational-professional fields gained significantly as compared to arts and sciences fields, with nearly two in three degrees awarded in occupational-professional fields in 1985–86. The arts and sciences rebounded from their nadir of the mid-1980s, but a decisive majority of degrees have continued to be awarded in occupational-professional fields since that time; in recent years, some 58% of bachelors' degrees have been awarded in occupational-professional fields. A more refined analysis can be made of these data by allocating subfields within the broad NCES disciplinary categories. Such an analysis suggests that a more accurate figure for the proportion of occupational-professional degrees awarded would be 2–3% higher.[5]

At the undergraduate level, the fastest-growing degree fields include a number that barely existed 30 years ago. Protective services and computer and information systems both experienced more than a ten-fold growth between 1970–71 and 2000–2001; fitness, recreation, and leisure studies experienced more than a five-fold growth; and communications grew more than three times larger. As Table 1 indicates, over the last three decades the fast-growing fields have been occupational in virtually every case.[6] The fastest-growing of all has been business, which now accounts for some one-fifth of all undergraduate degrees—up from one-seventh in 1970–71. As Adelman observed, business became in the 1980s "the empirical core curriculum" (Adelman, 1995, p. 229). By contrast, over the period only four liberal arts fields grew relative to other fields. Two of these fields—psychology and life sciences—are closely linked to health occupations. The other two fields are "liberal/general studies" and "interdisciplinary studies." These latter two fields—still quite small in numbers of graduates—illustrate one facet of another interesting trend in academe: the slow and still very limited erosion of disciplinary boundaries in the liberal arts. Performing and visual arts, fields which could be classified either as arts and sciences or as occupational-professional, have also grown a little relative to other fields.[7]

Every other arts and sciences field has declined not only proportionately, but also in absolute numbers. It is important to emphasize this point, because the American higher education system is substantially larger today than it was in 1970–71. More than 1.5 million students graduated with bachelors' degrees in 2000–2001 compared to about 840,000 in 1970–71. Under these circumstances, it is not easy for a field to decline in absolute numbers, however poorly it may fare in competition with other fields. In this context, it is necessary to underline the significance of a decline in absolute numbers: *During a period in which graduates nearly doubled, almost every field which constituted the old liberal arts core of the undergraduate college was in absolute decline as measured by numbers of graduates. This includes not only all of the humanities and social sciences (except psychology), but also the physical sciences and mathematics.* One could say that all of the traditional arts and sciences fields, except those closely connected to health careers, have a receding profile in today's colleges and universities.

From these new enrollment patterns arises the prevailing wisdom: "[In] recent decades, students . . . have been oriented chiefly toward gaining useful skills and knowledge rather than

TABLE 1
Growing, Stable, and Declining Degree Fields, 1970–2000

A. Growing Fields	B. Stable Fields	C. Declining Fields
Bachelor's Degree Fields		
I. Fields with Fewer than 1% of BA/BS Degrees in 2000		
Law/Legal Studies	Architecture	Library Science
Transportation Studies	Area/Ethnic Studies	Philosophy
	Communications Technology	Religious Studies
	Theology	
II. Fields with 1–5% of BA/BS Degrees in 2000		
Public Administration	Agricultural Science	English Literature
Visual/Performing Arts	Home Economics	Physical Sciences
Communications		Mathematics
Liberal/General Studies		Foreign Languages/
Interdisciplinary Studies		Literatures
Computer/Info. Systems		
Protective Services		
Recreation/Leisure/Fitness		
III. Fields with More than 5% of BA/BS Degrees in 2000		
Business	Engineering	Education
Health Professions		Social Sciences
Psychology		History
Biological/Life Sciences		
Master's Degree Fields		
I. Fields with Fewer than 1% of Master's Degrees in 1995–96		
Communications Tech.	Area/Ethnic Studies	Foreign Languages/
Engineering Tech.	Home Economics	Literature
Law/Legal Studies		Philosophy/Religion
Liberal Studies		
Interdisciplinary/ Multidisciplinary Studies		
Parks/Recreation/Fitness		
Protective Services		
II. Fields with 1–5% of Master's Degrees in 1995–96		
Communications	Agriculture/Nat. Resources	Biological/Life Sciences
Computer/Information Sciences	Theology	English Literature
Psychology	Visual/Performing Arts	Library Science
	Architecture	Mathematics
		Physical Sciences
		Social Science/History
III. Fields with More than 5% of Master's Degrees in 1995–96		
Business Administration	Engineering	Education
Health Professions		
Public Administration/Services		

SOURCE: Computed from NCES, 1998, p. 282–3.

membership in a cultural elite . . . " (Trow, 2000, p. 1), and the familiar but nevertheless arresting statistic from Astin's annual survey showing that the proportion of college freshmen interested in attending college to develop a "meaningful philosophy of life" dropped by 45% in the years between 1967 and 1987, while the proportion interested in attending to "become well-off financially" grew by 40% over essentially the same period (Astin, 1998).

Institutions, nevertheless, vary greatly in the extent to which they have embraced the "practical arts." Hundreds of institutions graduate nearly all of their students in occupational-professional fields. Hundreds more maintain a near-exclusive focus on the arts and sciences. And, of course, a very large number of institutions are located somewhere between these two extremes. We will turn now to an analysis of the sources of variation among American colleges and universities in the proportion of bachelor's degrees they award in occupational-professional as opposed to arts and sciences fields.

Institutional Bases of the "Practical Arts"

What factors explain this variation in curricular focus among American colleges and universities? Previous efforts to investigate this issue have focused on one or another of two institutional characteristics: Carnegie classification and average SAT scores (see Breneman, 1994; Gilbert, 1995; Morgan, 1998; and Turner & Bowen, 1990). Are these the most important influences? It is at least plausible that other factors, such as socioeconomic composition, size, religious affiliation, or regional location are also important explanatory factors. Our approach is to develop a set of explanatory models based on competing theoretical expectations about the relationship between institutional characteristics and curricular emphasis and to choose the most important explanatory variables from these models for further analysis. Specifically, we focus on four sets of hypotheses to account for levels of concentration in occupational-professional fields. These have to do with: (1) organizational functions and market segmentation, (2) status and selectivity, (3) historical traditions, and (4) the environmental context in which institutions are located.

The first set of hypotheses is based on the expectation that degree concentrations should be associated with differences in *organizational functions*. This is obviously true in the case of institutions specifically constituted for the purpose of occupational education, such as the Georgia Institute of Technology or the University of Texas Health Sciences campus. The Carnegie classification system was designed to reflect (and also to shape) the functional differentiation of the American higher education system circa 1970. The Carnegie categories distinguish between institutions that serve differing functions as marked by the level of degrees offered and the defined purposes of the institutions. Selective baccalaureate-granting institutions are functionally differentiated in this framework by their greater concentration on arts and sciences fields. In so far as they are oriented to the advance of basic science and scholarship, research universities might also be expected to produce comparatively high proportions of arts and sciences graduates. Campus size, whether measured by enrollment or budget, is another functional measure in so far as size reflects the likelihood that curricular activities will be more diverse than concentrated. Today, program diversification occurs primarily through the development of new occupational-professional programs (Breneman, 1994; Hashem, 2002). Functional analysis can be enhanced by drawing on the insights of market segmentation economics. Winston (1999) has argued that because of their small subsidy resources, the less prestigious baccalaureate and master's granting institutions face the largest incentives to reduce their cost structures or diversify their current revenue streams. This leads to the expectation that occupational-professional fields may be particularly strong at Carnegie BA II and Carnegie MA I and MA II (or Comprehensive) institutions. Thus, other factors held constant, we expect BA I colleges, Research I universities, and smaller institutions to award a higher proportion of degrees in arts and sciences fields, while technical colleges and universities, larger institutions, and the financially weaker BA II and MA I and II institutions to award a higher proportion of degrees in occupational-professional fields.

The second set of hypotheses is based on the expectation that degree concentrations should be associated with the *status and selectivity* of institutions. Higher education observers have long noted the dominant ideal of elite sectors of American higher education is that "students should do liberal arts work as undergraduates, postponing occupational training until they entered a graduate school or took a . . . job" (Jencks & Riesman, 1968, p. 263). Reputation and undergraduates' standardized test scores are indicators of academic status and selectivity. The socioeconomic composition of student bodies is a second dimension of status. Students from higher SES families may be expected to enroll in higher status curricula (Bourdieu & Passeron, 1977). The economic status of institutions is a third dimension of status. Institutions charging high tuitions and those with large operating budgets per student are out of reach of many lower and middle-class students. These institutions might also be associated with higher status curricula in the arts and sciences. Thus, we expect academically selective, socially elite, and expensive institutions to have higher proportions of graduates in the arts and sciences.

The third set of hypotheses is based on the expectation that *historical traditions* should make a difference in the proportion of occupational degrees awarded. Organizational sociologists since Stinchcombe (1965) have noted the constraining force of the institutional designs at the time of their foundings. Colleges founded earlier in the nation's history, denominational colleges connected originally to the liberal arts, and women's and historically black institutions might all be expected to cleave closely to the older traditions in undergraduate education, while state institutions, influenced throughout their history by the economic development concerns spelled out in the Morrill Acts, should be more likely to favor practical education as a means of serving their states and their generally less affluent student constituencies. Catholic colleges were founded to provide opportunities to members of then-subordinate religious and ethnic communities, and it is reasonable to expect that they might remain more attuned to occupational-professional education. Thus, we expect older, Protestant-affiliated, single-sex, historically black, and private institutions to retain a stronger focus on the arts and sciences.

The fourth set of hypotheses is based on the expectation that degree concentrations should be associated with the *socioeconomic and political context* in which institutions act. Institutional offerings may reflect more liberal or more conservative political cultures of states. States with more liberal political cultures may encourage a stronger emphasis on the arts and sciences because of citizen concerns with issues of intellectual and social development, whereas more conservative states may feel an affinity to the utilitarian outlooks of occupational-professional programs. Degree concentrations might also reflect variations in opportunities for postgraduate training within states. Where such opportunities are relatively plentiful, undergraduates can "afford" to major in arts and sciences fields, knowing that they can receive occupational education following college graduation. We might expect a correlation between economic growth and arts and sciences for similar reasons. Where average incomes are growing, more people will feel a degree of autonomy from the conditioning influence of market forces (Brint & Karabel, 1991). Even population growth alone might encourage a greater emphasis on traditionally higher status curricula, because population growth creates a sense of increasing opportunities. Thus, we expect variations in the proportion of arts and sciences graduates to reflect the area of the country in which institutions are located and changes in states' per capita incomes and population growth rates.

Data and Methods

The data used to construct the dependent variable in this analysis is drawn from the NCES annual survey of American colleges and universities, as reported in its Integrated Post-secondary Educational Survey (IPEDS). We have used data from 1997–98, the most recent data currently available on degree fields by institution. We have classified fields as either occupational-professional or arts and sciences and computed the proportion occupational-professional degrees awarded at each institution for 1997–98. All data is for bachelor's degrees only. Table 2 shows the categorization scheme used in this analysis. This categorization scheme is based on the 40 major discipline categories currently in use by NCES. To increase the accuracy of the analysis, we reallocated a small number of subfields in communications, law and legal studies, psychology, and visual and performing arts. (See Table 2.) The dependent variable is continuous and runs from under 10% to over 90% of degrees awarded in occupational-professional programs.

TABLE 2
Occupational/Professional and Arts and Sciences Degree Categories

Occupational/Professional	Arts and Sciences
Advertising (Communications)	Area, ethnic and cultural studies
Agricultural business & production	Biological sciences/Life sciences
Agricultural sciences	Communications (except those found under
Architecture and related programs	occ./prof.)
Arts management (Visual & Perform. Arts)	English language and literature/letters
Broadcast journalism (Communications)	Foreign languages and literatures
Business management & admin. services	History
Clinical psychology (Psychology)	Law and legal studies (except those found under
Communications Technologies (Communications)	occ./prof.)
Communications, other (Communications)	Liberal/general studies & humanities
Computer & information sciences	Mathematics
Commercial photography (Visual & Perform. Arts)	Multi/Interdisciplinary Studies
Communications, General	Philosophy and religion
Conservation & renew. natural resources	Physical Sciences
Construction trades	Psychology (except those found under
Counseling psychology (Psychology)	occ./prof.)
Education	Social Sciences
Engineering	Visual & performing arts (except those found under
Engineering related technologies	occ./prof.)
Fashion design (Visual & Perform. Arts)	
Film-video making/cinematography and prod.	
(Visual & Perform. Arts)	
Graphic design, commercial art and illus.	
(Visual & Perform. Arts)	
Health professions and related sciences	
Home economics	
Industrial design (Visual & Perform. Arts)	
Interior design (Visual & Perform. Arts)	
Journalism (Communications)	
Law (Law and legal studies)	
Library science	
Marketing opers./market & distribution	
Mechanics and repairers	
Military technologies	
Music bus. management & merchandising	
(Visual & Perform. Arts)	
Paralegal/legal asst. (Law and legal studies)	
Parks, recreation, leisure & fitness	
Personal & Miscellaneous services	
Precision production trades	
Protective services	
Public administration and services	
Public relations & Organizational comm. (Communications)	
Radio & television broadcasting (Communications)	
School psychology (Psychology)	
Science technologies	
Theological studies/religious vocations	
Transportation & material moving workers	
Vocational home economics	

The data set used in this analysis was constructed by combining the earned degrees data with variables collected from a wide variety of sources and archived in the Institutional Data Archive on American Higher Education (IDA). The analysis is based on data collected on every four-year college and university in the United States listed in the Higher Education Directory (1999). We will use sample statistics in reporting the results of our analyses, however, because not all institutions are included in the Higher Education Directory and because missing data do not allow us to make claims that the analyses are based on a complete representation of the underlying population.[8]

Table 3 provides an overview of the independent variables used in the analysis. The independent variables are grouped in relation to the four sets of hypotheses described above. Our analyses

TABLE 3
Independent Variables

Variable	Categories/Range	Level of Measurement
I. Function/Market Segment		
Technical Institution	Technical	Nominal
	Other (reference)	
Carnegie Classification	BA II	Nominal
	BA I (Reference)	
	MA II	
	MA I	
	Doctorate II	
	Doctorate I	
	Research II	
	Research I	
Enrollment	278–48,906	Interval
Log operating Budget	$3.1M–$3.03B	Interval
II. Status/Selectivity		
Combined (V+M) SAT/ACT Scores	623–1500 (SAT)	Interval
	ACT converted to SAT scale	
"National" Institution	National	Nominal
	Other (Reference)	
5-Year Graduation Rate	Very High: >75% (Reference)	Nominal
	High: 60–74% public; 65–74% private	
	Mid: 35–59% public; 40–64% private	
	Low: <35% public; <40% private	
	V. Low: <15% & > 25% part-time	
Log Tuition	$150–$32,164	Interval
III. Historical Tradition		
Date of Establishment	Before 1800 (reference)	Nominal
	1800–1850	
	1851–1875	
	1876–1900	
	1901–1925	
	1926–1950	
	1951–2000	

(Continued)

TABLE 3 *(Continued)*

Variable	Categories/Range	Level of Measurement
Control	Public	Nominal
	Private (reference)	
Religious Affiliation[1]	No Religious Affiliation (reference)	Nominal
	Christian Council Colleges	
	Other Protestant	
	Catholic	
Historically Black	Yes	Nominal
	No (reference)	
Women's College	Yes	Nominal
	No (reference)	
IV. Social/Political Context		
Region[2]	Northeast (reference)	Nominal
	West Coast	
	Mid-Atlantic	
	South Central	
	Southeast	
	Southwest	
	Industrial Midwest	
	Farm Midwest	
	Mountain	
Population Growth, 1990–2000	–34,841–4,111,627	Interval
Income Growth Per Capita, 1990–2000	$1,166–$5,281	Interval

SOURCES: *Carnegie Classification, Enrollment, Control, Religious Affiliation, Historically Black Colleges and Universities, Women's Colleges, Region:* Higher Education Directory (1999); *Technical Institution:* Derived from Higher Education Directory (1999); *Operating Budget, Operating Budget for Student:* National Center for Educational Statistics, IPEDS data file (1999); *SAT/ACT scores:* Higher Education Research Institute (1999); *National Institutions:* American Association of Universities membership list, Consortium for Financing Higher Education membership list, Breneman (1994), Goldberger, Maher, and Flattau (1995), Geiger (2002); *Five Year Graduation Rates:* College Board Institutional data file (1998); *Christian Council Colleges:* CCCU website (www.cccu.org); *Population Growth, 1990–2000, Income Growth Per Capita, 1990–2000:* United States Bureau of the Census data file (2002).

NOTES: [1]The Higher Education Directory data file was our primary source for determining religious affiliations. We also relied on the membership lists provided on websites for denominational colleges. These included: Christian Council (www.cccu.org), Congregationalist (www.naucc.org), Episcopal (www.cuac.org), Independent Baptist (www.bn66.com/churches/schools), Latter Day Saints (Mormon) (www.lds.org), Lutheran (www.lutherancolleges.org), Mennonite (www.mennoyouth.org), Methodist (www.gbhem.org), Nazarene (www.ptloma.edu/universityinformation/Nazarene colleges), Presbyterian (ww.apcu.net), Quaker (www.earlham.edu/-fahe), Roman Catholic (www.accunet.org), Seventh Day Adventist (www.sdanet.org), and Southern Baptist (www.baptistschools.org).
[2]Northeast region includes: Connecticut, Maine, Massachussetts, New Hampshire, Rhode Island, Vermont. Mid-Atlantic region includes: Delaware, Maryland, New Jersey, New York, Pennsylvania, Washington, DC. South Central region includes: Kentucky, North Carolina, Tennessee, Virginia, West Virginia. Southeast region includes: Alabama, Arkansas, Florida, Georgia, Louisiana, Mississippi, South Carolina. Industrial Midwest region includes: Indiana, Illinois, Michigan, Minnesota, Ohio, Wisconsin. Farm Midwest includes: Iowa, Kansas, Nebraska, Missouri, North Dakota, South Dakota. Southwest region includes: Arizona, Colorado, New Mexico, Oklahoma, Texas. Mountain states include: Alaska, Idaho, Montana, Nevada, Utah, Wyoming. West Coast includes: California, Hawaii, Oregon, Washington.

compare the explanatory power of these sets of independent variables. Variables in Model 1 (organizational function/market segment) include: (1) dummy-coded variables for each Carnegie classifications measured in 1994 with BA I institutions as the reference category; (2) student enrollment in 1997–98; and (3) log of operating budget in 1997–98, the latter two being measures of organizational size. This set also includes: (4) a variable dummy coded to isolate institutions dedicated to technical, business, or health sciences education.[9] Variables in Model 2 (status and selectivity) include: (1) average combined SAT/ACT scores; (2) a dummy variable for institutions of national reputation based on membership in the American Association of Universities, the Consortium for Financing Higher Education, and other measures of national reputation; (3) dummy variables for five categories of graduation rates—a measure correlated with the socioeconomic composition of student bodies; and (4) log of tuition. The first two of these variables are academic status variables, and the last measures economic status of institutions. In the absence of direct measures of the socioeconomic composition of student bodies, we have chosen to use five-year graduation rates, a measure correlated both with the academic status of institutions and the socioeconomic status of student bodies. Variables in Model 3 (historical traditions) include: (1) institutional age in 2002 coded in seven time periods with colleges established in the seventeenth and eighteenth centuries as the reference category; (2) a dummy variable for public institutions; (3) dummy variables for evangelical Christian, other Protestant, and Catholic colleges with independent, nonreligious colleges as the reference category; (4) a dummy variable for historically black colleges and universities; and (5) a dummy variable for women's colleges. Variables in Model 4 include: (1) dummy variables for nine regions of the country with New England as the reference category; (2) income growth per capita by state, 1990–2000; and (3) population growth by state, 1990–2000.[10]

Findings

We have used ordinary least squares multiple regression to determine the net effects of variables in each of our four models.[11] The regressions in Table 4 look successively at the models based on organizational function, status and selectivity, historical traditions, and socioeconomic and political context.

TABLE 4
Four Models of Percent Occupational-Professional Degrees, 1997–98

Variables	Model 1 Functional/ Market Segment		Model 2 Status & Selectivity		Model 3 Historical Traditions		Model 4 Socio-Political Contexts	
	B	Beta	B	Beta	B	Beta	B	Beta
BA 2	33.9	.702***						
MA 1	35.1	.728***						
MA 2	36.7	.397***						
D 1	32.8	.268***						
D 2	36.2	.325***						
R 1	19.5	.218***						
R 2	30.5	.224***						
Technical Institution	25.5	.158***						
Enrollment (in 0000s)	.6	.206***						
Log_Op Budget	−3.7	−.210***						
Ave. SAV. ACT (in 000s)			−5.8	−.309***				
National Reputation			−14.2	−.188***				
Very Low Grad Rate			5.5	.106***				
Low Grad Rate			−.7	−.007				
Mid Grad Rate			3.2	.065*				
High Grad Rate			−.8	−.011				
Log Tuition			−3.0	−.112***				

(Continued)

TABLE 4 *(Continued)*

Variables	Model 1 Functional/ Market Segment		Model 2 Status & Selectivity		Model 3 Historical Traditions		Model 4 Socio-Political Contexts	
	B	Beta	B	Beta	B	Beta	B	Beta
Established 1800–1850					14.5	.217***		
Established 1851–1875					25.2	.448***		
Established 1876–1900					29.5	.549***		
Established 1901–1925					28.4	.462***		
Established 1926–1950					27.3	.376***		
Established 1951–2000					26.5	.407***		
Public Institution					8.6	.182***		
Historically Black Institution					1.4	.015		
Women's College					−12.5	−.111***		
Christian Council College					8.2	.093***		
Other Protestant College					2.5	.047		
Catholic College/University					9.0	.138***		
Population Growth, 1990–2000 (in 000,000s)							−1.7	−.087*
Per Capita Inc Growth, 1990–2000 (in $0000s)							−2.3	−.084**
West Coast Region							2.1	.026
Mid Atlantic Region							6.4	.111*
South Central Region							8.8	.128***
Industrial Midwest Region							13.5	.230***
Southwest Region							15.3	.191***
Southeast Region							15.8	.239***
Farm Midwest Region							18.8	.238***
Mountain States Region							21.7	.135***
R2	.348		.301		.137		.074	
Adj.R2	.343		.297		.129		.068	
SEE	18.3		18.6		21.1		21.8	

***p < .001, **p < .01, *p < .05

This analysis indicates that an explanatory model built around functional variables explains nearly one-third of the variation in the proportion of occupational-professional degrees awarded by institutions in 1997–98. Not surprisingly, BA I institutions stand out for their commitment to the arts and sciences. Research I universities also award comparatively more arts and sciences degrees than other institutions. By contrast, nonselective baccalaureate institutions (BA II) and comprehensive institutions (MA I and MA II) are strongly associated with higher levels of occupational-professional degrees. These findings tend to confirm Winston's (1999) thesis that the weaker baccalaureate and master's granting institutions should be more market sensitive and, therefore, more occupationally oriented than other institutions. At the same time, institutions in all categories other than elite liberal arts colleges and research universities appear to be highly market sensitive and oriented to occupational-professional education. As expected, larger institutions as measured by student enrollment were also more occupationally oriented. However, our other measure of size, log operating budget, was connected with higher proportions of arts and sciences degrees and thus behaved more like a status variable than a functional variable.

The set of status and selectivity variables also provided a relatively good explanatory model, again explaining nearly one-third of the variation in proportion occupational degrees awarded. The variable measuring average SAT/ACT scores was by some measure the best predictor in this set, with each additional one-hundred points in SAT score being associated with a decrease of nearly 6% in the proportion of occupational as compared to arts and sciences degrees awarded. The national reputation variable also showed strong effects; it was associated with a decrease of 14% in the proportion of occupational degrees awarded. As expected, log tuition was also associated with lower proportions of occupational degrees. The variable measuring six-year graduation rates showed a less consistent predictive power.[12] In general, the findings indicate that the arts and sciences are strongly favored by prestigious institutions and that status includes at least two dimensions, academic and economic.

The models based on historical traditions and sociopolitical contexts were less powerful, although variables in these models (with the exception of historically black colleges and universities) do show the expected pattern of relationships: that is, higher proportions of arts and sciences degrees among older colleges and universities, women's colleges, and more liberal regions of the country (New England, the West Coast, and the Mid-Atlantic regions). They also show higher proportions of occupational degrees among public, Catholic, and evangelical colleges and in the "heartland" regions of the country (notably, the farm and industrial Midwest, the mountain states, and the Southeast). We have associated population and income growth with higher degrees of autonomy from the conditioning of the labor market. Consistent with this notion, these variables showed significant, albeit weak, net associations with higher proportions of arts and sciences degrees.

Regional variation in the proportion of occupational-professional degrees may be due to a number of possible influences. These include: more conservative political cultures, leading to an emphasis on practical pursuits; economies requiring fewer highly educated professionals; or simply fewer opportunities for postgraduate study. We were unable to find measures that perfectly capture these potential sources of variation, but our exploratory analysis using state data suggests that political culture—as measured by presidential vote in 2000—may be a surprisingly important influence.[13]

Our best-fitting model incorporates variables from each of the four models discussed above. We created this best-fitting model through stepwise deletion of nonsignificant predictors. Table 5 shows the coefficients and significance levels for the independent variables in our best-fitting model.[14]

The results for this model represent a clear improvement over the results obtained for any one of the four models in Table 4. The model explains nearly 60% of the variance in the percentage of occupational degrees awarded by four-year colleges and universities in 1997–98. Standardized regression coefficients indicate that Carnegie categories and average SAT/ACT scores are the strongest predictors of the proportion occupational-professional degrees awarded. These findings indicate that selective baccalaureate-granting institutions and other institutions with strong academic profiles, as measured by average SAT/ACT scores, are the core of support for the arts and sciences, while nonselective baccalaureate-granting institutions, master's granting institutions, and other institutions with weaker academic profiles are the core of support for occupational-professional education. Other variables also made an important net contribution to the explanatory power of the model. The most important of those associated with higher proportions of occupational-professional degrees were technical institutions, institutions established during the peak years of industrialization (1876–1900), larger institutions, and institutions located in heartland regions. The most important of those associated with higher proportions of arts and sciences degrees were public institutions, historically black institutions, women's colleges, and institutions located in the Northeast, Atlantic and Western seaboard states.

TABLE 5
Best-Fitting Model of Percent Occupational-Professional Degrees, 1997–98

A. Functional/Market Variables	B	Beta	C. Historical Identity Variables	B	Beta
BA 2	24.3	.501***	Established 1851–1875	4.5	.081***
MA 1	27.4	.574***	Established 1876–1900	6.2	.117***
MA 2	27.8	.313***	Public Institution	–8.0	–.172***
D 1	28.2	.238***	Historically Black	–15.6	–.113***
D 2	30.4	.274***	Women's College	–9.5	–.086***
R 1	25.8	.300***	Evang. Christian College	3.3	.041*
R 2	29.8	.234***			
Technical Institution	30.0	.195***	D. Socio-Political Context Variables		
Enrollment	.3	.109***	Population Growth, 1990–2000	–.2	–.079***
(in 0000s)			(in 000,000s)		
			Per Cap Inc Growth, 1990–2000	–2.0	–.077***
B. Status & Selectivity Variables			(in $0000s)		
Ave. SAT/ACT	–5.1	–.272***	West Coast Region	–7.2	–.091***
(in 000s)			Industrial Midwest Region	6.4	.112***
National Reputation	–6.7	–.089***	Southeast Region	6.1	.090***
Very Low Grad Rate	3.6	.068**	Farm Midwest Region	7.6	.102***
Mid-Level Grad Rate	2.4	.048*	R2		.585
Log Tuition	–2.9	–.107*	Adj. R2		.575
			SEE		14.5

***p < .001, **p < .01, *p < .05

Perhaps the most interesting finding is the net association between the arts and sciences and institutions created to serve socially disadvantaged groups (women's colleges, historically black colleges and universities, and public universities). It is particularly notable that state control is associated with a higher proportion of arts and sciences degrees net of other predictors—a finding at odds with popular images of state and land grant institutions. Although high proportions of arts and sciences graduates are the norm only among institutions serving academic and socioeconomic elites, some institutions designed to serve less advantaged groups do provide support for the arts and sciences. This is true of historically black institutions, women's colleges, and state colleges and universities, but not of religiously affiliated institutions. Evangelical Christian colleges are more likely to embrace occupational-professional fields than are otherwise comparable nondenominational institutions.

Discussion

The shift toward the practical arts in American colleges and universities cuts to the core of the competing values of educators in different sectors of the American higher education system. Many educators in the liberal arts sector endorse the view that shaping "the intellectual maturation of young people and widening their cultural horizons has traditionally been the strength and the mission of American undergraduate education" and agree with the assessment that the decline of the liberal arts tradition can only lead to a significant deterioration in "the vitality of intellectual life throughout the broad middle of the academic hierarchy" (Geiger, 1980, p. 54). Against this view, many educators in other sectors argue that colleges and universities have little choice but to adapt to the job-related interests of today's students, and in any event this adaptation allows higher education to contribute more effectively than it once did to the economic life of the country (see, e.g., Clark, 1998).

Whatever one concludes about the larger value issues at stake, there can be no doubt that the resurgence of the practical arts since 1970 has had important implications for the organization of academe. The growth of occupational-professional education is itself one support for the climate of utilitarianism on campus. It has also led to the migration of faculty toward the professional schools and indeed whole disciplines toward a professional model. In many institutions, arts and sciences disciplines have been transferred to colleges of professional studies to articulate more closely with career-oriented programs.[15] Psychology has become a clinical specialty at some universities and economics an arm of business administration. The smaller arts and sciences disciplines, particularly area studies and foreign languages and literatures, have faced significant downsizing and even elimination, while interdisciplinary majors in the arts and sciences have grown more popular among administrators, sometimes as much for economic as for intellectual reasons (Brint, 2002).

Kerr argued that "it may become increasingly difficult and misleading to talk about the future of 'higher education.' There will be many quite different segments, each with its own future . . . Institutions in the different segments will not know or care much about each other" (Kerr, 2002, p. 10). In contrast to contemporary forms of segmentation, Kerr foresaw a new classification of institutions emerging, which include today's research universities and liberal arts colleges, but also new categories of "professional school institutions" (presumably today's doctoral-granting institutions) and "polytechnic colleges" (today's comprehensive and less selective baccalaureate-granting colleges).

Our analysis indicates the plausibility of Kerr's vision of the future. The resurgence of the practical arts since 1970 has been largely driven by less prestigious institutions, which have also experienced the greatest growth in enrollments. The less selective baccalaureate and comprehensive institutions are now quite far along in the direction of transforming themselves into exclusively career-oriented polytechnics.[16] Prestigious institutions, by contrast, do not need to worry about competing for students and funds by providing job-related education, because they have a secure market position. They have, therefore, largely eschewed lower-level practical training and have instead competed for the highest status students and for research grants in the established disciplines. Indeed, some research universities have had an incentive to become markedly *more* liberal arts oriented, as they attempt to compete more exclusively in the "status goods" segment of the market for undergraduate students. Thus, Kerr's vision of the future may need to be adjusted just a little to separate out "liberal arts research universities," such as Duke and Harvard, from true "multiversities," such as the University of Florida and the University of Illinois, in which enrollments in occupational-professional have long been very strong among undergraduates (Morgan, 1998).

Because the current proportion of occupational-professional degrees is comparable to that found throughout much of the mid-twentieth century, it is possible to conclude that worries about the decline of the arts and sciences are overstated. If not for one important difference between the two eras, we would tend to agree with this assessment. That difference is as follows: Where arts and sciences degrees were once concentrated in both BA I and BA II institutions, they are now concentrated in elite segments of the system: the BA I institutions and a fraction of high-status R I institutions (Gilbert, 1995; Morgan, 1998). This suggests that what was once largely a functional divide—different kinds of institutions emphasize different curricula—has become largely a status divide. Kuh's (1999) concerns about changes in students' reports concerning their personal development and cultural awareness should be interpreted in the context of increasing stratification between undergraduates attending elite institutions and all others.

The most important finding of this paper is the connection between less prestigious institutions and high proportions of occupational-professional degrees. We find a particularly strong occupational emphasis in institutions enrolling high proportions of students with low test scores and, by implication, from lower socioeconomic backgrounds.[17] To the extent that these institutions represent the growth areas of academe, the practical arts are greatly favored. The broader institutional implications of this finding are also important: Just as secondary schools became vocationalized in the early twentieth century, when they were transformed from elite preparatory institutions into institutions the majority attended and did not go beyond (Trow, 1961), so colleges and universities became definitively oriented to occupational-professional education at the end of the twentieth century, at a time when they were becoming mass terminal institutions in the same sense.

A variety of circumstances can, as we have shown, provide freedom from the conditioning influence of the labor market, thereby encouraging higher enrollments in the arts and sciences. Clearly, institutions enrolling students with unusually good prospects in life are much more likely to emphasize the arts and sciences. For this reason, the stratum of selective liberal arts colleges and elite research universities, those that send large numbers of students on to postgraduate studies, will likely continue to be an exception. As environmental influences at the state level, growth in population and per capita income are associated with higher arts and sciences proportions for similar reasons, we believe, because they encourage a degree of freedom from the conditioning influence of the labor market.

However, these forces are not likely to reverse the rise of the practical arts, now that occupational fields have demonstrated their centrality over the last 30 years in both good economic times and bad. It is particularly notable that the growing earnings advantage of college-educated workers in the 1990s did not lead to a marked decline in occupational-professional degrees. This suggests that any rebirth of the arts and sciences as the center of undergraduate education probably lies well in the future, at a time when the bachelor's degree has become a preparatory degree for a majority of students who are planning to pursue postgraduate training, rather than the mass terminal degree it is today.[18] And even in this distant future it is possible that the arts and sciences will become the preserve of a still smaller number of students and faculty than they are today, if they are further devalued by a society that has turned away from the types of intellectualism they reflect and sustain.[19]

Notes

1. The pattern in Scotland and England is a bit different, and some other parts of the world, including India and Japan, have a variant of general education at the undergraduate level. Interestingly, a recent report of the World Bank's task force on higher education and society makes a case for introducing general education (Hopper, 2001).
2. The time series developed by Gilbert (1995) goes back only to 1956 and that developed by Turner and Bowen (1990) also begins in the 1950s.
3. The following fields were classified as "first professional degree" fields throughout the time series and excluded: dentistry, law, medicine, optometry, pharmacy, and veterinary medicine. The following fields were classified as arts and sciences: area studies, biological/life sciences (e.g., biology, biochemistry, ecology, microbiology), English and cultural studies, ethnic studies, foreign languages and literatures, history, legal studies (other than law as a first professional degree), liberal/general studies, mathematics, multi-/interdisciplinary studies, philosophy, physical sciences (e.g., chemistry, geology, physics), psychology, religious studies, social science (e.g., anthropology, economics, political science, sociology), visual and performing arts (e.g., art, dance, drama, music). The following fields were classified as occupational-professional: agriculture, architecture, business/commerce, communications, computer and information sciences, construction trades, education, engineering, forestry, health professions (other than first professional degree fields), home economics, industrial technology, journalism, library science, parks and recreation, precision productive trades, pre-dentistry, pre-law, pre-medicine, protective services, public administration, religious vocations (other than theology), and transportation.
4. This is an algebraic solution. We begin by plotting on a Cartesian coordinate system the proportion of occupational-professional to total degrees in arts and sciences for those years when official data makes that distinction. We then use the line formed by that plot to estimate the proportion occupational-professional for the earlier years in which some occupational-professional programs are contained within arts and science colleges. The line is a curve formed by a fourth-degree polynomial of the form: $y = 3Dax + bx^2 + cx^3 - dx^4$. For this reason, the line is frequently referred to as a polynomial spline.
5. This more refined analysis allocates occupational-professional subfields within arts and sciences categories to the occupational-professional category and vice versa. Thus, mass communication degrees are reallocated from occupational-professional to arts and sciences, while arts management degrees are reallocated from arts and sciences to occupational-professional. Similarly, clinical psychology degrees are reallocated from arts and sciences to occupational-professional.
6. Hashem (2002) has examined the development of eight fast-growing occupational fields, including computer and information science, legal studies, recreation and fitness, criminal justice, communications,

public administration, mental health, and health administration. Two of these fields (computer and information science and legal studies) were offshoots of well-established academic disciplines (mathematics and law) and here innovation occurred near the center of the system. One might expect that innovation in the other fields would have occurred in the weakest schools, those most exposed to market threat. But the innovating institutions were not, by and large, those most exposed to market threat. Instead, they were large, often urban, and less selective universities, such as New York University, Syracuse, Florida State, Wayne State, Kent State University, and San Jose State. In other words, innovation was led by institutions with discretionary resources at the fringes of the center. In two cases (mental health and criminal justice), another organization, the federal government, played a major role by providing funds for the development of new programs. This study illustrates the importance of looking at curricular change in organizational terms and not simply as a function of market forces.

7. Over the period, economics also grew slightly in absolute terms, perhaps due to its close connection to business, but it did not grow in relative terms.

8. Data is quite complete on the great majority of variables used in this analysis. No missing values exist for Carnegie classes, enrollment, national reputation, establishment date, public/private control, historically black colleges and universities, women's colleges, region, population growth, or average income growth. Several variables include 10 or fewer missing values: operating budget, operating budget per student, tuition, and graduation rate. Only two variables have larger numbers of missing values: average SAT/ACT scores (148) and religious affiliation (244).

9. These institutions are usually not exclusively occupational-professional. Both MIT and Cal Tech, for example, also offer degrees in arts and especially sciences.

10. Enrollment size and log of operating budget are strongly associated ($r=.82$). This raises concerns about multicollinearity. However, a high correlation between two variables in a multiple regression model does not violate the Gauss-Markov assumption concerning the limits of multicollinearity for multiple regression (Berry, 1993). Otherwise, the correlation matrix indicates moderate to low correlations for the independent variables, and we therefore conclude that the models are not compromised by problems of multicollinearity. Normal diagnostics were run to test for potential biases due to nonnormal distributions, skewness, and outliers. These diagnostic tests indicate that results of the analyses are unbiased.

11. Using a proportion for a dependent variable in ordinary least squares multiple regression can raise problems if the variable is nonnormally distributed and skewed. In this case, two solutions are possible: either the variable must be transformed or a different statistical model (such as logistic regression or general linear modeling) must be used. However, if the proportion is normally distributed and is mainly dispersed between .3 and .7, as is true of the dependent variable in our analyses, ordinary least-squares multiple regression remains a robust model.

12. Interestingly, institutions with both very low and mid-level retention rates were associated with higher proportions of occupational degrees, controlling for other variables in the model. Many institutions with very low graduation rates resemble community colleges and proprietary schools in their student base and objectives, while a number of institutions with mid-level graduation rates have adopted either a polytechnic model of post-secondary education or are former teacher's colleges which retain large education programs.

13. In our exploratory analysis, we used the percentage of each state's vote for George W. Bush in the presidential election of 2000 as an indicator of more conservative political cultures, and graduate degrees per capita as an indicator of postgraduate opportunities. The findings from this two-variable regression suggest that political culture deserves additional study as a potential influence on curricular emphasis. In this two-variable regression, state percentage vote for Bush was strongly associated with state-level variation in the proportion of occupational degrees awarded, while graduate degrees per capita was insignificant.

14. Again, normal diagnostics show no important biases in the model presented in Table 5.

15. Two examples of this phenomenon are the College of Science, Technology, and Health Professions at Western Kentucky University and the College of Business and Economics at California State University-Los Angeles. Although organization based on separate colleges of arts and sciences and professional schools remains the norm, such hybrids are now found at a number of institutions.

16. Our research does not answer one important question: How much of the change at less prestigious institutions is due to the growth of a new market composed of nontraditional, adult re-entry students? Clearly, these students are among the most likely to want courses and degrees that will help them with their careers. We think it likely that they are a very important source of support for occupational programs at comprehensive and doctorate-granting institutions, but a less important influence at BA II institutions, where 18–24-year-old students continue to predominate. This question merits additional study.

17. No direct measures of socioeconomic composition exist in this data set. One correlated measure, log tuition, was one of the last variables deleted from the best-fitting model, while another correlated measure, five-year graduation rates, showed relatively small net effects (cf. Goyette and Mullen, 2002). It is likely that more direct measures of socioeconomic composition would show stronger effects.
18. This forecast is based on the view that demographic movements and the inflationary pressures they encourage play major roles in structuring the higher education system at the most macro level. As the number of students entering college goes up, inflationary pressures encourage more students to differentiate themselves from their peers by pursuing still higher levels of education (Collins, 1979, 2002). Eventually, this pressure can encourage a "ratcheting up" of the normative level of education.
19. This possibility is suggested by Cohen (1998, p. 450).

References

Adelman, C. (1995). *The new college course map and transcript files: Changes in course-taking and achievement, 1972–1993.* Washington: Department of Education, Office of Educational Research and Improvement.

Allmendinger, J. (1989). "Educational systems and labor market outcomes." *European Sociological Review*, 5, 231–250.

Astin, A. W. (1998). "The changing American college student: Thirty-year trends, 1966–1996." *Review of Higher Education*, 21, 115–135.

Berry, W. (1993). *Understanding regression assumptions.* Newbury Park, CA: Sage Publications.

Bourdieu, P., & Passeron, J-C. (1977). *Reproduction in economy, society, and culture.* Beverly Hills: Sage Publications.

Bowen, W. G., & Bok, D. (1998). *The shape of the river: Long-term consequences of considering race in college and university admissions.* Princeton: Princeton University Press.

Breneman, D.W. (1994). *Liberal arts colleges—thriving, surviving, or endangered?* Washington: The Brookings Institution Press.

Brint, S. (2002). "The rise of the 'practical arts'." In S. Brint (Ed.), *The future of the city of intellect: the changing American university* (pp. 231–259). Stanford: Stanford University Press.

Brint, S., & Karabel, J. (1991). "Institutional origins and transformations: The case of American community colleges." In P. J. DiMaggio and W.W. Powell (Eds.), *The new institutionalism in organizational studies* (pp. 337–360). Chicago: University of Chicago Press.

Clark, B. R. (1983). *The higher education system: Academic organization in cross-national perspective.* Berkeley: University of California Press.

Clark, B. R. (1998). *Creating entrepreneurial universities: organizational pathways to transformation.* London: Pergamon.

College Board. (1999). *Institutional data, 1997–98.* New York: The College Board. (data file)

Collins, R. (1979). *The credential society: An historical sociology of education and stratification.* New York: Academic Press.

Collins, R. (2002). "Credential inflation and the future of universities." In S. Brint, (ed.), *The future of the city of intellect: The changing American university* (pp. 23–46). Stanford: Stanford University Press.

Cohen, A. M. (1998). *The shaping of American higher education: Emergence and growth of the contemporary system.* San Francisco: Jossey-Bass.

Federal Security Administration, Office of Education. (1949). *Biennial survey of education in the United States, 1942–44.* Washington: Government Printing Office.

Federal Security Administration, Office of Education (1950). *Biennial survey of education in the United States, 1948–49.* Chap. 4 ("Statistics of Higher Education"). Washington: Government Printing Office.

Federal Security Administration, Office of Education (1951). *Earned degrees conferred by higher education institutions.* Washington: Government Printing Office. Circular 282a.

Federal Security Administration, Office of Education (1952). *Earned degrees conferred by higher education institutions.* Washington: Government Printing Office. Circular 333a.

Freeman, R. (1976). *The overeducated American.* New York: Academic Press.

Geiger, R. L. (1980). "The college curriculum and the marketplace." *Change* (November/December), 17–23ff.

Geiger, R. L. (1998). "The rise and fall of useful knowledge: Higher education for science, agriculture and the mechanic arts, 1850–1875." *History of Higher Education Annual* 18, 47–65.

Gilbert, J. (1995). A "The liberal arts college—is it really an endangered species?" *Change* (September/October), 37–43.

Goldberger, M. L., Maher, B. A.,& Flatteau, P .E. (Eds.). (1995). *Research-doctorate programs in the United States.* Washington: National Academy Press.

Goyette, K. A., & Mullen, A. L. (2002). "College for what? The influence of social background on the choice of liberal arts or pre-professional fields of study." Paper presented at the annual meeting of the American Sociological Association.

Hashem, M. (2002). *Academic knowledge from elite closure to public catering: The rise of new growth fields in American higher education.* Unpublished Ph. D. dissertation, Department of Sociology, University of California, Riverside.

Higher Education Directory. (1999). *Higher education directory.* Falls Church: Higher Education Publications, Inc. (data file).

Higher Education Research Institute. (1999). *Selectivity index, 1997–98.* Los Angeles: HERI. (data file).

Hofstadter, R. (1962). *Anti-intellectualism in American life.* New York: Knopf.

Hopper, R. (Ed.). (2002). *Constructing knowledge societies: New challenges for tertiary education.* New York: World Bank.

Jencks, C., & Riesman, D. (1968). *The academic revolution.* New York: Doubleday.

Kerr, C. (2002). "Shock wave II: An introduction to the twenty-first century." In S. Brint (Ed.), *The future of the city of intellect: The changing American university* (pp. 1–22). Stanford: Stanford University Press.

Kuh, G. (1999). "How are we doing? Tracking the quality of the undergraduate experience, 1960s to the present." *Review of Higher Education* 22, 99–120.

Morgan, H. P. 1998. *Moving missions: organizational change in liberal arts colleges.* Unpublished Ph.D. dissertation. University of Chicago, Department of Sociology.

National Center for Educational Statistics. (1966). *Earned degrees conferred, 1963–64.* Washington: Government Printing Office.

National Center for Educational Statistics. (1967). *Earned degrees conferred, 1964–65.* Washington: Government Printing Office.

National Center for Educational Statistics. (1968). *Earned degrees conferred, 1965–66.* Washington: Government Printing Office.

National Center for Educational Statistics. (1969). *Earned degrees conferred, 1966–67.* Washington: Government Printing Office.

National Center for Educational Statistics. (1970). *Earned degrees conferred, 1967–68.* Washington: Government Printing Office.

National Center for Educational Statistics. (1971). *Earned degrees conferred, 1968–69.* Washington: Government Printing Office.

National Center for Educational Statistics. (1998). *Chartbook of degrees conferred, 1969–70 to 1993–94.* Washington: U.S. Office of Education.

National Center for Educational Statistics. (1999). *Integrated Post-secondary educational survey, 1997–98.* Washington: U.S. Office of Education (data file)

National Center for Educational Statistics. (2001). *Digest of education statistics, 2000.* Washington: U.S. Office of Education.

Shapiro, H . T. (1997). "Cognition, character and culture in undergraduate education: Rhetoric and reality." In R. G. Ehrenberg (Ed.), *The American University: National treasure or endangered species?* (pp. 58–97). Ithaca: Cornell University Press.

Shulman, L. S. (1997). "Professing the liberal arts." In R. Orrill (Ed.), *Education and democracy: Re-Imagining liberal learning in America* (pp. 151–173). New York: The College Board.

Slaughter, S. (1998). "Federal policy and supply side institutional resource allocation at public research universities." *Review of Higher Education* 21, 209–244.

Stinchcombe, A. (1965). "Social structure and organizations." In J. G. March (Ed.), *Handbook of Organizations* (pp. 142–193). New York: Rand McNally.

Trow, M. (1961). "The second transformation of American secondary education." *International Journal of Comparative Sociology* 2, 144–166.

Trow, M. (2000). "From mass higher education to universal access: The American advantage." *Minerva* 37 (Spring): 1–26.

Turner, S. E., & Bowen, W. G. (1990). "The flight from the arts and sciences: Trends in degrees conferred." *Science*, 250, 517–521.

U.S. Bureau of the Census. (2002). *Population statistics of the United States*, 2000. Washington: Bureau of the Census. (data file).

U.S. Department of Health, Education, and Welfare, Office of Education. (1954). *Earned degrees conferred by higher educational institutions*. Washington: Office of Education. Circular No. 360a.

U.S. Department of Health, Education, and Welfare, Office of Education. (1955). *Earned degrees conferred by higher educational institutions*. Washington: Office of Education. Circular No. 380a.

U.S. Department of Health, Education, and Welfare, Office of Education. (1956). *Earned degrees conferred by higher educational institutions*, 1953–54. Washington: Office of Education. Circular No. 418.

U.S. Department of Health, Education, and Welfare, Office of Education. (1958). *Earned degrees conferred, 1955–56*. Washington: Government Printing Office.

U.S. Department of Health, Education, and Welfare, Office of Education. (1960). *Biennial survey of education, 1956–58*. Washington: Government Printing Office.

U.S. Department of the Interior, Commissioner of Education. (1917). *Report 1917*. Chap. 4. (A Universities, colleges and technological schools, 1915–16"). Washington: Government Printing Office.

U.S. Department of the Interior, Bureau of Education. (1919). *Bulletin 1919*. Chap. 4. ("Statistics of universities, colleges, and professional schools"). Washington: Government Printing Office.

U.S. Department of the Interior, Bureau of Education. (1922). *Bulletin 1922*. No. 28 ("Statistics of universities, colleges, and professional schools"). Washington: Government Printing Office.

U.S. Department of the Interior, Bureau of Education. (1925). *Bulletin 1925*. No. 45 ("Statistics of universities, colleges, and professional schools"). Washington: Government Printing Office.

U.S. Department of the Interior, Bureau of Education. (1927). *Bulletin 1927*. No. 40. ("Statistics of universities, colleges, and professional schools"). Washington: Government Printing Office.

U.S. Department of the Interior, Office of Education. (1929). *Bulletin 1929*. No. 38. ("Statistics of universities, colleges, and professional schools"). Washington: Government Printing Office.

U.S. Department of the Interior, Office of Education. (1931). *Biennial Survey of Education, 1929–30*. Chap. 4. ("Statistics of universities, colleges, and professional schools"). Washington: Government Printing Office.

U.S. Department of the Interior, Office of Education. (1933). *Biennial Survey of Education, 1930–32*. Chap. 3. ("Statistics of universities, colleges, and professional schools"). Washington: Government Printing Office.

U.S. Department of the Interior, Office of Education. (1935). *Biennial survey of education, 1935*. Chap. 4. ("Statistics of universities, colleges, and professional schools"). Washington: Government Printing Office.

U.S. Department of the Interior, Office of Education. (1937). *Biennial survey of education, 1937*. Vol. 2, Chap. 4. ("Statistics of universities, colleges, and professional schools"). Washington: Government Printing Office.

U.S. Department of the Interior, Office of Education. (1939). *Biennial survey of education, 1936–38*. Chap. 4. ("Higher education"). Washington: Government Printing Office.

U.S. Department of the Interior, Office of Education. (1943). *Biennial surveys of education, 1939–40 and 1941–42*. Chap. 4. ("Higher education"). Washington: Government Printing Office.

Winston, G. C. (1999). "Subsidies, hierarchy, and peers: The awkward economics of higher education." *Journal of Economic Perspectives* 13, 13–36.

Acknowledgement

We would like to thank Philip Altbach, Mazen Hashem, John Mohr, Harriet P. Morgan, Ann Mullen, Craig Rawlings, Ann Swidler, and three anonymous reviewers for comments and/or bibliographic references that helped to improve the quality of this paper.

Vocationalism in Higher Education: The Triumph of the Education Gospel

W. Norton Grubb and Marvin Lazerson

At the beginning of the twenty-first century, a widely circulated Education Gospel has achieved worldwide influence. Communicating the good word about education, the Gospel's essential vision goes something like this: The Knowledge Revolution (or the Information Society, or the Communications Revolution, or the High-Tech revolution) has changed the nature of work, shifting away from occupations rooted in industrial production to occupations associated with knowledge and information. This transformation has both increased the skills required for new occupations and updated the three R's, driving work skills in the direction of "higher-order" skills including communications skills, problem solving, and reasoning—the "skills of the twenty-first century." Obtaining these skills normally requires formal schooling and training past the high-school level so that some college—though not necessarily a baccalaureate degree—will be necessary for the jobs of the future, a position that we and others label "College for All." The pace of change means that individuals are likely to find their specific work skills becoming obsolete. They must keep up with advances in technology and expect to change their employment often as firms and industries compete globally, adopt new technologies and new forms of work organization, and individuals must be able to engage in "life-long" learning. And, because no country wants to lose out in the global marketplace, every country is under pressure to increase its commitments to its educational system.[1]

In American higher education, the Education Gospel has led to a dramatic expansion of access and to a greater emphasis on vocational purposes. As higher education became a mass institution in the last half of the twentieth century, it simultaneously exalted its public purposes—benefits to the nation's economy, protection of the national defense, the creation of new knowledge, and the promise of equality of educational opportunity—and its private benefits in giving individuals access to income and professional status. Increasingly, the latter has come to dominate. Higher education is now the clearest embodiment of the American dream of getting ahead, especially getting ahead through one's own labor (Lazerson, 1998).

In this essay, we show how higher education converted to occupational education—called professional education to distinguish it from lower-level vocational training. The vocationalization process has always had dissenters, those who complain that the dominant focus on vocational goals undermines education's moral, civic, and intellectual purposes, a point of view that we suggest has become marginalized over time. More active forms of dissent, we argue, have come from those concerned about the inequities built into vocationalism, the differentiation of higher education institutions by occupational purposes with inequitably provided resources. A different kind of debate has occurred around what constitutes a genuine professional education, one that is inextricably linked to the vocationalism of formal schooling. We conclude the essay by arguing that vocationalism is now so deeply embedded in American higher education that it cannot be wished away and that reforms need to focus on ways to integrate vocational purposes with broader civic, intellectual, and moral goals.

Reprinted by permission from the *Journal of Higher Education* 76, no. 1 (January/February 2005).

From Moral to Vocational Purposes

America's colleges and universities did not begin as vocational institutions, at least not in the way we currently use the term. Instead there existed a deeply held conviction that the classical liberal arts were essential to prepare moral, civic, and intellectual public leaders who followed professional careers.[2] Interest in using college for explicitly vocational purposes began to be evident in the early and mid-nineteenth century, with the founding of West Point (1802), Rensellaer Polytechnic (1824), and some agricultural colleges in the 1850s. Passage by the U.S. Congress of the Morrill Act in 1862 formally recognized the role of higher education in preparing people for vocations. Each state received federal land to establish at least one institution "to teach such branches of learning as are related to agriculture and the mechanic arts . . . in order to promote the liberal and practical education of the industrial classes in the several pursuits and professions in life." The emphasis on "the liberal and the practical" was important, for it suggested that traditional notions of higher education—that it teach intellectual, moral, and civic values—should coexist with the newer expectation that learning be practical and vocational and that the state institutions had a responsibility to serve public needs (Eddy, 1957).

In practice, most of the land-grant institutions developed curriculums that paralleled those of existing colleges and universities, thereby leaving little to distinguish the Morrill Act schools from others. Many Americans doubted that college was the place to prepare for employment; college-based preparation for work was viewed as "academic," irrelevant, even sissified. For their part, the land-grants' leaders saw their institutions' future less as technical and trade training schools and more as universities with broad public responsibilities. In his inaugural address, President of the University of Wisconsin, Charles Van Hise (1904) articulated the fundamental rationale that would ultimately shape American higher education.

> Be the choice of the sons and daughters of the state, language, literature, history, political economy, pure science, agriculture, engineering, architecture, sculpture, painting or music, they should find at the state university ample opportunity for the pursuit of the chosen subject . . . Nothing short of such opportunity is just, for each has an equal right to find at the state university the advanced intellectual life adapted to his need. Any narrower view is indefensible.

The public universities were not alone in expanding the curriculum in the interests of public service and vocational purposes. During the nineteenth century a number of small "multipurpose" colleges adapted their curriculums to local labor market needs so that they would increase their students' job opportunities and would serve regional and local economic development. Often competing with one another in the same geographic area, the colleges established separate schools and departments of science, engineering, and agriculture, instituted short courses for commercial occupations, and prepared women for teaching (Geiger, 2000a).

Still, even as more vocationally oriented courses entered the curriculum, most colleges and universities continued to view their responsibilities in terms of broadly intellectual, ethical, and public service goals, for knowledge had a moral purpose. As new subjects, especially in the sciences, claimed greater weight, they were almost always justified as being congruent with the traditional values of moral and civic education. During the first three decades of the twentieth century, this view became attenuated and virtually disintegrated at the research universities that were fast becoming the cutting edge of American higher education. In simple terms, the search for scientific truth was best accomplished when scholars removed ethical concerns from their research. This separation meant that increasing numbers of faculty began to abide by formal research methodologies that required advanced professional training. And these same professors became more and more influential in preparing those who would enter the professions, training individuals to possess expert knowledge and a specialized vocabulary learned in college and in graduate school (Reuben, 1996).

The Rise of the Professions

Between 1880 and the 1930s, American higher education came to define itself in terms of its direct application to specific occupations. Nowhere was this more apparent than in the explosive growth of professional schools, in law, medicine, business, engineering, education, social work, nursing, and dentistry. What Joseph Kett (1994, chaps. 7–8) calls "quantum leaps" in the number of professional schools made clear that vocational education was the dominant mode of preparation for the professions and that the way for an occupation to become a profession was by connecting it to higher education.

Through the end of the nineteenth century, no profession—not medicine, law, or engineering—required college graduation to practice. The primary form of professional preparation took place on the job, sometimes under apprenticeship arrangements, but often on one's own, as individuals starting working in an occupation and moved in and out of formal schooling as necessary. Lawyers might attend lectures, but they were also likely to train by clerking; many physicians acquired degrees from medical schools after they began to practice medicine, and some never received any degree. In sharp contrast to the twentieth century pattern of spending extended periods of time in schooling before entering a profession, the basic pattern was to go to school as one found it necessary or thought it useful, but the lack of schooling did not stand in the way of practicing (Douglas, 1921, chap. I; Kett 1994;).

The pattern of interspersing school and work was partially due to a relatively dim view of school-based preparation, but it also reflected the absence of clear differentiation among educational institutions. Colleges, academies, and high schools were often interchangeable, and a high school diploma was rarely required to enroll in college. To reduce institutional chaos and to improve their status, a number of colleges and universities in the last decades of the nineteenth century established admissions agreements with local high schools. In return for meeting certain academic standards, the schools' graduates would be certified to enroll in college, formalizing a sequence that made secondary schools preparatory to college, a phenomenon that grew rapidly in the twentieth century (Johanek, 2001). A clear trajectory was being crafted, from high school to college and then on to a professional occupation, a sequential rather than interspersed pattern of school and work.

The movement of the professions into colleges and universities was also closely tied to the growing authority of science, in a broad sense (Reuben, 1996). Every profession created a liturgy about the importance of specialized knowledge. In turn, scientific knowledge brought with it the ability to benefit society and to serve one's clients better. While these claims seem self-serving in retrospect, they also had considerable substance. The requirements of structural engineering in building the modern city went beyond what could be learned on the job. As human anatomy and the nature of disease became more widely understood, treating patients required more than day-to-day practice could teach. Understanding economic principles and the techniques of accounting enhanced decisions among those responsible for assessing corporate balance sheets. The expansion of occupational preparation training in higher education—always called *professional* education to distinguish it from lower-level *vocational* education—had a substantial rational basis.

Since professional expertise required greater scientific understanding, school-based knowledge came to be more highly prized than work-based knowledge. In an example with widespread parallels, Cornell's engineering school, which began with a "shop" orientation and was originally named the Sibley College of the Mechanic Arts, was modified after 1885 to an academic model with higher admission standards and two years of required course work. The conception of the professional rooted in specialized knowledge and formal schooling rather than practical on-the-job experience stressed a deep conceptual understanding, not merely the manual skill or the procedural knowledge of vocational education. While the professions continued to stress the importance of character—many adopted a code of ethics, for example—increasingly success in school-based subjects became the necessary condition of entry (Bledstein, 1978; Geiger, 2000b; Sullivan, 1995).

Higher education provided the necessary expertise and increasingly standardized it by using easily recognized criteria to certify professional knowledge—entrance examinations, formal courses of study, degree requirements, and (in conjunction with national and state oversight boards) licensing examinations. Between 1870 and 1918 the scientifically trained mechanical engineer inexorably displaced the unschooled mechanic, as the proportion of engineers graduating from engineering schools grew from 11% to 50%. This shift, repeated in all the other professions, effectively changed America's traditional faith in self-education, or education on the job, into a belief that going to school was the most important form of education (Brown, 1995; Labaree, 1997).

By World War II, the essential elements of a mass higher education system were in place, with a large number of institutions emphasizing professional preparation to attract students, a majority of students in professional rather than liberal arts programs, and a quasi-market in higher education, with "consumers" choosing among competing institutions on the basis of the advantages they could confer. The growth in high school graduation rates, the monopoly that higher education could claim over routes into the professions, and the increasing adaptability of the college curriculum to labor market needs combined to give higher education a new prominence. The fact that going to college was becoming the route to greater earnings and higher status was muted because higher education was still relatively small, but that was about to change.

The Great Transformation

The expansion of higher education after World War II was nothing short of astounding. Following the G.I. Bill, the Cold War allowed higher education to claim a national purpose requiring federal investments. States rushed to create low-tuition public universities and community colleges (Douglass, 2000; Lowen, 1997). The clearest result of this was the expansion of public rather than private institutions. In 1947, 49% of enrollments were in public institutions; by the end of the century 76% were in public institutions, the overwhelming majority in public community colleges and in second-tier public colleges and universities.[3] The process of the expansion depended on the interaction of demand and supply: legislatures supplied increasing public funding to build them, and students began enrolling in public institutions because of their lower tuition relative to private colleges, forcing still further public investments.

While the post-World War II expansion drew upon a rhetoric of public purposes, the drive by students to attend college was overwhelmingly based upon the possibilities for individual gain. At the end of the century, some 74% of enrolled freshmen reported that it was very important or essential that they be well-off financially, a sharp change from the politically and socially involved 1960s, when less than 45% rated financial well-being that high and 80% rated developing a meaningful philosophy of life as their most important goal (Astin, 1998). Few today question a student's rationale to the *New York Times* that multiple majors is a good idea.

Vocationalism's success is most obvious in the prominence of explicitly occupational majors (Brint, 2002; Brint, Riddle, Turk-Bicakci, and Levy, 2002). While the 1960s, with its idealism and economic expansion, created a slight fall in the proportion of occupational majors, from 62% in 1959–60 to 58% in 1970–71, since then the proportion has gone back up to about 65% in 1987–88, before declining slightly during the expansionary period of the 1990s. These figures are probably underestimates;[4] at the beginning of the twenty-first century at least two-thirds of college undergraduates are in professional fields, with clearly vocational goals dominating their progression into higher education. Indeed virtually every field of study that grew over the last few decades has been occupational, including business, health professions and biology, computer systems, and various recreation studies. The only exceptions have been psychology and the life sciences, both closely linked to health occupations, and two small fields labeled "liberal/general studies" and "interdisciplinary studies." No liberal arts fields grew relative to other fields. The result, as Brint has emphasized, is a substantial shift in higher education: "*During a period in which the system grew by 50 percent, almost every field which constituted the old liberal arts core of the undergraduate college was in absolute decline as measured by numbers of graduates*" (2002, p. 235).

The vocationalization of higher education has given students enormous power. For the most part student choice drives what colleges and universities offer. They are not the only voices, to be sure; faculty still exert some control over what is taught, particularly in general education and in the majors, and professional organizations impose requirements on occupational majors. But the choices *among* institutions, and the choices of majors *within* institutions, determine most of the curriculum. The enormous expansion of student choice is consistent with the bewildering variety of occupations needing specialized preparation. It is also consistent with notions of development growth; students progress through levels of education with expanding choices until they become (supposedly) more sophisticated choosers, capable of making life decisions on their own behalf. But the dark side of student choice is the power it has given to vocational aspirations to mold higher education.[5]

The vocational transformation has also led to the expansion of a relatively new type of institution: the second-tier, comprehensive public university, especially attentive to regional labor market demands and to those occupations that gain social status by being embedded in a university program. Most of these universities emerged from teacher training colleges or technical and agricultural colleges, and therefore originated in explicitly occupational institutions; others emerged from multipurpose colleges, or junior colleges adding additional years of study.[6] They are overwhelmingly comprehensive institutions, providing a vast array of academic and professional offerings; almost none of them in the public sector has recreated the old liberal arts colleges (except for Evergreen State College in Washington and St. Mary's College in Maryland), and none of them has been a specialized professional school, like the schools of art, psychology, engineering, or culinary arts in the private sector. They are much less selective than the first-tier universities, often accepting 80–90% of students who apply; perhaps reflecting this fact, their graduation rates are often abysmally low, in the range of 25–50%. Every state has established such institutions: they are the California State Universities rather than the University of California system, the state colleges in Texas rather than the universities, the Universities of Western and Northern Illinois rather than the flagship University of Illinois at Champaign-Urbana, members of the American Association of State Colleges and Universities rather than the Association of American Universities. These regionally oriented comprehensive institutions account for about 57% of enrollments in all public four-year colleges and universities and about 37% of all public and private enrollment.[7] And, these institutions are explicitly occupational (or professional), with the majority of enrolling 60% or more of their students in professional fields. These are now the modal institutions of higher education.

Among private institutions, the great transformation has been the evolution of most liberal arts colleges into vocationalized institutions. When Breneman (1990, 1994) went in search of liberal arts colleges, he found that most had become "small professional schools with a liberal arts tradition, but little of the reality of a traditional liberal college." Defining liberal arts colleges as residential institutions awarding the baccalaureate degree in largely academic subjects, he concluded that only 212 of the 540 colleges classified by the Carnegie Commission as liberal arts colleges deserved the distinction. Of the liberal arts colleges as defined by Carnegie, the proportion of professional degrees increased between 1972 and 1988 from 11% to 24% in the elite colleges, and from 41% to 64% in the less-selective colleges. He concluded that "we are indeed losing many of our liberal arts colleges, not through closures but through steady change into a different type of institution"—driven, we should point out, by the combination of student choice and vocational pressure.

Even the elite liberal arts colleges, the Swarthmores, Wellesleys, and Amhersts, all private, all expensive and selective, have been transformed, since a high proportion of their students continue on to graduate school where they get their formal occupational training. The academic curriculum of the elite colleges thus also serves vocational purposes, even though it is a respite from immediate vocational pressures.

The development of the post-World War II mass system of higher education has been inextricably tied to its occupational purposes. Students come in order to get ahead, to get a credential and licensed, and be valuable in the labor market. Many believe, rightly, that they have no choice; the deterioration of the labor market for high school graduates, who have to settle for low-skilled, low-paid, and insecure work, has meant that going to college is a much better bet than finding a job right after high school. The dominant force that propels students to college is the belief that they can exchange a degree for professional status.

The Fragility of Liberal Education

The dissenters from rampant vocationalism have almost always concentrated on making the curriculum serve intellectual and civic purposes, particularly through general education courses, the re-creation of the humanities, and restatements of the case for civic purposes.[8] These efforts have generated little enthusiasm, partly because they have had to battle against the overwhelming trends we have already reviewed. The plain fact is that civic, intellectual, and moral purposes are not what most students think higher education is about.

The professoriate is itself divided on what higher education means. Business faculty vote along with philosophers, and medical faculty have equal standing with the English departments—indeed, in most institutions, the occupational faculty outweighs the academic faculty, and in many colleges and universities they have greater status and higher pay. Without faculty consensus, it is unclear where the defense of liberal education can come from—not from students with their increasingly utilitarian goals, not from policymakers with their concern with benefits compared to costs, and certainly not from the community of employers with its emphasis on the bottom line. When faced with the conflicts of trying to define a liberal education in a pluralist society, with competing interest groups and understandings of what knowledge matters, the tasks of constructing a liberal education seem almost insurmountable, and it is not surprising that universities have virtually abandoned the effort. As a committee of the Stanford University faculty put it in 1968,

> the University cannot in any event impress upon its students the total content of present knowledge, and it is impossible to choose what exactly it is that every student should know without imposing arbitrary constraints on the range of free inquiry.

Instead professors teach their specialties and students have the freedom "to discover new interests . . . and to explore the many fields and endeavors" available to them (Levine, 1996).

Patterns of student choice have further weakened the commitment to a coherent program of liberal education. Both the traditional college-age population and older students have shifted toward "swirling," taking courses in a variety of institutions and accumulating degrees credit by credit. Public postsecondary systems have even encouraged swirling by requiring common course numbering systems and transfers of credits among institutions. When this process works well, it leads to a consistent set of requirements in the major, plus general education requirements, that match the student's desires and culminates in a coherent degree. More often, however, the result is a patchwork of courses with little consistent rationale and little progress toward a degree, and a potpourri of general education courses from several institutions where the consistency that might emerge in a single institution has been destroyed (Smith, 1993).

The intellectual and moral traditions most closely associated with liberal education are still alive, of course, but they are most vibrant in those institutions in which occupational pressures are easily postponed, in the elite private and public colleges—Harvard and Stanford, Berkeley and Michigan, Swarthmore and Amherst. These institutions have the luxury of avoiding explicitly vocationalized undergraduate curriculums since for many of their students, a vocational curriculum awaits them in graduate school. For the most part, however, the defenders of intellectual and civic traditions in higher education have been reduced to sniping at the margins.

The Equity Effects of Vocationalism

A quite different challenge to vocationalism comes from the perspective of equity. The American *system* of higher education has become endlessly differentiated, along largely vocational lines. At the bottom level are the community colleges, with open access allowing second chances for students who did poorly in high school, who made mistakes in their earlier plans, or who have come to this country and need to start anew. With relatively low rates of completion, community colleges prepare students for the middle-level labor force—even though some students transfer to four-year colleges, preserving the option of moving to the next level. One step up are the second-tier public comprehensive universities and similar less-selective private universities for students with a little more money and somewhat better high school records, universities with minimal admissions standards and a great variety of occupational majors. These comprehensive universities prepare students for middle-level managerial positions in businesses and for the less prestigious, lower paid, and often predominantly female professions (like teaching and social work); like the community colleges, they have low graduation rates. The public universities and flagship campuses stand above them, and the elite research universities—most of them now private, with a few public institutions among them—rise triumphant at the apex, preparing their students for professional and graduate schools and access to well-paid, high-status professions. This system has simultaneously opened up college access for millions of Americans, while it has also allowed for a variety of elite institutions; equity and meritocracy can coexist within the same system. The repeated call for "College for All" does not mean that all colleges are the same nor that every one has the same shot at the best colleges.

The state systems of higher education created in the post-World War II period have reflected this duality of expansive opportunity and inegalitarian differentiation. California has one of the most formalized delineations.[9] When its Master Plan was developed in 1960, the California state system was divided so that the universities were designated for the top 12.5% of graduating high school students, and their graduate schools were responsible for professional education and Ph.D.s. The state colleges (now state universities) admitted those in the top 33% of the graduating class and provided baccalaureate degrees and a few master's degrees, but no PhDs; and community colleges were accessible to all, virtually without cost, and offered both occupational preparation and academic transfer to four-year institutions. The students in each of the three segments vary by design in the quality of their high school preparation, and because of the tight link with school achievement and income, they vary as well in their family backgrounds, with community college students most likely to come from low-income families, from families without a history of college, and from Latino and black families. The evident differences in status among institutions are reflected in sharp differences in spending: the public universities spend roughly $19,720 per student, the state colleges/universities spend about $10,116, and the community colleges—the level with the greatest variety of students and the greatest teaching challenges—spend about $4,557 per student (CPEC, 2000). California provides College for All, though now under substantial challenge, but not equal opportunity as measured by fiscal resources, by the likelihood of receiving a degree, or by the occupational destinations targeted by the different institutions. Other states have to a greater or lesser extent emulated California; even if the numbers of different institutions differ and the boundaries between elite and second tier universities are less precise, the three-part structure with different admissions standards, different levels of public support, and different occupational goals is typical. States thus provide equality of opportunity only in the sense of access to *some* form of postsecondary education for all.

The consequence is that debates about access and funding are pandemic. The most obvious point of conflict is affirmative action, which pits conceptions of meritocracy against equity, and clarifies our ambivalence about a relatively mass system of higher education, as individuals and groups struggle for entry into the preferred institutions and the preferred professions. Vitriolic debates have also taken place over outreach programs, standardized testing (especially the SAT) used in admissions, the extent of public funding and the levels of tuition, federal funding for grants, and loans and now its extension to the Hope and Lifelong Learning Tax Credits. Indeed, the funding issues are perhaps the ones where the gap between older conceptions of college—with high tuitions readily paid by the upper-middle class—and newer conceptions of College for All, of college as an entitlement, lead even the modest tuitions of public colleges to seem excessive and set off incendiary headlines— "Skyrocketing Public-College Tuition Renews Calls for Better Policies" (Heber, 2002). These are the issues where public policy takes the clearest stand on who will win and who will lose—or who will and who will not have access to college and postgraduate degrees, with the highly differentiated status and employment benefits.

These battles all depend on the triumph of vocationalism: if higher education was not the gateway to professional positions and higher individual status, little of this would matter. Little wonder that the bucolic and largely irrelevant college of the nineteenth century has become a battleground in the twenty-first Higher education's role in providing access to the American Dream is simultaneously its foundation and its burden, and conflict is the price it has to pay.

Professional Preparation, For and Against

Given the dependence of the Education Gospel upon assumptions of the Knowledge Revolution and the power of professional preparation in shaping higher education, we might expect schooling and employment to be most congruent at the level of professional education. However, the content of professional education has almost always been a source of unending complaint. In one profession after another, including both the high professions and the semiprofessions, there have been amazingly identical attacks on the quality of professional preparation.

Most obviously, critics have faulted professional schools for providing the wrong kinds of skills—plagued by a bloated curriculum, a surfeit of facts, an emphasis on rote memory and on the technical aspects of profession. Medical doctor and nursing education have seen almost the exact kinds of complaints (American Medical Colleges, 1998; Ludmerer, 1985, 1999; O'Neill and the Pew Health Professions Commission, 1998). In all cases, the remedy called for is to teach broader "higher-order" and interpersonal skills: "critical thinking, reflection, and problem-solving skills"; the use of "communication and information technology effectively and appropriately"; the ability to work in interdisciplinary teams; and the capacity to recognize "the multiple determinants of health in clinical care," rather than seeing health care as narrowly responsive to specific diseases or injuries. The legal profession has faced similar criticism. A 1981 report sponsored by the American Bar Association on "curricula for change" (Dutile, 1981) noted the lack of attention to competence in written and oral expression, analytic skills, and the kinds of interactive abilities with other people in such processes as interviewing, counseling, negotiation, and arbitration. A decade later, another report of the American Bar Association (MacCrate, 1992) restated the case for problem solving, legal analysis and reasoning, communication, counseling, and negotiation.

In business education, critics emphasize the need for "creative analytical power," including imaginative thinking and creative synthesis; interpersonal abilities like sensitivity to individual, ability to work with people, and awareness of group loyalties; communications skills; the capacity to plan, organize, and delegate; willingness to take responsibility and risks; and sound judgement over the kind of rote approach taken in many business schools (GMAC, 1990; Gordon and Howell, 1959; Pierson, 1959; Porter and McKibbin, 1988). Teaching has faced the same kind of criticism for being narrowly vocational. The Holmes Group (1986) called for making the preparation of all teachers intellectually more demanding and creating standards of entry in the profession that are intellectually defensible and professionally relevant. Similarly, the field of social work is embarking on a period of self-examination to clarify the skills required for a changing world of practice.[10]

Another strand of critique has pointed in quite different directions, persistently attacking professional schools for elevating research over practice and for emphasizing academic courses in which the demands of the job are virtually ignored. Again these views cut across all the professions. The American Bar Association regularly complains that new lawyers cannot draft contracts, have never seen a summons, cannot write in the forms required by courts, and have been taught by professors who have never practiced law (McCrate, 1992). In teacher education, the complaint about overly academic teaching—the teaching of theory, with few applications to the classroom, and with new teachers poorly prepared for issues like classroom management and discipline—has been common. The National League of Nursing has called for more collaboration between nursing programs and practice. In engineering education, the Olin Foundation was so disgusted with the distance of education from practice that it set up a new engineering school—Olin College—rather than trying to reform any existing schools (Marcus, 2002). The antidote in these and other examples has included efforts to have more practitioners teaching in professional schools, to incorporate more practice-oriented coursework, and to introduce early and more intensive internships in professional programs.[11]

The responses to these critiques have been quite similar, reflecting the structural limitations on educational institutions. The dominant change has been curricular reform, adjusting to changes in knowledge, updating the specific content of classes, but leaving the basic structure of professional preparation relatively unchanged—the reliance on classes, the lack of practice-based learning, the emphasis on cognitive abilities and particular forms of knowledge, the greater prestige of research over practice, the inevitable distance between educational institutions and the conditions of practice. Reformers have tended to blame the faculty—entrenched, conservative, in love with their research rather than teaching or the "real world" outside the academy—for the slow pace of change. But other institutional factors are also to blame: the unwillingness of much of the employer community to participate actively with colleges and universities; the system of funding higher education institutions, which supports enrollments within classes but not work-based learning or service learning outside the academy; the incentive structures of the research university, which reinforce the unwillingness of faculty to invest much in revising their teaching. Finally, what appears as conservatism and entrenchment is often allegiance to prevocational ideals of the university—to learning for its own sake rather than for instrumental reasons, to student development in broader forms other than employability, to public values rather than individualistic gain, to the value of the university as a haven from the acquisitiveness of commerce. The basic conflicts over the effectiveness of professionalism in the academy stem from the inherent logic of lodging occupational preparation in educational institutions with different values, different rhythms, and different goals compared to the employers they serve.

The similarity in the critiques of professional education is stunning. The same complaints have emerged about the need for new "skills for the twenty-first century" rather than narrow technical skills and a greater integration of schooling with practice as have occurred for more than a century. A mismatch between school skills and job requirements appears pervasive. Higher education thus faces what America's public elementary and secondary schools have faced for more than a century: the familiar process of "reforming again and again and again" in order to achieve greater integration between school and work (Cuban, 1990; Tyack and Cuban, 1995).

Renegotiating Higher Education

There has been no lack of recommendations for reforming higher education. Few, however, recognize just how powerful the vocational roles of schooling have become. Calls to resurrect the liberal arts almost always are undermined by faculty inability to define what they mean, by the reality of student choice, and by unwillingness to bring academic and vocational learning together.

The most common recent reform efforts have stressed the need for greater accountability, usually through calls for mandated assessments of learning, post-tenure reviews, state-by-state report cards, and greater commitments to teaching. These have tended to be more rhetorical than practical, and they thus far have produced little if any substantial change in the quality of teaching and learning (Lazerson, Wagener, and Shumanis, 2000). Efforts to create new kinds of institutions, e.g., the recent creation of Olin Engineering College by the Olin Foundation, and the expansion of new institutions like the University of Phoenix and National University have achieved a great deal of media attention. But these successes still remain only a small part of the higher education enterprise, and they almost invariably stress the narrower forms of vocational training that is regularly attacked and always in the process of being reformed. When new public institutions are created, they almost always follow the standard model of a comprehensive university. In the California system, for example, the attempt to establish Santa Cruz as a liberal arts institution with a series of smaller "colleges" and unconventional instructional practices (like the absence of grades) has given way to a much more conventional institution, and there has been no clamor for the new University of California at Merced to be a different type of institution.

Perhaps the strongest development of the last two decades has been the growing segmentation of higher education. In the process, the *system* of higher education has become dominated by market driven segments that don't compete or interact with one another, even as there is intense competition within each segment. Although there is a certain amount of integration—e.g., through transfer agreements between community colleges and four-year colleges—American higher education is essentially divided into a segment of highly selective private colleges, a segment of national private and a few public research universities, a segment of regional second-tier comprehensive universities without much local competition, a segment of low-quality private universities for those students limited in their choices, a segment of very localized public community colleges, and number of institutions oriented entirely to vocational training (Kerr, 2002). This trend, if it continues or accelerates, would leave most colleges and universities intensely professional and occupational, with a few remaining liberal arts institutions whose primary vocational role is to prepare students for graduate professional schools. The power of markets and choice would thus completely take over and most institutions of higher education would become high-level trade schools. This is vocationalism *in extremis*, and it is an unappealing vision, one that stands as a warning of what might happen if current directions continue (Kirp et. al., forthcoming).

We propose an alternative approach. It starts by acknowledging the vocationalization of American higher education and asserts that it is too late to reverse the developments of the past century. Failing to understand the occupational goals of most students, the segmentation of higher education around vocational goals, and the many faculty devoted to occupational preparation can only lead back to old, stale debates. By acknowledging the professional education trends of the past century, we can more readily turn to efforts to integrate nonvocational ideals with vocational realities. Taking a page out of John Dewey, trying to reject the new in order to go back to the old makes no sense, and simply adopting the new because it is the reality abdicates our aspirations for a better way.[12]

We deplore the tendency toward "narrow vocationalism," both because it undermines genuine occupational preparation and because it impoverishes the intellectual and civic roles that higher education can play. But professionalism broadly understood provides its own avenues back to liberal education. Ethical issues, central to every profession, provide a hook for the deeper study of ethical and philosophical issues. An understanding of the development of specific professions, and of professionalism in general, provides an approach to history, to the development of occupations and ideals in American society, to the conflicts over technological and social change, to the responsibilities of different groups (including professional groups) within society, and to conceptions of work and occupation and profession relative to other spheres of life. And students in colleges and universities become the middle class, with some responsibility for the political culture and the moral tone of the country as a whole. A frank introduction to civic responsibilities that incorporates their vocational responsibilities can and should be part of their education. Professionalism—the vocationalism of higher education—thus provides a logical entry to many elements of liberal education, one that can be exploited through interdisciplinary courses and general education courses that acknowledge the professional aspirations of students.[13]

At the same time it is important to recognize the complexity of work preparation. The critiques from professional associations criticize work preparation as too narrow, too concerned with facts and procedures without deeper understanding, too academic, too research-oriented, and too disconnected from the world of professional practice. These surprisingly consistent and contradictory criticisms, historically repeated, indicate some ways in which professional education needs to be reshaped. A first step is to make sure that students have a broad understanding of underlying theories and conceptions so that they can organize and understand "the rich confusion of ordinary experience," distinguishing professionalism from trade training. The constant complaints about university-based preparation drifting too far from the world of practice suggests a second necessary step, obvious in outline if difficult to execute: to integrate the concerns of practice more thoroughly into the professionalized university, through internships, co-operative education, and other forms of work-based learning that provide antidotes to the excessively "academic" elements of professional preparation. In many fields there are also ways of redirecting research so that it is less divorced from practice (Boyer, 1990). If the canons of what constitutes research were broadened, then the gulf between research and practice, the "academic" and the "vocational," might be more readily bridged.

Such modifications are likely to improve the quality of pedagogy, a chronic concern among those interested in professional education. One goal is to teach in more constructivist, meaning-centered, and contextualized ways, following the idea that students need to be better prepared to understand the deeper constructs underlying practice. Another goal is to incorporate nonacademic and nonstandard competencies into professional curricula—visual competency for architects and graphic designers, interpersonal skills for the helping professions, diagnostic abilities for engineers and computer scientists, problem-solving abilities for those in policy-oriented fields and many scientific areas, and nonstandard applications of reading, writing, and mathematics in many professional areas. As obvious as these pedagogical goals seem, little attention is directed to the preparation of instructors in professional fields, and therefore no clear way to improve the quality of instruction except through trial and error. Taking the nature of professional teaching more seriously, as a subject in its own right, would help diminish the distance between the academy and practice which remains so prevalent.[14]

Achieving the integration of the academic and the vocational, the intellectual and the practical, and creating the pedagogies necessary to achieve these ends will also require a much more substantial commitment to learning than currently exists in higher education. The multiple goals of colleges and universities are more easily approached when students are part of communities of learning. After a long period of increasingly large, impersonal, and anomic educational institutions, the ideal of smaller scale has begun to take hold—in high schools where there are major efforts to create small schools within larger settings; in community colleges, which celebrate their small classes and now are creating more learning communities and linked courses; and perhaps also in four-year colleges, which have been experimenting with freshman-year experiences, colleges-within-colleges, intellectual activities within residential settings, more seminars and tutorials, house systems, and other ways to break the large comprehensive university into smaller-scale learning communities. Doing so is more expensive, of course, since it is no longer possible to pack 500 freshman into large lectures, and it is made more difficult in institutions where students are commuters. But there are good reasons to think that smaller learning communities enhance retention and progress toward degrees and that students themselves value the support and the intellectual exchange possible in smaller learning communities.[15]

Finally, we as a society must confront the huge structure of inequality we have created in postsecondary education. The endless differentiation of postsecondary institutions, with their varied admissions standards and status differentials, leading to substantial homogeneity within most four-year colleges, constitutes the most extensive system of tracking in the entire educational system. In itself, there is clearly a place for more focused, mission-driven, differentiated educational institutions, and American higher education has probably been too disdainful of such differentiation. But the current forms of market-segmentation have had the pernicious effect of a differentiation among institutions in which resources flow in highly disproportionate ways to different types of institutions. Community colleges, which the neediest students attend, require more resources to make good on their promises to be teaching institutions and to provide more support to their nontraditional students. While the second-tier comprehensive universities receive more funding, they are still not equipped to provide the academic and social support (including smaller learning communities) and the student services that their students need. Some of the differentials among institutions will not be eliminated unless the distribution of income and wealth in the United States narrows considerably: high-income families will continue to seek advantages for their children (just as low-income families do and should), and if they want to spend more than $35,000 a year on an elite colleges, or a second-tier private university with the trappings of "college" that will remain their prerogative. But the public support of higher education should substantially narrow the differentials in revenues, as well as improving the support provided students in community colleges and second-tier public universities—income support, guidance and counseling in new forms, improvements in basic skills instruction, access to a broader array of community-based services.

While higher education has changed remarkably over the past century, our conceptions of "college" have changed remarkably little. Even as Americans created a mass higher educational system, the dominant conception of college remains embedded in the nineteenth century, in the image of 17 to 22 year olds in manicured residential colleges taking liberal arts courses for entry into professions, while engaging in wholesome and character-building extracurricular activities. This vision, artificial from the start, describes only a minority of students today, one which is almost certainly going to become proportionally smaller tomorrow. For substantial numbers of faculty hoping more prestigious universities will recruit them, and for countless administrators and trustees hoping to emulate the major research universities, the pot of gold at the end of the rainbow is to become like the selective colleges and the major research universities by ratcheting up admissions standards, creating honors programs, dropping remedial programs, adding doctoral degrees, and expanding research.[16] While it may be too late to undo this kind of institutional competition, a clear alternative is for institutions to be as good as they can *in their own terms*, creating multiple conceptions of excellence, based on more equitable distributions of resources. This would allow regional institutions and second-tier universities to focus on what they do well instead of trying to emulate the elite, to examine how best to serve their regions, to expand conceptions of applied research and useful knowledge, to see how best they could prepare the middle-level students they have rather than the students they would like to have, to develop faculty who are enthusiastic about their teaching roles and public service (and have possibly been prepared through teaching-oriented doctorates) rather than feeling like wannabe researchers. Then it might be possible to strengthen both occupational preparation and liberal learning, particularly by developing programs that integrate academic and professional learning and that connect classrooms to the workplace in mutually beneficial ways. By being honest about what higher education has become, it might be possible to acknowledge that not all occupations require a baccalaureate or graduate degree, and that preparation might be effectively done in a year or two. But without this kind of institutional redefinition, then all of higher education will continue to be dominated by the pressure at the top of the occupational hierarchy. This is a race that very few can win.

Notes

1. See Kwon's (2001) contention that "the idea of a knowledge-based economy is enthusiastically treated like a gospel among Korean people." See also Immerwahr and Foleno (2000) and on College for All see Boesel and Fredlund (1999) and Rosenbaum (2001).

2. Three excellent studies developing the changes we describe in this section are Reuben (1996) and Geiger (2000a, 2000b).

3. *Digest of Educational Statistics, 2001*, Tables 172–173, pp. 206–207.

4. See Brint, Riddle, Turk-Bicakci, and Levy, 2002, Table 1. On the reasons that these are under-estimates, see p. 7. Obviously, almost every aspect of post-baccalaureate schooling is professional education.

5. The parallel in secondary schools is explored in Powell, Farrar, and Cohen. (1985). *The Shopping Mall High School: Winners and Losers in the Educational Marketplace.* Boston: Houghton Mifflin.

6. Dunham (1969, p. 28) provides a useful table showing the origins of state colleges and universities belonging to the American Association of State Colleges and Universities: 59% originated as teachers' colleges, 14% as technical or agricultural colleges, 10% as multi-purpose colleges, 8% as junior colleges, 6% as academies, and 3% as religious or YMCA institutions.

7. There is some disagreement on these numbers. We have used data from the American Association of State Colleges and Universities (AASUC, *Findings and Trends*, 2002). If we rely instead on the Carnegie Classification of Institutions of Higher Education, then between 38% and 54% of all enrollments are in these second-tier institutions, depending on how one counts doctoral universities. The research and writing on these institutions is exceedingly sparse, but see Dunham (1969), now out of date because of the subsequent rapid expansion of the comprehensive universities; Kanter, Gamson, and London (1997), who call these colleges "non-elite, unselective, and neither research institutions nor true liberal arts colleges" (p. 2); and Selingo (2002).

8. For recent statements of the importance of general or liberal education in postsecondary education, see Bloom (1987); Gaff (1991); Westbury and Purves (1988); Kantor, Gamson, and London (1997). Many of these follow a similar pattern, bemoaning the decline of liberal education without acknowledging the rise of professional goals.

9. See Douglass (2000) on the historical background to the California Master Plan.

10. See especially the *Journal of Teaching in Social Work* during the 1990s.

11. Other efforts to overcome the separation of professional education from practice include calls to incorporate social and ethical dimensions, in place of an exclusive emphasis on scientific and technical dimensions, and to teach professionals to recognize the constellation of diverse economic, social, and cultural conditions in which their clients live.

12. Dewey's advice (1938, p. 22) was "the problems are not even recognized, to say nothing of being solved, when it is assumed that it suffices to reject the ideas and practices of the old education and then go to the opposite extreme."

13. We are not calling for all education to be rooted in work, a point we make more fully in our book. But in a vocationalized educational system, it is imperative to take work in its fullest dimensions into account.

14. Many of the professions have a journal devoted to pedagogical issues—for example, the *Journal of Teaching in Social Work, Journal of Engineering Education*, the *Journal of Nursing Education, Journal of Legal Education, Journal of Management Education, Management Learning*, and *American Medicine*. Our own work on the pedagogy of vocational education (Achtenhagen & Grubb, 2001) and occupational teaching in community colleges (Grubb & Associates, 1999, Ch. 3) indicates how little attention has been given to the pedagogy of occupational instruction, at least compared to instruction in conventional academic subjects.

15. See Tinto (1993), Tinto and Goodsell-Love (1995) and Tinto, Russo, P., & Kadel, S. (1994), as well as Tokina (1993) and Tokina and Campbell (1992).

16. See Dunham, 1969, p. 155. His conclusion is similar in spirit to ours, arguing that the state and regional colleges and universities should create a unique role for themselves instead of trying to emulate the elite institutions.

References

Achtenhagen, F., & Grubb, W. N. (2001). Vocational and occupational education: Pedagogical complexity, institutional indifference. In V. Richardson (Ed.), *Handbook of Research on Teaching* (4th ed.). Washington: American Educational Research Association.

American Association of Colleges of Nursing (1999). *Nursing education's agenda for the 21st century.* Washington: AACN.

American Association of Law Schools (2000). *Striving for equal justice: The AALS in its second century.* Washington: AALS.

Association of American Medical Colleges (1998). *Physicians for the twenty-first century.* Report of the Project Panel on the General Professional Education of the Physician. Washington: AAMC.

Astin, A. (1998). The changing American college student: Thirty-year trends, 1966–1996. *Review of Higher Education*, 21(2), 115–135.

Bledstein, B. (1978). *The culture of professionalism: The middle class and the development of higher education in America.* New York: W.W. Norton.

Bloom, A. D. (1987). *The closing of the American mind.* New York: Simon and Schuster.

Boesel, D., & Fredlund, E. (1999). *College for all: Is there too much emphasis on getting a four-year college degree?* Washington: U.S. Department of Education.

Boyer, E. (1990). *Scholarship reconsidered: Priorities of the professoriate.* Princeton: Carnegie Foundation for the Advancement of Teaching.

Breneman, D. (1990). Are we losing our liberal arts colleges? *College Board Review*, 156, 16–21, 29.

Breneman, D. (1994). *Liberal arts colleges: Thriving, surviving, or endangered?* Washington: The Brookings Institution Press.

Brint, Steven, Mark Riddle, Lori Turk-Bicakci, & Charles S. Levy (2002). "Colleges and universities of the 'practical arts': Correlates of a resurgent form," unpublished paper.

Brint, Steven (2002). "The Rise of the 'Practical Arts.'" In Steve Brint (Ed.), *The future of the city of intellect: The changing American university.* Stanford: Stanford University Press.

Brown, David K. (1995). *Degrees of control: A sociology of educational expansion and occupational credentialism.* New York: Teachers College Press.

Cheit, E. (1975). *The useful arts and the liberal tradition.* New York: McGraw-Hill for the Carnegie Commission on Higher Education.

Cuban, L. (1990, January). Reforming again, again, and again. *Educational Researcher* 19(1).

Dewey, J. (1938). *Experience and education.* New York: Macmillan Publishing.

Douglas, P. (1921). *American Apprenticship and Industrial Education.* Studies in History, Economics, and Public Law XCV(2). New York: Columbia University.

Douglass, John (2000). *The California idea and American higher education: 1850 to the 1960 master plan.* Stanford: Stanford University Press.

Dunham, E. A. (1969). *Colleges of the forgotten Americans: A profile of state colleges and regional universities.* Carnegie Commission on Higher Education. New York: McGraw-Hill.

Dutile, Fernand N. (Ed.). (1981). *Legal education and lawyer competency: Curricula for change.* Notre Dame: University of Notre Dame Press.

Eddy, E. D. (1957). *Colleges for our land and time: The land-grant idea in American education.* New York: Harper.

Gaff, J. G. (1991). *New life for the college curriculum: Assessing achievements and furthering progress in the reform of general education.* San Francisco: Jossey-Bass.

Geiger, Roger (2000a). "The era of multipurpose colleges in American higher education, 1850–1890." In *The American college in the nineteenth century*, Roger L. Geiger (ed.). Nashville: Vanderbilt University Press.

Geiger, Roger (2000b). "The rise and fall of useful knowledge: higher education for science, agriculture, and the mechanic arts, 1850–1875." In *The American college in the nineteenth century*, Roger L. Geiger (ed.). Nashville: Vanderbilt University Press.

GMAC. (Commission on Admission to Graduate Management Education) (1990). *Leadership for a changing world: The future role of graduate management education.* Los Angeles: Graduate Management Admission Council.

Gordon, R. & Howell, J. (1959). *Higher education for business.* New York: Columbia University Press.

Grubb, W. Norton & Marvin Lazerson (1988). *Broken promises: How Americans fail their children*. Chicago: University of Chicago Press.

Grubb., W. N., & Associates (1999). *Honored but invisible: An inside look at teaching community colleges*. New York and London: Routledge.

Heber, S. (2002, Oct. 25). Skyrocketing public-college tuition renews calls for better policies. *Chronicle of Higher Education* A20–A21.

Holmes Group (1984). *Tomorrow's teachers: A report of the Holmes Group*. East Lansing: School of Education, Michigan State University.

Immerwahr, J., & Foleno, T. (2000, May). *Great expectations: How the public and parents—White, African, and Hispanic—view higher education*. New York: Public Agenda Foundation.

Johanek, Michael (Ed.) (2001). *A faithful mirror: Reflections on the college board and education in America*. New York: College Entrance Examination Board.

Kantor, S. L., Gamson, Z. F., & London, H. B. (1997). *Revitalizing general education in a time of scarcity: A navigational chart for administrators and faculty*. Boston: Allyn and Bacon.

Kerr, C. (1991). The new race to be Harvard or Berkeley or Stanford. *Change*, 23(3), 3–8.

Kerr, C. (2002). Shock wave II: An introduction to the twenty-first century. In S. Brint (Ed.), *The Future of the city of intellect: The changing American university* (Pp. 1–22). Stanford: Stanford University Press.

Kett, Joseph F. (1994). *The Pursuit of Knowledge under Difficulties: From Self-Improvement to Adult Education in America, 1750–1990*. Stanford: Stanford University Press.

Kirp, David, et al. (forthcoming). *Higher education in the age of money*.

Koziol, K., & Grubb, W. N. (1995). Paths not taken: Curriculum integration and the political and moral purposes of education. In W. N. Grubb (Ed.), *Education Through Occupations in American High Schools*. Vol. II: *The Challenges of Implementing Curriculum Integration* (Pp. 115–140). New York: Teachers College Press.

Kwon, D. B. (2001). Adult Education in Korea. Unpublished paper. Seoul: College of Education, Korea University.

Labaree, David F. (1997). *How to succeed in school without really learning: The credentials race in American education*. New Haven: Yale University Press.

Larson, Magali Sarfatti (1977). *The rise of professionalism: A sociological analysis*. Berkeley: University of California Press.

Lazerson, Marvin, Wagener, U., & Shumanis, N. (2000). What Makes a Revolution: Teaching and Learning in Higher Education, 1980–2000. *Change*, May/June 2000.

Lazerson, Marvin (1998). The Disappointments of success: Higher education after World War II. *Annals of the American Academy of Political and Social Science, 559*(September), 64–76.

Levine, David (1986). *The American college and the culture of aspiration, 1915–1940*. Ithaca: Cornell University Press.

Levine, Lawrence W. (1996). *The opening of the American mind: Canons, culture, and history*. Boston: Beacon Press.

Lowen, R. S. (1997). *Creating the Cold War university: The transformation of Stanford*. Berkeley: University of California Press.

Ludmerer, Kenneth M. (1999). *A time to heal: American medical education from the turn of the century to the era of managed care*. New York: Oxford University Press.

Ludmerer, Kenneth M. (1985). *Learning to heal: The Development of American medical education*. New York: Basic Books.

MacCrate, R. (1992). *Legal education and professional development—An educational continuum report of the task force on law schools and the profession: Narrowing the gap*. Washington: American Bar Association, Section of Legal Education and Admissions to the Bar.

Marcus, J. (2002, Spring). An unknown quality: Olin College students, faculty and administrators create an innovative new university from scratch. *National Crosstalk, National Center for Public Policy and Higher Education, 20(2)*, 1, 14, 15.

McGrath, E. & Russell, C. (1958). *Are liberal arts colleges becoming professional schools?* New York: Teachers College, Columbia University.

National Center for Public Policy and Higher Education (2002). *Measuring Up 2002: The State-by-State Report Card for Higher Education*. San Jose: NCPPHE.

O'Neil, E. H., & The Pew Health Professions Commission (1998). *Recreating health professional practice for a new century*. San Francisco: Pew Health Professions Commission.

Orrill, R. (Ed.), (1997). *Education and democracy*. New York: The College Board.

Orrill, R. with Kimball, B. A. (1995). *The condition of American liberal education: Pragmatism and a changing tradition*. New York: College Entrance Examination Board.

Pierson, F. (1959). *The education of American businessmen*. New York: McGraw-Hill.

Powell, A., Farrar, E., & Cohen., D. (1985). *The shopping mall high school: Winners and losers in the educational marketplace*. Boston: Houghton Mifflin.

Porter, W., & McKibbin, L. (1988). *Management education and development: Drift or thrust into the twenty-first century?* New York: McGraw-Hill Company. 1988.

Reuben, Julie (1996). *The making of the modern university*. Chicago: University of Chicago Press.

Rosenbaum, J. (2001). *Beyond college for all: Career paths for the forgotten half*. New York: Russell Sage.

Selingo, J. (2002, May 31). Mission creep? More regional colleges start honors programs to raise their profiles and draw better students. *Chronicle of Higher Education,*, A19–A21.

Smith, V. (1993). Phantom students: Student mobility and general education. *AAHE Bulletin, 45*(10), 10–13, 7.

Sullivan, William M. (1995). *Work and integrity: The crisis and promise of professionalism in America*. New York: Harper Business.

Swift, J. (1995). *Wheel of fortune: Work and life in the age of falling expectations*. Toronto: Between the Lines.

Tinto, V. (1993). *Leaving college: Rethinking the causes and cures of student attrition* (2nd ed.). Chicago: University of Chicago Press.

Tinto, V., & Goodsell-Love, A. (1995). *a longitudinal study of learning communities at LaGuardia Community College* (ERIC Document ED 380 178). Washington: National Center on Postsecondary Teaching, Learning, and Assessment, Office of Educational Research and Improvement, U.S. Department of Education.

Tinto, V., Goodsell-Love, A., & Russo, P. (1994). *Building learning communities for new college students: A summary of research findings of the collaborative learning project*. Washington: National Center on Postsecondary Teaching, Learning, and Assessment, Office of Educational Research and Improvement, U.S. Department of Education.

Tinto, V., Russo, P., & Kadel, S. (1994, February/March). constructing educational communities: Increasing retention in challenging circumstances. *AACC Journal, 64*(4), 26–29.

Tokina, K. (1993). Long-term and recent student outcomes of freshman interest groups. *Journal of the Freshman Year Experience, 5*(2), 7–28.

Tokina, K., & Campbell. F. (1992). Freshman interest groups at the University of Washington: Effects on retention and scholarship. *Journal of the Freshman Year Experience, 4*(1), 7–22.

Tyack, David, & Larry Cuban (1995). *Tinkering toward utopia: A century of public school reform*. Cambridge: Harvard University Press.

Van Hise, Charles R. 1904. "Inaugural address of President Charles Richard Van Hise." *Science*, XX (August 12), 193–205.

Villeneuve, J. C., & Grubb, W. N. (1996). *Indigenous school-to-work programs: Lessons from Cincinnati's co-op education*. Berkeley: National Center for Research in Vocational Education.

Westbury, I., & Purves, A. G., eds. (1988). *Cultural literacy and the idea of general education*. Part II. Chicago: NSSE.

HISTORY, RATIONALE, AND THE COMMUNITY COLLEGE BACCALAUREATE ASSOCIATION

KENNETH P. WALKER

The first section of this article looks briefly at the evolution of higher education in the United States. The second section considers the rationale underlying the introduction and implementation of the community college baccalaureate. The third summarizes the fast pace of developments since 1997, including the emergence of the Community College Baccalaureate Association, a new international organization dedicated to advocacy for access to the baccalaureate. The article finishes with some policy recommendations and avenues for future research.

History

Early Colleges

Education has been important to American society from the first European colonization of North America to the twenty-first century. The colonists in New Netherland did not want their children to forget the decency and order of a civilized life. So, in 1649, the Nine Tribunes wrote to the States General in Holland about "the sad state into which learning had fallen in the colony and recommended a public school . . . so that the youth be well instructed, not only in reading and writing, but also in the knowledge and fear of the Lord" (Wright, 1957, p. 105).

Even vocational versus academic learning was a matter of disagreement and debate during early colonial times. William Penn was an "early advocate of adapting schools to the practical needs of humanity instead of slavishly following outworn methods" (Wright, 1957, p. 107). Pennsylvania emphasized practical over classical education.

Higher education in the colonies started at Harvard College in Cambridge, Massachusetts, in 1636. The preparation of ministers spurred establishment of many early colleges. In addition, such institutions provided instruction in the trivium (i.e., grammar, rhetoric, and logic) and the quadrivium (i.e., arithmetic, music, geometry, and astronomy). Colonists eager to prepare ministers and provide education comparable to that in England, established the College of William and Mary in Williamsburg, Virginia, in 1693 by British royal charter, and the Collegiate School in New Haven, Connecticut, in 1701, renamed Yale in 1718 for an early benefactor. Other than at seminaries, there was little academic training in the professions before 1763. Attorneys and doctors who were not able to travel to England for studies learned their trades through apprenticeships (Wright, 1957).

A pattern of evolution and change has characterized higher education in the United States throughout its history. The early colleges no longer primarily prepare ministers. Vertical expansion of college programs (so-called mission creep) has resulted in comprehensive universities. Some universities even offer certificates of completion and associate degrees. So, one might ask,

Reprinted from *The Community College Baccalaureate: Emerging Trends and Policy Issues*, edited by Deborah L. Floyd, Michael L. Skolnik, and Kenneth P. Walker (2005), by permission of Stylus Publishing.

what is the point of all this? The answer is simple: Community colleges, as well as all other colleges, evolve their missions and adapt their programs and services vertically to respond to changing needs in the communities that they serve. What is traditional today was not traditional 200, or even 50 years ago. There have been dramatic changes in who is educated and how they are educated.

Junior Colleges

In 1901, the first of a new type of college opened in Joliet, Illinois. This junior college was to provide access to college for poorly prepared students (Cohen & Brawer, 1996). U.S. society and the economy were based first on agriculture, then on industry, and today on information and knowledge. As society has evolved, so has education in response. It is again essential to expand educational opportunity to everyone in today's knowledge-based society. Just as community colleges democratized higher education through their open-door philosophy and associate degrees, so they must now democratize opportunity for higher education through the baccalaureate degree. Community colleges must not condone those who would, under the guise of maintaining quality and controlling competition, restrict access to higher education.

Higher Education for American Democracy (the Truman Commission Report) in 1947 called for a major expansion of education services. It proposed encouraging and enabling all Americans to explore their full educational potential, stating that "The American people should set as their ultimate goal an educational system in which at no level . . . will a qualified individual . . . encounter an economic barrier to the attainment of the kind of education suited to his aptitudes and interests" (Witt, Wattenbarger, Gollattscheck, & Suppiger, 1994, p. 131).

The commission suggested the name "community college" for colleges designed chiefly to serve local educational needs. "And it noted that it may have various forms of organization and may have curricula of various lengths. Its dominant feature is its intimate relations to the life of the community it serves" (Witt et al., 1994, p. 131). "The community college seeks to become the center of learning for the entire community. . . . It gears its programs and services to the needs and wishes of the people it serves" (Witt et al., 1994, p. 132).

Nowhere does the report limit community colleges to two-year programs; open-door access and responsiveness to community needs are to be their primary values. If community colleges are to be true to these fundamental values, they must respond anytime there is an identified need in the communities that they serve, including one for baccalaureate degrees. As Edmund Gleazer, Jr. has stated, "[t]he basic, inexorable, unmistakable fact and force to deal with is that of CHANGE— unparalleled and unprecedented change that perplexes the public, confounds the authorities, and demands response from education, one of its instigators" (1980, p. 2). Gleazer went on to say that "[t]he institution must be able to change as communities change with new conditions, demands, or circumstances" (pp. 4–5).

We build our present and future on the wisdom of scholars and leaders from earlier generations. We can measure a proposition's enduring value by the extent to which it remains relevant. Truly great minds live in the present and envision the future. Thus, the Truman Report and Gleazer were prophetic. The values that guided the junior colleges are relevant today even as community colleges consider offering bachelor's degrees.

Beginnings of the Community College Baccalaureate Degree

It is difficult to identify the first instance in which a community college offered the baccalaureate. Throughout the twentieth century it was not uncommon for a junior college to evolve into a four-year college. What began to happen in the 1980s, and more particularly in the late 1990s, was for some community colleges to decide to offer a few baccalaureate programs in selected areas in order to provide access to baccalaureate for students who would not otherwise be able to earn a four-year degree. In most cases, these contemporary community colleges have stated that their goal was to maintain emphasis on traditional community college values while at the same time adding baccalaureate programs that complemented their emphasis on access.

For instance, in 1985, Navarro College in Texas sought legislative approval to offer baccalaureate degrees.[2] Later, in 1993, Utah Valley Community College received legislative approval to offer baccalaureate degrees[1] and in 1997, the Arkansas legislature authorized Westark Community College to develop a bachelor's degree in manufacturing technology. In 1999, the Utah legislature authorized Dixie State College to offer a bachelor's degree in education. In 1999, Great Basin College in Reno, Nevada began offering a bachelor's degree in education. Colleges in Arizona, Kansas, and Oregon have unsuccessfully sought approval to offer baccalaureate degrees. The Florida Council of Community College presidents endorsed community colleges offering selected baccalaureate degrees in 1997[2] and later, in 2001, the Florida legislature greatly expanded the authority of the state's community colleges to offer four-year degrees.

The Florida legislation expands access to baccalaureate programs through community colleges; authorizes these institutions to offer a few baccalaureates to meet local workforce needs; prohibits them from terminating programs for associate in arts or associate in science degrees; and reinforces their primary mission as provider of associate degrees.

Very recently, in 2003, Texas and Hawaii authorized some community colleges in their states to add baccalaureate programs. Deborah L. Floyd describes these and other developments pertaining to the community college baccalaureate in the United States. From the increase in the number of states and colleges that have shown interest in the community college baccalaureate, especially since the 1990s, it is clear that the momentum for community colleges providing baccalaureate access has accelerated.

Rationale

The rationale for community colleges to add baccalaureate degrees to their offerings can be explained from both a societal perspective and an institutional perspective. From a societal perspective, a key factor is meeting the need for a baccalaureate educated workforce. Insofar as community college students experience barriers which limit baccalaureate attainment, the opportunity for them to complete their baccalaureate at the community college could likely increase their income and their contributions to society. From an institutional perspective, an issue for the community college is that many of the occupations for which it has been providing education have, in recent years, elevated their entry requirements to the baccalaureate level. Thus, if the community college is to continue to be a major provider of graduates for these occupations it is necessary for the community college to ensure that students in these programs have the opportunity to obtain the necessary credential—a baccalaureate.

Interest in the community college baccalaureate is in response to a variety of social and economic concerns. Three factors affect the motivation for community colleges to offer baccalaureate degrees: rising demand of employers and students, rising costs of universities, and limited programs and access to meet these demands. How will community colleges change to address these challenges, especially when students are demanding more access to opportunities for the bachelor's degree?

Community colleges are being confronted with competition from a variety of educational providers. Challenges to their survival will come from charter colleges, e-colleges, broker colleges, proprietary colleges, and private nonprofit institutions granting baccalaureate degrees. To be competitive, community colleges must develop new products and delivery systems, and shed the confining title of "two-year college."

The nation's social and economic foundations are at risk because more education is needed for productive employment, and access to college is being denied to millions of students (Commission on National Investment in Higher Education, 1997).

The national crisis in higher education calls for creative solutions. Traditional thinking, based on past experiences and limited by defensiveness and personal interests, does a disservice to the millions of students who need baccalaureate degrees, but who cannot attend a university. Community colleges can develop innovative ways to address rising demand, limited access, and increasing costs. If it is true that "widespread access to higher education . . . is critical to the economic health and social welfare of the nation" (Commission on National Investment in Higher Education, 1997, p. 2), community colleges must play a major role in the delivery of those degrees.

The facilities, faculty, staff, and programs are already in place at conveniently located community colleges across the nation. Expanding missions to include baccalaureate degrees without changing the open-door philosophy is a logical option. Missions should not reflect a bygone era, but rather respond, adapt, and grow in ways appropriate to changing communities.

The market for higher education is increasingly consumer driven, and it has become international in scope. The Internet enables colleges and universities to enroll students from anywhere in the world. Competition is increasing rapidly from private nonprofit and private for-profit institutions that now award degrees. There were 400 U.S. corporate universities in 1988, and there are more than 1,000 today (Meister, 1998), many of them now accredited by regional associations.

Such private competitors may transform higher education. According to the *Chronicle of Higher Education*, lawmakers and business leaders warned the annual meeting of the Education Commission of the States that "more and more companies are creating their own colleges or asking for-profit institutions like the University of Phoenix to train their employees because public colleges are too slow to respond to the corporations' needs" (Selingo & Basinger, 1999, p. A61). Business leaders also said that for-profit institutions have cutting-edge programs and move students through more quickly (Selingo & Basinger, 1999).

The three Cs—competition, cooperation, and collaboration—are becoming forces in the decision-making process for higher education. University centers and collaborative efforts between community colleges and universities have emerged on community college campuses across the country. Examples are Macomb Community College in Michigan; North Harris Montgomery Community College in Texas; and St. Petersburg College and Edison College in Florida. In addition, the Open University in Britain is exploring partnerships with community colleges to make baccalaureate degrees available through distance learning.

Given heightened demand and growing competition, the colleges that attract students will be those that best adapt to change. To remain relevant, community colleges must prepare to do new things and not simply do the same things differently. It is time for them to rethink their *raisons d'etre* and to assess the current competition. The complexities of the modern world require community colleges to adapt their services and forge a plan that should include the baccalaureate degree.

As student demand for the baccalaureate increases, community colleges have the capacity to accommodate this demand. Performing this role is a natural progression in the evolution of the mission of the community college.

A number of factors are reshaping higher education and have significant implications for the role of the community college with regard to the baccalaureate:

- The market has become international.

- A large proportion of students are older part-timers and are working.

- The baccalaureate is replacing the associate degree as the entry-level credential for many jobs that pay the best salaries and offer opportunities for promotions.

- The Internet has changed service area boundaries and resulted in a wide variety of new providers of baccalaureate programs.

In an age that places a premium on intellectual capital, a nation that fails to maintain first-rate education risks losing its economic and social position. Community colleges help to ensure that a nation's workforce remains globally competitive by addressing the rising demand for, limited access to, and increasing costs of baccalaureate education.

Distinctive Strengths

Widespread access to higher education is critical to the economic health and social welfare of any nation. Community colleges must expand their role in providing this access by offering baccalaureate degrees. By doing so, they will help promote the following:

- increased geographical, financial, and academic access to higher education;
- cost efficiencies through existing infrastructure;
- success among nontraditional or returning students through smaller classes, less-rigid sequencing, and greater scheduling options;
- ready matriculation and upward mobility for students with associate degrees;
- stable family and employment relationships for students while they complete their degrees;
- community college commitment to economic and workforce development; and
- responsiveness to community needs for specialized programs.

Community colleges are uniquely qualified to train and educate a workforce to the level necessary to meet future needs. Moreover, with their history of serving disadvantaged and minority students, they can open the door to greater access. Offering the baccalaureate is a logical next step—the community college can provide it to more learners, at convenient locations, in a more learner-centered environment, and at greatly reduced cost.

Increased demand for higher education is challenging community colleges. "Projected increases in the number of college-age students threaten to overwhelm many state public higher education systems during the next decade" (Ehrenberg, 2000, p. 34). Community colleges were designed to serve students not readily admissible to university because of limited financial means, poor academic records, language difficulties, or family concerns. They continue to serve those students well and to adapt and adjust their programs. Surveys and focus groups show that students, in addition to needing basic skills and short-cycle training and certification, want baccalaureate degrees. Transfer to traditional colleges or universities may not be suitable for them, and they would like to earn their bachelor's degree at their local community college.

Demographics may be an underlying force for change. Community college student demographics often mirror the communities they serve and they are becoming increasingly diverse. Having found success at the community college, more students want to pursue the baccalaureate and would prefer to do so locally in their communities. Community college leaders are fiercely loyal to these nontraditional students, and some ask: "Why we should give these students two years of education and then say, 'we can't serve you anymore—you're on your own—go to a university if you can afford it, and if you can overcome the obstacles that are in your way.'"

Facing the Critics

It is often said that students who start at a community college are significantly less likely to complete a four-year degree than students who begin at a four-year college or university. Completion rates at community colleges are elusive; many students do not seek a degree, much less pursue upper-division studies. In Florida, however, degree-seeking community college students in the upper division of the state university system traditionally do as well as or better than people who enroll there as freshmen (Florida Community College System, 1999). Indeed, permitting community colleges to offer selected baccalaureates could enhance access rates by making upper-division studies accessible to more students.

Critics argue that granting higher degrees implies an abandonment of the community college mission. According to Wattenbarger, "It would be difficult, if not impossible, to convince anyone that the bachelor's degree offered by a community college is as important as the one offered by a university or a four-year college" (Wattenbarger, 2000, p. 4). However, the regional accrediting associations hold such community colleges to the same standards as universities, so this criticism is questionable. Surely the quality of degrees varies among universities, so it could also be argued that degrees from some universities are not as respected as those from other universities. Adding the baccalaureate to the mission of the community college is not shifting focus; it is adding a focus in order to increase relevance. What proponents are saying is, "Keep the core values of the community colleges," and to the students, "We are not going to get you halfway there and then abandon you. We are going to take you all the way to the baccalaureate degree."

Future Directions: Building on Strengths

It is possible that students might pay less tuition for a baccalaureate at a community college than at a state university. Lower costs and convenient locations would increase opportunities for place-bound students, for whom community colleges may offer the only route to a bachelor's degree.

The rising cost of higher education is preventing many students from attaining a bachelor's degree. According to Chris Simmons, assistant director of government relations at the American Council of Education, low-income students remain underrepresented in college compared with middle- and upper-income students (Lane, 2003). Since community colleges enroll a large proportion of low- and moderate-income students, an obvious solution would be to authorize community colleges to confer baccalaureates. The infrastructure is already in place and adding two more years of education would be far less costly than building new universities.

Community colleges have played a major role in the higher education revolution of the twentieth century. Some educators believe that the revolution is almost over. "Two years of postsecondary education are within the reach—financially, geographically, practically—of virtually every American. . . . Open-admission policies and programs for everyone ensure that no member of the community need miss the chance to attend" (Cohen & Brawer, 1996, p. 31).

If associate degrees were enough to gain good jobs and advance in careers, then perhaps the revolution would be almost over. In the competition for the best jobs, however, the baccalaureate is an essential credential. Just as community colleges democratized access to the associate degree, they must now do the same for the baccalaureate. Education opens the door to success, and every person should have an equal opportunity to pursue the bachelor's degree at a minimum.

Whereas addition of the baccalaureate will change community colleges, there is no reason why their core values of open-door access, learner-centeredness, affordability, convenience, and responsiveness could not be maintained. Granting the bachelor's degree will take community colleges out of the undesirable position of offering "incomplete" education and transform them from halfway colleges on the way to a baccalaureate. With this transformation, community colleges could achieve recognition and respect for the quality that they have always provided. The beneficiaries would be the millions of students who would be able to gain more affordable access to a baccalaureate degree.

The Community College Baccalaureate Association

In the late 1990s, it became very apparent to the author that an organization was needed to serve as a convener and catalyst for the growing number of community college practitioners who were concerned about, and wanted to address, these challenges of baccalaureate access in their communities. Thus, The Community College Baccalaureate Association (CCBA) was founded in August, 1999 as a nonprofit organization to promote the development and acceptance of community college baccalaureate degrees as a means of addressing the national problems of student access, demand, and cost; to chronicle further progress in this arena; and to share information and facilitate networking. Florida incorporated the CCBA as a nonprofit organization on June 5, 2000, (CCBA, 2000).

Since its inception, the CCBA has served as a resource center, disseminating articles written by proponents, publishing and distributing a newsletter, and holding annual conferences. Information is available at www.accbd.org, such as articles with theoretical arguments for the community college baccalaureate. At present, CCBA's 130 members represent twenty-eight U.S. states, four Canadian provinces, Bermuda, and Jamaica, as well as research institutions, higher-education governing bodies, and private industry.

The CCBA's first annual conference was held in 2001 in Orlando, Florida, and there have been annual conferences with continually increased attendance. These conferences have featured presentations from practitioners, community college researchers, policy leaders, and others who are interested in issues of access to the baccalaureate. At the most recent conference in 2004, more than sixty institutions from the United States, Canada and other nations were represented.

It is important to note that when the CCBA was founded, its focus was exclusively on advocating for bachelor's degrees developed and awarded by community colleges. In 2004, the focus was expanded to include other models of enhancing baccalaureate access.

The current vision, philosophy, purpose, and mission of the Community College Baccalaureate Association are as follows:

> *Vision*: To be a catalyst for increasing access to the baccalaureate degree at community colleges.
>
> *Philosophy*: An educated populace is the foundation of a free and prosperous society. The baccalaureate degree is an important entry requirement for the better jobs and a better lifestyle. Therefore, every person should have an opportunity to pursue the baccalaureate degree at a place that is convenient, accessible, and affordable.
>
> *Purpose*: To promote better access to the baccalaureate degree on community college campuses, and to serve as a resource for information on various models for accomplishing this purpose.
>
> *Mission*: The purpose will be achieved by:
>
> 1. encouraging research, fostering dialogue, and sharing research data, publications, best practices, state legislation, and policies;
> 2. encouraging development of baccalaureate degrees conferred by community colleges;
> 3. encouraging development of university centers on community college campuses; and
> 4. encouraging joint degree programs with universities on community college campuses (CCBA, n.d.).

Clearly, the Community College Baccalaureate Association is meeting a need of community colleges in various countries that are addressing issues of providing baccalaureate programming through various models of delivery.

Issues for Research and Policy: Commentary

The purpose of this article has been to briefly describe the development of the community college baccalaureate within the context of the historical development of community colleges, to present a rationale or case for support of the community college baccalaureate, and to describe the Community College Baccalaureate Association. A great many issues for policy and research have arisen related to the community college baccalaureate and they are aptly identified and described in the following articles of this book.

The time has come to stop defining the community college as a two-year institution. Community colleges thrived in the last century because they were the hallmark of change and adaptation while they also remained responsive to their communities and core values. Community colleges should continue to lift the aspirations of ordinary people beyond two years of education and thus, the time is right for a new vision for community colleges, one that embraces a strong commitment to baccalaureate access.

In adding the baccalaureate to their mission, community colleges should heed the advice of Mark Milliron, President and Chief Executive Officer of the League for Innovation in the Community College. In his keynote address to the 2002 annual conference of the Community College Baccalaureate Association, he advised the audience to "be honest about whether you're ready to do this." He added, "do it for the right reasons, do it the community college way, and do it thoughtfully" (Milliron, 2002).

Notes

1. The author was president of Navarro College during this time. The bill, which did not leave committee, was authored by Tom Waldrop, a Texas state representative.
2. The author introduced the resolution of support to the Florida Community College presidents and it passed by a vote of twenty to one. (Florida Council of Presidents minutes, September, 1997.)

References

Cohen, A. M., & Brawer, F. B. (1996). *The American community college.* 3rd edition. San Francisco: Jossey-Bass, Inc.

Commission on National Investment in Higher Education (J. L. Dionne & T. Kean, Co-Chairs). (1997). Breaking the social contract: The fiscal crisis in higher education. Santa Monica, CA: Council for Aid to Education and Rand Corporation.

Community College Baccalaureate Association (CCBA). (June 5, 2000). Articles of incorporation. Florida Department of State Document No. N00000003823.

Community College Baccalaureate Association. (n.d.). Board of directors. Retrieved August 21, 2003, from www.accbd.org/boardofdirectors.html

Ehrenberg, R. G. (2000). Financial forecasts for the next decade. *Presidency.* Washington, DC: American Council on Education, 34.

Florida Community College System (April 1999). Articulation report. Tallahassee, FL: Florida Board of Education.

Florida Council of Presidents for Community Colleges (September 25–26, 1997). Minutes of meeting, 5.

Gleazer, E. J., Jr. (1980). *The community college: Values, vision, and vitality.* Washington, DC: Community College Press.

Lane, K. (September 1, 2003). Federal withholding. *Community College Week,* 7.

Meister, J. C. (1998). *Corporate universities: Lessons in building a world-class workforce.* New York: McGraw Hill.

Milliron, M. D. (March 17, 2002). Keynote address. Given at the Community College Baccalaureate Association Annual Conference, Boston.

Selingo, J., & Basinger, J. (July 23, 1999). At a meeting, education leaders talk of teacher quality and businesses' needs. *Chronicle of Education, 45,* A61.

Walker, K., & Zeiss, P. A. (December 2000/January 2001). Designs for change: Degrees and skills, baccalaureate degrees and skills certification. *Community College Journal, 71,* 8, 10.

Wattenbarger, J. (2000). Colleges should stick to what they do best. *Community College Week, 13*(18), p. 4–5.

Witt, A. A., Wattenbarger, J. L., Gollattscheck, J. F., & Suppiger, J. E. (1994). *America's community colleges: The first century.* Washington, DC: Community College Press.

Wright, L. B. (1957). *The cultural life of the American colonies.* New York: Harper and Brothers.

Acknowledgement

The author thanks and gratefully acknowledges the assistance of Ms. Laurie McDowell, District Director of the Edison University Center, Edison College District, Ft. Myers Florida. She assisted with the preparation of the section about the Community College Baccalaureate Association.

NEOLIBERAL IDEOLOGY IN COMMUNITY COLLEGE MISSION STATEMENTS: A CRITICAL DISCOURSE ANALYSIS

D. FRANKLIN AYERS

With more than 1,200 campuses serving nearly half of all undergraduate learners in the United States, the community college is a major institution of postsecondary education (Cohen & Brawer, 2003). Conventions of the community college up to late modernity have included public support as well as commitments to teaching, open access, an identified service area, community-based programs, comprehensive programs, and learning support services (Vaughan, 1997). The community college is particularly distinct among institutions of postsecondary education in that it serves learners through a variety of programs including student services, career education, developmental education, community education, transfer and liberal education, and general education (Cohen & Brawer, 2003). Another singularity of the community college is that it serves a unique student population, including high numbers of students from lower socioeconomic backgrounds; a disproportionately large share of learners who are African American, American Indian, Asian, Hispanic, and Pacific Islander; and nearly half of first-generation college students in the United States (Cohen & Brawer, 2003). Because the community college is often the only viable educational option for members of marginalized communities, the structural outcomes of its mission are of great consequence to educators, policymakers, and citizens concerned with social justice and participatory democracy.

Proponents of the community college, referred to by Kevin Dougherty (2001) as functionalist advocates (e.g., Cohen & Brawer, 2003), have identified this institution as "the People's college" and "Democracy's college." Citing its all-around accessibility, functionalist advocates contend that the community college facilitates the realization of the "American dream" for those of humble means and that the institution serves an egalitarian function in society. As one example of this function, advocates assert that the community college provides needed job training for those without the ability, means, or interest to attend four-year institutions. In this view, the community college affords the disadvantaged an opportunity for employment, financial independence, and personal development. Such an outcome may represent the ideal, perhaps; however, in this article, I contrast this vision against pervasive neoliberal discourses that threaten to engulf the mission and purpose of the community college.

The rising dominion of neoliberal ideology within the discourse of community college education diverges from the vision of the functional advocates because it promotes consumerism in lieu of participatory democracy and legitimates the world view of the upper strata of society to the exclusion of alternative perspectives (Chomsky, 2000; Engel, 2000; Giroux & Giroux, 2004; McChesney, 1999). In order to confront neoliberalism's opaque ideology, this critical discourse analysis reveals ideological-discursive practices that, when viewed tacitly from within the Western neoliberal hegemony, seem to be neutral and commonsensical but, when analyzed through a critical theoretical lens, refashion the meaning of community college education so that it serves the interests of those in the upper social strata.

Reprinted by permission from the *Review of Higher Education* 28, no. 4 (summer 2005).

Broadly conceived, the purpose of this analysis is to illustrate the downward transmission of ideological norms from the level of social formation to the level of the institution via ideological-discursive practices. My main thesis is that, insofar as the community college mission is represented through neoliberal discourse, the community college itself is instrumental in reproducing the class inequalities associated with advanced capitalism, thereby supporting the position of its instrumentalist Marxist critics (Clark, 1960; Karabel, 1972; Zwerling, 1976; see also Dougherty, 2001). While these researchers have discussed the community college's role in reproducing social inequality for more than 40 years, the analysis in this article is unique in explaining social reproduction as a discursive phenomenon. Doing so is not intended to discount the theories espoused by the aforementioned community college critics. Instead, following discourse theory, I contend that the social processes described by these theorists are a consequence of discourse. Lillie Chouliariki and Norman Fairclough (1999) elaborate on the instrumental nature of discourse:

> It is an important characteristic of the economic, social and cultural changes of late modernity that they exist as *discourses* as well as processes that are taking place outside discourse, and that the processes that are taking place outside discourse are substantively shaped by these discourses. (p. 4)

In other words, discourse is the medium through which economic, social, and cultural processes transpire. It is problematic, however, when the ideologies manifest in discourse are opaque, when unjust discourses proliferate uncontested, and when discursive alternatives are not considered. In these circumstances, it is of paramount importance for critical educators to reveal and confront such ideological-discursive practices through critical discourse analytical research.

On behalf of those who believe strongly in the egalitarian project of the community college, I aspire to reveal and challenge the discourse of neoliberalism, or market fundamentalism, and call for a counter-hegemonic discourse more fitting for an institution that, by virtue of its accessibility, is well positioned to serve the interests of a democratic society. I further suggest that, if the community college is to realize the vision of the functionalist advocates, its mission and purpose must be represented by a discourse of emancipation. That is, the term "community college" must come to signify an opportunity for people from all segments of society to realize their full potential. Furthermore, this potential must not be defined solely in terms of earnings and economic productivity but instead must address a broad range of human capacities.

Before proceeding to the analysis, I will provide an overview and critique of neoliberal ideology to situate the targeted discourse within its late modern context. Then I will explain how discourse analysis draws from linguistics and critical social science to explain how language constitutes meanings and exists in a dialectical relationship with social processes and material realities. Following this overview of the analytical framework, I will discuss ideological-discursive practices at the national level that promote a neoliberal world view. A full accounting of these widely circulated discourses is not possible, so I focus specifically on discourse fragments extracted from speeches by President Bill Clinton and President George W. Bush. Semiotic themes within the discourse of neoliberalism are then traced to discursive practices promulgated by well-known community college leaders and scholars. Finally, the manifestations of neoliberal discourse at the level of the institution become the center of focus. Specifically, I explain how certain language practices—as they appear in community college mission statements—represent the community college mission as an economic endeavor. I also examine the ideological effects on related social practices such as program planning, learning, and the negotiation of power relations and learner identities.

The Ascendancy of Market Fundamentalism

Classical liberal economics originated in 1776 with Adam Smith's *The Wealth of Nations*, "the Bible of capitalist economics" (Engel, 2000, p. 20). In this work, Smith proposed that prices of goods self-regulate through free trade as buyers and sellers bargain for a mutually beneficial exchange. In this exchange, prices automatically settle at an equilibrium, or the point at which the seller benefits in the form of profit and the buyer benefits from procurement of the good. As such, according to Smith, the materialistic, self-interested endeavors of the populace result in a utopian society, one managed not by government incompetence but instead by the "invisible hand" of the market.

In the latter part of the 20th century, these ideas gained renewed viability in the United States, particularly through the free-market doctrines of Friedrich A. von Hayek (1994). Hayek's resurrection of classical liberal economics differed in one fundamental aspect, however. Whereas Adam Smith advocated minimal government involvement in the free market, von Hayek argued that the government should, in fact, take deliberate steps to ensure the workings of the free market (Spring, 1998). Nobel laureate Milton Friedman's book *Capitalism and Freedom* (1962) precipitated further allegiance to Hayek's free-market ideals, particularly among policy makers in the United States and the United Kingdom. In this widely read treatise, Friedman argued that, in a free society, social problems are best resolved through market activity and not through government intervention. Manfred Steger (2002) summarizes these classical economic principles:

> The state should only provide the legal framework for contracts, defense, and law and order. Public-policy initiatives should be confined to those measures that liberate the economy from social constraints: privatization of public enterprises, deregulation instead of state control, liberalization of trade and industry, massive tax cuts, strict control of organized labor, and the reduction of public expenditures. (p. 12)

In consequence, advocates of these economic principles argue that the sole purpose of government is to provide a favorable climate for business and industry; thus, public well-being becomes less a civic endeavor and more a function of market activity. As the discourse of neoliberalism intensified, it gained the support of such political leaders as Ronald Reagan and Margaret Thatcher. In fact, the terms of these leaders marked the beginning of an era during which the markets were the primary interest of government, and challenges to the market's ascendancy were met with forceful defenses of neoliberal capitalism, particularly in Latin America (Chomsky, 1999; 2000; MacEwan, 1999).

Aligning more fully with neoliberal principles, national economic goals in the United States have shifted from full employment to technology as a proxy for labor (Aronowitz, 2001; Aronowitz & DiFazio, 1994), from the living wage to an all-out commitment to global competitiveness (Spring, 1998), and from democracy to the radical sovereignty of market forces (Chomsky, 1999; Giroux, 2001; Engel, 2000; MacEwan, 1999). Often captured in terms such as "market fundamentalism," the "new capitalism," "market ideology," and "turbo capitalism," this doctrine has drawn harsh criticism from grassroots activists, engaged scholars, and a few political leaders on both the right and the left (Steger, 2002). Robert McChesney (1999) describes neoliberalism in austere terms:

> Neoliberalism is the defining political economic paradigm or our time—it refers to the policies and processes whereby a relative handful of private interests are permitted to control as much as possible of social life in order to maximize their personal profit. (p. 7)

A principal argument against neoliberal policy is that it limits the power of citizens to advocate for social change through democratic processes. Arthur MacEwan (1999) articulates this criticism well:

> By reducing explicit social regulation of private economic activity and "leaving things up to the market," neo-liberalism prevents the implementation of programmes that would allow people to exercise political control over their economic affairs, involve people in solving their own economic problems, and serve the material needs of the great majority. (p. 5)

McChesney refers to neoliberalism as "the immediate and foremost enemy of genuine participatory democracy" (p. 11), and Henry Giroux (2001) refers to the current social order as a "dystopian culture of neoliberalism" (p. 426). Within the neoliberal regime, public education is reduced to two purposes: national defense and human capital development (Engel, 2000). To the extent that education is geared toward the latter, the purpose of education migrates from democratic ends to economic ends; that is, the discourse of education for participation and leadership in democratic society is overtaken by the economic discourse of production and consumerism. This recontextualization of educational discourse often emerges through endorsements of human capital theory.

Economists define human capital as "the stock of knowledge and skills possessed by the labor force that increases its productivity" (Engel, 2000, p. 24). As L. Steven Zwerling (1976) notes, human capital theory can be traced back to Adam Smith's classical liberal economics, although it was in a very basic form at the time. Accompanying the resurgence of free-market doctrines, however, human capital emerged as a keen interest of economists in the 1960s. This renewed interest in human capital began with the 1960 meeting of the American Economic Association when Theodore W. Schultz focused his presidential address on human capital accounting. Schultz (1977) noted in this speech:

> Although it is obvious that people acquire useful skills and knowledge, it is not obvious that these skills and knowledge are a form of capital, that this capital is in substantial part a product of deliberate investment, that it has grown in Western societies at a much faster rate than conventional (nonhuman) capital, and that its growth may well be the most distinctive feature of the economic system. It has been widely observed that increases in national output have been large compared with the increases of land, man-hours, and physical reproducible capital. Investment in human capital is probably the major explanation for this difference. (p. 313)

With this speech, Schultz initiated a flurry of research, the purpose of which was to account for various components of production, now to include human capital. The problem, however, was how to account for human capital in equations that explain production. Arising from this agenda were two prominent works, Gary Becker's (1964) *Human Capital* and Edward Denison's (1963) *Measuring the Contribution of Education to Economic Growth*.

Human capital accounting provided an economic rationale for allocating taxpayer dollars toward education. During this era, in fact, education ceased to be described as an expenditure but instead as an investment (Engel, 2000). Because education was an investment in capital, it promoted economic growth, so the argument ran, and economic growth is the primary aim of free market capitalism. Although human capital accounting resulted in increased expenditures for education, it reduced learning to its economic aspect.

The argument for public investment in education, when based on human capital theory, sanctions the idea that education is acceptable only to the extent that it yields a return on investment; therefore, non-commodified areas of study such as philosophy, literature, and others cannot be justified (Giroux, 2001; Giroux & Giroux, 2004; Engel, 2000). Educational investment based on this rationale, therefore, results in a "cost-benefit strait-jacket for curriculum development" (Engel, 2000, p. 30). Furthermore, human capital theory is less an empirical reality than an article of faith (Engel, 2000; Spring, 1998). Various studies (Berg, 1970; Machlup, 1970; Thurow, 1977) have exposed methodological flaws, unconfirmed assumptions, and ideological bias in human capital theory and its line of research. As such, within a few decades, interest in human capital theory as a line of research diminished substantially (Engel, 2000; Spring 1998). Its ideological underpinnings, however, continue to provide politicians and educators with a powerful discourse for garnering public support of educational initiatives that meet the interests of business and industry (Spring, 1998).

Indeed, despite its shortcomings, political and educational leaders often draw from human capital theory to justify the cost of education to taxpayers, citing its effect on overall economic development. The line of reasoning here is that the allocation of taxpayer dollars toward developing human capital results in higher levels of productivity, greater profits for private enterprise, and, thus, economic growth. This economic growth is said to yield higher levels of employment and eventually an improved quality of life for all.

Once again, the claims espoused through this discourse are not borne out in practice. Although, the minimum wage still exists today, it has declined 26% in real value since 1979 (Economic Policy Institute, 2004) despite increases in productivity and economic development, particularly in the 1990s. Furthermore, "in the 1990s, U.S. unemployment rates declined while the gap between the rich and poor increased" (Spring, 1998, p. 224), and income inequality is greater today than at any time in the past 70 years (Chomsky, 1999).

Given the rising levels of inequality since the mid-1900s—even during periods of high employment—one can reasonably conclude that economic development is not necessarily equivalent to wealth expansion. In fact, it is widely acknowledged by critics and proponents of neoliberalism alike that, in today's advanced capitalist society, the distribution of social goods typically associated with economic development is highly asymmetrical (Chomsky, 1999; Spring, 1998; Steger, 2002). Thus, a developed economy within a neoliberal state is not necessarily equivalent to a rise in the standard of living for all segments of society. Insofar as the community college joins with neoliberal discourses to represent its mission, it takes an active role in reproducing ideologies associated with structural inequality.

Critical Discourse Analysis

Critical discourse analysis (CDA), formerly critical linguistics, applies linguistic and semiotic analysis toward a social problem such as structures of dominance and oppression (Fairclough, 1995). It is based on understanding language as a force of dominance and ideology (Habermas, 1997). Furthermore, critical discourse analysts submit that powerful regimes produce discourses that shape the meanings of social and material processes in such a way as to secure their own interests. CDA offers critical theorists a way of understanding the production and consequences of dominant discourses. It is an approach to analyzing "opaque as well as transparent structural relationships of dominance, discrimination, power and control as manifested in language" (Wodak & Meyer, 2001, p. 2).

With roots in systemic functional linguistics (Halliday, 1978; Halliday & Hasan, 1989) CDA is grounded in a view of language not as a simple tool for communicating information but as a means of ordering social activity. In other words, language constitutes social action; it is the site where meanings are created and changed. For instance, I argue in this article that, within the neoliberal milieu, the meaning of community college education has shifted from a community-based social practice focused on the needs of learner systems (Boone, 1992) to a market-based social practice focused on the needs of business and industry. Once defined in this way by the neoliberal regime, community college education no longer signifies an opportunity for cognitive, intellectual, and leadership development as well as other types of personal growth typically associated with postsecondary education but instead becomes an investment in production. As a consequence of this semiotic change, related social practices such as program planning, teaching, learning, and assessment all realign with the demands of business and industry. Along with these shifts, the view of community college education as a means of human capital development becomes the norm. Critical theory is an attempt to understand how such a norm comes to be accepted even though it reproduces social inequality and threatens democratic culture. CDA is therefore a complement to critical theory in that it offers a way of studying the way power and language figure in the construction of meanings of social practices (Wodak & Meyer, 2001), particularly those enacted by social institutions.

Norman Fairclough (1995) positions social institutions such as the community college at the junction between two levels of social structuring. The highest and most abstract level of social structuring is that of the social formation, and the most concrete level is that of the particular social event or action. Fairclough contends that social institutions and their discourses are determined by the social formation, although it must be noted that the direction of determination is not inevitably unidirectional. Determination may transpire dialectically.

Because discourses are determined by higher levels of social structuring, texts—such as community college mission statements—and the discourses they represent are not created entirely by individuals. Instead, individual producers of text can only choose among the discursive options available at higher levels of social structuring. Because no ideology is monolithic, multiple discourses exist and are available to producers of text, although hegemonic discourses may make alternatives nearly imperceptible. Because discourses reflect ideologies of groups with unequal power resources and because the producer of text must choose among these discourses, he or she engages in a negotiation of power relations.

To the degree that powerful groups act upon discourses at various levels of social structuring, their ideologies and world views gain authority. Dominant discourses consequently determine the meanings assigned to social and materials processes, and they do this in ways that reinforce power inequities. One way that meanings may be determined is through recontextualization (Fairclough, 1995). Recontextualization is a process in which the discourse related to one social process dominates or colonizes the discourse related to another social process.

My analysis demonstrates how this progression works by explaining in linguistic terms how discourses related to community college education are recontextualized by discourses relating to neoliberal ideology. Consistent with Fairclough, I propose that the community college is an intermediary institution positioned between the highest and lowest levels of social structuring and that its discourses are determined largely by the social formation. In other words, language choices made at the level of the institution may be severely limited by the ideological-discursive options available at the level of social formation. This study, therefore, addresses a particular type of education in its semiotic aspect. By connecting dominant discourses at the level of the social formation with specific ideological-discursive practices at the level of the institution, this study reveals how education comes to signify economic processes that represent the interests of powerful groups.

Hegemony

According to Bernard McKenna (2004), "It is the facility of taken-for-granted 'common sense' that provides ideology with its strongest ideological effect" (p. 13). This analysis demonstrates how national political leaders, educational leaders, scholars, and producers of local institutional texts subscribe to the discourse of neoliberalism in representing the mission and purpose of the community college. These tacit, discursive endorsements of neoliberal ideology, perhaps by unsuspecting actors, illustrate McKenna's point: The discursive manifestations of neoliberal ideology in political speeches, publications by the American Association of Community Colleges, and community college mission statements represent common assumptions about the mission and purpose of the community college in late modernity. That these manifestations of an unjust ideology proceed largely uncontested suggests a hegemonic state of affairs. This Gramscian concept is fundamental to my argument, which Barry Burke (1999) defines:

> By hegemony, Gramsci meant the permeation *throughout* society of an entire system of values, attitudes, beliefs and morality that has the effect of supporting the status quo in power relations. Hegemony in this sense might be defined as an "organising principle" that is diffused by the process of socialisation into every area of daily life. To the extent that this prevailing consciousness is internalised by the population it becomes part of what is generally called "common sense" so that the philosophy, culture and morality of the ruling elite comes to appear as the natural order of things. (19)

Along similar lines, Gordon Marshall (1998) explains that hegemony "involves the production of ways of thinking and seeing, and of excluding alternative visions and discourses" (p. 272). Henry Giroux and Susan Searls Giroux (2004) connect the concept of hegemony to late modernity: "As the discourse of neoliberalism seizes the public imagination, there is no vocabulary for political or social transformation, democratically inspired visions, or critical notions of social agency to enlarge the meaning and purpose of democratic public life" (p. 251). Nothing the invasion of market discourses into social practices at all levels of society, no matter how inappropriate, Bernard McKenna (2004) observes that "the neoliberal hegemony in Western culture is very close to absolute" (p. 17). Noam Chomsky (1999, 2000) likens this development to the regimentation of minds, and Michael Engel (2000) claims that neoliberal ideology has become a secular religion.

Representations of the Community College within National Discourses

Central to my argument is the concept that discursive practices both reflect and construct a worldview in which the markets are seen as fundamental to the national interests when they are, in fact, of primary interest to those affiliated with power and wealth. Within this discourse, education is represented as a means toward economic development. The representation of education as an economic issue suggests a recontextualization of educational discourse. This recontextualization can be observed at various levels of social structuring. In this section, I will explain such a recontextualization as I comment on various discourses from prominent politicians, scholars, and community college leaders.

The discussion begins with the Clinton administration. When speaking at Miami-Dade Community College in 1996, President Clinton positioned market demands as the driver of educational programming in community colleges:

> If you just think about it, this is not a bureaucratic organization, it's a flexible, creative organization. You change from year to year the programs you offer. And you have to meet a high standard of excellence, otherwise you'll be punished for what you don't know in the marketplace. (Office of the Press secretary, 1996)

As this statement makes clear, Clinton is directing the community college with continuously realigning its programming to the impulses of the market. In this way, the community college abandons its commitment to community-based programming as planned through democratic processes (Boone, 1992) and instead becomes a servant of unfettered, free-market capitalism.

In his 2004 State of the Union Address, President George W. Bush reproduced this discourse when he pledged "support for America's community colleges to train workers for the industries that are creating the most new jobs" (State of the Union, 2004). The following day, Bush provided more information on this initiative in a speech at Owens Community College in Ohio. In this speech, Bush referred to the provost as the "guy who is responsible for making sure the curriculum actually adjusts and doesn't stay stuck." He further added, "If you're in the local community, you've got to ask this question to a provost, are you flexible? [Laughter.] In other words, if somebody shows up and says, we've got a demand for jobs, will the community college adjust?" (Office of the Press Secretary, 2004). Once again in connecting educational programming with the shifting markets, discursive practices portray the community college as a reactive institution that is dependent on market activity for its curriculum. Furthermore, the initiative Bush mentions will be managed, not by the Department of Education, but instead by the Department of Labor. The community college thus fulfills a purely economic role.

Furthermore, in the third presidential debate in 2004 President Bush responded to a question about the economy and job creation in purely educational terms. When asked how he would speak to an individual who had just lost his job, Bush responded:

> You know, there's a lot of talk about how to keep the economy growing. We talk about fiscal matters. But perhaps the best way to keep jobs here in America and to keep this economy growing is to make sure our education system works. . . . Education is how to make sure we've got a workforce that's productive and competitive. And so the person you talked to, I say, here's some help, here's some trade adjustment assistance money for you to go a community college in your neighborhood, a community college which is providing the skills necessary to fill the jobs of the 21st century. (Commission on Presidential Debates, 2004).

With these comments, the boundaries between educational and economic policy are razed. Government becomes responsible for unemployment only through its involvement in education. Consequently, the community college is reduced to an arm of economic policy, and other responsibilities traditionally associated with postsecondary education such as intellectual and social development become secondary.

As stated above, neoliberal ideology holds that the government should act in support of business and industry as a way of protecting national economic interests. One way of promoting a healthy business climate, therefore is to allocate government resources toward the production of human capital, and this is achieved to a great extent through community college education. Researchers Anthony Carnevale and Donna Desrochers (2001) acknowledge the role of the community college in providing human capital for employers, equating developing relationships between community college educators and employers with an "ongoing restructuring of the human capital development system" (p. 11). Indeed, through collaboration with members of the corporate world, community colleges nationwide are demonstrating increasing commitment to the production of human capital for accumulation by private enterprise (Zeiss, 1997). Reproducing the neoliberal principle that government activity should be limited to establishing a favorable business climate, Carnevale and Desrochers advocate community college education as a means of benefiting private enterprise at the public's expense: "We cannot expect employers to carry the costs of the growing need for career development among employed workers" (qtd. in Zeiss, 1997, p. viii).

Furthermore, representing the community college's focus on human capital development, the North Carolina Community College System has adopted the slogan, "preparing North Carolina's world-class workforce," and the University and Community College System of Nevada claims that the community college mission "encompasses a belief that education and training are the chief means of developing human capital for investment in the economic health of the state" Finally P. Anthony Zeiss (1997) recommends that "community college leaders, including trustees, should strongly consider positioning workforce development as a core mission" (p. 102). This discussion of the human capital development role of the community college exemplifies how the discourse of economics has colonized the discourse of higher learning.

The discourse above demonstrates the involvement of political leaders at the highest level, prominent researchers, and community college leaders in refashioning the purpose of education from one of cognitive and intellectual, spiritual, moral, and personal development to one of human capital development; thus, the learner is reduced to an economic entity (Levin, 2001). As represented through this discourse, the community college itself is instrumental in reproducing inequality. As such, the community college is complicit in what Joel Spring (1998) describes as the chasm between the nation's richest and its poorest citizens. In other words, the income of the wealthy has increased while the income of the poor has decreased, and this consequence of neoliberalism is both reflected and reinforced through the mission and impacts of the community college, at least to the extent that it is represented in purely economic terms.

The Discursive Construction of Inequality at the Level of the Institution

The Analytical Process

As part of a larger project, I gathered a systematic sample of 144 institutions located in the United States that are currently members of the American Association of Community Colleges. I retrieved mission statements—including statements of philosophy, purpose, goals, and objectives, as available—from the internet sites of each institution. With the analytical framework described above in mind, I examined these mission statements in search of discursive manifestations of human capital theory and neoliberal ideology. I subjected these ideological-discursive practices to semiotic and linguistic analyses with particular attention to evidence of recontextualization. Through this analytical process, two prominent ideological effects emerged. I present below the linguistic analysis and the ideological effects of neoliberal discourse as represented in these community college mission statements, illustrated by examples from these mission statements.

The first set of discursive practices revealed by this analysis yields the ideological effect of reducing learners to an economic entity whose responsibility to society is "to please employers" so that business and industry may remain competitive in the global economy. The second set of ideological effects revealed in this analysis is closely related. It deals with the restructuring of the curriculum so that it accommodates the demands of business and industry as they respond to the irregularities of the market. Through these discursive practices, education is justified primarily by its effect on economic conditions. In effect, both sets of discursive practices naturalize the incursion of neoliberal ideology into the domain of postsecondary learning in ways that reinforce and reproduce the differential distribution of power and other social goods in advanced capitalist societies.

The Learner as an Economic Entity

Reflecting and reinforcing the neoliberal social order in late modernity, the first set of discursive practices in the corpus of community college mission statements reduces the learner to human capital, an economic entity whose only role in society is to remain competitive in a perpetually adjusting labor market. Table 1 presents examples of such discursive practices, and a critical analysis follows.

TABLE 1
Discursive Practices that position the student as an Economic Entity

Location of Institution	Excerpts from Community College Mission Statements
1. Florida	Goals. . . . Promote economic development for the state through special education and training programs including technical courses, workshops, and services designed to enhance the competitiveness of individuals, businesses and industries in the local, state, national and global economies.
2. Indiana	Professional and technical education to prepare students with the knowledge, comprehension, and skills to achieve their goals, meet the needs of Indiana's employers, and be contributing members of the Indiana economy.
3. Ohio	We see [the college] as a dynamic and diverse institution offering accessible, affordable, lifelong learning opportunities to meet the educational, employment, and enrichment needs of our community as it participates in the global economy.
4. North Carolina	The college serves as an economic catalyst by assisting business and service sectors by training employees.
5. Massachusetts	The community colleges support the public system of higher education by . . . developing partnerships with business and industry to provide job training, retraining, and skills improvement to ensure a workforce equipped to meet the needs of a changing economy.

Selection 1 is taken from a list of college goals. Within the foreground of this excerpt, the stated goal is to develop the economy. This discourse, typically associated with economics, may seem unnatural within the mission of an educational institution, but it is naturalized here in that its end is said to be achieved through an array of educational programs. The intended outcome is economic competitiveness, a responsibility that is said to be shouldered by both individuals and private enterprise. Because the language restricts the educational needs of individuals to those that intersect the goal of economic competitiveness, the excerpt constrains the individual to an economic role. Learning needs relating to non-economic fields are not addressed. This discursive practice holds individuals and business and industry accountable only to their economic performance. Moral and ethical responsibilities to family, community, and democratic society are therefore excluded.

Selection 2 presents one item from a listing of educational programs offered at a community college in Indiana. The human subjects in this example—the learners—are directed to meet three obligations. The first is to meet individual needs. In the form of self-advocacy and an ethical pursuit of improved quality of life, this responsibility possibly relates to justice and democracy. A focus on individual needs may also reflect a doctrine of Machiavellianism. In this excerpt, there is no mention of ethical responsibility or obligation to that which exists beyond the self.

The following two goals do, in fact, indicate an obligation to a social collective, but this responsibility is defined in entirely economic terms. First, the student exists to meet the needs of the employers. This language assembles hierarchical power relations between learners and employers; it subordinates learners to employers. Second, the student exists as a subsystem of advanced capitalism whose responsibility to society is purely economic. Conspicuously absent from the mention of duty to society is the obligation of public service and participation in the democratic process.

I retrieved the third excerpt from a statement of philosophy. Until the final clause of this selection, the language reflects community college traditions such as open access, affordability, and learning throughout the lifespan. This language seems to represent a comprehensive educational agenda. The final clause, however, severely limits the purpose of educational programs. That is, the clause "as it participates in the global economy" restricts the focus of educational programs to its nexus with society's economic sphere. This clause renders all other possible learning objectives—particularly those in the public sphere (Giroux, 2001) imperceptible.

The fourth excerpt in Table 1 also positions learners as inferior to employers. Appearing in the foreground are the business and service sectors, which are explicitly identified as the beneficiaries of the community college enterprise. Relegated to the background is the reference to employees, who are positioned as human capital to be controlled by business and industry. This language portrays students as passive subjects whose only important needs are those consistent with the needs of private enterprise. This language also reflects and reinforces a passive role for learners and their communities in the planning, design, implementation, and evaluation of educational programs. Once again, the needs of learners and their communities are seen as inferior to the needs of employers.

The fifth selection is extracted from a list of institutional goals. This selection is a component of a local community college mission statement but is derived from the general Massachusetts Community College mission statement. The initial clause identifies community colleges as an integral component of the state system of higher education. Six subsequent gerund clauses detail how community colleges operationalize their service to the public system of higher education. Extracted from this list, Selection 5 demonstrates the role of language in positioning the student as an economic entity with the purpose of serving private enterprise. In the foreground is a commitment to serve the needs of business and industry through partnerships.

Following the initial gerund clause, an infinitive clause lists the purposes of such partnerships as "to provide job training, retraining, and skills improvement. . . . " The choice of the words "skills improvement," a nominalization, seems awkward. It renders the learner conspicuously absent. By choosing a nominalization, or the use of a noun to represent an action, the producers of this text are able to erase all recognition of learners as individuals (Fairclough, 1995). This impersonal reference to the learner parallels another impersonal reference in a subsequent clause. That is, the second infinitive clause cites the purpose of educational programming as to "provide a workforce equipped to meet the needs of a changing economy." The reference to learners as "a workforce" is common in community college mission statements, and it reduces the needs of learners to those deemed important by employers. By implication, the learner's purpose is to please future employers and learning needs tangential to this purpose are irrelevant.

In these examples, the discourse of economics colonizes the discourse of pedagogy. Because individual citizens are empowered only to meet the needs of employers and to promote their own self-interest, they fail to develop the critical citizenship skills that are requisite to a democratic society. Under such circumstances, a naive and acquiescent society may develop, deferring political decision making to an elite class of politicians who claim to act in the universal interest of a homogenous populace.

The Market-Driven Curriculum

A second theme relating to the development of human capital is language that escalates the market's role in determining educational objectives. The function of business and industry within this discourse strand is to make meaning of the erratic and ever-changing whims of the market. The resulting interpretations of market activity become the building blocks of the curriculum. As a result, curriculum foundations emanate from semiotic endeavors of business and industry representatives. Following discourse theory, these individuals make meaning of market activity through language and discourse; and because all discourse is laden with ideology, the resulting educational programs are likely to facilitate ideological indoctrination. The set of discursive practices analyzed below fails to recognize the needs of the community in the planning, design, and evaluation of educational programs.

Table 2 presents typical ideological discursive practices from representative texts in the corpus of mission statements. The first selection is extracted from a list of college purposes. It presents a string of three clauses. The first clause states one college purpose, which is economic development. The second clause identifies the means through which the goal is to be achieved, which is a collaboration or a partnership with business and industry. The human agents responsible for promoting economic development thus become community college educators and representatives from private enterprise. In the third clause, the purpose of the partnership is identified as restructuring occupational program offerings as dictated by the "job market." Thus, the market provides the rationale behind the renewal, creation, evaluation, or termination of educational programs. Accordingly, community college educators and business and industry representatives function simply to interpret market activity as they plan, design, implement, and evaluate educational programs.

TABLE 2
Discursive Practices That Condense Education to a Market Function

Location of Institution	Selected Excerpts from Community College Mission Statements
1. Arkansas	Goals:. . . . To promote economic development by working with business and industry to match the college's occupational programs with the needs of the job market
2. Missouri	[Curriculum, under "Objectives"] Provide academic opportunities that enable graduates to meet the changing needs of industry
3. Florida	Goal 3: Skilled Workforce and Economic Development *Strategic Imperative 6*: Appropriately aligning the workforce's education with the skill requirements of the new economy.
4. Illinois	Provide an educational delivery system that upgrades skill levels, enhances employability, and responds to changing needs of the local, regional and national labor markets.
5. Maryland	That business, government and industry in the community have an opportunity to enhance their operations through specially tailored educational programs developed in consultation with the college.

Also in the first selection, the goals statement contains the two sequential prepositional phrases: "with the needs of the job market." In this excerpt, the market is personified with the human quality of having needs. As Norman Fairclough (1995) points out, this discursive practice suggests that the market is the agent of change and that human agents are not. By implication, if human actors are not responsible for curricular change, then the tyranny of the market is, by default, a natural phenomenon that cannot be contested any more than bad weather can be contested. This language not only portrays change as an inevitability but also releases human actors from ethical responsibility for policies and practices that perpetuate distributive injustice and social inequality.

The second selection is extracted from a list of institutional objectives. The objective in focus in this excerpt is curriculum. It portrays the learners as passive, economic entities who exist to meet the demands of industry. The noun phrase in the foreground is "academic opportunities," which can refer to a wide variety of learning experiences. However, this array of possibilities is greatly restricted by the subsequent clause. Only the learning experiences that meet the needs of industry are deemed relevant; therefore, industry determines which skills, knowledge, and dispositions will be addressed through the curriculum. Once again, positioning industry representatives as the ultimate legitimators of knowledge invites an inculcation of market ideology into the learning experience. Finally, the needs of industry are described as "changing," which provides justification for constant disruptions in educational programming based on employers' preferences. From a different point of view, however, this practice indicates the short-term value of narrowly focused educational programs designed to meet specific production demands.

The third selection in Table 2 comes from a list of goals and strategic imperatives. The heading limits the described action to the economic and workforce development mission of the college. As is common within this discourse strand, the learners are dehumanized and referred to as a collective, in this case "the workforce." This discursive practice depicts a group of learners as a single entity with homogenous needs. It furthermore reflects and reinforces an industrial frame of mind that favors the standardization of components in the production process. Also, there is no acknowledgment that each individual learner may have unique needs nor that the needs of the individual may be markedly different from those of the employer. As in the example above, the genesis of curricular change is portrayed as a nonhuman entity: in this case, "the new economy." The effect is the same, however; societal changes that accommodate shifting markets and the demands of business and industry are portrayed as an innate, common-sense responses to natural phenomena. It is implied that, if the new economy is a force of nature, then it has no human agents and that the advanced capitalist economy is something that society must accommodate without question. As McKenna (2004) argues, blind acceptance of the status quo feeds power to an ideology and its proponents. However, the proponents of neoliberalism who are responsible for the new economy and its resultant social inequality are invisible in this text.

The fourth selection delineates one purpose of several of an Illinois community college. As in the examples above, the needs of the learner—or even that individual learners may have unique needs—are not acknowledged. What is acknowledged is that local, regional, and national labor markets are changing and that the role of educational programs is to accommodate these market vagaries. Once again, this language positions a nonhuman entity, the market, in control of the curriculum.

The final selection comes from a list of objectives of a Maryland community college. Its description of the purpose of educational programming is simply to benefit business, government, and industry. Educational programs are said to be specially tailored to the needs of external organizations. The needs of the learner are deemed irrelevant by virtue of their absence in the stated objective. Furthermore, the college and its faculty are reduced to a consultative role. As with the above excerpts from community college mission statements, this example positions noneducational entities as the primary designers of curricula.

In the above discourse fragments, control of the curriculum is placed largely within the domain of business and industry. That is, representatives of business and industry, although at times in concert with community college educators, are granted dominion over the curriculum in certain community college programs. As a result, the discourse of economics reconstitutes the meaning of education; the value and legitimacy of knowledge are determined purely by their market value. Non-commodified knowledge, skills, and wisdom addressed through civic and liberal education migrate from the core of higher education to a distant periphery (Engel, 2000; Giroux, 2001; Levin, 2001).

Conclusions

In summary, discourses promulgated by high-level politicians, scholars, community college leaders, and even community college mission statements demonstrate the recontextualization of the educational process by economic processes and their neoliberal ideological basis. In effect, the representation of community college education through neoliberal discourse (a) subordinates workers/learners to employers, thereby constituting identities of servitude, and (b) displaces the community and faculty in planning educational programs, placing instead representatives of business and industry as the chief designers of curricula.

This analysis supports Burton Clark (1960), Jerome Karabel (1972), and L. Steven Zwerling (1976) and other critics whose works describe the community college as an institution that serves the interests of the elite to the detriment of learners and workers. This analysis also parallels John Levin's (2001) claims that, in the 1990s, (a) community colleges shifted their focus from meeting the needs of learners to meeting the needs of business and industry, (b) the mission of the community college has become focused on economic ends rather than educational ends, and (c) that this transformation has occurred at the learner's expense.

The narrow educational focus on economic development is alarming because it places the market in control of the curriculum and because, as Engel (2000) states, "If the market is making the big decisions about the direction of education, then the community is not" (p. 30). One danger of this development is that the curriculum is likely to become heavily laden with a market ideology that reinforces and reproduces power asymmetries among learners, their communities, faculty, and representatives of the private sector. The colonization of the community college mission by a neoliberal regime should therefore arouse trepidation among functionalist advocates who view "the People's college" as a democratic institution that empowers individual learners and communities from all segments of society. The colonization of educational discourse by a neoliberal discourse is also troublesome because "the markets do not reward moral behavior" (Giroux, 2001, p. 32). On the contrary, the tyranny of the markets emphasizes "profit over people" as Chomsky (1999) asserts in the title of his book on neoliberalism and the global order. Finally, Giroux and Giroux (2004) summarize the consequences of the rising dominion of neoliberalism: "In short, private interests trump social needs, and economic growth becomes more important than social justice" (p. 250).

The community college mission is much more extensive than that represented in neoliberal discourses. In many instances, community college mission statements explicitly uphold the community college as an institution committed to democracy and justice. In his work on community-based programming, Edgar Boone (1992) points out that the community college occupies a unique position in society: With its close proximity to the people, the community college is capable of engaging individuals across America's communities in democratic decision-making processes that enhance community development. In this way, progress is not defined purely in terms of corporate interests but instead by the broad interests of a diverse society. Through community-based programming, individuals of different means have an equal voice in determining their shared future. Although empowering individuals with a voice equal to that of business and industry is quite the antithesis of neoliberal ideology, it is the basis of participatory democracy.

Community-based programming and civic programs such as service learning are gaining momentum within the community college, suggesting that, even though the neoliberal ideological norms of late modernity have permeated the discourse of community college education, this permeation is neither absolute nor universal. Perhaps the manifestations of neoliberalism in community college mission statements represent only one ideological discursive formation (Fairclough, 1995) within the institution. If so, then the evolution of the community college mission is both a semiotic endeavor and an ideological struggle between competing discourse regimes. Given this struggle, if the community college is to realize its egalitarian mission then functionalist advocates must mount alternatives to the discourse of neoliberalism. To the degree that alternative discourses are available, hegemony dissipates into choice, and this invites resistance to domination and oppression.

References

Aronowitz, S. (2001). *The last good job in America: Work and education in the new global technoculture.* New York: Rowman & Littlefield.

Aronowitz, S., & DiFazio, W. (1994). *The jobless future: Sci-tech and the dogma of work.* Minneapolis: University of Minnesota Press.

Becker, G. (1964). *Human capital: A theoretical and empirical analysis, with special reference to education.* New York: Columbia University Press.

Berg, I. (1970). *The great training robbery.* New York: Praeger.

Boone, E. J. (1992). Community-based programming: An opportunity and imperative for the community college. *Community College Review, 20*(3), 8–20.

Burke, B. (1999). Antonio Gramsci and informal education. *The encyclopedia of informal education.* Retrieved November 5, 2004, from http://www.infed.org/thinkers/et-gram.htm.

Carnevale, A. P., & Desrochers, D. M. (2001). *Help wanted . . . credentials required: Community colleges in the knowledge economy.* Annapolis Junction, MD: Community College Press.

Chomsky, N. (1999). *Profit over people: Neoliberalism and global order.* New York: Seven Stories Press.

Chomsky, N. (2000). *Chomsky on MisEducation.* Edited by D. Macedo. Lanham, MD: Rowman & Littlefield.

Chouliaraki, J., & Fairclough, N. (1999). *Discourse in late modernity: Rethinking critical discourse analysis.* Edinburgh, Scotland: Edinburgh University Press.

Clark, B. (1960). *The open door college: A case study.* New York: McGraw-Hill.

Cohen, A. M., & Brawer, F. B. (2003). *The American community college* (4th ed.). San Francisco: Jossey-Bass.

Commission on Presidential Debates. (2004). *The third Bush-Kerry presidential debate.* Retrieved November 3, 2004, from http://www.debates.org/pages/trans2004d.html.

Denison, E. (1963). *Measuring the contribution of education to economic growth.* Study Group in the Economics of Education. Paris: Organization for Economic Cooperation and Development.

Dougherty, K. J. (2001). *The contradictory college: The conflicting origins, impacts, and futures of the community college.* New York: State University of New York Press.

Economic Policy Institute. (2004). Minimum wage facts at a glance. Retrieved November 12, 2004, from http://www.epinet.org/content.cfm/issueguides_minwage_minwagefacts.

Engel, M. (2000). *The struggle for control of public education: Market ideology vs. democratic values.* Philadelphia: Temple University Press.

Fairclough, N. (1995). *Critical discourse analysis: The critical study of language.* Harlow, Eng.: Pearson Education, Ltd.

Friedman, M. (1962). *Capitalism and freedom.* Chicago: University of Chicago Press.

Giroux, H. A. (2001). Vocationalizing higher education: Schooling and the politics of corporate culture. In H. A. Giroux & K. Myrsiades (Eds.), *Beyond the corporate university: Culture and pedagogy in the new millennium* (pp. 29–44). New York: Rowman & Littlefield.

Giroux, H. A., & Giroux, S.S. (2004). *Take back higher education: Race, youth, and the crisis of democracy in the post-civil rights era.* New York: Palgrave Macmillan.

Habermas, J. (1977). *Erkenntnis und interesse.* Frankfurt, Ger.: Suhrkamp.

Halliday, M. A. K. (1978). *Language as social semiotic: The social interpretation of language and meaning.* Baltimore, MD: University Park Press.

Halliday, M. A. K., & Hasan, R. (1989). *Language, context, and text: Aspects of language in a social-semiotic perspective* (2nd ed.). Hong Kong: Oxford University Press.

Karabel, J. (1972). Community colleges and social stratification. *Harvard Educational Review, 42,* 521–562.

Levin, J. S. (2001). *Globalizing the community college: Strategies for change in the twenty-first century.* New York: Palgrave.

MacEwan, A. (1999). *Neo-liberalism or democracy?: Economic strategy, markets, and alternatives for the 21st Century.* New York: Zed Books.

Marshall, G. (1998). *Oxford dictionary of sociology* (2nd ed.). Oxford: Oxford University Press.

Machlup, F. (1970). *Education and economic growth.* Lincoln: University of Nebraska Press.

McChesney, R. W. (1999). Introduction. In N. Chomsky, *Profit over people: Neoliberalism and global order.* New York: Seven Stories Press.

McKenna, B. (2004). Critical discourse studies: Where to from here? *Critical Discourse Studies, 1,* 9–39.

Office of the Press Secretary. (1996, October 22). Remarks by the President to the people of the Miami area. Retrieved November 12, 2004, from http://www.clintonpresidentialcenter.org/legacy/102296-speech-by-president-at-miami-dade-community-college.htm.

Office of the Press Secretary. (2004, January 21). President discusses job training and the economy in Ohio. Retrieved November 12, 2004, from http://www.whitehouse.gov/news/releases/2004/01/20040121-2.html.

Schultz, T. W. (1977). *Investment in human capital.* In J. Karabel & A. H. Halsey (Eds.), Power and ideology in education (pp. 131–324). New York: Oxford University Press.

Spring, J. (1998). *Education and the rise of the global economy.* Mahwah, NJ:Lawrence Erlbaum Associates.

State of the Union 2004 Home Page. (2004). Retrieved February 12, 2004 from http://www.whitehouse.gov/stateoftheunion/2004/print/index.html.

Steger, M. B. (2002). *Globalism: The new market ideology.* New York: Rowman & Littlefield.

Thurow, L. C. (1977). *Investment in human capital.* In J. Karabel & A. H. Halsey (Eds.), Power and ideology in education (pp. 325–334). New York: Oxford University Press.

Vaughan, G. B. (1997). The community college's mission and milieu: Institutionalizing community-based programming. In E. J. Boone (Ed.), *Community leadership through community-based programming: The role of the community college* (pp. 21–58). Washington, DC: Community College Press.

Von Hayek, F. A. (1994). *The road to serfdom* (50th anniversary ed.). Chicago: University of Chicago Press.

Wodak, R., & Meyer, M. (Eds.). (2001). *Methods of critical discourse analysis.* Thousand Oaks, CA: Sage Publications.

Zeiss, T. (Ed.). (1997). *Developing the world's best workforce: An agenda for America's community colleges.* Washington, DC: Community College Press.

Zwerling, L. S. (1976). *Second best: The crisis of the junior college.* New York: McGraw-Hill.

RACE, RHETORIC, AND THE CONTEST OVER CIVIC EDUCATION

H.A. GIROUX AND S.S. GIROUX

The Liberal Arts in a Neoliberal Age

It is one of the more revealing paradoxes in contemporary liberal arts education that recent, cutting-edge discourses proffered in the service of democratic renewal—discourses frequently excoriated as trendy, postmodern, or ultra-radical by academics and the popular press alike—share, in many ways, the assumptions of some of the oldest theoretical justifications for higher education in America. Primarily concerned with reasserting the university's role in producing a literate and critical citizenry, recent progressive work in rhetorical and cultural theory has focused on the dynamic interconnections among the study of rhetoric and composition, the practice of democratic citizenship, and the politics of race. In doing so, such work speaks to the necessity of an educational discourse steeped in democratic principles at a time when neoliberal agendas redefine public goods such as schooling as private interests, and in doing so suggest that "we have no choice but to adapt both our hopes and our abilities to the new global market."

For those unfamiliar with the history of American universities or the social foundations of education, the relationship among terms such as *rhetoric, pedagogy, democracy, ethics,* and *race* are not immediately apparent. Nor will this particular combination of topics fall easily on the ears of those in academia who insist that education, even civic education, can somehow be abstracted from broader questions of politics in a multiracial and multiethnic society. Although recent theoretical work points to the necessity of taking up a fundamental commitment to democracy as an ongoing educational and ethical project within the field of rhetoric and composition, and liberal arts education in generals, such a call is not entirely new. Dedication to education for democracy, for example, can be traced as far back as the radical educational work of Thomas Jefferson, the Enlightenment philosopher and statesman who was one of the first to put forth a multitiered plan for free and universal public education as the primary means for safeguarding a young and fragile democratic nation. Of course, the Jeffersonian legacy is also central to any understanding of the nation's most vexing contradiction—a historical commitment to universal citizenship and free, public education that simultaneously excluded nonwhite races and women. We are not suggesting, however, that current progressive work is merely a recuperation of a forgotten rhetorical model of university education, but rather that it is an attempt to locate such work within a tradition of thought about the relationship between higher education and the practice of citizenship, while at the same time demonstrating where that work departs from tradition to engage its most critical theoretical weaknesses and exclusions.

Recently, there has been an odd convergence of rhetorics deployed by academics from left to right in the contest over the future of liberal arts education. The language of curricular reform has expanded. Whereas, "culture," or the more specific "canon," was *the* contested terrain in the academy a decade ago, battlelines are now being drawn around notions of "citizenship" and "civic education"

Reprinted from *Take Back Higher Education: Race, Youth, and the Crisis of Democracy in the Post-Civil Rights Era,* by Henry A. Giroux and Susan Searls Giroux (2004), Palgrave Publishers.

as well. The broadening of this theater of struggle is not necessarily a negative turn of events; it may even produce more rather than less latitude for negotiation among generally opposed ideological positions in the humanities. In contrast to the go-nowhere debates over culture—the Matthew Arnold-or-bust idiom of the right versus an often essentialized identity politics on the left—civic education offers a language of social responsibility and social change often lost in the allegiances to the individual cultivation of pure taste or narrowly defined group solidarities. Certainly this has been the case at dozens of schools such as Berkeley, University of Wisconsin, Harvard, Cornell, and George Mason University, where student and faculty protests against the growing corporate influence on research and curricular requirements have recently erupted. As Kevin Avruch, a professor of anthropology at GMU, noted, such restructuring has "actually united professors on the left and right." Avruch explains that although the faculty at GMU are often characterized as "overly liberal," they discovered that they had at least one thing in common with their colleagues on the Right: "we share a nineteenth-century view that our job is to educate well-rounded citizens." Thus, the rhetoric of civic education also provides a shared language informed by democratic—rather than market—traditions to fight the ongoing vocationalization and corporatization of higher education. At the same time, citizenship, like culture, is not a stable referent. As often as appeals are made to the education of future generations of citizens in a variety of academic venues, there is shockingly little attention given to the different ways in which citizenship as an ideal and as a set of practices is defined and negotiated both currently and historically. As Judith Skhlar aptly notes, "there is no concept more central in politics than citizenship, and none more variable in history, or contested in theory."

Hence, our continued reliance on war metaphors is not accidental; we use them to dramatize our efforts to shift the debate over liberal arts education, in Chantal Mouffe's terms, from the realm of antagonism to one of agonism. If, as Mouffe explains, an antagonism defines a "relation between enemies" in which each group wants to destroy the other, then agonism marks a relation among "adversaries" who struggle "in order to establish a different hegemony." Our goal, correspondingly, is not to wage a polemical war, the point of which is a simple dismissal of conceptions of citizenship and civic education other than our own; rather, it is an attempt to bring historical evidence to bear on an evaluation of different articulations of citizenship and corresponding forms of education. The purposes of this article, then, are threefold: first, it seeks to reaffirm critical citizenship as a core value and the centrality of civic education to democratic public life at a time when "visionary reform" has led to the corporatization of the university and capitalism has become synonymous with democracy itself. Second, it maps the history of various definitions of citizen—liberal, republican, and ascriptive Americanist—and the forms of education proper to their development in an effort to establish the centrality of race and rhetoric to current debates over the future of liberal arts education. Finally, it examines the necessary and historical linkages between educational theory and curricular development, the practice of citizenship, and the politics of race. Our interest in exploring the various definitions of citizenship and civic education at work in contemporary professional conversations is not to establish the objective equality of all positions. Although disparate understandings of these key notions demand due consideration, we will nonetheless provide a very specific interpretation of the social values different theoretical positions represent as we defend our own project as part of a broader effort to connect learning to the production of democratic values and the imperative of emancipatory social change.

Before we examine the current controversy over the role of a liberal arts education in the production of good citizens, it is necessary to first address the various ways in which the concept of the "good citizen" has been defined over time. Hence, in what follows, we will map different conceptions of American civic identity, indicating when, historically, each enjoyed a period of relative hegemony. In doing so, we will analyze how shifts in dominant notions of citizenship in the last decades of the nineteenth century correspond to significant changes in college curricula about the same time—changes that dramatically altered the nature and purpose of higher education for the next century. Our hope is to establish a relevant historical context for, and so a richer assessment of, the contemporary debates over these issues. Of course, it is impossible to render this extensive history in any nuanced or complete way here, so we offer only passing apologies for the necessary simplification involved.

Conflicting Visions of American Citizenship: Liberal, Republican, and Ascriptive

Since Alexis de Tocqueville's 1840 classic, *Democracy in America*, the traditions of American political philosophy have held that citizenship is not determined by birth or inherited traits, but rather by sworn adherence to a set of political ideals, principles, and hopes that comprise liberal democracy. According to the liberal perspective, to be an American citizen, a person did not have to be of any particular national, linguistic, religious, or ethnic background (though racialized minorities were not recognized as citizens until the twentieth century). All one had to do was to pledge allegiance to a political ideology centered on the abstract ideals of liberty, equality, and freedom, largely derived from the seventeenth-century philosopher John Locke. Conceived in opposition to the oppressive hierarchies of traditional or feudal societies—societies dominated by a monarchy, aristocracy, or the church—liberalism has always maintained "a contractual and competitive rather than ascriptive idea of social order." Rather than accept the rigid "social hierarchies characteristic of conservative social philosophies," liberalism has always been on the side of "change, dynamism, growth, mobility, accumulation and competition." Accordingly, liberalism has tended to stand for a commitment to individualism, upholding the moral, political, and legal claims of the individual over and against those of the collective. It vouchsafes universal rights applicable to all humans or rational agents, the force of reason, and so rational reform. Liberalism privileges equality and religious toleration rather than repressive medieval religious and intellectual orthodoxies, hence the defense of pluralism, the division of church and state, and progress through the promotion of commerce and the sciences. Citizenship in a liberal polity, then, is not a function of birthright or inheritance, but the right of any energetic individual who has achieved social standing and success through the pursuit of his own interests. Thus, as Philip Gleason argues, "the universalist ideological character of American nationality meant that it was open to anyone who willed to become an American." From Tocqueville to Louis Hartz's 1955 classic, *The Liberal Tradition in America*, the Lockean liberal foundation of American politics enjoyed an uncontested hegemony.

Beginning in the late 1960s, however, the received understanding of American political culture as overwhelmingly liberal democratic was significantly challenged in at least three ways. Following the lead of Bernard Bailyn and his groundbreaking 1967 publication, *The Ideological Origins of the American Revolution*, a number of historians such as Gordon Wood, John Pocock, Lance Banning, and others have claimed that American political philosophy was shaped by traditions of republicanism that were different from, and in significant ways opposed to, the liberalism of John Locke. According to Pocock, the origins of civic republicanism extend back to the works of Aristotle and Cicero, but it is in the fifteenth-century Florence of Machiavelli that such traditions find their apotheosis and go on to influence American political thought. In contrast to liberalism's conception of liberty as freedom from state interference in individual private pursuits, the common feature of the diverse strains of republican thought was "an emphasis on achieving institutions and practices that make collective self-governance in the pursuit of a common good possible for the community as a whole."

Against the liberal concern for the individual's universal rights and freedoms, the second critique ran in a similar vein to the first. Communitarian political theorists like Michael Sandel and Alasdair MacIntyre acknowledged the dominance of liberal philosophy in American thought, but they also argued that the liberal conception of the individual was an entirely atomistic one, leaving no room for a theory of political community or a notion of public good. In other words, because liberalism held the individual to be "naturally" driven by power, competition, self-interest, and security, it follows that the liberal concept of the good society was one in which individuals could pursue their private affairs with the least interference. The few constraints society imposed were necessary to ensure the equal protection of all in the common pursuit of their self-interests, to prevent individuals from destroying one another in the Hobbesian "war of all against all." Hence, liberalism had no way to engage the desire for, or necessity of, meaningful collective political life or pride in origin, let alone accommodate such notions as public-mindedness, civic duty, or active political participation in a community of equals.

In contrast to the liberal tension between the individual and the state, republican thought favors free popular government, requiring citizens to actively participate in their own self-rule. Although liberalism has contributed the notion of universal citizenship to American political thought, it has also reduced it to a mere legal status. Conversely, civic republicanism holds citizenship to be an ongoing activity or a practice. Moreover, "civic republicanism," as Adrian Oldfield has argued, "recognizes that, unsupported, individuals cannot be expected to engage in the practice [of self-governance]. This means more than that individuals need empowering and need to be afforded opportunities to perform the duties of the practice: it means, further, that they have to be provided with sufficient motivation." For Oldfield, the motivations for active political citizenship include the capacity to attain a degree of moral and political autonomy that a liberal rights-based citizenship cannot vouchsafe. Civic republicanism also maintains that direct participation in the political life of the nation creates the conditions for the highest form of moral and intellectual growth. In addition to full political participation, republicanism also requires that citizens acknowledge the goals of the political community and the needs of individuals as one and the same—hence Montesquieu's argument that citizens in a classical republic had to be raised "like a single family." Identification with one's political community is achieved through "a pervasive civic education in patriotism reinforced by frequent public rites and ceremonies, censorship of dissenting ideas, preservation of a single religion if possible, limits on divisive and privatizing economic pursuits, and strict restraints on the addition of aliens to the citizenry." Thus, a successful republic is characterized by considerable social homogeneity and must be composed of a relatively small number of citizens.

According to Rogers Smith, such demands have no small role to play in justifying a wide range of political exclusions and inequalities. "The demand for homogeneity," Smith concludes,

> could be used to defend numerous ethnocentric impulses including citizenship laws that discriminated on the basis of race, sex, religion and national origins. The second requirement helped generate and maintain America's commitment to federalism, to state and local autonomy—a commitment often used to justify national acquiescence in local inequalities.

Finally, scholars such as Smith and Judith Skhlar have recently extended the liberal critique by taking up the question of American civic identity from the perspective of historically excluded groups—women and minorities of color. Skhlar has demonstrated how institutionalized forms of servitude were not anomalous to but absolutely constitutive of a modern popular representative republic dedicated to liberty and freedom. For Skhlar, "The equality of political rights, which is the first mark of American citizenship, was proclaimed in the accepted presence of its absolute denial. Its second mark, the overt rejection of hereditary privileges, was no easier to achieve in practice for the same reason." Similarly, Smith set out to assess the civic republican critiques through an investigation of American citizenship laws, which both defined what citizenship was and who was capable of achieving it. The upshot was a 700-page tome entitled *Civic Ideals: Conflicting Visions of Citizenship in U.S. History* and a fundamental redefinition of American political culture. In short, Smith contends that though many liberal and republican elements were visible, much of the history of American citizenship laws did not fit the liberalism of Montesquieu and Hartz or the republicanism of Pocock and MacIntyre. Smith argues:

> Rather than stressing the protection of individual rights for all in liberal fashion, or participation in common civic institutions in republican fashion, American law had been shot through with forms of second-class citizenship, denying personal liberties and opportunities for political participation to most of the adult population on the basis of race, ethnicity, gender, and even religion . . . many of the restrictions on immigration, naturalization, and equal citizenship seemed to express views of American civic identity that did not feature either individual rights or membership in a republic. They manifested passionate beliefs that America was by rights a white nation, a Protestant nation, a nation in which true Americans were native-born men with Anglo-Saxon ancestors.

Accordingly, Smith boldly identifies yet another tradition in American political thought in addition to liberalism and civic republicanism, the "ascriptive tradition of Americanism." From the dawn of the republic, Smith explains, many Americans defined citizenship not in terms of personal liberties or popular self-governance but rather in terms of

> a whole array of cultural origins and customs—with northern European, if not English ancestry, with Christianity, especially dissenting Protestantism, and its message for the world; with the white race, with patriarchal familial leadership and female domesticity; and with all the economic and social arrangements that came to be seen as the true, traditional "American" way of life.

According to Smith, ascriptive Americanism, or the identification of American nationality with a particular ethnocultural identity, became a full-fledged civic ideology by the late nineteenth century, spurred by such events as the growth of racial science, the alarm over mass European immigration, and the desire to dismantle those social policies associated with Reconstruction. And formal institutions of education, as widely noted, have been one of the primary vehicles for producing a largely assimilationist version of American citizenship.

It is important to note that Smith's multiple traditions thesis is not an attempt to shift responsibility for the vast inequalities of American life onto its ascriptive traditions, exonerating liberal and republican values and institutions. To be sure, Matthew Frye Jacobson and David Theo Goldberg have insightfully demonstrated how republican and liberal traditions have been complicitous with racialized ideologies and exclusions. Jacobson argues, for example, that citizenship was a racially inscribed concept from the start of the new nation; "political identity was rendered racial identity"—thus establishing, at least implicitly, a European political order in the New World. Though the majority of scholarly opinion has decried a democracy built on both gender and racial exclusion as both a profound hypocrisy and a betrayal of its most sacred principles, Jacobson asserts that racial and gendered exclusions cannot be understood as a mere inconsistency in an otherwise liberal political philosophy; on the contrary, racialism is inseparable from, and in fact constitutive of, the ideology of republicanism. Both the tenets of classical republicanism and the racist practices that normalized the equation of whiteness with citizenship have deep roots in Enlightenment thought.

According to Jacobson, the Enlightenment experiment in democratic forms of government demanded "a polity disciplined, virtuous, self-sacrificing, productive, far-seeing, and wise—traits that were all racially inscribed in eighteenth-century Euro-American thought." In short, the shift from monarchic power to democratic power demanded of its participants a remarkable degree of "self-possession"—a condition that was already denied literally to Africans in bondage and figuratively to both "savage" or "non-white" peoples, as well as women, who were said to be lacking in reason, dispassionate judgment, and overall "fitness for self-government." And republicanism, with its emphasis on the common good, community, and self-sacrifice, also demanded from "the people" an extraordinary moral character. At a time when the Anglo-Saxon was hailed as a paragon of political genius, reflection, and restraint, Jacobson wryly notes that a definition of the word Negro in a Philadelphia encyclopedia could include "idleness, treachery, revenge, debauchery, nastiness, and intemperance."

Similarly, Goldberg has eloquently elaborated on liberalism as the preeminent modern—and modernizing—ideology and its central paradox: as modernity commits itself to the idealized principles of liberty, equality, and fraternity, as it increasingly insists upon the moral irrelevance of race, there is a proliferation of racial identities and sets of exclusions that they rationalize and sustain. "The more abstract modernity's universal identity," he explains, "the more it has to be insisted upon, the more it needs to be *imposed*. The more ideologically hegemonic liberal values seem and the more open to difference liberal modernity declares itself, the more dismissive of difference it becomes and the more closed it seeks to make the circle of acceptability." Accordingly, Goldberg traces the liberal impulse from Locke, Hume, Kant, and Mills, to contemporary theorists of rights, demonstrating where and how race is conceptually able to insinuate itself into the terms of each discursive shift.

Smith's argument assumes that American civic identity has always drawn from these three interrelated but analytically distinguishable ideologies. In this way Smith is able to address not only where these traditions mutually inform each other in the promotion of racist exclusions, but also where these traditions are in tension. For example, Smith acknowledges the ways in which a republican ideology, with its insistence on social homogeneity and small political communities, feeds racist exclusions. He also points to the crucial tension between liberalism's commitment to freewheeling individualism and the socially repressive elements of republican and ascriptive Americanist ideologies. Similarly, Smith highlights the tension between republicanism's emphasis on civic participation and duty to the polity and an ascriptive tradition that theorizes citizenship not in terms of one's capacities for "doing" but rather in terms of one's innate "being."

Of course, numerous scholars and critics have and will continue to protest that such ascriptive American impulses, like racisms in general, are more psychological than ideological—a mix of primal tribal loyalties with the fears and anxieties that accompany an encounter with the Other. What such theories of racism leave unexamined is the degree to which occurrences of racialized exclusion are in fact purposeful and quite rationally instituted for the aim of gaining political or economic power. Smith's insistence that ascriptive Americanism proved to be not only intellectually respectable but also a politically and legally authoritative discourse has been supported by historical evidence recently brought to light by John Higham, Reginald Horsman, George Fredrickson, David Theo Goldberg, Ivan Hannaford, Matthew Frye Jacobson, and others.

As these scholars make clear, the discourse of race has been in circulation since the seventeenth century, but its ascendancy in the nineteenth century to a form of legitimate science posed dramatic challenges to the central tenets of classical republican and liberal political traditions, effecting changes not only in American political thought but European thought as well. In his impressive *Race: The History of an Idea in the West*, Ivan Hannaford explains how the centuries-long intellectual history of race—a discourse that increasingly came to identify itself with natural history, science, and thus modernity's interest in scientific forms of social amelioration or social engineering—challenged those notions of citizenship and political community, derived from antiquity, that laid the foundation for modern political thought. According to Hannaford,

> the emergence of political life and law (*polis* and *nomos*) [in antiquity] was the outcome of a heated and controversial debate about words and letters (*logomachy*) in a public place (*agora*), which might lead to interesting solutions to the puzzles (*logogriph*) of human existence. One important suggestion arising from this discourse was that secular human beings might be persuaded to try a novel form of governance that provided options and alternatives to the prevailing forms of rule then surrounding them. *It was not a matter of Nature, but a difficult and original choice.*

In contrast, from the end of the seventeenth century to the dawn of the twentieth, Hannaford observes that natural history increasingly became the basis for inquiry into legitimate forms of government—meaning that emphasis was placed on the temperament and character of races and the discovery of their true origins, rather than on political histories and the vices and virtues of actual states. Writers like Montesquieu, Hume, Blumenbach, Kant, Herder, and Burke contributed to the emergence of a self-conscious idea of race, and with the work of Niebuhr in the early nineteenth century "history was not the history of historical political communities of the Greco-Roman kind, but . . . transmogrifications of peoples into 'races' on a universal scale." After the advent of Darwinism, Hannaford argues,

> it was generally agreed that classical political theory had little or nothing to offer Western industrial society. Notions of state drew support from the new literatures of nation and race. The tests of true belonging *were no longer decided on action as citizenship* but upon the purity of language, color, and shape. And since none of these tests could ever be fully satisfied, all that was left *in the place of political settlement* were ideas of assimilation, naturalization, evacuation, exclusion, expulsion, and finally liquidation.

It is in this sense that Hannaford, after Michael Oakeshott, suggests that race must be understood as the perfect antonym for politics.

Similarly, capturing the rise of mid-nineteenth-century faith in race thinking and the simultaneous decline in the modern liberal commitments, Reginald Horsman observes that it had become "unusual by the late 1840s to profess a belief in innate human equality and to challenge the idea that a superior race was about to shape the fates of other races for the future of the world. To assert this meant challenging not only popular opinion, but also the opinion of most American intellectuals." More recently, Matthew Frye Jacobson has addressed the ways in which racial science reformed common-sense understandings of the governing capacities of both nonwhite and white races. According to Jacobson, since the 1790 Naturalization Act, European immigrants had been granted entrance to the United States solely on the grounds of their whiteness. The unprecedented waves of immigrants in the mid-nineteenth century now caused concern that the policy was entirely too liberal and too inclusive. "Fitness for self-government," an attribute accorded exclusively to whiteness prior to the nineteenth century, now generated a "new perception of some Europeans' unfitness for self-government, now rendered racially in a series of subcategorical white groupings—Celt, Slav, Hebrew, Iberic, Mediterranean, and so on—white Others of a supreme Anglo-Saxondom." Jacobson explains:

> It was the racial appellation "white persons" in the nation's naturalization law that allows the migrations from Europe in the first place; the problem this immigration posed to the polity was increasingly cast in terms of racial difference and assimilablity; the most significant revision of immigrant policy, the Johnson-Reed Act of 1924, was founded upon a racial logic borrowed from biology and eugenics.

Thus, Jacobson further complicates the history of ascriptive Americanism as a civic ideology by reconceiving it as a response to the political crisis created by the over-inclusivity of the category "free white persons" in the 1790 naturalization law, and hence "a history of a fundamental revision of whiteness itself."

In short, democratic, republican, and ascriptive ideologies, Smith argues, have always appeared on the historical stage in various combinations, as opposed to the dominance of any one in its "pure" or "ideal" form. And as the above allusion to the impact of racial science on late-nineteenth-century American political thought would indicate, Smith contends that various combinations of "liberal republicanism" dominated political agendas up to the 1870s; then a "republican nativist" agenda became more prominent. The hegemony of republican nativism only increased through the 1920s and persisted until the 1950s, when contemporary liberal ideas gained greater authority.

We want to expand the implications of this important body of work on American civic identity by arguing that the reproduction of alternative conceptions of citizenship demands various forms of institutional support, particularly in educational apparatuses where the onus of responsibility for molding a competent and productive citizenry largely falls. If Smith is correct in his assessment of the general rearticulation of citizenship in the last decades of the nineteenth century, one would reasonably expect to see an equally profound curricular shift in higher education commensurate with the dramatic changes in the political thought that marked the era, especially given the university's historic role in the production of political and moral leadership. And in fact we do. Simultaneous with the transformation of the notion of citizenship and of political life more generally, American universities inaugurate a transition in the humanities from classical rhetoric to philology first, and then literary studies. The transition from rhetoric to English studies is significant, particularly when one considers how uniform and unchanging the college curriculum was until the late nineteenth century. Typically, undergraduate education centered on three to four years of required rhetoric courses in which students produced written essays and public addresses in the promotion of civic responsibility and political leadership. Yet, by the turn of the century the classical curriculum had all but disappeared, and English emerged as a new discipline. Overwhelmingly literary in orientation, the goals of the new curriculum were twofold: to produce an organic awareness of national cultural traditions that link Americanness with a specific version of whiteness, and to cultivate "discrimination," good taste, and moral sensibility—the latter objective as racially coded as the former. As curricular emphasis shifted from the production of texts to their consumption, the arrival of literature as an object of formal study inaugurated not only the end of the classical university, but also a dramatic decline in public discourse and the practice of citizenship as an educational imperative.

The task at hand, then, is to demonstrate in a clear and concise way the differences between the classical curriculum and its modern counterpart in terms of how each negotiates the demands of a broader culture of politics—and participates in a politics of culture, particularly with respect to race. To do this, we will contrast briefly the educational thought of Thomas Jefferson and Calvin Coolidge, both of whom wrote on the civic function of higher education, and more particularly of the role of language and literature in the production of specific models of civic identity and national cultural tradition. We thus argue that the transition from rhetoric to literary studies is in part a function of changing definitions of citizenship, politics, race, and national identity, by contrasting Jefferson's plans for university education, as representative of the "liberal republican" ideological interests prior to the late nineteenth century, and Coolidge's program for higher education, as representative of the "nativist republican" agenda that marked the era from the 1870s to the 1950s. In spite of our characterization of the rise of literary education as a "fall" from public grace, our point is not to argue for a simple "return" to rhetoric, but to demonstrate how forms of race consciousness informed both the classical curriculum and its literary counterpart.

Not only is race a central determination in the history of liberal arts education; it is also central to its future. Race cannot be addressed as a discourse removed from mainstream educational theory, a burden imposed from the outside by the forces of multiculturalism or "PC." First, in order to grasp the significance of the rise of literary studies in the liberal arts curriculum, it is important to understand the rhetorical tradition that was in place before its decline.

From Rhetorical to Literary Education

Progressive scholars such as Raymond Williams, Terry Eagleton, James Berlin, and Sharon Crowley have tended to explain the simultaneous decline of classical rhetoric and the rise of literary education in terms of emergent bourgeois class interests. Williams argues, for example, that the turn to literature is best understood as a major affirmative response, in the name of human creativity and imagination, to the socially repressive and mechanistic nature of the new capitalist order. To understand this profound curricular shift in the nineteenth-century college, scholars must address the advance of capitalism *and* the impact of mass immigration, the influence of the leading scientific discourses of the day such as social Darwinism, efficiency, eugenics, and the nation's commitment to racial segregation. These events, as we've already indicated, induced dramatic reconceptualizations of liberal political philosophy, national identity, citizenship, and race—all of which affected educational thought and practice. In other words, to the degree that the political order was rearticulated in terms of a natural order, citizenship became less contingent on one's performance in public life and more on an innate capacity determined by blood and heredity. This is not to suggest that civic education was altogether abandoned; rather we argue that the kind of citizen university curricula attempted to put into place was radically reconfigured. If the goal of classical rhetorical education was to enhance the practice of citizenship as a performance of duties and responsibilities to the political community in exchange for rights and entitlements in keeping with liberal and republican ideologies, the new educational mandate privileging literary study was, at least in part, an attempt to establish an ascriptive notion of citizenship—by redefining it not as a function of "doing," but one of "being." Thus it became the "duty" of students endowed with the appropriate class and racial inheritance simply to receive, appreciate, and protect their distinctive ethnocultural heritage.

According to historians of rhetorical and literary education such as James Berlin, S. Michael Halloran, and Gerald Graff, rhetoric was at the center of a relatively stable and unchanging college curriculum prior to the late nineteenth century. Since their appearance in the seventeenth and eighteenth century, American colleges followed the traditions established by Oxford, Cambridge, and the continental universities in the preparation of their overwhelmingly white male student body for law, ministry, medicine, and politics. Rhetoric was emphasized so heavily in these disciplines because, as Halloran explains,

> it was understood as the art through which all other arts could become effective. The more specialized studies in philosophy and natural science and the classical languages and literatures would be brought to focus by the art of rhetoric and made to shed light on problems in the world of social and political affairs. The purpose of education was to prepare men for positions of leadership in the community, as it had been for Cicero and Quintilian.

Investigating more specifically the various ways in which rhetorical education was conceived in the classical college, Halloran has argued that in contrast to the anticlassical bias in the seventeenth-century college, classical rhetoric as the art of public discourse flourished in the eighteenth century at Harvard and newer colleges such as William and Mary and Yale. For Halloran, the tradition of classical rhetoric gave "primary emphasis to communication on public problems, problems that arise from our life in political communities." The emergence of the classical impulse was reflected in the increasing curricular emphasis on the English language and on effective oral communication, which dealt with public issues and concerns, a shift Halloran attributes to the greater availability of works by Cicero and Quintilian during the second decade of the eighteenth century.

A graduate of William and Mary in the mid-1760s, Thomas Jefferson wrote extensively on the relationship between higher education and the political life of the nation, and his views are clearly reflective of the classical training he received there. In fact, Jefferson's vast educational plans for a free and universal, multi-tiered educational system including primary, grammar, and university training are central to his social and political thought. For Jefferson, education was the primary means for producing the kind of critically informed and active citizenry necessary to both nurture and sustain a democratic nation; he argued, in keeping with classical republican tradition, that democracy was the highest form of political organization for any nation because it provided the conditions for its citizens to grow both intellectually and morally through the exercise of these faculties. In addition to three legislative proposals—the Bill for the More General Diffusion of Knowledge; the Bill for Amending the Constitution of the College of William and Mary, and Substituting More Certain Revenues for Its Support; and the Bill for Establishing a Public Library—which constitute the core of his educational thought, Jefferson elaborated his educational vision in his *Notes on the State of Virginia* and in numerous private letters to his nephew Peter Carr and others. Jefferson's classic preamble to the 1776 Bill for the More General Diffusion of Knowledge bears the hallmark of his views on the relationship between education and public life:

> Whereas . . . certain forms of government are better calculated than others to protect individuals in the free exercise of their natural rights . . . experience hath shewn, that even under the best forms, those entrusted with power have . . . perverted it into tyranny; and it is believed that *the most effectual means of preventing this would be, to illuminate, as far as practicable, the minds of the people at large;* And whereas it is generally true that people will be happiest whose laws are best, and are best administered, and that laws will be wisely formed, and honestly administered, in proportion as those who form and administer them are wise and honest.

As this passage indicates, "illuminating" via formal education is central to Jefferson's liberal philosophical leanings and his republican agendas; it is both a means for preserving individual rights and property from all forms of tyranny and a means for enabling wise and honest self-government. What both traditions share, as is evident in Jefferson's prose, is a conception of education as a preeminently political issue—and politics as a preeminently educational issue. (As we will demonstrate shortly, Jefferson's thought was also reflective of his ascriptive agendas, as his role in the nation's legacy of racialized exclusion makes clear.) After his administration, he penned a Bill for Establishing a System of Public Education and the Report of the Commission Appointed to Fix the Site of the University of Virginia, commonly known as the Rockfish Gap Report. In this 1818 document, Jefferson maps the objectives for university education and provides an eloquent defense of higher education as a public good worthy of federal funding. According to Jefferson, the purpose of higher education is to provide the following (which we quote at length, if only to underscore how little in common the contemporary mission of the corporate university has with its historic counterpart):

> To form the statesmen, legislators and judges, on whom public prosperity and individual happiness are so much to depend;
>
> To expound the principles and structures of government, the laws which regulate the intercourse of nations, those formed municipally for our own government, and a sound spirit of legislation, which banishing all arbitrary and unnecessary restraint on individual action, shall leave us free to do whatever does not violate the equal rights of another;

> To harmonize and promote the interests of agriculture, manufactures and commerce, and by well informed views of political economy to give a free scope to the public industry;
>
> To develop the reasoning faculties of our youth, enlarge their minds, cultivate their morals, and instill into them the precepts of virtue and order;
>
> To enlighten them with mathematical and physical sciences, which advance the arts, and administer to the health, the subsistence, and the comforts of human life;
>
> And, generally, to form them to habits of reflection and correct action rendering them examples of virtue to others, and of happiness within themselves.

As these objectives indicate, the branches of higher education are responsible for producing effective moral and political leadership, not trained technicians; where professional interests are alluded to, they are always tied to the interests and well-being of the commonweal. In contrast to the current state of affairs, there is no confusion between education and training.

Jefferson divided the university curriculum into ten branches: ancient languages, modern languages, five branches of mathematics and the sciences, government, law, and finally "ideology," which included studies in grammar, ethics, rhetoric, and belles lettres. Private letters to his nephew and protégé, Peter Carr, indicated more specifically what the study of ideology entailed. He advised Carr to read ancient history including works by Herodotus, Thucydides, Xenophontis Hellenica, Xenophontis Anabasis, Quintus Curtius, and Justin; Roman history, then modern; Greek and Latin poetry including Virgil, Terence, Horace, Anacreon, Theocritus, and Homer; and moral philosophy. According to Jefferson, such readings provide ordinary citizens "knowledge of those facts, which history exhibiteth, that possessed thereby of the experience of other ages and countries, they may be enabled to know ambition under all its shapes, and prompt to exert their natural powers to defeat its purposes." The pedagogical emphasis here is on the production of an active and critical citizenry skilled not only in the protection of their individual rights but popular participation in the interests of self-governance. "If the condition of man is to be progressively ameliorated," Jefferson argued, "education is to be the chief instrument in effecting it." It is interesting to note, in light of the direction that rhetorical education would take, that Jefferson also advises his protégé to read Milton's *Paradise Lost*, Ossian, Pope, and Swift "in order to form your style in your own language." These literary works were recommended as models for the improvement of form in oral and written communication—and not, as they would later be proffered, for honoring one's racial heritage or asserting racial superiority.

Thus Jefferson inevitably looked to education as a means of social, moral, and political uplift, as well as an aid to the personal and professional advancement of individual citizens. He hoped that formal educational experience would lead, by force of habit, to learning as a lifelong practice. "Education generates," he insisted, "habits of application, of order, and the love of virtue; and controls, by the force of habit, any innate obliquities in our moral organization." In other words, education secured the progress of "man":

> We should be far, too, from the discouraging persuasion that man is fixed, by the law of this nature, at any given point; that his improvement is a chimera. . . . As well might it be urged that the wild and uncultivated tree, hitherto yielding sour and bitter fruit only, can never be made to yield better; yet we know that the grafting art implants a new tree on the savage stock, producing what is most estimable in kind and degree. Education, in like manner, engrafts new man on the native stock, and improves what in his nature was vicious and perverse into qualities of virtue and social worth.

But Jefferson was not interested in the rights, civic participation, or general progress of women in general and men of color. Jefferson's views on both women and African Americans are now well known. The statesman who penned the Declaration of Independence and proclaimed universal human rights and human equality also insisted that, unlike Native Americans, African Americans did not have the natural intellectual endowment necessary for self-government. In his *Notes on the State of Virginia*, Jefferson wrote that "Comparing them [African Americans] by their faculties of memory, reason, and imagination, it appears to me that in memory they are equal to whites: in reason much inferior, as I think one could scarcely be found capable of tracing and comprehending the investigations of Euclid; and that in imagination they are dull, tasteless, and anomalous." As if in anticipation of the eugenic vision of Coolidge a century later, Jefferson also argued that "amalgamation with the other color produces a degradation to which no lover of his country, no lover of excellence in the human character can innocently consent." All his major proposals for free public education excluded slaves. And, as in classical Greece, Jefferson held that women belonged in the private or domestic sphere and not in public life; as citizenship was a male privilege, females were provided schooling only at the elementary level.

As these exclusions make clear, Aristotle was correct in assuming that a good citizen is not the same as a good man; in fulfilling the demands of their polity, citizens are only as good as the laws that they frame and obey. Any attempt to reappropriate elements of a "classical" rhetorical education, with its emphasis on the responsibilities of citizenship and the importance of participation in public life, will have to engage the ways that citizenship and agency itself—defined in terms of fitness for self-government—have been both gendered as male and racially coded as white since the nation's inception.

Jefferson's 1818 commentary on higher education is in keeping with classical liberalism's faith in natural law, rationality, freedom, and the ameliorative force of social institutions such as education. Within the next hundred years these "classical" liberal tenets underwent a profound revision in response to rapidly changing social and political conditions, as well as the Darwinian revolution in scientific thought. Unlike Jefferson's faith in the average citizen's capacity to reason, debate, and take action in the interests of justice and the public good, the "modern" search for truth required scientific method and the intervention of expert knowledge. Jefferson's beliefs that human reason would triumph over the base instincts of human nature and that social progress was inevitable were significantly challenged by modern scientific findings. Influenced in part by Charles Darwin's observations that some species decline while the fit survive, and in part by the crises brought about by rapid urbanization and industrialization—overcrowding, poverty, disease, crime, revolt—modern liberals no longer believed that progress was inevitable, but that it required expert social planning and scientific management. Moreover, in contrast to Jefferson's commitment to intellectual and moral growth through education, modern thought held that such improvement was limited by genetic endowment.

Lawrence Cremin explains the influence of Charles Darwin and Herbert Spencer on educational thought and practice in the following terms:

> because the development of the mind followed evolutionary processes and because evolutionary processes worked themselves out over time, independent of immediate human acts, education could never be a significant factor in social progress. The only thing teachers could do was provide the knowledge that would enable people to adapt to their circumstances.

Specifically, Spencer's *Education: Intellectual, Moral and Physical* was used to legitimate the transition from the classical curriculum to a version of "progressive" education associated with the work of Harvard president Charles A. Eliot and the National Education Association's Committee of Ten. It was in part through Eliot's efforts that the classical curriculum was eventually replaced by a differentiated course of study designed to help the nation's youth adapt to their environment rather than shape or reform it. Alarmed at the increasing ethnic diversity of the school environment and convinced of the intellectual incapacities of all but "pure American stock" (which excluded all those white races that came to the United States in the second wave of European immigration), Eliot became a staunch advocate for vocational education.

In 1908 he suggested that modern American society was made up of four largely unchanging social classes: a small leading class, a commercial class devoted to business interests, skilled craftsman, and "rough workers." Failure to recognize these divisions, according to Eliot, resulted in an inefficient system in which "the immense majority of our children do not receive from our school system an education which trains them for the vocation in which they are clearly destined." Once an advocate of liberal education for all youth, Eliot pushed for a differentiated curriculum appropriate to the largely "innate" capacities of various classes and races. In the same year, fellow Spencerian Alfred Schultz captured the race consciousness so influential in educational reform as he bemoaned the limits of assimilation in the following analogy:

> The opinion is advanced that the public schools change the children of all races into Americans. Put a Scandinavian, a German, and a Maygar boy in at one end, and they will come out Americans at the other end. Which is like saying, let a pointer, a setter, and a pug enter one end of a tunnel and they will come out three greyhounds at the other end.

What Schultz's startling pronouncement reflects is an increasingly mainstream concern over the impossibility of Americanization for some (in this instance, white) immigrant races. In fact, some races were agents of de-Americanization, meaning that their presence threatened the purity of the gene pool of "real American stock." To understand how pervasive such race thinking was in the first decades of the twentieth century, it is interesting to note the similarity in thought between intellectuals like Eliot and Schultz and Klansmen like Imperial Wizard Hiram Wesley Evans, who over a decade later insisted that federal legislation must be passed to keep out delinquent and downtrodden races from the Mediterranean and Alpine regions in these terms: "We demand a return of power into the hands of the everyday, not highly cultured, not overly intellectualized but entirely unspoiled and not de-Americanized average citizens of the old stock."

Indeed, evidence of such race thinking would shortly find its way to the executive branches of government. In a 1921 article in *Good Housekeeping* entitled "Whose Country Is This?" Vice President Calvin Coolidge put the weight of his support behind ascriptive Americanist legislative agendas, rationalizing his endorsement by invoking the same rhetoric as Jefferson—the goal of inculcating good citizens. Now the production of good citizens was less a matter of civic education than one of social engineering—an attempt to govern through the logic of scientific management and efficiency. And what better place to issue advice in the national interest to American mommies and daddies than *Good Housekeeping*? In short, Coolidge's plan meant subjecting citizens to a process of Americanization, which was only possible with those groups, or "races," of people capable of self-government (and thus full assimilation) in the first place. Thus, with the racial science of the day behind him, Coolidge declared that "Biological laws tell us that certain divergent people do not mix or blend. The Nordics propagate themselves successfully. With other races, the outcome shows deterioration on both sides." He concluded in favor of legislation restricting the flow of immigrants of non-Nordic origins, stating, "Quality of mind and body suggests that observance of ethnic law is as great a necessity to a nation as immigration law." The ascriptive Americanist agendas to which Coolidge subscribes reduces the complexities of citizenship to the question of membership, which is determined on the basis of heredity and ignores altogether issues of citizens' rights, civic duties, and political participation in the community.

As we've already indicated, such a limited notion of citizenship is in part the result of the declining faith in civic institutions as a whole, which accompanied the growing influence of racial science. Though the origins of race thinking hardly begin with Darwin and Spencer, their work spawned an intellectual movement in which human society and politics were understood to be subject to the same rules of evolution that applied to the natural world. Thus, as Hannaford has argued, it provided a scientific rationale for decrying Aristotelian political theory and all aspects of the Greco-Roman polity as out of step with modernity. Society was now understood to be "a natural entity in a state of war in the classic Hobbesian sense, in which power and force in the hands of the classes or races, scientifically applied, would lead inevitably to the progressive ends of . . . 'industrial civilization.'" Accordingly, by the mid-1850s notions of legal right, treaty, compromise, settlement, arbitration, and justice, which constitute political community, were "eclipsed, and then obliterated" by a doctrine of "natural evolutionary course" that expressed itself in a language of "biological necessity, managerial efficiency, and effectiveness."

Coolidge did, however, argue for the necessity of higher education, though in vastly different terms than Jefferson. According to Coolidge, the "first great duty" of education was "the formation of character, which is the result of heredity and training." Whereas Jefferson's educational thought bore the legacy of Enlightenment racism, Coolidge's flirted with eugenics. While the passing of the Johnson Act was a great victory for Coolidge's administration, he told the National Education

Association that such legislation was, in the final analysis, of secondary importance. National progress depended not on the "interposition of the government" but on "the genius of the people themselves." Real appreciation of this "genius" required more "intense" study of our "heritage," and particularly "those events which brought about the settlement of our own land."

Curiously, Coolidge's referent was not the Revolutionary Era and the end of English colonial domination. "Modern civilization dates from Greece and Rome," he argued, and just as they were "the inheritors of a civilization which had gone before," we were now their inheritors. In answering the question, "What are the fundamental things that young Americans should be taught?" Coolidge responded, "Greek and Latin literature." Coolidge's response gives rise to two apparent contradictions: first, real "American stock" was not of Greek origin—though he locates the origins of national culture there—and, as if to keep it that way, the Johnson Act restricted the real descendants of classical Greece from U.S. citizenship. The latter contradiction is easily resolved. According to the *Dictionary of Races and Peoples*, which comprised volume nine of the Dillingham Commission's Report on Immigration and was presented to the sixty-first Congress in December 1910, modern Greeks were themselves a different race from the ancients, and now a "degenerate" population as a result of the Turkish invasion and subsequent amalgamation. Hence, the former contraction, insisting on our Greek origins, unfolds: Americans were the inheritors of civilization not because "we" descended racially from the ancient Greeks, but because we remained, as the Johnson Act would ensure, a pure race. Thus one witnesses in Coolidge's social and educational policy the same fear of racial amalgamation to which Jefferson gave voice. "Culture is the product of a continuing effort," Coolidge asserted, because "The education of the race is never accomplished." The process of educating the nation's citizenry to understand and take pride in their racial and cultural inheritance was ongoing because its purity was continually threatened by unassimilable races. In short, Coolidge's support for the study of Greek and Roman literature is for vastly different reasons than Jefferson's. For Jefferson it was about learning how to take an active and ongoing role in democratic public life; for Coolidge, it was about the appreciation and protection of one's racial endowment through the harnessing (or educating) of desire in the name of individual morality and patriotism.

David Shumway has situated the shift from rhetoric to literature in the period when "historians first produced the Teutonic-origins theory of American civilization, that Anglo-Saxonism and Anglophilia reached its peak among the American cultural elite and that concerted efforts were made to Americanize immigrants." In such a climate, the turn to literature was quite natural. As Shumway explains, "Literature was more than peripherally related to this racism since it was widely held that literature expresses the essential character of a race. This is true because language, the substance of literature, 'is an expression or function of race.'" But as we have attempted to show, "Anglo-Saxonism" did more than influence literary conversations; it also changed the ways in which broader concepts such as the nation, politics, civic duty, citizenship, and civic education were understood. Indeed, the forms of race thinking that gave rise to racist exclusions have flourished throughout the entire modern period, and continue to exert their influence today. Covering centuries rather than decades, the influence of racist thought and practice on civil institutions cannot be reduced to the "Anglo-Saxon mystic" or "Anglophilia" of the turn of the century, as if such institutions were now untouched by the politics of race.

What the comparison between Jefferson's and Coolidge's educational thought suggests is that different versions of citizenship—liberal democratic, civic republican, and ascriptive Americanist—presuppose a curricular and pedagogical model that puts into place subjectivities invested with specific notions of identity and community, knowledge and authority, values and social relations. Additionally, each pedagogical model makes claims on particular forms of consciousness, memory, and agency that influence not only individual subjects but the collectivity as a whole.

It is possible to assess critically each model as it circulates in contemporary conversations about the future direction of liberal arts education, analyzing how the relationship between pedagogy and politics is both theorized and enacted by posing the following questions. First, what are the conditions for the development of both individual and collective agency? Or, put in slightly different terms, how is learning linked to civic action or social change? Do citizens learn to take an active role in self-government, or is the educational agenda one of adaptation or subordination? Second, how is knowledge produced? Is it dialogical and open to critique or is it canonical and sacred, and so above criticism? Who controls the production of knowledge and who benefits from it? Third, how does each model of pedagogy legitimate different versions of social relations—democratic relations and hierarchical ones? Is the notion of political community that such curricular models and pedagogies give rise to marked by inclusion or exclusion? Fourth, does the pedagogical model make clear the grounds for its own authority or is it considered natural, innate, or prepolitical? Finally, what values are legitimated? Are social homogeneity and consensus privileged? Or are difference and dissent? Obedience, or the questioning of authority? With these issues in mind, and in light of the ways in which different versions of citizenship have been articulated to educational policy, we would like to turn to the contemporary debates over civic education.

The Contemporary Contest Over Civic Education

The narrative we've provided of the past and future of English studies is not what Bruce Robbins would rightly dismiss as a "narrative of the fall," of the discipline's (even the humanities') retirement from public life. Rather, our ongoing interest has been in demonstrating how changes in notions of liberal democratic politics, nationalism, citizenship, and always closely associated notions of race bring about corresponding shifts in educational thought and practice. The early transition from classical rhetoric to literary study, which shifted emphasis from civic to aesthetic concerns, is really about trading one form of citizenship for another—one participatory and public, the other nationalistic and privatized.

As the intellectual basis for theorizing civic capacities in terms of race faltered and gave way beginning in the 1930s, the discourse of literature, now grounded in theories of cultural value as opposed to racial heritage, was refashioned into a highly formalized, insular, and "professional" rhetoric that prided itself on its distance from public life. The "New Criticism," whose heyday spanned from the 1930s to the 1950s, no longer derived its authority from a direct socially ameliorative function, but rather from its withdrawal into disinterestedness. Of course, there remained a vast distance between the rhetoric of disinterestedness and professional neutrality and its actual practice in both scholarship and pedagogy. The social lessons of race-based literary study could be achieved, perhaps even more efficiently, with a rhetoric of pristine objectivity rather than social engineering. The privileged question of "value" within the New Critical lexicon still wielded its profoundly Eurocentric and exclusionary force, and the supreme legitimating discourse remained the rhetoric of science, purged of its former commitments to racial theory.

With the upheavals of the 1960s, needless to say, the era of high modernist hegemony came to a close and literature and its critics once again had to renegotiate their relationship to public life. To say the least, the task has been far from easy. While we won't recount here the myriad criticisms of the postmodern, multicultural academy, the upshot of these debates is to have produced a new genre of writing exclusively concerned with the future direction of English studies in particular, and the humanities more generally. Some of these debates have mourned the alleged passing of literature altogether. Former provost at Yale and dean of the graduate school at Princeton Alvin Kernan commenced the eulogistic theme popular among conservatives with *The Death of Literature* (1990). This was quickly followed by melancholy tomes like Harold Bloom's *The Western Canon*, with its opening "Eulogy" (1993); John Ellis's *Literature Lost: Social Agendas and the Corruption of the Humanities* (1997); Kernan's edited collection, *What's Happened to the Humanities?* (1997); and Roger Shattuck's *Candor and Perversion: Literature, Education and the Arts* (1999). Although the mood is unmistakably *in memoriam*, the arguments attempt to establish the rationale for a return to the good old days of aesthetic formalism and closed canonicity.

As space will not allow a full investigation of the claims made in the above literature, the general sentiment and mode of critique of this subgenre can best be captured in a pithy commentary in a September 1996 issue of the *National Review*. Senior editor and Dartmouth professor Jeffrey Hart announced that something was terribly amiss in higher education and had been for at least a decade. He likened the discovery to an occasion in W. H. Auden where a guest at a garden party senses disaster and discovers a corpse on the tennis court. What has so profoundly disturbed the country-club serenity of the Ivy League? To begin with, Hart attests, recent intellectual trends such as postmodernism and multiculturalism, as well as their corollary in policy, affirmative action. "Concomitantly," he adds, "ideology has been imposed on the curriculum to a startling degree." Nonetheless, Hart assures his readers that all is not lost. And as the title of the essay, "How to Get a College Education," forecasts, he offers the following advice to undergraduates:

> Select the ordinary courses. I use ordinary here in a paradoxical and challenging way. An ordinary course is one that has always been taken and obviously should be taken—even if the student is not yet equipped with a sophisticated rationale for so doing. The student should be discouraged from putting his money on the cutting edge of interdisciplinary cross-textuality.
>
> Thus, do take American and European history, an introduction to philosophy, American and European literature, the Old and New Testaments, and at least one modern language. It would be absurd not to take a course in Shakespeare, the best poet in our language. . . .
>
> I hasten to add that I applaud the student who devotes his life to the history of China or Islam, but that . . . should come later. America is part of the narrative of European history.
>
> If the student should seek out those "ordinary" courses, then it follows that he should avoid the flashy come-ons. Avoid things like Nicaraguan Lesbian Poets. Yes, and anything listed under "Studies," any course whose description uses the words "interdisciplinary," "hegemonic," "phallocratic," or "empowerment," anything that mentions "keeping a diary," any course with a title like "Adventures in Film."
>
> Also, any male professor who comes to class without a jacket and tie should be regarded with extreme prejudice unless he has won a Nobel Prize.

At first glance, it is easy to disregard Hart's polemical essay as so much right-wing hysteria. But the challenges posed to these academic "fads" are hardly confined to conservative circles alone and so cannot be dismissed as *merely* ideological. In the 1990s, for example, a number of progressives have denounced the cultural left, as Ellen Willis points out, for "its divisive obsession with race and sex, its arcane 'elitist' battles over curriculum, its penchant for pointy-headed social theory and its aversion to the socially and sexually conservative values most Americans uphold." In his *Professional Correctness*, Stanley Fish takes to task the literary critic who would conclude his analysis of *Sister Carrie* or the *Grapes of Wrath* with a commentary on homelessness rather than with an assessment of literary realism and assume it will find its way to the Department of Housing and Urban Development. Exposing as fallacious and insipid any academic pretense to social change, Fish advocates a return to the practical and professional criticism associated with John Crowe Ransom and the New Critics of the 1940s. In short, he argues that the contemporary push for English studies to become cultural studies threatens the integrity of the "kind of thing we [allegedly] do here," which, according to Fish, is about the aesthetic reading of canonical texts, a judgment with which Hart would agree. Further, the loss of "distinctiveness" of what "we do" in English threatens to undermine the discipline's *raison d'être*.

Similarly, in "The Inspirational Value of Great Works of Literature," Richard Rorty suggests that the current academic fervor for literary analysis of the "knowing, debunking, *nil admirandi* kind" drains the possibilities for enthusiasm, imagination, and hope from scholars and students alike. In place of critical analysis, Rorty urges an appreciation of "great" works of literature; by that he means seeking inspiration from works of literature that "inculcate the same eternal 'humanistic' values." What such an appeal to transcendent truth means coming from a philosopher committed to the notion of cultural relativism remains unclear, but the universalizing gesture has a profoundly Eurocentric pedigree. Decrying the rise of cultural studies in English departments and its cult of knowingness, Rorty contends that "You cannot . . . find inspirational value in a text at the same time you are viewing it as a product of a mechanism of cultural production." Pitting understanding against the romantic values of awe, inspiration, and hope, Rorty advocates a kind of intellectual passivity among readers in the name of hopefulness. Basically it is helplessness.

It is worth noting that Lynn Hunt made a similar claim that "cultural studies . . . may end up providing the deans with a convenient method for amalgamating humanities departments under one roof and reducing their faculty size." According to this logic, it is theoretical discourses associated with cultural studies rather than the logic of corporatization and downsizing that challenges the continued existence of the humanities. What both Rorty and Fish share with conservatives such as Hart, Bloom, Hunt, and others is a desire to narrow the field of intellectual inquiry, to reduce literary interest to what makes it most "distinctive": its capacity for formal aesthetic appreciation. Such a call is a retreat from the political in the name of professional survival. The moral and ethical imperative to engage the social implications of how students learn to read is traded for either a breathless romanticism (Rorty) or a cool-headed pragmatism (Fish). Edward Said is not the first intellectual to associate the call for professionalism and its attendant demands for specialization and expertise with intellectual inertia and laziness. In the study of literature, Said argues, "specialization has meant an increasing technical formalism, and less and less of a historical sense of what real experiences actually went into the making of a work of literature." The result is an inability to "view knowledge and art as choices and decisions, commitments and alignments, but only in terms of impersonal theories or methodologies."

Moreover, criticisms by Hart, Fish, Rorty and others resonate powerfully with the growing concerns of many undergraduate populations over politically correct curricula, diversity requirements, and teachers who assume that race, class, and gender are the only analytical tools for engaging cultural texts. These are the very students who are supposed to feel more empowered, critically literate, and socially conscious through their encounter with these discourses. So for the latter reason alone, it is necessary to engage Hart's depiction of the contemporary "multicultural turn" in university education as a kind of representative critique and offer a response.

While there is much to oppose in Hart's essay, some of his basic assumptions and concerns hold merit and warrant further analysis. First, Hart's repeated rant against courses like "Nicaraguan Lesbian Poets" and identity politics in general is one that—for vastly different reasons—gives intellectuals across the ideological spectrum some pause. While for conservatives such as Hart curricula gave way to the horror show of "political correctness" across university campuses in the 1980s and 1990s, progressives have critiqued its tendency, to reproduce facile, oftentimes reactionary, understandings of the complexities of identity and the politics of race and gender—hence Keith Gilyard's recent insistence that the necessity for *theorizing race* now be taken seriously in rhetoric and composition. Such practices not only undermine complex notions of identity as multiple, shifting, and in process; they parade under the banner of a form of multicultural education that Stuart Hall criticizes for reproducing "essentialized notion[s] of ethnicity," gender, and sexuality.

Second, the vast majority of scholars—even those in cultural studies, postcolonial studies, and women's studies—share Hart's commitment to providing students with an introduction to the intellectual traditions that have shaped contemporary culture. But unlike Hart, such scholars approach the question of content dialogically. That means, according to Stanley Aronowitz, they distinguish between the hegemonic culture, which constitutes the conventional values and beliefs of society, and subordinate cultures, "which often violate aspects of this common sense." Nor do they "assume the superiority of the conventional over the alternative or oppositional canon, only its power"; in short, they substitute the practice of critique for reverence. Homi Bhabha has described the necessity for educators to promote critical literacies by teaching students to

> intervene in the continuity and consensus of common sense and also to interrupt the dominant and dominating strategies of generalization within a cultural or communicative or interpretive community precisely where that community wants to say in a very settled and stentorian way: this is the general and this is the case; this is the principle and this is its empirical application as a form of proof and justification.

In contrast to Hart's emphasis on the transmission of "depoliticized" content, which rejects the need for educators to make explicit the moral and political thrust of their practices, real higher learning for Aronowitz and Bhabha takes up the task of showing how knowledge, values, desire, and social relations are always implicated in power. What these theorists share is an awareness that knowledge is not only linked to the power of self-definition, but also to broader social questions about ethics and democracy. Similarly, Paulo Freire insightfully argues that the "permanent struggle" that educators must wage against forms of bigotry and domination does not take the place of their responsibilities as intellectuals. He concludes,

> I cannot be a teacher without considering myself prepared to teach well and correctly the contents of my discipline, I cannot reduce my teaching practice to the mere transition of these contents. It is my ethical posture in the course of teaching these contents that will make the difference.

Thus, in spite of Hart's compulsive use of the term, there is nothing "ordinary," historically given, or apolitical about the course of study he and a score of others from Harold Bloom to Richard Rorty propose for undergraduate education. In fact, Hart's overzealousness betrays his efforts to legitimate such selections through an appeal to a version of common sense that is increasingly open to question; his obsessive iteration of "ordinary" reveals that such assumptions can hardly be taken for granted. Quite to the contrary, the selection of courses and topics Hart mentions have not "always" been taken; some, in fact, have been added to university curricula relatively recently. The study of Shakespeare, for example, is only as old as the English department itself, which has been around for slightly over one hundred years, when it displaced a much older tradition of classical rhetoric.

Finally, Hart's assessment of the essential function of a liberal arts education is a judgment with which few scholars could disagree. "The goal of education," he asserts, "is to produce the citizen." At first glance, Hart's insistence that citizenship is the goal of higher education seems paradoxical, particularly in light of his pronouncement that ideology has denigrated academic pursuits. How is it possible, after all, to decouple civic education from the broader culture of politics? The answer to this apparent irony lies in Hart's definition of "the citizen," which abstracts civic membership from active, public performance in the interests of the commonweal. According to Hart,

> the citizen should know the great themes of his civilization, its important areas of thought, its philosophical and religious controversies, the outline of its history and major works. The citizen need not know quantum physics, but he should know that it is there and what it means. Once the citizen knows the shape, the narrative, of his civilization, he is able to locate new things—and other civilization—in relation to it.

Hart's citizen is a passive bearer of national cultural traditions, here made identical to those of Western culture. It is a far cry from the Aristotelian model of the virtuous citizen who "lives in and for the forum," actively pursuing the public good with single-minded devotion—a model that has always haunted republican notions of American civic identity. She does not even have to master this knowledge, but rather, in game show–like fashion, be able to name it and know it's there. Republican emphasis on constant and direct involvement in governing as well as being governed, on duties and responsibilities in reciprocity, remain untheorized and, one assumes, unimportant to Hart's civic and educational vision.

Similarly, Hart's definition of citizenship is at odds with the liberal version of American civic identity. In contrast to most other nations for whom "national identity is the product of a long process of historical evolution involving common ancestors, common experiences, common ethnic background, common language, common culture, and usually common religion," American civic identity has historically been based on "political ideas," on an allegiance to the "American Creed" of liberal democracy. Yet Hart's definition of the citizen is precisely based on the "common ancestors, common experiences, common ethnic background, common language, common culture, and usually common religion" that Huntington ascribes to other renditions of national identity. It is thus a direct descendant of the ascriptive Americanism dominant at the turn of the twentieth century. As such, it is a form of citizenship that offers no theory of politics because it cannot deal with notions of conflict or antagonism. Insisting on a common culture that promotes harmony on the basis of social homogeneity, it requires the exclusion of dissent and difference.

In spite of its deviation from common republican and liberal conceptions of citizenship, the definition Hart relies upon has nonetheless been a popular one in the contemporary debate over liberal arts education. For example, the notion of citizen as bearer of common cultural knowledge has been powerfully articulated by such scholars as E. D. Hirsch and Roger Shattuck. In his now classic 1987 volume, *Cultural Literacy: What Every American Needs to Know*, Hirsch argues that:

> Literate culture has become the common currency for social and economic exchange in our democracy, and the only available ticket to full citizenship. Getting one's membership card is not tied to class or race. Membership is automatic if one learns the background information and . . . linguistic conventions.

The language Hirsch uses to describe national civic identity bears a striking resemblance to Hart's. Both scholars rely heavily on the criteria of common knowledge (and hence, common culture and experience) for civic membership, while at the same time claiming that conditions of inheritance—such as one's gender, race, or socioeconomic status, for in many ways the latter is inherited in spite of the myth of class mobility—are not prerequisites. Yet the knowledge Hart and Hirsch require of citizens is, nonetheless, race-and class-specific. Like the nativist arguments at the turn of the century, their understanding of national cultural identity not only privileges a Eurocentric perspective of history and culture but also silently equates Americanness with whiteness in the interests of promoting an allegedly time-tested, Western "Great Books" curriculum that in actuality has only been around for little more than 80 years. The similarity between the language conservatives like Harold Bloom uses to defend American cultural traditions with the eugenicist language of Calvin Coolidge is unmistakable:

> We [the United States of America] are the final inheritors of Western tradition. Education founded upon the *Iliad*, the Bible, Plato and Shakespeare remains, in some strained form, our ideal, though the relevance of these cultural monuments to life in our inner cities is inevitably rather remote.

Like that of Coolidge, Bloom's rhetoric not only summons up a genealogy that links ancient Greece to modern American culture, but also establishes the vast distance between the final inheritors of Western European cultural traditions and the "inevitable" remoteness of our inner cities as a racial, as opposed to spacial, divide.

More recently Roger Shattuck, former president of the Association of Literary Scholars and Critics, lambasted educators and school boards alike for attempts to foster critical thinking over instilling well-defined content requirements reflective of a "core tradition" in the humanities. In English, the arts, and foreign languages, Shattuck claims, "the emphasis falls entirely on what I call 'empty skills'—to read, to write, to analyze, to describe, to evaluate." How Shattuck proposes students engage a "core tradition" without recourse to such "empty skills" remains unclear—unless, like Hart, he feels that students "need not know" what (or how) texts like *Moby Dick* mean, only that they are simply "there."

Not only do the advocates of an Anglo common culture rely on transmission theories of pedagogy; they advocate, as Shattuck asserts, that "our schools will serve us best as a means of passing on an integrated culture, not as a means of trying to divide that culture into segregated interest groups." In fact, Shattuck juxtaposes the passing on of an integrated culture as the primary purpose of schooling with a view of education proposed by "Americans long ago" such as "Jefferson, Horace Mann, and John Dewey," who decided that education was "the best vehicle . . . to change society"—that "free public schools could serve to establish a common democratic culture." The kind of social change Shattuck envisions, however, is a form of cultural assimilation to forms of social and cultural hegemony for the purposes of adapting to existing social conditions. It is not about challenging abusive forms of power in the interests of social transformation, as Jefferson requires. Within Shattuck's rhetoric, the Jeffersonian view of civic education as a means for preserving individual rights and property and for enabling non-repressive self-government gets rearticulated as a deeply divisive, politicized mechanism that teaches "propaganda and advocacy" in the service of special interests such as "minority groups, feminists, gays and lesbians, Marxists, and the like." Here Shattuck capitalizes on a mainstream logic since the Reagan era, which suggests that politics in general, or what is now commonly referred to as "Big Government," uniformly works to protect special interest groups at the expense of individual, taxpaying (read: white) citizens. Though this is not what the author meant by "candor and perversion," such a recoding of civic education demands forceful engagement and challenge.

Perhaps most interesting for our purposes is Shattuck's reliance on biological evidence to forward his racist arguments against the Jeffersonian model of the political education of citizens. Confronting the problem of the purpose of higher education as either a means for socialization within an existing culture or for "challeng[ing] and overthrow[ing] that culture," Shattuck appeals to the following analogy between human biological reproduction and education. After fertilization, "the human embryo [apparently a metaphor for the college student] sets aside a few cells . . . sheltered from the rest of the organisms." These, we are reminded, have the special ability to reproduce sexually. "Our gonads," Shattuck continues, "represent the most stable and protected element in the body and are usually able to pass on unchanged to the next generation the genetic material we were born with." Thus "the sins of the fathers and mothers . . . are not visited upon their children." As no such biological process exists in cultures, the analogy continues, all cultures have nonetheless devised something similar—what "we call *education*. By education, we pass on to the young the customs, restrictions, discoveries, and wisdom that have afforded survival so far." And thus Shattuck draws the following conclusion: "There is good reason to maintain that, unlike other institutions—political, social, and artistic—which may criticize and rebel against the status quo, education should remain primarily a conservative institution, *like our gonads*." While we see no need to deconstruct what one might call Shattuck's "gonad theory of education," it is interesting to note that such appeals to biology—we might recall here Alfred Schulz's shameless greyhound analogy—are always on the side of the dominant order. Or more precisely, biologism is waged against politics itself, as natural law is repeatedly invoked to sanction racial inequality and exclusion. Thus it is imperative to challenge, as we've attempted throughout this article, the deeply antipolitical and racist sentiments that scholars such as Shattuck give voice to. Such commentaries, though ludicrous at times, nonetheless resonate with broader public discourses that are fundamentally an attack on political democracy—either through an assault on public spaces for deliberation and dissent like the university or on the notion of difference itself.

Conclusion

Recent progressive work in rhetorical and cultural theory takes aim primarily at notions of citizenship that denigrate individual and collective agency and forms of civic education that reinvent racist national traditions rather than expand the scope of individual freedoms and the conditions for democratic public life. In short, what such critics share is a commitment to education as, in Paulo Freire's words, an ethical and political act of "intervention in the world." Such a commitment, we have tried to demonstrate, is entirely in keeping with the historical responsibilities of the university, as Thomas Jefferson and others conceived it, to produce an active and critical citizenry. But as the above debates indicate, citizenship and civic education are highly and historically contested terms. Just as there is nothing self-evident (in spite of their rhetoric) about the largely ascriptive notion of citizenship that Hart, Hirsch, and others subscribe to, there is nothing self-evident about their concept of an appropriate college curriculum for producing good citizens. We have attempted to show that the very historical moment when the conception of citizen as bearer and protector of Anglo-American cultural traditions displaces the liberal-republican citizen as bearer of rights and duties is also the moment when the liberal arts curriculum shifts from classical rhetoric to literary studies and the subsequent racist invention of national cultural tradition. We have also tried to demonstrate, after Raymond Williams, how the pedagogical imperative of higher learning correspondingly shifts from the production of texts to their consumption, and from production of active citizens to passive consumers of high culture. Although we have been largely concerned with mapping the historical conditions—inflected by the politics of race— that led to these transformations, our purpose has been to demonstrate just how central race is to any understanding of past and present notions of citizenship and civic education and their relationship to the liberal arts. Just as any call to rethink notions of citizenship and civic education must consider a history of racialized exclusions in the United States, so too must it engage the problem of political agency in a neoliberal era. We will examine these questions more specifically in later articles.

A Nation at Risk After 20 Years: Continuing Implications for Higher Education

Timothy C. Caboni and Mitiku Adisu

On August 26, 1981, the secretary of education, T. H. Bell, created the National Commission on Excellence in Education (NCEE) with the charge of presenting a report on the quality of education in April 1983. The final report was titled *A Nation at Risk: The Imperative for Educational Reform (NAR)*. In it, the NCEE detailed issues facing American education and proposed possible solutions to the identified problems. In the 20 years since the release of *NAR*, the proposed solutions have driven much of the debate surrounding K-12 education reform in the nation. Although primarily focused on issues tangential to postsecondary education, the report did make several important recommendations for reform in the U.S. higher education system.

Also, because the majority of students engaged in postsecondary education have been prepared for college study in the nation's K-12 system, policies implemented in response to the report have influenced the quality and number of students entering higher education. The percentage of high school students entering U.S. colleges and universities is reaching record proportions. In 1994 over 75% of high school seniors enrolled in a post-secondary institution within 2 years of high school graduation (National Center for Education Statistics [NCES], 1997, Indicator 9). An examination of college admissions trends reveals that between 1994 and 1999 first time, first-year college enrollment increased by approximately 85,000 students (Breland, Maxey, Gernand, Cumming, & Trapani, 2002, pp. 2–3). This trend is projected to continue.

This article explores the continuing implications of *NAR* for U.S. post secondary education. First, we describe the report's initial recommendations for colleges and universities. Second, we addresses issues of continued importance for postsecondary education raised in *NAR* including (a) curricular alignment between K–12 and higher education, (b) remediation for entering college freshmen, (c) teacher preparation in schools of education, and (d) the climate of increased accountability demands for higher education. Finally, we discuss how these issues pose continuing challenges for higher education researchers, practitioners, and policymakers.

Findings and Recommendation from *A Nation at Risk (NAR)*

Within the findings and recommendations included in *NAR*, several pertain directly to higher education. These are divided into three categories: curriculum, remediation, and teaching.

Curriculum

One of the major findings of *NAR* was that students were departing high school without having taken basic coursework necessary to pursue a college degree. The report found that students in high school were enrolling in ever greater numbers in "general tracks" rather than in more rigorous "college preparatory" curriculum, and that many students were not enrolling in courses necessary for college work, such as intermediate Algebra (31%) and French I (13%; NCEE, 1983).

Reprinted from *Peabody Journal of Education* 79, no. 1 (2004).

As a potential remedy to this, the report suggested a revision of high school graduation requirements. This revised curriculum was comprised of new core courses referred to as the "New Basics." The NCEE recommended that high schools require students to enroll in 4 years of English, 3 years of mathematics, 3 years of science, 3 years of social studies, and half a year of computer science. Suggestions also included that students intending to pursue a college degree should take 2 years of a foreign language in addition to the proposed New Basics (NCEE, 1983).

To ensure enrollment of high school students in the new curriculum, colleges and universities were urged to revise expectations about the courses during their secondary schooling and to communicate these revised requirements to those students intending on pursuing postsecondary education. The report states that "Four-year colleges and universities should raise their admissions requirements and advise all potential applicants of the standards for admission in terms of specific courses required, performance in these areas, and levels of achievement on standardized achievement tests in each of the five Basics and, where applicable foreign languages" (NCEE, 1983, Recommendation B, No. 2).

Remediation

Connected to the revision of curricular requirements for entry into higher education institutions was the recommendation that colleges and universities test students to determine which of them were in need of remedial education before pursuing college-level course work. The NCEE recommended the implementation of a program of tests administered at important transition points, including from high school to college. It was suggested that students should be tested to certify credentials, identify remediation needs, and locate those students who would benefit from advanced or accelerated study (NCEE, 1983).

Teaching

Finally, of particular concern for the NCEE was the state of teaching at all levels of K–12 education. The NCEE focused primarily on the academic qualifications of those individuals choosing teaching as a career and the scope and quality of teacher education at the nation's professional schools of education. The report stated, "Too many teachers are being drawn from the bottom quarter of graduating high school and college students" (NCEE, 1983, p. 3). To encourage a more qualified group of students to enter the teaching professions, the NCEE suggested that incentives should be made available to students considering entering the teaching profession to attract those most able, especially in areas where there were shortages. Two possible incentives recommended included grants and loans for highly qualified students (NCEE, 1983).

The NCEE also devoted considerable attention to the curriculum in which future teachers were enrolled during college. Of particular concern was the lack of time spent mastering the subject area in which teachers would deliver instruction. At our nation's colleges and universities, the report stated, "the teacher preparation curriculum weighted heavily with courses in 'educational methods' at the expense of courses in subjects to be taught" (NCEE, 1983, p. 3). Students majoring in elementary education took 41% of their total courses in education, which reduced the number of available courses focused on subject matter in which those students could enroll (NCEE, 1983).

Also included within the report's recommendations was a call for colleges and universities to be accountable for the quality of the teachers they prepared. The NCEE proposed that institutions engaged in teacher preparation should be judged on several criteria. The report stated that students intending to enter the teaching profession should be expected "to meet high education standards, demonstrate an aptitude for teaching and display competence in an academic discipline. Colleges and universities which prepare future teachers should be judged by how well their graduates meet these criteria" (NCEE, 1983, Recommendation D, No. 1)

Current State of Reforms Proposed in *A Nation at Risk (NAR)*

In the three areas of emphasis for higher education described earlier, there have been multiple nationwide efforts to improve the integration of *NAR* recommendations into the relation between

K–12 and higher education. The current state of these reforms is now discussed including efforts to align K–12 and higher education curriculum, to reduce the number of students engaged in remedial coursework upon college enrollment, and to improve the state of teacher preparation. Additionally, this article addresses the issue of the drive toward increased accountability for higher education.

K–12 and Postsecondary Curriculum Alignment

The intensity and quality of students' high school curriculum often is the strongest predictor of bachelor's degree completion (Adelman, 1999). A total of 55% of first-generation college students who took a core curriculum in high school persisted to receive an undergraduate degree; for those who enrolled in a rigorous high school curriculum, 81% completed their studies (NCES, 2002). This pattern is similar for students who had at least one parent who received a bachelor's degree.

Several studies examining the relation between the curricula in which students are engaged during high school and college success are ongoing. These include (a) The National Commission on the Senior Year of High School and (b) Stanford University's Bridge Project. These two efforts are particularly important because of findings that suggest "rigorous academic preparation in high school narrows the gap in post secondary persistence between first generation students and their peers with a parent who has a bachelor's degree" (NCES, Section 3, Indicator 23, 2002). As postsecondary institutions attempt to increase the percentage of students who complete degrees after enrollment, an important piece of the persistence puzzle is the academic preparation of students who pursue college degrees.

Twenty years after the release of the NCEE's findings, school district requirements for graduation are frequently less than those required by colleges and universities for entry (The Education Trust, 1999). Although 42 states explicitly state the minimum required courses within content areas for students to receive a diploma, there is almost no consensus between K–12 and postsecondary education on the courses students should take in high school (National Association of System Heads, 2002). In some states there is agreement on the number of courses that should be taken within each area, but not on the topics of these courses.

According to the National Commission on the High School Senior Year (2001, p. 23), only 10 states have aligned their high school graduation requirements in English and only two states have done so in math. Additionally, only 20% of schools require students to take the "New Basics Curriculum" recommended by *NAR*.

There is a tendency to overlook the importance of preparing high school seniors for college-level education. The focus is often placed on successful completion of the high school program. Once in college students realize the inadequacy of their preparation (Kirst, 2000). There is also a failure on the part of policy makers and educators, who tend to view K–12 and postsecondary education as entities divorced from one another rather than as a seamless unit. This failure may explain why the percentage of high school seniors who eventually receive a bachelor's degree has remained steady since 1950 despite an increase in the percentage entering postsecondary education (Kirst, 2000).

The Stanford Institute for Higher Education Research's Bridge Project examined the barriers to student transitions from high school to postsecondary-level education in six states (Venezia, Kirst, & Antonio, 2003). One of the findings from the study outlines the gap between curricular standards in high schools and those required for entrance into colleges (Venezia et al., 2003).

Remedial Education in Higher Education

With the lack of alignment between higher education and K–12 education curriculum and the number of students engaged in college preparatory study, it is not surprising that remediation remains an important issue for colleges and universities. Adelman (1999) found that half of the first-year beginning students need to upgrade their math or English.

This has important implications for postsecondary institutions, especially in the climate of state budget cuts and increased pressure on the funding of higher education institutions. With such a large percentage of college students engaged in remediation, institutions are beginning to question the role of colleges and universities in providing developmental education for such enrollees. States have moved to bar 4-year colleges from offering remedial programs (e.g., Arizona, Colorado, Georgia, Florida), to not fund such programs (Colorado, New Mexico, and Utah), or simply limit enrollment to less than 10% (Massachusetts; Jenkins & Boswell, 2002).

For example, in *Defining Our Future*, the Tennessee Board of Education (2001) outlined cost-cutting opportunities that could be realized by reducing the number of remedial and developmental courses in which students could enroll from eight to no more than three, by ensuring that such programs help students move faster to college-level courses, and by transferring these program costs from 4-year colleges to community colleges within 5 years.

The increasing need for remedial and developmental courses and the rising costs of providing them is also defining community colleges in a new light. In 1999–2000, a total of 345,000 resident alien students enrolled in community college remedial programs while 4-year colleges enrolled 100,000 fewer of these students (Jenkins & Boswell, 2002, p. 1). Many of these students are either working adults and recent graduates or immigrants. Low-income and other disadvantages impinge on school performance of this population. Hence, enrollment in more than one remedial course tends to be higher among this group. However, taking more courses did not increase the rate of degree completion (Adelman, 1998).

Teacher Preparation Programs

Finding quality teachers for inner-city and rural schools has been a challenge to educators. Do students from low-income households, with low levels of parental education, achieve less, irrespective of what school they attended? This question has been at the heart of the debate over the role and impact of teachers. The 1966 Coleman Report, for example, answered that question in the affirmative. Current research, however, seems to indicate a reversal of those long-held views. According to Haycock (2003), nothing could substitute for good teaching. For example, the difference in achievement between students who attended classes taught by high-quality versus those taught by low-quality teachers for 3 consecutive years is sizeable: approximately 50 percentile points on standardized tests (Sanders & Rivers, 1996). Also, significant there is a significant relation between teacher experience and student achievement (Hanushek, Kain, & Rivkin, 1998).

But for "good teaching" to occur, persisting problems need to be identified. There are shortages of teachers in categories such as math and special education, training is not geared to meeting this need both in terms of content knowledge and skills, the manner of teacher transfers do not take into consideration schools with the greatest needs, and standards are not equally enforced for both teachers and students for fear teachers will resign (Haycock, 2003, McKeon, 2003). Further, "College students with low college entrance examination scores are more likely than students with high scores to prepare to become teachers, enter teaching, and remain in the profession" (U.S. Department of Education, 2002, p. 2).

There is now a growing recognition of the gravity and impact of poor-quality teaching. Teach for America, for example, has addressed this problem since 1990 (Raymond & Fletcher, 2002). More than 7,000 teachers have served as "missionaries" across the nation. Recruitment is based on a grade point average of 3.4 and leadership experience. Recruits are provided with the opportunity to earn low-cost certification while making a difference in the lives of students.

Higher Education Accountability Initiatives

The education reform debate, which was spurred by *NAR*, has spilled over into increased calls for accountability in postsecondary education. These calls for increased accountability have been tied to the spiraling costs of college tuition. Over the past 20 years, tuition and fees showed nearly a five-fold increase. There has been a decline in public revenues, and to offset the shortfall, institutions simply charged more in tuition and fees. No serious attempt was made to restructure prices as well as costs (The Institute for Higher Education Policy, 1999).

Additionally, over the past 20 years, criticism of higher education has gained attention from the mainstream media. Works such as Bloom's (1987) *The Closing of the American Mind: How Higher*

Education Has Failed Democracy and Impoverished the Souls of Today's Students, Sykes's (1988) *Prof-Scam: Professors and the Demise of Higher Education*, Sykes's (1990) *The Hollow Men: Politics and Corruption in Higher Education*, and Anderson's (1996) *Imposters in the Temple: American Intellectuals Are Destroying Our Universities and Cheating Our Students out of Their Futures* have influenced the popular perception of the nation's colleges and universities.

Since 1990, many states have begun to construct and implement accountability plans for their higher education systems. The State Higher Education Executive Officers web site lists accountability reports for 30 U.S. states. Although these institutional reports are useful for examining institutional effectiveness, they do not allow for cross-institutional comparison because of differences in data collection. States are pursuing different strategies to develop statewide accountability systems. These strategies "range from expansion of existing institutional information systems in public 'report cards,' to statewide performance standards and performance-based budgeting" (Wellman, 2002, p. 9). Report card systems aim to provide the public with additional information on which they can base college choices, but they are not tied to state budget decisions. Performance-based funding, however, links institutional performance with future funding streams.

Future Directions for Practitioners and Policymakers

Since *NAR* was released, postsecondary institutions have moved to address the issues raised in the report. Although colleges and universities have made progress, multiple areas for continued attention still exist. Possible avenues for continued efforts include developing partnerships between higher education institutions and K–12 systems at the state level; integrating preschool, K–12, and postsecondary systems to address issues spanning the entire educational careers of students; designing dual enrollment programs to smooth the transition between high school and college; continuing efforts to align K–12 curriculum and college admissions requirements; and implementing accountability systems focused on student outcomes.

Higher Education/K–12 Partnerships

Higher education institutions should become more fully engaged in the K–12 education discussion. The American Federation of Teachers College-School Task Force on Student Achievement (2000) suggested that for school reform to work, colleges and universities must become full partners in discussions about K–12 school reform. In their report, *Closing the Circle*, the American Federation of Teachers recommends that colleges establish working partnerships with the institutions from which most of their students are drawn. Particular attention should be focused on revising admissions requirements that reflect the curricular requirements in high school and on revising high school curriculum to more accurately prepare high school students for entering college. Admissions standards closely aligned with K–12 requirements would also provide a strong incentive for high school students to enroll in more rigorous college preparatory coursework.

Other suggestions for future efforts include publicizing college and university academic standards for admission so that "students, their parents, and educators have accurate college preparation information" (Venezia et al., 2003, p. 47) and examining the relation between state K–12 exit standards and postsecondary education placement examinations to determine if the two are compatible (Venezia et al., 2003).

Development of Integrated P–16 Systems

In the 21st century, ensuring educational success "will require policy-makers and educators to view education as an integrated system from birth to adulthood" (State Higher Education Executive Officers, 2003, p. 1). All of the previously mentioned recommendations will require multiple partnerships between preschool, K–12, and postsecondary education. For successful creation and implementation of these efforts, systems that frequently operate as separate and distinct will need to act cooperatively and in conjunction with each other. Currently, 24 states are engaged in some P–16 activity (Education Commission of the States, 2000). Such arrangements would improve student achievement by aligning curricular standards across a student's educational career, increase college access by clearly delineating pathways to college beginning early in the educational process, enhance teacher preparation by aligning the two partner systems in the effort, and ease student transitions from high school to college by matching exit examinations with admissions requirements (Van de Water & Rainwater, 2001).

Dual Enrollment Programs

A rapidly growing initiative that colleges and universities (especially community colleges) should explore is the creation of dual enrollment programs. Dual enrollment refers to allowing high school students to take college-level course before graduating from high school. Students earn both high school and college credit while also learning first-hand about performance expectations in college classrooms. While typically designed to offer those academically advanced students an opportunity to move beyond typical high school coursework, including both low and middle-achieving students, this initiative might facilitate the transition from high school to college for these students.

Developing Entry Standards for Colleges and Universities

One project underway that holds promise for understanding the nexus between college and high school is the Standards for Success program, which is a cooperative effort between the American Association of Universities (AAU) and the Pew Charitable trusts. The program examines the connection between the standards tested on K–12 exit examinations and the skill sets necessary for success in entry-level college courses and university entrance examinations (Conley, 2003). Through the project, researchers identified the knowledge and skills necessary for success in AAU institutions and are in the process of distributing these nationally, with an eye to aligning K–12 exit tests to measure those areas necessary for student success in postsecondary education. Several states are engaged in creating better articulation arrangements between secondary and higher education, including Maryland, which is developing evaluations given at the end of courses that will link to college admissions and placement, and Oregon, which created a proficiency-based admission standards system that will smooth the transition to college for students.

It is important for higher education to engage in this discussion with K–12 education, particularly as some states move to tie exit examinations to college admission. Administrators and policymakers have a responsibility to ensure that there is a connection between what is measured at the K–12 level. Continued avoidance or disengagement from this discussion on the part of higher education may potentially cast colleges and universities in the role of unwilling partners in the standards movement. This is particularly true as states begin to rethink the separation of K–12 and postsecondary systems and shift toward K–16 or K–20 organizations.

Accountability Systems

As demand increases for postsecondary education and competition for state funding dollars continues, higher education will continue to experience calls for accountability. Higher education needs to respond to these calls proactively. In testimony before Congress on the reauthorization of the higher education act, Charles Miller of the University of Texas system stated that although higher education is already accountable and collects data on multiple measures that are reported to federal, state, regional, and local agencies, current accountability systems are not highly useful, feedback is fragmented, and the gathered information is not communicated effectively (Miller, 2003). He proposed that "the challenge is to get the right information to the right people and to align accountability systems so that institutional, state level, and national systems use the same information" (Miller, 2003, Part 1, No. 1, para. 7).

Although there is great variation of student ability and background, institutional type, and mission across the system of higher education, colleges and universities must begin to grapple with the question "what is the 'value added' from attending college?" If higher education institutions do not begin to address this issue internally, forces from outside the system will surely begin to place their own, more punitive measurements onto higher education.

Conclusion

In the 20 years since *NAR* identified curriculum, teaching, and remediation as important issues for higher education, many efforts have been made to address these problems. Initiatives dealing with the issues outlined in *NAR* include attempts to align K–12 and postsecondary curriculum, reduce the number of students engaged in remedial courses, and improve teacher preparation. In the future, higher education policymakers and practitioners should continue their efforts to develop K–12 and higher education partnerships, create P–16 systems of education at the state level, create curricular standards bridging high school and college, and implement accountability systems focused on student outcomes.

References

Adelman, C. (1998). The kiss of death? An alternative view of college remediation. *National Crosstalk, 6*(3), 1–3.

Adelman, C. (1999). *Answers in the tool box: Academic intensity, attendance patterns, and bachelor's degree attainment.* Washington, DC: U.S. Department of Education, Office of Educational Research and Improvement.

Anderson, M. (1996). *Imposters in the temple: A blueprint for improving higher education in America.* Stanford, CA: Hoover Institution Press.

Bloom, A. (1987). *The closing of the American mind: How higher education has failed democracy and impoverished the souls of today's students.* New York: Simon and Schuster.

Breland, H., Maxey, J., Gernand, R., Cumming, T., & Trapani, C. (2002). Trends in college admission. *A Report of a Survey of Undergraduate Admissions Policies, Practices, and Procedures,* 35.

Conley, D. (2003). *Understanding university success: A project of the Association of American Universities and the Pew Charitable Trusts.* Eugene, OR: University of Oregon.

Education Commission of the States. (2000, August). *P–16 collaboration in the states.* Retrieved June 30, 2003, from http://www.ecs.org/clearinghouse/13/58/1358.pdf

The Education Trust. (1999, Fall). Ticket to nowhere: The gap between leaving high school and entering college and high-performance jobs, *Thinking K–16, 3*(2).

Hanushek, E. A., Kain, J. F., & Rivkin, S. G. (August, 1998). *Teachers, schools, and academic achievement* (NBER Working Paper No. w6691). Cambridge, MA: National Bureau of Economic Research.

Haycock, K. (May 20, 2003), Testimony before the U.S. House of Representatives Committee on Education and the Workforce Subcommittee on 21st Century Competitiveness. Washington, DC: The Education Trust.

The Institute for Higher Education Policy. (1999). *The tuition puzzle: Putting the pieces together,* Washington, DC: Author.

Jenkins, D., & Boswell, K. (2002). State policies on community college remedial education: Findings from a national survey. *Education Commission of the States,* 12 pp.

Kirst, M. W. (2000, Fall). *The senior slump: Making the most of high school preparation.* San Jose, CA: Stanford University, The National Center for Public Policy and Higher Education.

McKeon, H. P. (2003, May). Opening statement: Hearing on "America's teacher colleges: Are they making the grade?" [Chairman]. *Subcommittee on 21st Century Competitiveness.*

Miller, C. (2003, May). Is there a need for a new approach to higher education accountability? *Testimony before the U.S. House Committee on Education and the Workforce.*

National Association of System Heads. (2002, October). *Aligning K–12 and postsecondary expectations: State policy in transition.* Washington, DC: Author.

National Center for Education Statistics, (1997). *The condition of education in 1994.* Washington, DC: U.S. Department of Education, Office of Educational Research and Improvement.

National Center for Education Statistics. (2002). *The condition of education 2002 in brief.* Washington, DC: U.S. Department of Education, Office of Educational Research and Improvement.

National Commission on Excellence in Education (NCEE). (1983). *A nation at risk: The imperative for educational reform.* Washington, DC: U.S. Government Printing Office.

The National Commission on the High School Senior Year, (2001, October). *Raising our sights: No high school senior left behind.* Princeton, NJ: The Woodrow Wilson National Fellowship Foundation.

National Commission on the High School Senior Year, Final Report. (2001). Retrieved June 30, 2003, from http://www.woodrow.org/CommissionOnTheSeniorYear/index.html.

Raymond, M., & Fletcher, S. (2002, Spring). Teach for America, *Education Next.*

Sanders, W. L., & Rivers, J. C. (1996). *Cumulative and residual effects of teachers on future student academic achievement*, Knoxville, TN: University of Tennessee Value Added Research and Assessment Center.

State Higher Education Executive Officers. (2003). *Student success: Statewide P–16 systems.* Retrieved June 30, 2003, from http://www.sheeo.org/k16/P16.pdf

Sykes, C. J. (1988). *ProfScam: Professors and the demise of higher education*, New York: St. Martin's.

Sykes, C. J. (1990). *The hollow men: Politics and corruption in higher education*, Washington, DC: Regenery Gateway.

Tennessee Board of Education, (December 2001). *Defining our future.* A Report to the Tennessee General Assembly Assessing Impacts of Current and Future Budget Reductions and Reporting New Efficiency Measures for the TBRs System. Pursuant to HB 2038/SB 2000.

U.S. Department of Education, (2002). Indicator 31, Sec. 4, p. 2.

Van de Water, G., & Rainwater, T. (April 2001). *What is P–16 education? A primer for legislators: A practical introduction to the concept, language, and policy issues of an integrated system of public education.* Denver, CO: Education Commission of the States.

Venezia, A., Kirst, M., & Antonio, A. (2003), *Betraying the college dream: How disconnected K–12 and postsecondary education systems undermine student aspirations.* Stanford, CA: Stanford Institution for Higher Education Research.

Wellman, J. V. (2002). *Statewide higher education accountability issues, options and strategies for success*, Washington, DC: Institute for Higher Education Policy.

PART II

CURRICULAR CONVERSATIONS

Part II: Curricular Conversations

As the readings in the previous section demonstrate, there is no shortage of opinions and perspectives with regard to the forms and functions of college and university curricula. While much of this opinion and perspective is communicated through relatively private modes like curriculum committee meetings, institutional memoranda, and casual hallway discussions, a fair amount of conversation about curricular matters happens in much more public venues among influential people. This section brings into focus such "curricular conversations" by presenting a series of readings that include both primary sources and secondary analyses.

"Another Season of Discontent," an article from Christopher Lucas' *American Higher Education: A History*, provides an overview of the spate of criticism that colleges and universities have been subjected to since the early 1970s, and it reveals how much of the criticism has been targeted at curricular matters. From chronicling post-Vietnam efforts to inject more global perspective into general education to describing the phenomenon of "political correctness" in the 1980s and 1990s to documenting concerns expressed about declines in standards, Lucas' treatment of "discontent" across the higher learning landscape is a robust yet concise annotated bibliography of the so-called crisis literature genre and annotated register of critical issues that vex the public identities of American colleges and universities.

The two readings that follow provide a glimpse into a multi-sided curricular conversation that is typically remembered for one side in particular—namely, the *Yale Report of 1828*. Accompanying this oft-cited document known for its defense of Greek and Latin as cornerstones of a proper collegiate education—and essential building blocks of "the discipline and the furniture of the mind"—is a short essay by Henry Vethake, a Princeton professor whose views reflected an emerging approach to situating classical studies as complements to, not prerequisites for, studies in other areas of literature and science. Among the arguments on both sides are instances of commentary which illuminate how the complex contextual factors that weighed heavily on the minds of faculty in New Haven, New Jersey, and elsewhere at the time are not dissimilar from the challenges and opportunities identified by today's academy—that is, this conversation about the role of Greek and Latin in the curriculum pivots on questions about changing demographics in the student population and the relationship between higher education society as much as it turns on simple judgments about curricular content, per se.

The shift to the next trio of readings provides insight into another enduring curricular conversation nested in a complex web of historical circumstance and ideological predisposition. The debate between W.E.B. DuBois and Booker T. Washington regarding the best approach for educating African Americans in the wake of the abolition of slavery is an important historical artifact that provokes thoughtful reflection regarding what college and university curricula can do to address egregious socio-economic inequities. Washington is most often credited with advancing a vocational education agenda that would slowly but steadily bring about equality. In his words, "I would set no limits to the attainments of the Negro in arts, in letters or statesmanship, but I believe the surest way to reach those ends is by laying the foundation in the little things of life that lie immediately about one's door." DuBois responded by calling Washington "The Great Accommodator" and urged that attention be given to "the talented tenth" of the African American community so that they may become "men" and not merely "money-makers" or "artisans," both of which would be valuable positions but inherently unequal to those held by members of the white majority who obtain a collegiate education. In his *Journal of Negro Education* article, entitled "The Educational Philosophies of Washington, DuBois, and Houston: Laying the Foundations for Afrocentrism and Multiculturalism," Frederick Dunn summarizes their respective sides and adds to the mix the perspective of Charles Hamilton Houston, an education reformer who promoted integration/desegregation. In so doing, Dunn suggests how the views of Washington, DuBois, and Houston are a "living legacy" that continues to contribute to the fight for social justice through educational change.

Another set of three readings, two primary source texts and one contemporary analysis, reinforce the significance of individual voices and spirited debate in the development of college and university curricula and the importance of revisiting those voices in continually revisiting and revising the historical record. In "President Hutchins' Proposals to Remake Higher Education," John Dewey reviews Robert Maynard Hutchins' *The Higher Learning in America*, which was published the previous year (1936). While Dewey applauds Hutchins' diagnosis of "evils" ailing higher education (e.g., its "aimlessness," its willingness to cater to the public's "love of money"), he takes issue with the remedy he proposes—namely, a rededication to the modes of inquiry demonstrated by "Plato, Aristotle, and St. Thomas." One of Dewey's conclusions is that such a perspective calls for higher learning in seclusion, a move that is precisely (and ironically) counter to the modes of inquiry pursued by the great thinkers Hutchins invokes. In "Grammar, Rhetoric, and Mr. Dewey," Hutchins responds in a spirited manner, quoting lines from Dewey's appraisal of his book and methodically refuting his claims. With respect to his views toward Plato, Aristotle, and Aquinas, Hutchins suggests that he and Dewey actually agree: "My position as to the significance of these writers is precisely that (if I understand it) of Mr. Dewey. What they did was to restudy, rework, and revitalize the intellectual tradition they inherited for the purpose of understanding the contemporary world. We must do the same." Among the matters they're contesting is the relevance of the so-called "great books" curriculum, for which Hutchins was a well-known proponent. In "Reinterpreting the Roots of the Great Books Movement," Katherine Chaddock Reynolds challenges the common contemporary criticism of the "great books" as an effort to "support the politics of oppression" by arguing that Hutchins' colleagues at the University of Chicago and elsewhere "were determined to democratize liberal education by providing emblems of the elite to college students from varying socio-economic circumstances and to workers seeking adult continuing education." In a tone that is far from conciliatory, Reynolds reminds us that what we remember is not necessarily what was—and she invites us to revisit conversations like that between Hutchins and Dewey to develop more fully informed judgments of individuals' points of view from the past so that we can make better use of them now and in the future.

In "Theory of General Education," an article from *General Education in a Free Society* (also known as "Redbook"), members of the Harvard Committee begin by reviewing changes in the educational landscape since the time of the *Yale Report* and express an affinity for Dewey's belief in the importance of "the scientific method of thought" and how it "emphasizes that full truth is not known and that we must be forever led by facts to revise our approximations of it." Nested in this context, the authors then move on to distinguish general education ("that part . . . which looks first of all to his life as a responsible human being and citizen") from special education ("that part . . . which looks to the student's competence in come occupation"). Further, they circumscribe important "areas of knowledge" and "traits of mind" and conclude with a discussion of how "the good man and the citizen" must be educated with an emphasis on his "wholeness." The publication of the Harvard Committee's work elicited a series of critical reactions, including Alexander's Brody essay succinctly titled "The Harvard Report." Brody summarizes the report and raises questions which illuminate its context, including, for example, "Why is the question of education in a common heritage and common citizenship so persistent?"

Brody surmises answers to such questions. For example, he notes that the recent war highlighted the need to work for democracy—and the Redbook is further contextualized by the next reading, "Education for a Better Nation and a Better World," an article from *Higher Education for American Democracy*. Written by the Commission on Higher Education appointed by President Harry Truman, this reading offers insight into how American higher education writ large was envisioned at a time, which is now recognized as being the dawn of massive expansion in higher education with enrollments increased by the G.I. Bill and research fueled by increases in federal funding. Its myriad goals, such as a fuller realization of democracy, better relationships with other countries, solutions to social problems, are couched in a hopeful sense of urgency: "But to delay is to fail. Colleges must accelerate the normally slow rate of social change which the educational system reflects." In "Who

Calls the Tune?" Robert Lynd reviews the work of the Commission, praising its confidence yet criticizing its view of education "as an independent force in society" and its lack of recognition of the fact "that liberal democracy lives in unresolved conflict with capitalism." Brody complements his identification of ideological contradictions in the report with an analysis of fallacies in its concept of "general education:" ". . . it assumes that democratic values and procedures are essentially known and . . . it assumes that the creative experience of perceptive coming to grips with one's world can best be achieved in the crucial early years of college by funneling into all students the same subject-matter in substantially the same sequence."

Three particular threads running through the readings in this section are especially worth noting. First, there is certainly no shortage of opinions and perspectives with regard to the forms and functions of college and university curricula. Second, many of these opinions and perspectives endure through changes in context. Third, and not least, conversations about college and university curricula are strongly influenced by contemporary controversial public issues—and by extension, the curriculum itself sometimes becomes a controversial public issue. A series of questions arise from these readings as well. How do the texts and conversations that circulated about the President's Commission and the Harvard Redbook of the 1940s compare with the contemporary texts and conversations about Harvard's 2007 "Report on the Task Force of General Education" (http://www.fas.harvard.edu/curriculum-review/general_education.pdf), and the U.S. Department of Education's 2007 "A Test of Leadership: Charting the Future of U.S. Higher Education"http://www.ed.gov/about/bdscomm/list/hiedfuture/reports/final-report.pdf)? Who are the contemporary Washington, DuBois, Dewey, and Hutchins figures and what are they saying about the curriculum?

ANOTHER SEASON OF DISCONTENT: THE CRITICS

C. LUCAS

General Education Reconsidered

Once it became apparent that the era of collegiate turmoil in the sixties was over and relative tranquility had returned to the campuses of the nation's colleges and universities, there were signs in the early 1970s that the American academic community was now willing to take a fresh look at general education. Once again, official enthusiasm for liberal learning resurfaced. Once again there ensued a national debate, an outpouring of books and articles on the subject, a rash of curricular experiments, and a few new proposals which, in the public mind, came to epitomize the movement.

In the aftermath of the Vietnam war and the isolationism that swept the country, many pundits began calling for the development of curricula designed to foster a more global perspective, a larger world consciousness. New learning was called for at a time when it had grown obvious that the nation's destiny was linked inexorably with the fate of other peoples around the world. Others, in the wake of the Watergate scandal of the Nixon administration in Washington, urged more attention to moral training and ethics education. Environmental education took on new urgency. Above all, some sort of general education was argued for as an antidote to the narcissistic self-absorption allegedly characteristic of the college student generation of the 1970s. Liberal learning likewise was viewed as a palliative for rampant vocationalism and professionalism on campuses. Calls for common learning to counter the elimination of general requirements effected a decade or so earlier in the 1960s were repeatedly issued.

"Contemporary liberal education," declared Willis D. Weatherford, chair of the 1971 Commission on Liberal Learning of the American Association of American Colleges, "seems irrelevant to much of the undergraduate population and, more especially, to middle America. The concept of intellect has not been democratized; the humanities are moribund, unrelated to student interest, and the liberal arts appear headed for stagnation. Narrow vocational education has captured the larger portion of political interest." Weatherford placed the blame equally on faculty, students, and public officials. "The liberal arts college," he alleged, "are captives of illiberally educated faculty members who barter with credit hours and pacts of nonaggression among their fiefs and baronies. Illiberally educated politicians, who want a bigger gross national product with scant regard for whether the mind and lives of the persons who produce it are or are not gross, make their own negative contribution, as do illiberally educated students." As though to confirm Weatherford's indictment, half a dozen years later the Carnegie Council on Policy Studies in Higher Education reported that between 1967 and 1974 general-education requirements, as a percentage of undergraduate curricula, had dropped dramatically. "Today there is little consensus on what constitutes a liberal education," the Council found, "and, as if by default, the choices have been left to the student." General education, the report claimed, "is now a disaster area. It had been on the defensive and losing ground for more than 100 years."

Reprinted from *American Higher Education: A History*, Second Edition, by Christopher J. Lucas (2006), Palgrave Publishers.

Attempts at analyzing causes for the "disaster" dominated an ever-growing body of literature. Between the mid-seventies and mid-eighties, the total number of published books and articles treating relevant topics registered a tremendous increase, more than doubling the number for the preceding ten-year period, from 1965 to 1975. The same trend continued into the mid-1990s. Throughout, however, there was remarkable unanimity of opinion on what forces threatened to gut the substance of liberal and general education, leaving perhaps only an empty rhetorical shell. Commentators were agreed that the professionalization of scholarship in higher education had been a major factor contributing to fragmentation and specialization. A second factor inimical to the cause of the liberal arts was the modern tendency to treat knowledge as a commodity, something to be "used" or "consumed." Finally, the structural organization of the university itself was identified as a culprit. Such allegations had been heard before, of course. But they were given new clarity and force in analyses of the apparent decline of liberal educational values.

Clark Kerr, former president of the University of California at Berkeley, had argued in the opening years of the 1960s that the American university had become a "multiversity" under pressure from its many publics. Faced with an explosion of knowledge and rising demands that it serve the needs of business, government, the military, and other groups and causes, the character of the university had been transformed. Too harassed to lead, university administrators had become mediators among competing interests, trying to balance contradictory demands, treating students as consumers, knowledge as a factory product, and course offerings as supermarket wares. In the confusion, general learning was bound to be overlooked. For Kerr, the rise of the multiversity had come about as a result of the radical democratization of higher education and the colleges' inability to resist social, business, and governmental pressures.

Critic Robert Paul Wolff in *The Ideal of the University* (1969), Brand Blanchard in *The Uses of a Liberal Education* (1973), and Christopher Jencks and David Riesman in *The Academic Revolution* (1977) all tended to offer the same diagnoses. Universities, they alleged, had grown complacent, less reflective about their own practices. Bereft of any guiding intellectual vision, most institutions of higher learning had settled for hodgepodge curricula, which thinking students rightly disdained as "required irrelevance." Corrupted by populism, professionalism, and assembly-line scholarship, universities had allegedly given themselves over to turning students to specialized professional careers as quickly as possible. Having abandoned their integrity to marketplace flux and flow, such institutions had lost the will to insist upon any intellectual coherence or unity in their vast offerings. Universities, many further argued, had become knowledge factories. They were the principal manufacturers and retailers of knowledge as a commodity. Their buyers included students seeking credentials to guarantee themselves prosperous futures, industries in search of the skills and products of research, and governmental agencies needing an array of specialized services. In their quest for competitive advantage and prestige, such critics lamented, academic institutions had "sold themselves out" to the highest bidders.

In the absence of a scheme of values commanding broad assent within society, it was said, academic disciplines had sought to be value-free, each imitating the neutral discourse of the so-called "hard" sciences. The result, according to one anonymous wit, was the appearance of social sciences that were not terribly "social" and humanities that were not very "humane." The American university had committed itself to all that was objective, countable, precise, and verifiable. Its focus, once again, was upon knowledge as a commodity, packaged for consumption in tidy little bundles called credit units, hours, and courses. Further, given the standing assumption that larger questions of human meaning, purpose, or significance are unanswerable, and hence not worth asking seriously, universities had acceded to the popular belief that ultimate questions are nonintellectual, subjective, and not amenable to reasoned analysis or dispute. The proof, or so it was claimed, as Herbert I. London, dean at New York University, phrased it, was the degree to which a so-called cult of neutrality prevailed in academe. Combining behavioristic, reductionist, and positivist leanings, London alleged, it was a mentality or mind-set that had "created a Gresham's Law of curriculum design: That which is measurable will drive what is not measurable out of the curriculum." The "minimalists," he feared, if unopposed, would eventually destroy what was left of the liberal-arts tradition in higher education and make general learning impossible.

Historian Page Smith, founding provost of the University of California at Santa Cruz, later referred to the same phenomenon as a species of mindless reductionism. It was, he alleged, a kind of "academic fundamentalism" at work in the marketplace of ideas, where all ideas are considered equal and no value judgments are admitted or considered worthy of examination. The result, as he analyzed it, was a profound impoverishment of the human spirit within academe, exacerbated by the general demoralization of all of the non-scientific disciplines and a fragmentation of knowledge to the point where it no longer made sense to speak of a "community of learning." What was left, Smith alleged, was an aggregation of specialists scarcely able to communicate with one another, much less with any outside public.

Herbert London, writing in *Change* magazine in 1978, was not optimistic about prospects for liberal and general learning in the modern college or university. Efforts to find a shared view of appropriate undergraduate experiences, in his opinion, reflected compromise among faculty factions, not consensus. The issue of a possible "core curriculum," for example, had become particularly touchy at a time when many academic departments were more concerned with survival than principle. Behind the rhetoric of some holistic approach, specialists were pressing for a wider array of specialized courses. And in the intense competition for space, time, and resources, "a ballot to determine the complexion of the curriculum is very often simply a pork barrel bid." Anxious to preserve faculty jobs and bolster enrollments, one department votes for another's preferred course selection in exchange for support of its own required course in the general education program. "Of what value is debate about academic issues in this climate of academic backscratching?" London asked rhetorically.

Critics of American higher education from the late 1970s through the 1990s sensed the malaise affecting colleges and universities across the country, though less often were they in agreement over its meaning or significance. It had been brought on, it was said, by an economic crunch, by changing student enrollments, by curricular disagreements, and, more broadly, public skepticism over the practicality of any general education whatsoever. Writing in 1978 in *Change* magazine, Barry O'Connell felt college students would not easily be disabused of the persistent notion that general learning had nothing to do with career preparation. But he was inclined to offer a more charitable interpretation of students' expectations and desires. Taking their cues from their elders, he said, students were pressured to elect courses most directly relevant to their chosen careers. Told of the oversupply of graduates competing for fewer desirable jobs, it was understandable that they should feel compelled to hold everything else in abeyance as they prepared themselves for employment. "This process does not conduce to much self-respect among the current student generation," O'Connell commented. "Having lost their faith, as it were, they must now endure the excoriations of their teachers and the media for being narrowly obsessed with careers, and, if one believes most of the curricular reports, inept at writing, incompetent in mathematics, and moral barbarians." Students unquestionably needed a broad general education, he argued, but their disinclination to pursue it was entirely understandable.

Throughout the last two decades of the twentieth century, studies lamenting the state of general learning in collegiate curricula were issued with almost monotonous regularity. In all cases, recurrent themes included pleas for more stringent academic standards, demands that ethical values be given more attention in learning, reiteration of the need to restore citizenship education to a place of primacy, and arguments in defense of a common learning capable of supplying a more coherent unifying purpose and structure to undergraduate curricula.

Multiculturalism and the "Political Correctness" Controversy

Were it not for the fact that the so-called PC controversy of the late 1980s and early 1990s received so much attention in the public press, it would be tempting to dismiss it as just another short-lived if curious episode in the history of American higher education. But campus debates over affirmative action, the attempted proscription of "hate speech," and curricular "canonicity" pointed beyond themselves to a host of quite fundamental issues having to do, among other things, with the sociology of knowledge, with academic politics and equity, free speech, multiculturalism, ethnic separatism and feminist activism, textual criticism in the humanities, the role of general education in higher learning, and, more broadly still, with the very nature of the role of colleges and universities within the social order. To some observers, the various controversies and debates over "political correctness" lacked much sense or substance, amounting to little more than an intellectual tempest in an academic teapot, an exercise in overblown rhetoric soon to be forgotten. To others, the furor symbolized a long overdue protest against subversive professorial radicalism; misplaced egalitarianism; and the moral bankruptcy of academic institutions allegedly brought about by a wholesale politicization of higher learning. To still others of different persuasion, the conflict represented nothing less than a needed effort to expose once and for all the enduring "mystification" of the university's role in the reproduction of social, economic, and cultural inequality and injustice in American society.

National debate over political correctness began in the fall of 1990, with the appearance of a lengthy article in the *New York Review of Books* (December 6, 1990) authored by John Searle, a philosophy professor at Berkeley. A new postmodern generation of professors molded by the radicalism of the 1960s had finally come to power in American academe, he reported, and the results promised to be devastating to the world of conventional scholarship. The new breed of radicals, as he represented them, included radical feminists, gays and lesbians, Marxist ideologues, a diverse assortment of deconstructionists, structuralists, poststructuralists, reader-response theorists, new historicists, and a bewildering array of others. What they shared in common, Searle and others argued, was a desire to expose the facade of objectivity and critical detachment claimed by traditional bourgeois thought, and a programmatic disdain for all standards of judgment—intellectual, moral, and aesthetic—except their own ideologically-driven imperatives, which allegedly they held immune from criticism. Their precepts, according to the indictment, included the denial of any objective difference between truth and falsity, or between disinterested inquiry and partisan proselytizing. These new academic mandarins, or so it was claimed, were distinguished chiefly by a contempt for bourgeois rationality; and by their antipathy toward color-blind justice and advancement based on merit rather than according to gender, race, or ethnicity.

Having come to positions of influence and authority in academe, Searle and others claimed, campus radicals were now engaged in promoting an ideology informed by a conviction that all of Western civilization was hopelessly oppressive and reactionary. Their conviction, it was said, was that general studies had been dominated exclusively by treatments of the accomplishments of "dead white European males" to the virtual exclusion of all others, that the entire historical, literary, and cultural "canon" was "Eurocentric" and "elitist." Because traditional general education courses were racist, sexist, and homophobic, study of the classic works of Western civilization needed to be replaced with courses devoted to Third-World cultures and victims of oppression. Multiculturalism as a curriculum reform initiative thus implied the retrieval of minority cultural capital from the marginality to which it had historically been consigned. But in process, or so it was alleged, postmodern radicals had generated an atmosphere of fear and repression. In the name of sensitivity to others, under pain of being denounced as a sexist or racist, radicals were forcing everyone to adhere to their own codes of politically correct speech and behavior.

So arcane a controversy might have attracted little public attention beyond the precincts of the nation's ivory towers had it not been for the appearance in 1991 of a work entitled *Illiberal Education: The Politics of Race and Sex on Campus* by Dinesh D'Souza, former editor of a right-wing campus newspaper at Dartmouth, manager of a conservative public-policy quarterly, and a fellow at the American Enterprise Institute. His book, more than any other single work, served to focus and popularize the debate over political correctness in the first half of the decade of the 1990s. At the root of divisive, often bitter controversies over race and gender simmering on college campuses across the country, D'Souza argued, lay conflicting standards of excellence and justice. The problem as he saw it began with preferential treatment for ethnic minorities. Although university administrators might try to disguise the truth about affirmative-action plans with evasive verbal gymnastics, according to D'Souza, the truth of the matter was that Orwellian "doublespeak" could not mask the inherent unfairness of racial quotas and double standards, no matter how laudable the desire to enhance minority opportunity or to redress historical inequities. Whereas people were entitled to their own opinions about tinkering with standards, he declared, they were not entitled to their own facts: "It is unequivocally the case that affirmative action involves displacing and lowering academic standards in order to promote proportional representation for racial groups."

Precisely because affirmative action depended on unjust means to achieve its goal, he declared, it exacerbated racial tension and made authentic racial pluralism all the more unlikely. Only when measures that exalted group equality above individual justice were decisively repudiated, he judged, would interracial conflict abate. Administrative censorship of derogatory speech, mandated codes of discourse, and etiquette seminars would never suffice to eliminate campus racial tensions. Nor would acceding to the demands of special groups who sought to protect their own racial or ethnic identity on campus through separatist measures or institutions. "No community," he observed, "can be built on the basis of preferential treatment and double standards, and their existence belies university rhetoric about equality." He warned, "If the university model is replicated in the country at large, far from bringing ethnic harmony, it will reproduce and magnify the lurid bigotry, intolerance, and balkanization of campus life in the broader culture."

D'Souza assailed what he felt was a chilling tendency on the part of campus radicals and some liberals to circumscribe debate about race and ethnicity, to insist upon a special lexicon of words in reference to women and minorities, and to insist that all others adhere to their code—in short, that everyone be "politically correct" in speech and conduct. Worse yet, D'Souza and other like-minded critics alleged, there was something terribly disingenuous about the way leftist radicals obfuscated or obscured their own motives by loudly denying that their intent was to harass or intimidate anyone, or that, indeed, any such things as "political correctness" existed.

Those, in turn, who stood accused of intimidation from the left responded with criticisms of their own, scoffing at what they characterized as the "alarmist" posturing of a phalanx of dour political reactionaries and right-wing conservatives. The real problem, they argued, was that conservatives had willfully misrepresented their attempt to broaden or widen courses of study to reflect the differing needs and standards of marginalized groups formerly not adequately represented within the academy. To criticize the dominant curriculum as "Eurocentric," for example, was only to point out the obvious: that learning circumscribed by the culture and history of Europe and North America was limiting and no longer functional in a global community. As Catharine R. Stimpson, dean of the graduate school at Rutgers University, expressed it in her 1990 presidential address before the Modern Languages Association, "Multiculturalism promises to bring dignity to the dispossessed and self-empowerment to the disempowered, to recuperate the texts and traditions of ignored groups, to broaden cultural history." She professed not to understand why any such movement would arouse such strident opposition. "I am baffled," she declared, "why we cannot be students of Western culture and of multiculturalism at the same time, why we cannot show the historical and present-day relations among many cultures."

Dinesh D'Souza, for one, remained unconvinced. Multicultural courses, he charged in a television interview in June 1991, had "degenerated into a kind of ethnic cheerleading, a primitive romanticism about the Third World, combined with the systematic denunciation of the West." Roger Kimball, author of a widely-read work entitled *Tenured Radicals: How Politics Has Corrupted Our Higher Education* (1990), took much the same position. Multiculturalist ideologues, he argued, were engaged in the "aggressive politicization" of academic studies. He deplored what he saw as "a pervasive animus against the achievements and values of Western culture" and the "subjugation" of teaching and scholarship to political imperatives. Celebrating "diversity" would be unobjectionable, Kimball averred, were it not for the fact that the concept or general theme had been converted into a rigid multiculturalist orthodoxy, any deviation from which by dissidents was likely to lead to social ostracism and expressions of contempt.

Studying Western civilization as the appropriate core for general and common learning, defenders claimed, was justified, if by nothing else, by the ineluctable fact that contemporary American society *is* the product of the Western intellectual and cultural tradition, extending from classical antiquity down to modern times. If it was deemed too exclusionary, the remedy then was more inclusion—better representation of the achievements and works of non-European, non-male, non-white figures. Some opponents argued their objections had been misconstrued. Defenders of the Western canon, they argued, were advocating a narrow and specific aggregation of cultural capital and holding it up as a normative referent for everyone. Opening the canon of itself was not enough, not so long as a small and powerful caste was able to claim it for its own. Nor was it a matter of proprietorship alone. The internal history of Western civilization, leftist critics charged, internally is a chronicle of the oppression of women and minorities. Externally, the story is one of imperialism and colonialism. Specific debate over what is or is not hegemonic, patriarchal, or exclusionary was therefore held by radicals to be fruitless. The solution to a closed, privileged club is not to open it to new members, but to abolish the "club" itself. Likewise, authentic cultural and curricular pluralism could not be achieved until old structures had been demolished and new learning configurations erected in their place. The answer to the problem of exclusion, as leftist critics saw it, was the development of an entirely different order of knowledge, a new construction quite unlike anything known before in American higher education.

Curriculum theorist Michael Apple of the University of Wisconsin offered a leftist perspective on canonicity. Basically, his argument amounted to a categorical denial that there could be one textual authority, one definitive set of "facts" divorced from its context of power relations. A "common culture," he labored to show, could never be an extension to everyone of what a minority mean and believe. Rather, and crucially, an authentic shared culture would require not the stipulation and incorporation within textbooks of lists and concepts that make everyone "culturally literate," but the creation of "the conditions necessary for all people to participate in the creation and recreation of meanings and values." He concluded that a democratic process in which all people—not simply those who see themselves as the intellectual guardians of the "Western tradition"—nevertheless could be involved in the deliberation of what is important.

Inevitably, increased visibility for leftist professorial voices and groups led to the spawning of rightist organizations as well, most notably the National Association of Scholars, a group dedicated to opposing what it characterized as the radical left-wing political agenda being advanced on campuses. By 1983 the eight-year-old organizations had grown to nearly 3,000 members and claimed affiliated groups in 29 different states. William Pruitt, a literature professor from the City College of San Francisco, was quoted in the *Chronicle of Higher Education* (April 28, 1993), explaining the organization's rapid growth as a backlash to the criticism to which the NAS had been subjected. "A lot of these guys were hiding in carrels hoping the multicultural stuff would go away," he said. "Now they're coming out because they believe American democracy is at stake."

In the 1990s, academe remained deeply polarized over affirmative action, speech codes, the movement toward a more multicultural curriculum, and the treatment of women and members of minority groups. Nevertheless, as the United States approached the end of the millennium, some observes detected a certain muting of inflammatory rhetoric, a greater willingness on both sides to offer concessions, a lessening of extremism. Activists on the left had grown more wary of policies aimed at restricting offensive speech. Scholars on the right appeared to be more open-minded about revising courses of study to include minority perspectives. Cautious experimentation was under way in many colleges and universities with devising new courses incorporating a more pluralistic cultural outlook.

Gerald Graff, an English professor at the University of Chicago and founder of Teachers for a Democratic Culture, a professional group formed to combat charges that campuses were dominated by political correctness, foresaw no immediate or dramatic resolution of issues raised by the PC controversy. But as quoted in the April 23, 1993, issue of the *Chronicle of Higher Education*, Graff anticipated greater civility in the discussions to come. "We still haven't constructed regular channels for conflict resolution," he remarked, "and we don't even recognize the need for them. I've been arguing that the place to do that is in the curriculum." If nothing else, protagonists on all sides appeared more willing than formerly to explore the questions anew. In that respect, historically, they stood very much in the tradition of constant curricular revision that had characterized higher learning in America since its inception.

Diagnosing the Malaise

Despite its apparent robustness, some observers of American higher education in the last years of the twentieth century professed to detect a kind of pervasive "dis-ease" afflicting academe, what more than a few critics called a spiritual malaise, and others termed a peculiar "joylessness." George H. Douglas, a professor of English at the University of Illinois, writing in *Education Without Impact* (1992), agreed something was wrong with the nation's colleges and universities, though he dismissed claims they were in a state of "crisis." It seemed to him histrionic, alarmist even, to proclaim a crisis in higher education once again, for crisis had been the norm for decades on end.

With the advent of Sputnik in 1957, when the country's technological leadership seemed jeopardized, alarms were sounded proclaiming a state of crisis in education at all levels, higher education included. Toward the end of the sixties, when colleges and universities were under siege by youthful student radicals and dissidents and all forms of authority were being attacked as illegitimate, pundits loudly proclaimed yet another campus crisis of major proportions. Ten years later, crisis loomed anew amidst claims that academic standards from kindergarten to graduate school had been seriously eroded, that the traditional curricular canon had disintegrated, and that compulsory multiculturalism and media-manufactured hysteria over "political correctness" had seemingly transformed each and every pedagogical debate into a life-or-death ideological conflict, a brouhaha threatening to tear asunder the fabric of American intellectual culture and, with it, academic institutions of higher learning.

But crisis by definition cannot be chronic, as Benjamin R. Barber, a professor of political science at Rutgers, observed in his *An Aristocracy of Everyone: The Politics of Education and the Future of America* (1992). As he phrased it, "On tenth hearing, the alarm bells inspire despair rather than action. Tired out by our repeated crises, we roll over in bed." For Douglas, the condition afflicting American academe might have been better likened to a low-grade fever than to a terminal illness. America's colleges and universities, he judged, were suffering from "a kind of lethargy, a tediousness, a middle-age disease of some kind—something like arthritis, shall we say, or any disease that ebbs and flows."

Interpretations of *what* precisely was wrong differed. Critics disagreed over the causes of academic malaise, and still more in their prescriptions for a cure. There was remarkable unanimity, nonetheless, about the more obvious symptoms. Historian Page Smith, in his 1990 work *Killing the Spirit: Higher Education in America* claimed the current academic scene resembled nothing so much as a vast metaphorical "desert." Sketching out historically what he perceived to have gone awry, he cited as major themes an alleged flight from teaching by the professorate, the egregious neglect of undergraduate education, the meretriciousness of most academic research, and the alliance of universities with corporate and governmental agencies. Each in its own way, he argued, had contributed to "killing the spirit" of American higher education, leaving behind something that to all outward appearances might appear as vibrant as ever, but within was hollow or dead.

Comparable in its targets but far less temperate in tone was a diatribe unleashed by Charles J. Sykes, author of a widely read, muckraking work entitled *Profscam: Professors and the Demise of Higher Education* (1988) and a follow-up work, *The Hollow Men: Politics and Corruption in Higher Education* (1990). Professors, he claimed, were chiefly to blame for the ills afflicting academe; and in his opinion, they had a great deal to answer for. "Overpaid" and "grotesquely underworked," he alleged, they presided over a scandalous satrapy of inefficiency and waste. As a professional class, college and university teachers were typically neglectful of their teaching duties, "unapproachable, uncommunicative and unavailable" to the typical undergraduate, obsessed with research, and prone to turning over their classroom chores to an underpaid and overworked lumpen proletariat—graduate assistants—whenever expediency dictated.

Worse yet, as Sykes portrayed them, professors were guilty of inflicting thousands of useless articles and books upon the world, written in "stupefying and inscrutable jargon" that served only to mask the vacuous and trivial nature of their content. In their lust to fulfill their own professional careers, he claimed, professors were busily engaged filling up whole libraries with "masses of unread, unreadable and worthless pablum." American universities had degenerated to the point where they were now mere factories for "junk-think," their inhabitants devoted to woolly-headed, pettifogging theorizing of no conceivable value to anyone. The ubiquity of dull pedants raking over the dust heaps of learning, dispensers of tiny little packages of abstruse learning, Sykes declared, lay at the heart of almost everything wrong with American higher learning.

Careerism and the Entrepreneurial University

Often cited as a corrupting influence upon academe was its unholy alliance with business, industry, and government. Page Smith rehearsed the familiar story of the rise of the corporate university and its historic entanglement with business enterprise and the military-industrial establishment. "One must ask," he observed, "whether the university can, in the long run, preserve its freedom to carry on . . . in the face of . . . shameless huckstering. Who pays the piper calls the tune. There is no reason to believe that the university is immune to that law." Benjamin Barber's *An Aristocracy of Everyone* went even further: "We may moralize about the virtues of education," its author wrote, "but higher education has come to mean education for hire: the university is increasingly for sale to those corporations and state agencies that want to buy its research facilities and, for appropriate funding, acquire the legitimacy of its professorate." He emphasized, "I do not mean the university in service to the public and private sectors; I mean the university in servitude to the public and private sectors. I mean not partnership but a 'corporate takeover' of the university."

Barber judged that in the early 1990s the hegemony of markets in academe had grown virtually complete. Free inquiry in many fields had been subordinated to guided—which is to say, subsidized—research. Autonomous pedagogical standards had long since been displaced by market pressures from both immediate consumers (students) and long-term consumers (the private and public sectors). If established trends continued, he predicted, colleges and universities would end up becoming little more than pawns of the tastes, values, and goals of society at large, if they had not already become so. Faculty who acceded to the system would continue to share in the spoils; those who did not would find themselves on second-class career tracks or even out of work. Research, publications, and external grants and contracts were what counted. And where commerce encroached upon higher education so blatantly, he judged, it was not to be wondered at that professors more and more were thinking like capitalists, or more modestly, like proletarians.

Barber's analysis of what was wrong with American higher education hinged in part on two contrasting models of the university, each allegedly a mirror image of the other, neither of them in his view fully adequate or satisfying. The first—the so-called purist model—as Barber depicted it, calls always for refurbishing the ivory tower and reinforcing its monastic isolation from the world. The other, the "vocational," apes the marketplace and urges that the tower be demolished, overcoming its isolation by embracing servitude to the market's whims and fashions, which—*mirabile dictu*—then pass as its purposes and aims. The purist model, essentially an embellishment on the medieval university as favored by nostalgic scholastics, seeks to insulate the university from society at large. Its primary concern is the abstract pursuit of speculative knowledge for its own sake. Learning is for learning's sake, not for power or happiness or career, but for itself as a self-contained, intrinsic good. To the purist, knowledge is "radically divorced from time and culture, from power and interest . . . [and] above all, it eschews utility." The purist ideal of the university "knows a social context exists but believes the job of the university is to offer sanctuary from that context."

As Barber noted, the purist model in a sense was the old-fashioned liberal model of academe as a neutral domain in which free minds "engage in open discourse at a cosmic distance from power and interest and the other distractions of the real world." While he did not specifically allude to Robert Maynard Hutchins, the Chicago Plan of the 1930s might have come to mind as a prime example of some such model or ideal prominent in the history of twentieth-century American higher education.

The vocational model, in contrast, abjures tradition no less decisively than the purist model abjures relevance. Indeed, it is highly responsive to the demands of the larger society it believes education must serve. The vocationalist, according to Barber, wishes to see the university prostrate itself before the new gods of modernity. "Service to the market, training for its professions, research in the name of its products are the hallmarks of the new full-service university, which wants nothing so much as to be counted as a peer among the nation's great corporations, an equal opportunism producer of prosperity and material happiness." The vocationalist model looks with approval upon the image of the university forging alliances with research companies and with government, plying corporations for program funding and stalking the public sector in search of public "needs" it can profitably satisfy. "In each of these cases," Barber wrote, "it asks society to show the way and compliantly follows."

Again, Barber adduced no specific historical precedents to illustrate his second model. Had he elected to do so, he would have found an ample supply of illustrations, for example, in the rhetoric of post–Civil War proponents of the modern research university throughout the late 1800s, and again in public pronouncements of the role and mission of the American university in the late 1950s and early 1960s.

If the purist model ignores issues of power and influence, the vocationalist model ignores how a focus upon research adapted to the needs of society corrupts, Barber believed. Advocates of the "Entrepreneurial University," he claimed, were impervious to the dangers. They were perfectly willing to subsume teaching to research, and research itself to product-oriented engineering. They showed little concern over careerism in academe. As he phrased it, "If it requires that education take on the aspect of vocational training, and that the university become a kindergarten for corporate society where in the name of economic competition the young are socialized, bullied, and brainwashed into market usefulness, then the curriculum must be recast in the language of opportunism, careerism, and professionalism—in a word, commerce. Every course is affixed with a 'pre' (as in premedical, prelaw, prebusiness, and pre-professional). Academic departments hem in students' intellectual lives with a bevy of technical requirements, which leave no room for liberal or general education and which assume that education for living is in fact education for making a living. . . . Where the philosopher once said that all of life is a preparation for death, the educational careerist now thinks that all of life is a preparation for business—or perhaps, more bluntly, that life *is* business. "

Many critiques of American higher education in the 1990s, like Barber's, were strikingly reminiscent of Thorstein Veblen's indictment in *The Higher Learning in America* (1918), which had appeared three-quarters of a century earlier. Veblen's complaint then, it will be recalled, was that captains of industry (among them Johns Hopkins, Daniel Drew, Leland Stanford and James B. Duke) had captured the nation's sleepy little colleges with promises of largesse and proceeded to turn them—some of them, at any rate—into stone, granite, and marble monuments to themselves. They had inflicted upon the academy, Veblen complained, a certain cast of mind, a crude utilitarianism, an expectation that universities would become more productive and more attentive to output, after the fashion of the businesses through which they as industrial magnates had built up their own fortunes. Under the model prescribed by a business ethos, the university was transformed into a place whose style or mode of operation was shaped by the spirit of business management, that is, by an insistence upon salesmanship, boosterism, bureaucracy, cost-control measures, and public relations, by a constant seeking of competitive advantage within the academic marketplace. The tone set was one of activity, bustle, and intrigue.

The institutional environment thereby created, Veblen labored to show, was one in which professors were reduced to mere hirelings, hemmed in by rigid professional practices and the dictates of the guild, and set to clawing their way up a ladder of career advancement not unlike that prevailing in business and industry. Veblen's somewhat overblown characterization of professors as prisoners of an inhumane and debilitating system, in the final analysis, fully anticipated Barber's equally sweeping claim in the early 1990s that "the vast apathetic mass of faculty . . . do not give a damn one way or another about what goes in [the classroom]." Far too many professors on too many campuses, the latter alleged, "either do not care or cannot afford to. Certainly university administrators give them neither reason nor incentive. They have become 'employees' of corporate managers. . . . The demeaned status of teachers in the modern university gives scholars little reason to measure their career progress other than by how quickly they get tenure, how much they get paid, and how little time they have to spend in the classroom."

Specialization and Fragmentation

Robert Bellah, a professor of sociology at the University of California at Berkeley, who together with a number of associates authored a widely discussed analysis of American culture entitled *Habits of the Heart: Individualism and Commitment in American Life* (1985), linked the transformation of the nineteenth-century American college into the twentieth-century corporate university with a concomitant array of other social and cultural changes, none of them necessarily healthy for modern academe. Before the Civil War, as he pointed out, liberal-arts colleges were too small to be divided into departments. (In 1872 the entering freshman class at Harvard had only 200 students; Yale had 131; Princeton, 110; Dartmouth, 74; and Williams, 49.) As late as 1869, there were no more than two dozen faculty members at Harvard, and they mostly taught the traditional subjects of classical languages and mathematics. The antebellum college was organized on the assumption that higher learning constituted a single unified culture; and literature, the arts, and sciences were viewed as branches of that whole. It was the task of moral philosophy, often a required course in the senior year, usually taught by the college president himself, not only to integrate the various fields of learning, including science and religion, but even more importantly to draw out the implications for the living of a good life individually and socially. The social sciences, Bellah noted, so far as they were taught at all, were subsumed under the heading of moral philosophy.

Throughout the latter half of the nineteenth century the research university began to supplant the college as the model for higher education—contemporaneously with the rise of the business corporation. The two institutions were manifestations of the same social forces "Graduate education, research, and specialization, leading to largely autonomous departments, were the hallmarks of the new universities," Bellah and his colleagues noted. "The prestige of natural science as the model for all disciplined knowing and the belief that the progress of science would inevitably bring social amelioration in its wake partially obscured the fact that the unity and ethical meaning of higher education were being lost."

On balance, Bellah felt there had been "great positive achievements" in that transformation of higher education. The new academic system was better adapted to preparing vast numbers of people for employment in an industrial society; and it included as students those who, because of class, sex, or race, had formerly been excluded. In an undeniable sense, the research university and its many spinoffs in the twentieth century brought democratization. Though the full promise did not begin to be fulfilled until after World War II, from the very beginning there was the idea of institutions open to a much wider spectrum of the society than the old colleges had ever been. And the new university, rather than providing the final polish to an already-established upper class, would itself be an avenue of advancement in the world. As Francis H. Snow of the University of Kansas, in his inaugural address of 1890 put it, "Let it be everywhere made known that the University of the State, every son and daughter of the state may receive the special training that makes chemists, naturalists, entomologists, electricians, engineers, lawyers, musicians, pharmacists and artists, or the broader and more symmetrical culture which prepares those who receive it for that general, well-rounded efficiency which makes the educated man a success in any line of intellectual activity."

But there were costs also. Part of the price entailed by the rise of the modern research university and its attendant specialization and professionalism was, as Bellah put it, "the impoverishment of the public sphere." The new experts in science, in particular, exchanged general citizenship in society for membership within a smaller, more specialized community of experts. Within his field of expertise, the specialist's opinions would be judged henceforth not so much by the literate public at large as by his or her professional colleagues and peers. He was apt to become less intelligible to lay readers. Today's academic specialists, he observed, were writing within a set of assumptions and a vocabulary shared only by other experts. Specialization was inevitable. What was *not* inevitable, as Bellah judged it, was that discourse would tend to confine itself within the narrow limits of subcommunities of specialists without ever addressing any larger audience or informing public discussion beyond those subcommunities. Needless to add, in academe, any sense of integration, any moral dimension whatsoever, had disappeared.

In a later work entitled *The Good Society* (1991), Bellah and his colleagues cited a still more troubling consequence flowing from the enthronement of scientific knowledge as a cultural paradigm for the modern research university. "Within less than two decades of its founding the effort to create an integrated, democratic higher education had degenerated into an early form of what we have come to know as the multiversity cafeteria," he and his associates remarked. "The research university, the cathedral of learning, rather than interpreting and integrating the larger society, came more and more to mirror it. Far from becoming a new community that would bring coherence out of chaos, it became instead congeries of faculty and students, each pursuing their own ends, integrated not by any shared vision but only by the bureaucratic procedures of the 'administration.'" (As a university president was once heard to declare, "A university is an untidy constellation of academic and administrative units sharing in common little more than a heating plant.")

What Bellah referred to as the "multiversity cafeteria," and Barber the "full-service" university, George Douglas called the "giant bazaar" model of academe. "Since the end of the nineteenth century," he commented, "we Americans have gravitated toward the idea that the university is like a giant department store, an emporium, a bazaar of some kind, a place where people come to shop for things. People come to the university to purchase goods that are prepackaged or made to order. Students, for example, want to obtain degrees so that they can step out into a technologically complex world that requires specialized knowledge. They pay for those degrees and expect to receive them on time and at the right price, just like a person who buys a bolt of cloth in a dry goods store." Yet, as Douglas noted, just as buyers sometimes are shortchanged or cheated, today's students might not be receiving fair value for their investment. Further, there might be something quite fundamentally wrong with their being encouraged to think of knowledge as a consumable commodity, or education as something to be purchased off the shelf. Some such attitude, he felt, might be responsible for the tendency of many college students to consider their education as something simply to be endured, to be gotten over or gotten through, "as a cat shakes its paw to get rid of a few drops of water into which it has unfortunately been obliged to step."

Part of the problem also, as many critics discussed it, was the extent to which "credentialism" had come to dominate students' attitudes toward higher education. The college degree, as Pierre Bourdieu and Jean-Claude Passeron noted (*Reproduction in Education, Society and Culture*, 1979), might not function directly as a guarantee or affidavit of job competency in a given field, but its acquisition signified the acquisition of a certain "cultural capital" recognized by employers and society at large as symbolizing a rite of occupational initiation, and hence required of those aspiring to a certain occupational status. The academic system, in other words, to the extent that it had replaced guild and apprenticeship training, had now become the means of controlling access to jobs. It was not to be wondered at, therefore, that labor market considerations loomed large in students' interpretations of the meaning and purpose of their college education.

The "Publish or Perish" Syndrome

Bellah's analysis did not explicitly treat university research or discuss it as a social phenomenon. If it had, it could easily have accounted for the importance accorded research in many institutions of higher learning; for how the model of cumulative extension of knowledge as a product of scientific investigation historically gained currency and came to generate separate imperatives for "doing research" in the social sciences and humanities as well as the physical and biological sciences or mathematics; for the ways in which the Germanic research ideal, as peculiarly adapted to the American cultural milieu, had the unintended outcome ultimately of encouraging a "publish or perish" mentality within the professorate; and for the weighty, sometimes mixed consequences of the research emphasis on undergraduate education.

In any case, many critics of American higher education in the 1980s and 1990s seized upon research as another part of the problem plaguing academe. "If there is one thing that the general public has heard about college professors," observed Douglas, "it is that they are somehow burdened with the necessity of publishing the results of their research." He went on to note that in many small colleges the emphasis on research was much less compulsive and in some places virtually nonexistent. Lack of pressure to publish in some smaller institutions, he further observed, was sometimes taken as a token of their mediocrity or inferiority by those holding appointments in the more prestigious institutions—which might or might not be true. But conversely, claims by those in liberal-arts colleges or other smaller institutions that they stressed good teaching rather than publication also might or might not be true. Either way, all observers were agreed that research productivity had become the *sine qua non* of the activist, corporate university. The issue at stake was how to assess the meaning and significance of that emphasis upon research and publication, both on its own terms and as a controlling consideration for academic advancement.

Economics professor Henry Rosovsky, a former dean at Harvard, offered a characteristic defense for university research. University-level teaching is difficult without the new ideas and inspiration provided by research, he argued. Students are apt to interpret an interest in research as a symptom of lack of interest in teaching, and are encouraged to believe that teaching and research are a zero-sum game—that is, that more research leads to a neglect of teaching and vice versa. What they fail to understand, ran his argument, is that for faculty who find it congenial to work in research institutions, some combination of teaching and research is considered ideal. The university teacher is not a teacher who is expected to confine him- or herself to the transmission of received knowledge to generations of students, after the fashion perhaps of the old antebellum college teaching master. He or she is assumed to be a producer of new knowledge as well.

Rosovsky conceded that promotion, tenure, salary, and professional esteem were all closely associated with research and scholarship, and that pressures to publish in some cases could have adverse consequences. But he felt on balance that researchers tended to be "more interesting and better professors." His argument, of course, was a familiar one: that the best teachers are obviously the leaders in any field of academic endeavor, that people who are on the "cutting edge" of inquiry are more likely to be creative teachers as well. Further, because published research is subject to peer scrutiny, it serves as a useful "quality-control" on the scholarship behind classroom instruction.

It was precisely that article of faith that increasingly came under attack in criticisms of higher education in the eighties and nineties. As Page Smith saw it, academic research had come to be viewed in a perverse sort of way as its own justification, without any real-world referent, producing a corpus of literature "as broad as the ocean and as shallow as a pond." The vast majority of research turned out in a modern university, he alleged, is essentially worthless, does not result in any measurable benefit to anything or anyone, does not push back the frontiers of knowledge so confidently and frequently invoked, and does not contribute much of significance to the general populace or any particular segment thereof—with the possible exception of those external agencies that sometimes subsidize its costs. So far as Smith was concerned, it was all "busywork on a vast, almost incomprehensible scale." The pity of it all was that so many professors had been forced into becoming unwilling accomplices to a system that forced them to write when, it was painfully obvious, they had nothing of significance to say.

For Charles Sykes, research was an absurdly inflated boondoggle, an enterprise of doubtful worth carried on, often at public expense, without any real utility, cultural or otherwise. As for Rosovsky's argument and others like it that research and teaching are interdependent and mutually reinforcing, Barber remarked that the supposed synergy of the two amounted to a very dubious proposition lacking much supporting evidence. To talk about a "balance" between research and teaching, as he saw it, was an exercise in wishful thinking at best, and at worst, a lie. "The dirty little open secret of American higher education," he observed, "known to every faculty member who manages to gain tenure, is this: No one ever was tenured at a major college or university on the basis of great teaching alone; and no one with a great record of research and publication was ever denied tenure because of a poor teaching record. Teaching is the gravy, but research is the meat and potatoes."

Much criticism of academic research fastened on the character or quality of what was being produced. Some alleged that the system forced professors to become even more specialized than the demands of their respective disciplines required, given the common academic expectation that "serious" scholarship confine itself to small problems, narrowly drawn topics or issues, and in-depth analysis of subjects of microscopic proportions and sharply delimited boundaries. Large sweeping theories had become suspect; straying beyond one's accredited field of expertise was now more and more frowned upon—in short, as one commentator expressed it, the message was that professors were safe only as they became intellectual and scholastic miniaturists. Other critics, like Bellah, assailed the withdrawal of much academic scholarship from issues of large public import, its seeming isolation from the cultural mainstream, its abdication of responsibility for forging linkages to society as a whole.

Still others criticized scholars for their alleged preoccupation with method and technique; and their deliberate penchant for writing in specialized, inaccessible languages intelligible only to other specialists. "They feast," claimed George Douglas, "on a weak gruel of dead abstractions occasionally seasoned with obscure pomposities." Barber, for his part, felt that criticisms of academic scholarship were more than fully justified, and he felt they applied with special force to the new champions of democratic education no less than to others. The oddest feature about radical scholarship on race, ethnicity, and feminism, for example, he commented, "is how inaccessible it is to its purported constituencies. At least Marx's *Manifesto* was a good and popular read. . . . But a good deal of postmodernist criticism is intelligible only to insiders . . . and, trapped in its own metacritical jargon, is no less elitist than the canon it challenges."

Detractors of academic research and scholarship apportioned blame in equal measure. Researchers in the natural sciences, they alleged, had shut themselves up within their respective specializations, each hermetically sealed and locked apart from one another. Social scientists had just as willfully erected fixed barricades around their own disciplines. Plagued by feelings of inferiority to their colleagues in the physical sciences, they allegedly had drawn a cloak of near-impenetrable technicality over their work and, in a vain attempt to ape the conventions of the "hard" sciences, were engaged in dressing up their investigations with ponderous argot and spurious quantification. Humanists—teachers of literature, language, history, and philosophy—according to Douglas, had indulged themselves in a new and deadly form of scholasticism distinguished chiefly by its obscurantism, bombastic prose, and introspective solipsism. The assorted "perversities" of structuralism, post-structuralism, deconstructionism, and other "murky impostures" in literary and historical analysis, he felt, held full sway. The scholasticism of the humanities, Barber agreed, was well illustrated by its tendency to take the very culture that is its putative object of study and to turn it into the study of the study of culture. Thus, he observed, one no longer reads and interprets books; one studies what it means to read books; one does not interpret theories, but develops theories of interpretation. Overall, the constant refrain of a flood of books commenting on the state of American scholarship in the 1990s was that it appeared to have succumbed to a chilling form of "mandarism," that it had grown utterly remote and removed from the vital concerns with which academic inquiry had once been engaged. The ivory tower, it was said, had become a tower of babble.

Loss of Community

Loss of a sense of community figured as a recurrent theme in several late-twentieth-century analyses of American higher education. Once again, although there were many other studies of the same genre which emphasized much the same motifs, George Douglas's *Education Without Impact* supplied an incisive case in point. Americans, he argued at length, had long demanded the "wrong" thing of colleges and universities, and institutions of higher learning had responded by developing an educational style well adapted to meeting the technical and commercial needs of society but not necessarily the needs of individuals as human beings, and certainly not the fundamental civic needs of the republic. Universities, he judged, were failing to provide the type of human setting in which education worthy of the term could thrive. They were too big, too full of activity, too busy to be places of authentic learning. Instead they had become merely factories for producing specialized expertise or for imparting information, in both cases doing so in a relatively routine and unimaginative fashion.

For all of their primitivism, social isolation, stagnancy, and detachment, their limited curricula and autocratic paternalism, Douglas avowed, the old-style colleges that had their footing in colonial times were more authentic communities of learners. They offered little that was directly useful or practical; they prepared for an exceedingly narrow range of careers, and they were forced to make do with only a modicum of support, financial or otherwise. Nevertheless, for all their faults and shortcomings, at their best they provided an environment or an atmosphere in which genuine learning was possible. They afforded time and space for intellectual transactions between professors and students, opportunities for youthful learners to pose fundamental questions, chances to ponder and analyze and discuss issues of common interest. They took seriously the challenge to shape and inform character and to engage questions of normative judgment and standards. Their very smallness made for a type of cohesiveness and personal unity that was later lost. They were learning communities. Above all else, even when college authorities treated their charges as unruly schoolboys whose deportment had to be monitored and regulated in every particular possible, they did take them seriously as learners.

Douglas and other like-minded critics might have invoked as an example of the guiding ideal of the old-style college William Johnson Cory's address (*Eton Reform*, 1861) to a group of young men about to embark upon the next phase of their academic careers. "You are not engaged so much in acquiring knowledge as in making mental efforts under criticism," he told them. "A certain amount of knowledge you can indeed with average faculties acquire so as to retain; nor need you regret the hours that you have spent on much that is forgotten, for the shadow of lost knowledge at least protects you from many illusions. But you go to a great school, not for knowledge so much as for arts and habits; for the habit of attention, for the art of expression, for the art of assuming at a moment's notice a new intellectual posture, for the art of entering quickly into another person's thoughts, for the habit of submitting to censure and refutation, for the art of indicating assent or dissent in graduated terms, for the habit of regarding minute points of accuracy, for the habit of working out what is possible in a given time, for taste, for discrimination, for mental courage and mental soberness." Cory concluded, "Above all, you go to a great school for self-knowledge."

Something of that arcadian ambience of intimacy and leisured contemplation lingered on as formerly bucolic colleges and universities grew larger and were transformed into something else altogether. "Even when huge institutions grew up the years just before the turn of our century," as Douglas phrased it, "persistent efforts were made to keep something of that essence of the small, ivy-covered college—otherwise we wouldn't have erected universities with Georgian or 'collegiate Gothic' buildings, with quadrangles and shaded paths. We would have stopped planting ivy." (Interestingly, in another context altogether, historian Daniel Boorstin also discerned a special symbolic significance, albeit of a different sort, in collegiate architecture. If there was to be a new "religion of education," he observed, the universities would serve as its cathedrals, just as the high schools would become its parish churches. It was no accident, he felt, that American universities had adopted the architecture of the great age of European cathedral building. In short, for institutions that could afford it, "Collegiate Gothic" naturally became a standard.)

On balance, critics of American higher education in the nineties did not appear overly optimistic about prospects for re-creating the spirit of a genuine learning community in academe. Gigantism—the sheer size and complexity of the modern university—seemed to militate against recapturing the closeness and intimacy said to be characteristic of higher learning in former times. The likelihood that mega-universities could be downsized to any appreciable extent (even if some such scaling-down was deemed desirable or necessary) seemed remote. Another factor at work, it was pointed out, was a dramatic increase in the percentage of students in colleges and universities attending on a part-time basis. Unable or unwilling to invest in full-time instruction, many students had long since abandoned the traditional four-year time frame for completing requirements for a bachelor's degree. Campuses were now thronged with older, returning students, both graduate and undergraduate, nontraditional collegians in their middle years, men and women whose career and familial responsibilities competed with academic pursuits for their time and energy. Even among the traditional 18-to 22-year-old cohort, economic pressures demanded that many hold down part-time or even full-time jobs while going to school. Under these circumstances, it was observed, chances of reviving the leisurely environment of the old-time college as a tightly knit community seemed nil.

Academic Standards

Allegations that academic standards had dropped precipitously was a familiar refrain among observers of the American collegiate scene in the eighties and nineties. Similar complaints had been voiced many times before, of course, and were hardly novel, but they appeared more frequently and seemingly with greater force than ever before. Part of the problem, according to one line of analysis, was that America as a democratic society had set for itself the goal of ensuring that as many of its youth as possible should graduate from high schools and continue on to college. Unlike pyramidal European models in which schools traditionally were called upon to perform a "winnowing-out" function, sorting and screening students and passing on only those of exceptional academic talent to the next higher echelon, the American approach was more radically egalitarian.

No effort was to be spared in seeing to it that everyone completed secondary education, and, further, that virtually anyone desiring access to higher education was afforded an opportunity to pursue a college degree. However, in the absence of national standards of academic achievement, not to mention the prevalence of open admissions policies, or so it was claimed, colleges and universities could take very little for granted in terms of ability or achievement among entering students. The presence on campuses of increasing numbers of students of indifferent or mediocre ability, many of them having graduated from the bottom half of their high-school classes, was bound to affect the rigor of collegiate education.

What was indisputable, in any event, was the trend toward nonselectivity in admissions. Whereas in 1955 over half of the nation's colleges and universities had some type of selective admissions policies in place, three decades later, in 1985, according to the New York Times' *Selective Guide to Colleges*, out of almost 3,000 institutions surveyed, fewer than 175 institutions were classified as "selective." What constituted "selectivity" was always open to debate, but at the extremes, the differences were obvious enough. In 1985, for example, Stanford University accepted no more than 15 percent of those applying; in the same year the University of Arkansas accepted fully 99 percent of all applicants.

Considerable confusion continued to surround debates over the meaning and implications of egalitarian admission policies and practices. Some argued for an unabashedly "elitist" approach based on the concept of intellectual and academic meritocracy. Only the "best and brightest" ought to be admitted. Sometimes a proviso was added that special efforts be made, in the sports jargon popular in the nineties, to "level the playing field"—that is, to equalize opportunities for anyone to demonstrate his or her potential to profit from higher learning, especially those from disadvantaged backgrounds. But the principle that higher learning was not for everyone was to be preserved. Others argued that opening the gates of academe to anyone seeking entrance was entirely unobjectionable and innocuous, so long as the principle was kept clear that "opportunity" did not mean "entitlement"—that is, that everyone deserved a chance to succeed, but they would be held accountable to certain institutional standards of academic achievement as a condition for retention.

In response, opponents argued it was a cruel hoax to hold out hope for success by admitting masses of students who, by any predictive standard, were unlikely to succeed. Accordingly, some commentators continued to claim that lack of stringent admission standards threatened to undermine the integrity of the entire academic enterprise. Finally, a few radical egalitarians, possibly a minuscule number, went so far as to urge the abandonment of any proficiency standards whatsoever—in which case, of course, concerns about possible failure would be rendered moot. Everyone would succeed in some way, at some performance level.

Misplaced egalitarianism had contributed to the problem of confusion over standards. Some conservative critics, however, felt that a more important cause of the apparent erosion or loss of academic rigor in colleges and universities was traceable back to the period of campus turmoil of the 1960s and early 1970s. In an era when authority was suspect, when all standards and constraints were under attack, and everything traditional was assailed as undemocratic and elitist, academic administrators and faculty were anxious to sidestep confrontations with angry students. In the face of unrelenting pressure to relax requirements, professors ultimately capitulated. Because they lacked strong convictions of their own about which standards were defensible, professors surrendered by allowing students to decide. They acceded, in other words, to the substitution of easier, less demanding courses for more difficult ones. Additional choices and alternatives were created, even as expectations and workloads were lowered. Foreign language, mathematics, and science requirements were cut back or eliminated. Students were allowed greater freedom to shape their courses of study. The general curriculum became softer, more pliable. Withdrawing from courses became easier, and new pass/fail options were introduced to allow students to protect their academic grade-point averages.

Tacit acceptance of a "market model" for higher education exacerbated the tendency to relax standards. If students were "consumers" and education were a "commodity" available for purchase, ran the logic, then students were entitled to pick and choose as they saw fit. And if tuition-paying students were not to be denied good grades, more or less independently of their actual achievements, the inevitable result would be grade inflation—which, as critics hastened to point out, was precisely what happened in the 1970s. In the 1920s at Harvard, for example, no more than one student in five made the dean's list. By 1976, over three-quarters—76 percent—did so. In the 1950s the modal letter grade awarded undergraduates was a C. In the 1980s, three decades later, studies showed that among a national representative cross-section of public colleges and universities of varying sizes surveyed, the average grade awarded had risen to B. Because students were the beneficiaries of the new dispensation, they were least likely to complain, even if inflation implied a certain devaluation in the worth of their credentials.

Revelations of lax grading standards continued with depressing regularity well into the 1990s. At Harvard in 1992, for example, 91 percent of all undergraduate grades were B- or higher. At Stanford, no more than about 6 percent of all grades reported were C's. At Princeton, A's rose from 33 percent of all grades to 40 percent in four years. Harvard instructor William Cole diagnosed the cause of the problem as a loss of nerve. "Relativism is the key word today," he avowed. "There's a general conception in the literary-academic world that holding things to high standards—like logic, argument, having an interesting thesis—is patriarchal, Eurocentric, and conservative. If you say, 'This paper is no good because you don't support your argument,' that's almost like being racist and sexist." Similar in tone was the explanation offered in 1994 by Stephen Cahn, former provost and vice-provost at the Graduate Center of the City University of New York. The general reluctance of academics to award low grades, Cahn claimed, reflected the temper of the times in its wholesale rejection of the concept of comparative merit. The results, he concluded, were plain for all to see: lowered expectations, misguided egalitarianism, abandonment of standards of quality, and finally, what he characterized as an "eclipse of excellence."

Meanwhile, students seemed unaffected by debates over the quality of their education. For most consumers of collegiate training, their sojourn on campus was considered an entitlement and a rite of passage, almost implacable in its inevitability, something practically everyone was both allowed and obliged to pass through en route to something else—graduate school perhaps, or a job, or another rung on the career ladder. By the 1990s, the suggestion that a college education ought to be appreciated as an intellectual adventure to be savored and enjoyed instead of being merely endured as a conduit to some further destination point might have seemed to many students, literally, incomprehensible.

Neglect of Undergraduate Education

As some critics assessed the situation, the modern university, public or private, all too often had lost sight of the conditions needed for promoting genuine education. Traditionally, it was alleged, the task was conceived of by academic leaders as simply one of "imparting information," preferably in as expeditious a fashion as possible. But students entering college were not looking for, and did not need, yet another experience that only "imparted" data—they had had plenty of that in the lower schools. Whether they consciously realized it or not, they did not need some perfunctory or impersonal handing down of information, more often than not in large lecture classes, often taught by relatively inexperienced graduate teaching assistants or, often reluctantly and only under duress, by faculty members unlucky enough to be assigned responsibility for supervising lower-level courses. Nor was the cause of high-quality undergraduate education well served by framing introductory courses as intellectual antechambers to professional specialization, as devices for recruiting departmental majors to some particular discipline.

Students did not need to be talked "at," but conversed "with," preferably in small seminars and colloquia, recognizing that meaningful learning is inherently "labor intensive" and cannot be conducted on a large-scale, assembly-line basis. Undergraduates, some said, did not need competency testing, and outcomes assessments, and standardized computer-scored tests, or any of the other mechanistic appurtenances of corporate academe. They would not benefit from technological innovations employed in ways that made learning less meaningful and more impersonal. Students, critics asserted (perhaps unfairly), deserved something better than to be allowed by default to pass like stones through the intestinal tracts of the nation's colleges and universities, only to emerge as fundamentally unenlightened and illiterate as they were when they first entered.

What undergraduates allegedly needed in order to be truly educated, it was said, were opportunities to stretch their minds, to be provoked and challenged, to pose fundamental questions, to assess alternative answers, to integrate and synthesize and apply what they had learned. This they were unlikely to receive, unless or until undergraduate education was no longer neglected or devalued as an enterprise strictly ancillary to professional and graduate training. The real imperative for any self-respecting institution of higher learning, it was argued, was to enshrine undergraduate learning once again as the very raison d'être of the college or university. Left unclear in most of the discussions of the nineties were detailed analyses of what it would require in terms of altered priorities, changes in the professorial reward system, and the transformation of academic culture to effect that proposed restoration of undergraduate education to a position of centrality.

William D. Schaefer, a former vice-chancellor at the University of California at Los Angeles, ranked among those who attempted to offer a diagnosis of the problem. In his view, institutions of higher learning for years had "mindlessly mixed vocational and academic courses without continuity or coherence or anything approaching a consensus as to what really should constitute an education." To him, this was the crux of the problem—one that would need to be addressed with thought and deliberation, not dollars. "I believe," he remarked, "that we should be . . . deeply concerned about this confusion of purpose—a confusion that has led colleges and universities to make fraudulent claims about their goals and missions as they package a hodgepodge of unrelated courses and incoherent requirements."

Schaefer took note of the many national reports and studies on undergraduate education that had appeared throughout the eighties. Criticism of the baccalaureate degree had achieved the status of a national pastime amidst allegations that general education was a "disaster area," that colleges offered a smorgasbord of courses from which students were allowed to pick and choose their way to graduation, that the standards for a bachelor's degree had come to vary so greatly that no one could say what the degree was supposed to represent, that academe had sunk to the point where there was more confidence about the length of a college education than about its substance or purpose, and so on. What, he asked, would be the *least* a college or university should expect its undergraduates to attain in the way of knowledge and analytic skills? His proposed minimum for ensuring that students received a meaningful general education included the following: (1) the expectation that students could read, write, and converse in English at a level sufficient for serious academic discourse; (2) the ability to read and converse in at least one foreign language, and to understand in general how language works; (3) a basic understanding of the studio and performing arts (origins, historical development, theory, and so on); (4) a similar understanding of the world of letters, including sufficient literary criticism to enable one to read literature, including major works in the fields of philosophy, religion, and the social sciences; (5) awareness of the historical development of humankind, its roots, traditions, and achievements, and its civilizations—both West and East; (6) a solid grasp of the scientific approach to knowledge, a more than superficial awareness of the physical sciences, and an understanding of mathematics; and, finally, (7) a similar understanding of the human body and the workings of the human mind. Acknowledging that one might argue for other goals and different priorities, Schaefer insisted nonetheless that "not until such goals are identified and agreed upon can we talk intelligently about required courses and general education programs."

Schaefer concluded with a plea. "What is needed," he observed, "is a commitment on the part of each institution—without qualification, without reservation, without compromise—that through a carefully organized, coherent program of instruction it will share with its students what today it deems to be the best known and thought, through time and space, in this our world." A viable college education in the twenty-first century, he added, demanded a "complete rethinking" of what an educated person could and should know.

Integrating the Curriculum

In 1959 the English scholar C. P. Snow published a lecture delivered at Cambridge entitled *The Two Cultures.* His judgment at that time was that the university had divided into two camps, consisting of culturally illiterate scientists on the one side and scientifically-illiterate humanists on the other. Between the two, Snow alleged, there had grown up "a gulf of mutual comprehension . . . hostility and dislike, but most of all of lack of understanding." Scientists, as he portrayed them, showed little interest in the social, moral, or psychological dimensions of human existence, and tended to be indifferent to matters extending beyond the range of empirical science. Humanists, he felt, were even more indifferent to, and ignorant about, even the most basic scientific principles. But as regards general learning, Snow's judgment was that scientists and technologists bore the greater burden of responsibility for failing to address questions of how to integrate the college curriculum. Meanwhile, it was later observed, college students had since managed to bridge the "two-cultures" gap with indifference and universal shallowness. Equally ignorant of both, illiteracy and innumeracy had come together to create, as one wit put it, "a splendid egalitarianism of ignorance."

Thirty years after Snow's analysis, Allan Bloom, in *The Closing of the American Mind* (1989), returned to the same issues. The professorate, he claimed, had abandoned liberal learning because it was too difficult to conceptualize or administer. Having trashed the traditional curriculum without having anything coherent to replace it, faculties everywhere had given themselves, over to trendy intellectual fads or retreated inward to their specialties. The very idea of a shared general culture was forgotten, and undergraduates were left to their own devices. Universities, Bloom observed sarcastically, can do everything yet "cannot generate a modest program of general education for undergraduates."

Bloom's critique apparently hit some kind of nerve. Overshadowing practically all other issues in American higher education toward the end of the century was the search for an anchor or "center" for undergraduate liberal learning. Much of the national debate had begun a half dozen years earlier with the publication of a 1983 essay in the *American Scholar* entitled "Cultural Literacy" by E. D. Hirsch, Jr., a professor of English at the University of Virginia. In his essay and in a subsequent book bearing the same title, Hirsch argued that in the absence of a common curriculum, American society was drifting dangerously close to losing "its coherence as a culture." "We need to connect more of our students to our history, our culture, and those ideas which hold us together," he argued. Similar in tone was the declaration by philosopher Mortimer Adler and his associates in a 1982 work entitled *The Paideia Proposal*: "For mutual understanding and responsible debate among the citizens of a democratic community, and for differences of opinion to be aired and resolved, citizens must be able to communicate with one another in a common language."

Responding to the calumny heaped upon his suggestion that school curricula should share common elements, Hirsch took the offensive. Against those who claimed that celebrating multicultural diversity within American society was far more important than imposing "monoculturalism," and that the latter amounted to a form of "cultural imperialism," Hirsch declared, "American literate culture has itself assimilated many of the materials that those who favor multiculturalism wish to include." To those who accused him of ethnic elitism, he rejoined, writing in *NEA Today* in 1988, "It is true that many of the richest and best-educated Americans of the nineteenth and early twentieth centuries were white, Anglo-Saxon and Protestant, and it's true that the literate culture they possessed is still dominantly present in American literate culture. But to think that literate culture is Waspish and elitist just because the educated people who possessed it happened to be, is to reason *post hoc ergo propter hoc*, which an expert in critical thinking will quickly identify as a logical fallacy."

Hirsch's focus was primarily upon the secondary-school curriculum. But the basic terms of the argument played themselves out at the college level also. It reached a crescendo of sorts in 1988 in a pitched battle between then-Secretary of Education William Bennett and his critics over a decision by the faculty of Stanford University to replace a required freshman course, "Western Culture," with a course entitled "Cultures, Ideas, and Values." In its revised edition, the course de-emphasized fifteen "classic" texts and required inclusion of writings by "women, minorities, and persons of color." Bennett's charge that the faculty's action would "trivialize" the university's course of studies set off a storm of protest in the nation's magazines and newspaper op-ed pages.

Critics of so-called "monoculturalism" ridiculed Hirsch's suggestion that one could identify a discrete set list of topics, names, and ideas everyone should share in common. Others argued that in attempting to preserve an exclusionary past, Bennett and his disciples appeared to have fallen prey to a certain mean-spiritedness that was at root both antidemocratic and intellectually elitist. Some theorists took special exception to the notion of a common curricular canon. There can never be a fixed content at the core of liberal learning, they argued; it must be constantly revised, reformulated, reinvented, and then reacquired by the learning community as a function of balanced interests and shifting social values, all of which are dynamic rather than static and always in a state of flux.

The practical problem, as most observers saw it in the 1990s, was finding new and more creative ways of reconciling legitimate demands for diversity with the equally urgent need to find a unifying center—if not a common core, then a fund of experiences that would breathe life once again into the ideal of general or liberal learning. "General education," as Howard Lee Nostrand characterized it a half century ago in his introduction to José Ortega y Gassett's *Mission of the University* (1946), "means the whole development of an individual, apart from his occupation training. It includes the civilizing of his life purposes, the refining of his emotional reactions, and the maturing of his understanding about the nature of things according to the best knowledge of our time." Toward the end of the twentieth century, there was little to indicate there was much consensus on how to achieve that venerable goal of holistic development. Some had abandoned the effort as impossible. Other colleges and universities were still engaged in experiments to preserve the spirit of general learning in an era of rampant specialization and intellectual fragmentation.

Academic "Commodification"

Higher-education controversies in the waning years of the twentieth century had to do mostly with cultural diversity, multiculturalism, finance and governance, accountability, and the limits, of academic freedom, among other topics. In the decade following, pundits began to focus on quite different issues—in particular the escalating cost of a college education itself. At the same time, a growing number of critics were troubled by a much broader, overarching ethos that had begun to coalesce in academe, a mindset that promised to highlight several disquieting campus trends: the seeming loss of collegiate community, growing curricular incoherence, the virtual eclipse of the liberal arts, an alleged neglect of undergraduate education generally, and unchecked careerism among a new generation of decidedly non-traditional collegians.

A "foul wind" has blown over the campuses of our nation's institutions of higher learning, warned freelance journalist Jennifer Washburn in a 2005 work entitled *University Inc., The Corporate Corruption of American Higher Education*. Its source, she alleged, was the growing role of purely commercial values in academic life, "the intrusion of a market ideology into the heart of academic life." Rutgers historian Jackson Lears similarly spoke of the growing "menace" of market-driven managerial influence in colleges and universities: "the impulse to subject universities to quantitative standards of efficiency and productivity, to turn knowledge into a commodity, to transform open sites of inquiry into corporate research laboratories and job-training centers."

Lears traced the syndrome back to the early twentieth century when the Prussian ideal of productive scholarship within the university first began to meld with American vocationalism and anti-intellectualism—the love of the practical, the demand for short-term utility and cash value. (In point of fact he might have extended the analysis back to the land-grant college movement of the 1850s or even earlier.) Whatever its origins, the historic outcome underscored an enduring tension between two dissimilar institutional missions. The first was defined by the disinterested pursuit of truth and knowledge as intrinsically valuable ends. The other was constituted by the practical business of supplying technical expertise for government and corporate business.

Half a century later, with the advent of the Cold War, national security considerations lent renewed urgency to demands for a skilled, more highly-trained work force. Federal and state pressures for career-related learning and programming, together with urgings from corporate behemoths that higher education be run more "like a business," made for a potent, nearly irresistible combination. It virtually assured that higher education in the post-war era would be marked by a narrow technocratic orientation. Not without good reason did UC Berkeley Chancellor Clark Kerr in a 1959 commencement address characterize the modern American university as a "knowledge factory."

Traditionally, institutions of higher learning have tried to counterbalance the narrow careerism favored by students and some external constituencies by insisting that sufficient time and space be reserved for a more disinterested academic regimen as well, one consisting of the humanities and arts—the whole calculated to encourage the development of well-rounded persons instead of narrowly-trained technicians. The biggest problem today, Washburn alleged, was that those countervailing forces had been eroded to the point where for all practical purposes they no longer exist at all.

For Lears the inclination among educational leaders to invoke market pressure as an irresistible force and moral absolute demonstrated the same trend. Invoking the overwhelming power of the marketplace as a reason not to challenge its intrusion into academe (*We're just giving the public what it wants*), he judged, was tantamount to ethical bankruptcy, a form of rationalization that conferred on the "market" a standing resembling that accorded God in medieval theology—the Primum Mobile, the First Cause, the Unmoved Mover." So too for Washburn, in the absence of values capable of constraining how unregulated markets function when left to their own devices, she argued, universities were fast becoming little more than appendages of corporate business and industry, their leaders willfully blind to the deleterious effects of wholesale commercialism.

In higher education today, came the complaint, the liberal arts suffer for their presumed inutility and hence their inability to retain "market share." Professors nowadays, for their part, are rewarded more for garnering research monies and generating publications than for teaching or mentoring students. The all-important introductory courses in the arts and humanities are taught mainly by graduate teaching assistants (TAs), not by experienced academics with a genuine commitment to the task of molding and stimulating young minds. Meanwhile, academic research (most notably in the applied sciences and technologies) is conducted with an eye toward licensing and the short-term development of lucrative products and industrial processes. How long, critics like Washburn and Lears asked, would universities fund research that has no immediate practical application but might offer rewards on a longer-term basis in future? Similarly, it was asked, could disinterested inquiry be sustained in an institutional environment that encouraged professors to behave like entrepreneurs or hucksters?

Indications that the process of academic commodification was already well advanced were not difficult to detect in the early 2000s. The mechanistic discourse increasingly favored by collegiate administrators and academics themselves afforded one clear sign: a parlance that described learning as a commodity; information as a "product" to be packaged and marketed; knowledge bundled into credits and "delivered" via an instructional "system"; students as "consumers" or "resources" or "human capital" awaiting batch processing, and so on.

For Lears, the most egregious illustration of learning as commodity was higher education's preoccupation with the virtual classroom and the effort to substitute cyber-technology for live interaction between teacher and student. "Any use of computers that undermines face-to-face contact is potentially destructive to education," he insisted. "Distance learning is to learning as phone sex is to sex: it may be better than no learning at all, but you wouldn't want to confuse it with the real thing." Summing up, he observed:

> Good teaching is an investment in the minds of the young, as obscure in result, as remote from immediate proof as planting a chestnut seedling. But we have come to prefer ends that are entirely foreseeable, even though that requires us to shorten our vision. Education is coming to be, not a long-term investment in young minds and in the life the community, but a short-term investment in the economy. We want to be able to tell how many dollars an education is worth and how soon it will begin to pay.

Perhaps nothing else served so vividly to confirm Lears' claims than the growing presence in American higher education of a quite different type of postsecondary institution: the for-profit college and university. "They have distilled the business of higher education into its no-frills essence," alleged Richard Ruch, author of *Higher Ed, Inc.* (2001), himself a one-time administrator in a for-profit school. "They have taken a simple and straightforward approach to the business of education and applied tried-and-true business practices to meet the needs of a market niche. They are doing so," he continued, "with considerable success in terms of growing enrollments, improved retention, and impressive levels of graduate placement, not to mention high profitability and very good returns on invested capital . . ." Having aligned themselves with the fastest growing part of the American economy, the "knowledge sector of the service industry," Ruch was confident their continued success was virtually assured.

For-profit schools, he explained, do not seek to nurture civic literacy and good citizenship. They do not attempt to instill an appreciation for high culture or a love of the arts either. Their exclusive mission is to provide an efficient, cost-effective route to a degree and subsequent job placement in a high-demand field at a good salary. This essentially is what they do (besides enriching their stockholders). And their phenomenal growth record, he went on to observe, attested to the fact they were filling a popular demand for career- and employment-linked postsecondary education.

In 1991, for example, there was only one for-profit baccalaureate degree-granting, accredited institution listed on the stock exchange—DeVry, Inc., which became a public company that year. Over the course of the next ten years, the number of publicly-traded institutions more than quadrupled, to around 40, attracting more than 4.8 billion in private investment capital. By 1996 there were 669 for-profit degree-granting centers in operation, boasting a combined enrollment of around 305,000 students. Major players by 2005 or thereabouts included the University of Phoenix, the Argosy Education Group, DeVry Institutes of Technology, Corinthian Colleges, Strayer Education, Education Management Corporation, and Quest Education, each with multiple campuses or instructional sites.

All told, by the turn of the century, the number of for-profit campuses had registered a 112 percent growth rate over the preceding ten-year period, increasing from 350 to over 750 sites by 2001. If the for-profit sector continued to grow at anything resembling its previous growth rate, it did not appear unreasonable in the early 2000s to expect that within a foreseeable future, *one in every four or five students attending college would be enrolled in a for-profit institution.*

In an engaging *New Yorker* article entitled "Drive-Thru U," James Traub wrote that "the traditional American university occupies a space that is both bounded and pastoral—a space that speaks of monastic origins and a commitment to unworldliness." Comparing non-profit universities with their for-profit competitors, Traub offered a judgment: "The institution that sees itself as the steward of intellectual culture is becoming increasingly marginal," he declared, while "the others are racing to accommodate the new student."

Ruch, in common with many others, agreed. And in common with other proponents of vocational education, the value added of a college education, he declared, inheres in its capacity to help launch a person's career. The metric to be applied, ultimately, is the greater earning power the college degree affords. Hence, the major consideration shaping a student's decision to attend college, quite simply, is—or ought to be—an economic-return equation.

Having pressed his point, Ruch added a qualification however. "Those time-honored, laudable ideas—the life of the mind, learning for its own sake—sometimes haunt me in my dreams like a secret lover" he admitted. "Something ancient in my heart of hearts resists the notion that efficiency and practicality should define the greatest good. There are real losses in this shift in values, and I suspect that all of us in academia, regardless of our institutional affiliation, have felt them to some degree."

What that shift undergirding the ideology of the free market might portend long-term for American higher education was difficult to discern from the vantage point of the early twenty-first century. But at the very least, it was apparent that many factors were working together to render traditional notions of higher learning more and more obsolete. Which academic degree programs might benefit from an increasingly hard-nosed corporate environment and which might wither or even disappear entirely seemed difficult to predict. The continuing arrival of more and more "non-traditional" students promised one sort of transformational change within academe. So too did increasing reliance on computer technology to supply instruction to students far removed from the physical campus. With the advent of web-based courses and asynchronous learning as a pedagogical norm, bucolic images of the groves of academe as they once existed now seemed increasingly anachronistic and outdated. About all that could be said with real confidence about the state of higher learning in the United States was that major changes on an unprecedented scale were already underway. What the future might hold in store, as always, awaited its own unfolding.

HENRY VETHAKE PROPOSES CURRICULAR AND TEACHING CHANGES, 1830

R. HOFSTADTER AND W. SMITH (EDS)

Documents 12–18 are portions of addresses made to the Convention of Literary and Scientific Gentlemen in New York City in October, 1830. The convention was called partly to criticize the spirit of the Yale Report in 1828 (see Doc. II) and partly to lay the foundation of what was to become New York University. Some of the leading men of letters in the country attended or sent their advice. Although their discussions were far-ranging and lacking in central agreement on all matters having to do with higher learning, there did emerge from them a clear idea of the necessity for a university, rather than a college, in a great metropolis. Secretary of the convention, and the man responsible for publishing its proceedings, was John Delafield (1786–1853), New York banker and Columbia College graduate. See Richard J. Storr, *The Beginnings of Graduate Education in America*, pp. 33–43.

Born in British Guiana, Henry Vethake (1792–1866) taught mathematics and philosophy at several colleges. When he submitted this first paper read at the convention, Vethake was teaching at Princeton. Thereafter he held a professorship in the University of the City of New York, the short-lived institution that was the direct result of this convention; he won membership in the American Philosophical Society, served a brief term as president of Washington College, Virginia, then was connected with the University of Pennsylvania from 1836 to 1859. Dyspeptic and peppery in his later years, Vethake made his reputation as a thoroughly orthodox political economist. He did much to further the idea of economics as a separate academic discipline, but by the 1850's he doubted the wisdom of graduate and popular instruction and reversed the sentiments he expressed in 1830.

On Vethake see Joseph Dorfman and Rexford Guy Tugwell, *Early American Policy: Six Columbia Contributors* (New York, 1960), pp. 155–204.

The students of our colleges, it is well known, are almost universally divided into four different classes, viz: the Freshman, Sophomore, Junior, and Senior Classes. The course of study in each of them endures for a year, and is the same for every student, whatever may be his capacity or tastes. A candidate for admission to the Freshman or lowest class, besides possessing a competent knowledge of various branches of what is usually styled an *English* education, such as English Grammar, Geography, &c. must come prepared to be examined on a certain number, or on portions of a certain number of the classical (Greek and Latin) authors; and the Greek and Latin languages are also usually the principal subject of study during the first two years of the collegiate course, the sciences only becoming predominant objects of the students' attention in the Junior and Senior years. The instruction in the different sciences, Mathematical, Physical, and Moral, is, generally speaking, conducted almost entirely by recitation from a text book, with remarks, less or more extended, on the part of the teacher. At certain stated periods *distinctions* or *honours* are awarded to a certain number of the students who excel in scholarship; and, at the

Reprinted from *American Higher Education: A Documentary History*, edited by Richard Hofstadter and Wilson Smith (1961), University of Chicago Press.

close of his college career, every individual receives the first degree in the Arts. These are all the different circumstances which involve the points that will present themselves for my animadversion.

It is clear that our colleges are not institutions which are engaged in diffusing the blessings of knowledge among the community as generally as they have it in their power to do. They do not say to parents, send your children within our walls to make such acquirements in science, or letters, as their previous education may fit them to make. A young man desirous of obtaining a knowledge of Mathematics, Natural or Moral Philosophy, Chemistry, Natural History, or Political Economy, and who may possess all the preparatory information requisite for attending with advantage the course of instruction in any of those branches of knowledge, will yet find himself debarred from admission to college, if he have not provided himself with a certain stock of Latin and Greek. Our colleges do in fact say to such an individual, whatever your aspirations after knowledge may be, to you *we* are not the dispensers of it. It is true that we have it in our power to make you more useful members of society, and to exalt you in the scale of being; but, nevertheless, we condemn you, as far as lies with us, to comparative ignorance and a lower sphere of usefulness; and we reserve our instructions for those only who have the wealth necessary to enable them to consume many years of their lives in the exclusive, or nearly the exclusive, occupation of learning two complicated and difficult languages, very imperfectly, in most cases, after all. That the learned or dead languages should, some two or three centuries ago, have been made the study of every one having in view scientific information as his ultimate end, as well as by those whose lives were to be devoted to literary or philological pursuits, was natural enough; since at that period almost all useful knowledge was contained in books written in those languages, which for that reason then hardly deserved the epithet of dead. But that, at the present day, when men of science, with very few exceptions, and those chiefly among the Germans and the other northern nations of Europe, make use, in recording their speculations, of their vernacular tongues,—when every thing which antiquity has left us worth the perusal, for the sake of acquiring information, has been translated into the modern dialects, the English among the number,—when the progress of knowledge, more especially of mathematical and physical science, has been such as to render the older authors of no value, except in so far as the gratification of the curiosity of those who are interested in tracing the gradual advances made by the human mind gives them one,—and when, more particularly in the United States, the number of individuals desirous of gaining useful information, vastly exceeds that of those who have the time and money to enable them to go through the *whole* course of education prescribed by our colleges,—it does seem to me that the very general persistance of those institutions, in the *restricted* system above mentioned, is one of the most remarkable instances with which I am acquainted, of a persistance in error, merely because it has been long established. . . .

While I thus fully acknowledge the value of classical literature, I see no reason why an *artificial* preference should be given to it in our systems of education, and why young men should be told, that unless they learn Latin and Greek, they shall not be permitted to learn any thing else. Whilst I would have ample provision made in our colleges for instruction, and able instruction, in these languages, as well as in every branch of literature and science, I would leave the *supply* of instruction in all to be regulated by the proportional *demand* of the public for each. . . .

That the courses of instruction would become superficial if opened, as is proposed, to all who are *sufficiently* prepared, by their age and previous education, to attend them with advantage, is an assumption which seems to me, to be quite gratuitous. In the present state of things, as every one knows, a few of our colleges, in order to attract such students as are more anxious to get a degree, than an education, degrade their instruction below what is furnished by many of our gymnasiums, or academies of reputation, which, having no foreign or adventitious support from the power of operating on the imaginations of the public, and more particularly of the younger portion of it, by the magic of degrees and diplomas, are dependent for patronage on merit alone. So, no doubt, would this continue to be the case under the system of which I am an advocate. Some institutions would still think it for their interest to teach more superficially than others, or would not have it in their power to furnish as extensive and thorough an education as others; but I do not hesitate to assert, for reasons to be presently stated, that the fact would be found to be, that the changes proposed would have a tendency to elevate rather than to lower the scale of education. This is, indeed, implied in the next objection to be considered, and which is in direct contradiction with the one of which we have been speaking. . . .

The remark, so often made, that the object of that education which is communicated by one mind to another, is not intended to make men masters of any one science, but rather, in addition to the expanding and invigorating of their faculties, to give them an encyclopedic outline of human knowledge, to be afterwards filled up, by their own unassisted efforts, in such parts as they may then select for their particular provinces of intellectual labor, is one which I am not disposed to controvert; but I cannot but think its application to the case under consideration to be somewhat strained, and out of place. I presume it can hardly be intended by the friends of the new University scheme, to undertake to produce annually a number of *finished* scholars, and *accomplished* men of science. They will still leave the eminences of knowledge to be slowly attained by the strenuous and persevering efforts of the student, long after he shall have quitted the walls of the University. The several courses of instruction will certainly not be of a nature to require the whole time and attention of those who attend them; the students, with the exception of a few, of inferior capacities, or of inefficient habits of intellectual exertion, will have ample leisure to engage in the study of more branches of knowledge than one. The numerous relations, too, which apparently the remotest of the sciences bear to each other, and the frequent points of contact which many of them present, have a constant tendency to withdraw the mind from a limited field of study, and to induce it to waste its energies in ranging fruitlessly over too wide a surface. Hence there is no room for apprehending that young men at college will confine themselves, from inclination, to the acquiring of a single science alone. I see no objection, however, to render it obligatory on them to attend at the same period of time, a certain number of courses, unless specially exempted for sufficient reasons, as is now the arrangement in the University of Virginia. Such a regulation would, indeed, be highly expedient in reference to the *discipline* of an institution, by securing, as much as possible, a full employment of his time for every student. But independent of any measure of the kind, there will be no difficulty in acquiring an *outline* of human knowledge. Besides the effect naturally resulting from the discursive disposition of the mind above mentioned, the tendency of the present age, more especially in our own country, for reasons which it is unnecessary to adduce, since the fact will hardly be questioned, is to produce a state of things in which the most educated men are, in general, acquainted, to a certain extent, with all things under the sun, rather than with any one branch of knowledge thoroughly, so as to be able to be of much practical service to their fellow men, or to contribute in any striking degree, to the progress of invention or discovery. And it would be well, perhaps, for the interests of education, if our literary institutions were to administer some check to this prevalent evil, instead of encouraging it by teaching, as some of them do, a mere smattering of many things. . . .

The fact is that the existing state of things, which I am anxious to see altered, is the necessary result of the arrangement of the students into regularly organized bodies, and of the distribution among them of the usual distinctions and honors. The student who would frequently visit his instructer, or even exhibit, unasked for and unnecessarily in any way before his class, his information, or his desire to obtain information, would at once become an object of suspicion and jealousy. He would be charged by his fellow students with an intention to curry favor in order to obtain unfairly an honor. He is condemned by their esprit du corps to content himself with such displays of his knowledge or talent alone as can be fairly made in reply to the questions put to him, in the class by his teacher. For the confirmation of this statement I appeal to the professors and students of colleges generally. . . .

I am persuaded that the error is as frequently committed in this country of teaching almost entirely by hearing recitations from a text book, as in Europe by trusting to the delivery of lectures alone. Both these methods I regard as extremes to be avoided. The proper system seems to me to be a combination of lectures, on all the branches that admit of them, with close examinations on their subject, and on the correspondent parts of a text book to be put into the hands of the students. With these accompaniments I do think that lecturing is not only the most agreeable mode of communicating instruction but that there is no other public mode in which a taste and an enthusiasm for knowledge can be so readily excited. There is something peculiarly impressive in the tones and aspect of a public speaker which we can fully realize by reflecting on the very different effect produced by a written discourse read in the closet, and the same discourse delivered from the pulpit or the rostrum by a man of even ordinary powers of elocution. I would, therefore, oblige every professor to read a course of lectures, or to lecture without note if he pleased, on the subjects embraced in his department: if he can do the latter *well*, so much the better. There is, indeed, one case, and one case only, in which I would allow him to hear recitations from a book, and comment upon the text, to wit, when he is himself the author of the text-book; for there would then be evidently very little use in repeating to his hearers what they have before them in print; and there would be no danger of his comments being either spiritless or sparing.

THE YALE REPORT OF 1828

R. HOFSTADTER AND W. SMITH (EDS)

Yale's leadership in furnishing the largest number of college presidents and, with Princeton, faculty members to the new colleges of the South and West made this the most influential document in American higher education in the first half of the nineteenth century. It was written as the reply of the Yale Corporation and faculty to Connecticut critics of the classical college curriculum who, like exponents of vocational or "practical" studies elsewhere in the 1820's, were specifically opposing the retention of the "dead" languages. The two authors of the Report, which was somewhat shortened for publication in Benjamin Silliman's (see Doc. 17) famous magazine and to which was added a seven-page endorsement by a committee of the Yale Corporation, were President Jeremiah Day (1773–1867) and Professor James L. Kingsley (1778–1852). Day, who wrote the first part, was officially connected with Yale for sixty-nine years as tutor, professor, president, and member of the Corporation; his successful presidency was marked by its stability, conservatism, and caution. Kingsley, author of the second part, taught at Yale from 1801 to 1851; his outstanding scholarship made him eminent in the fields of classics, mathematical science, and New England history. Their work quieted the critics of the college and entrenched the classics at Yale for the rest of the century. Not until the 1850's did men such as Francis Wayland (see Doc. 21, and Part VI, Doc. 1) attempt to soften the impact of the Report in some other institutions by their efforts toward curricular change and expansion.

Modern discussions of the Report can be found in R. Freeman Butts, *The College Charts Its Course: Historical Conceptions and Current Proposals* (New York, 1939), pp. 118–25; George P. Schmidt, *The Liberal Arts College: A Chapter in American Cultural History* (New Brunswick, N.J., 1957), pp. 55–58; and Richard Hofstadter and C. DeWitt Hardy, *The Development and Scope of Higher Education in the United States* (New York, 1952), pp. 15–17.

Remarks by the Editor [Benjamin Silliman]

The following papers relate to an important subject, respecting which there is at present some diversity of opinion. As the interests of sound learning, in relation both to literature and science, and to professional and active life, are intimately connected with the views developed in the subjoined reports, they are therefore inserted in this Journal, in the belief that they will be deemed both important and interesting by its readers.

At a Meeting of the President and Fellows of Yale College, Sept 11th, 1827, The Following Resolution was Passed

That His Excellency Governor Tomlinson, Rev. President Day, Rev. Dr. Chapin, Hon. Noyes Darling, and Rev. Abel McEwen, be a committee to inquire into the expediency of so altering the regular course of instruction in this college, as to leave out of said course the study of the *dead languages*, substituting

Reprinted from *American Higher Education: A Documentary History*, edited by Richard Hofstadter and Wilson Smith (1961), University of Chicago Press.

other studies therefor; and either requiring a competent knowledge of said languages, as a condition of admittance into the college, or providing instruction in the same, for such as shall choose to study them after admittance; and that the said committee be requested to report at the next annual meeting of this corporation.

This committee, at their first meeting in April, 1828, after taking into consideration the case referred to them, requested the Faculty of the college to express their views on the subject of the resolution.

The expediency of retaining the ancient languages, as an essential part of our course of instruction, is so obviously connected with the object and plan of education in the college, that justice could not be done to the particular subject of inquiry in the resolution, without a brief statement of the nature and arrangement of the various branches of the whole system. The report of the faculty was accordingly made out in *two parts;* one containing a summary view of the plan of education in the college; the other, an inquiry into the expediency of insisting on the study of the ancient languages. . . .

Report of the Faculty, Part I

. . . We are decidedly of the opinion, that our present plan of education admits of improvement. We are aware that the system is imperfect: and we cherish the hope, that some of its defects may ere long be remedied. We believe that changes may, from time to time be made with advantage, to meet the varying demands of the community, to accommodate the course of instruction to the rapid advance of the country, in population, refinement, and opulence. We have no doubt that important improvements may be suggested, by attentive observation of the literary institutions in Europe; and by the earnest spirit of inquiry which is now so prevalent, on the subject of education.

The guardians of the college appear to have ever acted upon the principle, that it ought not to be stationary, but continually advancing. Some alteration has accordingly been proposed, almost every year, from its first establishment. . . .

Not only the course of studies, and the modes of instruction, have been greatly varied; but whole sciences have, for the first time, been introduced; chemistry, mineralogy, geology, political economy, &c. By raising the qualifications for admission, the standard of attainment has been elevated. Alterations so extensive and frequent, satisfactorily prove, that if those who are intrusted with the superintendence of the institution, still firmly adhere to some of its original features, it is from a higher principle, than a blind opposition to salutary reform. Improvements, we trust, will continue to be made, as rapidly as they can be, without hazarding the loss of what has been already attained.

But perhaps the time has come, when we ought to pause, and inquire, whether it will be sufficient to make *gradual* changes, as heretofore; and whether the whole system is not rather to be broken up, and a better one substituted in its stead. From different quarters, we have heard the suggestion, that our colleges must be *new-modelled;* that they are not adapted to the spirit and wants of the age; that they will soon be deserted, unless they are better accommodated to the business character of the nation. As this point may have an important bearing upon the question immediately before the committee, we would ask their indulgence, while we attempt to explain, at some length, the nature and object of the present plan of education at the college. . . .

What then is the appropriate object of a college? It is not necessary here to determine what it is which, in every case, entitles an institution to the *name* of a college. But if we have not greatly misapprehended the design of the patrons and guardians of this college, its object is to *lay the foundation* of a *superior education:* and this is to be done, at a period of life when a substitute must be provided for *parental superintendence.* The ground work of a thorough education, must be broad, and deep, and solid. For a partial or superficial education, the support may be of looser materials, and more hastily laid.

The two great points to be gained in intellectual culture, are the *discipline* and the *furniture* of the mind; expanding its powers, and storing it with knowledge. The former of these is, perhaps, the more important of the two. A commanding object, therefore, in a collegiate course, should be, to call into daily and vigorous exercise the faculties of the student. Those branches of study should be prescribed, and those modes of instruction adopted, which are best calculated to teach the art of fixing the attention, directing the train of thought, analyzing a subject proposed for investigation; following, with accurate discrimination, the course of argument; balancing nicely the evidence presented to the judgment; awakening, elevating, and controlling the imagination; arranging, with skill, the treasures which memory gathers; rousing and guiding the powers of genius. All this is not to be effected by a light and hasty course of study; by reading a few books, hearing a few lectures, and spending some months at a literary institution. The habits of thinking are to be formed, by long continued and close application. The mines of science must be penetrated far below the surface, before they will disclose their treasures. If a dexterous performance of the manual operations, in many of the mechanical arts, requires an apprenticeship, with diligent attention for years; much more does the training of the powers of the mind demand vigorous, and steady, and systematic effort.

In laying the foundation of a thorough education, it is necessary that *all* the important mental faculties be brought into exercise. . . . In the course of instruction in this college, it has been an object to maintain such a proportion between the different branches of literature and science, as to form in the student a proper *balance* of character. From the pure mathematics, he learns the art of demonstrative reasoning. In attending to the physical sciences, he becomes familiar with facts, with the process of induction, and the varieties of probable evidence. In ancient literature, he finds some of the most finished models of taste. By English reading, he learns the powers of the language in which he is to speak and write. By logic and mental philosophy, he is taught the art of thinking; by rhetoric and oratory, the art of speaking. By frequent exercise on written composition, he acquires copiousness and accuracy of expression. By extemporaneous discussion, he becomes prompt, and fluent, and animated. It is a point of high importance, that eloquence and solid learning should go together; that he who has accumulated the richest treasures of thought, should possess the highest powers of oratory. To what purpose has a man become deeply learned, if he has no faculty of communicating his knowledge? And of what use is a display of rhetorical elegance, from one who knows little or nothing which is worth communicating? . . .

No one feature in a system of intellectual education, is of greater moment than such an arrangement of duties and motives, as will most effectually throw the student upon the *resources of his own mind*. Without this, the whole apparatus of libraries, and instruments, and specimens, and lectures, and teachers, will be insufficient to secure distinguished excellence. The scholar must form himself, by his own exertions. The advantages furnished by a residence at a college, can do little more than stimulate and aid his personal efforts. The *inventive* powers are especially to be called into vigorous exercise. . . .

In our arrangements for the communication of knowledge, as well as in intellectual discipline, such branches are to be taught as will produce a proper symmetry and balance of character. We doubt whether the powers of the mind can be developed, in their fairest proportions, by studying languages alone, or mathematics alone, or natural or political science alone. As the bodily frame is brought to its highest perfection, not by one simple and uniform motion, but by a variety of exercises; so the mental faculties are expanded, and invigorated, and adapted to each other, by familiarity with different departments of science.

A most important feature in the colleges of this country is, that the students are generally of an age which requires, that a substitute be provided for *parental superintendence*. When removed from under the roof of their parents, and exposed to the untried scenes of temptation, it is necessary that some faithful and affectionate guardian take them by the hand, and guide their steps. This consideration determines the *kind* of government which ought to be maintained in our colleges. As it is a substitute for the regulations of a family, it should approach as near to the character of parental control as the circumstances of the case will admit. It should be founded on mutual affection and confidence. It should aim to effect its purpose, principally by kind and persuasive influence; not wholly or chiefly by restraint and terror. Still, punishment may sometimes be necessary. There may be perverse members of a college, as well as of a family. There may be those whom nothing but the arm of law can reach. . . .

Having now stated what we understand to be the proper *object* of an education at this college, viz. to lay a solid *foundation* in literature and science; we would ask permission to add a few observations on the *means* which are employed to effect this object.

In giving the course of instruction, it is intended that a due proportion be observed between *lectures*, and the exercises which are familiarly termed *recitations*; that is, examinations in a text book. The great advantage of lectures is, that while they call forth the highest efforts of the lecturer, and accelerate his advance to professional eminence; they give that light and spirit to the subject, which awaken the interest and ardor of the student. . . . Still it is important, that the student should have opportunities of retiring by himself, and giving a more commanding direction to his thoughts, than when listening to oral instruction. To secure his steady and earnest efforts, is the great object of the daily examinations or recitations. In these exercises, a text-book is commonly the guide. . . . When he comes to be engaged in the study of his *profession*, he may find his way through the maze, and firmly establish his own opinions, by taking days or weeks for the examination of each separate point. Text-books are, therefore, not as necessary in this advanced stage of education, as in the course at college, where the time allotted to each branch is rarely more than sufficient for the learner to become familiar with its elementary principles . . .

We deem it to be indispensable to a proper adjustment of our collegiate system, that there should be in it both Professors and Tutors. There is wanted, on the one hand, the experience of those who have been long resident at the institution, and on the other, the fresh and minute information of those who, having more recently mingled with the students, have a distinct recollection of their peculiar feelings, prejudices, and habits of thinking. At the head of each great division of science, it is necessary that there should be a Professor, to superintend the department, to arrange the plan of instruction, to regulate the mode of conducting it, and to teach the more important and difficult parts of the subject. But students in a college, who have just entered on the first elements of science, are not principally occupied with the more abstruse and disputable points. Their attention ought not to be solely or mainly directed to the latest discoveries. They have first to learn the principles which have been in a course of investigation, through the successive ages; and have now become simplified and settled. Before arriving at regions hitherto unexplored, they must pass over the intervening cultivated ground. The Professor at the head of a department may, therefore, be greatly aided, in some parts of the course of instruction, by those who are not as deeply versed as himself in all the intricacies of the science. Indeed we doubt, whether elementary principles are always taught to the best advantage, by those whose researches have carried them so far beyond these simpler truths, that they come back to them with reluctance and distaste. . . .

In the internal police of the institution, as the students are gathered into one family, it is deemed an essential provision, that some of the officers should constitute a portion of this family; being always present with them, not only at their meals, and during the business of the day; but in the hours allotted to rest. The arrangement is such, that in our college buildings, there is no room occupied by students, which is not near to the chamber of one of the officers.

But the feature in our system which renders a considerable number of tutors indispensable, is the subdivision of our classes, and the assignment of each portion to the particular charge of one man. . . .

The course of instruction which is given to the undergraduates in the college, is not designed to include *professional* studies. Our object is not to teach that which is peculiar to any one of the professions; but to lay the foundation which is common to them all. There are separate schools for medicine, law, and theology, connected with the college, as well as in various parts of the country; which are open for the reception of all who are prepared to enter upon the appropriate studies of their several professions. With these, the academical course is not intended to interfere.

But why, it may be asked, should a student waste his time upon studies which have no immediate connection with his future profession? . . . In answer to this, it may be observed, that there is no science which does not contribute its aid to professional skill. "Every thing throws light upon every thing." The great object of a collegiate education, preparatory to the study of a profession, is to give that expansion and balance of the mental powers, those liberal and comprehensive views, and those fine proportions of character, which are not to be found in him whose ideas are always confined to one particular channel. When a man has entered upon the practice of his profession, the energies of his mind must be given, principally, to its appropriate duties. But if his thoughts never range on other subjects, if he never looks abroad on the ample domains of literature and science, there will be a narrowness in his habits of thinking, a peculiarity of character, which will be sure to mark him as a man of limited views and attainments. Should he be distinguished in his profession, his ignorance on other subjects, and the defects of his education, will be the more exposed to public observation. On the other hand, he who is not only eminent in professional life, but has also a mind richly stored with general knowledge, has an elevation and dignity of character, which gives him a commanding influence in society, and a widely extended sphere of usefulness. His situation enables him to diffuse the light of science among all classes of the community. Is a man to have no other object, than to obtain a *living* by professional pursuits? Has he not duties to perform to his family, to his fellow citizens, to his country; duties which require various and extensive intellectual furniture? . . .

As our course of instruction is not intended to complete an education, in theological, medical, or legal science; neither does it include all the minute details of *mercantile, mechanical,* or *agricultural* concerns. These can never be effectually learned except in the very circumstances in which they are to be practised. The young merchant must be trained in the counting room, the mechanic, in the workshop, the farmer, in the field. But we have, on our premises, no experimental farm or retail shop; no cotton or iron manufactory; no hatter's, or silver-smith's, or coach-maker's establishment. For what purpose, then, it will be asked, are young men who are destined to these occupations, ever sent to a college? They should not be sent, as we think, with an expectation of *finishing* their education at the college; but with a view of laying a thorough foundation in the principles of science, preparatory to the study of the practical arts. . . .

We are far from believing that theory *alone,* should be taught in a college. It cannot be effectually taught, except in connection with practical illustrations. . . . To bring down the principles of science to their practical application by the laboring classes, is the office of men of superior education. It is the separation of theory and practice, which has brought reproach upon both. Their union alone can elevate them to their true dignity and value. The man of science is often disposed to assume an air of superiority, when he looks upon the narrow and partial views of the mere artisan. The latter in return laughs at the practical blunders of the former. The defects in the education of both classes would be remedied, by giving them a knowledge of scientific principles, preparatory to practice.

We are aware that a thorough education is not within the reach of all. Many, for want of time and pecuniary resources, must be content with a partial course. A defective education is better than none. If a youth can afford to devote only two or three years, to a scientific and professional education, it will be proper for him to make a selection of a few of the most important branches, and give his attention exclusively to these. But this is an imperfection, arising from the necessity of the case. A partial course of study, must inevitably give a partial education. . . .

A partial education is often expedient; a superficial one, never. . . .

But why, it is asked, should *all* the students in a college be required to tread in the *same steps*? Why should not each one be allowed to select those branches of study which are most to his taste, which are best adapted to his peculiar talents, and which are most nearly connected with his intended profession? To this we answer, that our prescribed course contains those subjects only which ought to be understood, as we think, by every one who aims at a thorough education. They are not the peculiarities of any profession or art. These are to be learned in the professional and practical schools. But the principles of sciences, are the common foundation of all high intellectual attainments. As in our primary schools, reading, writing, and arithmetic are taught to all, however different their prospects; so in a college, all should be instructed in those branches of knowledge, of which no one destined to the higher walks of life ought to be ignorant. What subject which is now studied here, could be set aside, without evidently marring the system[?] Not to speak particularly, in this place, of the ancient languages; who that aims at a well proportioned and superior education will remain ignorant of the elements of the various branches of the mathematics, or of history and antiquities, or of rhetoric and oratory, or natural philosophy, or astronomy, or chemistry, or mineralogy, or geology, or political economy, or mental and moral philosophy?

It is sometimes thought that a student ought not to be urged to the study of that for which he has *no taste or capacity*. But how is he to know, whether he has a taste or capacity for a science, before he has even entered upon its elementary truths? If he is really destitute of talent sufficient for these common departments of education, he is destined for some narrow sphere of action. But we are well persuaded, that our students are not so deficient in intellectual powers, as they sometimes profess to be; though they are easily made to believe, that they have no capacity for the study of that which they are told is almost wholly useless.

When a class have become familiar with the common elements of the several sciences, then is the proper time for them to *divide off* to their favorite studies. They can then make their choice from actual trial. This is now done here, to some extent, in our Junior year. The division might be commenced at an earlier period, and extended farther, provided the qualifications for admission into the college, were brought to a higher standard.

If the view which we have thus far taken of the subject is correct, it will be seen, that the object of the system of instruction at this college, is not to give a *partial* education, consisting of a few branches only; nor, on the other hand, to give a *superficial* education, containing a smattering of almost every thing; nor to *finish* the details of either a professional or practical education; but to *commence* a *thorough* course, and to carry it as far as the time of residence here will allow. It is intended to occupy, to the best advantage, the four years immediately preceding the study of a profession, or of the operations which are peculiar to the higher mercantile, manufacturing, or agricultural establishments. . . .

Our institution is not modelled exactly after the pattern of *European* universities. Difference of circumstances has rendered a different arrangement expedient. It has been the policy of most monarchical governments, to concentrate the advantages of a superior education in a few privileged places. In England, for instance, each of the ancient universities of Oxford and Cambridge, is not so much a single institution, as a large number of distinct, though contiguous colleges. But in this country, our republican habits and feelings will never allow a monopoly of literature in any one place. There must be, in the union, as many colleges, at least, as states. Nor would we complain of this arrangement as inexpedient, provided that starvation is not the consequence of a patronage so minutely divided. We anticipate no disastrous results from the multiplication of colleges, if they can only be adequately endowed. We are not without apprehensions, however, that a feeble and stinted growth of our national literature, will be the consequence of the very scanty supply of means to most of our public seminaries. . . .

Although we do not consider the literary institutions of Europe as faultless models, to be exactly copied by our American colleges; yet we would be far from condemning every feature, in systems of instruction which have had an origin more ancient than our republican seminaries. We do not suppose that the world has learned absolutely nothing, by the experience of ages; that a branch of science, or a mode of teaching, is to be abandoned, precisely because it has stood its ground, after a trial by various nations, and through successive centuries. We believe that our colleges may derive important improvements from the universities and schools in Europe; not by blindly adopting all their measures without discrimination; but by cautiously introducing, with proper modifications, such parts of their plans as are suited to our peculiar situation and character. The first and great improvement which we wish to see made, is an elevation in the standard of attainment for admission. Until this is effected, we shall only expose ourselves to inevitable failure and ridicule, by attempting a general imitation of foreign universities. . . .

It is said that the public now demand, that the doors should be thrown open to all; that education ought to be so modified, and varied, as to adapt it to the exigencies of the country, and the prospects of different individuals; that the instruction given to those who are destined to be merchants, or manufacturers, or agriculturalists, should have a special reference to their respective professional pursuits.

The public are undoubtedly right, in demanding that there should be appropriate courses of education, accessible to all classes of youth. And we rejoice at the prospect of ample provision for this purpose, in the improvement of our academies, and the establishment of commercial high-schools, gymnasia, lycea, agricultural seminaries, &c. But do the public insist, that every college shall become a high-school, gymnasium, lyceum, and academy? Why should we interfere with these valuable institutions? Why wish to take their business out of their hands? The college has its appropriate object, and they have theirs. . . . What is the characteristic difference between a college and an academy? Not that the former teaches more branches than the latter. There are many academies in the country, whose scheme of studies, at least upon paper, is more various than that of the colleges. But while an academy teaches a little of every thing, the college, by directing its efforts to one uniform course, aims at doing its work with greater precision, and economy of time; just as the merchant who deals in a single class of commodities, or a manufacturer who produces but one kind of fabrics, executes his business more perfectly, than he whose attention and skill are divided among a multitude of objects. . . .

But might we not, by making the college more accessible to different descriptions of persons, enlarge our *numbers*, and in that way, increase our income? This might be the operation of the measure, for a very short time, while a degree from the college should retain its present value in public estimation; a value depending entirely upon the character of the education which we give. But the moment it is understood that the institution has descended to an inferior standard of attainment, its reputation will sink to a corresponding level. After we shall have become a college in *name only*, and in reality nothing more than an academy; or half college, and half academy; what will induce parents in various and distant parts of the country, to send us their sons, when they have academies enough in their own neighborhood? There is no magical influence in an act of incorporation, to give celebrity to a literary institution, which does not command respect for itself, by the elevated rank of its education. When the college has lost its hold on the public confidence, by depressing its standard of merit, by substituting a partial, for a thorough education, we may expect that it will be deserted by that class of persons who have hitherto been drawn here by high expectations and purposes. Even if we should *not* immediately suffer in point of *numbers*, yet we shall exchange the best portion of our students, for others of inferior aims and attainments.

As long as we can maintain an elevated character, we need be under no apprehension with respect to numbers. Without character, it will be in vain to think of retaining them. It is a hazardous experiment, to act upon the plan of gaining numbers first, and character afterwards. . . .

The difficulties with which we are now struggling, we fear would be increased, rather than diminished, by attempting to unite different plans of education. It is far from being our intention to dictate to *other* colleges a system to be adopted by them. There may be good and sufficient reasons why some of them should introduce a partial course of instruction. We are not sure, that the demand for thorough education is, at present, sufficient to fill all the colleges in the United States, with students who will be satisfied with nothing short of high and solid attainments. But it is to be hoped that, at no very distant period, they will be able to come up to this elevated ground, and leave the business of second-rate education to the inferior seminaries.

The competition of colleges may advance the interests of literature: if it is a competition for *excellence*, rather than for numbers; if each aims to surpass the others, not in an imposing display, but in the substantial value of its education. . . .

Our republican form of government renders it highly important, that great numbers should enjoy the advantage of a thorough education. On the Eastern continent, the *few* who are destined to particular departments in political life, may be educated for the purpose; while the mass of the people are left in comparative ignorance. But in this country, where offices are accessible to all who are qualified for them, superior intellectual attainments ought not to be confined to any description of persons. *Merchants, manufacturers,* and *farmers*, as well as professional gentlemen, take their places in our public councils. A thorough education ought therefore to be extended to all these classes. It is not sufficient that they be men of sound judgment, who can decide correctly, and give a silent vote, on great national questions. Their influence upon the minds of others is needed; an influence to be produced by extent of knowledge, and the force of eloquence. Ought the speaking in our deliberative assemblies to be confined to a single profession? If it is knowledge, which gives us the command of physical agents and instruments, much more is it that which enables us to control the combinations of moral and political machinery. . . .

Can merchants, manufacturers, and agriculturists, derive no benefit from high intellectual culture? They are the very classes which, from their situation and business, have the best opportunities for reducing the principles of science to their practical applications. The large estates which the tide of prosperity in our country is so rapidly accumulating, will fall mostly into their hands. Is it not desirable that they should be men of superior education, of large and liberal views, of those solid and elegant attainments, which will raise them to a higher distinction, than the mere possession of property; which will not allow them to hoard their treasures, or waste them in senseless extravagance; which will enable them to adorn society by their learning, to move in the more intelligent circles with dignity, and to make such an application of their wealth, as will be most honorable to themselves, and most beneficial to their country?

The active, enterprising character of our population, renders it highly important, that this bustle and energy should be directed by sound intelligence, the result of deep thought and early discipline. The greater the impulse to action, the greater is the need of wise and skilful guidance. When nearly all the ship's crew are aloft, setting the topsails, and catching the breezes, it is necessary there should be a steady hand at helm. Light and moderate learning is but poorly fitted to direct the energies of a nation, so widely extended, so intelligent, so powerful in resources, so rapidly advancing in population, strength, and opulence. Where a free government gives full liberty to the human intellect to expand and operate, education should be proportionably liberal and ample. When even our mountains, and rivers, and lakes, are upon a scale which seems to denote, that we are destined to be a great and mighty nation, shall our literature be feeble, and scanty, and superficial?

Report of the Faculty, Part II

... The subject of inquiry now presented, is, whether the plan of instruction pursued in Yale College, is sufficiently accommodated to the present state of literature and science; and, especially, whether such a change is demanded as would leave out of this plan the study of the Greek and Roman classics, and make an acquaintance with ancient literature no longer necessary for a degree in the liberal arts. . . .

Whoever . . . without a preparation in classical literature, engages in any literary investigation, or undertakes to discuss any literary topic, or associates with those who in any country of Europe, or in this country, are acknowledged to be men of liberal acquirements, immediately feels a deficiency in his education, and is convinced that he is destitute of an important part of practical learning. If scholars, then, are to be prepared to act in the literary world as it in fact exists, classical literature, from considerations purely practical, should form an important part of their early discipline.

But the claims of classical learning are not limited to this single view. It may be defended not only as a necessary branch of education, in the present state of the world, but on the ground of its distinct and independent merits. Familiarity with the Greek and Roman writers is especially adapted to form the taste, and to discipline the mind, both in thought and diction, to the relish of what is elevated, chaste, and simple. . . .

But the study of the classics is useful, not only as it lays the foundations of a correct taste, and furnishes the student with those elementary ideas which are found in the literature of modern times, and which he no where so well acquires as in their original sources;—but also as the study itself forms the most effectual discipline of the mental faculties. This is a topic so often insisted on, that little need be said of it here. It must be obvious to the most cursory observer, that the classics afford materials to exercise talent of every degree, from the first opening of the youthful intellect to the period of its highest maturity. The range of classical study extends from the elements of language, to the most difficult questions arising from literary research and criticism. Every faculty of the mind is employed; not only the memory, judgment, and reasoning powers, but the taste and fancy are occupied and improved.

Classical discipline, likewise, forms the best preparation for professional study. The interpretation of language, and its correct use, are no where more important, than in the professions of divinity and law. . . .

In the profession of medicine, the knowledge of the Greek and Latin languages is less necessary now than formerly; but even at the present time it may be doubted, whether the facilities which classical learning affords for understanding and rendering familiar the terms of science, do not more than counterbalance the time and labor requisite for obtaining this learning. . . .

To acquire the knowledge of any of the modern languages of Europe, is chiefly an effort of memory. The general structure of these languages is much the same as that of our own. The few idiomatical differences, are made familiar with little labor; nor is there the same necessity of accurate comparison and discrimination, as in studying the classic writers of Greece and Rome. To establish this truth, let a page of Voltaire be compared with a page of Tacitus. . . .

Modern languages, with most of our students, are studied, and will continue to be studied, as an accomplishment, rather than as a necessary acquisition. . . . To suppose the modern languages more practical than the ancient, to the great body of our students, because the former are now spoken in some parts of the world, is an obvious fallacy. The proper question is,—what course of discipline affords the best mental culture, leads to the most thorough knowledge of our own literature, and lays the best foundation for professional study. The ancient languages have here a decided advantage. If the elements of modern languages are acquired by our students in connection with the established collegiate course, and abundant facilities for this purpose, have for a long time, been afforded, further acquisitions will be easily made, where circumstances render them important and useful. From the graduates of this college, who have visited Europe, complaints have sometimes been heard, that their classical attainments were too small for the literature of the old world; but none are recollected to have expressed regret, that they had cultivated ancient learning while here, however much time they might have devoted to this subject. On the contrary, those who have excelled in classical literature, and have likewise acquired a competent knowledge of some one modern European language besides the English, have found themselves the best qualified to make a full use of their new advantages. Deficiencies in modern literature are easily and rapidly supplied, where the mind has had a proper previous discipline; deficiencies in ancient literature are supplied tardily, and in most instances, imperfectly. . . .

Such, then, being the value of ancient literature, both as respects the general estimation in which it is held in the literary world, and its intrinsic merits,—if the college should confer degrees upon students for their attainments in modern literature only, it would be to declare *that* to be a liberal education, which the world will not acknowledge to deserve the name;—and which those who shall receive degrees in this way, will soon find, is not what it is called. A liberal education, whatever course the college should adopt, would without doubt continue to be, what it long has been. Ancient literature is too deeply in wrought into the whole system of the modern literature of Europe to be so easily laid aside. The college ought not to presume upon its influence, nor to set itself up in any manner as a dictator. If it should pursue a course very different from that which the present state of literature demands; if it should confer its honors according to a rule which is not sanctioned by literary men, the faculty see nothing to expect for favoring such innovations, but that they will be considered visionaries in education, ignorant of its true design and objects, and unfit for their places. The ultimate consequence, it is not difficult to predict. The college would be distrusted by the public, and its reputation would be irrecoverably lost. . . .

No question has engaged the attention of the faculty more constantly, than how the course of education in the college might be improved, and rendered more practically useful. Free communications have at all times been held between the faculty and the corporation, on subjects connected with the instruction of the college. When the aid of the corporation has been thought necessary, it has been asked; and by this course of proceeding, the interests of the institution have been regularly advanced. No remark is more frequently made by those, who visit the college after the absence of some years, than that changes have been made for the better; and those who make the fullest investigation, are the most ready to approve what they find. The charge, therefore, that the college is stationary, that no efforts are made to accommodate it to the wants of the age, that all exertions are for the purpose of perpetuating abuses, and that the college is much the same as it was at the time of its foundation, are wholly gratuitous. The changes in the country, during the last century, have not been greater than the changes in the college. These remarks have been limited to Yale College, as its history is here best known; no doubt, other colleges alluded to in the above quotations, might defend themselves with equal success.

INDUSTRIAL EDUCATION FOR THE NEGRO

BOOKER T. WASHINGTON

The necessity for the race's learning the difference between being worked and working. He would not confine the Negro to industrial life, but believes that the very best service which any one can render to what is called the "higher education" is to teach the present generation to work and save. This will create the wealth from which alone can come leisure and the opportunity for higher education.

Industrial Education for the Negro

One of the most fundamental and far-reaching deeds that has been accomplished during the last quarter of a century has been that by which the Negro has been helped to find himself and to learn the secrets of civilization—to learn that there are a few simple, cardinal principles upon which a race must start its upward course, unless it would fail, and its last estate be worse than its first.

It has been necessary for the Negro to learn the difference between being worked and working—to learn that being worked meant degradation, while working means civilization; that all forms of labor are honorable, and all forms of idleness disgraceful. It has been necessary for him to learn that all races that have got upon their feet have done so largely by laying an economic foundation, and, in general, by beginning in a proper cultivation and ownership of the soil.

Forty years ago my race emerged from slavery into freedom. If, in too many cases, the Negro race began development at the wrong end, it was largely because neither white nor black properly understood the case. Nor is it any wonder that this was so, for never before in the history of the world had just such a problem been presented as that of the two races at the coming of freedom in this country.

For two hundred and fifty years, I believe the way for the redemption of the Negro was being prepared through industrial development. Through all those years the Southern white man did business with the Negro in a way that no one else has done business with him. In most cases if a Southern white man wanted a house built he consulted a Negro mechanic about the plan and about the actual building of the structure. If he wanted a suit of clothes made he went to a Negro tailor, and for shoes he went to a shoemaker of the same race. In a certain way every slave plantation in the South was an industrial school. On these plantations young colored men and women were constantly being trained not only as farmers but as carpenters, blacksmiths, wheel-wrights, brick masons, engineers, cooks, laundresses, sewing women and housekeepers.

I do not mean in any way to apologize for the curse of slavery, which was a curse to both races, but in what I say about industrial training in slavery I am simply stating facts. This training was crude, and was given for selfish purposes. It did not answer the highest ends, because there was an absence of mental training in connection with the training of the hand. To a large degree, though, this business contact with the Southern white man, and the industrial training on the plantations, left the Negro at the close of the war in possession of nearly all the common and skilled labor in the

Reprinted from *The American Negro: His History and Literature* (1969), Random House.

South. The industries that gave the South its power, prominence and wealth prior to the Civil War were mainly the raising of cotton, sugar cane, rice and tobacco. Before the way could be prepared for the proper growing and marketing of these crops forests had to be cleared, houses to be built, public roads and railroads constructed. In all these works the Negro did most of the heavy work. In the planting, cultivating and marketing of the crops not only was the Negro the chief dependence, but in the manufacture of tobacco he became a skilled and proficient workman, and in this, up to the present time, in the South, holds the lead in the large tobacco manufactories.

In most of the industries, though, what happened? For nearly twenty years after the war, except in a few instances, the value of the industrial training given by the plantations was overlooked. Negro men and women were educated in literature, in mathematics and in the sciences, with little thought of what had been taking place during the preceding two hundred and fifty years, except, perhaps, as something to be escaped, to be got as far away from as possible. As a generation began to pass, those who had been trained as mechanics in slavery began to disappear by death, and gradually it began to be realized that there were few to take their places. There were young men educated in foreign tongues, but few in carpentry or in mechanical or architectural drawing. Many were trained in Latin, but few as engineers and blacksmiths. Too many were taken from the farm and educated, but educated in everything but farming. For this reason they had no interest in farming and did not return to it. And yet eighty-five per cent. of the Negro population of the Southern states lives and for a considerable time will continue to live in the country districts. The charge is often brought against the members of my race—and too often justly, I confess—that they are found leaving the country districts and flocking into the great cities where temptations are more frequent and harder to resist, and where the Negro people too often become demoralized. Think, though, how frequently it is the case that from the first day that a pupil begins to go to school his books teach him much about the cities of the world and city life, and almost nothing about the country. How natural it is, then, that when he has the ordering of his life he wants to live it in the city.

Only a short time before his death the late Mr. C. P. Huntington, to whose memory a magnificent library has just been given by his widow to the Hampton Institute for Negroes, in Virginia, said in a public address some words which seem to me so wise that I want to quote them here:

"Our schools teach everybody a little of almost everything, but, in my opinion, they teach very few children just what they ought to know in order to make their way successfully in life. They do not put into their hands the tools they are best fitted to use, and hence so many failures. Many a mother and sister have worked and slaved, living upon scanty food, in order to give a son and brother a "liberal education," and in doing this have built up a barrier between the boy and the work he was fitted to do. Let me say to you that all honest work is honorable work. If the labor is manual, and seems common, you will have all the more chance to be thinking of other things, or of work that is higher and brings better pay, and to work out in your minds better and higher duties and responsibilities for yourselves, and for thinking of ways by which you can help others as well as yourselves, and bring them up to your own higher level."

Some years ago, when we decided to make tailoring a part of our training at the Tuskegee Institute, I was amazed to find that it was almost impossible to find in the whole country an educated colored man who could teach the making of clothing. We could find numbers of them who could teach astronomy, theology, Latin or grammar, but almost none who could instruct in the making of clothing, something that has to be used by every one of us every day in the year. How often have I been discouraged as I have gone through the South, and into the homes of the people of my race, and have found women who could converse intelligently upon abstruse subjects, and yet could not tell how to improve the condition of the poorly cooked and still more poorly served bread and meat which they and their families were eating three times a day. It is discouraging to find a girl who can tell you the geographical location of any country on the globe and who does not know where to place the dishes upon a common dinner table. It is discouraging to find a woman who knows much about theoretical chemistry, and who cannot properly was and iron a shirt.

In what I say here I would not by any means have it understood that I would limit or circumscribe the mental development of the Negro student. No race can be lifted until its mind is awakened and strengthened. By the side of industrial training should always go mental and moral training, but the pushing of mere abstract knowledge into the head means little. We want more than the mere performance of mental gymnastics. Our knowledge must be harnessed to the things of real life. I would encourage the Negro to secure all the mental strength, all the mental culture—whether gleaned from science, mathematics, history, language or literature that his circumstances will allow, but I believe most earnestly that for years to come the education of the people of my race should be so directed that the greatest proportion of the mental strength of the masses will be brought to bear upon the every-day practical things of life, upon something that is needed to be done, and something which they will be permitted to do in the community in which they reside. And just the same with the professional class which the race needs and must have, I would say give the men and women of that class, too, the training which will best fit them to perform in the most successful manner the service which the race demands.

I would not confine the race to industrial life, not even to agriculture, for example, although I believe that by far the greater part of the Negro race is best off in the country districts and must and should continue to live there, but I would teach the race that in industry the foundation must be laid—that the very best service which any one can render to what is called the higher education is to teach the present generation to provide a material or industrial foundation. On such a foundation as this will grow habits of thrift, a love of work, economy, ownership of property, bank accounts. Out of it in the future will grow practical education, professional education, positions of public responsibility. Out of it will grow moral and religious strength. Out of it will grow wealth from which alone can come leisure and the opportunity for the enjoyment of literature and the fine arts.

In the words of the late beloved Frederick Douglass: "Every blow of the sledge hammer wielded by a sable arm is a powerful blow in support of our cause. Every colored mechanic is by virtue of circumstances an elevator of his race. Every house built by a black man is a strong tower against the allied hosts of prejudice. It is impossible for us to attach too much importance to this aspect of the subject. Without industrial development there can be no wealth; without wealth there can be no leisure; without leisure no opportunity for thoughtful reflection and the cultivation of the higher arts."

I would set no limits to the attainments of the Negro in arts, in letters or statesmanship, but I believe the surest way to reach those ends is by laying the foundation in the little things of life that lie immediately about one's door. I plead for industrial education and development for the Negro not because I want to cramp him, but because I want to free him. I want to see him enter the all-powerful business and commercial world.

It was such combined mental, moral and industrial education which the late General Armstrong set out to give at the Hampton Institute when he established that school thirty years ago. The Hampton Institute has continued along the lines laid down by its great founder, and now each year an increasing number of similar schools are being established in the South, for the people of both races.

Early in the history of the Tuskegee Institute we began to combine industrial training with mental and moral culture. Our first efforts were in the direction of agriculture, and we began teaching this with no appliances except one hoe and a blind mule. From this small beginning we have grown until now the Institute owns two thousand acres of land, eight hundred of which are cultivated each year by the young men of the school. We began teaching wheelwrighting and blacksmithing in a small way to the men, and laundry work, cooking and sewing and housekeeping to the young women. The fourteen hundred and over young men and women who attended the school during the last school year received instruction—in addition to academic and religious training—in thirty-three trades and industries, including carpentry, blacksmithing, printing, wheelwrighting, harnessmaking, painting, machinery, founding, shoemaking, brickmasonry and brickmaking, plastering, sawmilling, tinsmithing, tailoring, mechanical and architectural drawing, electrical and steam engineering, canning, sewing, dressmaking, millinery, cooking, laundering, housekeeping, mattress making, basketry, nursing, agriculture, dairying and stock raising, horticulture.

Not only do the students receive instruction in these trades, but they do actual work, by means of which more than half of them pay some part or all of their expenses while remaining at the school. Of the sixty buildings belonging to the school all but four were almost wholly erected by the students as a part of their industrial education. Even the bricks which go into the walls are made by students in the school's brick yard, in which, last year, they manufactured two million bricks.

When we first began this work at Tuskegee, and the idea got spread among the people of my race that the students who came to the Tuskegee school were to be taught industries in connection with their academic studies, were, in other words, to be taught to work, I received a great many verbal messages and letters from parents informing me that they wanted their children taught books, but not how to work. This protest went on for three or four years, but I am glad to be able to say now that our people have very generally been educated to a point where they see their own needs and conditions so clearly that it has been several years since we have had a single protest from parents against the teaching of industries, and there is now a positive enthusiasm for it. In fact, public sentiment among the students at Tuskegee is now so strong for industrial training that it would hardly permit a student to remain on the grounds who was unwilling to labor.

It seems to me that too often mere book education leaves the Negro young man or woman in a weak position. For example, I have seen a Negro girl taught by her mother to help her in doing laundry work at home. Later, when this same girl was graduated from the public schools or a high school and returned home she finds herself educated out of sympathy with laundry work, and yet not able to find anything to do which seems in keeping with the cost and character of her education. Under these circumstances we cannot be surprised if she does not fulfill the expectations made for her. What should have been done for her, it seems, to me, was to give her along with her academic education thorough training in the latest and best methods of laundry work, so that she could have put so much skill and intelligence into it that the work would have been lifted out from the plane of drudgery. The home which she would then have been able to found by the results of her work would have enabled her to help her children to take a still more responsible position in life.

Almost from the first Tuskegee has kept in mind—and this I think should be the policy of all industrial schools—fitting students for occupations which would be open to them in their home communities. Some years ago we noted the fact that there was beginning to be a demand in the South for men to operate dairies in a skillful, modern manner. We opened a dairy department in connection with the school, where a number of young men could have instruction in the latest and most scientific methods of dairy work. At present we have calls—mainly from Southern white men—for twice as many dairymen as we are able to supply. What is equally satisfactory, the reports which come to us indicate that our young men are giving the highest satisfaction and are fast changing and improving the dairy product in the communities into which they go. I use the dairy here as an example. What I have said of this is equally true of many of the other industries which we teach. Aside from the economic value of this work I cannot but believe, and my observation confirms me in my belief, that as we continue to place Negro men and women of intelligence, religion, modesty, conscience and skill in every community in the South, who will prove by actual results their value to the community, I cannot but believe, I say, that this will constitute a solution to many of the present political and social difficulties.

Many seem to think that industrial education is meant to make the Negro work as he worked in the days of slavery. This is far from my conception of industrial education. If this training is worth anything to the Negro, it consists in teaching him how not to work, but how to make the forces of nature—air, steam, water, horse-power and electricity—work for him. If it has any value it is in lifting labor up out of toil and drudgery into the plane of the dignified and the beautiful. The Negro in the South works and works hard; but too often his ignorance and lack of skill causes him to do his work in the most costly and shiftless manner, and this keeps him near the bottom of the ladder in the economic world.

I have not emphasized particularly in these pages the great need of training the Negro in agriculture, but I believe that this branch of industrial education does need very great emphasis. In this connection I want to quote some words which Mr. Edgar Gardner Murphy, of Montgomery, Alabama, has recently written upon this subject:

"We must incorporate into our public school system a larger recognition of the practical and industrial elements in educational training. Ours is an agricultural population. The school must be brought more closely to the soil. The teaching of history, for example, is all very well, but nobody can really know anything of history unless he has been taught to see things grow—has so seen things not only with the outward eye, but with the eyes of his intelligence and conscience. The actual things of the present are more important, however, than the institutions of the past. Even to young children can be shown the simpler conditions and processes of growth—how corn is put into the ground—how cotton and potatoes should be planted—how to choose the soil best adapted to a particular plant, how to improve that soil, how to care for the plant while it grows, how to get the most value out of it, how to use the elements of waste for the fertilization of other crops; how, through the alternation of crops, the land may be made to increase the annual value of its products—these things, upon their elementary side are absolutely vital to the worth and success of hundreds of thousands of these people of the Negro race, and yet our whole educational system has practically ignored them.

✳✳✳

"Such work will mean not only an education in agriculture, but an education through agriculture and education, through natural symbols and practical forms, which will educate as deeply, as broadly and as truly as any other system which the world has known. Such changes will bring far larger results than the mere improvement of our Negroes. They will give us an agricultural class, a class of tenants or small land owners, trained not away from the soil, but in relation to the soil and in intelligent dependence upon its resources."

I close, then, as I began, by saying that as a slave the Negro was worked, and that as a freeman he must learn to work. There is still doubt in many quarters as to the ability of the Negro unguided, unsupported, to hew his own path and put into visible, tangible, indisputable form, products and signs of civilization. This doubt cannot be much affected by abstract arguments, no matter how delicately and convincingly woven together. Patiently, quietly, doggedly, persistently, through summer and winter, sunshine and shadow, by self-sacrifice, by foresight, by honesty and industry, we must re-enforce argument with results. One farm bought, one house built, one home sweetly and intelligently kept, one man who is the largest tax payer or has the largest bank account, one school or church maintained, one factory running successfully, one truck garden profitably cultivated, one patient cured by a Negro doctor, one sermon well preached, one office well filled, one life cleanly lived—these will tell more in our favor than all the abstract eloquence that can be summoned to plead our cause. Our pathway must be up through the soil, up through swamps, up through forests, up through the streams, the rocks, up through commerce, education and religion!

THE TALENTED TENTH

PROF. W.E. BURGHARDT DUBOIS

A strong plea for the higher education of the Negro, which those who are interested in the future of the freedmen cannot afford to ignore. Prof. DuBois produces ample evidence to prove conclusively the truth of his statement that "to attempt to establish any sort of a system of common and industrial school training, without *first* providing for the higher training of the very best teachers, is simply throwing your money to the winds."

The Talented Tenth

The Negro race, like all races, is going to be saved by its exceptional men. The problem of education, then, among Negroes must first of all deal with the Talented Tenth; it is the problem of developing the Best of this race that they may guide the Mass away from the contamination and death of the Worst, in their own and other races. Now the training of men is a difficult and intricate task. Its technique is a matter for educational experts, but its object is for the vision of seers. If we make money the object of man-training, we shall develop money-makers but not necessarily men; if we make technical skill the object of education, we may possess artisans but not, in nature, men. Men we shall have only as we make manhood the object of the work of the schools—intelligence, broad sympathy, knowledge of the world that was and is, and of the relation of men to it—this is the curriculum of that Higher Education which must underlie true life. On this foundation we may build bread winning, skill of hand and quickness of brain, with never a fear lest the child and man mistake the means of living for the object of life.

***

If this be true—and who can deny it—three tasks lay before me; first to show from the past that the Talented Tenth as they have risen among American Negroes have been worthy of leadership; secondly, to show how these men may be educated and developed; and thirdly, to show their relation to the Negro problem.

***

You misjudge us because you do not know us. From the very first it has been the educated and intelligent of the Negro people that have led and elevated the mass, and the sole obstacles that nullified and retarded their efforts were slavery and race prejudice; for what is slavery but the legalized survival of the unfit and the nullification of the work of natural internal leadership? Negro leadership, therefore, sought from the first to rid the race of this awful incubus that it might make way for natural selection and the survival of the fittest. In colonial days came Phillis Wheatley and Paul Cuffe striving against the bars of prejudice; and Benjamin Banneker, the almanac maker, voiced their longings when

Reprinted from *The American Negro: His History and Literature* (1969), Random House.

he said to Thomas Jefferson, "I freely and cheerfully acknowledge that I am of the African race, and in colour which is natural to them, of the deepest dye; and it is under a sense of the most profound gratitude to the Supreme Ruler of the Universe, that I now confess to you that I am not under that state of tyrannical thraldom and inhuman captivity to which too many of my brethren are doomed, but that I have abundantly tasted of the fruition of those blessings which proceed from that free and unequalled liberty with which you are favored, and which I hope you will willingly allow, you have mercifully received from the immediate hand of that Being from whom proceedeth every good and perfect gift.

"Suffer me to recall to your mind that time, in which the arms of the British crown were exerted with every powerful effort, in order to reduce you to a state of servitude; look back, I entreat you, on the variety of dangers to which you were exposed; reflect on that period in which every human aid appeared unavailable, and in which even hope and fortitude wore the aspect of inability to the conflict, and you cannot but be led to a serious and grateful sense of your miraculous and providential preservation, you cannot but acknowledge, that the present freedom and tranquility which you enjoy, you have mercifully received, and that a peculiar blessing of heaven.

"This, sir, was a time when you clearly saw into the injustice of a state of Slavery, and in which you had just apprehensions of the horrors of its condition. It was then that your abhorrence thereof was so excited, that you publicly held forth this true and invaluable doctrine, which is worthy to be recorded and remembered in all succeeding ages: 'We hold these truths to be self evident, that all men are created equal; that they are endowed with certain inalienable rights, and that among these are life, liberty and the pursuit of happiness.'"

Then came Dr. James Derham, who could tell even the learned Dr. Rush, something of medicine, and Lemuel Haynes, to whom Middlebury College gave an honorary A. M. in 1804. These and others we may call the Revolutionary group of distinguished Negroes—they were persons of marked ability, leaders of a Talented Tenth, standing conspicuously among the best of their time. They strove by word and deed to save the color line from becoming the line between the bond and free, but all they could do was nullified by Eli Whitney and the Curse of Gold. So they passed into forgetfulness.

But their spirit did not wholly die; here and there in the early part of the century came other exceptional men. Some were natural sons of unnatural fathers and were given often a liberal training and thus a race of educated mulattoes sprang up to plead for black men's rights. There was Ira Aldridge, whom all Europe loved to honor; there was that Voice crying in the Wilderness, David Walker, and saying:

"I declare it does appear to me as though some nations think God is asleep, or that he made the Africans for nothing else but to dig their mines and work their farms, or they cannot believe history, sacred or profane. I ask every man who has a heart, and is blessed with the privilege of believing— Is not God a God of justice to all his creatures? Do you say he is? Then if he gives peace and tranquility to tyrants and permits them to keep our fathers, our mothers, ourselves and our children in eternal ignorance and wretchedness to support them and their families, would he be to us a God of Justice? I ask, O, ye Christians, who hold us and our children in the most abject ignorance and degradation that ever a people were afflicted with since the world began—I say if God gives you peace and tranquility, and suffers you thus to go on afflicting us, and our children, who have never given you the least provocation—would He be to us a God of Justice? If you will allow that we are men, who feel for each other, does not the blood of our fathers and of us, their children, cry aloud to the Lord of Sabaoth against you for the cruelties and murders with which you have and do continue to afflict us?"

This was the wild voice that first aroused Southern legislators in 1829 to the terrors of abolitionism.

In 1831 there met that first Negro convention in Philadelphia, at which the world gaped curiously but which bravely attacked the problems of race and slavery, crying out against persecution and declaring that "Laws as cruel in themselves as they were unconstitutional and unjust, have in many places been enacted against our poor, unfriended and unoffending brethren (without a shadow of provocation on our part), at whose bare recital the very savage draws himself up for fear of contagion—looks noble and prides himself because he bears not the name of Christian." Side by side this free Negro movement, and the movement for abolition, strove until they merged into one strong stream. Too little notice has been taken of the work which the Talented Tenth among Negroes took in the great abolition crusade. From the very day that a Philadelphia colored man became the first subscriber to Garrison's "Liberator," to the day when Negro soldiers made the Emancipation Proclamation possible, black leaders worked shoulder to shoulder with white men in a movement, the success of which would have been impossible without them. There was Purvis and Remond, Pennington and Highland Garnett, Sojourner Truth and Alexander Crummel, and above all, Frederick Douglass—what would the abolition movement have been without them? They stood as living examples of the possibilities of the Negro race, their own hard experiences and well wrought culture said silently more than all the drawn periods of orators—they were the men who made American slavery impossible. As Maria Weston Chapman once said, from the school of anti-slavery agitation "a throng of authors, editors, lawyers, orators and accomplished gentlemen of color have taken their degree! It has equally implanted hopes and aspirations, noble thoughts, and sublime purposes, in the hearts of both races. It has prepared the white man for the freedom of the black man, and it has made the black man scorn the thought of enslavement, as does a white man, as far as its influence has extended. Strengthen that noble influence! Before its organization, the country only saw here and there in slavery some faithful Cudjoe or Dinah, whose strong natures blossomed even in bondage, like a fine plant beneath a heavy stone. Now, under the elevating and cherishing influence of the American Anti-slavery Society, the colored race, like the white, furnishes Corinthian capitals for the noblest temples."

Where were these black abolitionists trained? Some, like Frederick Douglass, were self-trained, but yet trained liberally; others, like Alexander Crummell and McCune Smith, graduated from famous foreign universities. Most of them rose up through the colored schools of New York and Philadelphia and Boston, taught by college-bred men like Russworm, of Dartmouth, and college-bred white men like Neau and Benezet.

After emancipation came a new group of educated and gifted leaders: Langston, Bruce and Elliot, Greener, Williams and Payne. Through political organization, historical and polemic writing and moral regeneration, these men strove to uplift their people. It is the fashion of to-day to sneer at them and to say that with freedom Negro leadership should have begun at the plow and not in the Senate—a foolish and mischievous lie; two hundred and fifty years that black serf toiled at the plow and yet that toiling was in vain till the Senate passed the war amendments; and two hundred and fifty years more the half-free serf of to-day may toil at his plow, but unless he have political rights and righteously guarded civic status, he will still remain the poverty-stricken and ignorant plaything of rascals, that he now is. This all sane men know even if they dare not say it.

And so we come to the present—a day of cowardice and vacillation, of strident wide-voiced wrong and faint hearted compromise; of double-faced dallying with Truth and Right. Who are today guiding the work of the Negro people? The "exceptions" of course. And yet so sure as this Talented Tenth is pointed out, the blind worshippers of the Average cry out in alarm: "These are exceptions, look here at death, disease and crime—these are the happy rule." Of course they are the rule, because a silly nation made them the rule: Because for three long centuries this people lynched Negroes who dared to be brave, raped black women who dared to be virtuous, crushed dark-hued youth who dared to be ambitious, and encouraged and made to flourish servility and lewdness and apathy. But not even this was able to crush all manhood and chastity and aspiration from black folk. A saving remnant continually survives and persists, continually aspires, continually shows itself in thrift and ability and character. Exceptional it is to be sure, but this is its chiefest promise; it shows the capability of Negro blood, the promise of black men. Do Americans ever stop to reflect that there are in this land a million men of Negro blood, well-educated, owners of homes, against the honor of whose womanhood no breath was ever raised, whose men occupy positions of trust and usefulness, and who, judged by any standard, have reached the full measure of the best type of modern European culture? Is it fair, is it decent, is it Christian to ignore these facts of the Negro problem, to belittle such aspiration, to nullify such leadership and seek to crush these people back into the mass out of which by toil and travail, they and their fathers have raised themselves?

Can the masses of the Negro people be in any possible way more quickly raised than by the effort and example of this aristocracy of talent and character? Was there ever a nation on God's fair earth civilized from the bottom upward? Never; it is, ever was and ever will be from the top downward that culture filters. The Talented Tenth rises and pulls all that are worth the saving up to their vantage ground. This is the history of human progress; and the two historic mistakes which have hindered that progress were the thinking first that no more could ever rise save the few already risen; or second, that it would better the unrisen to pull the risen down.

How then shall the leaders of a struggling people be trained and the hands of the risen few strengthened? There can be but one answer: The best and most capable of their youth must be schooled in the colleges and universities of the land. We will not quarrel as to just what the university of the Negro should teach or how it should teach it—I willingly admit that each soul and each race-soul needs its own peculiar curriculum. But this is true: A university is a human invention for the transmission of knowledge and culture from generation to generation, through the training of quick minds and pure hearts, and for this work no other human invention will suffice, not even trade and industrial schools.

All men cannot go to college but some men must; every isolated group or nation must have its yeast, must have for the talented few centers of training where men are not so mystified and befuddled by the hard and necessary toil of earning a living, as to have no aims higher than their bellies, and no God greater than Gold. This is true training, and thus in the beginning were the favored sons of the freedmen trained. Out of the colleges of the North came, after the blood of war, Ware, Cravath, Chase, Andrews, Bumstead and Spence to build the foundations of knowledge and civilization in the black South. Where ought they to have begun to build? At the bottom, of course, quibbles the mole with his eyes in the earth. Aye! truly at the bottom, at the very bottom; at the bottom of knowledge, down in the very depths of knowledge there where the roots of justice strike into the lowest soil of Truth. And so they did begin; they founded colleges, and up from the colleges shot normal schools, and out from the normal schools went teachers, and around the normal teachers clustered other teachers to teach the public schools; the college trained in Greek and Latin and mathematics, 2,000 men; and these men trained full 50,000 others in morals and manners, and they in turn taught thrift and the alphabet to nine millions of men, who to-day hold $300,000,000 of property. It was a miracle—the most wonderful peace-battle of the 19th century, and yet to-day men smile at it, and in fine superiority tell us that it was all a strange mistake; that a proper way to found a system of education is first to gather the children and buy them spelling books and hoes; afterward men may look about for teachers, if haply they may find them; or again they would teach men Work, but as for Life—why, what has Work to do with Life, they ask vacantly.

Was the work of these college founders successful; did it stand the test of time? Did the college graduates, with all their fine theories of life, really live? Are they useful men helping to civilize and elevate their less fortunate fellows? Let us see. Omitting all institutions which have not actually graduated students from a college course, there are to-day in the United States thirty-four institutions giving something above high school training to Negroes and designed especially for this race.

Three of these were established in border States before the War; thirteen were planted by the Freedmen's Bureau in the years 1864-1869; nine were established between 1870 and 1880 by various church bodies; five were established after 1881 by Negro churches, and four are state institutions supported by United States' agricultural funds. In most cases the college departments are small adjuncts to high and common school work. As a matter of fact six institutions—Atlanta, Fisk, Howard, Shaw, Wilberforce and Leland, are the important Negro colleges so far as actual work and number of students are concerned. In all these institutions, seven hundred and fifty Negro college students are enrolled. In grade the best of these colleges are about a year behind the smaller New England colleges and a typical curriculum is that of Atlanta University. Here students from the grammar grades, after a three years' high school course, take a college course of 136 weeks. One-fourth of this time is given to Latin and Greek; one-fifth, to English and modern languages; one-sixth, to history and social science; one-seventh, to natural science; one-eighth to mathematics, and one-eighth to philosophy and pedagogy.

In addition to these students in the South, Negroes have attended Northern colleges for many years. As early as 1826 one was graduated from Bowdoin College, and from that time till to-day nearly every year has seen elsewhere, other such graduates. They have, of course, met much color prejudice. Fifty years ago very few colleges would admit them at all. Even to-day no Negro has ever been admitted to Princeton, and at some other leading institutions they are rather endured than encouraged. Oberlin was the great pioneer in the work of blotting out the color line in colleges, and has more Negro graduates by far than any other Northern college.

The total number of Negro college graduates up to 1899, (several of the graduates of that year not being reported), was as follows:

	Negro Colleges	*White Colleges*
Before '76	. . . . . . 137	. . . . . . 75 . . . . . .
'75–80	. . . . . . 143	. . . . . . 22 . . . . . .
'80–85	. . . . . . 250	. . . . . . 31 . . . . . .
'85–90	. . . . . . 413	. . . . . . 43 . . . . . .
'90–95	. . . . . . 465	. . . . . . 66 . . . . . .
'95–99	. . . . . . 475	. . . . . . 88 . . . . . .
Class Unknown . .	. . . . . . 57	. . . . . . 64 . . . . . .
Total	. . . . . . 1,914	. . . . . 390 . . . . .

Of these graduates 2,079 were men and 252 were women; 50 per cent. of Northern-born college men come South to work among the masses of their people, at a sacrifice which few people realize; nearly 90 per cent. of the Southern-born graduates instead of seeking that personal freedom and broader intellectual atmosphere which their training has led them, in some degree, to conceive, stay and labor and wait in the midst of their black neighbors and relatives.

The most interesting question, and in many respects the crucial question, to be asked concerning college-bred Negroes, is: Do they earn a living? It has been intimated more than once that the higher training of Negroes has resulted in sending into the world of work, men who could find nothing to do suitable to their talents. Now and then there comes a rumor of a colored college man working at menial service, etc. Fortunately, returns as to occupations of college-bred Negroes, gathered by the Atlanta conference, are quite full—nearly sixty per cent. of the total number of graduates.

This enables us to reach fairly certain conclusions as to the occupations of all college-bred Negroes. Of 1,312 persons reported, there were:

	Percent.	
Teachers, ...	. . . .53.4 . .	████████████
Clergyman, ...	. . . .16.4 . .	████
Physicians, etc., ...	. . . . 6.3 . .	██
Students, ...	. . . . 5.6 . .	██
Lawyers, ...	. . . . 4.7 . .	██
In Govt. Service, ...	. . . . 4.0 . .	██
In Business, ...	. . . . 3.6 . .	█
Farmers and Artisans, ...	. . . . 2.7 . .	█
Editors, Secretaries and Clerks, ...	. . . . 2.4 . .	▎
Miscellaneous	. . . . .5 . .	▎

Over half are teachers, a sixth are preachers, another sixth are students and professional men; over 6 per cent. are farmers, artisans and merchants, and 4 per cent. are in government service. In detail the occupations are as follows:

Occupations of College-Bred Men

Teachers:		
Presidents and Deans,	19	
Teacher of Music,	7	
Professors, Principals and Teachers,	675	Total 701
Clergymen:		
Bishop,	1	
Chaplains U.S. Army,	2	
Missionaries,	9	
Presiding Elders,	12	
Preachers,	197	Total 221
Physicians,		
Doctors of Medicine,	76	
Druggists,	4	
Dentists,	3	Total 83
Students,		74
Lawyers,		62
Civil Service:		
U.S. Minister Plenipotentiary,	1	
U.S. Consul,	1	
U.S. Deputy Collector,	1	
U.S. Gauger,	1	
U.S. Postmasters,	2	
U.S. Clerks,	44	
State Civil Service	2	
City Civil Service,	1	Total 53
Business Men:		
Merchants, etc.,	30	
Managers,	13	
Real Estate Dealers,	4	Total 47
Farmers,		26
Clerks and Secretaries:		
Secretary of National Societies,	7	
Clerks, etc.,	15	Total 22
Artisans,		9
Editors,		9
Miscellaneous,		5

These figures illustrate vividly the function of the college-bred Negro. He is, as he ought to be, the group leader, the man who sets the ideals of the community where he lives, directs its thoughts and heads its social movements. It need hardly be argued that the Negro people need social leadership more than most groups; that they have no traditions to fall back upon, no long established customs, no strong family ties, no well defined social classes. All these things must be slowly and painfully evolved. The preacher was, even before the war, the group leader of the Negroes, and the church their greatest social institution. Naturally this preacher was ignorant and often immoral, and the problem of replacing the older type by better educated men has been a difficult one. Both by direct work and by direct influence on other preachers, and on congregations, the college-bred preacher has an opportunity for reformatory work and moral inspiration, the value of which cannot be overestimated.

It has, however, been in the furnishing of teachers that the Negro college has found its peculiar function. Few persons realize how vast a work, how mighty a revolution has been thus accomplished. To furnish five millions and more of ignorant people with teachers of their own race and blood, in one generation, was not only a very difficult undertaking, but a very important one, in that, it placed before the eyes of almost every Negro child an attainable ideal. It brought the masses of the blacks in contact with modern civilization, made black men the leaders of their communities and trainers of the new generation. In this work college-bred Negroes were first teachers, and then teachers of teachers. And here it is that the broad culture of college work has been of peculiar value. Knowledge of life and its wider meaning, has been the point of the Negro's deepest ignorance, and the sending out of teachers whose training has not been simply for bread winning, but also for human culture, has been of inestimable value in the training of these men.

In earlier years the two occupations of preacher and teacher were practically the only ones open to the black college graduate. Of later years a larger diversity of life among his people, has opened new avenues of employment. Nor have these college men been paupers and spendthrifts; 557 college-bred Negroes owned in 1899, $1,342,862.50 worth of real estate, (assessed value) or $2,411 per family. The real value of the total accumulations of the whole group is perhaps about $10,000,000, or $5,000 a piece. Pitiful, is it not, beside the fortunes of oil kings and steel trusts, but after all is the fortune of the millionaire the only stamp of true and successful living? Alas! it is, with many, and there's the rub.

The problem of training the Negro is to-day immensely complicated by the fact that the whole question of the efficiency and appropriateness of our present systems of education, for any kind of child, is a matter of active debate, in which final settlement seems still afar off. Consequently it often happens that persons arguing for or against certain systems of education for Negroes, have these controversies in mind and miss the real question at issue. The main question, so far as the Southern Negro is concerned, is: What under the present circumstance, must a system of education do in order to raise the Negro as quickly as possible in the scale of civilization? The answer to this question seems to me clear: It must strengthen the Negro's character, increase his knowledge and teach him to earn a living. Now it goes without saying, that it is hard to do all these things simultaneously or suddenly, and that at the same time it will not do to give all the attention to one and neglect the others; we could give black boys trades, but that alone will not civilize a race of ex-slaves; we might simply increase their knowledge of the world, but this would not necessarily make them wish to use this knowledge honestly; we might seek to strengthen character and purpose, but to what end if this people have nothing to eat or to wear? A system of education is not one thing, nor does it have a single definite object, nor is it a mere matter of schools. Education is that whole system of human training within and without the school house walls, which molds and develops men. If then we start out to train an ignorant and unskilled people with a heritage of bad habits, our system of training must set before itself two great aims—the one dealing with knowledge and character, the other part seeking to give the child the technical knowledge necessary for him to earn a living under the present circumstances. These objects are accomplished in part by the opening of the common schools on the one, and of the industrial schools on the other. But only in part, for there must also be trained those who are to teach these schools—men and women of knowledge and culture and technical skill who understand modern civilization, and have the training and aptitude to impart it to the children under them. There must be teachers, and teachers of teachers, and to attempt to establish any sort of a system of common and industrial school training, without *first* (and I say *first* advisedly) without *first* providing for the higher training of the very best teachers, is simply throwing your money to the winds, School houses do not teach themselves—piles of brick and mortar and machinery do not send out *men*. It is the trained, living human soul, cultivated and strengthened by long study and thought, that breathes the real breath of life into boys and girls and makes them human, whether they be black or white, Greek, Russian or American. Nothing, in these latter days, has so dampened the faith of thinking Negroes in recent educational movements, as the fact that such movements have been accompanied by ridicule and denouncement and decrying of those very institutions of higher training which made the Negro public school possible, and make Negro industrial schools thinkable. It was Fisk, Atlanta, Howard and Straight, those colleges born of the faith and sacrifice of the abolitionists, that placed in the black schools of the South the 30,000 teachers and more, which some, who depreciate the work of these higher schools, are using to teach their own new experiments. If Hampton, Tuskegee and the hundred other industrial schools prove in the future to be as successful as they deserve to be then their success in training black artisans for the South, will be due primarily to the white colleges of the North and the black colleges of the South, which trained the teachers who to-day conduct these institutions. There was a time when the American people believed pretty devoutly that a log of wood with a boy at one end and Mark Hopkins at the other, represented the highest ideal of human training. But in these eager days it would seem that we have changed all that and think it necessary to add a couple of saw-mills and a hammer to this outfit, and, at a pinch, to dispense with the services of Mark Hopkins.

I would not deny, or for a moment seem to deny, the paramount necessity of teaching the Negro to work, and to work steadily and skillfully; or seem to depreciate in the slightest degree the important part industrial schools must play in the accomplishment of these ends, but I *do* say, and insist upon it, that it is industrialism drunk with its vision of success, to imagine that its own work can be accomplished without providing for the training of broadly cultured men and women to teach its own teachers, and to teach the teachers of the public schools.

But I have already said that human education is not simply a matter of schools; it is much more a matter of family and group life—the training of one's home, of one's daily companions, of one's social class. Now the black boy of the South moves in a black world—a world with its own leaders, its own thoughts, its own ideals. In this world he gets by far the larger part of his life training, and through the eyes of this dark world he peers into the veiled world beyond. Who guides and determines the education which he receives in his world? His teachers here are the group-leaders of the Negro people—the physicians and clergymen, the trained fathers and mothers, the influential and forceful men about him of all kinds; here it is, if at all, that the culture of the surrounding world trickles through and is handed on by the graduates of the higher schools. Can such culture training of group leaders be neglected? Can we afford to ignore it? Do you think that if the leaders of thought among Negroes are not trained and educated thinkers, that they will have no leaders? On the contrary a hundred half-trained demagogues will still hold the places they so largely occupy now, and hundreds of vociferous busy-bodies will multiply. You have no choice; either you must help furnish this race from within its own ranks with thoughtful men of trained leadership, or you must suffer the evil consequences of a headless misguided rabble.

I am an earnest advocate of manual training and trade teaching for black boys, and for white boys, too. I believe that next to the founding of Negro colleges the most valuable addition to Negro education since the war, has been industrial training for black boys. Nevertheless, I insist that the object of all true education is not to make men carpenters, it is to make carpenters men; there are two means of making the carpenter a man, each equally important: the first is to give the group and community in which he works, liberally trained teachers and leaders to teach him and his family what life means; the second is to give him sufficient intelligence and technical skill to make him an efficient workman; the first object demands the Negro college and college-bred men—not a quantity of such colleges, but a few of excellent quality; not too many college-bred men, but enough to leaven the lump, to inspire the masses, to raise the Talented Tenth to leadership; the second object demands a good system of common schools, well-taught, conveniently located and properly equipped.

The Sixth Atlanta Conference truly said in 1901:

"We call the attention of the Nation to the fact that less than one million of the three million Negro children of school age, are at present regularly attending school, and these attend a session which lasts only a few months.

"We are to-day deliberately rearing millions of our citizens in ignorance, and at the same time limiting the rights of citizenship by educational qualifications. This is unjust. Half the black youth of the land have no opportunities open to them for learning to read, write and cipher. In the discussion as to the proper training of Negro children after they leave the public schools, we have forgotten that they are not yet decently provided with public schools.

"Propositions are beginning to be made in the South to reduce the already meagre school facilities of Negroes. We congratulate the South on resisting, as much as it has, this pressure, and on the many millions it has spent on Negro education. But it is only fair to point out that Negro taxes and the Negroes' share of the income from indirect taxes and endowments have fully repaid this expenditure, so that the Negro public school system has not in all probability cost the white taxpayers a single cent since the war.

"This is not fair. Negro schools should be a public burden, since they are a public benefit. The Negro has a right to demand good common school training at the hands of the States and the Nation since by their fault he is not in position to pay for this himself."

What is the chief need for the building up of the Negro public school in the South? The Negro race in the South needs teachers to-day above all else. This is the concurrent testimony of all who know the situation. For the supply of this great demand two things are needed—institutions of higher education and money for school houses and salaries. It is usually assumed that a hundred or more institutions for Negro training are to-day turning out so many teachers and college-bred men that the race is threatened with an over-supply. This is sheer nonsense. There are to-day less than 3,000 living Negro college graduates in the United States, and less than 1,000 Negroes in college. Moreover, in the 164 schools for Negroes, 95 per cent. of their students are doing elementary and secondary work, work which should be done in the public schools. Over half the remaining 2,157 students are taking high school studies. The mass of so-called "normal" schools for the Negro, are simply doing elementary common school work, or at most, high school work, with a little instruction in methods. The Negro colleges and the post-graduate courses at other institutions are the only agencies for the broader and more careful training of teachers. The work of these institutions is hampered for lack of funds. It is getting increasingly difficult to get funds for training teachers in the best modern methods, and yet all over the South, from State Superintendents, county officials, city boards and school principals comes the wail, "We need TEACHERS!" and teachers must be trained. As the fairest minded of all white Southerners, Atticus G. Haygood, once said: "The defects of colored teachers are so great as to create an urgent necessity for training better ones. Their excellencies and their successes are sufficient to justify the best hopes of success in the effort, and to vindicate the judgment of those who make large investments of money and service, to give to colored students opportunity for thoroughly preparing themselves for the work of teaching children of their people."

The truth of this has been strikingly shown in the marked improvement of white teachers in the South. Twenty years ago the rank and file of white public school teachers were not as good as the Negro teachers. But they, by scholarships and good salaries, have been encouraged to thorough normal and collegiate preparation, while the Negro teachers have been discouraged by starvation wages and the idea that any training will do for a black teacher. If carpenters are needed it is well and good to train men as carpenters. But to train men as carpenters, and then set them to teaching is wasteful and criminal; and to train men as teachers and then refuse them living wages, unless they become carpenters, is rank nonsense.

The United States Commissioner of Education says in his report for 1900: "For comparison between the white and colored enrollment in secondary and higher education, I have added together the enrollment in high schools and secondary schools, with the attendance on colleges and universities, not being sure of the actual grade of work done in the colleges and universities. The work done in the secondary schools is reported in such detail in this office, that there can be no doubt of its grade."

He then makes the following comparisons of persons in every million enrolled in secondary and higher education:

	Whole Country	Negroes
1880	4,362	1,289
1900	10,743	2,061

And he concludes: "While the number in colored high schools and colleges had increased somewhat faster than the population, it had not kept pace with the average of the whole country, for it had fallen from 30 per cent. to 24 per cent. of the average quota. Of all colored pupils, one (1) in one hundred was engaged in secondary and higher work, and that ratio has continued substantially for the past twenty years. If the ratio of colored population in secondary and higher education is to be equal to the average for the whole country, it must be increased to five times its present average." And if this be true of the secondary and higher education, it is safe to say that the Negro has not one-tenth his quota in college studies. How baseless, therefore, is the charge of too much training! We need Negro teachers for the Negro common schools, and we need first-class normal schools and colleges to train them. This is the work of higher Negro education and it must be done.

Further than this, after being provided with group leaders of civilization, and a foundation of intelligence in the public schools, the carpenter, in order to be a man, needs technical skill. This calls for trade schools. Now trade schools are not nearly such simple things as people once thought. The original idea was that the "Industrial" school was to furnish education, practically free, to those willing to work for it; it was to "do" things—i. e.: become a center of productive industry, it was to be partially, if not wholly, self-supporting, and it was to teach trades. Admirable as were some of the ideas underlying this scheme, the whole thing simply would not work in practice; it was found that if you were to use time and material to teach trades thoroughly, you could not at the same time keep the industries on a commercial basis and make them pay. Many schools started out to do this on a large scale and went into virtual bankruptcy. Moreover, it was found also that it was possible to teach a boy a trade mechanically, without giving him the full educative benefit of the process, and vice versa, that there was a distinctive educative value in teaching a boy to use his hands and eyes in carrying out certain physical processes, even though he did not actually learn a trade. It has happened, therefore, in the last decade, that a noticeable change has come over the industrial schools. In the first place the idea of commercially remunerative industry in a school is being pushed rapidly to the background. There are still schools with shops and farms that bring an income, and schools that use student labor partially for the erection of their buildings and the furnishing of equipment. It is coming to be seen, however, in the education of the Negro, as clearly as it has been seen in the education of the youths the world over, that it is the *boy* and not the material product, that is the true object of education. Consequently the object of the industrial school came to be the thorough training of boys regardless of the cost of the training, so long as it was thoroughly well done.

Even at this point, however, the difficulties were not surmounted. In the first place modern industry has taken great strides since the war, and the teaching of trades is no longer a simple matter. Machinery and long processes of work have greatly changed the work of the carpenter, the iron-worker and the shoemaker. A really efficient workman must be to-day an intelligent man who has had good technical training in addition to thorough common school, and perhaps even higher training. To meet this situation the industrial schools began a further development; they established distinct Trade Schools for the thorough training of better class artisans, and at the same time they sought to preserve for the purposes of general education, such of the simpler processes of elementary trade learning as were best suited therefor. In this differentiation of the Trade School and manual training, the best of the industrial schools simply followed the plain trend of the present educational epoch. A prominent educator tells us that, in Sweden, "In the beginning the economic conception was generally adopted, and everywhere manual training was looked upon as a means of preparing the children of the common people to earn their living. But gradually it came to be recognized that manual training has a more elevated purpose, and one, indeed, more useful in the deeper meaning of the term. It came to be considered as an educative process for the complete moral, physical and intellectual development of the child."

Thus, again, in the manning of trade schools and manual training schools we are thrown back upon the higher training as its source and chief support. There was a time when any aged and wornout carpenter could teach in a trade school. But not so to-day. Indeed the demand for college-bred men by a school like Tuskegee, ought to make Mr. Booker T. Washington the firmest friend of higher training. Here he has as helpers the son of a Negro senator, trained in Greek and the humanities, and graduated at Harvard; the son of a Negro congressman and lawyer, trained in Latin and mathematics, and graduated at Oberlin; he has as his wife, a woman who read Virgil and Homer in the same class room with me; he has as college chaplain, a classical graduate of Atlanta University; as teacher of science, a graduate of Fisk; as teacher of history, a graduate of Smith,—indeed some thirty of his chief teachers are college graduates, and instead of studying French grammars in the midst of weeds, or buying pianos for dirty cabins, they are at Mr. Washington's right hand helping him in a noble work. [And yet one of the effects of Mr. Washington's propaganda has been to throw doubt upon the expediency of such training for Negroes, as these persons have had.]

✳✳✳

Men of America, the problem is plain before you. Here is a race transplanted through the criminal foolishness of your fathers. Whether you like it or not the millions are here, and here they will remain. If you do not lift them up, they will pull you down. Education and work are the levers to uplift a people. Work alone will not do it unless inspired by the right ideals and guided by intelligence. Education must not simply teach work—it must teach Life. The Talented Tenth of the Negro race must be made leaders of thought and missionaries of culture among their people. No others can do this work and Negro colleges must train men for it. The Negro race, like all other races, is going to be saved by its exceptional men.

THE EDUCATIONAL PHILOSOPHIES OF WASHINGTON, DUBOIS, AND HOUSTON: LAYING THE FOUNDATIONS FOR AFROCENTRISM AND MULTICULTURALISM

FREDERICK DUNN

Freedom is not won by a passive acceptance of suffering. Freedom is won by the struggle against suffering. By this measure, Negroes have not yet paid the full price for freedom. And whites have not yet faced the full cost of justice. (King, 1967, p. 20)

The Political and Social Struggle for Emancipation: The Aims of African American Philosophers of Education

The history of African American education in the United States dates back to the first arrival of African slaves on American shores, where, according to one researcher:

> . . . the education of the black race in the Virginia Colony was inexorably interwoven with the history of the church. The teaching of blacks by church missionaries began there in 1619, when the first twenty black indentured servants landed in Jamestown. (Holte, 1947, p. 4)

After Emancipation, and within the framework of "Jim Crow" segregation and racism, African Americans soon developed their own educational institutions that bore a distinctly ethnic character. As Bullock (1970) notes, the education of African Americans in the South was limited,

> . . . to a special kind considered suitable for their status . . . it directed the development of Negro children out of the mainstream of American culture. . . . If there is any period that can be said to mark the beginning of what is commonly called Negro education, this is it. (p. 74)

Thus were born scores of what are today known as the nation's historically Black colleges and universities (HBCUs) and other African American-owned and operated institutions of learning. To some extent, the enforced separateness of the African American community from that of Whites provided a cohesion and focus among African Americans that furthered the advancement of an ethic of self-help and self-reliance in education and other areas. These developments allowed the ex-slaves to fashion, to the extent that they could, an educational philosophy and pedagogy that would assist their quest for liberation. While their immediate educational goals and purposes differed from county to county and state to state, there was convergence on the fundamental thrust of African American educational philosophy—namely, it was aimed at the attainment, sooner or later, of social justice for all Americans regardless of race. However, in understanding the character of these emerging educational philosophies, one must always remember that the most prevalent condition of African Americans was that of a severely oppressed minority struggling to find a pathway through the thickets of a mounting racial hatred.

Reprinted by permission from the *Journal of Negro Education* 62, no. 1 (1993).

Several interrelated issues complicated the development of African American education during the half-century after the Civil War. These issues precipitated intense debate, among African Americans as well as Whites, on the aims of African American education. Among the questions addressed: What would be the main emphasis of education for African Americans? Would or should it include the full range of training, from elementary to graduate and professional education? Or would it consist of a smattering of basic elementary education and vocational/technical/agricultural training for a people who were mostly farmers and unskilled workers and who, in the opinion of most southern Whites, were not capable of higher education? The debate led to the development of distinctive philosophies to address educational policy and practice in and for the African American community.

Generally, educational philosophy has neither acknowledged the contributions of African American philosophers of education nor recognized the existence of an African American philosophy of education. However, in the continuing struggle of African Americans for full participation in United States society, three African American philosophical orientations to education have achieved prominence. These philosophies and their foremost proponents can be identified as: (1) the accommodationist or technical skills-oriented philosophy, as represented by Booker T. Washington (1856–1915); (2) the radical or liberationist and intellectual-oriented philosophy, as articulated by W.E.B. DuBois (1868–1963); and (3) the integrationist/desegregationist or reformist philosophy, as expounded by Charles Hamilton Houston (1895–1950). Although each of these perspectives and their proponents have a different relationship to education, they all have significant implications for the field. Washington's vocational/technical framework, with its emphasis on skills development, dominated the nature of the educational service extended to African Americans during the post-Reconstruction period. Although his position does not support the Afrocentric or multicultural thrusts prominent in African American education today, the combination of DuBois's and Houston's positions, advocated to a great extent in opposition to Washington's philosophy, do support these contemporary developments. DuBois's concern with the development of African American intellectual and critical competencies, along with Houston's concern for his race's attainment of high-quality education through the reduction of racial isolation, speak directly to the emerging purposes of multicultural education. Houston's push for the desegregation of America's public educational and other institutions opened the door for Afrocentric and multicultural thought in education by forcing into that arena the ideas of multicultural representation and inclusion.

As Pratte (1979) attests, before analyzing historic African American philosophies and philosophers of education, it is important that one thoroughly understand that concepts central to contemporary education were not addressed similarly in the past, and vice-versa. One of the interesting aspects about the educational philosophies of Washington, DuBois, Houston, and other African Americans of their eras is that their foci were highly particularistic; that is, most were ethnocentric in nature and did not even pretend to be universal. Their pronouncements did not focus on the broader nature of education or its normative components and practices (i.e., learning theories, curriculum selection, teaching strategies, classroom management techniques, etc.). Rather, they almost always focused on the ultimate purpose of education for African Americans: freedom from what was, for people of color, a debilitating and racially segregated political, economic, and legal system and society. In that regard, each man was at once both philosopher and activist. Underscoring Freire's (1985) contention that "there is no truly neutral education" (p. 102), Washington's, DuBois's, and Houston's educational philosophies were ultimately political in character, style, language, and aims. It is appropriate, then, to suggest that, while their educational philosophies differ in terms of their methods, audiences, tone, and character, they are markedly similar in their aims. They were all born out of the strife and alienation brought about by de jure and de facto discrimination and each philosophy was created to alleviate injustices and inequalities inherent in a racist society. Each sought to respond to the gross inequalities inherited from slavery and the host of oppressive Jim Crow laws that succeeded it. Washington's, DuBois's, and Houston's philosophies can thus be seen as fundamentally social philosophies that focus on education. In that vein, each can be called liberation philosophies.

The Accommodationist Philosophy of Education: Booker T. Washington

When Frederick Douglass died in 1895, he left a despairing and oppressed people to mourn his loss at a somber moment in their fortunes. Douglass had been for several decades the most prominent spokesperson and leader of African American people. His influence due to his long-term dedication and radicalism, characterized by his journalistic forcefulness and extraordinary oratorical power, served well the advancement efforts of African Americans. Relief from the ever-heightening violence of lynchings, the increasingly repressive "Black Codes" enacted in several southern states, the disenfranchisement of African American voters who had (by then) only recently been enfranchised, and the newly legalized system of Jim Crow (or so-called "separate-but-equal") segregation seemed nowhere in sight. Into this vacuum of leadership stepped Booker T. Washington, whose main instruction as a student at Hampton Institute was in "moral philosophy" (Bond, 1966, p. 118). As DuBois (1903/1961) once noted, even though he himself was known as one of Washington's staunchest philosophical opponents, "Easily the most striking thing in the history of the American Negro since 1876 is the ascendancy of Mr. Booker T. Washington" (p. 42). Washington's leadership was extraordinary in its breadth of influence. In matters pertaining to African Americans, his counsel was much sought by Whites of prominence and power. His archival papers give testimony to frequent communications between Washington and state and federal government officials, superintendents of school in both the North and the South, several wealthy philanthropists and directors of philanthropic organizations, and at least two U.S. presidents (Harlan, 1972). Washington's leadership, especially in education, marked an era in African American history that was thoroughly dominated by one man as the spokesperson for his race.

In 1881 Washington was invited to accept the presidency of Tuskegee Institute in Alabama. Under his direction the school soon became one of America's leading institutions for African Americans. Washington's educational philosophy, as embodied in what came to be touted as "the Tuskegee model," was aimed at improving African Americans' marketability in the segregated American workforce. The centerpiece of the Washingtonian philosophy of African American education was an emphasis on economic self-help through agricultural and industrial/vocational training and development. As Washington wrote:

> Almost from the first I determined to have the students do practically all the work of putting up the buildings . . . the lesson of self-help would be more valuable to them in the long run than if they were put into a building which had been wholly the creation of the generosity of some one else. (Harlan, 1972, p. 38)

Washington's educational philosophy was very much rooted in the pragmatic philosophical tradition, especially as it relates purpose to the resolution of difficulties that arise out of experience. In his view, the African American educational experience required a hard-headed, commonsensical approach. He was suspicious of the solutions posed by his Ivy League-trained antagonists (DuBois among them), dismissing them as too intellectual and theoretical for the masses of African American people.

Washington advocated vocational education for four reasons: (1) because he thought it was the wave of the future; (2) because he was a product of it at Hampton Institute, and he had internalized that experience; (3) because he strongly felt that African Americans could best develop a strong economic base through the acquisition of utilitarian skills; and (4) because he deeply believed a vocational education was all that the larger, White-dominated society would allow. It is this last point—Washington's ability to read the societal landscape, avoid the pitfalls, and achieve his objectives, limited though they were—that gained him the title "the Wizard of Tuskegee" (Harlan, 1983). When Washington coupled his educational ideas of manual training with his social philosophy of accommodationism, or acceptance by African Americans of second-class citizenship and legally mandated segregation, he was widely endorsed by southern and northern White philanthropists and politicians. He soon became recognized as an enormously powerful spokesperson for African Americans. As his fame quickened and solidified, efforts began in earnest to limit African American schooling to education for vocational, industrial, and agricultural utility and service.

Washington's educational philosophy had many shortcomings, and in many ways Washington remains an enigmatic historical figure. His focus on appeasing Whites (by promoting the illusion of a non-aspiring, accommodating African American populace) and his advocacy of the nonparticipation of African Americans in the political and social arenas of U.S. society failed to address the menial nature of African Americans' socioeconomic status. Much to his credit, Washington "sent out thousands of trained teachers, craftsmen, and businessmen to numerous rural Negro villages, always emphasizing his own version of 'learning by doing'" (Wish, 1974); yet, the thrust of the Washington program was to produce African American domestics and farmers who were polite and submissive in the face of what was frequently dehumanizing treatment from Whites. In this, Washington did nearly as much to reinforce the lasting image of the African American worker (specifically males) as a "Super Masculine Menial" (Cleaver, 1968, p. 162) as did those who championed the concept of White supremacy. Among Washington's critics were those who suspected that the philosophy of limiting African American education to manual training catered to the needs of Blacks' former oppressors. Many of them expressed doubts that Washington had any real understanding of the massive tide of industrialization that was sweeping and transforming the nation or of the role Tuskegee's students in particular or African Americans in general could play in the shifting labor markets and socioeconomic order of the Industrial Age.

The Radical Philosophy of Education: W.E.B. Dubois

DuBois, who followed the more militant tradition of Frederick Douglass, was Washington's primary critic. DuBois penned a scathing attack on Washington's social and educational philosophy entitled *The Souls of Black Folk* (1903/1961), which, while it lauded much of the work and sincerity of Washington and claimed that African Americans must "strive with" Washington in his endeavors, emphasized the following:

> The black men of America have a duty to perform. But so far as Mr. Washington apologizes for injustice, North or South, does not rightly value the privilege and duty of voting, belittles the emasculating effects of caste distinctions, and opposes the higher training and ambition of our brighter minds . . . we must increasingly and firmly oppose them. (pp. 53–54)

Thus, two rather distinct African American philosophies of education began to emerge, with educators and educational policymakers choosing to side with either the DuBois or the Washington camp.

During much of his long and extremely productive life, DuBois was driven by a need to reconcile the dualism inherent in the African American experience and identity. He contended that African Americans must develop their own distinct and "superior" culture within the context of the American social system while simultaneously fighting to eliminate "the color line"—the social, political, economic, and legal barrier of racial segregation. The core concept of DuBois's philosophy of African American education was his idea of the "Talented Tenth." In DuBois's view, those few African Americans (roughly estimated as a tenth of the African American populace) who had attended (or would attend in the future) the best colleges and universities in the land, were entrusted to return to African American communities to educate the masses of their race and ultimately lead African America out of economic, political, and social bondage. Was DuBois an elitist? By the standards of anti-intellectualism sometimes ascribed to the masses of African American people, he could be thus described. By intent, however, he was consistently egalitarian in his beliefs—favoring excellence in intellectual development initially for the few, yet ultimately committed to a high level of intellectual development for all. DuBois's focus on the African American intelligentsia was a social and educational tactic for advancing the race, not a goal in and of itself. Further, while DuBois believed, like Washington, that education for the masses of African Americans must be related to their daily and social realities, he stressed the importance of the liberal arts and sciences and viewed these academic areas as the critical focus of African American education. A people whose education led them to aspire to and achieve high levels of intellectual and conceptual competence, DuBois contended, could never be enslaved again.

Did DuBois advocate separate, segregated education for African Americans? The answer is yes, but with important qualifications. Given that the doctrine of "separate but equal" was the law of the land, DuBois had little choice but to urge African Americans to move forward under the limits of segregation while yet striving for educational excellence. However, it would be a gross misunderstanding to suggest that he favored separation of the races or segregated schools. Like Washington, DuBois was also something of a pragmatist; nonetheless, his advocacy of segregated education must be seen as an exhortation to African Americans to do the best they could with what they had—not to avoid antagonizing Whites. Unlike Washington, DuBois did not believe that African Americans had to accommodate White racism, accept second-class citizenship, or wait for Whites to ameliorate racial disparities.

Due to DuBois's long life and his involvement in the general leadership of African Americans for over 70 years, it is difficult to attach any label to him. At one time he was an assimilationist, at another a Pan-Africanist, at another a socialist and at still another, a Black Nationalist. He died a communist Pan-Africanist. Notwithstanding, his beliefs about African American education and its aims were clear. As civil rights leader Martin Luther King, Jr., pointed out in what turned out to be the last major speech of his life:

> Dr. DuBois was not only an intellectual giant exploring the frontiers of knowledge, he was in the first place a teacher. He would have wanted his life to teach us something about our tasks about emancipation. (quoted in DuBois, 1968, p. vii)

The Integrationist Philosophy of Education: Charles Hamilton Houston

The idea of integration generally suffers from a lack of clarity as it relates to the question of race relations, especially in the educational arena. It is inextricably interwoven with notions of equality, freedom, and democracy. It is also intimately connected with the concepts of desegregation, acculturation, assimilation, and amalgamation. For the purposes of this discussion, integration is the active participation by African Americans as equals in American life. This interpretation allows the inclusion of all the varieties and gradations of African American racial thought, save one: the strict separatist philosophy, or fundamentalist Black nationalism, which has represented only a small minority of the African American population since the days of Marcus Garvey in the 1920s.

America's first real experiment with integration came during the Reconstruction period with the passage of the 14th and 15th amendments to the U.S. Constitution. While the rights and recognitions gained as a result of these amendments are nothing to be scoffed at, they began eroding as early as 1871 and continued eroding for more than half a century due to the *Plessy V. Ferguson* Supreme Court decision in 1896. The second real attempt at integration occurred as a result of the 1954 *Brown V. Board of Education* decision.

One of the chief architects of the legal fight to end state-sponsored racial isolation and segregation in public education, Charles Hamilton Houston, was born one year before the *Plessy* decision. His most famous student, former Supreme Court justice Thurgood Marshall, described Houston as the "First Mr. Civil Rights Lawyer" (quoted in Logan, 1969, p. 140). Marshall, who is usually identified as the legal mind behind the civil rights movement's thrust toward school integration, made the following statement in 1979:

> When Brown against the Board of Education was being argued in the Supreme Court . . . there were some two dozen lawyers on the side of the Negroes . . . . Of those lawyers . . . only two had not been touched by Charlie Hamilton. That man was the engineer of all of it . . . (p. 276)

Like DuBois, Houston was extremely well-educated and held a deep-seated belief in the efficacy of using education as a focal point in the struggle for civil and human rights. However, Houston's philosophy of education was cultivated in the interpretation of the law. Therefore, he created, practiced, and communicated a model of "social engineering"—a framework for using law to effect social change—that proved integral to the transformation of the nation's educational system. According to his biographer, Gena Rae McNeil (1983), in Houston's view:

> . . . a social engineer was a highly skilled, perceptive, sensitive lawyer who understood the Constitution of the United States and knew how to explore it in the solving of "problems of . . . local communities" and in "bettering conditions of the underprivileged citizens. (p. 84)

The early development and expansion of Houston's philosophy of social engineering took place at Howard University in Washington, DC. During his years as a professor and administrator at that university's school of law from 1924 to 1935, his ideas were ingrained into the philosophy, curriculum, and methodology of the school. It was at Howard that Houston promulgated his belief that African American lawyers were obligated not only to understand the Constitution but to explore its uses, both in the solution of problems of local communities and the improvement of the conditions under which African American and poor citizens lived. According to McNeil (1983), Houston forthrightly believed that Howard could become "the school that would produce lawyers who would be excellent in their profession and fearless in their struggle against racial discrimination" (p. 65). Thus, he was adamant that lawyers trained at the Howard law school become active participants and leaders in the "struggle for liberty and the improvement of the quality of African American life in the United States" (p. 67). William H. Hastie, who served as dean of Howard's law school from 1939 to 1946, concurs, noting that Houston set out to deliver "superior professional training and extraordinary motivation . . . to prepare the professional cadres needed to lead successful litigation against racism as practiced by government and sanctioned by law" (cited in Robinson, 1977, p. 34). For example, as McNeil relates, "In the course on administrative law [Houston] stressed the elements of expedience, social interest, and spheres of influence to illustrate the growing importance of administrative law to black people" (p. 67).

Houston became vice dean of the Howard law school at a time when it had lost its accreditation. He was instrumental both in getting the school re-accredited as well as reorganizing its thrust along the lines of his social engineering model. Fundamental in this reorganization was Houston's emphasis on preparing students for the practice of constitutional law and advocacy with a focus on African American advancement. Houston set forth his goals in his "Personal Observations":

> . . . first, that every group must justify and interpret itself in terms of the general welfare; and . . . second, that the only justification for the Howard University School of Law, in a city having seven white law schools, is that it is doing a distinct, necessary work for the social good. (cited in Logan, 1969, p. 267)

In Houston's view, "necessary work for the social good" meant the education of lawyers in a particular way: toward supporting the African American movement for racial justice. As he asserted:

> . . . [the] Negro lawyer must be trained as a social engineer and group interpreter. Due to the Negro's social and political condition . . . the Negro lawyer must be prepared to anticipate, guide and interpret his group advancement. (cited in Logan, 1969, p. 267)

Houston's leadership of the Howard University School of Law transformed it from an unaccredited evening school to a fully accredited, nationally known and respected, civil rights-oriented institution of excellence—one committed to the elimination of social injustice in both the study of law and its usage in defense of African Americans' racial advancement and their pursuit of full freedom and justice (McNeil, p. 122). His implementation of the idea of social engineering into the culture and classroom of this HBCU law school marked a clear attempt to use education as a means of redressing social problems.

Houston's educational philosophy was one designed to meet the pressing social and political needs of the masses of African Americans. It embodied idealistic general aims as well as aims derived from a specific reality. If for no other reason than that he believed "separate" would always be unequal in the American racial scheme—a dilemma that remains problematic even today, at the close of the 20th century—Houston espoused a desegregationist philosophy of education and was an integrationist. However, his integrationist posture did not stop him from propounding the centrality of African American self-reliance in much the same vein as did Washington and DuBois.

In 1935 Charles Houston left Howard to accept the position of Special Counsel to the National Association for the Advancement of Colored People (NAACP), an organization DuBois had helped to found. His duties included directing that organization's national legal campaign, and in this capacity he began to outline his desegregationist philosophy of education in a way that had not and could not be shown at Howard due to its status as a segregated institution. In a memorandum to the NAACP Oversight Committee outlining his goals for the first year of his appointment, Houston proposed that the central thrust of the organization's legal campaign be the following:

> . . . [to] make segregation *with* inequality a target of litigation, make segregation *with* equality too expensive to maintain and use legal papers in every situation to make plain the desirability of the elimination of segregated dual systems [italics added]. (McNeil, 1983, p. 117)

Houston strategized that this process of systematically building one case upon another, and then linking seemingly separate and discrete cases into one colossal case, would ultimately slay the dragon of segregation. Indeed, it was this long-range view of a protracted struggle with the courts and other forces of segregation that brought about the eventual *Brown* decision, four years after Houston's death. Although the centerpiece of Houston's plan was an attack on the laws that supported segregation in education, his long-range strategy focused on the eradication of all forms of segregation:

> . . . equality of education is not enough. There can be no true equality under a segregated system. No segregation operates fairly on a minority group unless it is a d[o]minant minority. . . . The American Negro is not a dominant minority; therefore, he must fight for complete elimination of segregation as his ultimate goal. (McNeil, 1983, p. 134)

At the NAACP the Houstonian educational philosophy began to broaden and blossom. Houston, simultaneously the legal architect and litigator, became a mass educator as well. It could be said that Houston's motto during his tenure at the NAACP, from 1935 to 1940, was "educate (the community) before we litigate." He realized that African Americans in many communities, especially those in the South, were fearful and apathetic about taking radical action to ameliorate racism and discrimination. He also realized an important point about most Whites of his day: "The truth is there are millions of white people who have no real knowledge of the Negro's problem and who never give the Negro a serious thought" (Houston, 1936, p. 79). Thus, he urged the NAACP and other organizations to launch an extensive campaign in southern and border states to communicate the necessity of mass participation in support of desegregation efforts. This campaign utilized many social institutions to educate African American and White communities, with the goal of developing "a sustaining mass interest behind the programs . . . before the actual litigation commences" (Houston, 1935, p. 4). Writing in *Crisis*, the official magazine of the NAACP (edited by DuBois), Houston commented that "law suits mean little unless supported by public opinion," but "the really baffling problem is how to create the proper kind of public opinion" (Houston, 1936, p. 79).

The debate over the extent of the usefulness of *Brown* may rage on, but Houston's contribution to the American educational landscape is inestimable. In a real sense this historic decision, irrespective of how one evaluates it, was the culmination of Houston's educational philosophy. Yet, his greatest gift to the philosophy of education for African Americans was the formulation of a vision. That vision, in its applied form, translated academic and community concerns into a unique blend of liberating legal activism directed at ensuring more democratic access to education, the elimination of racial barriers in education, and the assurance of high-quality education for all Americans regardless of race.

Conclusion

In the heat of the current debate over Afrocentric and multicultural education, it is sometimes forgotten that the occasion for the debate, and certainly the opportunity to explore its rationale, exists in large measure because equally fundamental issues concerning the education of African Americans were debated in earlier periods. Struggles to transform the U.S. school system and its curriculum—to create a more inclusive educational environment and to counter the essentially Eurocentric character of the nation's schools—were initially waged in the names of African American students. Very prominent in these early debates and struggles were figures such as Booker T. Washington, W.E.B. DuBois, and Charles Hamilton Houston—three African American leaders whose philosophies of education ultimately have helped to shape the whole of schooling in U.S. society.

Washington's accommodationist philosophy and his consequent great popularity helped to make possible basic education for African Americans. In this contemporary period, however, the limited scope of the Washingtonian vision, which continues to dominate so much of the thrust of African American education, is nothing short of retrogressive. In his ongoing debates with Washington, as in much of his work, DuBois argued from a liberationist perspective. He stressed the importance of the liberal arts, humanities, and sciences in the education of African Americans, contending that, through intellectual development, African Americans would develop the cognitive and technical competencies necessary to achieve their true emancipation and full participation in the social order. Indeed, the DuBoisian legacy is represented today in the emergence of perspectivism as a major component of multicultural education. Then there is Houston's legacy, which, in its insistence on eliminating political and instrumental barriers to broader access to public education, forms part of the rationale for the present thrusts for a more broadly inclusive and representative curriculum. Perhaps the greatest of Houston's contributions was the formulation of a vision—one that was shared by DuBois—that, in its applied form, translated educational and community concerns into a unique blend of liberating legal activism. Viewed in total, the educational philosophies of Washington, DuBois, and Houston form a continuum, a living legacy, that points to the need for African American and other people of color to complete the task of liberation and freedom, through and beyond education, in ways that will ultimately lead to the transformation of the society and greater measures of social justice for all.

References

Bond, H. M. (1966). *The education of the Negro in the American social order.* New York: Octagon Books.

Bullock, H. A. (1970). *A history of Negro education in the South.* New York: Praeger.

Cleaver, E. (1968). *Soul on ice.* New York: Dell.

DuBois, W. E. B. (1961). *The souls of Black folk.* Greenwich, CT: Fawcett. (Work originally published 1903)

DuBois, W. E. B. (1968). *Dusk of dawn.* New York: Schocken.

Freire, P. (D. Macedo, Trans.). (1985). *The politics of education: Culture, power and liberation.* South Hadley, MA: Bergin & Garvey.

Harlan, L. R. (Ed.). (1972). *The Booker T. Washington papers* (Vols. 1 & 2). Urbana, IL: University of Illinois Press.

Harlan, L. R. (1983). *Booker T. Washington, The Wizard of Tuskegee, 1901–1915.* New York: Oxford University Press.

Holte, C. (1947). *Education of Blacks in America.* Norfolk, VA: Journal and Guide.

Houston, C. H. (1935, November 14). [Memorandum to the Joint Committee on the American Fund for Public Service, Inc.; NAACP Archival Records, New York City.]

Houston, C. H. (1936, March). Don't shout too soon. *Crisis,* pp. 79–91.

King, M. L., Jr. (1967). *Where do we go from here?* Boston: Beacon Press.

Logan, R. W. (1969). *Howard University: The first hundred years, 1867–1967*. New York: New York University Press.

Marshall, T. (1979, June–July). Amherst College honors Charles Houston. *Crisis*, p. 267.

McNeil, G. A. (1983). *Groundwork: Charles Hamilton Houston and the struggle for civil rights*. Philadelphia: University of Pennsylvania Press.

Pratte, R. (1979). Analytic philosophy of education. In J. Soltis (Ed.), *Philosophy of education since mid-century* (pp. 17–37). New York: Teachers College Press.

Robinson, S. W., III. (1977). No tea for the feeble: Two perspectives on Charles Hamilton Houston. *Howard Law Journal, 20*, 1–9.

Wish, H. (Ed.). (1964). *The Negro since emancipation*. Englewood Cliffs, NJ: Prentice–Hall.

PRESIDENT HUTCHINS' PROPOSALS TO REMAKE HIGHER EDUCATION

J. DEWEY

The Existing Disorder

President Hutchins' book[1] consists of two parts. One of them is a critical discussion of the plight of education in this country, with especial reference to colleges and universities. The other is a plan for the thorough remaking of education. This second part is again divided. It opens with an analysis of the meaning of general or liberal education, and is followed by an application of the conclusions reached to reconstruction of education in existing colleges and universities. The criticism of the present situation is trenchant. "The most striking fact about the higher learning in America is the confusion that besets it." The college of liberal arts is partly high school, partly university, partly general, partly special. The university consisting of graduate work for the master's and doctor's degree, and of a group of professional schools, is no better off. The universities are not only non-intellectual but they are anti-intellectual.

There then follows a diagnosis of the disease of "disunity, discord, and disorder." Fundamentally, the ailment proceeds from too ready response of universities to immediate demands of the American public. This public is moved by love of money, and the higher learning responds to anything that promises to bring money to the college and university whether from donors, student-fees, or state legislatures. The result is that these institutions become public service-stations; and as there is no special tide in public opinion and sentiment, but only a criss-cross of currents, the kind of service that is to be rendered shifts with every change in public whim and interest. Love of money results in demand for large numbers of students, and the presence of large numbers renders training even more indiscriminate in order to meet the demands of unselected heterogeneous groups.

Another symptom of our quick response to immediate and often passing public desires is seen in the effect upon higher education of the popular notion of democracy. This notion, although confused, encourages the belief that everybody should have the same chance of getting higher education, and everybody should have just the kind of education he happens to want. As against this view, President Hutchins holds that the responsibility of the public for providing education ends properly at the sophomore year of college, and after that point education should be given only to those who have demonstrated special capacity. (Incidentally, the author attributes to the false popular idea of democracy the existing perverse system of control of higher institutions by boards of trustees.)

The third major cause of our educational disorder is the erroneous notion of progress. Everything is supposed to be getting better, the future will be better yet. Why not then break with the past? Since in fact the "progress" that has taken place is mainly in material things and techniques, information, more and more and more data, become the demand; and higher learning is swamped by an empiricism that drowns the intellect. Somewhat strangely, the natural sciences are regarded by Mr. Hutchins as the cause and the mirror of this empiricism.

Reprinted from the *Social Frontier* 3, no. 22 (January 1937).

The Remedy

One may venture to summarize the evils in relation to their source by saying that they are an excessive regard for practicality, and practicality of a very immediate sort. The essence of the remedy accordingly, is emancipation of higher learning from this practicality, and its devotion to the cultivation of intellectuality for its own sake.

Many readers will share my opinion that Mr. Hutchins has shrewdly pointed out many evils attending the aimlessness of our present educational scheme, and will join in his desire that higher institutions become "centers of creative thought." So strong will be their sympathies that they may overlook the essence of the remedy, namely, his conception of the nature of intellectuality or rationality. This conception is characterized by two dominant traits. The first, as I pointed out in an article in the December number of this journal, is belief in the existence of fixed and eternal authoritative principles as truths that are not to be questioned. "Real unity can be achieved only by a hierarchy of truths which shows us which are fundamental and which are subsidiary." The hierarchy must be already there, or else it could not show us. The other point is not so explicitly stated. But it does not require much reading between the lines to see the remedy proposed rests upon a belief that since evils have come from surrender to shifting currents of public sentiment, the remedy is to be found in the greatest possible aloofness of higher learning from contemporary social life. This conception is explicitly seen in the constant divorce set up between intellect and practice, and between intellect and "experience."

I shall not stop to inquire whether such a divorce, if it is established, will be conducive to creative intellectual work, inviting as is the topic. I content myself with pointing out that—admitting that many present ills come from surrender of educational institutions to immediate social pressures—the facts are open to another interpretation with respect to educational policy. The policy of aloofness amounts fundamentally to acceptance of a popular American slogan, "Safety first." It would seem, on the other hand, as if the facts stated about the evil effects of our love of money should invite attention on the part of institutions devoted to love of truth for its own sake to the economic institutions that have produced this overweening love, and to their social consequences in other matters than the temper of educational institutions; and attention to the means available for changing this state of things. The immediate effect of such attention would probably be withdrawal of donations of money. But for an institution supposedly devoted to truth, a policy of complete withdrawal, however safe, hardly seems the way out. I have given but one illustration. I hope it may suggest a principle widely applicable. Escape from present evil contemporary social tendencies may require something more than escape. It may demand study of social needs and social potentialities of enduring time span. President Hutchins' discussion is noteworthy for complete absence of any reference to this alternative method of educational reconstruction. It is conceivable that educational reconstruction cannot be accomplished without a social reconstruction in which higher education has a part to play.

Authority and Truth

There are indications that Mr. Hutchins would not take kindly to labelling the other phase of this remedial plan "authoritarian." But any scheme based on the existence of ultimate first principles, with their dependent hierarchy of subsidiary principles, does not escape authoritarianism by calling the principles "truths." I would not intimate that the author has any sympathy with fascism. But basically his idea as to the proper course to be taken is akin to the distrust of freedom and the consequent appeal to *some* fixed authority that is now overrunning the world. There is implicit in every assertion of fixed and eternal first truths the necessity for some *human* authority to decide, in this world of conflicts, just what these truths are and how they shall be taught. This problem is conveniently ignored. Doubtless much may be said for selecting Aristotle and St. Thomas as competent promulgators of first truths. But it took the authority of a powerful ecclesiastic organization to secure their wide recognition. Others may prefer Hegel, or Karl Marx, or even Mussolini as the seers of first truths; and there are those who prefer Nazism. As far as I can see, President Hutchins has completely evaded the problem of who is to determine the definite truths that constitute the hierarchy.

In view of the emphasis given by our author to the subject of logic, it is pertinent to raise the question of how far institutions can become centers of creative thought, if in their management it is assumed that fundamental truths and the hierarchy of truth are already known. The assumption that merely by learning pre-existent truths, students will become even students, much less capable of independent creative thought, is one that demands considerable logical inquiry. President Hutchins' contempt for science as merely empirical perhaps accounts for his complete acceptance of the doctrine of formal discipline. But it is difficult to account for complete neglect of the place of the natural sciences in his educational scheme (apart from possible limitations of his own education) save on the score of a feeling, perhaps subconscious, that their recognition is so hostile to the whole scheme of prescribed antecedent first truths that it would be fatal to the educational plan he proposes to give them an important place. Considering, however, that their rise has already created a revolution in the old logic, and that they now afford the best existing patterns of controlled inquiry in search for truth, there will be others besides myself who will conclude that President Hutchins' policy of reform by withdrawal from everything that smacks of modernity and contemporaneousness is not after all the road to the kind of intellectuality that will remedy the evils he so vividly depicts.

The constant appeal of President Hutchins to Plato, Aristotle, and St. Thomas urgently calls for a very different interpretation from that which is given it. Their work is significant precisely because it does not represent withdrawal from the science and social affairs of their own times. On the contrary, each of them represents a genuine and profound attempt to discover and present in organized form the meaning of the science and the institutions that existed in their historic periods. The real conclusion to be drawn is that the task of higher learning at present is to accomplish a similar work for the confused and disordered conditions of our own day. The sciences have changed enormously since these men performed their task, both in logical method and in results. We live in a different social medium. It is astounding that anyone should suppose that a return to the conceptions and methods of these writers would do for the present situation what they did for the Greek and Medieval eras. The cure for surrender of higher learning to immediate and transitory pressures is not monastic seclusion. Higher learning can become intellectually vital only by coming to that close grip with our contemporary science and contemporary social affairs which Plato, Aristotle, and St. Thomas exemplify in their respective ways.

JOHN DEWEY

Note

1. *The Higher Learning in America*, by Robert Maynard Hutchins. The Yale Press, New Haven, 1936

GRAMMAR, RHETORIC, AND MR. DEWEY

R.M. HUTCHINS

Mr. John Dewey has devoted much of two recent articles in THE SOCIAL FRONTIER to my book, *The Higher Learning in America.* The editors of THE SOCIAL FRONTIER have asked me to reply to Mr. Dewey. This I am unable to do, in any real sense, for Mr. Dewey has stated my position in such a way as to lead me to think that I cannot write, and has stated his own in such a way as to make me suspect that I cannot read.

Mr. Dewey says (1) that I look to Plato, Aristotle, and Aquinas; (2) that I am anti-scientific; (3) that I am for withdrawing from the world; and (4) that I am authoritarian.

1. *"Mr. Hutchins looks to Plato, Aristotle, and Aquinas. . . ."*

   a. Mr. Hutchins also looks to Sir R. W. Livingstone, p. 25; Dean C. H. Wilkinson, p. 54; Newman, p. 63; Shorey, p. 64; Whewell, p. 73; Locke, p. 76; Nicholas Murray Butler, p. 80; De Tocqueville, p. 90; Judge Learned Hand, p. 92; Kant, p. 99; and Lenin, p. 105.

   b. If I had not already done so in an earlier book, I should have looked to Mr. Dewey. In *No Friendly Voice*, p. 39, I said, "Mr. C. I. Lewis had written that 'Professor Dewey seems to view such abstractionism in science as a defect—something unnecessary—but always regrettable.' Mr. Dewey replied: 'I fear that on occasion I may so have written as to give this impression. I am glad therefore to have the opportunity of saying that this is not my actual position. Abstraction is the heart of thought; there is no other way . . . to control and enrich concrete experience except through an intermediate flight of thought with conceptions, relata, abstractions . . . I wish to agree also with Mr. Lewis that the need of the social sciences at present is precisely such abstractions as will get their unwieldy elephants into box-cars that will move on rails arrived at by other abstractions. What is to be regretted is, to my mind, the tendency of many inquirers in the field of human affairs to be over-awed by the abstractions of the physical sciences and hence to fail to develop the conceptions or abstractions appropriate to their own subject-matter.'"

   c. If he had made it earlier I should also have looked to Mr. Dewey's address before the Progressive Education Association, November 13, 1936, in which he said, according to the New York *Herald-Tribune*, "Even social studies suffer greatly from that dead hand of worship of information that still grips the schools."

   d. In the second of his articles in THE SOCIAL FRONTIER Mr. Dewey refers to Plato, Aristotle, and Aquinas and their work as significant, genuine, profound, etc. He says: "Higher learning can become intellectually vital only by coming to that close grip with our contemporary science and contemporary social affairs which Plato, Aristotle and St. Thomas exemplify in their respective ways."

If we are to perform in our own day the work that Plato, Aristotle, and Aquinas performed in theirs, should we not know what they did and how they did it? My position as to the significance of these writers is precisely that (if I understand it) of Mr. Dewey. What they did was to restudy,

Reprinted from the *Social Frontier* 3, no. 23 (1937).

rework, and revitalize the intellectual tradition they inherited for the purpose of understanding the contemporary world. We must do the same.

2. *"President Hutchins' contempt for science as merely empirical . . . complete neglect of the place of the natural sciences in his educational scheme. . . ."*

   a. The faculty of natural science is one-third of the university I propose in *The Higher Learning in America*, Chapter IV.
   b. At least one-third of the great books of the western world proposed as the basis of general education in Chapter III are in the natural sciences. Mathematics and logic, two disciplines put forth as central in general education in Chapter III, are important to the understanding of natural science and intimately related to it.
   c. Chapter II criticizes engineering schools for their remoteness from departments of natural science and congratulates the newer medical schools on their close association with them.
   d. "I yield to no one in my admiration for and belief in the accumulation of data, the collection of facts, and the advance of the empirical sciences," p. 89.
   e. pp. 89–94 seem to me to make clear that I am arguing against a misconception of natural science, namely that it is merely collections of data, not against natural science as it actually is.

3. *"The remedy [proposed by Mr. Hutchins] is to be found in the greatest possible aloofness of higher learning from contemporary social life. This conception is explicitly seen in the constant divorce set up between intellect and 'experience.'*
   It is conceivable that educational reconstruction cannot be accomplished without a social reconstruction in which higher education has a part to play."

   a. "I agree, of course, that any plan of general education must be such as to educate the student for intelligent action." *The Higher Learning in America*, p. 67.
   b. "I know, of course, that thinking cannot proceed divorced from the facts and from experience." *Ibid*, p. 90.
   c. "We may say in behalf of the Marxists that they at least realize that there is no advance in the speculative realm which does not have practical consequences, and no change in the practical realm which need not be speculatively analyzed." *Ibid*, p. 91.
   d. "If we can secure a real university in this country and a real program of general education upon which its work can rest, it may be that the character of our civilization may slowly change. It may be that we can outgrow the love of money, that we can get a saner conception of democracy, and that we can even understand the purposes of education. It may be that we can abandon our false notions of progress and utility and that we can come to prefer intelligible organization to the chaos that we mistake for liberty. It is because these things may be that education is important. Upon education our country must pin its hopes of true progress, which involves scientific and technological advance, but under the direction of reason; of true prosperity, which includes external goods but does not overlook those of the soul; and of true liberty, which can exist only in society, and in a society rationally ordered." *Ibid*, pp. 118–119.
   e. One-third of the university I propose (*Ibid*, Chapter IV) is the faculty of social science. What does Mr. Dewey think that faculty will study?
   f. At least one-third of the books proposed for study in general education (*Ibid*, Chapter III) are in the social sciences and history. The discussion of contemporary problems would of course be an integral part of the discussion of these books.
   g. If I am a follower of Aristotle and Aquinas, I must be in Mr. Dewey's view a very poor one: "Lack of experience diminishes our power of taking a comprehensive view of the admitted facts. Hence those who dwell in intimate association with nature and its phenomena grow more and more able to formulate, as the foundation of their theories, principles such as to admit of a wide and coherent development; while those whom devotion to abstract

discussions has rendered unobservant of the facts are too ready to dogmatize on the basis of a few observations." Aristotle, *De Generatione et Corruptione*, 1, 2, 316a 5–12.

"The truth in practical matters is discerned from the facts of life." Aristotle, *Ethics*, 1179a.

"Knowledge in natural science must be terminated at sense in order that we may judge concerning natural things in the manner according to which sense demonstrates them . . . and he who neglects sense in natural questions falls into error." Aquinas, *De Trinitate Boetii*, Q. 6, Art. 2.

"For the human intellect is measured by things, so that a human concept is not true by reason of itself, but by reason of its being consonant with things, since *an opinion is true or false according as it answers to the reality*." Aquinas, *Summa Theologica*. Part I of part II, Q. 93, Art. 1, Reply Obj. 3.

4. *"Fixed and eternal authoritative principles [are regarded by Mr. Hutchins] as truths that are not to be questioned. . . . But any scheme based on the existence of ultimate first principles, with their dependent hierarchy of subsidiary principles, does not escape authoritarianism by calling the principles 'truths.' I would not intimate that the author has any sympathy with fascism. But basically his idea. . . is akin to the distrust of freedom and the consequent appeal to some fixed authority that is now overrunning the world. There is implicit in every assertion of fixed and eternal first truths the necessity for some human authority to decide . . . just what these truths are and how they shall be taught. This problem is conveniently ignored. . . ."*

   a. The words "fixed" and "eternal" are Mr. Dewey's; I do not apply them to principles or truths in my book.
   b. There is no suggestion anywhere in the book that principles are not to be questioned. On the contrary, "Research in the sense of the development, elaboration, and refinement of principles together with the collection and use of empirical materials to aid in these processes is one of the highest activities of a university and one in which all its professors should be engaged." *The Higher Learning in America*, p. 90.
   c. "I am not here arguing for any specific theological or metaphysical system. I am insisting that consciously or unconsciously we are always trying to get one. I suggest that we shall get a better one if we recognize explicitly the need for one and try to get the most rational one we can. We are, as a matter of fact, living today by the haphazard, accidental, shifting shreds of a theology and metaphysics to which we cling because we must cling to something." *Ibid*, p. 105.
   d. Today the faculties decide what the curriculum shall be. These human authorities would continue to do so.
   e. Is Mr. Dewey saying that there should not be a faculty of metaphysics? If so, is it because there is no such thing as metaphysics or because there are no metaphysicians? Would a university which had a faculty of philosophy be more or less authoritarian than one which had not and in which only the natural and social sciences were studied and taught?
   f. Mr. Dewey's dexterous intimation that I am a fascist in result if not in intention (made more dexterous by his remark that he is making no such intimation) suggests the desirability of the educational reforms I have proposed. A graduate of my hypothetical university writing for his fellow-alumni would know that such observations were rhetoric and that they would be received as such. As a matter of fact fascism is a consequence of the absence of philosophy. It is possible only in the context of the disorganization of analysis and the disruption of the intellectual tradition and intellectual discipline through the pressure of immediate practical concerns.

In *Reconstruction in Philosophy*, p. 24, Mr. Dewey says, "Common frankness requires that it be stated that this account of the origin of philosophies claiming to deal with absolute Being in a systematic way has been given with malice prepense. It seems to me that this genetic method of approach is a more effective way of undermining this type of philosophic theorizing than any attempt at logical refutation could be."

One effect of the education I propose might be that a philosopher who had received it would be willing to consider arguments. He would not assume that his appeal must be to the prejudices of his audience.

Mr. Dewey has suggested that only a defective education can account for some of my views. I am moved to inquire whether the explanation of some of his may not be that he thinks he is still fighting nineteenth-century German philosophy.

ROBERT M. HUTCHINS

A Canon of Democratic Intent: Reinterpreting the Roots of the Great Books Movement

K.C. Reynolds

This article investigates the earliest roots of the American "Great Books" movement by examining the intersecting lives and aims of individuals who were influential in grouping western classical texts in curriculums for adult education, self study, and undergraduate degree programs. It concludes that the educators involved in book listing and classical text programs had motivations far different from the building of an authoritative canon. In fact, the most persistent of them (e.g., Scott Buchanan, Richard Erskine, Stringfellow Barr, Mortimer Adler) were determined to democratize liberal education by providing emblems of the elite to college students from varying socio-economic circumstances and to workers seeking adult continuing education.

Lists of books, especially those emphasizing the "great" or ancient classic texts of Western culture, have been argued, published, maligned, recommended, and taught for centuries in Europe and the United States. Motivations for book listing can be located in a grab bag of intentions, including: education for the future cultural elite; demonstration of a literary and/or cultural tradition; organization of liberal arts learning; curricular convenience concerning texts and teachers; and democratization in education.

Clearly, the last of the above concepts is not what canon phobics of radical postmodern persuasions have in mind when they describe the "great books" as narrowly authoritative in content and politically incorrect in intention—a shifting but unidirectional canon of texts located in western European, white male traditionalism and replete with messages that support the politics of oppression. Classroom emphasis on these texts, typically beginning with Greek and Roman classical thought and moving on through a variety of important Western literature, is perceived as insensitive to the cultural diversity necessary for complete and meaningful learning. More valuable literature is viewed as writings that allow for positioning individual experience in the context of contemporary socio-political issues, rather than centuries-old texts that seek to illuminate universal conditions and themes. In these present terms, any organized curricular endeavor related to the classic literature of Western culture seems archaic, elitist, and epistemologically narrow at best; purposefully hegemonic at worst.[1]

Early twentieth century proponents of the great books of western literature—including educators John Erskine, Alexander Meiklejohn, Scott Buchanan, Mark Van Doren, Stringfellow Barr, Richard McKeon, Robert Maynard Hutchins, and Mortimer Adler—would be surprised by the stridency of these later interpretations. There is ample evidence that while devising and sometimes implementing curriculums based on lists of great books, they also sought to democratize education by increasing access to elements once reserved for the high brow few—albeit a seemingly anomalous end to be garnered from apparently elitist means. Not only would the realm of "haves" be expanded in terms of who was conversant with important literature, but also liberal education itself might become increasingly appealing and available across the socio-economic classes.

Reprinted from *History of Higher Education Annual* 22 (2002).

227

Investigation into early motivations at the root of the twentieth century American great books activities suggests intentions initially aimed at intellectual coherence and wide appeal in an educational program that could be foundational for all higher education students and all further areas of study, including continuing adult education. To achieve that coherence, the early canonists looked to the liberal arts; and to accomplish a liberal arts education, they looked to a set of books. Reading from important texts was viewed as an appropriate and accessible method both to promote learning in the wide-ranging subject matter of liberal education and to spark conversation that crossed disciplinary interests and class consciousness.

A historical examination of the roots of the great books movement quickly veers away from the notion that classical text promoters harbored a nefarious desire to share truths among elite gate keepers—a concept that early canonists themselves sometimes mistakenly fueled in debates that started at the point of the instruments (the books), rather than the intents, of liberal education.[2] Nor were the early canon loaders as inflexible about their ammunition as might be gathered from the suggestion by Lawrence W. Levine that the "inclusion of 'modern' writers from Shakespeare to Walt Whitman and Herman Melville came only after prolonged battles as intense and divisive as those that rage today."[3] In fact, reading lists of classical texts evolved with great regularity—generally in the direction of inclusion of more contemporary sources. "I'm not stuck on the classics at all," insisted Scott Buchanan some years after he devised and implemented the great books curriculum at St. John's College. " . . . I was immediately embarrassed when we got to be exclusively connected with the classics and the classical tradition."[4] Buchanan explained that he viewed the classic texts only as "scaffolding" to support an initial approach to liberal education, but not as the permanent structure of that education.[5]

The conundrum and inherent suspicion engendered by the idea of popular access to the distinguishing elements of elite culture is well known in American higher education. A 1922 editorial in the *New Republic* noted that the American college had opened to the masses by abandoning the aristocratic ideals reflected in the classical curriculum, but immediately found it could best attract the interest of its new middle-class students by retaining those ideals in its ivory tower reputation. "The college became one of those democratic institutions whose function seemed to be to give exclusiveness to the masses."[6]

The academy was not alone in its preference for both mass consumption and elite consumables. Caroline Winterer, noting that the general American embrace of classicism inspired by Greek and Roman antiquity was well suited to a late nineteenth century impulse for things both superior and democratic, observed, "In an expanding, commercial economy the middle classes through the acquisition of classical objects could simultaneously discredit the idea of inherited aristocracy while acquiring by purchase its stamp of authoritative nobility."[7] Industrialization and a swelling middle class coincided with similar occurrences in the arts, the information media, and elsewhere. James Sloan Allen aptly observed in early twentieth century high brows a group who "saw themselves joined in combat against cultural disintegration, dehumanization, and bad taste and who often found themselves deploying in battle the techniques of consumer commerce."[8]

This study of the roots of American great books education demonstrates that efforts to resolve the tension between two seemingly disparate notions (high culture curriculum and democratic access), as well as attempts to reconcile practical realities of individual and institutional contexts, resulted in a concept of great books that developed in two intertwined strands—undergraduate liberal arts curriculum and adult outreach education. These strands represented attempts to bring liberal education to youths and adults of many social and economic classes, in essence to democratize a type of learning that had been perceived as accessible only to the intellectually elite.

Key proponents of the great books movement, determined to prompt liberal arts alternatives to the late nineteenth century enthusiasm for professional higher education and research universities, undertook endeavors in both strands as they wrote about books and book lists, developed curricula for community education, shaped college programs, and founded institutions. Although these efforts relied heavily on reading texts that represented Western thought and literary traditions, they varied in both content and delivery as they became tempered by compromise, workable practice, and personal preferences. The stubborn dualisms of canon controversies soften in light of these early aims that sought the spread of liberal a cultured few, thus supporting the notion that universalism does not always align with conservative political thought, just as contextualism does not always align with liberal political thought.[9]

Antecedents in Early Practice

The earliest American practice in using texts of Western intellectual tradition toward liberal education was, simply, college education.[10] The undergraduate curriculum, emphasizing classical Greek and Roman works, quickly became the primary site for required reading in the Western tradition. For at least two centuries after the founding of Harvard, colleges were reluctant to deviate from the program defended in an 1858 student editorial in the literary journal of Erskine College in South Carolina: "The main object of an education is the training of the mind to think. As a means to this end, the ancient classics and the mathematics have been universally adopted. . . . We believe all praise due to these. By means of the classics, we are instructed in the peculiar structure of languages acknowledged to be the nearest perfection of any known language. We can thus hold converse with the mighty dead. . . ." Perhaps presaging canon debates to come, Henry Adams graduated from Harvard the year the Erskine editorial appeared and decided he had "wasted" time in classical studies that "taught little, and that little ill. . . . The student got nothing from ancient languages."[11]

The classical curriculum conveniently fit both the ends and means of the eighteenth and nineteenth century small colleges for boys that would later become Ivy League institutions and public research universities. The major books could be found in the upper crust homes that supplied the students, and they were available in their original Latin and Greek. Thus, the ancient classics could teach the discipline of acquiring languages (or at least words) and the precision of pondering precise grammatical nuances. They also could offer some European history and philosophy and provide the basis for disputations and debates necessary for the oratorical training of future civic leaders and clergy.

By the close of the nineteenth century, the liberal culture imparted by the Western literary icons was touted by classicists as a response to runaway enthusiasm for a curriculum aimed at careerism and financial gain. Classicists urged alternatives to utilitarian higher education by inferring that "classical study bestowed something higher than vocational or exclusively scientific preparation: it offered *culture*."[12]

However, even the most die-hard classicists found they needed to soften their stance, and strict adherence to ancient Greek and Roman classics adjusted to accommodate the humanities in general and historicism in particular. Winterer notes that the classical Western texts expanded to include a "modern literary canon" that had "taken shape out of this sense that literature properly historicized had cultivating powers. . . . This new canon hinged on the assumption not only that classical antiquity and the present were part of a continuous narrative, but that it behooved students to know such a narrative in order to be considered liberally educated."[13] By the late nineteenth century, American supporters of a Western canon recognized the need to reflect shifts in general social and intellectual preferences. The ancient classics were joined by works from later European literary figures: Chaucer, Rousseau, Milton, Moliere, and others. Eventually, they would expand to include social, economic, and philosophical thought by authors such as Jeremy Bentham, Karl Marx, John Stuart Mill, and Friedrich Nietzsche.

Although the classic texts soon fought an uphill battle to retain a toehold in the American college curriculum amidst enthusiasm for professional and vocational training, electives, and research, liberal culture aspirations were kept alive into the early twentieth century at resolute outposts like Williams and Amherst and reinvigorated in new forms such as the Swarthmore honors program. Efforts to retain Greek and Latin requirements or to teach a core of traditional liberal arts courses were more locally symbolic than widely influential. Their proponents were not so much in "revolt against mass education," as David O. Levine has suggested, as in revolt against curricular specialization and professionalization.[14] Swarthmore president Frank Aydelotte, still awash with the warm glow of his Rhodes Scholarship experience at Oxford, was happy to bring exclusive honors learning to middle-class scholarship students, as long as their interest and ability in learning merited the privilege. Alexander Meiklejohn, as president of Amherst and founder of the Experimental College at the University of Wisconsin, distinguished among students only on the basis of their immediate desires to pursue foundational intelligence versus their desires for career training.[15]

Other American educators of the late nineteenth and early twentieth centuries embraced the idea of heralding good reading and good books less for reasons concerning the college curriculum than for reasons of organizing for the general public the fruits of a swelling publishing industry. In this regard, they sewed seeds for the second strand of the great books movement, adult outreach education. Noah Porter led the way with advice to the reading public in his 1871 volume, *Books and Reading: Or What Books Shall I Read and How Shall I Read Them*. Charles W. Eliot selected a fifty-volume, "five foot shelf," published in a variety of cover colors by P.F. Collier and Son and mass marketed to the working class with the lofty label *The Harvard Classics*. With works from Homer and Cicero to Charles Darwin and Ben Johnson, the *Classics* attempted to package a self-taught liberal education that could be accomplished, according to the publisher's publicity, by devoting fifteen minutes each day to the task. The objective, according to Eliot, was to provide the literature "essential to the twentieth century idea of a cultivated man . . . ," because it introduced him to a "prodigious store of recorded discoveries, experiences, and reflections which humanity in its intermittent and irregular progress from barbarism to civilization has acquired and laid up."[16] Eliot's cousin, literary critic and Harvard professor Charles Eliot Norton, joined the impulse to select appropriate reading material by editing a series of "selected portions of the best literature" for children, published as *The Heart of Oaks Books*.[17] During a time when the American college classroom increased its attention toward career preparation, educators turned to the American home as the venue for foundational liberal education among young and old. There, they found middlebrow masses eager for the promise of the trappings, while not the reality, of high culture.

Book lists and reading advice for adults also found audiences in Europe. British writer and banker Sir John Lubbock published an essay entitled "The Choice of Books" in his 1896 general volume of life advise, *The Pleasures of Life*.[18] The pamphlet he developed soon after, titled *The One Hundred Best Books* and distributed by George Routledge and Sons, is generally recognized as the taproot for early American academic notions about the study of classic western texts. Lubbock's list was laden with ancient Greek and Roman works, as well as those of celebrated British authors like Swift, Shakespeare, Milton, Carlyle, and Tennyson. The Bible and the Koran also appeared. Motivated to spread educational advantages generally reserved for the upper classes to others who might benefit, Lubbock intended his list for the intellectual experience of working adults, especially those who participated in the mechanics institutes that had popularized the idea of continuing education groups for like-minded citizens.[19]

The efforts to commercialize classical texts with published lists and packaged sets had numerous critics who saw only vulgarity in alternatives to exclusivity. According to a 1909 editorial in *The Nation*, for example, the notion that the *Harvard Classics* could "transform anybody into a man of liberal education, is to turn the whole idea of our colleges into ridicule; and a final touch of grotesqueness is added when the five-foot shelf, instead of being vaguely indicated or left to the imagination, is expressly prescribed. . . ."[20] The "great books," like the elite among American colleges and universities, quickly found themselves walking a thin line between exclusivity and commercialism. Outcries that continued throughout the twentieth century were perhaps best summarized by Dwight Macdonald who named two of the most visible champions of great books when he charged, "It is one thing to bring High Culture to a wider audience without change; and another to 'popularize' it by sales talk in the manner of Clifton Fadiman or Mortimer J. Adler."[21]

Organizing the Two Strands: Early College and Community Outreach Programs

Columbia University literature professor and poet John Erskine, a skilled musician who eventually became president of Julliard School of Music, also joined the ranks of book advising educators with his 1928 volume *The Delight of Great Books*. However, unlike Eliot, Norton, and Lubbock, Erskine became one of a handful of educators whose taste for classic literature soon led them back to the undergraduate curriculum. As the first to fully test the impact of a Western classics curriculum in a twentieth century undergraduate classroom, Erskine in essence broke trail for those after him who would join the struggle to position great books at the intersection of liberal education content and educational access intentions.[22]

Before serving in France as an Army educator during World War I, Erskine had proposed to his Columbia University colleagues a plan for a two-year course of undergraduate study for all juniors and seniors, based on seventy-five volumes of great western literature—a semester each for ancient Greeks and ancient Romans, followed by two semesters to study works of European literature, history, and philosophy. Erskine drew from his own teaching experiences in his "desire to make up for the lack of acquaintance with the best literature that he noticed among the undergraduates in his classes. In addition, he thought that such a course would be useful the to students later on in life. . . ."[23] As innovative in pedagogy as in content, the plan called for discussion groups based on Socratic dialogue, so that students "having read the books . . . could form their opinions at once in a free-for-all discussion."[24] Erskine's colleagues in the Columbia English department, collectively moving toward curricular specialization at the time, turned down the idea in 1916. In 1919, when he returned from France and re-introduced a similar plan, Erskine found only grudging acceptance among faculty who "tried to protect the students—and themselves—from it by decreeing that my course should be open only to the specially qualified, who would take it as an extra, or as they like to say, as 'honors.'"[25] Erskine's proposal for a major program accessible to any student desiring it had effectively become minimal and meritorious. Unfortunately, reserving the texts for honors students seemed to support the general idea that great books were an elite notion. Nevertheless, although relegated to an elective seminar labeled "General Honors," the course attracted students and faculty from various disciplines for nine years, after which it was suspended for two years and then reconstituted in 1931 as "Colloquium on Important Books."

Erskine's initial proposed list of books had swelled to include 133 authors, but canon formation soon intersected with administrative reality; and the list was cut by more than half to accommodate the idea of reading a book a week for two academic years (see Appendix A).[26] Among the students whose continuing enthusiasm helped the honors program earn its reputation for keeping general education alive at Columbia and elsewhere were Jacques Barzun, Clifton Fadiman, Lionel Trilling, Mortimer Adler, Leon Keyserling, Henry Morton Robinson, Joseph Mankiewicz, and Whittaker Chambers. Perhaps the most important seed sewn by Erskine's honors course, however, occurred in the adult outreach strand by taking classic texts to the general community—utilizing what appeared to be a curriculum for and about high-culture, white males as the basis for stimulating education among newly arrived immigrants of mixed genders and ethnic backgrounds. Within five years of its inception as an honors class at Columbia, Erskine's idea became the model for a public reading and discussion program that occurred at Cooper Union and in the New York City public library system. The "great books" movement apparently was destined to gather into various waves that, depending on the locale and the individuals involved, could break on shore as popular adult education or college curriculum. A lifelong proponent of the movement and the architect of its enduring presence at St. John's College, Scott Buchanan saw both possibilities when he noted that the study of the classics of Western civilization seemed both "a sound basis for third-and fourth-year college work" and "indeed, for wise living."[27]

Buchanan began to place significant Western literature in the hands and minds of the adult citizenry of New York City when he became assistant director of the People's Institute, a community outreach program of lectures and seminars sponsored by Cooper Union. However, his inspiration came as much from his early mentor, Alexander Meiklejohn, as from John Erskine whose honors course seeded the idea.

Born in Washington and raised in Vermont and Massachusetts, Buchanan entered Amherst College in 1912, the year Alexander Meiklejohn left his professorship at Brown to assume the Amherst presidency.[28] Bringing to the college the somewhat disturbing quality of what Buchanan later recognized as a "very Socratic administration," Meiklejohn questioned students and faculty continually about why things were done as they were, searching for a way out of what he noted in his inaugural speech as the disarray in American colleges. Buchanan later noted, "This [questioning] was very catching. Students began doing it too. . . . Amherst was a very dialectical college. Just ordinary conversations took on a new quality and we were going after each other intellectually."[29]

Buchanan, who graduated with a triple major in Greek, French, and mathematics, participated in conversations and informal seminars with Meiklejohn, although he did not register for any classes with him. He credited those seminars, including a series on Kant with several young faculty members, with his idea that difficult subject matter could best be understood by groups that took charge of their own learning. "We'd get into the most complicated arguments and he [Meiklejohn] was really a Socratic character on those occasions. He was never bringing doctrine to us at all. This was all our own stuff."[30]

Buchanan also undoubtedly resonated well with Meiklejohn's penchant for enthusiastic dreaming and experimentation toward a unified and unifying liberal arts education that could prepare students for "intelligence . . . being able to see, in any set of circumstances, the best response which a human being can make to those circumstances."[31] At Amherst, where he railed against electives and specialized professional training, Meiklejohn met resistance from both faculty and trustees to his innovative ideas for an integrated liberal arts curriculum that would unite intellectual excellence and democracy in a community that included students of all races and religions.[32] Perhaps his most important contribution during his beleaguered eleven-year presidency was to involve Amherst in one of the country's first adult workers' education programs, gathering mill workers from nearby Holyoke, Massachusetts, for classes in the rudiments of reading, writing, history, and economics. Later, he founded the Experimental College, an undergraduate two-year liberal arts program within the University of Wisconsin. A lively, but controversial, residential learning community, with academic fare largely organized and united by required reading of ancient and modern classics, the Experimental College survived only from 1927 to 1933.[33]

During his stay at Oxford as a Rhodes Scholar, Buchanan wrote to his mentor and fellow experimenter, Meiklejohn, about his own fledgling plan for a new and distinctive liberal arts institution—a preparatory academy for future Amherst students that he characterized as "a much worthwhile experiment for Amherst and for the general educational needs of the country." Drawing from his Oxford experiences, he proposed a system of tutors and fellows; and drawing on aspirations about his own future, he proposed that administration be placed in the hands of several young Amherst alumni.[34] The proposal never moved beyond dreaming, and Buchanan soon came home to marry and to be funded by his new father-in-law in pursuit of a Harvard Ph.D. However, Meiklejohn's young student continued to seek opportunities for educational experimentation. That experimentation, while holding fast to the Western canon as a unified starting point, would more importantly reflect two other Meiklejohn emphases: 1) a commitment to libertarian freedoms and obligations; and 2) the use of Socratic teaching methods that Stringfellow Barr characterized in both Meiklejohn and Buchanan as the ability to ask "gentle, courteous questions that went off in one's mind like time bombs and caused a major illumination when they exploded."[35]

Buchanan received his Ph.D. at Harvard in 1925, after submitting a dissertation that constituted a philosophical inquiry into imaginative and scientific possibility and was published two years later by Kegan Paul as *Possibility*. In a circumstance that would later seem highly ironic, John Dewey reviewed the book for *The Nation* and found it "a significant intellectual achievement."[36] In 1925, Buchanan also became the assistant director of the People's Institute, a New York City educational outreach endeavor of Cooper Union that had been founded by Columbia University professor Charles Sprague Smith in 1895. Smith had, Buchanan later recalled, "wanted the immigrants of the lower East Side to meet the intellectuals of the Upper West Side, to make the 'melting pot' boil."[37] He initiated his vision by use of an article that Peter Cooper had inserted into the charter of Cooper Union calling for a balance of mechanical arts training with understanding of social and political ethics. This, as interpreted by Smith, was done with series of lectures that took place in the Cooper Union Great

Hall, eventually under the direction of former journalist and expert orator Everett Dean Martin. Buchanan, who was not at all surprised that Martin could draw crowds of over 1,000, often mostly Jewish immigrants but also college students, noted:

> The lectures, literary and academic as they might be in origin, took account of events here and abroad, so that by the time of World War I the Great Hall not only boiled; it often exploded verbally, on occasion violently, with issues of the times. It was a true forum. In 1925 there was an established schedule of three lectures a week: on Sunday evenings lectures on politics and morals, on Tuesday evenings lectures on natural and social science, and on Friday evenings a series of lectures by Everett Dean Martin. . . . Certain [of Martin's] lectures each year celebrated the same heroes, Socrates, Cicero, Rousseau, Tom Paine, and Jefferson. . . .
>
> Certain members of the audience were noticeable as underprivileged slum dwellers who found a free lecture a physically and socially warm place to take a nap. But the great body of the audience was first- or second-generation immigrants whose migration to this country had uprooted them from intellectual and educational traditions that they had come to fear they would lose in America . . . . There were also internal migrants, remnants of native American intellectual and political movements who spent their summers in harvesting on the Great Plains or in lumber camps and rode the rods back to New York for the winter. . . . They knew Jack London. . . . These two groups, the East siders and the Wobblies, as we used to call them, were, with the graduate students from local universities, probably the best read audience in America.[38]

The formative nature of the experience on Buchanan's personal philosophy of education was later explained by Stringfellow Barr as the effect of seeing "hungry adults of every class, of every age, of many races, of both sexes, who, like Aristotle's man, desired to know. Buchanan never forgot the uncollegiate drive for understanding at Cooper Union and the contrast between this and a certain coziness that well-endowed campuses readily acquire."[39]

Buchanan also began to prepare lectures he himself would deliver in the Great Hall, hoping to fill gaps he saw in the knowledge of the adult students. The two missing areas were mathematics and poetry; and as Buchanan prepared his lectures, they became more and more intertwined in their ability to illuminate one another. Buchanan was especially interested in exploring the relationship of their symbolic elements: words, in the case of poetry; ratios, in the case of mathematics. Eventually, Columbia philosophy professor Richard McKeon would suggest that by delving into these two, Buchanan was actually rediscovering and connecting the trivium (grammar, rhetoric, logic) and quadrivium (arithmetic, geometry, music, astronomy) of the seven liberal arts. With excellent reception and feedback, Buchanan expanded on the topics of these lectures for his 1929 book *Poetry and Mathematics*.[40]

When the Carnegie Corporation, interested in new forms of adult education, funded the People's Institute to set up additional lectures and seminars for smaller group instruction in extension locations, Buchanan was put in charge of taking this new program to the Manhattan Trade School, the Muhlenburg Branch of the public library system, and other meeting facilities throughout the city. He needed to develop a curriculum that would serve smaller, discussion-oriented groups with instruction that might complement the large lectures. Informally, discussion groups already regularly formed after the lectures to review and debate in a social setting. Buchanan had watched several such groups meet regularly in cafes and studios to discuss topics that he recalled as including "Greek tragedy, Stoic ethics, Aristotelian, atomic, and energetic physics, Dante's Divine Comedy, Milton's Paradise Lost, Newtonian and Einsteinian space, Humian and Kantian epistemology, Hegelian and Spenglerian theories of history. Russian novels and Oriental epics. . . . the man with the latest book under his arm usually took over."[41]

When one of the Institute's regular lecturers, Columbia University psychology instructor Mortimer Adler, suggested that Erskine's General Honors course might offer a model for the People's Institute instructional outreach efforts with the smaller discussion groups, Buchanan jumped at the idea. Adler would recall, "He regarded the [Columbia] great books course as a characteristically American extension of the 'ancient greats' and 'modern greats' that, in his day at Oxford, were the main undergraduate programs. He also thought he saw in the discussion method of the seminars something both akin to and askew from the Oxford tutorial."[42] Apparently, the first use of the great books in an American adult education curriculum happened not because they were so "great," but because they had an eager supporter in Adler and they reflected an important part of Scott Buchanan's own educational experience. Their early use at the People's Institute also undoubtedly had something to do with the availability of a pool of willing instructors made up of Columbia graduate students and faculty familiar with Erskine's course. By 1927, the People's Institute courses modeled on the Columbia honors course were held in public libraries throughout the city, drawing heavily on Columbia faculty and students as instructors. Adler, McKeon, and Mark Van Doren were among the most enthusiastic, and all three would become lifelong friends and long-term associates of Buchanan and one another.[43]

Only later, after he left the People's Institute, would Buchanan connect the great books with the idea of a unified education in the liberal arts. He believed immediately that the ancient classic texts could usefully spark discussion and teach multiple subject matters, but eventually also would decide that "a great book is the product of the liberal arts; the authors are liberal artists, masters of the arts."[44]

Exhausted with the administrative pressures of carrying on a city-wide adult education effort and hoping for an opportunity to more fully pursue research interests in philosophy, Buchanan accepted an appointment to the faculty of the philosophy department at the University of Virginia in 1929, leaving the People's Institute library seminars to continue under the guidance of Mortimer Adler and others.[45] He often wondered why he went to Virginia, where he was immediately discouraged to find "The college at the University was being squeezed, exploited, and reduced to the size and functions of a secondary preparatory school for the graduate schools, which were in turn losing their professional statuses and becoming handmaidens to the going concerns of science, technology, and business. . . . It was reported that an ad hoc Honors Course for the better students had been chosen by only two and a half students per year. . . . "[46]

The Virginia Plan: A Canon Aimed at a Comprehensive Liberal Arts Education

Within only two months of his arrival at the University of Virginia, Buchanan sorely missed the bustle of New York, especially his intellectually vigorous students and colleagues. He explained to Mortimer Adler that he was already pondering his departure, noting, "Virginia represents the country, eventually enough money, official ceremonies, bad students, an interesting but slow educational change, a brutal selection from a very poor variety of social types."[47] However, Buchanan quickly managed to become somewhat of a legend for his Socratic manner in seminars; and he soon found reward in teaching adults at an extension in Richmond, using a "great books" curriculum and dialectical method. He also quickly applied for several leaves of absence: the first for the 1931–32 academic year and the next for Spring Semester, 1933.[48]

In addition to the availability of off-campus teaching to adults and long absences for funded research projects, two other bright spots appeared on the Charlottesville landscape for Buchanan. The first of these was his renewed friendship with Stringfellow Barr (nicknamed "Winkie" all his life), a history professor at the University of Virginia who had become a close friend of Buchanan's when they were both Rhodes Scholars at Oxford. Barr, originally from Louisiana with degrees from Tulane and the University of Virginia, credited Buchanan with convincing him to switch from English literature to history at Oxford, a move that led Barr to finish his A.B. with honors in 1920. Buchanan, rushing his studies to return home before his slim financial resources ran out, failed his qualifying examinations for an Oxford degree. At Virginia, Barr and Buchanan once again enjoyed long conversations about history, philosophy, and the state of the liberal arts and higher education. Like Buchanan, Barr had studied Greek and Latin and had managed to read some of the ancient classics in their original languages.

The second event of note for Buchanan at Charlottesville was the appointment of both he and Barr to the University Committee on Honors Courses, along with four other faculty members. The committee was charged by president Edwin A. Alderman to review and recommend actions concerning honors courses, because, as Alderman remarked, "I think the University of Virginia should do more than it does now for the more favored college student." Chaired by Robert K. Gooch, also a former Rhodes Scholar, the committee quickly determined that the decline of the liberal arts was responsible for the "intellectual bankruptcy" of a typical undergraduate college education.[49] However, their deliberations about improving the situation for honors students faltered when Buchanan suggested the ancient classics as a remedy. Buchanan fumed to his friend Mortimer Adler that "the committee members are all wet except Winkie [Barr]. . . . The trouble is as usual that none of these people has read the books in my scheme, and any discussion becomes a meeting in the course when no one has read his lesson. One then discusses faculty opinion and the probability of approval."[50]

However, Buchanan found he could move the committee in his direction with the assistance of the more sanguine and patient Barr. Buchanan had already convinced Barr to incorporate in his classes some discussions of the historical works of Herodotus, Thucydides, and Plutarch; and Barr, who had earlier read ancient classics with no particular appreciation, eventually became an enthusiastic convert under his friend's tutelage when he realized "the extraordinary effects they had" on his students. Later, he would recall that after initial resistance, he realized, "Scott was right. . . . Something happened to the discussion that I had never seen happen before. These authors got under their hides." Barr then helped Buchanan guide their fellow committee members toward agreement on a report highly reminiscent of the major educational influences on Buchanan to date: Alexander Meiklejohn, Oxford, and the People's Institute. Like Meiklejohn's experimental college within the University of Wisconsin, a "college within the college" plan was proposed as the first two years for Virginia honors students. Small seminars and tutors echoed the Oxford system; and from the People's Institute, via Columbia's honors course, came the great books.[51]

The nature of the proposed list of books, however, deviated from the Lubbock and Erskine incarnations in a direction that reflected Buchanan's sense of missing educational elements in science and mathematics. Gone was Lubbock's emphasis on ancient philosophers mixed with British literary traditions. Greatly renovated was Columbia's balance of literature, political economy, governance, and philosophy. The Virginia proposal was based on the division of the seven liberal arts—language and literature of the trivium and science and mathematics of the quadrivium. The aim was liberal education in pursuit of the Aristotelian intellectual virtues of art, practical wisdom, scientific knowledge, intuitive reason, and philosophical wisdom. The means, described in an appendix to the committee report, were to be "the best subject matter that is at present available for passing on the tradition [of the liberal arts]. These materials have been found in their highest form in the literary and scientific classics of Europe. They are crystallization of the experience of the race, reminiscent of the past; clarifying for any present time. They project the unchanging problems of the future. They provide eminently formative studies."[52]

Where the People's Institute list of seventy-six books had been categorized into texts of "classic, medieval and Renaissance thought" and those of "modern thought," the Virginia list followed the liberal arts distinction by grouping texts in mathematics and science and in language and literature. Each area was further subdivided into expository reading, exemplary models, and materials for analysis and practice.[53]

The proposal suggested that honors students should spend their first two years in liberal arts study through the readings, seminars, formal lectures, tutorials, and laboratories. During that time they were also expected to master calculus and one ancient and one modern foreign language. During their junior and senior years, the students would select their own courses and work with tutors on special projects. Although their charge concerned only the most gifted students at the University of Virginia, the committee did manage to dip somewhat into the issue of wider access to the fruits of their deliberations. Their report noted that since the issues and needs concerning honors students were symptomatic of teaching and learning problems affecting all students, their recommendations should eventually be considered for a wider audience of all undergraduates.[54]

Perhaps predictably, the proposal quickly moved from committee to shelf at University of Virginia, although copies also were tucked into personal files for use as models in later experiments. Barr summarized the implementation vacuum succinctly: "The president of the University [then John L. Newcomb] pleaded lack of funds, and nothing happened."[55]

In fact, something had happened. The idea of the "great books" had moved beyond the notion of a long list of Western classics that would give honors students and interested adults good discussion while signifying good education. For the first time, a list of books and the various subsidiary requirements for mastering them were aimed at a balanced education in the liberal arts, inclusive of mathematics and science, that could undergird any later pre-professional and professional studies.[56] Buchanan friend and philosopher Richard McKeon would later eloquently characterize this integrative frame work as "liberating arts and regulating disciplines to guide men in the specification and in the use of the possibilities of imagination and the ideas of wisdom."[57] Perhaps defensively or perhaps to net additional supporters among Virginia traditionalists, the committee also added the "cultural inheritance" rationale for a goal of "comprehension of the main elements of Occidental thought."[58]

The University of Chicago: Big Ideals and Small Experiments

While Buchanan was struggling to recruit interest in the idea of the great books at the University of Virginia, Mortimer Adler was battling in a similar vein at the University of Chicago. There, with an eager new president willing to launch skirmishes on faculty turf, the classic texts met with at least some experimentation and publicity. However, the concept never played a key role in either of the two aims sought by president Robert Maynard Hutchins: bringing coherence to a fragmented and compartmentalized undergraduate curriculum or supporting the preparation of high school graduates whose education left them unprepared for college work.

Hutchins first heard about Adler and some of his philosophical work through mutual acquaintances, as well as through Adler's book, *Dialectic*, which Hutchins read when he was acting dean of Yale Law School. They met in 1927 to probe a possible mutual interest in law of evidence and quickly seeded an unlikely lifetime friendship between the elegant and charming Hutchins and the scrappy and outspoken Adler.[59] When Hutchins was appointed president of the University of Chicago in 1929, Adler followed immediately and, with sorely limited knowledge of academic appointment processes, began interesting his old New York pals Scott Buchanan and Richard McKeon in joining him. A year after his arrival, Adler assured McKeon, "It is quite clear Scott will be here next year and equally clear that you will, even if Bob [Hutchins] has to annihilate the Department of Philosophy to do it."[60]

Although Hutchins won a small initial victory in pushing Adler's appointment on the Chicago philosophy department, he would pay a high price in ill will and distrust from the faculty that acquiesced to having a newly minted Ph.D. graduate in a discipline outside their own—psychology—join them at a salary higher than their full professors. Eventually, Adler and Hutchins were forced to retreat—Adler to an appointment in Chicago's law school, which was more friendly to the president who was their colleague, and Hutchins to his attempts to create an undergraduate college that would become renown for breaking down disciplinary boundaries and for countering the general academic drift toward devoting resources and prominence solely to research and graduate education.[61]

The plan for the academic approach to the College at the University of Chicago, referred to as the New Plan or the Chicago Plan, was already on the drawing boards when Hutchins arrived. His predecessor, president Max Mason, had directed undergraduate dean Chauncey Boucher, to develop recommendations for reform, but Mason had resigned before their approval by the faculty senate. Among them were required survey courses to replace the array of electives during students' first two years and examinations by a board of examiners to replace grades and required credit hours for movement toward degree completion. Hutchins, as immediately as his inaugural day, supported the idea of "an experimental attitude" for the University and "a curriculum intelligently adjusted to the needs of the individual."[62]

Adler, still enthused about his experiences with the great books curriculum at Columbia and the People's Institute, suggested a Western texts concept as an organizing framework for the new Chicago program of study, noting to Hutchins that juniors and seniors could then engage in a reading program similar to Alexander Meiklejohn's new college within the University of Wisconsin.[63] Although the University of Chicago soon gained notoriety for its new undergraduate curriculum, especially in terms of greater emphasis on liberal arts and de-emphasis on required class attendance and credit hours, Adler's push for great books did not result in the adoption of any particular group of texts. Rather, the use of a Western canon at the University of Chicago occurred anecdotally and sporadically in some courses and classes throughout the Hutchins years. Even without any particular master plan or general faculty acceptance, however, study of the Western classical texts managed to demonstrate their persistence in both adult and undergraduate venues at Chicago and their ability to attract individuals of wide-ranging backgrounds and abilities.

The first of these venues was an undergraduate great books course co-taught as a two-year sequence by Hutchins and Adler. It was prompted first by Adler's encouragement and then by Hutchins' realization that a teaching commitment would cement his personal desire to study Greek and Roman classics. However, since the course was restricted to twenty students, it veered far from the ideal of democracy in education. While the students were not required to attend the Socratic seminars or to even do the reading, few failed to keep up. Discussions proved invigorating as Adler and Hutchins challenged each other as well as the students, and Hutchins' presence as an instructor generated extensive publicity. With visitors from on and off campus, there was usually standing room only in the seminar room, and the course helped to continue the University's reputation for putting intellectual activity first among student pursuits. Eventually, its designation as a "general honors" course was dropped, and the course was variously designated as "Great Books," or "The History of Ideas." After more than ten years, Hutchins reported, "Thanks to the kind cooperation of the students, I have made some progress with my education."[64]

The next outcropping of the great books notion occurred when Adler and law professor Malcolm Sharp taught a group of third-year pre-law students a year-long course in grammar, rhetoric, and logic using twenty books from the Columbia honors list. Among the students in the class were future University of Chicago law professors Edward H. Levi and Harry Kalven. In addition, Hutchins and Adler introduced a two-year great books seminar to juniors and seniors at University High School in 1934 as part of a plan to combine into a coherent liberal arts program the last two years of that school with the first two years of the undergraduate College. At the other end of the spectrum were several informal off-campus reading adult groups, formed by suburban alumni groups who invited Adler or Hutchins to speak and then tackled their class list of great books over a period of years. One, dubbed "the fat man's class," launched a group of noted Chicago executives into the Western canon after Hutchins took them to lunch and convinced them their educations were incomplete.[65]

In 1936 it appeared the idea of the great books might take hold in a more comprehensive form when Hutchins found funds to establish a Committee on Liberal Arts that was to study the issue of the liberal arts in the curriculum. He had long wanted to find a way to appoint Scott Buchanan to a university post, even though the philosophy department was unwilling to consider a faculty position for him; and the funding for the committee allowed the opportunity. Buchanan resigned from the University of Virginia and convinced Stringfellow Barr to join him, although Barr did so on a year-long leave of absence. He also tried unsuccessfully to convince his good friend Mark Van Doren to join the venture.[66]

Hutchins' appointments to the committee, charge to the committee, and administrative arrangements concerning the committee largely were verbal and confusing. Adler and Richard McKeon, who had come to Chicago from Columbia two years earlier and was by then Dean of Humanities, were among the University of Chicago representatives. Two other faculty members, Norman McLean and Ronald Crane, were verbally appointed, but attended no meetings. Barr and Buchanan were joined by two young research associates from Virginia. Barr pleaded with Hutchins to put the committee appointments in writing.[67] Buchanan urged him to give it an administrative home after McKeon fended off Hutchins' initial attempt to attach the group to the Division of Humanities. Four months after arriving in October, 1936, Buchanan found himself warning Hutchins of committee chaos that had "so far been occasioned, if not caused, by administrative timidity and confusion."[68]

A proposal for funding the Liberal Arts Committee stated its aim as "to achieve a common and communicable acquaintance with the European tradition for the sake of directing current educational pursuits in accordance with it."[69] Members of the committee immediately called upon the ancient classics as their source material for a study of the liberal arts, but they found they philosophically disagreed as to which classics were important and how to use them. Buchanan clung tightly to those books that had been hammered into the Virginia Plan, but Adler and McKeon were not enthusiastic about the inclusion of mathematics and the sciences. Finally, the group agreed to move on by simply discussing some works by Aristotle as "samples of subject matter and method in the application of the liberal arts." However, "the meetings ended invariably, not merely in explicit disagreement, but in passionate outrage, each at the others' distortion of the text."[70] Finally, committee members resorted to reading on their own without meeting; and it became apparent the ill-conceived committee would not last beyond its first year.

Perhaps the most important accomplishment to come from the attempted committee was three lengthy white papers by Buchanan, written as memos to Hutchins and titled "The Classics and the Liberal Arts." These marked the first time that a major proponent of great books formally clarified the aims of an education using such texts and ventured to define a "great" book. In doing so, Buchanan heartily supported the idea of the liberal arts and the great books as a means of democratic access to education, rather than a method of protective gate keeping among the intellectual elite. "I do not think this education should be aimed at merely the intellectual aristocaracy," he told Hutchins. "I doubt if there can be an American intellectual aristocracy unless the whole mass is somehow brought a little higher than it is being brought by our public education. I can think of no more effective way to accomplish this task than the general reading of the classics with as much of the liberal arts as can be recovered and made effective at present."[71]

Buchanan embraced several definitions for a "great" book, perhaps most surprisingly the simplest one, which had been offered by Mark Van Doren. "He [Van Doren] says that the great books are those that have the most readers. The numerical measure is a bit shocking, but Mark knows what he is saying. It assumes that men are rational and that if a book is read by many men, it must have the stuff that properly interests the most genuine men. It works on contemporary books as well as on ancient books. . . . " Buchanan also suggested several of his own criteria: "Great books are those that have the greatest number of possible interpretations. . . . Great books raise unanswerable questions. . . . They exercise the intuitive reason and its inevitable companion, the contemplative imagination. . . . The last intrinsic criterion is that they shall be works of fine art, as well as of liberal art."[72]

St. John's College: Socrates and Serendipity

With the Committee on the Liberal Arts adrift, the hopeful scholars who had come to Chicago from Virginia pondered their future. In an amazing coincidence of timing, the trustees of a little college quickly heading toward oblivion in Maryland also wondered about the future. In May, 1937, Scott Buchanan attended a small conference in Virginia where he renewed his acquaintance with Francis Pickens Miller, a new board member of the college in question who had been a Rhodes Scholar with Buchanan and Barr. Miller convinced Buchanan and Stringfellow Barr to meet with other trustees of St. John's College in Annapolis, Maryland, where a serious search had begun for a new president and any ideas that could turn the college around.

Barr later recounted the events that led him and Buchanan to St. John's: "When Scott came back from seeing Miller and talked to me, I said, 'For God's sake, don't talk this way. I know the place; I've been lecturing annually at the Naval Academy. That [St. John's College] is just a miserable fate.' He [Buchanan] right away knew that the fact that the college was in a frightful jam, as Miller reported, meant there was an opportunity there [for beginning a program based on great books]. He knew darned well that any college in America that was really thriving would say, 'It's an interesting idea, but we're busy.'"[73]

Eventually, the reluctant Barr consented not only to leave Chicago to attempt an untried curriculum at a failing college, but also to be named president of St. John's College, while Buchanan served as college dean. The small, all-male liberal arts school they took on boasted a worthy history, but little else. Founded in 1696 and first named King William's School, the college initially flourished as, according to its colonial charter, "a place of study of Latin, Greek, writing, and the like. . . ."[74] Three of its trustees signed the Declaration of Independence. It closed briefly during the Revolution, and reopened as St. John's College in 1784. A century later, amidst a general national embrace of professional and vocational training and graduate education, the small four-year liberal arts college began to fall victim to a changing marketplace for higher education. St. John's attempted to keep up by adopting an elective system that added courses in fairly narrow specialties and allowed students to build their own liberal arts curriculum, but the effort proved costly and failed to increase appeal to potential students.[75] The college eventually lost its regional accreditation. Enrollment, also hard hit by the Depression, dipped under 300 students in 1934 and under 250 in 1937.[76]

By the time Barr and Buchanan entered into discussions about coming to St. John's and installing a curriculum strictly tied to great books, they found the St. John's trustees willing to "just hold their noses and jump—because it was either that or close."[77] The two were appointed to their new posts only one month after Buchanan's initial discussions with Francis Miller. As president, Barr had primary responsibility for the college's financial problems and interactions with trustees, donors, and others. Buchanan concentrated on the curriculum and the students. Both also taught in the new Western texts curriculum labeled the New Program, Barr's opinion of the situation they encountered softened slightly as he came to know the place as, "shocking, decaying, crooked, in a mess, demoralized, beautiful, elegant, a civilized community. . . . A lot of the old South's rot and decay. Sort of a William Faulkner quality about it."[78]

With the New Program initially phased into practice but eventually encompassing the entire curriculum, St. John's became the singular representation of a traditional liberal arts curriculum accomplished through reading classic texts. Although Robert Maynard Hutchins' book *Higher Learning in America* had been published to considerable controversy a year earlier when it suggested a classic texts curriculum for college education, the New Program was more a product of Buchanan's work on the Virginia plan than a practice site for Hutchins' ideas.[79] The framework for the curriculum was a list of books nearly identical to the Virginia list (see Appendix B). Chronologically, the list started with works by Homer, Aeschylus, and Herodotus and concluded with works by William James, Sigmund Freud, Thorstein Veblen, and Bertrand Russell. Philosophy, history, theology, politics, economics, psychology, literature, science, and mathematics were represented by Western authors through the ages.

Barr and Buchanan were careful not to explain the texts as "the" great books, insisting in the 1937–38 catalogue that "any limited list of the classics must always remain open to revision. There is no better way of revising it than its continuous use in teaching in a college. The 'best hundred books' is a variable for collecting the values that satisfy its criteria."[80] Barr later recalled, "The public always thought we said 'the' great books or 'the' 100 great books, as if we knew just exactly. We never talked of 'the' great books. We were simple minded, but not that simple minded."[81]

Buchanan often described the book list as a work in progress, insisting "There's no magic about this."[82] However, he saw no room for evolutionary change in the key teaching methodology, the Socratic seminar. Starting with a question from a faculty leader, the seminar typically moved in the direction of student discussion and more questions. As Barr later described, "The rules of the dialectic are not unlike the rules of a game. You ask your question, get the answer and keep asking questions until you find where the argument leads. And too often it leads to a stupid remark. . . . This is a very special talent which I think we succeeded in cultivating to a rather remarkable degree at St. John's. It was our chief teaching instrument."[83] Other teaching methods included (and still continue to include) laboratory work in the sciences, lectures, and small group tutorials.

Buchanan and Barr agreed that although at the time St. John's did not attract what Barr referred to as "a very solid type of student," the studies of classic texts would still be relevant to all.[84] Buchanan, in particular, believed in the potential of all students, as Barr explained:

> Scott has an infinite faith in the human intellect and in the surprising motions of the human intellect. He wouldn't hesitate to say, "Jones is stupid"—not cruelly, just noting the fact. But if you say, "Well, then, why listen to him?" I think he would say, "Because the stupidest people sometimes come out with very good ideas."[85]

The St. John's program quickly demonstrated what Buchanan's experience with the People's Institute participants had earlier indicated: Rigorous study of difficult texts could be tackled by a wide range of minds. Barr insisted that during the ten years of his presidency at St. John's, students represented "a very typical cross-section. At the lower end we had some students most good colleges would not admit. And some of those turned out superbly."[86]

Buchanan became known as a student centered dean who more often than not sided with students in differences with faculty. His stand on academic suspension provided an example when he insisted that students should not be forced to leave campus; he reasoned that learning could only stop in the opinion of the student, not of the faculty.[87] For Buchanan, the variances of privilege had no place in college. Soon after arriving at St. John's, he initiated a successful effort to eliminate fraternities when he realized they were providing free housing to their members while those who did not pledge a fraternity had to pay for housing.

Reflecting both the deteriorating world political situation and his own educational ideals, Buchanan soon championed a liberal education as foundational for a free society. He reminded readers of the 1939–40 *St. John's Catalogue* that in an aristocracy, a liberal education would be reserved for the ruling class. However, in a democracy every citizen must be schooled in "intelligent free choice of the ends and means of both our common and individual life. This is a most glorious and most difficult proposition to which we are dedicated. Among other things it means that each man must have his measure of liberal education. . . . the end of teaching and learning is the production of good intellectual and moral habits which provide the basis for human freedom."[88]

With the installation of Western literature at St. John's College, the idea of great books had come full circle—from colonial college curriculums, through lists and programs aimed at continuing adult education, beyond honors courses and individual classroom experiments, and back to a full undergraduate liberal arts program. The program formulated at St. John's is particularly notable for demonstrating an ongoing preference among great books proponents to utilize the texts to increase access to liberal education and classical literature beyond the intellectual and/or socio-economic elite. Although Buchanan and Barr resigned from St. John's College in 1947 after breathing a second life into St. John's, the college continued to thrive (and add a second campus in Santa Fe, New Mexico) as the enduring evidence of a liberal arts curriculum fully committed to emphasizing fundamental knowledge, unifying ideas, and Western heritage through the study of great books.

Conclusion: An Idea Is Not a "Movement"

Efforts to promote reading of important Western literature among adults and college students may have spawned less of a "movement" than is generally credited for the "great books" in U.S. education. Early ideas for great books endeavors appear more as methods within possible movements, including the movement to retain liberal education (but not classical education) as part of the college curriculum and the movement to promote lifelong learning. In this regard, the evolving and changing lists of texts can be located in the neighborhood of instruments that, like Socratic dialogue, spark and support learning in a variety of areas that may or may not be organized into a comprehensive liberal arts education.

The lineage of the great books idea—perhaps fueled by the popular and misleading label that so easily rolls off the tongue as "the great books"—continues to hop scotch from continuing education outreach endeavors to college general education courses based on book lists and on to honors programs. It is institutionalized in the programs of the Chicago-based Great Books Foundation, founded by Hutchins and Adler in 1947. Initiated to promote lifelong learning through conversation about important literature, that foundation encourages local book groups and school-based "junior great books" programs and supports them with the publication of anthologies and discussion guides. The adult education and commercial strand of the idea received a boost in 1952 when Encyclopedia Britannica, Inc., published the fifty-four-volume set, *Great Books of the Western World*, edited by Mortimer Adler and Robert Maynard Hutchins. Stringfellow Barr was among those who rekindled the undergraduate curriculum strand when he returned to the University of Virginia as a visiting professor of political science from 1951 to 1953. His courses, "Origin and Development of American Political Thought" and "The Western Political Tradition," were based on discussions of Western political classics and included readings from Plato, Aristotle, Plutarch, Cicero, Euclid, Dante, Locke, and deTocqueville.[89] Scott Buchanan also returned to brief teaching stints and unrequited plans to found another liberal arts college. In 1958, he joined the Center for the Study of Democratic Institutions, a social issues think tank headed by Robert Maynard Hutchins in Santa Barbara, California.

While the "great books" have been soundly berated as an authoritative canon reeking of Western white-male elitism, post-structural interpretations aided by historical contexts support the notion that the roots of the concept are closer to Daniel Bell's argument that, starting with Erskine's proposal at Columbia, "the intention in reading the 'great books' was to inculcate in the student a humanistic rather than a professional orientation; to force him to confront a great work directly, rather than treat it with the awe reserved for a classic; and, in the contemporary jargon, 'to acculturate' a student whose background and upbringing had excluded him from the 'great traditions.'"[90]

Erskine, Meiklejohn, Buchanan, Barr, and others were democratic in intent in terms of both access to important literature and interpretations of that literature. Diverse interpretations and the ever-changing discussions they might engender were more sought after than universal truths in the classrooms at Columbia and St. John's and in the meeting halls of the People's Institute. Text selection in the courses and programs that got underway was always a living construct, albeit generally a construct guided by Western heritage. Before his death in 1968, Buchanan was called upon to defend the adherence to Western thinking, and he did so by positing a canon of convenience. Texts representing other cultures would be a welcome inclusion, he insisted to his friend Harris Wofford, but the Western texts and people who knew how to teach them were more available. Wofford recalled Buchanan's recognition that "Of course there are great things to teach beyond the Western—other civilizations and other points of view. But we don't know how to master them yet."[91]

Clearly, the early proponents of education through great Western texts went only so far. They stopped short of completely understanding the political and educational arguments that would occur later; although some understanding was implied in the evolution of book lists over time. Their contributions were foundational in terms of what we now sense about democracy in education. They helped to keep alive the possibility of liberal arts education and the efficacy of learning through intense and shared dialogue. And, importantly, they introduced and demonstrated in practice that instruments of education once reserved for upper class homes and elite boys colleges could be extended to diverse populations[92] and students of all ages.

Notes

1. Anti-canonist points of view are well expressed in, for example: Henry Louis Gates Jr., *Loose Canons: Notes on the Culture Wars* (New York: Oxford University Press, 1992); Stanley Fish, "Canon Busting: The Basic Issues," *National Forum* 69, no. 3 (Summer 1989); Lawrence W. Levine, *The Opening of the American Mind: Canons, Culture, and History* (Boston: Beacon Press, 1996); and Barbara Herrnstein Smith, *Contingencies of Value* (Cambridge: Harvard University Press, 1988).

    Earlier objections to using a set of predetermined classic texts to support for liberal education focused less on multi-culturalism and more on multi-curricularism, with John Dewey and other child-centered progressives railing against proponents of the great books for encouraging study of specific pre-selected (therefore, authoritative) texts. See, for example, John Dewey, "Challenge to Liberal Thought," *Fortune* (August 1944): 154–60.

2. Robert Maynard Hutchins was perhaps most open to charges of narrow curricular elitism and personal arrogance when he noted (in words still frequently quoted in canon debate literature): "Education implies teaching. Teaching implies knowledge. Knowledge is truth. The truth is everywhere the same. Hence education should be everywhere the same." In Robert M. Hutchins, *The Higher Learning in America* (New Haven: Yale University Press, 1936), 3.

3. Levine, *The Opening of the American Mind*, 15. Although Melville and Whitman were left off most of the notable early "lists" of great books, all such lists, dating back to Sir John Lubbock's 1887 model, included works by Shakespeare. Also typically included among more "modern" writers were John Stuart Mill, Darwin, Marx, Tolstoy, Nietzsche, and William James.

4. Scott M. Buchanan, quoted in Harris Wofford Jr., ed., *Embers of the World: Conversations With Scott Buchanan* (Santa Barbara, Calif.: Center for the Study of Democratic Institutions, 1969), 157.

5. Harris Wofford Jr., interview by Katherine Reynolds, 8 December 2000, transcript in possession of the author:

6. "The American College," *The New Republic*, 25 October 1922, p. 208. For discussions or cultural distance and aspiration in American life, see also Joan Shelley Rubin, *The Making of Middlebrow Culture* (Chapel Hill: University of North Carolina Press, 1992); and Dwight Macdonald, "Masscult and Midcult I," *Partisan Review* 27 (Spring 1960): 203–33; and "Masscult and Midcult II," *Partisan Review* 27 (Fall 1960): 589–631.

7. Caroline Winterer, *The Culture of Classicism: Ancient Greece and Rome in American Intellectual Life, 1780–1910* (Baltimore: The Johns Hopkins University Press, 2002), 144. See also Richard Bushman, *The Refinement of America: Persons, Houses, Cities* (New York: Vintage Books, 1993).

8. James Sloan Allen, *The Romance of Commerce and Culture: Capitalism, Modernism, and the Chicago-Aspen Crusade for Cultural Reform* (Chicago: University of Chicago Press, 1983), xiii.

9. For further exploration of the wide-ranging political stances that can align with anti-canon contextualism or pro-canon universalism, see William Casement, *The Great Canon Controversy: The Battle of the Books in Higher Education* (New Brunswick: Transaction Publishers, 1996), 76–82; and Russell Jacoby, *Dogmatic Wisdom: How the Culture Wars Divert Education and Distract America* (New York: Doubleday, 1994).

10. Casement, in *The Great Canon Controversy*, and others trace the teaching of a canon of "great" works to the Greek Sophists and Platonists, noting the European Enlightenment as the first occasion for controversy about the educational value of ancients v. moderns.

11. "Ought Erskine to Raise Its Standard of Admission?" *The Erskine Collegiate Recorder*, July 1858, 60. Henry Adams, *The Education of Henry Adams* (New York: Modern Library edition, 1931), 59.

12. Winterer, *The Culture of Classicism*, 110. See also Chapter IX, "The Resurgence of Collegiate Concerns" in Hugh Hawkins, *Between Harvard and America: The Educational Leadership of Charles W. Eliot* (New York: Oxford University Press, 1972), 263–89.

13. Winterer, *The Culture of Classicism*, 136–37.

14. David O. Levine, *The American College and the Culture of Aspiration, 1915–1940* (Ithaca, N.Y.: Cornell University Press, 1986), 102.

15. Frances Blanchard, *Frank Aydelotte of Swarthmore* (Middletown, Conn.: Wesleyan University Press, 1970). Alexander Meiklejohn, *The Experimental College* (New York: Harper and Brothers, 1932). "Alexander Meiklejohn, 1872–1964, President of Amherst College, 1912–1923," n.d., typescript by Scott Buchanan, Scott M. Buchanan Papers, Bms. Am. 1992, Houghton Library, Harvard University.

16. Charles W. Eliot, *The Editor's Introduction to the Harvard Classics* (New York: P. F. Collier and Son, 1910).

17. Noah Porter, *Books and Reading: Or What Books Shall I Read and How Shall I Read Them* (New York: Charles Scribner, 1871). For discussions of *The Harvard Classics* and their implications and influence, see Hugh Hawkins, *Between Harvard and America: The Educational Leadership of Charles W. Eliot* (New York: Oxford University Press, 1972) and Joan Shelley Rubin, *The Making of Middlebrow Culture* (Chapel Hill: University of North Carolina Press, 1992). Charles Eliot Norton, ed., *The Heart of Oaks Books: First Book* (Boston: D.C. Heath and Company, 1902), vi.

18. John Lubbock, *The Pleasures of Life* (London: Macmillan and Company, 1896).

19. For a thorough treatment of Lubbock and other early book lists, see Hugh S. Moorhead, *The Great Books Movement* (Ph.D. diss., University of Chicago, 1964). Moorhead traces the appearance of the adjective "great" to its use in several 19th century book advice volumes, including *The Choice of Books* by Charles F. Richardson (1881) and *Choice of Books* by Federic Harrison (1888).

20. "The American College and American Culture," *Nation*, 89 (1909): 321.

21. Dwight Macdonald, "Masscult and Midcult II," *Partisan Review* 27 (Fall 1960): 615. Macdonald characterized "masscult" as popular culture indicated by folk art and ranch houses. He saw "midcult," as more dangerously blurring the lines once separating high culture from the masses as huge numbers of the American middle class became interested the music, art, and literature that were once exclusive to high culture.

22. John Erskine, *The Delight of Great Books* (Indianapolis: The Bobbs-Merrill Company, 1928). Mortimer J. Adler, *How to Read a Book: The Art of Getting a Liberal Education* (New York: Macmillan, 1977).

23. Amy Apfel Kass, *Radical Conservatives for Liberal Education* (Ph.D. diss., Johns Hopkins University, 1973), 19.

24. John Erskine, *The Memories of Certain Persons* (New York: J. B. Lippincott Company, 1947), 343.

25. Ibid., 342.

26. Predictably, the list of books went through many changes as the notion navigated through various faculty committees. The list that launched General Honors in 1920 differed substantially from Lubbock's list by dropping the *Bible*, the *Koran* and many British poets and essayists.

27. "Report of the Committee on Honors Courses to the President of the University," March 1935, typescript of a University of Virginia faculty report, Adler Papers, Box 57, folder 5, University of Chicago, Joseph Regenstein Library.

28. Biographical information on the early life of Scott M. Buchanan is developed from: "Slightly Autobiographical—By Request," transcript of a taped interview with Buchanan by Frank Kelly, n.d., Tape 142, Box 5, Center for the Study of Democratic Institutions Papers, Davidson Library, University of California, Santa Barbara; "Socratic Teacher," transcript of taped interview with Stringfellow Barr by Frank Kelly, 14 March 1968, Tape 473, Box 5, Center for the Study of Democratic Institutions Papers, Tape 473, Box 5, Davidson Library, University of California, Santa Barbara; and Wofford, *Embers of the World*.

29. Wofford, *Embers of the World*, 45.

30. Ibid., 54.

31. Meiklejohn, *Experimental College*, 5.

32. Much to the unhappiness of many Amherst alumni, during Meiklejohn's presidency (1912–24), 17 African American students enrolled. He railed against Harvard's quotas to limit Jewish students and insisted that Amherst seek applicants of every socio-economic class, race, and religion. For a full account of Meiklejohn's educational philosophy, see Adam R. Nelson, *Education and Democracy: The Meaning of Alexander Meiklejohn, 1872–1964* (Madison: The University of Wisconsin Press, 2001).

33. "Biography." Typescript overview with inventory to finding guides, Meiklejohn Papers, Box 1, Wisconsin State Historical Society.

34. Scott M. Buchanan to Alexander Meiklejohn, 22 August 1920, Meiklejohn Papers, Box 6, Wisconsin State Historical Society.

35. Stringfellow Barr, "Scott Buchanan, Teacher," *The Center Magazine* 1, no. 7 (November 1968): 83.

36. Scott M. Buchanan, *Possibility* (London: Kegan Paul, Trench, Trubner & Company, 1927); John Dewey, review of *Possibility, The Nation*, 18 April 1928.

37. Scott M. Buchanan, "A New Introduction," *Poetry and Mathematics*, 2nd ed. (New York: J. B. Lippincott Company, 1962), 11.

38. Ibid., 13–14.

39. Barr, "Scott Buchanan, Teacher," 84.

40. See Buchanan, "A New Introduction," and Richard McKeon, "Memorial Minutes," *Proceedings of the American Philosophical Association, 1968–69*, 133.

41. Buchanan, "A New Introduction," 16.

42. Mortimer J. Adler, *Philosopher At Large* (New York: Macmillan Publishing Company, 1977), 87–88. Adler, who had been a student at Columbia, was on the Department of Psychology faculty and a frequent instructor for the General Honors course.

43. During 1926–27, readings and discussions covered 40 of the 76 authors on a list drawn up by Buchanan, in collaboration with Adler and other potential instructors, for the seminar program of the People's Institute. The ancient texts among these included works by Homer, Euripides, Herodotus, Aristotle, Plato, Virgil, St. Thomas Aquinas, and St. Augustine; more modern thought included books by Hume, Goethe, Hegel, Balzac, Darwin, Mill, Dostoevsky, Rousseau, Tolstoy, and William James. See Moorhead, *The Great Books Movement*, for inclusion and comparison of early lists of books used at Columbia and the People's Institute. For the full range of Buchanan's many influential friends and associates, see Charles A. Nelson, ed., *Scott Buchanan: A Centennial Appreciation of His Life and Work* (Annapolis: St. John's College Press, 1995).

44. Buchanan, "A New Introduction," 21.

45. Buchanan to Meiklejohn, 22 August 1920, Meiklejohn Papers, Box 6, folder 11, Wisconsin State Historical Society.
46. Buchanan, "A New Introduction," 23.
47. Scott M. Buchanan to Mortimer J. Adler, 30 October 1929, Box 27, unnumbered folder, Mortimer Adler Papers, Joseph Regenstein Library, University of Chicago.
48. Buchanan spent 1931–32 in England, funded by Mrs. Ethel S. Dummer of Chicago to research interpretations of George and Mary Boole related to both mathematics and the work of the human mind. One result of this study was Buchanan's book *Symbolic Distance in Relation to Analogy and Fiction* (London: Kegan Paul, 1932). During the first six months of 1934, Buchanan worked at John's Hopkins University School of Medicine, where a grant from the Josiah Macy Foundation allowed him to explore philosophic connections with medical theory and write *The Doctrine of Signatures: A defense of Theory in Medicine* (New York: Harcourt, Brace & Company, 1938).
49. Edwin A. Alderman, quoted in Scott M. Buchanan, "Report of the Committee on Honors Courses to the President of the University," March 1935. Typescript of a University of Virginia faculty report. Adler Papers, Box 57, University of Chicago, Joseph Regenstein Library; Barr, "Scott Buchanan, Teacher," 85.
50. Scott M. Buchanan to Mortimer J. Adler, 5 October 1934, Box 27, Mortimer Adler Papers, Special Collections, Joseph Regenstein Library, University of Chicago.
51. Stringfellow Barr quoted in Harris Wofford(ed.), *Embers*, p. 86 and quoted in Moorhead, *The Great Books Movement*, p. 146; Scott M. Buchanan, "Report of the Committee on Honors Courses to the President of the University," March 1935, 5–7. For a detailed discussion of the Virginia Plan, see William Noble Haarlow, *Great Books, Honors Programs and Hidden Origins: The Virginia Plan and the University of Virginia in the Liberal Arts Movement* (Ph.D. diss., University of Virginia, 2000).
52. Scott M. Buchanan, "The Proposed Course in General Honors," Appendix A of "Report of the Committee on Honors Courses to the President of the University," March 1935. Barr recalled in *Scott Buchanan Teacher*, that his major contribution to the committee's report was the early narrative material assessing the state of liberal arts education. Buchanan provided the liberal arts rationale and list of books, and Gooch wrote a section calling for third and fourth year independent readings and tutorials for honors students.
53. The proposed books totaled over 100 and included many of the literary and philosophical works common to earlier lists—from ancient Greece through 19th century England. Forty-one texts appeared in the mathematics and science category, most not appearing on previous lists, including those by Euclid, Nichomachus, Appollonius, Copernicus, Lavoisier, Leibniz, Faraday, Gauss, Boole, and Hilbert. See Scott M. Buchanan, "The Proposed Course in General Honors," Appendix A of "Report of the Committee on Honors Courses to the President of the University," March 1935, 3–5.
54. "Report of the Committee on Honors Courses to the President of the University," March 1935. See also Kass, *Radical Conservatives for Liberal Education*, 129–135.
55. Barr, "Scott Buchanan, Teacher," 85.
56. More than a century earlier, the Yale Report of 1828 called for adherence to a liberal education through the study of classical literature, as well as "scientific principles" and their "practical application." However, that report did not list particular texts or imply that the scientific studies could be under-girded by specific literature. See Committee of the Corporation and the Academical Faculty, *Reports on the Course of Instruction in Yale College* (New Haven: Hezekiah Howe, Printer, 1828).
57. Richard McKeon, quoted in Charles A. Nelson, ed., *Scott Buchanan: A Centennial Appreciation*, 50.
58. "Report of the Committee on Honors Courses to the President of the University," March 1935, 4.
59. Moorhead, *The Great Books Movement*, 244.
60. Mortimer Adler to Richard McKeon, n.d., 1931, Box 17, folder 2, Richard Peter McKeon Papers, Special Collections, Joseph Regenstein Library, University of Chicago. McKeon arrived at The University of Chicago in 1934 as a visiting professor of history and eventually became Dean of Humanities. Buchanan arrived in 1936 as a special non-faculty presidential appointee.
61. Sources for Hutchins' early years at the University of Chicago include several biographies and institutional histories: Adler, *Philosopher at Large*; Harry S. Ashmore, *Unseasonable Truths: The Life of Robert Maynard Hutchins* (Boston: Little, Brown & Company, 1989); Mary Ann Dzuback, *Robert M. Hutchins: Portrait of an Educator* (Chicago: University of Chicago Press, 1991); Henry D. Gideonse, *The Higher Learning in a Democracy* (New York: Farrar & Rhinehart, 1937); and William H. McNeill, *Hutchins'. University: A Memoir of the University of Chicago, 1929–1950* (Chicago: University of Chicago Press, 1991).
62. Speech at inaugural dinner. Box 19, folder 1, Robert M. Hutchins Papers, Special Collections, Joseph Regenstein Library, University of Chicago.
63. Mortimer Adler to Robert Maynard Hutchins, n.d., Sunday, 1930, Box 4, folder 2, Robert M. Hutchins Papers, Special Collections, Joseph Regenstein Library, University of Chicago.

64. Robert Maynard Hutchins, *Education for Freedom* (Baton Rouge: Louisiana State University Press, 1943), 14.
65. For a full account of the various great books classes introduced by Hutchins and Adler, see Moorhead, *The Great Books Movement*, 240–318.
66. Scott Buchanan to Dorothy Van Doren, 5 February 1937, Charles Nelson Collection, unprocessed, Greenfield Library, St. John's College.
67. Stringfellow Barr to Robert M. Hutchins, 21 October 1936, Stringfellow Barr Papers, Box 29, folder 4, Greenfield Library, St. John's College.
68. Scott Buchanan to Robert M. Hutchins, 12 February 1937, Scott Buchanan Collection, Bms. Am. 1992, item 642, Houghton Library, Harvard University.
69. "A Three Year Plan for the Liberal Arts Committee," n.d., typescript, Box 57, unnumbered folder, Mortimer Adler Papers, Special Collections, Joseph Regenstein Library, University of Chicago.
70. Scott Buchanan, "The Liberal Arts and the Great Books," 1952, typescript draft, 24, Meiklejohn Papers, Box 6, folder 14, Wisconsin State Historical Society.
71. Scott Buchanan, "The Classics and the Liberal Arts, Number I," 1936, 5, Stringfellow Barr Papers, Box 30, folder 4, Greenfield Library, St. John's College.
72. Scott Buchanan, "The Classics and the Liberal Arts, Number II," 1936, 7–8, Stringfellow Barr Papers, Box 30, folder 5, Greenfield Library, St. John's College.
73. Stringfellow Barr, interview by Francis Mason, 27 July 1975, transcript in Stringfellow Barr Audio Collection, Series 1, Box 2, Greenfield Library, St. John's College.
74. "A Petitionary Act for Free Schools," *Laws of Maryland, Session of July 1–9, 1696*.
75. "The New Program at St. John's College," in *Catalogue of St. John's College: 1937–38*, 17–30, St. John's Archives, Greenfield Library, St. John's College.
76. Stringfellow Barr, "President's Report to the Board of Visitors and Governors of St. John's College," 11 July, 1938, Stringfellow Barr Papers, Box 29, folder 6, Greenfield Library, St. John's College.
77. Stringfellow Barr, interview by Douglas W. Tanner, 12 September 1972, transcript in Stringfellow Barr Audio Collection, Box 2, Greenfield Library, St. John's College.
78. Stringfellow Barr, interview by Chauncey G. Olinger Jr., 1972, transcript in Stringfellow Barr Audio Collection, Series 1, Box 2, Greenfield Library, St. John's College.
79. Barr later noted that the clearest and most important connection between the Virginia plan and the St. John's New Program was the "really novel" inclusion in both of mathematics and science. See Stringfellow Barr, interview by Hugh Moorhead, 23 August 1958, in Moorhead, *The Great Books Movement*, 145.
80. "The New Program at St. John's College," in *Catalogue of St. John's College: 1937-38*, 25, St. John's Archives, Greenfield Library, St. John's College. Among the texts that have been added as the list evolved over decades are works by: Booker T. Washington, W.E.B. DuBois, William Faulkner, Joseph Conrad, Flanery O'Conner, Mark Twain, Virginia Woolf, Albert Einstein, T.S. Eliot, Wallace Stevens, and others.
81. Stringfellow Barr, interview by Frank Kelly, 14 March 1968, transcript in Stringfellow Barr Audio Collection, Series 1, Box 2, Greenfield Library, St. John's College.
82. Quoted in Wofford, *Embers of the World*, 157.
83. Ibid., 90–91.
84. Stringfellow Barr, "President's Report," 2.
85. Quoted in Wofford, *Embers of the World*, 92–93.
86. Barr, interview by Kelly.
87. Samuel Cutler, interview by Katherine Reynolds, 17 May 2002, transcript in possession of the author.
88. "Why a College Education Should be Liberal," in *Catalogue of St. John's College: 1939–40*, 21–22, St. John's Archives, Greenfield Library, St. John's College.
89. Haarlow, *Great Books, Honors Programs*, 314–316.
90. Daniel Bell, *The Reforming of General Education* (New York: Columbia University Press, 1966), 13–14.
91. Harris Wofford Jr., interview by Katherine Reynolds, 8 December 2000, transcript in possession of the author.
92. Although a wide range of colleges have utilized classic Western literature to at least some measure, their use has not been notable among highly selective elite institutions. Scott Buchanan, after leaving St. John's, was among the many who took the classic texts to diverse institutions. He introduced the great books idea at Springfield College, a YMCA affiliated school in Massachusetts, and at historically black Fisk University, where he was on the faculty from 1956 to 1957 and taught general humanities and logic as great books courses.

Appendix A

List of Authors/Books Developed for the Columbia Honors Course*

Homer
Herodotus
Thucydides
Aeschylus
Sophocles
Euripides
Aristophanes
Selections from Greek Art
Plato
Aristotle
Lucretius

Virgil
Horace
Plutarch
Marcus Aurelius
St. Augustine
The Song of Roland
The Nibelungenlied
St. Thomas Aquinas
Dante
Bacon
Descartes
Hobbes

Milton
Moliere
Locke
Montesquieu
Voltaire
Rousseau
Gibbon
Adam Smith
Kant
Goethe
American papers
    (Declaration of Independence,
    Constitution, Federalist Papers)

Victor Hugo
Hegel
Sir Charles Lyell
Balzac
Malthus
Bentham
Pasteur
Marx
Tolstoy
Dostoevsky
Nietzsche
William James

*From Moorhead, *The Great Books Movement*, 690

Appendix B

St. John's College, "A List of Great Books," 1938*

Homer: Iliad, *Odyssey*
Aeschylus: *Oresteia*
Herodotus: *History*
Sophocles: *Oedipus Rex*
Hippocrates: *Selections*
Hippocrates: *Selections*
Euripides: *Medea, Electra*
Thucydides: *History of the Pelopnnesian Wars*
Aristophanes: *Frogs, Clouds, Birds*
Aristarchus: *On Distance of the Sun and Moon*
Aristoxenus: *Harmony*
Plato: *Meno, Republic, Sophist*
Aristotle: *Organon, Poetics*
Archimedes: *Works*
Euclid: *Elements*
Appollonius: *Conics*
Lucian: *True History*

Plutarch: *Lives*

Virgil: *Aeneid*
Strabo: *Geography*
Tacitus: *History*
Cicero: *De Officiis*
Horace: *Arts Poetica*
Horace: *Arts Poetica*
Ovid: *Metamorphoses*
Quintilian: *Institutes*
Marcus Aurelius: *To Himself*
The Bible
Galen: *On the Natural Faculties*
Plotinus: *Enneads*
Justinian: *Institutes*
Augustine: *De Musica, De Magistro*
Song of Roland
Volsunga Saga
Bonaventura: *Reduction of the Arts
    to Theology*
Thomas: *Summa Theologica*

Lucretius: *On the Nature of Things*
Nicomachus: *Introduction to Mathematics*
Ptolemy: *Almagest*
Leonardo: *Notebooks*
Erasmus: *Colloquies*
Rabelais: *Gargantua*
Corpernicus: *De Revolutionibus*
Machiavelli: *The Prince*
Harvey: *On the Motion of the Heart*
Gilbert: *On the Magnet*
Kepler: *Epitome of Astronomy*
Galileo: *Two New Sciences*
Descartes: *Geometry*
Bacon: *Novum Organum*
Hobbes: *Leviathan*
Montaigne: *Essays*
Cervantes: *Don Quixote*
Shakespeare: *Hamlet*
Calvin: *Institutes*
Grotius: *The Law of War and Peace*
Corneille: *Le Cid*
Spinoza: *Ethics*
Racine: *Phédre*
Moliere: *Tartuffe*
Milton: *Paradise Lost*
Mill: *System of Logic*
Marx: *Capital*

Balzac: *père Goriot*

Thackeray: *Henry Esmond*
Dickens: *David Copperfield*
Flaubert: *Madame Bovary*
Dosteovski: *Crime and Punishment*
Zola: *Experimental Novel*
Ibsen: *The Doll's House*
Dalton: *A New System of Chemical Philosophy*
Clifford: *The Common Sense of the Exact Sciences*
Fourier: *Mathematical Analysis of Heat*
Faraday: *Experimental Research into Electricity*
Peacock: *Algebra*
Lobachevski: *Theory of Parallels*
Darwin: *Origin of the Species*

Dante: *Divine Comedy*
Bacon: *Opus Maius*
Chaucer: *Canterbury Tales*
Leibniz: *Mathematical Papers*
Newton: *Principia*
Lavoisier: *Elements of Chemistry*
Boyle: *Skeptical Chymist*
Montesquieu: *The Spirit of the Laws*
Swift: *Gulliver's Travels*
Locke: *Concerning Human Understanding*
Voltaire: *Candide*
Fielding: *Tom Jones*
Rousseau: *Social Contract*
Adam Smith: *Wealth of Nations*
Hume: *Treatise of Human Nature*
Gibbon: *Decline and Fall of the Roman Empire*
Constitution of the United States
Federalist Papers
Kant: *Critique of Pure Reason*
Goethe: *Faust*
Hegel: *Science of Logic*
Schopenhauer: *The World as Will and idea*
Coleridge: *Biographia Literaria*
Bentham: *Principles of Morals and Legislation*
Malthus: *Essay on Principles of Population*
Mendel: *Papers*
Bernard: *Introduction to Experimental Medicine*
Galton: *Enquiries into the Human Mind and its Faculties*
Joule: *Scientific Papers*
Maxwell: *Electricity and Magnetism*
Gauss: *Mathematical Papers*
Galois: *Mathematical Papers*
Hamilton: *Quaternions*
Riemann: *The Hypotheses of Geometry*
Cantor: *Transfinite Numbers*
Virchow: *Cellular Pathology*
Poincare: *Science and Hypothesis*
Hilbert: *Foundations of Geometry*
James: *Principles of Psychology*
Freud: *Papers on Hysteria*
Russell: *Principles of Mathematics*
Veblen & Young: Projective Geometry

*From Catalogue of St. John's College: 1937–38, 26–27.

Acknowledgement

The author wishes to thank Edward J. Brunet, Roger Geiger, George Keller, and L. Jackson Newell for their thoughtful comments and contributions.

THEORY OF GENERAL EDUCATION

HARVARD COMMITTEE

I

Heritage and Change

WE have tried so far to sketch in broad outline the growth of American education and to indicate the factors which have determined this growth. The very momentum of its development, like that which has marked American life generally, left a legacy of disturbance and maladjustment undreamed of in simpler times. A passage from Machiavelli's *Discourses* comes to mind in which, after asking why the Roman Republic showed signs of confusion in the period of its fastest growth, he observes that such confusion was inevitable in so vigorous a state. "Had the Roman Commonwealth," he concludes, "grown to be more tranquil, this inconvenience would have resulted that it must at the same time have grown weaker, since the road would have been closed to that greatness to which it came. For in removing the causes of her tumults, Rome must have interfered with the causes of her growth." Just so in the United States, the most ideally planned educational system would have found itself in conflict with the unforeseen forces set loose by the growth and development of the country. But this very growth, the source of the gravest problems to education, is at the same time the index of its strength and promise.

In order to pass judgment on the actualities of education and to make reasonable proposals for revising the present system, it is necessary to have an insight, however tentative, into the ideal aims of education in our society. The present article will accordingly consider what can, perhaps overformally, be called a philosophy of American education, and especially that part of it which is general education.

It was remarked at the end of the previous article that a supreme need of American education is for a unifying purpose and idea. As recently as a century ago, no doubt existed about such a purpose: it was to train the Christian citizen. Nor was there doubt how this training was to be accomplished. The student's logical powers were to be formed by mathematics, his taste by the Greek and Latin classics, his speech by rhetoric, and his ideals by Christian ethics. College catalogues commonly began with a specific statement about the influence of such a training on the mind and character. The reasons why this enviable certainty both of goal and of means has largely disappeared have already been set forth. For some decades the mere excitement of enlarging the curriculum and making place for new subjects, new methods, and masses of new students seems quite pardonably to have absorbed the energies of schools and colleges. It is fashionable now to criticize the leading figures of that expansive time for failing to replace, or even to see the need of replacing, the unity which they destroyed. But such criticisms, if just in themselves, are hardly just historically. A great and necessary task of modernizing and broadening education waited to be done, and there is credit enough in its accomplishment. In recent times, however, the question of unity has become insistent. We are faced with a diversity of education which, if it has many virtues,

Reprinted from *General Education in a Free Society: Report of the Harvard Committee* (1945), by permission of Harvard University Press.

nevertheless works against the good of society by helping to destroy the common ground of training and outlook on which any society depends.

It seems that a common ground between some, though not all, of the ideas underlying our educational practice is the sense of heritage. The word heritage is not here taken to mean mere retrospection. The purpose of all education is to help students live their own lives. The appeal to heritage is partly to the authority, partly to the clarification of the past about what is important in the present. All Catholic and many Protestant institutions thus appeal to the Christian view of man and history as providing both final meaning and immediate standards for life. As observed at the outset, it is less than a century since such was the common practice of American education generally, and certainly this impulse to mold students to a pattern sanctioned by the past can, in one form or another, never be absent from education. If it were, society would become discontinuous.

In this concern for heritage lies a close similarity between religious education and education in the great classic books. Exponents of the latter have, to be sure, described it as primarily a process of intellectual discipline in the joint arts of word and number, the so-called *trivium* (grammar, logic, rhetoric) and *quadrivium* (arithmetic, geometry, astronomy, music). But, since the very idea of this discipline goes back to antiquity and since the actual books by which it is carried out are in fact the great books of the Western tradition, it seems fairer, without denying the disciplinary value of such a curriculum, to think of it as primarily a process of opening before students the intellectual forces that have shaped the Western mind. There is a sense in which education in the great books can be looked at as a secular continuation of the spirit of Protestantism. As early Protestantism, rejecting the authority and philosophy of the medieval church, placed reliance on each man's personal reading of the Scriptures, so this present movement, rejecting the unique authority of the Scriptures, places reliance on the reading of those books which are taken to represent the fullest revelation of the Western mind. But be this as it may, it is certain that, like religious education, education in the great books is essentially an introduction of students to their heritage.

Nor is the sense of heritage less important, though it may be less obvious, a part of education for modern democratic life. To the degree that the implications of democracy are drawn forth and expounded, to that degree the long-standing impulse of education toward shaping students to a received ideal is still pursued. Consider the teaching of American history and of modern democratic life. However ostensibly factual such teaching may be, it commonly carries with it a presupposition which is not subject to scientific proof: namely, the presupposition that democracy is meaningful and right. Moreover, since contemporary life is itself a product of history, to study it is to tread unconsciously, in the words of the hymn, where the saints have trod. To know modern democracy is to know something at least of Jefferson, though you have not read him; to learn to respect freedom of speech or the rights of the private conscience is not to be wholly ignorant of the *Areopagitica* or the *Antigone*, though you know nothing about them. Whether, as philosophers of history argue, being conditioned by the present we inevitably judge the past by what we know in the present (since otherwise the past would be unintelligible) or whether human motives and choices do not in reality greatly change with time, the fact remains that the past and the present are parts of the same unrolling scene and, whether you enter early or late, you see for the most part the still-unfinished progress of the same issues.

Here, then, in so far as our culture is adequately reflected in current ideas on education, one point about it is clear: it depends in part on an inherited view of man and society which it is the function, though not the only function, of education to pass on. It is not and cannot be true that all possible choices are open to us individually or collectively. We are part of an organic process, which is the American and, more broadly, the Western evolution. Our standards of judgment, ways of life, and form of government all bear the marks of this evolution, which would accordingly influence us, though confusedly, even if it were not understood. Ideally it should be understood at several degrees of depth which complement rather than exclude each other. To study the American present is to discern at best the aims and purposes of a free society animating its imperfections. To study the past is immensely to enrich the meaning of the present and at the same time to clarify it by the simplification of the writings and the issues which have been winnowed from history. To study either past or present is to confront, in some form or another, the philosophic and religious fact of man in history and to recognize the huge continuing influence alike on past and present of the stream of

Jewish and Greek thought in Christianity. There is doubtless a sense in which religious education, education in the great books, and education in modern democracy may be mutually exclusive. But there is a far more important sense in which they work together to the same end, which is belief in the idea of man and society that we inherit, adapt, and pass on.

This idea is described in many ways, perhaps most commonly in recent times, as that of the dignity of man. To the belief in man's dignity must be added the recognition of his duty to his fellow men. Dignity does not rest on any man as a being separate from all other beings, which he in any case cannot be, but springs from his common humanity and exists positively as he makes the common good his own. This concept is essentially that of the Western tradition: the view of man as free and not as slave, an end in himself and not a means. It may have what many believe to be the limitations of humanism, which are those of pride and arise from making man the measure of all things. But it need not have these limitations, since it is equally compatible with a religious view of life. Thus it is similar to the position described at the end of the last article as coöperation without uniformity, agreement on the good of man at the level of performance without the necessity of agreement on ultimates. But two points have now been added. First, thus stated, the goal of education is not in conflict with but largely includes the goals of religious education, education in the Western tradition, and education in modern democracy. For these in turn have been seen to involve necessary elements in our common tradition, each to a great extent implied in the others as levels at which it can be understood. Certainly no fruitful way of stating the belief in the dignity and mutual obligation of man can present it as other than, at one and the same time, effective in the present, emerging from the past, and partaking of the nature not of fact but of faith. Second, it has become clear that the common ground between these various views—namely, the impulse to rear students to a received idea of the good—is in fact necessary to education. It is impossible to escape the realization that our society, like any society, rests on common beliefs and that a major task of education is to perpetuate them.

This conclusion raises one of the most fundamental problems of education, indeed of society itself: how to reconcile this necessity for common belief with the equally obvious necessity for new and independent insights leading to change. We approach here the one previously mentioned concept of education which was not included under the idea of heritage: namely, the views associated with the names of James and Dewey and having to do with science, the scientific attitude, and pragmatism. This is hardly the place to try to summarize this body of thought or even to set forth in detail its application by Mr. Dewey to education. To do so would be virtually to retrace the educational controversies of the last forty years. But, at the risk of some injustice to Mr. Dewey's thought as a whole, a few points can be made about it. It puts trust in the scientific method of thought, the method which demands that you reach conclusions from tested data only, but that, since the data may be enlarged or the conclusions themselves combined with still other conclusions, you must hold them only tentatively. It emphasizes that full truth is not known and that we must be forever led by facts to revise our approximations of it. As a feeling of commitment and of allegiance marks the sense of heritage, so a tone of tough-mindedness and curiosity and a readiness for change mark this pragmatic attitude.

Here, then, is a concept of education, founded on obedience to fact and well disposed, even hospitable, to change, which appears at first sight the antithesis of any view based on the importance of heritage. Such hostility to tradition well reflects one side of the modern mind. It is impossible to contemplate the changes even of the last decades, much less the major groundswell of change since the Renaissance, without feeling that we face largely new conditions which call for new qualities of mind and outlook. Moreover, it is obviously no accident that this pragmatic philosophy has been worked out most fully in the United States. Yet, in spite of its seeming conflict with views of education based on heritage, strong doubt exists whether the questioning, innovating, experimental attitude of pragmatism is in fact something alien to the Western heritage or whether it is not, in the broadest sense of the word, a part of it.

The rest of the present volume would hardly suffice for this sweeping subject. But it can be observed even here that we look back on antiquity not simply out of curiosity but because ancient thought is sympathetic to us. The Greek idea of an orderly universe, of political freedom under rationally constructed laws, and of the inner life itself as subject to the sway of reason, was certainly not achieved without skepticism, observation, or the test of experience. The ancient atomists and medical writers and, to a large extent, Socrates himself relied precisely on induction from observed facts. Socrates, the teacher and the gadfly of the Athenian city, impressed on his pupils and the public at large the duty of man to reflect on his beliefs and to criticize his presuppositions. Socrates was an individualist proclaiming that man should form his opinions by his own reasoning and not receive them by social indoctrination. And yet, it was this same Socrates who died in obedience to the judgment of the state, even though he believed this judgment to be wrong. Again, historical Christianity has been expressly and consistently concerned with the importance of this life on earth. The doctrine of the Incarnation, that God took the form of man and inhabited the earth, declares this concern. While perhaps for Greek thought, only the timeless realm had importance, in Christian thought the process of history is vested with absolute significance. If the ideal of democracy was rightly described above in the interwoven ideas of the dignity of man (that is, his existence as an independent moral agent) and his duty to his fellow men (that is, his testing by outward performance), the debt of these two ideas to the similarly interwoven commandments of the love of God and the love of neighbor is obvious.

These evidences of a consistent and characteristic appeal throughout Western history to the test of reason and experience are not adduced for the purpose of minimizing the huge creativeness of the modern scientific age or of glozing over its actual break from the past. In the well-known opening chapters of his *Science and the Modern World* in which he inquires into the origin of modern science, Mr. Whitehead pictures it as inspired by a revolt against abstract reasoning and a respect for unique fact. So considered, the first impulse of modern science was antirational or, better, antitheoretical, in the sense that it was a reaction against the most towering intellectual system which the West has known, namely, scholasticism. But be this question of origin as it may, there is no doubt that the modern mind received one of its characteristic bents in the empiricism, the passion for observation, and the distrust of abstract reasoning which have attended the origin and growth of science.

But there also seems no doubt that what happened was a shift, perhaps to some degree a restoration, of emphasis within the Western tradition itself rather than a complete change in its nature. It is a mistake to identify the older Western culture with traditionalism. Classical antiquity handed on a working system of truth which relied on both reason and experience and was designed to provide a norm for civilized life. Its import was heightened and vastly intensified by its confluence with Christianity. But when, in its rigid systematization in the late Middle Ages, it lost touch with experience and individual inquiry, it violated its own nature and provoked the modernist revolt. The seeming opposition that resulted between traditionalism and modernism has been a tragedy for Western thought. Modernism rightly affirms the importance of inquiry and of relevance to experience. But as scholasticism ran the danger of becoming a system without vitality, so modernism runs the danger of achieving vitality without pattern.

While, then, there are discontinuities between the classical and the modern components of our Western culture, there are also continuities. For instance, it would be wrong to construe the scientific outlook as inimical to human values. Even if it were true that science is concerned with means only, it would not follow that science ignores the intrinsic worth of man. For the values of human life cannot be achieved within a physical vacuum; they require for their fulfillment the existence of material conditions. To the extent that classical civilization failed to mitigate the evils of poverty, disease, squalor, and a generally low level of living among the masses, to that extent it failed to liberate man. Conversely, to the extent that science, especially in its medical and technological applications, has succeeded in dealing with these evils, it has contributed to the realization of human values. Thus science has implemented the humanism which classicism and Christianity have proclaimed.

Science has done more than provide the material basis of the good life; it has directly fostered the spiritual values of humanism. To explain, science is both the outcome and the source of the habit of forming objective, disinterested judgments based upon exact evidence. Such a habit is of particular value in the formation of citizens for a free society. It opposes to the arbitrariness of authority and "first principles" the direct and continuing appeal to things as they are. Thus it develops the qualities of the free man. It is no accident that John Locke, who set forth the political doctrine of the natural rights of man against established authority, should have been also the man who rejected the authority of innate ideas.

Students of antiquity and of the Middle Ages can therefore rightly affirm that decisive truths about the human mind and its relation to the world were laid hold of then, and yet agree that, when new application of these truths was made through a more scrupulous attention to fact, their whole implication and meaning were immensely enlarged. Modern civilization has seen this enlargement of meaning and possibility; yet it is not a new civilization but the organic development of an earlier civilization. The true task of education is therefore so to reconcile the sense of pattern and direction deriving from heritage with the sense of experiment and innovation deriving from science that they may exist fruitfully together, as in varying degrees they have never ceased to do throughout Western history.

Belief in the dignity and mutual obligation of man is the common ground between these contrasting but mutually necessary forces in our culture. As was pointed out earlier, this belief is the fruit at once of religion, of the Western tradition, and of the American tradition. It equally inspires the faith in human reason which is the basis for trust in the future of democracy. And if it is not, strictly speaking, implied in all statements of the scientific method, there is no doubt that science has become its powerful instrument. In this tension between the opposite forces of heritage and change poised only in the faith in man, lies something like the old philosophic problem of the knowledge of the good. If you know the good, why do you seek it? If you are ignorant of the good, how do you recognize it when you find it? You must evidently at one and the same time both know it and be ignorant of it. Just so, the tradition which has come down to us regarding the nature of man and the good society must inevitably provide our standard of good. Yet an axiom of that tradition itself is the belief that no current form of the received ideal is final but that every generation, indeed every individual, must discover it in a fresh form. Education can therefore be wholly devoted neither to tradition nor to experiment, neither to the belief that the ideal in itself is enough nor to the view that means are valuable apart from the ideal. It must uphold at the same time tradition and experiment, the ideal and the means, subserving, like our culture itself, change within commitment.

2

General and Special Education

IN the previous section we have attempted to outline the unifying elements of our culture and therefore of American education as well. In the present section we shall take the next step of indicating in what ways these cultural strands may be woven into the fabric of education. Education is broadly divided into general and special education; our topic now is the difference and the relationship between the two. The term, general education, is somewhat vague and colorless; it does not mean some airy education in knowledge in general (if there be such knowledge), nor does it mean education for all in the sense of universal education. It is used to indicate that part of a student's whole education which looks first of all to his life as a responsible human being and citizen; while the term, special education, indicates that part which looks to the student's competence in some occupation. These two sides of life are not entirely separable, and it would be false to imagine education for the one as quite distinct from education for the other—more will be said on this point presently. Clearly, general education has somewhat the meaning of liberal education, except that, by applying to high school as well as to college, it envisages immensely greater numbers of students and thus escapes the invidium which, rightly or wrongly, attaches to liberal education in the minds of some people. But if one cling to the root meaning of liberal as that which befits or helps to make free men, then general and liberal education have identical goals. The one may be thought of as an earlier stage of the other, similar in nature but less advanced in degree.

The opposition to liberal education—both to the phrase and to the fact—stems largely from historical causes. The concept of liberal education first appeared in a slave-owning society, like that of Athens, in which the community was divided into freemen and slaves, rulers and subjects. While the slaves carried on the specialized occupations of menial work, the freemen were primarily concerned with the right and duties of citizenship. The training of the former was purely vocational; but as the freemen were not only a ruling but also a leisure class, their education was exclusively in the liberal arts, without any utilitarian tinge. The freemen were trained in the reflective pursuit of the good life; their education was unspecialized as well as unvocational; its aim was to produce a rounded person with a full understanding of himself and of his place in society and in the cosmos.

Modern democratic society clearly does not regard labor as odious or disgraceful; on the contrary, in this country at least, it regards leisure with suspicion and expects its "gentlemen" to engage in work. Thus we attach no odium to vocational instruction. Moreover, in so far as we surely reject the idea of freemen who are free in so far as they have slaves or subjects, we are apt strongly to deprecate the liberal education which went with the structure of the aristocratic ideal. Herein our society runs the risk of committing a serious fallacy. Democracy is the view that not only the few but that all are free, in that everyone governs his own life and shares in the responsibility for the management of the community. This being the case, it follows that all human beings stand in need of an ampler and rounded education. The task of modern democracy is to preserve the ancient ideal of liberal education and to extend it as far as possible to all the members of the community. In short, we have been apt to confuse accidental with fundamental factors, in our suspicion of the classical ideal. To believe in the equality of human beings is to believe that the good life, and the education which trains the citizen for the good life, are equally the privilege of all. And these are the touchstones of the liberated man: first, is he free; that is to say, is he able to judge and plan for himself, so that he can truly govern himself? In order to do this, his must be a mind capable of self-criticism; he must lead that self-examined life which according to Socrates is alone worthy of a free man. Thus he will possess inner freedom, as well as social freedom. Second, is he universal in his motives and sympathies? For the civilized man is a citizen of the entire universe; he has overcome provincialism, he is objective, and is a "spectator of all time and all existence." Surely these two are the very aims of democracy itself.

But the opposition to general education does not stem from causes located in the past alone. We are living in an age of specialism, in which the avenue to success for the student often lies in his choice of a specialized career, whether as a chemist, or an engineer, or a doctor, or a specialist in some form of business or of manual or technical work. Each of these specialties makes an increasing demand on the time and on the interest of the student. Specialism is the means for advancement in our mobile social structure; yet we must envisage the fact that a society controlled wholly by specialists is not a wisely ordered society. We cannot, however, turn away from specialism. The problem is how to save general education and its values within a system where specialism is necessary.

The very prevalence and power of the demand for special training makes doubly clear the need for a concurrent, balancing force in general education. Specialism enhances the centrifugal forces in society. The business of providing for the needs of society breeds a great diversity of special occupations; and a given specialist does not speak the language of the other specialists. In order to discharge his duties as a citizen adequately, a person must somehow be able to grasp the complexities of life as a whole. Even from the point of view of economic success, specialism has its peculiar limitations. Specializing in a vocation makes for inflexibility in a world of fluid possibilities. Business demands minds capable of adjusting themselves to varying situations and of managing complex human institutions. Given the pace of economic progress, techniques alter speedily; and even the work in which the student has been trained may no longer be useful when he is ready to earn a living or soon after. Our conclusion, then, is that the aim of education should be to prepare an individual to become an expert both in some particular vocation or art and in the general art of the free man and the citizen. Thus the two kinds of education once given separately to different social classes must be given together to all alike.

In this epoch in which almost all of us must be experts in some field in order to make a living, general education therefore assumes a peculiar importance. Since no one can become an expert in all fields, everyone is compelled to trust the judgment of other people pretty thoroughly in most areas of activity. I must trust the advice of my doctor, my plumber, my lawyer, my radio repairman, and so on. Therefore I am in peculiar need of a kind of sagacity by which to distinguish the expert from the quack, and the better from the worse expert. From this point of view, the aim of general education may be defined as that of providing the broad critical sense by which to recognize competence in any field. William James said that an educated person knows a good man when he sees one. There are standards and a style for every type of activity—manual, athletic, intellectual, or artistic; and the educated man should be one who can tell sound from shoddy work in a field outside his own. General education is especially required in a democracy where the public elects its leaders and officials; the ordinary citizen must be discerning enough so that he will not be deceived by appearances and will elect the candidate who is wise in his field.

Both kinds of education—special as well as general—contribute to the task of implementing the pervasive forces of our culture. Here we revert to what was said at the start of this article on the aims of education in our society. It was argued there that two complementary forces are at the root of our culture: on the one hand, an ideal of man and society distilled from the past but at the same time transcending the past as a standard of judgment valid in itself, and, on the other hand, the belief that no existent expressions of this ideal are final but that all alike call for perpetual scrutiny and change in the light of new knowledge. Specialism is usually the vehicle of this second force. It fosters the open-mindedness and love of investigation which are the wellspring of change, and it devotes itself to the means by which change is brought about. The fact may not always be obvious. There is a sterile specialism which hugs accepted knowledge and ends in the bleakest conservatism. Modern life also calls for many skills which, though specialized, are repetitive and certainly do not conduce to inquiry. These minister to change but unconsciously. Nevertheless, the previous statement is true in the sense that specialism is concerned primarily with knowledge in action, as it advances into new fields and into further applications.

Special education comprises a wider field than vocationalism; and correspondingly, general education extends beyond the limits of merely literary preoccupation. An example will make our point clearer. A scholar—let us say a scientist (whether student or teacher)—will, in the laudable aim of saving himself from narrowness, take a course in English literature, or perhaps read poetry and novels, or perhaps listen to good music and generally occupy himself with the fine arts. All this, while eminently fine and good, reveals a misapprehension. In his altogether unjustified humility, the scientist wrongly interprets the distinction between liberal and illiberal in terms of the distinction between the humanities and the sciences. Plato and Cicero would have been very much surprised to hear that geometry, astronomy, and the sciences of nature in general, are excluded from the humanities. There is also implied a more serious contempt for the liberal arts, harking back to the fallacy which identifies liberal education with the aristocratic ideal. The implication is that liberal education is something only genteel. A similar error is evident in the student's attitude toward his required courses outside his major field as something to "get over with," so that he may engage in the business of serious education, identified in his mind with the field of concentration.

Now, a general education is distinguished from special education, not by subject matter, but in terms of method and outlook, no matter what the field. Literature, when studied in a technical fashion, gives rise to the special science of philology; there is also the highly specialized historical approach to painting. Specialism is interchangeable, not with natural science, but with the method of science, the method which abstracts material from its context and handles it in complete isolation. The reward of scientific method is the utmost degree of precision and exactness. But, as we have seen, specialism as an educational force has its own limitations; it does not usually provide an insight into general relationships.

A further point is worth noting. The impact of specialism has been felt not only in those phases of education which are necessarily and rightly specialistic; it has affected also the whole structure of higher and even of secondary education. Teachers, themselves products of highly technical disciplines, tend to reproduce their knowledge in class. The result is that each subject, being taught by an expert, tends to be so presented as to attract potential experts. This complaint is perhaps more keenly felt in colleges and universities, which naturally look to scholarship. The undergraduate in a college receives his teaching from professors who, in their turn, have been trained in graduate schools. And the latter are dominated by the ideal of specialization. Learning now is diversified and parceled into a myriad of specialties. Correspondingly, colleges and universities are divided into large numbers of departments, with further specialization within the departments. As a result, a student in search of a general course is commonly frustrated. Even an elementary course is devised as an introduction to a specialism within a department; it is significant only as the beginning of a series of courses of advancing complexity. In short, such introductory courses are planned for the specialist, not for the student seeking a general education. The young chemist in the course in literature and the young writer in the course in chemistry find themselves in thoroughly uncomfortable positions so long as the purpose of these courses is primarily to train experts who will go on to higher courses rather than to give some basic understanding of science as it is revealed in chemistry or of the arts as they are revealed in literature.

It is most unfortunate if we envisage general education as something formless—that is to say, the taking of one course after another; and as something negative, namely, the study of what is not in a field of concentration. Just as we regard the courses in concentration as having definite relations to one another, so should we envisage general education as an organic whole whose parts join in expounding a ruling idea and in serving a common aim. And to do so means to abandon the view that all fields and all departments are equally valuable vehicles of general education. It also implies some prescription. At the least it means abandoning the usual attitude of regarding "distribution" as a sphere in which the student exercises a virtually untrammeled freedom of choice. It may be objected that we are proposing to limit the liberty of the student in the very name of liberal education. Such an objection would only indicate an ambiguity in the conception of liberal education. We must distinguish between liberalism in education and education in liberalism. The former, based as it is on the doctrine of individualism, expresses the view that the student should be free in his choice of courses. But education in liberalism is an altogether different matter; it is education which has a pattern of its own, namely, the pattern associated with the liberal outlook. In this view, there are truths which none can be free to ignore, if one is to have that wisdom through which life can become useful. These are the truths concerning the structure of the good life and concerning the factual conditions by which it may be achieved, truths comprising the goals of the free society.

Finally, the problem of general education is one of combining fixity of aim with diversity in application. It is not a question of providing a general education which will be uniform through the same classes of all schools and colleges all over the country, even were such a thing possible in our decentralized system. It is rather to adapt general education to the needs and intentions of different groups and, so far as possible, to carry its spirit into special education. The effectiveness of teaching has always largely depended on this willingness to adapt a central unvarying purpose to varying outlooks. Such adaptation is as much in the interest of the quick as of the slow, of the bookish as of the unbookish, and is the necessary protection of each. What is wanted, then, is a general education capable at once of taking on many different forms and yet of representing in all its forms the common knowledge and the common values on which a free society depends.

3

Areas of Knowledge

WE have gradually moved from the less to the more specific, until now we have reached the topic of actual outcomes of education. In this section we shall deal with general education only; and our question will take two forms: what characteristics (traits of mind and character) are necessary for anything like a full and responsible life in our society; and, by what elements of knowledge are such traits nourished? These two questions, these two aspects, are images of each other. We have repeatedly found ourselves until now describing general education, at one time, as looking to the good of man in society and, at another time, as dictated by the nature of knowledge itself. There is no escape from thus shifting from one face of the same truth to the other. But temporarily and for the sake of clarity it may be useful to separate the two questions and consider first the elements of knowledge, and later the characteristics.

Tradition points to a separation of learning into the three areas of natural science, social studies, and the humanities. The study of the natural sciences looks to an understanding of our physical environment, so that we may have a suitable relation to it. The study of the social sciences is intended to produce an understanding of our social environment and of human institutions in general, so that the student may achieve a proper relation to society—not only the local but also the great society, and, by the aid of history, the society of the past and even of the future. Finally, the purpose of the humanities is to enable man to understand man in relation to himself, that is to say, in his inner aspirations and ideals.

While all this is obvious and even trite, it is hardly adequate. Subject matters do not lend themselves to such neat distinctions. To consider only one example, psychology, which has been classified as a natural science in the above list, surely has, or ought to have, something to say about human nature. A more serious flaw of this classification is that it conceives of education as the act of getting acquainted with something, and so as the acquiring of information. But information is inert knowledge. Yet, given this limitation, such an approach has its merits because it directs the student's attention to the useful truth that man must familiarize himself with the environment in which nature has placed him if he is to proceed realistically with the task of achieving the good life.

A much better justification of the way in which the areas of learning are divided is in terms of methods of knowledge. Let us start with the difference between the natural sciences and the humanities. The former describe, analyze, and explain; the latter appraise, judge, and criticize. In the first, a statement is judged as true or false; in the second, a result is judged as good or bad. The natural sciences do not take it on themselves to evaluate the worth of what they describe. The chemist is content to state the actual structure of his compound without either praising or deploring the fact. Natural science measures what can be measured, and it operates upon its materials with the instruments of formal logic and mathematics. Yet these latter are not themselves science or even the final arbiters of science. Science serves a harsher master—the brute facts of physical reality. Logic and mathematics are triumphs of abstraction. These are the media by which a scientific argument is pursued. But when the argument has by these means yielded a solution, this in turn must meet the question, "is it real?" "is it true?" By this final appeal to things as they are, or as they appear to be, the argument stands or falls.

In contrast to mathematics and the natural sciences, the humanities explore and exhibit the realm of value. For example, in literature the student is presented with various ways of life, with the tragic and the heroic outlook, or with the merely pathetic and ridiculous. His imagination is stirred with vivid evocations of ideals of action, passion, and thought, among which he may learn to discriminate. The intelligent teacher will explore the great arts and literatures in order to bring out the ideals toward which man has been groping, confusedly yet stubbornly. And of course the arts have done as much through form as through content; they disclose varying standards of taste.

Although techniques have been developed for the study of natural phenomena, no comparable progress has been made in our insight into values. We can measure a physical body, but we cannot measure an ideal, nor can we put critical standards under a microscope so as to note all their elements with precision. Science aims at precision and gets it. This is true, partly because science will not bother itself with facts when these do not lend themselves to the methods of exact observation. It limits itself to events that recur and to things which permit measurement. To the extent that an object is truly unique and occurs only once it is not the stuff of science. For example, every society is to a degree unique; hence the student of social phenomena is still baffled in his search for strict uniformities.

To admit that a difference exists between the methods of science and our insight into values is one thing; to go on from there and assert that values are wholly arbitrary is a different and wholly unjustified conclusion. It has been thought that, since the words right and wrong as applied to ethical situations do not have the same meaning as right and wrong when applied to mathematical propositions, no rational criteria are involved; and that one is at liberty to choose any set of standards more or less from the air and apply them to the problems which come to hand. Or by way of reaction some persons have gone to the opposite extreme of setting up fixed dogmas and imposing them by sheer authority. But standards are the reflection neither of personal whims nor of dogmatic attitudes. In the realm of values, critical analysis of complex situations is possible by rational methods and in the light of what other men have thought upon such matters. Here we return to what was said earlier in this article about the twin contribution of heritage and innovation to human beliefs. Starting with a few premises, for instance with those involved in our commitment to a free society, the mind can proceed to analyze the implications of these premises and also to modify their initial meaning by the aid of experience. While there can be no experimenting with ideals, there is experience of values in application, and there is heaping up of such experience. While there can be no precise measurement, there is intelligent analysis of codes and standards. While there are no simple uniformities, there are moral principles which command the assent of civilized men. Of all this more presently; our conclusion is that value-judgments are, or at least can be, rational in so far as they are informed and disciplined; they are communicable and can become matters of intelligent discussion and persuasion.

Finally, on this basis the social studies may be said to combine the methods of the natural sciences and of the humanities, and to use both explanation and evaluation. For instance, the historian is obviously concerned with facts and events and with the causal relations between happenings; yet he is no less concerned with values. A historical fact is not merely a fact: it is a victory or a defeat, an indication of progress or of retrogression, it is a misfortune or good fortune. We do not mean by this that a historian passes moral judgments on events and nations. We do mean that a historian is selective; that out of the infinity of events he chooses those that have a bearing on man's destiny. A similar situation is disclosed in economics, which is a judicious mixture, not always acknowledged or even realized, of factual objective study and normative judgment. The classical, if not the contemporary, economist is engaged on the one hand in a description and analysis of this or that economic institution, and on the other hand with a criticism of what he describes and analyzes in the light of the norm of a sound economy. From this point of view the object of philosophy would appear to be the bringing together of both facts and values. Philosophy asks the question: what is the place of human aspirations and ideals in the total scheme of things?

The method of science can be set off against the method of social studies and humanities taken together in the following way. In science, new findings are constantly being made in such a way that the sum of these findings constitutes the current view of truth. Science is knowledge for which an exact standard of truth exists; as a result, within any particular present there is common agreement about what is scientific truth; or if the agreement is lacking there are determinate criteria commonly agreed upon, by the application of which the issue can be settled. But in the other two fields there is often no common agreement as to what is valid within any given present; there is diversity of schools and doctrines, the reason being that a standard of exact truth or exact rightness is lacking. In the sciences, thought is progressive; the later stage corrects the earlier and includes the truth of the earlier. Were Galileo able to return to the land of the living, who doubts that he would regard later changes in physical theory as an improvement on his own? In consequence, the history of its thought is strictly irrelevant to science. But it is impossible to say with the same assurance that our philosophy or art, thought presumably better than the cave man's, is better than that of the Greeks or of the men of the Renaissance. The work of any genius in art or philosophy or literature represents in some sense a complete and absolute vision. Goethe does not render Sophocles obsolete, nor does Descartes supersede Plato. The geniuses that follow do not so much correct preceding insights as they supply alternative but similarly simple and total insights from new perspectives. For this reason historical knowledge has a special importance in philosophy, and the achievements of the past have a significance for the arts and literature which is certainly not true of science.

At this point the impatient reader will interject that the distinctions which we have made do not really distinguish. We have said that literature exhibits life as it might be; yet is it not a fact that literature also depicts life as it is? We have said that economics is concerned with norms as well as actualities; yet surely mathematical economics is an analytical study and nothing else. And conversely, the reader may add, it is false that science is wholly restricted to the techniques of measurement. The very method of science, the way in which it defines a fact and its essential presuppositions, is not subject to scientific proof. All this we admit without reservation. The distinctions we have made are rough and inexact; the total area of learning is more like a spectrum along which the diverse modes of thought are combined in varying degrees, approximating to purity only at the extreme ends.

Nevertheless, these distinctions retain their importance at least for pragmatic, that is, educational reasons. If it is true that in questions of government the words right and wrong, true and false, lack the exactitude which they have in questions of mathematics, the fact must be of the essence of teaching government and history. Clearly, education will not look solely to the giving of information. Information is of course the basis of any knowledge, but if both the nature of truth and the methods of asserting it differ as between the areas, the fact must be made fully apparent. As Mr. Whitehead has said, a student should not be taught more than he can think about. Selection is the essence of teaching. Even the most compendious survey is only the rudest culling from reality. Since the problem of choice can under no circumstances be avoided, the problem becomes what, rather than how much, to teach; or better, what principles and methods to illustrate by the use of information. The same conflict between the factual aspects of a subject and the need of insight into the kind of truth with which it deals arises in an acute form in that most factual of disciplines, natural science itself. While a heaping up of information is peculiarly necessary in the teaching of science, information is not enough. Facts must be so chosen as to convey not only something of the substance of science but, also and above all, of its methods, its characteristic achievements, and its limitations. To the extent that a student becomes aware of the methods he is using, and critically conscious of his presuppositions, he learns to transcend his specialty and generates a liberal outlook in himself.

4

Traits of Mind

AT the time of his examination the average student hardly remembers more than 75 per cent of what he was taught. If he were a sophomore when he took the course, how much does he recall by the time of his graduation, how much five years later, how much, or how little, when he returns on his twenty-fifth reunion? Pondering on all this, the pessimist might well conclude that education is a wholly wasteful process. He would of course be wrong, for the simple reason that education is not a process of stuffing the mind with facts. Yet he would be partly right because the student soon forgets not only many facts but even some general ideas and principles. No doubt we are exaggerating. Those students particularly who have been able to unite what they learned in school or college with later studies or with their jobs do retain a surprising amount of information. Nevertheless, the real answer to the pessimist is that education is not merely the imparting of knowledge but the cultivation of certain aptitudes and attitudes in the mind of the young. As we have said earlier, education looks both to the nature of knowledge and to the good of man in society. It is to the latter aspect that we shall now turn our attention—more particularly to the traits and characteristics of mind fostered by education.

By characteristics we mean aims so important as to prescribe how general education should be carried out and which abilities should be sought above all others in every part of it. These abilities, in our opinion, are: *to think effectively, to communicate thought, to make relevant judgments, to discriminate among values.* They are not in practice separable and are not to be developed in isolation. Nor can they be even analyzed in separation. Each is an indispensable coexistent function of a sanely growing mind. Nonetheless, since exposition requires that one thing be discussed at one time, our description of these abilities must take them up in turn.

By *effective thinking* we mean, in the first place, logical thinking: the ability to draw sound conclusions from premises. Yet by logical thinking we do not mean the equipment of the specialist or what a student would learn by taking a course in formal logic. We are concerned with the student who is going to be a worker, or a businessman, or a professional man, and who does not necessarily look forward to a career in scholarship or in pure science. As a plain citizen he will practice his logical skills in practical situations—in choosing a career, in deciding whom to vote for, or what house to buy, or even in choosing a wife. But perhaps the last case is just the point where logical skills fail, although European parents might disagree.

Logical thinking is the capacity to extract universal truths from particular cases and, in turn, to infer particulars from general laws. More strictly, it is the ability to discern a pattern of relationships—on the one hand to analyze a problem into its component elements, and on the other to recombine these, often by the use of imaginative insight, so as to reach a solution. Its prototype is mathematics which, starting with a few selected postulates, makes exact deductions with certainty. Logical thinking is involved to a degree in the analysis of the structure of a painting as well as in that of a geometrical system. In moving toward a solution, the trained mind will have a sharp eye for the relevant factors while zealously excluding all that is irrelevant; and it will arrange the relevant factors according to weight. For instance, in voting during a presidential election our citizen should consider whether the candidate has sound policies, whether he has the ability to get on with Congress, whether he has a good grasp of international relations, and, in these troubled times, whether he has an understanding of military strategy. These are some of the factors which are relevant to the problem in hand. But the looks of the candidate most probably, and his religious denomination surely, are irrelevant. Prejudice brings in irrelevancies and logic should keep them out.

Effective thinking, while starting with logic, goes further so as to include certain broad mental skills. Thus an effective thinker is a man who can handle terms and concepts with skill and yet does not confuse words with things; he is empirical in the widest sense of the word, looking outward to nature. He is not satisfied merely with noting the facts, but his mind ever soars to implications. He knows when he knows and when he does not; he does not mistake opinion for knowledge. Furthermore, effective thinking includes the understanding of complex and fluid situations, in dealing with which logical methods are inadequate as mental tools. Of course thinking must never violate the laws of logic, but it may use techniques beyond those of exact mathematical reasoning. In the fields of the social studies and history, and in the problems of daily life, there are large areas where evidence is incomplete and may never be completed. Sometimes the evidence may be also untrustworthy; but, if the situation is practical, a decision must be made. The scientist has been habituated to deal with properties which can be abstracted from their total background and with variables which are few and well defined. Consequently, where the facts are unique and unpredictable, where the variables are numerous and their interactions too complicated for precise calculation, the scientist is apt to throw up his hands in despair and perhaps turn the situation over to the sentimentalist or the mystic. But surely he would be wrong in so doing; for the methods of logical thinking do not exhaust the resources of reason. In coping with complex and fluid situations we need thinking which is relational and which searches for cross bearings between areas; this is thinking in a context. By its use it is possible to reach an understanding of historical and social materials and of human relations, although not with the same degree of precision as in the case of simpler materials and of recurring events. As Aristotle says, "It is the mark of an educated man to expect no more exactness than the subject permits."

A further element in effective thinking is the imagination, by which we mean whatever is distinctive in the thinking of the poet. Logical thinking is straight, as opposed to crooked, thinking; and that of the poet may be described as curved thinking. Where the scientist operates with abstract conceptions the poet employs sensuous images; imagination is the faculty of thinking in terms of concrete ideas and symbols. Instead of reading a prosaic analysis of exuberant vitality, we may get a direct vision of it in Manet's portrait of the boy with the flute. We may study human nature in the psychologist's abstract accounts of it, or we may see it in the vivid presentations of imagined individuals like Othello, Becky Sharp, Ulysses, and Anna Karenina. The reader might demur that imagination has little to do with effective thinking. Yet the imagination is most valuable in the field of human relations. Statistics are useful, but statistics alone will not carry us very far in the understanding of human beings. We need an imagination delicately sensitive to the hopes and the fears, the qualities and the flaws of our fellow man, and which can evoke a total personality in its concrete fullness. In practical matters, imagination supplies the ability to break with habit and routine, to see beyond the obvious and to envisage new alternatives; it is the spur of the inventor and the revolutionary, no less than of the artist.

It may be noted that the three phases of effective thinking, logical, relational, and imaginative, correspond roughly to the three divisions of learning, the natural sciences, the social studies, and the humanities, respectively.

Communication—the ability to express oneself so as to be understood by others—is obviously inseparable from effective thinking. In most thinking, one is talking to oneself; and good speech and writing are the visible test and sign of good thinking. Conversely, to speak clearly one must have clear ideas. You cannot say something unless you have something to say; but in order to express your ideas properly you also need some skill in communication. There is something else too: the honest intent to make your ideas known, as against the desire to deceive or merely to conceal. Communication is not speaking only but listening as well; you cannot succeed in communicating your ideas unless the other person wishes to hear and knows how to listen. As there are two kinds of language, oral and written, communication breaks up into the four related skills of speaking and listening, writing and reading.

Communication is that unrestricted exchange of ideas within the body politic by which a prosperous intellectual economy is secured. In its character as the sharing of meanings it is the instrument by which human beings are welded into a society, both the living with the living and the living with the dead. In a free and democratic society the art of communication has a special importance. A totalitarian state can obtain consent by force; but a democracy must persuade, and persuasion is through speech, oral or other. In a democracy issues are aired, talked out of existence or talked into solution. Failure of communication between the citizens, or between the government and the public, means a breakdown in the democratic process. Nevertheless, whereas people have been brought together nearer than ever before, in a physical sense, by the improvement of mechanisms of transportation, it cannot be said that mutual understanding among individuals and among peoples has made a corresponding advance. Skills, crafts, professions, and scholarly disciplines are apt to surround themselves by high walls of esoteric jargon. Other barriers are erected through the tendency to convert communication into propaganda, whether it be political propaganda, or economic propaganda, as for instance in some types of advertising. Thus, effective communication depends on the possession not only of skills such as clear thinking and cogent expression but of moral qualities as well, such as candor.

In older days, a course on rhetoric was a normal part of the curriculum. Rhetoric to us suggests oratory, and today we are suspicious of or at least indifferent to oratory. Yet the art of rhetoric meant the simple skill of making one's ideas clear and cogent; it did not necessarily mean high-flown speeches. The simplest example of communication is conversation. It is a truism to say that conversation is a lost art. The question is, where was it lost? If we carry on less, or less good, conversation than our ancestors did, is it because we have lost the art, or because, having become technicians, we have little to say that is suitable for general conversation, or because we are much more interested in doing things—driving, for example, or playing bridge? Learned persons are apt to disparage conversation as trivial or frivolous, but unjustly so. If you are looking for the uncovering of important truths during a dinner party, of course you may be disappointed; but that is because you will be looking for the wrong thing. The contribution of general conversation is the revelation and impact of personality. While nothings are being bandied about and trivial words, like the lightest balloons, are launched into the air, contact with personalities is being achieved through characteristic inflections and emphases, through readiness or shyness of response. In conversation the idea is inseparable from the man; conversation is useful because it is the most unforced and natural means of bringing persons together into a society. Beyond its social function, conversation is a delight in itself. It is an art, yet it loses its value if it becomes artificial. Its essence is spontaneity, impetus, movement; the words of a conversation are evanescent, things of the moment, while written words are formalized, rigid, and fixed. Starting with simple things like the weather and minor personal happenings, it proceeds to weave a pattern of sentiments and ideas, and through these of persons, which is fugitive just because it is alive.

Perhaps we have wandered too far from the serious—or should we say the ponderous—aspects of our problem. Yet we had a point to make: that language needs to be neither high learning nor high literature in order to be communication. What we have in mind is the language of a businessman writing a plain and crisp letter, of a scientist making a report, of a citizen asking straight questions, of human beings arguing together on some matter of common interest.

The *making of relevant judgments* involves the ability of the student to bring to bear the whole range of ideas upon the area of experience. It is not now a question of apprehending more relationships within ideas but of applying these to actual facts. The most competent instructor of military science is not necessarily the best officer in the field. An adequate theory of ball playing is conceivable, but an abstract knowledge of it would not make a good ballplayer any more than a course on poetics, however good, would make a good poet. It is not the power to distinguish or state the universal formula, for separated contemplation, which heightens our skill. It is the power to use the formula in the new concrete situations as they fleet past us which education aims to advance. In Plato's myth the philosopher who has obtained the vision of the good must return to the cave and use his vision in order to guide himself among the shadows. Initially and inevitably he is confused; only after long habituation is he able to find his way around and properly to apply his concepts to his concrete experience. There is no rule to be learned which could tell the student how to apply rules to cases; the translation from theory to practice involves an art all its own and requires the skill which we call sagacity or judgment.

To some degree every school or college is separated from life by high walls, visible or invisible; it holds reality at arm's length. And up to a point this is necessary and proper. While it is true that the present is our only fact, nevertheless we cannot see the present so long as we are immersed in it; we need the perspective afforded by distance in time and in space. One of the aims of education is to break the stranglehold of the present upon the mind. On the other side is the fact that youth is instinctive and ardent; to subject youth to a steady diet of abstractions alone would be cruel and unnatural. Moreover, abstractions in themselves are meaningless unless connected with experience; and for this reason all education is in some sense premature. The adult who rereads his great authors realizes how much he had missed of their meaning when he read them in school or college. Now his reading is more rewarding because his range of experience is greater. One might conceive fancifully of another scheme of life in which work comes first and education begins later, say at forty-five. The advantages of this scheme are obvious. Not only would the mature student be amply equipped with the depth of experience necessary for the understanding of the great authors, but the financial problem would be solved. The student would have saved enough money from his work, or perhaps his children would support him.

But such utopias are not for us; we have to deal with harsh realities. Education must be so contrived that the young, during the very process of their schooling, will realize the difference between abstractions and facts and will learn to make the transition from thought to action. A young man who has been nourished with ideas exclusively will be tempted by the sin of intellectual pride, thinking himself capable of dealing with any problem, independently of experience. When he later comes into contact with things, he will stumble or perhaps in self-defense withdraw into sterile cleverness. As we have seen, the aptitude of making relevant judgments cannot be developed by theoretical teaching; being an art, it comes from example, practice, and habituation. The teacher can do a great deal nonetheless; he can relate theoretical content to the student's life at every feasible point, and he can deliberately simulate in the classroom situations from life. Finally, he can bring concrete reports of actual cases for discussion with the students. The essential thing is that the teacher should be constantly aware of the ultimate objectives, never letting means obscure ends, and be persistent in directing the attention of the student from the symbols to the things they symbolize.

Discrimination among values involves choice. The ability to discriminate in choosing covers not only awareness of different kinds of value but of their relations, including a sense of relative importance and of the mutual dependence of means and ends. It covers also much that is analogous to method in thinking; for example, the power to distinguish values truly known from values received only from opinion and therefore not in the same way part of the fabric of experience. Values are of many kinds. There are the obvious values of character, like fair play, courage, self-control, the impulse of beneficence and humanity; there are the intellectual values, like the love of truth and the respect for the intellectual enterprise in all its forms; there are the aesthetic values, like good taste and the appreciation of beauty. As for the last, people are apt to locate beauty in picture galleries and in museums and to leave it there; it is equally, if not more, important to seek beauty in ordinary things, so that it may surround one's life like an atmosphere.

Add to all this that the objective of education is not just knowledge of values but commitment to them, the embodiment of the ideal in one's actions, feelings, and thoughts, no less than an intellectual grasp of the ideal. The reader may object that we are proposing a confusion, that we are suggesting the turning of school or college into a moral reformatory or a church. For is not the purpose of educational institutions to train the mind and the mind only? Yet it is not easy, indeed it is impossible, to separate effective thinking from character. An essential factor in the advancement of knowledge is intellectual integrity, the suppression of all wishful thinking and the strictest regard for the claims of evidence. The universal community of educated men is a fellowship of ideals as well as of beliefs. To isolate the activity of thinking from the morals of thinking is to make sophists of the young and to encourage them to argue for the sake of personal victory rather than of the truth. We are not so naive as to suggest that theoretical instruction in the virtues will automatically make a student virtuous. Rather, we assert that the best way to infect the student with the zest for intellectual integrity is to put him near a teacher who is himself selflessly devoted to the truth; so that a spark from the teacher will, so to speak, leap across the desk into the classroom, kindling within the student the flame of intellectual integrity, which will thereafter sustain itself.

The problem of moral values and character is more complex. Here the college does not play quite the same role as the school. Clearly we have a right to expect the school to be engaged directly in moral education. But although the college shares in this responsibility, it cannot be expected to use the same direct approach. The college will have to confine itself to providing a proper discrimination of values and will trust to the Socratic dictum that the knowledge of the good will lead to a commitment to the good. Nevertheless, we must recognize a difference between the responsibility of both school and college to train the intellect and their responsibility to form character. In some sense, the former responsibility is a unique one for the educational institution. But in the sphere of moral instruction the school shares its responsibilities with numerous other institutions, of which the family is the most important. Moreover, the school's responsibility is less than that of the family in this field. To use an earlier figure there is danger in regarding the school as a modern Atlas to whom is entrusted the bearing of the whole task of the formation of man. To change the metaphor, a wise society does not put all its eggs in one basket. By the same token, the school cannot remain uninterested in the task of moral education. Just as liberal education, while strictly liberal, must somehow be oriented toward vocationalism, so in this general way will school and college be oriented toward moral character.

Discrimination in values is developed by the study of all the three areas of learning. We have seen that the humanities point both to moral and to aesthetic values. It may be true, as we have said earlier, that ethical neutrality is a guiding rule for the historian as scholar. Nevertheless, the historian or social scientist, as *teacher*, should probably go further and present to the student the human past and human institutions not merely as facts but as attempted embodiments of the good life in its various phases. In the natural sciences facts are studied in abstraction from values. But this separation, while pragmatically valid, leads to disaster if treated as final. Values are rooted in facts; and human ideals are somehow a part of nature.

5

The Good Man and the Citizen

General education, we repeat, must consciously aim at these abilities: at effective thinking, communication, the making of relevant judgments, and the discrimination of values. As was noted earlier, one of the subtlest and most prevalent effects of specialism has been that, through its influence, subjects have tended to be conceived and taught with an eye, so to speak, to their own internal logic rather than to their larger usefulness to students. In a course in history, for example, little concern will be felt for a student's ability to express himself, which will be left to English, or for his ability to think logically, which will fall to mathematics. Good teachers will, to be sure, always say of their subject that it subserves these higher aims, and to their great credit many do seek these aims. But the organization of knowledge into rigid, almost autonomous units, works against them. One of the few clear facts about the unclear and much disputed question of the transfer of powers from one subject to another is that it will tend not to take place unless it is deliberately planned for and worked for. Again, every course, whether general or special, may be expected to contribute something to all these abilities. Doubtless some courses will contribute more to some traits and others to others, but these abilities are after all of quite universal importance. Communication is basic to science as well as to literature; the power to think effectively is as essential to all forms of speech as it is to mathematics. Indeed, it will not be fostered as it should even by mathematics, unless the logical movements which find their purest form in theorems and equations are expressly given wider use. The power to discriminate between values is involved in this very act of wider application. Finally, the mastery of any one of the three large areas of learning will be of little use to the student unless he can relate his learning to the realities of experience and practice.

Human personality cannot, however, be broken up into distinct parts or traits. Education must look to the whole man. It has been wisely said that education aims at the good man, the good citizen, and the useful man. By a good man is meant one who possesses an inner integration, poise, and firmness, which in the long run come from an adequate philosophy of life. Personal integration is not a fifth characteristic in addition to the other four and coördinate with them; it is their proper fruition. The aim of liberal education is the development of the whole man; and human nature involves instincts and sentiments as well as the intellect. Two dangers must be mentioned. First, there is the danger of identifying intelligence with the qualities of the so-called intellectual type—with bookishness and skill in the manipulation of concepts. We have tried to guard against this mistake by stressing the traits of relevant judgment and discrimination of values in effective thinking. Second, we must remember that intelligence, even when taken in its widest sense, does not exhaust the total potentialities of human nature. Man is not a contemplative being alone. Why is it, then, that education is conceived as primarily an intellectual enterprise when, in fact, human nature is so complex? For instance, man has his emotions and his drives and his will; why should education center on the training of the intellect? The answer is found in the truth that intelligence is not a special function (or not that only) but a way in which all human powers may function. Intelligence is that leaven of awareness and reflection which, operating upon the native powers of men, raises them from the animal level and makes them truly human. By reason we mean, not an activity apart, but rational guidance of all human activity. Thus the fruit of education is intelligence in action. The aim is mastery of life; and since living is an art, wisdom is the indispensable means to this end.

We are here disputing the doctrine, sometimes described as the classical view, that in education, reason is a self-sufficient end. Yet it was Plato himself who urged that the guardians of the state should be courageous as well as wise, in other words, that they should be full-blooded human beings as well as trained minds. We equally oppose the view at the other extreme that vitality and initiative, unregulated by the intellect, are adequate criteria of the good man. Whenever the two parts of the single aim are separated, when either thought or action is stressed as an exclusive end, when the teachers look only to scholarly ability and the students (and perhaps the public too) only to proficiency in activities and to "personality" (whatever that may mean), then indeed wholeness is lost. And what is worse, these qualities themselves, in proportion as they are divorced from each other, tend to wither or at least to fall short of fulfilling their promise.

We are not at all unmindful of the importance of religious belief in the completely good life. But, given the American scene with its varieties of faith and even of unfaith, we did not feel justified in proposing religious instruction as a part of the curriculum. The love of God is tested by the love of neighbor; nevertheless the love of God transcends merely human obligations. We must perforce speak in purely humanistic terms, confining ourselves to the obligations of man to himself and to society. But we have been careful so to delimit humanism as not to exclude the religious ideal. Yet we are not arguing for an education which is student-centered. As man is the measure of the abstract values, so in their turn do these values measure man. Like an ellipse, an educational institution has two centers, not one. And although the geometrical metaphor forbids it, truth compels us to add a third, namely, society.

Just as it is wrong to split the human person into separate parts, so would it be wrong to split the individual from society. We must resist the prevalent tendency, or at any rate temptation, to interpret the good life purely in terms of atomic individuals engaged in fulfilling their potentialities. Individualism is often confused with the life of private and selfish interest. The mandate of this committee is to concern itself with "the objectives of education in a free society." It is important to realize that the ideal of a free society involves a twofold value, the value of freedom and that of society. Democracy is a *community* of free men. We are apt sometimes to stress freedom—the power of individual choice and the right to think for oneself—without taking sufficient account of the obligation to coöperate with our fellow men; democracy must represent an adjustment between the values of freedom and social living.

Eighteenth-century liberalism tended to conceive the good life in terms of freedom alone and thought of humanity in pluralistic terms (like matter in Newtonian physics) as an aggregate of independent particles. But a life in which everyone owns his home as his castle and refrains from interfering with others is a community in a negative sense only. Rugged individualism is not sufficient to constitute a democracy; democracy also is fraternity and coöperation for the common good. Josiah Royce defined the good life in terms of loyalty to a shared value. Of course when union is stressed to the exclusion of freedom we fall into totalitarianism; but when freedom is stressed exclusively we fall into chaos. Democracy is the attempt to combine liberty with loyalty, each limiting the other, and also each reinforcing the other.

It is important, however, to limit the idea of the good citizen expressly by the ideal of the good man. By citizenship we do not mean the kind of loyalty which never questions the accepted purposes of society. A society which leaves no place for criticism of its own aims and methods by its component members has no chance to correct its errors and ailments, no chance to advance to new and better forms, and will eventually stagnate, if not die. The quality of alert and aggressive individualism is essential to good citizenship; and the good society consists of individuals who are independent in outlook and think for themselves while also willing to subordinate their individual good to the common good.

But the problem of combining these two aims is one of the hardest tasks facing our society. The ideal of free inquiry is a precious heritage of Western culture; yet a measure of firm belief is surely part of the good life. A free society means toleration, which in turn comes from openness of mind. But freedom also presupposes conviction; a free choice—unless it be wholly arbitrary (and then it would not be free)—comes from belief and ultimately from principle. A free society, then, cherishes both toleration and conviction. Yet the two seem incompatible. If I am convinced of the truth of my views, on what grounds should I tolerate your views, which I believe to be false? The answer lies partly in my understanding of my limitations as a man. Such understanding is not only the expression of an intellectual humility but is a valid inference from the fact that wise men have made endless mistakes in the past. Furthermore, a belief which does not meet the challenge of criticism and dissent soon becomes inert, habitual, dead. Had there been no heterodoxies, the orthodox should have invented them. A belief which is not envisaged as an answer to a problem is not a belief but a barren formula.

How far should we go in the direction of the open mind? Especially after the first World War, liberals were sometimes too distrustful of enthusiasm and were inclined to abstain from committing themselves as though there were something foolish, even shameful, in belief. Yet especially with youth, which is ardent and enthusiastic, open-mindedness without belief is apt to lead to the opposite extreme of fanaticism. We can all perhaps recall young people of our acquaintance who from a position of extreme skepticism, and indeed because of that position, fell an easy prey to fanatical gospels. It seems that nature abhors an intellectual vacuum. A measure of belief is necessary in order to preserve the quality of the open mind. If toleration is not to become nihilism, if conviction is not to become dogmatism, if criticism is not to become cynicism, each must have something of the other.

THE HARVARD REPORT

ALEXANDER BRODY

I. In Search of Unity

The Persian Wars, according to the history textbooks, produced a division among the Athenians between the innovators and the conservatives. A "fierce and tumultuous individualism" released by increased opportunities for wealth, leasiure, and political power weakened civic loyalty, while the growth of knowledge and the critical spirit challenged the institutional basis of social and moral life. The impact of social change was reflected also in the educational system. A demand arose for a new education—an education that would fit the individual for expanding opportunities and personal achievement. A new class of teachers, the Sophists, appeared in the land. They professed knowledge in all fields, opposed nature to custom and taught that man is the measure of all things. The conflict between the new and the old produced intellectual uncertainty and the problem of the reconciliation of the individual and society became acute. Educational theorists or philosophers sought to formulate a new basis for social and moral life—one which would conserve the worth of the individual and at the same time, the worth of society. Socrates arrived at the fundamental principle that knowledge is virtue. Plato accepted the Socratic notion of rational knowledge as the guide for belief and conduct, but sought to pattern knowledge after preexisting and absolute ideas. Aristotle derived the idea of good from concrete particulars, and made happiness or goodness, rather than knowledge, the aim of life and the basis of the reconciliation between the new and the old.

It would be reading history backwards to trace the components of the modern social and educational problems in the crisis which faced fifth-century Athens. Today it is industrialism, science, and the pervasive influence of technology which make the reconciliation between the individual and the social so acute. Nevertheless, each age offers a striking example of the formal continuity of certain problems arising out of the relations of the individual to society. These problems, although with considerable change of content, assume a conceptual form as the problem of the particular and the universal, unity and diversity, authority and freedom, stability and change. The unity of the Middle Ages rested upon membership in a universal community under immutable law. The men of the Renaissance found the principle of unity in the humanistic ideal of the individual. Eighteenth-and-nineteenth-century liberalism sought in competition the mechanism by which to equate individual and social interest. In natural reaction to individualistic liberalism in America in the early twenties, Dewey and his followers went to the opposite extreme. Politics and ethics were to be judged by the test of social consequences, and mind and character became mere attitudes of participating responses to social situations. Today we know that competitive individualism operated to the advantage of the few at the expense of the many, while the overemphasis on the social obliterates the individual. Democracy must avoid the chaos of individualism and the tyranny of totalitarianism. The crucial problem of Democracy is to discover and adopt a via media between the values of freedom and social control.

This problem of democracy furnishes the starting point for the Harvard Report on Education. The Harvard educators are deeply concerned over the clash of interests between opposing groups

Reprinted from *Social Forces* 25, no. 2 (1946).

and classes in America. They would like to resolve the contradiction between the traditional American ideals of individualism, born of days of the pioneer and the frontier, and the contemporary age of science and economic interdependence. Hence they emphasize those aspects of democracy which make for common values, common standards, and common responsibilities. But unity must be conditioned by diversity, and the necessity for common belief must be reconciled with "the equally obvious necessity for new and independent insights leading to change." That is, the sense of pattern and direction deriving from heritage is to be balanced with the sense of experiment and innovation deriving from science. For the habit of forming objective, disinterested judgments based upon exact evidence is "of particular value in the formation of citizens for a free society."

The Harvard professors are in search for some "over-all logic," some strong "not easily broken frame" within which American culture and education may fulfill their at once diversifying and uniting tasks. This logic must be wide enough "to embrace the actual richness and variegation of modern life" and "it must also be strong enough to give goal and direction to this system." It is evidently to be looked for in the character of American society, "a society not wholly of the new world since it came from the old, not wholly given to innovation since it acknowledges certain fixed beliefs." This logic must further embody certain values which American life predicates, namely, cooperation without uniformity, and "agreement on level of operation without the necessity of agreement on ultimates."

The ideal of unity in democratic society must be implemented by intellectual unity. For democracy is peculiarly dependent on a common view on life and on the integrative work of the schools. This is the basic theme of the Harvard Report. But how is unity in the educational system to be achieved? What method or substance gives meaning and coherence to all parts of the curriculum? By what fields of study can the proper traits of mind and character be developed? Here one meets a multitude of conflicting solutions. There are those who insist that religion is the source of intellectual unity. Others seek the solution in the tradition of western culture as embodied in the great writers of the European and American past. A third solution is the functional approach. It casts off the formal divisions of knowledge and tries to organize knowledge around actual problems of contemporary life. Finally, the pragmatist solution sees in science and the scientific outlook this saving unity, urging that what is common to modern knowledge is not so much any over-all scheme as a habit of meeting problems in a detached experimental, observing spirit. Is the concept of education to be torn asunder in these divisive ways?

II. The Nature of the Social Sciences

The line of reasoning in the Harvard Report thus far, may be put as follows. American education, or, more broadly our culture, is at present a centrifugal one "in extreme need of unifying forces." In the tension between the opposite forces of heritage and change, between those who view education as committed to the past and those who view education as committed to change and innovations, there lies a dichotomy which threatens "to cut us off from the past and therefore from one another." What is wanted, then, is general education representing in all its forms "the common knowledge and the common values on which a free society depends." But knowledge is "dangerous" and "illiberal" if it does not embrace as fully as possible "the mainsprings of our culture." For example, education though compatible with religious values, "can not be safely left to those who see our culture solely through the eyes of formal religion." Neither is this culture wholly reflected in any one list of great books, which, important as they may be in setting forth standards, "necessarily neglect the relevance of these standards to the present." But equally suspicious are those empiricists who believe the truth is to be found only in experiment, "a position that finally implies the denial of any stable truth." The main task of education is, rather "to interpret both the common sphere of truth and the specific avenues of growth and change." The traditional heritage is the source of the first, and science the vehicle of the second. These two contrasting but complementary forces in our culture are the coordinates upon which and by which the character of education is to be tested. Education must be as it were at once vertical in the sense of uniting us with the past and horizontal in the sense of being relevant to the present.

Why has this concern for intellectual unity and social integration become so strong of late? Why is the question of education in a common heritage and common citizenship so persistent? The following factors stand out. In the first place, the war, and now the winning of the peace, have made ideological unity very real and urgent. It is now clear to all that democracy cannot be taken for granted, that it cannot be regarded as something already attained and to be passed on. That democracy depends peculiarly on the work of the schools is of course not new. The prewar controversy between the traditionalists and the progressives focused attention on the intimate connection between education and a democratic social order. But the implications of this interdependence was not fully recognized until the threat of totalitarianism before and during the war. Today, we know that educational objectives cannot exist apart from the kind of society to which America is committed. And the educational problem today is not so much how to teach but what to teach.

In the second place, the serious conflict between capital and labor has made the need for unity more explicit and real. Democracy implies fraternity and cooperation. Can the ideological ties which bind Americans transcend the class struggles?

In the third place, there is a growing concern over the effect of science, technology, and specialization on social cohesion and stability. This is a recurrent theme in the Harvard Report. A technological age encourages specialization, division of effort, competitive success, and vocationalism. Therein lies the danger of a split between specialized knowledge and humanistic concern and welfare. Specialism sponsors the centrifugal forces in our society in that it puts a premium on individual achievement, diversity of interest, and worldly success. The problem is to "humanize" science, that is, to make science (technology) subservient to proper social ends. While the structure of theoretical science may go on without a social reference, applied science, i.e. technology, always implies the ends which a community is concerned to achieve. Isolated from such ends, it is a matter of indifference whether the disclosures of science are used to sustain life or to destroy it; whether scientific inventions and techniques are to be exploited for profit or whether these are to be used for democratic social ends. Hence the idea of a common body of training and knowledge. The task of education in liberalism is to unify the mental disposition of all members of society, so that every one irrespective of his bent will owe a duty "to his general sharing in the culture and to his membership in society."

Finally, the demand for a 'total' attitude to man and to the world has arisen from the fact that "religion is not now, for most colleges a practicable source of intellectual unity." Less than a century ago, the conviction generally prevailed that religion gives meaning and ultimate unity to all parts of the curriculum, and that it provides both the ultimate and immediate standards of life. The great expansion of the educational system, the profusion of courses, new methods, masses of new students and the demands of vocationalism seem to have absorbed the energies of schools and colleges. In recent times the question of replacing the unity which the foregoing factors have helped to destroy has become insistent. "Unless (the mandate to the Harvard Committee reads) the educational process includes some continuing contacts with those fields in which value judgments are of prime importance, it must fall short of the ideal. The student must be concerned, in part at least, with the words 'right' and 'wrong' in both the ethical and the mathematical sense." The problem, then, is to safeguard the ethical idea in the western religious tradition in an age when sectarian teaching in most schools has become impracticable.

What, then, is the scheme of education which follows from these premises? What fields of study represent a common discipline or can give anything like a unified view of life? General education (i.e. liberal education for all) is a scheme of relationships between courses in the three areas of knowledge; natural sciences (man's corporate life) and humanities (ideals and inspirations). Each of these areas has a unique contribution to make to general education, both from the standpoint of content (subject matter) and form (method and outlook). The method of science as the method of getting knowledge is "both the outcome and source of the habit of forming objective disinterested judgments based upon exact evidence." But science according to the Harvard view, has its own limitations. Science as a method of inquiry involves "highly restricted aspects of reality." Science is prepared to deal only with those aspects of reality which lend themselves to its methods of exact observation and measurement. The natural sciences are value free. By this is meant that science deals only with naked facts. Science is tentative, changing, dynamic and hence lacks, according to the Harvard Report, the framework of permanent direction.

On the other hand, the humanities "explore and exhibit the realm of value." They point to both moral and aesthetic values. The humanities are based on value judgments; they embody presuppositions which are not subject to scientific proof and for which an exact standard of measurement does not exist.

Finally, the social sciences are defined as combining the method of natural science and of the humanities. The social scientist may employ the method of collecting data, forming hypotheses, and testing these in action, but such findings can have meaning only in the light of our value judgments, i.e. with the need of an insight into the kinds of truth with which such facts deal. The natural scientist studies facts in abstraction from values, but the function of the social scientist is interpretative. Thus an historian or social scientist is not merely interested in human past and human institutions as facts, but also "as the attempted embodiments of the good life in its various phases." From this point of view the object of social science would be to bring together both norms and actualities.

The basic idea underlying the Harvard conception of general education is that there is a mutual relationship among the humanities, social sciences, and natural sciences, "however great may be the aptitudes and opportunities which each singly possesses." They identify science with change and innovation, and the humanities with permanence and stability. In general education, the immediate and instrumental values of science and the intrinsic and ultimate values in the humanities will achieve an ideal balance.

The Harvard Report is an effort to mitigate the current conflict in social and educational philosophy. The Committee rejects the views of pragmatism which would base the social sciences on the same procedures as the natural sciences. This, in the view of the Harvard educators, would reduce social life to mechanistic and quantitative terms. Nor would they pattern natural science after the social sciences; for this would make physical science teleological. But they are equally critical of the "Great Books" theory which would depreciate science into a mere convention. Science, the Harvard educators hold, gives us an insight into reality. Their own modest evaluation aptly characterizes their efforts. They say: "An extreme and one-sided view easily calls attention to itself and gains fervent adherents; but a balanced view is apt to be less striking. Reasonableness does not lead to exciting conclusions because it aims to do justice to the whole truth in all its shadings. By the same token reasonableness may legitimately hope to attain at least part of the truth."

THE WISDOM TREE. By Emma Hawkridge. Boston: Houghton Mifflin Company, 1945. 486 pp. $3.50.
    CHRISTIAN BEHAVIOR. By C. S. Lewis. New York: The Macmillan Company. 1944. 70 pp. $1.00.

The Wisdom Tree is an honest, factual, and impressive survey of the major religious faiths. The book found its start in an attempt to tell a twelve-year old boy the story of the beginnings of the earth's great religious systems and grew, as he grew, until it went far beyond its first difficult task to the even more ambitious effort to trace for the adult reader the human quest for emotional security through a faith that could thrust itself beyond the frontier of human knowledge. The story is a pathetic tale of a "yearning after God" by those so "shut in by fear" as to find everywhere "trust in signs and omens" until the "sad after-time" brought doubt. *The Wisdom Tree* is well-fruited by wide reading and the vast gathering of a discerning, scholarly mind. Although obviously impartial, in such a spatial panorama of human experience there are undoubtedly details that would be differently stated or interpreted by specialists through whose field of knowledge the portrayal passes. The reviewer, with a more modest insight, represents the general reader who will welcome this book for its quantity of information, its catholic spirit, and its sympathy with the human searching for spiritual confidence. Nothing seems more certain to the reviewer than that man's mind and outward life are out of balance and that science, which has worked so magnificently for the latter, must for the safety of even the material wealth it has created explore and understand the former, and provide man a reasonable basis for his emotional need and well-being (p. 481). Then the record of religious striving will have a different meaning and we shall see that racial wisdom concerning human emotions was an approximation of truths which, cleared of archaic habit in their religious contexts (p. 486), "grow too great

For narrow needs of right and wrong which fade
Before the unmeasured thirst for good; while fear
Rises within them ever more and more"
                                (Paracelsus)

Christian Behavior is a very practical and a very modern application of Christian principles adapted to broadcast talks which were originally given over the British Broadcasting System. In secular words it is propaganda, although of a righteous sort, and in theological terminology would be given the more dignified description of Christian apologetics. As the reader should expect, the author depends in part for the gaining and holding of his audience upon the unexpected form of his assertions, the dramatic appeal which is so well illustrated by the sermons of Laurence Sterne and at times by those of the American preacher, Charles Parkhurst. It is interesting to wonder how the apostle Paul would react to this attempt to adjust Christian faith and practices to the conditions of contemporary western culture. The following brief statements, both drawn from the article on sexual morality, the most controversial perhaps of all the discussions, give the flavor of the book.

"The biological purpose of sex is children, just as the biological purpose of eating is to repair the body. Now if we eat whenever we feel inclined and just as much as we want, it's quite true that most of us will eat too much: but not terrifically too much." "The appetite goes a little beyond its biological purpose, but not enormously. But if a healthy young man indulged his sexual appetite whenever he felt inclined, and if each act produced a baby, then in ten years he might easily populate a small village."

"If anyone thinks that Christians regard unchastity as *the* great vice, he is quite wrong. The sins of the flesh are bad, but they are the least bad of all sins. All the worst pleasures are purely spiritual."

ERNEST R. GROVES

EDUCATION FOR A BETTER NATION AND A BETTER WORLD

U.S. PRESIDENT'S COMMISSION ON HIGHER EDUCATION

Education is an institution of every civilized society, but the purposes of education are not the same in all societies. An educational system finds its guiding principles and ultimate goals in the aims and philosophy of the social order in which it functions. The two predominant types of society in the world today are the democratic and the authoritarian, and the social role of education is very different in the two systems.

American society is a democracy: that is, its folkways and institutions, its arts and sciences and religions are based on the principle of equal freedom and equal rights for all its members, regardless of race, faith, sex, occupation, or economic status. The law of the land, providing equal justice for the poor as well as the rich, for the weak as well as the strong, is one instrument by which a democratic society establishes, maintains, and protects this equality among different persons and groups. The other instrument is education, which, as all the leaders in the making of democracy have pointed out again and again, is necessary to give effect to the equality prescribed by law.

The Role of Education

It is a commonplace of the democratic faith that education is indispensable to the maintenance and growth of freedom of thought, faith, enterprise, and association. Thus the social role of education in a democratic society is at once to insure equal liberty and equal opportunity to differing individuals and groups, and to enable the citizens to understand, appraise, and redirect forces, men, and events as these tend to strengthen or to weaken their liberties.

In performing this role, education will necessarily vary its means and methods to fit the diversity of its constituency, but it will achieve its ends more successfully if its programs and policies grow out of and are relevant to the characteristics and needs of contemporary society. Effective democratic education will deal directly with current problems.

This is not to say that education should neglect the past—only that it should not get lost in the past. No one would deny that a study of man's history can contribute immeasurably to understanding and managing the present. But to assume that all we need do is apply to present and future problems "eternal" truths revealed in earlier ages is likely to stifle creative imagination and intellectual daring. Such an assumption may blind us to new problems and the possible need for new solutions. It is wisdom in education to use the past selectively and critically, in order to illumine the pressing problems of the present.

At the same time education is the making of the future. Its role in a democratic society is that of critic and leader as well as servant; its task is not merely to meet the demands of the present but to alter those demands if necessary, so as to keep them always suited to democratic ideals. Perhaps its most important role is to serve as an instrument of social transition, and its responsibilities are defined

Reprinted from *Higher Education for American Democracy: A Report of The President's Commission on Higher Education* (1946).

in terms of the kind of civilization society hopes to build. If its adjustments to present needs are not to be mere fortuitous improvisations, those who formulate its policies and programs must have a vision of the Nation and the world we want—to give a sense of direction to their choices among alternatives.

What America needs today, then, is "a schooling better aware of its aims." Our colleges need to see clearly what it is they are trying to accomplish. The efforts of individual institutions, local communities, the several States, the educational foundations and associations, and the Federal Government will all be more effective if they are directed toward the same general ends.

In the future as in the past, American higher education will embody the principle of diversity in unity: each institution, State, or other agency will continue to make its own contribution in its own way. But educational leaders should try to agree on certain common objectives that can serve as a stimulus and guide to individual decision and action.

A Time of Crisis

It is essential today that education come decisively to grips with the world-wide crisis of mankind. This is no careless or uncritical use of words. No thinking person doubts that we are living in a decisive moment of human history.

Atomic scientists are doing their utmost to make us realize how easily and quickly a world catastrophe may come. They know the fearful power for destruction possessed by the weapons their knowledge and skill have fashioned. They know that the scientific principles on which these weapons are based are no secret to the scientists of other nations, and that America's monopoly of the engineering processes involved in the manufacture of atom bombs is not likely to last many years. And to the horror of atomic weapons, biological and chemical instruments of destruction are now being added.

But disaster is not inevitable. The release of atomic energy that has brought man within sight of world devastation has just as truly brought him the promise of a brighter future. The potentialities of atomic power are as great for human betterment as for human annihilation. Man can choose which he will have.

The possibility of this choice is the supreme fact of our day, and it will necessarily influence the ordering of educational priorities. We have a big job of reeducation to do. Nothing less than a complete reorientation of our thinking will suffice if mankind is to survive and move on to higher levels.

In a real sense the future of our civilization depends on the direction education takes, not just in the distant future, but in the days immediately ahead.

This crisis is admittedly world-wide. All nations need reeducation to meet it. But this fact does not lessen the obligation of colleges and universities to undertake the task in the United States. On the contrary, our new position in international affairs increases the obligation. We can do something about the problem in our own country and in occupied areas, and hope that by so doing we will win the friendly cooperation of other nations.

The fundamental goal of the United States in its administration of occupied areas must be the reeducation of the populations to the individual responsibilities of democracy. Such reeducation calls for the immediate removal of authoritarian barriers to democratic education, and inculcation of democratic ideals and principles through the guidance, example, and wisdom of United States occupation forces. The primacy of the objective of reeducation, however, appears too often to have been lost sight of in the press of day-to-day administrative problems. Yet every contact by Americans with Germans or Japanese either strengthens or retards the achievement of the goal. Evidence reaching this Commission indicates that while many specific existing barriers to democratic reform have been removed, new obstacles are being created daily by inadequacies of educational personnel and policy. Cognizant of the great responsibility of American education to promote democratic ideals in occupied areas, this Commission recommends the formation of a special committee to appraise progress and offer advice to the Departments of State and National Defense on educational policy and administration in occupied areas.

The schools and colleges are not solely or even mainly to blame for the situation in which we find ourselves, or that the responsibility for resolving the crisis is not or can not be entirely theirs.

But the scientific knowledge and technical skills that have made atomic and bacteriological warfare possible are the products of education and research, and higher education must share proportionately in the task of forging social and political defenses against obliteration. The indirect way toward some longer view and superficial curricular tinkering can no longer serve. The measures higher education takes will have to match in boldness and vision the magnitude of the problem.

In the light of this situation, the President's Commission on Higher Education has attempted to select, from among the principal goals for higher education, those which should come first in our time. They are to bring to all the people of the Nation:

Education for a fuller realization of democracy in every phase of living.

Education directly and explicitly for international understanding and cooperation.

Education for the application of creative imagination and trained intelligence to the solution of social problems and to the administration of public affairs.

Toward a Fuller Realization of Democracy

The dramatic events of the last few years have tended to focus our attention on the need for a world view, for global vision, for international-mindedness. This is an urgent necessity; but it would be unwise to let this necessity blind us to the fact that America's leadership in world affairs can be effective only as it rests upon increasing strength and unity at home.

Understanding Among Men

Harmony and cooperation among peoples of differing races, customs, and opinions is not one thing on the regional or national level and another on the international. The problem of understanding among men is indivisible, and the mutual acceptance and respect upon which any reliable international cooperation must depend, begin at home.

If we cannot reconcile conflicts of opinion and interest among the diverse groups that make up our own Nation, we are not likely to succeed in compromising the differences that divide nations. If we cannot make scientific and technological progress contribute to the greater well-being of all our own citizens, we shall scarcely be able to exercise leadership in reducing inequality and injustice among the other peoples of the world. If we cannot achieve a fuller realization of democracy in the United States, we are not likely to secure its adoption willingly outside the United States.

A century ago even political thinkers who did not approve the trend toward democracy accepted its eventual triumph as inevitable. Today we cannot be so sure that the future of the democratic way of life is secure. Within recent decades democratic principles have been dangerously challenged by authoritarianism, and World War II did not by any means resolve the conflict. The issue of a free society versus totalitarianism is still very much with us. It has been called "the critical and supreme political issue of today."

It is the American faith that the ultimate verdict in this conflict will go to that form of human association and government which best serves the needs and promotes the welfare of the people. We firmly believe that democracy is this form, but we shall convince others only by demonstration, not by words.

It is certainly to be hoped that we of America will continue to give democracy, and not its opponents, our full moral and economic support wherever efforts toward freedom appear, but we can do most to strengthen and extend the democratic ideal in the world by increasing the vigor and effectiveness of our achievement at home. Only to the extent that we make our own democracy function to improve the physical and mental well-being of our citizens can we hope to see freedom grow, not vanish, from the earth.

"To preserve our democracy we must improve it." Surely this fact determines one of today's urgent objectives for higher education. In the past our colleges have perhaps taken it for granted that education for democratic living could be left to courses in history and political science. It should become instead a primary aim of all classroom teaching and, more important still, of every phase of campus life.

Development of the Individual

The first goal in education for democracy is the full, rounded, and continuing development of the person. The discovery, training, and utilization of individual talents is of fundamental importance in a free society. To liberate and perfect the intrinsic powers of every citizen is the central purpose of democracy, and its furtherance of individual self-realization is its greatest glory.

A free society is necessarily composed of free citizens, and men are not made free solely by the absence of external restraints. Freedom is a function of the mind and the spirit. It flows from strength of character, firmness of conviction, integrity of purpose. It is channeled by knowledge, understanding, and the exercise of discriminating judgment. It consists of freedom of thought and conscience in action. Free men are men who not only insist on rights and liberties but who of their own free will assume the corresponding responsibilities and obligations.

If our colleges and universities are to graduate individuals who have learned how to be free, they will have to concern themselves with the development of self-discipline and self-reliance, of ethical principles as a guide for conduct, of sensitivity to injustice and inequality, of insight into human motives and aspirations, of discriminating appreciation of a wide range of human values, of the spirit of democratic compromise and cooperation.

Responsibility for the development of these personal qualities cannot be left as heretofore to some courses or a few departments or scattered extracurricular organizations; it must become a part of every phase of college life.

Social Responsibility

Higher education has always attempted to teach young people both spiritual and material values. The classroom has imparted the principle of collective responsibility for liberty—the rule that no one person's right to freedom can be maintained unless all men work together to make secure the freedom of all.

But these efforts have not always been effective. All too often the benefits of education have been sought and used for personal and private profit, to the neglect of public and social service. Yet individual freedom entails communal responsibility. The democratic way of life can endure only as private careers and social obligations are made to mesh, as personal ambition is reconciled with public responsibility.

Today, all are agreed, we need as never before to enlist all the abilities and energies we can command in the conduct of our common affairs. Today less than ever can we afford the social loss that occurs when educated men and women neglect their obligations as citizens and deliberately refrain from taking part in public affairs.

To preserve everybody's right to life, liberty, and the pursuit of happiness, then, we need first to become aware of the fact that there is no longer room for isolationism in any successful life, personal or national. No man can live to himself alone, expecting to benefit from social progress without contributing to it.

Nor can any *group* in our society, organized or unorganized, pursue purely private ends and seek to promote its own welfare without regard to the social consequences of its activities. Business, industry, labor, agriculture, medicine, law, engineering, education . . . all these modes of association call for the voluntary development of codes of conduct, or the revision of such codes as already exist, to harmonize the special interests of the group with the general welfare.

Toward these ends, higher education must inspire its graduates with high social aims as well as endow them with specialized information and technical skill. Teaching and learning must be invested with public purpose.

Meaning of Democracy

Basic to the practice of democracy is a clear understanding of its meaning. This resides in the human values and ethical ideas on which democratic living is based.

Democracy is much more than a set of political processes. It formulates and implements a philosophy of human relations. It is a way of life—a way of thinking, feeling, and acting in regard to the associations of men and of groups, one with another. The assumption, judgments, values, and necessities of this way of life have been set down by many great minds of the Western tradition and they are embodied in the documents that make up the American bible of democracy: such documents as the Declaration of Independence, the Constitution and its Bill of Rights, the papers of Thomas Jefferson, the addresses of Abraham Lincoln, the Atlantic Charter.

The fundamental concept of democracy is a belief in the inherent worth of the individual, in the dignity and value of human life. Based on the assumption that every human being is endowed with certain inalienable rights, among which are life, liberty, and the pursuit of happiness, democracy requires of its adherents a jealous regard, not only for their own rights, but equally for the similar rights of others.

From this basic tenet have derived the specific ingredients in the American idea of democracy; the right of all men to equality of opportunity, the equal right of all citizens to vote and to hold office, the rights of religious liberty, freedom of speech and all forms of expression, freedom of association, freedom from want and from fear and ignorance; the obligation of the majority in power to respect and protect the rights of the minority.

The Government of our country embodies the effort to express these principles and to effect them in practice. Its institutions and agencies are based on the ground plan of the Constitution, amended by experience and modified in form and function through trial and error. Modifications are made whenever the people come to feel that changes are necessary in order to realize more effectively the ends of human betterment and individual development which democratic government is intended to serve.

The processes and institutions of democracy are not static or fixed; it is essential that they be flexible, capable of adaptation to the changing needs and conditions of men. The everlasting moral essence of democracy lies in its fundamental principles, not in its means and methods of the moment.

To educate our citizens only in the structure and processes of the American Government, therefore, is to fall far short of what is needed for the fuller realization of the democratic ideal. It is the responsibility of higher education to devise programs and methods which will make clear the ethical values and the concept of human relations upon which our political system rests. Otherwise we are likely to cling to the letter of democracy and lose its spirit, to hold fast to its procedures when they no longer serve its ends, to propose and follow undemocratic courses of action in the very name of democracy.

Processes of Democracy

Young people will be better fitted to perform the duties of citizenship with wisdom and vision if to an understanding of democratic principles they join a realistic knowledge of the actual processes by which the political, economic, and social life of the people is carried on.

It will help little toward the fuller realization of democracy to have our colleges and universities turn out a generation of impractical visionaries. Youth certainly should possess inspiring vision, but it should also be familiar with the procedures and institutions through which long-range social goals are achieved in our democracy. Citizens need to understand thoroughly the functioning of political parties, the role of lobbies and pressure groups, the processes of ward and precinct caucuses. They need to know not only the potential greatness of democracy, not only the splendor of its aspirations, but also its present imperfections in practice.

These imperfections are no cause for cynicism. In the relatively short span of our history we have made tremendous strides toward equity, justice, and freedom for all. We have deepened and widened our social conscience. We have come to demand and support programs of social action designed to free common men from poverty and insecurity and make them participants in the benefits of social and cultural progress.

We do not undervalue these accomplishments when we admit that they stop far short of our purpose. The discrepancies between America's democratic creed and how Americans live are still many and serious.

Democracy's Unfinished Business

Democracy rests upon a belief in the worth and dignity of human life, yet democratic nations within a generation have had forced upon them two world wars taking millions of human lives. Democracy is dedicated to the proposition that all men are entitled to an equal chance to be free and to seek happiness, yet our society is plagued with inequalities, even in so fundamental a right as education. Democracy insists on freedom of conscience and expression, yet Americans often seek to deny this freedom to those who do not agree with the majority opinion of the moment. Democracy is designed to promote human well-being, yet many thousands of our citizens continue to live in poverty, disease, hunger, and ignorance. Democracy sets up reason as the final arbiter in human relations, yet the appeal to emotion and prejudice is more common and often more effective among us than the appeal to reason.

Only by seeing today's democracy in the light of our vision of democracy as it can be will we come to appreciate the size of the job that remains to be done. It is a task to challenge the energies of young people and one that is worthy of their passionate devotion. It must be so presented to them.

To recognize and admit defects is not to disparage democracy. It is merely to see clearly the extent of its unfinished business.

Allegiance to Democracy

Many thoughtful observers are convinced that one of America's urgent needs today is a continued commitment to the principles of democracy. These Americans are troubled by a seeming lack of purpose in our national life. They feel we have lost our sureness of the way toward a better tomorrow.

If we have lost our sense of direction, it is a serious matter in this period of rapid and revolutionary change. Societies, like men, need a sound core of clear purpose to keep them stable in the midst of swirling uncertainties. Only with a sure view of the goal toward which they are moving can they adapt wisely and well to changing conditions along the way, and upon a society's capacity for such adaptation rests its chance of survival.

The democratic ideal will provide this core of purpose for our people if we keep it a warm and living thing. When it is a vital vision of future good, it engages the passionate loyalties of youth. But young people will not dedicate themselves to a version of democracy whose vitality and whose results for the common man they believe to be in doubt.

It becomes, then, an urgent task for our scholars and our teachers to restate and revivify the ideals of democracy. Clearing away whatever has become outworn or been debased by tawdry uses, they must rephrase in dynamic form for our day the vision of free men in a free society, so that it may remain a living faith and an inspiring dream for the American people.

But putting the democratic faith into words, no matter how new or how vital they are, is not enough. When the democratic spirit is deep and strong in a society, its expression is not limited to the sphere of government; it animates every phase of living: economic and social and personal as well as political, relations between man and man and among groups as well as within and among nations.

This integration of democratic principles into the active life of a person and a people is not to be achieved merely by studying or discussing democracy. Classroom teaching of the American tradition, however excellent, will not weave its spirit into the innermost fiber of the students. Experience in the give and take of free men in a free society is equally necessary. Democracy must be lived to be thoroughly understood. It must become an established attitude and activity, not just a body of remote and abstract doctrine—a way for men to live and work harmoniously together, not just words in a textbook or a series of slogans.

To achieve such practice in democratic action the President's Commission recommends a careful review of administrative policies in institutions of higher education. Revision may be necessary to give students every possible experience in democratic processes within the college community. Young people cannot be expected to develop a firm allegiance to the democratic faith they are taught in the classroom if their campus life is carried on in an authoritarian atmosphere.

Admittedly there is danger in seeking to inculcate in youth a passionate loyalty to one way of life. Rededication to democracy will necessarily involve the emotions as well as the intellect. Yet the allegiance we want dare not be unreasoning and intolerant, fanatic and self-righteous. If it is, it will only aggravate excessive nationalism that is at the root of current failures in international cooperation. The task of college faculties is to inspire in our young people a consuming enthusiasm for the democratic way of life and at the same time develop in them an active appreciation of different cultures and other peoples.

To state the seeming dilemma is to point the way out of it. The heart of democracy is a constant regard for the rights and freedoms of others, and this regard cannot stop short at national boundary lines. In the measure that our renewed commitment is to the fundamentals of democracy, it will set up no barrier to international understanding; it can only further cooperation among nations.

Toward International Understanding and Cooperation

That citizens be equipped to deal intelligently with the problems that arise in our national life is important; that they bring informed minds and a liberal spirit to the resolution of issues growing out of international relations is imperative.

Defense of Peace

Education for peace is the condition of our survival, and it must have a high priority in all our programs of education. In the words of the constitution of the United Nations Educational, Scientific, and Cultural Organization, wars begin in the minds of men and it is in the minds of men that the defenses of peace must be constructed. However much the political and economic arrangements of governments may contribute to world union, the peace must be founded upon the intellectual and moral union of mankind.

In a world in which technology is acting as a solvent of cultures, the historic conception of international relations—political, economic, and cultural—will have to be modified if contemporary civilization is to survive. No longer can peoples hope to build their security and the peace of the world on national strength and balance of power arrangements.

The competitive principle, so long dominant in international relations, must give place, if nations are to survive, to the principle of cooperation. Men will have to invent and perfect institutional forms—such as the United Nations, UNESCO, the International Monetary Fund, and yet others— through which this cooperation can effectively take place. But these institutional arrangements will have to be built upon and buttressed by an understanding among people—an understanding that embraces cultural heritage, value premises, political ideology, legitimate national interests, folkways, and patterns of sentiment and feeling.

If the peoples of the world are to work together to build a unified, prosperous, and peaceful world, there must be freedom of communication. And this freedom must include both the *agencies* and the *subject matter* of communication. Freedom of the press, of the radio, and of reporting must be maintained in all parts of the world if we are really to understand one another. Full and free discussion of all aspects of national and international life—including the basic facts involved in diplomatic relations—is essential in a world society of free men.

American institutions of higher education have an enlarged responsibility for the diffusion of ideas in the world that is emerging. They will have to help our own citizens as well as other peoples to move from the provincial and insular mind to the international mind.

This will involve providing expanded opportunity in colleges and universities for the study of all aspects of international affairs: the nature and development of other civilizations and cultures; nationalism in its relation to internationalism; the tensions leading to war as well as war itself; the ways in which war has been used as an instrument of national policy and the attitudes which nations have had in each war with respect to the justice of that war as they saw it—in other words, an analytical study of war and its causes as these have developed in the past.

Development of the international mind will also involve study of the effect of technology on the present world situation and analysis of the structure and operation of the various new world organizations designed to further international security and the peaceful solution of common problems.

Peace today is indivisible. Never again can war anywhere in the world be dismissed as a "local conflict" or a matter of "domestic jurisdiction." A threat to peace anywhere menaces the security of people everywhere. But we shall not achieve a stable and lasting peace if we think of it negatively as the mere absence of armed conflict. The creation and preservation of an affirmative peace demands the establishment of just and humans relationships among the peoples of the world, the development of a state of solidarity and mutual confidence in which men and women may live secure and satisfying lives.

Preparation for World Citizenship

In speed of transportation and communication and in economic interdependence the nations of the globe already are one world; the task is to secure recognition and acceptance of this oneness in the thinking of the people, so that the concept of one world may be realized psychologically, socially, and in good time politically. It is this task in particular that challenges our scholars and our teachers to lead the way toward a new way of thinking.

Traditionally the United States, having the conquest of a continental wilderness to occupy its energies and two mighty oceans to protect it, has sought to remain aloof from "foreign entanglements." But now foreign affairs are no longer foreign. The airplane and the radio have wiped out the ocean barriers; they have brought us next door to our neighbors overseas. And World War II and its aftermath have committed us to a responsible role in world affairs beyond any possibility of turning back to the illusive safety of detachment.

But the American people are not adequately prepared for world citizenship. The new role has come upon us so suddenly that we approach it with hesitation instead of with an exciting vision of its possibilities. Our thinking still bears marks of provincialism. We tend to see other countries and peoples in our own image and to view them with suspicion or dismiss them as inferior and backward when we find them different from ourselves.

For effective international understanding and cooperation we need to acquire knowledge of, and respect for, other peoples and their cultures—their traditions, their customs, and attitudes, their social institutions, their needs and aspirations for the future. We must learn to admit the possible worth of human values and ways of living we ourselves do not accept.

In the past the liberal arts college has stressed the history, arts, and institutions of Western culture, without giving much time or attention to the kinds of civilization that exist in other parts of the globe. In the new world it is not enough to know and understand our own heritage. Modern man needs to sense the sweep of world history in order to see his own civilization in the context of other cultures.

We need to perceive the rich advantages of cultural diversity. To a provincial mind cultural differences are irritating and frightening in their strangeness, but to a cosmopolitan and sensitive mind they are stimulating and rewarding. They are colorful elaborations on the common humanity of men everywhere. We must develop a deep sensitivity to the emotions, the hopes, and the needs of human beings everywhere and so come to accept, not merely in abstract terms but in concrete forms, the brotherhood and interdependence as well as the individuality of all men.

To fit ourselves for the world leadership that has fallen to America in this crucial moment of history, we shall have to acquire quickly a sympathetic understanding of the values and aspirations that move men in the vast areas of eastern Europe, Asia, Africa, South America, and the islands of the sea. We can gain this understanding both through a study of their historical development and through knowledge of their contemporary culture. Information about their current activities in science, industry, literature, and the arts will be an invaluable aid and can be secured in part through the exchange of persons and goods.

It is especially important that we acquaint ourselves with the oriental world. Asiatics constitute the largest single segment of the human race. Yet American undergraduates and graduates know little or nothing about the history, the present problems, or the future needs of these millions with whom our relations are certain to increase. We must study the Orient—not as a remote and static display of artifacts in a museum, but as a living and dynamic factor in our own society. The East is shaking off its traditional passive attitude toward the West and more than ever we shall feel the impact of its cultures.

American students should be encouraged to discover why the Oriental properly considers himself as much a person of refinement, of ethical standards, and of religious values as any citizen of Western society. East and West are coming together in one world order. We could not stem this development if we wanted to; we can only prepare to deal with it intelligently.

It is equally important that we learn the ways of thinking and living of the Russian people. The vast Russian state, part European, part Asiatic, is one of the world's greatest powers and her policies and deeds are of supreme importance. Yet the average American college graduate knows almost nothing about Russia. The study of the U.S.S.R., in a sincere attempt to understand it, must be given an important place in American education.

Instruments of International Cooperation

Every effort should be made to secure free and uncensored communication among the peoples of the world, so that they may come to understand one another, recognize their interdependence, and accept the rule of life that personal and national rights are extended and made more secure through international agreement and the progress of world-wide well-being.

International understanding and cooperation cannot be expected to elimiate disagreement and conflict among nations. But no well-ordered or civilized society permits a conflict of interests among its individual citizens to be settled by violent assault. National societies have outlawed killing by accepting a code of laws and a system of courts to which the strong as well as the weak are subject. International society must follow the same course to the same goal.

The nations of the world now have a new agency for effecting international amity and cooperation. It remains for the peoples of the world to make a United Nations work—by insisting that their governments shall use it and shall strengthen it step by step, supporting it by international law and international courts to which all nations, the strong as well as the weak, shall be subject.

Toward achievement of this ultimate goal UNESCO promises much, because its work lies largely in those areas in which international communication has been characteristic from the beginning. National boundaries have never been maintained effectively in the world of letters, art, music, and science. The citizens of that world are all people of all nations to whom words and images and music and mathematical formulas have meaning. Through widening the citizenship in that world, UNESCO can make a great contribution to effective communication between peoples who are still separated by the boundaries of national states.

Helpful too will be actual experience wherever possible, within our own Nation and among nations, in working with people of different races and cultures on measures for human betterment and world brotherhood. The exchange of persons between nations—experts and scholars in all fields, teachers and students, writers and artists, businessmen and farmers, clubwomen and labor leaders—will further understanding also, if these individuals go and come, not as casual sightseers, but as coworkers seeking to learn.

The radio, the motion picture, newspapers, magazines, books—all the mediums of mass communication that proved so effective in creating unity and morale during the recent war—can be equally effective in creating unity and the will for peace.

But the major part of the task will still devolve upon the schools and colleges. Education has taught the concept of common humanity and brotherhood; the schools and colleges have tried to create world-wide understanding; teachers have presented the ideal of peace and cooperation among men and nations. But in the past these things have been done too indirectly; now we must do them directly, explicitly, and urgently.

Unfortunately we are handicapped by the lack of appropriate tools and materials. Studies have revealed how inadequate and prejudiced many of our elementary and secondary school textbooks are in their treatment of other nations and peoples. At the college level many of our disciplines and courses bear incidentally on the problem, but rarely do we educate systematically and deliberately for world-wide understanding.

The geographic area study programs that are being set up in a number of universities are a commendable development in this direction, but as yet higher education in America does not even approximate adequate presentation of any of the major Eastern and Middle Eastern civilizations. For no one of these cultures is our supply of trained scholars adequate, and for many of them we have virtually no competent teachers at all. Any considerable improvement or extension of foreign-area studies in the colleges is dependent upon the creation of an adequate teaching personnel.

In addition, this personnel must be provided with the necessary tools. For example, it is estimated that any college contemplating serious study of Russian culture must have in its library a basic collection of at least 500 specified books, and there will be no adequate development of Russian studies in this country until 200 or 300 American colleges possess these books or their equivalent. But these books cannot be bought; they do not exist; it will take a major publishing enterprise to make them available. And the same obstacle to serious scholarship exists in many other areas of non-European culture.

Nor are these difficulties of scholarship the whole of the problem. Specialized area studies are too limited in scope and touch too small a part of the student body to accomplish the necessary diffusion of intercultural understanding. For this purpose, courses of broader scope and more general interpretation and synthesis are required. And for these again, the teachers are yet to be trained and the textbooks are yet to be written.

There is urgent need for a program of education for world citizenship that can be made a part of every person's general education. No one scholar, no one group of scholars, possesses the comprehensive knowledge needed to devise this kind of educational program. Men trained in many different areas must pool their knowledge—not arranging their fragmentary contributions in a loose sequence, but organizing them into an integrated pattern.

The task is not easy; it demands imaginative thinking, exceptional ingenuity, and concerted effort. But it must be done; we dare not again risk being too late with too little.

Toward the Solution of Social Problems

It is essential that we apply our trained intelligence and creative imagination, our scientific methods of investigation, our skill in invention and adaptation, as fully to the problems of human association as to the extension of knowledge about the physical world. This is what is meant by the development of *social invention* and *social technology*.

Human Relations

We have worked wonders by the application of technology to the problems of our physical environment, but we have scarcely touched the fringes of its possibilities in the realm of human relations. In fact, we hardly recognize the existence of inventiveness in the social sphere. Yet the United Nations and UNESCO are inventions no less than the atom bomb, and they are just as capable of technical improvement.

As a people, Americans have come to appreciate the need for experimental research and technical training in the physical and natural sciences, but we tend still to think that good will, tolerance, and the cooperative spirit are all we need to make society function. These attitudes are vitally necessary; we shall make little progress without them; and, as has already been emphasized, education should concern itself with developing them. But alone they are not enough. Social techniques and social mechanisms must be found to express and implement them.

One often hears or reads, for example, puzzled questioning as to why man's intense desire for security and his fear of another war have produced so little actual progress toward peace in the world. But man's fear of smallpox did not eliminate that scourge until medical science and technology had invented and improved the technique of vaccination. Nor did man's desire to fly enable him to accomplish the feat until scientific ingenuity and engineering skill had produced the necessary mechanism and had trained men to use it.

In comparable fashion it will take social science and social engineering to solve the problems of human relations. Our people must learn to respect the need for special knowledge and technical training in this field as they have come to defer to the expert in physics, chemistry, medicine, and other sciences. Relieving the tensions that produce war, for example, will require methods as specific and as technical as are those of aeronautics or electronics.

The development of social technology is an imperative today because of the remarkable advances we have made in natural science. Scientific discoveries and their technological application have altered our physical environment profoundly in the space of only a few generations, but our social institutions have not kept pace with the changes—although by applying the methods of science we have achieved marked success in some forms of social organization.

Understanding of Self

Man's capacity to subdue nature to his will has raced far ahead of his ability to understand himself or to reconstruct his institutions. This is true in spite of the fact that higher education itself traditionally has followed the Socratic prescription of putting the study of man first. We have grown strong in the mastery of our physical world, but by no means equally strong in the ability to manage and direct the social forces that shape our lives.

The gap between our scientific know-how and our personal and social wisdom has been growing steadily through the years, until now with the release of atomic energy it has become too wide to be safe.

It is imperative that we find not only the will but the ways and means to reorder our lives and our institutions so as to make science and technology contribute to man's well-being rather than to his destruction. We need to experiment boldly in the whole area of human relations, seeking to modify existing institutions and to discover new workable patterns of association. We must bring our social skills quickly abreast of our skills in natural science.

The irony is that the very developments which have precipitated this critical situation seem likely to aggravate it. The spectacular achievements of natural science, especially during World War II, are certain to bring increased pressure for scientific advance. Already it is suggested that "scientific preeminence will be the keystone of national security." But will it? Can we depend solely, or even primarily, on natural science for our national safety?

In the recent war the margin of our scientific and technical superiority over our enemies was dangerously narrow at times, and the scientists themselves are warning us at every opportunity that they can provide no defense against the new weapons. It is they who are proclaiming most vigorously that this defense can be found only in the realm of social and political organization on a world-wide scale. To quote Albert Einstein for one: "Being an ingenious people, Americans find it hard to believe there is no foreseeable defense against atomic bombs. But this is a basic fact. Scientists do not even know of any field which promises us any hope of adequate defense. . . . Our defense is in international law and order."

Leadership Needed

Upon leadership in social invention, then, as much as upon superiority in natural science and engineering, rests our hope of national survival. Unfortunately, the uneasy state of the world leads us to discuss these matters in terms of national defense. The ultimate justification for progress in science, social and natural, is the contribution it can make to the welfare of people everywhere. Continued advance in natural science will give strength to democracy in the eyes of other peoples because of the improvement it makes possible in our standard of living, and the development of a more effective social science will contribute to a fuller realization of the democratic principles of justice and freedom for all.

The colleges and universities, the philanthropic foundations, and the Federal Government should not be tempted by the prestige of natural science and its immediately tangible results into giving it a disproportionate emphasis in research budgets or in teaching programs. It is the peculiar responsibility of the colleges to train personnel and inaugurate extensive programs of research in social science and technology. To the extent that they have neglected this function in the past they should concentrate upon it in the decades just ahead.

We cannot pin our faith on social drift, hoping that if each individual pursues his own ends with intelligence and good will, things will somehow right themselves. We cannot rely on the processes of automatic adjustment. We must develop a positive social policy, both within and among nations. We must plan, with intelligence and imagination, the course we are to take toward the kind of tomorrow we want.

It Can Be Done

In emphasizing education for democracy, for international understanding, and for more effective social science as objectives for higher education in America today, the President's Commission has no desire to suggest limitations on progress and experimentation in other directions. Diversity in purpose is a potential source of strength in democratic institutions. From the innovative and experimental approach of today may well come the general objective of tomorrow.

These three goals are stated as the minimum essentials of the program to be developed in all institutions of higher education. And they pose a truly staggering job for the colleges and universities. But it can be done. The necessary intelligence and ability exist. What we need is awareness of the urgency of the task, the will and the courage to tackle it, and a wholehearted commitment to its successful performance.

But to delay is to fail. Colleges must accelerate the normally slow rate of social change which the educational system reflects; we need to find ways quickly or making the understanding and vision of our most farsighted and sensitive citizens the common possession of all our people.

To this end the educational task is partly a matter of the numbers to be educated and partly one of the kind of education that is to be provided. We shall have to educate more of our people at each level of the educational program, and we shall have to devise patterns of education that will prepare them more effectively than in the past for responsible roles in modern society.

WHO CALLS THE TUNE?

BY ROBERT S. LYND

"Establishing the Goals," Volume I of the "Report of the President's Commission on Higher Education"

Educators, of all people, should be most apt at seeing things whole, with parts observed in relation to the biasing overall thrust of the whole system. It is we who are most vocal about the "total situation," the "whole personality," the continuities involved in "activity leading to further activity," and similar emphases on wholeness, interaction of parts, and the dynamics of growth, movement, and change.

Of course, anything must be temporarily abstracted and in some sense distorted in order to be studied at all. One fixates upon any given thing under discussion, precisely as one focuses a camera or a microscope; and this process in some sense temporarily plays down the rest of the universe. Any field of science or action gets ahead with its proper business largely by concentrating on things interior to itself. This is why we must have division of labor among our specialties. But recurrently, and especially at the times when one resets goals for future work, it is relevant to ask: How does the rest of what is going on in the social universe outside my specialty impinge upon what I am trying to do and upon the way I state my problems?

The significance of the interrupting pressure of the rest of the social world upon the component parts of a social system and its culture varies with time and location. For long stretches of time in earlier eras, peasants off the main trade routes lived and died in what to our hurtling institutional world seems an incredible localization and homely fixity of circumstances; one's life was pressed very close to the exigent immediacies of nature, with few interruptions from without. Even those of us in our fifties who grew up in Middle Western small towns can remember the quiet, leisurely tempo of a largely self-contained world of local affairs. Progress was manifestly happening, but it was a benign progress, with the scenery cut to the size of ordinary people. Democracy, too, was surely happening, unchallenged and here to stay. And business was the great wheel that bore everything forward. One did not hear the word *ideology* in those days, and while there was occasional "labor trouble," were we not all Americans and would not each of us get "his turn" if he worked hard? Today we are living in an ideological devil's cauldron, with ourselves and all our values tossed about and obscured. This, we are beginning reluctantly to realize, is one of the great historic eras of institutional change, one of the decisive moments of human history. It is a time when the institutional chunks of our culture grind against each other in a movement so vast as to dwarf the individual. Never before in our national life have the will and the voice of the single man of integrity and good will seemed so impotent; only group action any longer counts for social change, and the middle-class man can find no group with whom to move except those carrying old banners in dubious directions.

In times like these, what is the case with those who assay to talk about education? Can one in these days talk about things of the mind and spirit as worthy in themselves? Surely one must—now more than ever! And yet one has an eerie sense of whistling in the wind. Education, we say, must be related to life. But to which part of this roaring hurricane of reality that besets us? Deep in our cultural tradition is the conception of "natural order" and a "higher sanction" underlying the

Reprinted by permission from the *Journal of Higher Education* 19, no. 4 (April 1948).

daily circumstances of social living. On such an assumption "education" makes sense; for one learns about things that are surely there, in place, moving with one to appointed, though perhaps not yet entirely apparent, goals. One can teach and one can learn, even as one can "belong," in a world so conceived. Education can view itself as in some real sense belonging to itself, an autonomous permanent force authorized to state values for society and to work steadily to make those values real in daily life. In a world so conceived there is "sin" and there are "good" people and "bad" people; but the universe is neither sinful nor aimless, and democracy is not at stake; and the grand adventure of education, working with the tide of the universe and of democracy, is to make more and more people more rational (that is, "better") until the underlying drive toward orderliness comes to pervade all men's affairs. Here is a setting for confidence for the educator.

And it is this kind of confident statement of its own goals that the opening volume on *Establishing the Goals* of the "Report of the President's Commission on Higher Education" makes—and makes superbly. I happen not to be an enthusiast for the new gospel of "general education," and I became somewhat restless when the Report moved on to that specific recommendation, for reasons I shall state later in this paper. But the first two chapters on the broad aims of education state better than I have ever seen them stated before what every imaginative educator dreams of at his healthiest, most rested, professional best. Here it all is.

American society is a democracy. [And law and education are the two instruments that establish, maintain, and protect] . . . equal freedom and equal rights for all its members, regardless of race, faith, sex, occupation, or economic status.

. . . Within recent decades democratic principles have been dangerously challenged by authoritarianism. . . . To preserve our democracy we must improve it.

[Education] should not get lost in the past, [for it] is the making of the future. . . . Perhaps its most important rôle is to serve as an instrument of social transition, and its responsibilities are defined in terms of the kind of civilization society hopes to build.

. . . the colleges [have] not kept pace with changing social conditions.

. . . we are living in a decisive moment of human history.

. . . Colleges must accelerate the normally slow rate of social change which the educational system reflects.

In a real sense the future of our civilization depends on the direction education takes, not just in the distant future, but in the days immediately ahead.

. . . The indirect way toward some longer view and superficial curricular tinkering can no longer serve.

What America needs today, then, is "a schooling better aware of its aims".

The first goal in education for democracy is the full, rounded, and continuing development of the person.

[The] first [goals for contemporary] higher education [should be] a fuller realization of democracy in every phase of living . . . education directly and explicitly for international understanding and cooperation . . . [and] education for the application of creative imagination and trained intelligence to the solution of social problems. . . .

. . . men are not made free solely by the absence of external restraints.

. . . individual freedom entails communal responsibility. . . . Nor can any *group* in our society, organized or unorganized, pursue purely private ends and seek to promote its own welfare without regard to the social consequences of its activities.

The gap between our scientific know-how and our personal and social wisdom has been growing steadily through the years.

. . . For the great majority of our boys and girls, the kind and amount of education they may hope to attain depends, not on their own abilities, but on the family or community into which they happened to be born, or, worse still, on the color of their skin or the religion of their parents.

. . . Even in State-supported institutions we have been moving away from the principle of free education to a much greater degree than is commonly supposed.

The importance of economic barriers to post-high school education lies in the fact that there is little if any relationship between the ability to benefit from a college education and the ability to pay for it.

Segregation lessens the quality of education for the whites as well [as for the Negroes].

[The quota system] is a violation of a major American principle and is contributing to the growing tension in one of the crucial areas of our democracy.

. . . If the ladder of educational opportunity rises high at the doors of some youth and scarcely rises at all at the doors of others, while at the same time formal education is made a prerequisite to occupational and social advance, then education may become the means, not of eliminating race and class distinctions, but of deepening and solidifying them.

The time has come to make public education at all levels equally accessible to all, without regard to race, creed, sex or national origin .

I read these pages with the sustained inner excitement that accompanies the clear public affirmation in an important document of the values one affirms most deeply in a time of controversy. But even as I read, I had a troubled sense of indulgence in unreality, of something vital left out. The experience reverberated other similar experiences—college chapel services that had caught me up momentarily into singleness of focus, and a memorable service on the day of the Assumption in Chartres Cathedral from which it had been a shock to come out into the August sunlight of the "other world" outside.

It Is this bifocal quality about reading such contemporary statements of the "goals of education" that worries me; the insistent presence of "another world outside"; and the persistent, interrupting sense that our fine educational talk, honest as it is, is turned into "double-talk" by things beyond the control of us educators.

I have already said that, if one can assume a natural goodness and orderliness in the universe directly related to men's constructive efforts, it makes sense for education to state its own orderly, autonomous aims and to seek to realize them. But this assumption does not hold. There is no basic orderliness in social living; our institutions have no "higher" validation, but are what they have come to be—man-made and subject to all the vicissitudes of time and circumstance; and education, far from occupying an ordained place in the human procession, is only what it can contrive to be in the jostling throng of interests that seek to have things their own way in society.

It is good to be confident. Chapter I of the "Report of the President's Commission" is headed "Education for a Better Nation and a Better World," and the closing subhead of the chapter is "It Can Be Done." The only hindrances seen by the Commission are internal to education itself:

> [These goals] pose a truly staggering job for the colleges and universities. But it can be done. The necessary intelligence and ability exist. What we need is awareness of the urgency of the task, and the will and courage to tackle it, and a wholehearted commitment to its successful performance.

But the sober fact dogs the work of all of us who value democracy and the sensitive aspects of human living that "intelligence," "awareness of the urgency of the task," and "will and courage" on the part of us educators still may not be enough to force the door through which we must pass to achieve our goals. It is, therefore, the stark realities of the institutional setting in which education, the family, democracy, and our other institutional foci of values are caught today that must be studied first by those who seek to state and to realize values.

The weakness of the "Report of the President's Commission on Higher Education" is that it states a program for education apart from a realistic appraisal of the nature and drive of power in the contemporary United States.

The simple fact—to which we educators pay formal lip service in our troubled private discussions among ourselves—is that education may not look upon itself as an independent force in society. We non-Catholics worry about the case of education forced to operate within the political goals of the organization ramifying from the Vatican. But we do not, in the main and in public, recognize the possibility that there are other constraints upon education no less coercive and determined to have their way within our own cultural system. Our general confidence about education in America stems from the fact that we assume the dominant characteristic of our society to be that it is a political democracy; that is, that the front door is open to Americans to do anything with our common life that the majority of us elect. But we must face the further question as to whether political democracy is, in fact, master in its own house. As Harold J. Laski points out in his *Democracy in Crisis:*

> The Industrial Revolution brought the middle classes to power, and they evolved a form of state—capitalist democracy—which seemed most suited to their security . . . . It offered a share in political authority to all citizens upon the unstated assumption that the equality involved in the democratic ideal did not seek extension to the economic sphere. The assumption could not be maintained.
>
> [For the citizens, having won formal political power], realized that the clue to authority lay in the possession of economic control. When they sought to move by the ordinary constitutional means to its conquest as well, they found that the fight had to be begun all over again. Not only was this the case, but the essential weapons lay in their opponents' hands. The Courts, the Press, the educational system, the armed forces of the state, even, in large degree, the bureaucracy, were instruments operating towards their defeat. If they maintained law and order, they maintained that subtle atmosphere upon which the security of economic privilege depended.[1]

What this suggests is that liberal democracy lives in unresolved conflict with capitalism. Charles A. Beard pointed out this basic ambivalence between our political and economic institutions in his *An Economic Interpretation of the Constitution of the United States.*[2] Our middle-class revolution, like the English revolution of the seventeenth century, failed to go clear through from the political to the economic sector, but ended in a makeshift compromise. This compromise has never been resolved, but has persisted as a more or less disguised guerilla warfare between the two fundamentally opposed segments of the culture.

Under the surface of our national life this irrepressible conflict has grown in violence with the unchecked increase in economic monopoly. Arthur Schlesinger, Jr.'s *The Age of Jackson*[3] deals with one of the occasions on which the issue broke into the open. It describes the re-forming of the fighting front of the predecessors of the present Republican party after their defeat by Andrew Jackson. The blunt emphasis of the financial and industrial upper class upon the fact that the masses were dangerous to property had proved in Jackson's campaign a double-edged weapon; for the masses, come to power, could claim that property was dangerous to the masses. So the aristocratic Whig party did a smart ideological face-lifting job, commencing in the 1830's. Central in this was the emphasis that America is different from Europe, class differences do not apply here, and the interests of all elements in our American population are identical. And, ever since, this line has proved a useful propaganda weapon for big business. One follows this struggle between democracy and capitalism through the fruitless effort to curb the monopoly tendency; the three revealing lobby investigations which have resulted in no check on the growing power of business lobbies; the fiasco of NRA which revealed that, when business is given its head even in a national emergency, it proceeds to have a field day for its own profit; the Nye Committee munitions investigation; the LaFollette Committee investigation of the anti-labor tactics of big business; the business sabotaging of conversion to a wartime footing; the colossal profits of both World Wars; the killing of OPA by the National Association of Manufacturers; and so on.[4]

Today, big business, better organized than ever before and commanding all the best manipulative brains-for-sale in America, has launched an all-out campaign to shatter organized labor and to control political democracy through gaining command over public opinion at the grass roots. Central in this campaign is the false assertion that democracy and the "private enterprise system" are but two aspects of the same thing, and that democracy itself will collapse if the private-enterprise system is impaired. According to *Management News*, the organ of the American Management Association, . . . probably more millions are being spent on public relations on behalf of the free enterprise system than management and stockholders realize. Virtually every industry in the United States—even the smallest companies—is involved in some effort to sell "economic truths" to the public.[5]

On February 1 of this year, a detailed plan, worked out by the best public-relations talent in the country, was thrown into gear to capture local communities for big business. This program calls for the systematic organization, first, of all the leaders at the local community level, from business through religion and education to labor; and then, through them, the organization of all the organizations in each community behind the purposes of business. What all of this means is that business is out to destroy the *private* character of everything except property. We educators may smile at *Trends in Education-Industry Cooperation*, sent us monthly by the NAM. But we do not smile at the systematic encirclement of free opinion that has put liberal commentators off the air, that suppresses and distorts important news in our press and periodicals,[6] or at the growing aggressiveness of businessmen alumni and members of school boards and the organized heresy-hunting that is reaching shamelessly into our schools.

Here is the hard core of contemporary power that we educators must try to appraise and to hold relentlessly before ourselves as we look ahead. The issue does not concern "good" men and "bad" men. As William Allen White wrote in 1943 of the disenchanting spectacle in Washington:

> For the most part these managerial magnates are decent, patriotic Americans. . . . If you touch them in nine relations of life out of ten, they are kindly, courteous, Christian gentlemen.
> But in the tenth relation, where it touches their own organization, they are stark mad, ruthless, unchecked by God or man, paranoiacs, in fact, as evil in their design as Hitler.[7]

And it so happens that this tenth relation is the one that dominates American life. As educators confront it, the issue is not, as I say, one of "good" and "bad" men, but of private business as an *organized system of power*. It is the dynamic purposes of this system that confront us as we attempt to state the goals of education.

Why have Americans, proud as we are of our democracy, allowed this conflict within our house to go unresolved and now to mount to its present pitch of intensity? From the beginning of our national life we have leaned back upon natural law, natural rights, and progress. Having set up the external forms of democracy, we turned to the vast private adventure of growing rich. A great continent rich in resources beckoned, and the new power of machinery born of the Industrial Revolution lay ready to hand. With no threatening neighbors on this hemisphere, it seemed that we could almost literally throw the reins on the back of the democratic nag and let political progress happen, while we all attended to growing rich. Cheap European labor came here at its own expense, and we fed their bodies into the industrial furnace as we broke the plains, rolled steel rails, and built our cities.[8] Actually, all down through our national life, until only two decades ago, we were borne forward by a favoring tail wind. We did not appraise this as a sheer stroke of good fortune, but as a continuing vindication of the rightness and essential finality of our "American way" and its institutions. Only since 1929 have many Americans begun to suspect that progress is not a permanent, built-in part of the American scene.

Meanwhile, the depression of 1929 and after has alerted business power to the fact that all is not well with the private-enterprise system. The depression really hurt it, hurt it as nothing had hurt it before. And when the government moved in on business in the New Deal, business became thoroughly aroused. Government sponsorship of labor organization was a body blow; but, as noted in the Report to Executives on "Management Looks at the Labor Problem," it was government under the New Deal that had hurt property more than had labor.[9] So, today, government is the prize, the game is "for keeps," and business is in Washington to stay, with the armed forces as its closest ally. I do not believe that business will allow another New Deal, with its freewheeling populist sentiment, to happen. As to the new strength of organized labor, this should be borne in mind: Next to, and as an adjunct to, control of the government, organized business today is out to destroy organized labor power; and despite the growth of organized labor from less than four million in 1932 to fourteen to fifteen million today, I believe the estimate may be hazarded that the *relative* position of labor in the power struggle today is weaker than it was twenty years ago. The development of labor-management training centers in our universities is a deceptive device aimed at pulling the teeth of potential leaders. This is industry's answer to the dangerous dilemma pointed out by Gunnar Myrdal in his *An American Dilemma*.[10] According to Myrdal, vertical mobility of able men out of the working class is being slowed up in America, but meanwhile increasing popular education is making these men better equipped to exercise leadership. If, he says, they are blocked from moving up in the industrial structure, they will in time turn to leadership of their own class.[11]

What all this means for education is serious in the extreme. It looks as though the old liberal middle way is out from here on: either democracy will arouse itself and move in on our economy and democratize it, or business will swallow up democracy—in which event we shall have an American version of fascism. There is evidence that, while the broad middle-class element in America has failed to learn any clear thing from the last two decades and still repeats mechanically and uncritically the slogans "freedom," "equality," and "competition," big business has been learning rapidly; and central in this new learning is a fundamental administrative contempt for democracy as too slow, too unreliable, and too wasteful for the purposes of big business.[12]

The basis for my uneasiness about the goals for higher education stated in the "Report of the President's Commission" will by now be quite apparent. These goals are stated in the expansive mood of nineteenth-century liberalism. They are stated as education's own contribution to progress. And only the atom bomb is allowed to creep into the Report as a possible interruption of that progress. As a matter of fact, we Americans, including the President's Commission, have allowed ourselves to be stampeded by the atom bomb. Of course it has horrifyingly dangerous potentialities, but so do other achievements of modern science. It is also one of the great potentials for doing the work of men more quickly and economically. The thing that makes atomic energy dangerous is not the fact of its discovery, but the fact that a capitalist society views it primarily as a weapon in the world-wide struggle for power. And it is the failure of the President's Commission to identify correctly the prime destructive agent in the present scene that worries me.

The Commission is careful, with one exception, not to use the word *class*. We are a class-stratified society, as every capitalist society is, but the Commission struggles to avoid saying so. It hints at the problem when it says, "all too often the benefits of education have been sought and used for personal and private profit, to the neglect of public and social service" and "nor can any *group* in our society, organized or unorganized, pursue purely private ends and seek to promote its own welfare without regard to the social consequences of its activities" and it identifies the fact of class by name in the passage quoted earlier from page 36 of the Report.

> Throughout the volume, the implication is that our American system is essentially sound and requires only to be extended and corrected in respect to details. We are told that
> . . . citizens need to understand thoroughly the functioning of political parties, the role of lobbies and pressure groups, the processes of ward and precinct caucuses. They need to know not only the potential greatness of democracy, not only the splendor of its aspirations, but also its present imperfections in practice.

And if students are taught that, despite the copious revelations of three Congressional lobbying investitions, lobbying flourishes in Washington and in our state capitals as never before and dominates legislation, then what? And when students seeking to "understand thoroughly the functioning of political parties" are confronted with a university or college administration that hesitates to let Henry Wallace speak on the campus, then what?

The Commission states that "perhaps" [and the qualification is significant] education's "most important role is to serve as an instrument of social transition". And what are liberal students and faculty members to make of the obvious anxiety with which their administrative officers view their activities?

Again, the Commission speaks of the obvious fact that "the gap between our scientific know-how and our personal and social wisdom has been growing steadily through the years." I wish the Commission had gone on to ask why this is happening. It is not just a matter of the gap between the discovery and control of the use of atomic energy. No social scientist who believes in the need to close this gap and effect social change works on any campus without some degree of real anxiety as to the relation of his research and teaching to his chances of promotion; and this anxiety is directly mediated to him through the administration of the institution in which he teaches. I wish the Commission had read the first twenty-five pages of the TNEC Monograph 26 on *Economic Power and Political Pressures*.[13] This states better than any other source I know, the fact of the monopoly over science, both pure and applied, enjoyed by private business, and the resulting key political power in American life this gives to business. What I am trying to say is that the cause of the "gap" between what we know and what we elect or are able to apply is not the inadequacy of scientists in our colleges and universities, but the power of private business. In this connection, the Commission might also have read with profit pages 39 to 66 of the National Resources Committee's *Technological Trends and National Policy*, dealing with such things as business' resistance to the use of new scientific knowledge.[14]

Discrimination within American society is viewed by the Commission as a matter requiring changed attitudes. Of course it does. But how are we to bring about this change? There is good reason for saying that as long as the Negro is a marginal economic man in our society, to be used in times of labor shortage and fired when the labor market gets "easy," he will be discriminated against; and that the "Jewish problem" is a function of an economy of artificial scarcity in which the Jew is a convenient scapegoat. As an educator and scientist, I feel "sold short" by a commission of my colleagues that leaves a problem like this hanging on the easy, vague basis of "changing attitudes."

And finally, the failure of the Commission boldly to "go to town" on the cause of the class basis for current higher education leaves me limp. Do they actually believe that within a class-stratified society there is any possibility of meeting their pious goal? They say that "even in the State-supported institutions we have been moving away from the principle of free education to a much greater degree than is commonly supposed." If this is the case, it reflects strong pressures within our kind of society. Then how does the Commission conceive of a reversal of this tendency? Here again we face the puny strength of exhortation in the face of economic power.

A basic weakness of the Commission lies in its assumption that problems are discrete things to be "reconciled" one at a time, whereas the essence of the problem education confronts is a related *system* of power directives. We are told that "effective democratic education will deal directly with current problems." But it makes no sense to tackle the subsidiary aspects of our culture apart from the central source of our dilemma.

The preceding discussion also provides a part of the basis for my belief that "general education" is inadequate as a solution for our educational problem. "General education" strikes me as but another example of the "curricular tinkering" which the Commission itself rejects. If, as the Report says, "present college programs are not contributing adequately to the quality of students' adult lives either as workers or as citizens", is "general education" a direct road to the remedying of this lack? Rather, it seems to be a retreat from reality. It appears to assume, as the Commission in fact assumes throughout the Report, that democratic principles have all been already worked out, that our institutions are basically sound, and that the problem is to stretch the student to their content. This I believe to be an evasion of the necessary task of facing up to the inherent contradictions within our hybrid institutional system and to the need fundamentally to re-think and to re-structure democracy. It says in effect that, if we only give the student a broad and standardized enough approach, the going system can be made to work. I believe that it is no accident that the clamor of businessmen for a return to "teaching the fundamentals" coincides with the new gospel of "general education."

To the Commission, "the failure to provide any core of unity in the essential diversity of higher education is a cause for grave concern." But how does a "core" come about in the process of becoming educated? "General education" assumes that such a core of unity can be achieved by the wholesale process of putting every student through required general courses, in the hope that the neat order of the college catalogue will unroll itself in the student. Actually, what matters is not whether a student has "taken" a given course, but whether the course "takes" with the student. But this depends upon the student's building his own integration, and no faculty curriculum committee can do this for him by setting up formal requirements.

So "general education" rests upon two fallacies: first, it assumes that democratic values and procedures are essentially known and ready to be learned *in extenso*; and second, it assumes that the creative experience of perceptive coming to grips with one's world can best be achieved in the crucial early years of college by funneling into all students the same subject-matter in substantially the same sequence.

In our society, youth and adult life are discontinuous. The two disparate worlds begin to mesh in earnest in college; and college, particularly the important first two years, may be viewed either as the time to "housebreak" youth to the ways of the outside world, or as a critical time for genuinely exploratory discovery of oneself in one's world. If the latter is accepted as the responsibility of education, the lack of order involved in discovering oneself in a new and urgent situation must be accepted as both a necessary and a richly potential part of this transition process. And if one is a good enough democrat to believe that the complicated experience of attempting to make democracy work must be re-created afresh in each generation in the person of each young citizen, then, too, one must accept, and not short-circuit, the unavoidable discontinuities of trial and error as the student lives himself into awareness of the potentialities of the democratic process. For the meaning of democracy as well as its necessary institutions can only in part be "handed on" from generation to generation, and must be ever discovered afresh in the growing experience of each new person.

The new curriculum of "general education" may be an administratively easier and cheaper way to provide mass education at the college level, but it is not the most effective way to bring into live synthesis the very real needs of the individual student and a rapidly changing institutional scene. If, as the Commission says, the gap between what we might do and what we manage to do is widening, if the colleges are lagging, and if education's most important rôle is the speeding up of social change, then let the Commission ponder this: Any "general" pattern of education for all students inevitably operates at the level both of teachers and of students to smooth out the rebel grain of each new generation in the academic planing mill.

If all of this seems somewhat sharp in its critical stance, let me simply say this in conclusion: I write as a professor in a graduate school, and my central drive is to attempt to make "education" mean the responsibility of trained men and women to address themselves to fundamentally needed social change, whether as teachers or researchers or both. As such a teacher, I work constantly under the shadow of the pliancy of American university administrators to business pressures, though I am fortunate in the case of my immediate university connection. It is just because I am so keenly aware of the need for more and more legislative appropriations and endowments, and aware of what this does to anxious administrators, that the failure of the Commission to address itself squarely to the problems of power in our society leaves me with a feeling of having been let down by my professional colleagues on the Commission.

The prospect ahead, as the reader will have gathered, seems to me more than a little dark and threatening. I see no ready solution to the dilemma of American education, caught, as I believe it is, ever more firmly in the vise of big-business power. As an educator and one who believes that democracy is one of the great social inventions glimpsed by man and, as such, worth fighting to preserve and perfect, I nevertheless believe that our first task is to try unflinchingly to understand and to state the full measure of the danger in which democracy and education lie. It helps neither democracy nor education to play the ostrich or to rest back upon optimism in a time like this.

The administrative echelons in our colleges and universities are most immediately the captives of business. This exposed position of the men who must deal directly with businessmen alumni, legislative committees, and private donors must be faced in all understanding and sympathy by the rest of us.

Next in the hierarchy come we members of the teaching staffs. Shorn of the defenses of administrative expediency which the officers above us may invoke, and directly pledged to the inner integrities of teaching as a profession, we face, for the most part one by one, the full brunt of outside opposition. Our defenses as teachers are not by any means negligible, but I believe that they are growing weaker. If we elect so to do, we can pull in our necks and teach the safe, non-political aspects of our respective subject-matters. Without minimizing our desperate need for all the generous and courageous support and protection administrators above us can give us, we may not rely on such support; nor may we take our color from our administrators. To do the latter of these is to quitclaim our central responsibility as teachers. Regardless of what administrators may do, courage must dig itself in at the level of the teaching ranks. And those of us who are full professors and in major institutions must be prepared to carry a disproportionate share of the fight in behalf of our less secure younger colleagues in the lower academic ranks and in behalf of those in smaller and more exposed institutions. Meanwhile, those of us who as social scientists work in the full heat of current issues require all of the understanding and assistance we can get from our colleagues in less controversial fields like the humanities and the natural sciences. One of the ominous symptoms on many campuses today is the quiet withdrawal from colleagues who get the increasingly easy label, "radical."

Along with teachers come the students. It is my definite impression that this postwar student body, as I meet them in the graduate school, is the best I have ever known—with an extraordinary level of social realism and readiness to face the facts. I have never before had so many students ready to ask, "All right, if this is the situation, where can I go out and get to work on the problem of democracy?" The answer to that one wrings the vitals of the candid professor! It is my belief that education must rely as never before upon the fresh thrust of energy and courage of our students as an indispensable ally. Our respect for our students and what they can contribute must rise in these critical times to levels perhaps never before reached.

And now, turning the Commission's affirmation into a question: Can it be done? None of us knows, but none of us can afford to quit the fight. Each time an administrator stands unwaveringly between a professor or students and outside attack, the democratic tradition survives in that action. A teacher stands before his class or confers with a student in his office and gives his whole self—his doubts, his lack of knowledge, as well as his affirmations—and, again, the democratic process is at work. The climactic issue of our time will be fought out by great blocs of organized power beyond our campuses, and for the immediate future the decision may go against the mass of the people. But over the long future, it is my belief that man will fight his way back toward more and more democracy. Meanwhile, we educators can be sure that our classrooms have a great rôle to play as one of the few potential active focal points for that longer future.

Notes

1. Chapel Hill, North Carolina: University of North Carolina Press, 1933. pp. 52–53.
2. New York: Macmillan Company, 1913.
3. Boston: Little, Brown, and Company, 1945.
4. Parts of the story are told in such books as Engelbrecht and Hanighen's *Merchants of Death*, Lundberg's *America's 60 Families*, I. F. Stone's *Business as Usual*, Carl Dreher's *The Coming Showdown*, George Seldes' *One Thousand Americans*, the LaFollette Committee reports, and the publications of the Temporary National Economic Committee, especially Monograph 26 on *Economic Power and Political Pressures*.
5. "The President's Scratch-Pad," Sept. 30, 1947.
6. *See* the weekly issues of *In Fact*.
7. From the *Emporia Gazette*. Quoted in Seldes, *op. cit.*, p. 150.
8. *See* Sprague's *The Battle for Chicago* for the mood of this vast era of predation.
9. *Business Week*, September 26, 1942.
10. New York: Harper and Brothers, 1944. p. 715.
11. Of interest in this connection is the recent Luckman proposal that a million dollars a year be spent by industry on the education of labor-management leaders in colleges and universities, under an arrangement whereby labor and management would each nominate five hundred likely leaders annually for such indoctrination training.
12. The new business tactic of the administrative by-passing of democracy at the level of government action is suggested in Walton Hamilton's "The Smoldering Constitutional Crisis," *New Republic*, January 18, 1943.
13. United States Government Printing Office, 1941.
14. United States Government Printing Office, 1937.

PART III
CURRICULAR DESIGN

Part III: Curricular Design

The readings in this third section of the volume take a pragmatic turn by focusing on a range of models and approaches for planning and building programs and courses. It is important to note that the readings included here are by no means intended to be taken as a sequential set of "how-to" instructions. While the readings can certainly be utilized in such hands-on endeavors, each selection presented here stands on its own as a robust resource for charting college and university curricula.

In "Organizing Principles," Clifton Conrad advances a three-step framework for curriculum planning originally presented in his book entitled, *The Undergraduate Curriculum: A Guide to Innovation and Reform*. The first step involves "choosing an organizing principle" that will serve as a touchstone or theme of the design process. Conrad notes five common organizing principles: academic disciplines, student development, great books and ideas, social problems, and selected competences, and then sketches the historical influences, lines of scholarly inquiry, and advantages and challenges associated with each of the organizing principles. The second step of Conrad's framework for curriculum planning calls for "establishing curricular emphases," a process in which curriculum planners determine where the curriculum will be grounded along four continua: "locus of learning," "curriculum content," "design of program," and "flexibility of program." Following an explication of these continua and considerations for working along them, he details the third step, "building a curricular structure," which consists of making choices among an expansive menu of components, including but not limited to how the curriculum is implemented in terms of length of time, size of enrollment, location of learning environment, and responsibility for oversight.

Another classic contribution to the literature on curriculum design is "Curriculum Perspectives and Frameworks," an article from *Shaping the College Curriculum* by Joan Stark and Lisa Lattuca. In light of their circumscription of the "vaguely-defined concept called curriculum" as "a plan for students' academic development," Stark and Lattuca lay groundwork for advancing a theory of curriculum that will be useful to faculty and administrators engaged in designing courses and programs. They contend that a theory of this kind has not yet been developed but that many of the pieces of it are present in the extant scholarship. In this article, they review two decades' worth of literature—particularly works that put forward "comprehensive frameworks concerning what is taught and why"—and identify the contributions and shortcomings therein with respect to the theory of curriculum that they envision.

In the third article of this section, Charlotte Briggs, Joan Stark, and Jean Rowland-Poplawski illuminate further the formidable challenge of establishing and maintaining a wide-angle focus on the curriculum. In their *Journal of Higher Education* article entitled "How Do We Know a 'Continuous Planning' Academic Program When We See One?" they report on a multi-year study to learn whether, to what degree, and how academic departments incorporate "continuous improvement" principles and processes akin to the "total quality management (TQM)" or "continuous quality improvement (CQI)" trends that gained popularity in corporations and, subsequently, higher education administration in the 1990s. While such movements have largely become outmoded, they observe, the need for departments to engage in continuously planning processes remains as demands for curricular outcomes have not ceased. Based on a synthesis of the practices of "exemplary" departments, they advance four criteria (i.e., "continuous and frequent curricular planning processes," "awareness and responsiveness," "participation and teamwork," and "use of evaluation for adaptive change") and five indicators for each criterion that faculty and researchers can use to cultivate and test models of continuous curricular planning.

The following is an article by John Braxton, Deborah Olsen, and Ada Simmons entitled "Affinity Disciplines and the Use of Principles of Good Practice for Undergraduate Education," offers additional insight into challenges and opportunities inherent in program-level curriculum design.

The authors identify a factor, a level of "paradigmatic development," that helps to predict the likelihood of academic departments' adoption of "principles of good practice" in undergraduate education. A department's level of paradigmatic development is determined by the discipline for which it has the strongest affinity and "the extent to which members of [that] discipline agree about theory, methods, techniques, and the importance of problems for the discipline to pursue." In this light, according to the authors, disciplines like physics and chemistry have "high" paradigmatic development, and disciplines like history and sociology have "low" paradigmatic development. The consequence is that faculty in departments with an affinity for the latter type of discipline are more likely to be afforded more flexibility in how and what they teach and what curricular elements may constitute a program. To understand the contours of this "affinity discipline hypothesis," Braxton, Olsen, and Simmons studied the correlation between departments' paradigmatic development along the "seven principles for good practice in undergraduate education," a highly regarded heuristic developed by Arthur Chickering and Zelda Gamson, and found that the hypothesis holds for most but not all of the principles. An implication of this study is that, while the level of a department's paradigmatic development cannot be changed, those engaged in curriculum design can develop an awareness of this variability among affinity disciplines and determine goals and objectives accordingly.

In addition to discipline-specific challenges and opportunities encountered in curricular design, there may be considerations that arise depending on what unit of curriculum is being engaged. In "Tensions and Models in General Education Planning," Robert Newton argues that general education reformers are routinely confounded because they are unaware of relatively common themes in deliberations over general education change and fairly common attributes of the final products of such efforts. He explains that there are four areas of tension that are characterized by polarized interests: knowledge (unity vs. fragmentation), student learning (breadth vs. depth), faculty competence (generalist vs. specialist), and content (Western culture vs. cultural diversity). After elaborating on these tensions, he presents and describes how the aforementioned tensions play out in three basic models—Great Books, Scholarly Discipline, and Effective Citizen—that typically emerge from institutions' general education reform processes. Newton contends that efforts to review and redesign general education will be more informed and ultimately more successful if those involved in the process become familiar with these tensions and models.

An issue that has become increasingly important when considering the design of general education and degree programs as a whole is remedial (or "compensatory") education. In "Remedial Education in Colleges and Universities: What's Really Going On?" Jamie Merisotis and Ronald Phipps aim "to bring some clarity" to recent discussions regarding compensatory education. They remind us that remedial education has always been a part of collegiate education in the U.S. and that very few (20 percent or less) institutions offer no remedial courses. Complicating the matter, they argue, is the fact that many colleges and universities are hesitant to offer remedial courses due to concerns about negative effects it might have on their reputations. In turn, they suggest that there is likely a greater need for remediation than what is currently being acknowledged. Following a review of literature concerning the demographics, effectiveness, and costs of remedial education, Merisotis and Phipps conclude with recommendations for, first and foremost, recognizing remedial education as a "core function" of higher education so that it may be funded properly and made more effective. In turn, the implications for curriculum design are clear: Remedial education ought to be embraced and incorporated systematically, not shunned and added reluctantly.

The next reading introduces an element that may be incorporated into an undergraduate program alongside any combination of general, specialized, and remedial education. Called "the Option," this curricular building block is described by Roger Baldwin and Melissa Baumann in their *Innovative Higher Education* article entitled "Options for Change: A Flexible Vehicle for Curriculum Evolution and Reform." Developed at Michigan State University, the Option "is a technique other institutions could adapt to increase the flexibility and responsiveness of their educational programs in an era of fiscal constraint and unprecedented change." Put simply, the Option is a specialized program of study— a combination of courses from any number of departments and co-curricular learning experiences— that differs from traditional major and minor courses of study because it is a less formal institutional arrangement. In turn, the Option is "more malleable" because it is subject to fewer institutional policies (including State review in Michigan's case) and fosters "creative" change that meets the interests of multiple stakeholders. Following a description of the Option and a presentation of examples (e.g., a combination of engineering and orthopedics studies for a "joint replacement" Option), Baldwin and Baumann conclude their curricular design showcase with recommendations for implementation, including considerations for quality control and weighing its advantages and disadvantages in comparison to creating new courses or degree programs.

Among the most common elements of contemporary curriculum design are courses and programs that are dubbed "interdisciplinary" and are intended to introduce students to scholarly knowledge and equip them with skills in such ways that they are better prepared for participating in a world that does not align itself lock-step with disciplinary boundaries. According to the author of the next reading, however, components of curriculum design often fall short of their good intentions because they are based on ill-defined notions of interdisciplinarity. In "'Comprehensive' Curricular Reform: Providing Students with a Map of the Scholarly Enterprise," Rick Szostak articulates a definition of interdisciplinarity that, he argues, can serve to ameliorate the problems with interdisciplinary curriculum design: "*Openness* to the application of *all* theories and *all* methods to *any* set of phenomena." By asserting a definition of interdisciplinarity that reflects the disposition of an "interdisciplinarian," he implicitly makes the central concern of curriculum design the cultivation of that disposition. In light of this end, Szostak contends that "comprehensive" curriculum design is necessary—that is, whatever topic or question is taken up as a subject of study must be located "within a comprehensive map of the scholarly enterprise." Designing curricula in this way involves organizing phenomena of interest "hierarchically" (he delineates or "disaggregates" the phenomenon of "culture" as an example), presenting theories within a comprehensive typology of theories, always naming the research method (he notes there are essentially "twelve distinct methods") and ethical perspective (he notes there are five types) employed. Following observations he makes regarding the implementation of comprehensive curricular reform, Szostak discusses what he sees as its benefits, which include but are not limited to students making better sense of scholarly terrain, a transformation of "the major," a more defensible liberal arts concept, and a stronger basis for educating citizens.

Citizenship education is the primary subject of the final reading in this section on designing college and university curricula. In "Pedagogical Strategies for Educating Citizens," Anne Colby, Thomas Ehrlich, Elizabeth Beaumont, and Jason Stephens, authors of *Educating Citizens: Preparing America's Undergraduates for Moral and Civic Responsibility*, identify components of curricular design that help and hinder moral and civic learning. Rather than using lectures and textbooks as the primary means of communicating with students, Colby et al. suggest using "pedagogies of engagement" like service learning and other forms of experiential education, problem-based learning, and collaborative learning to facilitate the complex learning required for educating citizens. They close the article with specific guidelines for teaching ethics and details of curriculum design from four exemplary courses.

The readings in this section provide useful starting points for understanding how the design of courses and programs has been conceptualized and enacted to date and for thinking about how research and practice related to curricular design may be approached in the future. To be sure, there are elements of curriculum design that may well be timeless, and reviewing older texts provides insight into the enduring—and passing—qualities of curriculum design. To illustrate, we might ask the following question: How might Conrad's third step of curriculum planning be revised, if at all, to reflect contextual factors of higher education today? With some of the readings we get a glimpse at the role that theory plays in curriculum design, a matter that can compel a variety of questions. What are the implications of defining curriculum as an "academic plan" as Stark and Lattuca do? How, if at all, does sharpening the definition of curriculum in this way exclude other conceptualizations of curricula? If a sixth "indicator" was added to each "criterion" in the article by Briggs et al., what would they be and why? The use of the concept of "paradigmatic development" by Braxton et al. appears relatively straightforward with respect to disciplines like physics, chemistry, history and sociology; what about English or communications or education? Questions about the application of curriculum design scholarship also arise. Will becoming aware of Newton's "models and tensions" help curriculum planners or is becoming aware of them through exploration and running up against them a part of the process that he overlooks? Merisotis and Phipps argue that the faculty and administrator attitudes toward remedial education are inhibiting, but what about students' attitudes? What issues may need to be identified if Michigan State University's "Option" were to be successfully implemented at, say, a small private college or a public university in a different state? If you were in charge of implementing Szostak's model of "comprehensive" curricular reform, where would you start, and who do you think should be responsible for the hierarchical disaggregation of knowledge? Could Szostak's model be used to implement the citizenship education envisioned by Colby et al.? Entertaining these questions, of course, generates even more questions, and an object lesson in the never-ending possibilities and critical stakes inherent in curricular design.

ORGANIZING PRINCIPLES

C.F. CONRAD

Let us assume that a college or university is faced with the challenge of undertaking a comprehensive review of the undergraduate curriculum. We will also assume that there is some acceptance of the view that the curriculum operates as a system, whether we like it or not. Furthermore, we will assume that a rational approach to planning is possible, at least to some degree, and that the planning process is more than a political game, whereby department and divisional chairpersons work out agreements which express the self-interest of their various faculties. Granted these assumptions, is it possible to develop a framework for planning which is at once theoretical and specific?

A Framework for Planning

Figure 1 suggests three major steps involved in planning the curriculum. The first and most important step involves the selection of an organizing principle on which to base the curriculum. As the figure indicates, five major organizing principles have been identified: academic disciplines, student development, great books and ideas, social problems, and selected competences. Let us examine each one briefly.

Perhaps unwittingly, the majority of postsecondary institutions organizes its curriculum around the academic disciplines. Since the organization of knowledge has taken place through self-contained disciplines, it is usually assumed that knowledge should be communicated in the same pattern. By force of tradition, this principle will probably continue as the basis of most curricular structures. However, in the last few decades, at least four alternative ways of organizing the curriculum have gained a foothold in American higher education.

The curriculum can be organized so that its major goal is the facilitation of student development. A curriculum organized around this axis assumes that the development of the "whole person" is central to planning the undergraduate program. The main purpose of the curriculum is to promote both the affective and cognitive growth of students.

A third approach organizes the curriculum around great books and ideas. While persons favoring this approach do not necessarily downgrade the contributions of the academic disciplines or take issue with the goal of student development, they are in agreement that the major contributions in human thought can be captured in a selection of great books and great ideas—classics considered essential to Western civilization. Accordingly, they argue that the important issues facing mankind are timeless, and that the curriculum can best be structured around a series of carefully selected works.

The social problems approach is most concerned with the organization and communication of knowledge most needed to solve current problems. This approach is based on the premise that knowledge can best be communicated through a study of social problems—such as pollution, population control, and transportation—rather than through traditional disciplines or through the classics. It is both contemporary and futuristic in orientation, stressing the importance of the application of knowledge.

Reprinted from *The Undergraduate Curriculum: A Guide to Innovation and Reform*, by Clifton Conrad (1978), by permission of Westview Press.

Step 1: Choosing an Organizing Principle

1. Academic Disciplines
2. Student Development
3. Great Books and Ideas
4. Social Problems
5. Selected Competences

Step 2: Establishing Curricular Emphases

Four Continua:

1. Locus of Learning:
   Campus-Based   Experiential
       Classroom Learning — Learning
2. Curriculum Content:
   Breadth ——————————— Depth
3. Design of Program:
   Faculty —— Contractual —— Student
4. Flexibility of Program:
   Required — Distribution — Elective

Step 3: Building a Curricular Structure

Some Considerations:

1. Requirements for the total degree program, probably including general education, concentration, and electives.
2. Alternative degree programs, including accelerated degree programs, external degree programs, and student-designed programs.
3. Arrangements for concentration, including discipline-based majors, interdisciplinary majors, student-designed majors, and career-oriented majors.
4. Components of general education, including core programs, interdisciplinary programs, competence-based programs, and freshman seminars.
5. Experiential learning opportunities, including work-learning and service-learning programs, cross-cultural experiences, academic credit for prior learning, and individual growth experiences.
6. Calendar arrangements, including daily, weekly, and annual schedules as well as modular and interim arrangements.
7. Formal and informal structural arrangements for learning, ranging from the traditional classroom to cluster colleges and living-learning centers.
8. Individual course experiences, including the number and subject area of courses to be offered.
9. Overall course structure, ranging from structured classroom courses to seminars and independent study.
10. Methods of student evaluation, ranging from grades and comprehensive examinations to written evaluations and external assessment.
11. Selection and advising of students.
12. Administrative and financial responsibilities for organizing and managing the curriculum.

Figure 1 A Framework for Curriculum Planning

Finally, a major new way of organizing the undergraduate curriculum is to provide educational experiences that will enable students to develop selected competences. Emphasis is placed on the achievement of certain levels of competence such as the ability to read with high levels of comprehension, to write and speak fluently, and to use statistics and computers. Thus in contrast to the other approaches, which usually evaluate student performance only in terms of passage through a number of courses and the accumulation of credits, the selected competences approach places major emphasis on the identification of skills and abilities and on the process of assessing student progress toward the achievement of specific educational goals.

It should be emphasized that these organizing principles are not primarily distinguished from one another at a broad philosophical level. Persons favoring the academic disciplines or a great books and ideas approach, for example, may have similar educational philosophies. The crucial distinctions, instead of residing at the philosophical level, lie in the way knowledge is organized and communicated. To the extent that institutions can find agreement on one or more of these bases for planning, within the broad context of overall institutional goals, a solid foundation can be laid for building the curriculum.

After choosing an organizing principle, the second step in curriculum planning is the selection of emphases. Figure 1 exhibits four continua which curriculum planners need to consider. The first continuum refers to the locus of learning by comparing campus-based classroom learning with experiential learning. Historically, college and university curricula have favored one end of the continuum: traditional classroom learning. In recent years, however, many institutions have moved closer to the middle of the continuum by offering a variety of experiential learning opportunities.

The second continuum refers to the content of the curriculum and compares *breadth* and *depth*. For our purposes, breadth refers to a basic knowledge of some of the essential facts and concepts in all major areas of knowledge and, in addition, some understanding of the structure, concepts, and modes of thought utilized in academic inquiry. Accordingly, breadth is achieved through the use of various modes of knowing to illustrate the foundations as well as the substance of the major areas of knowledge. While most curricula emphasize breadth through the general education program, it can also be achieved through the manner in which a subject is introduced. For example, a course in a student's major may emphasize breadth because the subject is placed within the context of a larger body of knowledge.

The concept of depth can be an even more difficult term, usually referring to study in a field of concentration. For our purposes, depth will be defined as a detailed knowledge of the concepts, terminology, and methodology of a particular way of organizing knowledge—such as through the academic disciplines. Although study in breadth and study in depth may seem mutually exclusive, they are but two points on a continuum and can complement one another. The critical issue is the relative weight given to study across various fields of knowledge (breadth) versus the intensive study of a particular approach to organizing and communicating knowledge (depth). Most institutions fall somewhere in the middle on this continuum, but there is some evidence that breadth may have been receiving less emphasis in the last several years through the reduction of general education requirements.

The third continuum refers to the design of the program; that is, whether the program is faculty-designed, student-designed or is a contract between faculty and student. In most institutions, of course, faculty retain complete control over the design of a student's program, usually through a broad set of requirements agreed upon by the faculty as a whole. In recent years, as students have demanded a greater share in planning their own programs, there has been a marked shift in a number of institutions moving toward the midpoint on the continuum. Usually this position on the continuum is represented by a contract where the student more or less designs his own program, subject only to faculty approval. While a totally student-designed program is conceivable, only a handful of institutions surrenders to students the final approval over their plan of study. The distinction between faculty designed and contractually-designed programs is an important one, with many students today playing an important role in the design and evaluation of their academic program.

The last continuum refers to the flexibility of the program and compares a highly structured or required program to a wide-open or elective program. The issue here is not who designs the content, but what is required. There are three distinct types of courses, or sets of experiences, that can be represented on this continuum. Required courses are defined as those specific courses and experiences that students must present for graduation; distribution courses are defined as those within a content division, department, or group, where some freedom of choice is allowed the student; elective courses are those which can be taken from among the listing of courses of the institution without any restrictions, except the meeting of prerequisites. In practice most institutions offer all three types of courses, but many schools choose to emphasize one end of the continuum or the other.

The establishment of curricular emphases should not be viewed as a needless exercise. Indeed, the conscious selection of various points on the continua will have important implications for the expression of the organizing principles.

Only after the curricular emphases have been wedded to one or more of the organizing principles should attention be turned to the building of a curricular structure. This third step in curriculum planning involves the translation of these principles and emphases into an integrated curriculum plan. Figure 1 lists the various tasks which must be undertaken to develop the curriculum into a fully elaborated undergraduate program. Unfortunately, most curriculum planning begins with Step 3 rather than Steps 1 and 2.

This framework for curriculum development can be used in a variety of ways. It can serve as a tool for analyzing a total institutional curriculum or parts of the undergraduate program such as general education, the major, and various special programs. In addition, it can serve as a device for analyzing new curricular innovations. It also provides a stimulus for imagining new curricular arrangements based upon alternative combinations of organizing principles and emphases. Most important, it can serve as a tool for planning all or part of the undergraduate program. By forcing curriculum planners to think in terms of organizing principles and curricular emphases, it encourages the construction of a curriculum that reflects a systematic approach to the undergraduate program instead of a hodgepodge of unrelated courses and experiences. With those goals in mind, the underlying purpose of this volume is to develop and demonstrate the model so that it can be easily utilized by those involved in curriculum planning.

In order to expand upon the framework, it is necessary to develop in detail the five organizing principles. For each of the latter, I will look at the background and basic premises of the approach and the combinations of curricular emphases that are often associated with that organizing principle. An example of how one or more institutions have organized their curricula around each principle will be presented. Finally, some strengths and weaknesses associated with each principle will be considered.

The Academic Disciplines as an Organizing Principle

It has long been argued that the way in which the curriculum is formulated depends on the way in which the structure of knowledge is conceived. Central to this issue are at least three questions that have concerned philosophers for centuries: How do we define knowledge? How do we "get" knowledge? How do we verify what is or is not knowledge? Beginning with fundamental Platonic and Aristotelian differences over the definition of knowledge and how knowledge can be verified, philosophers such as Locke, Hume, Berkeley, and Kant have addressed these critical issues.

The purpose here is only to raise these epistemological issues, for a primary concern of this analysis is the ways in which man has organized knowledge for academic study, particularly through the academic disciplines. Before discussing the academic disciplines as an organizing principle, we might ask: What are some of the other ways in which man has organized knowledge in recent times? John Dewey developed ten categories which have served as the primary tool for organizing college and university libraries. They have been superseded recently by the classification system of the Library of Congress with its thirty-one basic categories. Mortimer Adler developed an organizing tool for the Encyclopedia Britannica which also uses ten categories, although they are different from those of Dewey. Some conception of the structure of knowledge is consciously or unconsciously employed in defining the nature and extent of the curriculum. But which of the different conceptions of the structure of knowledge, if any, should provide a unifying principle for the curriculum?

One response to that question is the academic disciplines. From an historical viewpoint, the organization of the disciplines is a recurring issue. Aristotle, for example, delineated three classes of disciplines: the theoretical disciplines (such as metaphysics, mathematics, and the natural sciences), the practical disciplines (such as ethics and politics), and the productive disciplines (such as fine arts, the applied arts, and engineering). Other well-known schemes have been put forward by such diverse persons as Plato, Auguste Comte, and, more recently, Philip Phenix. Each of these schemes has at various times influenced the organization and definition of the disciplines.

A number of definitions of the term "discipline" have been suggested. For our purposes, the definition developed by Arthur King and John Brownell is most useful. They suggest that a discipline is: a community of persons; an expression of human imagination; a domain; a tradition; a syntactical structure—a mode of inquiry; a conceptual structure; a specialized language or other system of symbols; a heritage of literature and artifacts and a network of communications; a valuative and affective stance; and an instructive community (King and Brownell, 1966, p. 95).

The organization of the disciplines within higher educational institutions has always been subject to change. The history of curriculum development in the American college and university illustrates the changes that have taken place in the organization of the disciplines. Neither the number nor the structure of acceptable disciplines for college and university studies has ever been static. New disciplines have emerged, providing the basis for new traditions. Many of the contemporary social and natural science disciplines were gradually included within the curriculum in the late nineteenth and early twentieth century and only after considerable controversy. The concomitant growth of the academic department has further led to the strengthening of various disciplines.

Persons espousing the academic disciplines as a major organizing principle suggest that the curriculum should reflect the existing state of knowledge as defined through the departmental and disciplinary structure. Put simply, the curriculum should be structured around the academic disciplines. King and Brownell, among others, suggest that the major way of organizing and communicating knowledge is through an acquaintance with the concepts and modes of inquiry provided by the disciplines (King and Brownell, 1966, pp. 146–149).

While the structure and organization of knowledge have not remained static, the American undergraduate curriculum today reflects the dominance of well-established academic disciplines and departments. Indeed, the organizational structure of most colleges and universities, by perpetuating the authority of academic departments, is a powerful force for maintaining the status quo in curricular organization.

Applying this organizing principle to the framework for curriculum planning, it can be seen that several emphases (refer to Step 2 of Figure 1) are often associated with a discipline-based approach. For obvious reasons, the locus of learning is almost invariably campus-based—in the classroom—with few, if any, provisions for experiential learning. The content may emphasize breadth through the general education program, but is also likely to emphasize depth to the extent that general education is based upon courses in particular disciplines. The concentration portion of a student's program usually represents depth by definition, and even the elective portion is likely to be based in a few disciplines. The design of the program will likely reflect faculty control, although its flexibility may range from highly prescriptive or required to elective courses. These trends on the various continua notwithstanding, there is considerable variation in the curricular structures (refer to Step 3) that are utilized by postsecondary institutions.

Because the majority of undergraduate curricula is based on this organizing principle, it is unnecessary to provide an institutional example of a discipline-based curriculum. It is more appropriate to identify some of the possible strengths and weaknesses of such an approach to organizing the undergraduate program.

A number of advantages to organizing the academic program around the disciplines have been noted. Perhaps the most compelling argument is that knowledge in the modern world is principally organized around the disciplines and can thus best be understood and communicated through the disciplines. As Philip Phenix (1964) states it:

> The most impressive claim the disciplines have upon the education is that they are the outcome
> of learning that has actually been successful. A discipline is a field of inquiry in which learning

has been achieved in an unusually productive way. Most human efforts at understanding fail. A very few succeed, and these fruitful ways of thought are conserved and developed in the disciplines. Every discipline is simply a pattern of investigation that has proved to be a fertile field for the growth of understanding [p. 36].

Put simply, one major advantage is that this approach is based on a widely accepted epistemology, namely that the disciplines are the single best way of organizing and communicating knowledge.

There are also a number of practical advantages in planning the undergraduate program around the academic disciplines. Since most colleges and universities are organized by academic departments based on the various disciplines, it is administratively efficient to organize the curriculum around the department rather than another organizing principle which cuts across the existing academic organization. Also, since the majority of postsecondary institutions rely on the disciplines as the basis of curricular formation, a similar curriculum allows students to transfer easily from one institution to another.

Although most planners would agree that the curriculum should impart to the student some understanding of the disciplines, many persons raise serious questions about the hegemony enjoyed by discipline-based programs. Some people have attacked the very classification of knowledge by academic discipline, pointing out that there are a number of sound alternative schemes which offer distinct advantages. Still others suggest that given the development of so many disciplines it is difficult, if not impossible, to structure the curriculum in a way that incorporates the major concepts and modes of inquiry common to the disciplines.

While the epistemological issues will likely remain unresolved, a more concrete criticism is that even if the structure of knowledge should be based on disciplines, the structure of the curriculum should still be based on educational goals and designated learning experiences. Robert Pace (1966) observes:

> In higher education today knowledge is organized around academic disciplines. This organization has a special relevance for scholars and researchers and it is certainly not irrelevant for the ordinary student. It is nevertheless a clerical organization of knowledge which serves most directly the interests of the academic priesthood . . . [pp. 39–40].

Many persons today share Pace's concern with the dominance of the academic discipline. Some go a step further, however, and argue that alternatives to the narrow, knowledge-consumption view reflected in the disciplinary approach call for other organizing principles such as student development or competence-based curricula. In particular, a discipline-based curriculum may indicate a lack of concern for the affective development of students as well as for their individually preferred educational goals.

Oddly enough, some of the strongest criticisms of the disciplinary approach are coming from within the disciplines themselves. The rigid boundaries and specialized language of the disciplines hamper both the application of knowledge to contemporary problems and the extension of basic research. The biologist today must know what the chemist and physicist are talking about to carry on more penetrating investigations within the field of biology. Furthermore, all three must be able to talk to political scientists and sociologist if what they have discovered is ever going to "do the world any good." Requests for mechanisms for carrying on the interdisciplinary studies often come from the most advanced and specialized scholars within the disciplines.

While the academic disciplines are likely to continue to dominate the structure of undergraduate curricula, attention is being given to other organizing principles.

Student Development as an Organizing Principle

There have always been proponents of the view that the proper foundation for curriculum planning should be the development of students as persons. In the early years of the Republic, this viewpoint was often referred to as the "character building" conception of the college. In spite of its widespread acceptance, this organizing principle has not historically provided the underpinnings of many college and university curricula.

In the last several decades, however, there has been a "developmental" movement that has attracted widespread attention and has led, in a number of institutions, to the adoption of a curriculum based upon some conception of students' developmental needs. The modern roots of this approach can be traced to the work of such developmental psychologists as Nevitt Sanford and Joseph Katz.

Attacking the grip of the professions or disciplines, Sanford and Katz view the development of personality as the prime meaning of undergraduate liberal education (Sanford and Katz, 1962, p. 424). Their main argument is that in planning the curriculum, educators should

> . . . ignore conceptions of what college students "ought to know," whether the concern be with their preparation for more advanced courses or with a suitable sampling of organized knowledge, and that we ought to concentrate instead on giving these students experiences that set in motion the developmental changes in which we are interested [p. 434].

Operating out of a Freudian developmental framework, Sanford and Katz offer some general guidelines for organizing the curriculum around student developmental needs—such as allowing the entering student freedom to indulge in those interests that he already has and teaching subjects in a way that addresses the student's existential concerns. More recently, other developmentalists, such as Arthur Chickering and Kenneth Keniston, have charted the stages and tasks which most undergraduates must confront.

While there are often major differences among developmentalists regarding the particular definition of the developmental tasks facing adolescents and young adults during their college years, the developmentalists are united by their basic approach. Most important, they usually agree that the curriculum should not be organized around preparing people to enact social roles, but around helping students "put themselves together internally," that is, encouraging developmental growth. They also see a need for the integration of emotion and feeling with intellectual and cognitive growth. College should be a place and time for students to have a psycho-social moratorium from making decisions, so that they can find out who they are and where they are going.

Arthur Chickering integrates much of the developmental literature by demonstrating how college can make a difference along seven major vectors of change: developing competence, managing emotions, developing autonomy, establishing identity, freeing interpersonal relationships, finding purpose, and developing integrity (Chickering, 1969, pp. 9–19). Not only does Chickering identify the commonalities in the developmental tradition, he also draws upon the existing literature to try to identify the institutional conditions that make a difference to student development. With regard to the curriculum, Chickering (1969) suggests:

> The principal curricular change would be increased flexibility. Increased flexibility could be achieved by adding opportunities for independent study and for groups of students to work together with an instructor in a large and amorphous area—which could take more definite shape as these students defined more clearly their own interests and as the significant components of the area itself became known. Flexibility could be enhanced by opportunities to put together courses from diverse domains, or to pursue fewer courses more exhaustively. Time units might also be loosened. Some students and faculty members might develop an area for study and then fit the time to the study—putting the horse before the cart, in proper fashion for a change—rather than the other way around, where a fixed time unit is set and all subjects cut to fit it [pp. 285–286].

Although Chickering's *Education and Identity* is viewed as a classic by many espousing a developmental perspective, there are a number of other sources. *The Student in Higher Education* (1968), for example, a volume representing the Report of the Committee on the Student in Higher Education, includes some general recommendations regarding the curriculum.

To summarize briefly, proponents of this approach are united by a conviction that the curriculum should be organized around student developmental growth. The curriculum should not be viewed as an aggregate of discipline-based courses, but rather as a flexible set of experiences designed with the students' developmental growth as the guiding principle.

Applying this organizing principle to the framework for curriculum planning, it can be seen that several curricular emphases on the four continua (refer to Step 2) are often associated with this approach, and further, that most of these emphases tend toward the ends of the continua opposite to the academic disciplines. The third and fourth continua are particularly critical in clarifying this approach. Significantly, the developmentalists argue that a student's program should be individually designed, usually through a contract with the faculty. Student growth and curricular flexibility, in terms of the design of the program, are viewed as inseparable by the developmentalists. It generally follows that the program should also be highly flexible through an emphasis in the major program on elective courses. Also following from the notion of curricular flexibility and student-designed programs, most developmentalists would argue that the locus of learning should not be confined to campus-based activities; provisions should be made for off-campus experiential learning. Finally, with regard to curriculum content, the developmental viewpoint seems to emphasize neither breadth nor depth, although many programs tend initially to steer students in the direction of breadth.

An interesting example of a curriculum conceived to facilitate developmental growth is the Goddard College undergraduate program. In explaining the "Goddard idea," this excerpt from the college catalog suggests the developmental focus of the curriculum:

> The Goddard idea about education is offered as a reasonable basis for seeking answers, not as an answer in itself.
>
> The idea is that learning takes place as persons discover their needs and move to meet them.
>
> Need-meeting experiences can give an individual a growing body of resources to draw on in identifying and meeting new needs. They may also be of such a nature as to make clear the value of earlier experiences.
>
> A learning experience is so defined here: it is vital to the student's present needs, illuminating of his past experience, and useful as a resource in his future life.
>
> Such experience, it must be added, is in the nature of a transaction. The learner takes from her environment what will be useful in meeting her needs—information, skills she may observe and practice, advice, instruction—and gives back to her environment a newly modified, developing, and growing behavior which becomes, in turn, part of the environment of resources for other learners. So this transactional learning is social as well as personal: many of the needs each individual must meet derive from the human fact that she is interdependent with others; and her behavior sums with the behaviors of millions of other persons to become society, cultures, civilizations, the human world [*Goddard College: The Resident Undergraduate Program, 1975–1976*, pp. 9–10].

The curriculum at Goddard emphasizes flexibility, a contract-designed program, and a diverse offering of courses and experiences. Within guidelines established by the faculty, each student plans his own educational program, including at least two nonresident semesters.

At Goddard "curriculum" is defined as the whole life of the student, with particular emphasis not only on formal study activities but also on the student's ability to live cooperatively in a college residence, on performance in a college work program, and on participation in college governance. There are six main kinds of formal study activities: 1) group courses, which generally meet as discussion groups; 2) independent studies, which are planned by individual students with faculty who help them find resources and evaluate their work; 3) studio and workshop activities, in which the emphasis is on practical work with the assistance of faculty; 4) off-campus field-service work, in which students learn through serving in hospitals, schools, social agencies, and elsewhere in the community; 5) nonresident term studies, which usually involve apprenticeships, internships, or short-term enrollment in other educational institutions or programs under sponsorship of the college and faculty; 6) special summer sessions at Goddard, where a student devotes twelve weeks to working on a single issue or topic chosen from a limited number of offerings. A typical program for a student in a resident semester includes three study activities. Students are counselled to choose group courses during the first year, although they may include studio work and field-service experience. Additional study activities are utilized as the student moves through the program.

At the end of each term, a Goddard student writes evaluative reports about each activity. Reports are also written by a student's teachers, nonresident-term supervisors, counsellors, and others who share responsibility for the program. These reports become the basic materials for the periodic reviews that faculty members make of each student. Four such reviews take place during a student's eight terms at Goddard.

The first two years of the program are viewed as exploratory study. While Goddard has no "majors" in the traditional sense, at the end of the second year each student is asked to define her interests in an application for degree candidacy. With the assistance of a counsellor and other faculty members, the student outlines the proposed area of study she wishes to make the core of studies during the last two years at Goddard. Usually in the next-to-last term, a candidate for the degree chooses a Senior Study committee made up of at least three faculty members, one of whom is her advisor. With the help of the committee, the student plans her Senior Study in considerable detail. As the Study nears completion, a final review focuses on the student's execution of the Senior Study plan against the background of her entire Goddard education. If the student's plan is carried out to the satisfaction of the committee and the document or product resulting from the Study meets the approval of committee members (and an additional person appointed by the Dean's office), the student will be graduated. The description of the various stages in a student's progress through Goddard suggests the importance attached to thorough evaluative reports written by students and their teachers. Goddard does not use letter or number grades; the reports are the sole basis for the preparation of transcripts of Goddard study.

The academic program at Goddard College is one example of organizing the undergraduate curriculum around student developmental needs. From its philosophical statements to the practical implementation of the curriculum—including a wide variety of nonconventional learning opportunities— the Goddard program represents a concrete alternative to many existing curricular arrangements.

The Goddard example suggests some of the potential advantages of organizing the curriculum around student development. The curriculum structure is likely to be highly flexible, thereby promoting the creativity of students and enhancing their motivation. Most of all, its proponents argue that such a curriculum will encourage colleges to once again nurture the "whole person." Regardless of whether or not one subscribes to this organizing principle, the overall contributions of the developmental movement in the last decade have been widely heralded. The movement has fostered the trend toward stripping away the last vestiges of *in loco parentis*, by encouraging greater freedom of choice and making students assume responsibility for planning their educational program.

While many persons acknowledge these contributions, some are quick to point out some of the potential deficiencies in this approach. Perhaps the most biting criticism is that it places insufficient attention on the acquisition of knowledge. As a consequence, it is myopic and overlooks a fundamental mission of the college and university: the transmission of knowledge. Charges of elitism are also leveled at this approach. Is college the appropriate institution for promoting development? Or is this a psychological luxury for privileged students? Should we encourage the "new students" in higher education (especially the disadvantaged) to be interested in personal development at the expense of preparing for a career?

Other criticisms focus more directly on the application of a developmental framework for planning the curriculum. For example, some argue that students need more guidance than freedom, and a developmental approach clearly emphasizes the latter. Some are simply critical of any developmental framework, while others, who are perhaps more sympathetic, admit that there is little agreement regarding the particular developmental needs of college students; it is difficult to design a program without substantial agreement on those needs, however. In spite of these criticisms, some of which are met in the Goddard program, curricular formation based on student developmental needs is one alternative for organizing the curriculum.

Great Books and Ideas as an Organizing Principle

Among those most deeply committed to the liberal arts, there has long been a disdain for many of the developments in the American undergraduate curriculum. From this viewpoint the elective system is often seen as a device which led to the multiplication of subject matters, the effect of which was hardly alleviated by the introduction of majors. The curriculum, through the dominance of the academic disciplines, has often been conceived in reference to the requirements of graduate and professional schools or to changing conditions of employment in the contemporary world, rather than to the pursuit of knowledge for its own sake. In short, liberal education has been undermined as the college curriculum has become fanatically preparatory.

In the past four decades, one attempt to recover the true meaning of the liberal arts has involved a new approach to the vast tradition of Western thought as embodied in the "great books." Proponents of this approach argue that the wisdom of the past is distilled in selected great books which have come to be known as classics. Although our knowledge of the world is always expanding, the important problems confronting man and man's responses to them are those which have been dealt with by the great minds through the ages. While the form of the central problems confronting mankind may change, the substance of the problems will not. Thus, the content of the great books should be the foundation of learning.

This approach most emphatically rejects the domination of undergraduate education by the academic disciplines and the concomitant emphasis on specialization at the undergraduate level. Because the disciplines depend completely on a detailed understanding of the particular, attention is confined to a special subject matter. Discipline-based learning entails a fragmentation of the students' attention, a multiplication of special problems, instead of addressing the perennial problems of mankind—the hallmark of a liberal education.

The most ardent defenders of the great books call for the organization of the entire curriculum around selected classics. Academic departments, with their disciplinary base, should assuredly not occupy a position in the academic organization of a college committed to the great books approach.

Applying this organizing principle to the framework for analyzing curricular emphases, it is obvious that this approach stresses the left end of each of the four continua. Learning should principally occur in a classroom setting through the serious consideration of the great books; experiential learning, which is rooted in the present, is an anomaly to an approach that emphasizes the past. By implicitly denouncing the emphasis placed on discipline-based curricula, this approach almost exclusively emphasizes breadth in the content of the program. The faculty, who are obviously better prepared than students to select the great books, assume total responsibility for the design of the program. It follows that the program will probably be highly rigid, with at best only a few electives.

St. John's College, which began its great books program in 1937, is the only institution which has applied this principle to the organization of the entire academic program. The examination of a program which has survived and prospered for four decades provides some interesting insights into the development of a great books curriculum. The College's organizing principle is explained in its catalog:

> St. John's College believes that the way to liberal education lies through the books in which the greatest minds of our civilization—the great teachers—have expressed themselves. These books are both timeless and timely; they not only illuminate the persisting questions of human existence, but also have great relevance to the contemporary problems with which we have to deal. They can therefore enter directly into our everyday lives. Their authors can speak to us almost as freshly as when they spoke for the first time, for what they have to tell us is not something of merely academic concern, remote from our real interests. They change our minds, move our hearts, and touch our spirits.
>
> The books speak to us in more than one way. In raising the persisting human questions, they lend themselves to different interpretations that reveal a variety of independent and yet complementary meanings. And, while seeking the truth, they please us as works of art with a clarity and a beauty that reflect their intrinsic intelligibility. They are therefore properly called great, whether they are epic poems or political treatises, and whether their subject matter is scientific, historical, or philosophical. They are also linked together, for each of them is introduced, supported, or criticized by others. In a real sense they converse with each other, and they draw each reader to take part, within the limits of his ability, in their large and unending conversation [*St. John's College Catalog, 1976–1977*, p. 5].

Although the list of books may vary slightly from year to year, all students take the same required program of great books—classics from Plato and Aristophanes to Marx and Freud. There is no departmental structure, and all faculty are simply referred to as tutors. Except for preceptorials (nine week in-depth studies), there are no electives.

There are three principal curricular vehicles for the implementation of the St. John's program: seminars, tutorials, and preceptorials. Students attend seminars based on the great books for each of the four years. Two tutors meet twice weekly for several hours with fifteen to twenty students. The seminar begins with a question asked by one of the tutors, and thereafter consists almost entirely of student discussion. The course of the session is not fixed in advance; it is determined by the process of discussing, of facing the crucial issues, or of seeking bases upon which a line of reasoning can be pursued.

The conversational methods of the seminar are carried over into the tutorials. For four years a student attends one language tutorial and one mathematics tutorial, usually four mornings a week. Three times a week sophomores also attend a music tutorial. As in the seminar, students talk freely with one another and the tutor, but the discussion focuses on assigned tasks. In addition, there are four years of laboratory science. Groups of students meet with a tutor twice a week for science laboratory to study such topics as theory of measurement and atomic structure.

Preceptorials were added to the program in 1962. For roughly nine weeks in the middle of the year the seminars of the junior and senior classes are replaced by preceptorials. These are small groups of students engaged in the study of one book or the exploration of one subject in several books. Although many preceptorials study one of the books on the seminar lists, or a theme suggested by the seminar reading, some preceptorials may deal with books and themes the students would not otherwise encounter in the program. The preceptorial is the only part of the curriculum which offers the student some choice, since he may choose from among the fifteen or twenty topics offered each year. One additional component of the program is the weekly formal lecture presented by an outside tutor. The lecture is followed by a discussion with both faculty and students participating.

In their study of undergraduate education, Arthur Levine and John Weingart conducted a number of interviews with students and faculty at St. John's College. They concluded that in spite of several drawbacks associated with the current organization of the program, there was widespread approval of the overall thrust of the great books program (Levine and Weingart, 1973, p. 48). In a broader context, however, what are some of the possible strengths and weaknesses of a program based on the great books?

On the plus side, a great books program may represent one of the most integrated courses of study offered in the entire nation. While using the great books as the principal vehicle for promoting the liberal arts, such a program can provide a firm foundation for further advanced study. Contrasted with the potpourri of disparate courses and experiences that characterizes most undergraduate programs, such a program may be highly appealing to those most committed to a vision of true liberal learning. While no institution other than St. John's has chosen to base its entire program on the great books, the attractiveness of this approach has led many educational reformers to devote part of their curriculum, especially in the general education program, to selected classic books in the history of Western civilization.

Yet the absence of support for the great books as an organizing principle for the entire curriculum suggests that there are some disadvantages. Foremost among them is the failure of the study of classical volumes to include new developments, a serious deficiency given the speed of knowledge expansion. Especially in the sciences it is argued, the increase in knowledge during the last twenty years has contributed more than in the entire previous history of mankind. A second criticism is that the program is primarily oriented toward the past rather than the present and the future. A third notes that at St. John's, the program tends to favor the humanities over the sciences and focuses exclusively on Western civilization, ignoring the intellectual contributions of the non-Western world. Also, it has been observed that such a program is necessarily rigid, allowing the student little choice to pursue his own interests. Finally, some persons suggest that while the concept may be attractive, it is impractical; students pay a price in terms of immediate job prospects and perceived readiness to engage directly in graduate work, because the majority of institutions focus on the preparation of students for graduate school and preprofessional training.

Regardless of whether or not one favors a great books approach, it deserves serious consideration, for in presenting an alternative to discipline-based curricula it raises some important issues regarding the more traditional academic program.

Social Problems as an Organizing Principle

Since education is largely a function of society, increasingly paid for by society, the focus of collegiate education, it is sometimes argued, ought to be on societal problems. The most pressing problems today are social problems; without their resolution, individuals, however gifted and talented, will not be able to develop to their fullest. This point of view has led to a new basis for planning the curriculum, a social problems approach.

A curriculum utilizing this approach is broadly organized around one or more themes such as environmental problems, urban problems, or world order. Most of these programs are characterized by a problem orientation, a concern for social responsibility, and a belief in the need to integrate knowledge. Several distinctive program emphases have generally evolved from these principles: flexibility and student initiative in curriculum development, an orientation toward emphasizing the present and future instead of the past, and off-campus learning through community action and practical experience. In utilizing a social problems approach, institutions do not usually organize their program around traditional academic disciplines. A larger university, for example, might be organized in colleges concerned with various social problem themes, rather than in colleges grouped according to disciplines.

Applying the framework, it is clear that using a social problems approach may lead to many different combinations of curricular emphases. For example, in terms of the locus of learning, in the advanced stages the program will probably emphasize experiential learning, where the student deals directly with a pertinent social problem; before that, however, traditional classroom learning will probably be emphasized. In terms of the content of the curriculum, the program, almost by definition, includes both breadth and depth: breadth through the delineation of a problem area within the context of a larger theme, but depth in the sense of pursuing the problem with the aid of a limited number of methodological approaches. Similarly, the program is likely to be flexible, although designated introductory courses may be required.

Possibly the best single example of a social problems approach is the curriculum at the University of Wisconsin—Green Bay. The focus of the program is man and his environment. (At UWGB, "environment" is defined to include the biophysical, social, cultural, and aesthetic spheres.) The aim of the program is to help student, instructor, and community member to relate more effectively to, and do something constructive about, the environment.

The four colleges of UWGB are organized around environmental themes rather than traditional academic disciplines. They are the College of Human Biology, the College of Environmental Sciences, the College of Community Sciences, and the College of Creative Communication. The names suggest the focus of each college and its particular area of teaching, research, and community outreach activity. A School of Professional Studies complements the theme colleges and is responsible for professional programs that relate to them.

Under the UWGB academic plan, each student builds his program around a broad problem of the physical or social environment rather than around a standard disciplinary area. He may take courses in a variety of fields, but must relate the knowledge acquired in those courses to the environmental problem chosen for the focus of study. The UWGB faculty have identified twelve broad problems, including such areas as environmental control, man's use of the natural environment, and the processes of modernization. The student chooses one of these concentration areas as his major. Within the concentration, the student may select a single subject field, such as political science, as a comajor. In addition, a concentration in almost any field may be accompanied by a professional minor that leads to a teaching certificate or credentials in business administration or other professional fields. In addition to concentration requirements, there are two major categories of

All-University requirements: distribution courses and the liberal education seminar. Through the former, the University requires a student to earn a minimum of five credits in each of the four theme colleges. In some areas, concentration courses may be used to fulfill the distribution requirement.

The academic core at UWGB is the liberal education seminar (LES), a program which engages every student in a variety of learning experiences relating classic and contemporary concepts of values to contemporary environmental problems and to perennial human concerns. As a freshman, the student chooses four seven-week modules from a list of topics such as the human condition in world perspective, technology and human values, resource utilization and the American character, and crises in communication.

During the intermediate years (sophomore and junior), the student learns how to become usefully involved in the community and in other cultures. Usually there is a project associated with this portion of LES, and the learner is its designer, taking major responsibility for the content and for developing skills in working with other persons outside the University. At the senior level, the student attempts to integrate his knowledge and experiences with those of students working in many other concentrations. Working with themes such as "social consciousness and the scientist," the student can apply what has been learned to continuing issues in our culture and the world. According to the catalog, "Students begin by analyzing common values and assumptions and synthesizing them into a generalized conceptual overview; return to the concrete by applying such conceptualizations to the theme; and, finally, go beyond prior assumptions by examining the nature and quality of the human condition from new perspectives." Altogether, LES is an eighteen-credit required program: freshman—six credits (two semesters); intermediate—nine credits (thematic packages, usually running two semesters plus January); senior—three credits (one semester).

In addition to UWGB, a number of other institutions have adopted a social problems thematic approach. One interesting example is the University of California at Santa Cruz. The institution is made up of eight small, self-contained, distinctive liberal arts colleges. While one of the colleges is viewed as an arts and sciences college, several of the colleges are loosely organized around a theme or social problem (e.g., science and technology, issues that confront Third World societies and the poor and powerless within this country, and development and change). Newly created colleges will address new problems. Several possible topics have been identified to serve as the basis for emerging colleges: regional planning, Pacific studies, public life, oceanographic studies, and health services.

There are some obvious advantages in using social problems as the basis for organizing the curriculum. Most important, such a problem may be a powerful force for motivating students. By having a major responsibility for designing one's own program (UWGB) or by having the option of selecting a thematic program from among several major social problems (Santa Cruz), students may become more self-directed learners than they would in more traditional discipline-based programs. Coupled with experiential learning, which is usually an important component of these programs, a social problems approach is relevant to the "real world" in a way that many students desire.

Unlike most other programs, this approach tends to be heavily oriented toward the present and future. The problem orientation emphasizes a breadth of preparation that requires moving beyond the narrow sanctuaries of the academic disciplines. Such a holistic approach, which does not deny the contributions of the disciplines but rather refuses to make them the foundation of education, is appealing to those who decry the increasing fragmentation of knowledge.

At the same time, some searching questions have been raised about a social problems approach. Above all, such an approach contradicts the notion of education as a "value-free" process. Social responsibility involves a cultivation of commitment. While proponents of a social problems approach argue that value-free education is a myth, the notion persists in some circles that such an approach is inimical to a liberal arts education. In addition, critics argue that a social problems approach tends to ignore the rich historical foundations of the liberal arts in the humanities and sciences through a futuristic vision of education. Furthermore, problem-solving is only one academic skill. A curriculum that exclusively emphasizes problem-solving runs the risk of becoming excessively preoccupied with the practical. Education should be useful, but perhaps it should be much more than that. Thus, while a problems approach may be broad in its focus on issues that cut across the disciplines, it may also be excessively narrow in its emphasis on the future. Nevertheless, at the very least a social problems focus offers another major alternative approach to organizing the undergraduate program.

Selected Competences as an Organizing Principle

Some educators believe that a discipline-based approach to planning the undergraduate program is too narrow, that a "here and now" focus on developmental needs is short-sighted, that a great books approach is too past-oriented, and that a social problems focus is too value-laden. Proponents of a competence-based approach contend that the main focus of a college education should be functional; that is, the emphasis should be placed on the utility of education in later life. What should graduates be able to do? What competences should they have? And most important for our purposes, what types of curricula will assure that certain behavioral outcomes will result?

The concept of educating for competence is not new to higher education. In the 1920s, for example, the concept of a formalized competence-based curriculum for teacher education was formulated by W. W. Charters. Today, many colleges require comprehensive exams for seniors, while others utilize performance criteria in the fine arts and in technical skill areas. In recent years, however, the term "competence-based curriculum" has been given a new significance as attempts have been made to construct the entire undergraduate curriculum in terms of an explicit competence base. Bob Knott (1975) offers a useful definition of the term:

> A competence-based curriculum does not differ from other curricula in its goals. It differs in the assumption that the basic desired outcomes of an educational process can be stated in terms of defined and recognizable competences and all students can be held responsible for achieving these competences. Under a competence-based curriculum, mastery learning and not time is the major criterion of performance.
>
> Further clarification of the concept of a competence-based curriculum can be gained by a closer examination of the joint use of the terms competence and curriculum. Competence may be defined as "the state of having requisite abilities or qualities." A curriculum is a set of designed courses or experiences. A competence-based curriculum then is one where the competences expected of all graduates are agreed upon and defined, and courses or experiences are designed to assist the student in becoming competent. If a curriculum is to have a competence base, there must be a clear statement of both what the competences are and how a student may attain them. A curriculum designed around competences would consist of three basic elements; first, an overall statement of competences to be acquired for a successful completion of the program; second, sets of evaluative criteria for each competence which define the proficiency levels required for successful attainment, and third, sets of experiences designed to assist the student in attaining the required competences [p. 28].

Put simply, competence-based programs focus on the outcomes of rather than the inputs to the learning process. A competence-based program is concerned with three central issues: identifying competences, building a curriculum which will facilitate student progress toward the achievement of those competences, and developing adequate procedures for assessing competence.

In terms of the four curricular emphases, competence-based programs are likely to range across the entire length of all four of the continua. With regard to the locus of learning, most competence-based curricula emphasize experiential learning as much as classroom learning. Many programs, for example, give credit for previous life experience, and most programs offer a wide variety of experiential learning opportunities that are compatible with identified competences. At some colleges the program is highly individualized and largely student-designed. In consultation with a faculty member, the student identifies a range of competences that he wishes to pursue, develops a course of study designed to meet those competences, and proposes means for assessing his progress. Other programs, however, are faculty-designed and allow the student considerably less freedom in identifying individual competences to be developed.

Most competence-based programs organize their curriculum around specific behavioral goals and objectives. Learners are evaluated on the results of their educational experiences in terms of the identified competences. Demonstrable evidence, not grades, is the sole criterion for "credit" or certification. A competence-based program can look very much like a traditional program or can be non-traditional in a literal sense. Because the nature of the curriculum may depend to a large extent on whether it is faculty-designed or student-designed, several examples will be discussed to suggest a range of possibilities for developing a competence-based curriculum.

Mars Hill College in North Carolina has recently started a competence-based curriculum wherein the college has restated its curricular requirements in terms of competences rather than simply in terms of required courses and credit hours. All bachelor degrees awarded are based on student mastery of seven basic competences. The development of the seven competence units was drawn largely from Philip Phenix's *Realms of Meaning*, (1964) and also makes use of Arthur Chickering's *Education and Identity* (1969). According to the college catalog, a graduate of Mars Hill College

1. . . . is competent in communication skills;
2. . . . can use knowledge gained in self-assessment to further his/her own personal development;
3. . . . comprehends the major values of his/her own and one foreign culture, can analyze relationships of values between the cultures and can appraise the influence of those values on contemporary societal developments in the cultures;
4. . . . understands the nature of aesthetic perception and is aware of the significance of creative and aesthetic dimensions of his/her own experience which he/she can compare to other cultures;
5. . . . understands the basic elements of the scientific method of inquiry, applies this understanding by acquiring and analyzing information which leads to scientific conclusions and appraises those conclusions;
6. . . . has examined several attempts to achieve a unified world view and knows how such attempts are made. The graduate is aware of the broad questions that have been posed in the history, philosophy and religion of western civilization and can assess the validity of answers given to these broad questions in terms of internal consistency, comparative analyses, and his/her own position;
7. . . . is competent in an area of specialization [*Mars Hill College Emphasis, 1976*, p. 6].

Proficiency in the seven areas is demonstrated by the achievement of competence units, as attested by assessment teams specializing in each of the areas, and the successful achievement of at least thirty-five course credits (or their equivalent). The assessment teams are responsible for certifying that students have demonstrated the required knowledge and skills with respect to each of the seven competences. These teams consist variously of faculty, community persons, students, and administrators according to the scope of the particular competence. They publish a list of requirements and procedures for demonstrating competence in each area. In those cases where a student successfully demonstrates competence without the use of college-designed learning experiences, the credit received is noted on the student's transcript as Credit by Examination.

In the early 1970s, Alverno College in Milwaukee, Wisconsin, fit almost perfectly the profile of a small, Catholic women's college. The majority of its students came from middle-class Catholic homes in the surrounding area. In 1973, Alverno adopted a new competence-based program that marked a radical shift in the curricular organization of the college.

To graduate from Alverno, a student must amass "competence-level units" that indicate how well she can perform tasks considered essential to a liberally educated person. Alverno has identified eight areas of competence that are required outcomes for each student who seeks a liberal education at the institution:

Communications ability
Analytic ability

Problem solving ability
Valuing in decision making
Effective social interaction
Understanding of the environment
Understanding of the contemporary world
Knowledgeable response to the arts and humanities [*Alverno College Bulletin, 1976–77*, p. 13].

To encourage students to structure and pace their learning as a process, each competence has six developmental levels. All students develop all eight competences through level four. In addition, they develop selected competences through level five or six, depending on their area of concentration.

At Alverno the development of competence means an individually-paced process in which the student makes use of multiple resources in multiple contexts. Her courses provide a structure to assist her in using a network of learning resources that extend through the entire campus environment and beyond. The student is provided with a considerable amount of practice as well as ongoing evaluation and feedback at Alverno. Texts and library sources, media presentations, and live lectures provide information. Laboratories, group tasks, and off-campus sessions provide practice. Instructors and other trained assessors provide evaluation and feedback. Syllabi for each course specify the possible means of learning and the method and criteria for assessing each competence level offered in the course.

When a student is assessed for a given competence level, she receives feedback on how she performed in relation to the criteria specified for that level. If her performance meets the criteria, the specific ability is added to her record. Students are not assigned grades to describe their performance; verbal statements specify what they have achieved. If the performance is not sufficient, the student receives an explanation including suggestions for learning experiences to improve her skills before applying for reassessment.

To receive a bachelor degree from Alverno, students demonstrate attainment of knowledge and competence by their successful completion of forty competence-level units. The forty units include the first four levels of all eight competences, for thirty-two units, plus eight advanced level units, including at least one unit at level six. Prior to beginning advanced level work students participate in a seminar which enables them to evaluate their ability in the eight general competence areas. A major area of concentration requires the successful completion of at least four advanced level units. Attaining eight advanced level units enables students to complete an interdisciplinary area of concentration, or the integration of two major areas or a major area and support areas. From this brief description of the program, it is clear that Alverno College provides an excellent example of how a competence-based program might be conceived and implemented.

In contrast to Mars Hill and Alverno, Metropolitan State University (formerly Minnesota Metropolitan State College) has a competence-based program that is designed primarily by the student. The University consciously avoided replicating existing approaches to educating adults. In addition to being competence-based, the program has a major experiential emphasis, is student-centered, and is highly individualized.

Metropolitan State University (Metro U) has a number of fairly unique features: the absence of a traditional campus, a faculty which is drawn primarily from persons with professional backgrounds in the community, B.A. degrees awarded on the basis of demonstrated competences rather than credit hours, and a student body of which 80 percent are employed on a full-time basis. Metro U is an upper division university serving persons who wish to continue their education in times and places compatible with their lifestyles. Students enter the university after completing the first two years of college or through university recognition of learning acquired through such prior life experiences as public service, work, homemaking, or nursing education. Persons with less than two years of college or its equivalent may enroll in Metro U's model lower division competence-based programs which were developed with six area community colleges.

Metro U students must first enroll in an Individualized Educational Planning Course (IEPC) which is designed to assist students to 1) understand University policies, including assessment policies and practices; 2) learn the principles of self-directed, independent study; 3) identify their current competences and their learning needs; and 4) design their upper-division degree plans. The degree plan specifies the competences the student wants included in his upper-division program, including those gained prior to admission and those the student plans to attain while enrolled at Metro U. In addition, the degree plan specifies the learning strategies used to attain prior competences or to be used to attain future competences, the techniques that will be employed to assess the competences, and the names and qualifications of the "expert judges" who will evaluate each of the competences. Thus, the identification and articulation phases of the assessment process are accomplished through the IEPC and the development of the degree plan.

Once the IEPC is successfully completed, the student is accepted as a candidate for the Bachelor of Arts Degree, the only degree awarded by Metro U. At this point, the student assumes responsibility for and authority over his education. As a degree candidate, the student receives a faculty advisor and begins to implement the degree plan using a contract learning model. Students are encouraged to use both community-based learning activities and those sponsored by the University. To facilitate the development of the University's learning resources, three Academic Conferences (Administration, Human Services, and Arts and Sciences) have been established. The Conferences coordinate the learning activities sponsored by the University and generate additional learning opportunities. Each term there is a wide variety of learning experiences offered by Metro U which may fit into a student's contract learning model, such as independent studies, internships, workshops, regular courses, and group learning opportunities. In preparation for the degree, the student must generate documentation in support of each of the competences in the degree plan. The documentation must meet the University's standards of adequate evidence and evaluators must meet the University's criteria for "expert judge." When the student has successfully demonstrated attainment of each of the competences listed in the degree plan, he is ready for graduation. In place of a credit-based letter grade transcript, Metro U uses a narrative transcript that includes the titles of the competences demonstrated, the learning strategies employed, the name and qualifications of each evaluator, and a narrative evaluation prepared by each expert judge.

Metro U offers an interesting example of an individualized competence-based curriculum. While all of the individually-designed educational programs are couched in terms of competence, they may be achieved in many ways: through prior learning, fairly traditional courses, creatively designed nonconventional experiences, or through some combination of the above. As implemented at Metro U, a competence-based curriculum is very different from the typical program of undergraduate study.

Because most of the competence-based programs are relatively new, there have been few major evaluative studies. However, proponents of such an approach have pointed out several advantages. Most significantly, they state that by clearly defining educational goals, and by stating explicitly how competences will be assessed, education can be more accountable to students and the public. By focusing on "competences" or "educational outputs," time or "credit hours" will no longer be the major evaluative mechanism for students pursuing the baccalaureate degree. The degree, in other words, will come to represent certain levels of competence rather than four years of accumulated credit hours.

Critics of such an approach are united by a nagging suspicion that one simply cannot adequately measure competence levels. After all, they say, much of learning is serendipitous and it is impossible to measure such effects. Put differently, education is a dynamic process and quantitative measurement will never capture the important qualitative learning that may be taking place. Furthermore, educational programs designed in this way run the risk of becoming just as routine and unimaginative as those where students gather credit hours. Students, being students, will learn only what they have to learn to attain certain levels of competence. They will know what they need to know, but possibly little more. As years pass and the future makes new demands, students in competence-based programs may discover that they have traded away an education for the accumulation of a handful of skills.

Nevertheless, there has been widespread acceptance of the competence-based approach and it will probably serve as one major organizing principle for the college curriculum in the foreseeable future. At the very least, such an approach has sensitized faculty and students to the importance of establishing clearly defined educational goals.

Implications for Planning

By comparing and contrasting the different organizing principles, relating them to the four curricular emphases, and illustrating them with concrete examples, it has been demonstrated that there can be substantial differences among the resultant curricula. There are major differences in the five organizing principles and the four curricular emphases, and the model developed here can be a useful tool for assisting academic planners in analyzing and designing various approaches to undergraduate education. The framework is an attempt to provide a lens through which the undergraduate curriculum can be brought into focus and viewed more clearly.

Confronted with these different approaches to planning the curriculum, how can faculty members and administrators utilize the model for planning their total undergraduate program? This model can be employed four distinct ways. First, it can be used as a device for analyzing an institution's existing curriculum. What is the main organizing principle and what are the major curricular emphases reflected in the current curricular structure? Second, the model serves as a tool for comparing and contrasting alternative curricular arrangements—programs which reflect combinations of organizing principles and curricular emphases that are different from those currently used. Such a comparison sensitizes planners to alternative methods of organizing the curriculum.

Third, the model can be used as a heuristic device to encourage planners to think of curricular arrangements implied by combinations of organizing principles and curricular emphases which are not currently in vogue. For example, combining a great books approach with a student-designed curricular emphasis suggests a curricular structure which may not be employed currently in a college or university. Thus, using the model serves as a device for creating new curricular possibilities. Then by using the model a fourth time, planners can finally begin to construct an integrated curriculum which is based on a specified organizing principle and selected curricular emphases. Therefore, by identifying one or more organizing principles, and by consciously choosing curricular emphases and structural components which are compatible with those principles, those who plan the undergraduate curriculum will be able to develop programs which meet identified institutional needs. Surely that institution in our society which values rationality so highly must be capable of moving beyond happenstance and political gerrymandering in the development of the undergraduate curriculum.

References

Alverno College Bulletin, 1976–77. Milwaukee, Wisconsin: Alverno College, 1976.

Chickering, Arthur W. *Education and Identity.* San Francisco: Jossey-Bass, 1969.

Goddard College: The Resident Undergraduate Program, 1975–1976. Plainfield, Vermont: Goddard College, 1975.

Katz, Joseph, and Nevitt Sanford. "The Curriculum in the Perspective of the Theory of Personality Development." In Nevitt Sanford (ed.), *The American College.* New York: John Wiley, 1962: 418–444.

King, Arthur R., and John A. Brownell. *The Curriculum and the Disciplines of Knowledge.* New York: John Wiley, 1966.

Knott, Bob. "What Is a Competence-Based Curriculum in the Liberal Arts?" *Journal of Higher Education,* 46 (1975): 25–39.

Levine, Arthur, and John Weingart. *Reform of Undergraduate Education.* San Francisco: Jossey-Bass, 1973.

Mars Hill College Emphasis. Mars Hill, North Carolina: Mars Hill College, 1976.

Pace, C. Robert. "New Concepts in Institutional Goals for Students." In Earl J. McGrath (ed.), *The Liberal Arts College's Responsibility for the Individual Student.* New York: Teachers College Press, Columbia University, 1966: 38–47.

Phenix, Philip H. *Realms of Meaning.* New York: McGraw-Hill, 1964.

St. John's College Catalog, 1976–1977. Annapolis, Maryland: St. John's College, 1976.

The Student in Higher Education. New Haven, Connecticut: Hazen Foundation, 1968.

CURRICULUM PERSPECTIVES AND FRAMEWORKS

J.S. STARK AND L.R. LATTUCA

Curricular Frameworks

We have stressed that the vaguely-defined concept called *curriculum* can be viewed more concretely when discussed as a *plan* for students' academic development. Because this academic plan includes several elements, from purpose to evaluation and adjustment, nearly all literature written about topics such as college mission, teaching and learning, or educational evaluation is in some way relevant to our definition of curriculum. In this article we selectively review ideas that focus on one or more of the eight elements we have included in our definition of the academic plan. We hope to show how we came to think of the curriculum as an academic plan and to compare and contrast this comprehensive approach with those of others who have taken more limited approaches. Finally, we will discuss more fully why we believe curricular theory is a useful guide for faculty in constructing and analyzing curriculum plans.

Our view of curriculum as an academic plan builds on the thinking of earlier scholars. Perhaps it is because higher education is so complex and diverse that few scholars have attempted to develop comprehensive frameworks concerning what is taught and why. Much college curriculum literature focuses on specific disciplines and is published in specialty journals, making it difficult for generalists to access and synthesize. Relatively few higher education scholars have outlined frameworks that assist faculty and administrators in classifying, developing, or evaluating the ideas about curriculum from varied sources. In contrast, among those interested in elementary and secondary school curriculum, where it is assumed most practitioners are familiar with the subject matter to be taught, educational psychologists and teacher educators have generated a large body of expository literature about curriculum, curriculum development, and curriculum theory (see, e.g., Jackson, 1992; Posner, 1992; Walker, 1990). We have found some of this literature useful in developing systematic ways to view the college curriculum as well.

In this article, therefore, we review work of influential scholars from all levels of education, including those few who have tried to bring order to a limited but increasing set of curricular studies in higher education (see, e.g., Conrad & Pratt, 1983, 1986; Dressel, 1971, 1979b, 1980; Dressel & Marcus, 1982; Levine 1978; Stark & Lowther, 1986; Toombs, 1977–1978).

An ideal framework for thinking about college curriculum would allow us to identify the elements of an academic plan and the relationships among them, as well as to examine how various types of influence interact to affect the elements and the entire plan. The elements and influences specified should be sufficiently general to fit diverse disciplines and diverse types of colleges and students. We should avoid value judgments about what should be taught, to whom, or how, if the framework is to be generally applicable. To the extent that some value judgments or assumptions cannot be avoided, we should recognize them and make them explicit.

We find that existing approaches to studying curricula generally are either not value-neutral or not comprehensive. Indeed, some scholars believe all curricular decisions are implicitly value-laden (Walker, 1990). Surely, much current discourse about the college curriculum is undertaken to persuade,

Reprinted from *Shaping the College Curriculum: Academic Plans in Action*, by Joan S. Stark and Lisa R. Lattuca (1996), Allyn and Bacon, a Pearson Education Company.

rather than to analyze. Even ostensibly neutral perspectives often conceal tacit assumptions about what should be taught or how it should be taught; for example, some writers incorporate support for either culturally pluralistic content or a common core of knowledge for all students. They may extol education based on special instructional strategies or urge the involvement of specific interest groups in curriculum planning. The influence of constituencies is important, as we shall show, but tends to obscure attention to basic educational assumptions that should under-gird curriculum development.

Many considerations of curriculum by educational leaders seem less than comprehensive because they avoid any substantive definition or discussion of important curriculum elements. They may merely defer to the presumed wisdom of the faculty in developing the curriculum, report how many students are studying in what types of colleges or majors, or even suggest that curriculum does not exist because each student experiences education in his or her own way. Another typical approach involves the construction of lists, histories, or typologies of "innovative" programs and attempts at curricular change, such as those occurring periodically in general education or specific academic majors. Because such typologies usually are based on only one or two elements of curriculum, they may provide little information that helps in curriculum planning, generally.

Many educators try to describe the curriculum as they see it in their institutions or to highlight innovative approaches as they emerge, rather than advocating a specific content or educational process. Their conceptual schemes frequently represent attempts to classify their observations. Among the diverse conceptions, we will review only those we have found most useful and relevant to developing our emerging theory. In our discussion, we note what we believe are the underlying assumptions of the perspectives we review. We will organize our review by discussing the simplest curriculum perspectives first, then the more complex. Most writers focus on only one or two elements of the academic plan, so "single-element" perspectives are very common. We first summarize these single-element approaches, beginning with discussions of educational purpose and ending with those primarily concerned with evaluation and adjustment. Next, we discuss perspectives that consider several elements. Only a few writers in higher education have tried to view several elements of curriculum simultaneously or examine how the elements are interrelated—that is, how each element is influenced, implemented, and enhanced by the others. These come closer to representing general curricular frameworks because they propose relationships to connect some elements of the academic plan. Finally, we show how our own thinking about curriculum as a plan builds on the work of these others and extends it.

None of the literature we have reviewed purports to constitute a theory—that is, a framework that encourages analysis or prediction of relationships between the various curriculum elements or guides practice. Indeed, some previous theorists (Dressel, 1980; Toombs, 1977–1978) have doubted that it was possible to build such a theory for postsecondary curriculum. We agree that the diversity of collegiate educational settings, programs, and learners certainly makes it very difficult to generate a simple framework with wide applicability. We believe, however, that this difficulty may stem from the tendency of scholars to take normative approaches. In viewing curriculum as an academic plan, we deliberately maintain an analytical stance. As we identify and hypothesize relationships among elements of the plan and between the plan elements and the varied influences, we will approach a general theory of college curriculum.

Because most other writers have separated the academic plan from the influences upon it, we will only occasionally mention influences on the plan in this review of the work of others. Later, we will turn our attention to influences and outline how our framework emerges in the context of changes in society.

Single-Element Curricular Perspectives

Analysts and advocates alike have focused, not on all elements of the curriculum plan but, rather, on one or two key elements or on the processes and politics of curriculum change. Some elements of the academic plan have received more attention than others. The most commonly discussed elements, those that most people consider the foundation of curriculum, are the elements we call purposes, content, and sequence. Discussions of purpose and content are often intricately linked by academic writers, whereas considerations of sequence usually take the form of "structural" curriculum discussions, emphasizing student progression through an entire college program or the formal listing and sequencing of courses. In these structural discussions, writers typically state obvious relationships among the curriculum elements, then proceed to disregard these linkages in their analysis. For example, although studies of postsecondary students have a long tradition and are clearly relevant to the structural view of curriculum, authors seldom relate discussions of students to the proposed sequences. Similarly, discussions of instructional processes often focus on the activities or development of faculty members but seldom consider the relation of these concerns to subject content and the learner. Although it is important to understand the actors in higher education, the focused interests of scholars in studying *either* learners *or* teachers have led to research that artificially separates who teaches and who learns from the context of what is taught, how, and in what order.

Perspectives on Educational Purpose

Many curricular perspectives involve a single element of the academic plan, namely educational purpose. The literature advocating specific missions and objectives is especially extensive. Often these speakers are college presidents, scholars, and educational statespersons, and thus they may represent one of at least four different sets of stakeholders who hold varying purposes: society, colleges, faculty members, and students. Some writers fail to specify which stakeholder group is represented, leaving the implicit and erroneous assumption that the purposes of these groups are congruent. Such congruence can usually be achieved only if the statements of purpose are very broad indeed.

College presidents frequently write and talk about educational purposes and missions, and their words, in speeches and college catalogs, have enjoyed strong credibility and provoked useful discussions. Howard Bowen (1977), a university president and scholar of higher education, collected and classified many such college goal statements. Other illustrations of this genre are the writings of Derek Bok (1974), former president of Harvard University, Donald Kennedy of Stanford University (1991), and community college presidents Robert McCabe (1988) and Judith Eaton (1988). Usually such statements emphasize broad principles but lack the specificity needed to translate them into functional curriculum objectives. Often, too, they relate to specific societal and institutional contexts.

Usually college presidents advocate that students should acquire information and knowledge, skills and habits of thought, judgment, and values (Bok, 1974) that will prepare them for participation in society as citizens, workers, technocrats, businesspersons, scholars, or a combination of such roles. Or they may advocate developing various types of literacy for civic and occupational purposes (Eaton, 1988). Often they avoid grappling with the important questions of *which* "information and knowledge," *which* "skills and habits of thought," and *which* "values" should be taught or how these learnings should be achieved. The pronouncements of college presidents tend to reflect their interpretation of what society demands of their colleges and what is suitable for their students. But minefields of unacknowledged dissent and disagreement lie ahead of the college that seeks to use only the broad and neutral presidential view of purpose to achieve a curriculum plan in its own environmental context or to assess its success as the other elements of the academic plan come into play.

Arthur Levine (1978), in a report for the Carnegie Commission, saw faculty members as the primary architects of curriculum and summarized a typology of purposes that he believed illustrated faculty views on U.S. campuses. Levine identified four general educational purposes or "philosophies" that potentially underlie curriculum decisions.

1. *Perennialism*—training the rational faculties of the mind
2. *Essentialism*—learning a prescribed knowledge, cultural heritage
3. *Progressivism*—building on life experience—student-centered, problem-oriented
4. *Reconstructionism*—reconstructing society

Levine left out such purposes as vocational preparation and value development, which we have found to be especially important to faculty members in community colleges and denominational colleges, respectively. But the typology is useful in reminding us that an appropriate model for curriculum planning must provide for multiple faculty viewpoints of educational purpose.

Although presidential views may be too broad to guide curriculum development, faculty may express educational goals too narrowly, based on their discipline and the type of college where they teach.

Students' voices are often expressed through the voices of researchers who have queried them. Based on surveys of entering college students over many years, researchers have reported that educational goals of students have become increasingly vocational (Dey, Astin, & Korn, 1991). Our own studies, asking enrolled students to answer surveys about college and course goals, confirm this strong vocational purpose, but find that it usually coexists with broader purposes such as those expressed by presidents and faculty.

During the 1960s and early 1970s, students asked that education be made relevant to their lives and interests. In the 1980s and 1990s, some have been asking for greater consideration of diversity in higher education. Today's spokespersons for students feel that a list of educational purposes must include the goal of granting legitimacy and higher status to those with diverse lifestyles, particularly underrepresented ethnic groups and gay students. As yet, few educational theorists have incorporated these student views into their expressions of educational purpose.

Traditionally, society sought college graduates with well-developed cultural tastes, the habit of continuing to learn, and the ability to think critically (Kaysen, 1974, p. 180). Recently, a more technologically complex society has preferred a view of the educated person as a specialized and professionally competent worker, able to make rational decisions in "the application of organized knowledge" (p. 184). Yet, as debate about the purpose of an undergraduate college education emerged again in the 1980s, varied blue-ribbon commissions and educational statespersons wrote opinions that returned to traditional purposes.

There are many views of collegiate purposes, ranging from transmission of a shared culture to the position that no shared culture exists, and ranging from the view that cultural development is the primary purpose of education to the view that students must achieve scientific-rational decision-making capabilities to serve the economy or achieve full employment. At any single point in time, great diversity exists even within primary groups of higher education constituents because of the wide diversity of missions that college and disciplines define for themselves. In our view, therefore, the extensive rhetoric that expounds on the "appropriate" college mission nonetheless fails to resolve the "correct" purposes of the curriculum in any specific context. A general framework for careful discussion of curriculum will help decision makers in a specific context recognize how essential it is to achieve agreement on their plan's purpose. But purpose does not automatically help decision makers select content, process, or sequence. Rather, attention to these other elements of the academic plan must follow and extend discussions of purpose to make them more concrete. We turn next to frameworks that focus on the selection of content.

Perspectives on Content Selection

The general goals that educators or society's spokespersons advocate could be achieved by selecting many different types of content to teach. However, general and specific educational purposes are typically embedded in some content area of learning. Thus, selecting subject matter to help students achieve educational objectives is crucial in shaping accepted views of educational purposes into the actual academic plan. In this process, faculty purposes become very important since content is traditionally selected according to faculty interests and scholarly preparation in specific disciplines or professional fields.

Embedding educational objectives in the disciplines is based on the assumption that these divisions of knowledge are appropriate vehicles by which to simultaneously develop specific knowledge and general learned abilities, such as thinking skills. For example, among those whose educational goals include transmitting the cultural heritage (described by Levine as "essentialism"), certain disciplines and classic reading materials are assumed to promote such general abilities as effective thinking and the ability to make value judgments. For those who view the development of problem-solving abilities as a key educational purpose, other types of study, including philosophy, the logical structure of mathematics, and language, are often cited as essential vehicles. In fact, most colleges try to ensure students' exposure to the varied disciplines, rather than focusing on other objectives such as general abilities.

Conceivably, however, educators who view the learner's intellectual development as the most important goal of the academic plan may successfully challenge the monopoly of the traditional disciplines. Currently, some are urging attention to different purposes and other bases for selecting content to be learned in college. One such purpose is to develop generic skills or "general learned abilities" that cross disciplines. Another is to embed the achievement of educational objectives in the study of societal problems from the perspective of several disciplines. Faculty members teaching in area studies, ethnic studies, or women's studies programs frequently challenge traditional views and propose other rationales for content selection. They claim, for example, that both the great books and the traditional disciplines of knowledge have excluded important segments of our population. Thus, while educators debate not only what Americans should know to participate meaningfully in a common culture and also what content should be used as the teaching vehicle, other educators challenge the idea that such a "common" culture even exists. In short, the question is not only *which* cultural heritage is to be learned but *how* and *why*. To solve the problem of exclusiveness, these groups advocate departure from the traditional disciplines as the appropriate content to teach.

Even those who agree that reading classic works of literature, philosophy, and history should be the primary way to learn the cultural heritage disagree on important issues. This debate especially centers on the best ways to achieve the educational purpose Levine called "perennialism"—that is, cultivation of the ability to think effectively. According to one view, reading the great works is assumed inherently to promote effective thinking. But, a second view holds that important outcomes like effective thinking are generic; the content chosen is distinctly secondary to the end itself. In still a third view, no content promotes effective thinking unless it is linked with explicit pedagogical attention to developing this ability. The following types of questions characterize this discussion: What topics should a student be able to think effectively about? Which academic subjects best develop critical thinking? What ways of learning will most likely strengthen effective thinking, regardless of topic? How do we evaluate whether the desired ways of thinking have been achieved? In these arguments, adversaries make clear their positions but tend to make some connections among curricular purpose, content, and educational process on faith.

The connection between educational purpose and the content chosen is a key issue as we think of the curriculum as an academic plan. While some might try to separate these two elements, we believe that their linkage is so well entrenched in our culture that it is not possible at present to do so.

Perspectives on Learners

In addition to mirroring educators' interpretations of society's goals, college goals may reflect the goals of the students who attend. These sets of goals may be out of phase. The educators' curriculum may not quite match the students' curriculum. The separation between students' and faculty's goals especially persists when one examines the relative importance of vocational goals to the two groups. In studies of both faculty and students in all types of colleges, vocational goals are very important for enrolled students but quite unimportant to most of their teachers, particularly in introductory courses (Stark, Lowther, Ryan, et al., 1988). Whether one agrees that colleges should be responsive to students' vocational orientation, the fact remains that enrolled students may have different educational purposes from those of the college and its faculty. In the vocational realm, student demands for specific career majors tend to reflect society's demand more quickly than the college's response; thus, colleges frequently seem to lag in changing curricula to meet student interests.

Educators expect that the curriculum plans they construct will guide students' learning activities. They also traditionally evaluate the success of the curriculum by looking at operational aspects of the faculty members' plan (syllabus, reading list, activities, and exam questions) and whether students achieve goals specified in the plan. As we have argued elsewhere (Stark, Shaw, & Lowther, 1989), it is also necessary to examine the learners' abilities, goals, and effort to predict how appropriate and successful an academic plan may be for them. Scholars such as Thomas F. Green, Alexander W. Astin, K. Patricia Cross, Arthur W. Chickering, and William G. Perry have focused attention on learners as a key element of the academic plan and, to some extent, have linked them with other elements of academic plans such as purposes and educational processes.

Thomas Green described learner development in terms of broad processes like "developing competence" that lead learners to both maturational and intellectual goals of service and judgment. He asserted that acquired information, skills, habits, qualities of mind and understanding, judgments, and values should interact and operate to structure the attitudes and behavior of the educated person (Green in Chickering & Associates, 1981, pp. 543–555). Green used the idea of professional "competence" to illustrate the ideal interaction of processes and outcomes, showing that competence is self-reinforcing. That is, the person who experiences a sense of developing competence in any field is encouraged to continue learning. Humanistic frameworks such as that proposed by Green are useful in creating an appropriate academic plan because they link purpose and process with notions of continuing learner development. The stance is neutral, but there is clear emphasis on the learner as an important entity.

K. Patricia Cross has directed educators' attention to the diversity of learners whose goals and talents academic plans must accommodate. She has been concerned with "new students"—that is, adult, underprepared, and members of underrepresented groups of learners who began to enter higher education in the 1970s (Cross, 1976a, 1976b, 1981)—and has reinforced the importance of considering student's talents and capabilities when constructing a curricular plan.

In Alexander Astin's scheme, which he calls the "talent development model," the purpose of the curriculum is to move the student toward acquiring specified improved qualities (Astin, 1985, 1988, 1993). To Astin, the specific absolute standard of "quality of mind" is less important than how far the student progresses toward this quality during college. Yet his work has become more closely linked with evaluation than with learners.

William Perry studied the intellectual development of Harvard students over a lengthy period and developed a scheme showing how students progress in cognitive and ethical development. Perry's work helps to illuminate the interaction between the student's level of thinking and the types of content and instructional activities that are likely to be successful curriculum components. Although there is much discussion of Perry's "scheme" among college educators, examples of its successful use in curriculum planning are not abundant.

These few scholarly frameworks focusing on learners amply illustrate the diversity of such emphases. Both Cross and Astin have been concerned with fostering development of individual learner talents. Without being specific about desired outcomes, Astin has developed a model that local educators can use to think of how learners develop in ways that they desire. Perry, in contrast, merely described learner intellectual development and, by his own report, did not intend his description to be a model (Perry in Chickering and Associates, 1981, pp. 76–116). Each of these scholars would make learners a central element in constructing an academic plan. Their contribution to our thinking is to show the impossibility of constructing an effective academic plan without considering the learners who will pursue it. Our awareness of student development processes makes it impossible for us to continue to define curriculum as a set of courses or structures that exist in a catalog or policy book, independent of the learner.

Curriculum Sequence Perspectives

Sequences and structures result from decisions about arranging content in the academic plan. Curriculum sequences occur at all levels. At the course level, making such decisions is usually called "arranging content," or "sequencing." At the program level, making functional decisions about sequence is often called "creating curriculum structure." Teachers make deliberate decisions to sequence course content in certain ways—for example, from simplest to most complex or chronologically (Posner & Strike, 1976). At the college program level, the type and extent of structure created may depend on how much consensus exists on a discipline paradigm (Lattuca & Stark, 1994). Unfortunately, when taken alone, decisions about sequencing and structure do not always include attention to the learner and may be based on unwarranted assumptions about relations of content, its sequencing, and desired outcomes.

Curricular structures at the college level may be policies or rules intended to ensure that students are exposed to a variety of educational beliefs, a variety of learning processes, and varied critical perspectives, as well as varied subject matter. In fact, the sequencing structures that college educators have created to guide student progress have typically been so prominent that many think of college curriculum at the program or college level primarily in terms of credit hour structure, perhaps because such structure comes to be a surrogate for educational philosophy. This definition has led to research studies that gather information manually from catalogs or transcripts or electronically from student data files to describe the structural aspects of the curriculum and the presumed educational results (see, e.g., studies by Blackburn et al., 1976; Dressel & DeLisle, 1970; Ratcliff, 1992b; Zemsky, 1989).

A useful analysis of the influence of curriculum structure directed at the program level, rather than at specific courses, was completed by Bergquist, Gould, and Greenberg, who proposed six generic dimensions of all college curricula and attempted to show how they can be used in curricular design:

1. *Time:* Duration and schedule of instructional units
2. *Space:* Use of instructional and non-instructional areas both on and off the college campus
3. *Resources:* Instructional use of people, situations, and materials, both on and off campus, from instructional and non-instructional areas
4. *Organization:* Arrangement and sequencing of instructional units and arrangement of academic administrative units
5. *Procedures:* Planning, implementing, evaluating, and crediting instructional units
6. *Outcomes:* Defining the intended desired results of a particular instructional unit or academic program (1981, p. 5; emphasis in original)

The authors propose that these dimensions are arranged in a hierarchy of importance, from lower order (time) to higher order (outcomes) and that their importance is inversely proportional to the ease with which changes can be made. That is, it is relatively easy to change the time dimensions of the academic program but relatively difficult to change the intended outcomes. The three lower level dimensions (time, space, and resources) require only structural changes, whereas the three higher level dimensions (organization, procedure, and outcomes) require increasingly greater changes in processes and attitudes as well as structure (pp. 6–7). This framework is extremely useful because it exposes the erroneous assumption that curriculum reform consists of changing relatively unimportant structural dimensions. Viewing curriculum as an academic plan requires that all dimensions be examined and potentially changed, but the emphasis is directed to the top three levels: arrangements, procedures, and especially intended outcomes.

Instructional Process Perspectives

The common definition of curriculum as a set of courses or structural dimensions artificially separates instructional processes from curriculum. However, by viewing curriculum as an academic plan, we necessarily ally instructional process to other elements of the plan. Faculty base decisions about instructional processes on expectations that certain strategies will help students achieve the desired purposes better than others. Often we think of instructional processes as concerned only with decisions made when curriculum is planned at the course level, but similar decisions are made at the program and college level. For example, a course-level decision would be to use lecture or seminar presentations. The suitability of the process depends on whether the purpose is to transmit information to students (lecture) or to engage students in active problem-solving behavior (discussion). At the program level, a parallel example is the use of the "freshman seminar." Not only may the content of the seminar be carefully chosen to involve students, capture their interests, and build on their goals and backgrounds, but the seminar instructional process may be deliberately chosen to augment and enhance students' problem-solving abilities. (Upcraft, Gardner & Associates, 1989). Such links between process and the goal of effective thinking have been advocated by many who discuss active learning or "learning to learn" (see, e.g., Bonwell & Eison, 1991; McKeachie et al., 1986; Weimer, 1990).

Perspectives on Evaluation and Adjustment

Traditionally, broad mission statements have received more attention and publicity in higher education than have lists of specific intended learner outcomes. Examination of student achievement has typically been a semiprivate interaction between an instructor and a group of students; the instructor's expert judgment of student learning is rarely questioned. In colleges, all instructors evaluate students, but few talk much about the process except when several instructors teach multiple-section courses with common syllabi and examinations.

The assumption that learning can be measured and attributed to specific courses has not been popular among college faculty; they frequently assert that, as learning objectives become more complex, learning is intangible or "ineffable" (Ewell, 1991b). In the 1980s, however, interest in evaluating college student learning more broadly than course-specific achievement increased because of a crisis in public confidence, pressures from government leaders for accountability, and responses of voluntary accreditors. Advocates of this recent assessment movement believe that "general learned abilities" and broad college outcomes can be measured or documented along with course-specific outcomes.

A well-established evaluation framework is based on "the Tyler rationale," named after Ralph Tyler, known to elementary and secondary educators as the father of educational evaluation (see Madaus & Stufflebeam, 1989). Steps in this framework include: establishing goals, objectives, and desired outcomes; identifying the learning processes intended to teach them; choosing measures to see if the learners have achieved them; collecting performance data; and finally comparing the data with the original goals and objectives. The assumption underlying these steps is that what is learned can be measured and also can be reasonably attributed to the instructional process. Depending on which step is in progress, curriculum development under the Tyler rationale can variously be viewed as goal setting, instructional planning, or evaluation.

In the higher education assessment movement, Alexander Astin's "input, environment, and outcome" framework (sometimes known as "value-added assessment") is the counterpart to the Tyler rationale (Astin, 1991a). Whereas Tyler defines excellence as the achieving the stated objectives at a predetermined level, in Astin's broader scheme educational effectiveness is documented by observing appropriate changes in the students after considering pretests to account for their initial level of knowledge, development, and other relevant characteristics. As with the Tyler rationale, Astin's ideas about assessment are popular but not wholly accepted among college faculty and educational researchers (for a contrary view, see Warren, 1984).

Like the notion of an academic plan, value-added assessment can be used to assess outcomes at several levels: for individual students, courses, programs, and whole colleges (Ewell, 1991b). Although the value-added perspective leaves the specific objectives and related content unspecified, it comes close to a general framework because it helps to specify desired outcomes, focuses attention on both the learner and the instructional environment, and encourages feedback that can be used to revise the curriculum plan.

A different perspective on evaluation is called "classroom assessment" (Angelo & Cross, 1993; Cross & Angelo, 1988), a scheme to gather evaluation information informally and regularly in the classroom and use it to improve teaching and planning. This idea, capturing what many good teachers may always have done, has become popular among college teachers, who typically guard autonomy and privacy in the classroom (Angelo, 1991). Recent evaluation perspectives like those developed by Angelo and Cross and by Astin seem likely to concentrate on more elements of the academic plan and their relationships. Noting this possible trend, we move to consider more general curriculum frameworks.

General Curriculum Frameworks

A general framework for viewing curriculum should consider all or most of the elements that constitute an academic plan and, ideally, should show that these elements are frequently interdependent. This is because decisions about educational purpose, selection of content, and choice of instructional processes are often based on related assumptions about learning and the learner. The elementary and secondary school literature recognizing these links is more fully developed than that in higher education, and we have found some of it particularly useful. Therefore, as our first general curriculum framework we will review a set of models from the precollege literature.

Precollegiate Curriculum Frameworks

The four-model curricular framework set forth by Geneva Gay (1980) is worth discussing in detail because it illustrates the tensions or conflicts between several strong sets of beliefs that cause dissent among faculty members as they plan curriculum. Ideas similar to Gay's have been discussed by other educational theorists; Eisner and Vallance (1974) aptly called them "conflicting conceptions" of the curriculum. We chose Gay's models from among the many possible configurations because they capture dimensions familiar to college educators.

Although focusing strongly on educational purposes, Gay's four models link purposes with instructional processes, indicating a tendency for educators to adopt purpose and process concomitantly. Indeed, as we shall show shortly, we also found this temporal and conceptual link between purpose and process in the college literature (Chickering, 1969; Dressel, 1980) and demonstrated it empirically among college faculty in studies of course planning (Stark, Lowther, Ryan, et al., 1988). The expression of the link may indicate the planner's assessment of the relative importance of learners in the discipline. Several such links among at least three elements of the academic plan in each of Gay's hypothetical models, summarized below, render them reasonably close to being a full curriculum framework.

The *academic-rational model*, a "systematic" view of curriculum, assumes that choices of curriculum content are based on scholarly logic and a clear view of what knowledge is worth knowing. In this model, the curriculum planners strive for a balance among five tensions, the learner, the society, the subject matter and disciplines, philosophy of education, and psychology of learning. They also seek a balanced emphasis on physical, psychological, intellectual, and moral dimensions of learning. The academic-rational design assumes that curriculum development is a linear process in which decisions are made sequentially about objectives, content, learning activities, teaching techniques, and evaluation processes.

The *experiential model* is more subjective and learner-centered than the academic-rational model. In this model, the planner engages students in planning their own active, self-directed learning experiences. Because of student involvement, the planning steps for this model cannot be specified in advance. The desired outcomes include intellectual, emotional, social, physical, aesthetic, and spiritual development; self-control; and a sense of personal efficacy.

The *technical model*, derived from systems management and production, assumes that education is a rational process. If the process is carefully controlled, the nature of the products can be predicted and determined. Like the Tyler model, the technical curriculum development process requires specifying desired objectives in advance, constructing activities to achieve these objectives, and evaluating their success, primarily as observed changes in learner behavior. Frequently, the purposes are linked with preparing the learner for life's functions.

The *pragmatic model* is neither systematic nor rational; rather, it is a dynamic political and social interaction model, reacting to events and stakeholders who wield power in determining both the purpose and process of curriculum. In this model, curriculum development is often localized and pluralistic. Planning is a consensual process, responsive to constituencies and seeking to distribute influence and resources and to exert pressure on various sources to develop and sustain the negotiated curriculum.

Faculty always espouse a philosophy of education (purpose) and a related view of the psychology of learning and teaching, each of which is related to their discipline. Often, however, they do not recognize or make explicit these concepts. Evidence indicates that faculty in different disciplines generally support different purposes, thus choosing related views of learning and planning according to different models among those mentioned by Gay. For example, science faculty tend to espouse the academic-rational model, while faculty in English and some other humanities are likely to espouse the experiential model. Generally, only faculty who teach career-directed courses endorse the technical model; this model is congruent in some respects with the emphasis on skill development in the new assessment movement.

College faculty acknowledge but do not endorse the pragmatic model. Yet they often report the types of influences in curriculum development suggested by the pragmatic model, including graduate schools, the media, suppliers of instructional materials, federal aid programs that support specific curricula, the courts, lobbies, unions, scholarly societies, and accreditors. Observation of curriculum development at the department level leads us to believe that, depending on the discipline(s) involved, each of the other planning models may be combined with the pragmatic model. This phenomenon is consistent with Gay's observation that the models do not exist in pure form. The process of college curriculum development may begin with one of the first three models but, as diverse views are considered, pragmatic concerns influence the final results. At the public school level, where Gay's models originated, political tension and value conflicts occur in the local community. In the college or university community, these same tensions affect curriculum development, resulting in political compromise within and between curriculum committees or departmental groups, or among the entire faculty. Just as faculty do not recognize other assumptions that direct their curriculum thinking, we believe they often fail to recognize the political aspects of curriculum planning and development. The pragmatic model helps us to recognize that the framework of the academic plan is incomplete without considering the internal and external influences on it.

Frameworks from Higher Education

Chickering has helped scholars develop an effective understanding of the learner through his work on vectors of student growth and maturation (Chickering, 1969; Chickering & Reisser, 1993). Consideration of the changes that traditional-age college students undergo in seven areas—competency, emotions, autonomy, identity, personal relationships, purpose, and integrity—clarifies the multidimensional nature of student development in college. Chickering believed that connections could be made between these dimensions of student change and the educational policies and practices in both formal instruction and less formal learning situations such as residential life. Linking learner development with instructional processes is an appropriate step toward a more complete model of an academic plan that includes student maturation. To use Chickering's words, "Curriculum arrangements, teaching practices, and evaluational procedures are systematically linked. To consider one element in isolation from the others is unwise; to modify one part without threatening the others is impossible" (1969, p. 196). Chickering tried to relate several curriculum models much like those Gay described to all seven dimensions of student development. In the end, however, only some of the models could be closely connected to some of the student development dimensions (1969, pp. 196–219).

In considering curriculum from multiple perspectives over a career of sixty-five years, Paul Dressel seems to have moved steadily toward a conceptualization of curriculum as a comprehensive academic plan (1971/1968, 1976, 1980; Dressel & DeLisle, 1970; Dressel & Marcus, 1982). Dressel created numerous frameworks within which to examine curriculum, but he regularly took normative positions on most of the plan's elements, making his work more of a prescriptive treatise on curriculum than an open framework to guide thinking.

Dressel addressed the "purpose" element of curriculum plans directly. While acknowledging affective development as an important correlate, he argued that the primary purpose of college instruction is to promote students' *cognitive* growth. Further, the primary objective of emphasis on cognitive growth is to make learners self-sufficient thinkers and continuing learners.

Dressel also addressed the "content" element. He believed that attention to the structure of the disciplines is essential in achieving appropriate educational outcomes and, therefore, in devising instructional plans. In his view, the disciplines, artifacts of human intellectual development, have emerged as organizers of human history and experience. Consequently, they represent useful and essential classifications for organizing teaching and learning. Since disciplines and their methods are seen as tools for achieving understanding and gaining meaning in relation to one's environment, the educated person must know about the objectives, methods, concepts, and structures of disciplines and their interrelationship.

With respect to "learners," Dressel believed that individuals are unlikely to acquire knowledge, values or abilities, unless they attach some importance to them (although the term *active learner* had not yet become fashionable in his lifetime). He hoped therefore that students would read classical works because they got satisfaction from them, not only because someone viewed them as "good for you." In a nutshell, his framework called for education to be simultaneously useful, individualized, eclectic, and beneficial to the student. Dressel did not say, however, how he would entice to the fount of knowledge a student who found little satisfaction in learning or who did not see its benefits.

Dressel also discussed educational structures and "processes." Structure, in his view, is intrinsic either to the learning process or the content. Although his writing took place before recent developments in cognitive psychology, Dressel clearly presaged the need for the learner to associate new experiences with prior experiences. He felt the college must provide structures and arrangements for learning that help the learner integrate the topics of a course and relate them to other courses and experiences. The process of studying a discipline must therefore involve assimilating previous learning and may involve the creation of new concepts, relationships, and organizational patterns of knowledge.

Dressel also addressed the instructional process element of the academic plan. His view of the psychology of learning, however, seemed to contain an unresolved tension between the development of the individual and the development of society. In their book *On Teaching and Learning in College* (1982), Dressel and co-author Dora Marcus departed from the disciplines and leaned more toward individual student development, outlining a model they called "humanizing education." Humanizing education transcends the disciplines and suggests six humanizing competences directed toward achieving the common interests of the community (pp. 62–63). The model focuses on educational purpose but the use of the verbs *humanizing, socializing,* and *individualizing* imply a process to which the learner is to be subjected or led.

Dressel devoted much attention to the evaluation of students, teachers, and programs. In *Improving Degree Programs,* he observed,

> An ongoing program evaluation that transcends courses should attempt to find out what students have gained from a course or program, what elements of the program have been successful or unsuccessful in promoting this development, and what aspects of the course, content, resource materials, and experiences need to be revised to maintain vigor and enthusiasm. This form of evaluation produces information that tends to modify instructional materials and processes and also the manner in which they are conjoined into courses. In an integrated, cumulative curricular experience, evaluation must be a major structural component, but it cannot be the sole instrument for developing or maintaining such a program. (1980, p. 57)

Carrying this thought further, Dressel added that "Ultimately, evaluation becomes a review of the actual outcomes and a reflection upon the processes, content, and instructional patterns used to determine whether alteration is needed," and he portrayed the relationships among these academic plan elements in a pyramid with objectives as the apex and content, instruction, evaluation, and procedures as the base (1980, p. 146). He also constructed a flow model of steps in course and program development and evaluation (1980, pp. 145–146). This flow model incorporates most fully Gay's academic-rational model, which Dressel believed most popular among faculty, but it also includes some attention to internal, organizational, and external influences on the college curriculum. Finally, Dressel noted that not only intended objectives should be examined in evaluation but also that information about unintended outcomes of curriculum programs should enter into the adjustment process.

Clearly, as we try to conceptualize curriculum and build models to guide research and practice, our debt to Dressel is great, as was his to theorists from other educational levels. While some theorists, like Chickering, have developed the association between two or three elements of the academic plan, Dressel discussed almost all of the eight elements in detail, as well as acknowledging some of the important influences on curriculum development.

We also acknowledge the achievement of Clifton Conrad and Anne Pratt (1983), who attempted to develop a nonprescriptive model of curriculum just before we began to outline the academic plan. After an extensive search of the literature on college curriculum, Conrad and Pratt (1986) identified a few conceptual frameworks that refine terminology or suggest potential avenues for organizing future research about the curriculum. They emphasized the lack of a comprehensive view of

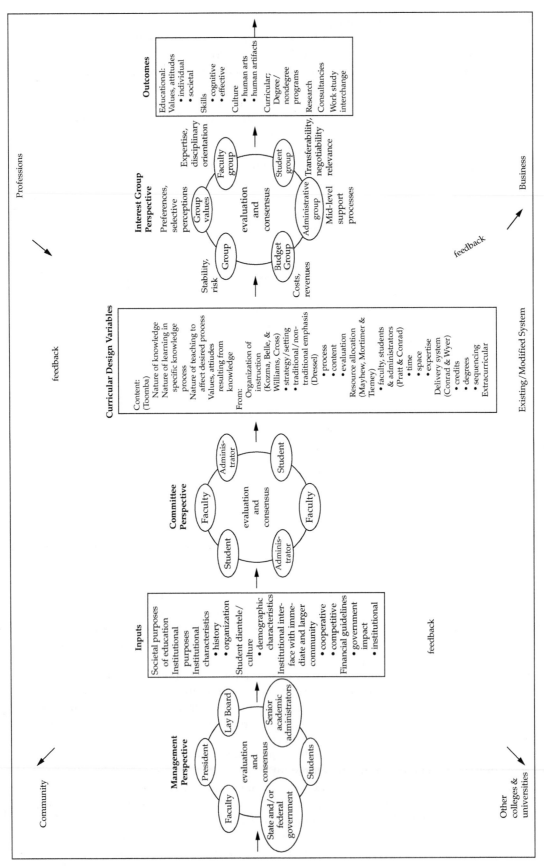

Figure 1 Conrad and Pratt's Framework for Curricular Decisions

SOURCE: Figure 2 from "Making Decisions about Curriculum" by Clifton F. Conrad and Anne M. Pratt, *Journal of Higher Education*, Vol. 54, no. 1 (January–February 1983) is reprinted by permission. Copyright 1983 by the Ohio State University Press. All rights reserved.

curriculum in any of the sources they examined. Indeed, lack of agreement on basic terms describing the relationship between the arrangements for learning and the substance of learning constricts vision of the dimensions along which variations may be introduced. Specifically, they noted that the curriculum was frequently viewed as a structure, but they failed to find views of the curriculum that also included consideration of educational outcomes for which the structure was devised.

Like us, Conrad and Pratt saw curriculum as a series of decisions or "options." Some options they called "curricular design variables" and, following Toombs, divided these variables into content and form. Context, presumably, was subsumed under the internal and external influences on curriculum and produced an effect they called "input variables." Finally, Conrad and Pratt described two types of outcome variables—curriculum design outcomes and educational outcomes. In our terms, curriculum design outcomes designate the plan itself and the shape it takes after the decisions are made; educational outcomes are linked to purpose (see Figure 1).

Conrad and Pratt, noting that decisions depend on professors' behavior, recognized the importance of the disciplines and the fact that college professors do not plan in a linear way. Our primary concern with this model is that we believe it may be overly specific, thus limiting its potential external validity for the wide range of curriculum-decision situations. Thus, we have tried to simplify our own emerging theory for greater utility in guiding practice.

Curriculum Planning and Design

As they discuss the process of developing curriculum, most higher education writers (except for Dressel and Conrad & Pratt) have used frameworks quite different from that which we are developing in this book. According to Conrad and Pratt (1986), who exhaustively reviewed curriculum literature, many curriculum studies are case study reports of programs or colleges deemed innovative by the writer. This genre, best illustrated by reports of new colleges or those that adopted experimental programs during periods of educational reform (Levine, 1978; Cardozier, 1993), continues to attract researchers' interest and attention. As a result, several planning frameworks have stressed the political nature of curriculum development or have been based on theories of change, innovation, and diffusion (Lindquist, 1974) or the administrative climate within a college (Seymour, 1988). In emphasizing innovations, writers seem to focus on change for change's sake rather than seek to understand how academic plans are continually evaluated and the evaluations used to improve the original plan. Such approaches bring a few colleges that have made broad changes into the limelight and foster a "bandwagon effect" as change diffuses to other colleges. We believe that studies of innovation, rather than continual and systematic curriculum adjustment, are appropriate primarily when researchers study change at the program and collegewide levels, where the pragmatic model of conflicting ideas (as outlined by Gay) becomes visible. These approaches do not, however, provide much assistance to colleges with established programs that wish to improve or respond with less radical restructuring.

Political frameworks decrease in usefulness—and analytical frameworks increase in usefulness—as one moves to individual courses. Toombs contended (and our studies confirmed) that while courses are meaningful to faculty, programs are typically courses "strung together"—and are not easily comprehended or defended (1977–1978, p. 19). At the course level of curriculum development, faculty make regular small adjustments and occasional drastic overhauls of their academic plans and usually can state their rationale for doing so very clearly (Lowther & Stark, 1990). Because faculty are directly involved, improving the way courses are incrementally adjusted may have greater impact on students than the dramatic changes at the program and college level so frequently heralded in case studies and touted in conference presentations.

Because of these very different levels of faculty involvement, we believe an appropriate curriculum development framework should include a perspective in which to view both extensive and incremental change at several levels: course, program, and the college. The framework can then equally well serve to analyze and guide the broad-scale changes of reform eras when external influences are strong and the smaller scale changes of more "normal" times as faculty intermittently respond to both internal and external influences on the curriculum. To some extent, writers who view construction of academic plans as a systematic design process already take such dual perspectives.

By definition, both *design* and *plan* imply deliberate decisions incorporating some desired relationship among setting and students, purpose, and process or, using Toombs's terminology, context, content, and form (Toombs, 1977–1978). Curriculum designs or plans are far more complex than simple statements of goals or descriptions of instructional processes. Accordingly, the process of creating the design is more elaborate than getting a few people with different views to compromise. A few frameworks exist that serve as lenses through which to examine both the current attempts at systematic curriculum design and critiques of them.

Toombs (1977–1978) and Toombs and Tierney (1993) used the idea of design to discuss both curriculum planning and curriculum analysis. They argued that *design* is a process that involves deliberate decisions about curriculum and can be understood by faculty members in diverse fields ranging from art to engineering. By curriculum *analysis*, Toombs (1977–1978) meant design in reverse—that is, the process of analyzing the curriculum plan to determine whether it contains the assumptions, structures, and activities necessary to meet the objectives.

Although directed primarily at elementary and secondary education, George Posner's (1992) recent work on analyzing curricula complements his earlier work on sequencing (more recently, he calls it "organization") and on course design. At least for illustrative purposes, Posner's work on course design portrays the development of a course as a linear process. Even so, it allows the developer to iterate portions of the process when fine-tuning the academic course plan as faculty typically do in practice. When Posner speaks of curriculum analysis, he means the close examination of academic plans—their origins, their ideological basis, the way the components fit together, and their implications (1992, p. 12).

Robert Diamond (1989), a long-time college-level instructional developer, sees curriculum development as a dynamic process but emphasizes systematic design. In Diamond's process, a discipline-neutral consultant leads a faculty member or group of faculty through the development process, making the process explicit, questioning their assumptions and helping them associate educational objectives with instructional strategies. Typically, Diamond's development process emphasizes student learning gains over content transmission. Curriculum developers like Posner and instructional developers like Diamond come relatively close to implementing in practice a view of curriculum as an academic plan. In these frameworks, faculty are planners and the focus is on their activities as planners rather than on the plan itself. The extent to which they carry out the process systematically depends on the guide they follow.

David Halliburton (1977a, 1977b) also focused on curricular design and developed another useful framework for viewing curriculum planning in higher education. Halliburton pointed out that curricula need adjustment because (1) the role of education changes with respect to broad historical and social needs, (2) new trends occur within the higher education system itself, and (3) the disciplines undergo paradigmatic shifts (or changes in accepted assumptions (1977a, p. 37). He categorized curricular change as typically occurring according to one or more of three processes of curriculum planning: (1) mechanism or statics (a process of tinkering or curriculum maintenance rather than overhaul); (2) dualism (curriculum change that swings from one popular trend or focus to another), and (3) knowledge-ism (a focus on changes in disciplinary content). Each of these processes, according to Halliburton, is associated with a different assumption about education. Mechanism (tinkering) assumes that the student is an empty vessel to be filled; the question is how to organize the filling process. Dualism assumes that teaching is separate from learning. Knowledge-ism is based on content acquisition rather than learner development. Halliburton emphasized that the disciplines, which reflect the assumptions, values, and habits of their practitioners, play a large part in determining which process is used. We concur. Like Halliburton, we have found that curriculum change processes vary at several levels of the academic plan and among the disciplines. But there is also reason to believe that the local context acts as a "filter" for the disciplinary frameworks in the curriculum development process at both the course level and the program level (Stark, Lowther, Ryan, et al., 1988). At the program level, resource allocations, structures, and leadership may constitute the contextual filters. (Posner, 1992; Seymour, 1988). Finally, at broader levels, such as that of an entire college, this contextual filtering may translate into competing societal and political interests. Thus, it is possible that the discipline orientations are potent at all levels of curriculum planning but manifest themselves differently and with different visibilities at different levels of the academic plan.

Drawing on the work of others, Halliburton (1977a, p. 47) saw that systematic curriculum planning needs a built-in process for change, should be articulated across levels, and should include evaluation. He stated that current curriculum development processes, bound as they are to assumptions about teaching and learning, limit our ability to create effective academic plans. Escape from these assumptions "will depend upon our learning to see the curriculum as a process that is subject to change, and our discovery of how to bring about change" (1977a, p. 45). Conrad and Pratt apparently endeavored to use these same ideas in their framework incorporating influences from inside and outside the collegiate institution.

These ideas about planning bring us full cycle in our process of considering curriculum itself as an academic plan based on unwritten and often unrecognized assumptions. At every turn we see that observers have noted the important associations between educational purpose, instructional processes, and change processes. They have also noted the strong impact of the disciplines on each of these, not separately but interdependently. In considerations of planning, the influences of forces both external and internal to the university become more visible than when curriculum is considered a static entity. How, then, can these ideas, repeated throughout the literature on curriculum, be tied together meaningfully? We believe that planning, however haphazard, occurs in all cases. A theory is essential to encourage faculty members and leaders to carry out curriculum planning as an intentional and informed design process.

In addition to varying in comprehensiveness, the frameworks we have examined vary in other ways. For example, they vary in origin—that is, the phenomena that have been observed to create them and the perspective of the educators who wrote about curriculum. Some are primarily descriptive, telling the story of what has been observed in colleges; others not only report these stories but attempt to interpret them through classifying and categorizing elements and processes. Still other frameworks are normative, taking a strong point of view about what should be taught, how it should be taught, or how curriculum change should be engineered. In such normative frameworks, how the theorists views linkages among the parts of the curriculum definition and the importance they give to each constitute a philosophy of education. Such frameworks cannot accommodate views stemming from contrary philosophies.

Each of the frameworks we have described has helped us to identify important elements that enter into academic plans and important influences on the plans educators make. The greatest number of prescriptive frameworks focus on questions like: "How will we define an educated person?" "How much is it necessary to study the established disciplines?" "How many great books must students read to appreciate our heritage?" Frameworks that include similar questions about the learner, the structure, and the types of activities to be used helped us to broaden these questions and recognize that the questions of purpose do not stand alone.

We believe that Dressel was closer to a theory of curriculum than he realized; his progress was limited, however, because he took a prescriptive position on many elements of the academic plan. A theory must be complex enough to accommodate uniqueness and diversity; it cannot take a normative stance. Conrad and Pratt's framework was also close to a theory but lacked a parsimonious set of curriculum elements and influences. Now, given our definition of curriculum as an academic plan, we are attempting to derive a coherent, linked framework for analyzing curriculum. There could be many ways of developing such a framework, and our choices reflect both our own perspectives and those of others whose work we have reviewed.

Linking the Elements: Toward a Theory of Curriculum

Why is a theory of the college curriculum important to such educational practitioners as faculty members and administrators? A curriculum theory permits the "careful systematic use of a well-defined set of ideas" and "provides an intellectual foundation or grounding for practice" (Walker, 1990, p. 133). Thus, a theory is first and foremost important in identifying curriculum elements and providing a way for faculty groups to systematically analyze curricular questions. For college faculty members, a theory may be particularly useful in eliminating pointless ideological debates that ensue when elements and assumptions are not distinguished. Theory can help ensure that systematic thinking replaces common sense, folklore, and disciplinary biases in developing the curriculum.

Second, we need theory to recognize and explore the interdependence of the elements within the complex phenomenon we call curriculum. Theory helps us appreciate that changes in one element of the plan are not independent from changes in other elements. Dressel indicated that we also needed a theory of curriculum to guide us in generating a set of interrelated and testable hypotheses (see also Kerlinger, 1973, p. 9).

Third, we need theory to help develop methods of detecting changes in the societal environment, cultivating a supportive institutional climate, and developing appropriate planning processes for curriculum at different levels. In particular, theory can help us to recognize the varied influences on curriculum planning and to estimate their influence on particular elements of the academic plan at specific levels.

Fourth, we need theory to help us understand how information about various elements of the curriculum plan is diffused among faculty within and between colleges and departments. This knowledge can help decision makers develop meaningful faculty development programs for improving all aspects of the curriculum.

Fifth, we need theory to recognize and assess the recursiveness of curriculum planning and its relation to society. The curriculum is shaped by the forces of society, true, but the curriculum also shapes society by shaping the knowledge, attitudes, and skills of the educated populace.

Making the best use of theory requires identifying and defining as many important elements (variables) related to curriculum as possible. It further requires that theorists speculate or hypothesize about relationships among elements that are sufficiently general to apply to a wide variety of cases and that can be observed or otherwise subjected to empirical test. Ultimately, we need theory to help us answer the most important question about curriculum: What is the relationship between desired educational outcomes and curriculum elements, alone and in combination? This question and others like it have only begun to be explored. We will present evidence for some of the connections within our emerging theory and point to others about which little is known. Later, we will return to the proposed theory to discuss its extension, testing, and limitations. The usefulness of our attempt to generate theory will be determined as we further specify the relationships between the steps, writing the propositions for each step, and verifying that the relationships hold. The ultimate test of usefulness will be in how well the theory of the academic plan can guide practice.

How Do We Know a "Continuous Planning" Academic Program When We See One?

Charlotte L. Briggs, Joan S. Stark
and Jean Rowland-Poplawski

Introduction

In the early 1990s, following numerous reports criticizing colleges and universities for inadequate responsiveness, a number of higher education leaders began advocating "total quality management" (TQM) principles borrowed from business (Chaffee & Sherr, 1992; Change, 1993; Seymour, 1993; Sherr & Teeter, 1991). Feeling squeezed between declining public opinion on one side, and cuts in public funding on the other, they hoped TQM might resolve the difficult question: How can higher education continue to meet new societal demands without the ability to expand? Throughout the postwar period, public funding for higher education had increased to cover the costs of rising enrollments and new branches of learning. More often than not, dissatisfaction with the status quo had been remedied by adding new options rather than by making difficult choices among competing priorities. By the late 1980s, however, most college administrators and national leaders had become convinced that retrenchment, which had begun with the oil crisis of the early 1970s, was a permanent condition, not merely a short-term aberration. This meant that emergency belt-tightening measures, no matter how necessary or painful, would not be sufficient over time because they failed to address the more fundamental question of how to survive, let alone thrive, in a zero-growth economy.

TQM appeared promising as a strategy for improving effectiveness under steady state conditions because it focused on setting very clear priorities for investing resources and reducing waste. It advocated organizing personnel into teams committed to a mission that focused on the needs and preferences of external stakeholders, and it called on the teams to base their decisions on objective data rather than on subjective assumptions.

Many academic personnel, however, responded negatively to TQM. Among other reasons, they were put off by the application of business language to education, such as calling students "customers," and graduates "products." They believed that quality was already their goal and that more management was not needed to achieve higher levels of excellence. Furthermore, many were suspicious that in practice TQM initiatives would emphasize increased productivity and cost cutting rather than quality.

Nonetheless, a number of higher education leaders saw benefits to TQM if it could be adapted for the higher education environment. Some called this adapted approach continuous quality improvement (or initiative) (CQI) (Marchese, 1991, 1992). CQI encouraged colleges and universities to place a greater emphasis on constituent input and satisfaction, in essence, defining excellence in more service-oriented terms than it had been defined previously. The words "continuous" and "improvement" (or "initiative") fit better with academic sensibilities and expectations than did the heavy-handed sound of "total" and "management."

Reprinted by permission from the *Journal of Higher Education* 74, no. 4 (July/August 2003).

During a burst of CQI initiatives on various campuses in the mid-1990s, my colleagues and I began to notice that few were drawing parallels between the need to continuously improve various administrative systems and the need to continuously reshape the curriculum to meet changing conditions and interests. It seemed to us there could be no function within the academy that called for more continuous vigilance and responsiveness than the college curriculum. Research by Stark and colleagues (1988) had found that the majority of faculty members constantly adjusted their individual courses to keep them up-to-date and to improve their effectiveness, but we wondered whether we could find examples of similar ongoing adaptation at the program level. That is, could we find models of department-level curriculum planning that engaged groups of faculty members in frequent reappraisal of the content, processes, resources, and outcomes of their program curricula? Previous interview studies suggested that faculty members were not accustomed to thinking about curriculum planning as a program level activity and often reverted to describing their own individual course planning when asked to discuss program planning in their departments (Stark et al., 1997). Had recent assessment initiatives changed that? Were there some departments that pursued program planning as a group responsibility on a regular basis rather than waiting for external pressures to force a major overhaul? If so, what were these departments like? What motivated them? What kind of leadership did they have? And in what ways did faculty members collaborate in program planning? In the spring of 1996, these were the questions that launched the study we now call Project CLUE, Curriculum Leadership for Undergraduate Education.

Judging from research and news reports, both in the mid-1990s when we began Project CLUE and now in the year 2002, it seems that colleges and universities have applied continuous planning principles primarily to their administrative units and seldom to the curriculum. In fact, even during the initial phases of our study we began to hear that the continuous improvement movement had become passé in business and, subsequently, had failed in higher education as well. While all accredited institutions now face mandates to assess student outcomes, regional and specialized accreditors are only just beginning to press institutions to actually use outcomes data to inform their academic decisions and to do so as part of an ongoing, cyclical planning process. Many faculty members continue to resist these efforts to promote a systems approach requiring programs to assess outcomes in light of explicit goals and objectives and then to initiate improvements. Wergin (1999), for instance, reported that departments recently have engaged in a great deal of evaluation activity, but that its cumulative impact has not been constructive change in departmental planning practices nor a stronger culture of collective responsibility. Indeed, he said "Most departments and most faculty failed to see the relevance of program evaluation and assessment to the work that they did."

Yet, despite faculty resistance to external mandates, we began this inquiry noting that some department faculties do work in teams to develop curricula, define departmental vision, measure student progress, and make changes they believe to be quality-driven (though they are more likely to use the term "excellence" than "quality"). Without a doubt, many also engage in the practice of "benchmarking," which is basic to continuous improvement models, when they identify other departments or programs they view as excellent and then attempt to emulate them.

It appears that principles associated with continuous improvement enjoy varying degrees of adoption within higher education. Some, such as a commitment to excellence, have been enduring features of academic culture for as long as anyone can remember. Others, such as using student satisfaction data in planning, have recently been accepted by some departments and are still rejected by others. While an economic boom in the late 1990s spelled a brief reprieve from intense pressure for rational planning, recent financial declines suggest that accountability mandates are likely to multiply again and never to be very far from the campus gates. If few faculty members view as helpful either the language of TQM or the strategies of assessment mandated by accreditors and policymakers, what types of ideas, standards, or guidelines would be more useful for supporting voluntary continuous planning efforts or for making program reviews more genuinely formative?

The researchers of Project CLUE conducted interviews with department chairs and faculty members in 44 departments around the country who might, through their own practices, provide some answers. These departments were nominated by their provosts as being especially attentive to curriculum planning at the program level. This article describes some ways to recognize "continuous program planning" as it already exists, to varying degrees, in the group of exemplary departments we studied. We present our findings as a set of 4 criteria and 20 indicators to assess the extent to which a department's program-level curriculum-planning efforts occur on a regular rather than sporadic basis. All criteria are derived directly from discussions about the experiences and practices of these actual academic departments, which are situated in a wide variety of institutional and disciplinary settings. Our goal was to develop "authentic" criteria that would take into account differences in context and make sense to faculty members in varied departments. Although we developed these criteria for research purposes, we believe they will be useful as well to academic administrators, department chairs, and faculty members as a tool for departmental self-study. It is in this spirit that we describe them in our article.

Project CLUE

We developed the criteria and indicators to aid several of our analyses for Project CLUE, so it will be helpful to provide a brief sketch of our study before discussing them. The CLUE Project aims to identify and study academic departments employing program planning practices that emphasize ongoing improvement. While most studies of curricular change have spotlighted radical reforms or major innovations, we were interested in describing models of program development that demonstrate continuous reflection, reappraisal, and adjustment of the curriculum. This process may lead to either major or minor changes, or even to informed decisions to maintain the status quo. The emphasis, however, is on frequent information gathering and group discussions that may lead to especially responsive decision making and implementation.

The goal of Project CLUE is to explore exemplary departments' processes of curriculum decision making, including the challenges they face and the roles played by department chairs and other leaders. We also hope to learn how these departments build expertise in academic planning, how technology has influenced their program planning, and the extent to which they gather and use information in the curriculum-planning process. In addition, we intend to explore the relevant influences of institutional culture, departmental culture, and disciplinary culture. As we have begun analyzing the data, we have found that the departments in our study vary greatly in the extent to which their planning appears to be ongoing. We suspect some of the provosts may have nominated departments as especially attentive to curriculum planning because of a recent major revision rather than for truly continuous planning practices. Therefore, in order to investigate how continuous planning is associated with various other process and context variables, it has been necessary for us to develop criteria to group the departments by how continuously they plan. The criteria constitute a framework for looking at various aspects of departmental practice that may provide evidence of continuous program planning.

Project CLUE Sample

Our continuous program planning criteria derive from analyses of Project CLUE data. To identify departments to include in the project, we used a two-stage sampling process. First we asked provosts at 253 randomly selected two- and four-year colleges and universities to nominate departments with at least seven full-time faculty members[1] that were "especially effective" in reviewing and planning their undergraduate curricula. We supplied eight possible, but optional, effectiveness indicators and invited provosts to contribute relevant others (see Table 1). Through these procedures, we developed a pool of 213 departments from 81 institutions that appeared to be especially attentive to curriculum planning.

In the second stage, we arrayed the nominated departments in a 28-cell matrix by institutional type and field of study (four Carnegie classifications by seven broad groups of pure and applied

TABLE 1

Optional Criteria for Provost Nominations of Departments for Project CLUE

The nominated department:

A.   Gives frequent attention to appraising the curriculum for renewal and redirection.

B.   Has identifiable curriculum leaders who encourage systematic appraisal.

C.   Gathers and uses relevant information about program successes and failures in the planning process.

D.   Implements curriculum plans in a timely and effective way.

E.   Maintains a high level of faculty involvement in curriculum issues.

F.   Is attuned to internal issues that may influence curriculum.

G.   Is attuned to external issues that may influence curriculum.

NOTE: Space was also provided for provosts to indicate alternative criteria used for nominations.

TABLE 2

Number of Departments Interviewed by Institutional and Discipline Type

Institutional Type		Discipline Type						
	Humanities	*Social Services*	*Sciences and Math*	*Enterprising Services*	*Human Services*	*Information Services*	*Artistic Services*	*Total*
Research	1	1	3	2	0	2	1	10
Doctoral	1	2	1	0	1	1	0	6
Master's	2	3	7	2	2	1	0	17
Associate	1	1	2	3	1	2	1	11
Total	5	7	13	7	4	6	2	44

SOURCE: *Carnegie Classification*, 1994 ed.

academic fields) and selected 50 departments for study. The applied field categories are those proposed by Stark (1998), who has suggested that the typical practice of lumping all professional preparation fields together is no more appropriate when studying influences on curriculum planning than failing to acknowledge at least some broad distinctions among the arts and science divisions.

Table 2 shows the distribution of the 44 departments for which we obtained usable interviews from the chair and at least one faculty member. The cell distributions represent our best effort to achieve a purposeful sample that would allow us to explore a wide variety of institutional and disciplinary contexts. We could not include all cells since some fields received no nominations or did not exist in some types of institutions. The science and math category is especially large because we received many nominations in math and computer science, perhaps due to calculus reform and to the introduction of new computer technology.

Data Collection

Three researchers developed, refined, and field tested a semistructured interview protocol, then interviewed chairs and faculty members in the sample. The interviews covered a wide range of questions designed to elicit descriptions, attitudes, and attributions of influence about the contexts, department member roles, processes, and types of curricular decisions made at a group level within each department. In all, the study yielded 127 usable 60-to-90-minute interviews representing 44 department cases, including 44 interviews with department chairs and 83 with faculty members from those same departments.[2]

Development of the Four Criteria

We initially analyzed interviews of 24 departments, seeking potential ways to define a continuous planning department. Each researcher listened to interviews with the chairpersons of 7 unique departments, one from each field-of-study category but within a single institutional type (Research and Doctoral, Master's, or Associate of Arts) and three departments in common, one from each institutional type. Based on the interviews, we each proposed general criteria for recognizing a continuous planning department. From overlapping lists, we selected three criteria we believed represented continuous effort to pursue responsive curriculum planning. We selected a fourth (participation and teamwork) because our own interest in Project CLUE is program planning by departmental groups rather than course planning by individual faculty members. The four broad criteria derived from the interviews are listed in Table 3.

Development of the Twenty Indicators

For each of the four general criteria, we identified 5 indicators representing manifestations of the criterion that at least some of the department chairs and faculty members mentioned when they described their program planning practices to us (a total of 20 indicators). We then used a three-step process to determine the stability of the indicators for rating a department's level of continuous planning. First, two higher education doctoral students studying curriculum, but not involved in the study, independently rated the interviews of 6 department chairs, taped their extensive discussions about their ratings, and suggested wording changes in the indicators to eliminate ambiguity. Second, the three researchers revised the indicators based on this feedback, and then independently rated the same 6 interviews and 3 additional ones on a 5-point scale for each indicator (5 = strong positive evidence, 4 = some positive evidence, 3 = insufficient evidence, 2 = some negative evidence, 1 = strong negative evidence).[3] We used the qualitative data analysis program QSR NUD*IST Vivo 1.1 to identify and archive quotations from the interviews that informed the ratings. We then summed the ratings of all 20 indicators for each department, and rank ordered the departments by those total scores. Each of the researchers ranked the same three departments as falling within the top, middle, and bottom tiers based on the 20 indicators for continuous curriculum planning. Despite this congruence, we spent an entire "training" day discussing the differences and similarities in our ratings in an effort to improve consistency, to reduce conceptual overlap among the indicators, and to make the indicators more broadly applicable to ways of collecting data other than interviews. Third, as a final stability check, we used the revised indicators and what we had learned from our training discussion to independently rate an additional three full department cases (comprising nine interviews). Again, we arrived at a high degree of agreement in our ratings.

TABLE 3
Criteria for Continuous Planning Departments

1. Continuous and Frequent Curricular Planning Processes: A continuous planning department gives frequent attention to appraising the curriculum for renewal and redirection and engages in on-going planning efforts. It uses organizational structures and processes that facilitate curriculum planning as an on-going routine.

2. Awareness and Responsiveness: A continuous planning department is attuned to and responsive to internal and external factors that may influence curriculum and is proactive with respect to future influences.

3. Participation and Teamwork: A continuous planning department maintains a high level of faculty involvement in curriculum issues.

4. Use of Evaluation for Adaptive Change: A continuous planning department gathers and uses relevant information about program successes and failures in the curriculum development process.

Description of the Criteria and Indicators

The following sections offer a brief description and rationale for each criterion and indicator. Definitions for the criteria can be found in Table 3, and for the indicators in Tables 4–7.

Criterion 1: Continuous and Frequent Curricular Planning Processes

Table 4 shows the 5 indicators for the first criterion "continuous and frequent curricular planning processes." These indicators capture evidence that program planning is a frequent and ongoing activity in the department.

The first indicator (1.1) takes as evidence the fact that department members tell us—either directly or by example—that they discuss or otherwise engage in curriculum planning activities as a regular and routine feature of departmental life. The second indicator (1.2) highlights committees and leadership as identifiable elements of departmental administration that keep curriculum on the front burner and help those with curricular ideas to move them to fruition, or at least to a departmental decision. It is not the mere existence of leadership or committees within the department that matters when it comes to this indicator, however, but whether they devote significant attention to curricular issues, and whether they clearly facilitate program planning efforts rather than hinder them. To be sure, curriculum committees are common in departments of all types, and most departments discuss curriculum at least when a pressing matter arises, but many curriculum committees meet only sporadically, and many departments make time for curricular discussions only on an ad hoc basis. Stark and colleagues (1997) found that program planning may be rare in the absence of a strong external catalyst or explicit internal leadership. The CLUE interviews support this conclusion, and therefore the inclusion of leadership (by individuals or committees) as a worthwhile avenue for gathering evidence of ongoing curriculum planning.

The third indicator (1.3), the extent to which departments routinely schedule specific occasions for curricular reflection and action, provides additional evidence that curriculum is, in fact, planned, and that curriculum planning is considered an important departmental responsibility. This indicator and several others focus on organized planning efforts, because our aim is to distinguish not only continuous from sporadic program development, but also curriculum renewal that is the result of planning from what some have called "random acts of improvement." This point is really the heart of what distinguishes our intended contribution to the scholarship on curriculum change from

TABLE 4
Criterion 1. Continuous and Frequent Curricular Planning Processes

A continuous planning department gives frequent attention to appraising the curriculum for renewal and redirection and engages in on-going planning efforts. It uses organizational structures and processes that facilitate curriculum planning as an on-going routine.

Specific indicators:

1.1 The extent to which the chair and/or faculty members report on-going planning activities and discussions as regular practice.

1.2 The extent to which committees and leaders facilitate the flow of faculty suggestions and get them on the agenda for discussion.

1.3 The extent to which the department schedules "dedicated time" to discussing curriculum issues: department meetings, committee meetings, special retreats, course coordinating meetings.

1.4 The extent to which the chair and/or faculty members view curriculum planning as an on-going process of continuous improvement.

1.5 The extent to which the department has an articulated mission to guide its curriculum and clarifies the mission periodically.

previous studies that focus on reform movements or major innovations and only recognize curriculum decisions as "successful" if they lead to dramatic changes that are "adopted" and "institutionalized." By focusing on routine practices, we hope to identify program planning approaches that are especially well informed, that respond to emerging needs and opportunities for incremental improvement, and that are sustainable despite very real limits on faculty time and stamina, both for meetings and for change itself.

The fourth indicator for the "continuous and frequent planning" criterion (1.4) is the extent to which department members view program planning to be an ongoing process of continuous improvement. In comparison to the first indicator's focus on reported planning behaviors, this indicator captures expressions of shared belief about how curriculum ought to be approached by the department. In the CLUE interviews, evidence for this indicator often arose as statements of educational philosophy or professional responsibility, particularly in response to a question we asked about what the department might tell a new faculty member about curriculum planning.

The fifth and final indicator for this criterion (1.5) is the extent to which a department shares an articulated mission to help guide its curricular decisions, and whether or not it periodically revisits that mission to decide if it is still appropriate. The existence of a mission statement, however, is insufficient as evidence of continuous program planning unless there is also evidence that the mission is a vital and adaptable agreement among departmental colleagues that has a real impact on curricular decisions. When department members readily paraphrase their mission as it relates to the curriculum, we are more convinced that the mission is meaningful as evidence of continuous planning than if they search their desktops to find a sheet of paper from which to read it. When faculty members and chairs point to the mission as an important influence on program planning without being asked, we are even more convinced. Again, we do not assume a mission is necessary for continuous planning, however, our interviews for Project CLUE indicate that departments that have clear curricular missions often view active, ongoing program planning as synonymous with carrying out that mission. Therefore, we have found departmental mission to be a criterion worth examining as a possible source of evidence for continuous program planning.

Criterion 2: Awareness and Responsiveness

The second criterion for assessing continuous program planning is awareness and responsiveness to factors, both internal and external to the department, that are relevant to program-level curriculum decisions (see Table 5). In our interviews with faculty members and chairs of departments nominated as especially attentive to curriculum planning, we found that awareness and responsiveness tended to motivate consideration of potential changes to the curriculum more frequently than did reactions to external catalysts. This is the rationale for our first indicator (2.1), which asks whether recent curriculum discussions were self-initiated by the department (i.e., proactive or responsive) rather than the result of external pressure (i.e., reactive or resistant). Departments that actively look for opportunities to experiment and improve find those opportunities fairly frequently. In contrast, departments that take the attitude that "if it ain't broke, don't fix it," tend to discuss revisions as discrete efforts they either are doing, are planning, or are done with. From these departments we get the impression there is little or no discussion of the curriculum during periods between major revisions, in other words, curriculum revision is a time-limited project, not an ongoing departmental function.

The second indicator of awareness and responsiveness (2.2) is closely related to the first. This indicator is the extent to which the department has used mandated reviews and accrediting visits as opportunities for genuine self-study. Generally, departments have no choice in whether to participate in such reviews, but they do have a choice whether or not they try to learn something from the process that might benefit their curriculum. Since reviews and assessment requirements tend to recur in cycles, self-study efforts that go beyond pro forma compliance can be a form of ongoing attention to the curriculum. When departments fail to make the most of such opportunities for curricular review and renewal, issues of department leadership or culture may be at fault. Alternatively, the problem may be that the institution has failed to coordinate multiple reporting

TABLE 5
Criterion 2. Awareness and Responsiveness

A continuous planning department is attuned to and responsive to internal and external factors that may influence curriculum and is proactive with respect to future influences.

Specific indicators:

2.1 The extent to which recent planning discussions are self-initiated by the department in response to needs or opportunities they identity (proactive or responsive) versus stimulated by pressure (reactive or resistant).

2.2 The extent to which faculty and/or chair have used university mandates, reviews, and accreditation visits as opportunities for self-study and planning.

2.3 The extent to which the department senses perceptions of faculty and students concerning program aspects, recent changes, and needs.

2.4 The extent to which the department senses the external environment, including changes in the discipline or field, and/or employer needs.

2.5 The extent to which the department develops linkages with other relevant departments or institutions.

requirements, leading to a burdensome paper chase that leaves little time for meaningful reflection. Faculty members and chairs often told us that the information required by their institution or external evaluating body was not the type of information that the department itself found useful to inform its curricular decisions. Therefore, it may be inappropriate to interpret negative evidence on this indicator as proof that planning is not ongoing. Nonetheless, this indicator represents a potentially worthwhile area of information gathering for evidence of continuous planning, as well as for gauging some of the challenges facing departments that might wish to plan more continuously.

The third and fourth indicators of "awareness and responsiveness" (2.3, 2.4) concern internal and external environmental scanning. Some departments told us they talk with their students "all the time" about the curriculum and use student input to identify problems and opportunities for improvement. Frequent conversations between the curriculum committee chair and a group of adjunct instructors is another example of internal scanning. Some departments maintain relationships with businesses or other agencies that employ their graduates and use those relationships to keep in touch with external developments in occupations associated with their field of study. Sharing curriculum experiences with faculty members at other institutions through participation in disciplinary or professional associations is another example of external scanning we frequently heard about in our interviews.

The final indicator of "awareness and responsiveness" is the extent to which departments develop linkages with other relevant departments or institutions (2.5). Some departments hold a lunch meeting once or twice a year with other campus departments for whom they provide service courses. Some community college departments meet annually with faculty members of nearby universities to discuss curriculum articulation issues that affect their students. By their nature, some departments require or benefit from such linkages more than others, therefore it is important to take disciplinary and institutional contexts into account when considering this indicator. For instance, a large sociology department at a research university where sociology is a popular major may have fewer linkages than a sociology department in a master's granting institution that primarily provides service courses to programs such as criminal justice, nursing, and social work. Nonetheless, some sociology departments in either situation may develop more or fewer linkages than other departments in similar settings. One of the science/math departments in our study went out of its way to make extensive linkages with other academic departments and with co-curricular living-learning communities on campus. It was clear the faculty members and chair viewed these linkages as an expression of the department's commitment to curricular development.

Criterion 3: Participation and Teamwork

The third criterion of continuous planning is "participation and teamwork" (see Table 6). While this criterion is a common element of TQM and CQI models, we did not assume it to be essential for program planning to be continuous. Indeed, as we stated earlier, Stark and others have found that the adjustments most faculty members continuously make to their individual courses do not require teamwork or departmental coordination (Stark, et al., 1997). The aim of Project CLUE, however, is to extend our knowledge of curriculum planning beyond the level of the individual faculty member and course to the level of the department and program. The "participation and teamwork" criterion clarifies whether curricular efforts described by faculty members and chairs are the result of departmental program planning or of individuals acting autonomously.

Some institutions achieve continuous program renewal through centralized planning that excludes department-level personnel from participation in curricular decisions. Examples of this model are some military and for-profit institutions that employ expert curriculum developers to create detailed materials for instructional staff to implement, as well as some technical programs at community colleges that are designed and closely controlled by state coordinating agencies. While this type of curriculum planning is worthy of further study, our interest in Project CLUE is to identify models of continuous program planning that are faculty driven, because in most departments the faculty does have primary responsibility for program curricula and would prefer to keep it that way. The faculty members and chairs in our study asserted repeatedly that faculty members are the most qualified people to make curricular decisions because they are the most knowledgeable about their fields and their students.

The first indicator for "participation and teamwork" (3.1) is the extent to which curriculum is considered "everybody's job." This indicator helps distinguish departments with widespread participation in curriculum renewal from those in which curriculum is the work of only one or two faculty members with a particularly strong interest in it. In most of the departments we studied, there appear to be some faculty members who play more of a leadership role than others in initiating and following through on program-planning efforts. Nonetheless, the expectation that curriculum is everybody's job, when reported as a departmental norm, is a strong indicator that program planning is an ongoing departmental concern. The second indicator for "participation and teamwork" (3.2) is the extent to which faculty members other than the chair are able to talk about curriculum planning for the program as a whole. The faculty members we interviewed for Project CLUE seldom had difficulty providing a program-level perspective on curriculum. This was in marked contrast to earlier findings that faculty members often revert to talking about their own courses when asked about program planning (Stark, et al., 1997). In departments nominated for being especially attentive to program planning, the chair is not the only one who understands how the curriculum fits together and

---

TABLE 6
Criterion 3. Participation and Teamwork

A continuous planning department maintains a high level of faculty involvement in curriculum issues.

Specific indicators:

3.1 The extent to which curriculum is considered "everybody's job," reflecting a strong sense of faculty responsibility and involvement.

3.2 The extent to which faculty members other than the chair are able to talk about curriculum planning for the program as a whole, or substantial program segments, rather than merely about their own courses.

3.3 The extent to which faculty ideas are welcomed and a culture of experimentation exists regarding the curriculum.

3.4 The extent to which participatory processes result in curriculum decisions.

3.5 The extent to which faculty collaborate in curriculum planning.

what the most pressing issues are. Where program planning is a vital departmental activity, all faculty members can describe how it is carried out through formal and informal processes.

The third indicator of "participation and teamwork" (3.3) is the extent to which faculty members' ideas are welcomed and a culture of experimentation exists regarding the curriculum. Most faculty members in the CLUE study told us they enjoy great freedom to pursue projects that excite them. More importantly, they said their chairs actively encourage new ideas, and their colleagues pitch in to help them develop curricular proposals. CLUE participants often told us they encourage new faculty members to bring ideas to the group. It is important to gain the group's consent, but equally importantly the group provides useful feedback to improve the proposal and to get it through the institution's curriculum approval process. Faculty members in CLUE departments also report freedom to run experiments with new curricular topics and instructional approaches. In fact, a number of faculty members described curricular experiments they had carried out that had required extensive cooperation from other faculty members in the department. In some departments experiments are quite common, and their outcomes are carefully monitored and discussed as part of the curriculum-planning process. The culture of a continuous planning department goes beyond mutual toleration of each other's pet projects to include valuing new ideas as a departmental asset.

The fourth indicator of "participation and teamwork" (3.4) is the extent to which participatory processes result in curricular decisions. The unique contribution of this indicator is that it differentiates between program-planning processes that result in decisions and those that do not. Departments abound that debate issues continuously without ever making a decision. Continuous planning should not be confused with continuous debate. Faculty members in continuous planning departments report that they occasionally have long debates but usually do not, because they gather enough information ahead of time to address anticipated questions. Faculty members in the CLUE study seldom spoke disparagingly of their department's curriculum planning process. Continuous planning departments avoid burnout on curricular discussion by bringing issues to closure in an efficient manner.

The final indicator of "participation and teamwork" is the extent of faculty collaboration in curriculum planning (3.5). Collaboration is another indicator that faculty members are thinking about the curriculum beyond the level of their own courses. Faculty members may collaborate on formal proposals, but this indicator helps identify informal planning activities as well, such as meeting over lunch to discuss pedagogical techniques. Among the CLUE departments, we found a wide variety of curricular collaborations. Often collaboration takes place in course teams (such as the precalculus faculty in a large mathematics department), in cohort teams (such as the first-year faculty in a nursing program), or among faculty members who represent a specialty within the department (such as the Americanists in a history department). At other times faculty members reach across subgroup boundaries to better integrate their program into a coherent whole. Examples of curricular collaboration include selecting a textbook for an introductory course, forming a seminar to develop a new cluster sequence, and sharing ideas for using technology in the classroom. Collecting examples of curricular collaboration may be especially helpful to departments that want to become more continuous program planners.

Criterion 4: Use of Evaluation for Adaptive Change

Our fourth criterion is the "use of evaluation for adaptive change" (see Table 7). This criterion is another that is common to TQM and CQI models, which assume that ongoing evaluation drives continuous improvement. Project CLUE interviews suggest that data collection and evaluation can be a vital part of ongoing program planning. In our interviews, use of evaluation distinguished between departments that innovate frequently without regard to documented needs or outcomes, and those that make curricular decisions clearly grounded in relevant information about potential benefits for students. When departments fail to bring evaluation into the process, program planning tends to be motivated disproportionately by what excites individual faculty members. In such cases, assumptions about what students want or need are tested only through their subsequent enrollments. While evaluation has its limitations, it is more encompassing than waiting for students to "vote with their feet."

TABLE 7
Criterion 4. Use of Evaluation for Adaptive Change

A continuous planning department gathers and uses relevant information about program successes and failures in the curriculum development process.

Specific indicators:

4.1 The extent to which program evaluation procedures are formally organized and implemented.

4.2 The extent to which curriculum decisions are based on relevant information gathered about program successes and failures.

4.3 The extent to which information about program successes/failures collected to assist in curriculum decisions includes data from a variety of sources within the program, from varied points in time and from varied perspectives.

4.4 The extent to which information about program successes/failures collected to assist in curriculum decisions includes data from a variety of sources external to the program, from varied points in time and from varied perspectives.

4.5 The extent to which the department critically examines curriculum trends in other programs before adapting, adopting, or rejecting them.

Our first indicator for "use of evaluation" (4.1) is the extent to which program evaluation procedures are formally organized and implemented. Data collection need not be formally organized to be continuous, but when faculty members described formal systems of data collection to us, they tended to be ongoing.[4] Common examples of formal evaluation are annual surveys of students or alumni, exit interviews with graduating seniors, annual review of student achievement, and faculty evaluation scores in core courses.

The second indicator for the "evaluation" criterion (4.2) is the extent to which curriculum decisions are based on relevant information gathered about program successes and failures. This indicator provides evidence that program planning is genuinely responsive to stakeholders, but it also provides a check against counting data collection as a program-planning activity when it is actually disconnected from the department's curriculum decision-making processes. Wergin's (1999) finding that departments collect much data without using it is an important warning in this regard, and proved prophetic even for our sample of departments that were nominated for being especially active in program planning. Some departments in our study routinely discussed the data they collected, but others reported that they did not. Likewise, when a new curricular issue arose, not all departments gathered information on which to base their decisions. A few faculty members and department chairs in our sample were unable to provide any examples either of data collection or of decisions made on the basis of information. Many expressed dissatisfaction or even embarrassment at their perceived weakness in evaluation. This finding suggests that departments that are especially attentive to curriculum planning may be in transition toward higher levels of data collection and use. That is to say, faculty members and chairs in the CLUE sample viewed evaluation as an important component of good planning practices, but few expressed comfort in their current level of evaluation expertise.

The third and fourth indicators of "evaluation" (4.3, 4.4) are the extent to which information to assist curricular decisions is collected from a variety of internal and external, sources, respectively, and from varied points in time and varied perspectives. When departments described a wide variety of data collection activities to us, our research team felt more convinced that their program planning was ongoing. However, we quickly discovered that it was necessary to follow up each question about a particular type of data with a question about its use. A good example of curriculum data that most departments said they collected is course evaluation data. Yet most, when probed, admitted that these data were used only by individual faculty members to improve their own courses, or by the department chair for faculty performance reviews.[5] A few departments discussed course evaluation data as a group for the purpose of program planning, but not many.

Some examples of internal data that continuous planning departments often collect and use are enrollment trends, student satisfaction measures, and comparisons of grades in one course or section with grades in a subsequent course in the major. Some examples of external data that continuous planning departments often use are employer surveys, government data on occupational trends, and scores on graduate placement and professional licensure examinations.

The last indicator of "evaluation" (4.5) is the extent to which departments critically examine curricular trends in other programs before adapting, adopting, or rejecting them. It is common for departments to look to peers for curricular ideas. In fact, one of the more common types of external data the CLUE departments reported was information they collected from the World Wide Web or conferences about what peer programs were doing. However, many stressed that their department seldom "jumps on the bandwagon" of popular curricular trends. A number described their departments as "ahead of the curve, but not exactly on the cutting edge." In fields that had experienced widespread movements to adopt particular innovations, such as "reform calculus" in the field of mathematics, departments that had not chosen to adopted the reform often told us they had nonetheless spent considerable time researching and evaluating the proposed change before rejecting it.

First Application of the Indicators

Following development and stability testing, the first author employed the indicators for the first time by applying them systematically to all 127 CLUE interview transcripts to score the 44 departments on each indicator. First, she coded the interviews to mark all passages that appeared to provide any direct or even contextual evidence that might inform the scoring of an indicator. Next, she reviewed the passages from interviews with all members of the same department to arrive at a single departmental score for the indicator on the 5-point scale described above (5 = strong positive evidence, 4 = some positive evidence, 3 = insufficient evidence, 2 = some negative evidence, 1 = strong negative evidence).

Using this generous 5-point scoring method, a department with no confirmatory or disconfirmatory evidence for any of the twenty indicators would receive a composite score of 60 out of a possible 100 points. A department with some negative evidence could receive less than 60 points; one with some positive evidence more than 60 points. The departments are arranged in rank order of their composite scores in Table 8. Composite scores for the CLUE departments ranged from 50 to 95 points, with a mean of 78.5. Only 3 departments out of 44 received continuous program planning scores of 60 points or below, which is consistent with our sample of departments that were nominated as especially active in their program-planning efforts. In subsequent analyses, the first author compared the departments that scored in the top quartile on the combined indicators to those in the bottom quartile and found substantial differences in the types of practices identified in the interview transcripts. Compared to departments in the bottom quartile for continuous program planning, those in the top quartile were more likely to:

- consider a wide array of curricular issues in their planning process;
- make an ongoing effort to increase departmental expertise in curricular matters;
- behave as a curriculum discourse community within the department;
- participate in curriculum related discourse communities beyond the department.

Table 9 shows the mean scores of the 44 departments for each criterion and indicator score.[6] Mean scores above 3 indicate a preponderance of explicit positive evidence based on the indicator. Mean scores below 3 indicate a preponderance of explicit negative evidence based on the indicator. Scores were highest for the first two criteria, "Continuous and Frequent Curricular Planning Processes" and "Awareness and Responsiveness," which seem to exhibit greatest face validity for the concept of continuousness in planning. The highest scores on indicators of these criteria were for departmental self-initiative (Indicator 2.1) and external scanning (Indicator 2.4). This finding, coupled with the low

TABLE 8
Department Composite Scores for Continuous Program Planning

Department	Score	Institution Type*	Field of Instruction	Department	Score	Institution Type	Field of Instruction
Case 29	95	A	Business Administration	Case 46	81	D	Biological Systems Engineering
Case 01	94	A	Fine Arts	Case 04	79	M	Chemistry
Case 28	93	M	Nursing	Case 17	79	M	Biology
Case 32	92	R	Math & Computer Science	Case 33	79	A	Engineering Technologies
Case 22	91	A	Nursing	Case 42	79	R	Mathematics-Calculus program
Case 30	91	M	English	Case 34	77	M	Sociology/Anthropology
Case 03	88	D	Nursing	Case 18	75	M	Mathematics
Case 19	87	R	Curriculum & Instruction	Case 45	75	R	Accounting & Information Systems
Case 35	87	M	Nursing	Case 14	74	M	Chemistry
Case 40	87	M	Chemistry	Case 21	73	R	Microbiology
Case 16	85	M	Industrial Technology	Case 41	73	M	Geography, Political Science, and Sociology
Case 07	84	D	Communication	Case 44	73	A	Electronics & Electronics Engineering
Case 11	84	D	Math & Computer Science	Case 15	72	M	Psychology
Case 25	84	A	Biology	Case 12	71	D	Sociology/ Anthropology
Case 05	83	M	Applied Engineering & Technology	Case 13	68	M	Biology
Case 06	83	M	Communication Studies	Case 38	67	R	Communication
Case 24	82	A	Math & Computer Science	Case 39	67	R	Sociology
Case 31	82	M	Math & Computer Science	Case 20	66	R	Art
Case 02	81	A	Humanities/English	Case 36	64	R	History
Case 23	81	A	Communications Media	Case 10	59	D	Psychology
Case 26	81	A	Communications/Humanities	Case 09	58	D	English
Case 27	81	A	Social/Behavioral Sciences	Case 43	50	M	English

*R = Research, D = Doctoral, M = Master's, A = Associate of Arts

TABLE 9
Continuous Curriculum Planning Criteria and Indicators Mean Scores

Criteria and Indicators	Mean	Score
Continuous and Frequent Curricular Planning Processes		4.07
1.1 Direct reports of ongoing curriculum planning processes	4.18	
1.2 Committees and leaders facilitate flow of suggestions to agenda	4.11	
1.3 Dedicated time for discussing curricular issues	3.98	
1.4 View curriculum planning as ongoing process	3.93	
1.5 Department has articulated mission, reviews it periodically	4.16	
Awareness and Responsiveness		4.13
2.1 Recent planning self-initiated, proactive, responsive, not resistant	4.25	
2.2 Mandates, reviews, accreditation used for genuine self-study	3.89	
2.3 Internal sensing of faculty and student perceptions	4.20	
2.4 External sensing of environment	4.27	
2.5 Develops linkages with other relevant departments and institutions	4.02	
Participation and Teamwork		3.64
3.1 Curriculum considered everybody's job	2.66	
3.2 Faculty other than chair can discuss curriculum as whole	3.68	
3.3 Ideas welcome and culture of experimentation	4.18	
3.4 Participatory processes result in decisions	3.55	
3.5 Faculty collaborate in curriculum planning	4.14	
Use of Evaluation for Adaptive Change		3.86
4.1 Program evaluation procedures are formally organized	3.93	
4.2 Curriculum decisions are based on relevant information gathered	3.75	
4.3 Internal data used in decision making is varied	3.75	
4.4 External data used in decisions making is varied	3.98	
4.5 Critical examination of trends before adapting, adopting, rejecting	3.91	
Mean for all indicators		3.93

NOTE: Departments were rated on each indicator on a 5-point scale: 5 = strong positive evidence, 4 = some positive evidence, 3 = insufficient evidence, 2 = some negative evidence, 1 = strong negative evidence

mean score for using mandates as genuine self-study opportunities (Indicator 2.2), suggests that departments that are not fully responsive to external mandates may, nonetheless, be proactive in curriculum planning through responsiveness to stakeholders they deem most important.

While the indicator scores on the fourth criterion, "Evaluation for Adaptive Change," were somewhat lower on average, they also reflect fairly strong departmental interest in using external sources of input in curriculum planning. One would expect a positive relationship between external sensing (Indicator 2.4) and use of external data (Indicator 4.4), but the lower score for the use of data suggests that evidence of external scanning was not always accompanied by evidence that the department sought external information about its successes and failures from a variety of sources, varied points in time, and varied perspectives. This discrepancy may suggest the need or potential for more varied external data collection, or it may simply reflect disciplinary and institutional differences in the number of relevant external sources.

The lowest mean score was for evidence that departments considered curriculum to be everybody's job (Indicator 3.1). Indeed this was the only indicator for which, on average, we found little explicit positive evidence among the CLUE departments. Possibly, this indicator may not be a necessary or important component of continuous program planning. In contrast, the other indicators for the third criterion, "Participation and Teamwork," received affirmative scores, particularly Indicator 3.3, indicating a culture that welcomes ideas and experimentation, and Indicator 3.5, faculty collaboration in curriculum planning. We noted that the three departments receiving the top composite scores for continuous program planning all received the highest score (5) for strong evidence that "curriculum is considered everybody's job." Yet, other departments that scored high on most other aspects of continuous program planning described extensive curricular collaboration in an atmosphere that encouraged such activities but allowed a few department members the prerogative to opt out. Possibly the absence of extremely disinterested, or even disruptive, faculty members can facilitate curriculum planning in some cases. Further research is needed to determine if unanimous participation in curriculum planning is associated with more continuous (or effective) program planning than is widespread participation, or if continuous planning departments simply vary in their need for faculty coordination and input.

Although most indicators were relatively easy to score for the CLUE interviews, several of the indicators caused some difficulty. For example, Indicator 1.2 highlights the role of leaders and committees by asking if they "facilitate the flow of *faculty* suggestions and get them on the agenda for discussion" (emphasis added). In scoring this indicator, evidence frequently arose of department chairs or curriculum committees that spurred curricular discussion by initiating their own proposals, as well as, or instead of, only facilitating those of colleagues. For the purpose of scoring the CLUE departments, only evidence for the original wording of Indicator 1.2 was considered, however a broader definition or the addition of another indicator might be useful.

The terms "internal" and "external" as descriptors of the scanning process and data origin (Indicators 2.3, 2.4, 4.3, 4.4) proved problematic as well. The problem is not so much the question of what defines the boundary between internal and external sensing or decision making, but rather that those boundaries legitimately differ from one department to another depending on disciplinary type, departmental mission, linkages, and various other factors. As with so many measures in higher education, context helps determine what is good practice.

The most problematic indicator to score for the CLUE departments was "the extent to which participatory processes result in decisions" (3.4). We developed this indicator from interview statements that indicated curriculum planning can bog down if discussion is permitted to continue indefinitely or if a few individuals are allowed to stall the process. However, it is very difficult for an outsider to judge from interview data how well a department functions as a decision-making body unless participants explicitly state whether debate frequently or seldom bogs down. Within collegial groups the length and emotional intensity of debate that can be deemed constructive varies tremendously. This particular indicator is surely meaningful in the assessment of continuous program planning, however its validity for general use probably will require a different approach to data collection than we used in Project CLUE.

Discussion

From analysis of the Project CLUE interviews, we have come to believe that continuous planning is a useful concept for academic programs. We have also identified a good number of "indigenous" examples that other departments can learn from distributed among a wide variety of disciplinary and institutional settings. In the preceding pages we have described a set of criteria and indicators that we offer as a framework for assessing continuous program planning in academic departments. These indicators of continuous program planning should have authenticity because they were derived from actual statements of department chairs and faculty members. They should have trustworthiness because of the variety of academic planning contexts included in the Project CLUE sample and because of the rigor of our process for developing them.

As researchers we have begun to use these criteria and indicators to identify multiple models of continuous program planning and to explore how matters of context, leadership, collaboration, and curriculum expertise relate to curriculum planning at the program level. We encourage others to test their usefulness in research, and adapt them where necessary. While we cannot prejudge the optimal weight that should be given to each criterion and indicator for any particular type of department, we do believe the criteria can be used, as we are currently doing, to compare and contrast departmental practices in order to learn more about internal and external influences on program planning.

In addition, we believe these criteria and indicators can be useful to departments for self-study and to suggest avenues for development of more responsive program-planning practices. At the beginning of our study, we encouraged provosts to nominate up to six departments from their campuses, but few nominated more than two or three. A significant number declined to make any nominations because they said they had no departments that attend to program planning particularly often. If this is true (and not just a lack of awareness on the part of provosts), the academic department, as an institutional unit, may hold considerable untapped potential for curricular improvement. It is our impression that many departments are looking for ways to improve their undergraduate programs. However, most have lacked a way to think and talk about curriculum planning at the program level except in terms of sporadic overhauls that exhaust most participants and make them reluctant to discuss program planning for a number of years to come. The continuous search for incremental improvements need not stand in the way of transformational changes when they are called for. However, too keen a focus on dramatic change can cause many smaller problems and opportunities to go unnoticed until only dramatic measures will suffice. We hope this article spurs other higher education researchers and departmental faculty to explore models of program planning that are more continuous than traditional practices and therefore more responsive and sustainable as well.

Limitations and Future Research

We developed these criteria to rate a particular set of research interviews, and only application to other data will confirm their generalizability. We have identified indicators we believe apply to most departments in which the faculty holds primary responsibility for the curriculum. However, some indicators may be easier to observe in larger, more complex departments where curriculum planning structures and practices tend to be more formally organized. Others may be more obvious in smaller departments where informal, collegial processes predominate. The first author has used the indicators to code passages in the full set of 127 interview transcripts in preparation for rating the 44 departments according to their level of continuous program planning. For the purpose of placing the departments into broad groupings representing high, medium, and low levels of continuous program planning, we are confident the criteria work well, however we do not believe finer grained comparisons would be an appropriate use of the criteria and indicators.

The indicators would benefit from testing with more departments to further assess their stability, and from direct feedback from faculty members, chairs, and academic administrators to determine if, indeed, they are understandable and meaningful to the practitioners whose activities and beliefs they describe. More importantly, if the criteria and indicators do prove stable and appear valid, we then must determine their relevance to the lives of students. Does continuous program planning lead to better educational experiences for students? We do not know. But by making it possible to capture variation in a sample of departments, the indicators should enable us to correlate planning patterns with various educational outcomes. Thus it may be possible to determine if continuous program planning truly benefits students by "adding value" over sporadic program planning, or whether continuous planning by the department as a group has benefits over the frequent adjustments that individual faculty members make to their individual courses.

Notes

1. We focused our study on departments with at least seven full-time faculty members to make it easier to study curriculum leadership and collaborative planning processes, which, we conjectured, might be more idiosyncratic in smaller departments.
2. Our intention was to interview two faculty members from each department.
3. We developed this scale to judge the evidence for the following reason. Because our research team developed the indicators inductively from the interview data, we had not—and could not have—designed

the interview protocol to assess all of the indicators equally well, and some we had not directly addressed at all. Consequently, for this initial group of departments, the amount and quality of the evidence for each indicator varied and was sometimes insufficient for determining a score. Therefore, a scale to gauge the strength and direction of evidence that accorded the benefit of the middle score (3 points) to departments without clear evidence for the presence or absence of an indicator seemed appropriate for this initial scoring task. As these indicators are more fully validated in further research, researchers using interviews or surveys obviously would include questions to tap each indicator. In other situations, such as a departmental self-study, researchers or evaluators might take a different approach to gathering data and scoring the indicators.

4. Formalized data collection processes that are the result of a department coming under extraordinary institutional scrutiny are not what we intend to capture with this indicator, since they do not reflect ongoing attention to the curriculum.

5. Only the rare department connects its faculty review process with its program planning in any systematic way, but there were one or two examples of this practice in our sample.

6. A table showing all 880 individual departmental scores for each indicator is available from the first author.

References

Carnegie Foundation for the Advancement of Teaching. (1994) *A classification of institutions of higher education* (1994 ed.). Princeton, NJ: The Foundation.

Chaffee, E. E., & Sherr, L. A. (1992). Quality: Transforming postsecondary education (ASHE-ERIC Higher Education Report no. 3). Washington, DC: The George Washington University.

Change: The Magazine of Higher Learning. (1993). Special Issue on Continuous Quality Improvement Principles for Higher Education Administrators. (May–June 1993).

Marchese, T. (1991). TQM teaches the academy. *AAHE Bulletin, 44*(3), 3–9.

Marchese, T. (1992). AAHE and TQM (. . .*Make that "CQI"*). *AAHE Bulletin, 45*(3), 11.

Seymour, D. T. (1993). *On Q: Causing quality in higher education.* Phoenix, AZ: Oryx Press.

Sherr, L. A., & Teeter, D. J. (Eds.). (1991). *Total quality management in higher education.* (New Directions for Institutional Research no. 71). San Francisco: Jossey-Bass.

Stark, J. S. (1998). Classifying professional preparation programs. *Journal of Higher Education, 69*, 353–383.

Stark, J. S., Lowther, M. A., Ryan, M. P., & Genthon, M. (1988). Faculty reflect on course planning. *Research in Higher Education, 29*(3), 219–240.

Stark, J. S., Lowther, M.A., Sharp, S., & Arnold, G. (1997). Program-level curriculum planning: An exploration of faculty perspectives on two different campuses. *Research in Higher Education, 38*(3), 99–130.

Wergin, J. F. (1999). Assessment of programs and units: Program review and specialized accreditation. In *Architecture for change: Presentations from the 1998 AAHE Assessment Conference.* Washington, DC: AAHE.

Affinity Disciplines and the Use of Principles of Good Practice for Undergraduate Education

John M. Braxton, Deborah Olsen and Ada Simmons

Academic disciplines with soft paradigmatic development tend to have an affinity for more readily enacting practices designed to improve undergraduate education than do hard paradigmatic development disciplines. This study extends the affinity discipline hypothesis to Chickering and Gamson's seven principles of good practice. The affinity discipline hypothesis garners empirical support for four of the seven principles of good practice: encouragement of faculty-student contact, encouragement of active learning, communication of high expectations, and respect for diverse talents and ways of knowing. Implications for theory and practice are suggested by the findings of this study.

The improvement of undergraduate education receives much attention from the lay public—state legislatures, students, and parents. National associations such as the American Association of Colleges and the National Endowment for the Humanities and various scholars also voice concern about undergraduate education in U.S. colleges and universities. Various recommendations to improve undergraduate education have been advanced. Posited recommendations focus on alterations to the undergraduate curriculum (Gaff, 1991; Association of American Colleges, 1985), organizational approaches to improving undergraduate teaching (Eble and McKeachie, 1985; Weimer, 1991), and enhancement of the teaching and learning process (Chickering and Gamson, 1987; Katz, 1985; McKeachie, 1986; National Institute of Education, 1984).

Chickering and Gamson's (1987) seven principles for good practice in undergraduate education offer a particularly promising approach to improving teaching and learning given that a robust base of research undergirds these principles (Sorcinelli, 1991). The first of these principles pertains to the *encouragement of student-faculty contact*. Student motivation and involvement are fostered by frequent student-faculty interactions in and out of class (Chickering and Gamson, 1991). The *encouragement of cooperation* among students is the second principle. Chickering and Gamson (1991) contend that collaboration among students heightens learning. Thinking and understanding are enhanced by sharing one's ideas and responding to the ideas of others. The third principle concerns the *encouragement of active learning*. Learning is increased if students actively participate in their courses by discussing and writing about course content (Chickering and Gamson, 1991). The *provision of prompt feedback* constitutes the fourth principle of good practice. Appropriate feedback on course performance helps students assess their knowledge and skills. Students should be provided with frequent opportunities to perform and receive feedback or ways to improve their work (Chickering and Gamson, 1991). The fifth principle stipulates that *time on task should be emphasized*. Time on task refers to the amount of time students spend learning course material (Chickering and Gamson, 1991). The *communication of high expectations* is specified by the sixth principle. This

Reprinted from *Research in Higher Education* 39, no. 3 (1998).

principle requires that faculty not only hold students to high standards but also expect that students will meet them. The seventh principle entails faculty *respect for diverse talents and ways of knowing*. Students have different skills and abilities and ways of learning. Faculty should provide students with opportunities to demonstrate their skills and use their styles of learning to their best advantage (Chickering and Gamson, 1991).

The implementation of these seven principles depends on faculty for their enactment, yet faculty enjoy considerable autonomy in their teaching role performance. Given such autonomy, a question emerges: What assures successful enactment of these seven principles by faculty? Chickering (1991) postulates that an organizational culture that values continued improvement in the professional practice of its faculty, inertia, traditional values concerning undergraduate education, and institutional structures and rewards affect faculty performance of the seven principles of good practice.

However, some academic disciplines demonstrate an affinity for practice designed to improve undergraduate education (Braxton, 1995). Hence, the academic discipline in which a faculty member holds membership may influence his or her performance of the seven principles of good practice in undergraduate education.

Conceptual Framework

Distinctions among academic disciplines are "profound and extensive" (Braxton and Hargens, 1996, p. 35). Such differences range from the level of the academic discipline to the day-to-day professorial activities of faculty.

These distinctions occur between disciplines of high and low paradigmatic development. Paradigmatic development refers to the extent to which members of a discipline agree about theory, methods, techniques, and the importance of problems for the discipline to pursue (Kuhn, 1962, 1970). Biology, chemistry and physics are examples of disciplines high in paradigmatic development, whereas history, psychology and sociology are disciplines showing low paradigmatic development (Biglan, 1973).

Hard paradigmatic fields display higher levels of agreement on course content and degree requirements than do their low field counterparts (Lodahl and Gordon, 1972). However, low paradigmatic discipline faculty tend to value student character development, emphasize the development of critical thinking skills (analysis and synthesis), use discursive or student-centered teaching practices, and favor the use of program review and student assessment to improve teaching and learning more than do their counterparts in disciplines exhibiting high paradigmatic development (Braxton, 1995; Braxton and Hargens, 1996). Moreover, low paradigmatic development faculty behave more frequently in ways that encourage student participation than do their colleagues in high paradigmatic disciplines who more frequently exhibit behaviors that facilitate structuring and organization of subject matter (Murray and Renaud, 1995).

The normative preferences for teaching practices existing in disciplines of high and low paradigmatic development account for the pattern of differences in teaching practices. High paradigmatic development leads to the promulgation of strong, narrowly prescribed norms for appropriate teaching practices, whereas low paradigmatic development results in weakly held norms for appropriate teaching practice. Thus, faculty in high paradigmatic fields are less willing to explore new teaching methods or techniques that deviate from those that are customarily used within the discipline. In contrast, faculty in fields exhibiting low paradigmatic development allow more latitude to use a wide range of approaches to teaching. Such wide latitude stems from lower levels of agreement on course content and degree requirements. Consequently, faculty in academic disciplines exhibiting low paradigmatic development tend to show an affinity for practices designed to improve undergraduate education (Braxton, 1995).

From these formulations, the following hypothesis emerges: Faculty in academic disciplines of low paradigmatic development apply the seven principles of good practice more frequently than faculty in academic fields of high paradigmatic development. This hypothesis can be labeled the "affinity discipline hypothesis."

Previous research has assessed the relationship of faculty research performance and the seven principles of good practice (Olsen and Simmons, 1996). However, little or no research has focused on the influence of the paradigmatic development of a his or her faculty member's discipline on his or her performance of these good practices. Consequently, this research focused on the influence of the paradigmatic development of faculty discipline on use of the seven principles of good practice described by Chickering and Gamson (1987).

A robust test of the affinity discipline hypothesis entails an assessment of whether the influence of paradigmatic development—high and low—on the seven principles of good practice is mediated by various personal and organizational characteristics. The hypothesized effects of paradigmatic development on the application of the seven principles of good practice may be mediated, or even overwhelmed, by the characteristics of individual faculty members and academic departments. Research suggests that such faculty characteristics as academic rank, gender, and personal preference for teaching or research affect teaching role performance (Blackburn and Lawrence, 1995). The individual faculty member's satisfaction with teaching also is posited to affect teaching role performance (Bess, 1977, 1997). Teaching load may influence the enactment of the seven principles of good practice. Faculty with heavier teaching loads may be less likely to adhere to the seven principles of good practice because they require more effort than do more traditional instructional practices. Moreover, the support faculty members receive from their academic department for teaching also affects teaching role performance (Blackburn and Lawrence, 1995). Thus, academic rank, gender, teaching load, personal preference for teaching, teaching satisfaction, and departmental support for teaching were held constant in this study in order to rigorously test the affinity discipline hypothesis.

The findings of this study should contribute to our understanding of factors that facilitate or impede faculty application of Chickering and Gamson's seven principles of good practice. Moreover, if this study's findings provide empirical support for the affinity discipline hypothesis, then such backing would augment an already existing body of knowledge that indicates that faculty in disciplines of low paradigmatic development tend to have an affinity for practices designed to improve undergraduate education. From such a knowledge base, approaches to altering the social structure and social processes of academic disciplines evincing high paradigmatic development could be developed so that faculty in such disciplines would be more likely to engage in teaching practices designed to improve undergraduate college teaching.

Methods

Data Collection

A random sample of 167 faculty from the population of faculty in the College of Arts and Sciences and School of Business at large, public Research I University, were selected to participate in this study. Of these 167 faculty, 114 individuals in the College of Arts and Sciences and the School of Business agreed to take part in this study. Thus, a response rate of 83% was realized. Study participants had taught at least one undergraduate course within the last two years; average class size was 63. Of the sample, 85% were male and 92% were white. Whites and males were overrepresented in the sample. Assistant, associate, and full professors made up 30%, 30%, and 40% of the sample, respectively, mirroring the overall distribution of faculty by rank of the institution. Eighty-seven percent of the sample was from the College of Arts and Sciences and 13% was from the School of Business. More precisely, the breakdown of participants from the College of Arts and Sciences included 41% Arts and Humanities, 29% Social Sciences, and 31% Hard Sciences—proportions that closely approximate those found in the college as a whole. Faculty had spent a mean of 12 years at the university. Thus, the obtained sample appears to be representative of the population of faculty at the focal university.

Members of the sample were interviewed about their undergraduate teaching. The semistructured interview agenda included questions about course load, methods used to improve teaching, peer and departmental support for teaching, and personal interest and satisfaction with teaching, as well as other topics not relevant to this inquiry. Privately, either before or after the interview itself, faculty also completed a 70-item paper-and-pencil questionnaire on their use of seven "best" teaching practices (Chickering et al., 1989). The Appendix exhibits the specific items measuring each of the seven practices. Using a 5-point scale ranging from Never to Very Often, faculty indicated how often they used these practices in their undergraduate teaching. Items on the "best practices" questionnaire were not clustered by each of the seven practices but were randomly ordered so that, for example, an item on active learning might follow one on prompt feedback.

Measures

To test this study's general hypothesis, a research design composed of seven independent variables and seven dependent variables was used. The independent variables were gender, academic rank, teaching load, preference for teaching over research, satisfaction with teaching, departmental support for teaching, and the level of discipline paradigmatic development.

Discipline paradigmatic development was measured using the hard (high)-soft (low) dimensions of Biglan's (1973) classification schema for academic subject matter areas.[1] Disciplines low in paradigmatic development were coded 1, whereas disciplines high in paradigmatic development were coded 0.

Academic rank was computed by assigning the value of 1 to assistant professor, 2 to associate professor, and 3 to full professor. *Gender* was coded so that 1 = male and 2 = female. For the purposes of the multiple regression analysis, gender was dummy coded so that males (coded as 0) were the reference group. *Teaching load* was computed by summing the courses taught during the academic year of the interview.

Preference for teaching was measured using the following question: "On balance, how would you characterize your professional interests at present—equally divided between research and teaching or inclining more toward one than the other?" Faculty being interview used the following scale to respond: 1 = heavily toward research; 2 = both, lean to research; 3 = both, equal and complementary; 4 = both, lean to teaching; and 5 = heavily toward teaching.

Teaching satisfaction was constructed from four items tapping global and specific aspects of satisfaction. One global item asked faculty to rate their overall satisfaction with teaching based on their own standards and objectives. Other satisfaction items asked faculty to rate personal enjoyment of teaching, student interest, and student performance ($a = 75$).

Departmental support was computed by summing five items that assessed the extent of conversation about teaching-related issues at the departmental level: (1) the number of individuals with whom faculty regularly discussed teaching; (2) whether their chair gave them teaching feedback (1 = no, 2 = yes); (3) whether other faculty besides their chair gave them teaching feedback (1 = no, 2 = yes); (4) the number of faculty they gave their syllabi to; and (5) the number of faculty they received syllabi from. Individual scores on each item were standardized by converting to t-scores to accommodate the lack of a common metric among the response categories of the six items comprising *departmental support*. The Cronbach alpha estimate of internal consistency reliability for this composite variable is $r = .59$.

The seven dependent variables correspond to the seven principles of good practice: (1) *encouragement of student-faculty contact*, (2) *encouragement of cooperation among students*, (3) *encouragement of active learning*, (4) *provision of prompt feedback*, (5) *enhancement of time on task*, (6) *communication of high expectations*, and (7) *respect for diverse talents and ways of knowing* (Chickering and Gamson, 1987). Faculty respondents used a 5-point Likert scale (1 = never to 5 = very often) to indicate how often they engaged in each of 70 practices. These 70 practices are subsumed under seven 10-item subscales (all alphas > .75) that represent the seven principles of good practice.[2] The specific items subsumed under these seven scales are exhibited in the Appendix.

Data Analysis Design

Hierarchical multiple linear regression was used to test the affinity discipline hypothesis above and beyond the influence of gender, academic rank, teaching load, preference for teaching over research, satisfaction with teaching, and departmental support for teaching. Separate equations were solved for each of the seven principles of good practice. The regression analyses used to solve these equations were conducted in two steps. The first step entailed the regression of the focal principle of good practice on gender, academic rank, teaching load, preference for teaching over research, satisfaction with teaching, and departmental support for teaching. The second step added discipline paradigmatic development to the first equation solved. Two steps were conducted to estimate the percent of explained variance accounted for by discipline paradigmatic development.

The 0.05 level of statistical significance was applied. A two-tailed test of statistical significance was used for assessing the statistical significance of each of the seven regression equations solved and for all the independent variables except discipline paradigmatic development. However, a one-tailed test of statistical significance was used for appraising the statistical significance of the influence of discipline paradigmatic development on each of the seven principles of good practice if the sign of the obtained regression coefficient was positive. In such cases, a one-tailed test is appropriate because a positive relationship between low paradigmatic development and enactment of each of the seven principles of good practice is predicted by this study's general hypothesis (Mohr, 1990).[3]

Findings

Table 1 contains means and standard deviations for each of the variables used in this inquiry's research design. Intercorrelations among these variables are exhibited in Table 2.[4] The results of the multiple regression analyses used to test the affinity discipline hypothesis are shown in Table 3.

TABLE 1
Means and Standard Deviations (in parentheses)

	Mean (Standard Deviation)					
Variable	Total Sample		Soft Disciplines		Hard Disciplines	
Rank	2.09	(.83)	2.02	(.86)	2.28	(.75)
Courseload	3.68	(1.10)	3.88	(1.02)	3.07	(1.13)
Professional interest	2.78	(1.07)	2.82	(1.11)	2.64	(.95)
Departmental support for teaching*	249.88	(28.93)	252.15	(30.39)	242.26	(22.29)
Student-faculty contact	2.96	(.63)	3.04	(.60)	2.73	(.68)
Student cooperation	2.76	(.80)	2.82	(.81)	2.58	(.75)
Active learning	3.18	(.79)	3.29	(.67)	2.86	(1.01)
Student feedback	3.16	(.55)	3.17	(.56)	3.13	(.55)
Time on task	3.63	(.68)	3.66	(.70)	3.52	(.60)
High expectations	3.97	(.53)	4.06	(.51)	3.72	(.49)
Respect for diverse learning styles	3.20	(.69)	3.28	(.69)	2.94	(.66)

*Reported as standardized scores (t-scores).

TABLE 2
Correlation Matrix (two-tailed test of significance)

	Gender	Rank	Course Load	Discipline	Student Contact	Student Cooperation	Active Learning
Gender	1.00						
Rank	-.332***	1.00					
Course load	.033	-.094	1.00				
Discipline	-.078	.133	-.323***	1.00			
Student contact	.129	-.103	.038	.215*	1.00		
Student cooperation	.091	-.125	.027	.132	.630***	1.00	
Active learning	.182	-.202*	.099	.242*	.708***	.772***	1.00
Student feedback							
Time on task							
High expectations							
Respect for diversity							
Departmental support							
Professional interest							
Teaching satisfaction							

	Student Feedback	Time On Task	High Expectations	Respect for Diversity	Departmental Support	Professional Interest	Teaching Satisfaction
Gender	.157	.085	.141	.140	.081	.062	-.031
Rank	-.092	-.191*	-.224*	-.340*	.027	.003	.137
Course load	.126	.101	.212*	.099	-.112	.017	-.042
Discipline	.034	.094	.283**	.217*	.145	.073	-.008
Student contact	.515***	.350***	.504***	.627***	.331***	.320***	.562***
Student cooperation	.524***	.392***	.546***	.707***	.325***	.128	.430***
Active learning	.528***	.386***	.619***	.785***	.220*	.157	.358***
Student feedback	1.00	.597***	.524***	.503***	.169	.285**	.290**
Time on task		1.00	.591***	.432***	.116	.091	.160
High expectations			1.00	.591***	.246*	.279**	.288**
Respect for diversity				1.00	.145	.179	.380***
Departmental support					1.00	.012	.193
Professional interest						1.00	.491***
Teaching satisfaction							1.00

*$p \leq .05$, **$p \leq .01$, ***$p \leq .001$.

TABLE 3
Effects of Paradigmatic Development on the Seven Principles

		Student Contact		Student Feedback		Student Cooperation		Active Learning	
		Step 1	Step 2	Step 1	Step 2	Step 1	Step 2	Step 1	Step 2
Gender	β	.074009	.071349	.114707	.115818	.033323	.032013	.112030	.109055
	b	.104146	.100402	.140825	.142188	.059028	.056708	.196888	.191661
Rank	β	-.142125*	-.127091	-.067682	-.073957	-.172627*	-.165224*	-.203478*	-.186668*
	b	-.106915	-.095606	-.044420	-.048538	-.163467	-.156458	-.191169	-.175376
Load	β	.066691	.013859	.139241	.161294*	.051877	.025862	.106476	.047402
	b	.037639	.007822	.068560	.079418	.036855	.018373	.075050	.033412
Preference	β	.055155	.040954	.172258*	.178186*	-.106801	-.113794	-.038663	-.054541
	b	.032276	.023966	.087945	.090971	-.078673	-.083824	-.028257	-.039862
Dept. support	β	.226923**	.200721**	.130953	.141890	.248487**	.235585**	.158455*	.129157
	b	.005316	.004702	.002677	.002900	.007328	.006948	.004636	.003779
Satisfaction	β	.514828***	.521968***	.202353*	.199372*	.463696***	.467212***	.382560***	.390543***
	b	.131514	.133338	.045097	.044433	.149107	.150237	.122051	.124598
Discipline	β	—	.160209*	—	-.066875	—	.078888	—	.179136*
	b	—	.227587	—	-.082881	—	.141066	—	.317816
R^2		.39117	.41305	.16737	.17118	.28046	.28576	.23051	.25785
ΔF		11.45803***	3.94973*	3.58478***	.48737	6.95094***	.78699	5.34219***	3.90546*

		High Expectations		Time On Task		Respect Diversity	
		Step 1	Step 2	Step 1	Step 2	Step 1	Step 2
Gender	β	.040498	.037833	.012104	.011677	.018673	.016214
	b	.047453	.044330	.018183	.017541	.028832	.025035
Rank	β	-.217086**	-.202028*	-.200017*	-.197604*	-.376485***	-.362588***
	b	-.135980	-.126548	-.160629	-.158691	-.310753	-.299282
Load	β	.222501**	.169581*	.097841	.089360	.089389	.040550
	b	.104562	.079693	.058949	.053839	.055354	.025111
Preference	β	.165081*	.150857	.003656	.001377	-.030039	-.043166
	b	.080440	.073509	.002284	8.6003^{-04}	-.019288	-.027717
Dept. Support	β	.214379**	.188133*	.097355	.093149	.098474	.074253
	b	.004182	.003670	.002435	.002330	.002531	.001909
Satisfaction	β	.210198*	.217350*	.169488	.170634	.426730***	.433331***
	b	.044711	.046232	.046221	.046533	.119609	.121459
Discipline	β	—	.160474*	—	.025719	—	.148098*
	b	—	.189818	—	.039003	—	.230839
R^2		.25204	.27399	.08520	.08577	.30355	.32224
ΔF		6.00939***	3.20375*	1.66099	.06535	7.77285***	2.92294*

*$p < .05$, one-tailed test.
**$p < .01$, one-tailed test.
***$p < .001$, one-tailed test.

Student Contact. Discipline paradigmatic development ($b = .23$, $p < .05$) exerts a statistically significant influence on faculty encouragement of student-faculty contact. Put differently, faculty in disciplines of low paradigmatic development are more likely to apply this principle of good practice than are their counterparts in disciplines of high paradigmatic development. Discipline paradigmatic development accounts for 2% of the variance in the application of this principle of good practice.

In addition, departmental support for teaching ($b = .005$, $p < .01$) and satisfaction with teaching ($b = .13$, $p < .001$) enhance the performance of this principle of good practice. Moreover, 41% of the variability in the encouragement of faculty-student contact is explained by the seven variables included in the regression analysis.

Student Feedback. Disciplinary paradigmatic development ($b = -.08$, $p < .49$). fails to wield a statistically reliable influence on the provision of prompt feedback to students. Moreover, none of the other six variables included in the regression analysis attain statistical significance at the .05 level.

Student Cooperation. The encouragement of cooperation among students appears' uninfluenced by discipline paradigmatic development ($b = .14$, $p < .38$). However, faculty who derive satisfaction from teaching ($b = .15$, $p < .001$) and faculty who perceive that their department supports teaching ($b = .01$, $p < .01$) tend to encourage cooperation among students.

Active Learning. Faculty in disciplines exhibiting low paradigmatic development encourage active learning in their students to a greater extent than their colleagues in disciplines of high paradigmatic development ($b = .32$, $p < .05$). Moreover, discipline paradigmatic development accounts for 2.7% of the variance in faculty encouragement of active learning.

In addition, academic rank ($b = -18$, $p < 04$) negatively affects faculty use of this particular principle of good practice. The higher the academic rank of a faculty member ($b = -.18$, $p < .05$), the less frequently active learning is encouraged.

High Expectations. The communication of high expectations for students tends to occur more frequently in disciplines of low paradigmatic development ($b = .19$, $p < .05$) than in disciplines of high paradigmatic development. Discipline paradigmatic development also explains 1.9% of the variability in communication of high expectations.

Academic rank, course load, departmental support for teaching, and satisfaction with teaching also affect in a statistically reliable way the use of this principle of good practice. As faculty academic rank increases ($b = -.13$, $p < .05$), the communication of high expectations decreases. However, increments in faculty course load ($b = .08$, $p < .05$) increase their communication of high expectations. Increments in satisfaction with teaching ($b = .05$, $p < .05$) and in departmental support for teaching also tend to increase the frequency of communication of high expectations.

Time On Task. The regression equation solved for this principle of good practice failed to reach statistical significance at the .05 level. Consequently, neither discipline paradigmatic development nor any of the other six variables exert statistically reliable influences on time on task.

Respect for Diversity. Faculty in disciplines showing low paradigmatic development more frequently demonstrate respect for diverse talents and ways of knowing than their counterparts in disciplines of high paradigmatic development ($b = .23$, $p < .05$). Discipline paradigmatic development explains 1.9% of the variance in the use of this principle of good practice.

Satisfaction with teaching and academic ranks also influence showing respect for diverse talents and ways of knowing. Satisfaction with teaching affects the use of this principle in a positive way ($b = .12$, $p < .001$), whereas academic rank negatively influences faculty application of this principle ($b = -.29$, $p < .001$).

Limitations

This study is limited in four primary ways. Although the "best practices" questionnaire was not administered in person to participants, other information about teaching practices was collected in a face-to-face setting. Consequently, the tendency of respondents to give socially desirable responses may have influenced some of our findings. Different findings might result if all the data were collected without face-to-face contact, such as by mail. Second, the measures of enactment of the seven principles of good practice are self-reported estimates made by faculty. Students' perceptions of the extent to which faculty enact the seven principles of good practice may be different from faculty self-reports. Thus, students' perceptions might have provided more objective and independently derived measures of faculty performance of these principles. Third, this study was conducted in a single institution. Therefore, the findings may not be generalizable to either research universities or other types of colleges and universities. Fourth, a faculty member's typical class size and intended level of courses taught might influence the application of the seven principles of good practice. However, these two possible sources of influence were not available for this study. Thus, their absence constitutes a limitation to this study.[5] The findings, discussion, implications for practice, and conclusions of this study are tempered to some extent by these two limitations.

Discussion

The findings of this study indicate that faculty in low paradigmatic disciplines are no more likely than faculty in high paradigmatic disciplines to provide prompt feedback, encourage cooperation among students, or emphasize time on task. What accounts for the failure of the affinity discipline hypothesis for these three principles of good practice is unclear, but some possible explanations are advanced below.

Because faculty in disciplines with low paradigmatic development tend to be more student centered in their instructional goals and practices (Braxton and Hargens, 1996; Smart and Elton, 1982; Stark et al., 1990), the failure to confirm the affinity discipline hypothesis is surprising. Sorcinelli (1991) points out the similarities between the principle of active learning and encouraging cooperation between students. Perhaps faculty in academic fields of either high or low paradigmatic development are unable to make the distinctions between these two principles. To faculty in fields of low paradigmatic development, active learning may resonate more with their preferences than fostering cooperation between students as defined by Chickering and Gamson (1987).

Braxton, Eimers, and Bayer (1996) observe that faculty subscription to a norm supportive of providing prompt feedback to students is invariant across type of institution—Research I Universities and Comprehensive Universities and Colleges II—and hard and soft academic disciplines. Faculty adherence to such a norm in both academic fields of high and low paradigmatic development may account for the failure to confirm the affinity discipline hypothesis for the provision of prompt feedback.

The management of classroom time presents a problem to faculty regardless of their academic discipline. More specifically, faculty in all academic disciplines face such issues as the allocation of time, the management of time, and the amount of time spent on the learning of course content. Insofar as giving direction about time on task to students, faculty in this study indicated a general reluctance to articulate estimates of time on task, given the wide variation in students' capabilities and levels of academic preparation. Thus, faculty place similar degrees of emphasis on time on task regardless of the extent of paradigm development extant in their academic discipline.

Implications for Practice

Support for the affinity discipline hypothesis for four of the seven principles of good practice has practical significance for colleges and universities wishing to implement Chickering and Gamson's seven principles of good practice. Such institutions may wish to encourage faculty in disciplines of low paradigmatic development to use four of the seven practices—encouragement of student-faculty contact, encouragement of active learning, accentuation of high expectations, and respectfulness of diverse talents and ways of knowing—before encouraging their use by faculty in fields showing high paradigmatic development. Successful implementation is more likely to occur in such disciplines.

However, successful implementation of these four principles of good practice may be problematic in fields having high paradigmatic development. These principles must come to be viewed by faculty in such disciplines as being appropriate teaching practices before their more frequent use is likely to take place. Nevertheless, the remaining three principles can be fully institutionalized without piloting them in either disciplines of high or low paradigm development.

Satisfaction with teaching and departmental support for teaching also have implications for practice. Departments known for the support they give to teaching could be targeted for pilot programs designed to implement the seven principles of good practice. Faculty who espouse satisfaction derived from teaching might also be asked to participate in trial efforts to implement the seven principles.

Conclusions

The findings of this study accord partial support for the affinity discipline hypothesis. Disciplines having low paradigmatic development tend to have a greater affinity for engaging in four of the seven practices designed to improve college teaching than do disciplines exhibiting high paradigmatic development. Although together the six moderating personal and organizational characteristics account for more explained variance than discipline paradigmatic development, backing for this hypothesis obtains above and beyond the influence of these six possible moderating personal and organizational characteristics.

Thus, the findings of this study add to our understanding of the ways in which academic disciplines differ in teaching role performance. We already know from reviews of empirical research that academic disciplines of high and low paradigmatic development vary on such facets of teaching role performance as teaching goals, teaching practices, course examination questions, and the relationship between teaching and research (Braxton, 1995; Braxton and Hargens, 1996). The current study augments such knowledge by suggesting that disciplines of high and low paradigm development also vary on four of the seven principles of good practice delineated by Chickering and Gamson (1987). Given that these findings were obtained in a single institutional setting, the current study needs to be replicated in not only other research-oriented universities but in other types of colleges and universities such as comprehensive colleges and universities, liberal arts colleges, and two-year colleges.

Chickering (1991) contends that the single most important force for the institutionalization of the seven principles of good practice is an organizational culture that values continued improvement in the professional practice of its faculty. He also points to inertia, the tendency of faculty to view undergraduate education in traditional terms, and institutional structures and rewards as barriers to the institutionalization of these practices. The influence of departmental support for teaching on three principles—encouraging faculty-student contact, encouraging student cooperation, and communicating high expectations—tends to corroborate Chickering's contention that institutional structure and rewards facilitate the institutionalization of the good practices.

The findings of this study also suggest that the characteristics of faculty—academic rank, teaching load, and satisfaction derived from teaching—at the level of the individual are of importance. Academic rank poses a barrier to the institutionalization of four principles, whereas teaching load and teaching satisfaction appear to be opportunities rather than barriers for institutionalization of the principles of good practice.

Although the efficacy of the seven principles is robustly backed by empirical investigations (Sorcinelli, 1991), little or no research, the current study not withstanding, has focused on the identification of factors affecting their implementation. Consequently, future research on the improvement of undergraduate education in general and the institutionalization of the seven principles of good practice in particular should include such factors as the paradigmatic development of the faculty member's discipline, research, departmental support for teaching, and satisfaction with teaching, academic rank, and teaching load. Moreover, studies concentrating on forces that shape faculty satisfaction with teaching and departmental support for teaching should also be conducted.

Appendix: Faculty Inventory of "7 Principles for Good Practice in Undergraduate Education"

Good Practice Encourages Student-Faculty Contact

1. I advise my students about career opportunities in their major field.
2. Students drop by my office just to visit.

3. I share my past experiences, attitudes, and values with students.
4. I attend events sponsored by student groups.
5. I work with student affairs staff on issues related to student extracurricular life and life outside of school.
6. I know my students by name by the end of the first two weeks of the term.
7. I make special efforts to be available to students of a culture or race different from my own.
8. I serve as a mentor or informal advisor to students.
9. I take students to professional meetings or other events in my field.
10. Whenever there is a conflict on campus involving students, I try to help in its resolution.

Good Practice Encourages Cooperation Among Students

1. I ask students to tell each other about their interests and backgrounds.
2. I encourage my students to prepare together for classes or exams.
3. I encourage students to do projects together.
4. I ask my students to evaluate each other's work.
5. I ask my students to explain difficult ideas to each other.
6. I encourage my students to praise each other for their accomplishments.
7. I ask my students to discuss key concepts with other students whose backgrounds and viewpoints are different from their own.
8. I create "learning communities," study groups, or project teams within my courses.
9. I encourage students to join at least one campus organization.
10. I distribute performance criteria to students so that each person's grade is independent of those achieved by others.

Good Practice Encourages Active Learning

1. I ask my students to present their work to the class.
2. I ask my students to summarize similarities and differences among different theorists, research findings, or artistic works.
3. I ask my students to relate outside events or activities to the subjects covered in my courses.
4. I ask my students to undertake research or independent study.
5. I encourage students to challenge my ideas, the ideas of other students, or those presented in readings or other course materials.
6. I give my students concrete, real-life situations to analyze.
7. I use simulations, role-playing, or labs in my classes.
8. I encourage my students to suggest new readings, research projects, field trips, or other course activities.
9. My students and I arrange field trips, volunteer activities, or internships related to the course.
10. I carry out research projects with my students.

Good Practice Gives Prompt Feedback

1. I give quizzes and homework assignments.
2. I prepare classroom exercises and problems that give students immediate feedback on how well they do.
3. I return examinations and papers within a week.

4. I give students detailed evaluations of their work early in the term.
5. I ask my students to schedule conferences with me to discuss their progress.
6. I give my students written comments on their strengths and weaknesses on exams and papers.
7. I give my students a pretest at the beginning of each course.
8. I ask students to keep logs or records of their progress.
9. I discuss the results of the final examination with my students at the end of the semester.
10. I call or write a note to students who miss classes.

Good Practice Emphasizes Time on Task

1. I expect my students to complete their assignments promptly.
2. I clearly communicate to my students the minimum amount of time they should spend preparing for classes.
3. I make clear to my students the amount of time that is required understand complex material.
4. I help students set challenging goals for their own learning.
5. When oral reports or class presentations are called for I encourage students to rehearse in advance.
6. I underscore the importance of regular work, steady application, sound self-pacing, and scheduling.
7. I explain to my students the consequences of nonattendance.
8. I make it clear that full-time study is a full-time job that requires 40 or more hours a week.
9. I meet with students who fall behind to discuss their study habits, schedules, and other commitments.
10. If students miss my classes, I require them to make up lost work.

Good Practice Communicates High Expectations

1. I tell students that I expect them to work hard in my classes.
2. I emphasize the importance of holding high standards for academic achievement.
3. I make clear my expectations orally and in writing at the beginning of each course.
4. I help students set challenging goals for their own learning.
5. I explain to students what will happen if they do not complete their work on time.
6. I suggest extra reading or writing tasks.
7. I encourage students to write a lot.
8. I publicly call attention to excellent performance by my students.
9. I revise my courses.
10. I periodically discuss how well we are doing during the course of the semester.

Good Practice Respects Diverse Talents and Ways of Learning

1. I encourage students to speak up when they don't understand.
2. I use diverse teaching activities to address a broad spectrum of students.
3. I select readings and design activities related to the background of my students.
4. I provide extra material or exercises for students who lack essential background knowledge or skills.
5. I integrate new knowledge about women and other underrepresented populations into my courses.

6. I make explicit provisions for students who wish to carry out independent studies within my own course or as separate courses.

7. I have developed mastery learning, learning contracts, or computer-assisted learning alternatives for my courses.

8. I encourage my students to design their own majors when their interests warrant doing so.

9. I try to find out about my students' learning styles, interests, or backgrounds at the beginning of each course.

Notes

1. Biglan (1973) provides a table displaying the classification of academic subject matter areas using three dimensions: hard-soft, pure-applied, and life-nonlife. However, only the hard-soft dimension was used in this study, as the other two dimensions are irrelevant to this study's hypothesis. Moreover, this study does not test Biglan's model; it only tests the influence of paradigmatic development on the performance of the seven principles of good practice.
2. Pilot testing of the survey instrument indicated that one item on the *Respect for Diversity* scale was ambiguous; consequently, it was dropped from this scale.
3. A one-tailed test requires that the two-tailed probability value of a t statistic be split in half (Mohr, 1990).
4. An examination of these zero-order correlations indicates that high multicollinearity between any of the independent or control variables does not pose a problem for the interpretation of the regression coefficients obtained.
5. We wish to express our appreciation to an anonymous reviewer for *Research in Higher Education* for suggesting these two possible sources of influence.

References

Association of American Colleges (1985). *Integrity in the College Curriculum: A Report to the Academic Community*. Washington, DC: Association of American Colleges.

Becher, T. (1989). *Academic Tribes and Territories: Intellectual Enquiry and the Cultures of Disciplines*. Milton Keynes, England: Open University Press.

Bess, J. L. (1977). The motivation to teach. *Journal of Higher Education* 48: 243–258.

Bess, J. L. (1997). Introduction. In J. L. Bess (ed.), *Teaching Well and Liking It: Motivating Faculty to Teach Effectively* (pp. ix–xv). Baltimore, MD: The Johns Hopkins University Press.

Biglan, A. (1973). The characteristics of subject matter in different academic areas. *Journal of Applied Psychology* 57(3): 195–203.

Blackburn, R. T., and Lawrence, J. H. (1995). *Faculty at Work: Motivation, Expectation, Satisfaction*. Baltimore, MD: The Johns Hopkins University Press.

Blackburn, R. T., Behymer, C. E., and Hall, D. E. (1978). Research note: Correlates of faculty publications. *Sociology of Education* 5: 132–141.

Boice, R. (1992). *The New Faculty Member*. San Francisco, CA: Jossey-Bass.

Braxton, J.M. (1995). Disciplines with an affinity for the improvement of undergraduate education. In N. Hativa and M. Marincovich (eds.), *Disciplinary Differences in Teaching and Learning: Implications for Practice* (pp 59–64). San Francisco, CA: Jossey-Bass.

Braxton, J. M., and Hargens, L. L. (1996). Variation among academic disciplines: Analytical frameworks and research. In J. C. Smart (ed.), *Higher Education: Handbook of Theory and Research* (pp. 1–46). New York: Agathon Press.

Braxton, J. M., Eimers, M., and Bayer, A. E. (1996). The implications of teaching norms for the improvement of undergraduate education. *Journal of Higher Education* 67: 603–625.

Chickering, A. W. (1991). Institutionalizing the seven principles and the faculty and institutional inventories. In A. W. Chickering and Z. F. Gamson (eds.), *Applying the Seven Principles of Good Practice in Undergraduate Education* (pp. 51–61). San Francisco, CA: Jossey-Bass.

Chickering, A. W., and Gamson, Z. E. (1987). Seven principles for good practice in undergraduate education. *AAHE Bulletin* 39: 3–7.

Chickering, A. W., and Gamson, Z. E. (1991). Appendix A: Seven principles of good practice in undergraduate education. In A. W. Chickering and Z. F. Gamson (eds.), *Applying the Seven Principles of Good Practice in Undergraduate Education* (pp. 63–69). San Francisco, CA: Jossey-Bass.

Chickering, A. W., Gamson, Z. E., and Barsi, L. M. (1989). *Seven Principles for Good Practice in Undergraduate Education: Faculty Inventory*. Milwaukee, WI: The Johnson Foundation.

Eble, K. E., and McKeachie, W. J. (1985). *Improving Undergraduate Education Through Faculty Development*. San Francisco, CA: Jossey-Bass.

Gaff, J. G. (1991). *New Life for the College Curriculum*. San Francisco, CA: Jossey-Bass.

Katz, J. (1985). Teaching based on knowledge of students. *New Directions for Teaching and Learning* 21: 3–11.

Kuhn, T. S. (1962, 1970). *The Structure of Scientific Revolutions*. Chicago: University of Chicago Press.

Lodahl, J. B., and Gordon, G. (1972). The structure of scientific fields and the functioning of university graduate departments. *American Sociological Review* 37: 57–72.

McKeachie, W. J. (1986). *Teaching Tips: A Guide for the Beginning College Teacher*. San Francisco, CA: Jossey-Bass.

Mohr, L. B. (1990). *Understanding Significance Testing*. Newbury Park, CA: Sage Publications.

Murray, H. G., and Renaud, R. D. (1995). Disciplinary differences in classroom teaching behaviors. In N. Hativa and M. Marincovich (eds.), *Disciplinary Differences in Teaching and Learning: Implications for Practice* (pp. 31–39). San Francisco, CA: Jossey-Bass.

National Institute of Education (1984). *Involvement in Learning: Realizing the Potential of American Higher Education*. Washington, DC: National Institute of Education.

Olsen, D., and Simmons, A. (1996). The research versus teaching debate: Untangling the relationship. In J. M. Braxton (ed.), *Faculty Teaching and Research: Is There a Conflict*. New Directions for Institutional Research, no. 90. San Francisco, CA: Jossey-Bass.

Smart, J. C., and Elton, C. F. (1982). Validation of the Biglan model. *Research in Higher Education* 17: 213–229.

Sorcinelli, M. D. (1991). Research findings on the seven principles. In A. W. Chickering and Z. F. Gamson (eds.), *Applying the Seven Principles of Good Practice in Undergraduate Education* (pp. 13–25). San Francisco, CA: Jossey-Bass.

Stark, J. S., Lowther, M. A., Bentley, R. J., and Martens, G. G. (1990). Disciplinary differences in course planning. *Review of Higher Education* 13: 141–165.

Weimer, M. (1991). *Improving College Teaching*. San Francisco, CA: Jossey-Bass.

Received November 18, 1996.

Tensions and Models in General Education Planning

Robert R. Newton

A Perennial Planning Issue

Discussions of general education have become a permanent fixture in American higher education, reflecting the perennial struggle between general education and specialization. The undergraduate curriculum, originally a unified, common, prescribed program in virtually all colleges, has been eroded in various historical periods by the rise of electives, the need for specialized programs, and the emergence of new knowledge. As these centrifugal forces strengthened, periodic counterattacks were mounted by those who wished to restore unity and coherence in the form of a resuscitated core curriculum or general education program (Rudolph, 1977). The battlefield of undergraduate education is strewn with the skeletons of well-meaning but unsuccessful reformers who attempted to stem the tide of specialization in defense of general education. The revival of interest in general education over the past two decades is in part a recognition that the forces of departmentalization and specialization continue in the ascendancy and are advancing virtually unopposed; this recognition is to the dismay of those for whom breadth is the essential foundation of an effective undergraduate education (Association of American Colleges, 1985).

In spite of the extensive time and effort that continues to go into reexamining general education programs, frequently only a few members of blue ribbon general education reform committees are well prepared for the task. More often than not they have little background in the history of general education, insufficient understanding of the underlying pedagogical issues, or minimal acquaintance with competing models of general education.

A useful context would be one in which busy faculty, unfamiliar with general education trends, might understand the issues surrounding general education reform and the assumptions of competing models. This context would include:

- the tensions and issues which will likely emerge in a general education exploration,
- the competing models of general education a committee is likely to encounter both among its own members and in surveying the programs of other institutions, and
- an analysis of how the different models might fit into different kinds of institutions.

Four Tensions in General Education

Contemporary tensions that confront general education reformers involve four issues:
- unity versus fragmentation (*knowledge*),
- breadth versus depth (*student learning*),

Reprinted from the *Journal of General Education* 49, no. 3 (2000), by permission of Pennsylvania State University Press.

- generalist versus specialist (*faculty competence*), and
- Western culture versus cultural diversity (*content*).

Knowledge

Reflection on the purposes of general education inevitably exposes a fundamental disagreement on the nature of a college or university. Some emphasize the clear distinctions embodied in the foci and methods of the different disciplines and see the university as a loose collection of sharply defined departments drawn together under a broad institutional mission. Others stress a unity and coherence in the pursuit of knowledge that transcends departmental divisions and view the university as a common enterprise based on a coherent set of widely accepted assumptions.

The former would expose students to many disciplines, and assume that students themselves will construct a coherent understanding of the world from these separate experiences. The latter would design an integrated set of courses that brings together the disciplines either through blurring the lines among disciplines or insisting on a structure that promotes an underlying unity and greater coherence among general education courses. On the one hand, the emphasis on a broad sampling of the various disciplines reflects the rich, diverse interests and shape of a contemporary university, but it may suffer, as many complain the university itself does, from the defect of its virtue—fragmentation. On the other hand, striving for the realization of a genuine academic community based on shared interests, a common body of knowledge, and a concern for common problems may seek an elusive unity that has diminishing significance to an increasingly specialized and discipline-oriented faculty.

Student Learning

In the beginning, American colleges provided a broad common education for their students. This approach eroded over time because of three developments: the introduction of new disciplines, the enormous increase in the amount of knowledge, and the emphasis on faculty research and publication. These movements have resulted in a chronic tension between breadth and depth in undergraduate education, a tension usually resolved by further reduction of general education requirements to make additional room for courses in the major. In pre-professional undergraduate curricula especially, the prescriptions of outside accrediting agencies have left less and less room for general education or electives.

General education requirements are often viewed by students (and sometimes faculty advisors) as obstacles to be overcome as early as possible in their undergraduate careers in order to concentrate on what is genuinely important—the major. Though few would champion the cause of narrowness in undergraduate education, some argue that students, supported by an effective academic advisement system, should be allowed greater freedom to design programs based on their own talents and interests rather than be forced into predetermined general education requirements. They are skeptical whether, in the modern university and in contemporary society, there can be a common body of knowledge that every educated person should possess.

Faculty

The general education program is a reflection of a college faculty's perceptions, interests and ambitions. The rise of specialization and departmentalization has had a profound effect on faculty roles in leading universities nationwide. Primary identification and loyalty have shifted from the university to the professional specialty. The most significant reference group has become other members of one's discipline rather than one's university colleagues, and the department has supplanted the university as the primary source of authority and rewards. Researching teachers have been replaced by teaching researchers. Specialists with only passing interest in knowledge outside their disciplines have supplanted faculty who were not intimidated by involvement in integrative programs that took them beyond their specialties.

A view of the university as a set of separate schools or departments only loosely joined under a vague general purpose has pushed aside the perception of the university as an organic whole pursuing a common purpose. Departmental search committees more often than not seek narrow expertise with little concern whether the candidate is broadly educated or has an interest in general education. In such an environment, the concerns of general education are at the bottom of the list. With little attraction and few rewards for junior or senior faculty, especially in larger universities, general education courses have often become the domain of graduate students and part-time teachers. As university citizens retire, they are replaced by departmental members, and the importance and effective implementation of general education diminishes.

Content

In the contemporary controversy swirling around general education, no issue has been more passionately argued than the content of general education. The traditional importance of communicating the Western cultural heritage is challenged by those who demand expansion of general education to incorporate cultures and voices not represented in the canonical works and authors of the Western tradition.

Advocates of the centrality of Western culture argue that this tradition has been the dominant force in the development of American institutions and values and has had a major influence on the emergence of similar values in other cultures. They bemoan the cultural illiteracy of modern day college graduates and the curriculum's substitution of the contemporary issues for perennial concerns. Critics of Western cultural dominance in general education argue that it represents the disembodied ideas and values of an elite in one culture to the virtual exclusion of the contributions of other cultures or theoretical perspectives (Tierney, 1989). They propose that it is time for a radical revision of general education that emphasizes diversity and multicultural and gender concerns, not only to offer students a more balanced education, but also to prepare them to live in a world where an understanding of cultural differences will be essential for survival and success.

Models of General Education

In the midst of these tensions, general education programs are being examined, debated, and revised in colleges and universities across the country. The decentralized character of American higher education has meant and will continue to mean that there will be almost as many different general education programs as there are colleges—each responding to its own idiosyncratic history, organizational culture, and special mission. At the same time, if one emulates Procrustes and reduces the blurring detail and multiplicity of literally thousands of programs, certain illuminating assumptions and patterns emerge. Below are three approaches that I propose can provide a context for general education planning—both for understanding the nature of the current program and for envisioning how that program might be changed. The three models are the Great Books Model, the Scholarly Discipline Model, and the Effective Citizen Model.

Great Books Model

Proponents of the Great Books Model complain that the segregation of knowledge into discrete disciplines introduces artifical divisions in the understanding of reality and the pursuit of knowledge. As the disciplines enforce fragmentation, so a general education curriculum that follows the disciplinary structure leaves the student with a general education that is disjointed and incoherent. Disciplines as such should recede into the background since genuinely important problems cannot be fully and effectively explored if chopped artificially into disciplinary pieces. Rather, the most effective general education takes an interdisciplinary approach. The focus of general education becomes not the latest ideas or discoveries of contemporary scholars but an in-depth historical review of the works of pivotal thinkers whose ideas changed human history.

The aim of education, right living, is neither vocational nor pragmatic. Encounters with works that have stood the test of time by raising questions central to human existence and striving confront students with the fundamental questions of life, questions that have and will continue to preoccupy and perplex humanity at all times and in all places. In exploration of the tradition, students develop the intellectual habits, interests, and values that enable and insure the preservation and advancement of their cultural heritage (Association of American Colleges, 1985; Bennett, 1984; Bloom, 1987; Cheney, 1989; Hutchins, 1936).

Knowledge

The Great Books Model offers a clear position on the four tensions described above. Unity of knowledge is prized, while the fragmentation introduced by a disciplinary approach is eschewed. Reminiscent of early American colleges, the general education program reduces the blur of the knowledge explosion by focusing on a common body of universally accepted works that represent the essence of the students' cultural heritage. Coherence is further supported by the historical arrangement of the curriculum.

Student Learning

Emphasis is on the breadth of student learning while avoiding premature concentration on one discipline. Students are allowed to immerse themselves in specialized learning only after they possess the broader context provided by an integrated general education curriculum. They confront problems simultaneously in all their complexity rather than serially and from the disjointed perspectives of independent disciplines. Students are active learners, immersed in the careful reading and rigorous discussion of the classic texts themselves rather than the study of textbooks that repackage the insights of the classical authors.

Faculty

The competence of the faculty in a Great Books Model is broad rather than specialized. Faculty are at ease with the classic works of Western civilization and, as broadly educated scholars, are willing to step outside their home disciplines. They are committed to the premise that general education should concentrate on fundamental human questions rather than narrower and more artificial disciplinary concepts and methods. Usually such programs require a high level of cooperation among faculty—both for initial and ongoing curriculum and for faculty development.

Content

The content of the Great Books Model emphasizes the universality of the questions raised in the classics of Western culture and maintains the importance of the canon. At the very least, the study of other traditions or perspectives and critical evaluation of the Western tradition should follow a thorough acquaintance with the ideas and values that, whatever their strengths and weaknesses, are the basis of the culture in which we live. Great Books advocates have sometimes responded to the challenge of multiculturalism by devising supplementary courses that focus on the great books of other cultures.

The Great Books Model often flourishes in small liberal arts colleges where specialization and departmentalization are less pronounced. Programs also emerge in enclaves within larger institutions where reform-minded faculty have rejected the view of education implicit in overspecialization and excessive emphasis on research. Great Books programs have been established for whole curricula; in other settings, Great Books courses stand, usually in the humanities, as a required or alternative sequence for part of the general education curriculum. Among the more publicized recent proposals of the Great Books Model are Bennett's *To Reclaim a Legacy* (Bennett, 1984) and the National Endowment for the Humanities' *50 Hours* proposal (Cheney, 1989).

Scholarly Discipline Model

Advocates of the Scholarly Discipline Model complain that Great Books Model approaches look backwards to an era when knowledge was less voluminous, specialized methods of inquiry were less developed, and mastery in more than one field was more attainable. The Scholarly Discipline Model proposes that general education should be basically an introduction to the disciplines that comprise and give shape to the college. Today, the amount of knowledge and level of sophistication required for serious achievement in any scholarly area requires a concentration and specialization possible only through dedication to a single discipline. Faculty who stray into areas where they lack specialized training risk an amateurism they would be quick to condemn if intruders without disciplinary expertise invaded their disciplines.

The scholarly disciplines are the storehouses of human knowledge and the ways which humanity has developed over the centuries to understand the world. The organization of the university into disciplines mirrors this intellectual heritage and supports its ongoing development. General education should be derived from and draw on the strength of the disciplines. Consequently, the strongest general education is comprised of a series of rigorous introductory courses in the disciplines. General education teachers are specialists in the discipline and the content of courses emphasizes the insights and methods of the best contemporary scholars in the discipline (Phenix, 1964; Bruner, 1960).

Knowledge

The emphasis of the Scholarly Discipline Model is less on the coherence and unity of knowledge as it is on a series of intensive experiences in discrete disciplines. The source of integration is not a blending of the substance of the different disciplines but the students themselves who, with a solid grounding in the fundamental concepts and scholarly methods of the individual disciplines, can reflectively make their own connections.

Student Learning

The curriculum emphasizes both breadth and depth through an intensive introduction to a wide range of basic disciplines. The general education course is not a watered down presentation *about* the discipline for nonspecialists, but a rigorous introduction to the discipline designed to make even students who will not specialize in the discipline understand its basic concepts and how the scholars in the discipline analyze and solve problems. The student emerges from the general education program with a solid knowledge of the most important disciplines and an intelligent grasp of the way scholars discover knowledge in these disciplines. Their concentration in a particular discipline in their majors is enhanced by the intensive introduction they have received in a variety of disciplines.

Faculty

Scholarly Discipline faculty are specialists committed primarily to their disciplines and to the expansion of knowledge in these disciplines. While recognizing the value of a broad-based general education, they respect the integrity of the other disciplines and the special expertise of scholars in other fields. They are reluctant to venture outside the discipline and are often suspicious of those who, in an era when knowledge is increasingly complex and specialized, claim to be generalists. The level of cooperation among faculty of different disciplines is minimal since the basic assumption is that general education courses in the different disciplines are independently planned and executed. Once the disciplines to be included in the general education program are determined, scholars within departments decide what should be taught.

Content

In the debate between Western culture and cultural diversity, Scholarly Discipline proponents reject both sides. The content of courses should be the best contemporary understanding of the key concepts and their interrelationship in a discipline. If, in certain disciplines, this principle leads to the incorporation of the classic authors or concepts of Western civilization or the addition of other voices not given adequate attention in the past, then their inclusion is based on the merit and importance of their contributions to the discipline rather than the need either to be faithful to the tradition or to be more inclusive.

The Scholarly Discipline approach is at home in larger, complex universities with strong departments with a commitment to research and with hiring and promotion practices that encourage specialization. The Scholarly Discipline approach, controlled in large measure by the departments, usually results in a set of distribution requirements that spreads the general education program across disciplines. In some instances, the distribution requirements rigorously implement a commitment to communicating the key concepts and methods of inquiry of the disciplines that underlies the Scholarly Discipline approach; in other cases, the distribution program may represent a political compromise rather than a pedagogical position and may be simply acceptable lists of courses from competing departments.

Effective Citizen Model

Proponents of the third approach, the Effective Citizen Model, argue that the Scholarly Discipline approach focuses more on the university's ivory tower than the demanding and rapidly changing society into which students will graduate. Both the preoccupation of the Scholarly Discipline advocates to turn out beginning practitioners of the disciplines and the nostalgic attempts of Great Books advocates to resuscitate an early American collegiate ideal are misguided. These models reflect more the interests of college faculties than the needs of contemporary students or of a modern democratic society.

The primary question is what kind of general education is required to live well and participate fully in the world of the 21st century. The general education curriculum is that special component of undergraduate education providing the comprehensive context for more specialized study in the major and for further exploration of knowledge through electives. General education courses are not introductions for those who will major in the discipline; rather, they are special offerings aimed at students who will likely have minimal additional formal coursework in these disciplines. Courses are designed to communicate relevant information, to spell out its implications for life in modern society, and to develop the skills and values required for effective citizenship.

Knowledge

Coherence and unity in the Effective Citizen Model are promoted by building the curriculum around the issues and problems graduates will be expected to confront in order to lead productive lives. The curriculum is drawn from the disciplines because the disciplines contain the knowledge future citizens will require. But rather than, for example, giving students a rigorous introduction to basic chemistry, a general education course should develop an understanding of what chemistry is, how it interprets and shapes the modern world, and what critical challenges it poses to humanity. The objective is not to train a scientist but to educate graduates with the scientific literacy essential to be effective citizens.

Student Learning

General education should address a coherent and relatively comprehensive set of questions and issues so that graduates possess a general understanding of their world, its problems and opportunities. The emphasis is on a broad understanding of the important ideas and approaches of the disciplines and their societal implications rather than on an in-depth introduction to the discipline more appropriate to specialists. Students do not learn the discipline as much as they learn *about* the discipline and its importance both in modern society and for them as citizens of the next century.

Faculty

In the Effective Citizen Model, faculty set aside their preoccupation with training neophyte practitioners of their disciplines and develop courses intended for nonspecialists, in which relevancy and societal implications are pivotal concerns. The faculty recognize that, while committed to producing well-trained specialists in their majors, their obligation to the student body in general requires them to play a quite different, though also important role: educating informed citizens. In some instances, general education courses in this model remain within the discipline; in others, general education courses may be interdisciplinary, constructed around themes like "living in a social context" or "living in a scientific and technological world."

Content

The substance of general education in the Effective Citizen Model is significantly influenced by the debate over the canon of Western culture and cultural diversity. Preparation of students for today's world, and even more for tomorrow's, demands that the curriculum reflect the multicultural reality of American and global society. Courses should not only raise neglected issues of cultural and gender diversity but also promote the attitudes and values needed to address societal problems in these areas. Today's graduates will be ill prepared for the future if they graduate lacking an understanding and experience of cultures significantly different from their own.

There are two variations of this model worth noting. First, the recent emphasis on competencies and learning outcomes promoted by the assessment movement can give a particular character to the Effective Citizen Model. In this context, the goal of effective citizenship is defined in terms of a series of specific competencies necessary for productive membership in society. Sharp articulation of the objectives and careful assessment of outcomes are at the center of a competency-based interpretation of the Effective Citizen Model (Hutchings, Marchese, & Wright, 1991).

Second, the Effective Citizenship Model can be interpreted in the philosophical tradition of Dewey, for whom the aim of education was not to produce graduates who would fit into the existing society but to develop individuals who would emerge from their education with the skills, habits of inquiry, and attitudes they needed to change society for the better (Childs, 1950; Cremin, 1961; Dewey, 1916). In this view, colleges prepare graduates for their civic responsibility to rediscover, reorganize, and remake their democratic society.

The Effective Citizen Model can emerge in a variety of settings, such as comprehensive universities or small colleges. The model requires a varying level of cooperation and coordination among faculty, dependent on whether the courses remain within a particular discipline or merge material from various disciplines. In either case, courses must be reworked for a more comprehensive clientele and, since relevancy is emphasized, regularly reformulated as student or societal needs change. College-wide commitment to the Effective Citizen Model is required, as is cooperation within and, in the case of interdisciplinary courses, among departments to select the content and experiences appropriate for the nonspecialist.

Different General Education Programs for Different Settings

As noted at the outset, controversy over general education is a reflection of different perceptions of the nature of a university. Few would disagree that the decentralization of American higher education and the resulting myriad initiatives and idiosyncratic institutional histories has promoted great diversity. Local community colleges and international research universities are both institutions of higher learning, yet they differ dramatically in mission, goals, norms, values, faculties, clienteles, organizational structures, levels of faculty or administrative control, and complexity of organization. The differences among the 3,600 institutions of higher education emerge clearly in the design of general education programs.

In some institutions, the dominant metaphor is the university as a community of scholars that introduces the new generation to their cultural heritage and that trains and inspires them to advance this heritage. In other institutions, the metaphor is that of an educational service center, part of the higher education industry, providing the knowledge and skills that the individual and society need.

The characteristics of the student body and the degree to which the institution is explicitly oriented towards serving the career aspirations of its students will influence the design of its general education program. Students seeking a traditional college education will be attracted to colleges with Great Books or Scholarly Discipline models. Students more oriented toward careers will be less patient with Great Books and Scholarly Discipline approaches. They would likely be better served with a variation of the Effective Citizen Model.

Faculty are a key determinant of the appropriate model of general education for their institution. Faculty hired with the expectation of strong research productivity in their disciplines will be reluctant to adopt a model that distracts them from their disciplines by requiring teaching outside their home departments. It is also unlikely that the universities hiring such faculty will expect them to teach outside their specialties. Further, some faculty will reject the concept of courses for nonspecialists as a betrayal of standards and mission. On the other hand, faculty in colleges or universities whose mission and programs are more sensitive to the changing societal needs and clienteles will likely be more responsive to the "real world" concerns of their students. Courses will be more heavily influenced by students' aspirations than by a predetermined notion or ideal of what should be learned. General education in "traditional" universities whose programs change slowly will differ from general education in more "entrepreneurial" institutions that constantly scan the environment for emerging needs, opportunities, and clienteles.

Colleges differ in their need and their ability to establish an explicit sense of integration in general education, whether it be by blending the content in interdisciplinary courses, creating a special set of general education courses different from regular departmental courses, or insisting on a common form or structure for all general education courses. Small colleges where the whole faculty can fit into a modest auditorium have more of a chance to develop models that require substantial faculty planning, agreement, and coordination. Enclaves within larger institutions may separate themselves to establish special working groups to develop more coherent general education sequences. Larger universities may see explicit integration as unattainable or may devise a "common approach" that both conceptually and in practice pursues greater integration by establishing a common structure for general education courses, without forcing faculty to leave their disciplines.

Though the three models are presented above as distinct, the implementation of any particular general education program is likely to be an eclectic process with elements of the three models being selected in idiosyncratic ways by different faculty and departments. In a number of universities, Great Books programs for certain disciplines may be mixed with departmental programs that involve no interdisciplinary thrust. Some departments may build their courses around the Scholarly Discipline Model, while others in the same institution promote the Effective Citizen Model. Variation within universities is likely to be a function of the strength of the departments vis-à-vis university-wide governance structure and the willingness to commit resources to a general education program rather than to strengthening departmental programs.

Even though the models may have different assumptions, pedagogical approaches, and perceptions of the ideal graduate, that does not mean their implementation will exclude entirely the concerns of the other models. Great Books advocates might argue that developing a familiarity with the perennial questions is the best way to produce effective citizens. Scholarly Discipline proponents may incorporate classical authors and historical development of the discipline as essential components of their general education courses. Effective Citizen advocates may argue that life in modern society requires an understanding of relevance of the key concepts of the disciplines. So it is likely that each model, while sufficiently different to represent a distinct approach, will in varying ways seek to incorporate aspects of the two other models.

Finally, the models define the ideally educated person in different ways. The graduate of the Great Books program is familiar with the classical works and authors of Western culture (and perhaps other cultures) and has grappled with perennial questions of human existence. The Scholarly Discipline graduate has become a beginning practitioner of the basic disciplines and understands both the key concepts and the methods of inquiry scholars use in these disciplines. The Effective Citizen graduate is familiar with the important ideas of the disciplines and their implications for contemporary society and is prepared to live in and work for the improvement of it.

Summary Conclusion

The initial premise of this presentation was that general education revision committees are more often than not unprepared for their task. To provide a broad, albeit preliminary, context for general education planners, this analysis identified four key issues confronting reformers, outlined three models of general education, proposed how these models respond to the four issues, and described the factors that might make the various models more appropriate for different types of institutions (see table 1).

Though the decentralization of American education promotes idiosyncratic rather than uniform general education programs, these models provide relatively coherent sets of assumptions around which general education programs can and have been conceptualized, implemented, and assessed. A familiarity with these models can also provide a context against which the institution's current general education program can be analyzed and evaluated and can allow general education reformers to identify more sharply and quickly both their own presuppositions and the assumptions of their colleagues.

TABLE 1
Three Models of General Education

	Great Books	Scholarly Discipline	Effective Citizen
Key insight	Focus on the perennial human questions	Disciplines as the accumulated wisdom and ways of understanding the world humankind has developed over the centuries	Education in the service of self-reforming democracy
Role of the university	Handing on the tradition	Vigorous developer/extender of the knowledge and methods of the academic disciplines	Progressive force for democratic change
Substance of curriculum	Pivotal ideas/authors of Western tradition	Key concepts and methods of inquiry as defined by the disciplines	Knowledge/skills vital to living in and improving modern society
Ideal graduate	Classically educated through encounters with classic works and authors	Beginning practitioner of the disciplines	An effective citizen
Emphasis	Unity	Method	Action
Breadth/depth	Broad review of the substance of the Western tradition	Sharp introduction to the range of basic disciplines	Comprehensive introduction to current knowledge
Source of coherence	Unified by a historical review of key responses to the perennial questions	The individual student piecing together the mosaic of the disciplines	The focus on preparing graduates with skills/knowledge for modern society
Faculty	Broadly educated generalists	Disciplinary experts	Instructors committed to educate nonspecialists in their areas of specialty
Likely locations	Liberal arts colleges/special programs in larger universities	Research-oriented universities with strong departments	Institutions with strong client-centered orientation and sense of public mission
Orientation	Looks to past for enduring ideas and values to form and guide students in the present	Instills an understanding of the intellectual treasures and scholarly methods that are society's intellectual heritage	Develops the tools and commitment needed to shape the future
Inspiration/ advocates	Hutchins/Adler/Bennett Cheney/Bloom	Bruner/Phenix/professional disciplinary societies	Dewey/Childs

References

Association of American Colleges. (1985). *Integrity in the college curriculum: A report to the academic community.* Washington, DC: Association of American Colleges.

Bennett, W. J. (1984). *To reclaim a legacy: A report on the humanities in higher education.* Washington, DC: National Endowment for the Humanities.

Bloom, A. (1987). *The closing of the American mind.* New York: Simon & Schuster.

Bruner, J. (1960). *The process of education.* Cambridge: Harvard University Press.

Cheney, L. V. (1989). *50 hours: A core curriculum for colleges.* Washington, DC: National Endowment for the Humanities.

Childs, J. L. (1950). *American pragmatism and education.* New York: Henry Holt.

Cremin, L. A. (1961). *The transformation of the school.* New York: Knopf.

Dewey, J. (1916). *Democracy and education.* New York: Macmillan.

Hutchings, P., Marchese, T., & Wright, B. (1991). *Using assessment to strengthen general education.* Washington, DC: American Association of Higher Education.

Hutchins, R. M. (1936). *The higher learning in America.* New Haven: Yale University Press.

Phenix, P. H. (1964). *Realms of meaning: A philosophy of the curriculum for general education.* New York: McGraw-Hill.

Rudolph, F. (1977). *Curriculum: A history of the American undergraduate course of study since 1636.* San Francisco: Jossey-Bass.

Tierney, W. G. (1989). Cultural politics and the curriculum in postsecondary education. *Journal of Education, 171*(3), 72–88.

REMEDIAL EDUCATION IN COLLEGES AND UNIVERSITIES: WHAT'S REALLY GOING ON?

JAMIE P. MERISOTIS AND RONALD A. PHIPPS

Offering coursework below college level in higher education institutions is coming under increased scrutiny. Variously referred to as "remedial education," "developmental education," "college prep," or "basic skills," it constitutes a field about which policy makers are asking: Why are so many students in institutions of higher learning taking basic reading, writing, and arithmetic—subjects that should have been learned in high school, if not junior high school?

Over the past several years, some states—including Arkansas, Louisiana, Oklahoma, Tennessee, and Virginia—are attempting to limit remedial education. In 1998, the trustees of the City University of New York (CUNY) voted to phase out most remedial education in the system's 11 four-year institutions, and the CUNY plan has moved ahead steadily since its implementation in September 1999. Following similar patterns, some states such as Florida have moved virtually all remediation to community colleges. Legislators in Texas and other states are expressing concern that tax dollars are being used in colleges to teach high school courses. In response, the legislatures in the states of New Jersey, Montana, Florida, and Oregon, among others, are considering proposals that would require public school systems to pay for any remedial work that a public school graduate must take in college.

A survey of state legislators showed that they were split three ways on the topic. In response to the statement that colleges and universities should give remedial education more attention, 34% disagreed, 32% agreed, and 32% were neutral. While state legislators agree that the problem is inherited from the K-12 sector, they are less clear about who to hold responsible (Ruppert, 1996). Educators mirror this ambivalence. Proponents and opponents alike point to the effects of remedial education on the quality, accountability, and efficiency of higher education institutions. The quality of discussions on the effect of remediation on diversity, educational opportunity, and enrollment is diminished by the lack of agreement on the nature of remediation. There is little consensus and understanding about what remedial education is, whom it serves, who should provide it, and how much it costs. Consequently, this lack of fundamental information and imprecision of language often renders public policy discussions ill informed at best.

This article, which is adapted from a recent publication on remediation by The Institute for Higher Education Policy (1998a), seeks to bring some clarity to the policy discussions. It includes an analysis of remediation's core function in the higher education enterprise, a review of the current status of remedial education at the college level, a discussion of financing remedial education, an argument about the costs of not providing remedial education, and a set of recommendations intended to reduce the need for remediation while also enhancing its effectiveness.

Remediation's Core Function in Higher Education

Given the increased attention to remedial education, it may be easy to conclude that efforts providing compensatory education to underprepared students in colleges and universities are recent events

Reprinted by permission from *Review of Higher Education* 24, no. 1 (fall 2000).

that somehow reflect the present condition of U.S. postsecondary education. Although some individuals may argue that the quality of the higher educational enterprise has decreased over the years, the fact remains that remedial education has been part of higher education since early colonial days. Dating back to the 17th century, Harvard College provided tutors in Greek and Latin for those underprepared students who did not want to study for the ministry. The middle of the 18th century saw the establishment of land-grant colleges, which instituted preparatory programs or departments for students below average in reading, writing, and arithmetic skills (Payne & Lyman, 1998). In 1849, the first remedial education programs in reading, writing, and arithmetic were offered at the University of Wisconsin (Breneman & Haarlow, 1998). By the end of the 19th century, when only 238,000 students were enrolled in all of higher education, more than 40% of first-year students college participated in precollegiate programs (Ignash, 1997).

Due to increased competition for students among higher education institutions at the beginning of the 20th century, underprepared students continued to be accepted at growing rates. For instance, over half of the students enrolled in Harvard, Princeton, Yale, and Columbia did not meet entrance requirements and were placed in remedial courses. The vast influx of World War II veterans taking advantage of the G.I. Bill created another surge in the need for remedial education. Then thousands of underprepared students enrolled in colleges and universities from the 1960s to the 1980s in response to open admissions policies and government funding following the passage of the Civil Rights Act of 1964 and the Higher Education Act of 1965 (Payne & Lyman, 1998).

In short, those halcyon days when all students who enrolled in college were adequately prepared, all courses offered at higher education institutions were "college level," and students smoothly made the transition from high school and college simply never existed. And they do not exist now. A comprehensive survey of remediation in higher education, conducted by the National Center for Education Statistics (NCES) for fall 1995, provides evidence of this reality. Remedial courses were defined as courses in reading, writing, and mathematics for college students lacking skills necessary to perform college-level work at the level required by the institution. Thus, what constituted remedial courses varied from institution to institution. Here are NCES's major findings (U.S. Department of Education, 1996):

- Over three-quarters (78%) of higher education institutions that enrolled first-year students in fall 1995 offered at least one remedial reading, writing, or mathematics course. All public two-year institutions and almost all (94%) institutions with high minority enrollments offered remedial courses.

- Twenty-nine percent of first-time first-year students enrolled in at least one remedial reading, writing, or mathematics course in fall 1995. First-year students were more likely to enroll in a remedial mathematics course than in a remedial reading or writing course, irrespective of institution attended.

- At most institutions, students do not take remedial courses for extended periods of time. Two-thirds of the institutions indicated that the average time a student takes remedial courses was less than one year, 28% one year, and 5% more than one year.

Because NCES conducted similar surveys for the academic year 1983–1984 and for fall 1989, it is possible to compare the intensity of remedial education course offerings over the past decade. The consistency is striking. In 1983–1984, 82% of the institutions offered remedial education in all three areas (reading, writing, and mathematics), compared to 78% in fall 1995. Sixty-six percent provided remedial reading courses in 1983–1984 compared to 57% in fall 1995; for remedial writing, 73% and 71%; and remedial mathematics, 71% and 72%, respectively.

Statistics for first-year students enrolled in remedial courses were not estimated for the academic year 1983–1984; however, comparisons can be made between fall 1989 and fall 1995. Thirty percent of first-year students enrolled in all three remedial courses in fall 1989 compared to 29% in fall 1995. Thirteen percent of first-year students enrolled in remedial reading for both years. Remedial writing courses were taken by 16% of the first-year students in fall 1989 compared to 17% in fall 1995. In remedial mathematics, the percentages were 21% and 24%, respectively. Interestingly, although little change resulted in the percentage of students enrolling in remedial courses from fall 1989 to fall 1995, college and university enrollment increased by approximately a half million students.

Institutions that Do Not Offer Remediation

Twenty-two percent of the institutions in the NCES survey indicated that they did not offer remedial education courses. Of that percentage, two-thirds noted that their students did not need remediation. Approximately a quarter reported that those students needing remediation take such courses at another institution and/or that institutional policy prohibits the offering of remedial courses on their campus.

There is some reason to believe that the percentage of institutions not offering remedial courses is much lower than reported and, conversely, that the percentage of students requiring remedial courses is higher. This conclusion, based on the nature of the higher education enterprise, is supported by anecdotal evidence. For example, many institutions do not find it in their best interests to acknowledge that they enroll students who require remediation. In a paper presented to the American Council on Education, Astin (1998) posits that an institution's "excellence" is defined primarily by resources and reputation. A major boost to an institution's reputation is the enrollment rates of students with the highest GPAs, the top test scores, and the strongest recommendations. Astin states:

> It goes without saying that the underprepared student is a kind of pariah in American higher education, and some of the reasons are obvious: since most of us believe that the excellence of our departments and of our institutions depends on enrolling the very best-prepared students that we can, to admit underprepared students would pose a real threat to our excellence. (1998, p. 11)

However, there is a disproportionate emphasis on the credentials and the abilities of the *applicants* compared to the knowledge and skills of the *graduates*—as evidenced by virtually every national ranking publication (Astin, 1998, p. 11).

Steinberg, as cited in Breneman and Haarlow, refers to the National Assessment of Educational Progress and the Third International Math and Science Study to suggest that more high school students than we would like to admit are unprepared for college-level work (Breneman & Haarlow, 1998). Even in high-performing states, only one-third of American high school students meet or exceed levels of grade-appropriate proficiency in mathematics, science, reading, and writing. The country's 12th graders perform as poorly on standardized math and science tests as their counterparts from the worst-performing industrialized countries in the world. Steinberg states:

> Even if we assume that none of these sub-proficient students graduating from American high schools goes on to postsecondary education (surely an untenable assumption), the fact that somewhere close to 60% of U.S. high school graduates do attend college suggests that a fairly significant number of college-bound young people cannot do, and do not know, the things that educators agree that high school graduates ought to know and be able to do. (Qtd. in Breneman & Haarlow, 1998, p. 46)

The purpose of this analysis is not to place blame or point fingers at the nation's K-12 system or the higher education community. It is merely to suggest that there is validity behind the hypothesis that more remedial activities are occurring than meet the eye. Therefore, it is reasonable to say that a portion of the 22% of institutions reporting that they do not offer remedial education courses enroll underprepared students and provide some sort of remedial service. Also, it is likely that *at least* 78% of higher education institutions enroll underprepared students and that, in all probability, more than 30% of the students require remediation.

The Many Faces of Remedial Education

The discussion of remedial education evokes the image of courses in reading, writing, and mathematics whose content is below "college-level." The term "college-level" suggests that agreed-upon standards exist, or at least enjoy a consensus by educators. A reasonable assumption would be that the academic community has identified specific knowledge and skills that are required of students to be successful in a college or university. Conversely, if students do not possess the specified knowledge and skills, remedial education is needed for academic success.

The fact is that remedial education is in the eye of the beholder. Rather than being based on some immutable set of college-level standards, remedial education, more often than not, is determined by the admissions requirements of the particular institution. Obviously, remediation at a community college with open admissions is not the same as remediation at a doctoral research institution. As Astin points out: "Most remedial students turn out to be simply those who have the lowest scores on some sort of normative measurement—standardized tests, school grades, and the like. But where we draw the line is completely arbitrary: lowest quarter, lowest fifth, lowest 5%, or what? Nobody knows. Second, the 'norms' that define a 'low' score are highly variable from one setting to another" (Astin, 1998, p. 13). A case in point is the 21-campus California State University (CSU) System. Although state policy in California mandates that students entering CSU are supposed to be in the top third of their high school graduating class, the *Los Angeles Times* reported that 47% of the fall 1997 first-year class required remedial work in English and 54% needed remedial work in mathematics (National Center, 1998).

Furthermore, remediation standards vary even for institutions with similar missions. A 1996 study by the Maryland Higher Education Commission found that policies, instruments, and standards used by Maryland colleges and universities to identify and place remedial students differed, even within the community college sector. Institutions employ various approaches toward the particular subject areas of remediation, including locally developed norms, nationally developed norms, grade-level equivalences, and specific deficiencies and/or competencies.

Another study conducted in 1998 by the Maryland Higher Education Commission illuminates the relationship between high school preparation and the need for remediation in college. The conventional wisdom is that students who complete college preparatory courses in high school will not need remedial education in college, while students who have not taken a college preparatory curriculum in high school will probably need remediation. This particular study measured the college success rates of recent high school graduates. The basic findings of the report agree with common sense. Students who completed college-preparatory courses in high school performed better in college than students who did not complete college-preparatory courses in high school. College-preparatory students earned higher grades in their initial math and English courses and had higher grade point averages after their first year in college than students who did not complete the college-preparatory curriculum. Also, fewer college-preparatory students required assistance in math, English, and reading.

It is helpful, however, to examine these data further. First, a significant number of students who took college-preparatory courses in high school needed remediation in college. For students who completed college-preparatory courses in high school and immediately attended a community college, 40% needed math remediation, one out of five required English remediation, and one of four needed remedial reading. At one community college, 73% of college-preparatory students needed math remediation, 79% English remediation, and 76% reading remediation. At the public four year institutions, 14% of college-preparatory students needed math remediation, 7% English remediation, and 6% reading remediation.

Some disconnect exists between what high schools consider college-preparatory, particularly in mathematics and English, and what colleges are requiring of their entering students. But a more interesting question emerges from these data. The percentages of *college-preparatory* students requiring remediation at the community colleges is dramatically higher than the percentage of *college-preparatory* students at the public four-year institutions. How can that be? Conventional wisdom would suggest that the percentages would be approximately the same for both higher education sectors because all of the students have completed a state-mandated college preparatory curriculum. Or, for those who contend that community colleges are less academically rigorous than four-year institutions with selective admissions (a debatable argument), the expectation would be that the percentages would be reversed. That is, since all students have enjoyed the benefit of a college-preparatory curriculum, those enrolling in community colleges would be quite prepared for the easier curriculum compared to those enrolling in four-year institutions with the more academically rigorous curriculum.

There can be many explanations for this intriguing issue. One could argue that the college-preparatory students admitted by the four-year institutions are academically superior to the college-preparatory students admitted by the community colleges and therefore need less remediation. Also, it could be that community colleges, because of their open-door mission, have more structured procedures than four-year colleges for determining which students require remedial courses. Critics of the quality of high schools may posit that college preparatory students from high schools that lack academic rigor, in spite of the college preparatory label, choose to attend a community college because they are concerned about their academic preparation. Whatever the explanation, this example helps to affirm the essential point made by Astin and others: remedial education in colleges and universities is relative and arbitrary.

Remedial Education's Diverse Client Population

The examination of remedial education is incomplete if it focuses only on recent high school graduates. According to several studies, a substantial proportion of postsecondary education students are 25 years of age or older, and many of these adult students are enrolled in remedial courses. The exact proportion or number of older students requiring remedial education, however, is difficult to discern and the data on age distribution of remedial students vary widely from state to state.

One important source of national data in the composition of students in remedial courses is provided by the National Center for Developmental Education (NCDE). NCDE data indicated that approximately 80% of remedial students in the country's colleges and universities are age 21 or younger (Breneman & Haarlow, 1998). However, other data suggest that a much higher proportion of older students is taking remedial courses and that the remediation population is bipolar in terms of age and time elapsed between secondary and postsecondary experiences. According to NCES, 31% of entering first-year students who took a remedial education class in 1992–1993 were 19 or younger. In contrast, 45% of the entering first-year students who took a remedial course were over twenty-two years of age, the traditional age of the baccalaureate degree graduate. Another study found that one-quarter (27%) of entering first-year students in remedial courses were 30 or older (Ignash, 1997).

Data from individual states support the NCES findings. For instance, Maryland found that more than three-fourths of remedial students in the community colleges in 1994–1995 were 20 years of age or older (Maryland Higher Education Commission, 1996). In Florida, a reported 80% of the students in remedial classes were not recent high school graduates but older students who needed to brush up their skills, usually in mathematics, before entering the higher education mainstream (National Center, 1998). First-year students also are not the only students who take remediation. NCES data show that 56% of students enrolled in remedial courses were first-year students, 24% were sophomores, 9% were juniors, and 9% were seniors (Ignash, 1997).

The policy debate about remediation in higher education must address not only first-year students who recently graduated from high school but also students of all ages and levels of undergraduate progress. In fact, it appears that, in the future, older students will attend colleges and universities in record numbers and will require remedial education. According to a recent report, between 1970 and 1993, the participation in higher education by students age 40 and over increased from 5.5% of total enrollment to 11.2%—the largest jump of any age cohort (Institute for Higher Education Policy, 1996). Policies addressing remediation must recognize that the demand for remedial education is being fueled in part by older students who need refresher courses in mathematics or writing.

How Successful Is Remedial Education?

Research about the effectiveness of remedial education programs has typically been sporadic, underfunded, and inconclusive. For instance, a study of 116 two-and four-year colleges and universities revealed that only a small percentage conducted any systematic evaluation of their remedial education programs (Weissman, Bulakowski, & Jumisco, 1997). The Southern Regional Education Board has observed that, because few states have exit standards for remedial courses, it is unclear whether many states know whether their programs work (Crowe, 1998). Adelman (1998) examined college transcripts from the national high school class of 1982 and, not surprisingly, found an inverse relationship between the extent of students' need for remedial courses and their eventual completion of a degree. Of the 1982 high school graduates who had earned more than a semester of college credit by age 30, 60% of those who took no remedial courses, and 55% of those who took only one remedial course, had either earned a bachelor's or associate's degree. In contrast, only 35% of the students who participated in five or more remedial courses attained either a bachelor's or associate's degree.

Focusing upon reading remediation reveals another perspective. Sixty-six percent of students required to take remedial reading were in three or more other remedial courses, and only 12% of this group earned bachelor's degrees. Among students who were required to take more than one remedial reading course, nearly 80% were in two or more other remedial courses, and less than 9% earned bachelors' degree. When reading is at the core of the problem, the probability of success in college appears to be very low.

According to Adelman, the need to take remedial education courses reduces the probability of achieving a degree. Yet it is also instructive to look at the ratio of students who did not need remedial education and those who did. Students who did not take remediation courses had a graduation rate of 60%. But even the least academically prepared students—those who took five or more remedial education courses—had a 35% graduation rate. Therefore, remediation allowed the academically weakest students to perform almost three-fifths as well as the students who did not need any remediation. Further, students who needed two remedial courses performed almost three-quarters as well as the academically strongest students. These data seem to indicate that remediation is, in fact, quite effective at improving the chances of collegiate success for underprepared students.

Financial Costs

Hard evidence regarding the costs of remediation nationwide is elusive. The most recent analysis of the cost, authored by Breneman and Haarlow (1998) suggest that nationally remedial education absorbs about $1 billion annually in a public higher education budget of $115 billion—less than 1% of expenditures. This estimate, derived by conducting a survey of all 50 states along with individual site visits to five states, includes the costs associated with remediation for both traditional age first-year students and returning adult students.

Among states and between higher education segments, the percentage of remedial education expenditures to the total budget showed wide variance. In FY 1996, 1.1% of the direct salary budget of public universities in Illinois was dedicated to remediation, while it took 6.5% of the community college direct salary budget. In FY 1995, the percentage of expenditures for remediation in Maryland was 1.2% of the total expenditures for the public campuses. In Washington, 7% of total expenditures was earmarked for remedial education in 1995–1996. Focusing on the appropriation per full-time equivalent (FTE) student for individual states, the cost to California for remediation is about $2,950 per FTE student and the cost to Florida is about $2,409.

It is important to note what the total national cost estimate of $1 billion does *not* entail. First, this estimate does not include the remediation budget of private colleges and universities. Second, costs borne by students through foregone earnings and diminished labor productivity were not calculated. Third, there was no effort to figure the costs to society as a whole by failing to develop the nation's human capital to its fullest potential. These limitations notwithstanding, the Breneman and Haarlow report compiles the most comprehensive, accurate information to date.

There are several impediments to collecting reliable data about the costs of remediation:

- There is no universally accepted definition of what constitutes remedial education within the academic community.
- How "costs" are distributed among the several activities within a college or university can, and do, vary widely.

- Even if the functions to be included in determining the cost of remediation were understood, higher education institutions have difficulty supplying precise breakdowns of remediation costs.

- It is not always clear whether reported cost figures include expenditures or appropriations. As Breneman and Haarlow point out, "These are two different measures of cost, and ideally, one would want all the figures on both bases, but what one gets is a mix of the two" (1998, pp. 12–13).

- Because states do not compute remediation education costs regularly, financial data can either be relatively current or several years old.

Perhaps the most intractable barrier to collecting valid and reliable data on remediation is that noted by commentators like Astin and Steinberg: Official estimates of the extent and cost of remediation are often understated for a variety of reasons—not the least of which is the perceived damage to the "reputation" of a college or university. Unfortunately, there are many incentives for agencies and institutions to underreport remediation. Thus, we can reasonably conclude that the costs of remediation are higher than reported. Our estimate is that the figure is probably closer to $2 billion. However, if $2 billion—which amounts to 2% of higher education expenditures—is the actual cost of remediation, it is still a relatively modest amount to be spent on an activity of such importance to the nation. If remedial education were terminated at every college and university, it is unlikely that the money would be put to better use.

A useful case study is the Arkansas Department of Higher Education's comprehensive study over several years that compares direct and indirect instructional costs of academic programs for the state's public colleges and universities. In 1996–1997, the total cost of remediation in Arkansas colleges and universities was $27 million—approximately 3% of the total expenditures. At community colleges, 9% of the total expenditures went to remedial education compared to 2% at four-year institutions. The total state subsidy for remedial education was almost $14 million. The state subsidy for community colleges was 59% of the total expenditures compared to 40% at four-year institutions. These data show that, although remediation is provided at both four-year and two-year institutions, community colleges commit substantially more resources toward remedial education—which is not surprising given their open-admissions policies.

The Arkansas cost study shows that the cost per FTE student for remedial education at the four-year institutions was $7,381. The average program costs per FTE student at four-year institutions ranged from $7,919 for psychology, to $8,804 for English, to $9,320 for mathematics, to $12,369 in music. The cost per FTE student for remedial education at the community colleges was $6,709. The average program costs per FTE student at the community colleges ranged from $6,163 for general studies, to $7,730 for business, to $8,235 in nursing.

These data illustrate that remediation costs per FTE student generally are lower than the costs per FTE student for core academic programs—English, mathematics, etc.—that lead to an associate or bachelor's degree. Knowing the cost per FTE student for remediation vis-à-vis the cost per FTE student for academic programs provides another viewpoint in the remediation debate. One issue that most institutions grapple with is resource reallocation: How can the institution use limited resources to the greatest benefit? What is the cost/benefit of providing remediation? Many institutions are targeting "low-demand programs"—programs with few graduates—for elimination. How does the cost of low-demand programs compare to remedial education costs, and can resources be better used elsewhere? How is the cost per FTE student in academic programs affected by remedial students who are successful and who participate in college-level courses? These and other questions can frame the public policy debate regarding the cost of remediation.

In addition to examining the financial cost of providing remedial education in higher education, it is helpful to look at the other side of the coin. More explicitly, what are the financial gains of a successful remedial education program for a specific institution? A remedial education program that enables a significant proportion of remedial students to continue their education after completing remedial courses is beneficial for the institutional bottom line since it enhances revenue that can partially offset costs associated with providing remediation.

Social and Economic Costs of Not Providing Remediation

What does the nation get for its $1 to $2 billion investment in remedial education? There is considerable evidence that the nation cannot afford to disfranchise even a small portion of the population who has the potential of succeeding in college from participating in some form of postsecondary education. Therefore, the costs and benefits associated with providing access to underprepared students and helping them succeed in higher education must be measured accurately.

Ponitz, as cited in Breneman and Haarlow, points out that 80% of sustainable jobs today require some education beyond high school (Breneman & Haarlow, 1998). Currently, 65% of the nation's workers need the skills of a generalist/technician, including advanced reading, writing, mathematical, critical thinking, and interpersonal group skills. Twenty years ago, that figure was only 15% (Breneman & Haarlow, 1998).

According to a Lehman Brothers report (citing Bureau of Labor Statistics data), the growth rate in jobs between 1994 and 2005 will be the greatest for categories that require at least an associate's degree (Ghazi & Irani, 1997). Jobs requiring a master's degree will grow the fastest (at a rate of 28%), followed closely by those requiring a bachelor's degree (27%), and an associate's degree (24%). "All jobs requiring postsecondary education and training of an associate's degree or better are projected to grow significantly higher than the average, and all those with lesser levels of training are expected to grow below the average," summarizes the Lehman Brothers' report. "In our opinion, this is a clear indication that the transformation to a knowledge-based economy will require a more highly skilled, more adept, and more knowledgeable work force" (Ghazi & Irani, 1997, p. 71).

A report from The Institute for Higher Education Policy (1998b) summarizes four types of benefits of going to college: private economic benefits, private social benefits, public economic benefits, and public social benefits. While much of the recent public policy focus has been on the private benefits, the public benefits of going to college are extensive. Since going to college results in greater benefits to the public as a whole—increased tax revenues, greater productivity, reduced crime rates, increased quality of civic life, etc.—then students who benefit from the remedial instruction provided by higher education also must be contributing to the public good.

However, not all agree with these findings. Rubenstein (1998) argues that the economic return of higher education to the graduate is an illusion. Significant factors relating to higher wages of college graduates when compared to high school graduates include the higher socioeconomic background of college graduates, in addition to their higher motivation and, probably, higher IQs. He further notes that too many colleges are chasing many marginal students and that the United States has an abundance of college graduates, not a deficit. As a consequence, in 1995 approximately 40% of people with some college education—and 10% of those with a college degree—worked at jobs requiring only high school skills. In 1971, the figures were 30% and 6% respectively. Rubenstein concludes that functionally literate graduates are in short supply. College graduates who do not have the functional literacy traditionally associated with college degrees are taking jobs that had previously gone to employees with high school diplomas.

Rubenstein's argument is alarming and, if accurate, poses a challenge to educators in both the K-12 and higher education sectors. The obvious challenge is to ensure that college graduates are functionally literate and possess the skills necessary to compete in a global society. Few would argue, it seems to us, that there can be too many functionally literate people, whether they are college graduates or not. As a society, we have little choice about providing remediation in higher education, with the goal of increasing functional literacy. Abandoning remedial efforts in higher education and therefore reducing the number of people gaining the skills and knowledge associated with postsecondary education is unwise public policy. Thus, it is appropriate to confront the causes of underpreparation and try to reduce the necessity for remediation as much as possible. In addition, policies should be explored to improve the effectiveness of remediation programs, and cost efficiencies should be implemented wherever needed.

Recommendations

The evidence is compelling that remediation in colleges and universities is not an appendage with little connection to the mission of the institution but rather represents a core function of the higher education community that it has performed for hundreds of years. Although the financial data are not as reliable as some would like, there is sufficient reason to assume that the cost is minimal when compared to the total higher education budget. Also, the case has been made that attempts to eliminate remediation completely from higher education are both unrealistic and unwise public policy. Realizing this, where do we go from here?

It is important to recognize that not all remediation is delivered effectively or efficiently. Like any educational process, remedial education must be continuously examined and revised to meet prevailing conditions and needs. Therefore, good public policy must focus upon two mutually reinforcing goals: (1) implementing multiple strategies that help to reduce the need of remediation in higher education, and (2) improving the effectiveness of remedial education in higher education. It is evident that a piecemeal approach to addressing the problem of remediation in higher education has not worked. Intermittent schemes to "correct" remedial education are stop-gap solutions at best. Only a systemic design at the state level comprised of a set of interrelated strategies will succeed.

The discussion below presents a set of strategies that states and institutions can use to achieve the public policy goals. Outlined here. We emphasize that there is a positive relationship between the number of implemented strategies and the probability of meeting the public policy goals. Implementing one or two of the strategies may be helpful, but fundamentally addressing the issue requires using the entire range of strategic options.

The importance of collaboration cannot be understated. Borrowing the realtor's mantra—location, location, location—reducing the need for remediation in higher education will require collaboration between and among: colleges and universities and high schools; states and their colleges and universities, as well as state departments of education, K-12 public and private schools, public and private two-and four-year colleges and universities, businesses, and philanthropies. We have no illusions that the various players in the educational enterprise will welcome cooperation and abandon their traditional turf. We simply state that a lack of a true, invested collaborative effort among the parties will doom any effort to fully address the issue of remediation.

Reducing the Need for Remediation in Higher Education

Strategies for reducing the need for college remediation include: (a) aligning high school requirements and course content with college competency and content expectations; (b) offering early intervention and financial aid programs that target K–12 students by linking mentoring, tutoring, and academic guidance with a guarantee of college financial aid; (3) tracking students and providing high school feedback systems; and (4) improving teacher preparation. Many of these approaches are found in the K–16 movement occurring in many states.

1. *Aligning High School Requirements with College Content and Competency Expectations.* Several state initiatives are underway to define specifically what a first-year college student needs to know and be able to do. These initiatives often are identified in terms of content and competency levels rather than Carnegie units or high-school class rank. College entry-level content standards and competencies apply across the curriculum to all first-year students who are recent high school graduates. They do not target students enrolling in a specific course or a specific major. The competency categories parallel college general education categories and align with the content standards being adopted in school districts.

2. *Early Intervention and Financial Aid Programs.* Some states have developed, or are considering developing, early intervention strategies in the high schools, often beginning in the ninth grade. These techniques are designed to correct student academic deficiencies before the students reach college. Also, a number of states have established early intervention financial aid programs

modeled after the Taylor Plan in Louisiana, which in addition to enhancing access, contain provisions to increase the ability of students to succeed in college. Although details vary from state to state, the programs guarantee low-income K-12 students admission to college if they meet certain criteria, including completion of a college-preparatory curriculum, achieving a minimum grade point average, and participating in a counseling program. The federal government has enacted the Gaining Early Awareness and Readiness for Undergraduate Programs (GEAR UP) for low-income students. This program encourages states and university-school partnerships to provide support services to students who are at risk of dropping out of school by offering them information, encouragement, and the means to pursue postsecondary study.

3. *Student Tracking and High School Feedback Systems.* An effective tool for enhancing collaboration between high schools and colleges, in addition to identifying areas of mutual concern, is to provide feedback to high schools regarding the success of their students in college. Several states provide high schools with information on student admission exemptions; remedial course work in mathematics, English, and reading; performance in the first college-level courses in English and mathematics; cumulative grade point average; and persistence (Wallhaus, 1998).

4. *Improved Teacher Preparation.* Teacher education reform is now on the national agenda, as evidenced by the 1998 reauthorization of the Higher Education Act of 1965. The legislation replaces several small teacher education programs—which were not funded—with a three-part grant: 45% of the funding will go to states to improve the quality of its teachers; 45% will go to partnerships between colleges and secondary schools; and 10% will go to recruiting more students to teach in low-income school districts (Burd, 1998).

Initiatives in several states include: (a) reexamining teacher certification and licensure requirements based on specific standards of what teachers should know and be able to do, (b) emphasizing academic disciplines in the teacher education curricula, and (3) establishing performance-based career advancement opportunities for veteran teachers.

Improving the Effectiveness of Remediation in Higher Education

What can be done to improve the effectiveness of remediation in higher education? We have identified three core strategies: (a) creating interinstitutional collaborations, (b) making remediation a comprehensive program, and (c) utilizing technology.

1. *Interinstitutional Collaboration.* Astin makes a strong case for interinstitutional collaboration between institutions of higher education in a region or state. The opportunities for collaborative research—given that there are hundreds of remedial programs of all types and perhaps thousands of individual courses—are remarkable. Research on programs for under-prepared students and faculty preparation to teach such students should be a collaborative effort among colleges and universities in a system or state. Although admitting that such collaboration would be difficult to achieve because of threats to institutional "reputation," interinstitutional conversations hopefully would be successful in leading the participants to agree that (a) "developing effective programs for lower-performing students at *all levels of education* is of vital importance not only to our education system, but also to the state and the society at large" and (b) "finding and implementing more effective programs for under-prepared students is a 'systems' challenge that must be accepted and shared by all institutions at all levels of education" (Astin, 1998, pp. 29–30; emphasis ours).

2. *Making Remediation a Comprehensive Program.* Substantial research has been conducted to identify essential components of an effective remedial education program. One recent study by the Massachusetts community colleges provides an excellent overview of best practices in remedial education (Massachusetts, 1998). These practices include:

   • *Assessment and Placement.* All incoming students are evaluated and, where necessary, placed in remediation according to a mandatory comprehensive instrument for assessing reading, writing, and mathematics.

- *Curriculum Design and Delivery.* The goals and objectives of the remedial program must be defined clearly so that all students understand them.
- *Support Services.* Underprepared students require individualized help. Effective programs use "intrusive" advising to identify and solve problems early.
- *Evaluation.* The remedial education program's effectiveness is assessed according to how many students complete remedial education programs, how many excel continue on to college-level courses, how many complete college-level courses, and how many reach their academic goals.

3. *Utilizing Technology.* In the past decade or so, computers have enhanced the teaching-learning process, particularly in remedial courses that are hierarchical, linear, and stable in their structure and content. Many private companies have developed, or are developing, remedial software. One such company, Academic Systems Corporation, has generated computer-assisted remedial courses in mathematics and writing that are being used in hundreds of colleges and universities nationwide. Several controlled studies in colleges and universities have indicated that this type of pedagogy has great potential for remedial education (Academic Systems, 1997). The applied nature of the courses and the fact that the software is geared to adults is especially appropriate for students in remedial courses. Although the student can work at his or her own pace, mediated learning allows the instructor to intervene whenever the student is having difficulty.

Next Steps

The previous strategies promote the two public policy goals of reducing the need for remediation in higher education while at the same time improving its effectiveness. In effect, these strategies provide a checklist of initiatives that have a positive effect on the two policy objectives. If our thesis is correct, the degree to which a state or region implements these strategies will determine the extent to which it will meet the policy goals.

One way to test this premise would be to conduct a set of case studies in key states. The strategies in the checklist can be used as criteria for making objective judgments about a state's commitment to reducing and improving remediation. Correlating a state's "score"—the extent of its active strategies—with its success in attaining the dual public policy objectives would contribute illuminating information to the national dialogue on remediation. The case study method could further the dialogue about what works in remedial education and could address the need for more accurate and timely data.

The need for remediation and its core function in higher education will not be eliminated by controversy and criticism. Unfortunately, much of the recent discussion on remedial education has tended to produce more heat than light. Public policy efforts would be more productively focused on determining what works in remedial education, for whom, and at what cost. These efforts would propel the nation's higher education institutions toward reaching the dual goals of reducing the need for remediation while ensuring its continued effectiveness.

References

Academic Systems. (1997). *Working paper: The economics of mediated learning.* Mountain View, CA: Academic Systems. From the Academic Systems website <www.academic.com>.

Adelman, C. (1998, Summer). The kiss of death? An alternative view of college remediation. *National Crosstalk,* 6(3), p. 11. San Jose, CA: National Center for Public Policy and Higher Education.

Arkansas Department of Higher Education. (1998). *Arkansas academic cost accounting.* Little Rock: Arkansas Department of Higher Education.

Astin, A. (1998, June 19). *Higher education and civic responsibility.* Paper presented at the American Council on Education's Conference on Civic Roles and Responsibilities, Washington, DC.

Breneman D., & Haarlow, W. (1998). *Remediation in higher education.* Washington, DC: Thomas B. Fordham Foundation.

Burd, S. (1998, October 16). The higher education amendments of 1998: The impact on college and students. *Chronicle of Higher Education*, A39. From the Chronicle of Higher Education website <www.chronicle.com>.

Colorado Commission on Higher Education. (1998). *K-12/postsecondary linkage initiatives*. Denver: Colorado Commission on Higher Education.

Crowe, E. (1998). *Statewide remedial education policies*. Denver, CO: State Higher Education Executive Officers.

Ghazi K., & Irani, I. (1997). *Emerging trends in the $670 billion education market*. New York: Lehman Brothers.

Ignash, J. (1997, Winter). Who should provide postsecondary remedial/developmental education? In J. Ignash (Ed.), *New Directions for Community Colleges, no. 100* (pp. 5–19). San Francisco: Jossey-Bass.

The Institute for Higher Education Policy. (1996). *Life after 40: A new portrait of today's—and tomorrow's—postsecondary students*. Boston: Institute for Higher Education Policy and The Education Resources Institute.

The Institute for Higher Education Policy. (1998a). *College remediation: What it is. What it costs. What's at stake*. Washington, DC: Institute for Higher Education Policy.

The Institute for Higher Education Policy. (1998b). Reaping the Benefits: Defining the public and private value of going to college. *The new millennium project on higher education costs, pricing, and productivity*. Washington, DC: Institute for Higher Education Policy.

Maryland Higher Education Commission. (1996). *A study of remedial education at Maryland public campuses*. Annapolis: Maryland Higher Education Commission.

Maryland Higher Education Commission. (1998). *College performance of New Maryland high school graduates*. Annapolis: Maryland Higher Education Commission.

Massachusetts Community College Development Education Committee (MCCDEC). (1998). Access and quality: Improving the performance of Massachusetts community college developmental education programs. Boston: MCCDEC.

National Center for Public Policy and Higher Education. (1998, Summer). The remedial controversy. *National Crosstalk, 6*(3), p. 2.

Payne, E., & Lyman, B. (1998). *Issues affecting the definition of developmental education*. From the National Association of Developmental Education website <www.umkc.edu/cad/nade/index.htm>.

Rubenstein, E. (1998, Fall). The college payoff illusion. *American Outlook*, 14–18. (Published in New York by the Hudson Institute).

Ruppert, S. (1996). *The politics of remedy: State legislative views on higher education*. Washington, DC: National Education Association.

U. S. Department of Education. National Center for Education Statistics (NCES). (1996). *Remedial education at higher education institutions in fall 1995*. NCES 97–584. Washington, DC: U.S. Government Printing Office.

Wallhaus, R. (1998). *Statewide K-16 systems: Helping underprepared students succeed in postsecondary education programs*. Denver, CO: State Higher Education Executive Officers.

Weissman, J., Bulakowski, C., & Jumisco, M. (1997, Winter). Using research to evaluate developmental education programs and policies. In J. Ignash (Ed.), *New Directions for Community Colleges, no. 100* (pp. 73–80). San Francisco: Jossey-Bass.

Acknowledgement

The authors thank Christina Redmond, Research Assistant, and Mark Harvey, Project Assistant, for editorial and research support for this article and the prior report.

OPTIONS FOR CHANGE: A FLEXIBLE VEHICLE FOR CURRICULUM EVOLUTION AND REFORM

ROGER G. BALDWIN AND MELISSA J. BAUMANN

ABSTRACT: In this article we examine a flexible curricular approach known as the "Option." The Option enables students to supplement traditional majors with a coherent set of courses and other educational experiences in a related, often interdisciplinary field. Options can act as curricular bridges between mainstream academic fields and problems of professional practice. They can also give students experience with emerging subject areas (e.g., biomedical engineering). Options serve as laboratories for experimenting with new subject areas before incorporating them fully into the curriculum as majors and minors. Hence, Options promote creativity and risk-taking by providing a proving ground for potential new academic programs.

In a time of rapid change, academic programs must experiment and evolve in order to keep pace with advances in knowledge, changes in professional practice, and shifting conditions in society. The need for malleable, responsive academic programs is particularly a concern in scientific and technological fields where the growth of knowledge is exponential. However, education in every academic field must adapt to accommodate changing student interests, new approaches to teaching and learning, and new interpretations and applications of the discipline. Educational programs designed to prepare students for a dynamic future must be dynamic themselves, or they will become increasingly unpopular and irrelevant.

This article describes an approach Michigan State University employs to adapt its curriculum to emerging fields and shifting student interests. It is a technique other institutions can adapt to increase the flexibility and responsiveness of their educational programs in an era of fiscal constraint and unprecedented change.

Critics of higher education (e.g., Association of American Colleges, 1991; Barr & Tagg, 1995; Boyer, 1987; Guskin, 1997; Levine, 1989, 1990, 2001; Marcy & Guskin, 2003; Wingspread Group on Higher Education, 1993) have complained that college curricula are slow to change, mired in tradition, and designed more for the convenience of professors rather than to meet the needs of students, employers, or the larger society. Traditionally colleges have revised their educational programs through accretion—by adding new courses and degree programs, by designing new majors and minors, and by setting up additional departments or other academic units to manage and deliver new fields of study that have won a place in the curriculum (Cohen, 1998; Gaff & Ratcliff, 1996; Stark & Lattuca, 1997). Rarely is curriculum reformed by deleting courses or programs or by reassembling existing learning opportunities in new ways.

The process for adapting the college curriculum is typically slow, laborious, costly, and cautious (Levine, 1978; Stark & Lattuca, 1997). Institutions carefully weigh the costs and consequences of a move in a new academic direction before they commit limited resources to new academic programs or educational reform proposals. This very deliberate process has led to the charges that higher education is slow, out-of-touch, and unresponsive (Zemsky & Massy, 1995).

Reprinted from *Innovative Higher Education* 30, no. 2 (2005).

In dynamic times, higher education must think "outside the box" imposed by the standard curriculum structure (e.g., majors, minors, rigid and complex decision making processes). New options are needed to make educational programs more flexible and adaptive in a dynamic environment where change is a constant and rigid, one-size-fits-all programs and procedures are inefficient and impede needed reforms. Additional ways of fostering curriculum innovation and experimentation are needed if higher education is to serve a diverse society effectively.

"The Option": A Creative Approach to Curriculum Change

Michigan State utilizes a non-traditional approach in the curriculum change process which has the capacity to encourage experimentation, enhance curricular flexibility and responsiveness, and lower barriers to major curriculum change. At MSU, this mechanism is called "an Option."[1] An Option[2] is "a discrete set of courses or courses and other academic requirements within or supplementary to the major" (Registrar's Office, Michigan State University, 2002). Options appear on a student's transcript and document educational experiences in a defined subject area such as biomedical engineering or information technology. For example, an Option in biomedical engineering can supplement a major in mechanical engineering and give students a wider array of educational and employment opportunities upon graduation. The student would graduate with a major in mechanical engineering and an Option in biomedical engineering. Her transcript would record both her major and her Option.

At MSU, Options can be defined by a single department, collaborating departments, or by a college as a whole. In addition, more than one college can also sponsor an Option jointly (e.g., MSU's Option in Information Technology is co-sponsored by the Colleges of Engineering, Business, and Communication Arts and Sciences).

Frequently, Options are defined in emerging fields (e.g., biomedical engineering, global studies, health promotion) that have not yet been fully integrated into the curriculum as a major or program area. The "Option" option (no pun intended) allows departments or colleges within the University to define a coherent set of courses that provide a foundation of knowledge and skills in a specialized, often interdisciplinary subject field. Usually, Options are comprised of courses and other learning opportunities that are already available at the institution. Sometimes supplementary courses (e.g., a survey course, a capstone course) in the Option field are added to integrate this academic component more fully. Packaging discrete courses as an Option provides a carefully coordinated exposure to a field rather than the random exposure that may result when students make individual elective and distribution requirement choices. An Option not only allows a student to complete a widely recognized and broad-based major like civil engineering but also to demonstrate interest and acquire a core knowledge base in a related specialized subject field (e.g., environmental studies). In this respect, Options parallel traditional academic minors. (See Table 1 for sample Options in Michigan State's College of Engineering).

However, Options differ from minors in key ways that account for their greater flexibility and responsiveness. First, Options are not rigidly defined by predetermined requirements. They are defined by their sponsoring unit (i.e., department(s), college(s)) and, unlike many majors and minors, require no fixed number of courses or credit hours. Options can be any number of courses plus other types of educational experiences (e.g., clinical practice, internships, research experience) as long as the sponsoring entity makes a compelling case for the package of educational experiences it wishes to include in the Option.

Second, to be listed on a transcript,[3] an Option does not require review at the state level as majors frequently do. The Option must be approved by the appropriate department and college curriculum committee(s) as well as the University curriculum committee. However, the absence of a state-level review requirement simplifies and accelerates the approval process. This allows Options to be developed and approved more quickly with less bureaucratic red tape. It also allows an institution to make a more qualified commitment to a new or changing subject area before it chooses to seek state-level approval for a new academic program or major. Furthermore, the Option's flexibility makes it relatively simple to modify its content and structure over time as the Option's subject area develops

TABLE 1
**Sample "Options": Michigan State University College
of Engineering**

Chemical engineering: Environmental option (18 credits)
    Required courses
        Introduction to Environmental Engineering
        Biochemical Engineering
        Fundamentals of Microbiology
    Complete three of the following courses:
        Environmental Engineering Chemistry
        Water and Wastewater Treatment
        Solid and Hazardous Waste Management
        Microbiology for Environmental Health Engineering
Materials science and engineering: Biomaterials engineering option (27 Credits)
    Required courses
        Human Gross Anatomy & Structural Biology
        Quantitative Human Biology
        Organic Chemistry I
        Tissue Mechanics
        Biomaterials & Biocompatibility
    Complete one of the following courses
        Ceramics and Refractory Materials
        Fracture and Failure Analysis
        Physical Metallurgy of Ferrous & Aluminum Alloys
Technical electives
        Nine credits from an approved list of technical electives

and as related employment and/or post graduate opportunities evolve. Hence, the Option encourages more educational and programmatic experimentation and more risk-taking because it consumes less time to design, test, and revise a potential new program. It also requires a lower initial investment of limited resources to try out a new academic program idea with uncertain enrollment potential or only tentative support from some key academic stakeholders.

In a nutshell, Options can be more quickly designed and assembled than traditional majors and minors. Due to the absence of fixed course or credit-hour requirements, Options are more malleable than standard majors and minors. Essentially, Options can be tailored to the distinctive nature of a subject area and the specific purposes for which the Options are designed (e.g., preparation for graduate school, professional school, employment opportunities).

Likewise, Options can be used to supplement basic (and more traditional) academic programs. Options can provide students with specialized knowledge and skills in interdisciplinary areas that bridge traditional academic disciplines. They can also be employed to address key problem areas in professional practice (e.g., joint replacement in medicine [a marriage of engineering and orthopedics]). In an era when academic disciplines are often faulted for their narrow focus on complex problems (see, for example, Wulf and Fisher, 2002, "A Makeover for Engineering Education"), Options offer a means to overcome the sharp segmentation of knowledge that is both a strength and a weakness of higher education today. Options are a creative way to respond to the educational challenge of connecting theory to real world problems and professional practice. For example, an English major could take an Option in technical writing or a nursing major could take an Option in environmental/interior design. Each Option would enhance students' knowledge of their major field while expanding their professional expertise and career opportunities.

Stakeholder Support

At Michigan State, Options have proven to be attractive to three important constituencies—faculty, students, and administrators—for different reasons. Among engineering faculty members, for example, Options are viewed as non-threatening to the standard academic majors. As supplementary education and credentialing, they leave the core of existing academic programs intact. They achieve some of the objectives of curriculum change without uprooting well-established programs. Options also permit faculty and academic units to experiment with new program initiatives before launching a major new educational program or even a department which may require substantial resource reallocation and potentially jeopardize program enrollments and reputations. For faculty, a new program Option may be seen as a trial balloon. If the Option sets sail and remains afloat for a lengthy period, a new major, program, or department in the same area may seem like a far less risky venture.

In addition, faculty like Options because they can serve as recruiting tools for mainstream subject fields. For example, an Option in superconductivity can enhance students' interest and enrollment in underlying core fields such as chemistry, physics, and engineering. Likewise, Options in fields such as biomedical engineering can also attract students from underrepresented groups (e.g., women) to disciplines like engineering.

Students like the Option opportunity because it gives them a means to flesh out their educational program in areas of specialized or topical interest within the time constraints of a standard 4-year degree program. It also provides an added credential that may be beneficial to one's career. Options can make a traditional degree more current and adaptable in today's ever more competitive job market. For instance, a graduate with a major in history and an Option in museum studies may have an advantage when competing for jobs with other liberal arts majors.

At Michigan State, students are pleased with the Option label as long as the Option they have pursued is recorded specifically on their transcript. Some of the new Biomedical Options approved for implementation in MSU's College of Engineering are analogous to existing biomedical engineering (BME) programs and degrees at other institutions. For example, Ohio State University offers a minor in BME that consists of a core that integrates engineering, biomedical and life science courses worth 20 credit hours. The BME Option in Biomedical Materials at MSU is comparable in scope (at 23–24 credits) to the Ohio State Minor (at 20 credits). Although MSU does not offer a Biomedical major or minor in engineering at present, the BME Option enables MSU engineering students to have an educational experience comparable to BME programs at other institutions.

Options receive a friendly reception from administrators and university-wide committees because they do not appear to create too much change too fast and generally do not increase the time needed for graduation beyond 4 years. Most of the courses and other appropriate learning experiences included in an Option are already available at the institution. Some Options involve the addition of one or more new courses (e.g., survey of the field, a capstone experience) designed to make the Option a coherent learning experience. However, Options usually do not require major new staffing and resource commitments before trying out a new program initiative. Because of their limited scope, Options provide a less threatening opportunity to experiment with curriculum reform.

Furthermore, academic administrators like Options because they are easier to abolish than majors, minors, and stand alone programs if they prove to be unpopular or too costly to maintain. Students in an abolished Option would still reside in a core major program. Hence, their basic educational program would remain intact. Furthermore, most courses within an abolished Option would still count as elective credits toward a degree.

Essentially, Options can serve as a proving ground or a test kitchen for innovative educational programs. If an Option proves successful, it may eventually move into the curriculum as a major. Alternatively, the Option may eventually take on a different identity as related mainstream academic fields mutate and take on new features and subject matter by absorbing aspects of successful Options. The history of higher education is rich with fields that emerged at the intersection of other disciplines.

Psychology, ecology, and chemical engineering are a few examples. Options provide an interim mechanism to nurture and test the viability of cutting-edge and innovative subject areas. Like an apprenticeship, an Option provides a probationary phase where novel academic initiatives can be refined and strengthened before potentially entering the curriculum as full-fledged academic programs.

Quality Control

The Option offers an attractive supplement to more traditional means of curriculum change and reform. Options are not without risks, however. Careful monitoring and management are necessary to insure that Options provide a positive learning experience for students and a high quality educational outcome. We recommend the following actions to make sure that Options are carefully implemented and maintained:

- Approve only Options that are well-designed and build upon sufficient existing resources. A coherent package of educational experiences (courses, other learning opportunities) is necessary for an Option to provide a credible educational product. Options that are merely a collection of discrete, uncoordinated courses are not likely to succeed. Likewise, Options must be built upon adequate resources. If a department or institution lacks appropriate courses and other resources (e.g., faculty expertise and teaching time) to implement a quality Option, it should not be approved.

- Manage and supervise Options carefully. Responsible management and supervision are necessary to implement and sustain quality Options. A department chair, director, or coordinator should be assigned responsibility for monitoring an Option's implementation and performance. At the very least, the responsible party should keep track of the number of students who select an Option over time, assess student satisfaction with the educational experience their Option provides, and gather information on the placement and performance of graduates who complete the Option. Before converting an Option to a more traditional academic program, it is important to know how well the Option is performing. It is also important to assess the level of demand for the Option from students, employers, and post-graduate institutions.

- Communicate with key stakeholders concerning the nature, objectives, and status of Options. Ongoing communication is necessary for an Option to work effectively. Options represent a novel curricular approach. Stakeholders such as faculty members, administrators, and students must understand the purpose and goals of Options in order to give them serious consideration and make them priority concerns. All stakeholders need to know why Options are available. Students need to know how they can benefit from selecting an Option. Faculty need to know why supporting an Option can benefit both them and their students. Potential employers and graduate and professional schools also need to understand what an Option is and how completing an Option can enhance a student's education and career preparation. At minimum, Options must be clearly defined in catalogs, on academic program websites, and on material accompanying transcripts. Clear explanations of Options and their uses can help to legitimize this curricular device and encourage its adoption on a wider scale.

Conclusion

Table 2 summarizes where Options can fit into the curriculum development process by comparing Options to two standard curriculum change vehicles—new courses and new degree programs. As Table 2 demonstrates, Options offer a middle course through the complex, and often dangerous, curriculum change process. Options are more ambitious and integrated than the piecemeal addition of single new courses. Yet Options are less risky and less resource driven than major new initiatives like new majors and new degree programs. Due to their more cautious and experimental approach to educational program development, Options can foster creative responses to changing educational

TABLE 2
The Option as a Vehicle for Change

New single course	New "Option"	New degree program
Minimal change	Coherent but cautious change	Major change
Requires additional resources (e.g., faculty time, expertise)	Requires modest new resources (faculty time, expertise; money)	Requires a great deal of resources (faculty resources; money)
Not explicitly linked/integrated with other aspects of curriculum/program	Draws upon and integrates existing courses, other learning opportunities	May stand alone or be well integrated with other programs
Easy to institute but course tends to be tied to/dependent on the instructor	Experimental; easy to implement and abolish	Hard to implement
	Little resistance to change; does not threaten existing programs	May threaten established programs; hence, difficult to garner support
	Tests viability of larger changes/reforms, new majors/programs	

needs without generating substantial resistance from stakeholders and programs that feel threatened by major new program initiatives that require extensive resource investments. In some cases, Options may represent an alternative to major curriculum change while still responding to a defined educational need. In other cases, Options may represent an experimental step on the path to a major new program housed in its own department or cross-disciplinary unit.

Many powerful forces require higher education institutions to re-think their missions and how they can best serve society. Business as usual is no longer a viable option. As colleges and universities search for effective strategies to make their educational programs more flexible and responsive, the Option is a curricular tool they can employ judiciously. This device is helping Michigan State University to cope creatively in a turbulent educational environment where major new academic program investments are costly, contentious, and often risky. Other higher education institutions can also benefit by experimenting with the Option option.

Notes

1. Other labels for this curriculum technique/vehicle are also appropriate provided they are meaningful and useful in the disciplinary and institutional context where they are employed.
2. We capitalize the word Option whenever it refers to the specific curricular approach we are discussing. When option is not capitalized, we are using it in the more conventional way.
3. To be "transcriptable" is the terminology used at Michigan State.

References

Association of American Colleges, Project on liberal learning, study-in-depth, and the arts and sciences major (1991). *The challenge of connecting learning*. Washington, DC: Association of American Colleges.

Barr, R. B., & Tagg, J. (1995). From teaching to learning: A new paradigm for undergraduate education. *Change*, 27(6), 12–25.

Boyer, E. L. (1987). *College: The undergraduate experience in America*. Princeton, NJ: Carnegie Foundation for the Advancement of Teaching.

Cohen, A. M. (1998). *The shaping of American higher education: Emergence and growth of the contemporary system*. San Francisco, CA: Jossey-Bass.

Gaff, J. G., & Ratcliff, J. L. (1996). *Handbook of the undergraduate curriculum: A comprehensive guide to purposes, structures, practices, and change*. San Francisco, CA: Jossey-Bass.

Guskin, A. E. (1997). Restructuring to enhance student learning (and reduce costs). *Liberal Education*, *83*(2), 10–19.

Levine, A. (1978). *Handbook on undergraduate curriculum*. San Francisco, CA: Jossey-Bass.

Levine, A. (1989). Undergraduate curriculum 2000. In C. H. Pazandak (Vol. Ed.), *Improving undergraduate education in large universities* (pp. 77–84). *New Directions for Higher Education, Vol. 66*. San Francisco, CA: Jossey-Bass.

Levine, A. (1990). Curriculi-Curricula. *Change*, *22*(2), 46–51.

Levine, A. (2001). The remaking of the American university. *Innovative Higher Education*, *25*, 253–267.

Marcy, M., & Guskin, A. (2003). Project on the future of higher education: Teaching and learning in a climate of restricted resources. *Liberal Education*, *89*(2), 22–29.

Registrar's Office. (2002). *Academic program terminology*. East Lansing, MI: Michigan State University.

Stark, J. S., & Lattuca, L. R. (1997). *Shaping the college curriculum: Academic plans in action*. Needham Heights, MA: Allyn and Bacon.

Wingspread Group on Higher Education. (1993). *An American Imperative: Higher expectations for higher education*. Racine, WI: The Johnson Foundation and others.

Wulf, W. A., & Fisher, G. M. C. (2002). A makeover for engineering education. *Issues in Science and Technology*, *18*(3), 35–39.

Zemsky, R., & Massy, W. F. (1995). Toward an understanding of our current predicaments: Expanding perimeters, melting cores, and sticky functions. *Change*, *27*(6), 40–49.

Acknowledgement

This article is based upon work supported by the National Science Foundation under Grant No. 0230058.

"Comprehensive" Curricular Reform: Providing Students with a Map of the Scholarly Enterprise

Rick Szostak

Introduction

The Association of American Colleges and Universities has published a series of discussion papers under the rubric, "The Academy in Transition." The series is motivated by a desire to take stock of and guide the variety of curricular reform initiatives underway at North American universities. In the first two papers in the series Schneider & Schoenberg, 1999; Gaff, 1999), interdisciplinarity is listed as one of a handful of key characteristics of reform initiatives. The third paper in the series (Klein, 1999), is devoted to 'mapping' interdisciplinary curricular reforms. Various rationales for the renewed emphasis on interdisciplinarity are given in these papers. Both scholarly research and social problems increasingly require an interdisciplinary focus. Interdisciplinary courses can better prepare students for lifelong learning, especially as the problems they face in life will generally be interdisciplinary in nature.

Students, however, have difficulty drawing connections across courses from different disciplines. In response, faculty have a tendency to rethink distributional requirements in terms of perspectives rather than content, and thus desire students to integrate across these perspectives. Gaff (1999), for example, speaks of integrated alternatives to traditional distribution models. It is hardly surprising, given the discussions around interdisciplinarity, that a recent AAC&U survey of 479 administrators found that interdisciplinary courses were a part of a majority of general education programs (Ratcliff et al., 2001).

There is also an increased emphasis on skill acquisition by students, and a feeling that interdisciplinary coursework can aid with this acquisition. More broadly, there is a growing dissatisfaction with an inherited ideal of disciplines as self-contained bodies of knowledge:

> The point to be made here is that the rhetoric and curricular organization associated with inherited concepts of 'the discipline' invite students to think of themselves as pursuing a specific and well-defined competence when the entire ethos of the contemporary world calls for the capacity to cross boundaries, explore connections, move in uncharted directions. (Schneider & Schoenberg, 1999, p. 14)

We shall see that a 'comprehensive' curriculum can chart much of the uncharted.

Defining Interdisciplinarity

But what is interdisciplinarity? Salter and Hearn (1996) identify several types of interdisciplinarity, while Klein (1996) supplies numerous definitions. These definitions have all been developed

Reprinted from the *Journal of General Education* 52, no. 1 (2003), by permission of Pennsylvania State University Press.

inductively from observation of what some interdisciplinarians do. Yet observations of scholars performing different types of interdisciplinarity can too easily yield differing and unnecessarily limiting definitions. Salter and Hearn (1996, p. 174), indeed, bemoan the fact that most or all definitions of interdisciplinarity apply only to a subset of interdisciplinary activities. Interdisciplinarity, however, must start from a feeling that we need something more than disciplinary research and teaching. "An understanding of disciplines sets the context for an appreciation of interdisciplinarity" (Salter & Hearn, 1996, p. 124). We can, then, develop a superior definition of interdisciplinarity by asking about the nature of disciplines, and in what precise ways they might limit scholarly understanding.

Klein (1990) and Salter and Hearn (1996), have specified several characteristics of disciplines. That is, a particular "community of scholars" can be identified at a particular point in time in terms of these characteristics, though characteristics may change as a discipline evolves, and there will always be some in the discipline who operate outside of these characteristics.[1] These characteristics can be grouped under five headings:

a. A set of phenomena to be studied. Every discipline takes a certain subject matter to be its own. Sometimes, this subject area is defined narrowly in terms of a handful of phenomena, and other times more broadly, as for example in anthropology, the study of humanity. Even when the discipline is defined broadly, there will be certain subjects that are favored and receive considerable attention.

b. A set of (evolving) theories. Every discipline at any point in time will have a set of theories that are widely accepted. The bulk of research will be devoted to extending these or examining various implications of them. These theories in many cases are combined in an overarching paradigm (sometimes with related methods), which may guide research in the discipline for decades.[2]

c. A set of preferred method(s). Many disciplines countenance only one method of inquiry. Some disciplines are open to two or three distinct methods, but none display openness to all of the methods employed by scholars that are enumerated below. Alternatively, some disciplines not only favor a particular method, but have strong preferences for narrowly defined 'tools' or 'procedures' (see Salter & Hearn, 1996).

d. A 'worldview.' While there is widespread agreement that disciplines can be identified by a distinctive worldview, there has been little consensus on the components of a disciplinary worldview. Confusion here must inevitably lead to confusion about the purpose and conduct of interdisciplinarity. Some components of worldview are identified below.

e. "Rules of the game." There is a structure of rewards within every discipline. Since these rewards are primarily structured around research, they will not be reprised here in detail.

Integrating Phenomena, Methods, and Theory

A definition of interdisciplinarity should encompass an attitude toward each of these five disciplinary characteristics. However, the first three are arguably of central importance, and thus a core definition of interdisciplinarity can be derived that focuses on these characteristics. This core definition of interdisciplinarity reflects the fact that every discipline privileges a subset of the full body of theories, methods, and subject matter (phenomena):

> Definition of interdisciplinarity: *Openness* to the application of *all* theories and *all* methods to *any* set of phenomena.[3]

Disciplinarity, in contrast, would be defined as: the application of a subset of theories and methods to a constrained set of phenomena of interest.

A person qualifies as interdisciplinary by being open to diverse theories, methods, and subjects of study, but may at times find themselves engaged in teaching or research that does fit comfortably within a particular discipline. The word 'openness' in the definition serves an important purpose;

otherwise, one would cease being an interdisciplinarian at every moment when one undertook a disciplinary analysis. Klein (1990) asks if one can be both disciplinary and interdisciplinary; if these are defined in terms of attitude, the answer is 'no.'

Nevertheless, a piece of teaching or research qualifies as interdisciplinary only if it involves utilizing theories *and/or* methods *and/or* studying phenomena which are the province of more than one discipline (at the time it was produced). An interdisciplinarian may present a lecture that is disciplinary. A disciplinarian could not present an interdisciplinary lecture, for to do so would require some openness to theories, methods, and/or phenomena from other disciplines.

Note that this definition does not require an *a priori* judgment of the role of disciplines, as many inductive definitions do. Some interdisciplinarians see disciplinary teaching and research as a useful complement to, or base for, interdisciplinary teaching and research, while others see interdisciplinarity as a substitute for disciplinarity; each could accept this definition. The definition does, however, guide us to ask: can we gain a full and complete understanding of complex issues if we constrain our analysis to the theories, methods, and phenomena encompassed by any one discipline?[4]

Miller (1999) notes that interdisciplinarians often talk about 'integration' without defining what and how to integrate. This lack of definition leaves interdisciplinarity open to charges of "serious conceptual confusion." The definition of interdisciplinarity above speaks more directly to 'what' than 'how' scholars should integrate, but nevertheless provides an answer to the problem raised by Miller.

- Interdisciplinarians integrate theories by comparing and contrasting and/or combining theories from more than one discipline and/or
- Interdisciplinarians integrate methods by combining methods from more than one discipline and/or
- Interdisciplinarians integrate phenomena by examining the linkages between phenomena considered the province of different disciplines

The definition thus also provides an answer to the vexed question of whether interdisciplinarity and integration are the same thing.

Integrating Worldview/Ethics

While it is relatively straightforward to define interdisciplinarity with respect to phenomena, theories, and methods, it is much more difficult to understand what integration of disciplinary worldviews should look like. This reflects the simple fact that worldview itself is much harder to define. Of the five characteristics of disciplines identified above, worldview is by far the most ambiguous. As such, it has likely played a disproportionate role in the fuzziness about the meaning of integration of which Miller (1999) complained.

Much of what is meant by worldview both reflects and is reflected in the three characteristics of disciplines already discussed. While integrating theories, methods, and phenomena, then, interdisciplinarians should discuss how these reflect and are reflected in disciplinary worldviews. For example, the worldview of economists is operationalized in theoretical preferences (rational individuals, markets that generally work), methodological preferences (which exclude hard-to-qualify complexities of individuals and societies), and limits to subject matter (so that social norms, for example, are excluded); pressure to operate within acceptable disciplinary guidelines in turn encourages economists to adopt this worldview. Moreover, one component of worldview is a discipline's openness to ideas from other disciplines, reflecting in large part the degree to which it sees its theories and methods as superior.

Interdisciplinary scholarship has increasingly emphasized the integration of worldview, precisely because of a recognition that disciplines do not choose theories, methods, and subject matter randomly, but that these tend to be mutually supportive: the favored method analyses the phenomena deemed important by the favored theory. Disciplines may use a particular theory or method in a particular way in order to fit this within the disciplinary worldview.

As noted above, there is little scholarly consensus on the other components of worldview. Reference is often made, though, to common differences in philosophical outlook across disciplines. If scholars differ in what they think should be the goals of human societies, and/or on the criteria by which to determine whether a particular outcome or act is 'good' or 'better,' then they will be driven both to ask different questions and reach different conclusions. This will occur even when they believe that they are performing pure scholarship uncontaminated by philosophical concerns. Note also that judging acts in terms of their consequences is conducive to the use of quantitative methods, while concern with, say, justice or virtues, likely encourages qualitative analysis.

An example that demonstrates differences in worldview may be useful. Economists tend for the most part to be supportive of free trade initiatives, while political scientists tend to be much more suspicious. How might we attempt to explain this difference in (the expression of) worldview? We could first observe that the theories used by economists point to advantages of increased market size. The preferred methods guide them to look only at that which can be quantified. Economists look at only the effect on economic variables. The theories and methods used by political scientists suggest that abuse of power, unforeseen consequences, and special interests are integral parts of most/all political negotiations. Political scientists are likely to focus on implications for national sovereignty. Typically, the two groups use different philosophical standards: political scientists stress consequences for autonomy rather than incomes, value traditions more highly, stress virtues of self-reliance rather than innovation, and emphasize collective over individual rights—at least relative to the average economist. Finally, some scholars would include statistical differences in participation by discipline as a component of worldview; in this respect it might be noteworthy that economists are more conservative than political scientists and thus more confident of the beneficial impact of market exchange, though we must be wary of stereotyping.

While further exploration of elements of worldview is desirable, the existence of differing philosophical perspectives is of great importance, and should thus be reflected in both our definition of interdisciplinarity and curricula. Moreover, while there are innumerable ethical perspectives, there are only five broad (and complementary) types of these, grounded respectively in consequences, virtues, deontology (rules), traditions, and intuition (we will return to this in more detail below). The core definition of interdisciplinarity can thus be supplemented:

- Interdisciplinarians are open to applications of each of the five types of ethical perspective.

Integration and Rules of the Game

What, finally, should integration mean with respect to rules of the game—the fifth characteristic of disciplines? Stanley Fish (1998) has worried that any scholarly enterprise inevitably develops a set of rules, and thus interdisciplinarity, if successful, would itself serve to constrain scholarly effort. But arguably scholars can and should strive for 'rules of the game' that serve exclusively to distinguish good from bad research. The rules should embrace respect and open-mindedness, and an ideal of a shared pursuit of understanding. Publications should be evaluated solely in terms of whether they enhance our understanding, weighted by the importance of the question addressed, not by their adherence to any disciplinary standards. Scholars should be encouraged to pursue their curiosity, and both theory and empirics should be valued. Such rules of the game are necessary if integration is not to be arbitrarily constrained.

While integration of phenomena, theories, methods, and philosophical perspectives was urged above, with respect to 'rules of the game' the wholesale replacement of disciplinary rules that serve to artificially constrain scholarly effort is implied. Scholars should embrace common 'rules of the game' that can be justified in terms of sound philosophical principles. The definition of interdisciplinarity can, therefore, be further supplemented:

- Interdisciplinarians believe that research should be evaluated solely in terms of whether it contributes to our collective understanding.[5]

At this point, an academic example of the application of this definition of interdisciplinarity may be helpful. A disciplinary approach to the study of economic growth would be constrained to look only at economic phenomena, apply economic theory (including the development of new versions of that theory), use mathematical/statistical techniques, and judge the goodness of policies consequentially. An interdisciplinary approach would be open to cultural and political influences, non-quantitative techniques, theories from other disciplines, and evaluation of acts and outcomes in terms of virtues, rules, traditions, or institutions. Such an approach ignores the 'rules of the game' of the discipline of economics. An interdisciplinary analysis can provide us with important insights that will be neglected by a disciplinary analysis. Accordingly, interdisciplinary researchers should strive to familiarize themselves with a wide range of theory, method, and phenomena. Interdisciplinary education should likewise take as one of its goals the exposure of students to the widest possible range of theory, method, phenomena, and philosophical perspectives.

Nature and Feasibility of "Comprehensive" Curricular Reform

The first step in any integrative endeavor must involve the identification of the phenomena, theories, methods, and philosophical perspectives relevant to a particular topic or question. Only then can theories, methods, and perspectives be compared and contrasted, and integrated—generally after being amended—into a more complete and complex understanding. A useful way to facilitate this first step, whether by students or scholars, is to provide a comprehensive overview of the full range of phenomena, theories, methods, and perspectives. Such comprehensive material has further advantages; in particular, it allows students to place all of their coursework within a comprehensive map of the scholarly enterprise. This in turn provides a powerful antidote to the tendency, bemoaned by Graff (1992), for students to compartmentalize their knowledge by course, and thus fail to recognize when different instructors reach opposing conclusions about the same subject.

Phenomena

How could we possibly give students a comprehensive overview of the diverse subject matter of interest to scholars? Surely the list of relevant phenomena would be unmanageably large? In fact, it is quite feasible to give students a useful *and detailed* overview. The enterprise is manageable because the phenomena of interest to scholars can be organized hierarchically: broad categories of phenomena can be disaggregated (or 'unpacked', to use the terminology of realist philosophers) into sets of phenomena of interest, and these further disaggregated. Each phenomenon has only one place in this hierarchical structure. Students can thus master the broad outlines of this structure, and then readily locate where any particular phenomenon fits within it. Parsons (1966), Brady (1989), and Barber (1993) have pursued the goal of developing a list of phenomena, and each recognized the advantages, feasibility, and necessity of doing so hierarchically, though none of them proceeded much beyond identifying a set of very broad categories.

For the purpose of this paper, a disaggregation of one of ten categories ("culture") within human science research is provided. (See Szostak (2000) and Szostak (2003) for a complete scheme of the hierarchical list of phenomena of interest to human scientists.)[6] While the phenomena labeled third-level—a nomenclature which indicates merely their place in the schema, not any estimate of their importance—in Table 1 can often be disaggregated further into hundreds on thousands of other phenomena, the Table nevertheless illustrates the point that there is a manageably small number of second and third level phenomena. Students can readily see where phenomena of interest 'fit,' and they are easily exposed to the full range of phenomena of interest. The list of phenomena provides a structure for organizing the analysis of a complex issue or subject, without restricting theoretical or methodological flexibility (see Szostak 2000a, 2001, 2001a, 2003).

TABLE 1
The List of Cultural Phenomena

Second level Phenomena	Third Level Phenomena
Languages	By descent
Religions	Providence, revelation, salvation, miracles, doctrine
Stories	Myths, fairy tales, legends, family sagas, fables, jokes and riddles
Expressions of culture	Rituals, dance, song, cuisine, attire, ornamentation of buildings, games
Values (Goals:)	Ambition, optimism, attitudes toward wealth, power, prestige, beauty, honor, recognition, love, friendship, sex, incest, marriage, time preference, physical and psychological wellbeing
(Means:)	Honesty, ethics, righteousness, fate?, work valued intrinsically, violence, vengeance, curiosity, innovation, nature
(Community:)	Identity, family vs. community, openness to outsiders, trust, egalitarianism, attitude to young and old, responsibility, respect for individuals, authoritarianism
(Everyday Norms:)	Courtesy, manners, proxemics, tidiness, cleanliness, punctuality, conversational rules, locomotion rules, tipping

Theory

Given that new theories are developed every day, a comprehensive survey of theory cannot be performed as with phenomena. Students can, however, be exposed to a comprehensive typology of theory, so that they will at least understand what types of theories are possible. A comprehensive typology of theory types could rely on asking the *Who, What, Why, Where,* and *When* questions of each theory (Szostak, 2003a) and can be briefly summarized as follows:

Who is the agent(s) within the theory? We can first distinguish agents in terms of whether they can exhibit intentionality or not, and within these two types distinguish individuals, groups, and relationships.

What does the agent do? There are three broad answers, which map imperfectly onto the six types of agency: passive action, active action, and changes in attitude.

Why does the agent do this? With non-intentional agents, only their inherent nature can be investigated. With intentional agents, five distinct types of decision-making can be explored: rational, intuitive, process (virtue) oriented, rule-based, and tradition-based. For groups and relationships, we can also ask how individual preferences are aggregated.

Where does the causal process occur? The concern here is with the generalizability of the theory on a continuum between nomothetic (very generalizable) and idiographic theory.

When does the causal process occur? There are four broad time paths that a causal process might follow: return to the original equilibrium, movement to a new equilibrium, change in a particular direction, or stochastic/uncertain.

Since complex social problems involve multiple types of agency, decision-making, and so on, the typology illustrates that any one theory will give us incomplete guidance. Familiarity with the typology encourages recognition of the weaknesses of a particular theory, and identification of other theories with compensating strengths. For example, rational choice theory focuses on individuals, actions, rational decision-making, and equilibrium outcomes within a nomothetic orientation; if groups, attitudes, non-rational decision-making, or non-equilibrium outcomes are deemed important for a particular question, other theories should be considered. Placing existing theories within the typology highlights the fact that many human science theories are ambiguous about their answers to some questions. Action theory, for example, gives firm answers to 'Who?' and 'What?', but action theorists debate 'Where?' while systems theory answers 'Where?' but not 'Who?' This highlights a weakness in these theories and also helps us to appreciate the key differences across and within theories.

Many scholars, especially self-styled positivists, have long emphasized the study of only actions, in large part because, being observable, it was felt that these could be studied objectively. Other scholars, often termed interpretivists, have in turn urged an exclusive focus on attitudes, arguing that we could only make sense of people's behavior by comprehending the meaning they attached to their circumstances. Potter (2000) reprises both arguments and urges a compromise in which scholars are open to both. He notes in particular that scholarship can never be perfectly objective, no matter what its subject. Our students deserve some acquaintance with both positivist and interpretivist perspectives, and the possibility of compromise.

Methods

If our students are to be provided with a comprehensive overview of the methods employed by scholars, these methods must first be identified. I am aware of no comprehensive list in the literature. There are several books that detail the methods in social science, including Nachmias and Frankfort-Nachmias (1996), Hartman and Hedblom (1988), and Ellis (1994). The methods used in the natural sciences are a subset of those used in social science. Sadly, the methods of the humanities are rarely juxtaposed with those of the social sciences, and social science authors are generally dismissive of the 'ways of knowing' common in the humanities. Some attention is given to qualitative analysis, but the preponderant focus in these books is quantitative. Statistical analysis is generally treated at great length, and other methods treated in an article or part thereof. Classification, mapmaking, and textual analysis receive scant attention. The focus is on how to use the methods, though some attention is paid to the drawbacks of each method. A more explicitly comparative approach that identifies the pros and cons of each method is warranted.

It is nevertheless possible to derive a list of methods inductively, by reading across a wide range of disciplines. Inevitably, it is possible that some methods will be missed or that methods that deserve separate treatment have been grouped together. Even so, the primary result of these efforts is robust: *the number of distinct methods used by scholars is manageably small.*

Broadly speaking, some twelve distinct methods are employed by scholars, often in combination:

- experiments (including natural or quasi-experiments)
- surveys
- interviews
- mathematical models (and simulations)
- statistical analysis (often, but far from always, associated with models) including secondary data analysis
- ethnographic/observational analysis (some would distinguish 'interactional' analysis in which the investigator interacts with those under observation)
- experience/intuition (some would treat this method as an important subset of observational analysis, since we are in effect 'observing' ourselves here)
- textual (content, discourse) analysis
- classification (including evolutionary analysis)
- mapmaking
- hermeneutics/semiotics (the study of symbols and their meaning)
- physical traces (as in archaeology)
- some would treat 'evaluation' (say, of programs) as distinct, though it can be seen as a combination of some of the above methods. Similar arguments can be made with respect to 'demography' and perhaps also hermeneutics.

Mastering any of these methods takes time, and most scholars or students could hardly be expected to be adept at more than a couple. Since people are exposed in their lives to applications of each, however, they should be acquainted with their pros and cons, the biases that can creep into results of inquiries utilizing each method, and the guidelines that might be used to evaluate the quality of a particular piece of research (Szostak, 2003c). For example, experiments are particularly useful with non-intentional agents, but with intentional agents we must worry that these agents will act differently in an experimental set-up. Interviews, alternatively, are at best indirectly useful in the study of non-intentional agents. Statistical techniques—at least those most commonly used—tend to assume some sort of equilibrium outcome. Particular methods are *biased* toward justifying particular types of theory, in this case those which posit equilibrium outcomes. Likewise, methods focused on attitudes, such as interviews, are more likely to justify interpretivist theories, while those emphasizing actions, like secondary data analysis, are most likely to justify positivist theories. And, as Ragin (2000) notes, various types of case study research are most likely to support idiographic theory while statistical analysis favors nomothetic. In discussing such biases our students are inevitably exposed to the important principle that they should always seek evidence from more than one method.

A method's inductive potential can also be queried: is it likely to alert the researcher to relevant phenomena not included in their theory? Some methods, like mathematical modelling, are inherently closed to influences not in the original theory. Others, like participant observation, are quite likely to alert researchers to hitherto unappreciated influences. Our students should be acquainted with the mutually supportive roles of induction and deduction in scholarly research. This, of course, provides yet another justification for methodological flexibility.

Ethical Perspectives (Worldview)

It was argued above that the most important element of worldview not captured in disciplinary preferences is the philosophical perspectives of scholars. How should students be introduced to the diverse ethical perspectives that guide not just scholars but all individuals? A dominant 'philosophical outlook' might be identified by discipline. Political theories can be categorized as: conservatives emphasizing tradition, classical liberals deontology, and socialists consequences (Szostak, 2003b). The possibility that disciplines can be to some extent similarly categorized should not be dismissed. For example, anthropologists like tradition, and economists favor consequentialism. Given the inherent difficulty of this task, and the diversity within disciplines, it seems much better to expose students to a comprehensive philosophical survey, similar to our comprehensive surveys of theory, method, and subject. Students then discern which philosophical perspective may be driving a particular research agenda, and also when scholarly disagreement reflects philosophical differences.

While there are innumerable ethical perspectives, there are only five broad (and complementary) types, grounded respectively in consequences, virtues, deontology (rules), traditions, and intuition. These reflect the five types of decision-making processes identified above. All philosophical speculation on the goals of human societies or individuals, and the means to achieve these, can be placed in one of these categories—except perhaps the eclectic approach of existentialism which urges us to each find our own path (Szostak, 2003b).

One point to be emphasized in an ethical survey is that each type of ethical perspective can be and has been justified in terms of the others. Advocates of a rights-based approach, for example, appeal variously to our intuition (we have an inherent distaste of murder), tradition (almost all societies have rules against murder), consequences (people will feel happier and safer, and be more productive, in a society that respects rights), and virtues (it is not virtuous to violate the freedom of another) (Almond, 1998). While the five types of ethical perspective are still largely independent, they can thus be seen as essentially complementary. Moreover this complementarity is a powerful justification for not relying exclusively on any one ethical approach. By exposing students to this argument we encourage the personal development and self-esteem that come from developing one's own balanced philosophical perspective.

Implementing "Comprehensive" Curricular Reform

The "comprehensive" material can be integrated readily into existing curricula. While human scientists care about hundreds of phenomena, these can be organized into a manageable table. This may seem overwhelming at first, but can easily be mastered during a college education. The list of methods used by scholars is even less difficult; we can reasonably hope to acquaint students with the major advantages and disadvantages of each. Likewise, it is certainly quite feasible to discuss each of the five broad ways in which ethical evaluation can proceed. The typology of theory may be the most difficult element in this package, but since each of the five broad dimensions of the typology yields a handful of possibilities, it too is certainly manageable in scope. Resources have been cited that could be used in developing each facet of comprehensive curricular reform.

Elements of the "comprehensive" curriculum might be integrated into existing introductory courses, or new courses might be created. A 'methods' course that compared different methods could be invaluable, though methods are best appreciated when applied to something. An introductory course structured around diverse causal links among the list of phenomena could help students choose the area in which they wished to concentrate, as well as provide a base from which to integrate later material. An ethical survey course might be especially valuable, given the limited philosophical content of most other courses. Such a course would provide students with some valuable guidelines on how to live their lives, while also preparing them to appreciate the ethical issues relevant to their other courses. Courses could also be structured around a typology of theory. In all cases, though, it is critical that the "comprehensive" material not be isolated in any one course, but rather reinforced throughout the curriculum.

Gaff (1999) argues that all programs of curricular reform should have an assessment component. While there is no one ideal method of assessment, experts in the area often advocate methods that can be employed in-class during a student's final year. If we take as a primary goal of our curriculum the exposure of students to "comprehensive" material, it would be relatively straight forward to test their mastery of the material during their final year, in part because it is hoped that all students acquire the same "comprehensive" body of knowledge. Moreover, the very exposition of the comprehensive material in this paper allows program administrators to readily gauge the breadth of coverage of existing or proposed programs.

Consequences of "Comprehensive" Curricular Reform

Mapping Scholarship

As suggested, the "comprehensive" material not only facilitates interdisciplinary analysis but provides students with a map of the scholarly enterprise. Students at present find it very difficult to draw connections across material from different courses. This problem is most severe in institutions where general education involves taking courses from a variety of disciplines, but occurs even in interdisciplinary programs. Students are often left to figure out on their own how the course in political economy is connected to the course on sociology of art or the course on race and gender issues. The hierarchical list of phenomena gives them a cognitive map on which they can locate the subject matter of diverse courses. Even if links between particular subjects are not covered, they can see that such links exist. And a course or set of courses structured around the list of phenomena could guide students on how to explore such links on their own (see Szostak, 2003). Without recognition of what they have *not* studied, students may artificially constrain their lifelong learning. Moreover, they will fail to appreciate the links between different courses that rely on the same—or different— theories, methods, and ethical perspectives.

Graff (1992) worries that students compartmentalize knowledge, and thus do not even attempt to draw connections between courses. They may fail to appreciate that different instructors have reached different conclusions about the same issue. This, in conjunction with the common failure of individual instructors to 'teach the conflicts,' leaves students unaware of and ill-prepared to cope with scholarly disagreements. If students actually place new material within a broader map of the scholarly enterprise, they become more aware of conflicts. Moreover, their appreciation of the strengths and weaknesses of different theory types and methods helps them appreciate the source of these conflicts. Instructors in turn, especially if encouraged to be explicit about the phenomena, theories, methods, and philosophical perspectives being addressed, are encouraged to teach the conflicts.

Enhancing the Major

"Campus leaders must attend not merely to the coherence of the general education program but also to the interrelation of general education and the majors" (Gaff, 1999, p. 4). Exposure to the "comprehensive" material may help students choose their major. Students can identify topics, theories, methods, and/or philosophical perspectives that they wish to pursue in greater detail. Moreover, if general education courses provided an introduction to the various sorts of comprehensive material outlined above, then courses in the major thereafter can continually reference what theory type, method, phenomena, and ethical approach are being discussed. Such a practice makes both instructors and students more aware of potential limitations and biases, while permitting students to place their major in a wider perspective. Thus, "comprehensive" material can be introduced without requiring any diminution in attention devoted to the major, can help students find the right major for them, and can enhance teaching within the major.

One further advantage of the "comprehensive" curriculum is that it enhances the ability of a student to choose a problem-oriented rather than discipline-determined area of specialization. While a handful of small curricular changes have been entertained above, further changes can result in upper-level coursework explicitly focused on particular linkages among specified sets of phenomena, rather than being constrained by disciplinary boundaries. Degree programs themselves could be organized more readily around interdisciplinary problems. A student interested in inner city poverty, for example, might struggle to stitch together the appropriate courses from several disciplines, whereas a question-driven curriculum would facilitate such a task.

Educating for Citizenship

One goal of a liberal education is to prepare students for democratic citizenship, including learning how to evaluate public policy issues. The "comprehensive" curriculum outlined here, aided perhaps by a capstone course or seminar with a policy focus, supports this goal in many ways. According to Vaughn and Buss (1998), errors in policy analysis come from three main sources: failure to properly specify goals; reliance on faulty scientific analysis of means; and, perhaps most commonly, failure to appreciate potential side effects of a proposed policy. These errors in turn reflect inadequate philosophical analysis, reliance on a limited set of theories and methods, and failure to contemplate a variety of causal linkages. Exposure to "comprehensive" material would help to prevent these errors.

In addition, exposure to the five ethical perspectives encourages students to appreciate the diverse philosophical bases on which opposing policy views (and political ideologies) may rest. This exposure guides them to respect the views of others and also guides them to seek consensus where possible. Policies that accord with all five types of ethical perspective should be preferred. Just as scientific theories should be tested by diverse methods, an ethical statement that can be justified (albeit imperfectly; no ethical argument is impervious to attack) in terms of all five types of ethical argument, is one that we should place great confidence in. Since the five types of ethical argument are found across the world's philosophical traditions, such statements may apply across diverse societies. And by applying all five types of ethical perspective to the phenomena of interest to human scientists we can identify a broad 'ethical core' of such statements. Some half of the 150 statements analyzed in Szostak (2002) belonged in the 'ethical core'; our collective tendency to focus on controversial issues diverts us from a realization of the extent of philosophical consensus. Students thus gain an answer to the ethical challenge of our times: how to respect the views of others while still believing that some behaviors are unethical.

Exposure to a comprehensive list of phenomena would guide students to appreciate the complexity of human society, and thus the diverse effects that any policy initiative may have. They may resist being seduced by oversimplification, while not abandoning hope that they and others can evaluate alternatives. Too often, expert policy advice ignores the links with which the expert is unfamiliar; citizens should be aware of this tendency. Finally, recognition of the true complexity of human societies should encourage us all to seek out the views of people with diverse perspectives. Fish (1998) has argued that reform of the academy can and should directly inform attempts to reform the wider world. A curriculum that embraces complexity through comprehensiveness enhances both our ability and will to cope with the complexity of our times.

Responding to Recent Critiques of the Liberal Arts

The "comprehensive" material allows much more powerful responses to many modern critiques of the Liberal Arts. Gaff (1991) noted an unfortunate ideological element in curricular debates. Those on the 'right,' who bemoan the lack of a 'core of knowledge,' can be told that there is a core: a comprehensive overview of theory, methods, phenomena, and philosophical perspectives that we should provide to all students. This core, unlike alternative 'cores of knowledge,' such as a focus on Western Civilization, does not privilege any one societal perspective. Gaff (1991) notes that proponents of core programs are often driven by a fear that college curricula are no longer coherent, and that there is no obvious way to achieve the goal of coherence without losing the benefits of specialization. The comprehensive curriculum allows us to provide a core that serves to place specializations in context, helps students to choose their area of specialization, and shows students how to learn outside of that area. At present, students are often not told what the Liberal Arts is about; the comprehensive core greatly facilitates that task as well.

Those on the 'left' urge a greater focus on issues of diversity. Scholars of diversity increasingly appreciate that one or two isolated required courses do not teach students that diversity is important to their individual concerns. Unless the subject matter is directly related to their area of specialization, students too easily view learning about diversity as a requirement to be forgotten as soon as possible. The list of phenomena includes a category of social divisions by race, gender, class, and family type, and thus a "comprehensive" curriculum must inevitably acquaint students with the fact that such divisions are causally related to all other phenomena. Cornwell and Stoddard (1999), notably, urge both the study of causal links and the unpacking of culture as a category. Moreover, exposure to the full range of theory, method, and ethical perspectives is a powerful antidote to narrowmindedness. An ethical survey course, in particular, develops an appreciation of the validity of alternative viewpoints. Recall that each of the five types of ethical argument can be found across a wide range of philosophical traditions.

Concluding Remarks

A deductively derived definition of interdisciplinarity guides us to focus on integrating across phenomena, theories, methods, and worldviews while recognizing the interrelationships among these. Interdisciplinary analysis can only occur if we first identify relevant phenomena, theories, methods, and worldviews. An overview of "comprehensive" material will greatly aid students in the process of integration, both while in college and thereafter. The comprehensive material also provides a map of the scholarly enterprise, so that students can relate different courses and topics to each other and no longer compartmentalize knowledge. Identifying the strengths and weaknesses of particular theories and methods allows students to be better judges of expert arguments. Each element of the "comprehensive" curriculum better prepares students for democratic citizenship. Finally, the comprehensive material will allow educators to better respond to diverse modern criticisms of a Liberal Education.

Author Note

I thank participants at conferences of the Association for General and Liberal Studies, Association for Integrative Studies, and Association of American Colleges and Universities, for much advice and encouragement. I thank Bill Newell for inspiring me to think about a definition of interdisciplinarity, and Marion Brady for pointing me toward the advantages of asking the Who, What, Where, When, and Why questions. I thank Elizabeth A Jones for encouraging me to write this paper. Last but far from least, I owe a great debt of gratitude to Marilyn Amey and anonymous referees for many helpful suggestions.

Notes

1. The definition of interdisciplinarity will be derived deductively rather than inductively. Nevertheless, it should be clear that the characteristics of disciplines from which it is derived were themselves derived inductively. Of course, some elements of induction can be discerned in (virtually?) any deductive endeavor. We are better off grounding our definition in an observation of what disciplines cannot do than in an observation of how diverse scholars have responded to what they perceive as the limitations of disciplines.

2. Some still hope that disciplines, at least in human science, can be unified by some grand theory. They thus define interdisciplinary as the search for such a grand theory. I share with others the view that past failures to develop all-encompassing grand theories have dimmed the attraction of interdisciplinarity (Parsons, 1966, Barber, 1993). All existing, and I suspect all future, grand theories will inevitably do a better job of illuminating causal linkages among some subset of phenomena than among others. I thus advocate theoretical flexibility as a core attribute of interdisciplinarity.

3. This definition accords well with one of the earliest and most comprehensive inductive definitions of interdisciplinarity, developed by the Organization for Economic Cooperation and Development in 1970 (see Klein, 1990, p. 63). They too emphasized the integration of theory, method, and phenomena. They also spoke of integration of data, procedures, concepts, and epistemology. Note that data are proxies for phenomena, procedures a subset of methods, concepts a component of theories, and epistemology—an element of worldview.

4. One implication of complexity theory is that any complex system (such as human science) has emergent properties, and thus *cannot* be reduced to a system of subsystems (such as disciplines). See Newell (2001).

5. This definition may seem to exclude those who do not believe that we can enhance our understanding and/or those who stress style over substance. It could be rewritten so that, instead of urging a standard, it opposes disciplinary biases toward particular methods, theories, styles, etc. Arguably, though, those who outline (reasons for) limits to our understanding are themselves adding to our understanding. And if it is accepted that enhanced understanding is possible, style must be viewed as the servant of substance (though style will be more important in some endeavors than others).

6. There is, of course, a possibility that the scholarly enterprise as a whole, or my reading of it, will have missed some phenomena. With regard to the first, it is unlikely that scholars will have completely missed phenomena that people have recognized, or that humanity will have failed to recognize phenomena that exert an important influence on our lives. With respect to the second, I read very widely in pursuing this project, and would note that any phenomenon I might have missed could be added readily.

References

Almond, B. (1998). *Exploring Ethics: A Traveller's Tale*. Oxford: Blackwell.

Barber, B. (1993). *Constructing the Social System*. New Brunswick NJ: Transaction Publishers.

Brady, M. (1989). *What's Worth Teaching?: Selecting, Organizing, and Integrating Knowledge*. Albany: SUNY Press.

Cornwell, G., & Stoddard, E. (1999). *Globalizing Knowledge: Connecting International and Intercultural Studies*. Washington: Association of American Colleges and Universities.

Ellis, L. (1994). *Research Methods in the Social Sciences*. Madison WI: Brown and Benchmark.

Fish, S. (1998). Being Interdisciplinary Is So Very Hard to Do. William H. Newell (Ed.), *Interdisciplinarity: Essays From the Literature*. New York: College Board.

Gaff, J. G. (1991). *New Life for the College Curriculum*. San Francisco: Jossey-Bass.

Gaff, J. G. (1999). *General Education: The Changing Agenda*. Washington: Association of American Colleges and Universities.

Graff, G. (1992). *Beyond the Culture Wars: How Teaching the Conflicts Can Revitalize American Education*. New York: Norton.

Hartman, J., & Hedblom, J. (1988). *Methods for the Social Sciences*. Westport CT: Greenwood.

Klein, J. T. (1990). *Interdisciplinarity*. Detroit: Wayne State University Press.

Klein, J. T. (1996). *Crossing Boundaries: Knowledge, Disciplinarities, and Interdisciplinarities*. Charlottesville: University Press of Virginia.

Klein, J. T. (1999). *Mapping Interdisciplinary Studies*. Washington: Association of American Colleges and Universities.

Miller, R. C. (1999). Review of the AAC&U 'Academy in Transition' Series. *Newsletter of the Association For Integrative Studies*, Fall.

Nachmias, D., & Frankfort-Nachmias, C. (1996). *Research Methods in the Social Sciences* (5th ed.). New York: St.Martin's.

Newell, W. H. (2001). A Theory of Interdisciplinary Studies. *Issues in Integrative Studies*, 1–26.

Parsons, T. (1966). *Societies: Evolutionary and Comparative Perspectives*. Englewood Cliffs NJ: Prentice-Hall Publishers.

Potter, G. (2000). *The Philosophy of Social Science*. Harlow UK: Prentice-Hall.

Ragin, C. F. (2000). *Fuzzy-Set Social Science*. Chicago: University of Chicago Press.

Ratcliff, J., Johnson, D. K., LaNasa, S. M., & Gaff, J. L. (2001). *The Status of General Education in the Year 2000: Summary of a National Survey*. Washington DC: Association of American Colleges and Universities.

Salter, L., & Hearn, A. (1996). *Outside the Lines: Issues in Interdisciplinary Research*. Montreal: McGill-Queen's University Press.

Schneider, C. G., & Schoenberg, R. (1999). *Contemporary Understandings of Liberal Education*. Washington: Association of American Colleges and Universities.

Szostak, R. (2000) Toward a Unified Human Science. *Issues in Integrative Studies*. 115–57.

Szostak, R. (2000a) Unifying Human Science Schematically: The Case of Art. *NSSA Perspectives Journal, 17:1*, 139–51.

Szostak, R. (2001). Putting Social Structure in Its Place. *Issues in Integrative Studies*. 171–220.

Szostak, R. (2001a). *A Schema For Unifying Human Science: Application to Health and Population*. Electronic journal, American Association for Behavioral and Social Sciences. 22msp

Szostak, R. (2002). *Unifying Human Ethics*. Ms. under review.

Szostak, R. (2003). *A Schema For Unifying Human Science: Interdisciplinary Perspectives on Culture*. Selinsgrove PA: Susquehanna University Press.

Szostak, R. (2003a) Classifying Natural and Social Scientific Theories. *Current Sociology, 51:1*.

Szostak, R. (2003b) Politics and the Five Types of Ethical Theory. *International Journal of Politics and Ethics, 3:1*.

Szostak, R. (2003c) Classifying Scientific Theories and Methods. *Knowledge Organization*. Forthcoming.

Vaughn, R., & Buss, T. (1998). *Communicating Social Science Research to Policy Makers*. Thousand Oaks: Sage.

PEDAGOGICAL STRATEGIES FOR EDUCATING CITIZENS

A. COLBY, T. EHRLICH, E. BEAUMONT AND J. STEPHENS

ON THE GENERAL LEVEL the challenges of teaching for moral and civic development are the same as the challenges of any good teaching—to help students achieve deep understanding of difficult ideas, impart knowledge and skills they can really use, and reach them on an emotional level, exciting passion and fostering commitment. More particular challenges arise from the wide-ranging complexity of moral and civic development, its multiple dimensions, and the special dilemmas it presents.

The moral domain is full of ideas that are multilayered, subtle, and often confusing. Many of these ideas conflict with students' preconceptions, making them even harder to grasp. Students predictably find it very difficult to understand moral pluralism, for example, or the grounds for evaluating a moral claim. They often ask questions like these: If there is more than one valid moral framework, how can anyone claim that some principles and values are morally preferable to others? How can I be tolerant of others yet question their moral beliefs? How can a moral claim be anything other than someone's personal opinion?

Issues of altruism, self-interest, and human nature may also be confusing and raise similarly complex questions: Is there really such a thing as altruism? If people get personal satisfaction from helping others, doesn't that mean they are helping for selfish reasons? Doesn't social science show that all people are really out for themselves and that to pretend otherwise is hypocritical?

And civic life presents puzzles of its own: With rare, heroic exceptions, how can it matter whether any particular individual is politically active? Isn't it better for a few knowledgeable people to run things and for everyone else to stay out of it? Is it always best to question authority, as some bumper stickers recommend?

Teachers also confront the challenge of getting students to relinquish stereotypes and oversimplified explanations that may seem to work for them in rough and ready ways and so persist in the face of contrary evidence—poor people don't have enough drive and ambition; politicians are crooks; wars and other conflicts are caused by the actions of a few bad people.

Teaching knowledge and skills that students can really use is no easier. How can teachers help students understand history or democratic or ethical theory in their own terms but also ensure that what they learn is usable in practice—that they can bring these theoretical schemes, rooted in centuries of scholarship, to bear on the messy, emotionally charged, and immediately pressing ethical and political problems of contemporary life? How can teachers encourage personal connections with course material without sacrificing analytical distance? How can teachers ensure that students learn to practice reasoned and respectful discourse not only in the classroom but also in more complicated and heated situations?

If classroom teaching is to support the full range of moral and civic development, it must connect with students on the emotional level as well as the intellectual level. This raises additional challenges and dilemmas: How can students come to admire and be inspired by moral leaders past and present when they are all too aware that everyone has feet of clay? How can teachers help them become less

Reprinted from *Educating Citizens: Preparing America's Undergraduates for Lives of Moral and Civic Responsibility*, by Anne Colby, Thomas Ehrlich, Elizabeth Beaumont, and Jason Stephens (2003), Jossey-Bass Publishers, Inc.

cynical about politics when their skepticism so often seems warranted? How can teachers foster both open-mindedness and conviction? If students do begin to tackle complicated social problems, what can teachers do to help them maintain resilience and hope in the face of inevitable setbacks?

These challenges mirror problems for education generally, not just for moral and civic education. Research clearly shows that students have a lot of trouble fully understanding difficult concepts, often do not know how to use what they do learn, and perhaps because they are not using that learning, tend to forget what they once knew. The experience of recalling information for a final exam but being unable to remember it later is familiar to everyone. In fact many college graduates cannot even remember what college courses they took. And sometimes students appear to remember the concepts they learned, but when asked to explain them, they reveal fundamental and persistent misconceptions (Clement, 1982; Perkins & Simmons, 1988). Students are known to hold these *naive theories* not only before but also after instruction in every discipline, and these misconceptions continue to impede consolidated understanding. Students often learn interpretations that conflict with their naive theories, but they learn them in the narrow context of the classroom and on a superficial level. When they are asked to explain or are confronted with a comparable issue outside that narrow context, their original misconceptions emerge intact. They have not achieved any real understanding of the ideas they believe they have learned but instead have learned to use heuristics or rough strategies that work much of the time in the classroom but that do not confront and uproot their misconceptions (Perkins & Martin, 1986).

Howard Gardner's review of this research in *The Unschooled Mind* (1991) offers illustrations from virtually every discipline. Some of these misconceptions are directly relevant to moral and civic development. For example, students may learn in a history course that wars result from multiple and complex forces, but they revert to a simplistic "bad man" explanation when asked to explain a contemporary conflict. And college students who have studied economics offer incorrect explanations of market forces that are essentially identical to those of college students who have never taken an economics course. Many students also continue to hold internally inconsistent ethical views even after taking courses in ethics. This persistence of stereotypes, oversimplified explanations, and erroneous naive theories seriously undermines the value of academic learning for educating citizens. To make matters worse, students often have knowledge they can recall when prompted but they do not think to use it, or do not know how to use it, in new situations where it could be helpful (Bransford, Franks, Vye, & Sherwood, 1989; Perkins & Martin, 1986). In many cases students cannot apply what they know even in a slightly different context. The research on this lack of *transfer* of learning is often startling, calling into question the subsequent usefulness of much academic learning.

Conventional modes of instruction, especially listening to lectures and reading textbooks, are especially vulnerable to producing fragile and superficial understanding. As a result students forget much of what they have learned, are unable to use in a new context what they do remember, and retain fundamental misconceptions that are inconsistent with what they seemed to have learned (Bligh, 1972; Gardiner, 1994). This has been shown in both natural settings and in the laboratory (Bransford et al., 1989). Lecture courses often do not support deep and enduring understandings of ideas and are even less well suited to developing the range of problem-solving, communication, and interpersonal skills toward which moral and civic education (and liberal education more generally) aspire. And the development of the motivational dimensions of moral and civic maturity—dimensions like a sense of identity as a responsible and engaged person; a passion for social justice; sympathy with others, including those who are different from oneself; and an enduring sense of hope and empowerment—is often beyond even the aspirations of this kind of teaching.

Student-Centered Pedagogies

Although a majority of college and university faculty use primarily lectures and discussion in their teaching (indeed, 74 percent of college courses rely on lectures, according to a recent survey, Shedd, 2002), a growing number are adopting an array of other strategies, including service learning, experiential education, problem-based learning, and collaborative learning (Sax, Astin, Korn, & Gilmartin, 1999). Many of these strategies represent models for teaching that if used well can support deep understanding, usable knowledge and skills, and personal connection and meaning. The pedagogies in this expanded and varied repertoire share a commitment to student learning as the central criterion of good teaching and conceive of learning as a more active process than it was once thought to be.

Faculty using these approaches, which are often called *pedagogies of engagement*, typically address a wider range of goals and attempt to match learning experiences more closely with those goals than do faculty using traditional approaches. These pedagogies are classified and named somewhat differently by different writers, so any given list is unavoidably somewhat arbitrary. The pedagogies also tend to intersect with each other, so the categories are not mutually exclusive. In addition, most existing lists include a number of approaches that we do not address here, such as undergraduate research and teaching methods based in information technology. For the sake of simplicity and focus, we limit our discussion to four well-known approaches that are particularly appropriate to moral and civic education.

Service Learning

In the last decade, *service learning*, also called *community-based learning*, has emerged as the most widespread and closely studied of the various student-centered, or engaged, pedagogies. It has become one of the most popular ways to integrate moral and civic learning into academic coursework. In service learning, students participate in organized, sustained service activity that is related to their classroom learning and meets identified community needs. They then reflect on that experience through activities such as journal writing and class discussions, connecting the service experience with the substantive content of the course and with various dimensions of personal growth, including civic responsibility (Bringle & Hatcher, 1995). Faculty teaching these courses provide the larger intellectual and ethical context for students' service work, helping them connect scholarship with practice and articulating grounds for commitment and action (Zlotkowski, 1999).

Other Experiential Education

Service learning is a subset of the broader category of *experiential education*, which includes many different kinds of direct, hands-on activities that are meant to help students connect theory with practice and represent and experience theoretical concepts in practical, behavioral modes and real-life settings. Experiential education employs a wide range of pedagogies, including simulations, role playing, internships and other fieldwork, and action research (Moore, 2000). Students often receive direct supervision and feedback in the field settings, which generally require the students to address complex and open-ended problems and projects. Faculty help students put their experiences into practical, theoretical, and ethical contexts and integrate the fieldwork with the course's academic content, rethinking theories in light of applied experiences.

Problem-Based Learning

In *problem-based learning*, students' work, occurring either individually or in groups, is organized around studying, evaluating, and often proposing possible solutions for concrete, usually real-world problems (Barrows, 1980). At the college level, students generally work on rich, complex, and relatively unstructured problems. The teacher serves as a resource and guide, helping students find and integrate information from many sources and assisting in their efforts to bridge theory and practice and put knowledge to work in applied situations.

Collaborative Learning

In *collaborative learning* students work together in teams on projects, group investigations, and other activities aimed at teaching a wide range of skills and improving students' understanding of complex substantive issues (Kadel & Keehner, 1994). The groups take collective responsibility for working together on assignments, often creating both joint and individual products. Student groups organize their own efforts, negotiating roles and resolving conflicts themselves. When differences of opinion arise, group members have opportunities to compare and evaluate their ideas and approaches, allowing more complex understandings to emerge. In collaborative learning the locus of authority is shifted from the teacher to the group, and the teacher acts as a coach and resource.

Why Engaged Pedagogies Support Complex Learning

The research literature on the effectiveness of pedagogies of engagement is extensive; it is also complicated because their impact depends on the quality and conditions of their use and the specific outcomes chosen to be assessed. A review of that literature is beyond the scope of this book, but taken as a whole the research indicates that if used well these student-centered, or active, pedagogies can have a positive impact on many dimensions of moral and civic learning as well as on other aspects of academic achievement. Teaching methods that actively involve students in the learning process and provide them with opportunities for interaction with their peers as well as with faculty enhance students' content learning, critical thinking, transfer of learning to new situations, and such aspects of moral and civic development as a sense of social responsibility, tolerance, and nonauthoritarianism (McKeachie, Pintrich, Yi-Guang, & Smith, 1986; Pascarella & Terenzini, 1991; Pederson-Randall, 1999).

Principles of Learning

There are good reasons for these positive learning outcomes—these pedagogies embody powerful research and theory about the nature of learning that has emerged in recent years from the fields of education, developmental psychology, and cognitive science. This research presents a picture of the nature of learning that explains why these pedagogies are so important for promoting deep academic learning and effective moral and civic education. It also forms the basis for our confidence that including moral and civic goals in coursework does not require a trade-off with other academic goals. As Lee Shulman (1997) has said, if one understands the implications of this research for resolving the major difficulties people experience with liberal learning (forgetting or misunderstanding what they learn or being unable to use it), it becomes clear that the kinds of pedagogy we associate with moral and civic education, service learning for example, are not curricular extravagances but rather ways to strengthen the very heart of liberal education. Here (necessarily oversimplified) are some of the central ideas from this research literature:

1. Learning is an active, constructive process. In order to achieve real understanding, learners must actively struggle to work through and interpret ideas, look for patterns and meaning, and connect new ideas with what they already know (Greeno, Collins & Resnick, 1996; Resnick, 1987).

2. Genuine and enduring learning occurs when students are interested in, even enthusiastic about, what they are learning, when they see it as important for their own present and future goals. In life outside the classroom, knowledge and skills are most often developed through efforts to make progress on tasks that need doing. Although almost any approach to teaching will stimulate interest and enthusiasm in some students, rich and authentic tasks (like those performed in real life) are more likely to be intrinsically interesting for most. This is important, because intrinsic motivation tends to support more sustained, self-motivated effort and therefore greater learning (Lepper & Green, 1978).

3. Thinking and learning are not only active but also social processes. In most work and other nonacademic settings, people are more likely to think and remember through interaction with other people than as a result of what they do alone. Working in a group can facilitate learning as participants work through the complexities of a task together, comparing and critiquing different perspectives and building on each other's proposed solutions (Newman, Griffin, & Cole, 1989).

4. Knowledge and skills are shaped in part by the particular contexts in which they are learned; they are qualitatively different as a result of different learning contexts (Brown, Collins, & Duguid, 1989; Lave, 1988). Few skills are truly generic and equally applicable across very different contexts. For this reason, transfer of knowledge and skills to very different contexts is difficult. Despite this difficulty, transfer is essential if knowledge and skills are to be usable.

5. There are two key ways to increase the likelihood that transfer will be successful. The first is to make the context in which skills and knowledge are learned more similar to the settings in which they will be used. This can raise problems for traditional modes of instruction, because classroom learning is in some sense *decontextualized* (Greeno et al., 1996). Traditional classrooms are of course contexts in themselves, but in most cases they are notably artificial, bearing little resemblance to the contexts in which educators hope the skills and knowledge can be used. The second way to support transfer of learning is to consciously, reflectively draw out principles that can guide and support that transfer, making them explicit and articulating their implications for the new situation or context (Brown, 1989; Salomon & Perkins, 1989). Therefore, genuine, usable learning depends not only on activity but also on carefully guided reflection on that activity.

6. Thoughtful, aware (reflective) practice, accompanied by informative feedback, is essential to learning. Because knowledge and skills are context specific, it is not usually sufficient for students to practice a performance that is assumed to be analogous to, though is actually quite different from, the one they will ultimately need. Too often schools and colleges do not teach what they want their students to know, instead asking students to practice distant substitutes. So, for example, if teachers want students to understand an idea well enough that they can explain it, represent it in new ways, apply it in new situations, and connect it to their lives, then students need to practice doing these things and not simply recall the concept in an abstract form. Students are more likely to develop understanding when they practice understanding (Perkins, 1992).

7. Students have different profiles of ability. Some are most expert with language; others are most skilled at logical and quantitative thinking or spatial representation; still others are especially insightful in understanding themselves or in understanding and managing other people (Gardner, 1983). Broadening the array of skills, tasks, and modes of representation used in a course increases the likelihood that students with different strengths will be able to connect productively with the work. It also provides opportunities for students to progress in areas where they are not yet strong, expanding the range of their competencies.

8. The development of genuine understanding is supported by the capacity to represent an idea or skill in more than one modality and to move back and forth among different forms of knowing (Gardner, 1991). Thus learning benefits when courses provide experience with a wider array of modalities than those that usually dominate higher education (namely the linguistic and logical/mathematical).

Pedagogical Implications

The connections between these principles of learning and student-centered pedagogies of engagement are clear. All these pedagogies build on the premise that learning requires students to be active and emotionally engaged in their work. This can happen in the context of a lecture course if the lectures are provocative enough to engage students actively in seeking answers to puzzles the readings or lectures raise, stimulating them to reflect, make connections, and organize and draw conclusions from some body of knowledge. But too often the active reflection, interpretation, and connecting are done by the lecturer, not by the students, and being an observer to this process does not suffice (Finkel, 2000). The more student-centered pedagogies ask students to do this work, although they are not expected to do it alone, and expert guidance from the teacher supports and shapes productive inquiry.

Recognition of the importance of students' practicing what it is hoped they will learn is behind many teachers' commitment to an expanded pedagogical repertoire that includes collaborative learning, simulations, internships, service learning, and problem-based learning. These all provide direct (and directed) practice of a wide array of performances. All attempt to create authentic, intrinsically interesting tasks for students. Often they allow students to create or choose these tasks themselves, increasing their investment in the work. In addition, these varied pedagogies tend to offer many different modes of representation, providing more entry points to engagement and reinforcing learning through integration across different modalities. In addition to these shared characteristics of engaged pedagogies, each approach also capitalizes in particular ways on some aspects of what is currently known about learning.

Experiential learning, including service learning, centrally acknowledges the context specificity of learning, providing educational settings that are less artificial than the classroom and much closer to the contexts in which students will later perform. When these settings are explicitly civic, as they are in service learning and many internships and other field experiences, they provide stronger support for moral and civic development than most lectures or seminars can. Service learning and other field experiences place students in contexts that involve social and conceptual complexity and ambiguity and often elicit emotional responses as well as unexamined stereotypes and other assumptions. Because the field contexts are so dissimilar from the classroom, learning to operate in those contexts, confronting the stereotypes and other misconceptions they raise, and being called on to trace ideas and principles across academic and applied settings can be a very effective means of deepening and extending learning. Reflective writing and discussions are essential components of high-quality service learning and other forms of experiential education in part because they provide opportunities for students and faculty to extract principles that facilitate the transfer of learning to new contexts.

Of course the essence of problem-based learning is inquiry into rich, complex, and authentic problems of real concern to the students. This can have a dramatic impact on their motivation and emotional engagement with the work. If students need the knowledge and skills they are learning in order to address or solve some problem with which they are preoccupied, especially a problem that is closely connected with their own interests and concerns, they will not ask the familiar question, Why do I have to learn this? (Finkel, 2000). Problem-based learning is also invaluable in providing opportunities for students to practice and receive feedback on intellectual capacities such as integrative thinking that might otherwise only be hoped for as a side effect of academic study and not actually taught.

Collaborative learning builds directly on what research has shown about the facilitative effect of social processes. This is why it is valuable in supporting students' learning of the many subtle and difficult concepts that are inherent in the moral and civic domains. Equally important, collaborative learning provides experience with a wide array of interpersonal skills, many of which are critical to civic participation. Among other things, students can practice cooperation, persuasion, negotiation, compromise, and fair distribution of efforts and rewards. When teams are composed of students with complementary strengths, participants can learn how to build on diversity in working toward a common goal. When students from different backgrounds work together closely over a period of time, they can achieve the cross-cultural competencies that are best learned through relationships and practice.

It may seem that the principles of learning we have discussed here are more relevant for acquiring moral and civic understanding and skills than for developing the motivational dimensions of moral and civic maturity, but this is not true. If anything, the development of values and goals, moral and civic identity, and a sense of efficacy, hope, and compassion is even more dependent on active engagement, complex and authentic contexts, social exchange, regular practice, and informative feedback than is the development of more traditional dimensions of academic understanding. Compassion and outrage become much more intense when students develop personal connections with those who have experienced hardship or injustice. When students work closely with inspiring people, they can internalize new images of what they want to be like more deeply and vividly than they are likely to do through reading. Students develop a love of the game only by playing it. The more students take civic or political action, especially if they enjoy it, the more they will see themselves as the kind of people who can and want to act civically and politically. If they see that their actions can make a difference, their sense of efficacy is strengthened. Of course they also need ways to maintain their commitment during the many times when their actions do not seem to have much effect. By weaving service into academic coursework, faculty can help students develop lenses for interpreting inevitable obstacles and failures in a way that will support rather than undermine their stamina. This connection between ways of understanding and dimensions of motivation is typical of the multiple and dynamic connections among understanding, skills, and motivation that become particularly real and salient through active educational experiences.

The skill with which these diverse pedagogies are implemented is critically important because experiential, problem-based, and collaborative approaches to learning do not automatically inspire interest or provide the kind of feedback that is required for learning. They are often harder to do well than traditional lectures precisely because the teacher is not "in control" of many of the student experiences. Nor do they spontaneously yield ideas that build cumulatively or principles that can guide transfer of learning. For this reason teachers must play a very active role in guiding and facilitating students' learning even in these student-centered forms of teaching. Among other things, teachers must make their specific learning goals clear, not only in their own minds but also to the students.

We have been defining the pedagogies of engagement on a global level, examining general pedagogical categories. But faculty shape what they do and ask students to do on a more *micro* level, and there are wide variations in what each pedagogy may involve for a given course. In addition, the broad categories intersect in practice, so it is not unusual for a particular classroom strategy to employ a combination of collaborative, problem-based *and* service learning and to be interdisciplinary as well.

All teaching, but especially teaching that takes full advantage of these more complex strategies, begins well before the teacher walks into the classroom and continues beyond the conclusion of the course. Teachers have an underlying, often implicit, conception of teaching and learning that guides the many choices they make. Selecting texts, planning student activities, designing and implementing assessments, all are important elements of teaching, as is shaping and guiding the work that students do, including reading, writing, classroom discussions and projects, simulations or field placements (if they are used), and test taking or other demonstrations of learning. For this reason, we use the term *pedagogy* to refer to all the things teachers do and ask their students to do to support students' learning. Teaching in this comprehensive sense can also include the things that teachers do to assess their own performance and the impact of their courses—reviews or evaluations of a course while it is ongoing and after it is over, involving student comments, student work, peer reviews, and other information. These reflections on course effectiveness may be quite informal or more systematic. Either way they can support teachers' capacity to learn from their own experience and, when they are shared, make it possible for teachers to learn from each other's experience. Writing about the teaching of elementary school mathematics, Maggie Lampert (1985) proposed an image of teachers as managers of dilemmas. In any given course the teacher holds multiple, conflicting aims and must find ways to balance those aims as the course proceeds. We find this image equally appropriate to teaching for moral and civic responsibility at the college level.

Teaching Ethics

In this section, we discuss the many ways faculty grapple with the challenges and dilemmas of teaching students about ethics and ethical issues, a key arena of moral and civic learning. Ethics is not the only issue we could have chosen to consider in detail, though it is among the most important. Some of the most difficult challenges of teaching ethics include working to move students beyond moral relativism, supporting deep understanding of and personal connections with ethical concepts, teaching the skills of moral discourse, promoting the values and themes that are central to the institution's goals for moral and civic education, and supporting transfer of learning to contexts beyond the classroom.

Moving Beyond Moral Relativism

In the area of ethics one of the naive theories, or fundamental misconceptions, that surfaces over and over in college classrooms is student moral relativism. This is the belief that no moral position is more valid than any other and that therefore (illogically) one should be tolerant of moral beliefs different from one's own (Ricks, 1999). Student moral relativism is connected with another phenomenon that is widely reported by faculty teaching all kinds of student populations—students' tendency to avoid engaging with moral disagreement. If any answer is as good as any other, why think hard about these questions, why make a serious effort to justify your position? A corollary is many students' reluctance to subject their own moral beliefs to serious scrutiny. Ironically, student moral relativism, which reflects humility and tolerance (as well as intellectual laziness in some cases), can get in the way of open-minded consideration of others' views. As Ricks (1999) puts it, "The phrase 'Well, it's all a matter of opinion anyway,' when uttered during a conversation about ethical topics, is usually a clear sign that the discussion, for all intents and purposes, is over" (p. 3).

A central dilemma for faculty who teach about ethical issues is how to help students see the problems with this kind of thinking without implying that there is one clearly right answer to hard ethical questions. This is not easy, and many teachers do not succeed in moving students beyond relativism. In fact, standard approaches to teaching ethics may inadvertently contribute to the problem. The two most common approaches to teaching ethics, which are often combined, are presentation and critique of the major ethical theories (deontology, utilitarianism, and virtue theory) and discussion of very difficult cases in which moral goods conflict and there is no consensus on how best to resolve the conflict.

Any responsible introduction to ethics must teach students about the major ethical theories that frame the field. And the kind of analytical thinking involved in working out the limitations of these theories lies at the heart of what it means to engage in philosophy. On the one hand, teaching this kind of analytical thinking is itself an important aim, because understanding the modes of inquiry that underlie different disciplines is a central goal of liberal education (Schneider & Shoenberg, 1998). On the other hand, if schools are to educate citizens, it is important for students to develop convictions—a place to stand morally even if only tentative and subject to change. Too heavy a focus on critical analysis gives students the impression that because each theory is flawed, the major ethical theories are all equally valid (or invalid), and none provides a useful basis for actual moral decisions.

The second standard approach, discussion of very difficult cases, can give the impression that ethics concerns only serious and ultimately irresolvable disagreements. Sharon Rowe (2001), who teaches introduction to moral philosophy at Kapi'olani Community College, points to these and other unfortunate consequences of this approach. In her experience the cases typically used are likely to concern issues that are unfamiliar to most students, making it hard for them to feel connected with the debate. Even more problematic is the fact that the cases tend to generate conversations that polarize quickly, with students becoming entrenched and defensive. Students who are more articulate or passionate dominate these discussions, and the others retreat. The dynamic is exacerbated by the cultural backgrounds of the students at Kapi'olani, because many students of Asian or Pacific Islander ancestry consider it rude to criticize others publicly.

Making Personal Connections

Like many other faculty perplexed by these dilemmas, Rowe has found it more useful to focus on issues that are personally relevant for her students, helping them explore more fully the ethical implications of those issues. Two topics she has found especially fruitful are lying and sexual behavior. Exploration of these familiar issues can help students see the relevance of the major theoretical perspectives for their lives. For example, Rowe asks students to engage in small-group discussions to address the potentially sensitive issue of sexual ethics and asks the groups to develop a "Sexual Ethic for the 21st Century" and give it a solid conceptual foundation. In the course of these discussions students are forced to confront the implications of moral relativism and the merits of a stronger ethical perspective.

Although there are clear advantages in connecting ethics teaching with students' personal experience, this strategy presents dilemmas of its own. Too strong a focus on everyday morality may lead students to conceive of ethics as concerned primarily with issues of private life and focused on people with whom they already have a relationship. An understanding of the moral dimensions of social and political issues will remain beyond their grasp (Beerbohm, 1999). This argues for using a variety of approaches, including strategies for extending issues of personal relevance and concern beyond the immediate, private sphere. One way to do this is to focus on a complex social problem that is familiar to students, such as poverty or racial justice, and to draw from multiple disciplines, using ethical analysis as a central theme. These problem-based ethics courses draw from applied fields of particular interest to the students and often require them to keep journals or participate in community service. A challenge in these courses is to ensure that they provide adequate theoretical grounding and require students to treat problems analytically through persuasive reasoning and argumentation. Otherwise they may teach students to formulate their own beliefs and debate with others but not to ground their views in reason and principle or to see why this grounding is important.

This kind of academic weakness is not unusual. Surveying the syllabi of ethics courses at many colleges and universities, we found that too often the courses ask students to read only brief secondary source summaries of moral philosophy rather than primary sources. Often these courses, especially those that aspire toward "values clarification," fail to provide experience with the rigorous argumentation that is so critical to ethical problem solving. Students are encouraged to clarify what they believe, but little attempt is made to ground this reflection in larger scholarly debates or to consider and debate the relative merits of other values and ethical perspectives.

Teaching Skills of Moral Discourse

Recognizing how important it is for students to learn and practice moral argumentation, many courses and programs focus directly on these skills. This is a central component of The Reflective Woman, for example, a course at the College of St. Catherine. This required, first-year course includes a lengthy section in which students participate in *structured controversies*. Collaborating in small groups, they work out both sides of a controversial topic, conducting research, writing position statements, debating, and switching positions at various points in the process. Using the experience of thinking through opposing viewpoints to refine their arguments, the groups then present their structured controversies to the class. After the presentations each student in the group writes a paper from her own viewpoint, supporting her position with a thorough consideration of contrary evidence and viewpoints. Students also reflect on the experience of conflict, any uncertainties about their own views, and the experience of being challenged by opposing views. Because all freshmen are participating in structured controversies at the same time, the residence halls are able to sponsor dialogues that connect with and support the process.

Teaching moral argumentation is also a central goal of Stanford University's Ethics in Society Program. Students practice these skills in introductory courses in ethics, political philosophy, and "the ethics of social (including governmental) decisions." In support of this goal a section on the program's Web site (www.stanford.edu/eis) outlines the basics of moral argumentation. This Web resource, titled *Arguing About Ethics*, offers guidelines on how to make a moral case and presents short excerpts from articles and books by distinguished (often contemporary) moral and political philosophers. The selections are meant to convey "a sense of the range and diversity of moral arguments—how they are made and what makes them compelling." They include brief excerpts from Ronald Dworkin, T.M. Scanlon, and Peter Singer on the value and nature of theorizing in moral and political philosophy and other respected thinkers commenting on "the essential tools of moral and political philosophy." The Web site also provides examples of different modes of moral argument, such as employing theory to explain confused intuitions; drawing upon material from the world, to supply an essay not just with empirical facts but also with reasons; preempting objections to one's position; giving reasons for one's intuitions that an argument is "implausible"; acknowledging agreement where it exists; considering alternative positions to common debates; and avoiding simple dichotomies. Of course students are not expected to learn these forms of argumentation simply from reading examples, but the site does provide useful reference material for courses in which students practice moral argumentation through a wide range of pedagogies.

"Distinctive Definitions" in the Teaching of Ethics

At some colleges the mission and special perspective of the institution may permeate the teaching of ethics—providing a *distinctive definition* of moral and civic responsibility. For example, Haverford College, which is strongly rooted in Quaker values, requires all students to take a course on ethics as social justice. The ethics requirement at Shaw University, a historically black college in North Carolina, places special emphasis on the ethics of influential African Americans such as Booker T. Washington, W.E.B. Du Bois, Malcolm X, and Martin Luther King Jr. At many religious colleges, ethical issues and theories are connected with theological and other religious issues. This can be valuable as long as these courses encourage open inquiry and debate, critical evaluation, and skills of analysis.

Most educators would agree that students need to develop clear convictions and a commitment to certain values, such as honesty, courage, and mutual respect, and also learn to think through subtle and ambiguous moral issues. Debates about the appropriate balance between these two goals emerge from the distinctive definition of moral and civic development at the United States Air Force Academy. The academy's task is to instill professional ethics within the military structure, which is characterized by a tension between obedience to legitimate authority and personal responsibility for ethical choices. Among other things, academy faculty are teaching a code of professional ethics. To some extent they are teaching a set of rules—making sure cadets understand what is right and why. Some express concern that this kind of clarity is rare in higher education. Faculty we met at the academy referred to a recent public television special in which a small group of students and professors talked about whether it would be acceptable to cheat on a five-page paper if students were given only a few days to write it when they were already over-whelmed with work. In the televised discussion, only two of the students and one professor thought that it was clearly wrong, a judgment very much at odds with the norms about cheating reflected in the academy's strict honor code.

Many faculty teaching ethics at the academy believe it is important for them to take clear positions on some of the ethical issues likely to arise in the cadets' later careers in the military, including corruption, such as over-charging for supplies or falsifying equipment maintenance records. They believe cadets need to learn the realities of the serious, even life-threatening situations that have resulted from cutting corners in a military context, even in cases where the violation seemed a fairly trivial matter when it occurred. Because many of the faculty are military officers themselves and have witnessed unethical behavior and its impact at some point in their careers, they can incorporate vivid stories into their teaching and help cadets connect lessons from these examples with difficult situations they are already beginning to face. Others at the academy believe it is more important to prepare cadets to make autonomous judgments about situations in which there are no obvious right or wrong answers. "Officers need the courage to constructively dissent—they may well be called upon to do this," one professor told us. This alternative point of view is in part a different prediction about what challenges cadets are likely to face as Air Force officers and in part a pedagogical claim that students gain more from working through dilemmas themselves than from being shown the implications of rules they are being asked to follow.

Although the academy no doubt feels a stronger need to establish clear ethical norms than most liberal arts programs do, many introductory ethics courses would probably benefit from consideration of the many basic values and beliefs around which moral philosophers substantially agree. Introductory science courses typically begin by studying the many areas in which there is wide agreement before moving to controversies or unresolved cutting-edge issues. When a version of this approach is used in ethics courses, it can reduce students' confusion about moral relativism (Ricks, 1999).

Supporting Transfer of Learning Beyond the Classroom

Recognizing how difficult it is to transfer skills learned in a classroom setting to the more complicated and emotionally charged contexts of life, many faculty incorporate experiential approaches into the teaching of ethics. When students face difficult moral issues in personal or public life, it will be important for them to consider multiple points of view and alternative courses of action and to appreciate the moral complexity of the issues. Moreover, sometimes difficult moral dilemmas require an answer urgently when there is no clear consensus on how they ought to be resolved.

Simulations can help students learn to make judgments in the face of uncertainty as they will need to do many times in the future. At the College of St. Catherine, students in health care fields participate in a number of ethical simulations: for example, they might sit on the board of a fictitious insurance company, making decisions about whether to cover certain kinds of experimental medical treatment. Guest experts such as attorneys and health care managers provide background information and varying perspectives on the issues, and then students must decide whether, for example, a patient with Parkinson's disease should receive coverage for his experimental implant.

Service learning plays an important role at many colleges because it offers an effective way for students to engage the complexity of ethical issues in the press and ambiguity of actual situations. This reflects the understanding that context and content matter—that real moral dilemmas are not solved by learning and applying an abstract moral algorithm. Debra Satz (2001), director of the Ethics in Society Program at Stanford University at the time of our visit, speaks to this issue:

> As a political philosopher, and as the head of an interdisciplinary ethics program, I have frequently been struck by how ill equipped much moral and political philosophy is to deal with the "limits of the possible." By the limits of the possible, I have in mind the non-ideal aspects of our world: that people don't always do the right thing, that there can be very high costs to doing the right thing when others do not, that information is imperfect, resources are limited, interests are powerful, the best options may not be politically or materially feasible, and that collective action problems are everywhere. We need a moral and political philosophy that integrates theoretical reflection on values with practical knowledge about how the world sets limits on what we can do and what we can hope for.

Satz and others in this program believe that making ethical judgments within the limits of the possible, that is, within the constraints and practical complexities of real life, is qualitatively different from "doing" academic moral philosophy or even applied ethics, and that service learning plays a vitally important role by placing students in contexts that give them necessary experience with this kind of contextual thinking.

Pedagogical Strategies in Four Courses

Teaching for moral and civic responsibility along with other aspects of academic learning requires faculty to address many different areas of understanding and foster a variety of skills while maintaining a course's coherence and building learning cumulatively across varied topics and tasks. In powerful courses the whole is greater than the sum of the parts. In order to convey a sense of some of these "wholes," we devote the rest of this article to describing the teaching strategies that make up the fabric of four quite different courses, all of which centrally address moral and civic learning. One of these courses prepares students for learning and service in the community, and another attempts to deepen and extend a service experience students have just completed. A third incorporates service preparation, action, and reflection on the action into a single semester, and the last of the four combines the challenge of conducting a course with these phases condensed with another challenge—attempting to reach students who begin the course with skepticism about and alienation from politics and civic life.

The Ethics and Politics of Public Service

The Ethics and Politics of Public Service is a course that grew out of a faculty service-learning institute organized by Stanford University's Haas Center for Public Service. It reflects the participants' conviction, consistent with research findings, that community service and service learning are more likely to help the community and to support student learning when students are well prepared before they embark on the work. The course serves as a gateway for students who plan to participate in service activities or enroll in courses with service-learning components. Rob Reich, an assistant professor in the Department of Political Science who was a member of the group, developed and teaches the course, which is cross-listed in six additional departments or programs—Human Biology, American Studies, Ethics in Society, Urban Studies, Public Policy, and Comparative Studies in Race and Ethnicity.

Ethics and Politics, which is aimed primarily at freshmen and sophomores, has two overarching goals: to prepare students for responsible service and to integrate their service experiences with their academic life. Reich believes that in preparing to engage with the community, students need to understand the history of the relationship between Stanford University and the surrounding communities; learn about socioeconomic, demographic, and political changes in the San Francisco Bay Area; and become aware of experiences, perceptions, dilemmas, and challenges that Stanford have encountered previously while engaged in community service.

Because an important goal is to expand students' appreciation of cultural differences and the very different perspectives they can entail, the course naturally raises some of the same issues of moral and cultural relativism that arise in ethics courses. The challenge for Reich is to help students develop a deep respect for diverse cultural understandings yet also appreciate the importance of fundamental human rights. He hopes that in the process they will come to see the value of ethical pluralism, which acknowledges legitimate differences in moral perspective without giving up the belief that there are boundaries around what is morally acceptable and valid grounds for evaluating moral claims. Among the other dilemmas that Reich must negotiate are how to instill humility without triggering paralysis and how to help students maintain a sense of efficacy even though they can expect only limited success in many of their service endeavors.

Ethics and Politics meets twice a week, generally with one class each week devoted to discussing broad philosophical questions raised in the assigned readings such as: What does it mean to "do service"? Would service be necessary in a just world? Can service do harm? The other meeting explores the same questions in connection with examples of actual service experiences, often through case studies written for the class by former course participants who have subsequently taken part in community service. During class, Reich alternates among small-group exercises; full-group discussions in which he actively questions, probes, and pushes the students; and *mini-lectures* in which he introduces or summarizes a set of issues. In addition to class participation and extensive reading, students write four papers exploring the history, dilemmas, and complexities of public service.

PHASE 1: TO HELL WITH GOOD INTENTIONS. The first several weeks of Ethics and Politics are designed to challenge the facile notion that service is automatically a good thing. The challenge begins with readings and discussions concerning various motives for doing service. Some students think only people who are motivated by altruism are "good" service providers, whereas others think that serving for self-interested reasons (for example, wanting to build a better résumé) is acceptable. Reich pushes students to recognize the prevalence of mixed motives and then asks the class to consider the sufficiency of thinking only about motives. Reich assigns several readings that illustrate how good intentions, even though a desirable starting point, may lead to bad consequences. Most provocative on this point is the well-known essay "To Hell with Good Intentions," by Ivan Illich (1968). In an address to a group of U.S. volunteers who were about to embark on a summer of service in Mexico, Illich tells his audience:

> You will not help anybody by your good intentions. . . . I am here to tell you, if possible to convince you, and hopefully, to stop you, from pretentiously imposing yourselves on Mexicans. . . . By definition, you cannot help being ultimately vacationing salesmen for the middle-class "American Way of Life," since that is really the only life you know. . . . All you will do in a Mexican village is create disorder. . . . At worst, in your "community development" spirit you might create just enough problems to get someone shot after your vacation ends and you rush back to your middle-class neighborhoods [pp. 1–4].

This paradox of good intentions yielding harmful outcomes is further explored in Anne Fadiman's *The Spirit Catches You and You Fall Down: A Hmong Child, Her American Doctors, and the Collision of Two Cultures* (1997). An investigation of a true story, the book explores the treatment of Lia Lee, a young Hmong girl with epilepsy, by her Hmong parents and her American doctors. Although the child's parents did not want their daughter to suffer any pain during her epileptic seizures, they did not want her to be "cured" of the disease—as the Hmong believe people with epilepsy are closer to divinity, and consequently these individuals hold an exalted status in the community. Lia's

American doctors, however, believed the severity of her seizures would result in long-term brain damage, and they wanted to treat her with medication. As the clash of views and cultures played out, the outcome for Lia was tragic, despite the good intentions on both sides. As Reich sees it: "The virtue of the book is that it portrays the motives, intentions, and actions of everyone involved—the parents, the community organizations, the doctors, the hospital administrators—from a sympathetic point of view. There's no villain in the book, yet the outcome is tragic."

Both Illich and Fadiman make clear to students that good intentions alone do not ensure a good outcome, that cultural differences can be too great to bridge, and that well-intentioned people can sometimes unknowingly do harm when they try to help. Readings like these might lead to a class-room full of disheartened moral relativists who have come to see community or public service as an irresponsible endeavor fraught with insurmountable perils. But these readings are only the beginning of the conversation, not the final word. Through the use of further readings, classroom discussions, and written assignments, Reich attempts to move students to a place where they are conscientious but also able to "embrace the ambiguity" that is inherent in public service. Ultimately, he wants students to see themselves as intentional, reflective service providers—even "interventionists":

> I use [these readings] as a way to talk to about cultural differences in doing service work and to talk about good intentions. One lesson I try to draw out of [Fadiman's] book is what it would mean to be a cultural broker or interpreter and what kind of preparation or knowledge one needs to play that role. . . . Is [the students' role] as a service provider or service agent simply to for-ward the interests of the organization they're working with, however they see it, or can you can be interventionist and attempt to show [misguided individuals in the organization], tell them, explain to them, come into dialogue with them, to say why you think what they're doing is wrong or inappropriate or ineffective.

Questions concerning moral relativism inevitably emanate from these discussions. Reich uses strategic probing and challenges to confront students who take relativistic or dogmatic positions, drawing out the implications of both. With thoughtful and difficult questions, he tries to bring these students to an appreciation of the plurality of moral values and the ways values can conflict as they do in *The Spirit Catches You and You Fall Down*:

> If students are pressing a line of, "Well, you've got to respect cultural beliefs," I'll press back with, "Does the state have an interest here?" Or if people are saying, "The parents are going to kill Lia— if they don't do anything about her epilepsy, she's going to have seizures and die," I'll press more about parental interests. Ultimately, what I'm most interested in is trying to get an appreciation of how both perspectives need to be considered and of how values can conflict in a particular case, as they do in this one.

Reich would like his students to be able to take multiple perspectives on a given issue and to form reasoned positions in the face of difficult ethical dilemmas. He is quick to challenge students who try to avoid the hard work of making moral judgments by simply saying, "Well, the Hmong parents have their culture and I have mine, and they're entitled to raise their kid the way they want."

PHASE 2: THE HISTORICAL AND SOCIOCULTURAL CONTEXTS OF SERVICE. Describing the second phase of Ethics and Politics, Reich says:

> The goal is really to give Stanford students an understanding about some of the local conditions. . . . So, if they do any volunteer service they have some concrete knowledge about the history of the university and the community. The goal is to prevent the stereotype of your average sophomore who shows up at Stanford and thinks, "Oh, it'd be great to do some service work." He goes over and signs up for ten hours of tutoring in East Palo Alto; logs in the ten hours and comes back home; and thinks he's struck some blow for goodness in the world simply by having spent ten hours [tutoring], completely unaware of the rafts of Stanford students who have gone over there for twenty or thirty years and the ill-will that might exist for good reason: the sense in which these tiny, episodic kinds of service are the least effective ones in terms of establishing an ongoing relationship and a real sense of connection between Stan-ford and East Palo Alto, not to mention that they are unlikely to provide meaningful help to the students.

Service learning does not happen in a vacuum, so this part of the course helps students understand the local context as well as the difficulties they may face as they attempt to negotiate between two different worlds. Among other things, students read Chuck Carlson's *Bled Dry by the Cutting Edge: A Short History of Silicon Valley*, and the U.S. Department of Housing and Urban Development report *Gentrification Forces in East Palo Alto* in order to better understand Bay Area demographic and socioeconomic conditions. Work during this three-week period addresses questions about privilege and the ways that being a student at an elite university can be a kind of stigma in the eyes of some who are less privileged. The sense of their own privilege and the magnitude of the gulf between them and the people they would like to help is paralyzing for some students. One young woman described how active she was in high school (she started a human rights club, for example, and worked with the Red Cross) but then said that since coming to Stanford she has not been very involved in service. She described feeling paralyzed by the Stanford name and struggling with what it means to come from such an elite community. Through discussions of cases and other course readings, Reich tries to help students see how they can maintain a sense of humility and realism about the complicated politics of their local situation without succumbing to this paralysis.

PHASE 3: "PUSHING THE PEANUT FORWARD." In the last week of Ethics and Politics, students reflect on what they have learned and look forward to applying it. Service learning is highlighted, as students discuss its meaning, what one should know in order to be successful in service-learning courses, and specific courses offered at Stanford. Many of the students will go on to take these courses together, and Reich encourages them to see each other as resources, not only for information but also for support. The group talks about how to survive the "moral quicksand" of public service. Even though service is fraught with difficult moral questions, Reich does not want students to be immobilized by the ethical dilemmas they will face. He tells them they must "embrace ambiguity" and advises them "to strive for moral *decency* rather than moral *perfection*." In discussing pieces by Robert Coles, bell hooks, and Parker Palmer, students acknowledge the importance of being reflective about their engagement and willing to accept (even seek) constructive criticism.

The course ends on an inspiring note as students discuss "Pushing the Peanut Forward," an article from Peter Singer's book (1998) on Henry Spira and the animal rights movement. Spira reminds students that "it's crucial to take a long-term perspective. . . . And when a particular initiative causes much frustration, I keep looking at the big picture while pushing obstacles out of the way. . . . It's like this guy from the *New York Times* asked me what I'd like my epitaph to be. I said, 'He pushed the peanut forward.' I try to move things on a little" (p. 198).

Integrating Community and Classroom: Internship Reflection

Effective service learning requires not only preparation before the field placement but also reflection and integration during and after it. The next course we consider follows a service experience, helping students extend and deepen their learning. Most service-learning courses are more condensed than this one, integrating academic learning with a service experience and reflection on that experience within the span of a semester or in a few cases an academic year. In Duke University's Service Opportunities in Leadership (SOL) Program, these basic elements are addressed in three phases that take a full year to complete. In the spring, students take a preparatory half-credit course, Civic Participation/Community Leadership, in which they participate in a service project and explore the ways in which values conflicts in local communities can affect civic participation and public policy.

After completing this course, students participate in the second phase—summer internships in which they work on projects for community-based organizations in the United States, Central America, or South Africa. About half the students choose to conduct optional service-learning research projects in conjunction with their internships. These research projects are designed collaboratively with the agency in which the students are working so that they address a real need and result in reports or other products that are genuinely useful to the agency. Research outcomes might take the form of survey data, documentary articles, oral history interviews, feasibility studies and business plans, or program manuals. Some recent project titles have been "Micro-Enterprise Development: Business, Job Creation, and Community Building in the New South Africa," "Child Care and Education: Barriers to Self-Sufficiency for Participants in the Supportive Housing Program," and "Tradeswomen's Stories, Tradeswomen's Lives: Oral Histories of Women in Blue Collar Trades." In addition to teaching valuable research skills, these projects can significantly strengthen students' sense of civic and political efficacy, because they serve such important functions for the agencies.

Following their summer internships, SOL students begin the third phase of the program, the one-semester full-credit course Integrating Community and Classroom: Internship Reflection. This seminar, taught by Alma Blount, a lecturer in Public Policy Studies, grapples with a number of issues, including some of the same ones Rob Reich addressed with Stanford students. Like many courses that attempt to foster long-term commitment to public service, this course takes up the question of how to support students' sense of efficacy when the outcomes of their work are sure to be mixed, so that students maintain resilience and hope rather than becoming cynical in the face of the realities of civic and political life. The course also builds on the students' summer field experiences, connecting them with deeper substantive knowledge and careful thought about the systemic dimensions of the social problems students confronted. The course allows students to place their service and research experiences in the context of related research and policy analysis and to deepen their commitment to civic participation.

Each week for seven weeks students read a diverse collection of texts around a different theme, writing a reflective essay each week that explores the ideas in the readings and their meaning in light of each student's field experiences and ideas and the students' questions about the theme. These essays are meant to be a cumulative investigation, laying the groundwork for a final essay on service leadership. Subgroups of students share essays each week so that preparation for class discussion involves not only doing the course reading and writing an essay but also at least skimming the essays of several other students. This practice builds community among the student groups, enriches the discussion, and stimulates discussion of course-related issues outside the classroom. The themes around which the readings and essays are organized are carefully designed to touch on key issues in developing and sustaining responsible engagement and commitment. They illustrate the interconnectedness of intellectual understanding and motivational factors such as cynicism versus hope, the values making up one's moral compass, and personal models of inspiration. The theme for Week 3, for example, is Facing Realities. Readings include selections from Paul Rogat Loeb's *Soul of a Citizen: Living with Conviction in a Cynical Time* (1999) and the same Ivan Illich essay ("To Hell with Good Intentions") that Reich uses. Later weeks focus on the themes Perspectives and Principles; Integrity, Congruence, and the Inner Work of Leadership; and Mentors, Models, and the search for a Compass of Values, for which students read and write about the life of a Nobel Peace Prize winner.

In addition to this intensive reading, writing, and discussion, each student investigates an issue relating to the internship experience—thus pursuing problem-based, inquiry learning that builds directly on the summer field placements. Students also create portfolios based on the investigation, using research, reflections, and other resources to illuminate and focus the issue. Although these investigations and portfolios are individual projects, students have regular, structured opportunities for peer learning in connection with the projects. Each is assigned to a small group that meets regularly to discuss the ongoing social issue investigations, offering suggestions and feedback and helping plan presentations to the class. Then students spend the last seven weeks of the course learning from each other as they take turns presenting their research to the full group. Two elements in the social issue investigation are an interview with an admired practitioner in the student's field of interest and a memo laying out policy or action recommendations. The memo must grapple with questions like these: "What are the underlying structures or systems that need to change in order to make serious progress on this issue? Who are the key players that need to be involved in the change process? What social policy options do you see? Which option seems most viable? Where do you locate yourself in these proposed actions?"

Alma Blount continues to refine what she calls the *pedagogy of service leadership* that underlies not only the course but the full SOL experience. Among other things, she is working with others at Duke to articulate the parameters of community-based research as a teaching strategy and to assess its impact on students. This systematic reflection on the pedagogies represented in the program feeds back into ongoing course development and provides a basis for national conversations with faculty at other institutions who are doing related work.

Ancients and Moderns: Democratic Theory and Practice

Sequences that connect one or more courses with service experiences over the course of a year, or even longer in some cases, offer students a powerful set of experiences, but these extended sequences are the exception rather than the rule. Most faculty who teach for moral and civic development take on the challenge of preparing students, facilitating their service or other action projects, and helping them reflect and build on those experiences within a single semester. A political science course at Providence College illustrates how rich and demanding this kind of teaching and learning can be. Rick Battistoni, professor of political science, is clear about the goals of his political theory course, Ancients and Moderns: Democratic Theory and Practice. He expects students to develop a beginning understanding of democratic theory as represented in ancient Athens, eighteenth-century Europe and the United States, and the United States today, reading contemporaneous critics of democratic practices in each of these times and places as well as historical accounts and theoretical analyses. In addition to introducing important disciplinary concepts and other substantive content, the course is meant to create a set of lenses, or conceptual frames, through which the students can interpret their own experiences and contemporary social and political issues; to provide experience applying those lenses or modes of analysis; and to help students develop a more examined and systematic sense of their own convictions about democracy and their own role in it.

Battistoni uses a wide array of strategies to accomplish these goals. He gives lectures periodically to provide an overview for each new section of the course. The course also requires extensive reading and discussion, with texts as wide ranging as Plato's *Republic*, Jean-Jacques Rousseau's *On the Social Contract*, selected writings of Thomas Jefferson, and Amy Gutmann and Dennis Thompson's *Democracy and Disagreement*. Because many aspects of the course concern the active use of theory and the relation of theory and practice, Battistoni stimulates students to begin thinking about the meaning of theory even before the course begins by articulating some of the key ideas in the syllabus:

> The course is about democracy, but it is also about *theory* (and, as a result of theorizing, ultimately about practice). Political theory, simply stated, is reflective discourse on the meaning of the political, delving underneath the surface of political practice to ask questions and understand the meaning of politics. In ancient Greek usage, *theoria* was a journey taken by statesmen (yes, as we all know, women were excluded from public life) or citizens to other places and cultures. The person making this journey would go study other governments, cultures, customs, and practices, and report back to leaders of the homeland. The "theorist" was thus a person who was able to examine these other cultures and abstract from his own experiences more general understandings and standards of political behavior and action. These could then be applied in criticizing, justifying, or amending institutions and practices in the home community. In this sense, then, political theory is both a critical and a creative activity, for each generation to participate in a continuous tradition. And in this sense, we are all theorists. So, I want you to read about theories and practices of democracy in these three periods, but with a view to your own theorizing about democracy.

The strategic use of simulations provides an experiential connection with the democratic process. The course opens, for example, with a simulation in which half the students are asked to design and act out a thoroughly undemocratic classroom and the other half to design and act out a perfectly democratic classroom. Predictably, the undemocratic group creates a form of dictatorial structure, and in the ensuing discussions students indicate that their representation not only draws on textual and other depictions of illegitimate authority systems but also represents an extreme version of their own experiences in school. Interestingly, the democratic group presentations tend to depict "inefficiency, disorder, even anarchy and chaos." In the discussions that follow the simulation, students in both groups indicate their lack of experience with democracy, and many express "their feeling that 'real' democracy is a nice idea, but utterly unrealistic, and at some level, undesirable" (Battistoni, 2000, p. 2). This introductory simulation uncovers on the first day of class some unexamined assumptions about democracy that might not have surfaced in a more general discussion of democracy.

As the course goes on, Battistoni uses a number of devices to bring democratic practices into the way the course operates. In a sense he makes the hidden curriculum visible and intentional, making the "medium part of the message." Research indicates that this kind of approach can be an important part of civic education. In fact an extensive review of the political socialization literature concluded that the most positive contribution a teacher at any level can make to the acquisition of democratic values is to foster democratic practices in the classroom and that this form of pedagogy was more important than any particular curricular component (Ehman, 1980). However, partly because this approach is so unfamiliar to students, it is sometimes difficult to introduce. Battistoni found, for example, that he and the students had to work through together what it would mean for the students to have some input into their grades for class participation. In Battistoni's mind, class participation includes more than how much or how well students speak in class:

> If we interpret democratic class participation to mean active engagement in the classroom, this includes not only giving voice to one's thoughts and opinions, but also what Langston Hughes once called "listen[ing] eloquently." It might also include preparation for class or discussions between students about course material outside of class. . . . To the extent that our definition of class participation includes things beyond the vocalizations that the faculty member can evaluate, then the student should have input, not only as a power-sharing arrangement but also because the student is the only one positioned to evaluate these other things [Battistoni, 2000, p. 6].

Throughout the course, students keep an ongoing *theory journal*, in which they respond to questions posed by Battistoni or derived from class discussions, using the readings and discussions to evolve their own theories of democracy. This writing involves the active interrogation of the assigned texts, analysis of the texts' meaning in a cumulative and recursive way, and connection with a developing sense of what the students themselves believe. The journal writing, on which students receive regular evaluation and feedback from Battistoni, results in a document of seventy to one hundred typed pages by the end of the course.

Finally, the students choose between two kinds of large course projects. The most popular option is the Democratic Theory in Action Project. Students are then grouped by project, and each group is instructed to organize itself democratically (whatever this means for the group), then create and implement some "democratic action." The nature of the action is up to the group, but it must exemplify the democratic ideals and theories the students have read about and discussed. The group submits a narrative report that summarizes the action in light of democratic theory and also chronicles the process followed by the group and the group's reflections on that process in light of democratic theory and principles. In addition, each individual writes a paper explicating his own conclusions about democracy and democratic theory in light of the experience of carrying out the project. For one recent democratic action project, students chose to address a perceived lack of democracy on the Providence College campus and sought to increase student input into decision making. The group organized a forum that brought together representatives from the college's major institutions (faculty senate, student congress, student affairs, and academic administration) to discuss student influence in decision making.

Alternatively, students can choose a more research-oriented option in which they study an organization of their choice from the standpoint of democratic theory, ideals, and values and their own understanding of what is at stake with respect to the governance and operation of this organization. Students are expected to spend a significant amount of time participating in the work of the organization and interviewing key informants. The students write a *Democratic Organizational Biography* based on this research, using democratic theory to analyze the particular patterns exhibited in the chosen organization. One student studied the Providence College Student Congress, another examined the democratic governance (or lack thereof) of her church, and a third chose to compare the practices and ideals of the college's Political Science Department.

For Rick Battistoni, as for Alma Blount, pedagogy extends beyond the end of the course. Each year Battistoni critically examines this course, assessing the quality of student work and considering student evaluations and comments. This assessment has led to important modifications and continual strengthening of the course. When he first introduced the Democratic Organizational Biography project, for example, Battistoni provided a list of organizations to be studied, and he found both the process and outcomes of the projects to be disappointing. Students were not really engaged, and unless they had had previous contact with the organization they studied, they had no stake in the outcome of their findings. When he gave students another choice for a major project (the democratic action project), so that writing the organizational biography was optional, and allowed students to choose organizations that matched their own interests, student engagement and the quality of the outcomes improved dramatically.

In addition to adjusting his teaching strategies, Battistoni also connected his teaching more broadly with his scholarship and used his classroom experiences as one source for "rethink[ing] the relationship between democratic theory, democratic pedagogy, and undemocratic power relations as they manifest themselves in higher education" (Battistoni, 2000, p. 4). He has shared his reflections on teaching democratic theory and practice with colleagues by presenting papers about the work at meetings of the American Political Science Association and at other conferences.

Social and Environmental History of California

The courses we have considered so far are all directed primarily toward students who bring a preexisting interest in community service or politics. Courses that build on these interests and develop them further can help sustain these students' commitment and increase its effectiveness. But undergraduate education also has the potential to awaken an interest in social issues in students who have not experienced that interest before, helping these students begin to see that they can and want to contribute to something beyond their immediate personal sphere.

Gerald Shenk, associate professor of history, and David Takacs, associate professor of earth systems science and policy, take on this challenge in their course Social and Environmental History of California, at California State University, Monterey Bay (CSUMB). The course is geared toward juniors and seniors, particularly natural and behavioral science majors, many of whom enroll in order to satisfy the CSUMB learning requirements in the areas of Democratic Participation and U.S. Histories as well as the state requirements in U.S. and California history. This multidisciplinary course looks at the way the geography of California has shaped the evolution of the state's diverse cultures and how the choices people made have shaped the physical landscape. In a way that is reminiscent of Rick Battistoni's aspirations regarding political theory, Shenk and Takacs hope students will learn not only about history but also about how to use historical analysis and knowledge to illuminate contemporary issues and to clarify what they believe in and are prepared to act on. Shenk and Takacs want students to understand themselves as "historical beings in relationship to each other and to the Earth" and to "come to see history as a tool they can use to understand and shape the world they live in." "Our primary goal," they say in their syllabus, "is for students to use what they learn in our class to become historically informed, self-aware, ethical participants in the civic lives of their communities."

Shenk and Takacs use a wide array of strategies to accomplish this, including reading assignments, periodic short lectures, discussions in which the forty students in the course frequently break into small groups and then come back together, journal writing, research on historical issues, and ambitious projects that include action in the community. "Every minute is precious," and Shenk and Takacs must make hard choices between content and process. Their answer to this dilemma has been to teach for thematic understanding, usable skills, and personal growth rather than mastery of large bodies of content knowledge.

The centerpiece of the course is the Historically Informed Political Project (HIPP). Constituting 75 percent of students' final grade, the HIPP brings together history, ecology, personal values, and political action. Projects must address a California issue that has both environmental and social dimensions. Students conduct historical research as background to the project, articulate the values and assumptions they bring to it, and reflect on how those values and assumptions have changed as a result of engaging in the project. The project must involve at least ten hours of community work and lead to a set of policy recommendations informed by the historical research and community experience. Students can choose to work together on a joint project or do their work independently, but even those doing individual projects have many opportunities to work through with others the questions their projects raise. By centering on the HIPP, the course takes advantage of the pedagogical strengths of multidisciplinary, project-based, collaborative, and service learning. These projects are extremely challenging for students. CSUMB students are accustomed to doing service-related projects and reflecting on that service, but the HIPP demands in-depth historical research and extensive analysis, synthesis, and evaluation. Students must place their political projects in a larger social and environmental context and make policy recommendations based on what they learn through their research and political action.

WHAT IS POLITICS? Because they recognize how difficult the projects are, Shenk and Takacs organize course readings and activities to help students construct them one step at a time. The first important milestone in doing a HIPP is defining politics. Students write a one-page thought piece on the following questions: "What is politics?" "What counts as politics for you?" "Do you ever act politically?" This seemingly simple task initially proves more a stumbling block than a cornerstone in constructing a HIPP, because most of the students begin the course uninterested in or disgusted by politics. With few exceptions, students in the course describe politics in negative terms: for example, "a corrupt system driven by people pursuing their own self-interest." Few students have any desire to become politically active. As one student put it: "I don't do anything political because I see anyone who makes a living at doing politics, usually one in government or in a position of power, as a little kid who is just squabbling over getting more money or more power. I do not want to be any way a part of that mess . . . so I don't do anything."

In an effort to broaden and reframe the meaning of politics by connecting it with things the students do care about, Shenk and Takacs ask students to consider the 1960s slogan: "The personal is political." They suggest to students that "virtually everything you do has some kind of impact on others"—from the way you get to class to the toilet paper you buy. To illustrate this point, Shenk and Takacs have students read Frank Bardacke's *Good Liberals and Great Blue Herons* (1994) and then take them to the nearby town of Watsonville to meet with Bardacke and discuss his life and political commitments. A veteran of the civil rights, free speech, and antiwar movements of the 1960s, Bardacke's recent efforts have focused on land use and labor issues in Watsonville. Referring to an exchange that speaks to the perennial challenge of maintaining stamina in the face of hard political realities, Takacs recalls with fondness Bardacke's response to a student who asked how many of his political battles he has actually won. "I have never won," he answered. "Well," she replied, "then how can you go on?" His answer: "You have to find joy in the struggle." In this, he echoes our comment that part of what students need to sustain a sense of efficacy is a love of the game.

The idea that politics can be defined more broadly than students initially thought and that many seemingly apolitical matters have political implications intrigues most students, and they come to enjoy discussing their conceptions of what counts as politics. In fact these discussions are among the most dynamic of the semester as students grapple with defining politics in ways that reflect their personal values and ask each other provocative questions: What forms of political participation are valid for you, and what aren't? What do you approve of others doing, and what don't you approve of? Is protesting or boycotting a valid a form of political participation? Is breaking the law?

CYCLES OF ACTION AND REFLECTION. Shenk and Takacs use the image of a triangle to help students think about the relationship between their definition of politics, their personal values, and the political action they would like to engage in for the HIPP. Students begin filling in the three points of this triangle and discussing them in class early in the course, and they repeat the exercise over and over as their historical and political understandings grow and their projects progress. This repeated exercise helps students learn to articulate, revise, and refine the values and other assumptions that inform their beliefs about their responsibilities as citizens, and allows them to see how the three points in the triangle connect to shape the political projects they are pursuing. The hope is that they will internalize habits of mind that involve careful reflection, followed by action, which is followed by a return to reflection on the action and possible changes in values and other assumptions as a result of the cycle of action and reflection.

As Shenk and Takacs describe it, the cycle consists of four steps: (1) reflection about oneself (that is, one's assumptions, beliefs, and values) in relation to one's world, in order to understand what is important to one; (2) exploration of various perspectives through study, research, and discussion with others on one or more of the issues identified as important; (3) action that is informed by one's understanding of oneself and by study, research, and discussion; and (4) further reflection about the whole process, and preparation to move through the cycle again.

Shenk and Takacs recognize the importance of students' practicing the skills and habits the course is intended to teach, so students engage in many cycles of action and reflection over the course of the semester. Although the HIPP itself can be viewed as one big cycle, it can also be seen as made up of several smaller cycles. For example, defining and redefining politics does not take place through a single discussion or journal entry. It begins with students setting out their own assumptions about politics. Then they read Bardacke's book, which "helps broaden students' conception of political work and gets them thinking about how they might act politically in the world in a way that is consistent with their values." Following those discussions, students begin to design a HIPP and contemplate taking action that reflects their current conceptions of politics. This leads to further reflection and a reexamination of the question of what politics is. The changes in understanding of and feelings toward politics can be striking for some students, although for others it is only the beginning of what Shenk and Takacs hope will be an ongoing broadening of perspective. As Shenk said: "I think all we can do is introduce the cycle to them. It clicks for some, and maybe for the others—in five, ten, or twenty years—it'll click. . . . A lot of students are not ready for this—they're not ready for deep introspection—and we can't require it. . . . You can't force it to be the deep kind of introspection you imagined people would go through that would cause great transformation."

The HIPPs for the year we visited focused on a wide range of topics, including improving the health of a river, establishing an alternative campus newspaper, and changing the logging practices of a major lumber company. A theme that emerged in several projects was the connection between economic booms (surrounding, for example, the gold rush, oil, aerospace, and, most recently, electronics and the Internet) and unforeseen environmental and social effects. Building on this theme and his longstanding love of surfing, one student, Charles Tilley, used his project to look at the extent to which natural surf breaks have been lost to development on the California coast near CSUMB. At a nearby beach in Santa Cruz, for example, the construction of a jetty has eroded the ocean floor that produced surfable waves. Tilley's project involved assessing the costs and likely effects of building an artificial reef at the site, which would improve the quality of waves. As he lobbied for the construction of the reef, Tilley learned a great deal about local and state laws and policies as well as relevant court cases elsewhere in California. The same theme—the unintended consequences of development—informed the HIPPs of three students whose collaborative project worked toward the passage of a local ballot initiative (Measure E) designed to control urban sprawl and its negative effects on the environment. These students identified a candidate (Bruce Delgado) who favored the initiative and who was running for a seat on the Marina City Council. Among other things, they created signs and went door-to-door campaigning for this initiative and this candidate. On election day the students were delighted to learn that Measure E had been approved (54.2 percent of the vote) and that Delgado had won by seven votes.

It is noteworthy, however, that this project was the only one that tackled electoral politics. Although there is no doubt that the course helped students reconsider politics and find a way to think about politics that was consonant with their values, electoral politics was still viewed by most of them as "a real turn-off." In order to better understand this and other aspects of the course, Shenk and Takacs undertook a careful review of their teaching and the students' learning, which included systematic analysis of the HIPPs. They developed two taxonomies to describe the range of student outcomes, one consisting of ten ways in which students used history to inform their political projects, the other of eight ways in which students thought or acted politically. They found that students were able to use history in many different ways to inform their projects, including analyzing systems of power relationships, seeing themselves as both products of history and actors in history, and drawing parables or lessons from history. Students were most successful in identifying and using historical themes to inform their action projects. Analyses of the ways students thought and acted politically supported Takacs and Shenk's impression that students did develop politically in the course, even if many retained some of their skepticism toward electoral politics: "Our initial reading and subsequent analyses of the HIPPs confirms our impression that students did seem to become less afraid of politics, more sophisticated in their understanding of politics, more committed to political work, and more aware of the connections between themselves and their communities" (Takacs & Shenk, 2001, p. 6).

Building Moral and Civic Learning into the Curriculum

At California State University, Monterey Bay, graduation requirements press students who might otherwise not do so to take courses such as Social and Environmental History of California that broaden their perspectives on moral and civic issues. Takacs and Shenk's course thus highlights one of the central challenges of undergraduate moral and civic education—how to reach students who are not already inclined toward civic participation. CSUMB accomplished this by establishing a set of learning outcomes that all students must meet in order to graduate. Alverno and Tusculum Colleges also use variants of this outcomes-based or abilities-based approach. Other campuses we visited use different approaches. But all struggle with the same dilemmas: how to integrate moral and civic learning throughout the academic curriculum in ways that will strengthen both moral and civic learning and other aspects of intellectual and personal development, how to ensure that work in academic majors and electives as well as in general education will contribute to moral and civic development, and how to reach the widest possible group of students.

PART IV

CURRICULUM CHANGE

Part IV: Curriculum Change

In the previous section we examined various perspectives regarding curriculum design, including components of curricular change. In this section, we move to readings which take up curricular change as a phenomenon and as a process. As with the preceding readings, the selections included here are not intended to serve as a step-wise, how-to guide. Rather, their purpose here is to induce—and in some respects, inspire—critical and creative thinking about one of the most formidable challenges facing faculty and administrators alike—namely, enriching student learning through meaningful curriculum change.

In "Habits Hard to Break: How Persistent Features of Campus Life Frustrate Curricular Reform," Carol Geary Schneider and Robert Shoenberg empathize with the would-be undergraduate education reformer by enumerating several familiar obstacles to changing courses, programs, and institutions. Among the hindrances discussed are the insularity of departments, the unnecessary bifurcation of the curriculum into breadth and depth in the form of general education and the major, the constraint of standardized course credits and units, the mismatch between credits transferred and actual learning experiences, the divergence between campus goals and faculty rewards, and the lack of definition for the baccalaureate degree as a whole. Lest the reader be left in despair, Schneider and Shoenberg conclude with a hopeful view of the future: "The groundwork for success has already been laid in the form of an emerging consensus about what matters in undergraduate education and some promising pedagogical strategies for getting there. We need to seize the opportunity for building the more purposeful, powerful, and integrative forms of undergraduate education that the consensus now makes possible."

Margaret Andersen intensifies the discussion of obstacles to curriculum change in her feminist critique of the curricular status quo in "Changing the Curriculum in Higher Education," an article from *Signs: Journal of Women in Culture and Society*. In one sobering conjecture about the colossal task of including women and women's perspectives in all avenues of the academy, she asks: "How would the discipline need to change to reflect the fact that women are half the world's population and have had, in one sense, half the world's experience?" She contemplates several such questions while methodically outlining considerations for building an inclusive curriculum (including many references to the work of specific institutions), five phases of curriculum change (beginning with the recognition that women have a history and concluding with the redefinition of categories and values of male-centric history), and discipline-specific appraisals (e.g., arts and humanities, science and technology, social sciences).

According to Parker Palmer, the project of the sort pressed for by Andersen calls for a "movement sensibility" rather than an "organizational mentality." In "Divided No More: A Movement Approach to Educational Reform," he insists that too often efforts at colleges and universities to achieve substantial change are brought to a standstill by the norms and values of the organization itself. When adopting a movement approach, individuals working together for major change can use the organization's inherent resistance in a productive way because movements are energized by antagonistic forces. "Opposition validates the audacious idea that change must come," he says, adding that "The genius of movements is paradoxical: They abandon the logic of organizations in order to gather the power necessary to rewrite the logic of organizations." Palmer proceeds to describe how movements evolve through four progressive stages and offers perspective on how movements may be brought about intentionally.

Though not necessarily a movement by Palmer's standards, the endeavor to make college and university curricula more "learning-centered" has become increasingly visible in recent years. Harry Hubball and Helen Burt "provide a critical review of the motivating factors, processes and outcomes" of this curriculum reform trend in the volume's next readings, "An Integrated Approach to Developing and Implementing Learning-Centred Curricula." Motivated by an interest similar to the one expressed by Robert Newton in the previous section, Hubball and Burt presume that people involved in such curricular change can benefit from a summary of common characteristics—including but not limited to "tensions and models"—identified among various efforts to make curricula more learning-centered. Based on a case study of a pharmaceutical sciences department's learning-centered curriculum initiative at the University of British Columbia, they detail assumptions made about learning-centered curricular emphases and benefits, outline strategic frameworks and objectives utilized by participants in the reform, describe developmental stages that the reform goes through, and recount the unanticipated challenges and consequences of the initiative. Hubball and Burt conclude by underscoring the complexities of learning-centered curriculum development—that is, it "cannot be considered simply as a series of non-problematic and discrete steps."

Thus far the readings in this section have conceptualized large-scale curricular change as a massive undertaking that more often than not fails to achieve its goals. That is, despite the best efforts of reformers, the hoped-for outcomes become diluted through the change process and the curriculum ends up remarkably unchanged. In "Symbolic Politics and Institutional Boundaries in Curriculum Reform: The Case of National Sectarian University," Gordon Arnold acknowledges that minimal change is more likely than major change but does not accept the premise assumed by previous authors in this section—namely, that a lack of aspired-to change constitutes a failure. He criticizes such a judgment as overly rational and argues that the symbolic value of the change process and outcomes— even if the outcomes appear to be only nominal or incremental in light of original goals—should not be underestimated. To make this case he reports on his multi-year study of a general education reform initiative at National Sectarian University (NSU—a pseudonym). At the conclusion of a two-year effort to revise its general education program an NSU task force presented a set of general education requirements that, with the notable exception of a new "cultural diversity" requirement, were nearly identical to the existing requirements. Nevertheless, Arnold maintains that this was not an all-for-naught result. On the contrary, while the general education program looked similar, "different meanings" were ascribed to its parts and, moreover, the process instilled confidence with internal and external stakeholders that NSU was doing the right thing. And the installation of a cultural diversity requirement was particularly laudable even though it relied primarily on existing courses in its execution. Lest he be understood as an apologist for inadequacies of colleges and universities, Arnold notes that the implication of adopting a symbolic sensibility toward curricular reform is not that it shouldn't be pursued so magnificently—rather, it compels us "to be mindful of the underlying matrix of values and organizational constraints" and to accept that we "may find smaller changes are more appropriate."

The significant "depth of change" that is concomitant with curricular reform is examined in the next reading by Susan Awbrey, entitled "General Education Reform as Organizational Change: Integrating Cultural and Structural Change." Adding a wrinkle to the idea of learner-centeredness, Awbrey observes that "although campus-wide general education efforts may focus on what is best for students, recognizing why faculty hold the beliefs they do about what is best is a much deeper task that involves systematic examination of the cultural context in which the change is taking place." By drawing connections with extant literature, she defines and sketches a model of organizational culture which she then applies to the case of general education reform. She concludes by identifying "potholes" on the general education reform road and advising that such reform should integrate both cultural and structural change guided by "cultural inquiry" throughout the process.

Whereas the readings up to this point in this section have approached the idea of curricular change largely at the institutional level through the program level, the three final readings that follow approach the idea of curricular change more at the course level through the program level. Also in common among these three articles is a focus on the promise and limitations of especially popular trends in curricular reform—namely, service-learning, learning communities, and interdisciplinary courses. In "The Limits of Service-Learning in Higher Education," Dan Butin critically examines the claims made by proponents of service-learning by identifying what he sees as the pedagogical, political, and institutional limits of the movement. His conclusion includes an observation that echoes issues explored by Margaret Andersen: "Rather than continuing to think *about* service-learning as a politics to transform higher education and society, we might more fruitfully reverse the terminology and begin to think *through* service-learning about the politics of transforming higher education and society." In "Reconsidering Learning Communities: Expanding the Discourse by Challenging the Discourse," Susan Talburt and Deron Boyles acutely assess "fundamental tenets underlying the idea and practice of learning communities" (e.g., claims made about their "progressive" history, the "idealized" ways they are talked about). They conclude that the idea of learning communities—freshman learning communities (FLCs in particular)—is a good one, yet they may have undesirable effects, due not least to the tendency of institutions to use them to their own benefit. And finally, in "Does Interdisciplinarity Promote Learning? Theoretical Support and Researchable Questions," Lisa Lattuca, Lois Voigt, and Kimberly Fath similarly challenge the presumed benefits of a highly regarded curricular innovation: interdisciplinary courses and programs. They review definitions of interdisciplinarity (or lack thereof—an expression of an affinity with Rick Szostak's point of view in the previous section) and related scholarship, analyze theoretical perspectives in light of two case studies, and pose a series of questions for further research, including: "Are gains in students' knowledge and skills attributable to the interdisciplinary nature of courses?" From their perspective, despite the eagerness of many to strive for curricula inspired by interdisciplinarity, this remains an open—and very difficult—question.

Curriculum change is hard. All of this volume's authors and readers would surely agree. The readings in this section well document the myriad reasons why it is hard, including the fact that it is often a deeply personal endeavor for those who are involved. Many of the readings imply that curriculum change is an "us against them" struggle. Who are "we" and who are "they" in the readings, and do the actors change from reading to reading? Several of the readings argue for the importance of reforming the perspective of the reformer, if curriculum is to be changed successfully. What would Schneider, Shoenberg, Andersen, and Palmer think about each other's points of view in that regard? Moreover, what would they think about Arnold's suggestion that reformers would do well not to overlook the contributions of incremental change? Thinking of Arnold's argument in particular, what role does striving for big goals play in the production of incremental change, and is the latter even possible without the former? Whatever the dispositions toward change held by individuals may be, the readings in this section also suggest that our collective attitude toward change is, perhaps, more celebratory than it ought to be at times. Be it learner-centeredness drawing attention away from faculty perspectives (Awbrey), the way service-learning (Butin) and learning community initiatives hold sway (Talburt & Boyles), or the promise of interdisciplinarity (Lattuca et al.), curricular change, like any other, is not without unintended consequences. What does the future hold for such curricular innovations? Will they evolve in such a way that "the curriculum" is simply a learning-centered, service-oriented, communal and interdisciplinary phenomenon? To what extent, if at all, does the educational power of such innovations depend on them being counter to "the curriculum?" To be sure, with questions like this, the pursuit and realization of curricular change will forever be a source of frustration and inspiration.

HABITS HARD TO BREAK

HOW PERSISTENT FEATURES OF CAMPUS LIFE
FRUSTRATE CURRICULAR REFORM

CAROL GEARY SCHNEIDER AND ROBERT SHOENBERG

As we write, hundreds of colleges are struggling to update or reform the liberal arts component of their curricula. Often there is excitement about this: during this decade, a sense has emerged that hands-on, inquiry-oriented strategies for learning, built around professor-created, often collaborative materials, may be the approach we need for undergraduate rejuvenation.

Over and over again, however, faculty design teams soon come face-to-face with organizational realities that frustrate their high hopes. Almost whatever plan for integrative, practice-oriented learning they envision, there are structural features of the academic environment that work silently but powerfully to undo it. This article takes up several of the most formidable of these obstacles, and looks at a remedy.

The Discipline as Silo

The 20th-century educational model is ostensibly—indeed was originally—built on a conceptualization of knowledge structured by "discipline." Each emergent discipline eventually came to be represented by an academic department; then, departments in the arts and sciences fields were organized into "colleges" according to rough principles of common subject matters and epistemologies.

If "department" and "discipline" ever were synonymous in the ways the model implies, they certainly are no longer so. The degree to which a discipline represents a paradigmatic structure of knowledge that provides, in and of itself, a viable organizational principle for undergraduate learning is called into question by the increasing "interdisciplinarity" of both student interests and faculty behaviors, not only in their teaching but in their research as well.

The scholarly concerns of individual faculty members within almost any academic department encompass a wide diversity of topics and methods, often including those primarily associated with other disciplines. One anthropologist may be studying evidence derived from analysis of tooth enamel in different cultures; another working in the same department may be producing a history of ideas about race and biology. One economist may study principles of supply and demand across all markets, even as a colleague pursues a cultural analysis of family economic decision-making.

Above and beyond the migration of scholarly topics and approaches from one discipline to another, new and avowedly interdisciplinary fields of study are springing up everywhere. In the arresting image of the historian John Higham, the contemporary academy is like "a house in which the inhabitants are leaning out of the many open windows gaily chatting with the neighbors, while the doors between the rooms stay closed."

Yet even as scholarship reconfigures knowledge in increasingly intersecting and polycentric designs, students in arts and sciences fields are still socialized not only into the rhetoric of "the

Reprinted from *Change* 31, no. 2 (March/April 1999), Change Magazine.

discipline" but also into the operational assumption that they have no need or responsibility to integrate their learning across multiple domains of inquiry and practice.

To enter into a discussion of what constitutes a discipline—that is, a distinctive mode of inquiry, as opposed to a subject matter or a community of scholars with overlapping interests—would lead this discussion too far afield. The point to be made here is that the rhetoric and curricular organization associated with inherited concepts of "the discipline" invite students to think of themselves as pursuing a specific, well-defined competence when the entire ethos of the contemporary world calls for the capacity to cross boundaries, explore connections, and move in uncharted directions. Discipline-based conceptions of advanced study become deeply problematic when they allow a student to burrow into only one corner of, say, literature or political science, rather than exploring the field's complex byways and neighboring communities.

Such insularity can be equally problematic for the two-thirds of American undergraduates who choose pre-professional fields. Students in these fields are too seldom invited to connect their vocational studies with larger societal, cultural, historical, or ethical questions. Why ask of the accounting major (a pre-professional field) what is not asked of the biology major (a discipline)? The result, as Ernest Boyer observed a decade ago, is all too often a neglect of the social and ethical responsibilities inherent in the work of any field. As Boyer noted in *College: The Undergraduate Experience in America*,

> [I]n many fields, skills have become ends. Scholars are busy sorting, counting, and decoding. We are turning out technicians. But the crisis of our time relates not to technical competence, but to a loss of social and historical perspective, to the disastrous divorce of competence from conscience. . . . And the values professionals bring to their work are every bit as crucial as the particularities of the work itself.

Lee Shulman, Boyer's successor at the Carnegie Foundation for the Advancement of Teaching, argues that all fields—disciplinary and professional—ought to be guided by an ethic of social obligation and service, and that espousing such an ethic would revitalize the basic conception of a liberal education.

This critique of inherited disciplinary assumptions does not negate the collegial importance of departments. Both faculty and students are sustained by structures that provide small communities of common interest, intellectual "homes" for learning, mentoring, and the give and take of collaborative exploration. As Alexander Astin reports in his 1993 *What Matters in College?* experience and research alike attest to the importance of close relationships between students and faculty in fostering students' intellectual growth and educational attainment. Something like the departmental home seems a necessity in any complex institution.

What we do question is the equating of department with unitary and self-contained courses of study, segregated by catalog design and powerful traditions from all the other parts of student learning. There is no inherent reason why the learning fostered in a departmental community need be narrowly bounded. Many of the newer fields, such as environmental studies, women's studies, or policy studies, not only model but require a problem-centered, multidisciplinary, and integrative approach to learning. The challenge for more traditional departments, disciplinary or pre-professional, is that of rethinking their educational aims and of asserting their own accountability for forms of learning that prepare students to navigate a kaleidoscopically complex world.

In some fields, broadening the recommended course of study to include larger societal perspectives and issues will require challenging and uprooting the encrusted educational assumptions of professional accrediting associations. In other fields, the accrediting associations are already broadening their expectations for student learning in ways that encourage inquiry and interpretive learning.

General Education and the Major

As long as general education was conceived predominantly as study of a range—or "breadth"—of subject matters, with study in a designated major providing "depth," the conventional sharp division between general education and the major made some sense. But with today's educational focus on helping students develop intellectual skills, understand a range of epistemologies, and increase their ability to negotiate intellectual, cultural, civic, and practical topics and relationships, the assumed dividing line between general education and the major is no longer useful.

On the one hand, the usual fraction of the curriculum allocated to general education is simply inadequate for developing, practicing, and integrating—at a reasonable level of proficiency—the complex analytical and inquiry-oriented skills that faculties aim for today. On the other, the development of those abilities requires a full four years of practice and application, which necessarily implicates the major. Developing such abilities, then, is just as much the business of the major as of general education—and it is just as essential to a baccalaureate-level mastery of a field.

Put another way, the logic of today's ambitions for undergraduate education forces us to think about that education as a whole. This whole should include communication skills; analytic, critical, and scientific thinking; and societal perspective and responsibility.

Goals for learning in the major, then, ought to deal at a high level of intentionality with the development of general and integrative as well as field-specific understandings, perspectives, and skills. This blending of general skills with field-specific approaches can already be seen in writing-across-the-curriculum programs and in similar efforts focused on skills such as oral communication, quantitative reasoning, and second-language acquisition. Some departments are introducing diversity content into their curricula in ways appropriate to their field; others are emphasizing issues of social responsibility and global engagement. But such efforts remain for the most part sporadic and elective.

The advantage to major programs of assuming this kind of instructional responsibility for students' integrative learning is a greater share of the attention of their students. What it takes is much clearer formulation of the purposes of the major and a willingness to teach with an intentionality that thoughtfully addresses the goals of the department and of the college, not just those of the individual faculty member.

Courses and Credits

The dysfunctional dichotomy between general and specialized education is discernibly beginning to erode. The challenge, of course, is to replace it with an educationally viable alternative. But standing in the way is another familiar structure, the system of courses and credit hours, which remains in place as strongly as ever.

Use of the word "course"—a shortening of the phrase "course of lectures"—traces its origin to the very beginnings of universities, when students registered and paid for a particular number of lectures by one of the learned men who "professed" at a school. In American higher education, beginning in the early part of this century, the course became standardized in terms of credit hours or an easily translatable equivalent. The modal course, as all know, is three credit hours, which usually implies a set number of class meetings spread over a given term. All sorts of modifications or equivalents are possible, but the three-credit course is the standard coin of the realm.

Equally standard, despite many familiar variants, is the notion of a bachelor's degree as the equivalent of four years of undergraduate study, defined as 40 three-credit courses or 120 credit hours. There is no particular reason why a bachelor's degree should take four years of full-time study, arbitrarily defined as five three-credit courses per semester, to complete. Nor is there any particular reason why all bachelor's degrees should take the same amount of time to complete, or why students in some programs should complete "free electives" to fill out the 120 credits, or why some programs— notably engineering—should try to squeeze themselves into the canonical 120 hours.

This standard for the degree emerged early in the 20th century as a counterweight to diploma mills and other sorts of ventures that awarded degrees on the basis of little or no effort on the part of recipients. The notion of the credit hour was born of the same impulse. Moreover, to a degree probably unforeseen by its inventors, the credit hour, by becoming the standard unit of academic currency, has made possible the American system of student transfer. In fact, transfer has become so pervasive that at many public institutions, both two-and four-year, the transfer process now controls the academic program.

As convenient as this standardization is, it has led—to say the least—to some questionable results . . . some so familiar that their dubiousness seldom occurs to us. For example, instructors have grown used to allowing the size of the package to control the treatment of the subject matter. No matter that some topics might benefit from being taught over a longer period of time, or some a shorter, or that others do not deserve a full course at all: each will appear on the course schedule for the same number of class hours and term time.

This uniform and separate packaging of learning experiences leads both faculty and students to treat courses in isolation from each other. Very seldom—unless courses are explicitly part of a sequence of two or three—do instructors make an effort to relate one course to another, either in terms of the content addressed or the analytical tasks assigned to students.

These problems, however, pale in contrast to the damage done by allowing course titles and credits to stand as surrogates for learning. The establishment of "interchangeable" course units and of declared "equivalencies" has led everywhere to a stunning neglect of what a student is supposed to be able to know and do at the completion of any particular course, and of how capacities fostered in any particular course do or should prepare students for work yet to come.

The result, as many faculty members pioneering with capstone courses and/or portfolios of student work well know, is that significant numbers of students ascend to the final year of study with analytical, problem-solving, and communicative competencies that are at best only shallowly developed.

Credit Transfer Practices

The equating of course titles with learning becomes even more problematic in the context of student transfer, a process increasingly the subject of state mandate in public systems of higher education. Student transfer is built on the presumption that courses with equivalent titles and credits will represent the same learning experience—of content and developed competence—across all institutions.

The flip side of this, of course, is that courses with different titles but equally valid learning experiences will not be accepted in transfer, a practice that enrages transfer students, community colleges, and state legislators alike. All around, the illogic of the practice is patent.

State coordinating boards and, increasingly and notoriously, state legislatures have sometimes responded by establishing a standard set of general education courses for all public institutions, which once completed, must be accepted by the receiving institution in satisfaction of all lower-division general education requirements.

The resulting general education package is frequently a thoroughly retrograde system of distribution requirements in their least intellectually defensible form. This lowest-common-denominator standardization certainly helps reduce barriers to transfer, but it also results in fragmented study and widespread student cynicism about the curriculum while imposing a severe restriction on the curricular and pedagogical imagination of faculties at both two-and four-year institutions.

The Undefined Baccalaureate Degree

The ultimate problem with this entire system of courses and credits is the way it comes to define the baccalaureate degree itself. As course credits become a surrogate for learning, we allow ourselves to shirk responsibility for developing a rigorous definition of what the baccalaureate degree should mean.

This is another way of saying that the academy is insufficiently focused on the kinds of educational outcomes it is trying to achieve. Progress in assessment notwithstanding, colleges and universities have a long way to go in developing functioning frameworks for expected outcomes, let alone in finding adequate ways of judging students' achievement of them.

True, hundreds of campuses have developed statements of their goals for student learning. But these statements are too frequently the stated goals only for that fraction of the curriculum devoted to general education. Seldom are the goals presented as charges to the departments as well.

Thus, having assigned most of the important educational goals to a fraction of the curriculum—often on a principle of a courses or two per goal—faculty assessment committees struggle unsuccessfully to figure out some way of assessing these general education outcomes "across the curriculum." One result is that campuses increasingly fall back upon satisfaction surveys as evidence that they are meeting their stated general education goals . . . proof again of how far the academy has to go in developing credible expectations for student performance as an outcome.

Many institutions have noted the powerful example of Alverno College and have sent teams of faculty members and administrators to that college's workshops to learn about assessing entire curricula. In the end, though, few have taken up the challenge of emulating Alverno's system of learning assessments. The example is there; Alverno and a handful of other campuses are pioneers in showing that educational goals can guide the curriculum, that assessment can be done well, and that the combination of faculty-led assessment and student self-assessment can be a powerful spur to demonstrable learning.

Why have so few other institutions shown the will to develop their own performance expectations and assessments? Part of the reason lies in our next topic.

The Faculty Reward Question

Hanging over all this need for rethinking inherited structures is the thorny question of how faculty members will be rewarded for the considerable efforts required to change and assess educational programs. Exhortations abound about the compelling need to change campus reward structures so that curricular and teaching innovations are duly recognized and faculty can devote time to these efforts without fear of jeopardizing their promotion and tenure.

Administrators and sometimes even faculty leaders encourage talented faculty to participate in renewal efforts, but so far, most faculty don't believe them. They've heard too many horror stories about colleagues who spent time on a teaching innovation and curricular reform, only to have it discounted by colleagues or administrators when it came time for promotion or merit increases.

Right now, neither institutions nor faculty members are willing to disarm unilaterally by honoring teaching and service efforts equally with research accomplishments. With the exception of two-year institutions and a fair number of regional liberal arts colleges, the prestige and rewards in higher education continue to lie with published research.

Reforms in teaching and curricula will be absolutely necessary for our colleges to survive and thrive in contexts of technological revolution and multiplying educational providers. But making those reforms will be difficult if not impossible until it becomes the norm for institutions to recognize and honor the intellectual work involved. Faculties will need to know that time spent on creative curricula and teaching will be as well rewarded as equivalent time spent on research. Since much of this work will necessarily be cross-disciplinary and integrative, departments and colleges will have to develop entirely new abilities to assess faculty work.

In short, the disciplinary hold on curriculum, a course-and-credit system of academic bookkeeping, and the atomism of faculty reward systems all stand as formidable impediments to the educational renewal to which campuses aspire. Perfectly reasonable desires to facilitate student transfer and curricular choice serve to keep a number of the more questionable structures in place, indeed to entrench them even more solidly.

Moving From Here to There

Yet these timeworn systems clearly are not total impediments to reform. We could not talk as we have about emerging new practices in baccalaureate education if they were not in fact present and thriving in enough places to attract attention. Whether or not they are involved in such practices, most faculty members are familiar with experiential and service learning, collaborative and cooperative learning, learning communities, capstone courses and projects, and performance assessments. It is not concepts and practices we lack, but a practical consensus about the purposes of baccalaureate education that will encompass them.

We believe an emerging framework for such a consensus exists. It emphasizes a range of intellectual skills; epistemological and research sophistication; global, societal, and self-knowledge; relational learning; and making intellectual connections. It requires seeing undergraduate education as a whole as opposed to splitting it between general and specialized learning. It also argues strongly for aligning the goals and emphases of K-12 education more intentionally with those of collegiate education.

This emerging direction for undergraduate learning is well served by instructional strategies that reflect the resurgent emphasis on the student as learner, with the teacher as mentor rather than sage. The development of problem-solving skills, both as an individual and in collaboration with others, is essential to this pattern, as is experiential learning in its many forms. Institutions' choices of educational technologies ought to reflect this learning-centered, intensively "hands-on" approach.

Connecting Goals with Practice

What we need next for collegiate reform is the parallel embodiment—in a variety of four-year undergraduate programs—of curricula purposely directed toward goals campuses avow. These models should do more than simply reorganize existing individual courses: they should be integrated structures of carefully related learning experiences that pay systematic attention to developmental sequencing and concomitant student assignments. For a variety of practical reasons, the curricula may need to be presented in the standard form of semesters and courses and credits, but the rationale for and instruction within ought to become far less atomistic than in current practice.

To meet fully the challenges of this approach, faculty members will have to give up some old habits of thinking, most significantly the idea that they are sole owners of the courses they teach. Offering their courses within integrated, intentional sequences will require them to acknowledge the stake that their departments and the institution as a whole have in each course and in the student outcomes it is intended to produce. Faculty will have to teach toward some goals about which there has been mutual agreement and around which there is some sense of collective accountability.

This need not mean what faculty most fear—externally imposed constraints on the actual content of a course. But it should mean that designated categories of courses work intentionally and accountably, through the kinds of assignments students undertake, to foster specific capacities and intellectual skills. Models for this combination of flexibility and focus already exist in some fields (the health sciences, for example). The challenge is to build on available examples.

Given the transience of students, particularly within regions or state systems of higher education, some broad agreements within the higher education community about educational goals and what they mean operationally will also be important. If the emphasis is on the mastery of particular intellectual practices rather than on a simple passing of named courses, then faculties within institutions among which students regularly move should be able to negotiate some common understandings about appropriate assignments. Educational goals should not simply be imparted to students; they need to become a continuing framework for students' educational planning, assessments, and self-assessment.

The difficulty of articulating important educational goals across institutions and getting faculty to acknowledge them in what and how they teach, while maintaining a high level of institutional and faculty autonomy, is not to be underestimated. Such coordination requires enormous amounts of educational insight, negotiating skill, and good will. Yet making sense of education for the large numbers of students who increasingly move from institution to institution, and for whom a coherent, purposeful curriculum can never be predesigned at a single campus, would seem to require the effort.

This emphasis on student outcomes rather than on course credits and curricular features implies a wider use of assessment. The assessment will be more appropriate and effective if it is embedded in coursework or grows naturally out of it, rather than taking the form of short-answer instruments created solely for the purpose of external reporting. Ideally, assessment should provide opportunities for students to advance, integrate, and correct their understandings at key junctures in their course of study. Assessments that provide no useful feedback to students themselves defeat what should be an important goal of the assessment effort.

Moving forward with a framework for learning that expects broad, deep, and complex accomplishments for every student is a challenge that invites the participation of the entire array of higher education stakeholders, from the public and its elected representatives to each individual institution, and including accreditors, state higher education agencies, university system offices, learned societies in the disciplines, testing agencies, federal education agencies, and so on. The ground-work for success has already been laid in the form of an emerging consensus about what matters in undergraduate education and some promising pedagogical strategies for getting there. We need to seize the opportunity for building the more purposeful, powerful, and integrative forms of under-graduate education that the consensus now makes possible.

CHANGING THE CURRICULUM IN HIGHER EDUCATION

MARGARET L. ANDERSEN

In Susan Glaspell's short story, "A Jury of Her Peers," a man is murdered, strangled in his bed with a rope. The victim's wife, Mrs. Wright, formerly Minnie Foster, has been arrested for the crime. The men investigating—the sheriff, the county attorney, and a friend—think she is guilty but cannot imagine her motive. "It's all perfectly clear, except the reason for doing it. But you know juries when it comes to women. If there was some definite thing—something to make a story about. A thing that would connect up with this clumsy way of doing it," the county attorney says.[1]

When the three men go to the Foster house to search for evidence, two of their wives go along to collect some things for the jailed Minnie Foster. In the house the men laugh at the women's attention to Minnie's kitchen and tease them for wondering about the quilt she was making. While the women speculate about whether she was going to quilt it or knot it, the men, considering this subject trivial, belittle the women for their interest in Minnie's handwork. "Nothing here but kitchen things," the sheriff says. "But would the women know a clue if they did come upon it?" the other man scoffs.[2] The three men leave the women in the kitchen while they search the rest of the house for important evidence.

While in the kitchen, the women discover several things amiss. The kitchen table is wiped half-clean, left half messy. The cover is left off a bucket of sugar, while beside it sits a paper bag only half filled with sugar. Mrs. Hale and Mrs. Peters see that one block of the quilt Minnie Foster was making is sewn very badly, while the other blocks have fine and even stitches. They wonder, "What was she so nervous about?" When they find an empty bird cage, its door hinge torn apart, they try to imagine how such anger could have erupted in an otherwise bleak and passionless house. Remembering Minnie Foster, Mrs. Hale recalls, "She—come to think of it, she was kind of like a bird herself. Real sweet and pretty, but kind of timid and—fluttery. How—she—did—change."[3] When the women pick up her sewing basket, they find in it Minnie's dead canary wrapped in a piece of silk, its neck snapped and broken. They realize they have discovered the reason Minnie Foster murdered her husband. Imagining the pain in Minnie Foster's marriage to Mr. Wright, Mrs. Hale says, "No, Wright wouldn't like the bird, a thing that sang. She used to sing. He killed that too."[4]

Soon the men return to the kitchen, but the women have tacitly agreed to say nothing of what they have found. Still mocking the women's attentiveness to kitchen details, the men tease them. The county attorney asks, "She was going to—what is it you call it, Ladies?" "We call it, knot it, Mr. Henderson."[5]

"Knot it," also alluding to the method of murder, is a punning commentary on the relative weights of men's and women's knowledge in the search for facts and evidence. Women's culture—"not it" to the men—is invisible, silenced, trivialized, and wholly ignored in men's construction of reality. At the same time, men's culture is assumed to present the entire and only truth.[6]

Reprinted from *Signs: Journal of Women in Culture and Society* 12, no. 2 (winter 1987), by permission of University of Chicago Press.

Glaspell's story suggests the social construction of knowledge in a gender-segregated world. In her story, women's understandings and observations are devalued and women are excluded from the search for truth. How might the truth look different, we are asked, were women's perspectives included in the making of facts and evidence? What worlds do women inhabit and how do their worlds affect what they know and what is known about them?

The themes of Glaspell's story are at the heart of women's studies, since women's studies rests on the premise that knowledge in the traditional academic disciplines is partial, incomplete, and distorted because it has excluded women. In the words of Adrienne Rich, "As the hitherto 'invisible' and marginal agent in culture, whose native culture has been effectively denied, women need a reorganization of knowledge, of perspectives and analytical tools that can help us know our foremothers, evaluate our present historical, political, and personal situation, and take ourselves seriously as agents in the creation of a more balanced culture."[7] Women's studies was born from this understanding and over the past two decades has evolved with two goals: to build knowledge and a curriculum in which women are agents of knowledge and in which knowledge of women transforms the male-centered curriculum of traditional institutions.[8] Curriculum change through women's studies is, as Florence Howe has said, both developmental and transformative: it is developmental in generating new scholarship about women and transformative in its potential to make the traditional curriculum truly coeducational.[9]

Since women have been excluded from the creation of formalized knowledge, to include women means more than just adding women into existing knowledge or making them new objects of knowledge. Throughout this essay, including women refers to the complex process of redefining knowledge by making women's experiences a primary subject for knowledge, conceptualizing women as active agents in the creation of knowledge, including women's perspectives on knowledge, looking at gender as fundamental to the articulation of knowledge in Western thought, and seeing women's and men's experiences in relation to the sex/gender system. Because this multifaceted understanding of "including women in the curriculum" is an integral part of the new scholarship on women and because we have not developed language sufficient to reflect these assumptions, readers should be alert to the fact that phrases like "scholarship on women," "including women," and "learning about women" are incomplete but are meant to refer to the multidimensional reconstruction of knowledge.

Women's studies has developed from feminists' radical critique of the content and form of the academic disciplines, the patriarchal structure of education, the consciousness education reproduces, and the relation of education to dominant cultural, economic, political, and social institutions. Women's studies seeks to make radical transformations in the systems and processes of knowledge creation and rests on the belief that changing what we study and know about women will change women's and men's lives.[10] Hence, curriculum change is understood as part of the political transformation of women's role in society because all teaching includes political values. As Florence Howe has written,

> In the broadest context of that word, teaching is a political act: some person is choosing, for whatever reasons, to teach a set of values, ideas, assumptions, and pieces of information, and in so doing, to omit other values, ideas, assumptions, and pieces of information. If all those choices form a pattern excluding half the human race, that is a political act one can hardly help noticing. To omit women entirely makes one kind of political statement; to include women as a target for humor makes another. To include women with seriousness and vision, and with some attention to the perspective of women as a hitherto subordinate group is simply another kind of political act. Education is the kind of political act that controls destinies, gives some persons hope for a particular kind of future, and deprives others even of ordinary expectations for work and achievement.[11]

This discussion raises important questions about how we define women's studies in the future and how, especially in this conservative political period,[12] the radicalism of women's studies can be realized within institutions that remain racist and sexist and integrally tied to the values and structures of a patriarchal society. But, as Susan Kirschner and Elizabeth Arch put it, women's studies and inclusive curriculum projects are "two important pieces of one work."[13] Feminists in educational institutions will likely continue working for both women's studies and curriculum change, since both projects seek to change the content and form of the traditional curriculum[14] and to contribute to social change through curriculum transformation. It is simply impossible, as Howe has put it, "to move directly from the male-centered curriculum to what I have described as 'transformation' of that curriculum into a changed and co-educational one—without passing through some form of women's studies."[15]

Building an Inclusive Curriculum

Peggy McIntosh estimates that since 1975 there have been at least eighty projects that, in various ways, examine how the disciplines can be redefined and reconstructed to include us all.[16] This estimate gives some idea of the magnitude of the movement to create new curricula that include women. Moreover, according to McIntosh, although fewer projects are now being funded through sources external to the institutions that house them, internal funding for such projects seems to be increasing.

Curriculum-change projects in women's studies have varied widely in their purposes, scope, institutional contexts, and sources of funding. For example, projects at Wheaton College and Towson State University (both funded through the Fund for the Improvement of Post Secondary Education [FIPSE]) are university-wide projects engaging faculty in the revision of courses across the curriculum. Other projects involve consortia of several campuses, such as those at Montana State University, the Southwest Institute for Research on Women (SIROW) at the University of Arizona, and the University of Massachusetts—Amherst.

The SIROW project has several dimensions, including course development and revision at the University of Arizona and a three-year project for integrating women into international studies and foreign language courses at several universities in Arizona and Colorado. Funded by the Women's Educational Equity Act program (WEEA), the Montana State project began as a two-year faculty development project intended to reduce bias in the curriculum; it was later renamed the Northern Rockies Program on Women and was expanded to develop curriculum resources in a twenty-five school consortium in Montana, Utah, Wyoming, and Idaho. The project "Black Studies/Women's Studies: An Overdue Partnership," funded by FIPSE, includes faculty from the University of Massachusetts, Smith College, Hampshire College, Mount Holyoke College, and Amherst College; twenty-nine faculty from this project met to create new courses and build theoretical and curricular connections between black studies and women's studies. The Mellon seminars at the Wellesley College Center for Research on Women, funded through the Andrew W. Mellon Foundation, have drawn together faculty from the New England area to apply feminist scholarship to curriculum transformation.

At the University of Delaware, the university provided funds for a development project for faculty in the social sciences who were revising introductory and core courses to make them inclusive of gender and race; faculty in the project met in an interdisciplinary faculty seminar on feminist scholarship, followed by a day-long conference on curriculum change and a one-year program for visiting consultants who gave public lectures and advised faculty on the reconstruction of their courses. The Women's Research and Resource Center at Spelman College, funded by the Ford Foundation, has emphasized curriculum revision in freshmen courses in English, world literature, and world civilization with the purpose of building a cross-cultural perspective that would illuminate both the contributions and experiences of Afro-American women and women in the Third World. Still other projects are designed primarily for resource development, such as the project of the Organization of American Historians that produced curriculum packets designed to integrate material on women in the United States and Europe into survey courses at both the college and secondary school level. The Geraldine R. Dodge seminars also focus on the secondary school level. Involving teachers from public and private secondary schools in three regions of the country, these seminars are intended to help teachers become better acquainted with feminist scholarship and to develop high-school curricula that reflect women's history, experiences, and perceptions.

There arc so many of these projects that it is impossible to describe all of them here. These few examples do, however, give an idea of the range of activities and the different institutional contexts of inclusive curriculum projects. All of them rest on the concept of faculty development since building faculty knowledge of new interdisciplinary scholarship from feminist studies is an integral and critical part of curriculum transformation.

Directors of these projects typically begin with the recognition that women's studies scholarship has not fully made its way into the "main" curriculum of colleges and universities and that, without programs designed to bring the new scholarship into the whole curriculum, most students— male and female—will remain untouched by scholarship on women and therefore unprepared to understand the world. Elizabeth Minnich suggests that, though liberal arts advocates claim that a liberal arts education instills in students the perspectives and faculties to understand a complex world, instead, students learn about a detached and alienating world outside their own experiences. Were we honest about traditional education, she says, we would teach them the irony of the gap between stated educational missions and actual educational practices. Schools do not typically teach a critical view of the liberal arts we have inherited; we seem to have forgotten that, historically, liberal arts education was an entrée into ruling positions for privileged males. Liberal arts education taught privileged men the language of their culture, its skills, graces, principles, and intellectual challenges, modeled on one normative character. It thus emphasized sameness over difference, even in a world marked by vast differences of culture, race, class, ethnicity, religion, and gender.[17] Consequently, there is now entrenched in the liberal arts a curriculum claiming general validity that is, however, based on the experience, values, and activities of a few.

Curriculum-change projects designed to bring the scholarship on women into the whole curriculum have been variously labeled "mainstreaming," "integrating women's studies into the curriculum," and "gender-balancing the curriculum." There are problems with each of these labels, since they may imply that curriculum change through women's studies follows some simple programmatic scheme when women's studies cannot be merely assimilated into the dominant curriculum. McIntosh says the label "mainstreaming" trivializes women by implying that we have been out of, and are only now entering, the mainstream. The term implies that there is only one mainstream and that, by entering it, women will be indistinguishable from men. It makes the reconstructive work of curriculum change seem like a quick and simple process, whereas women's studies builds its understanding on the assumption that there are diverse and plural streams of women's and men's experience.[18]

The use of the terms "integration" and "balance" to describe these projects is also problematic. Feminist scholarship has rested on the assumption that the exclusion of women leads to distorted, partial, and false claims to truth, yet "balancing" may imply that all perspectives are equally accurate or significant. Certainly, women's studies instructors do not want room in the curriculum for all perspectives, thereby including those that are racist, anti-Semitic, ethnocentric, class-biased, and sexist. Furthermore, liberal calls for balance often cloak an underlying appeal for analyses that are detached and dispassionate, as if those who are passionately committed to what they study cannot be objective. Gloria Bowles and Renate Duelli-Klein, among others, argue that it is unrealistic to seek a balanced curriculum in a world that is unbalanced.[19] Their concern reflects the understanding that most educational curricula mirror the values and structure of the dominant culture, yet they may underestimate the power of education to generate change.

Similarly, "integration" implies that women's studies can be assimilated into the dominant curriculum, when women's studies scholarship demonstrates that women cannot be simply included in a curriculum already structured, organized, and conceived through the experience of men. Critics of curriculum-integration projects, including Bowles and Duelli-Klein, caution that these projects might dilute the more radical goals of the women's studies movement by trying to make women's studies more palatable to those who control higher education. Integration is inadequate if it means only including traditionally excluded groups in a dominant system of thinking. So, if integration is interpreted as assimilation, these critics are right, but the history of the black protest movement in America indicates that the concept of integration cannot be dismissed merely as assimilation. Advocates of integration in the black protest movement understood that integration required a major transformation of American culture and values, as well as radical transformation of political and economic institutions. In the development of black studies, integration and separatism have not been either/or strategies, though they do reflect different emphases in black political philosophy and have been used strategically for different, yet complementary, purposes. If we take its meaning from black culture and politics, integration is a more complex idea and goal than assimilation; movements for integration in black history reflect a broad tolerance for diverse efforts to make radical transformations of educational institutions and the society at large.[20]

This controversy is more than a semantic one because the debate about terminology reflects political discussion among feminists who sometimes disagree about the possibilities and desirability of including women's studies in the curriculum. Because women's studies rejects the assumptions of the dominant culture and finds the traditional compartmentalization of knowledge inadequate for the questions women's studies asks, both the language and the work of curriculum change by necessity must maintain that what is wrong with the dominant curriculum cannot be fixed by simple addition, inclusion, and minor revision.[21] Feminist critics of curriculum-integration projects fear that these projects change the primary audience of women's studies to "academics who wish to reform the disciplines but see no need to challenge the existing structure of knowledge based on the dominant androcentric culture."[22] Other feminist criticisms reflect a concern that the political radicalism of feminism will be sacrificed in order to make women's studies scholarship more acceptable to nonfeminists.[23] As Mary Childers, former associate director at the University of Maine at Orono project, states it, curriculum-integration projects may transform feminist work more than they transform the people at whom the projects are directed.[24]

The debate about women's studies and curriculum-change projects has been described as a debate between autonomy and integration,[25] and it reflects the origins of women's studies as both an educational project and as a part of broader societal efforts for emancipatory change. Those who argue for autonomy worry that integration projects compromise women's studies by molding it to fit into patriarchal systems of knowledge. Developing women's studies as an autonomous field is more likely, they argue, to generate the new knowledge we need because it creates a sustained dialogue among feminists working on common questions and themes.[26] Integrationists see a dialectical relationship between women's studies and inclusive curriculum projects and recognize that curriculum-revision projects are not a substitute for women's studies.[27] They see curriculum projects as both growing out of women's studies and fostering its continued development (pointing out that on many campuses where inclusive curriculum projects preceded women's studies, the projects resulted in the creation of women's studies programs). Developers of inclusive curriculum projects know that the projects cannot replace women's studies programs and, in fact, rest on the continued development of women's studies programs and research. Moreover, the presence of inclusive curriculum projects in institutions has typically strengthened women's studies programs.[28]

Projects to balance the curriculum also raise the question of what it means to have men doing feminist studies, since curriculum-revision projects are typically designed to retrain male faculty. Elaine Showalter discusses this in the context of feminist literary criticism where a number of prominent men have now claimed feminist criticism as part of their own work. She asks if men's entry into feminist studies legitimates feminism as a form of academic discussion because it makes feminism "accessible and subject to correction to authoritative men."[29] And, does it make feminism only another academic perspective without the commitments to change on which feminist studies have been grounded? The radical shift in perspective found in women's studies stems, in large part, from the breach between women's consciousness and experience and that of the patriarchal world.[30] Merely having men study women as new objects of academic discourse does not necessarily represent a feminist transformation in men's thinking. Showalter concludes that, in literature, only when men become fully aware of the way in which they have been constituted as readers and writers by gender systems can they do feminist criticism; otherwise, she says, they are only engaging in a sophisticated form of girl-watching. By further implication, transforming men through feminist studies must mean more than their just becoming aware of new scholarship on women or understanding how their characters and privileges are structured by gender; it must include their active engagement in political change for the liberation of women.

For women and for men, working to transform the curriculum through women's studies requires political, intellectual, and personal change. Those who have worked in curriculum-revision projects testify that these are mutually reinforcing changes—all of which accompany the process of curriculum revision through women's studies.[31] Understanding the confluence of personal and intellectual change also appears to help women's studies faculty deal with the resistance and denial—both overt and covert—that faculty colleagues in such projects often exhibit.[32] Women's studies scholarship challenges the authority of traditional scholarship and, as a consequence, also challenges the egos of those who have invested their careers in this work. Revising the curriculum is therefore also a process of revising our personalities since our work and our psyches have been strongly intertwined with our educations.[33]

The reconstruction of the curriculum through women's studies is occurring in a context of significant change in the demographic composition of student populations. Women now represent a majority of the college population, and by the year 1990 it is projected that minorities will constitute 30 percent of the national youth cohort.[34] In a report to the Carnegie Foundation, Ernest Boyer and Fred Hechinger conclude that "from now on almost all young people, at some time in their lives, need some form of post-secondary education if they are to remain economically productive and socially functional in a world whose tasks and tools are becoming increasingly complex."[35]

At the same time, current appeals for educational reform threaten to reinstate educational privilege along lines determined by race, class, and sex. Various national reports conclude that there is a crisis in education defined as the erosion of academic standards and the collapse of traditional values in education. In all of these appeals, the decline of academic standards is clearly linked to the proliferation of scholarship and educational programs in women's studies and black studies.[36] And, though seemingly different in tone and intent, conservative academic arguments about the need to "return to the basics" and to reclaim the legacy of "the classics" are actually attempts to reinstate patriarchal authority.[37] The assumption is that, if we do not reclaim the classical legacy of the liberal arts, we will lose the academic rigor on which such forms of education are seen as resting.[38] By implication, women's studies and black studies are seen as intellectually weak and politically biased, while study of the classics is seen as both academically rigorous and politically neutral.

One of the goals of women's studies is to insure that education becomes democratic. Women's studies practitioners know that the skills acquired through education cannot be merely technical and task-oriented but must also address the facts of a multiracial and multicultural world that includes both women and men. Case studies from universities that have had inclusive curriculum projects show that students do learn through women's studies to enlarge their worldviews and to integrate academic learning into their personal experience even though the process by which this occurs is full of conflict, resistance, and anger.[39] Other research shows that, following women's studies courses, students report increased self-esteem, interpret their own experiences within a larger social context, increase their identification with other women, expand their sense of life options and goals, and state more liberal attitudes about women.[40] Moreover, faculty in inclusive curriculum projects often report that students are most captivated by the material that focuses specifically on women and gender; students in these projects also report that their classmates and their instructors are more engaged in class material where women are included as agents and subjects of knowledge.[41]

However, given the brief history of inclusive curriculum projects and the fact that balanced courses are still a small percentage of students' total education, evaluating student responses to such projects reveals only part of their significance. Equally important are the opportunities for revitalizing faculty when faculty positions are threatened by budget cuts, retrenchment, and narrowed professional opportunities.[42] Faculty in inclusive curriculum projects report new enthusiasm for their work and see new research questions and directions for their teaching as the result of this work.[43] After her review of inclusive curriculum projects around the country, Lois Banner reported to the Ford Foundation that the projects are also particularly impressive in the degree to which participants discuss and share course syllabi, pedagogical problems and successes, attitudes about themselves, and the changes they are experiencing. She finds this especially noteworthy since college faculty do not ordinarily share course materials with ease and regard their teaching as fundamentally private.[44]

The Phases of Curriculum Change

Several feminist scholars have developed theories to describe the *process* of curriculum change. These are useful because they provide a conceptual outline of transformations in our thinking about women and because they organize our understanding of curriculum critique and revision as an ongoing process. These phase theories also help unveil hidden assumptions within the curriculum and therefore help move us forward in the reconceptualization of knowledge.[45]

An important origin for phase theories is Gerda Lerner's description of the development of women's history.[46] Lerner describes the theoretical challenges of women's history as having evolved in five phases. The first phase was the recognition that women have a history, which led to the second phase, conceptualizing women as a group. In the third phase, women asked new questions about history and compiled new information about women. In the fourth phase, women's history challenged the periodization schemes of history that had been developed through the historical experiences of men, leading them, in the final phase, to redefine the categories and values of androcentric history through consideration of women's past and present.

Lerner's description of the evolution of feminist thought in history showed feminist scholars in other disciplines that scholarship on women was evolving from simply adding women into existing schemes of knowledge into more fundamental reconstructions of the concepts, methods, and theories of the disciplines. She was not the first to see this, but her articulation of these phases of change provided a map for the process through which women were traveling.

McIntosh has developed an analysis of phases in curriculum change that is unique in that it relates patterns of thought in the curriculum to human psyches and their relation to the dominant culture.[47] McIntosh calls phase 1 in the curriculum "womanless" (for example, "womanless history," "womanless sociology," or "womanless literature"). Only a select few are studied in this phase of the curriculum, and highly exclusionary standards of excellence are established. Since the select few in a womanless curriculum are men, we come to think of them as examples of the best of human life and thought. In turn, the curriculum reproduces psyches in students that define and exclusive few as winners and all the rest as losers, second-rate, or nonexistent.

Phase 2 of curriculum change maintains the same worldview as phase 1, since women and a few exceptions from other excluded groups are added in, but only on the same terms in which the famous few have been included. McIntosh defines this phase as "women in history," "women in society," or "women in literature," to use examples from the disciplines. In this phase of curriculum change the originally excluded still exist only as exceptions; their experiences and contributions are still measured through white, male-centered images and ideas. This phase can suggest new questions about old materials, such as, What are the images of women in so-called great literature? Also, this phase raises new questions like, Who were the best-selling women novelists of the nineteenth century? However, while this phase leads to some documentation of women's experience, it tends to see a few women as exceptions to their kind and never imagines women and other underclasses as central of fundamental to social change and continuity.

McIntosh calls the third phase of curriculum change "women as a problem, anomaly, or absence." In this phase, we identify the barriers that have excluded so many people and aspects of life from our studies, and we recognize that, when judged by androcentric standards, women and other excluded groups look deprived. As a result this phase tends to generate anger, but it is also the phase in which feminist scholars begin to challenge the canons of the disciplines and seek to redefine the terms, paradigms, and methods through which all of human experience is understood. Thus, it leads to more inclusive thinking in which class, race, gender, and sexuality are seen as fundamental to the construction of knowledge and human experience. Moreover, we recognize that inclusive studies cannot be done on the same terms as those preceding, thereby moving us to phase 4—"women on their own terms."

Phase 4, exemplified by "women's lives as history" or "women as society," makes central the claim that women's experiences and perspectives create history, society, and culture as much as do those of men. This phase also departs from the misogyny of the first three phases wherein women are either altogether invisible or are seen only as exceptional, victimized, or problematic relative to dominant groups. Phase 4 investigates cultural functions, especially those involving affiliation; understudied aspects of men's lives, such as their emotional lives and nurturant activities, become visible in this phase. In phase 4, according to McIntosh, boundaries between teachers and students break down as the division between the expert and the learner evaporates and teachers and students have a new adjacent relationship to the subjects of study. This phase also leads to a search for new and plural sources of knowledge.

Phase 5, McIntosh says, is harder to conceive because it is so unrealized—both in the curriculum and in our consciousness. She imagines this as a radical transformation of our minds and our work, centered on what she calls "lateral consciousness"—attachment to others and working for the survival of all.

Marilyn Schuster and Susan Van Dyne see curriculum change evolving from recognizing the invisibility of women and identifying sexism in traditional knowledge, to searching for missing women, then to conceptualizing women as a subordinate group, and, finally, to studying women on their own terms.[48] Through these first steps, women's studies poses a challenge to the disciplines by noting their incompleteness and describing the histories that have shaped their developments. Schuster and Van Dyne add women's studies as a challenge to the disciplines to their phase theory and define the last phase as one that is inclusive of human experience and appropriates women's and men's experience and the experiences generated by race and class as relational. The final phase of curriculum transformation, therefore, would be one based on the differences and diversity of human experience, not sameness and generalization. Schuster and Van Dyne identify the implied questions, incentives for change, pedagogical means, and potential outcomes for each of the six phases they identify, and they ask what implications each phase has for changed courses. They also provide a useful index of the characteristics of transformed courses.

In another analysis of curriculum change, Mary Kay Tetreault defines the phases of feminist scholarship as male scholarship, compensatory scholarship, bifocal scholarship, feminist scholarship, and multifocal or relational scholarship.[49] The first phase she identifies, like the first phases described by McIntosh and by Schuster and Van Dyne, accepts male experience as universal. Phase 2 notices that women are missing but still perceives men as the norm. The third phase, bifocal scholarship, defines human experience in dualist categories; curricula in this phase perceive men and women as generalized groups. This phase still emphasizes the oppression of women. Tetreault calls phase 4 "feminist scholarship"; here women's activities, not men's, are the measure of significance, and more attention is given to the contextual and the personal. Sex and gender are seen within historical, cultural, and ideological contexts, and thinking becomes more interdisciplinary. Tetreault's fifth phase, multifocal scholarship, seeks a holistic view in which the ways men and women relate to and complement each other is a continuum of human experience. In this phase, the experiences of race, class, and ethnicity are taken fully into account.

Tetreault suggests that understanding these different phases of curriculum change can be useful for program and course evaluation since they provide a yardstick for measuring the development of feminist thinking in different disciplines. Nevertheless, none of the authors of phase theories intends them to represent rankings or hierarchies of different kinds of feminist scholarship, and it is important to note that these phases have fluid boundaries and that their development does not necessarily follow a linear progression. Still, organizing women's studies scholarship into phases demonstrates how asking certain kinds of questions leads to similar curricular outcomes. As one example, adding black women into the history of science can reveal patterns of the exclusion of black women scientists and can then recast our definition of what it means to practice science and to be a scientist; this shows the necessity of seeing science in terms other than those posed by the dominant histories of science.[50] Furthermore, Showalter points out that different phases of thinking can coexist in our consciousnesses,[51] so for purposes of faculty development, it is important to recognize that certain phases are appropriate as faculty awareness progresses in different institutional, disciplinary, and course contexts.

Finally, identifying the phases of curriculum change is helpful in developing feminist pedagogy. Drawing from work by Blythe Clinchy and Claire Zimmerman[52] on cognitive development among undergraduate students, Francis Maher and Kathleen Dunn[53] discuss the implications of different phases of curriculum change for pedagogy. Clinchy and Zimmerman describe the first level of cognitive functioning for college students as dualist, meaning that students posit right and wrong as absolute and opposite. Maher and Dunn say the pedagogical complement to this phase of student development is the lecture format in which students are encouraged to see faculty members as experts who impart truth by identifying right and wrong.

Multiplism is the second phase in Clinchy and Zimmerman's analysis. This phase of cognitive development describes knowledge as stemming from within; in this phase, students discover the validity of their own experience. According to Maher and Dunn, this produces among students a highly relativistic stance—one in which they accept the legitimacy of different worldviews and experiences, thus opening themselves up to experiences that vary by class, race, and gender but seeing all experiences and perspectives as equally valid. Contextualism is the third phase of cognitive development identified by Clinchy and Zimmerman; according to Maher and Dunn, we can encourage this phase of student development through the creation of a pluralistic curriculum in women's studies.

Like those who have articulated phase theories of curriculum change, Maher and Dunn see the ultimate goal of women's studies as developing a curriculum that is inclusive in the fullest sense— taking gender, race, class, and sexuality in their fullest historical and cultural context and developing an understanding of the complexities of these experiences and their relatedness. Such a curriculum would no longer rest on the experiences and judgment of a few. Since phase theories help us move toward this goal, they are an important contribution to faculty and student development through women's studies.

Critique of the Disciplines

The new enthusiasm that participants in women's studies faculty development projects report for their work is a sign that the insights of feminist scholarship are on the theoretical and methodological cutting edge of the disciplines. Working to build a balanced curriculum has renewed faculty and brought them and their students a new level of awareness about women in society, culture, and history. In fact, the revisions in the disciplines that this literature stimulates are so extensive that it is reasonable to conclude that "whether or not you are in women's studies, its scholarship will affect your discipline."[54]

As Schuster and Van Dyne argue,[55] there are invisible paradigms within the educational curriculum that represent tacit assumptions that govern what and how we teach, even when we are unaware of these ruling principles. The feminist movement exposes these unexamined standards by showing their relation to the ideology, power, and values of dominant groups, who in our culture most often are white, European-American men. Thus, although women's studies is often accused of being ideological, it is the traditional curriculum that is nested within the unacknowledged ideology of the dominant culture. The more coherent and tacitly assumed an ideology is, the less visible are the curricular paradigms that stem from it and the more unconsciously we participate in them.

Feminist criticism is generated by the fact that women are both insiders and outsiders to the disciplines; the contradictions imposed by their status create a breach between their consciousnesses and their activity, generating critical dialogue and producing new sources of knowledge.[56] Feminist criticism across the disciplines reveals that what is taken to be timeless, excellent, representative, or objective is embedded within patriarchal assumptions about culture and society. Consequently, recentering knowledge within the experience of women unmasks the invisible paradigms that guide the curriculum and raises questions that require scholars to take a comprehensive and critical look at their fields.

Creating an inclusive curriculum means more than bringing women's studies into the general curriculum because it also means creating women's studies to be inclusive so that women's studies does not have the racist, class, heterosexist, and cultural bias that is found in the traditional curriculum.[57] Feminist curriculum change, then, must not exclude the voices of women of color in posing the research questions, defining the facts, shaping the concepts, and articulating theories of women's studies. How would the work be enriched, both cognitively and emotionally, by listening to the voices and fully including the experiences of women of color? What kind of knowledge is made by ignoring not only class and gender but also race as origins for and subjects of scholarship? If the curriculum—both inside and outside of women's studies—is focused on white cultures, it will continue to define women of color as peripheral and to see white experience as the norm and all others as deviant or exceptional. It will, in effect, reproduce the errors of classical education.[58]

Esther Chow[59] suggests three strategies for incorporating the perspectives of women of color into courses: the comparison method, special treatment, and mainstreaming. The comparison strategy brings materials on women of color into courses for purposes of comparison with the dominant group experience, and it exposes students to a wide range of materials by examining women's experiences from different perspectives. Chow suggests, however, that it can perpetuate the marginality of women of color by leaving white women at the center of the major paradigm for analysis. Alternatively, the special-treatment approach makes women of color the topic of general survey courses, special topic courses, or independent reading. The advantage to such courses is that they allow for in-depth understanding of themes in the lives of women of color, although, since these courses tend to be electives, they do not make an impact on a wide range of students. The mainstreaming strategy incorporates materials on women of color into existing courses so that they appear throughout, not just in segregated areas of courses or the curriculum. Chow is careful to point out that the substance of these courses should not be divided along clear racial and gender lines. And she concludes that the effectiveness of these different strategies is dependent on the needs and goals of particular courses, the institutional setting, and interaction between teachers and students of various racial-ethnic backgrounds.

Creating an inclusive curriculum both within women's studies and within traditional disciplines is initiated by asking two questions: What is the present content and scope and methodology of a discipline? and How would the discipline need to change to reflect the fact that women are half the world's population and have had, in one sense, half the world's experience?[60] Those who work in women's studies know that women's studies scholarship cannot be simply added into the existing curriculum, as it challenges the existing assumptions, facts, and theories of the traditional disciplines, as well as challenging the traditional boundaries between the disciplines. The identification of bias in the curriculum is the first step in analyzing the multiple implications of the fact that women have been excluded from creation of formalized knowledge.[61] But as feminist scholarship has developed, more fundamental transformations can be imagined.

Several volumes specifically address the impact of feminist scholarship on the disciplines[62] and, were this essay to review fully the impact of feminist scholarship on the disciplines, the whole of women's studies literature would need to be considered. Of course, this essay cannot possibly do this; instead, it addresses the major themes that emerge from consideration of curriculum change effected through women's studies.

The Arts and Humanities

Feminist criticism shows that the arts and humanities have in the past created and reinforced definitions of life that exclude the experiences of, deny expression to, and negate the creative works of the nonpowerful, even though the humanities claim to take the concerns of all humanity and the human experience as their subject matter.[63] Women have been excluded from literary and artistic canons on the grounds that their work does not meet standards of excellence,[64] though, as Paul Lauter suggests, "standards of literary merit are not absolute but contingent. They depend, among other considerations, upon the relative value we place on form and feeling in literary expression as well as on culturally different conceptions of form and function."[65]

The exclusion of women from literary and artistic canons suggests that the canons themselves are founded on principles embedded in masculine culture, even though many literature teachers and critics will say that great literature and art speak to universal themes and transcend the particularities of sociocultural conditions like race, class, and gender. In tracing the development of the canon of American literature, Lauter has shown that the exclusion of white women, blacks, and working class writers from the canon of American literature was consolidated in the 1920s when a small group of white elite men professionalized the teaching of literature and consolidated formal critical traditions and conventions of periodization.[66] Since then, the aesthetic standards of the canon have appeared to be universal because without revealing their history, the learned tastes and common experiences of certain academic men are exaggerated as universal. And, as Annette Kolodny argues, once a canon is established, the prior fact of canonization tends to put works beyond questions of merit.[67]

Other feminist critics in the arts and humanities have identified the chronological presentation of materials as deeply problematic. Natalie Kampen and Elizabeth Grossman, for example, say that the idea that time is fundamentally linear and progressive—fundamental in the study and teaching of art history through chronology—produces accounts of the development of human culture that are more linear than the actual historical evolution of the culture has been. Chronological presentation also assumes competition as a part of human creativity and suggests that hierarchical arrangements are inevitable in all organization of cultural reality.[68]

Including women in the curriculum has been especially difficult in fields like the history of philosophy where the canon is fixed and relatively small. Even in ethics, where it is more difficult to ignore variations in human values, the subject tends to be studied from the vantage point of those in power, lending the impression that only elites can understand cultural norms.[69] In the humanities, when women do appear in texts and as artistic objects, their own experiences are seldom primary. In American literature, for example, women, native Americans, and blacks sometimes "inhabit" texts but are rarely given primary voices within them. This reveals a deep sex, class, and race bias in the teaching of the arts and humanities.

Were we to begin study in the arts and humanities through the experience of traditionally excluded groups, new themes would be revealed. Gloria Hull, for example, in her account of reading literature by North American women of color, identifies several themes that arise from immersion in this literature on its own terms.[70] An acute awareness of racial and sexual oppression pervades this literature, but so do themes of bicultural identity (especially expressed through language), alternative understandings of sexuality, and the importance of preserving cultural tradition in forms of expression.

History, like literature and the arts, has tended to focus on the historical experience of a few. Because historians tend to concentrate on heroes, they ignore the lives of ordinary men and women. Thus, much of the impact of feminist scholarship in history has been to expand the "characters" of historical accounts. But, more than adding in new characters, feminist scholarship in history shows how the traditional periodization of historical accounts is organized through the experience of bourgeois men.[71] From a feminist perspective, including women means not only including those who have been left out but rethinking historical paradigms to generate new frameworks in which women are agents of history and that examine the lives of women in their own terms and bring them into accounts of historical change. Feminist revisions of history do more than expand the subjects of history; they introduce gender relations as a primary category of historical experience. So, although the narrative style of history has tended to produce singular tales of historical reality, feminist scholarship in history produces accounts that reflect the multiple layers of historical experience.[72] As one example, in American studies, scholars have focused on a singular myth of the physical and metaphysical frontier of the new world as a place to be conquered and possessed. In contrast, Kolodny's work on women's consciousness and westward expansion shows that women imagined the frontier as a garden to be cultivated.[73]

Feminist scholars suggest that how excellence is produced and defined by literary and cultural institutions should become part of the study of the arts and humanities. This requires methodological self-consciousness, asking, for example, what social conditions are necessary for certain female images to emerge? Whose interests are served by these images? How do they affect women? And what are the varieties of women's tastes, working methods, ideas, and experiences?[74]

These questions help us identify bias in the curriculum and ultimately reveal more deeply embedded habits of thought. In her analysis of foreign language textbooks, Barbara Wright shows that the texts ignore most social classes, except for educated, upper middle-class surgeons, professors, and businessmen.[75] She identifies several phases of critique of the curriculum in foreign language instruction by examining the images of women and girls in textbooks, then studying women's place in the culture being presented, and, finally, developing a critical look at language itself. This last phase of questioning helps us see the value judgments that inform decisions to include or exclude certain semantic and syntactic possibilities in the language and, therefore, reveals ways in which gender, class, and race are embedded in the language of a culture and in our language teaching. Feminist criticism understands that the "circumstances in which culture is produced and encountered, the functions of culture, the specific historical and formal traditions which shape and validate culture—these all differ somewhat from social group to social group and among classes. In this respect, the problem of changing curriculum has primarily to do with learning to understand, appreciate and teach about many varied cultural traditions."[76]

Carolyn Heilbrun writes, "The study of literature cannot survive if it cannot . . . illuminate human experience; and human experience cannot today be illuminated without attention to the place of women in literature, in the textuality of all our lives, both in history and in the present."[77] From feminist work in these fields we begin to see past and present cultures as "multi-layered, composites of men's and women's experiences, and rich in complexity and conflict."[78] This vision of cultural multiplicity explored through feminist scholarship would help the humanities to present a full account of human experience.

The Social Sciences

As in the arts and humanities, the exclusion of women from the social sciences leads to distortion and ignorance of their experience in society and culture.[79] Whereas the social sciences claim to give accurate accounts of social reality, the exclusion of women's experiences and perspectives has produced concepts and theories that, while allegedly universal, are, in fact, based on gender-specific experiences, and so these theories often project the assumptions of masculine, Western culture into the social groups under study.[80]

As a result, feminist scholars suggest that core concepts in the social sciences are gender biased. As one example, the assumed split between public and private spheres is reproduced in social science concepts that tend to be grounded in public experience and that ignore private experience and the relation between public and private dimensions of social life. Focus on the public sphere as the primary site for social interaction omits women's experience and much of men's.[81] Economic activity, for example, is defined as taking place only in the public sphere, leading to the total omission of household work as a measurable category of economic activity in economics. Thus, caring for the sick, elderly, or young is productive economic activity when performed for wages but not when performed by persons in the privacy of the household. Moreover, by assuming white Western male experience as the norm, mainstream economists assume that economic activity is based on rational choice and free interaction. A feminist approach, however, would develop economic analyses that identify constraints on choice and the process of choosing.[82]

Likewise, in political science, textbooks describe political activity only as it occurs in formal public political structures. The representation of women and minority groups in elected offices is typically included, as is some recognition of federal legislation on civil rights. But always omitted are such topics as women's and minority groups' participation in community politics, ethnic identity as a dimension of political activity, or sexuality as the basis of organized political movements. Were we to rely on these texts for our understanding of political systems and behavior, as do most faculty and students, the virtual omission of race, sex, gender, class, and ethnicity would lead us to believe that none of these has been significant in the development of political systems and behavior.[83]

The location of social science concepts within the public and masculine realm reflects the dichotomous thinking that prevails in both social science content and method. Dorothy Smith's work in the sociology of knowledge investigates the implications of the fact that men's experience in the public world has been segregated from that of women in the private sphere. She posits that men are able to become absorbed in an abstract conceptual mode because women take care of their everyday, emotional, and bodily needs. As a result, concepts in the social sciences, as they have been developed by men, are abstracted from women's experience and do not reflect their realities or worldviews.[84] Others have also argued that social science research methods polarize human experience by forcing respondents into either/or choices to describe their social experiences and attitudes. This is especially the case in experimental and survey research and in research on sex differences.[85] Furthermore, research methods in the social sciences routinely isolate people from the social contexts in which they are studied. And, in empirical research, race and sex, if mentioned at all, are treated as discrete categories and are reported as if they were separate features of social experience. It is an exceptional study that even presents data by race and by sex, and, when this is done, race and sex are most often reported separately. For example, sociologists comparing income by race and by sex typically report blacks' and whites' incomes and, in another table, compare men's and women's incomes. In reporting race and sex separately, the particular experiences of black women, white women, black men, and white men disappear from view. This practice produces false generalizations, perpetuates the invisibility of women of color, and denies that women of color have unique historical and contemporary experiences.

One of the greatest obstacles to curriculum change in the social sciences is the disciplines' search to establish themselves as sciences. The scientific method, as adopted in the social sciences, generates hierarchical methodologies in which the knower is seen as expert in the lives of others and produces research methodologies that deny that social relationships exist between researchers and those they study. Since the relationship between the knower and the known is part of the knowledge produced through research, denial of this relationship distorts the accounts produced by social science. Judith Stacey and Barrie Thorne conclude that, in sociology, positivist epistemology prohibits the infusion of feminist insights because positivism sees knowledge in abstract and universal terms that are unrelated to the stance of the observer. Feminist transformation has been more possible, they argue, in disciplines where interpretive methods are used. Interpretive methods are reflexive about the circumstances in which knowledge is produced and see researchers as situated in the action of their research; thus, they are better able to build knowledge in the social sciences that takes full account of social life.[86]

Feminist methodologies in the social sciences begin from the premise that the relationship between the knower and the known is a socially organized practice. The assumed detachment of scientific observers from that which they observe is, as feminists see it, made possible through organized hierarchies of science where, for example, women work as bottle washers, research assistants, or computer operators.[87] Moreover, feminists argue that the assumption of scientific detachment and rationality is a masculine value, one that is made possible only by ignoring the role of women in the practice of science. Additionally, Shulamit Reinharz suggests that feminist research in the social sciences should see the self-discovery of the researcher as integral to the process of doing research; consequently, it is ludicrous in her view to imagine the act of "data gathering" as separate from the act of "data analysis."[88]

In response to the preoccupation with scientific method in the social science disciplines, feminist scholars suggest that critiques of the scientific method should be a primary concern in feminist revisions of social science courses. In developing, for example, a feminist approach for teaching methods of psychology, Michelle Hoffnung suggests including a variety of approaches and methods and investigating in each case their assumptions about scientists' relations to the worlds being investigated.[89] Similarly, in teaching courses like the history of psychological thought, we need to recognize that women are more active in the history of psychology and social science disciplines than texts lead us to believe. When texts focus only on the internal development of a science, histories of the discipline wrongly ignore the external social and historical conditions that create scientific investigations.[90] As in the arts and humanities, putting women into social scientific courses requires this more reflexive approach—one that puts women and men in the full context of their historical and cultural experiences and that does not assume the universality of concepts, theories, and facts.

Science and Technology

Of all the disciplines, the natural and physical sciences have the closest connections to political and economic structures, yet they make the strongest claims to academic neutrality. For feminist scholars in the sciences, seeing how scientific studies reflect cultural values is a good starting point for understanding the interwoven worlds of science, capitalism, and patriarchy.

To begin with, scientific descriptions project cultural values onto the physical and natural world. Ruth Hubbard explains that kingdoms and orders are not intrinsic to the nature of organisms but have evolved in a world that values hierarchy and patrilineage.[91] Though it is often claimed that scientific explanations run counter to the widely shared beliefs of society, it is also true that scientific explanations are often highly congruent with the social and political ideology of the society in which they are produced.[92] Research on brain lateralization, for example, reflects a seeming intent to find a biological explanation for sexual differences in analytical reasoning, visual-spatial ability, and intuitive thought that cannot itself be clearly and consistently demonstrated in scientific investigations.[93] And perhaps nowhere else are culturally sexist values so embedded in scientific description and analysis as in discussions of sexual selection, human sexuality, and human reproduction.[94]

The feminist critique of science, as in the humanities and social sciences, looks at cultural dualisms associated with masculinity and femininity as they permeate scientific thought and discourse.[95] Some question whether the scientific method is even capable of dealing with collective behavior due to the fact that it parcels out behaviors, cells, categories, and events. In science, like the humanities and social sciences, explanations thought to be true often do not stand up when examined through women's experiences. For example, whereas medical researchers have typically described menopause as associated with a set of disease symptoms, new research by feminist biologists finds that the overwhelming majority of postmenopausal women report no remarkable menopausal symptoms.[96]

The feminist critique of science can be organized into five types of studies: equity studies documenting the resistance to women's participation in science; studies of the uses and abuses of science and their racist, sexist, homophobic, and class-based projects; epistemological studies; studies that, drawing from literary criticism, historical interpretation, and psychoanalysis, see science as a text and, therefore, look to reveal the social meaning embedded in value-neutral claims; and feminist debates about whether feminist science is possible or whether feminists seek simply a better science—undistorted by gender, race, class, and heterosexism.[97]

Building the feminist critique of science can therefore begin from several questions, including, Why are women excluded from science? How is science taught? What are the scientific research questions that, as feminists, we need to ask? How is difference studied in scientific institutions? Or, how is the exclusion of women from science related to the way science is done and thought? Some of these questions are similar to those asked in social studies of science. But feminist discussions of science specifically examine what Evelyn Fox Keller calls the science/gender system—the network of associations and disjunctions between public and private, personal and impersonal, and masculine and feminine as they appear in the basic structure of science and society. Keller argues that asking "how ideologies of gender and science inform each other in their mutual construction, how that construction functions in our social arrangements, and how it affects men and women, science and nature" is to examine the roots, dynamics, and consequences of the science/gender system.[98]

Science bears the imprint of the fact that, historically, scientists have been men. Therefore, asking how and why women have been excluded from the practice of science is one way to reveal deeply embedded gender, race, and class patterns in the structure of scientific professions and, consequently, in the character of scientific thought. As a consequence, while encouraging the participation of women in science is an obvious question of equity, it also reaches deeply into the social construction of science and provides insights about why some concepts gain legitimacy in science while others do not. So, important as it may be, women's experience is excluded from biological theory because it is considered to be subjective and therefore is considered to be outside the realm of scientific inquiry. Moreover, since it cannot be measured in scientific ways, the topic, not the method, is seen as illegitimate.[99]

Collectively, the work of feminist scientists raises new possibilities for the way science is taught[100] and conceived. By making us more conscious of the interrelatedness of gender and science, this work underscores the connection between science and the sex / gender system. Moreover, a feminist view of science would take it as only one of a number of ways to comprehend and know the world around us so that the hegemony of science as a way of knowing would be replaced with a more pluralistic view.

Resource Materials in the Disciplines

New scholarship on women does not automatically get translated into new teaching within the disciplines. Therefore, several of the professional organizations have sponsored projects that have produced guidelines for integrating new material on women into courses in the disciplines. These are especially valuable for assisting faculty teaching core courses in the disciplines and teaching new courses about women. The series published by the American Political Science Association[101] is a five-volume set with review essays, sample syllabi, field exercises, and suggested reading. The authors review explanations for the underrepresentation of women as public officials and examine sex discrimination against women as attorneys, judges, offenders, and victims. Moreover, they examine the traditional assumption that women are apolitical by looking at the political activity of women in community organizations and grassroots movements that are organized around such issues as sexual harassment, women's health, and violence against women.

Other professional groups have developed materials that focus particularly on integrating the study of women into the introductory curriculum; such materials are available in sociology, psychology, American history, and microeconomics.[102] These collections typically include a sample syllabus for introductory courses, with suggestions for new topics, examples, and readings in the different areas usually included in introductory courses. One collection from Feminist Press, *Reconstructing American Literature*, contains sixty-seven syllabi for courses in American literature. The American Sociological Association has recently published an excellent collection that includes syllabi for courses on sex and gender with suggested student assignments and exercises, lists of film resources, and essays on teaching women's studies, dealing with homophobia in the classroom, integrating race, sex, and gender in the classroom, and the experience of black women in higher education.[103]

The appendix of Schuster and Van Dyne's book, *Women's Place in the Academy: Transforming the Liberal Arts Curriculum,* is especially useful because it is organized by disciplines and separates suggested readings into those for classroom use and those more appropriate for teacher preparation. Faculty working to integrate scholarship on women into their courses would be wise to consult the various review essays published in *Signs* that summarize major research and theoretical developments in the academic fields and to consult the papers on curriculum change in the working papers series published by the Wellesley College Center for Research on Women. Newsletters from campuses with inclusive curriculum projects often include essays on revising courses written by faculty who are working to revise their courses.[104] Finally, women's caucuses within the professional associations of the disciplines can typically provide bibliographies and other resources designed to assist in the process of curriculum change.

A wealth of other materials are available to assist faculty specifically in the process of integrating women of color into the curriculum of women's studies and disciplinary courses. Gloria Hull, Patricia Bell Scott, and Barbara Smith's collection, *All the Women Are White, All the Blacks Are Men, But Some of Us Are Brave* is a classic and invaluable source. It includes not only essays on different dimensions of black women's experiences and contributions to knowledge and culture but also a superb selection of syllabi incorporating the study of women of color into courses and bibliographies and bibliographic essays of print and nonprint materials by and about black women.[105]

The Center for Research on Women at Memphis State University publishes a bibliography in the social sciences that is an excellent review of research about women of color;[106] their other projects include summer institutes on women of color and curriculum change, a visiting scholars program, faculty development seminars, and a working papers series. Maxine Baca Zinn's review essay in *Signs* includes an excellent bibliography for including Chicana women in the social sciences,[107] and *Estudios Femeniles de la Chicana* by Marcela Trujillo includes a proposal for Chicana Studies and course proposals and outlines that are useful for curriculum development.[108] Anne Fausto-Sterling and Lydia English have produced a packet of materials on women and minorities in science that is a collaborative project by students enrolled in a course at Brown University on the history of women and minority scientists; their collection includes essays written by the students about their experiences in science. In addition, Fausto-Sterling and English have printed a course materials guide that is an extensive bibliography of books, articles, bibliographies, visual aids, and reference works on the subject of women and minorities in science.[109]

The journal *Sage* is also an invaluable resource for scholars. *Sage* publishes interdisciplinary writing by and about women of color; recent issues have highlighted the topics of education, women writers, and mothers and daughters.[110] Other journals have published special issues devoted to studying women of color.[111] In addition to this growing primary research literature by and about women of color, there are numerous review essays that provide a guide to this important area of research.[112]

Such a wealth of material about women of color invalidates teachers' claims that they would include material on and by women of color if it were available. It also underscores the need to reeducate by recentering toward the lives of those who have been excluded from the curriculum and to do so by changing the materials and experiences we use in constructing classroom contents. Including the study of women of color in all aspects of the curriculum is rooted in a fundamental premise of women's studies: that there is great variation in human experiences and that this diversity should be central to educational studies. Although, as Johnella Butler notes, reductionist habits in the classroom make teaching about multiplicity difficult,[113] if the classrooms are more pluralistic both teachers and students will be better able to understand the pluralistic world.

Materials to assist in the process of curriculum change are abundant—so much so that one of the problems in faculty development projects is that faculty who have not followed the development of feminist scholarship over the past two decades must now learn an entirely new field of scholarship. Obviously, this cannot be accomplished quickly and, although we may sometimes feel discouraged by the magnitude of the needed changes, it is useful to remember that we are trying to reconstruct systems of knowledge that have evolved over centuries. Small changes, while obviously incomplete, do introduce larger changes—both in course content and in the political, intellectual, and personal transformations that this process inspires. Although it is also sometimes difficult to imagine what a revised curriculum would look like, Butler reminds us that working to build an inclusive curriculum requires a willingness to be surprised.

All of the materials reviewed above help us assess the climate for change in particular disciplines and devise appropriate strategies for the different fields in which we work and teach. With this information in mind and with the underlying philosophies of different projects specified, we can better analyze the context for curriculum change in various disciplines and imagine multiple ways of accomplishing educational change within them.

Conclusion

Adrienne Rich pointed the way to curriculum change through women's studies when she distinguished between claiming and receiving an education. Receiving an education is only "to come into possession of; to act as receptacle or container for; to accept as authoritative or true," while claiming an education is "to take as the rightful owner; to assert in the face of possible contradiction."[114] For women, Rich said, this means "refusing to let others do your thinking, talking, and naming for you."[115]

For women's studies to realize Rich's vision means we must develop women's studies itself to be inclusive; building an inclusive curriculum means both working to build women's studies into the curriculum and doing the work and thinking that makes women's studies multicultural and multiracial. These two dimensions will also strengthen women's studies as a field of its own, since they ask us to examine our own assumptions, methods, and relationship to the society in which we live. In this sense, changing the curriculum has three dimensions: changing our selves, changing our work, and changing society.

These are sobering times for women's studies scholars who seek through education an end to the injustices and patterns of exclusion that have characterized our culture. In the current political climate, one in which we are experiencing a serious backlash in educational change, women's studies and the feminist movement will meet new resistance.[116] Current appeals to return to the basics and to stabilize the curriculum threaten once again to exclude women, people of color, and gays and lesbians from the center of our learning, but Home provides us with hope for change when she writes, "It is essential to revelatory learning to see the opposition clearly. . . . In a period when the opposition will be most visible, we may be able to do our best work."[117]

DEPARTMENT OF SOCIOLOGY
UNIVERSITY OF DELAWARE

Notes

1. Susan Glaspell, "A Jury of Her Peers," in *The Best American Short Stories*, ed. Edward J. O'Brien (Boston: Houghton Mifflin Co., 1916), 371–83.
2. Ibid., 376.
3. Ibid., 381.
4. Ibid., 383.
5. Ibid., 385.
6. Building from Simone de Beauvoir's work, Catherine MacKinnon discusses this point. De Beauvoir writes, "Representation of the world, like the world itself, is the work of men; they describe it from their own point of view which they confuse with the absolute truth" (cited in MacKinnon, 537). MacKinnon continues the point by saying that "men create the world from their own point of view which then becomes the truth to be described." As a result, the male epistemological stance is one that is ostensibly objective and uninvolved and does not comprehend its own perspective; it does not take itself as subject but makes an object of all else it looks at. See Catherine MacKinnon, "Feminism, Marxism, Method, and the State: An Agenda for Theory," *Signs: Journal of Women in Culture and Society* 7, no. 3 (Spring 1982): 515–44, esp. 537.
7. Adrienne Rich, "Toward a Woman-centered University," in *On Lies, Secrets, and Silence* (New York: W. W. Norton & Co., 1979), 141.
8. Betty Schmitz, *Integrating Women's Studies into the Curriculum* (Old Westbury, N.Y.: Feminist Press, 1985).
9. Florence Howe, *Myths of Coeducation* (Bloomington: Indiana University Press, 1984).
10. Marilyn J. Boxer, "For and About Women: The Theory and Practice of Women's Studies in the United States," *Signs* 7, no. 3 (Spring 1982): 661–95.
11. Howe, 282–83.
12. Deborah Rosenfelt, "What Women's Studies Programs Do That Mainstreaming Can't," in "Special Issue: Strategies for Women's Studies in the 80s," ed. Gloria Bowles, *Women's Studies International Forum* 7, no. 4 (1984): 167–75.
13. Susan Kirschner and Elizabeth C. Arch, "'Transformation' of the Curriculum: Problems of Conception and Deception," in Bowles, ed. 149–51.
14. Florence Howe, "Feminist Scholarship: The Extent of the Revolution," in *Liberal Education and the New Scholarship on Women: Issues and Constraints in Institutional Change: A Report of the Wingspread Conference*, ed. Anne Fuller (Washington, D.C.: Association of American Colleges, 1981), 5–21.
15. Howe, *Myths of Coeducation*, 280.
16. The 1985 directory of such projects from the Wellesley College Center for Research on Women is reprinted in Schmitz. Although such a directory is quickly outdated, it is useful for seeing the diversity of projects that have been undertaken on different campuses across the country, as well as by professional associations. *Women's Studies Quarterly* periodically publishes reports from various projects; see vol. 11 (Summer 1983) and vol. 13 (Summer 1985). See also Peggy McIntosh, "The Study of Women: Processes of Personal and Curriculum Re-vision," *Forum* 6 (April 1984): 2–4; this issue of *Forum* and the vol. 4 (October 1981) issue of *Forum* also contain descriptions of curriculum-change projects on twenty-six campuses. *Forum* is available from the Association of American Colleges, 1818 R Street N.W., Washington D.C. 20009.
17. Elizabeth Kamarck Minnich, "A Feminist Criticism of the Liberal Arts," in Fuller, ed., 22–38.
18. Peggy McIntosh, "A Note on Terminology," *Women's Studies Quarterly* 11 (Summer 1983): 29–30.
19. Gloria Bowles and Renate Duelli-Klein, eds., *Theories of Women's Studies* (Boston: Routledge & Kegan Paul, 1983).
20. Margaret Andersen, "Black Studies/Women's Studies: Learning from Our Common Pasts/Forging a Common Future," in *Women's Place in the Academy: Transforming the Liberal Arts Curriculum*, ed. Marilyn Schuster and Susan Van Dyne (Totowa, N.J.: Rowman & Allanheld, 1985), 62–72.

21. Johnella Butler, "Minority Studies and Women's Studies: Do We Want to Kill a Dream?" in Bowles, ed., 135–38.
22. Bowles and Duelli-Klein, eds., 9.
23. Marian Lowe and Margaret Lowe Benston, "The Uneasy Alliance of Feminism and Academia," in Bowles, ed. (n. 12 above), 177–84.
24. Mary Childers, "Women's Studies: Sinking and Swimming in the Mainstream," in Bowles, ed., 161–66.
25. This debate can best be reviewed in Bowles, ed. (n. 12 above).
26. Sandra Coyner, "The Ideas of Mainstreaming: Women's Studies and the Disciplines," *Frontiers* 8, no. 3 (1986): 87–95.
27. Peggy McIntosh and Elizabeth Kamarck Minnich, "Varieties of Women's Studies," in Bowles, ed., 139–48.
28. See Myra Dinnerstein, Sheryl O'Donnell, and Patricia MacCorquodale, *How to Integrate Women's Studies into the Traditional Curriculum* (Tucson: University of Arizona, Southwest Institute for Research on Women [SIROW], n.d.); JoAnn M. Fritsche, ed., *Toward Excellence and Equity* (Orono: University of Maine at Orono Press, 1984); and Schmitz (n. 8 above). See also Betty Schmitz, *Sourcebook for Integrating the Study of Women into the Curriculum* (Bozeman: Montana State University, Northwest Women's Studies Association, 1983); and Bonnie Spanier, Alexander Bloom, and Darlene Boroviak, eds., *Toward a Balanced Curriculum: A Sourcebook for Initiating Gender Integration Projects* (Cambridge, Mass.: Schenckman Publishing Co., 1984).
29. Elaine Showalter, "Critical Cross-Dressing: Male Feminists and the Woman of the Year," *Raritan* 3 (Fall 1983): 130–49; quotation is from Gayatri Spivak, "Politics of Interpretations," *Critical inquiry* 9 (September 1982): 259–78, cited in Showalter, 133.
30. Marcia Westkott, "Feminist Criticism of the Social Sciences," *Harvard Educational Review* 49 (November 1979): 22–30.
31. Peggy McIntosh, "WARNING: The New Scholarship on Women May Be Hazardous to Your Ego," *Women's Studies Quarterly* 10 (Spring 1982): 29–31; and McIntosh, "The Study of Women," (n. 16 above).
32. Dinnerstein et al.
33. Peggy McIntosh, "Interactive Phases of Curricular Re-Vision: A Feminist Perspective," Working Papers Series, no. 124 (Wellesley, Mass.: Wellesley College Center for Research on Women, 1983).
34. Marilyn Schuster and Susan Van Dyne, "Curricular Change for the Twenty-first Century: Why Women?" in Schuster and Van Dyne, eds. (n. 20 above), 3–12.
35. Ernest L. Boyer and Fred M. Hechinger, *Higher Learning in the Nation's Service* (Washington, D.C.: Carnegie Foundation for the Advancement of Teaching, 1981), 28.
36. Michael Levin, "Women's Studies, Ersatz Scholarship," *New Perspectives* 17 (Summer 1985): 7–10. *New Perspectives* is published by the U.S. Commission on Civil Rights.
37. The Family Protection Act, proposed by the New Right, and introduced to Congress on September 24, 1979, would prohibit "any program which produces or promotes courses of instruction or curriculum seeking to inculcate values or modes of behavior which contradict the demonstrated beliefs and values of the community" or any program that supports "educational materials or studies . . . which would tend to denigrate, diminish, or deny role differences between the sexes as it has been historically understood in the United States" (Senate Bill 1808, 96th Congress, first session, title 1, sec. 101; cited in Rosalind Petchesky, "Antiabortion, Antifeminism, and the Rise of the New Right," *Feminist Studies* 7 [Summer 1981]: 225). The Family Protection Act would return moral authority to the heterosexual married couple with children and would eliminate women's studies and any other educational programs that suggest homosexuality as an acceptable life-style; it would also severely reduce federal jurisdiction over desegregation in private schools.
38. Nan Keohane, "Our Mission Should Not Be Merely to 'Reclaim' a Legacy of Scholarship—We Must Expand on It," *Chronicle of Higher Education* 32 (April 2, 1986): 88.
39. In Fritsche, ed. (n. 28 above): Christina L. Baker, "Through the Eye of the Storm: Feminism in the Classroom," 224–33; Jerome Nadelhaft, "Feminism in the Classroom: Through the Eye of the Storm," 235–45; and Ruth Nadelhaft, "Predictable Storm in the Feminist Classroom," 247–55.
40. Karen G. Howe, "The Psychological Impact of a Women's Studies Course," *Women's Studies Quarterly* 13 (Spring 1985): 23–24. In addition to a discussion of her own research, Howe includes an excellent review of literature on this topic.
41. Betty Schmitz, Myra Dinnerstein, and Nancy Mairs, "Initiating a Curriculum Integration Project: Lessons from the Campus and the Region," in Schuster and Van Dyne, eds., 116–29.
42. Marilyn Schuster and Susan Van Dyne, "Placing Women in the Liberal Arts: Stages of Curriculum Transformation," *Harvard Educational Review* 54 (November 1984): 413–28.
43. Dinnerstein et al. (no. 28 above).

44. Lois Banner, The Women's Studies Curriculum Integration Movement: A Report to the Ford Foundation" (New York: Ford Foundation, March 1985, typescript).

45. For a discussion of phase theories see Mary Kay Thompson Tetreault, "Women in the Curriculum," 1–2; Peggy McIntosh, "Women in the Curriculum," 3; Peggy McIntosh, "Convergences in Feminist Phase Theory," 4; all in the vol. 15 (February 1986) issue of *Comment. Comment* is available from RCI Communications, 680 West 11th Street, Claremont, Calif. 91711.

46. Gerda Lerner, "The Rise of Feminist Consciousness," in *All of Us Are Present*, ed. Eleanor Bender, Bobbie Burk, and Nancy Walker (Columbia, Mo.: James Madison Wood Research Institute, 1984), and "Symposium: Politics and Culture in Women's History," *Feminist Studies* 6 (Spring 1980): 49–54.

47. Peggy McIntosh, "Interactive Phases of Curricular Re-vision" (n. 33 above).

48. Schuster and Van Dyne, eds. (n. 20 above), 27–28.

49. Mary Kay Thompson Tetreault, "Feminist Phase Theory," *Journal of Higher Education* 56 (July/August 1985): 363–84.

50. Evelyn Hammonds, "Never Meant to Survive: A Black Woman's Journey: An Interview with Evelyn Hammonds by Aimee Sands," *Radical Teacher* 30 (January 1986): 8–15. Evelyn Fox Keller, *Reflections on Gender and Science* (New Haven, Conn.: Yale University Press, 1985).

51. Elaine Showalter, *A Literature of Their Own* (Princeton, N.J.: Princeton University Press, 1977).

52. Blythe Clinchy and Claire Zimmerman, "Epistemology and Agency in the Development of Undergraduate Women," in *The Undergraduate Woman: Issues in Educational Equity*, ed. Pamela Perun (Lexington, Mass.: D.C. Heath & Co., 1982), 161–81.

53. Frances Maher and Kathleen Dunn, "The Practice of Feminist Teaching: A Case Study of Interactions among Curriculum, Pedagogy, and Female Cognitive Development," Working Papers Series, no. 144 (Wellesley, Mass.: Wellesley College Center for Research on Women, 1984).

54. F. Howe, *Myths of Coeducation* (n. 9 above), 256.

55. Schuster and Van Dyne, "Placing Women in the Liberal Arts" (n. 42 above).

56. Westkott (n. 30 above).

57. Patricia Bell Scott, "Education for Self-Empowerment: A Priority for Women of Color," in Bender, Burk, and Walker, eds. (n. 46 above), 55–66.

58. Maxine Baca Zinn, Lynn Weber Cannon, Elizabeth Higginbotham, and Bonnie Thornton Dill, "The Costs of Exclusionary Practice in women's Studies," *Signs* 11, no. 2 (Winter 1986): 290–303.

59. Esther Ngan-Ling Chow, "Teaching Sex and Gender in Sociology: Incorporating the Perspective of Women of Color," *Teaching Sociology* 12 (April 1985): 299–312.

60. McIntosh, "Interactive Phases of Curricular Re-vision" (n. 33 above).

61. Mary Childers, "Working Definition of a Balanced Course," *Women's Studies Quarterly* 11 (Summer 1983): 30 ff.

62. See Ellen Carol DuBois, Gail Paradise Kelly, Elizabeth Lapovsky Kennedy, Carolyn W. Korsmeyer, and Lillian S. Robinson, eds., *Feminist Scholarship: Kindling in the Groves of Academia* (Urbana: University of Illinois Press, 1985); Diane L. Fowlkes and Charlotte S. McClure, eds., *Feminist Visions: Toward a Transformation of the Liberal Arts Curriculum* (University: University of Alabama Press, 1984); Elizabeth Langland and Walter Gove, eds., *A Feminist Perspective in the Academy: The Difference It Makes* (Chicago: University of Chicago Press, 1981); Julia A. Sherman and Evelyn Torton Beck, eds., *The Prism of Sex: Essays in the Sociology of Knowledge* (Madison: University of Wisconsin Press, 1979); Eloise C. Snyder, ed., *The Study of Women: Enlarging Perspectives of Social Reality* (New York: Harper & Row, 1979); Dale Spender, ed., *Men's Studies Modified: The Impact of Feminism on the Academic Disciplines* (New York: Pergamon Press, 1981); Marianne Triplette, ed., *Women's Studies and the Curriculum* (Winston-Salem, N.C.: Salem College, 1983).

63. Elizabeth Abel, ed., "Writing and Sexual Difference," *Critical Inquiry* 8 (Winter 1981): 173–403.

64. Lillian Robinson, "Treason Our Text: Feminist Challenges to the Literary Canon," Working Papers Series, no. 104 (Wellesley, Mass.: Wellesley College Center for Research on Women, 1983).

65. Paul Lauter, ed., *Reconstructing American Literature* (Old Westbury, N.Y.: Feminist Press, 1983), xx.

66. Paul Lauter, "Race and Gender in the Shaping of the American Literary Canon: A Case Study from the Twenties," *Feminist Studies* 9 (Fall 1983): 435–64.

67. Annette Kolodny, "Dancing through the Minefield: Some Observations on the Theory, Practice, and Politics of a Feminist Literary Criticism," in Spender, ed., 23–42.

68. Natalie Kampen and Elizabeth Grossman, "Feminism and Methodology: Dynamics of Change in the History of Art and Architecture," Working Papers Series, no. 121 (Wellesley, Mass.: Wellesley College Center for Research on Women, 1983); and Norma Broude and Mary Garrard, *Feminism and Art History: Questioning the Litany* (New York: Harper & Row, 1982).

69. Linda Gardiner, "Can This Discipline Be Saved? Feminist Theory Challenges Mainstream Philosophy," Working Papers Series, no. 118 (Wellesley, Mass.: Wellesley College Center for Research on Women, 1983).

70. Gloria Hull, "Reading Literature by U.S. Third World Women," Working Papers Series, no. 141 (Wellesley, Mass.: Wellesley College Center for Research on Women, 1984).

71. Joan Kelly-Gadol, "The Social Relations of the Sexes: Methodological Implications of Women's History," *Signs* 1, no. 4 (Summer 1976): 809–24.

72. Susan Armitage, "Women and Western American History," Working Papers Series, no. 134 (Wellesley, Mass.: Wellesley College Center for Research on Women, 1984).

73. Phyllis Cole and Deborah Lambert, "Gender and Race in American Literature: An Exploration of the Discipline and a Proposal for Two New Courses," Working Papers Series, no. 115 (Wellesley, Mass.: Wellesley College Center for Research on Women, 1983); Annette Kolodny, *The Land before Her: Fantasy and Experience of the American Frontiers, 1630–1860* (Chapel Hill: University of North Carolina Press, 1984).

74. Broude and Garrard.

75. Barbara Drygulski Wright, "Feminist Transformation of Foreign Language Instruction: Progress and Challenges," Working Papers Series, no. 117 (Wellesley, Mass.: Wellesley College Center for Research on Women, 1983).

76. Lauter, ed., *Reconstructing American Literature*, xxi.

77. Carolyn G. Heilbrun, "Feminist Criticism in Departments of Literature," *Academe* 69 (September–October 1983): 14.

78. Carroll Smith-Rosenberg, "The Feminist Reconstruction of History," *Academe* 69 (September–October 1983): 26–37.

79. Marcia Millman and Rosabeth Moss Kanter, eds., "Editorial Introduction," *Another Voice* (Garden City, N.Y.: Doubleday & Co., Anchor Press, 1975); Margaret L. Andersen, *Thinking about Women: Sociological and Feminist Perspectives* (New York: Macmillan Publishing Co., 1983); Carolyn Sherif, "Bias in Psychology," in Sherman and Beck, eds. (n. 62 above), 93–134.

80. Rayna Reiter, ed., *Toward an Anthropology of Women* (New York: Monthly Review Press, 1975).

81. Millman and Kanter, vii–xvi.

82. Barbara Bergmann, "Feminism and Economics," *Academe* 69 (September–October 1983): 22–25.

83. James Soles, "Recent Research on Racism" (paper presented at the University of Delaware, 1985 Lecture Series on Racism, Newark, January 1985).

84. Dorothy Smith, "Women's Perspective as a Radical Critique of Sociology," *Sociological Inquiry* 4 (1974): 7–13, and "Toward a Sociology for Women," in Sherman and Beck, eds., 135–88; Sandra Harding and Merrill B. Hintikka, eds., *Discovering Reality: Feminist Perspectives of Epistemology, Metaphysics, Methodology and Philosophy of Science* (Dordrecht: D. Reidel Publishing Co., 1983).

85. Michelle Hoffnung, "Feminist Transformation: Teaching Experimental Psychology," Working Papers Series, no. 140 (Wellesley, Mass.: Wellesley College Center for Research on Women, 1984); Sherif, 93–134.

86. Judith Stacey and Barrie Thorne, "The Missing Feminist Revolution in Sociology," *Social Problems* 32 (April 1985): 301–16.

87. Marian Lowe and Ruth Hubbard, eds., *Woman's Nature* (New York: Pergamon Press, 1983).

88. Shulamit Reinharz, "Experiential Analysis: A Contribution to Feminist Research," in Bowles and Duelli-Klein, eds. (n. 19 above), 162–91.

89. Michelle Hoffnung.

90. Laurel Furumoto, "Placing Women in the History of Psychology Courses," Working Papers Series, no. 139 (Wellesley, Mass.: Wellesley College Center for Research on Women, 1984).

91. Ruth Hubbard, "Feminist Science: A Meaningful Concept?" (paper presented at the annual meeting of the National Women's Studies Association, Douglass College, New Brunswick, N.J., June 1984).

92. Ruth Hubbard, "Have Only Men Evolved?" in *Biological Woman: The Convenient Myth*, ed. Ruth Hubbard, Mary Sue Henifin, and Barbara Fried (Cambridge, Mass.: Schenckman Publishing Co., 1982), 17–46; Ethel Tobach and Betty Rosoff, eds., *Genes and Gender*, vol. 1 (New York: Gordian Press, 1979); also see the four subsequent volumes of *Genes and Gender*.

93. Ruth Bleier, *Science and Gender* (New York: Pergamon Press, 1984).

94. Mina Davis Caulfield, "Sexuality in Human Evolution: What Is `Natural' about Sex?" *Feminist Studies* 11 (Summer 1985): 343–63.

95. Helene Longino and Ruth Doell, "Body, Bias, and Behavior: A Comparative Analysis of Reasoning in Two Areas of Biological Science, " *Signs* 9, no. 2 (Winter 1983): 206–27; Nancy Hartsock, "The Feminist Standpoint: Developing the Ground for a Specifically Feminist Historical Materialism," in *Money, Sex and Power*, ed. Nancy Hartsock (New York: Long-man, Inc., 1983), 231–51; Elizabeth Fee, "Woman's Nature and Scientific Objectivity," in Lowe and Hubbard, eds., 9–28.

96. Anne Fausto-Sterling, *Myths of Gender: Biological Theories about Women and Men* (New York: Basic Books, 1985), 117.

97. Sandra Harding, *The Science Question in Feminism* (Ithaca, N.Y.: Cornell University Press, 1986).

98. Keller (n. 50 above).

99. Patsy Schweickart, lecture presented at Mellon Faculty Development Seminar, Wellesley College Center for Research on Women, Fall 1985.

100. Dorothy Buerk, "An Experience with Some Able Women Who Avoid Mathematics," *For the Learning of Mathematics* 3 (November 1982): 19–24; Anne Fausto-Sterling, "The Myth of Neutrality: Race, Sex, and Class in Science." *Radical Teacher* 19:21–25, and *Myths of Gender*; see also the special issue, "Women in Science," ed. Pamela Annas, Saul Slapikoff, and Kathleen Weiler, *Radical Teacher*, vol. 30 (1986) for several excellent pieces evolving from the feminist critique of science.

101. American Political Science Association, *Citizenship and Change: Women and American Politics*, 9 vols. (Washington, D.C.: American Political Science Association, 1983).

102. Judith M. Gappa and Janice Pearce, "Sex and Gender in the Social Sciences: Reassessing the Introductory Course: Principles of Microeconomics" (San Francisco: San Francisco State University, 1982, mimeographed); Barrie Thorne, ed., *Sex and Gender in the Social Sciences: Reassessing the Introductory Course: Introductory Sociology* (Washington, D.C.: American Sociological Association, 1983); Nancy Felipe Russo and Natalie Malovich, *Sex and Gender in the Social Sciences: Reassessing the Introductory Course: Introductory Psychology* (Washington, D.C.: American Psychological Association, 1982); Bonnie Lloyd and Arlene Rengert, "Women in Geographic Curricula," *Journal of Geography* 77 (September–October 1978): 164–91; Organization for American Historians, *Restoring Women to History: Materials for U.S. I and II*, 2 vols. (Bloomington, Ind.: Organization of American Historians, 1983).

103. Barrie Thorne, Mary McCormack, Virginia Powell, and Delores Wunder, eds., *The Sociology of Sex and Gender: Syllabi and Teaching Materials* (Washington, D.C.: American Sociological Association Teaching Resources Center, 1985).

104. See especially newsletters from the Center for Research on Women, Memphis State University, and "Re-Visions," the newsletter from the Towson State curriculum project funded by the Fund for the Improvement of Post-Secondary Education.

105. Gloria Hull, Barbara Smith, and Patricia Bell Scott, eds., *All the Women Are White, All the Blacks Are Men, But Some of Us Are Brave* (Old Westbury, N.Y.: Feminist Press, 1983).

106. Memphis State University Center for Research on Women, "Selected Bibliography of Social Science Readings on Women of Color in the U.S." (Memphis, Tenn.: Memphis State University Center for Research on Women, n.d.).

107. Maxine Baca Zinn, "Mexican-American Women in the Social Sciences," *Signs* 8, no. 2 (Winter 1982): 259–72.

108. Marcela Trujillo, *Estudios Femeniles de la Chicana* (Los Angeles: University of California Press, 1974).

109. Anne Fausto-Sterling and Lydia L. English, *Women and Minorities in Science: Course Materials Guide*. Pamphlet and other materials are available from Anne Fausto-Sterling, Department of Biology, Brown University, Providence, R. I. 02921.

110. *Sage: A Scholarly Journal on Black Women*, Box 42471, Atlanta, GA. 30311.

111. See *Journal of Social Issues*, vol. 39 (Fall 1983); *Conditions*, vol. 5 (1979); *Spelman Messenger*, vol. 100 (Spring 1984); *Sinister Wisdom*, vols. 22–23 (1983).

112. Marilyn Jimenez, "Contrasting Portraits: Integrating Materials about the Afro-Hispanic Woman into the Traditional Curriculum," Working Papers Series, no. 120 (Wellesley, Mass.: Wellesley College Center for Research on Women, 1983); Baca Zinn (n. 107 above).

113. Johnella Butler, "Complicating the Question: Black Studies and Women's Studies," in Schuster and Van Dyne, eds. (n. 20 above), 73–86.

114. Adrienne Rich, "Claiming an Education," in *On Lies, Secrets, and Silence* (n. 7 above), 231.

115. Ibid., 231.

116. Banner (n. 44 above).

117. F. Howe (n. 9 above), 28.

Acknowledgment

This essay has been developed through the many discussions I have had with people working in women's studies curriculum projects around the country. I am particularly grateful for having been able to participate in the Mellon seminars at the Wellesley College Center for Research on Women. Although I cannot name all of the participants in these seminars, their collective work and thought continuously enriches my thinking and teaching; I thank them all. I especially thank Peggy McIntosh, director of these seminars, for her inspiration and ongoing support for this work. She, Valerie Hans, Sandra Harding, and the anonymous *Signs* reviewers provided very helpful reviews of the earlier drafts of this essay. And I appreciate the support of the Provost's Office of the University of Delaware for providing the funds for a curriculum revision project in women's studies at the University of Delaware; working with the participants in this project contributed much to the development of this essay.

DIVIDED NO MORE

A MOVEMENT APPROACH TO EDUCATIONAL REFORM

PARKER J. PALMER

As I travel the country talking with faculty about the reform of teaching and learning, I meet many people who care about the subject and who have compelling visions for change. But after we have talked a while, our conversations take an almost inevitable turn. "These are wonderful ideas," someone will say, "but every last one of them will be defeated by the conditions of academic life."

The claim is usually followed by a litany of impediments to institutional reform: Teaching has low status in the academy, tenure decisions favor those who publish, scarce dollars will always go to research (or to administration, or to bricks and mortar), etc. No matter how hopeful our previous conversation has been, these reminders of institutional gridlock create a mood of resignation, even despair—and the game feels lost before play has begun.

The constancy of this experience has forced me to think more carefully about how change really happens. I have found myself revisiting an old but helpful distinction between an *organizational* approach and a *movement* approach to change. Both organizations and movements are valuable, worthy of leadership, and channels for change—and a healthy society will encourage symbiosis between the two (indeed, reform-minded administrators often welcome movement energies). But when an organizational mentality is imposed on a problem that requires movement sensibilities, the result is often despair. I believe that some of us are making precisely that mistake when it comes to the reform of teaching and learning.

The organizational approach to change is premised on the notion that bureaucracies—their rules, roles, and relationships—define the limits of social reality within which change must happen. Organizations are essentially arrangements of power, so this approach to change asks: "How can the power contained within the boxes of this organization be rearranged or redirected to achieve the desired goal?" That is a good question—except when it assumes that bureaucracies are the only game in town.

This approach pits entrenched patterns of corporate power against fragile images of change harbored by a minority of individuals, and the match is inherently unfair. Constrained by this model, people with a vision for change may devote themselves to persuading powerholders to see things their way, which drains energy away from the vision and breeds resentment among the visionaries when "permission" is not granted. When organizations seem less interested in change than in preservation (which is, after all, their job), would-be reformers are likely to give up if the organizational approach is the only one they know.

But our obsession with the organizational model may suggest something more sinister than mere ignorance of another way. We sometimes get perverse satisfaction from insisting that organizations offer the only path to change. Then, when the path is blocked, we can indulge the luxury of resentment rather than seek an alternative avenue of reform—and we can blame it all on external forces rather than take responsibility upon ourselves.

Reprinted from *Change* 24, no. 2 (March/April 1992), Change Magazine.

There is a part of human nature that would rather remain hopeless than take the risk of new life. It is not uncommon for academics to be driven by this "death wish," even (and perhaps especially) the most idealistic among us. The most vigorous resistance to the movement model may come from reformers who have been defeated on one front and are too weary to open another. Sometimes it is easier to live with the comfort of despair than with the challenge of knowing that change can happen despite the inertia of organizations.

The Movement Way

But there is another avenue toward change: The way of the movement. I began to understand movements when I saw the simple fact that nothing would ever have changed if reformers had allowed themselves to be done in by organizational resistance. Many of us experience such resistance as checkmate to our hopes for change. But for a movement, resistance is merely the place where things begin. The movement mentality, far from being defeated by organizational resistance, takes energy from opposition. Opposition validates the audacious idea that change must come.

The black liberation movement and the women's movement would have died aborning if racist and sexist organizations had been allowed to define the rules of engagement. But for some blacks, and for some women, that resistance affirmed and energized the struggle. In both movements, advocates of change found sources of countervailing power outside of organizational structures, and they nurtured that power in ways that eventually gave them immense leverage on organizations.

The genius of movements is paradoxical: They abandon the logic of organizations in order to gather the power necessary to rewrite the logic of organizations. Both the black movement and the women's movement grew outside of organizational boundaries—but both returned to change the lay, and the law, of the land. I believe that the reform of teaching and learning will happen only if we who care about it learn to live this paradox.

What is the logic of a movement? How does a movement unfold and progress? I see four definable stages in the movements I have studied—stages that do not unfold as neatly as this list suggests, but often overlap and circle back on each other:

- Isolated individuals decide to stop leading "divided lives."
- These people discover each other and form groups for mutual support.
- Empowered by community, they learn to translate "private problems" into public issues.
- Alternative rewards emerge to sustain the movement's vision, which may force the conventional reward system to change.

I want to explore these stages here, but not simply in remembrance of things past. By understanding the stages of a movement, some of us may see more clearly that we are engaged in a movement today, that we hold real power in our hands—a form of power that has driven real change in recent times. Knowing our power, perhaps we will have less need or desire to succumb to the sweet despair of believing that organizational gridlock must have the last word.

Choosing Integrity

The first stage in a movement can be described with some precision, I think. It happens when isolated individuals make an inner choice to stop leading "divided lives." Most of us know from experience what a divided life is. Inwardly we feel one sort of imperative for our lives, but outwardly we respond to quite another. This is the human condition, of course; our inner and outer worlds will never be in perfect harmony. But there are extremes of dividedness that become intolerable, and when the tension snaps inside of this person, then that person, and then another, a movement may be underway.

The decision to stop leading a divided life, made by enough people over a period of time, may eventually have political impact. But at the outset, it is a deeply personal decision, taken for the sake of personal integrity and wholeness. I call it the "Rosa Parks decision" in honor of the woman who decided, one hot Alabama day in 1955, that she finally would sit at the front of the bus.

Rosa Parks' decision was neither random nor taken in isolation. She served as secretary for the local NAACP, had studied social change at the Highlander Folk School, and was aware of others' hopes to organize a bus boycott. But her motive that day in Montgomery was not to spark the modern civil rights movement. Years later, she explained her decision with a simple but powerful image of personal wholeness: "I sat down because my feet were tired."

I suspect we can say even more: Rosa Parks sat at the front of the bus because her soul was tired of the vast, demoralizing gap between knowing herself as fully human and collaborating with a system that denied her humanity. The decision to stop leading a divided life is less a strategy for altering other people's values than an uprising of the elemental need for one's own values to come to the fore. The power of a movement lies less in attacking some enemy's untruth than in naming and claiming a truth of one's own.

There is immense energy for change in such inward decisions as they leap from one person to another and outward to the society. With these decisions, individuals may set in motion a process that creates change from the inside out. There is an irony here: We often think of movements as "confrontational," as hammering away at social structures until the sinners inside repent—and we contrast them (often invidiously) with the "slow, steady, faithful" process of working for change from within the organization. In truth, people who take an organizational approach to problems often become obsessed with their unyielding "enemies," while people who adopt a movement approach must begin by changing themselves.

I meet teachers around the country who are choosing integrity in ways reminiscent of Rosa Parks. These faculty have realized that even if teaching is a back-of-the-bus thing for their institutions, it is a front-of-the-bus thing for them. They have realized that a passion for teaching was what animated their decision to enter the academy, and they do not want to lose the primal energy of their professional lives. They have realized that they care deeply about the lives of their students, and they do not want to abandon the young. They have realized that teaching is an enterprise in which they have a heavy investment of personal identity and meaning—and they have decided to reinvest their lives, even if they do not receive dividends from their colleges or from their colleagues.

For these teachers, the decision is really quite simple: Caring about teaching and about students brings them health as persons, and to collaborate in a denial of that fact is to collaborate in a diminishment of their own lives. They refuse any longer to act outwardly in contradiction to something they know inwardly to be true—that teaching, and teaching well, is a source of identity for them. They understand that this refusal may evoke the wrath of the gods of the professions, who are often threatened when we reach for personal wholeness. But still, they persist.

What drives such a decision, with all its risks? The difference between a person who stays at the back of the bus and "sits on it" and one who finally decides to sit up front is probably lost in the mystery of human courage. But courage is stimulated by the simple insight that my oppression is not simply the result of mindless external forces; it comes also from the fact that I collaborate with these forces, giving assent to the very thing that is crushing my spirit. With this realization comes anger, and in anger is the energy that drives some people to say: "Enough. My feet are tired. Here I sit."

These people have seized the personal insight from which all movements begin: No punishment can possibly be more severe than the punishment that comes from conspiring in the denial of one's own integrity.

Corporate Support

But the personal decision to stop leading a divided life is a frail reed. All around us, dividedness is presented as the sensible, even responsible, way to live. So the second stage in a movement happens when people who have been making these decisions start to discover each other and enter into relations of mutual encouragement and support. These groups, which are characteristic of every movement I know about, perform the crucial function of helping the Rosa Parks of the world know that even though they are out of step, they are not crazy. Together we learn that behaving normally is sometimes nuts but seeking integrity is always sane.

Often, when I offer a workshop on the reform of teaching and learning, a professor will come to me privately and say: "I agree with you about these things—but I am the only one on this campus who feels that way." Later in the day, two or three more faculty will take me aside and say the same thing. By evening I have spoken to eight or ten people who are committed to good teaching but are quite sure they are alone in these convictions on their campus.

While stage one is strong on many campuses, stage two is less well developed. Faculty who have decided to live "divided no more" are often unaware of each other's existence—so weak are the communal structures of the academy, and so diffident are intellectuals about sharing such "private" matters. It is difficult for faculty to seek each other out for mutual support. But it is clear from all great movements that mutual support is vital if the inner decision is to be sustained—and if the movement is to take its next crucial steps toward gathering power.

Where support groups do exist, they assume a simple form and function. Six or eight faculty from a variety of departments agree to meet on a regular but manageable schedule (say, once every two weeks) simply to talk about teaching. (The mix of departments is important because of the political vulnerability faculty often feel within their own guild halls.) They talk about what they teach, how they teach, what works and what doesn't, and—most important of all—the joys and pains of being a teacher. The conversations are informal, confidential, and, above all, candid. When you ask these people how they manage to add one more meeting to their crowded schedules, the answer often is: "This kind of meeting is not a burden, but a relief. It actually seems to free up my time."

Some of these groups have evolved ground rules for conversation, and—on the evidence of other movements—such rules are vital if these groups are to flourish. Rules may be especially vital in the academy, where real conversation is often thwarted by a culture that invites posturing, intimidation, and keeping score. Ground rules cannot create new attitudes, but they can encourage new behavior.

For example, the ground rules may say that each person gets an opportunity to speak—but when the others respond, they may respond only with questions that will help the speaker clarify his or her inner truth. They may not criticize, give advice, offer pity, or say "tsk, tsk" when it turns out one has not read the latest book. The questions-only rule encourages real listening by banning one-upping, amateur psychoanalysis, quick "fixes," and all the other ways we have of walling ourselves off from each other. Of course, people are always free to ask for help with the problems they face. But problem-solving is not the primary purpose of these gatherings. Their purpose is to wrap the individual's inner decision in a resolve that can only come from being heard by a supportive community.

At the moment, I suspect, more women than men are coming together on campus in support groups of this sort. The reason, I think, is simple: Women who care about teaching are involved in two movements at once—one in support of teaching, another in support of women in the academy—so they have double need of communal sustenance. Perhaps they have heard and heeded the admonition of Margaret Mead: "Never doubt that a small group of thoughtful, committed citizens can change the world; indeed, it's the only thing that ever has."

Going Public

The third stage of a movement has already been implied. As support groups develop, individuals learn to translate their private concerns into public issues, and they grow in their ability to give voice to these issues in public and compelling ways. To put it more precisely, support groups help people discover that their problems are not "private" at all, but have been occasioned by public conditions and therefore require public remedies.

This has been the story of the women's movement (and of the black liberation movement as well). For a long time, women were "kept in their place" partly by a psychology that relegated the pain women felt to the private realm—grist for the therapeutic mill. But when women came together and began discovering the prevalence of their pain, they also began discerning its public roots. Then they moved from Freud to feminism.

The translation of private pain into public issues that occurs in support groups goes far beyond the analysis of issues; it also empowers people to take those issues into public places. It was in small groups (notably, in churches) that blacks were empowered to take their protest to the larger community—in songs and sermons and speeches, in pickets and in marches, in open letters and essays and books. Group support encourages people to risk the public exposure of insights that had earlier seemed far too fragile for that rough-and-tumble realm.

I am using the word "public" here in a way that is more classical than contemporary. The public realm I have in mind is not the realm of politics, which would return us to the manipulation of organizational power. Instead, to "go public" is to enter one's convictions into the mix of communal discourse. It is to project one's ideas so that others can hear them, respond to them, and be influenced by them—and so that one's ideas can be tested and refined in the public crucible. The public, understood as a vehicle of discourse, is pre-political. It is that primitive process of communal conversation, conflict, and consensus on which the health of institutionalized power depends.

Many would argue, of course, that our public process is itself in poor health and cannot be relied upon for remedies. These critics claim that there is no longer a public forum for a movement to employ. But historically, it is precisely the energy of movements that has renewed the public realm; movements have the capacity to create the very public they depend on. However moribund the public may be, it is reinvigorated when people learn how to articulate their concerns in ways that allow—indeed, compel—a wider public to listen and respond.

Today, educational reform is becoming a focus of public discourse, and will become an even sharper focus if the movement grows. Many books have been written on the subject, and some—for better or for worse—have become best-sellers. Speakers roam the land planting seeds of change in workshops and convocations. New associations advance the cause of change in national and regional gatherings (and faculty who feel isolated on their own campuses seek them out as desert nomads seek oases). Well-established national associations have taken reform as an agendum.

Even more remarkable, the movement for educational reform has been joined by publics far beyond the walls of the academy. Parents, employers, legislators, and columnists are calling for more attention to teaching and learning, and their calls are insistent. Recently, a coalition of major accounting firms used the language of collaborative learning to press the agency that accredits business schools toward the reform of business education. At moments like that, one knows that "going public" can make a difference.

Because this activity does not always have direct political impact, some skeptics may call it "mere words." But this criticism comes from an organizational mentality. By giving public voice to alternative values we can create something more fundamental than political change. We can create cultural change. When we secure a place in public discourse for ideas and images like "collaborative learning," we are following those reformers who minted phrases like "affirmative action" and made them the coin of the realm. When the language of change becomes available in the common culture, people are better able to name their yearnings for change, to explore them with others, to claim membership in a great movement—and to overcome the disabling effects of feeling isolated and half-mad.

Alternative Rewards

As a movement passes through the first three stages, it develops ways of rewarding people for sustaining the movement itself. In part, these rewards are simply integral to the nature of each stage; they are the rewards that come from living one's values, from belonging to a community, from finding a public voice. But in stage four, a more systematic pattern of alternative rewards emerges, and with it comes the capacity to challenge the dominance of existing organizations.

The power of organizations depends on their ability to reward people who abide by their norms—even the people who suffer from those norms. A racist society depends on a majority who are rewarded for keeping the minority "in its place"—and on a minority willing to stay there. But as members of either group discover rewards for alternative behavior, it becomes more difficult for racism to reign. An educational system that ignores human need in favor of a narrow version of professionalism depends on a reward system that keeps both faculty and students in their place. But as soon as rewards for alternative behavior emerge for either group, it becomes more difficult for reform to be denied its day.

What are the alternative rewards offered by a growing movement? As a movement grows, the meaning one does not find in conventional work is found in the meaning of the movement. As a movement grows, the affirmation one does not receive from organizational colleagues is received from movement friends. As a movement grows, careers that no longer satisfy may be revisioned in forms and images that the movement has inspired. As a movement grows, the paid work one cannot find in conventional organizations may be found in the movement itself.

Ultimately, as a movement grows, conventional organizations are more and more likely to create spaces where movement-style work can be done. Forty years ago, anyone working openly for "equal opportunity" might have had a hard time getting paid work of any sort. Today, many organizations are required to pay someone to serve as their Equal Employment Opportunity officer. Similarly, black and feminist scholars whose insights have long been unwelcome in the academy are not only employable today, but are often recruited with vigor.

In stage one, people who decide to live "divided no more" find the courage to face punishment by realizing that there is no punishment worse than conspiring in a denial of one's own integrity. That axiom, inverted, shows how alternative rewards can create cracks in the conventional reward system and then grow in the cracks: People start realizing there is no reward greater than living in a way that honors one's own integrity. Taken together, the two axioms trace a powerful vector of a movement's growth—from rejecting conventional punishments to embracing alternative rewards.

These alternative rewards may seem frail and vulnerable when compared to the raises and promotions organizations are able to bestow upon their loyalists. So they are. Integrity, as the cynics say, does not put bread on the table. But people who are drawn into a movement generally find that stockpiling bread is not the main issue for them. They have the bread they need and, given that, they learn the wisdom of another saying: "People do not live on bread alone." We live, ultimately, on our integrity.

As we explore this fourth stage, where movements return to intersect with organizations, it is important to recall that a healthy society is one in which organizations and movements are related symbiotically—as the case of black and feminist scholars will show. Without movements, such scholars would not be bringing new life to organizations; without organizations, such scholars would not have found ways to sustain careers.

But now that black and feminist scholars have found an academic niche, the need for the movement is not gone. Organizations often employ critics in order to contain them. By placing these scholars in air-tight departments, the academy may yet be able to keep them from breathing new life into the places where education is oxygen-starved. Indeed, the academic culture often inhibits black and feminist scholars themselves from teaching in ways that honor their own insights. The movement has succeeded, but the movement is still needed.

Of course, the educational reform movement is not fulfilled when the academy grants a toehold to non-traditional scholars, any more than the black liberation movement is fulfilled by a society that "allows" blacks to make a life on its margins. The movement will persist until the obvious is acknowledged: Teaching has as much right to full status in the academy as any other academic function—research, athletics, administration, lobbying, fund-raising—and it may have even more right than some! Teaching simply *belongs* in the academy, and there is no need to defend that claim.

The defense, if any, must come from those who have promoted a concept of higher education so bizarre that it can ignore the question of how and why we teach and learn. We are at a moment in the history of education when the emptiness of that concept is clear—a moment when real progress on reform is possible. There is much to be done that I have not named here, from revisioning teaching as a legitimate form of scholarship (building on the superb work of the Carnegie Foundation) to developing more sophisticated strategies for change. But in the midst of those complexities, we must remember that all great movements start simply: A few people feel the pain of the divided life and resolve to live it no more. In that resolve is the power to live our moment to its full potential.

Postscript

Though the stages I have sketched here have historical warrant, they obviously comprise an "ideal type," a schematic version of how movements happen that is smoother and more hopeful in the writing than in the living. Movements offer no guarantees of success. But neither do organizations, nor life itself. What movements *do* offer is a creative channel for energies that might otherwise be extinguished. They offer us an alternative to the despairing cynicism that is the constant snare of contemporary professional life.

Different people will find themselves at different stages of a movement. Some will want to make a decision against dividedness, some will need to join with others for support, some will have to learn how to "go public," and some will try to find alternative rewards. Every stage has a contribution to make—not only to the cause, but to the person.

At every stage of a movement there is both power to help change happen and encouragement for disheartened souls. Wherever we are on this journey, a step taken to renew our spirits may turn out to be a step toward educational renewal—once we understand the movement way.

An Integrated Approach to Developing and Implementing Learning-centred Curricula

Harry Hubball and Helen Burt

The purpose of this article is to provide a critical review of the motivating factors, processes and outcomes pertaining to learning-centred curriculum reform in higher education. A case study example is provided from the Faculty of Pharmaceutical Sciences at the University of British Columbia. Although academic units on university campuses tend to present many unique contextual challenges, and are at different stages in curriculum re-design, useful lessons can be learned across settings without "re-inventing the wheel," or falling into similar implementation problems. A flexible framework, guiding principles and strategic approach to developing and implementing learning-centred curricula are provided to assist academic developers. Curricular reform has implications for learning communities, planning, assessment and programming in higher education.

Introduction: Curricular Reform as a Process of Transition in Higher Education

Over the past decade, in many parts of the world, universities, faculties, schools and departments in higher education have been undergoing significant curricular reform (Ganderton, 1996; Gibbons, 2000; Green, 1995; Mok, 1999). Globally, critical factors around university campuses influencing this process, include:

- social and economic challenges which call for increasing efficiency and accountability, while responding to the pressures of increasing student enrolment, shrinking budgets, competition and "having to do more with less" in higher education (Daniel, 1993; Schneider & Shoenberg, 1999);
- significant pedagogical shifts from teaching-centred to learning-centred approaches (Barr & Tag, 1995; Jansen & Christie, 1999);
- increasing importance of Prior Learning Assessment (PLA), attributes of graduates and learning outcomes, interdisciplinarity, interprofessionalism, internationalisation, work-based learning, educational technologies, and credit accumulation and transfer (Shulman, 1999; Trowler, 1996);
- "triggering opportunities" (Ewell, 1997; Knight & Trowler, 2000). For example, university initiatives to re-define the purpose of undergraduate education, external reviews, staffing/funding/programming crisis.

The sheer nature and scope of these factors continue to pose considerable challenges to institutions, curriculum committees and faculty members responsible for curricula design and implementation. Not surprisingly, therefore, there have been a wide range of interpretations, practices and reactions to learning-centred curricula reform (Drummond, Nixon, & Wiltshire, 1998; Green, 1999;

Reprinted from *International Journal for Academic Development* 9, no. 1 (May 2004), Taylor & Francis, Ltd.

Kemp & Seagraves, 1995). At the University of British Columbia (UBC), Canada, for example, prompted by a strategic institutional visioning process and subsequent development of an Academic Plan (VP Academic and Provost, 2000), all academic units on campus have been challenged to re-examine their curriculum and pedagogical practices in the context of the University's explicit goals and commitment toward learning and undergraduate education. Although academic units on university campuses tend to present many unique contextual challenges, and are at different stages in curriculum re-design, useful lessons can be learned across settings without "re-inventing the wheel," or falling into similar implementation problems. This paper provides a case study example of the motivating factors, processes and outcomes pertaining to curriculum reform within the UBC Faculty of Pharmaceutical Sciences. A flexible framework, guiding principles and strategic approach to implementing learning-centred curricula are provided to assist academic developers in higher education.

Learning-centred Curricula

Although not an entirely new concept in higher education, a learning-centred approach to curricular reform is part of a larger process of educational change (Hubball & Poole, 2003). In order to meet the diverse needs and circumstances of learning communities, no singular curriculum model, implementation strategy, nor approach to learning will suit all academic settings. The underlying assumptions about a learning-centred approach to curricular reform are that: representative students, faculty, and stakeholders in the broader context should be active participants in the curricular reform process; that academic units are at different stages in curricular reform and progress at different rates; that curricular reform should honour inclusion of a wide range of teaching and learning strategies; and that curricular reform within an academic unit is both an individual and social contextual process (Barab & Duffy, 2000; Barr & Tag, 1995; Gold, 1997; Kupperschmidt & Burns, 1997; Schneider & Schoenberg, 1999; Shulman, 1999).

Essentially, learning-centred curricula place emphases on *learning communities, curriculum integration, diverse pedagogies* and *clearly defined learning outcomes*. Learning outcomes focus on what students are expected to know and be able to do (for example, demonstrate critical thinking, responsible use of ethical principles, problem-solving skills) in the context of a field of study, and are designed to be assessable, transferable, and relevant to learners' lives as workers and citizens in a diverse world (Baron, 1996; Battersby, 1997; Clanchy & Ballard, 1995; Kanpol, 1995). In addition, the following benefits present a compelling rationale for curricula developed from a learning-centred approach:

1. informs learners of what they can expect to achieve from a program, so they can organise their time and efforts;

2. communicates curriculum/program goals in a meaningful way to a broader community;

3. outcomes-based curriculum helps to determine the extent to which learning has been accomplished;

4. guides curriculum committees (within resource constraints) to determine program(s) of study and course offerings;

5. guides instructors when they are designing course objectives, content, delivery and assessment strategies.

In practice, learning-centred curricula require a community of students/learners to be able to make choices within a responsive (that is, to diverse learners' needs, critical teaching and learning issues and available resources) carefully structured, and guided learning environment. Thus, in the broader context of significant educational reform, and in order to respond to the diverse needs and circumstances of students, faculty and society, the UBC Faculty of Pharmaceutical Sciences, embarked on a process to re-design and implement a learning-centred curriculum.

An Integrated Approach to Developing and Implementing Learning-centred Curricula

The processes of developing and implementing learning-centred curricula are complex and intricately inter-related, that cannot be treated as discrete entities, nor can they each be considered the responsibility of completely different people. Kupperschmidt and Burns (1997) suggested that focusing on curriculum revision as a process of transition (that is, requires a period of incremental adaptation) rather than radical change may help alleviate faculty anxiety or resistance. An integrated approach to developing and implementing learning-centred curricula combines both pedagogical and organisational change strategies (Diamond, 1997, 1998; Erickson, 2002; Fullan, 2001; Green & Kreuter, 1999; Murphy, 1997; Perrier, Stinson, & Milter, 1996; Pietersen, 2002; Wiles & Bondi, 2002; Winslade, Pugsley, Lavack, & Strand, 1995).

A conceptual framework (Figure 1) and a strategic approach was applied to curriculum reform in the UBC Faculty of Pharmaceutical Sciences. This flexible and iterative organisational framework takes into account the learning context, and integrates comprehensive strategies for curriculum reform in higher education.

Practical strategies (Tables 1–4) for each component of the framework were drawn from a combination of literature sources and specific experiences (focus group interviews, workshop assignments, discussion fora) with curriculum committees from a wide range of UBC faculties engaged in curriculum reform. Essentially, this framework provides (i) a benchmark for an analysis of needs to determine the current status of curriculum within an academic unit, (ii) guidelines for direction and progression in the curriculum re-design process, and (iii) strategies for implementation.

Learning context strategies refer to critical implementation initiatives (for example, adequate support; leadership qualities; teamwork; representative input; responsiveness, incentives and sources of reward) that empower the learning community (collectively and individually) to engage in curriculum re-design (Baker, 1999; Barab & Duffy, 2000; Cox, 2001; Gold, 1997; Middendorf, 1999; Nolinske, 1999). *Planning strategies* refer to the development of global (overall curriculum)

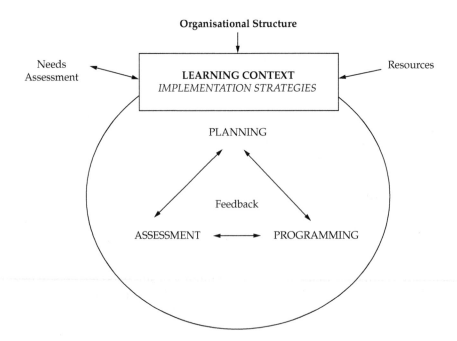

Figure 1 An Integrated Framework for Developing and Implementing Learning-centred Curricula in Higher Education: Implications for Learning Communities, Planning, Assessment and Programming

TABLE 1
Implementing Learning-centred Curricula: Practical Strategies for Learning Context

Learning Context Strategies

Curriculum redesign requires active support (financial, organisational, political) from Heads/administration. Effective leadership qualities of the Chair to engage the learning community are critical. Re-examine institutional visioning documents, accreditation requirements and/or expectations of the field regarding ability-based outcomes. Develop strong rationale and priority for curriculum re-design. Elevate status, reward and accountability for effective teaching within the academic unit.

Chair should seek input from stakeholders and conduct a comprehensive "needs assessment" to record current status of curriculum, available resources, vision, challenges, and input regarding expected learning outcomes on completion of a program of study. The "buy-in"—ownership. Ensure curriculum re-design is an open and inclusive process versus closed process administered by a select few. If necessary, consider a new, interactive and influential committee (inclusive of stakeholders), provide adequate support/time & workshop assistance. Develop short, intermediate and long-term curriculum goals.

Develop overall integration (vertical and horizontal) model for program "specializations", as well as provide autonomy for specializations to develop appropriate course offerings within curriculum. Reinforce learning-centred principles and benefits for graduates of faculty. Acknowledge complexity/challenge of curriculum re-design. Make visible available resources, constraints, and progress (e.g., notice board in lobby, website, e-mail communications, verbal presentation at faculty meetings). Provide adequate assistance/support for change.

Address unit-specific factors that influence well-being in the university workplace. Provide collective strategies and individual opportunities to enhance a healthy academic workplace environment.

Acknowledge past history and efforts regarding curriculum development. Engage faculty in dialogue regarding a rationale, benefits, significant differences and examples of real changes that occur from a learning-centred approach to curriculum re-design.

"Making Teaching Count." Convey commitment of academic unit toward teaching excellence (e.g., hiring priorities, reward system). Provide informational resources and open meetings/workshop support.

Provide faculty with interactive communication access to curriculum reform process (e.g., web-site, e-mail, suggestion boxes in key locations, interactive curriculum committee representatives).

Engage faculty in identifying and acknowledging barriers (individual and collective) and developing potential solutions for curricular reform. Provide adequate support and on-going workshop assistance for faculty regarding learning-centred approaches to course design, assessment of student learning, and teaching methods in higher education.

Integrate curriculum development and scholarship of teaching into tenure/promotion process.

Use multiple communications to update and to elicit faculty input. Provide visible curriculum notice-board with flow chart events, progress reports, challenges/issues etc.

Consider curriculum development as an on-going multifaceted process. Revisit and utilise faculty input, monitor progress, critically evaluate, refine.

and specific (program-specialization) learning outcomes (for example, critical thinking, responsible use of ethical principles, communication skills) which, in part, drive the curricula, teaching and learning process (Baird, 1996; Clanchy & Ballard, 1995; Lockhart & Borland, 2001). *Assessment strategies* refer to the development of a range of methods (for example, capstone projects, portfolios, student presentations, exams) and procedures used to assess and evaluate student learning and curriculum effectiveness (processes, impact and outcomes) (Adamcik, Hurley, & Erramouspe, 1996; Brown, Bull, & Pendlebury, 1997; Diamond, 1998; Shavelson & Huang, 2003); and *programming strategies* refer to the development and integration of diverse learning strategies (for example, interdisciplinary/core learning modules, intra-program specialization modules, and individual course work modules—learning technologies, problem-based learning, lectures, independent study and field experiences) in which students can acquire, integrate and apply knowledge in diverse settings (Brandt, Clements, & Piascik, 1998; Clarke & Hubball, 2001; Poindexter, 2003; Raman-Wilms, 2001).

TABLE 2
Implementing Learning-centred Curricula: Practical Strategies for Planning

Planning Strategies

(Developing clearly defined curriculum-wide learning outcomes)

- Develop/brainstorm desirable learning outcomes—compare with other departments. Adapt learning outcome templates to suit needs and circumstances, versus "re-invent wheel" or rigid compliance.

- Develop responsive, higher order and accountable learning outcomes versus narrow/simplistic measurement-driven outcomes or, in contrast, lofty outcomes without due consideration for assessment and evaluation. Consider global (related to core program) and specific (related to program streams) learning outcomes from the cognitive, affective and psychomotor domains. For example, nine ability-based global outcomes in the faculty of pharmaceutical sciences included: critical thinking, scientific inquiry, mathematical skills, independent learning skills, information access and evaluation skills, ethical behaviour, communication skills, social awareness, interpersonal and teamwork skills, and apply and integrate knowledge.

- Overly rigid, narrow or prescriptive curriculum learning outcomes are often undesirable, and unlikely to be faithfully implemented in practice. Curricular learning outcomes, therefore, should be developed in response to the needs of faculty, students and society, and be sufficiently flexible so that they can be realistically accountable and adapted to local situations and changing circumstances (Battersby, 1997; Green & Kreuter, 1991; Kanpol, 1995).

- Integrate learning outcomes with evaluation, programming and contextual factors.

- Seek workshop support if required.

TABLE 3
Implementing Learning-centred Curricula: Practical Strategies Assessment

Assessment Strategies

(Range of methods used to assess curriculum-wide learning outcomes)

- Integrate learning outcomes with evaluation, programming and contextual factors.
- Consider a variety of authentic assessment techniques (e.g., presentations, portfolios, projects, exams).
- Develop criteria and standards to differentiate levels of achievement.
- Develop formative and summative evaluations, informal and formal evaluations, teacher-centred and learner-centred evaluations.
- Develop an assessment and evaluation framework to monitor curriculum learning outcomes. For example, in the faculty of pharmaceutical sciences all courses are required to implement curriculum learning outcomes; course syllabi is required for submission to curriculum committee; formal feedback is elicited from students, faculty and external peer-review at key stages of the curriculum; core learning modules are placed strategically in the curriculum (i.e., interdisciplinary caps courses, capstone project, portfolio module).
- Provide time/workshop support for faculty regarding learning-centred approaches to assessment and evaluation.

TABLE 4
Implementing Learning-centred Curricula: Practical Strategies for Programming

Programming Strategies

(Program streams, teaching methods/learning experiences driven by curriculum-wide learning outcomes)

- Integrate learning outcomes and evaluation strategies to overall program(s) of study.
- Develop program(s) of study including: sequencing, time phases, core courses, pre-req./electives.
- Apply learning outcomes and evaluation strategies to program(s) of study.

(Continued)

TABLE 4 *(Continued)*

Programming Strategies

- Consider a variety of teaching/delivery strategies (teacher-centred, learner-centred, combined).
- Consider innovative learning modules and broad-based pedagogies (e.g., cohort learning experiences, interdisciplinary study, portfolio development, problem-based and case-based learning, lecture/lab, self-directed research, collaborative research, web-based learning, community-based and field experiences, peer-teaching modules, student conferences) that are applied in an integrated manner.
- Develop individual course offerings and apply learning outcomes and evaluation strategies.
- Provide time/workshop support for faculty regarding learning-centred approaches to course design, assessment and instructional skills.
- Curriculum development is an on-going process—revisit data, encourage input, monitor effectiveness, refine, seek workshop support if required.

Stage-specific Intervention Strategies

While the curriculum development team was sensitive to addressing all components of the curriculum re-design framework at all times during the reform process, it is important to note that the UBC Faculty of Pharmaceutical Sciences (like various other UBC faculties, schools and departments) progressed through critical stages of curriculum reform, albeit at different rates. There was firstly an *awareness stage* (aware of groundswell of curricular reform in alternative settings though no real energy or resources committed to curriculum change) Secondly there was an *initiative stage* (interest and commitment toward curriculum reform, initiate Chair and key personnel to spearhead process); then a *mobilisation stage* (mobilise and empower learning community for curriculum reform, establish curriculum committee, and sub-committee working groups for strategic planning). This was followed by an *action plan stage* ('buy-in' readiness and integration of responsive outcomes, assessment strategies and learning modules developed); and, finally a *practice stage* (on-going systematic analysis, refinement, further development and dissemination of curriculum reform process).

Figure 2 illustrates the progressive, though cyclical and messy realities of curriculum reform, from the *awareness stage* through to the *practice stage*.

In addition to understanding the unique context in which an academic unit operates, therefore, it is also important for academic developers to recognise the unit's readiness and stage of curriculum reform. Generally, learning context strategies were especially important during the *awareness, initiative and mobilisation stages*, whereas emphases on planning, assessment and programming strategies tended to be more relevant during the *action plan stage*. Rigorous reflection and feedback strategies, in the form of program evaluation data, is most informative during the *practice* stage. Stage-specific intervention strategies, however, were particularly useful for assisting this academic unit through each of the stages of curriculum reform.

During the *awareness stage*, curriculum leaders (Deans, committee personnel) across campus were exposed to a wide range of resources and current literature about the benefits of learning-centred curricula and best practice models, and encouraged to identify internal and external motivation (contextual) factors for curriculum reform. For example, the learning context in the UBC Faculty of Pharmaceutical Sciences includes 30 full-time equivalent faculty and 550 undergraduate students in a four-year B.Sc. (Pharm) Program. Within the Pharmaceutical Sciences program, there are five sub-disciplinary streams: Pharmaceutics, Pharmacology, Pharmaceutical Chemistry and Drug Metabolism, Clinical Pharmacy, and Pharmacy Practice. Students are required to complete at least one year of general sciences prior to admission to the B.Sc. program. In conjunction, and influenced by the institutional Academic Plan, the UBC Faculty of Pharmaceutical

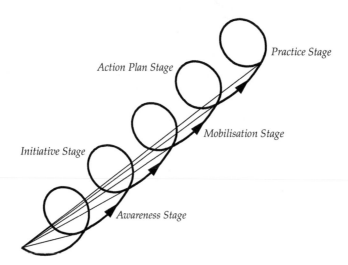

Figure 2 Diagram Showing the Progressive, though Cyclical and Unpredictable Realities of Curriculum Reform

Sciences in 1997/98 faced additional pressures for a major curriculum reform. These pressures originated from several sources:

- *Accreditation*—the current curriculum did not meet the requirements of the Canadian Council on Accreditation of Pharmacy Programs (CCAPP) that Pharmacy curricula be structured around ability-based outcomes.

- *Students and Pharmacy Practitioners*—excessive student workload and general dissatisfaction with a content-driven curriculum that did not prepare them well for Pharmacy practice.

- *Faculty*—faculty dissatisfaction with a highly traditional curriculum. The traditional approach to curriculum development within the faculty (not unlike most other faculties on campus) tended to focus on a teaching-centred model driven by content and instructional objectives with very tenuous links between these objectives, curriculum integration, and ad-hoc "evolved" course offerings. The overloaded, fragmented, and inflexible curriculum provided very limited opportunity for different teaching and learning strategies to be employed, and did not meet the learning needs and required abilities for graduates of the program.

During the *initiative stage*, a chair was elected to assemble a committee, to engage the whole Faculty through open-dialogue and various communications, and to spearhead the re-design and implementation of a learning-centred curriculum to enable undergraduate students to acquire, integrate and apply knowledge, abilities and skills. To ensure that the curriculum redesign process in the Faculty of Pharmaceutical Sciences was grounded in pedagogy and best practices, the curriculum Chair sought the assistance of a faculty member from Education with research and practical expertise in curriculum development, and teaching and learning in higher education. The curriculum consultant had worked with a variety of multidisciplinary units on the UBC campus (for example, Agricultural Sciences, Dentistry, Forestry, Human Kinetics, Law, Integrated Life Sciences, Pharmaceutical Sciences, Plant Sciences, Senate Curriculum Committee, *UBC Faculty Certificate Program on Teaching and Learning in Higher Education*, Wood Sciences). The consultant's role in this context was not to tell the curriculum committee how to re-design its curriculum (neither would this have been possible, especially in terms of content). Rather, by working collaboratively with the chair and curriculum committee, a conceptual framework and strategic approach was applied to engage the academic unit in creating a learning community, to determine analysis of needs and collectively define, rationalise, re-design and implement a learning-centred curriculum.

Typically, university faculties and academic units embrace several sub-disciplines, each with their own distinct sub-culture and perspective of the main discipline. Thus, during the *mobilisation stage*, the entire faculty were engaged collectively, and through disciplinary streams, in open-dialogue and needs analysis pertaining to the curriculum reform process. This was particularly effective through "Town hall" meetings (that is, discussion fora about curriculum issues for faculty, administrators, students and professionals in the field), noticeboard information about on-going issues and progress with the curriculum reform process, individual and focus group interviews with faculty members, and e-mail surveys and consultation with student and professional groups.

To ensure a well-designed and cohesive program among various sub-disciplines requires specific attention to vertical and horizontal curriculum integration. During the *action plan stage*, therefore, faculty members were organised by specific groupings and challenged to develop flexible and responsive learning modules within the curriculum. For example, following development of the global (and specific) learning outcomes document within the UBC Pharmaceutical Sciences program, disciplinary-based 'working groups' were established to develop course streams over the four years of the program and integrate (vertical integration) outcomes with learning experiences and assessment strategies within the sub-disciplinary field (Purkerson Hammer & Paulsen, 2001). Horizontal integration of knowledge and skills across the disciplines was co-ordinated by the curriculum committee and chair by designing case-based learning modules (entitled Cases in Pharmaceutical Sciences, CAPS) which students take continuously throughout the four-year program. The goal of CAPS modules is to give the students opportunities to apply and integrate knowledge, skills and attitudes being learned in the individual disciplinary streams to the solving of multidisciplinary cases and problems. The complexity of the cases and problems in CAPS increases as the students progress through the program. Figure 3 is a model that conceptualises

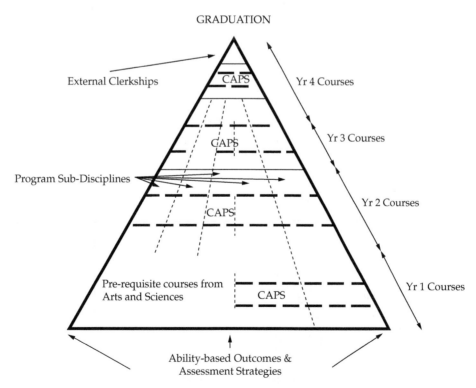

Figure 3 A Model Conceptualizing Vertical and Horizontal Integration throughout the Four-year Pharmaceutical Sciences Program

TABLE 5
Ability-based Outcomes, Assessment Strategies and Learning Modules
in the Four-year Pharmacy Curriculum

Outcome	Assessment tools	
Critical thinking skills	- In class, take home, exam cases - Written reports - Problem sets - Case presentations - Debates - Self, peer, assessment - Program Portfolio	**LEARNING MODULES** **TO ADDRESS OVERALL** **ABILITY-BASED** **OUTCOMES** ↑
Information access and evaluation	- Library assignments - Critical review of literature - Debate of literature - Mini lecture	
Communication skills	- Written exams - Written reports - Oral presentations - Videotape counseling - Practical lab exams - Essays - Self, peer evaluations - Program portfolio	**Problem-based Learning** **Web-based Learning** **Lectures** **Laboratories**
Scientific inquiry skills	- Analysis of evidence and data - Laboratory results and reports - Written evaluations of literature	**Practica** **Learning Portfolios** **CAPS (case-based learning)**
Self-directed learning skills	- Program Portfolio - Quizzes, exams, reports, assignments - Self, peer evaluation - Case analysis	
Mathematical skills	- Quizzes - Problem sets - Lab reports - Assignments - Exams	
Interpersonal and teamwork skills	Self and peer assessments Program portfolio	
Ethical behaviour & social awareness	- Case studies - Portfolio - Self and peer assessments	↓
Apply and integrate knowledge	- Written cases - Written problems to solve	

how vertical and horizontal integration was conceived for student learning throughout the four-year Pharmaceutical Sciences program. This model indicates the importance given to the core CAPS courses in years 1–4. These CAPS courses not only draw upon the expertise and issues of the sub-disciplines but they also build upon one another in each progressive year throughout the program. In addition, all nine ability-based outcomes are assessed throughout all four years of the curriculum. Table 5 provides examples of how ability-based learning outcomes are connected to authentic methods of assessment and diverse learning modules within the learning-centred curriculum.

The *practice stage* of curriculum reform is on-going and will result in a formal and detailed review of the curriculum within a three-year period. These data will be comprised of process, impact and follow-up evaluations. Such evaluations provide a broad and long perspective through which to investigate contextually-bound program processes and outcomes (Fullan, 2001; Green & Kreuter, 1999; Hubball & Clarke, 2004; Kreber & Brook, 2001; Mills, 2000; Stark et al., 1997; Priest, 2001). Process evaluations focus on periodic assessments of issues of importance that occur throughout the duration of a program (for example, to what extent are program goals reflected in individual course learning experiences?). Impact evaluations focus on issues of importance that occur as a result of a program (for example, how did students apply their learning? What were the main strengths and weaknesses of the program?). Follow-up evaluations focus on issues of importance that occur as a result of the longer term (months, year) impact of a program (for example, how did the program contribute to your current development as a professional pharmacist?). Prior to the three-year review, disciplinary stream leaders are charged with collecting informal evaluation data (for example, self-reflections, feedback from colleagues, student evaluations of individual courses) and providing on-going feedback to the curriculum chair. In this way, progress with the whole program is co-ordinated and continually monitored.

Early Reflections on the Process of Learning-centred Curriculum Reform

Despite a thorough, well-coordinated and systematic approach to curriculum reform in the UBC Faculty of Pharmaceutical Sciences, change was typically incremental and, at various times throughout each stage created a great deal of anxiety for many faculty members as they intermittently engaged with this challenging process, in addition to an otherwise demanding academic workload. As would be expected by experienced educational developers, initial resistance was expressed by some individual faculty members who perceived student learning in the curriculum to be driven exclusively by exposure to required content (usually quantity), versus adopt general ability-based outcomes (divorced of content) to drive the curriculum. Through various faculty meetings, discussions and workshop experiences, it became more clear to them that content and ability-based outcomes in a learning-centred curricula are interdependent. Content is clearly that which differentiates one course from another, however, in a learning-centred curriculum, content is integrated with ability-based outcomes as the driving force for teaching and learning.

The lack of release time for the committee chair contributed to periods of lost ground and momentum during the process which had a significant effect on the time-lines for completion of various stages of curriculum reform. The chair's leadership qualities, commitment, and ability to mobilise the faculty learning community, as well as the external program threat of non-accreditation (and by extension to job security), were critical factors for developing and implementing a learning-centred curriculum during this overly long (five-year) time frame. At the *practice stage* of curriculum reform, however, the UBC Pharmaceutical Sciences program was granted accreditation by the Canadian Council on Accreditation of Pharmacy Programs (CCAPP), as well as being successfully approved by the university senate curriculum committee. Although it is recognised that on-going refinements and adjustments to the curriculum are inevitable, preliminary survey feedback data and focus group interviews suggest that the new curriculum has been met very favourably by

TABLE 6
**Implementing Learning-centred Curricula: Lessons Learned in the UBC Faculty
of Pharmaceutical Sciences**

- Strong leadership qualities required.
- Release time and support required for committee chair.
- Inclusive committee design required.
- Outside expertise and professional development required.
- Open-mind and flexibility toward a broad range of pedagogies and integration of program specializations and fields required (i.e., maintain faculty's comfort-level with disciplinary knowledge, as well as focus on pedagogical implications of ability-based outcomes).
- Integrated approach to curriculum redesign AND implementation process required.
- Continuous reporting of progress and open dialogue required with faculty and students (e.g., town hall meetings, faculty retreats, faculty meetings, notice board/website displays).
- Individual faculty required to implement ability-based outcomes within individual courses.
- Conduct action research, on-going monitoring, and dissemination.
- Endurance!

students and faculty members thus far. Table 6 identifies the critical lessons learned from the UBC Pharmaceutical Sciences experience.

Conclusion

Curriculum reform is a complex, multifaceted, and iterative process, in which ideas, expressed as policy, are transformed into behaviour, expressed as a social action (Ottoson & Green, 1987; Wenger, McDermott, & Snyder, 2002). Thus, curriculum reform is shaped by many factors (social, political, economic, organisational, cultural and individual) and involves people at various institutional levels (administrators, curriculum development committee personnel, instructors and learners). Clearly, learning context factors play a central role in curricular reform (Angelo, 2000). In the Pharmaceutical Sciences' experience, the extent to which a learning community (that is, the academic unit) was empowered, as well as the commitment of adequate resources and the power to influence people required during this process, had a significant effect on the outcome. Timing is also crucial, not only in terms of the urgency, or the stimulus and support for curriculum reform, but also in terms of an analysis of long-term, intermediate and short-term goals and clarifying when, where, and who is responsible for achieving these goals.

Implementing learning-centred curricula cannot be considered simply as a series of non-problematic and discrete steps. It is not surprising, therefore, that inherent complexities in curriculum re-design can present significant pedagogical, as well as implementation challenges, for academic units in higher education. By implication, these challenges also extend to individual faculty who need to re-examine their course design, assessment and learning strategies to meet the objectives of the learning-centred curriculum (Adamcik et al., 1996; Beaudry & Schaub, 1998; Diamond, 1998; Hubball & Levy, 2004; Lawler & King, 2000; Purkerson Hammer & Paulsen, 2001). This article provides a flexible framework that takes into account context and integrates comprehensive strategies to assist academic units with re-designing and implementing learning-centred curricula. Ultimately, the success of re-designing and implementing a learning-centred curriculum, is contingent on the attention that is paid to integrating appropriate stage-specific learning context, planning, assessment and programming strategies.

Note

1. This paper uses the term "curriculum" as referring to the accredited program offered by an academic unit in higher education.

Notes on Contributors

- Harry Hubball PhD has provided curriculum development consultancy for multidisciplinary units at the University of British Columbia, Vancouver, Canada. His research interests include teacher education, curriculum development, and pedagogy in university settings. He co-ordinates the *UBC Faculty Certificate Program on Teaching and Learning in Higher Education*.
- Helen Burt PhD chaired the Faculty of Pharmaceutical Sciences Curriculum Review Committee from 1997–2001 to design and develop an outcomes-based curriculum. Her research interests include the development of novel polymer-based drug delivery systems.

References

Adamcik, B., Hurley, S., & Erramouspe, J. (1996). Assessment of pharmacy students' critical thinking and problem-solving abilities. *American Journal of Pharmaceutical Education, 60*, 256–265.

Angelo, T. A. (2000). Transforming departments into productive learning communities. In A. F. Lucas & Associates (Eds.), *Leading academic change: Essential roles for department chairs* (pp. 74–89). San Francisco: Jossey-Bass.

Baird, L. L. (1996). Documenting student outcomes in graduate and professional programs. In A. E. Bilder & C. F. Conrad (Eds.), *Challenges in assessing outcomes in graduate and professional education, New Directions For Institutional Research, 92*, 77–87.

Baker, P. (1999). Creating learning communities: The unfinished agenda. In B. A. Pescosolido & R. Aminzade (Eds.), *The social worlds of higher education* (pp. 95–109). Thousand Oaks, CA: Pine Forge Press.

Barab, S. A. & Duffy, T. (2000). From practice fields to communities of practice. In D. Jonassen & S. M. Land (Eds.), *Theoretical foundations of learning environments* (pp. 25–56). Mahwah, NJ: Erlbaum Associates.

Baron, M. A. (1996). Dispelling the myths surrounding outcome-based education. *Phi Delta Kappan, 77*, 574–576.

Barr, R. B. & Tag, J. (1995). From teaching to learning: A new paradigm for undergraduate education. *Change, 27(6)*, 13–25.

Battersby, M. (1997). Outcomes-based education: A college faculty perspective. *Learning Quarterly*, February, *1*, 6–11.

Beaudry, M. L. & Schaub, T. (1998). The learning-centred syllabus. *The Teaching Professor, 12(2)*, 5.

Brandt, B. F., Clements, M., & Piascik, P. (1998). Problem-solving activities for first-year pharmacy students. *American Journal of Pharmaceutical Education, 62*, 450–457.

Brown, G., Bull, J., & Pendlebury, M. (1997). *Assessing student learning in higher education*. London: Routledge.

Clanchy, J. & Ballard, B. (1995). Generic skills in the context of higher education. *Higher Education Research and Development, 14*, 155–166.

Clarke, A. & Hubball, H. T. (2001). Physical education methods course as an immersion experience in an elementary setting. *Avante, 7(2)*, 11–27.

Cox, M. (2000). Faculty learning communities. Change agents for transforming institutions into learning organisations. In D. Lieberman & C. Wehlburg (Eds.), *To improve the academy*, (vol. 19, pp. 69–93). Boston, MA: Anker.

Daniel, J. (1993). The challenge of mass education. *Studies in Higher Education, 18*, 197–203.

Diamond, R. M. (1998). *Developing and assessing courses and curricula*. San Francisco: Jossey-Bass.

Drummond, I., Nixon, I., & Wiltshire, J. (1998). Personal transferable skills in higher education: The problems of implementing good practice. *Quality Assurance in Education, 6*, 44–58.

Erickson, L. (2002). *Concept-based curriculum and instruction*. Thousand Oaks, CA: Corwin Press, Sage Publications.

Ewell, P. T. (1997). Organizing for learning: A new imperative. *AAHE Bulletin, 50(4)*, 3–6.

Fullan, M. G. (2001). *The new meaning of educational change* (3rd ed.). New York: Teachers College, Columbia University.

Ganderton, P. S. (1996). Concepts of globalisation and their impact upon curriculum policy making: Rhetoric and reality a study of Australasian reform. *International Journal of Educational Development, 16*, 393–405.

Gibbons, M. (2000). Universities of the new production of knowledge: Some policy implications for government. In A. Kraak (Ed.), *Changing modes: New knowledge production and its implications for higher education in South Africa*. Pretoria: HSRC.

Gold, P. (1997). Faculty collaboration for a new curriculum. *Liberal Education, 83*, 46–49.

Green, A. (1999). Education and globalisation in Europe and E. Asia: Convergent and divergent trends. *Journal of Educational Policy, 14*, 55–71.

Green, M. F. (1995). Transforming British higher education: A view from across the Atlantic. *Higher Education, 29*, 225–239.

Green, L. W. & Kreuter, M. (1999). *Health promotion planning: An educational and ecological approach*. Palo Alto, CA: Mayfield Publishing.

Hubball, H. T. & Poole, G. (2003). A learning-centred faculty certificate programme on university teaching. *International Journal for Academic Development, 8*, 11–24.

Hubball, H. T. & Clarke, A. (2004). Assessing faculty learning communities. In M. D. Cox and L. Richlin (Eds.), *Building Faculty Learning Communities. New Directions for Teaching and Learning (the "Journal"), 97*, 87–100.

Hubball, H. T. & Levy, A (2004). Graduate course design in Health Care and Epidemiology: A learning-centred approach. *Journal for Faculty Development, 20*(1).

Jansen, J. & Christie, P. (Eds.) (1999). *Changing curriculum: Studies on outcomes-based education in South Africa*. Cape Town: Juta.

Kanpol, B. (1995). Outcomes-based education and democratic commitment hopes and possibilities. *Educational Policy, 9*, 359–374.

Kemp I. J. & Seagraves L. (1995). Transferable skills—can higher education deliver? *Studies in Higher Education, 20*, 315–328.

Knight, P. T. & Trowler, P. R. (2000). Department level cultures and the improvement of learning and teaching. *Studies in Higher Education, 25*, 69–83.

Kreber, C. & Brook, P. (2001). Impact evaluation of educational development programs. *International Journal for Academic Development, 6*, 96–108.

Kupperschmidt, B. R. & Burns, P. (1997). Curriculum revision isn't just change: It's transition! *Journal of Professional Nursing, 13*, 90–98.

Lawler, P. A. & King, K. P. (2000). *Planning for effective faculty development: Using adult learning strategies*. Malabar, FL: Krieger Publishing Company.

Lockhart, M. & Borland, K. W. (2001). Critical thinking goals, outcomes, and pedagogy in senior capstone courses. *The Journal of Faculty Development, 18*, 19–25.

Middendorf, J. K. (1999). Finding key faculty to influence change. *To Improve the Academy, 18*, 83–93.

Mills, G. E. (2000). *Action research: A guide for the teacher researcher*. Upper Saddle River, NJ: Merrill Prentice Hall.

Mok, K. H. (1999). Education and the market place in Hong Kong and mainland China. *Higher Education, 37*, 133–158.

Murphy, S. E. (1997). Eight components of program implementation. *Performance Improvement, 36*, 6–8.

Nolinske, T. (1999). Creating an inclusive learning environment. *Teaching Excellence, 11*(4), 1–3.

Ottoson, J. M. & Green, L. W. (1987). Reconciling concept and context: Theory of implementation. *Advances in Health Education and Promotion, 2*, 353–382.

Perrier, D. G., Winslade, N., Pugsley, J., Lavack, L., & Strand, L. M. (1995). Designing a pharmaceutical care curriculum. *American Journal of Pharmaceutical Education, 59*, 113–125.

Pietersen, W. G. (2002). *Re-inventing strategy: Using strategic learning to create and sustain breakthrough performance*. London: John Wiley and Sons.

Poindexter, S. (2003). Holistic learning. *Change, January/February*, 25–30.

Priest, S. (2001). A program evaluation primer. *Journal of Experiential Education, 24*, 34–40.

Purkerson Hammer, D., & Paulsen, S. M. (2001). Strategies and processes to design an integrated, longitudinal professional skills development course sequence. *American Journal of Pharmaceutical Education, 65*, 77–85.

Raman-Wilms, L. (2001). Innovative enabling strategies in self-directed, problem-based therapeutics: Enhancing student preparedness for pharmaceutical care practice. *American Journal of Pharmaceutical Education, 65*, 56–64.

Schneider, C. G. & Shoenberg, R. (1999). Habits hard to break: How persistent features of campus life frustrate curricular reform. *Change, March/April*, 30–35.

Shulman, L. (1999). Taking learning seriously. *Change, 31(4)*, 11–17.

Shavelson, R. & Huang, L. (2003). Responding responsibly to the frenzy to assess learning in higher education. *Change, January/February*, 11–18.

Stark, J. S., Lowther, M. A., Sharp, S., & Arnold, G. L. (1997). Program-level curriculum planning: An exploration of faculty perspectives on two different campuses. *Research in Higher Education, 38*, 99–130.

Stinson, J. E. & Milter, R. G. (1996). Problem-based learning in business education: Curriculum design and implementation issues. In L. Wilkerson & W. H. Gijselaers (Eds.), *Bringing problem-based learning to higher education: Theory and practice. New Directions for Teaching and Learning, 68*, 33–42.

Trowler, P. R. (1996). Angels in marble? Accrediting prior experiential learning in higher education. *Studies in Higher Education, 21*, 17–30.

VP Academic and Provost. (2000). *UBC Academic Plan: Trek 2000*. Strategic visioning document developed by the Academic Plan Advisory Committee, The University of British Columbia, Canada.

Wenger, E., McDermott, R., & Snyder, W. (2002). *Cultivating communities of practice*. Boston, MA: Harvard University Press.

Wiles, J. & Bondi, J. (2002). *Curriculum development: A guide to practice* (6th ed.). Upper Saddle River, OH: Merrill Prentice Hall.

Symbolic Politics and Institutional Boundaries in Curriculum Reform: The Case of National Sectarian University

Gordon B. Arnold

Introduction

In recent years, many colleges and universities have set out to reform or revisit their general education curricula. These efforts often have failed to achieve the comprehensive change that reformers originally had envisioned (Kanter, Gamson, & London, 1997). Using the example of one case, this paper explores how institutionalized organizational elements and politics can shape the scope and limits of programmatic change, while increasing the importance of these reform efforts as symbolic action.

The perception of failure in the reform of a general education curriculum is often rooted in the desire for comprehensive change. Lesser change is frequently seen as inadequate and has been described in dismissive language, such as "piecemeal" or "rearranging the deck chairs." Although worthwhile curricular improvements can be found in change that is smaller in scale and more nuanced, reformers often find such results disappointing. Change that can be described as "symbolic" is particularly maligned. Often, it is not viewed as "real change." However, symbolic aspects of curriculum reform can serve useful organizational purposes, such as reorienting and repositioning general education within an academic community and among an organization's field of peers. As Rudolph (1977, p. 3) has observed, "the curriculum is . . . a locus and transmitter of values," and an especially powerful use of the reform process can be found in the symbolic action of articulating, defining, and ordering the values of a university or college.

Still, it is true that overarching change in general education is often what is sought. When these results do not materialize, reform advocates often attribute "failure" to organizational politics and the dampening effects of parochial interests and political trade-offs. This "rational" view emphasizes actors' intentional action and the motivations of self-interest. From this perspective, participants in a reform process are said to raise side issues (matters that seem only tangentially related, if they are related at all) to general education because they are seeking to advance their own, apparently unrelated, agendas within the organization. On the macroorganizational level, the introduction of such "side issues" seems to be a failure of rational decision making, and this state of affairs has been called a "garbage can" (Cohen, March, & Olsen, 1972).

As Birnbaum (1988) notes, such political aspects of the academic decision making are usually viewed as unwanted, intrusive, and extraneous forces that serve as a hindrance to orderly, planned change. Reformers with this picture in mind often become disenchanted with the process of curricular change at their campuses since in practice it is difficult to steer clear of organizational politics (Kanter, Gamson, & London, 1997). Indeed, from the point of view of individual actors in their roles within the organizational structure, it would be difficult to imagine collective decision without the introduction of side issues.

Reprinted by permission from the *Journal of Higher Education* 75, no. 5 (September/October 2004).

Looking beyond individual organizations, the national debate about the undergraduate curriculum, centering on overarching philosophies of general education and the purposes of undergraduate education, constitutes the arena in which the reform actions of individual colleges and universities are played out. The national rhetoric is abstract and idealized, focusing on what the curriculum should be and on what it means to be an educated person. Such rhetoric, however, is largely disconnected from the organizational realities of specific colleges and universities.

Within organizations, advocates of various curricular perspectives often fail to take into account how organizational factors, internal and external, may influence and significantly structure their proposals. At a deeper level, the organizational basis of politics—and thus of the supposedly irrelevant side issues—tends not to be considered (March & Olsen, 1989). Consequently, reform advocates are often surprised to find side issues influencing the planning process, ultimately leaving curricular aspirations unrealized, or only partially fulfilled.

However, the situation can be viewed from a different perspective that attends to how reform processes and outcomes are influenced by institutionalized, taken-for-granted assumptions among organizational actors. Such a perspective also can help us understand more fully the importance of symbolic outcomes in reform projects. To explore organizational and institutional dimensions in general education reform, this article examines a reform process at one university. As part of this investigation, special attention is paid to three major components of the reform effort: (1) the relationship of planners with academic departments; (2) the decision of how cultural diversity would be integrated into a new general education program; and (3) the creation of a general education oversight body.

Framework for Examining Reform

The curriculum reform process typically involves a major planning effort by organizational actors. Curricular change is regarded as an important activity since it is change to a major function of a college or university. The undergraduate curriculum is a central technology by which these organizations fulfill their purposes, and the general education component of the curriculum, because it is putatively common to all undergraduate students, is viewed as having particular importance.

The value of rationality is thoroughly ingrained in academic culture, and when colleges and universities set out to reform their curricula, it is assumed that only rational decision-making processes are legitimate and will be employed. The usual view adopted for analyzing a major planning effort such as curriculum reform, therefore, stresses the "rational" capabilities and behaviors of participants in the process (e.g., Keller, 1983). Taking cues from this approach, many planning practitioners and commentators infer that a goal of successful planning should be to insulate the change process from extraneous political factors that might undermine its rationality.

Change advocates with this perspective negatively view the introduction of side issues. In general education reform, examples of side issues include matters such as the effects of new curricular designs on departmental enrollments and faculty slots, or admissions and marketing considerations in a new general education program, or use of general education to validate newer academic perspectives (e.g., Kanter, Gamson, & London, 1997). To rational planners, such complications are off-topic and evidence of a poorly designed or executed process. Such judgments, however, may fail to consider adequately implications arising from the fact that academic organizations are complex polities, and in political contexts one would expect "rational" actors to build coalitions and to seek advantage through deliberate calculation (e.g., Allison, 1971; Becker, 1986; Birnbaum, 1988).

Thus, although planning leaders might seek to construct orderly change processes that isolate planning from "extraneous" issues, decision making and planning activities in academe frequently exhibit characteristics that seem to be less the result of such purposeful, rational planning. Despite intentions of leaders to the contrary, various side issues do become entwined in decision making, giving rise to the "garbage can" and "organized anarchy" images of choice in academic organizations (Cohen & March, 1986; Cohen, March, & Olsen, 1972).

Organizational boundaries and symbolic politics. Although there are aspects of strategic calculation in organizational politics, an overemphasis on this point obscures other organizational influences on the decision making of actors (e.g., Halperin, 1974). A different approach is taken by the neoinstitutional perspective in organizational analysis, which focuses attention on the importance of institutionalized elements within an organization and within its field(s) of peer organizations (March & Olsen, 1989).

As students of this perspective note, organizations are oriented to externally originating institutional arrangements—aspects of organization such as structural configurations, values, routines, rules, and beliefs that are "taken for granted" (i.e., institutionalized) across a field of similar organizations (Meyer & Rowan, 1977; DiMaggio & Powell, 1983). Institutions, from this perspective, are "symbolic systems" (Friedland & Alford, 1991, p. 243) that channel human behavior because they define the perceived limits of action and the meaning(s) attached to action (Douglas, 1986; Zucker, 1991). Institutionalized elements of organization therefore play an important role in providing legitimacy to an organization, which is important to the organization's continued viability.

Because they are taken for granted by actors, however, institutionalized aspects in an organization often are not fully recognized as having an effect on organizational activity. Yet, institutionalized organizational elements have significant influence on how an organizational change process flows and on what courses of action are considered and taken (March & Olsen, 1989). Because those facets of organizational life that are institutionalized are those that tend to be perceived as being the most legitimate, the boundaries of legitimacy can have a *de facto* influence on boundaries of action.

The similarity of organizational structure across U.S. colleges and universities is one example of a highly institutionalized element of academic organization. The hierarchies inherent in the configurations of subunits within a university—e.g., those of the academic departments, schools, divisions—can be seen as the result of prior "political contests" in which those subunits that are perceived as having the greatest capacity to aid an organization's stability and survival attain the greatest power and influence (Pfeffer, 1978, p. 38). From this perspective, then, political elements are already deeply embedded within an existing configuration of subunits and in the dispersal of power and legitimacy within the organization. This is important since, as Mintzberg (1994, p. 177) notes, "organizations develop their plans in terms of the sub-units they already have."

Thus, between the constraining influences of peer organizations and the internalized institutional arrangements within an organization, in many circumstances the scope of organizational action will have limitations. This highlights the importance of symbolic action, which can serve a useful function in communicating to external and internal audiences that an organization is taking the appropriate course(s) of action. Symbolic action can enhance perceptions of prestige and legitimacy, which are of particular use to academic organizations in extracting necessary resources from the environment. Beyond the merits or demerits of technical outcomes in academic decision making, then, it is important how actions are interpreted by actors in other settings (Habermas, 1970). Symbolic displays of attention and intention have useful political purposes (Edelman, 1964).

Symbolic outcomes are important in other ways as well. Control of meaning is a central element of politics (Bourdieu, 1991). The idea of coherence, which is normatively thought to be important in general education curricula, can be seen itself as socially constructed. An articulation of the sense that an organization asserts should be made of a curricular plan, which would be a symbolic outcome, is an essential part of the social construction of curricular coherence, and thus a useful result. More generally, embedded within the process of reform can be found specification, revelation, and explanation of values held by the organization. The process of reform, in bringing these to the surface, can help an organization maintain an alignment between its mission and practices and could be especially useful in making institutional aims clearer to organizational actors whose daily activities may focus largely on specialized or compartmentalized activities.

Data and Methods

Context and detail are important in discerning the role of politics and institutionalized organizational forms and processes in curricular reform. In this study, qualitative data were collected relating to a general education reform effort at a large, sectarian university, here given the pseudonym National Sectarian University [NSU]. The reform process under consideration began in 1989 and extended until 1991. NSU was chosen as the case site because it is a prominent, but not elite, university. Although the selection of NSU is not intended to represent universities or colleges generally and the specific details vary from organization to organization, some of the following may have applications to other settings.

The most important source of data was the extensive documentary record of the curricular reform process. The record consists of material housed in the university archives, as well as documents kept in the offices of key actors. In the case of the latter, extensive files were made available for inspection, with no apparent restrictions in access to the relevant material on the part of those maintaining the records. The types of material examined included reports, memoranda, private notes, correspondence, meeting minutes, official publications, and the like. Several thousand pages of documents were reviewed for this study.

Although the documentary record was the primary data source, this was cross-checked in a small number of retrospective interviews. A short list of 12 key actors, representing various positions and perspectives, was constructed. In addition to cross-checking the picture that emerged from the documentary record, these interviews were used to fill in gaps in the record. Particular care was taken throughout to assure that multiple points of view were examined, in order to avoid both an overly "official" and potentially cloudy picture and one too reliant upon critics of the process. The interviews were loosely structured, giving respondents wide latitude in shaping the direction of their comments. This heuristic structure allowed respondents to recall events and actions in a manner that was in accordance with their own perceptions of importance and with their unique frames of interpretation.

Using standard historical procedures (Barzun & Graff, 1992), data from the various sources were next synthesized and triangulated. This process yielded a reconstruction of events during NSU's reform effort.

Case Setting: National Sectarian University

Founded by members of a religious sect in the mid-nineteenth century, the original mission of National Sectarian University (NSU) was to provide a higher education for young men consistent with its religious values. More than a century later, NSU grew from a small college into a large, coeducational university that attained a strong financial situation and greatly increased enrollments in both undergraduate (about 10,000 students by the 1990s) and graduate programs (about 5,000 students).

The distribution of students and faculty at NSU provides some insight into the dispersal of power and prestige in the university, particularly the dominance of Arts and Sciences. During the period under consideration for this study, the undergraduate population was divided among four undergraduate schools: the College of Arts and Sciences (CAS), with about 5500 students; the College of Management (about 2000 students); the College of Education (about 700 students); and the College of Nursing (about 350 students).

During the same period, members of the faculty numbered about numbered about 600, with nearly 70% ranked at the Associate Professor level or higher. Arts and Sciences was the largest faculty body, with about 350 faculty members, while the School of Management had about 75 faculty, and the Schools of Education and Nursing had about 50 faculty each. (The remainder was affiliated with graduate schools having no undergraduate degree offerings.) Despite apparent attempts to increase faculty diversity, however, the faulty remained relatively homogenous and most faculty members were white males. In a break with earlier tradition, however, by 1990 many faculty members were not affiliated in any way with the founding religious sect.

General Education at National Sectarian University

Background. Following the norms of the founding sect's educational philosophy, undergraduate education at NSU traditionally was heavily prescribed, with emphasis on theology, philosophy, and similar "classical" subjects. Originally, almost the entirety of study was prescribed, but as the small college evolved into a large university, this picture changed. Though CAS gradually was joined by the other undergraduate schools, each of these organizational subunits maintained largely separate identities. Although a similar educational philosophy permeated all the undergraduate schools, each went about establishing its own curriculum, and it was not until the early 1970s that NSU, in the modern era, established a truly university-wide undergraduate general education program.

The founding sect's ecumenical explorations during the 1960s, combined with serious campus discontent at about the same time (e.g., a student strike which paralyzed NSU in the early 70s), resulted in NSU's move to a university-wide general education program. It was an attempt to become more relevant and to address fragmentation on campus. The university-wide general education program provided a common general education curriculum for all NSU undergraduates, and the faculty of the College of Arts and Sciences absorbed many of the faculty teaching general education who had previously been attached to the other colleges of NSU. In this way it became the university's sole provider of general education.

NSU's general education curriculum consisted of a set of distribution requirements. A Council on General Education (CGE), representing the various undergraduate schools, was established to oversee the program, but much power concerning the general education program remained squarely within the participating departments of CAS. Essentially departmentalized early in its life, the curriculum proved very long-lived and continued in essentially the same form for two decades. (Very minor changes were made 10 years later.)

After this success, what caused the university to launch a full-scale revision effort? Since common belief in American higher education is that the curriculum is the province of the faculty, (Kerr, 1963) it might be assumed that faculty discontent over the issue was responsible for the curricular revision effort. However, this was not the case; general education did not become a subject for campus-wide decision due to any concerted effort on the part of displeased faculty members. While some faculty, by the mid-1980s, certainly thought that NSU should revisit the issue, it was not viewed as a pressing concern. Indeed, many faculty seemed more or less pleased with the 1970s curriculum and even 20 years after its inception wondered why anyone should want to change it.

In any case, there was no viable mechanism where such personal opinions could have been translated into a formal organizational agenda item. As one member of the faculty observed:

> [by the early 1990s] the faculty . . . were no longer calling their own meetings . . . and so we had to wait for the deans or some other body to put something on the agenda for us.

Two facts of organizational history are important to the explanation for this general lack of urgency. First, the reputation of the Council on General Education, originally established by the university senate, was questionable. As a member of the COM faculty stated:

> [the] impression that I got was that the [Council on General Education] really had lost its credibility and lost its ability to enforce or to delete . . . . [W]hat we were seeing was the result of that.

The CGE had little prestige on campus, then, and regardless of the efforts of some individual members, it was perceived as a weak and rather ineffectual body. Consequently, it was not in a position to call for a revisiting of general education with any great authority.

Second, a university senate—originally a prime sponsor of CGE—had passed out of existence. Emerging onto the scene during the era of Vietnam and student activism, the senate had come to be viewed as increasingly irrelevant, and by the early 1980s it was discontinued, with little or no protest from the faculty. A long-time CAS faculty member, reporting a view heard from several sources, recalled the Senate as follows:

> When I first came here I was on the Senate for a few years, and at first it was interesting. But after three or four years it was the same people saying the same things over and over again— and endlessly. It became exasperating. . . . Yet, I think in a way they often weren't saying anything new or different; they weren't really engaging productively with the structures that are in the university. [The Senate was seen as] a place to go and [it was] a support group and a place to complain and gripe.

The Senate never became institutionalized within the NSU structure, and when the conditions that surrounded its original founding faded from the scene, so, too, did the senate itself. Moreover, the culture at NSU was such that most persons were comfortable with (or at least tolerant of) a situation in which the administration would take care of many things. (This, in turn, mirrored the way that the sect manages its affairs in noneducational arenas, as well.) The upshot of these conditions was that with no campus-wide faculty representative body and a poorly regarded CGE, the issue of general education instead reached the university's agenda by way of administratively driven committees.

In 1984, NSU's president, a strong advocate of central planning, initiated steps to produce overall goals for the university in the coming decade of the 1990s. To this end, he established a University Goals Committee (UGC) which included 20 persons representing a broad cross-section of the university, including administrators, faculty, and students. In going about their task, the UGC planners gathered information about various issues from each of the schools in the university. Many issues were raised, including some directly relating to general education at the university. For example, a position paper submitted by a College of Arts and Sciences committee (chaired by the Academic Vice President) asked "a complex and difficult question: How can the College of Arts and Sciences, while strengthening its academic dimensions and responding to changes in the society, remain faithful to its [religiously inspired] origin and mission?"

This question raised important issues. One was the changing profile of NSU students, which the document linked with the steady improvement of the university's ranking in the national arena. Students choosing NSU were more academically qualified than ever before according to the standard scales of measurement, especially SAT scores. However, university planners in the mid-80s projected that NSU would encounter increasingly stiff competition for these high-caliber students in the near future. These and other issues called attention back to the aging general education curriculum.

The UGC finally produced a document by 1986 that addressed six areas of the university. These included general education, about which it stated that UGC had "discerned a widespread sense that [general education] could be strengthened further by addressing a variety of issues." Specifically, the document cited the following concerns: (1) that general education courses were of uneven quality; (2) that general education was not sufficiently coordinated; and (3) that the attitudes of both students and faculty were of concern since both groups tended to view [general education] too much as something "to be completed as quickly as possible."

Surprisingly, having raised these apparently serious concerns, the university initially did not take action. Some concerns may have been voiced, but there was no identifiable crisis, and so other issues—particularly the need to search for a new Academic Vice President upon the retirement the incumbent—were instead pushed to the fore. As for the general education issue, there is little evidence that the delay was the cause of much concern within the university, and while the heavily politicized debate about general education was by then in the air nationally, no protests were forthcoming at NSU when the issue was not taken up.

Instead, several years passed until 1989, when the Council of Deans issued its own statement concerning academic goals and objectives. This document highlighted concerns that reflected those of the UGC and listed as one goal the need for NSU to achieve "more effective" general education. To this end, the Deans recommended the appointment of "a panel of distinguished [NSU] scholars" to review general education at National Sectarian University. At this time, the new Academic Vice-President took up the suggestion. General education had reached the university's agenda.

The choice of a decision-making process. The work of administratively organized central planners and senior academic administrators was clearly instrumental in pushing the issue of general education to the university's agenda. The immediate issue was the mechanism that would be used to make a decision about general education. On paper, the Council on General Education appeared to have had the right (perhaps obligation) to deal with general education. It had been created to deal with precisely such issues, but it had since become concerned primarily with the day-to-day administration of the existing general education curriculum and with more or less routine course approvals. Furthermore, selection of CGE for this task would have presented difficult problems, not only because of the group's questionable stature within the university, but also because the University Goals Committee had explicitly suggested that the Council on General Education was part of the problem with the "drifting" general education curriculum.

By this time the campus-wide senate no longer existed and the weakness of the CGE was apparent. In this void, the Academic Vice President took action. Following the suggestion of the Council of Deans (of which he was a key member), he established a General Education Task Force, thereby successfully sidestepping the issue of the Council on General Education.

The General Education Task Force included faculty from various ranks (with many senior members) and, as noted above, appears purposefully to have been designed with some attention to diversity as an organizing principle, although most members were white males, as was true of the university faculty and administration overall. Membership was predominantly from the faculty, but key administrators were also included. In the end, the sometimes overlapping interests that were represented included members of NSU's founding religious sect (including the Academic Vice President), members from each of the undergraduate schools (weighted in favor of CAS), and two students. (It is interesting to note that the students played little discernible role in the decision process as it would subsequently unfold.)

The Academic Vice President officially chaired the Task Force, but the Associate Dean of Faculties largely coordinated its daily operations. Subsequently, it was announced that the Task Force's final report was to be advisory and also that it would be submitted to the Academic Vice President, who would then consult with the President prior to any implementation. All of this indicated the strong tendency toward central coordination in the NSU approach to university-wide general education revision.

Flow the decision process. Over the next two years, the Task Force went about its work in regular meetings. These were usually every other week, but sometimes were held more frequently. The members of the Task Force appear to have taken their assignment seriously, and they devoted substantial attention to the revision task.

As one of its first activities, members of the Task Force reviewed then-current articles about the state of general education in American colleges and universities, as were very common at the time. They then examined the general education programs of leading institutions with a view to compare NSU's practices with those held in high regard nationally. Thus, from the outset Task Force members were well aware of national rhetoric and trends and of what the "competition" was doing.

As they settled into their working routine, the Task Force's major activities were: (1) establishing a model for general education at NSU; (2) meeting with representatives from departments that had courses in the existing general education curriculum; (3) meeting with representatives from departments and programs that were interested in offering general education courses in the future (ranging from Music to African-American Studies); (4) holding a series of open faculty forums to gather opinion about general education at NSU; (5) redesigning the general education program; and (6) presenting its findings to the faculty as a whole.

Three Episodes in the Curricular Reform Process

At the end of two years, a new general education program was proposed by the Task Force (See Table 1). Perhaps not surprisingly, the proposed curriculum closely resembled what already existed. The only major change was the addition of a new, one-course requirement in the area of cultural diversity, but (see below) even this addition was substantially less of a change than it might appear at first glance. Episodes from the reform process, discussed below, reveal that structural and institutionalized elements within NSU were instrumental in the close resemblance of the new curriculum to the old.

Task Force interactions with academic departments. Gathering information was the first major undertaking of the Task Force. As this process unfolded, it soon became apparent that departmental participation in the general education sequence was of great concern to the faculty. In part, it appears that the enrollment windfalls resulting from required study in a department were a factor in this. One Arts and Sciences faculty member recalled that in Task Force's deliberations:

> There was some . . . blunt and frank discussion of the impact of a new general education curriculum on certain departments and the fact that we live by this. One or two people, rather surprisingly to me, said outright that we're going to protect our turf as best we can because this is a "life-or-death" issue for us.

The Task Force took care to develop full-blown written rationales for the precise formula of proposed course requirements. Regardless of this apparently exhaustive task, the final result maintained roughly the same balance of departmental offerings as before, raising the credit requirements for general education from 42 to 45 of the 120 credits necessary for the baccalaureate degree. One source candidly described the outcome as "rearranging the deck chairs."

TABLE 1
General Education Requirements at National Sectarian University,
Before and After General Education Reform

General Education Requirements, est. CA. 1971, with Additions in Early 1980s		New General Education Requirements, 1991	
Theology	2 courses	Theology	2 courses
Philosophy	2 courses	Philosophy	2 courses
European History	2 courses	History	2 courses
English	2 courses	Writing	1 course
		Literature	1 course
Natural Science	2 courses	Natural Science	2 courses
Social Science	2 courses	Social Science	2 courses
Cluster Requirement (added early 1980s)		Mathematics	1 course
Mathematics	2 courses	Arts	1 course
OR BOTH:		Cultural Diversity	1 course
Fine Arts	1 course		
Speech/Communications	1 course		
TOTAL	16 courses	TOTAL	15 courses

*Added in early 1980s:

In the course of reaching a decision, the Task Force undertook an elaborate series of exchanges with representatives of various interests, typically disciplinary departments (especially in the case of Arts and Sciences), but sometimes the individual professions represented by the NSU professional schools (i.e., nursing, management, and education). Although much effort was expended on these activities, the actual message communicated to some of the participants seems to have been contrary to what was intended by the Task Force. The chair of one Arts and Science department, for example, recalled:

> We . . . were called to make a presentation. I went to that with another member of the department, and as it happened, there were several other departments there. Toward the end of the meeting we had a chance for a short presentation of our point of view about the role of [the department] in the . . . curriculum. But I didn't come away with a feeling that the Task Force was terribly engaged in what we had to say. They didn't seem to see any issues that required probing or extensive discussion. So I thought of it as sort of a *pro forma* thing.

Yet this appears to be an opposite interpretation from how Task Force members themselves saw these interactions. As one Task Force member stated:

> You always hear at the beginning that there were questions to whether this was a ritual, or whether we were going through the motions, or whether this was truly going to be something we were going to create by ourselves, as opposed to basically figuring out what we were "supposed" to do. Was there some secret plan that we would discover as went along? . . . I didn't really care if anyone else had a plan. As far as my goal was concerned, I wanted it to be creative and just open up any can of worms that might need to be opened.

Although at least one member of the Task Force suggested that the time had come for a reassessment of the departmental and school structure, particularly in relation to the general education curriculum, such action was carefully avoided. Importantly, the overall stature of Task Force membership was such that a suggestion of this sort could probably have been made, but the Task Force did not meddle with the established order. One participant recalled:

> to do something really radical would . . . require so many changes and would be so drastic. . . . [W]e would have to have a lot of confidence to do something like that.

Ultimately, the Task Force took care to reassure the Arts and Sciences departments, in particular, that departmental rights in matters of general education under their purview would not be challenged. This does not mean that the Task Force failed to take action about the role of departments (and to some extent, schools) in the matter of general education. Indeed, by retaining the established order the Task Force was taking an action; that action was a reaffirmation of traditional values, which were embedded deeply within the university's structure. Because it was widely understood that the Task Force could have chosen to make such a recommendation if it has so chosen, this reaffirmation was communicated in a symbolic fashion by the very fact that the existing order was instead left unaltered (Edelman, 1964).

Thus, little thought was given to reorganizing the structural basis for general education at NSU through the creation of a new organizational unit (e.g., a general education department or freestanding program) that would have primary authority for it. In the end, a new oversight committee was established to coordinate and give approval to core courses (see below), but from the outset the Task Force acknowledged the primacy of the departments. No action that would have infringed on this was seriously entertained.

The prestige hierarchy among the various department and professional school interests was not violated. Instead, the character of Task Force interactions with the departments appears to have been shaped by this unspoken, taken-for-granted "ranking" of the departments. For example, the departments of philosophy and theology—cornerstones in the founding sect's educational philosophy—were treated gingerly, even timidly, by the Task Force, with the result that no discernible thought was given to reducing their combined portion of the general education curriculum. By contrast, in the interactions between the Task Force and some of the social science departments (which were perceived as weaker and assumedly lower in the prestige hierarchy) it was apparent here that it was sometimes the departments, not the Task Force, which proceeded gingerly. This was especially true of the sociology department, which had a long history of strained relations with the administration.

Creating a cultural diversity requirement. By 1989, the conventional wisdom in U.S. higher education was that cultural diversity should be included in undergraduate study. On this point, some Task Force members explicitly stated that they saw this as inevitable, given the way that they perceived the environment. The reformed general education plan did include a one-course cultural diversity requirement, but a focus on this end result obscures a more complicated story.

In developing working models for a revised general education program, the Task Force was the object of intensive lobbying efforts. The most comprehensive and best organized of these efforts was made by proponents of a new general education requirement in the area of African-American Studies. Proponents of this idea organized strong attendance and participation in a Task Force public hearing on this question and orchestrated a vigorous letter writing campaign. Despite these efforts, however, the Task Force did not adopt the proposal.

This outcome can be traced, at least in part, to the fact that African-American Studies at NSU was a classified at the level of a program, and not as a department. In fact, the African-American Studies Program had no full-time faculty member solely affiliated with that program, and even its director held a joint appointment in a traditional Arts and Sciences department. Existing below the level of a department, the African-American Studies program at NSU was accorded substantially less prestige than the established disciplines.

More generally, the Task Force had difficulty deciding how to deal with the "cultural diversity" question in a way that would be acceptable to the university community overall. (One member noted that after almost two years and until just a few weeks before the final deadline, they were still unsure what to do.) Within the Task Force, there was disagreement about how to proceed. A Task Force member recalled:

> You've got a lot of strange things raised in that issue as to what it means. I remember one person saying that we should have the required a multicultural course for everybody except the minorities [sic]. . . . Or that the minorities should not be allowed to take certain courses. . . . I thought that generally it was just not handled very well. . . . There never really was a very clear statement as to what it [cultural diversity] was, and I worried what it would become if we set up courses that were multicultural—basically taken by the minorities—and [whether] they would basically become ghettoized [sic]. . . .

Eventually, a loose cultural diversity requirement was adopted. It required one course from among many offerings across many departments, rather than in African-American Studies only. Courses from traditional Arts and Sciences departments comprised the vast majority of the options, with African-American Studies courses relegated to but a few of the possibilities for fulfilling the requirement. Indeed, the departments, especially in Arts and Sciences, were not seen as likely to cooperate with a new general education plan that infringed too much in their perceived domain(s). Along these lines, a member of the Task Force stated:

> The departments had a lot of power and input. They didn't have so much power in determining what the core would look like, but they had power of acceptance or non-compliance.

To proponents of African-American Studies, requirements for "diversity" or "multicultural" course work implied study that centered on African-American issues and perspectives. To many, if not most, members of the traditional arts and sciences departments, however, what was meant by "diverse" or "multicultural" was much more broadly construed, including non-Anglo-Saxon components of European culture, as well as cultures from throughout other parts of the world. At NSU, the latter view prevailed. For courses later proposed to fulfill the diversity requirement, proponents of traditional disciplinary perspectives largely retained the established, conventional analytic lenses of their disciplines. In the end, although members of the Task Force assumed that cultural diversity would be included in the final proposal to reform general education, institutional pressures influenced the available ways in which that would be accommodated.

Creating a new general education oversight structure. A proposed new general education oversight body obviously could influence the program that would be implemented. As noted above, the Council on General Education was the existing oversight committee for the general education program at NSU, but by 1989 it was almost universally seen as ineffective. A main complaint was that although the committee had dealt adequately with individual courses and the minutiae of general education, the overall picture had become blurry and coherence had been lost. This line of argument mirrored a familiar criticism offered by those advocating curriculum reform (see Rudolph, 1977).

Accordingly, the Task Force was charged to make a decision about what sort of governance structure should be used to coordinate the new general education plan that it devised. It was quickly assumed that a new structure for faculty governance of general education was needed. However, some members of the faculty had already expressed apprehension about the nonrepresentativeness of the Task Force itself. This raised somewhat dormant issues about the lack of faculty participation in the overall governance of the university. One Task Force member, who otherwise seemed quite sympathetic to the administration, made the following observation:

> It would probably have been a good idea [if the faculty had been allowed to elect their representatives to the Task Force]. I think sometimes on the part of the administration there is a little nervousness about whether they are then going to have to deal with some crackpot who has totally got one issue or one agenda. . . . [but] I think is pretty much unfounded. I'm not sure that the faculty would elect crackpots to deal with university business. In university committees which I have served on where the faculty are elected, I really haven't had that experience too much. But when the appointments were made to the [Task Force] I think that the administrators doing the appointing tried to represent the kinds of moods and interest that they thought the faculty would have. And I think they did a fairly good job in doing that, but I think it would have made it a stronger statement of support for faculty involvement if they had allowed some delegates to be elected by the faculty.

Once the issue was raised, many NSU faculty asserted the view that control over the curriculum was most legitimately the province of the faculty. Proposals to delegate that authority elsewhere—in other words, to put the matter solely in the hands of the administration—were not seriously considered by the Task Force.

The various proposals for a new general education governance committee composed of faculty representatives varied only by degree of representation among the various schools and departments. The point is that there was no talk of representation other than along these existing structural lines. This structure, which is reflected throughout American higher education and into which future faculty are socialized during graduate training (Becher, 1987), is largely taken-for-granted and consequently was viewed as the most legitimate way to organize academic activity.

Institutions and the Politics of Meaning

The events in this case suggest that taken-for-granted institutions—manifest in such organizational features as structure, routines, and shared beliefs—significantly influenced the planning and decision making involved in NSU's general education reform effort. The course of events followed institutionalized elements embedded within the organization, especially the organizational structure and the prestige hierarchy arising from utilization of disciplinary departments and professional schools as the building blocks of the university. In addition, the importance of the academic major and the legitimacy of faculty sovereignty over curricular matters—which have deep roots in American college and university life—were boundaries that shaped the process and outcomes.

Although university leaders had moved the item to the agenda and retained considerable control over the course of decision making, there was no observable effort to forward curricular proposals that would violate the norms of the various disciplinary departments as institutionalized on campus. At the conclusion of the process, the general education program that was advanced by the Task Force was reflective of the university's underlying institutional-normative order, in both its secular and sectarian aspects. Some actors believed that more comprehensive change would be a real possibility in the outcome of the deliberations, but institutionalized structures and practices provided the framework upon which a more limited technical outcome was to be built. And so philosophy and theology maintained their special emphases, and newer imperatives, such as the inclusion of a cultural diversity requirement, were devised using the existing departmental frameworks, even though specialized programs were available.

Still, it would be a mistake to view the reform effort as an empty or meaningless enterprise that merely ended where it began. Although the curriculum and the power structure beneath it were relatively unchanged, the reform effort did serve organizationally useful symbolic purposes. The acts of attending to the general education curriculum and devoting substantial time and resources to the issue sent visible signals that were important to external and internal audiences. Since general education reform was in the air nationally, and since peer universities and colleges had addressed the issue, it was important for NSU seriously to examine its practices. To external audiences, NSU was shown to be in conformity with what a national university should be doing, reaffirming its consonance with values shared by other organizations. This was important for the maintenance of legitimacy among peer organizations.

To internal audiences—faculty, administrators, students, and alumnae/i—the general education reform effort symbolically communicated a sense of seriousness with which NSU regarded undergraduate education. For a previously teaching-oriented university that was aspiring to increase its reputation as a research institution, this was of special importance. By focusing attention on an important dimension of undergraduate education, the process provided an important context in which members of the community could participate in discussion about general education. Moreover, the adherence to process and organizational routines throughout this reform project meant that when side issues were raised, some common understandings about how to proceed (though not necessarily what decision to reach) helped prevent political interests from derailing the project.

As this case reveals, an important element in organizational politics involves the struggle to attach meaning to events and actions. Indeed, in this process of contextualization, entirely different meanings can be affixed to the same aspect of an organization (e.g., its general education curriculum). Diversity, for example, may be a widely shared organizational goal, but what that means, and how one gauges whether it has been achieved, may yet be contested. Reform projects can be as much about reasserting the legitimacy of organizational practice as they are about technical change.

Implications

What can we learn from NSU's experience? Advocates of reform need to be mindful of the underlying matrix of values and organizational constraints within their settings. In practice, reformers seem tempted to call for comprehensive reform, with the hope of bringing significant change to existing practice. With these lofty aims stated at the outset, failure to achieve highly visible, dramatic change then makes a reform effort appear to be a failure. Perhaps some organizations might find that extensive changes are necessary, but others, upon investigation and reflection, may find smaller changes more appropriate. However, given the realities of modern colleges and universities as political organizations, in which many perspectives are in close proximity, one should caution against being prematurely fixated on the degree of change that must be obtained, especially when it obscures or belittles the importance and worthiness of symbolic outcomes. NSU was largely successful in its efforts because actors in the process developed proposals that took into account the often conflicting (and largely taken-for-granted) values and norms of secular and sectarian higher education.

Symbolic results are often not seen as "real" outcomes. Yet, symbolic outcomes can play an important role in helping to maintain and bolster the sometimes-fragile underpinnings of academic organizations. Although arguments might be made regarding the need to shake up the balance of academic power within a university, a general education reform effort may not be the best venue for that project. Assumptions about power, preference, and privilege may be too important to be left as side issues in a reform effort about something else. They are also powerful and often emotional issues that can sidetrack general education reform. Although a highly educated elite, it cannot be assumed that faculty members of a modern academic organization have a solid understanding of why it is that colleagues trained in other disciplines see the facts of university life the way that they do. The professoriate is, after all, a fragmented group of specialists whose members sometimes have difficulty seeing things from the perspectives of others in their own disciplines, let alone across disciplinary lines. The diversity issue at NSU, for example, would probably have been more easily and more successfully resolved if the overarching diversity question had been explicitly addressed prior to the general education project.

Following this line, the events at NSU suggest that academic leaders would be wise to consider the state of academic politics on their campuses prior to undertaking a reform effort. For faculty who feel marginalized, disempowered, or unheard, it can be inviting to use a general education reform process as a venue for resolving those situations. Although NSU negotiated (more or less successfully, to many actors) around the side issues that were encountered, this was largely due to specific campus culture that largely acquiesced to administrative views on nondepartmental matters, undoubtedly a legacy of NSU's sectarian origins. In the absence of these, the outcome elsewhere could be much more acrimonious. Nonetheless, even at NSU some faculty were unhappy with an outcome that failed to legitimize their interests and perspectives, especially in newer and not-then institutionalized academic fields such as African-American Studies and Women's Studies. For some of these faculty members, the legacy of curriculum reform at NSU included disappointment.

Conclusion

A two-year effort to reform of general education at National Sectarian University resulted in minimal technical change. Yet, this can be viewed as a successful outcome. There have long been shifting ideas about what the undergraduate curriculum should strive to do (Rudolph, 1977), and as Bok (1986) noted, there is little agreement on what an educated person should know. Curriculum reform outcomes, on a technical basis, often can seem to be only trivially different from earlier curricula. Technical change, however, may be less important than symbolic action for some important organizational purposes. What can be important to colleges and universities is the political need to address seriously those issues regarded as important within the field of peer organizations and in society generally.

On a broader scale, the national rhetoric calling for comprehensive reform in general education seems to imply that U.S. colleges and universities are in crisis, and the implication is that catastrophic failure of this important social institution either has occurred or is impending. Although crisis rhetoric is sometimes employed, however, the negative state of affairs it implies is not necessarily self-evident. As with much in U.S. higher education, the state of general education remains ambiguous. Even if negative claims are taken at face value, it is by no means evident that there would a clear, objectively valid course of action that should be taken. As cultural constructs, general education curricula remain linked to shifting articulations and orderings of values. The national rhetoric is largely about the contesting of those competing interpretations.

In situations where ambiguous and contested rhetoric leads to calls for comprehensive reform of general education curricula, then, the process of attending to the issue has value, apart from technical, programmatic changes. Rather than a meager outcome of dubious utility, an outcome that has minimal technical change but is rich in symbolic action can enhance an organization, particularly in the maintenance of prestige and legitimacy. The symbolic act of renewing or establishing connection between meaning and a general education curriculum is itself an important result in a reform effort.

References

Allison, G. T. (1971). *Essence of decision: Explaining the Cuban missile crisis.* Boston: Little, Brown.

Barzun, J., & Graff, H. F. (1992). *The modern researcher* (5th ed.). New York: Harcourt, Brace, Jovanovich.

Becher, T. (1987). The disciplinary shaping of the profession. In B. Clark (Ed.), *The academic profession: National, disciplinary and institutional settings* (pp. 271–303). Berkeley: University of California Press.

Becker, G. (1986). The economic approach to human behavior. In J. Elster (Ed.), *Rational choice* (pp. 108–122). New York: New York University Press.

Birnbaum, R. (1988). *How colleges work: The cybernetics of academic organization and leadership.* San Francisco: Jossey-Bass.

Bok, D. (1986). *Higher learning.* Cambridge: Harvard University Press.

Bourdieu, P. (1991). *Language and symbolic power.* Cambridge: Harvard University Press.

Cohen, M. D., & March, J. G. (1986). *Leadership and ambiguity: The American college president,* 2d ed. Boston: Harvard Business School Press.

Cohen, M. D., March, J. G., & and Olsen, J. P. (1972). A garbage can model of organizational choice. *Administrative Science Quarterly, 17,* 1–25.

DiMaggio, P. J., & Powell, W. W. (1983). The iron cage revisited: Institutional isomorphism and collective rationality in organizational fields. *American Sociological Review, 48,* 147–60.

Douglas, M. (1986). *How institutions think.* Syracuse: Syracuse University Press.

Edelman, M. (1964). *The symbolic uses of politics.* Urbana: University of Illinois Press.

Friedland, R., & Alford, R. R. (1991). Bringing society back in: Symbols, practices, and institutional contradictions. In W. W. Powell & P. J. DiMaggio (Eds.), *The new institutionalism in organizational analysis* (pp. 232–263). Chicago: University of Chicago Press.

Habermas, J. (1971). *Toward a rational society: Student protest, science, and politics.* Boston: Beacon Press.

Halperin, M. (1974). *Bureaucratic politics and foreign policy.* Washington, DC: The Brookings Institution.

Kanter, S., Gamson, Z., & London, H. (1997). *Revitalizing general education in a time of scarcity: A navigational chart for administrators and faculty.* Boston: Allyn & Bacon.

Kerr, C. (1963). *The uses of the university.* Cambridge: Harvard University Press.

Keller, G. (1983). *Academic strategy: The management revolution in American higher education.* Baltimore: The Johns Hopkins University Press.

March, J. G., & Olsen, J. P. (1989). *Rediscovering institutions: The organizational basis of politics.* New York: The Free Press.

Meyer, J. W., & Rowan, B. (1977). Institutionalized organizations: Formal structure as myth and ceremony. *American Journal of Sociology, 83,* 340–363.

Mintzberg, H. (1994). *The rise and fall of strategic planning: Reconceiving roles for planning, plans, planners.* New York: Free Press.

Pfeffer, J. (1978). The micropolitics of organizations. In M. W. Meyer (Ed.), *Environments and organizations* (pp. 29–50). San Francisco: Jossey-Bass.

Rudolph, F. (1977). *Curriculum: A history of the American undergraduate course of study since 1636.* San Francisco: Jossey-Bass.

Zucker, L. G. (1991). The role of institutionalization in cultural persistence. In W. W. Powell & P. J. DiMaggio (Eds.) *The new institutionalism in organizational analysis* (pp. 83–107). Chicago: University of Chicago Press.

General Education Reform as Organizational Change: Integrating Cultural and Structural Change

Susan M. Awbrey

"I died on the hill of general education reform." This adage is repeatedly heard from faculty and administrators who have fought to bring a renewed vitality to undergraduate education but who were defeated by the process. The reform of general education is one of the most prevalent and complex challenges facing colleges and universities. General education is embedded in the culture of the institution. Its meaning and symbolism permeate the organization and extend beyond to external constituencies. Yet the task of reform is often assigned to a faculty committee or task force made up of individuals from a variety of disciplines who have little experience in examining institutional-level issues or in examining such issues from an organization-wide perspective. Faculty members focused on research, teaching, and service are often not aware that general education reform thrusts them into the unfamiliar role of agents of cultural change.

A significant impediment to effective organizational change, including general education reform, is failure to recognize the extent to which the change process is vulnerable to powerful cultural influences (Dooley, 1995). Information that assists faculty and administrators who are charged with general education reform to understand the nature of the issues, problems, and resistances that they will encounter—within the academic community and among themselves—can help them to work more effectively. This paper examines how higher education administrators and faculty can obtain more successful and sustainable reform outcomes by applying knowledge derived from literature and research on organizational change and by recognizing the importance of systematically integrating cultural and structural approaches to change.

An overview of the evolution of general education in the United States provides a backdrop for the discussion. The advantages of including the cultural perspective in change initiatives are identified and a model of organizational culture change is introduced and illustrated through application to the process of general education reform. The relationships of culture to learning and of learning to continuous institutional improvement are described. The paper concludes with the theoretical and practical integration of cultural and structural change processes.

The Changing Landscape of General Education

General education was not always a part of higher learning in the United States. When universities were first founded in the United States, classical education provided unity and coherence within the confines of a single canon. However, as the curriculum changed, faculty faced the challenge of integrating new forms of knowledge with older forms and defining what is essential to the education of undergraduate students. One of the first attempts to define what general education should

Reprinted from the *Journal of General Education* 54, no. 1 (2005), by permission of Pennsylvania State University Press.

be took place at Yale in 1828 (Kanter, Gamson, & London, 1997). The evolution of general education continued with the Harvard model and later with the rise of research institutions. But the development of general education did not unfold smoothly (Rudolph, 1977). In 1977 the Carnegie Foundation for the Advancement of Teaching (1977) issued a report that called general education a disaster area. This report gave impetus to a new and intense round of general education reform during the 1980s. Numerous national associations received funding for the study and improvement of general education and also issued reports during the mid-1980s indicating that undergraduate education had lost its liberal arts roots and that "students lack exposure to fundamental subjects and . . . basic intellectual skills" (Kanter et al., 1997, p. 9).

Gamson, Kanter, and London (1992) identified internal and external catalysts leading to general education reform during the 1980s. According to these authors, internal catalysts for change included: changes in academic leadership and vision, declining or under-enrollment, sagging university reputations, faculty dissatisfaction with current working conditions, faculty desire to educate students in a way that reflects faculty views, and departmental competition. External catalysts included the impact on reputation of declining enrollments, drops in the academic ability of students, and meeting accreditation standards.

Gaff & Wasescha (1991) studied 305 colleges and universities that underwent general education reform during the 1980s. They found that 67% of the institutions under study increased interdisciplinary coursework, 68% tightened their distribution requirements, 73% added upper division courses, and 93% increased writing across the curriculum requirements. In addition to programmatic changes, some institutions reported that the process focused the college's identity, brought people together from across the institution, and made faculty more aware of the environment beyond the confines of their department. However, potentially damaging effects of unsuccessful general education processes were also reported, including deeply divided and embittered faculty and increased tensions between faculty and administration (MacDonald, 2003).

Johnson (2002) studied how general education changed between 1989 and 2000 in a national survey of over 500 chief academic officers and directors responsible for general education at various Association of American Colleges and Universities institutions. He found that "the majority of reform activities consisted of changes to structural aspects of general education programs. Furthermore, institutions did not often assess broad aims for general education nor did they involve students in forming these aims" (p. 121). He notes that some of the primary strategies for changing curricula included more prescription of general education courses, the addition of interdisciplinary sequences, and thematic organization of general education programs. Although one of the major reasons for undertaking general education reform during the 1990s was to increase program coherence, Johnson found that the structural strategies used to create more coherence had not "achieved their aim of a more coherent curriculum." He concludes that " achieving coherent curricula may require more than academic planning and structure reorganization" (p. 109).

Results of a survey on the status of general education in 2000 conducted by Ratcliff, Johnson, La Nasa, and Gaff (2001) indicated that 57% of the institutions studied were engaged in the process of reviewing general education and that many more were planning to begin the process. Nevertheless, the authors indicate that "despite the high level of interest in general education from campus and external sources, there is little evidence that academic leaders have made much advancement in the science or art of developing shared educational values and embedding them in the life of institutions" (sp. 18).

Depth of Change

A mistake that faculty and administrators sometimes make when beginning the reform of general education is to believe that they are simply engaged in the overt structural task of curricular reform. Yet general education change is not just a task of curricular change: it is also cultural change. As Ratcliff writes, "The educational program of the institution reflects the norms, values, and behavior of the organizational culture" (Ratcliff, 1997b, p. 9). Fuhrmann and Grasha concur that what is or is not thought to be quality curriculum "is largely the result of our educational philosophies, beliefs, values, and normative positions (Cited in Ratcliff, 1997b, p. 152)." Although campus-wide general education efforts may focus on what is best for students, recognizing why faculty hold the beliefs they do about what is best is a much deeper task that involves systematic examination of the cultural context in which the change is taking place.

Regarding organizational change as involving just the task at hand is not unique to higher education. Selfridge and Sokolik (1975) have described this organizational problem as the iceberg phenomenon. The tip of the iceberg is the everyday, apparent operations of any organization. These include elements that are observable, rational, and related to the structure of the organization, including span of control, hierarchy, mission, goals, objectives, operating policies, procedures, programs, and practices. This is the formal, visible organization. It is in this realm that organizations focus most of their time and energy when dealing with change.

However, Selfridge and Sokolik note that there is a deeper, covert level of the iceberg that is crucial to the success of systemic organizational change. This level is made up of elements that are affective and that relate to the psychological and social characteristics of the organization. This is the informal organization that is made up of elements such as power and influence patterns, personal views and interpretations of the organization, interpersonal relationships, norms, trust, risk-taking, values, emotions, and needs. It is the level at which institutional culture operates. It is necessary to address this deeper level if change is to succeed and be maintained (Farmer, 1990). Organizations are not just operations: they have meaning for the individuals who inhabit them (Smircich, 1983b) and understanding the meaning that the organization has for its members is critical to facilitating successful change. Organization members enact shared meaning as culture (Morgan, 1986).

Defining Organizational Culture

The role of culture in organizations has long fascinated researchers from many disciplines both as a description of the life of the organization and in relation to an organization's effectiveness (Kezar & Eckel, 2002; Smircich, 1983a). There is no one definition of organizational culture. Many definitions reflect Peterson and Spencer's view that culture consists of "deeply embedded patterns of organizational behavior and the shared values, assumptions, beliefs, or ideologies that members have about their organization or its work" (1991, p. 142) or Farmer's conception that it is "what is done, how it is done, and who is doing it" (1990, p. 8). Anthropologist Clifford Geertz views culture as a web of significance—"a pattern of meanings embodied in symbols" (1973, p. 89). Culture has also been defined as the way organizational members enact shared reality (Morgan, 1986). J. Steven Ott notes that organizational culture "provides organization members with a way of understanding and making sense of events and symbols" and that "organizational culture is a powerful lever for guiding organizational behavior" (1989, p. 52).

Within higher education, early explorations of culture focused on describing the culture of specific segments of higher education such as students and faculty (Becker 1963; Bushnell 1960, Clark 1963) and on institutional distinctiveness (Clark 1970, Reisman, Gusfield & Gamson, 1970). Subsequent works focused on institutional improvement (Chaffee 1984; Freedman 1979) and on categorizing types of academic culture (Bergquist 1992; Cameron and Ettington 1988).

Tierney's work identifies the advantages of becoming aware of organizational culture. He notes that the cultural perspective encourages members of academe to: (1) consider conflicts "on the broad canvas of organizational life"; (2) recognize how tensions in the organization are played out in operational and structural issues; (3) make decisions with "keen awareness" of their impact on groups within the institution; (4) understand the symbolic nature of seemingly instrumental actions; and (5) consider why different groups in the organization have different perspectives on how the organization is performing (1988, p. 6). Having this deeper recognition also allows faculty and administrators to approach change initiatives such as general education reform with greater understanding of how the change process can best be facilitated and how the implementation of change can be sustained.

A Model of Organizational Culture

Given the amorphous nature of organizational culture, how can faculty and administrators form a useful picture of institutional culture? Based on decades of research, organizational theorist Edgar Schein developed one of the most useful models for cultural inquiry. Schein identifies three levels of organizational culture: artifacts, values and beliefs, and basic assumptions (Schein, 1984, 1985).

Level 1: Artifacts

Artifacts are visible behavior patterns and the results of behaviors, including language, jargon, programs, and policies. Because these elements are tangible and it is possible to "get your arms around them," so to speak, change strategies are often focused on changing artifacts, for example, changing policies or changing operational systems (Ott, 1989). However, artifacts are symbols of the deeper level of "the values and beliefs that lie behind" (Davis, 1984, p. 12). If artifacts are changed without likewise reaching to the values and beliefs that give them meaning, the change is unlikely to be lasting.

Level 2: Values and Beliefs

The second level of Schein's model involves organizational values and beliefs, "how people communicate, explain, rationalize, and justify what they say and do as a community—how they make sense of the first level of culture" (1985, p. 10). This level also includes elements such as philosophies, ideologies, ethical codes, and attitudes that help the individual make interpretations (Ott, 1989).

However, Schein acknowledges that the values that people espouse are not always the values that they enact in everyday life, which are called values-in-use (Argyris & Schon, 1978). Values-in-use actually guide everyday behavior, whereas espoused values are symbolic. Vision is the embodiment of our values. When we create a vision we are abstracting an ideal derived from our view of current reality. However, if that abstraction is not used to do something to improve reality it can become a utopian idealization, an idol that we espouse but fail to act upon.

Unfortunately, we often inhabit organizations that do not encourage us to disclose or discuss discrepancies between espoused values and those we actually use to guide our actions (Bergquist, 1993). Under conditions of uncertainty or threat, such as those that occur in times of change—including the reform of general education—individuals are more likely to use hidden value systems that are not aligned with the values they espouse (Dooley, 1995).

Level 3: Basic Assumptions

The final level of Schein's model involves basic assumptions. Basic assumptions are beliefs that are tacit—no longer fully conscious because they are so taken for granted (Schein, 1985). They are used to guide behavior without reflection and represent the deepest level of culture.

Change is more likely to be lasting if it reveals and reflects on the basic values and assumptions actually used to guide behavior—if it arises from examination of one's personal constructs or mental models of the world. Altering the basic beliefs and assumptions of organizational members can actually change their internal images of what the organization is and its purpose. Smircich has stated that "the success of strategic change efforts depends not only on the organization's ability to undergo a significant shift in direction, vision, and values, but also the ability of stakeholders to understand and accept a new conceptualization of the organization" (quoted in Gioia, Thomas, Clark, & Chittipeddi, 1994, p. 363). Barnett translates this view to higher education when he states, "What we mean by, and intend by, 'quality' in the context of higher education is bound up with our values and fundamental aims in higher education . . . what we take higher education ultimately to be" (quoted in Ratcliff, 1997a, p. 152).

Applying Schein's Model to General Education Reform

Schein's three-level model can help to illustrate how academic culture interacts with change initiatives such as general education reform. The following illustrates how deeper levels of cultural change may be achieved by examining the values, beliefs, and assumptions of the reformers and their decisions about general education.

Level 1: Artifacts

The general education literature discussed above shows that much of the focus of general education reform has been on overt, structural changes at the program level. Reforms such as tightened distribution requirements, addition of upper division courses, increased interdisciplinarity, and increased writing across the curriculum represent Level 1 artifact changes. They are structural and observable, often taking place within a specific accepted model of general education. When change takes place within the prevailing model of general education, reformers sometimes grapple with cultural issues as an aside or miss the step of examining the values and assumptions that underlie structural changes. This paper encourages reformers to systematically unveil cultural perspectives prior to undertaking discussion of structural change.

Level 2: Values and Beliefs

Although implementations vary widely, Newton (2000) described the three dominant models of general education in the United States as the *great books model*, the *scholarly discipline model*, and the *effective citizen model*. It is important to note that the adherents of each model hold a different set of values and beliefs about what it means to be an educated person and about the purpose of higher education. Newton's descriptions of the models illustrate the tensions and differences that derive from their underlying values and beliefs. According to Newton (2000), the great books model defines an ideally educated person as someone who is familiar with classic works and who has struggled with fundamental questions of human existence. This model strives to provide a context within which students confront fundamental questions of life, the perennial questions of humanity. These questions are introduced through "in-depth historical review of the works of thinkers whose ideas changed human history" (p. 170). Criticisms of this model include the lack of attention to current knowledge and the heated debate over what the canon should contain in order for it to represent cultural heritage. This model focuses on the unity of knowledge within a single framework, and those who take issue with this model point to its lack of diverse voices. The beliefs that underlie the great books model include the importance of introducing students to questions that transcend the disciplines and integrating knowledge through discussion of fundamental questions viewed from the perspective of Western civilization.

In Newton's description of the scholarly discipline model (Newton, 2000), the ideally educated person is a beginning practitioner of the basic disciplines who has an understanding of the key concepts and the methods of inquiry that scholars use. In its purest form, this model is an introduction to the separate disciplines. It views scholarly disciplines as the developers and "storehouses of human knowledge" (p. 172), and it focuses on the importance of specialization. According to Newton, this model became popular with the advent of the research universities where undergraduate students were viewed as novice practitioners of the disciplines. Its greatest advantage is that it offers a rigorous introduction to the basic concepts of the chosen discipline and the methods by which scholars analyze and solve problems in the discipline. Major criticisms include its fragmentation, the absence of an attempt to effectively communicate the relevance of the disciplines to students and society, and its focus on what is taught instead of what is learned. The scholarly discipline model is still the dominant model of general education among liberal arts faculty in universities in the United States.

Newton (2000) writes that an ideally educated person in the effective citizen model of general education is someone who is familiar with the important ideas and discoveries of the disciplines *and* who also understands their relationship to and implications for society. The effective citizen model focuses on the student and what the student should learn in order to live well and engage fully in society. Its major advantage is the combined focus on understanding important ideas and approaches of the disciplines and their social implications: it makes relevancy pivotal. This model is becoming more prevalent because of its focus on student learning. According to Newton, there are two roots of the effective citizen model. The first grows out of the assessment movement and the desire for accountability through student learning outcomes. It is based on development of the competencies needed to become a productive member of society. The other stems from the philosophy of John Dewey, which links theory and practice. It is based on learning the competencies needed to lead societal change.

There are several drivers that are moving higher education toward the effective citizen model. The focus on relevance to the "real world" makes the effective citizen model attractive to external constituents and to faculty within community colleges. Administrative culture favors the accountability of the model and marketability of the model to external constituencies. The effective citizen model also appeals to faculty concerned with giving voice to segments of academe previously marginalized by the Western intellectual tradition. The model supports the integration of multiculturalism and diversity into the curriculum.

The effective citizen model is often favored by external higher education accrediting agencies. Cecila Lopez (1999) completed a study of 100 randomly selected reports written by North Central Association (NCA) Evaluation Teams for comprehensive institutional reaccredidation visits from 1994–95 to 1997–98. These teams used regional accreditation standards to examine general education in each of their visits. The teams identified elements of good general education practice with a "high level of agreement." These included elements such as coherence, common learning experiences, integration and application of information, inclusion of multiculturalism and diversity, inclusion of skills and values, ongoing assessment and review, learning outcomes, and interdisciplinarity. Such elements of good practice are based on the values that underlie the effective citizen model of general education. The NCA's Higher Learning Commission Statement on General Education (2003) declares: "Understanding and appreciating diverse cultures, mastering multiple modes of inquiry, effectively analyzing and communicating information, and recognizing the importance of creativity and values to the human spirit not only allow people to live richer lives but also are a foundation for most careers and for the informed exercise of local, national, and international citizenship" (2003, p. 3–4–3).

The major criticism of the effective citizen model has been how it has been implemented. In many cases, programs teach only about the disciplines rather than rigorously teaching the substance of the disciplines. The effective citizen model is designed to develop values and teach skills in addition to knowledge. This has raised fears among adherents of the discipline-based model that only one particular set of values will be taught. Within the Western intellectual tradition that underlies the discipline-based model there is also a separation between theory and practice, where practice is seen as a more base pursuit. Skills equate to practice and applied knowledge is seen, in this view, as a lesser form of education. Thus, the emphasis on relevance in the effective citizen model is seen as suspect by many adherents of the discipline-based model of general education.

A fourth, less researched model of general education is emerging (Ratcliff, 2000; Stark & Lattuca, 1997). The *communicative model* focuses on the relationship between student and instructor and the connection between general and specialized education.

Level 3: Basic Assumptions

Underlying the models of general education are the basic assumptions that guide behavior and actions. This is the deepest level of culture. Judgments about what constitutes the "core" knowledge every educated person should know are based on paradigms that define what can be known and how we develop knowledge (Toma, 1997). Such paradigms also determine how higher education institutions are structured to pursue knowledge.

During the Renaissance, the well-educated person was defined as someone who was not only learned in one particular specialization, but who was also conversant within a broad range of knowledge, that is, a generalist. Renaissance assumptions regarding the unity of knowledge are foundational to the Great Books model of general education.

Since Descartes, the dominant inquiry paradigm has been positivism (Guba, 1990, pp. 19–27). Positivism subscribes to a realist ontology that believes reality is "out there" and is governed by natural laws. Positivists take an objectivist epistemological stance, whereby the appropriate methodology for inquiry is empirical experimentalism. The Industrial Revolution, the rise of science, and advent of research institutions have led to the development of specialization and the disciplines. The positivist paradigm underlies the discipline-based model of general education and also the departmental structure of research universities, making a shift away from the discipline-based model difficult. General education, when viewed from the discipline-based perspective, is often seen as a set of service courses that are delivered by individual departments or a set of courses with individual purposes (Levine, 1978). This can lead faculty to a course-by-course view of the change needed to revise general education rather than an overall assessment of general education as a curriculum. Agreement within this context of general education is often difficult because disciplines impart their own individual processes for inquiry, norms, and modes of learning.

Positivism has now been challenged by a resurgence of pragmatism, which values relevance, by critical theory, which seeks to eliminate "false consciousness" through "ideologically oriented inquiry" whereby values mediate inquiry (Guba, 1990, pp. 23–25), and by constructivism, in which "inquirer and inquired into are fused into a single entity—reality is created through their interaction" (p. 27). These are the paradigms that undergird the effective citizen and communicative models of general education.

Discussion of the major inquiry paradigms provides a lens for understanding the tacit underlying assumptions that shape the values and beliefs of academic culture. These paradigms help us to understand faculty adherence to the various models of general education, along with the corresponding resistances to change.

Learning to Change

The sustainability of change initiatives for an organization is related to the depth of self-examination and learning that takes place within its culture. Learning within organizations has been studied extensively (Argyris & Schon, 1996; Crossan & Guatto, 1996; Dodgson, 1993; Easterby-Smith, Snell, & Gherardi, 1998; Miller, 1996). Still, there are disagreements about whether learning is an individual process or can take place in groups (Brown & Duguid, 1991; Burgoyne, 1976; Elkjaer, 1999; Jones & Hendry, 1994; Pedler, Burgoyne & Boydell, 1991). Nevertheless, many scholars do agree that there are different levels of organizational learning (Argyris, 1991; Argyris & Schon, 1978; Bateson, 1972; Hawkins 1991, 1994; Swieringa & Wierdsma, 1992.)

Level 1 learning has been variously termed single-loop learning, adaptive learning, assimilation, or first-order learning (Perin & Sampaio, n.d.) This level of learning adds to knowledge but does not alter the values, beliefs, or rules that underlie it (Dodgson, 1993). Level 2 learning, which Argyris calls double-loop learning, is reflective. It reshapes patterns of thinking and reorganizes mental models and examines values and beliefs to reframe the situation (Probst & Buchel, 1997). Finally, Argyris and Schon (1978) extended Bateson's (1972) idea of deutero learning, which they term triple-loop learning. This is Level 3 learning, which shifts how organization members view themselves and how they view the organization. It restructures the context and creates new environments that allow both Level 1 and Level 2 learning to take place. The three-level model of learning is analogous to Schein's model of culture.

TABLE 1
Levels of Organizational Culture and Learning

	Cultural Levels (Schein)	Learning Levels (Argyris)	Organizational Levels (Adapted from Selfridge and Sokolik)
Level 1	Artifacts	Single Loop Adaptive	Formal Organization
Level 2	Values and Beliefs	Double Loop Reflective	Informal Organization
Level 3	Tacit Assumptions	Triple Loop Transformational	Informal Organization

The deeper the learning reaches, the more profound and lasting is the change it elicits (Boyce, 2003). Thus, change that reaches only to the formal, operational level of the organization usually involves only single-loop learning and is often short-lived. Change that is deeper, that involves examining the values and beliefs of the participants through interactive dialogue, and that fits better with the organization's culture and sometimes changes the culture (Farmer, 1990) involves double-loop learning. Change that is transformative, that changes both the structure of the organization and the way the organization is conceptualized by its members, involves triple-loop learning (Gioia et al., 1994). As members of the organization reach deeper levels of learning, they are more open to self-examination and the change they initiate becomes more lasting and sustainable because it is embedded in the culture through dialog. In this view culture is not something an organization has—it is something an organization is (Smircich, 1983a), and sustainable change is not something that is imposed on the culture—it emerges from the culture's self-examination.

Potholes on the Road to General Education Reform

The various ways that general education initiatives can get off track and end up in failure are described by Gaff (1980) as potholes in the road to change. He identified 47 such "potholes." If Gaff's potholes are examined in light of the above discussion, most can be shown to have cultural roots. For example, a disregard for cultural fit can lead to searching for the one best general education program, attempting to borrow a program whole-cloth from another institution, reform committees that work in isolation, or assuming that any opposition to attempted change is irrational. Miscalculating the depth of change that is needed can lead to beliefs that general education change is only curricular change, that general education change should be revolutionary, that change should take only a short time, or that the resources needed to support the change process will be minimal. Not reflecting on the underlying values of the culture and the model of general education that the institution embodies can result in a failure to understand the source of problematic beliefs, for instance, that there is only one true meaning of general education, that general education deals only with knowledge and not skills and values, that general education is only cognitive, that integration of what is learned is the responsibility of the students, and that general education reform is a strictly rational process. Engaging the organization's culture and attempting to understand it can help to steer the process of general education reform around Gaff's potholes.

Resistance is a normal part of the change process (Keup, Walker, Astin, & Lindholm, 1997; Simsek & Louis, 1994.) Individuals engage in active or passive forms of resistance. Trader-Leigh (2002) identifies several factors that contribute to resistance to change, including: (1) change threatens perceived self-interest; (2) changes in status and security have negative psychological impacts; (3) ingrained traditions present barriers; (4) fear of loss of job responsibility; (5) destabilization of the status quo; (6) change doesn't fit the organization's values and beliefs; and (7) change threatens individuals or groups with a loss of power.

Cultural inquiry helps those involved in reform to recognize that resistance can also exist as a group phenomenon and that it can operate below the level of conscious awareness resulting in what Argyris terms "organizational defense mechanisms" that are designed to sustain existing cultural norms. Organizational defense can manifest itself as rejection, procrastination, indecision, sabotage, and regression (Argyris, 1990). Understanding the values, beliefs, and assumptions that underlie the culture and dominant subcultures of an organization can assist in understanding the institution's patterns of resistance to change.

Culture can also create or reinforce structural problems. Organizations that do not reach the levels of double- and triple-loop learning can maintain organizational structures that pose barriers to change and to further learning. For example, faculty may support the discipline-based model of general education not only because they agree with its underlying paradigm and assumptions, but also because of the practical barriers presented by the structure of the university. Resources flow to departments based on credit-hour delivery. Change that affects credit hour delivery elicits fears about the survival of the department. These concerns may make it hard for faculty worried about department survival to focus on student learning, to consider the value of interdisciplinary courses, or to consider models of delivery other than the dominant discipline-based model on which much university structure is founded.

A Call for Integrative Change Process

Ultimately, effective change cannot be achieved by replacing structural change with cultural change. The goal is to overcome the penchant for seeing change as an either/or process, either structural or cultural. Schein's model illustrates that structure (artifacts) and culture are parts of the same whole. It focuses on the variables (artifacts, values and beliefs, and assumptions) that make up that whole, but it does not address the dynamic interaction between the variables. Hatch (1993) extended Schein's model by adding a fourth variable, symbols, and by describing the dynamic processes that take place between the variables. These processes include:

> *manifestation* (assumptions manifested in beliefs and values), *realization* (values materialized into artifacts), *symbolization* (artifacts acquiring surplus meaning and coming to stand for something more than they actually are), and *interpretation* (acting back upon and changing the initial assumptions). (Bates, Khan, & Pye, 2000, p. 198)

Based on Hatch's work, Bates, Khan, and Pye (2000) created a four-phase change process that integrates cultural and structural change. Phase I, cultural framing, involves mapping out the culture and hidden challenges by examining people's expectations and aspirations regarding the subject of change. Phase II, soft structuring, involves building new connections and trust between groups involved in the change. It involves overcoming the tensions identified in Phase I that exist between groups. This phase constructs a social foundation for the new program that will result from the change process. Phase III, hard wiring, brings together the expertise of relevant specialists to create a single, integrative design for the new program. Phase IV, retrospecting, is reflecting on what was learned, reexamining assumptions, and reconceptualizing—consciously creating new assumptions.

Applying Bates, Khan, and Pye's process to general education reform involves consciously unveiling the cultural frame and building a social foundation for the change prior to undertaking discussions of changes in program structure. It involves systematically reflecting on what has been learned and reconceptualizing general education once the renewed program is in place.

Conclusion

Making a conscious effort to undertake cultural inquiry and to integrate cultural and structural change from the outset of a systemic change initiative such as general education reform can lead to the possibility of implementing a more sustainable change. Structural change and cultural change are not separate, but are two parts of a whole. Administrators and faculty attempting to facilitate organization-wide change will be more likely to be successful and to develop sustainable change if they recognize that all members of the organization, including those attempting to make change, have values, beliefs, and tacit assumptions that guide their behaviors. Organization-wide change, such as the reform of general education, is not just a change in the operations of the institution. It is cultural change that is rooted in the meaning that the organization has for its members—including its students.

Cultural aspects of change are often overlooked in systemic change initiatives such as general education reform because of the time that it takes to unveil the values, beliefs, and assumptions of the institution's members and to engage in dialogue that leads to reflective, deep-level learning. It is estimated that successful, deep-level systemic change takes three to five years (Dooley, 1995). Nevertheless, it is this deeper change that fosters future growth and development, and that can open the institution to continuous learning and improvement. Therefore, the success of initiatives such as general education reform should be assessed not only by the structural, operational changes achieved but also by the cultural change and learning that takes place within the organization. The deeper the level of cultural awareness and learning, the richer the change process and the more likely the organization is to continue learning.

References

Argyris, C. (1990). *Overcoming organizational defenses.* Boston: Allyn and Bacon.

Argyris, C. (1991). Teaching smart people how to learn. *Harvard Business Review, 69*(3), 99–109.

Argyris, C., & Schon, D. A. (1978). *Organizational learning: A theory of action perspective.* Reading, MA: Addison-Wesley.

Argyris, C., & Schon, D. A. (1996). *Organizational learning II: Theory, method, and practice.* Reading, MA: Addison-Wesley.

Bates, P., Khan, R. & Pye, A. (2000). Towards a culturally sensitive approach to organizational structuring: Where organizational design meets organizational development. *Organization Science, 11*(2), 197–211.

Bateson, G. (1972). *Steps to an ecology of mind.* New York: Ballantine.

Becker, H. S. (1963). Student culture. In T. F. Lumsford (Ed.), *The study of campus cultures.* Boulder, CO: Western Interstate Commission for Higher Education, 11–26.

Bergquist, W. H. (1992). *The four cultures of the academy: Insights and strategies for improving leadership in collegiate organizations.* San Francisco: Jossey-Bass.

Bergquist, W. H. (1993). *The postmodern organization: Mastering the art of irreversible change.* San Francisco: Jossey-Bass.

Boyce, M. E. (2003). Organizational learning is essential to achieving and sustaining change in higher education. *Innovative Higher Education, 28*(2), 119–136.

Brown, J. S., & Duguid, P. (1991). Organizational learning and communities-of-practice: Toward a unified view of working, learning, and innovation. *Organization Science, 2*(1), 40–57.

Burgoyne, J. (1976). The nature, use, and acquisition of managerial skills and other attributes. *Personnel Review, 5*(4), 19–29.

Bushnell, J. (1960). Student values: A summary of research and future problems. In M. Carpenter (Ed.), *The larger learning.* Dubuque: Brown, 45–61.

Cameron, K. S., & Ettington, D. R. (1988). The conceptual foundations of organizational culture. In J. C. Smart (Ed.), *Higher education: Handbook of theory and research,* vol. 4. New York: Agathon Press, 356–396.

Carnegie Foundation for the Advancement of Teaching. (1977). *Missions of the college curriculum: A contemporary review with suggestions.* San Francisco: Jossey-Bass.

Chaffee, E. E. (1984). *After decline, what? Survival strategies at eight private colleges.* Boulder, CO: National Center for Higher Education Management Systems.

Clark, B. R. (1963). Faculty culture. In T. F. Lumsford (Ed.), *The study of campus cultures.* Boulder, CO: Western Interstate Commission for Higher Education, 39–54.

Clark, B. R. (1970). *The distinctive college: Antioch, Reed, and Swarthmore.* Chicago: Aldine.

Crossan, M. M., & Guatto, T. (1996). Organizational learning research profile. *Journal of Organizational Change Management, 9*(1), 107–112.

Davis, S. M. (1984). *Managing corporate culture.* Cambridge, MA: Ballinger.

Dodgson, M. (1993). Organizational learning: A review of some literatures. *Organizational Studies, 14*(3), 375–394.

Dooley, J. (1995). Cultural aspects of systemic change management. Retrieved March 4, 2005, from http://www.well.com/user/dooley/culture.pdf

Easterby-Smith, M., Snell, R., & Gherardi, S. (1998). Organizational learning: Diverging communities of practice? *Management Learning, 29*(3), 259–272.

Elkjaer, B. (1999). In search of a social learning theory. In M. Easterby-Smith, L. Araujo & J. Burgoyne (Eds.), *Organizational learning and the learning organization: Developments in theory and practice.* London: Sage.

Farmer, D. W. (1990). Strategies for change. In D. W. Steeples (Ed.), *Managing change in higher education* (pp. 7–18). (New Directions in Higher Education No. 71). San Francisco: Jossey-Bass.

Freedman, M. (1979). *Academic culture and faculty development.* Berkeley: University of California Press.

Gaff, J. G. (1980). Avoiding the potholes: Strategies for reforming general education. *Educational Record, 61*(4), 50–59.

Gaff, J. G., & Wasescha, A. (1991). Assessing the reform of general education. *Journal of General Education, 40,* 51–68.

Gamson, Z., Kanter, S., & London, H. (1992). General education reform: Moving beyond the rational model of change. *Perspectives: The Journal of the Association of General and Liberal Studies, 22*(1), 58–68.

Geertz, C. (1973). *The interpretation of cultures*. New York: Basic Books.

Gioia, D. A., Thomas, J. B., Clark, S. M., & Chittipeddi, K. (1994). Symbolism and strategic change in academia: The dynamics of sense making and influence. *Organization Science, 5*(3), 363–383.

Guba, E. G. (Ed). (1990). *The paradigm dialog*. Newbury Park: Sage Publications.

Hatch, M. J. (1993). The dynamics of organizational culture. *Academy of Management Review, 18*(4), 657–693.

Hawkins, P. (1991). The spiritual dimension of the learning organization. *Management Education and Development, 22*(3), 166–181.

Hawkins, P. (1994). Organizational learning: Taking stock and facing the challenge. *Management Learning, 25*(1), 71–82.

Higher Learning Commission, NCA. (2003). *Handbook of accreditation*. Chicago: Higher Learning Commission.

Johnson, D. K. (2002). *General education 2000—A national survey: How general education changed between 1989 and 2000*. Ph.D. dissertation, Pennsylvania State University. Retrieved March 10, 2005, from http://etda.libraries.psu.edu/theses/approved/WorldWideFiles/ETD-201/thesis.pdf

Jones, A. M., & Hendry, C. (1994). The learning organization: Adult learning and organizational transformation. *British Journal of Management, 5*(2), 153–162.

Kanter, S. L., Gamson, Z. F., & London, H. B. (1997). *Revitalizing general education in a time of scarcity*. Boston: Allyn and Bacon.

Keup, J. R., Walker, A. A., Astin, H. S., & Lindholm, J. A. (1997). *Organizational culture and institutional transformation*. ED464521.

Kezar, A. & Eckel, P. (2002). The effect of institutional culture on change strategies in higher education. *Journal of Higher Education, 73*(4), 435–460.

Levine, A. (1978). *Handbook on undergraduate curriculum*. San Francisco: Jossey-Bass.

Lopez, C. (1999). General education regional accreditation standards and expectations. *Liberal Education, 85*(3), 46–51.

MacDonald, W. B. (2003). *Trends in general education and core curriculum: A survey*. Retrieved January 28, 2003, from http://www.erin.utoronto.ca/~w3asc/trends.htm

Miller, D. (1996). A preliminary typology of organizational learning: Synthesizing the literature. *Journal of Management, 22*(3), 485–505.

Morgan, G. (1986). *Images of organization*. London: Sage Publications.

Newton, R. R. (2000). Tensions and models in general education planning. *Journal of General Education, 49*(3), 165–181.

Ott, J. S. (1989). *The organizational culture perspective*. Chicago: Dorsey Press.

Pedler, M., Burgoyne, J., & Boydell, T. (1991). *The learning company*. London: McGraw-Hill.

Perin, M. G., & Sampaio, C. H. (nd). *The relationship between learning orientation and innovation*. Retrieved April 4, 2003, from http://read.adm.ufrgs.br/read36/artigos/Article%2006.pdf

Peterson, M., & Spencer, M. (1991). Understanding academic culture and climate. In M. Peterson (Ed.), *ASHE reader on organization and governance* (pp. 140–155). Needham Heights, MA: Simon & Schuster.

Probst, G., & Buchel, (1997). *Organizational learning*. London: Prentice-Hall.

Ratcliff, J. L. (1997a). Quality and coherence in general education. In J. G. Gaff, J. L. Ratcliff & Associates (1997). *Handbook of the undergraduate curriculum: A comprehensive guide to purposes, structures, practices and change* (pp. 141–169). San Francisco: Jossey-Bass.

Ratcliff, J. L. (1997b). What is a curriculum and what should it be? In J. G. Gaff, J. L. Ratcliff & Associates (1997). *Handbook of the undergraduate curriculum: A comprehensive guide to purposes, structures, practices and change* (pp. 5–29). San Francisco: Jossey-Bass.

Ratcliff, J. L. (September 2000). A model for understanding curricular coherence and transparency. Paper presented at the Annual European Association for Institutional Research Forum, Freie Universitat, Berlin, Germany.

Ratcliff, J. L., Johnson, D. K., La Nasa, S. M., & Gaff, J. G. (2001). *The status of general education in the year 2000: Summary of a national survey*. Washington, DC: Association of American Colleges and Universities.

Reisman, D., Gusfield, J. & Gamson, Z. (1970). *Academic values and mass education: The story of Oakland and Monteith*. New York: Doubleday.

Rudolph, F. (1977). *Curriculum: A history of the American undergraduate course of study since 1636*. San Francisco: Jossey-Bass.

Schein, E. (1984). Coming to a new awareness of organizational culture. *Sloan Management Review, 25*(2), 3–16.

Schein, E. (1985). *Organizational culture and leadership: A dynamic view*. San Francisco: Jossey-Bass.

Selfridge, R. J. and Sokolik, S. L. (1975). A comprehensive view of organizational development. *Business Topics,* 47.

Simsek, H., & Louis K.S. (1994). Organizational change as a paradigm shift: Analysis of the change process in a large, public university. *Journal of Higher Education, 65*(6), 670–695.

Smircich, L. (1983a). Concepts of culture and organizational analysis. *Administrative Science Quarterly, 28*(3), 339–358.

Smircich, (1983b). Organizations as shared meanings. In L. R. Pondy, P. Frost, G. Morgan, and T. Dandridge (Eds.), *Organizational Symbolism* (pp. 55–65). Greenwich, CT: JAI press.

Stark, J. S., & Lattuca, L. R. (1997). *Shaping the college curriculum: Academic plans in action*. Boston: Allyn & Bacon.

Swieringa, K., & Wierdsma (1992). *Becoming a learning organization: Beyond the learning curve*. Wokingham: Addison-Wesley.

Tierney, W. G. (1988). Organizational culture in higher education: Defining the essentials. *Journal of Higher Education, 59*(1), 2–21.

Toma, J. D. (997). Alternative inquiry paradigms, faculty cultures, and the definition of academic lives. *Journal of Higher Education, 68*(6), 679–705.

Trader-Leigh, K. E. (2002). Case study: Identifying resistance in managing change. *Journal of Organizational Change Management, 15*(2), 138–155.

THE LIMITS OF SERVICE-LEARNING IN HIGHER EDUCATION

DAN W. BUTIN

Introduction

The service-learning movement has become a major presence within higher education. More than 950 colleges and universities are Campus Compact members, committed to the civic purposes of higher education. Tens of thousands of faculty engage millions of college students in some form of service-learning practice each and every year. Major federal and private funding sustains and expands an increasingly diverse K-16 service-learning movement.

The substantial spread of service-learning over the last ten years mirrors a larger development in the academy—namely, higher education has begun to embrace a "scholarship of engagement" (Boyer, 1990; Shulman, 2004), be it manifested as experiential education, service-learning, undergraduate research, community-based research, the scholarship of teaching and learning movement, or stronger relationships with local communities. A scholarship of engagement is seen to link theory and practice, cognitive and affective learning, and colleges with communities. Such a paradigm of teaching and learning seemingly breaches the bifurcation of lofty academics with the lived reality of everyday life to promote critical inquiry and reflective practice across complex and contested local, national, and international issues.

Yet even as the idea of service-learning moves into the academic mainstream, its actual institutional footprint appears uncertain. Service-learning is all too often positioned as a co-curricular practice, funded through "soft" short-term grants, and viewed by faculty as "just" an atheoretical (and time-consuming) pedagogy that may be detrimental for traditional tenure and promotion committees to take seriously. It is in this context that service-learning advocates have begun to devote intensive efforts to institutionalize service-learning within higher education. As service-learning practice and theory has reached a critical mass, attention has turned in the last few years to ensuring its institutional longevity.

In this article, I take a critical look at the attempted institutionalization of service-learning in higher education. I query whether service-learning can become deeply embedded within the academy; and, if so, what exactly it is that becomes embedded. Specifically, this article suggests that there are substantial pedagogical, political, and institutional limits to service-learning across the academy. These limits, moreover, are inherent to the service-learning movement as contemporarily theorized and enacted. As such, I argue, there may be a fundamental and unbridgeable gap between the rhetoric and reality of the aspirations of the present-day service-learning movement.

It should be noted that the goal of this article is not to dismiss, denigrate, or derail the immense work put in by two generations of service-learning scholars and advocates. Service-learning has immense transformational potential as a sustained, immersive, and consequential pedagogical practice (Butin, 2005a). Yet such potential, I suggest, can be fostered only by explicating the limits of present-day theoretical foundations and pedagogical practices that may inadvertently inhibit and constrain service-learning scholars and practitioners. As the concluding section makes clear, such

Reprinted by permission from the *Review of Higher Education* 29, no. 4 (summer 2006).

an explication may in fact offer substantial alternative possibilities for institutionalizing service-learning in higher education.

This article situates the service-learning movement through an analysis of its drive towards institutionalization. Such an analysis reveals some of the fundamental and underlying assumptions of the service-learning field. I then show how these assumptions harbor significant pedagogical, political, and institutional impediments for the authentic institutionalization of service-learning. I conclude by suggesting how a reframing of such assumptions may allow service-learning to be repositioned as a disciplinary field more suitable for becoming deeply embedded in higher education.

Institutionalizing Service-Learning

After a heady decade of exponential growth, the service-learning movement appears ideally situated within higher education. It is used by a substantial number of faculty across an increasingly diverse range of academic courses; administrative offices and centers are devoted to promoting its use; and it is prominently cited in college and university presidents' speeches, on institutional homepages, and in marketing brochures.

Yet as the recent Wingspread statement (2004) put it: "The honeymoon period for engagement is over; the difficult task of creating a lasting commitment has begun" (p. 4). For underneath the surface, the service-learning movement has found its institutionalization within higher education far from secure. Fewer than half of all service-learning directors are full-time, and 46% of all service-learning offices have annual budgets below $20,000 (Campus Compact, 2004). While the idea of service-learning is given high support across the academy, it is infrequently "hard wired" into institutional practices and policies. Service-learning is overwhelmingly used by the least powerful and most marginalized faculty (e.g., people of color, women, and the untenured), by the "softest" and most "vocational" disciplines and fields (e.g., education, social work), and with minimal exchange value (e.g., tenure and promotion prioritization) (Antonio, Astin, & Cross, 2000; Campus Compact, 2004). Recent research (Bell et al., 2000) suggests that even institutions at the top of the "service-learning pyramid" consistently have to revisit and rework service-learning implementation and institutionalization.

More troubling still is that the academy's "buy in" to service-learning may be much easier said than done, with few political or institutional costs for failing to achieve substantial goals. Rhetoric may be winning over reality. It is thus that the Wingspread Statement "call[s] the question": "Is higher education ready to commit to engagement?" (Brukardt et al., 2004, p. ii). This can be framed in poker parlance of calling the bluff. Does higher education have the desire, the long-term fortitude, and the resources to remake itself? Is higher education able, for the sake of itself, its students, and American society more generally, to embrace a more engaged, democratic, and transformative vision of what it should be, should have been, and was before? (Benson, Harkavy, & Hartley, 2005). If so, then it had better ante up.

There is thus a burgeoning literature on the institutionalization of service-learning. I want to focus on Andy Furco's work (2001, 2002a, 2002b, 2003; Furco & Billig, 2002) and on the Wingspread statement because each takes a diametrically opposed stance on the *means* of institutionalizing service-learning; both, however, carry exactly the same assumptions of what the *outcomes* of such institutionalization should be. While the literature is ever-growing and far from singular in perspective (Bell et al., 2000; Benson, Harkavy, & Hartley, 2005; Bringle & Hatcher, 2000; Gray, Ondaatje, & Zakaras, 2000; Hartley, Harkavy, & Benson, 2005; Holland, 2001; Kramer, 2000), Furco's work and the Wingspread statement are emblematic of the dominant vision and goals for service-learning institutionalization and the two primary and divergent paths to achieving such goals.

Specifically, Furco's work offers a systematic rubric for gauging the *incremental* progress of service-learning institutionalization; the Wingspread statement, in contrast, promotes a *transformational* vision for service-learning in higher education. Educational historian Larry Cuban (1990, 1998) has cogently referred to this distinction as first- versus second-order change and has explored the historical contexts and conditions that support one form of educational reform over another. More interesting for this article is that, irrespective of the divergent means propounded, both perspectives have a vision of service-learning as a meta-text for the policies, practices, and philosophies of higher education. Thus, irrespective of how it is to be institutionalized, service-learning is seen as the skeleton key to unlock the power and potential of postsecondary education as a force for democracy and social justice. By further explicating the divergent means propounded by incrementalist and transformationalist perspectives, it becomes possible to grasp the overarching assumptions and implications of the service-learning movement.

Furco (2002b) has developed a rubric for viewing the institutionalization of service-learning. The rubric acts as a road map that individuals and institutions committed to embedding service-learning throughout their campuses may follow. It further works as a formal or informal assessment mechanism to gauge progress along the institutionalization path. Furco operationalizes institutionalization across five distinct dimensions "which are considered by most service-learning experts to be key factors for higher education service-learning institutionalization" (p. 1): (a) philosophy and mission, (b) faculty support and involvement, (c) student support and involvement, (d) community participation and partnerships, and (e) institutional support. While Furco argues elsewhere (2001, 2002a, 2003) that research identifies the key institutional factors as faculty and institutional support, the rubric makes clear that "What is most important is the overall status of the campus's institutionalization progress rather than the progress of individual components" (p. 3).

The real value and usefulness of the rubric is that it clearly and succinctly lays out the step-by-step increments by which a campus can institutionalize service-learning. Faculty support for and involvement in service-learning, for example, moves from "very few" to "an adequate number" to "a substantial number" of faculty who are knowledgeable about, involved in, and leaders of service-learning on a campus. Staffing moves from "no staff" to "an appropriate number . . . paid from soft money or external grant funds" to "an appropriate number of permanent staff members" (p. 13). The rubric does not suggest how such incremental progress is to be achieved; each campus culture and context is different. Instead, it lays out an explicit framework for (in Cuban's terminology) "tinkering" toward institutionalization.

The Wingspread participants (Brukardt et al., 2004) have a fundamentally different agenda: "Our goal in calling the question is nothing less than the transformation of our nation's colleges and universities" (p. ii). Six specific practices are articulated to institutionalize engagement and accomplish this goal: (a) integrate engagement into mission, (b) forge partnerships as the overarching framework, (c) renew and redefine discovery and scholarship, (d) integrate engagement into teaching and learning, (e) recruit and support new champions, and (f) create radical institutional change. Many of these practices mirror Furco's rubric and are possible to implement without radical transformation: integrating engagement into a mission statement, forging stronger partnerships, fostering more engaged pedagogy, and recruiting new voices to speak for engagement are all doable without fundamentally altering the structure and practices of higher education.[1]

What *is* radically different are the third and sixth practices. Redefining scholarship and creating radical institutional change by, for example, overturning higher education's "hierarchical, elitist and competitive environment" (p. 15) is a revolutionary call to arms. And the Wingspread participants are well aware of this. Each specific practice in the statement has a "What Is Needed" section that offers concrete action steps. For example, it recommends "expanded assessment and portfolio review options for faculty" (Brukardt et al., 2004, p. 14) to integrate engagement into teaching and learning. This seems eminently reasonable. Yet under the "Create Radical Institutional Change" section, what is needed is "Courage!", "New models", "Serious . . . funding", "New links between academic work and critical public issues", and "Institutional flexibility and willingness to experiment—and to fail." These are not action steps. They are a battle cry.

Thus, where Furco's rubric offers a deliberate and deliberative procession of rational increments, the *Wingspread Statement* provides a fiery manifesto for reinvention. Irrespective of which model is better (or whether, perhaps, both are necessary), of relevance is that both assume that, by whichever means necessary, service-learning should become an overarching framework for higher education. This framework, moreover, should be embedded both horizontally across departments and vertically throughout all levels of an institution's pronouncements, policies, and practices. Both presume that service-learning can and should be done from accounting to women's studies; that all students, faculty, administrators, and community partners can be involved; and that everything from line-item budgets to institutional webpages have the imprint of service-learning.

Such a scenario is nothing less than a grand narrative for higher-education-as-service-learning, for it positions service-learning *as a politics* to transform higher education and society. The implications are both prominent and problematic. Such a perspective presumes that service-learning is a universal, coherent, cohesive, ameliorical, and liberatory practice. It further presumes that service-learning is not somehow always already a part of the institutional practices and norms it is attempting to modify and overcome. Yet as the following sections clarify, such presumptions are unfounded.

The Limits of Institutionalization

In this section I question the notion of service-learning as an overarching and transformative agent of social change and social justice in higher education and society more generally by focusing on three specific claims made by the service-learning movement—that service-learning is a means (a) to transform pedagogy, (b) to usher in a more democratic and socially just politics in higher education, and (c) to redirect postsecondary institutions outward toward public work rather than inward toward academic elitism.

These claims, it should be noted, are premised on an inherent compatibility between service-learning and the academy. This seeming compatibility indexes assumptions that civic engagement and "real world" learning are hallmarks of the future of higher education. Yet such assumptions are, of course, open to contestation and critique, perhaps the most biting of which has come from Stanley Fish. Fish (2004) has opined that we should stick to questions about the truth and not bother with issues of morality, democracy, or social justice: "We should look to the practices in our own shop, narrowly conceived, before we set out to alter the entire world by forming moral character, or fashioning democratic citizens, or combating globalization, or embracing globalization, or anything else" (p. A23; see also Butin, 2005b, for a contextualization of this argument). Fish was responding directly to a publication from a group of scholars at the Carnegie Foundation's Higher Education and Development of Moral and Civic Responsibility Project (Colby et al., 2003), but his critique has general resonance for those who see the academy as primarily a site of knowledge production and dissemination rather than of something as nondefinable and potentially partisan as moral and civic betterment.

I am sympathetic to Fish's arguments and have elsewhere explicated the theoretical limits of service-learning as beholden to a teleological and ethical stage theory framework in which students and faculty are supposed to move from a perspective of "service-learning as charity" to "service-learning as social justice" (Butin, 2003, 2005b, in press-a). Yet such larger theoretical debates about the values and purposes of service-learning vis-à-vis higher education are ultimately beyond the scope of this article, for the question today is no longer *if* service-learning is to become a part of the academy so much as *how* it is already becoming a part of it and the resulting implications.

Pedagogical Limits to Service-Learning

Advocates see service-learning as a transformative pedagogy that links classrooms with the real world, the cognitive with the affective, and theory with practice, thereby disrupting a banking model of education premised on passive students, expert faculty, and the "simple" transfer of discrete and quantifiable knowledge (Freire, 1994; hooks, 1994). Service-learning is supposed to foster respect for and reciprocity with the communities that colleges and universities are all too often in but not of.

But is this possible? Campus Compact's (2004) annual membership survey shows the following departments with the highest offering of service-learning courses: education (69%), sociology (56%), English (55%), psychology (55%), business/accounting (46%), communications (46%), and health/health related (45%). In a now-classic formulation, Becher (Becher & Trowler, 2001) argued that academic disciplines can be differentiated along two spectra: hard/soft and pure/applied. Hard-pure fields (e.g., chemistry and physics) view knowledge as cumulative and are concerned with universals, simplification, and quantification. Hard-applied fields (e.g., engineering) make use of hard, pure knowledge to develop products and techniques. Soft-pure fields (e.g., English) view knowledge as iterative and are concerned with particularity and qualitative inquiry. Soft-applied fields (e.g., education, management) make use of soft, pure knowledge to develop protocols and heuristics. What becomes immediately clear is that service-learning is overwhelmingly used in the "soft" disciplines. Biology is the highest "hard" field (at number 10 with 37%), with the natural sciences next at number 18 (with 25%).

I, of course, acknowledge that the hard/soft and pure/applied distinctions are socially constructed typologies that carry longstanding ideological baggage and serve as proxies for contestations surrounding the power, legitimacy, and prestige of any particular discipline. Scholars in the sociology of knowledge and history of science have shown not simply the ambiguity and permeability of the boundaries between so-called "soft" and "hard" disciplines, but have fundamentally questioned the (to use Foucault's terminology) "scientificity" of claims to the objective and neutral practice of mapping reality (Hacking, 1999; Lather, 2005; Latour, 1979). Yet what is at issue here is not whether there is "really" a distinction between the hard and soft sciences, but how such a socially constructed distinction is ultimately determined and practiced in our day-to-day life. As Cornel West (1994) once wryly noted, taxicabs in Harlem still didn't stop for him even if race was a social construction. Likewise, there is a plethora of empirical evidence (Biglan, 1973; Lueddeke, 2003; NCES, 2002) that teaching practices differ significantly across disciplines; as such, these disciplinary distinctions serve as useful heuristics for understanding how service-learning may or may not be taken up across the academy.

The service-learning field acknowledges that soft disciplines are much more apt to make use of service-learning, yet proponents presume that this is simply a consequence of *either* poorly marketing what service-learning can offer the hard sciences (from an incrementalist perspective) or the inability of the hard sciences to transform themselves into useful public disciplines (from a transformational perspective). What both perspectives miss is that Becher's typology demonstrates that each grouping of disciplines manifests "its own epistemological characteristics . . . [of] curriculum, assessment and main cognitive purpose . . . [and] the group characteristics of teachers, the types of teaching methods involved and the learning requirements of students" (Neumann & Becher, 2002, p. 406).

Of most salience here are divergent concepts of teaching styles and assessment procedures between hard and soft disciplines. I will focus only on the hard disciplines here to make vivid their antipathy to service-learning assumptions. Given the sequential and factual nature of the hard disciplines, lecturing predominates as the teaching style. Moreover, the cumulative nature of knowledge makes moot any notion of student perspectives or "voice" in the field. It is simply not relevant how students "feel" about subatomic particles. As such, "in keeping with their atomistic structure [hard/pure knowledge fields] prefer specific and closely focused examination questions to broader, essay-type assignments" (Neumann & Becher, 2002, p. 408). "Objective" tests, norm-referenced grading, and lack of rubrics (given the right/wrong nature of what constitutes knowledge) are typical.

U.S. Department of Education statistics support these theoretical insights. The most recent available data (NCES, 2002, Table 16) show that the social sciences and humanities use apprenticeships and fieldwork much more often (10–15% depending on the discipline) than the natural sciences (2–3%). Humanities and social sciences faculty are almost twice as likely to use research papers than natural science faculty (70–85% versus 40–50%, respectively), and half as likely to grade on a curve (20–30% versus 40–50%) (Tables 18, 22). While some of these data are confounded by the type of institution (e.g., doctoral versus nondoctoral institutions), fairly distinct patterns and differences among disciplines are visible.

Above and beyond these disciplinary differences, though, emerges a more troubling realization. Fully 83% of all faculty use lecturing as the primary instructional method in college classrooms. This percentage does not drastically change across the type of institution, faculty rank or tenure status, or discipline (NCES, 2002, Tables 15, 16). Thus, irrespective of disciplinary and epistemological differences, the vast majority of faculty in higher education see themselves as embodying the normative (read: non service-learning-oriented) model of teaching and learning.[2] This dominant trend is further exacerbated by the reality that non-tenure track faculty by now constitute almost half of all teaching faculty in higher education (Snyder, Tan, & Hoffman, 2004). A normative model of teaching is thus reinforced by the marginal and transitory status of faculty. There thus appears to be a very low upper limit to the use of service-learning across higher education.

If faculty demographics do not conform to who should make use of service-learning, then student demographics do not align with the type of students supposedly doing service-learning. I have argued elsewhere that the service-learning field assumes an "ideal type" of service-learning student: one who volunteers her time, has high cultural capital, and gains from contact with the "other" (Butin, 2003). The service-learning literature is replete with discussions of how students come to better understand themselves, cultural differences, and social justice through service-learning. The overarching assumption is that the students doing the service-learning are White, sheltered, middle-class, single, without children, un-indebted, and between ages 18 and 24. But that is not the demographics of higher education today, and it will be even less so in 20 years.

NCES (Snyder, Tan, & Hoffman, 2004) data show that the largest growth in postsecondary enrollment will be in for-profit and two-year institutions; already today, fully 39% of all postsecondary enrollment is in two-year institutions (Table 178). Moreover, 34% of undergraduates are over 25 years of age; 40% of undergraduates are part-time. Even considering just full-time undergraduates, more than 18% are over 25 years of age (Tables 176, 177). Additionally, college completion rates continue to be low: fewer than half of all college entrants complete a baccalaureate degree, with graduation percentages dipping much lower for two-year institutions and among part-time, lower-class, and/or non-White students. Finally, U.S. census data forecast that White youth will become a numeric minority in our K-12 schools within a generation; this changing demographic wave is already impacting the makeup of higher education.

These statistics raise three serious pedagogical issues for the service-learning field. First, service-learning is premised on full-time, single, non-indebted, and childless students pursuing a "liberal arts education." Yet a large proportion of the postsecondary population of today, and increasingly of the future, views higher education as a part-time, instrumental, and pre-professional endeavor that must be juggled with children, family time, and earning a living wage. Service-learning may be a luxury that many students cannot afford, whether in terms of time, finances, or job future.

Second, service-learning is premised on fostering "border-crossing" across categories of race, ethnicity, class, (im)migrant status, language, and (dis)ability. Yet what happens when the postsecondary population *already* occupies those identity categories? The service-learning field is only now beginning to explore such theoretical and pragmatic dilemmas (e.g., Henry, 2005; Henry & Breyfogle, in press; Swaminathan, 2005, in press), and these investigations are already disrupting some of the most basic categories within the service-learning field (e.g., the server/served binary, student/teacher and classroom/community power dynamics and reciprocity).

Third, there is a distinct possibility that service-learning may ultimately come to be viewed as the "Whitest of the White" enclave of postsecondary education. Given changing demographics and the rise of the "client-centered" postsecondary institution, service-learning may come to signify a luxury available only to the privileged few. Educational research has clearly shown how inequities across K-12 academic tracks (in e.g., teacher quality, adequate resources, and engaging curricula) correlates to youth's skin color and socioeconomic status. Such hierarchies within service-learning in higher education are not unthinkable.

Arguments can, of course, be made from both incrementalist and transformationalist perspectives. The former will argue that these issues will simply take more time to work through while the latter will argue that, in transforming higher education, such issues will become irrelevant. Perhaps. The goal here is not to be defeatist, presentist, or conservative; it is not to argue that higher education is a static and unchangeable monolith. Rather, my goal is simply to map out the structures and norms that inhibit the institutionalization of a viable and powerful service-learning pedagogy.

Political Limits to Service-Learning

Even if service-learning succeeds in overcoming the pedagogical barriers just described, what exactly is it that will become institutionalized? By framing service-learning as a politics, advocates may in fact be undermining their most valued goal. Specifically, by viewing service-learning as a universal transformative practice, advocates may allow it to become misappropriated and drained of its transformative potential.

Service-learning has a progressive and liberal agenda under the guise of a universalistic practice. The *Presidents' Declaration on the Civic Responsibility of Higher Education* (Campus Compact, 2000), for example, declares:

> Higher education is uniquely positioned to help Americans understand the histories and contours of our present challenges as a diverse democracy. It is also uniquely positioned to help both students and our communities to explore new ways of fulfilling the promise of justice and dignity for all . . . . We know that pluralism is a source of strength and vitality that will enrich our students' education and help them learn both to respect difference and to work together for the common good. (p. 1)

This is a noble and neutral sounding statement. Who could be against "the common good"? Yet clearly, the "diversity" and "dignity" being spoken are not those belonging to political conservatives. Rather, the reference is to the multiple populations within the United States who have suffered historically (and many still do today) due to social, cultural, economic, and educational marginalization, degradation, and destruction.

This view has a certain natural-seeming quality within the academy, as higher education is supposed to expand its participants' perspectives about how to think and act differently in becoming a public citizen. Yet while this goal also has a deep resonance with the service-learning field (and, some might say, is at the heart of the service-learning field [see Stanton, Giles, & Cruz, 1999]), it is certainly not the norm in our highly divided red state/blue state America. The most obvious example of this division is David Horowitz's (n.d.) "academic bill of rights."

Horowitz, the president of the Center for Study of Popular Culture, has crafted a seemingly neutral policy declaration demanding that colleges and universities not discriminate against political or religious orientations, thus enabling "academic freedom and intellectual diversity" to flourish in the academy. "Academic freedom," the document states,

> consists in protecting the intellectual independence of professors, researchers and students in pursuit of knowledge and the expression of ideas from interference by legislatures or authorities within the institution itself. This means that no political, ideological or religious orthodoxy will be imposed on professors and researchers through the hiring or tenure or termination process, or through any other administrative means by the academic institution. (p. 1)

The document goes on to enumerate numerous principles and procedures that flow from this statement of principle. These include, among others, that a faculty member cannot be "hired or fired or denied promotion or tenure on the basis of his or her political or religious beliefs," that "students will be graded solely on the basis of their reasoned answers," and that "exposing students to the spectrum of significant scholarly viewpoints on the subjects examined in their courses is a major responsibility of faculty. Faculty will not use their courses for the purpose of political, ideological, religious or antireligious indoctrination" (p. 2). These proposals sound eminently reasonable until one realizes that Horowitz is deliberately attempting to dismantle what he sees as the liberal orthodoxy permeating higher education.

Horowitz and Lehrer (n.d.) have shown, and social science research confirms (Lindholm et al., 2005; Klein & Stern, 2005; Rothman, Lichter, & Nevitte, 2005), that higher education faculty are overwhelming registered as Democrats, with (according to his data) an overall ratio of 10 to 1 across departments and upper-level administrations. On some campuses (e.g., Williams, Oberlin, Haverford), Horowitz could not find a single registered Republican faculty member. This, Horowitz (2003) argues, is not diversity:

> What is knowledge if it is thoroughly one-sided, or intellectual freedom if it is only freedom to conform? And what is a "liberal education," if one point of view is for all intents and purposes excluded from the classroom? How can students get a good education, if they are only being told one side of the story? The answer is they can't. (p. 1)

The attack on the liberal leanings of higher education is not new. What is new, though, are Horowitz's (2003) proposed strategies:

> I have undertaken the task of organizing conservative students myself and urging them to protest a situation that has become intolerable. *I encourage them to use the language that the left has deployed so effectively in behalf of its own agendas.* Radical professors have created a "hostile learning environment" for conservative students. There is a lack of "intellectual diversity" on college faculties and in academic classrooms. The conservative viewpoint is "under-represented" in the curriculum and on its reading lists. The university should be an "inclusive" and intellectually "diverse" community. I have encouraged students to demand that their schools adopt an "academic bill of rights" that stresses intellectual diversity, that demands balance in their reading lists, that recognizes that political partisanship by professors in the classroom is an abuse of students' academic freedom, that the inequity in funding of student organizations and visiting speakers is unacceptable, and that a learning environment hostile to conservatives is unacceptable. (pp. 2–3; emphasis mine)

Service-learning is not explicitly on the list of Horowitz's grievances, but it very well could (and might) be. The service-learning literature is replete with students' resistance to the implicit and/or explicit social justice emphasis. Susan Jones (2002; Jones, Gilbride-Brown, & Gasorski, 2005), for example, has carefully shown how student resistance manifests itself in service-learning experiences and how instructors might—through a "critical developmental lens"—begin to overcome such resistance. Yet what is clear is that such resistance is not about liberals resisting a conservative agenda; as one resistant student wrote in Jones's end-of-semester evaluation: "I don't enjoy the preaching of a debatable agenda in the first hour. Perhaps teaching from a more balanced perspective would be better than 'isms [that] are keeping us down'. . . . More emphasis on community service. Less on ideologically driven readings and lessons" (qtd. in Jones, Gilbride-Brown, & Gasorski, 2005, p. 14).

The point is not that service-learning should stop having an ideological agenda, nor that service-learning should now embrace conservative service-learning to provide "balance." Rather, it is that service-learning embodies a liberal agenda under the guise of universalistic garb. As such, it is ripe for conservative appropriation; to date, close to two dozen states have either proposed or are about to propose legislation patterned on the academic bill of rights.[3] In Pennsylvania, where I teach, the state legislature has approved a committee to investigate potential bias in the academy. Leading higher education organizations have recently released their own responses of what constitutes academic freedom (AACU, 2005). An era of legislative and public scrutinizing of higher education's political practices has begun.

Horowitz (or any university president under public pressure) can thus very easily raise the specter of service-learning offices that are indoctrinating first-year students into biased, unscientific, and indefensible liberal groupthink practices through, for example, daylong conferences about capital punishment or women's rights. The solutions? Horowitz would argue that either the entire service-learning office needs to be dismantled to avoid such blatant political abuse of public funds or that the university needs to completely rethink and redo how it helps students to think about such issues—by allowing undergraduates to work, for example, with a pro-life group to send out mailings or picketing with a retentionist organization committed to keeping the death penalty.

Service-learning is in a double-bind. If it attempts to be a truly radical and transformative (liberal) practice, it faces potential censure and sanction. If it attempts to be politically balanced to avoid such an attack, it risks losing any power to make a difference. At the root of this double-bind and the reason it cannot escape from this dilemma is that service-learning has positioned itself as a universalistic and thus neutral practice.

But as Stanley Fish (1999) has pointed out, there is no such thing.[4] "If, for example, I say 'Let's be fair,' you won't know what I mean unless I've specified the background conditions in relation to which fairness has an operational sense" (p. 3). No statements or positions are value-free; they come saturated with particular historical, social, and cultural baggage. Thus, not only do genuinely neutral principles not exist, but when seemingly neutral principles *are* articulated, it is a blatantly political and strategic move. Fish continues:

> Indeed, it is crucial that neutral principles not exist if they are to perform the function I have described, the function of facilitating the efforts of partisan agents to attach an honorific vocabulary to their agendas. For the effort to succeed, the vocabulary (of "fairness," "merit," "neutrality," "impartiality," mutual respect," and so on) must be empty, have no traction or bite of its own, and thus be an unoccupied vessel waiting to be filled by whoever gets to it first or with the most persuasive force. (p. 7)

Seemingly neutral principles are thus used strategically to promote one's specific ideological agenda, irrespective of political orientation. This is exactly what Horowitz has done with "intellectual diversity" and what the service-learning movement is attempting to do with "civic engagement." But in attempting to hold the (imaginary) center, such strategizing in fact politicizes the term in question through binary extremism. In the former case, "intellectual diversity" becomes a stalking horse for right-wing conservatism; in the latter case, "civic engagement" becomes linked to radical left-wing demands for "social justice" (Butin, in press-a).

Service-learning thus finds itself positioned as attempting to deliver a very specific and highly political notion of the truth under the guise of neutral pedagogy. Its overarching stage theory of moving individuals and institutions from charity-based perspectives to justice-oriented ones, in fact, maps directly onto our folk theories of what constitutes Republican and Democratic political positions: Republicans believe in individual responsibility and charity while Democrats focus on institutional structures and social justice (Westheimer & Kahne, 2004).

To claim service-learning as a universalistic practice available to all political persuasions is thus to ignore its politically liberal trappings as presently conceptualized and enacted. To cite just one obvious counter-example, is it service-learning if Jerry Falwell's Liberty University requires as a graduation requirement that all undergraduates spend a certain amount of time helping to blockade abortion clinics and thus saving the lives of the unborn? What if this activity was linked to reflection groups and learning circles and students had to create portfolios showing how such community service was linked to their academic courses?

Few service-learning advocates, I suggest, would quickly or easily accept that this is service-learning, much less service-learning committed to social justice. But to not accept such a counter-example is to admit that service-learning is not a universalistic practice. It is to admit that service-learning is an ideologically driven practice. And in so doing, service-learning falls neatly into the "intellectual diversity" trap. Once trapped, there is no way out. Service-learning, in order to survive in higher education, will have to become "balanced."

Institutional Limits to Service-Learning

I have suggested so far that service-learning faces major pedagogical and political barriers to becoming institutionalized. Yet if service-learning could overcome these pedagogical and political barriers, would it then be the truly transformative movement envisioned? Again, sadly, I doubt it, for higher education works by very specific disciplinary rules about knowledge production, who has the academic legitimacy to produce such knowledge, and how (Messer-Davidow, Shumway, & Sylvan, 1993). The very institution that service-learning advocates are trying to storm, in other words, may drown them.

The clearest example of this already-ongoing process is what I'll term the "quantitative move" in the service-learning field. Put otherwise, service-learning scholarship is becoming adept at using the "statistically significant" nomenclature. The idea is to show that service-learning can, holding all other variables constant, positively impact student outcomes. Thus, a wide variety of scholarly studies has shown service-learning to be a statistically significant practice in impacting, among other things, students' personal and interpersonal development, stereotype reduction, sense of citizenship, and academic learning. (See Eyler et al., 2001, for a comprehensive summary.) Much of this research has very low betas (i.e., the actual impact is not, statistically speaking, profound); nevertheless, service-learning has been "proven" to make a measurable difference in a positive direction vis-à-vis other pedagogical and institutional variables.

The idea behind this quantitative move is obvious. Service-learning advocates want to show that service-learning is a legitimate practice with legitimate, consequential, and measurable outcomes in higher education. When in Rome, the thinking goes, do as the Romans. The problem is that Rome has burned. There are three distinct reasons why the quantitative move ultimately will not help to institutionalize the kind of service-learning hoped for.

The first reason is that quantifying the value-added of service-learning is methodologically impossible. There are simply too many variables commingling and interacting with each other to allow for valid and reliable conclusions. The number of variables, from type of sites to types of interactions to types of reflection to types of teaching styles, becomes too unmanageable to accurately quantify and measure. In this way service-learning is analogous to teaching and other "wickedly" complex problems defying quantitative solutions.

For example, educational researchers have for 30 years been trying to adequately quantify the most basic principle in the field: what makes a high-quality teacher. Yet as the research supporting the No Child Left Behind legislation and the push for alternative certification pathways shows, there are no such data (at least none that can be agreed upon).[5] While on its face such uncertainty is absurd, it is also the end result and consequence of a quixotic search for absolute and quantifiable surety. None exists, and attempts to find it quickly become beholden to political pressures about which variables are measured and how. I do not deny that the quantitative move offers some basic guidance on some basic proxy variables. This is an important development. But to pin the legitimacy of service-learning on its quantification is to misunderstand how legitimacy ultimately works.

This strategy of legitimization is, in fact, the second reason why the quantitative move falters in the academy—namely, the paradigms by which we see the world are inextricably linked to our value systems as legitimate scholars. Thomas Kuhn, in his classic *The Structure of Scientific Revolutions* (1996), posited that paradigms shift, not because of rational discourse among objective scientists but because the old guard dies away and is replaced by the young turks with their own particular paradigm. While the conservative status-quo nature of this view has been roundly critiqued, the underlying psychological framework seems sound (see, e.g., Gardner, 2004): the more contested and revolutionary an issue, the stronger our resistance to it.

To again use an example from teacher education, a recent review of the literature on teacher change argued: "What we see expressed in these current studies of teacher education is the difficulty in changing the type of tacit beliefs and understandings that lie buried in a person's being" (Richardson & Placier, 2001, p. 915). Thus after four years of coursework, field experiences, and self-selective dispositions toward becoming a good teacher, the vast majority of teacher candidates leave their programs believing pretty much what they came in with.

It is thus naive for service-learning advocates to believe that a large number of academics will be persuaded to accept service-learning simply because data show it to have a statistically significant impact on any particular student outcome. As I have argued elsewhere (Butin, 2005b), a simple thought experiment puts this lie to rest: If data showed that students' work with terminally ill AIDS patients negatively impacted student understanding of the social health system, would that be reason enough to stop the program? Probably not. Service-learning advocates would instead

> question the validity and reliability of such data: How is "understanding" being measured? Is success defined instrumentally (i.e., test grades) or holistically (i.e., emotional intelligence, long-term changes)? What was the timeframe of my assessment procedures? Did I use pre- and post-tests or interviews? Was there an adequate control group? (p. 102)

Of course, if such data were consistent and long-term there might be good reasons to desist or substantially modify the service-learning component. But not only are most data not rigorous enough to warrant immediate acceptance, they also function as only a small part of how we marshal evidence to support our views of the world. The quantitative move toward statistically significant measurement thus cannot, on its own, convince scholars to embrace or reject service-learning.

The third reason that the quantitative move in service-learning undermines, rather than promotes, the institutionalization of service-learning is because it *is* quantitative. David Labaree (2004) has used Becher's typology of academic disciplines to point out the decidedly problematic implications of a soft discipline (in this case educational research) in search of a hard disguise:

> In order to create a solid ground for making hard claims about education, you can try to drain the swamp of human action and political purpose that makes this institution what it is, but the result is a science of something other than education as it is experienced by teachers and students. As I have argued elsewhere [Labaree, 1997], such an effort may have more positive impact on the status of researchers (for whom hard science is the holy grail) than the quality of learning in schools, and it may lead us to reshape education in the image of our own hyper-rationalized and disembodied constructs rather than our visions of the good school. (p. 75)

The scientific quantification of any human practice is what Max Weber (Sica, 2000) termed "rationalization." It is the attempt to order and systematize, for the sake of efficiency and (thus supposedly) progress, practices that were formally intuitive, haphazard, and grounded in heuristics rather than science. The point again is not that we should avoid scientific inquiry; rather, simply put, the point is that this is not at the heart of service-learning, nor should it be. To promote service-learning in the academy through quantification is to buy into a paradigm not of its own making. The quantitative move may helps service-learning scholars gain a certain legitimacy in the academy. What it will not do is expand the boundaries of how to think about the academy, and it will not provide a decidedly different discourse of how service-learning should be institutionalized.

Possibilities for Service-Learning in Higher Education

Thinking about service-learning as a form of politics has deep rhetorical resonance. Service-learning advocates argue that its practices and policies are uplifting and transformational for all involved. Yet as I have argued in the sections above, such rhetorical resonance also has limited and limiting possibilities for institutionalizing service-learning in the academy. Such an approach cannot overcome the deep and specific pedagogical, political, and institutional barriers.

It is beyond the scope of this article to provide a comprehensive alternative to the problematics just outlined. Rather, what I want to make clear is that the limits just outlined are fundamentally linked to the undergirding theoretical presuppositions of contemporary service-learning theory and practice. I want to thus briefly explicate such presuppositions in order to rethink and reframe how service-learning may be otherwise institutionalized.

Fundamentally, advocates presume service-learning to be a politics by which to transform higher education. As such, service-learning becomes positioned within the binary of an "oppositional social movement" embedded within the "status quo" academy. Moreover, this perspective reifies (and thus assumes) service-learning as a coherent and cohesive pedagogical strategy, able to see its own blind spots as it pursues liberal and always liberatory agendas.

But such is not the case. The service-learning movement is an amalgam of, among other things, experiential education, action research, critical theory, progressive education, adult education, social justice education, constructivism, community-based research, multicultural education, and undergraduate research. It is viewed as a form of community service, as a pedagogical methodology, as a strategy for cultural competence and awareness, as a social justice orientation, and as a philosophical worldview (see, e.g., Butin, 2003; Kendall, 1990; Lisman, 1998; Liu, 1995; Morton, 1995; Westheimer & Kahne, 2004). An immense diversity of ofttimes clashing perspectives thus cohabits under the service-learning umbrella.

Likewise, the service-learning movement has often downplayed or glossed over the minimal social justice outcomes of service-learning practices. For all of the human, fiscal, and institutional resources devoted to service-learning across higher education, there are, in fact, very minimal on-the-ground changes in the academy, in local communities, or in society more generally.

I do not dispute that, in isolated situations with unique circumstances, profound changes have occurred. What I am simply pointing out is that service-learning should not have to bear the burden (nor the brunt) of being the social justice standard-bearer. To do so would be to set up an impossible causal linkage between service-learning and social betterment. Much scholarship, for example, can be marshaled to show that the divisions in our society based on categories of race, class, ethnicity, and language have, in many cases, become worse, not better; that democracy for all intents and purposes has become a spectator sport as most of us (and particularly youth) have disengaged from the public sphere; and that the United States is the worst offender in the developed world of human principles and ethical norms for the treatment of its incarcerated population. Is this service-learning's fault? If service-learning succeeds as hoped in higher education and if these conditions continue to deteriorate, does this mean that service-learning is to blame? The issues cited have much more to do with a host of interconnected economic, social, political, and legal policies than they do with the percentage of faculty implementing service-learning on any particular campus.

What this realization makes clear is that thinking about service-learning as a politics to transform higher education is a theoretical cul-de-sac. I do not doubt that service-learning may in fact become deeply embedded within higher education. Yet I suggest that, service-learning scholars do not account for the pedagogical, political, and institutional limits enumerated, service-learning will have a minimal and unstable foundation for its longterm sustenance. Service-learning will become embedded only by giving up any analytic opportunity to understand how and why it is ultimately deeply limited.

All of the theoretical assumptions of the service-learning movement that I have just enumerated position it as a gleaming grand narrative. Service-learning scholars and activists want service-learning to be all things to all people. Service-learning wants to roam free across disciplines, across institutions, across society. It wants to change and transform any and all obstacles in its path. It wants freedom.

But that is not how things work in academia. Higher education is a disciplining mechanism, in all senses of the term. And that is a good thing. For to be disciplined is to carefully, systematically, and in a sustained fashion investigate whatever one is interested in doing, whether that is building bridges, changing communities, or understanding Kant. Positioning service-learning as a grand narrative is a set-up for implosion—from a vision to a mirage—for there is no mechanism by which a grand narrative can prevent itself from being questioned and critiqued once it has become a part of the academy. That is the basis of higher education and that is where, for better or worse, service-learning wants to be positioned.

The possibilities for service-learning, I thus suggest, lie in embracing rather than rejecting the very academy the service-learning movement is attempting to transform. More precisely, it is to speak about service-learning as akin to an academic discipline with the ability to control its knowledge production functions by internally debating and determining what issues are worthy of study, by what modes of inquiry, and to what ends. This approach assumes a plurality of perspectives of what service-learning is and should be. It assumes that the scholarship surrounding service-learning is not solely centripetal or convergent in focus.

Rather than continuing to think *about* service-learning as a politics to transform higher education and society, we might more fruitfully reverse the terminology and begin to think *through* service-learning about the politics of transforming higher education and society. (See Butin, in press-b, for a detailed explication of this argument.) I take this distinction from Robyn Wiegman's (2005; see also her 1999, 2002) analysis of the future of women's studies, specifically because I find the arc of institutionalization of women's studies in higher education instructive and applicable to the service-learning movement.

What women's studies has done over the last quarter century—through reasoned discourse and political pressure—has been to expand the academy's notion of what constitutes the "academic." Weigman argues that so long as women's studies and feminism were (and are) conflated with social activism, they risked being dismissed as yet another form of identitarian politics beholden to the unquestioned uplifting of an essentialized category (e.g., race, ethnicity, and gender). What makes women's studies an academic discipline and the gender(ed) subject the mode of inquiry is that its scholarship is able to both look outward (to examine an issue, such as education or the criminal justice system) and inward (to internally debate and determine what issues are worthy of study, by what modes of inquiry, and to what ends).

Women's studies, for example, was able to weather the storm of second-wave feminist critique (of being a White, middle-class and Western-centric enclave [see, e.g., DuBois, 1985; Moraga & Anzaldúa, 1981]) precisely *because* it could accommodate and appropriate such criticism within its academic purpose of teaching and research on the gendered subject. Wendy Brown (1997) could write an article entitled "The Impossibility of Women's Studies" only *because* such a critique was made possible by the academy's norms of what disciplines and the scholars within them are allowed to do.

There is no doubt that women's studies was disciplined in its institutionalization. It distanced itself from the "street" and from the fervent activism therein; it had to devote attention to bureaucratic maneuverings for funds and faculty rather than for institutional change and transformation; it had to settle for yearly conferences instead of round-the-clock activism. As Messer-Davidow (2002) phrases it, women's studies became routinized. Yet by becoming "disciplined," women's studies was able to produce the domains of objects and rituals of truth to be studied and recast. As such, I would argue, disciplinary institutionalization is not the negation of politics but the condition of its possibility. For it allows, in the safety of disciplinary parameters, scholars to debate and define themselves and their field.

Women's studies accomplished this goal by reversing its terminology to make the gender(ed) subject the mode of inquiry rather than using gender as the political project. I suggest that the service-learning field can do likewise by making community studies the mode of inquiry rather than using the community as a political project (Butin, in press-b). By reversing the terminology, by making community studies the disciplinary field, an entirely new model of practice becomes possible. It becomes possible to use all of the tools of the academy to analyze a very specific and bounded issue. Service-learning may no longer claim that it will change the face of higher education. But women's studies does not do that either anymore. Instead, women's studies scholars carefully and systematically elaborate how feminist perspectives are slowly infiltrating and modifying the ways specific disciplines and sub-disciplines work, think, and act (see, e.g., Stanton & Stewart, 1995). This is not radical and transformational change. This is disciplined change. It is the slow accretion, one arduous and deliberate step at a time, of contesting one worldview with another. Some of this contest is blatantly political. Some of it is deeply technical. Much of it is debatable, questionable, and modifiable—just like any good academic enterprise. And it is this process which is truly transformational.

At present, though, such heteroglossic analysis and critique is largely absent in the service-learning field. If service-learning is assumed to be "simply" a universal, coherent, and neutral pedagogical practice, then such an absence is understandable. But such is not the case, as this article makes clear. It thus becomes incumbent on scholars committed to a scholarship of engagement in general and to service-learning specifically to probe the limits of service-learning in higher education. For without an explicit articulation of its own limits, service-learning may be doomed to a limited and limiting model of transformation.

Notes

1. Of course such changes *shouldn't* be doable without fundamentally altering the structures and practices of higher education. The Wingspread statement is premised exactly on the notion that these practices would be taken up in "thick" ways. Unfortunately, these practices as articulated are all too easily misappropriated within the world of higher education. This is not to suggest that these practices are not important. In fact, they may actually be the most sustainable aspects of service-learning as presently conceived. The point here is simply that they are not at the heart of what the Wingspread statement really *means* when it talks about institutionalizing service-learning. What it really means, and what the third and sixth practices make vivid, is the desire to transform higher education through service-learning.
2. The NCES data have numerous methodological ambiguities. For example, the lack of a distinctive service-learning category may obscure its use, the lack of Likert-scales may distort actual use of instructional methods, and lecturing may be conflated with discussion. The primary point of the data, though, is the unambiguous marginality of non-lecturing pedagogical methods across higher education.
3. See the website of Students for Academic Freedom, <www.studentsforacademicfreedom.org>, for the most up-to-date tracking of these developments.

4. I am very well aware of the animosity of the service-learning field to Stanley Fish. Not many people have an entire Campus Compact website devoted exclusively to attacking them (http://www.compact.org/newscc/fish.html). Yet while I acknowledge the highly personal nature of some of Fish's attacks (Ira Harkavy, personal communication, 3/30/05), I suggest that his insights into this political dilemma are critical for understanding the issues at stake.
5. The data and debate around this issue are legion. See, for example, Cochran-Smith, 2001, 2003; Goldhaber & Brewer, 1999; NCDTF, 2004; NCTQ, 2004. The basic point, though, is this: If the educational field, after all this time and research, is still this stuck, woe to service-learning.

References

AACU. Association of American Colleges and Universities. (2005, December 21). *Academic freedom and educational responsibility*. Washington, DC: AACU.

ACE. American Council on Education. (2005, June 23). *Statement on academic rights and responsibilities*. Washington, DC: ACE.

Antonio, A. L., Astin, H. S., & Cross, C. (2000). Community Service in higher education: A look at the faculty. *The Review of Higher Education, 23*(4), 373–398.

Becher, T., & Trowler, P. (2001). *Academic tribes and territories: Intellectual enquiry and the culture of disciplines* (2nd ed.). Philadelphia: Open University Press.

Benson, L., Harkavy, I., & Hartley, M. (2005). Integrating a commitment to the public good into the institutional fabric. In A. Kezar, T. Chambers, & J. Burkhardt, J. (Eds.), *Higher education for the public good* (pp. 185–216). San Francisco: Jossey-Bass.

Bell, R., Furco, A., Ammon, M. S., Muller, P., & Sorgen, V. (2000). *Institutionalizing service-learning in higher education*. Berkeley, CA: University of California.

Biglan, A. (1973). Relationship between subject matter characteristics and the structure and output of university departments. *Journal of Applied Psychology, 57*, 204–213.

Boyer, E. L. (1990). *Scholarship reconsidered: Priorities of the professoriate*. Stanford, CA: Carnegie Foundation for the Advancement of Teaching.

Bringle, R. G., & Hatcher, J. A. (2000). Institutionalization of service learning in higher education. *Journal of Higher Education, 71*(3), 273–291.

Brown, W. (1997). The impossibility of women's studies. *Differences: A Journal of Feminist Cultural Studies, 9*(3), 79–102.

Brukardt, M. H., Holland, B., Percy, S. L., Simpher, N., on behalf of Wingspread Conference Participants. (2004). *Wingspread Statement: Calling the question: Is higher education ready to commit to community engagement*. Milwaukee: University of Wisconsin-Milwaukee.

Butin, D. W. (2003). Of what use is it? Multiple conceptualizations of service-learning in education. *Teachers College Record, 105*(9), 1674–1692.

Butin, D. W. (2005a). Preface: Disturbing normalizations of service-learning. In D. W. Butin, (Ed.), *Service-learning in higher education: Critical issues and directions* (pp. vii–xx). New York: Palgrave.

Butin, D. W. (2005b). Service-learning as postmodern pedagogy. In D. W. Butin (Ed.) *Service-learning in higher education: Critical issues and directions* (pp. 89–104). New York: Palgrave.

Butin, D. W. (in press-a). Anti-anti-social justice: Academic freedom and the future of justice-oriented pedagogy in teacher preparation. *Equity and Excellence in Education, 40*(2).

Butin, D. W. (in press-b). Disciplining service-learning: Institutionalization and the case for community studies. *International Journal of Teaching and Learning in Higher Education, 17*(3). Available at http://222.isetle.org/ijtlhe/index.cfm.

Campus Compact. (2000). *Presidents' declaration on the civic responsibility of higher education*. Providence, RI: Campus Compact.

Campus Compact. (2004). 2003 *service statistics: Highlights of Campus Compact's annual membership survey*. Available at: http://www.compact.org/news-cc/2003_Statistics.pdf.

Cochran-Smith, M. (2001). Constructing outcomes in teacher education: Policy, practice and pitfalls. *Educational Policy Analysis Archives, 9*(11). Retrieved on February 3, 2004, from http://epaa.asu.edu/epaa/v9n11.html.

Cochran-Smith, M. (2003). Standing at the crossroads: Multicultural teacher education at the beginning of the 21st century. *Multicultural Perspectives, 5*(3), 3–11.

Colby, A., Ehrlich, T., Beaumont, E., & Stephens, J. (2003). *Educating citizens: Preparing America's undergraduates for lives of moral and civic responsibility.* San Francisco: Jossey-Bass.

Cuban, L. (1990). Reforming again, again, and again. *Educational Researcher, 19*(3), 3–13.

Cuban, L. (1998). How schools change reforms: Redefining reform success and failure. *Teachers College Record, 99*(3), 453–477.

DuBois, E. C. (1985). *Feminist scholarship: Kindling in the groves of academe.* Urbana: University of Illinois Press.

Eyler, J., Giles, D., Stenson, C., & Gray, C., (2001). At a glance: *What we know about the effects of service-learning on college students, faculty, institutions and communities,* 1993–2000. Washington, DC: Learn and Serve America National Service Learning Clearinghouse. Available at http://servicelearning.org.

Fish, S. E. (1999). *The trouble with principle.* Cambridge, MA: Harvard University Press.

Fish, S. E. (2004, February 13.). "Intellectual diversity": The Trojan horse of a dark design. *Chronicle of Higher Education,* pp. B13–B14.

Freire, P. (1994). *Pedagogy of the oppressed.* New York: Continuum.

Furco, A. (2001). Advancing service-learning at research universities. In M. Carada & B. W. Speck (Eds.), *Developing and implementing service-learning programs.* New Directions for Higher Education (no. 114, pp. 67–68). San Francisco: Jossey-Bass.

Furco, A. (2002a). Institutionalizing service-learning in higher education. *Journal of Public Affairs, 6,* 39–47.

Furco, A. (2002b). *Self-assessment rubric for the institutionalization of service-learning in higher education.* Berkeley, CA: University of California.

Furco, A. (2003). Issues of definition and program diversity in the study of service-learning. In S. H. Billig & A. S. Waterman, (Eds.), *Studying service-learning: innovations in educational research methodology* (pp. 13–34). Mahwah, NJ: Lawrence Erlbaum Associates.

Furco, A., & Billig, S. (2002). *Service-learning: The essence of the pedagogy.* Greenwich, CT: Information Age.

Gardner, H. (2004). *Changing minds: The art and science of changing our own and other people's minds.* Boston, MA: Harvard Business School Press.

Goldhaber, D. D., & Brewer, D. J. (1999). A three-way error components analysis of educational productivity. *Education Economics, 7*(3), 199–208.

Gray, M., Ondaatje, E., & Zakaras, L. (2000). *Combining service and learning in higher education.* Santa Monica, CA: RAND.

Hacking, I. (1999). *The social construction of what?* Cambridge, MA: Harvard University Press.

Hartley, M., Harkavy, I., & Benson, L. (2005). Putting down roots in the groves of academe: The challenges of institutionalizing service-learning. In D. W. Butin, (Ed.), *Service-learning in higher education: Critical issues and directions* (pp. 205–222). New York: Palgrave.

Henry, S. E. (2005). "I can never turn my back on that": Liminality and the impact of class on service-learning experiences. In D. W. Butin (Ed.) *Service-learning in higher education: Critical issues and directions* (pp. 45–66). New York: Palgrave.

Henry, S. E., & Brayfogle, M. L. (in press). Toward a new framework of "server" and "served": De(and re) constructing reciprocity in service-learning pedagogy. *International Journal of Teaching and Learning in Higher Education, 17*(3).

Holland, B. A. (2001). A comprehensive model for assessing service-learning and community-university partnerships. In M. Carada & B. W. Speck (Eds.), *Developing and implementing service-learning programs.* New Directions for Higher Education (no. 114, 51–60). San Francisco: Jossey-Bass.

hooks, b. (1994). *Teaching to transgress: Education as the practice of freedom.* New York: Routledge.

Horowitz, D. (n.d.). *Academic bill of rights.* Retrieved on January 7, 2005, from www.studentsforacademicfreedom.org/abor.html.

Horowitz, D. (2003). *The campus blacklist.* Retrieved on January 7, 2005, from www.studentsforacademicfreedom.org/essays/blacklist.html.

Horowitz, D., & Lehrer, E. (n.d.). Political bias in the administrations and faculties of 32 elite colleges and universities. Retrieved on January 7, 2005, from http://www.studentsforacademicfreedom.org/reports/lackdiversity.html.

Jones, S. R. (2002). The underside of service learning. *About Campus, 7*(4), 10–15.

Jones, S. R., Gilbride-Brown, J., & Gasorski, A. (2005). Getting inside the "underside" of service-learning: Student resistance and possibilities. In D.W. Butin (Ed.), *Service-learning in higher education: Critical issues and directions* (pp. 3–24). New York: Palgrave.

Kendall, J. (Ed). (1990). *Combining service and learning: A resource book for community and public service.* Raleigh, NC: National Society for Internships and Experiential Education.

Klein, D. B., & Stern, C. (2005). Political diversity is six disciplines. *Academic Questions, 18*(1), 40–52.

Kramer, M. (2000). Make it last forever: *The institutionalization of service learning in America.* Washington DC: Corporation for National Service.

Kuhn, T. (1996). *The structure of scientific revolutions.* (3rd ed.) Chicago: University of Chicago Press.

Labaree, D. F. (1997). *How to succeed in school without really learning: The credentials race in American education.* New Haven, CT: Yale University Press.

Labaree, D. F. (2004). *The trouble with ed schools.* New Haven, CT: Yale University Press.

Lather, P. (2005). *Scientism and scientificity in the rage for accountability: A feminist deconstruction.* Paper presented at the American Educational Research Associates, April 14.

Latour, B. (1979) *Laboratory life: The social construction of scientific facts.* Los Angeles: Sage.

Lindholm, J. A., Szelényi, K., Hurtado, S., & Korn, W.S. (2005). *The American college teacher: National norms for the 2004–2005 HERI faculty survey.* Los Angeles: Higher Education Research Institute, UCLA.

Lisman, C. D. (1998). *Toward a civil society: Civic literacy and service learning.* Westport, CT: Bergin & Garvey.

Liu, G. (1995). knowledge, foundations, and discourse: Philosophical support for service-learning. *The Michigan Journal of Community Service-Learning, 2,* 5–18.

Lueddeke, G. (2003). Professionalising teaching practice in higher education: A study of disciplinary variation and "teaching-scholarship." *Studies in Higher Education, 28*(2), 213–228.

Messer-Davidow, E. D. (2002). *Disciplining feminism: From social activism to academic discourse.* Durham, NC: Duke University Press.

Messer-Davidow, E., Shumway, D., & Sylvan, D. J. (Eds.). (1993). *Knowledges: Historical and critical studies in disciplinarity.* Charlottesville, VA: University of Virginia Press.

Moraga, C., & Anzaldúa, G. (1981). *This bridge called my back: Writings by radical women of color.* Watertown, MA: Persephone Press.

Morton, K. (1995). The irony of service: Charity, project, and social change in service-learning. *The Michigan Journal of Community Service-Learning, 2,* 19–32.

NCES. National Center for Educational Statistics (2002). *Teaching undergraduates in U.S. postsecondary institutions: Fall 1998.* Washington, DC: U. S. Department of Education.

NCDTF. National Collaborative on Diversity in the Teaching Force. (2004). *Assessment of diversity in America's teaching force.* Washington, DC: National Education Association. Retrieved on December 4, 2004, from http://www.nea.org/teacherquality/images/diversityreport.pdf.

NCTQ. National Council on Teacher Quality (2004). *Increasing the odds: How good policies can yield better teachers.* Washington, DC: NCTQ. Retrieved on December 4, 2004, from http://www.nctq.org/nctq/images/nctq_io.pdf.

Neumann, R., & Becher, T. (2002). Teaching and learning in their disciplinary contexts: A conceptual analysis. *Studies in Higher Education, 27*(4), 405–417.

Richardson, V. & Placier, P. (2001). Teacher change. In V. Richardson, & American Educational Research Association (Eds.), *Handbook of research on teaching* (4th ed., pp. 905–950). Washington, DC: American Educational Research Association.

Rothman, S., Lichter, S., & Nevitte, N. (2005). Politics and professional advancement among college faculty. *The Forum, 3*(1), 1–16.

Shulman, L. (2004). *Teaching as community property.* San Francisco: Jossey-Bass.

Sica, A. (2000). Rationalization and culture. In S. P. Turner, *The Cambridge companion to Weber* (pp. 42–58). New York: Cambridge University Press.

Snyder, T. D., Tan, A. G., and Hoffman, C. M. (2004). *Digest of education statistics 2003* (NCES 2005–025). U.S. Department of Education, National Center for Education Statistics. Washington, DC: Government Printing Office.

Stanton, D. C., & Stewart, A. J. (1995). *Feminisms in the academy.* Ann Arbor: University of Michigan Press.

Stanton, T., Giles, D., & Cruz, N. I. (1999). *Service-learning: A movement's pioneers reflect on its origins, practice, and future*. San Francisco: Jossey-Bass.

Swaminathan, R. (2005). "Whose school is it anyway?" Student voices in an urban classroom. In D. W. Butin (Ed.). *Service-learning in higher education: Critical issues and directions* (pp. 25–44). New York: Palgrave.

Swaminathan, R. (in press). Educating for the "real world": Perspectives from the community on youth, service-learning, and social justice. *Equity and Excellence in Education, 40*(2).

West, C. (1994). *Race matters*. New York: Vintage.

Westheimer, J. & Kahne, J. (2004). What kind of citizen? The politics of educating for democracy. *American Educational Research Journal, 41*(2): 237–269.

Wiegman, R. (1999). Feminism, institutionalism, and the idiom of failure. *Differences: A Journal of Feminist Cultural Studies, 11*(3), 107–136.

Wiegman, R. (2005). The possibility of women's studies. In E. L. Kennedy & A. Beins (Eds.), *Women's studies for the future: Foundations, interrogations, politics* (pp. 34–51). Piscataway, NJ: Rutgers University Press.

Wiegman, R. (2002). Academic feminism against itself. *NWSA Journal, 14*(2), 18–34.

Acknowledgment

Thanks to Eric Bredo, Gitte Wernaa Butin, Sean Flaherty, Ira Harkavy, and two anonymous reviewers, whose very useful comments helped me clarify the arguments I was making.

RECONSIDERING LEARNING COMMUNITIES: EXPANDING THE DISCOURSE BY CHALLENGING THE DISCOURSE

SUSAN TALBURT AND DERON BOYLES

At postsecondary institutions across the United States, concern has risen over the quality of undergraduate instruction, particularly for first-year students. Critics of undergraduate education cite the use of large lecture classes, incoherent curriculum, inconsistent quality of advising, and instruction by graduate teaching assistants and parttime instructors. Since the mid-1990s, numerous institutions have responded to these concerns by examining their first-year students' academic and social experiences and implementing programs designed to enhance their learning and integration into campus life. These programs are intended to raise retention rates, promote college student development, and cultivate academic success. One of the most significant efforts to improve freshman learning has been the development of residential and nonresidential "freshman learning communities" (FLCs) on campuses. FLCs typically link two or more of a group of students' classes during their first semester or year, emphasizing small class sizes, curricular cohesion, collaborative teaching, interdisciplinary learning, instruction by tenured and tenure-track faculty, the formation of peer networks, and out-of-class support.

The higher education literature on learning communities is replete with research and anecdotal accounts that support learning communities. Among the themes that undergird the positive view of FLCs are students' academic success, community building, student retention, and successful transitions from high school to college (Gabelnick, MacGregor, Matthews, & Smith, 1990; Kuh, 1995; Lenning & Ebbers, 1999; Shapiro & Levine, 1999; Tinto, 1998). Recent literature also asserts that changes in traditional student populations, including increasing diversity of age, race, and ethnicity, justify changing traditional teaching approaches via learning communities. These changes include faculty collaboration as well as the rejection of what is said to be individual, isolated study in hierarchically structured classrooms in favor of approaches that promote active learning with teachers as facilitators and an emphasis on "interdisciplinary and democratic collaboration, reflective practice, and relations between theory and practical applications" (DeMulder & Eby, 1999, p. 893; see also Barr & Tagg, 1995). Even with these innovations, the literature relies heavily on traditional measures of college student and college program success in evaluating learning communities: student retention, grade point averages (GPAs), the development of cognitive skills, satisfaction, positive peer social networks, student-faculty interaction, and increased learning outcomes (see Braunstein & McGrath, 1997; Gabelnick et al., 1990). However, the specifics within the literature establish a discourse on learning communities that seems to reify the learning community itself. That is, the literature seems to assume without question that learning communities are, by their nature, worthy enterprises. There appears to be little space in the overall discourse for questions about learning communities themselves.[1]

Reprinted from the *Journal of General Education* 54, no. 3 (2005), by permission of Pennsylvania State University Press.

In this article, we question some fundamental tenets underlying the idea and practice of learning communities: that they develop and demonstrate community, that learning is improved via less or nontraditional formats, and that learning communities are "better" than typical or traditional freshman experiences. We approach these doctrinal assumptions through three lenses. First, we examine claims about the historical background (or legacies) and philosophical justifications for learning communities, dating back to the Progressive Era. Second, we inquire into the normative assumptions about what it means to be a first-year college student underlying FLCs and their implications for actual practice. Third, we bring these questions to bear on our own experiences as coadvisers of an FLC as well as interviews we conducted with six students in the group. Our article, then, incorporates elements of philosophical, historical, and interpretive analyses of existing literature and our actual practice. Our goal is not to argue against learning communities per se but to bring to the discourse and practice of FLCs some critical questions regarding their value and application. These questions often reveal inconsistencies that the literature and general narratives on FLCs appear to overlook or ignore. We seek to understand the meaning of those inconsistencies and the motives behind offering FLCs. Do the stated motives correspond to FLCs in practice? If, for example, FLCs are claimed to be "progressive" and less bureaucratic but in practice are neither, what meaning might we glean? If FLCs are claimed to be supportive environments for interaction but risk sequestering students from the larger college or university sphere, what might FLC advocates do differently?

Historical and Philosophical Foundations

Integral to reconsidering learning communities is an elucidation of the historical and philosophical background frequently cited in the higher education literature. Specifically, the language often used in calling for FLCs appears to be "progressive" rather than traditional, and advocates trace learning communities to Alexander Meiklejohn and John Dewey.[2] Proponents of FLCs, for example, use the terms *collaborative* and *active* as a contrast to their interpretation of the isolation and passive learning that characterize contemporary college life (e.g., Gabelnick et al., 1990). In defining learning communities, Gabelnick et al. (1990) note the following:

> Large, impersonal, bureaucratic, and fragmented, the American college is often an educational community only in theory. A variety of factors make the notion of meaningful educational community—the root of the word "college"—elusive in many of our institutions. The vision of the collegiate learning community refers to an idealized version of the campus of the past, where students and faculty shared a close and sustained fellowship, where day-to-day contacts reinforced previous classroom learning, where the curriculum was organized around common purposes, and the small scale of the institution promoted active learning, discussion, and individuality. Such a vision remains nostalgic at best, except in small colleges such as Reed, Bard, and St. John's. (p. 9)

And Evenbeck and Williams (1998) explain, "The term *learning community* is refreshing. It suggests another time and place, far removed from the reality of university life as it is experienced by most students, faculty, and staff, and it connotes images of intimate conversations with faculty" (p. 35). It is interesting to note that ongoing nostalgia for close-knit communities itself dates to the Progressive Era. Rudolph (1977) describes the University of Wisconsin's expectations of Meiklejohn's experiment: "By 1927, when the college opened, a mythology had developed around the vanished small college of the nineteenth century, and Meiklejohn was willing to see himself as enlisted in an effort to bring back their vanished mystique of learning" (pp. 276–277).

In order to recuperate this idea of shared community and purpose, advocates of FLCs (e.g., Gabelnick et al., 1990; Lenning & Ebbers, 1999; Shapiro & Levine, 1999, pp. 17–18) attribute the practical origins of FLCs to Alexander Meiklejohn and a philosophical lineage to John Dewey. In Meiklejohn's Experimental College at the University of Wisconsin (which lasted from 1927 to 1932), students studied a two-year curriculum based on ancient Greece (freshman year) and contemporary U.S. society (sophomore year). The students also lived together in a shared dorm. Professors were "advisers" and were expected to be able to teach all of the courses that constituted the program of study. There were no grades until the end of the sophomore year, but the curriculum was avowedly perennialist. That is, "Great Books" were used as the foundation for a kind of intellectual inquiry that, to Meiklejohn, was essential to critically analyzing American democracy. Careers and specialized training were anathema to his educational vision.[3] Known for his civil libertarianism, Meiklejohn had a vision for what he called "liberal learning" (classical liberal arts), which meant developing students who merged their liberal arts study with their free speech rights to criticize society. Indeed, Brennan (1998) writes that during his presidency of Amherst College from 1912 to 1923, Meiklejohn clashed with alumni, trustees, and some faculty because of his insistence on representing multiple viewpoints in the curriculum and extracurriculum, such as including antiwar perspectives during a campus "readiness" event as the United States entered World War I and hiring faculty with leftist leanings. Ostensibly, the point was to bring about democracy by challenging democracy. Like Dewey, Meiklejohn (1932) rejected the idea that teaching and learning are worthy when done mechanically, procedurally, and without regard to change, interest, and context (see pp. 138–139).[4]

For his part, Dewey's progressivism meant criticizing society as well, and the criticism was directed at the daily lives of citizens. Dewey argued for educative experiences that are necessarily different and contextual. Like Meiklejohn, Dewey recognized that teaching and learning done by rote or done procedurally would yield the very kind of traditional schooling that had students bored with school in the first place. The point of learning was not "preparatory" for Dewey (1916), and he saw democracy as one mode of associated living (p. 87, see also pp. 81–110). Such a mode of living requires experiential learning-by-doing, and the approach uses students' background experiences as beginning points. Social interaction was necessary in Dewey's view of schooling because the projects students engaged in to solve problems were not done in isolation. There was no "rugged individualism" for Dewey. Still, for all of the similarities between Meiklejohn and Dewey, those who invoke the two thinkers in their discussions of learning communities appear to include little more than the idea that education is a "social process" vaguely linked to democracy and community—and ignore some fundamental ironies and contradictions of aligning these educators with the ideals of FLCs.[5]

Unlike Dewey, Meiklejohn held to idealist (some say elitist) principles and rejected much of what would come to be known as pragmatic or progressive educational theory (see, e.g., Meiklejohn, 1942). Unlike Meiklejohn, Dewey rejected "Great Books" programs and elitism. He was, after all, on the forefront arguing against curricular humanists who wanted schools to prepare students for college via liberal arts programs of study. Although Meiklejohn's experiment at Wisconsin is often cited as an example of a learning community, it should be noted that the faculty were the ones to develop the themes, and Meiklejohn eschewed electives (something Dewey embraced). Given that Meiklejohn's experiment focused on democracy and participation, it seems ironic that power was concentrated in the hands of Meiklejohn and the faculty. Moreover, as we have demonstrated, the compatibility of the educational ideas of Alexander Meiklejohn and John Dewey is debatable at best. This is particularly true given Meiklejohn's curricular prescriptiveness and Dewey's (1902, 1938) stance that educators should combine the "logical" and the "psychological," or content and the situations of learners, in formulating educational experiences and purposes. Although both men had concerns with cultivating habits of citizenship, their educational practices for democracy and community have very different implications for what a learning community might look like. On one hand, Meiklejohn's commitment to a "Great Books" curriculum means that the goals are preexistent and student interests need to match or adapt themselves to those goals. On the other hand, Dewey's commitment to students' experiences as the building blocks for further inquiry means that the community, itself, develops as the members of the community identify (and continually modify) their interests.

To the degree that Meiklejohn and Dewey *are* aligned (as with their agreement that teaching and learning are not easy and should not be mechanical and that participation in society requires criticality), we wonder about the connection of those similarities to current learning communities. To what degree is the teaching in learning communities actually different from that in non–learning community classes? Are students developing the kind of criticality that would, for example, allow for criticism of the learning communities themselves? To what degree are learning communities developing "better" students—where "better" means students who are more likely to fit traditional expectations for student success? Is there irony in the possibility that learning communities may not be democratic or reflective of a simplified curriculum, as Meiklejohn and Dewey might have come together to champion? Along a related line of irony, when Gabelnick et al. (1990) note that the learning community is an effort to confront the large, bureaucratic qualities of many universities and colleges, we wonder whether the bureaucracy is simply not moved to the level of the learning community itself (rather than being confronted and simplified). In order to consider these questions, we first analyze contemporary assumptions regarding first-year students, "community," and "success." We then explore our students' accounts of their experiences in an FLC.

Contemporary Assumptions Underlying Learning Communities

The nostalgia for small, close-knit communities that offer social and academic coherence maps onto contemporary theories of who students are and what they need in "the bustling, often impersonal environment of the modern campus" (Evenbeck & Williams, 1998, p. 35). Defined as a curricular and pedagogical response to concerns about student retention that follows Tinto's (1993, 1997; Tinto & Goodsell, 1993) and Astin's (1984, 1993) conceptualizations of "persistence" and "involvement," the FLC is constructed as meeting the needs of students as they make the difficult "transition and adjustment to the social and academic demands of college life, a time when the likelihood of drop-out and the possibility of transformative learning is greatest" (Tinto & Goodsell, 1993, p. 8). Tinto's theories of student departure and Astin's idea of involvement point to the need for the integration of students' social and academic lives to improve academic success and retention and suggest the power of FLCs to support student persistence (Lenning & Ebbers, 1999, p. 46). FLCs, then, are designed to respond to needs based on research that constructs the first year of college as a risky developmental passage from which students can be protected in small, safe, interactive communities. Writers who follow these models cite a range of benefits of FLCs for students that combine principles and outcomes of academic and psychosocial development: seeing the same people across classes, experiencing large universities as "small" (often by avoiding large lecture classes), engaging in social networks that support academic integration, cultivating interdisciplinary skills, developing purposeful identities, and gaining voice in the construction of knowledge (Gabelnick et al., 1990, pp. 63–72; Guarasci, 2001; Tinto, 1997).[6] Rarely questioned in this discourse are the construction of the first-year student as "at risk" and the construction of student participation that ignores cultural difference (Tierney, 1992). Moreover, "community" as an idea and an ideal appears to be beyond critique.

Lenning and Ebbers (1999) cull a comprehensive definition of community from writings about FLCs and education generally that "involves inclusiveness, commitment, consensus that allows differences to be acknowledged and processed, vulnerability, and `graceful fighting,' where conflict is not avoided, minimized, or disregarded" (p. 5). Included as well are purposefulness, "shared values, caring for one another, and appreciation for cooperation" (Lenning & Ebbers, 1999, p. 5). Community, they explain, has become "an end as much as a means to an end, in the same vein as the 'furniture of the mind' emphasized in the Yale Report of [1828]" (1999, p. 7). Community, then, is embedded as a normative ideal, presumed to be process and product, as are the benefits of FLCs. Raymond Williams (1976) contrasts two 20th-century uses of the word *community* that underscore tensions in its meanings:

> Community can be the warmly persuasive word to describe an existing set of relationships, or the warmly persuasive word to describe an alternative set of relationships. What is most important, perhaps, is that unlike all other terms of social organization (*state, nation, society,* etc.), it seems never to be used unfavorably, and never to be given any positive opposing or distinguishing term. (p. 66)

Read as an a priori assumption, *community* can take on a coercive, prescriptive tone rather than one that describes emerging identifications and purposes.

What happens to the student who does not make connections with others in the FLC or who is alienated by both the micro community and the larger university community? And what about the potential for the protections of FLCs to foster dependence on others rather than the independence and healthy "interdependence" (Chickering & Reisser, 1993, p. 47) they seek to cultivate? Questions of whom FLCs benefit, why, and how have largely been ignored in a discourse that zealously embraces integrating social and academic community without consideration of the potential for insularity, isolation, and dependence. For example, Tinto and Goodsell (1993) take as evidence of a desire for community a student's description of himself as "alienated" but fail to interrogate how that alienation could be a product of the structure of the FLC itself: "Even negative comments about the FIGs [freshman interest groups] support the idea that students wanted to meet people; in fact, students expressed disappointment if that did not happen for them" (p. 17). Although few critiques of or problems in learning communities are noted in the literature, Sapon-Shevin and Chandler-Scott (2001) point to the potential for the development of exclusionary cliques and conflicts that begin outside the classroom and are brought into it. And Strommer (1999) mentions faculty concerns that FLCs can segregate students from upper-class students from whom they could learn socially and academically and that segregation may reinforce a "'secondary school' mentality" of adversarial roles toward instructors, the formation of cliques, and even "negative" community behaviors such as cheating, rudeness, or skipping class (p. 43).

The predominantly positive depictions of communities lead us to wonder whether learning communities are surreptitiously used by universities as marketing tools under the guise of "community building." Although the research literature speaks repetitively of "students' needs," equally repetitive is an emphasis on retention related to economic exigencies, including "decreasing enrollments, greater competition among colleges for students, and the demand for accountability in institutions of higher education" (Johnson, 2000–2001, p. 219)—not to mention university and college rankings and classifications (indeed, they are not mentioned).[7] This marketing issue is linked to a question of the degree to which learning communities are socializing agents that support—and play on—particular narratives about what it means to be a student, particularly one who may be "at risk" during the first, "critical" year of college.

A Specific Case of an FLC

Our point is to consider questions about learning communities in general, but our analysis also extends the critique to our own experiences as codirectors of an FLC, "School and Society." We are not claiming that the general literature does not represent our circumstance. We wish to argue, on the contrary, that our experiences may be more common than the general literature indicates, particularly given the foundational assumptions behind learning communities and the way they are generally being used in institutions of higher education.

This FLC took place at a large, urban research university that has traditionally served part-time students but is moving toward attracting full-time students by, for example, constructing residential facilities and improving its general education offerings. As part of this move, the university introduced FLCs in 1999, when 295 students enrolled in 11 FLCs, and by 2001 it had doubled this number to enroll 600 students in 25 FLCs across the university's colleges. In 2002, the university had space for 800 students in 32 FLCs. The institution seemed to be approaching the learning community in an inverted manner. That is, whereas most learning communities appear to develop out of a sense of changing demographics (where those demographics indicate a pattern of movement from a traditional to a not-so-traditional student body), the university began with a nontraditional population and seems to see learning communities as a way to attract more traditional students.

An informational pamphlet on FLCs handed out to incoming first-year students at a pre-orientation begins with several letters to students. In the first, the associate provost for undergraduate studies addresses students:

> Freshman Learning Communities allow you to join a small group of students, faculty and student leaders. Joining the FLC will give you an opportunity to get to know the faculty, to become involved in a group and to participate in projects designed around the theme of your FLC. Most important, when you register for a Freshman Learning Community, you enroll in a strong academic program consisting of core curriculum courses. . . . Our research shows that students who enroll in an FLC earn a higher grade point average than their counterparts who do not participate in the program.

On the next page, the director of freshmen studies addresses another letter to students:

> FLC courses are taught by committed faculty with interdisciplinary backgrounds. The faculty members have been hard at work planning the curriculum, and you can be assured of taking the right courses for your first semester. The FLCs contain the best courses, offered at the best times, and taught by some of the best faculty. . . . Simply pick an FLC that sounds interesting and your first semester schedule is complete.

If these administrative "welcome letters" were not enough, a two-page "fact sheet" on FLCs reinforces these messages of getting the best, doing the best, and streamlining an intimidating process of registering and becoming a college student. In a section entitled "What Are Freshmen Learning Communities?" the fact sheet reiterates, "You will only have to register for the learning community of your choice to be assigned to each of the sections in the course cluster." After explaining that this course cluster would include "students who share your interests," the fact sheet promises that "this group creates a small, friendly community within a large research university." A following section, "Benefits of Joining an FLC," explains,

> First-year college students deserve a formative, integrative academic experience on which to build lifelong strengths and perspectives. This experience should include not just the courses they take, but the combination, sequence, and fit of those courses . . . Each FLC course builds on the other by exploring unique yet related fields of knowledge. . . . Although located in the heart of a fast-paced city, [the institution] is an ideal place to develop lifelong skills and build relationships . . . . Joining an FLC allows a student to:
>
> > Register more easily for Fall semester
> > Study and make friends with other freshmen
> > Connect with faculty in a learning community
> > Benefit from an enriched academic experience
> > Learn what [the university] has to offer in the classroom and beyond.

Despite assurances of a seamless bureaucratic, social, and academic transition for students, as faculty, we faced practical difficulties that render idealized notions of learning communities highly problematic. Indeed, once we set the FLC in motion, the institution seemed to reinforce the opposite of the antibureaucratic, anticentralized ethos associated with idealized notions of FLCs as benefiting not only students but also faculty. Advocates claim that faculty collaboration creates integrated and meaningful FLC courses and enhances faculty development and teaching satisfaction (Soldner, Lee, & Duby, 1999, p. 119; see also Gabelnick et al., 1990, pp. 79–82). However, although the literature speaks of addressing "challenges," such as administrative and institutional support, it ignores very real issues of departmental budgetary and staffing demands, that, in our experience, resulted in last minute enrollment increases in two of the five classes, and that hindered our ability to create collaborative assignments and integrated courses with the other faculty. Thus, ideas that FLCs "have a dynamic quality that arises naturally as a result of putting several teachers together to build a new curriculum" (Gabelnick et al., 1990, p. 54) or that interdisciplinary connections would become explicit and systematic in the course of teaching and learning became impossible to sustain. We thus question whether nonspecialized, interdisciplinary teaching and learning are possible in institutions that require core curricula. What happens in "successful" learning communities, when the nexus of student action, student voice, and student learning is faced with mandated course requirements (such as a required "Freshman Orientation" course), learning community classes within larger sections of the same class, and requirements beyond the scope of learning community faculty or student interests? What, in relation to their own desires and the promises of FLCs, did students articulate of their experiences?

To learn of our students' reasons for and perspectives about participating in the FLC, we conducted interviews with six students who were part of our FLC. We selected students whom we hoped would represent a diversity of perceptions in a class of 25 students comprising 18 white females, one Asian American male, three African American females, and three white males. We selected one white male, two African American females, and three white females, one of whom was the only student who had not come directly from high school. The semistructured interviews (LeCompte & Preissle, 1993; Seidman, 1998), which lasted less than an hour each, were designed to elicit the students' thoughts about what it was like for them to be first-year students, their perceptions of college life, their choice to participate in the FLC, and their experiences of the FLC. Because of the potentially sensitive nature of an instructor (Talburt) interviewing students about their learning experiences while they were in class with her, the interviews were carefully structured to include only general questions. As we did not conduct intensive interviews, our analysis consisted of inductive analysis of each interview transcript as an independent narrative, in which we distilled salient themes from each and then compared these themes across participants to uncover consistencies and inconsistencies. Finally, we also sought to examine these themes in relation to the literature on FLCs.

Though students echoed many of the recurring, positive themes of the literature on FLCs, they also offered some insights that are obscured in the literature. These include (1) feelings of alienation and isolation from, and even boredom with, their peers, which led to eagerness to move into classes in the larger university community; (2) an inchoate sense that the next semester would be the "test" of whether they could "make it" at college after the FLC had offered them something of a protective bubble from selecting their own "uncoordinated" classes, making their own social contacts, and navigating the university's bureaucratic structures; and (3) a lack of urgency to explore campus life, join clubs, or look for social interactions elsewhere, despite articulated statements of a need to cultivate independence. They considered the FLC a comfortable haven where much of the "work" of students' social and academic life was "done" for them.

Developing Needs

In the students' narratives, their choice to participate in the "School and Society" FLC was illuminating. While five of the six had declared majors in education and wanted to become teachers, their choices to enter an FLC were also influenced by such factors as ease of registration, parents' desires, and their own concerns about adapting socially and academically to college life. Keisha, for example, offered dual motivations: "I thought it would be easier to register for classes, and I thought it would give me a better perspective on education."[8] Angela, who was interested in exploring education as a career option, narrated an initial ambivalence about the social aspects of the FLC:

> I didn't know what it would be like to have classmates the same in every class, 'cause I was kind of thinking it would be cool to meet more people by having different classmates, but at the same time it would be cool to know the people better.

And Linda's mother chose the FLC for her:

> 'Cause she thought it would be good to have the same people in the same class and have you interact in a community at college, don't just jump into it. Just have the same people. People that, you know, help you study, understand college life.

After Carrie's mother pressed her daughter to join the FLC (contrary to Carrie's desires and intentions), Carrie came to hope that it would

> ease me into the college process. You know, it's a lot different from high school, so maybe just being with the same group of freshmen and the same professors, you know, that it would just make the transition a lot easier.

When asked to describe the transition, she cast it in academic terms, saying, "Mainly the academic, just because I wasn't sure how professors do stuff differently as far as exams and, you know, homework. . . . I wasn't sure, you know, a little scared about what to expect." It is interesting to note, however, that Carrie was a straight-A, 4.0 GPA student in high school. When asked whether, even with her high school record, college was still intimidating, she responded,

> Not academically, I mean, it was a little bit, because I'd hear these horror stories in high school about the professors. . . . Professors don't care about you at all, they don't want to know your name, you're just a thing, you're another person in their class, they're not sympathetic at all.

While Carrie explained that this fear was quickly allayed in the FLC, she also suggested that a benefit of FLCs is the possibility of studying with others, yet it was one she would not pursue: "I'm more of an independent studier."

Partially resonant with research that calls for small communities, it appears that a folklore about large, impersonal classes created anxieties for a number of these students. Marcy explained,

> I like the idea [of FLCs] because you get closer to your professors. . . . You get to know your professors better, which is good for a freshman, instead of them being scary and I can't go ask them any questions sort of thing.

She continued,

> I know a lot of my friends who are at [another large research university], they're in like lecture classes with like a hundred or plus people, and I was not looking forward to that at all, and everyone made it sound like, "Oh, you're definitely going to have these huge lecture classes, and you just take notes, and your professors won't know your name." I like the small classes a lot.

Keisha also sought small classes, based on what she had been told:

> I was scared of going into classes with 200 kids. You know, this lady was telling me, "You're going to go to college, and the professors, all they're going to want to know about you is your social security number."

A developmental narrative in which the FLC would support the future was evident in the students' articulations. Marcy, for example, explained the FLC's benefits: "Getting to know those people will make it easier to talk to people next semester when you're in classes with different people every day. You won't be afraid to approach them so much." Brad explained,

> I was nervous about the transition from high school to college. . . . And I know I don't do transitions well. Like moving from one period in my life to another, and I have this anxiety about it. Like I had some serious anxiety about coming to college, like I was leaving my small little community . . . and coming to downtown where there would be so many different kinds of people.

Indeed, when asked if the FLC had provided the continuity he was looking for, Brad responded,

> We'll find out next semester, I guess. Because after I cross the bridge, we'll see if it helped me. After I get over-this transitional period, then I'll know. . . . But I don't know about next semester when I'm thrown into random classes. Like I had a little anxiety about signing up for classes, because with the FLC it was done for me.

Brad, more than the other students, reiterated his anxieties through-out the interview. When asked whether he was less anxious now, he said,

> Not quite. I'm a little anxious about next semester, what it's going to be like to move from the comfort—again, comfort—of the FLC into this. I feel like I'm going from a smaller community in the college to like the big college community.

In fact, Brad painted the bridge of the FLC as one that was only temporary:

> And I think above and beyond the FLC to try in that first semester to reach out into the bigger realm of [the university]. That might make the transition easier. That might be what I should have done. And I kind of regret not doing that now, getting involved, auditioning for a play or something. Because the theater people are kind of like a family when they do the plays and stuff like that, so that when the FLC experience was over, you still would have a group that you belong to instead of having to go out and look for something, starting all over.

Brad was acutely aware of his position in a developmental narrative, one he was not taking control of:

> I haven't gone out and done anything to get myself involved, which I think might hinder my ability to make that step. But I feel like in the FLC I feel like part of the group. . . . I kind of feel like I belong at [the university], but I don't know if that'll change next semester.

The homogeneity of this FLC in particular may have provided Brad with a buffer from the larger student population. Brad spoke of his discomfort in an urban environment: "I feel an anxiety of being the minority. Because I've never in my life had to think about race . . . and sometimes I feel out of place." Yet Linda, too, wanted to reach out to broader communities in the university: "I haven't done any clubs yet, but next semester I'm going to get into a club just to get to know other people." And Angela described herself as concerned with what the next semester would bring, as she left her friends in the FLC and began taking required courses that she did not feel confident in:

> I'm worried about next semester because I'm worried that my teachers aren't going to be as cool as the ones I've got now. That's going to suck because I like every single teacher that I have. . . . I'm not looking forward to next semester as much as I was this one.

The protection of the FLC may have actually kept students from exploring other facets of the university, developing networks, and cultivating a sense of autonomy. In her analysis of developmental theories, Lesko (2001) takes up Erikson's enduring influence on conceptions of adolescence and youth, suggesting that his work sets up an idea of adolescence as a "developmental moratorium," in which young people are positioned in an expectant mode, protected as they passively await a future of responsibility and power. This "expectant time" is constructed by adults, institutions, and "theories that tell us that youth need dependency because they are confused about their identities" (Lesko, 2001, p. 130). We would extrapolate her discussion of Erikson to theorists who are frequently represented in the higher education literature, such as Chickering, given his use of aspects of Erikson's developmental tasks or stages (see Chickering & Reisser, 1993, pp. 2, 23). Lesko describes theories stemming from Erikson's work as perpetuating "dominant concepts regarding youth's position in the western societies," which position young people as "not fully developed or socialized" (2001, p. 123) and thus as needing guidance and protection. The college student whose needs and outcomes research would make knowable and known is positioned as passive, despite developmental theories' normative calls for young people to work for active mastery of the environment and a unified sense of self. Authoritative social scientific discourses, then, institutionalize structures in which college students exercise a pseudoautonomy directed to a desired future as they "are expected to measure up to finely attuned assessments of productivity, learning, morality, and achievement while remaining in a social position that is dependent and watched over not only by adults but also by their age-peers" (Lesko, 2001, p. 129). FLCs may be supporting a discourse of development and empowerment in which students are not active but passive, are told what they need, and as a result internalize their roles accordingly.

Failed Community

Students' naming social interaction as a benefit of FLCs was belied by their own lack of access to social interaction and by the lack of diversity in the FLC group. Marcy, for example, spoke of the study groups students formed as beneficial, enabling exchange of information and mutual support. Yet, when asked about this exchange, she said, "I don't go because they're always in the village [student dorms], and I don't live in the village, but everyone, like . . . they get together before exams. But I can't get down there in the evening." It appears that she learned to internalize a discourse of the benefits of FLCs as community without experiencing those benefits. And Angela, even as she embraced the close network, described herself as outside of it:

> Not superclose friends, you know, but we talk, we're cool. I think a lot of them get together and hang out on the weekends and after school, but I don't really do that stuff. I'm living at home, so I drive here every day, it takes about 45 minutes.[9]

Equally, if not more significant, was the sense of confinement in the FLC that several students described. Linda commented, "It's the same people. I'm ready to get out. Just seeing the same faces, just seeing the same people, going to the same classes with the same people." When asked about friendships she had made, Linda said, "Just one in particular, Heather . . . but like there's only like three African American people in the class." She framed the racial homogeneity of the class in terms of questions of comfort:

> I don't like to go to a restaurant and be like the only black person. Not that I'm a racist or nothing, I just feel uncomfortable. I don't know. I just would feel more comfortable, equal. . . . If there were more black people, you'd have more friends that you could talk to.

Another African American student, Keisha, commented,

> It's kind of annoying seeing everyone every single day. That's why I'm looking forward to second semester. I feel kind of like I'm in a little cage. . . . When I walk around, and I see these different people on campus, and I'd like to be in class with them, just to get the whole diversity of the campus.

Carrie, a self-proclaimed Christian, spoke of exclusions in the FLC:

> It's really hard me being a big Christian coming here, and just people aren't really as accepting as I thought they would be, this being such a diverse school. But I know my classmates, I mean they just make it clear that they don't want anything to have to do with my religion . . . . It's more the ethnic and racial diversity that's accepted, and that's great, but you're in the Bible Belt, and so there needs to be a lot of religious tolerance.

She perceived the group as exclusionary: "I see them walking around in little clumps, people from our FLC, and that's just fine that they're making new friendships, but if you have someone like me who's different from the rest of them, it's not okay." She offered an example from our class in which she was in a group preparing to lead a debate about teaching evolution in public schools:

> When I was doing the presentation for your class and we were going to do the debate thing, everybody wanted to be on the other side. And they're like, "Oh, you want to do that, that's great, because we don't really want to." Or, about 10 minutes before we were going to do the presentation, you know, they drew the fish, and they put the Darwin in there, and they just kept going on about how that was the best, and so I'm like, "What about the other fish?" and they're like, "Who cares?" So, I know it's just the little things, but they know how I feel, and so I think it's a little disrespectful. And so I just feel out of place. Really I haven't met anybody in my FLC that I know of with my views, and I don't feel like I fit in much. And they all like to party and get drunk, and that's okay, but I don't, so the social life is kind of hard.

The "buffer" Carrie found was outside the FLC:

> I have another class outside the FLC, and people are really nice in there. It's actually music appreciation class, but we talk, I've talked to some people about religion and about the church I go to, and they're like, "You go there, that's great," you know; they just seem a lot more accepting.

Carrie had investigated student organizations but found that she could not participate in them because of their evening meetings. She was considering transferring to another university in an outlying county near her home but wanted to try one more semester without the FLC:

> I'm hoping maybe things'll change next semester once I'm out of the FLC. . . . I just think maybe if I get with a bunch of different people, because right now I have five classes with the same people, and I don't get to meet a lot of different people I think. If I have a variety, then maybe.

Carrie's concerns about feelings of isolation and limited options regarding other people's ideas represent part of a discourse that challenges dominant views on learning communities. For example, some students felt that having the same classes with the same people meant that they already sensed what people were going to say in response to particular questions. When Carrie raised her hand to speak, students often rolled their eyes, presumably because they felt they already knew what kinds of ideas she was going to express. Could such familiarity as having the same people in all of one's classes breed a kind of contempt FLC advocates never imagined? And could the reality of specially selected, small classes be more problematic than the literature indicates? When students are told that FLCs develop friendships and a close-knit community, they appear to accept idealized notions of the concepts friendship and community. But when students indicated, like Angela did, that they rarely if ever actually engaged with their peers outside of class, we wonder whether there is a form of hegemony in evidence: students willingly engaging in a narrative about their FLC experience that supports FLCs even if the FLCs fail to provide individual students with some or much of what they promote. If FLC promotional literature, university FLC administrators, and FLC faculty establish and reinforce a discourse about what is beneficial about FLCs without engaging in questions about what might be problematic about FLCs, it appears to be a natural extension to have students say positive things about FLCs, even if their experiences contradict some or much of the larger discourse.

A significant concern that emerges from juxtaposing student, research, and institutional narratives is that although we are able to consider a student such as Carrie's views as part of a deliberation about FLCs, it becomes clear that individual student interests, problems, and possibilities are actually not the driving force behind current efforts to adopt, promote, and expand FLC programs. We wonder whether, in place of the interests of students and the historical, progressive narrative about developing community and democratic engagement, institutional motivations like retention rates and enrollments are actually the primary motivations behind learning communities.

Challenging the Discourse

In questioning the discourse on FLCs, we recall three major lenses we use to explore FLCs: (1) the nostalgic legacies frequently used to provide historical justification for FLCs, (2) the normative assumptions of FLCs, and (3) our experiences as codirectors of an FLC and our students' experiences within the FLC. By revisiting these lenses, we wish to craft a challenge to the dominant discourse in order that we (and others) might expand our understandings of FLC initiatives and practices. In so doing, we find ourselves increasingly worried that the dominant discourse on FLCs camouflages underlying, and arguably ominous, reasons for the recent proliferation of FLCs in the United States.

We worry, for example, that the progressive history attributed to Meiklejohn and Dewey is used to romanticize ideas like community and democracy in order to "sell" the idea of FLCs both to faculty on campuses and to students interested in coming to those campuses. The legacy of Meiklejohn and Dewey is, ironically, one exemplification of a problem we see with the movement toward FLCs: unquestioning attribution. That is, by not knowing or acknowledging the sometimes bitter feuds between Meiklejohn and Dewey, FLC advocates seem to advance an ahistorical and uncritical rationale as part of the justification for FLCs. This is symbolically important given the assumption that "community," "citizenship," and "individual development" are primarily based in "consensus" and "shared values," such that arguments within and among communities are not highlighted as important, valuable, or even existing. It is as though citizens can only be citizens if they do not disagree with one another. But Meiklejohn and Dewey not only disagreed with one another, they maintained that free speech rights for criticizing society are sacrosanct. Because the oft-cited historical justification for FLCs contradicts the assumptions of the very "community," "citizenship," and "individual development" that FLC advocates highlight, we argue that such inconsistency indicates that the historical background cited is cited uncritically. We are concerned that a lack of criticality and a lack of reflection reflect FLC practice and do not meet the expectations of citizenship and democracy frequently cited in the FLC literature.

Gabelnick et al. (1990) contend that a "sense of responsible citizenship is often present and purposefully cultivated in learning communities. . . . Group processes can be powerful in a learning community, and group norms for tolerance, inclusion, and support are important factors for success" (p. 59). We wonder what Gabelnick et al. mean by "responsible citizenship." We encourage educators to take seriously differing notions of citizenship, such as those embraced by Meiklejohn and Dewey. Similarly, markers of success should not be tied to institutional measures, such as GPAs and retention, but, rather, should entail questioning, collaborative development of classroom processes and purposes, and respectful dissensus.

Regarding the establishment of norms, Chickering and Reisser (1993) argue that when students form friendships and "participate in communities that become meaningful subcultures, and when diversity of backgrounds and attitudes as well as significant interchanges and shared interests exist" (p. 275), development is fostered. Yet they warn that student culture "can affect the development of identity and purpose by encouraging wide-ranging exploration or curtailing it. . . . [W]hen the community validates a limited set of roles, development of identity suffers" (1993, p. 276). Though a community is optimally diverse,

> it serves as a reference group, where there are boundaries in terms of who is "in" and who is "out." It has norms that inform those with different roles, behaviors, and status that they are "good" members or that what they are doing is unacceptable. (Chickering & Reisser, 1993, p. 277)

The norms to which Chickering and Reisser (1993) refer do not appear to emerge from student interaction but, in fact, are prescribed, as are the a priori assumptions of community. The challenge for educators and advocates of FLCs is to avoid preexistent norms that determine discourse of a particular type—one, say, that limits criticality, the raising of questions about taken-for-granted assumptions about curricular content and structure, and the format of classes.

We believe it is conceivable, if not likely, that institutions are using FLCs for purposes other than developing students' criticality. We believe it is likely that students and parents are provided with an idealized, normative version of FLCs that masks some very real problems that exist within and result from FLCs. Aside from the irony of their history, the lack of reflection that exists in the dominant discourse on (and in) FLCs becomes highly problematic when advocates assert that the goals and purposes of FLCs are focused on students and their needs and interests. Rather, the goals and purposes of FLCs may be directly related to the economic situation of institutions of higher education. In order to "survive," colleges and universities increase their focus on initiatives like FLCs in order to retain students and stay in business (Francis & Hampton, 1999; Slaughter, 1998).

Our critique of FLCs and the dominant discourse surrounding them should not suggest that such criticism has not existed in the past. Indeed, in responding to criticism that freshman seminars are often characterized as "holding students' hands," Gardner (1989) writes that

> the argument that freshman seminars coddle or hand hold students is true. Acknowledge it, then ask, "So what?" A certain amount of hand holding and coddling can be combined with legitimate academic work. If all this leads to a demonstrable increase in freshman learning and persistence rates, how is that disadvantageous to the institution? (p. 244)

Gardner dismisses the critique about "hand holding" first-year students, but the way he does so is what we find interesting. In his rationale for downplaying the critique, Gardner appears, in effect, to ignore the effects of hand holding on students that we have pointed to and suggests that as long as learning and persistence rates "increase," the *institution* should be content. By asking the question, "How is that disadvantageous to the institution?" Gardner reinforces a criterion that reifies the university and puts students in positions to support the institution. FLC advocates need to reframe the dominant discourse about universities' support of students to entail more than easing their bureaucratic experiences. Further, educators should be mindful that university administrations often "sell" FLCs based on enticements like easy registration and preplanned courses.

When the dominant discourse appears to focus on students, it has the potential to infantilize them. When, for example, registration is "taken care of" for students, when courses are selected for students, and when, as was the case in our experience, a required course ("New Student Orientation") was offered that stipulated that students play "name-learning" games, "team build," go through perfunctory campus tours, and fill out work sheets having to do with financial aid, "time management," and the essential parts of a syllabus, we wonder about the degree to which the FLC establishes expectations for students that, while well intentioned, often yield resentment about being treated less like a college student and more like a "baby." For example, in evaluating the FLC overall, Brad commented,

I know a lot of their policies and a lot of the stuff that goes along with the FLC is a little cheesy and some of the stuff that we have to go through with the ["New Student Orientation"], like the diversity training and whatever that guy is, team building. I think the idea, the concept, of an FLC is a good idea. I think that in theory it does kind of work because it makes people feel comfortable.

When asked what he would change, he said,

The team building and the diversity training. I think the . . . class is a good class in theory, but it's not really necessary. I think that it could be a weeklong course. I don't think we should have to learn about time management for two and a half hours a week, you know, that's really a waste of time.

In sum, then, our analysis of three elements of FLCs—historical antecedents, contemporary norms and discourses, and a case from our own practice—suggests that although the idea of an FLC has merit, a number of cautions are in order, including (1) consideration of who would benefit from an FLC and why, rather than the use of discourses of risk and community as a marketing tool to benefit institutions; (2) questioning the viability of administrative centralization of the FLC machinery, including courses and their content requirements; and (3) consideration of what historical traces are at work (and how) in FLCs as educators seek to cultivate student voice and autonomy through small communities. If FLCs are to continue to proliferate nationally, educators must attend to the nuances of the assumptions underlying them, their potential effects on faculty and students, and ultimately FLCs themselves as democratic learning communities.

Notes

1. Even where critique surfaces, the discourse is fashioned uncritically. Where "strengths" are listed for learning communities, there are no "weaknesses," only "challenges." Where there are claims to "collaboration," there is no "dissent" but, rather, "negativism." See, for example, DeMulder & Eby, 1999; Radencich et al., 1998.
2. For example, Temple University provides a bibliography regarding what the institution takes to be the historical and philosophical foundations for the learning communities it offers. Included in its list of nine historical sources are John Dewey's *Democracy and Education* (1916) and Alexander Meiklejohn's *The Experimental College* (1932). See www.temple.edu/LC/bibliography.html (retrieved September 11, 2003).
3. Meiklejohn (1924) outlined the importance of cultivating intellectual life and insight through the liberal arts in his 1912 inaugural address as president of Amherst College, in which he eschewed the practical demands of society and commerce, arguing that technical and professional education are "dominated by an immediate practical interest which cuts them off from the intellectual point of view of the scholar" (p. 35).
4. Meiklejohn (1932) argues, "It does mean that a democracy such as ours, by confusing the special and the general, has an infinite capacity for defeating its own deeper purposes. It means that the teachers of a democracy must be its critics, that in the training of its youth they must fight an unending battle against the blindly hostile forces of its popular drift. Their task is not so much to teach lessons whose value is recognized as to create the recognition of value for insights which are essential to individual and social well-being" (pp. 138–139).
5. Indeed, there may be an irony in aligning these two thinkers at all, particularly given their well-known disagreements in the 1940s over St. John's College's move to a classical, or "Great Books," curriculum. Gerald Grant and David Riesman (1978) point out that as educators nationally debated over Progressives' fear that a new curricular authoritarianism was overtaking American colleges and universities, "the high point of the debate was an exchange between John Dewey and Alexander Meiklejohn" (p. 49). Where the two men did agree was, as Dewey (1944) asserted, "that an overloaded and congested curriculum needs simplification" (p. 155). But their remedies differed, as Dewey argued against "the traditional view of truth as a fixed structure of eternal and unchanging principles already in our possession to which everything else should be made to conform" (1944, p. 188) and the isolation of vocational learning, scientific inquiry, and daily life from intellectual work. See also Meiklejohn's (1945) response to Dewey.

6. See Lenning and Ebbers (1999) for a list that includes GPA, retention, academic skills, self-esteem, engagement in learning, ability to meet academic and social needs, intellectual empowerment, complex thinking, openness to ideas different from one's own, and increased quality and quantity of learning (p. 52).
7. See also Soldner et al. (1999) on FLCs as many institutions' response to "the tremendous internal and external pressures to improve undergraduate education, student satisfaction, but most importantly, student persistence" (p. 115).
8. All names are pseudonyms.
9. FLCs have been suggested as a support through social and academic involvement for commuter students (Chickering & Reisser, 1993, p. 399; Pascarella & Terenzini, 1991, pp. 639–640), who have been labeled a "high-risk retention group" (Gordon, 1989, p. 196).

References

Astin, A. W. (1984). Student involvement: A developmental theory for higher education. *Journal of College Student Personnel, 25*(5), 297–308.

Astin, A. W. (1993). *What matters in college? Four critical years revisited.* San Francisco: Jossey-Bass.

Barr, R. B., & Tagg, J. (1995, November–December). From teaching to learning: A new paradigm for undergraduate education. *Change,* 13–25.

Braunstein, A., & McGrath, M. (1997). The retention of freshman students: An examination of the assumptions, beliefs, and perceptions held by college administrators and faculty. *College Student Journal, 31*(2), 188–200.

Brennan, R. T. (1998). The making of the liberal college: Alexander Meiklejohn at Amherst. *History of Education Quarterly, 28*(4), 569–597.

Chickering, A. W., & Reisser, L. (1993). *Education and identity* (2nd ed.). San Francisco: Jossey-Bass.

DeMulder, E. K., & Eby, K. (1999). Bridging troubled waters: Learning communities for the 21st century. *American Behavioral Scientist, 42*(5), 892–901.

Dewey, J. (1902). *The child and the curriculum.* Chicago: University of Chicago Press.

Dewey, J. (1916). *Democracy and education.* New York: Free Press.

Dewey, J. (1938). *Experience and education.* New York: MacMillan.

Dewey, J. (1944, August). Challenge to liberal thought. *Fortune, 30,* 155–158, 181–182, 184, 186, 188.

Evenbeck, S., & Williams, G. (1998). Learning communities: An instructional team approach. *Metropolitan Universities, 9*(1), 35–46.

Francis, J. G., & Hampton, M. C. (1999). Resourceful responses: The adaptive research university and the drive to the market. *Journal of Higher Education, 70*(6), 625–641.

Gabelnick, F., MacGregor, J., Matthews, R. S., & Smith, B. L. (1990). *Students in learning communities: Engaging with self, others, and community* (New Directions for Teaching and Learning, 41). San Francisco: Jossey-Bass.

Gardner, J. N. (1989). Starting a freshman seminar program. In M. L. Upcraft, J. N. Gardner, & Associates (Eds.), *The freshman year experience: Helping students survive and succeed in college* (pp. 238–249). San Francisco: Jossey-Bass.

Gordon, V. P. (1989). Origins and purposes of the freshman seminar. In M. L. Upcraft, J. N. Gardner, & Associates (Eds.), *The freshman year experience: Helping students survive and succeed in college* (pp. 183–197). San Francisco: Jossey-Bass.

Grant, G., & Riesman, D. (1978). *The perpetual dream: Reform and experiment in the American college.* Chicago: University of Chicago Press.

Guarasci, R. (2001). Recentering learning: An interdisciplinary approach to academic and student affairs. *New Directions for Higher Education, 116,* 101–109.

Johnson, J. L. (2000–2001). Learning communities and special efforts in the retention of university students: What works, what doesn't and is the return worth the investment? *Journal of College Student Retention, 2*(3), 219–238.

Kuh, G. D. (1995). Out of class experiences associated with student learning and personal development. *Journal of Higher Education, 66*(2), 123–155.

LeCompte, M. D., & Preissle, J. (1993). *Ethnography and qualitative design in educational research.* San Diego: Academic Press.

Lenning, O. T., & Ebbers, L. (1999). *The powerful potential of learning communities: Improving education for the future* (ASHE-ERIC Higher Education Report, 26[6]). Washington, DC: George Washington University.

Lesko, N. (2001). *Act your age! A cultural construction of adolescence.* New York: Routledge.

Meiklejohn, A. (1924). The aim of the liberal college. In M. G. Fulton (Ed.), *College life: Its conditions and problems* (pp. 32–52). New York: Macmillan.

Meiklejohn, A. (1932). *The experimental college.* New York: Harper and Row.

Meiklejohn, A. (1942). *Education between two worlds.* New York: Harper and Collins.

Meiklejohn, A. (1945, January). A reply to John Dewey. *Fortune, 31,* 207–219.

Pascarella, E. T., & Terenzini, P. T. (1991). *How college affects students: Findings and insights from twenty years of research.* San Francisco: Jossey-Bass.

Radencich, M. C., Thompson, T., Anderson, N. A., Oropallo, K., Fleege, P., Harrison, M., et al. (1998). The culture of cohorts: Preservice teacher education teams at a southeastern university in the United States. *Journal of Education for Teaching, 24*(2), 109–127.

Rudolph, F. (1977). *Curriculum: A history of the American undergraduate course of study since 1636.* San Francisco: Jossey-Bass.

Sapon-Shevin, M., & Chandler-Scott, K. (2001). Student cohorts: Communities of critique or dysfunctional families? *Journal of Teacher Education, 52*(5), 350–364.

Seidman, I. (1998). *Interviewing as qualitative research: A guide for research in education and the social sciences* (2nd ed.). New York: Teachers College Press.

Shapiro, N. S., & Levine, J. H. (1999). *Creating learning communities: A practical guide to winning support, organizing for change, and implementing programs.* San Francisco: Jossey-Bass.

Slaughter, S. (1998). Federal policy and supply-side institutional resource allocation at public research universities. *Review of Higher Education, 21*(3), 209–244.

Soldner, L., Lee, Y., & Duby, P. (1999). Welcome to the block: Developing freshman learning communities that work. *Journal of College Student Retention, 1*(2), 115–129.

Strommer, D. W. (1999). Teaching and learning in a learning community. In J. H. Levine (Ed.), *Learning communities: New structures, new partnerships for learning* (Monograph no. 26, pp. 39–49). Columbia: University of South Carolina, National Resource Center for the First-Year Experience and Students in Transition.

Tierney, W. G. (1992). An anthropological analysis of student participation in college. *Journal of Higher Education, 63*(6), 603–618.

Tinto, V. (1993). *Leaving college: Rethinking the causes and cures of student attrition.* Chicago: University of Chicago Press.

Tinto, V. (1997). Classrooms as communities. *Journal of Higher Education, 68*(6), 599–623.

Tinto, V. (1998). Colleges as communities: Taking research on student persistence seriously. *Review of Higher Education, 21*(2), 167–177.

Tinto, V., & Goodsell, A. (1993). Freshman interest groups and the first-year experience: Constructing student communities in a large university. *Journal of the Freshman Year Experience, 6*(1), 7–27.

Williams, R. (1976). *Keywords: A vocabulary of culture and society.* New York: Oxford University Press.

Does Interdisciplinarity Promote Learning? Theoretical Support and Researchable Questions

Lisa R. Lattuca, Lois J. Voigt and Kimberly Q. Fath

Do students in interdisciplinary courses and programs learn better or learn more than those in discipline-based curricula? Advocates portray interdisciplinary courses as more engaging than disciplinary courses because they capture students' intellectual interest and help them connect information from discrete disciplines. Some argue that interdisciplinary study better prepares students for work and citizenship by developing higher-order cognitive skills such as problem-solving, critical thinking, and the ability to employ multiple perspectives (e.g., Hursh, Hass, & Moore, 1983; Newell, 1990; Newell & Green, 1982). William Newell (1994) claimed that interdisciplinary courses could increase students' ability to evaluate experts' testimony; tolerance for ambiguity; sensitivity to ethical issues and disciplinary, political, or religious bias; creative or original thinking; and humility or listening skills.

Today, nearly 40% of faculty report having taught an interdisciplinary course (Lindholm et al., 2002), but evidence of the impact of these courses on student learning is sparse. Only a few studies at the college level lend support to the idea that interdisciplinary study has positive effects on learning. Australian students in an interdisciplinary course that used scientific evidence in decision making and problem solving improved their independent judgment and decreased their scores on a measure of dogmatism (Barnett & Brown, 1981). Newell (1992) found that students in the School of Interdisciplinary Studies at Miami University (Ohio) performed better than students in disciplinary programs on a set of ACT/COMP assessments. Alexander Astin (1993) reported that enrolling in an interdisciplinary course was positively correlated with self-reported growth in three areas: knowledge, critical thinking skills, and preparation for graduate or professional school.

Newell (1994) suggested that some of the beneficial outcomes of interdisciplinarity "stem as much from the way in which the courses are taught as they do from their interdisciplinary nature" (p. 35). More recently, Lisa Tsui (1999) used CIRP data to explore the effects of different kinds of courses and instructional techniques on students' self-reported critical thinking skills. She found that students' gains in critical thinking skills in interdisciplinary (and other kinds of courses) could be partially attributed to their association with the instructional variables measured in the study.

In addition to a lack of empirical evidence to support claims about interdisciplinary courses, there is little theorizing about how interdisciplinarity might encourage learning. Deborah Vess (2001) wrote:

> Although interdisciplinarians are building on an exceptionally strong foundation in the scholarship of teaching and learning, . . . [m]ore work needs to be done to better chart the connections among theory, pedagogy, course enactment, and student perceptions of the learning environment; further, we need to explore connections between the enactment of various models of interdisciplinarity and actual learning as reflected in coursework and later performance. (p. 96)

Reprinted by permission from the *Review of Higher Education* 28, no. 1 (fall 2004).

In this article, we take two steps toward a remedy. First, we use theories of learning and cognition to explore how and why interdisciplinary courses might promote specific learning outcomes. Next, we use these insights to build a research agenda that would encourage systematic study of the effects of interdisciplinarity on student learning.

Moving Targets: Defining Interdisciplinary Courses

Interdisciplinarity is often defined as the integration of existing disciplinary perspectives. If we accept this definition, then to understand the teaching and learning that occurs in an interdisciplinary course, we might explore the course's disciplinary pedigree, consulting, for example, Janet Donald's (2002) synthesis of 25 years of research on the influence of disciplinary epistemologies on teaching and student learning. If interdisciplinarity is, however, more differentiated—sometimes combining disciplines, but at other times critiquing and/or transcending the disciplines—then an exploration of a course's disciplinary contributions is insufficient, and another approach is required.

In one of the few empirical studies of interdisciplinarity in practice, Lisa Lattuca (2001) derived a typology of four different forms of interdisciplinarity based on the questions or issues that motivate the interdisciplinary research or teaching approach. (See Table 1.)

In *informed disciplinarity*, instructors focus instruction primarily on a single discipline but call upon other disciplines to illuminate course content. For example, a psychologist teaching a course on learning may discuss how social interactions and environments influence learning. If the instructor believes that learning is primarily determined by developmental structures, the discussion of social interactions informs the course but does not substantially alter the dominant view of learning.

Now consider a course on learning team-taught by a cognitive psychologist and a cultural anthropologist. Each instructor brings a different perspective on learning. The psychologist sees learning primarily as an individual activity; the anthropologist contends that learning is dramatically influenced by social and cultural systems. In *synthetic interdisciplinarity*, instructors combine theories, concepts, and perhaps even research methods from different disciplines; but the contributing disciplines remain clearly identifiable, revealing relatively bounded content areas and perhaps distinctive methods of inquiry.

In contrast, *transdisciplinarity* mutes the disciplinary sources of theories and methods, applying them across disciplines so that they are no longer associated with a single discipline or field. Transdisciplinary concepts, theories, and methods are tested in one discipline, then another. The course we have been describing would be transdisciplinary if the instructor argued that all learning, whether by humans or animals or organizations, could be explained by a single, overarching theory. The disciplines are not the focus of this type of course—the transdisciplinary theory is; and it is applied in domains that have traditionally been considered the realm of distinctive disciplines.

Finally, imagine a course taught by an instructor seeking a comprehensive view of learning in humans. The course explores perspectives on learning from different fields—for example, cognitive psychology, anthropology, education, sociology, and human development—but the instructor urges students to critique the disciplinary theories and research presented to expose their limitations. Her goal is to preserve the complexity of the phenomenon of learning; and although a *conceptual interdisciplinary* course like this one includes disciplinary perspectives, it has no compelling disciplinary focus. Conceptual interdisciplinarity also accommodates poststructural, postmodern, and feminist

TABLE 1
Types of Interdisciplinary Teaching

Name	Characteristics
Informed disciplinarity	Courses and instruction informed by other disciplines
Synthetic interdisciplinarity	Courses and instruction that link disciplines
Transdisciplinarity	Courses and instruction that cross disciplines
Conceptual interdisciplinarity	Courses and instruction without a compelling disciplinary basis

forms of inquiry, which explicitly critique the disciplines and may contend that *all* questions require interdisciplinary answers.

Researchers can generalize about disciplinary epistemologies because individuals within a discipline *tend* to rely on shared epistemologies, methods, concepts, and teaching practices. (For discussions, see Braxton & Hargens, 1996; Donald, 2002; Lattuca, 2001.) Interdisciplinary courses are more difficult to characterize, not only because they may include an underfined number of possible disciplinary combinations, but also because instructors' epistemologies are not necessarily consistent with those of the disciplines. Lattuca (2001) found that faculty using scientific paradigms tended to engage in synthetic interdisciplinarity and transdisciplinarity that respected methods of inquiry used in their home disciplines. Faculty in interpretative disciplines more often practiced conceptual interdisciplinarity, apparently feeling less constrained by disciplinary conventions. Because more research is needed to confirm these patterns, we chose to ground our discussion of interdisciplinary teaching and learning in two actual courses.

Two Illustrative Cases

It is not our intention to make claims about all interdisciplinary courses and teaching. Nor do we contend that the instruction we describe is unique to interdisciplinary courses. On the contrary, much of the instruction we highlight could be practiced in disciplinary courses. Our purpose, simply, is to examine interdisciplinarity in practice to explore why it might encourage student learning. We rely on examples from two courses, representing two types of interdisciplinarity: synthetic and conceptual. Each course spans a variety of disciplines in the sciences, social sciences, and humanities.

The courses are offered at two institutions known for interdisciplinary teaching: the University of Chicago and Miami University. Using the internet we identified courses (a) from undergraduate interdisciplinary programs (b) that spanned a range of disciplines and (c) that offered a clear description of course content and pedagogical methods. We contacted the course instructors and requested a telephone interview to gather additional information and to clarify our understanding of instructional purposes and teaching methods. The instructors gave us permission to include their names, affiliations, and descriptions of their courses. Descriptions of these focal courses, "Introduction to Environmental Studies" and "Kid's Stuff: Toys and Modern American Society," follow.

Environmental Studies: Synthetic Interdisciplinarity

The "Introduction to Environmental Studies" course at the University of Chicago serves as the foundational class for the undergraduate Environmental Studies concentration. Students typically take the course at the beginning of their third year, but nearly half of the students in the class are nonmajors. At the time of our interviews in 2000, the course materials included one textbook, the World Resources Institute's 1994–1995 almanac, and supplemental readings. The class met three times a week, and the short essays due each week accounted for 50% of the course grade. Class attendance (25%) and class participation (25%), including chat room dialogue comprised the balance of the requirements and grading scheme. The official course description stated:

> We analyze the impact of the human enterprise on the natural world that sustains it. Topics include human population dynamics; the role of economic and industrial activity in human well being; our use of natural resources (e.g., energy, soil, and water); biodiversity; prospects for sustainable development; and the role of cultural institutions and values in these matters. The format includes reading and discussing diverse sources and writing a short paper each week (Steck, 2000).

The instructor, who had taught the course for six years at the time of this interview, reported in an interview that his primary goal was to enable students to understand the relationship of human beings to the natural environment, including relevant events and their causal factors, and to gain "some sense of what can be brought to bear to make a difficult situation better." The primary guiding questions for the course included, "What is happening to our environment? What are the mechanisms driving environmental crises, and what are the remedies and the obstacles to resolving the crises?" (Steck, 2000). Typically, the professor lectured for approximately two-thirds of each class period utilizing questions and dialogue in the Socratic tradition, and reserved the remainder of the session for class discussion. Students also participated in chat room dialogue, and occasionally organized supplementary discussion sessions.

An example of synthetic interdisciplinarity, this course links disciplines to respond to organizing questions about the relationship between human-kind and the environment. Students encounter a variety of disciplines in the sciences, social sciences, and humanities, including, philosophy and ethics, human development, economics, biology, and political science.

Kid's Stuff: Conceptual Interdisciplinarity

"Kid's Stuff: Toys and Modern American Society" is a four-credit course offered at Miami University that uses toys and the concept of play to "explore human creativity and its codification in diverse situations" (Metcalf, 1999). "Kid's Stuff" was the required humanities course for second-year students in the School of Interdisciplinary Studies. The fall 1999 syllabus explained:

> This course will examine the development and cultural significance of modern American toys. Beginning with what has been called the "modern toy culture" in the late 19th century, it will conclude with an examination of Christmas, a consumer ritual in which toys have become a social sacrament. The class will use a variety of approaches in the humanities to consider how toys represent, and help influence, who we are and how we react to others. (Metcalf, 1999)

Questions guiding this course included "What is childhood?" "What are notions of play?" "How does popular culture influence the meaning we give toys?" (Metcalf, 1999). Thematic units included: Toys, Play, and the Invention of Childhood; Boy Culture, Aggression, and Toys; and "Bah Humbug": Unwrapping Christmas. The instructor would explore these themes using sociology, developmental psychology, art criticism, and history, as well as perspectives on gender and power.

Students in this course attended two seminar sessions and a one-hour lecture each week. The instructor rarely lectured, instead using a variety of instructional approaches—primarily discussion and active learning—in the seminar sessions. Students also viewed films about toys and play, visited the university's Child Studies Center to observe children, simulated play, and explored the impact of merchandizing on perceptions of toys through optional field trips to toy stores and shows.

The main assignment, accounting for 60% of a student's grade, consisted of an in-depth study of a toy, person, or toy-related phenomenon. Participation and attendance was worth 10% of the final grade, while the remaining 30% of the course grade was earned through the completion of exercises or written applications of the class readings.

"Kid's Stuff" is an example of a conceptual interdisciplinary course. As such courses often do, this one focused on issues related to human society. Although classified as a humanities course, the class used information from the sciences and social sciences as well. The instructor did not emphasize the use of disciplinary perspectives but rather stressed the development of critical perspectives on culture, gender, and power, which tend to signal conceptual interdisciplinarity.

Does Interdisciplinarity Promote Learning? Theoretical Perspectives

To understand how and why interdisciplinarity might promote learning we call upon on a number of theories of learning and cognition. James Greeno and his group (1997) identified three general perspectives on the nature of knowing, thinking, and learning that have shaped American educational thought and practice: the associationist/behaviorist perspective, the domain-structural / cognitive perspective, and the situative perspective. Each perspective, he noted, foregrounds different aspects of learning:

> The associationist/behaviorist perspective emphasizes the development of skills; the domain-structural/cognitive perspective emphasizes conceptual understanding and strategies of problem solving and reasoning; and the situative perspective emphasizes participation in practices of inquiry and sense-making of a community, and development of individual's identities as thinkers and learners. (p. 87)

Greeno and his colleagues argued that all of these perspectives contribute to our understandings of educational practices. Furthermore, while different perspectives may encourage particular practices, practices do not belong exclusively to a cognitive, situative, or behaviorist perspective, although the different perspectives correspond to significantly different emphases in practice. In this spirit, we analyze our focal courses through a variety of theoretical lenses to examine how interdisciplinarity might promote learning.

Engaging Students' Prior Knowledge and Experience

Psychologists use *cognition* to mean how people acquire information. Cognitive theories view learning as an active, constructive, goal-oriented process that depends on the learner's mental activities (Schuell, 1986). These activities include processes such as planning and goal setting; active selection of stimuli; and learners' attempts to organize the material they are learning.

Researchers have studied how knowledge is organized and stored in cognitive structures in individual memory (e.g., Ausubel, Novak, & Hanesian, 1978; Shavelson, 1974). Although they conceptualize cognitive structures somewhat differently, theorists and researchers agree that how new information is organized and linked to previous knowledge in memory is an important influence on learning: what a learner already knows, and the extent to which that knowledge is activated, has implications for what will be learned and what will make sense to the learner (e.g., Piaget, 1952; Vygotsky, 1978). The organized, structured, and abstract bodies of knowledge (schemas) that learners bring to bear when learning novel material determine how they interpret the learning task and what they will understand (Bransford, 2000; Schuell, 1986).

Instructors can promote learning by helping students access prior knowledge and connect new information to their existing knowledge and understandings. Does interdisciplinarity offer learners more opportunities to organize and to store their learning? In both of our sample courses, the instructors help students to make explicit connections between what is to be learned and what they have already learned through schooling and other experiences. The environmental studies instructor, in the phone interview, explained that to promote effective thinking he "meets students where they are":

> I will ask them a question, "Why do we breathe oxygen?" or something . . . and they'll know a little something because they've been to high school, and so we start there and we just work on it. And I fill in the gaps and correct them and we take the next step.

David Rumelhart and D. Norman (1978) labeled the encoding of new information in terms of existing schemas, *accretion*, and the process of constructing new schemas, *restructuring*. By beginning with students' existing knowledge this focal instructor may encourage either accretion or restructuring. Rumelhart and Norman postulated a third kind of learning that occurs when individuals "tune" existing schemas, refining or modifying them for use in different situations. In "Kid's Stuff," the encoding of information depends heavily on the restructuring of prior knowledge. Students are asked to incorporate their own experiences with toys and play into their interpretation of course readings. One class exercise asked students to "Recall a fond (or awful) experience related to Christmas or to this 'holiday' time of year, and consider it in light of issues arising from this week's readings" (Metcalf, 1999).

Interdisciplinarity may succeed because it provides individuals with more opportunities to connect new knowledge to existing knowledge. This process might occur as instructors and students call upon disciplinary information to solve complex, boundary-spanning problems or as they access relevant memories and experiences that facilitate understanding of new concepts and ideas. In either case, learners are integrating new ideas with ideas in working memory. Do interdisciplinary courses help students develop rich networks that connect knowledge and experience? Are instructors' efforts to evoke students' prior academic and experiential knowledge equally effective in promoting learning?

Encouraging Effective Thinking

James Davis (1995) argued that students in an information society need "considerably more help than they usually get" to find, retrieve, understand, and use information. Synthesis, analysis, and application, he claimed, "are best carried out . . . in interdisciplinary courses, where the focus is on developing critical thinking skills, employing multiple perspectives, and relating information to some larger conceptual framework than the concerns of a single discipline" (p. 38). To explore this claim, we focus here on the development of thinking skills, such as problem solving, reflective judgment, and critical thinking.

Newell (1994) argued that the learning processes used in interdisciplinary courses effectively develop students' abilities to synthesize and to evaluate the testimony of experts. In our focal courses, instructors took students on an intellectual journey that required them to develop factual understandings and to use such thinking skills as analysis, synthesis, and evaluation. In "Kid's Stuff," assignments required students to analyze objects of popular culture through various theoretical lenses. For example, one assignment asked students to use the gender critique explained in their readings to deconstruct the website of an action figure they had chosen.

Students in "Introduction to Environmental Studies" studied ecosystems. In doing so, they explored human nature and human culture to understand how relationships between humans and the environment have changed over time. For their first assignment, students developed "a succinct thoughtful essay" on this topic: "(a) After America was reached by European explorers, should Europe have respected the priority of its 'native' inhabitants and left it in peace? (b) Apply your answer to present initiatives to commercialize the Amazon rainforest." Students were asked to apply the principles they developed in response to an historical issue to a present-day problem. The juxtaposition requires students to evaluate their responses for logical consistency. In his well-known taxonomy of educational outcomes, Bloom (1956/1984) classified evaluation as the most challenging of the cognitive skills expected of students.

Most of the assignments in the focal courses stressed analysis, synthesis, and evaluation. Are assignments that require such thinking common in interdisciplinary courses or did we simply locate two exceptional courses? How common are such assignments in discipline-based college courses? How common are they in introductory courses such as "Kid's Stuff" and "Introduction to Environmental Studies"? In a study of the relationship between postsecondary teachers' prior knowledge, beliefs about teaching, and teaching effectiveness, Robert Ruddell and Pauline Harris (1989) found that influential teachers approached instruction as a learner-centered problem-solving process, mentally engaging students in a process of intellectual discovery by raising questions and using examples related to students' own experiences and understandings. Ruddell and Harris defined "influential" teachers as those who had a significant impact on their students' subsequent academic achievement and who had the reputation among former students and colleagues of being an expert teacher. Our focal instructors similarly tapped students' prior knowledge and experiences, and each drew students into a process of inquiry built on these prior understandings.

Each focal course was organized around a series of guiding questions. The instructor in "Kid's Stuff" asked questions such as: "What is childhood from a historical and sociological perspective? How does popular culture influence the meaning we give toys?" The instructor for "Introduction to Environmental Studies" organized his course around the questions, "What is happening to our environment? What are the mechanisms driving environmental crises? What are the remedies and the obstacles to resolving the crises?" In addition to posing questions, influential teachers explored the social, historical, and ideological contexts of issues (Ruddell & Harris, 1989). In our focal courses, contextualization was an essential aspect of learning. For example, the final project for "Kid's Stuff" was an in-depth study of a toy, person, or toy-related phenomenon that included a description and an analysis of the subject, emphasizing its social, cultural, and individual meaning.

Situated learning theories suggest that complex, real-world problems, such as those associated with interdisciplinarity, may enhance learning because they engage students in authentic tasks similar to those they will be expected to perform as workers or as citizens. Information embedded in a structured context—that is, in a set of meaningful relationships—is easier to recall (Rogoff, 2003). The real-world examples and problems that abound in our focal courses create meaningful contexts that students should find helpful as they consider abstract ideas. Such problems may also aid students' meaning-making because the tasks associated with the problem replicate the data gathering, analysis, and problem solving that students expect to encounter in everyday life and work.

Real-world problems may promote learning in additional ways. An assignment for "Introduction to Environmental Studies" requires students to utilize population trend data from developing and industrialized nations. The goal was to "turn numbers into concepts" by writing a brief essay describing and contrasting population trends. To accomplish this task, students completed calculations using prescribed formulas. In his description of the assignment, the instructor wrote, "Being real life, the story may not be a tidy one: so itemize the evidence which supports and that which confounds your position." This assignment prescribed a sequence of steps, but it also required students to use the data to make informed judgments that supported their opinions or courses of action.

Pollution, population growth, alternative energy sources, global warming, and sustainable development, to name just a few of the topics covered in "Introduction to Environmental Studies," are examples of ill-structured problems. Ill-structured problems cannot be completely described because the available data are incomplete. There is uncertainty about the "rightness" of solutions, and more than one solution is often possible. In many cases, ill-structured problems require analysis through multiple frames of reference. Individuals must consider alternative arguments, seek out evidence, evaluate its trustworthiness, and construct a solution that is itself open to question and further evaluation. Patricia King and Karen Kitchener (1994) contrast these with "well-structured" problems that can be solved through a given decision-making procedure. Well-structured problems have single correct answers that can be found, whereas ill-structured problems require, in King and Kitchener's terminology, the use of reflective judgment/thinking. They differentiate between reflective and critical. In their definition, critical thinking involves different kinds of reasoning (e.g., deductive and inductive) and is often characterized as a set of skills that can be improved by learning a set of rules or behaviors. Reflective judgment, in contrast, is "the outcome of an interaction between the individual's conceptual skills and environments that promote or inhibit the acquisition of these skills" (p. 18).

When courses like "Introduction to Environmental Studies" address real-world problems, they present students with opportunities to develop and to practice reflective judgment. They may therefore promote sophisticated forms of learning that serve students in college and beyond. The instructors for our sample courses said they were less concerned with covering content than with developing students' thinking skills. Are these instructors representative of the instructors who teach interdisciplinary courses or who gravitate to interdisciplinary programs? Do the goals of interdisciplinary courses systematically differ from the goals of disciplinary courses? Are interdisciplinary courses more likely to require, and thus enhance, problem solving, critical thinking, and reflective judgment?

Earlier we noted that people try to understand new information in terms of what they already know. Robert Glaser (1984) argued that it is therefore useful to teach problem solving in terms of the knowledge domains with which individuals are familiar. If instructors understand students' current state of knowledge, they can improve students' learning by providing overt organizational schemes or teaching temporary models that scaffold new information. When students are asked to interrogate these organizational schemes and models—and in the process either instantiate or falsify them—they are organizing their knowledge. The models also provide a basis for problem solving that leads to the formation of more complete and expert schemas.

The pedagogical implication is that effective instructors use a process of interrogation and confrontation to build new knowledge. This process is often presented through case, discovery, or Socratic methods of inquiry. The instructor for "Introduction to Environmental Studies" lectures approximately 65% of class time, and punctuates his lectures with what he describes as a Socratic dialogue:

> I do the lecturing by asking them questions . . . and so I will say, "What's the problem with capitalism?" and whatever they say, I will lead them by asking them questions. I will try to draw on what they should know, do know, could imagine. And it isn't then a factual discourse, but it's an attempt to digest the issues and integrate things and have them thinking. And then I hope that they'll be better prepared in time then to confront the issues.

Linda Kay and Jerry Young (1986) defined Socratic teaching as an open-ended question-answer format that encourages students to think independently; but others contend that this method bears only superficial resemblance to the often ironic and provocative strategy employed by Socrates (Fishman, 1985; Rud, 1997). Socratic dialogue can be confrontational, as the "Environmental Studies" instructor acknowledges: "I'm pretty provocative . . . I'm sparring with them, I'm challenging them, I'm even needling them a little bit. I want to take a perverse position to challenge them." More importantly, the Socratic and discovery methods take their cues from students' preconceptions and questions. Rather than performing a script of predetermined questions, the instructor begins with students' thinking, developing relevant questions to move the process to a fruitful end. Such dialogue is not unique to interdisciplinary classes, but researchers might explore the nature of dialogue in interdisciplinary and disciplinary courses.

Developing Multiple Perspectives

Davis (1995) claimed that students in an information society need to develop the capacity to cope with multiple perspectives on issues and problems, and that interdisciplinary courses are well suited to this task: "Problems come in 'layers' that need to be separated and analyzed, but solutions usually need to be comprehensive, addressing the problem as a system, not as pieces" (p. 39). Interdisciplinary courses, Davis suggested, emphasize the development of comprehensive perspectives. But knowing where to find the answers is only a first step toward understanding. Students must also be able to see, evaluate, and select from among differing perspectives that bear on a problem.

Students' social and educational experiences influence the ways they think about knowledge and, thus, their capacity to appreciate and choose among multiple perspectives. Adults' educational experiences appear to influence people's beliefs about the nature of knowledge and learning (i.e., their epistemologies). Reflecting on 25 years of research on college students' epistemological beliefs, Michael Paulsen and Charles Wells (1998) noted that studies have consistently found that "as students advance in their coursework and experience other aspects of the academic environment over the years of college (and graduate school), they develop more sophisticated epistemological beliefs" (p. 367).

Most studies of epistemological development owe a debt to William Perry (1968) who theorized that in late adolescence individuals move through several different views of knowledge; they progress from simplistic views (things are right or wrong, good or bad, true or false; knowledge comes from authorities) to multifaceted ones (there are multiple opinions and perspectives in the world). The urge and ability to resolve conflicting ideas and opinions, and to evaluate evidence supporting or refuting them occurs in a position Perry called relativism. In relativism, students are able to consider multiple perspectives and to assess their relative worth; ultimately, students not only assess others' perspectives, but also commit to a personal perspective (Perry, 1968, 1981). In a longitudinal study of young men and women in college and beyond, Marcia Baxter Magolda (1992) extended Perry's work and demonstrated young adults' increasing capacity to contend with and choose among multiple perspectives.

While some believe that epistemological beliefs evolve through developmental structures (Baxter Magolda, 1999), others argue that beliefs about knowledge and learning are strongly influenced by cultural and social interactions (Schommer, 1998; Schommer-Aikins & Hutter, 2002). Research reveals correlations among epistemological beliefs and contextual factors such as home environments, pre-college schooling, and major fields (Jehng, Johnson, & Anderson, 1993; Paulsen & Wells, 1998; Schommer, 1993, 1998; Schommer & Dunnell, 1994; Schommer & Walker, 1995). Despite differing assumptions about the sources of epistemological beliefs, researchers agree that pedagogy can promote the development of sophisticated views of knowledge—and should therefore challenge students to learn to recognize, evaluate, and choose among multiple perspectives.

The instructor of "Kid's Stuff" challenges traditional views of what makes art "good." In his classroom, multiple disciplinary perspectives (e.g., sociology and developmental psychology) are brought to bear on the topic. This approach is consistent with the goals of the School of Interdisciplinary Studies, where first-year courses present a variety of disciplinary perspectives that students will be expected to utilize in their second year. But the instructor of "Kid's Stuff" also expects his students to view toys through the lenses of power and gender, and he uses toys like Barbie dolls and action figures to address these issues.

According to the instructor, this class includes a wide variety of perspectives because of the nature of the subject matter and because of the ideas and opinions that students bring to the class: "I stay open to engaging students wherever they're coming from and having them, hopefully, see the opposite side of whatever attitude they have." He presents a broad set of ideas various disciplines and fields. During the first week of the course, he provided an overview of ecosystems and introduced questions of human nature and culture. In the next week, the discussion turned to classical economic concepts, like markets, and how these impact the environment. Once that background was laid, the class considered problems like energy use and alternative energy, pollution of water and air, agriculture, and food supplies. The focus was on quantitative analysis and technical issues, which the instructor juxtaposed against the philosophical base laid in the first week of the course. In the next section of the course, students studied developed and developing nations and discussed issues like sustainable development, industrialization, alternatives to industrialization, and demography. Finally, the course moved to an examination of politics, geopolitics, and policy.

Interdisciplinary courses may be especially well suited for encouraging complex views of knowledge among students; such courses, by definition, include multiple perspectives. But this assumption must be explored. There is some evidence that epistemologies are domain specific. A number of studies reveal correlations between students' academic majors and epistemological beliefs (Jehng, Johnson, & Anderson, 1993; Schommer & Walker, 1995; Paulsen & Wells, 1998). If further research confirms these findings, researchers will want to study learning outcomes of students in interdisciplinary programs to understand how such learning environments compare with discipline-based programs in terms of their influence on students' epistemological beliefs.

Many of the theories we have discussed thus far originated in schools of thought that conceptualize learning as an act of individual cognition. Situated or sociocultural views of learning, in contrast, frame cognition as a social interaction, and thus argue that cognition is powerfully shaped by the multidimensional and overlapping social and cultural contexts in which it occurs (Rogoff & Lave, 1984/1999; Vygotsky, 1978). A situated or sociocultural analysis of our focal courses would foreground the instructors' attempts to guide students in the use of the particular intellectual tools associated with American higher education and in the practice of particular kinds of academic discourse. It might also investigate the influence of these traditional methods of discourse and discovery on the range of problem solutions that the students and instructor can imagine. Importantly, this kind of analysis underscores the potential that differently organized learning experiences have for promoting learning. Our focal instructors appear quite purposeful in structuring and nurturing a particular kind of learning experience for students. Are all interdisciplinary course instructors as attentive to classroom and interactional contexts and dynamics?

Motivating Students to Learn

A number of studies have demonstrated significant relationships between students' epistemological beliefs and motivational constructs. Michael Paulsen and Kenneth Feldman (1999a, 1999b) found that students with more sophisticated beliefs about knowledge (i.e., that knowledge is tentative, interwoven, and acquired gradually, and that the capacity to learn can be changed and enhanced) were more likely to self-regulate their learning, have intrinsic goal motivations, appreciate the value of learning tasks, feel in control of their learning, and have a sense of self-efficacy than students who believed in simple knowledge (knowledge consists of unrelated, isolated facts), quick learning (either you "get" it right away, or not at all), and that the ability to learn is fixed at birth. The latter are also more likely to have an extrinsic goal orientation. In this section, we explore whether interdisciplinary courses, with their emphasis on creating holistic views of reality through the use of multiple perspectives, might be particularly effective in motivating students to learn and to self-regulate their learning.

Motivation and goal orientations are interrelated concepts. Both vary depending on the nature of the academic task, and can change over time (Hagen & Weinstein, 1995). Intrinsic motivation is characterized by personal interest and internal rewards: reading a book for the pleasure of doing so, or learning for the sake of learning (McKeachie et al., 1990). Extrinsic motivations represent external or secondary goals, usually rewards or punishments, such as learning in order to attain a good grade or to avoid a bad one, or to qualify for an occupation. A students might begin a course with only extrinsic motivations (to fulfill a distribution requirement), but eventually develop deep interests and intrinsic motivations. Mastery and performance goal orientations represent similar concepts. Students with a mastery orientation work hard in order to learn, while those with a performance orientation work to earn a high grade (Ames, 1992; Pintrich & Schunk, 1996). A student may demonstrate a goal orientation in a class in his or her major, and a performance orientation in a general education course in which he or she has little personal interest.

Interest is an intrinsic motivator that "emerges from an individual's interaction with his or her environment" (Krapp, Hidi, & Renninger, 1992, p. 5). Researchers often distinguish between situational interest, which is transitory and may be elicited by surprise or novelty, and individual interest, a more enduring preference for certain topics or tasks (Tobias, 1995). Schiefele's (1991) review of studies of high school and college students suggests that while varying levels of interest may not affect recall of details in a text, greater interest positively affects the ability to comprehend and remember complex concepts.

Whether by design—because they recognize motivational differences in their students, or simple professorial preference—the instructors of our focal courses appeal to different motivational and interest factors. The creator of "Kid's Stuff" used novelty (situational interest) to capture students' attention. He opened the course with a screening of the film *Star Wars* and a discussion of the five-inch figurines inspired by the film. He then moved to the topics of childhood, power, gender, and symbolism in culture. In contrast, the instructor for environmental studies attempted to tap students' self-interest. He demonstrated the impact of the environment on their lives and then sought to dialogue with them, both in class and in writing, about possible solutions.

Paul Pintrich (1995) defined self-regulated learning as the "active, goal-directed, self-control of behavior, motivation, and cognition for academic tasks by an individual student" (1995, p. 5). Self-regulated learners can select appropriate learning strategies to achieve desired outcomes and adjust those strategies in response to internal and external feedback. Studies suggest that mastery goals (discussed earlier) contribute to self-regulated learning, and that both self-efficacy (belief in one's ability) and self-regulation predict cognitive engagement and academic performance (Pintrich & DeGroot, 1990).

The environmental studies instructor encouraged self-efficacy and self-regulated learning when discussing the IDS program's senior thesis requirement with students:

> I say, "Well, it's not really a requirement because I can guarantee you will pass, so you don't have to do anything, but if you take it seriously and write the paper, that—you know—work on, do something that means something to you, it will be the most important thing you've ever done, and it will be a life experience for you. And it all depends on you asking yourself, "Why am I in this major? Why do I want to write on this topic? What does this mean to me?'" and delving and letting it come from within.

Citing studies that examined autonomy-supportive and controlling learning environments, Edward Deci (1992) concluded, "When people experience the context as supporting their autonomy—as encouraging their initiation and choice—they will maintain their interest and intrinsic motivation" (p. 59).

Offering students options or choices can also increase their intrinsic motivation and interest, improve self-efficacy, and foster self-regulated learning (Ames, 1992; Paris & Turner, 1994; Pintrich & Schunk, 1996). In "Kid's Stuff," students were given choices in written class exercises and the final project (collectively, 90% of their grade). To a lesser degree, the environmental studies instructor offered alternative assignments and encouraged majors to begin thinking about their senior project—a research paper on a topic of their choosing. Neither of our focal instructors used tests as the primary method of assessment. Instead, they based students' grades primarily on written projects and class participation. Theories of motivation and interest suggest that whereas tests are perceived as a controlling mechanism, writing not only promotes conceptual learning, but also gives students some personal control over their learning agendas.

We reiterate here that none of the pedagogical strategies used by our focal instructors is unique to interdisciplinary courses. Instructors of disciplinary courses can and do introduce the concepts of choice, novelty, challenge, and authentic assessment in their courses, and they attempt to maintain students' interest by appealing to both intrinsic and extrinsic motivators. If there is something unique about interdisciplinary courses, it may be a matter of degree. The questions raised by interdisciplinary courses may be more interesting to students, and thus motivate their learning. In-depth study of the real-world implications of different environmental issues may promote deeper learning better than a lecture on the same concepts. Similarly, the organizing framework of toys integrates information from the disciplines of history, sociology, psychology, and marketing, and may thus produce different learning outcomes than covering the topics of childhood and gender in separate disciplinary courses.

Schommer (1994) argued that college instructors should help students understand learning as a process of seeing connections among ideas and noting their evolving nature. If interdisciplinary courses encourage students to develop sophisticated views of knowledge, they may also promote effective learning strategies. Nonetheless, researchers should investigate whether some students benefit more than others from interdisciplinary courses. Are self-regulated learners and those with sophisticated views of knowledge more likely to feel efficacious in interdisciplinary courses than students with less developed metacognitive skills and naive epistemologies? How much challenge is too much?

Constructing Meaning in the Classroom

If interdisciplinary courses are potentially more interesting for students, and if they motivate students by engaging their interest, are instructors in interdisciplinary courses student centered? Do instructors of interdisciplinary courses purposefully design their courses to achieve high levels of engagement? Do they rely on active learning more than instructors in disciplinary courses?

Constructivist approaches to teaching place the student at the center of learning. Constructivist learning theory has two basic premises: "(1) learning takes as its starting point the knowledge, attitudes, and interests students bring to the learning situation, and (2) learning results from the interaction between these characteristics and experience in such a way that learners *construct* their own understanding, from the inside, as it were" (Howe & Berv, 2002, pp. 30–31; emphasis theirs). Constructivist instructors see themselves as facilitators rather than as transmitters of knowledge and view their students as active participants who interpret and create knowledge. There are, however, different varieties of constructivism that rely on differing beliefs about the nature of reality, the role of experience in learning, and differing understandings of the process of meaning-making (Steffe & Gale, 1995). Some constructivists favor models of learning that are rooted in individual cognition, while social constructivists argue that knowledge is constructed through the interactions of individuals engaging in talk or in action about shared tasks or problems (Driver et al., 1994; Steffe & Gale, 1995).

Sociocultural and cultural-historical theories of learning are often contrasted with cognitivist versions of constructivism because they focus not only on the individual's acquisition of information or knowledge, but simultaneously on the social interactions that mediate learning (e.g., Engeström 1999; Resnick, 1991; Wertsch, 1995; Wertsch, Del Rio, & Alvarez, 1995). This view of learning is consistent with an evolving theory of constructivism which rejects the assumption that what we know is a direct reflection of what we perceive in the physical world and which instead argues that most knowledge is an interpretation of experience, influenced by the cultural, social, and historical contexts in which it occurs. Interpretations of experience are expressed as idiosyncratic schemas that both enable and constrain an individual's processes of sense making. Cognitive and sociocultural approaches, therefore, are not necessarily oppositional and can offer different insights into how and why students learn.

Regardless of the type of constructivism an instructor practices, the shift to a focus on the learner introduces opportunities to include new sources of knowledge in a classroom. Students' values and experiences become as important to learning as the instructor's expertise and the knowledge contained in texts. The characteristics common to most (but not all) constructivist pedagogical approaches include:

> Active construction of knowledge based on experience with and previous knowledge of the physical and social worlds; an emphasis on the influence of human culture, where individuals construct the rules and conventions of the use of language; recognition of the social construction of knowledge through dialogue; emphasis on the intersubjective construction of knowledge, in that knowledge is socially negotiated between significant others who are able to share meanings and perspectives of a common lifeworld. (Jaworski as quoted in Stage et al., 1998, p. 39)

Do interdisciplinary courses facilitate learning within a constructivist framework? The instructors of our focal courses stress discussion in their classes. In "Kid's Stuff," the twice-weekly seminars were discussion driven because the instructor wanted to hear what students had to say about the topic and course readings. He reported lecturing only on rare occasions when students were asked to read a particularly difficult theoretical piece for class. Because students were actively engaged in the construction of meaning through dialogue and shared activity, students in the three discussion sections were in different places in their learning at different times in the term even though they were reading the same course materials. The instructor regarded this variance as both acceptable and expected.

An emphasis on dialogue that develops intersubjective understanding is also apparent in "Introduction to Environmental Studies." The instructor described his students as active learners: "They're not sitting there writing down my words. They are actually thinking, and speaking . . . . I'm not telling them 'Memorize this and it will come in handy later.' They are sort of building from within and I believe very strongly in that." In addition to opportunities to participate in class, talk about topics and issues spilled over into an optional chat room. The chat room had the added benefit of inviting students who were not comfortable speaking in class to contribute to the discussion on course topics.

Arguments for active learning can be inferred from both cognitive and constructivist learning theories. Cognitivists assert that active learning provides students with an immediate opportunity to incorporate new knowledge into existing schemas, increasing the chances that it will be stored in long-term memory and available for subsequent recall. Constructivist pedagogy emphasizes active learning because it is believed to encourage students, whether alone or with peers, to participate in the act of meaning- making.

The constructivist framework also emphasizes the importance of experience in the process of learning. In "Kid's Stuff," students played with toys and video games throughout the course. They also participated in field trips. Several class exercises required students to reflect on their own experiences with play and toys in light of course readings. In a unit on childhood, students analyzed a toy they still had from childhood and observed children at play. Current and prior experiences with toys and play were intended to provide students with a richer understanding of the meaning of childhood.

Our focal instructors, like constructivist teachers, contextualized course content for their students. For example, in "Kid's Stuff," the instructor situated toys in a larger cultural context, as is evident from the course units: "Barbie and the Politics of Gender and Doll Play in Twentieth Century America," "Boy Culture, Aggression, and Toys," and "Toys, TV, and Mass Market Culture." All imply the primacy of social contexts and explore current understandings of gender and power. The instructor's emphasis on cultural contexts in this course is more than a pedagogical strategy; it also reflects his theoretical commitment to power and gender as analytical frameworks that will stimulate particular kinds of shared insights among students. Contextualizing information in this way shapes, at least to some extent, the meanings students construct regarding course topics and organizing questions.

The strong emphasis on dialogue, experience, and active learning in the focal interdisciplinary courses raises the question of whether instructors are more likely to use constructivist methods in interdisciplinary courses. And if so, why are they so inclined? Are interdisciplinary instructors more attuned to the process by which students make meaning? If we were to assess student learning in the sample interdisciplinary courses, could we disentangle the relative contributions of the interdisciplinary topics, the student-centered nature of the course, and the collaborative nature of learning that occurs as students make meaning together?

Two additional questions emerge from our examination of the focal courses. The first question is: "What constitutes truly active learning?" Each of our focal instructors incorporated activities that could be classified as active learning into their courses, but only one spoke explicitly about the importance of active learning. If the goal of active learning pedagogy is to engage the students in meaning-making (a constructivist view), then active learning is present in our examples. If the goal of active learning is to facilitate the arrangement of knowledge (a cognitivist view), then evidence of it in the focal courses is limited; the instructors' selection of topics, concepts, and theories *may* suggest organizing frames for students. The choice to adopt these frames or produce one's own may be the difference between rote learning and active learning. A second question to consider is whether interdisciplinary courses make it easier to create an environment where students are actively learning.

A Proposed Research Agenda on Interdisciplinarity

Julie Thompson Klein and William Newell (1996) challenged researchers "to probe the precise mechanisms though which interdisciplinary study has such widespread effects" (p. 411). We agree that researchers need to explore the mechanisms by which interdisciplinarity succeeds. But there are also fundamental questions about interdisciplinary teaching and learning yet to be answered. We conclude with a preliminary research agenda on interdisciplinary teaching and learning.

Outcomes of Interdisciplinary Courses and Programs

Because we know little about teaching and learning in interdisciplinary courses, a survey of the landscape is needed. Our questions about teaching are tied to questions about student learning.

1. What are the educational outcomes of interdisciplinary courses? What behavioral, cognitive, and affective outcomes do students report? What do assessments of student learning reveal? Do learning outcomes vary by the type of interdisciplinary course (synthetic, transdisciplinary, or conceptual) or program (general education, concentration, science-based, humanities-based, etc.)? If they vary, why do they vary?

2. How do these outcomes compare to those of students in discipline-based courses? Are there educational outcomes that are achieved more frequently in interdisciplinary courses than in discipline-based courses, and vice versa? What accounts for any differences found?

    Comparative studies of student outcomes within and across institutions and academic programs are needed. Student demographics, institutional and program selectivity, instructional and other resources, and teaching styles are among the variables that should be considered in such comparative studies.

3. What types of students experience the greatest success in interdisciplinary courses? Researchers may define success differently depending on their interests but should study how academic preparation, affective responses, and behavioral characteristics contribute to student success in interdisciplinary (and disciplinary) courses and programs. To what do students attribute their success or difficulty in interdisciplinary courses and programs?

Course Planning and Pedagogy

This set of questions focuses on how faculty plan and teach interdisciplinary courses. It extends the survey of the landscape proposed above but also recommends exploring the broad philosophical, theoretical, and pedagogical commitments of faculty who teach interdisciplinary courses.

1. What theories of learning, explicit or implicit, do instructors of interdisciplinary courses espouse? Do perspectives on learning vary by type of interdisciplinary program or course? Are any perspectives more common in either interdisciplinary or disciplinary courses or

programs? What goals and objectives for learning do instructors who teach interdisciplinary courses develop and implement? Do these goals and objectives differ from those that guide discipline-based courses? Do faculty who teach both interdisciplinary and disciplinary courses espouse similar goals and objectives for their different courses? If not, why do their goals and objectives differ?

2. What kinds of guiding or organizing questions drive these courses? Are interdisciplinary courses more often organized around ill-structured problems? Do their organizing questions differ from questions that drive discipline-based courses? Do these guiding questions suggest that additional categories of interdisciplinarity should be added to those existing in the literature?

3. What pedagogical strategies do instructors in interdisciplinary courses use? Are any pedagogical strategies more common in interdisciplinary courses than in disciplinary courses? Do faculty who teach both interdisciplinary and disciplinary courses use similar pedagogical strategies in their courses? If they differ, why do they differ? Do pedagogical strategies vary by the type of course or the type of program involved?

Does Interdisciplinarity Promote Learning?

In analyzing our focal courses, we generated questions related to particular theories and instructional approaches in the hope of identifying the mechanisms by which interdisciplinary courses may encourage student success. These hypothesized routes to learning require systematic study. Rather than restating the questions posed in earlier sections, we suggest a set of overarching questions that connect pedagogy with student learning. These questions focus on how interdisciplinary courses and the instruction practiced by instructors in these courses might (a) forge connections to students' prior knowledge and experience; (b) assist students in developing complex understandings in particular subject areas; (c) promote the development of sophisticated views of knowledge and learning; (d) influence thinking skills; (e) build students' capacity to recognize, evaluate, and use differing (multiple) perspectives; (f) engage student interest and increase motivation; and (g) enact constructivist and active learning strategies. For each topic, the following questions can be posed:

1. How is a given learning goal translated into instructional practice in interdisciplinary courses?

2. Does the interdisciplinary nature of the course influence how it is taught?

3. How is a given learning goal and related instructional practice distributed across disciplinary and interdisciplinary courses? How do goals and teaching practices correlate with student achievement in interdisciplinary and disciplinary courses? Does the success of a given instructional practice vary between interdisciplinary and discipline-based courses?

4. We saved the most difficult question in our research agenda for last: Are gains in students' knowledge and skills attributable to the interdisciplinary nature of courses? Research and theory suggest that learning will vary depending on how content, pedagogy, and learner characteristics intersect in a course. Our theory-based analysis of the focal courses suggests that the combination of interdisciplinary topics and intentional pedagogy may promote learning better than either in isolation. For researchers, understanding—and possibly, untangling—the contributions of interdisciplinarity and pedagogy in actual educational settings will provide an exceptional challenge. Research designs that capture the contributions of content, pedagogy, and learner characteristics will require researchers to simultaneously explore multiple influences on learning—and may themselves demand interdisciplinary methods of inquiry.

References

Ames, C. (1992). Classroom: Goals, structures, and student motivation. *Journal of Educational Psychology, 84*(3), 261–271.

Astin, A. W. (1993). *What matters in college: Four critical years revisited.* San Francisco: Jossey-Bass.

Ausubel, D. P., Novak, J. D., & Hanesian, H. (1978). *Educational psychology: A cognitive view* (2nd ed.). New York: Holt, Rinehart and Winston.

Barnett, S. A., & Brown, V. A. (1981). Pull and push in educational innovation: Study of an interfaculty programme. *Studies in Higher Education, 6*(1), 13–22.

Baxter Magolda, M. (1992). *Knowing and reasoning in college: Gender-related patterns in students' intellectual development.* San Francisco: Jossey-Bass.

Baxter Magolda, M. (1999). *Creating contexts for self-authorship: Constructive-developmental pedagogy.* Nashville, TN: Vanderbilt University Press.

Bloom, B. S. (1956/1984). *Taxonomy of educational objectives: Handbook 1: Cognitive domain.* New York: Longman.

Bransford, J. D., Brown, A. L., & Cocking, R. R. (2000). *How people learn: Brain, mind, experience, and school.* Washington, DC: National Academy Press.

Braxton, J. M., & Hargens, L. L. (1996). Variation among academic disciplines: Analytical frameworks and research. In J. C. Smart (Ed.), *Higher Education: Handbook of theory and research* (Vol. 11, pp. 1–46). New York: Agathon Press.

Davis, J. R. (1995). *Interdisciplinary courses and team teaching: New arrangements for learning.* Phoenix, AZ: American Council on Education/Oryx Press.

Deci, E. L. (1992). The relation of interest to the motivation of behavior: A self-determination theory perspective. In K. A. Renninger, S. Hidi, & A. Krapp (Eds.), *The role of interest in learning and development* (pp. 43–70). Hillsdale, NJ: Lawrence Erlbaum Associates.

Donald, J. G. (2002). *Learning to think: Disciplinary perspectives.* San Francisco: Jossey-Bass.

Driver, R., Asoko, H., Leach, J., Mortimer, E., & Scott, P. (1994). Constructing scientific knowledge in the classroom. *Educational Researcher, 23*(7), 5–12.

Engeström, Y. (1999). Activity theory and individual and social transformation. In Y. Engeström, R. Miettinen, & R. Punamäki (Eds.), *Perspectives on activity theory* (pp. 19–38). Cambridge, MA: Cambridge University Press

Fishman, E. M. (1985). Counteracting misconceptions about the Socratic method. *College Teaching, 33*(4), 185–88.

Glaser, R. (1984). Education and thinking: The role of knowledge. *American Psychologist, 39*, 93–104.

Greeno, J. G., & The Middle-School Mathematics through Applications Project Group (1997). Theories and practices of thinking and learning to think. *American Journal of Education, 106*, 85–126.

Hagen, A. S., & Weinstein, C. E. (1995). Achievement goals, self-regulated learning, and the role of classroom context. In P. R. Pintrich (Ed.). *Understanding self-regulated learning.* New Directions for Teaching and Learning (Vol. 63, pp. 43–55). San Francisco: Jossey-Bass.

Howe, K. R., & Berv, J. (2000). Constructing constructivism, epistemological and pedagogical. In D. C. Phillips (Ed.), *Constructivism in education: Opinions and second opinions on controversial issues* (pp. 19–40). Chicago: University of Chicago.

Hursh, B., Haas, P., & Moore, M. (1983). An interdisciplinary model to implement general education. *Journal of Higher Education, 54* (1), 42–49.

Jehng, J. J., Johnson, S. D., & Anderson, R. C. (1993). Schooling and students' epistemological beliefs about learning. *Contemporary Educational Psychology, 18*, 23–35.

Kay, L. H., & Young, J. L. (1986). Socratic teaching in social studies. *Social Studies, 77*(4), 158–61.

King, P. M., & Kitchener, K. S. (1994). *Developing reflective judgment: Understanding and promoting intellectual growth and critical thinking in adolescents and adults.* San Francisco: Jossey-Bass.

Klein, J. T., & Newell, W. T. (1996). Advancing interdisciplinary studies. In J. G. Gaff and J. L. Ratcliff (Eds.), *Handbook of the undergraduate curriculum: A comprehensive guide to purposes, structures, practices, and change* (pp. 393–415). San Francisco: Jossey-Bass.

Krapp, A., Hidi, S., & Renninger, K. A. (1992). In K. A. Renninger, S. Hidi, & A. Krapp (Eds.). *The role of interest in learning and development* (pp. 3–25). Hillsdale, NJ: Lawrence Erlbaum Associates.

Lattuca, L. R. (2001). *Creating interdisciplinarity: Interdisciplinary research and teaching among college and university faculty.* Nashville, TN: Vanderbilt University Press.

Lindholm, J. A., Astin, A. W., Sax, L. J., & Korn, W. S. (2002). *The American college teacher: National norms for the 2001–02 HERI faculty survey.* Los Angeles: Higher Education Research Institute.

McKeachie, W. J., Pintrich, P. R., Lin, Y., Smith, D. A. F., & Sharma, R. (1990). *Teaching and learning in the college classroom: A review of the research literature.* Ann Arbor, MI: National Center for Research to Improve Postsecondary Teaching and Learning.

Metcalf, E. (1999). *Course Syllabi—CC II [WWW]*. Retrieved September 21, 2000, from http://wcp.muohio.edu/academics/ccii.html.

Newell, W. H. (1990). Interdisciplinary curriculum development. *Issues in Integrative Studies, 8,* 69–86.

Newell, W. H. (1992). Academic disciplines and undergraduate education: Lessons from the School of Interdisciplinary Studies at Miami University, Ohio. *European Journal of Education, 27*(3), 211–221.

Newell, W. H. (1994). Designing interdisciplinary courses. In J. T. Klein & W. G. Doty (Eds.), *Interdisciplinary studies today*. New Directions for Teaching and Learning (Vol. 58, pp. 35–51). San Francisco: Jossey-Bass.

Newell, W. H., & Green, W. J. (1982). Defining and teaching interdisciplinary studies. *Improving College and University Teaching, 30*(1), 23–30.

Paris, S. G., & Turner, J. C. (1994). Situated motivation. In P. R. Pintrich, D. R. Brown, & C. E. Weinstein (Eds.), *Student motivation, cognition, and learning: Essays in honor of Wilbert J. McKeachie* (pp. 213–237). Hillsdale, NJ: Lawrence Erlbaum Associates.

Paulsen, M. B., & Feldman, K. A. (1999a). Epistemological beliefs and self-regulated learning. *Journal of Staff, Program, and Organizational Development, 16*(2), 83–91.

Paulsen, M. B., & Feldman, K. A. (1999b). Student motivation and epistemological beliefs. In M. Theall (Ed.), *Motivation from within: Approaches for encouraging faculty and students to excel*. New Directions for Teaching and Learning (Vol. 78, pp. 17–25). San Francisco: Jossey-Bass.

Paulsen, M. B., & Wells, C. T. (1998). Domain differences in the epistemological beliefs of college students. *Research in Higher Education, 39*(4), 365–384.

Perry, W. (1968). *Forms of intellectual and ethical development in the college years*. New York: Holt, Rinehart, and Winston.

Perry, W. (1981). Cognitive and ethical growth: The making of meaning. In A. W. Chickering (Ed.), *The modern American college* (pp. 76–116). San Francisco: Jossey-Bass.

Piaget, J. (1952). *The origins of intelligence in children*. (M. Cook, trans.) New York: International Universities Press.

Pintrich, P. R. (1995). *Understanding self-regulated learning*. New Directions for Teaching and Learning, no. 63. San Francisco: Jossey-Bass.

Pintrich, P. R., & DeGroot, E. V. (1990). Motivational and self-regulated learning components of classroom academic performance. *Journal of Educational Psychology, 82*(1), 33–40.

Pintrich, P. R., & Schunk, D. A. (1996). *Motivation in education: Theory, research, and applications*. Englewood Cliffs, NJ: Prentice-Hall.

Resnick, L. B. (1991). Shared cognition: Thinking as social practice. In L. B. Resnick, J. M. Levine, and S. D. Teasley (Eds.), *Perspectives on socially shared cognition* (pp. 1–20). Washington, DC: American Psychological Association.

Rogoff, B. (2003). *The cultural nature of human development*. New York: Oxford University Press.

Rogoff, B., & Lave, J. (Eds.). (1984/1999). *Everyday cognition: Development in social context*. Cambridge, MA: Harvard University Press.

Rud, A. G. (1997). The use and abuse of Socrates in present day teaching. *Education Policy and Analysis Archives, 5*(20), 1–14.

Ruddell, R. B., & Harris, P. (1989). A study of the relationship between influential teachers' prior knowledge and beliefs and teaching effectiveness: Developing higher order thinking in content areas. In S. McCormick and J. Zutell (Eds.), *Cognitive and social perspectives for literacy research and instruction: Thirty-eighth yearbook of the national reading conference* (pp. 461–472). Chicago: National Reading Conference.

Rumelhart, D., & Norman, D. (1978). Accretion, tuning, and restructuring: Three modes of learning. In J. W. Cotton & R. L. Klatzky (Eds.), *Semantic factors in cognition* (pp. 37–53). Hillsdale, NJ: Erlbaum.

Schiefele, U. (1991). Interest, learning, and motivation. *Educational Psychologist, 26*(3–4), 299–323.

Schommer, M. (1993). Comparisons of beliefs about the nature of knowledge and learning among postsecondary students. *Research in Higher Education, 34*(3), 355–370.

Schommer, M. (1998). The influence of age and education on epistemological beliefs. *British Journal of Educational Psychology, 68,* 551–562.

Schommer-Aikins, M., & Hutter, R. (2002). Epistemological beliefs and thinking about everyday controversial issues. *Journal of Psychology, 136*(1), 5–20.

Schommer, M., & Dunnell, P. A. (1994). A comparison of epistemological beliefs between gifted and non-gifted high school students. *Roeper Review, 16*(3), 207–210.

Schommer, M., & Walker, K. (1995). Are epistemological beliefs similar across domains? *Journal of Educational Psychology, 87*(3), 424–432.

Schuell, T. (1986). Cognitive conceptions of learning. *Review of Educational Research, 56,* 411–436.

Shavelson, R. J. (1974). Methods for examining representations of a subject matter structure in students' memory. *Journal of Research in Science Teaching, 11,* 231–250.

Stage, F. K., Muller, P. A., Kinzie, J., & Simmons, A. (1998). *Creating learning centered classrooms: What does learning theory have to say?* ASHE-ERIC Higher Education Report, Vol. 26, no. 4. Washington, DC: The George Washington University, Graduate School of Education and Human Development.

Steck, T. (2000). Introduction to environmental studies course homepages. Retrieved September 22, 2000, from http://environment.uchicago.edu/studies/courses.html.

Steffe, L. P., & Gale, J. (Eds.). (1995). *Constructivism in education.* Hillsdale, NJ: Erlbaum.

Tobias, S. (1995). Interest and metacognitive word knowledge. *Journal of Educational Psychology, 87*(3), 399–405.

Tsui, L. (1999). Courses and instruction affecting critical thinking. *Research in Higher Education, 40,* 185–200.

Vess, D. (2001). Navigating the interdisciplinary archipelago: The scholarship of interdisciplinary teaching and learning. In M. T. Huber & S. P. Morreale (Eds.), *Disciplinary styles in the scholarship of teaching and learning: Exploring common ground* (pp. 87–106). Washington, DC: AAHE/Carnegie Foundation for the Advancement of Teaching.

Vygotsky, L. S. (1978). *Mind in society: The development of higher psychological processes.* Cambridge, MA: Harvard University Press. (Originally published 1930, New York: Oxford University Press.)

Wertsch, J. V. (1995). The need for action in sociocultural research. In J. V. Wertsch, P. Del Rio, & A. Alvarez (Eds.), *Sociocultural studies of mind* (pp. 56–74). New York: Cambridge University Press.

Wertsch, J. V., Del Rio, P., & Alvarez, A. (1995). Sociocultural studies: History, action, and mediation. In J. V. Wertsch, P. Del Rio, & A. Alvarez (Eds.), *Sociocultural studies of mind* (pp. 1–34). New York: Cambridge University Press.

PART V

TEACHING, LEARNING, AND THE CURRICULUM

Part V: Teaching, Learning, and the Curriculum

As the readings in the previous sections make clear, a curriculum is not simply a blunt instrument that can be fashioned and implemented without regard for the ways in which it is entangled with the human condition. Even the most thoroughly deliberated, philosophically well-grounded, carefully designed and innovative curriculum is at best a rigorous thought experiment unless it is enacted through mutually reinforcing teaching and learning. Lines of inquiry running the gamut of methodological approaches, the readings in this section provide a variety of perspectives on how teaching and learning may be defined, modeled, and experimented with.

In "Meaning Making and 'The Learning Paradigm': A Provocative Idea in Practice," Frank Fear, Diane Doberneck, Carole Robinson, Kathleen Fear, Robert Barr, and other colleagues provide a glimpse into how an abstract idea about teaching, learning, and curricula is made concrete when assimilated into a campus community. In the mid-1990s, one of this article's authors (Barr) and John Tagg introduced a concept called "the Learning Paradigm" and set it against "the Instruction Paradigm" by suggesting that it was a propitious time for colleges and universities to move from being instruction-centered to being learning-centered. The article here by Fear et al. reports on a study of how the Learning Paradigm concept had been interpreted and implemented at the campus level—particularly Olivet College and Michigan State University, just two of scores of colleges and institutions that have used the Learning Paradigm as an organizing principle in curriculum reform initiatives. At the crux of their study is their observation that the Learning Paradigm was introduced in a single text, yet it was being made sense of in a variety of markedly different ways. Nested in this context, Fear et al. explicate the discourse—particularly metaphors—surrounding the Learning Paradigm. In their conclusion, they suggest that the multiplicity of interpretations adds vitality to the teaching-to-learning movement and they invite others to further adapt the Learning Paradigm idea.

In the second chapter of this section, we (the two co-editors of this volume) along with our colleague, Divya Gupta, introduce a more practice-oriented idea into the discourse on teaching, learning, and assessment. In light of ideas like the Learning Paradigm and the widespread recognition of the enduring challenge of enhancing the learning of all students—including a growing number of students representing diverse racial, ethnic, and socioeconomic backgrounds—we observe that there has been a profusion of literature on teaching, learning, and assessment in higher education. With many promising new ideas notwithstanding, we contend that individual faculty in higher education are still left wanting for a model to help them engage in a systematic and continuous process of exploring and testing various teaching and assessment practices. To address this lacuna, we introduce Teaching-for-Learning (TFL), a model that may be used, adapted, and tested.

In "Teaching Excellence, Teaching Expertise, and the Scholarship of Teaching," Carolin Kreber takes on the challenge of making sense of the wave of terminology borne by the flood of research related to teaching, learning, and curriculum in recent years. In addition to sharing commentary on the ambiguity of labels in the literature, she cites research that indicates a lack of clarity among faculty with respect to the meaning of these various terms. Building on the work of others who have similarly sought to make the waters less muddy, in this article Kreber intends "to provide faculty and academic administrators with a language and an understanding that permits them to distinguish the various ways of practicing post-secondary teaching: excellence in teaching, expertise in teaching, and the scholarship of teaching." Through an analysis of the predominant uses of these terms, she establishes parameters around what it means to be a "scholar of teaching," an "excellent teacher," and an "expert teacher," and then argues that all three deserve consideration in revisions to faculty reward systems.

Following Kreber's focus on sharpening ideas about teachers' identities, Ian Baptiste turns our attention to the matter of students' identities in his article entitled "Educating Lone Wolves: Pedagogical Implications of Human Capital Theory." Specifically, as the title suggests, he seeks to develop an understanding of the influence human capital theory has had on educators' views toward students (he refers to "adult students" in particular, though his analysis holds for the population of undergraduate students as a whole, if not for all students in the American education system) and, moreover, how educators can reverse the negative consequences of doing so. Following an overview of human capital theory and its philosophical foundations, Baptiste argues that it is damaging in an educational environment because it treats students like "lone wolves": "radically isolated hedonists, creatures of habit (not intentions) who temper their avarice with economic rationality." Given that such a view runs counter to goals of educating students to be "interdependent, social beings," he concludes by urging educators to be wary of human capital theory and all its manifestations in colleges and universities.

The value of educating students to not be wolf-like is a fundamental premise of the next reading. In "Embracing Change: Teaching in a Multicultural World," bell hooks describes her first experiences with attempting to "approach the multicultural classroom and curriculum" when she was a new professor at Oberlin College. She writes about being frustrated with her colleagues' "unwillingness to approach teaching from a standpoint that includes awareness of race, sex, and class," yet she empathized with them because she recognized that such unwillingness was "often rooted in the fear that classrooms will be uncontrollable, that emotions and passions will not be contained." She shares that she herself was "unprepared" to teach in such a way, despite her "progressive politics, and [her] deep engagement with the feminist movement." She concludes with the observation that it is essential to "recognize our complicity in accepting and perpetuating biases of any kind" in order to "give students the education they desire and deserve."

In "Advocacy Education: Teaching, Research, and Difference in Higher Education," like hooks, authors Becky Ropers-Huilman and Denise Taliaferro engage in critical self-reflection and disclosure with respect to their own teaching and learning in a shared curricular experience. Both participants in a Louisiana State University seminar entitled "Women of Color in College," Ropers-Huilman and Taliaferro each share first-person accounts of their experiences in the seminar in order to "explore the ways scholars' positions in the academy influence their abilities to effectively act as advocates, teachers, and researchers in multicultural environments." Grounded in "feminist, womanist, critical, and poststructural approaches to knowledge," they each grapple with their own identities (Taliaferro, an African-American female graduate student originally from Detroit, and Ropers-Huilman, a White female professor [and the seminar's organizer] new to the South) and they conclude together that, as demonstrated by their own divergent points of view, higher education has much work to do and "it is in everyone's best interests to foster dialogic communities in which we can see, hear, and feel (at least partially) the material effects of each other's life experiences."

In "Seeking Self-Authorship: The World of Educators," Marcia Baxter Magolda accentuates the importance of faculty understanding the life experiences of students if they are to "create the conditions in which students learn to construct knowledge" rather than continuing higher education's seeming penchant for disregarding how what it teaches interacts with students' beliefs, thoughts, and feelings. The intended outcome is, according to Magolda, cultivating "self-authorship" in a student, "simultaneously an ability to construct knowledge in a contextual world, an ability to construct an internal identity separate from external influences, and an ability to engage in relationships without losing one's internal identity." She specifies how developing self-authorship necessitates that attention be given to cognitive, interpersonal, and intrapersonal facets of teaching, learning, and curricula. More specifically, she elucidates elements of "constructive-developmental pedagogy" by sharing her own experiences with it and her observations from her study of three classrooms at Miami University in Ohio.

The author of the next chapter, Douglas Reimondo Robertson, would say that there are contradictions implicit in Magolda's depiction of the professor's aim as cultivating self-authorship in students—not contradictions in her logic, but in the teacher role itself. In "Generative Paradox in Learner-Centered College Teaching," Robertson argues that there are at least six contradictions inherent in the push for faculty to be learner-centered (rather than knowledge-centered) in their teaching because doing so requires that they must be in control yet flexible, trusted by students while evaluating them, dedicated to their own learning as much as their students' learning, a subject expert and a teaching expert, capable of caring for themselves and their students at the same time, and attentive to individual students and the students as a group simultaneously. He describes how each contradiction is inextricably linked with learner-centered teaching and how each has the potential to stifle faculty as a result, particularly if they produce what he calls "conflicts" or "generative paradoxes." With the former, "the two sides of the contradiction fight each other," and with the latter, "the two sides . . . co-exist by taking turns." These two possibilities represent just two along a continuum, however, for there is a third possibility—namely "generative paradoxes" in which "the two sides of the contradiction feed each other" and "the teacher achieves a win/win relationship." Teachers should strive for generative paradox to fully reap the benefits of learner-centered teaching, contends Robertson, and he illustrates how this may be done with each contradiction.

In "Maximizing What Students Get Out of College: Testing a Learning Productivity Model," Shouping Hu and George Kuh conclude this section by offering additional perspective on how student learning may be brought to full force. Utilizing data from the College Student Experience Questionnaire (CSEQ)—an institutional research tool closely related to another instrument developed at Indiana University, the National Survey of Student Engagement (NSSE)—Hu and Kuh present evidence to support their hypothesis that "some colleges are more efficient than others in promoting student learning." This hypothesis is based in the view that colleges and universities cannot only offer resources that support student learning but that they can configure those resources (e.g., curriculum, libraries, tutoring) in such a way that students use them more efficiently and, in turn, improve their learning. They conclude with recommendations for faculty and administrators, including the need to pay attention to how students perceive the college environment.

Each of the readings in this section underscore the notion that simply putting professors and students in the same learning environment may surely result in teaching and learning but quality teaching and learning is far from an inevitable outcome. The classroom—whatever form it may take—is a space where teachers' and learners' identities are negotiated and changed, where knowledge is transmitted, challenged, and created, and the curriculum is a mediating force throughout. Many of the readings in this section called our attention, explicitly and implicitly, to various metaphors for teaching and learning. Based on the readings in this section and your own experiences in higher education, what metaphor would you use to capture the relationship among teaching, learning, and the curriculum?

Meaning Making and "The Learning Paradigm": A Provocative Idea in Practice

Frank A. Fear, Diane M. Doberneck, Carole F. Robinson, Kathleen L. Fear, Robert B. Barr with Heather Van Den Berg, Jeffrey Smith, and Robert Petrulis

ABSTRACT: Amidst the considerable literature published on institutional change in undergraduate teaching and learning, an article co-authored by Robert Barr and John Tagg in 1995 stands out. The authors offered a vision and—perhaps most importantly—gave it a memorable name, the **Learning Paradigm.** "From Teaching to Learning—A New Paradigm for Undergraduate Education" is the most frequently cited article in the history of *Change*. In this article, Barr blended his voice with colleagues who helped initiate Learning Paradigm programs at a public university and in a liberal arts college setting. Through multiple forms of inquiry, including discourse and metaphor analysis, they interpreted the shift from teaching to learning and speculate about its future.

An essay about teaching and learning in higher education was published in the November/December 1995 issue of *Change: The Magazine of Higher Education.* Co-authored by Robert Barr and John Tagg and entitled "From Teaching to Learning—A New Paradigm for Undergraduate Education," this article would become the most frequently cited article in the publication's history (AAHE, personal communication). The text begins:

> A paradigm shift is taking hold in American higher education. In its briefest form, the paradigm that has governed our colleges is this: A college is an institution that exists to provide instruction. Subtly but profoundly we are shifting to a new paradigm: A college is an institution that exists to produce learning. This shift changes everything. It is both needed and wanted. (1995, p. 13).

Barr and Tagg defined a college governed by the Learning Paradigm as one which conducts an organized and systematic effort to "create environments and experiences that bring students to discover and construct knowledge for themselves, to make students members of communities of learners that make discoveries and solve problems . . . and . . . to create a series of ever more powerful learning environments" (p. 15). The authors contrasted the Learning Paradigm with the Instruction Paradigm in a variety of domains:

- Institutional mission and purposes (from delivering instruction to producing learning)
- Success criteria (from producing student credit hours to achieving student learning outcomes)
- Teaching-learning structures (from organizing classes in 50-minute lecture blocks to having flexibly structured learning arrangements)
- Learning theory (from viewing students as passive recipients to encouraging them to be active knowledge constructors)

Reprinted from *Innovative Higher Education* 27, no. 3 (spring 2003).

- Productivity and funding (from focusing on inputs, such as enrollment size, to focusing on outcomes, such as student learning)
- Nature of faculty and student roles (from declaring faculty-staff as knowers and students as knowledge recipients to reframing all involved as learners).

Emergence of the Learning Paradigm

Although Barr and Tagg created the label and image of a "learning paradigm," there is a longstanding, deep, and diverse literature about learner- and learning-centered education (see, for example, Bruffee, 1999; Cross, 1999; Weaver, 1990; Whitlock, 1984; Wingspread Group, 1993). Barr and Tagg helped stimulate the spread of learner- and learning-centered education *for institutional change* by effectively summarizing core ideas and presenting them in an easy to read manner. They presented a framework, proposed a new way of proceeding, and gave that way a memorable name—Learning Paradigm.

How did the article come about? Barr, then director of institutional research and planning at Palomar College, a San Diego-area community college, articulated the concept for himself in a reflective moment in the spring of 1991 as he grappled with two concerns. First, he had been concerned for some time about the lack of innovation associated with core educational practices of institutions of higher education. He asked constantly, "Why don't educational practices evolve and lead to improved outcomes over time?" Put another way: "Why aren't colleges getting better and smarter at their work?" Second, as leader of a major planning effort at his college, he sought a powerful and concise way to express Palomar's core mission. "What is the essential mission of this college?" he asked. Providing a rigorous curriculum wasn't satisfactory. He searched for an impassioned expression, along the lines of declaring, "We have a dream!" rather than reporting, "We have a strategic plan."

Then it hit him. The focus of his college (and most other higher education institutions) was not on learning, it was on instructing—what he and Tagg later conceptualized as being governed by the Instruction Paradigm. This paradigm has influenced colleges and universities in function and form for hundreds of years. It is expressed, for example, when colleges market themselves as America's "premier *teaching* colleges" and when university core functions are described as "*teaching*, research, and service."

With this insight, Barr began charting the differences between the dominant paradigm (Instruction) and an alternate paradigm (Learning). He shared his thinking with John Tagg, an associate professor of English at Palomar. Tagg saw the relevance immediately and the co-authorship emerged. The article made a immediate splash with Barr and Tagg receiving numerous speaking and consultation requests. Soon, Palomar College produced a companion educational video, conducted national teleconferences, and initiated an annual conference on the Learning Paradigm.

The Learning Paradigm in Practice

Like many other readers, we—Barr's co-authors of this article—responded enthusiastically to the Learning Paradigm concept. We were delighted to find an article that expressed so elegantly and clearly many of the ideas we held with conviction. We immediately shared the article with colleagues and began drawing on the ideas in our respective campus change efforts. More than anything, we felt as though Barr and Tagg were speaking to us personally in the challenge they posed at the end of the article:

> Try this . . . experiment. Take a team of faculty at any college—at your college . . . Tell the faculty team, "We want you to create a program for these students so that they will improve significantly in . . . learning. . . .In doing so, you are not constrained by any of the rules or regulations you have grown accustomed to. You are free to organize the environment in any way that you like. The only thing you are required to do is to produce the desired result—student learning." (1995, p. 25).

Our experimental work took place in two very different campus settings. Michigan State University is a large, public, land grant, research-intensive university with international obligations. Learning Paradigm ideas were used to create a specialization in whole-person development—The Liberty Hyde Bailey Scholars Program—in one of the University's colleges, the technically-focused College of Agriculture and Natural Resources. Olivet College, a private liberal arts institution located in Michigan, was established in 1844. From inception, Olivet has offered access to women, people of color, and students of limited economic means. It has a distinctive mission, reframed in contemporary terms in the 1990s as "Education for Individual and Social Responsibility," with an ethos proclaimed publicly in the "Olivet College Compact" (see The Faculty, the Staff Senate, Student Senate, 1994, and the Board of Trustees, 1997, Olivet College).

As these campus efforts moved forward, we developed a relationship with Barr—communicating with him about our work and hosting him at our respective institutions. In turn, we joined Barr at the annual conference on the Learning Paradigm, sharing lessons learned from our campus experiments.

Purpose

As the relationship deepened, our group—the originator of the Learning Paradigm concept and practitioners in two campus settings—began engaging in dialogue about the Learning Paradigm. A provocative question held our attention: *"How is the 1995 article being interpreted by campus change agents as they conceive and enact Learning Paradigm efforts in diverse practice settings?"* Over time we viewed this as a researchable question and began undertaking activities with the intent of sharing what we found.

In this essay, we share the outcomes of discourse on the Learning Paradigm and describe how the original article was interpreted and applied in our respective campus contexts. We also report the interpretations attributed to the Learning Paradigm by colleagues who work at other institutions. These interpretations are discussed and analyzed through imagery, namely, metaphors of the Learning Paradigm in context. We end the article by drawing on discourse and metaphor analysis to speculate about the future of the movement to shift higher education from the Instruction to the Learning Paradigm.

Meaning Making Sharpened Through Discourse

A fascinating dynamic emerged early in our conversations with Barr. He pointed out passages from the article that we had either overlooked or underemphasized in our change work. With time, we realized that we had "read what we already believed," using the article to validate prior thinking and confirm the prior direction of our work. When re-reading the article with fresh eyes, we also found ourselves reacting negatively to some of its language, such as the words "producing learning" (conjuring up a factory image). These unexpected conflicts ultimately led to deeper understanding of the Learning Paradigm.

The work of Jack Mezirow (1991, 1994, 1996) sheds light on why a disruptive circumstance can represent a threshold of opportunity.[1] Mezirow believed that

> We resist learning anything that does not comfortably fit our meaning structures, but we have a strong urgent need to understand the meaning of our experience so that, given the limitations of our meaning structures, we strive toward viewpoints that are more functional. A more functional frame of reference is more inclusive, differentiating, permeable, critically reflective, and integrative of experience. (1996, p. 163).

Mezirow contended that transformations in meaning structures could occur over time through incremental change, a disorienting experience, or a confounding dilemma. Transformative learning—that is, learning that results in fundamentally changing one's perspective—can follow when a person is introspective, thinks critically about underlying beliefs, recognizes the existence of alternative perspectives, and begins exploring new options for understanding and action.

Discourse is a potential pathway to transformative learning. Discourse is "a special type of dialogue in which we focus on content and attempt to justify beliefs by giving and defending reasons and by examining the evidence for and against competing viewpoints." (Mezirow, 1994 p. 223). Through discourse, we moved with Barr toward a deeper and shared understanding of the Learning Paradigm.

The Shift from Teaching to Learning as Educational Movement

Why did the Learning Paradigm concept "catch fire?" We thought it likely that the time was simply right. The article's release may have been a precipitating event in a fertile environment with multiple predisposing factors, such as copious literature on learning and learner- centered education and considerable experimentation by faculty members and administrators who were primed to take action. One way to interpret this social dynamic is in terms of an *educational movement*. Palmer (1998) believes that movements abandon the logic inherent in the system as it operates currently and, instead, imagine and enact a radically different logic.

Potential Pitfalls in Interpreting the Learning Paradigm

We often complained to Barr about how we felt others in the movement were *mis*interpreting what we saw as the essence of the Learning Paradigm. Through these discussions we began to see how preferred learning theories and approaches affected the way different people interpreted the article. We recognized how important it was to refrain from making—and often overlaying—partisan interpretations of (and on) the Learning Paradigm. Over time, it became apparent just how much we had to learn from colleagues whose work and practices are informed by different theories of learning and who walk different practice paths. It is not a matter of definitive interpretation, we concluded, it is an issue of remaining open to learning.

The Learning Paradigm at Olivet College and Michigan State University

With these insights, we began seeing the Learning Paradigm as a simple concept that has profound implications for practice. Although there are fundamental questions associated with shifting from instruction-based to learning (and learner)-centered education, the answers are anything but straightforward. The questions include learning about what, for what purpose and toward what end, with whom, where, when, and how. The more we talked with Barr, the more we realized how we—colleagues who work at institutions less than fifty miles apart—answer these questions differently.

At Olivet and in the Bailey program at Michigan State, broad frames of reference guide practice, including matters of institutional context (mission, history, need) and preferences for certain philosophic and scholarly traditions. Both expressions are influenced heavily by work associated with connected knowing (e.g., Belenky, Clinchy, Goldberger, & Tarule, 1997) with its emphasis on relational learning in learning communities. However, there are profound differences. Olivet seeks to be a learning college, and all involved—faculty, students and even staff—are participants in a shared endeavor. At Michigan State, the impact of the Bailey program is limited because participation is voluntary and restricted (e.g., available only to students matriculating in the College of Agriculture and Natural Resources).

Olivet College was founded in 1844 in response to questions about access to higher education and the purpose of higher learning. Founded by Abolitionists, Olivet was the first college by charter to challenge the practice of excluding woman, people of color, and students with limited economic means from receiving a college education. The Campus Square, with well-worn paths by early "freedom fighters," is a reminder of a tradition of access to higher education.

The institutional vision was expressed in an early college catalogue (Olivet Institute, 1846) with the words, "the future of humanity rests in the hands, hearts, and minds of those who accept the responsibility for themselves and others in an increasingly diverse society." Today, members of the

Olivet campus community carry on this legacy by assuming individual and social responsibility as articulated in the Olivet College Compact.

As a member of this community, I affirm the following commitments:

I am responsible for my own learning and personal development. We recognize the critical importance of taking ownership for our learning.

I am responsible for contributing to the learning of others. Every learner benefits when each shares ideas, insights and experiences with others.

I am responsible for service to Olivet College and the larger community. People working together for the common good are a key to growth for both the individual and the community.

I am responsible for contributing to the quality of the physical environment. Enhancing environmental quality is critical to the College, the community and ultimately to the survival of our planet.

I am responsible for treating all people with respect. We aim to create a positive and inclusive campus culture celebrating both the individual and cultural differences that make each of us unique and the similarities that bond us together.

I am responsible for behaving and communicating with honesty and integrity. We build trust when we communicate openly, when we seek justice and fairness for all people, regardless of role or position, and when we honor our values and commitments in our private as well as our public behavior.

I am responsible for the development and growth of Olivet College. We reach outward and seek to inform, involve and recruit new students, employees and friends who share the vision and principles of Olivet College.

In joining this community, I commit myself to these principles and accept the obligation entrusted to me to foster a culture of responsibility at Olivet College.

Living examples of this ethos are expressed in service projects undertaken by students, on-campus and off. For example, education majors learn to recognize differences and similarities among cultural backgrounds of school children and to understand how these backgrounds impact schooling. Criminal Justice students work in community policing programs. Business students calculate insurance risk and work on problems of insurability and risk with and for community agencies and groups.

The focus of the curriculum is clear—individual and social responsibility. By working collaboratively, community members, students, staff, and faculty put into practice what it means to be socially responsible and how individual action can influence the common good. By documenting and sharing in portfolios what they have accomplished and learned, members of the campus community give public testimony to what it means to say, "People working together for the common good are a key to growth for both the individual and the community."

Multicultural faculty and students (approximately 30% of the campus community) conduct these service projects in culturally diverse settings. Celebrating the bond of human similarity and the wealth of human difference is more than a curricular focus at Olivet. It is a critically conscious way of knowing and being. For many members of the campus community, the work of multicultural and feminist scholars speaks to the ways that the Learning Paradigm is lived at Olivet (see, for example, Belenky, Bond, & Weinstock, 1997; Delpit, 1995; hooks, 1994; Noddings, 1984; West, 1993).

At Michigan State University, interest in the Learning Paradigm began as faculty and administrators explored ways of balancing technical specialization in undergraduate education with self-directed learning, including character development. What emerged was The Liberty Hyde Bailey Scholars program in the College of Agriculture and Natural Resources, launched in 1998 and named in honor of the father of modern horticulture and an early proponent of learner-centered expressions in agricultural education. The Bailey program is organized as a 21-credit undergraduate elective specialization with abundant opportunities for co-curricular learning. The program complements—rather than replaces—students' majors by fusing technical education with leadership development and character education. It also offers an opportunity for faculty members to experiment with alternative pedagogical forms.

All learning activities—curricular and co-curricular—are guided by the Declaration of Bailey, developed collaboratively by faculty and students, which hangs in large block letters around the ceiling of the program's main meeting room. The Declaration states:

> We seek to be a community of scholars dedicated to lifelong learning. All members of the community work toward providing a respectful, trusting environment where we acknowledge our interdependence and encourage personal growth.

To promote character development, each learner (students and faculty alike) is encouraged to interpret what "developing as a whole person" means. Then, together, students and faculty design and undertake curricular and co-curricular learning experiences with wholeness in mind.

The pedagogical foundation for the Bailey program is collaborative learning. Cross (1999) perceives collaborative learning to be a radical expression of engaged learning, where through interaction and consensus students and faculty work together as knowledge co-constructors. Bruffee (1999) understands collaborative learning as "education as conversation," a consummately social phenomenon (Geertz, 1973) where reflective thought is social conversation internalized (Vygotsky, 1962).

The organizational foundation of the Bailey program is complex adaptive systems theory (see, for example, Caine & Caine, 1997; Stacey, 1992). Complex adaptive systems are different from conventional organizational systems, the latter of which is characterized by persistent structure, management for stability and preconceived outcomes, and with leadership exercised by authority figures. Networks of relationships—that emerge, evolve, and persist for ad hoc purposes—distinguish complex adaptive systems in organizational settings. Key characteristics include connectedness, creativity, and open possibilities (Youngblood, 1997).

In the Bailey program, collaborative learning in complex adaptive systems involves students and faculty organizing curricular and co-curricular experiences around shared learning interests. An example of such an experience is the collaborative writing of this article. At any point in time, the program resembles what Wenger (1998) describes as "communities of practice," independent groups working on matters that capture the common interest of respective group members. For example, Bailey courses have generic descriptions and official course numbers, but what learners explore together in any course depends on who is around the table and what common learning interests emerge.

Toward a Practice-Informed Interpretation of the Learning Paradigm

Conversations about how we were making the teaching to learning shift on our respective campuses motivated Barr to start thinking about how he might newly articulate the essence of the Learning Paradigm so as to capture the realities of practice. After considerable thought, he offered a minimalist response—**enabling deep learning and getting better at it over time.** As we engaged in discourse about this emergent understanding, it became clear that "deep learning" for us referred to engaging and transforming the individual on multiple levels—emotionally, spiritually, and cognitively (McLeod, 1986; Ramsden, 1992). "Getting better at it over time" shines the spotlight on how we, as faculty and in our work institutionally, seek to continually improve the capacity to stimulate deep learning in our students and ourselves.

Attempts to foster deep learning, we concluded, must be informed by scholarship on learning (see, for example, Biggs, 1999; Dart, Burnett, & Purdie, 2000; Entwhistle, 1987; Grauerholz, 2001). From experience, we understand what Cross & Steadman (1996, 122) report about deep learning—that deep learners have an internal emphasis on learning, driven more by a curiosity to understand than by the need to meet others' learning objectives. We also recognize in our students what Hart (2001) writes about as the dynamic of personal engagement in learning, cultivated through relevance and resonance. Relevance pertains to the matter of personal importance. Resonance pertains to the matter of personal meaning.

"Getting at it better over time" starts with understanding the complexities associated with deep learning. Drawing on Ramsden's work in Australia, Cross & Steadman point out that the same learner may take different approaches in different learning situations—deep learning at one time and surface learning at another time, depending on the situation and context. Having said that, the Oxford Centre for Staff Development (1992) in Great Britain reports that deep learning can be stimulated when learning environments and experiences align with learners' interests and when learning situations afford active learning and interaction among learners.

Meaning Making and Metaphor

Because this evolving understanding emerged from our discourse and experiences only, we sought to explore others' interpretations. To do that, we organized a session at the 5th North American Conference on the Learning Paradigm held in San Diego in March 2001. Forty colleagues from the U.S. and Canada participated in our session.

As participants entered the conference session, they were invited to take a chair in one of four circles. Each person was asked to provide a response to the question: "What is the single most powerful metaphor of the Learning Paradigm on your campus?" Individual responses were shared with other members in the small groups, followed by twenty minutes of small group discussion. Each of the four groups then reported on their individual and group interpretations. That sharing set the stage for three follow-up questions to the full group: What do you see as the range of metaphors? What (if any) themes emerge from the metaphors? What does the Learning Paradigm look like "in action" across our campuses?

We selected metaphor as a means to explore conferees' interpretation of the Learning Paradigm because it evokes imagery, offers a relatively easy way to communicate complex ideas, and enables expressive communication. Palmer (1993) uses metaphor as a tool for encouraging faculty to talk about teaching and learning:

> Metaphors can make us available to ourselves, and to each other, in fresh and surprising ways. They are antidotes, if you will, to our "theories" . . . which—as valuable as they are—are also subject to sophisticated self-deceptions that mask who we really are and what we're really up to. The gift of honest metaphor is that it comes to us rough and raw and full of psychic energy, unedited by the conventions of the rational mind. If I give you my metaphor, I am likely to be speaking honestly about myself—in ways that even I do not understand until I have listened carefully to what the metaphor is trying to teach me. (1993, p. 12).

Session participants mentioned metaphors such as mining for gold, a swamp, a voice crying in the wilderness, pushing a boulder up an incline, a shopping center, and a diver on a diving board. Exploration, choice making, and struggle emerged as several of the core themes (see Table 1 for a summary of the outcomes).

Conferees acknowledged the diversity of meaning as expressed in the metaphors and the emergent themes. Amidst lively discussion about the third question (what the Learning Paradigm looks like in action on campus), a point of tension emerged. Several participants expressed discomfort with the flow of the discussion and the implication that the Learning Paradigm was open to multiple interpretations. "We know what it is!" It is absolutely essential, they contended, to put parameters on what it means to be "a learning college," to be clear about how one proceeds in design and execution, and to know when you have achieved desired outcomes. With such an understanding, the Learning Paradigm is *destination, mapped as route*.

In contrast, some participants interpreted this work as a journey where one has mental pictures but no map. Some expressed the feeling that the journey is the reward and that the Learning Paradigm is better understood as a verb rather than as a noun. One person expressed it this way: "There is no 'it' and there is 'no there, there.'" Some saw the work as an expression of reaching out, as a yearning, and as a quest to travel to "a new place." Some asserted that it feels like moving into the unknown, propelling you "out of your comfort zone." It can prompt visceral responses such as joy, fear, or dissonance, and the feeling that you are "on and at the edge." In this image, the Learning Paradigm is *pathway of discovery—a journey*.

TABLE 1
Themes and Metaphors

Themes	Metaphors
Exploration & Discovery	Mining for gold; ships passing in the night; intrepid explorer; revealing the sculpture that's already there; journey—a process of discovery; Ah-ha's
Dynamics of Natural Systems	A tree with leaves as learning outcomes; a swamp with a rich ecosystem, but with sinkholes, quicksand, poisonous snakes (policies) and alligators (the reward system); a galaxy with shooting stars that are dynamic and dying bodies; popcorn popping from the heat—creating an environment where "what's already inside" can burst forth
Relationships ·	Learning community; mentoring; team-building; coaching; conversations at a table
Struggle & Tension	A voice crying out in the wilderness; riding a bicycle with a few tacks on the ground; pushing a boulder up an incline; swimming and sinking in a lake; a sky-diver jumping out of a plane; looking over a picket fence with the learning paradigm on the other side
Choices & Content	A portfolio; a shopping center with professors offering wares in different shops; an adult helping a child learn how to cross the road—holding hands at first and then letting go; baking a muffin—what emerges depends on the chef, baking pan, the heat of the oven, and the recipe; a diver and a diving board—flexibility of the board, wind speed, and motivation, intent, and ability of the diver make the dive

From a session at the 2001 Learning Paradigm Conference, Palomar College, San Diego, California.

The Evolution from Teaching to Learning

We struggled in conversations about the Learning Paradigm because multiple opinions were revealed, often voiced in contentious and conflicted manner. That left us asking: Are we talking about the same Learning Paradigm? Through what Habermas (1971) refers to as communicative knowing, we were able to listen beyond such disagreements to hear profoundly different ways of thinking about matters fundamental to the rubric called "the Learning Paradigm." We collectively drew a conclusion about the Learning Paradigm in practice. Higher education administrators and faculty members work in diverse institutional settings, face a variety of organizational challenges, represent a range of views about higher education and its role in society, and come from differing philosophic and scholarly traditions. These differences lead to varying views on the shift from teaching to learning. With diversity as key, we believe that the shift to the Learning Paradigm is likely to *inspire diverse interpretations and spawn multiple expressions about deep learning and getting better at it over time.*

Based on this understanding, we offer four observations about the evolving shift from the Instruction to the Learning Paradigm.

Beyond "Implementing" the Learning Paradigm

We believe there is no final answer for what works best to enable our students to learn deeply and for our institutions and programs to get better at what they do over time. Declaring any particular way of conceiving and expressing learning as "best" or "preferred" holds back the robust development of the shift from teaching to learning. Even though the notion that there is no one right way may provoke some, it is the most compelling outcome of our discourse. The Learning Paradigm is not an "it" to be implemented.

Moments in the Shift from Teaching to Learning

Denzin and Lincoln (2000) use the concept "moment" (rather than phase) to chronicle the evolution of qualitative research.[2] We adapt the term moment here as a way to understand the evolution of the shift from teaching to learning. In the **First Moment**, Barr and Tagg provided a language and definition for a newly coalescing perspective on higher education. In the columns of "to" and "from," they compared the paradigms through juxtaposition and contrasting dualisms. In posing a "set of new questions and a domain of possible responses," Barr and Tagg laid the groundwork for reconceptualizing the core mission of institutions as learning rather than teaching. In their conclusion, they challenged us to imagine beyond our traditional institutional constraints and to experiment with producing learning. This invitation in the First Moment engendered a new way of thinking. Over time, this new way of thinking spawned a movement.

After more than five years of practice and experimentation, we believe that a **Second Moment** has arrived. In the Second Moment, the shift is characterized by diverse interpretations of learning that are being expressed in a variety of ways and forms. We believe that the complexity associated with the Second Moment includes, but extends beyond (as important as they are), matters of specific institutional context and history. The Second Moment is also an expression of diverse frames of reference, made visible through metaphor.

Interpreting Metaphors

Through vivid imagery, metaphor has the power of making explicit what it means to learn deeply and to get better at it over time. Explicitness is further revealed by exploring multiple frames of reference associated with metaphor—the *conceptual* frame, the *philosophic* frame, and the *scholarly* frame. By using metaphors to reveal the conceptual, philosophic, and scholarly frames of reference, we can become more sensitive to different ways of conceptualizing and enabling "deep learning and getting better at it over time." Metaphor allows us to view the evolving interpretations and expressions of the Learning Paradigm, even as they differ in philosophy and practice. We found all of this to be true as we articulated and discussed metaphors about learning at Olivet and in the Bailey program.

The conceptual frame is the metaphor's reference point. For example, Bailey is *learning to ride a bicycle* refers to the process entering Bailey Scholars and faculty experience when undergraduates learn "under their own power." At Olivet, *the midwife* metaphor expresses viscerally alive learning. Partners work together, encourage learning to unfold naturally, push ideas along, and experience the pain and joy when a "healthy idea" comes forth.

Any metaphor also reflects a philosophic preference in language expressions (rhetoric), values (axiology), perceptions of reality (ontology), ways of knowing (epistemology), and modes of engagement (methodology). In the Bailey program, a *swamp* metaphor recognizes the messiness associated with learning how to learn together; when all aspects of the learning agenda are co-created, and faculty and student roles are blurred by the reality that "we are all learners, learning together." Reflecting this ontology, the Bailey Declaration affirms both interconnectedness and individuality in the salient phrase, "we acknowledge our interdependence and personal growth." At Olivet, *windows and mirrors* reflect a critical connection between ontology and epistemology, namely, that what we see externally is inseparable from who we are and what we know. Teaching and learning, then, is a truly human activity that emerges from the inwardness of diverse ethnic, racial, and cultural differences of colleagues who reflect together. By discussing their reflections, all involved gain a richer understanding of the complexity that surrounds them.

The metaphor of a *jazz improv* in the Bailey program suggests a link to its scholarly underpinnings. In form and function, Bailey is what Dee Hock (1999) calls "chaordic," that is, an adaptive and self-governing organism that harmoniously blends characteristics of order and chaos. Olivet's metaphor of *voice* flows from a 160-year intellectual tradition. Learners blend voices to address matters of power, privilege, and the struggle to overcome oppression. Resonating with the voices of the College's founding mothers and fathers, they also seek to sustain Olivet as an example of multicultural vitality.

In conceptual, philosophic, and scholarly juxtaposition, these metaphors reveal profoundly important aspects of the Learning Paradigm-informed programs at Michigan State and Olivet. Metaphor helped us better understand the essence of each program—what we share in common and, more importantly, how, in what ways, and why our campus expressions differ. Recognizing that, we conclude that respecting, understanding, and learning from persons who embrace different interpretations and engage in different practices may be the most important contribution made in the Second Moment.

The Power of Prototyping

Creating powerful learning environments implies that an institution must itself become a learning organization. In other words, we must assume that we do not have the final answers about what works best for learning; therefore, we must continually question our own fundamental assumptions and beliefs, and experiment with promising new alternatives. By becoming learning organizations, our institutions will be able to adjust to changing expectations and "learn our way" into the future.

San Francisco Design firm, IDEO, believes that prototyping is the shorthand of innovation (Kelly, 2001). Lead designers encourage playful, iterative problem-solving approaches that **move quickly** from idea into experimental practice. By adopting a prototyping culture, we may begin to create institutional cultures comfortable with continuous exploration and change.

Valued as a research and development strategy in business, higher education tends to eschew prototyping as a change strategy, preferring instead, singular and longer-term change platforms that stretch across the entire institution. Think about the dynamic exchanges that might occur, with all the learning involved, if—at the same institution—faculty and administrators were encouraged to experiment with multiple and diverse expressions of learning-centered education. In today's complex world, is it prudent to invest in a single approach? Even if we get that way "right," an enduring issue in a changing world is what comes next. Prototyping is a way for higher education to become an incubator for learning.

Toward a Third Moment in the Shift from Teaching to Learning

We perceive a "many flowers blooming" environment in what we interpret as a Second Moment in the shift from teaching to learning. To encourage vitality of the movement, we offer this invitation— a re-interpretation of Barr and Tagg's 1995 closing statement—as a potential gateway to a "Third Moment":

> We encourage you to experiment. Bring together teams of students, staff, faculty, administrators, parents, residents, public officials, and employers. Tell the teams: "We want you to create a variety of ways to stimulate 'deep learning,' undertaken so that any means is self-renewing. That way, we can constantly improve our effort and outcome." Tell the teams that they need not be constrained by any of the rules or regulations they have grown accustomed to in higher education. Make sure they understand their charge: this is not about fixing what isn't working. Challenge them to be practical visionaries, to create fresh and forward ways of enabling deep learning.

Notes

1. Michigan State colleague Ron Whitmore helped us discover the link between discourse and transformative learning with application to the Learning Paradigm.
2. Denzin and Lincoln suggest that "moments" overlap and simultaneously operate in the present.

References

American Association for Higher Education (2002). Personal communication.

Barr, R., & Tagg, J. T. (1995). From teaching to learning: A new paradigm for undergraduate education. *Change, 27* (November/December), 12–25.

Belenky, M. F., Clinchy, B.B., Goldberger, N.R., & Tarule, J.M. (1997). *Women's ways of knowing: The development of self, voice, and mind* (10th anniversary ed.). New York: Basic Books.

Belenky, M., Bond, L., & Weinstock, J. (1997). *A tradition that has no name: Nurturing the development of people, families, and communities.* New York: Basic Books.

Biggs, J. (1999). *Teaching for quality learning at university.* Buckingham: SRHE and Open University Press.

Bruffee, K. A. (1999). *Collaborative learning: Higher education, interdependence, and the authority of knowledge* (2nd ed.). Baltimore: The Johns Hopkins University Press.

Caine, R., & Caine, G. (1997). *Education at the edge of possibility.* Alexandria, VA: Association for the Supervision of Curriculum Development.

Cross, K. P. (1999). What do we know about students' learning, and how do we know it? *Innovative Higher Education, 23,* 255–270.

Cross, K. P., & Steadman, M. H. (1996). *Classroom research: Implementing the scholarship of teaching.* San Francisco: Jossey-Bass.

Dart, B. C., Burnett, P. C., & Purdie, N. M. (2000). Students' conceptions of learning, the classroom environment, and approaches to learning. *The Journal of Educational Research, 93,* 262–70.

Delpit, L. (1995). *Other people's children: Conflict in the classroom.* New York: The New Press.

Denzin, N., & Lincoln, Y. (2000). *Handbook of qualitative research.* Thousand Oaks, CA: Sage Publications.

Entwhistle, N. (1987). *Understanding classroom learning.* London, England: Hodder and Stoughton.

Geertz, G. (1973). *The interpretation of cultures: Selected essays.* New York: Basic Books.

Grauerholz, E. (2001). Teaching holistically to achieve deep learning. *College Teaching, 49,* 44–50.

Habermas, J. (1971). *Knowledge and human interests.* Boston: Beacon Press.

Hart, T. (2001). *From information to transformation. Education for the evolution of critical consciousness.* New York: Peter Lang.

hooks, b. (1994). *Teaching to transgress: Education as the practice of freedom.* New York: Routledge.

Hock, D. (1999). *Birth of the chaordic age.* San Francisco: Berrett-Koehler.

Kelly, Tom. (2001). *The art of innovation: Lessons in creativity from IDEO, America's leading design firm.* New York: Doubleday.

McLeod, A. (1986). Discovering and facilitating deep learning states. *The National Teaching and Learning Forum 5,* 1–7.

Mezirow, J. (1991). *Transformative dimensions of adult learning.* San Francisco: Jossey-Bass.

Mezirow, J. (1994). Understanding transformative theory. *Adult Education Quarterly, 44,* 222–232.

Mezirow, J. (1996). Contemporary paradigms of learning. *Adult Education Quarterly, 46,* 158–172.

Noddings, N. (1984). *Caring, a feminine approach to ethics and moral education.* Berkeley University of California Press.

Olivet Institute (1846). *Olivet Institute catalogue.* Olivet, MI: Olivet Institute.

Oxford Centre for Staff Development. (1992). *Improving student learning.* Oxford, England: Brookes University.

Palmer, P. J. (1993). Good talk about good teaching. *Change, 25* (November/December), 8–13.

Palmer, P. J. (1998). *The courage to teach: Exploring the inner landscape of a teacher's life.* San Francisco: Jossey-Bass.

Ramsden, P. (1992). *Learning to teach in higher education.* London, England: Routledge.

Stacy, R. (1992). *Managing the unknowable: Strategic boundaries between order and chaos in organizations.* San Francisco: Jossey-Bass.

The Faculty, the Staff Senate and the Student Senate (1994) and the Board of Trustees (1997), Olivet College. *The Olivet College Compact* http://www.olivetcollege.edu/catalog/cat_i_compact.htm.

Vygotsky, L. S. (1962). *Thought and action.* Cambridge, MA: Harvard University Press.

Weaver, C. with Stephens, D., & Vance, M. (1990). *Understanding whole language: From principles to practice.* Portsmouth, NH: Heinemann.

Wenger, E. (1998). *Communities of practice: Learning, meaning, and identity*. New York: Cambridge University Press.

West, C. (1993). *Race matters*. New York: Vintage Books.

Whitlock, G. E. (1984). *Person-centered learning: Confluent learning processes*. New York: University Press of America.

Wingspread Group on Higher Education. (1993). *An American imperative: Higher expectations for higher education. An open letter to those concerned about the American future*. Racine, WI: The S.C. Johnson Foundation.

Youngblood, M.D. (1997). *Life at the edge of chaos: Creating the quantum organization*. Dallas, TX: Perceval Publishing.

Acknowledgement

Several Olivet College colleagues participated in the conference session on metaphor discussed in this article. They include June Hein, Linda McWright, and Kim Thayer. Several Michigan State University colleagues helped prepare for the conference session. They include Ben Chaffin, Howard Person, Lori Preston, and Ron Whitmore.

TEACHING-FOR-LEARNING (TFL): A MODEL FOR FACULTY TO ADVANCE STUDENT LEARNING

CLIFTON F. CONRAD, JASON JOHNSON AND DIVYA MALIK GUPTA

ABSTRACT: In light of the widespread recognition of the enduring challenge of enhancing the learning of all students—including a growing number of students representing diverse racial, ethnic, and socioeconomic backgrounds—there has been an explosion of literature on teaching, learning, and assessment in higher education. Notwithstanding scores of promising new ideas, individual faculty in higher education need a dynamic and inclusive model to help them engage in a systematic and continuous process of exploring and testing various teaching and assessment practices to ensure the learning of their students. This paper introduces a model—Teaching-for-Learning (TFL)—developed to meet this need.

Key words: Teaching, Learning, Assessment

Those of us who teach at colleges and universities have at least one thing in common regardless of differences among our fields of study and the courses we teach: there are well-worn paths between our offices and the classrooms in which we teach, and we can each trace much of our growth as teachers to the thoughts and feelings we have had while traveling those paths. Approaching the classroom, we often review our plans and make last-minute adjustments. Returning to the office, we reflect on what transpired in class. Sometimes we are filled with the spirited satisfaction of knowing that we helped to advance our students' learning. Other times, frustrated or pleasantly surprised by having experienced the unexpected yet again, we try to make sense of what happened and begin to consider the implications for future classes. Such is the dance of teaching and learning.

While college and university teaching has traditionally been a relatively private matter, accountability initiatives in the last few decades have emphasized the importance of student learning outcomes and drawn attention to the fact that little has been done to intentionally prepare faculty to teach. In turn, the last few years have seen robust conversation about teaching and learning; scholarly journals and other volumes contain scores of promising ideas for how teaching, assessment, and learning can be improved, and small-scale campus initiatives of every sort boldly pursue large-scale change. Nevertheless, the vast majority of us who teach at colleges and universities are left to persist with our own devices. When we do feel compelled to turn to the literature for guidance, we are reminded about how much is known about teaching, learning, and assessment, respectively, and yet how little is known about their interrelationships. In short, scholarly work in this area has still not produced a widely-accepted—much less widely accessible—model that systematically connects teaching and assessment practices with student learning.

In this article, we advance a model that can at once serve as a guide for individual teachers and extend the substantial work underway on the scholarship of teaching and learning. Specifically, we introduce Teaching-for-Learning (TFL), an inquiry-based approach to enhancing the learning of all students through systematically connecting teaching practices, assessment practices, and

Reprinted from *Innovative Higher Education* 32, no. 3 (2007).

student learning experiences in light of course-specific challenges. This focus on course-specific challenges is the principal distinction between TFL and classic instructional design models; in contrast to those models, TFL invites teachers to view course challenges not as friction in a well-oiled input-throughput-output model of instructional design but as the fuel for helping teachers to ensure teaching-for-learning along the bumpy roads that teachers confront in their everyday lives. As we elaborate in our discussion of the definition and scope of TFL, we propose that TFL invites faculty to recognize and address the ongoing "mystery of teaching" through a dynamic framework for constantly replenishing their teaching practices to enrich the learning of all students.

We begin by reviewing recent scholarship on teaching, learning, and assessment and then define TFL and its six major components. We then illustrate through a vignette how TFL can be used by teachers in their everyday practice and conclude with a brief discussion of the possibilities of TFL for enhancing the learning of all students. In so doing, we propose that TFL is best viewed as a heuristic device that can be used by individual faculty, by those who support faculty in instructional training and development, and by researchers who wish to test and improve TFL.

Scholarship of Teaching and Learning

Ernest Boyer's *Scholarship Reconsidered: Priorities of the Professoriate* (1990) provided the foundation for the movement termed the Scholarship of Teaching and Learning (SoTL). Circulated by the Carnegie Foundation for the Advancement of Teaching as a part of its CASTL (Carnegie Academy for the Scholarship of Teaching and Learning) initiative, this text is but one of the Carnegie Foundation's dozens of publications that are concerned with recasting the concept of "scholarship" in such a way that legitimates professors' research on teaching and learning in their own classrooms (e.g., Glassick et al. 1997; Huber 2005; Huber and Hutchings 2005; Huber and Morreale 2002; Hutchings 2000, 2002). Further evincing the influence of CASTL and SoTL are the many offices, centers, and initiatives using the "scholarship of teaching and learning" moniker at colleges and universities, including several holding no formal affiliation with the CASTL initiative. As Huber and Morreale noted, "The scholarship of teaching and learning in higher education currently belongs to no single national association and has no unique campus address" (2002, p.1).

The rapid growth of the scholarship of teaching and learning has also brought forth a profusion of ideas accompanied by an explosion of new terminology. As classrooms have come to be viewed more and more as "laboratories for learning" as predicted by Cross (1996, p.5), we have been presented with a variety of ways for viewing teaching, learning, and assessment—and a growing collection of categories and sub-categories. There have been numerous ideas for addressing various dimensions of learning: learning styles (Lewthwaite and Dunham 1999), problem-based learning (Jones 2002; Savin-Baden 2000), active learning (Johnson and Malinowski 2001), alternative learning approaches (Scovic 1983), and taxonomies of learning objectives (Bloom et al. 1956; Krathwohl 2002). Aspects of teaching such as teacher research (Cochran-Smith and Lytle 1999), teaching practices (Nilson 2003), action research (Collins and Spiegel 1995; Marion and Zeichner 2001), inquiry-based teaching and learning (Brew 2003), scientific teaching (Handelsman et al. 2004), and teaching and research (Jenkins et al. 2002) have likewise been advanced. Especially in the last few years, assessment has become increasingly prominent as scholars have addressed formative evaluation (Smith 2001), classroom research (Cross 1996; Cross and Steadman 1996), and student evaluation of teaching (Bastick 2001).

Scholars have also advanced a wide range of specific strategies and techniques for individual faculty to use in their courses—such as classroom assessment techniques (Angelo and Cross 1993), strategies for adventurous and critical thinking (Barell 1995), technology-based teaching strategies (Palaskas 2002) and learning-centered assessment (Huba and Freed 2000). Discipline-specific approaches have also been developed to advance teaching, learning, and assessment across many areas of knowledge, ranging from medicine (Anderson 1999) to statistics (Kirk 2002) to Spanish (Cabedo-Timmons 2002) to psychology (McCann et al. 2001). And, of course, journals in the field of higher education have presented sustained conversations about teaching, learning, and assessment.

In the last ten volumes of *Innovative Higher Education* alone, no less than 110 articles can be found with emphases on teaching (e.g., Hansen 1998; Justice et al. 2007; McDaniel and Colarulli 1997), learning (e.g., Ash and Clayton 2004; Cross 1999; Rogers et al. 2001), or assessment (e.g., Beaman 1998; C. B. Myers and S. M. Myers 2007; Quarstein and Peterson 2001). Inquiry related to teaching, learning, and assessment is no less prominent in the other leading journals in the field of higher education (e.g., Colbeck et al. 2000; Fairweather 2005; Lattuca et al. 2004; Wright 2005).

In summary, there is a rapidly growing body of promising ideas regarding approaches, strategies, and techniques for enhancing teaching, learning, and assessment. The sheer volume of this work can be taken as evidence of what Barr and Tagg (1995) observed in their oft-cited *Change* magazine article: higher education is in the midst of a "paradigm shift" as its aims, structures, and theories are moving from being instruction-centered to being learning-centered. Perhaps needless to say, this shift has produced conceptual overlaps, competing ideas, and a flood of terms and phrases that, overall, provide a wellspring of ideas through which faculty may sift and winnow.

The flip side of having such an abundance of ideas for teaching, learning, and assessment is having to make sense of these ideas in practice. Put simply, how do these three domains of literature stand in relation to one another conceptually and how should they be operationalized in practice? Faculty are currently left to intuit or infer an answer to these questions as they attempt to make sense of the complex web that constitutes the scholarship of teaching and learning. To address this lacuna, we advance Teaching-for-Learning (TFL)—a model to help orient faculty to basic principles and practices drawn from the scholarship of teaching and learning (though without the element of *doing* the scholarship of teaching and learning) and guide them in a systematic process of exploring and testing teaching and assessment practices to achieve course learning goals.

Teaching-for-Learning (TFL): Definition and Scope

Teaching-for-Learning (TFL) is a systematic and inclusive model for teachers to explore and test teaching and assessment practices in order to ensure learning experiences that enhance the learning of all students. The model places teachers in an investigative role and allows them to draw from their background, skills, and dispositions to advance their own "theories-in-practice" within the context of their discipline or field of study, course goals, learning environment, and student population. In advancing TFL, we invite readers to scrutinize it, test it, and modify it as appropriate within the context of their courses, their students, and their respective learning contexts.

Before turning to the model itself, it is important to elaborate on the definition and scope of TFL, particularly in relation to the extant literature. To begin with, a signature contribution of the scholarship of teaching and learning movement has been its characterization of teaching as an inquiry-based activity. As the movement has evolved, Hutchings and Shulman (1999) have drawn a meaningful distinction in the ongoing scholarship of teaching and learning, namely, between the "scholarship of teaching" and "scholarly teaching"—with the latter focused on teaching to enhance student learning and the former focused more broadly on developing and disseminating knowledge about teaching and learning while, at the same time, enhancing student learning. As an inquiry-based model, TFL may be used by faculty to share their findings with a scholarly audience—as in the "scholarship of teaching." That said, such external concerns are secondary to TFL's primary focus on student learning—that is, teaching for the sake of learning. Unlike "scholarly teaching," which precludes by definition "scholarship of teaching," TFL does not draw such a boundary.

Because TFL neither fits squarely within nor precludes the existing rubrics of "scholarly teaching" and the "scholarship of teaching," we propose that it be viewed as a generic model with generative potential. We suggest that TFL is generic because it reflects what we see as a genre that has emerged in the teaching, learning, and assessment literature. Indeed, we developed the TFL model in our review of these texts, identifying and giving expression to points of convergence regarding teaching, learning, and assessment. In other words, TFL—a heuristic model—stands as both an interpretation of extant texts and a guide for further interpretation. We suggest that TFL is generative because the simple, dynamic, and inclusive approach of the model builds capacity for continuous experimentation and discovery grounded in the experiences of individual faculty. To illustrate, TFL can be thought of as a model which facilitates professors' ongoing experiences in what Parker Palmer observed as the "mystery" of teaching:

> Good teachers dwell in the mystery of good teaching until it dwells in them. As they explore it alone and with others, the insight and energy of mystery begins to inform and animate their work. They discover and develop methods of teaching that emerge from their own integrity—but they never reduce their teaching to technique (Palmer 1990, p. 11).

In light of the notion of faculty "living the mystery" of teaching, we make a distinction between TFL and other models which also explicitly advocate a systematic approach to teaching, learning, and assessment. For example, Diamond (1998) described in great detail a two-phase systematic design model consisting of "project selection and design" and "production, implementation, and evaluation" (p. 17). Although TFL is not wholly dissimilar in comparison to Diamond's emphasis on engaging in a step-wise process of developing goals and identifying ways to reach and evaluate them, it differs significantly from his and other models informed by systems and quality approaches (e.g., Cornesky 1993; Dick et al. 2001) in two major ways. First, TFL is primarily animated by *classroom experiences* (both anticipated and unanticipated), including teachers' experiences, students' experiences, and the interaction among them rather than by a "vision" (Shulman 1998) and other instructional design "inputs" that are associated with systems models. Second, whereas systems models are usually focused on the whole of a course, TFL can be used not only for planning a course at the outset but also for mid-course adjustments (e.g., course modules spanning multiple class sessions, a single class session, a portion of a single class session) made by faculty in response to unfolding classroom experiences. We elaborate on these qualities as we explicate the major components of the TFL model in the section that follows.

The Teaching-for-Learning Model

Six components make up the Teaching-for-Learning model. Figure 1 is a diagrammatic representation of these six components.

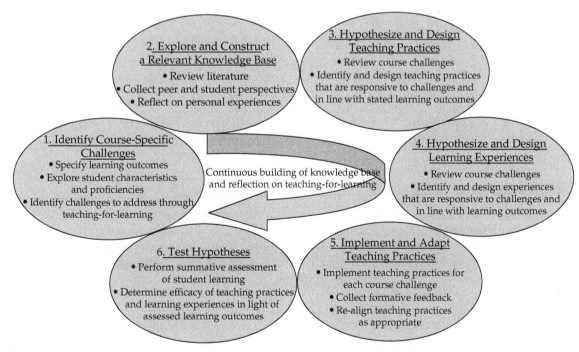

Figure 1 Teaching-for-Learning: A Systematic Approach for Teachers to Identify and Enact—through Exploring and Testing—Teaching Practices that Enrich Learning Experiences Leading to the Enhancement of Learning for all Students

Identifying Course-specific Challenges

Arguably the most important component of the TFL approach is identifying the major challenges that need to be addressed in a course. As teachers we usually know what we expect our students to achieve in terms of learning by the end of a course; but more often than not, we give relatively little thought to what invisible hindrances—and missed opportunities—might come along the way. TFL begins by urging us to identify and articulate the major challenges we need to address within our course—challenges that might arise from factors as varied as the learning environment, diverse student demographics, and course content. This emphasis on the early identification of challenges encourages us to work backwards from the learning goals we have set for our students and anticipate the factors that could hinder attainment. In effect, TFL explicitly reminds us of the need to make a direct connection between our teaching and our students' learning by identifying and addressing the impediments that may militate against closing the gap between the two.

Because they not only give direction to the teacher in designing the course but also provide a foundation for assessing student learning, identifying specific learning outcomes expected of all students is a critical initial step in TFL. Learning outcomes may range from the mastery of a specific skill to the understanding of a concept to the cultivation of greater appreciation for a particular way-of-knowing. In identifying learning goals, it is important not only that they reflect teacher expectations for the course; they should also be in alignment with the mission, purpose, and culture of the program in which the course is nested.

A follow-up step in the process of identifying key course-specific challenges is teacher exploration of the backgrounds and characteristics of students in the course—collectively and, insofar as possible, individually—in concert with entry-level assessment of their subject matter proficiency. Alternatively, teachers might choose to begin the TFL process by exploring student characteristics and establishing learning goals based on a preliminary judgment of their proficiency. Put simply, studying the student population invites the teacher to begin thinking about potentially valuable learning experiences and teaching practices that seem likely to match the needs of a diverse student group. Optimum learning experiences for a heterogeneous student cohort will likely differ from a cohort of a more homogenous group of students. An enhanced understanding of the student population can also provide a foundation for subsequent assessment of student learning.

Anchored in the context of student learning goals and an understanding of the backgrounds, characteristics, and subject matter expertise of students in the course, faculty members can begin to identify specific challenges that may hinder the achievement of the intended learning outcomes. These may include a lack of students' preparation for certain course expectations, limited time available to teach content matter, or even the instructor's own struggle with specific subject matter. The challenges that have been identified provide the foundation for TFL, for the remainder of the TFL process is centered on the identification of teaching practices that will help foster learning experiences consonant with each of the challenges specified.

Constructing a Knowledge Base

Developing a foundation of knowledge is an important part of the inquiry-based TFL process: what is known about teaching, learning, and assessment can go a long way in helping faculty systematically connect teaching and learning. To take but one example, the literature on Classroom Research (Cross and Steadman 1996)—with its focus on "how students learn" and attendant classroom challenges—can be a valuable resource. By drawing in part on such literature and then testing it within the context of their courses, TFL is a tool that encourages individual faculty to navigate systematically through myriad teaching techniques advanced in the literature in order to enhance the learning of all of their students.

To construct a knowledge base, the teacher, guided by the course-specific challenges identified, explores potentially effective learning experiences in light of student diversity in background and learning styles, reflects on alternative teaching practices for cultivating these experiences, and considers alternative approaches to assessing the teaching and learning in the course. As suggested earlier, reviewing the literature on teaching, learning, and assessment both across and within disciplines and fields of study can help a teacher construct a knowledge base for TFL. For example, an enormous amount of research has been done on learning styles and learner needs in the fields of psychology, education, and engineering. One might also draw from research in such fields as educational psychology which have identified and explored the efficacy of diverse teaching and instructional styles in varying circumstances. And, of course, peers and colleagues can be a valuable source of ideas as can one's own reflections on previous teaching experiences.

To be sure, most faculty members do not have the time and energy to explore directly the literatures on teaching, learning, and assessment. Fortunately, most colleges and universities now have faculty development offices with highly-skilled faculty developers who have easy access to the literature and, in our experiences, can be of great assistance to faculty in developing a knowledge base. Underscoring the generative potential of TFL, we encourage faculty to seek out faculty development experts. The reality of implementing the TFL model almost requires their services and expertise.

Hypothesizing and Designing Relevant Learning Experiences

Based on literature reviews and perspectives from peers and students as well as knowledge of student characteristics, the teacher then identifies and designs learning experiences that seem most conducive to addressing the major course challenges and, in turn, achieving the intended learning outcomes for the student population. Learning experiences—which deserve explicit attention lest they be over-looked—represent the ways in which students are engaged (e.g., memorizing, thinking, reasoning, applying, doing) or otherwise. In short, the teacher hypothesizes relationships between learning experiences and outcomes, choosing those experiences that seem most likely to match the intended learning goals and course challenges. TFL invites faculty to recognize the salience of identifying and designing learning experiences that help link teaching with learning. These learning experiences provide the means through which TFL strives to accomplish the end-goal: enhanced learning outcomes. The focus on learning experiences encourages faculty as teachers-qua-researchers to deliberate over the ways in which students learn and what specifically can be done to bring about such learning. They guide the selection and use of teaching practices that we think will foster experiences that enhance learning.

Designing learning experiences is at the heart of the TFL process because it is these experiences—shaped by teaching practices—that influence what students learn. To be sure, the teacher must be mindful that some learning experiences may work better for certain students than others and hence a variety of experiences may have to be created in order to address the needs of all students. TFL encourages teachers to learn about their students and consciously think about experiences and teaching practices. In short, TFL encourages faculty members to acknowledge and respond to varied learning styles, abilities, and interests among students and seeks to create a range of experiences that may facilitate the learning of a diverse student body.

Hypothesizing and Designing Teaching Practices

Having identified course-specific challenges and designed learning experiences aimed at addressing those challenges, teachers can now explore relationships between teaching practices and students' learning experiences. More precisely, this involves the teacher selecting (from the knowledge base constructed) teaching practices most likely to lead to learning experiences which will enhance learning. To illustrate, in order to strengthen students' writing skills (course challenge), a teacher might hypothesize that employing small group discussions (teaching strategy) to share students' in-class writing would encourage them to apply their critical thinking and analytic skills (learning experience) which, in turn, will help them attain the desired learning outcome.

As Palmer (1998) has suggested, "good teaching" cannot be reduced to technique; in his words, good teaching also comes from the "identity and integrity" of the teacher. In selecting teaching practices in the TFL model, it is important to reflect not only on teaching techniques per se but also on "who" the teacher is as a person. Selection of teaching practices should be in alignment with one's own personality and disposition.

Implementing and Adapting Teaching Practices

Once learning experiences have been identified and teaching practices have been selected, teaching practices are implemented. Formative assessment—ongoing assessment of both teaching practices and students that, in turn, provides information to guide instruction and improve student performance—provides the teacher with insight into the effectiveness of teaching practices as well as ideas for adjustments in teaching practices. Such assessment may be carried out directly through students' feedback and testing students and/or indirectly through observations of students' engagement in class and responses to teaching practices. In turn, teaching practices are adapted as appropriate.

Hypotheses-testing

Until this point in the TFL process, the teacher will have made two hypotheses for each course challenge, namely, that the selected learning experiences will lead to desired learning outcomes and that the selected teaching practices will enhance the selected learning experiences. Hypotheses-testing is the final stage in the TFL process whereby the teacher explores the efficacy of the various teaching practices. Summative assessment—a conclusive evaluation to record student achievement and gauge student learning in light of the entry-level assessment carried out at the beginning of the course—is then carried out.

The teacher may invite student feedback on the effectiveness of teaching strategies used in the course and can then decide if the methods should be adopted for future use or if they need to be modified. If a teaching strategy is found appropriate for meeting a particular challenge, the teacher can add this learning to her knowledge base and begin again with another challenge and teaching method; alternatively, the experiment may be tried again with another teaching strategy or learning experience for the same challenge. Of course, TFL can be used by teachers to address multiple learning outcomes and/or challenges at the same time.

Engaging in Teaching-for-Learning: A Vignette

She began this first session of her qualitative methods course as she always had, namely, by briefly discussing her learning outcomes with her students in order to identify any major course-specific challenges that she might need to address. In order to get a sense of her students' backgrounds and other notable characteristics, she asked them to indicate why they enrolled in the course and what they expected to learn from it. Without exception, every student in the class communicated that they were there to learn "methodologically correct" qualitative research techniques. She understood, of course, that they likely had come to embrace this goal for many reasons, not the least of which was because "technique" was a predominant concern in courses elsewhere in the school and, indeed, the field at large. Yet, for these same reasons she was deeply troubled because she believed that spirited engagement with ideas was the hallmark of exemplary inquiry and ought to trump methodology concerns, per se. As she communicated in several of her learning outcomes for the course, she expected students to identify and crystallize meaningful problems to guide their inquiry and to "seize their own voice" throughout their research.

After reflecting on that first night of class, she determined that the most formidable challenge she faced was to get her students to place ideas at the center of their inquiry and to seize ownership of their inquiry by developing and maintaining fidelity to a meaningful research question that had both personal and professional significance. She considered the option of entering the next class meeting with a plan to engage in a single didactic and passionate commentary; but she suspected that such an approach would either be seen as a footnote to her earlier presentation of class objectives, as an annoyance, or both. Instead, she began to explore and construct a relevant knowledge base to address this challenge. After discussing the matter with several colleagues, including two faculty developers, the best idea they could come up with was to have class members form "research groups" in which they were asked to generate an agreed-upon research question and approach to answering it. The animating intent of having the students do this was to demonstrate that determining the appropriateness of a research question and methodology is as much a matter of satisfying groups of individuals as it is a matter of adhering to transcendent truths.

In the first few weeks of the course, she remained conscious of the challenge she had identified at the outset and made a variety of efforts to modify the direction of the conversation in subtle ways and not to allow the exclusively technique-centered sensibilities of the first week continue to dominate the classroom discourse. The harsh reality was that provisional project proposals from the students showed her that she was hardly making a dent, for they were heavy on methods and light on the ideas and messy complications associated with conducting meaningful research. She then turned to major texts and the most recent journal articles regarding graduate education in an attempt to identify promising practices she might implement. She didn't find much that she could use; neither the literature nor her peers had many promising suggestions.

However, by sheer coincidence she then came across a chapter in a book on research that caught her attention. Entitled "The Challenge of Framing a Problem: What Is Your Burning Question" (Harter 2006), the chapter was written in first person and in lively and invitational prose that communicated the importance of taking ownership of a research question at once meaningful to self and others. After reading the chapter, she hypothesized that the metaphor of the "burning question" might help individuals—and groups—to take ownership of their inquiry, beginning with their research question. Consonant with that metaphor, she asked each research group to reorganize their group "learning experiences" around developing and maintaining fidelity to their burning question. More specifically, she asked each group to come up with their burning question and, in turn, to conduct their inquiry in the spirit of the metaphor.

As she engaged in implementing and adapting her teaching practices in light of the challenge that she had identified that first night of the course, she solicited a great deal of informal feedback on the impact of the "burning question" intervention. Somewhat to her surprise, the chapter and the metaphor seemed to be doing more than she could have ever imagined in terms of encouraging students to personally invest in the pursuit of ideas as much as they were focused on technique and methodological rules and procedures. And in class, she found herself using the burning question approach (she was mindful that it, too, could simply become another "rule" if it were not treated as a metaphor) as they reflected on various research studies that they read during the term.

She was able further to test her hypothesis on the occasion of reviewing her students' final papers. While she did not use an experimental design, she did compare students' in-class presentations of their final papers and the papers themselves with those of other qualitative research classes she had taught previously. To her delight, the group papers were among the best she had ever received; and in the class presentations students communicated an ownership of their problems with a passion she had rarely seen before. In short, the evidence strongly suggested that the simple intervention of a "reading," in concert with inviting students to apply the message of that reading throughout their research project, had made a significant difference in her students' learning. To come full circle, students consistently placed ideas at the center of their inquiry through seizing ownership and developing and maintaining fidelity to a meaningful research question that had personal as well as professional significance. Moreover, the papers displayed a fierce intellectuality and rigor in comparison to many previous classes. She was delighted with some unexpected outcomes: students were more imaginative, self-directed, curious, and engaged inquirers than had often been the case in her previous classes.

Conclusion

Triggered by the identification of course-specific challenges in light of intended learning outcomes and student characteristics, we advance TFL as an inclusive and dynamic approach in the search for teaching and assessment practices to enhance the learning of all students. More specifically, TFL invites faculty to engage in a dynamic process of constructing a knowledge base, designing learning experiences and teaching practices, hypothesizing their effect on students' learning experiences (and, in turn, learning outcomes), applying these teaching practices within the course and testing their effectiveness in enhancing student learning.

TFL is inclusive of what have traditionally been discrete areas of research and innovations in practice. While most approaches found in the literature focus mainly on teaching, learning, or assessment, TFL incorporates all three of these domains in concert with other elements that are salient in the literature: student characteristics and learning styles, learning experiences, teaching practices, and assessment techniques. Moreover, the model is inclusive because it represents both teachers and learners, perhaps most importantly by encouraging teachers to select teaching practices in concert with their students' needs as well as their own personality and disposition. And not insignificantly, the model encourages teachers to explore and test a wide range of so-called "best practices"—not only those advanced in the literature but also those suggested by colleagues and peers as well as those drawn from their own experiences—for enhancing student learning.

TFL invites faculty to engage in the dynamic process of teaching-for-learning and continuously revitalize their teaching in ways that ensure student learning in widely differing contexts—including learning environment, diversity in student populations, and course learning goals. As higher education continues to change, experimentation and innovation in our teaching and learning practices will clearly be needed for the foreseeable future. The TFL model provides a heuristic for faculty members to reexamine their teaching in order to determine what teaching practices are meaningfully contributing to student growth and development and what alternative teaching practices might be introduced within the context of the ever-changing challenges that we face in teaching-for-learning.

References

Anderson, M. B. (1999). In progress: Reports of new approaches in medical education. *Academic Medicine, 74*, 561–618.

Angelo, T. A., & Cross, K. P. (1993). *Classroom assessment techniques: A handbook for college teachers* (2nd ed.). San Francisco, CA: Jossey-Bass.

Ash, S. L., & Clayton, P. H. (2004). The articulated learning: An approach to guided reflection and assessment. *Innovative Higher Education, 29*, 137–154.

Barell, J. (1995). *Teaching for thoughtfulness: Classroom strategies to enhance intellectual development* (2nd ed.). White Plains, NY: Longman.

Barr, R. B., & Tagg, J. (1995). From teaching to learning: A new paradigm for undergraduate education. *Change, 27*(6), 13–25.

Bastick, T. (2001, August). *Relationships between in-course alignment indicators and post-course criteria of quality teaching and learning in higher education.* Paper presented at the Biennial Meeting of the European Association for Research in Learning and Instruction, Fribourg, Switzerland.

Beaman, R. (1998). The unquiet . . . even loud, andragogy! Alternative assessment for adult learners. *Innovative Higher Education, 23*, 47–59.

Bloom, B. S., Engelhart, M. D., Furst, E. J., Hill, W. H., & Krathwohl, D. R. (1956). *Taxonomy of educational objectives: The classification of educational goals. Handbook 1: Cognitive domain.* New York, NY: David McKay.

Boyer, E. (1990). *Scholarship reconsidered: Priorities of the professoriate.* Princeton, NJ: The Carnegie Foundation for the Advancement of Teaching.

Brew, A. (2003). Teaching and research: New relationships and their implications for inquiry-based teaching and learning in higher education. *Higher Education Research & Development, 22*, 3–18.

Cabedo-Timmons, G. (2002). *Teaching Spanish subject matters to college students in the USA.* Macomb, IL: Western Illinois University. (ERIC Document Reproduction Service no. ED468881)

Cochran-Smith, M., & Lytle, S. L. (1999). The teacher research movement: A decade later. *Educational Researcher, 28*, 15–25.

Colbeck, C. L., Cabrera, A. F., & Terenzini, P. T. (2000). Learning professional confidence: Linking teaching practices, students' self-perceptions, and gender. *The Review of Higher Education, 24*, 173–191.

Collins, A., & Spiegel, S. A. (1995). *So you want to do action research?* Retrieved October 29, 2004, from Eisenhower National Clearinghouse (ENC) website: http://www.enc.org/professional/learn/research/journal/-science/document.shtm?input=ENC-002432-2432.

Cornesky, R. (1993). *The quality professor: Implementing TQM in the classroom*. Madison, WI: Magna Publications.

Cross, K. P. (1996). Classroom research: Implementing the scholarship of teaching. *American Journal of Pharmaceutical Education, 60*, 402–407.

Cross, K. P. (1999). What do we know about students' learning, and how do we know it? *Innovative Higher Education, 23*, 255–270.

Cross, K. P., & Steadman, M. H. (1996). *Classroom research: Implementing the scholarship of teaching*. San Francisco, CA: Jossey-Bass.

Diamond, R. M. (1998). *Designing and assessing courses and curricula: A practical guide*. San Francisco, CA: Jossey-Bass.

Dick, W., Carey, L., & Carey, J. (2001). *The systematic design of instruction*. New York, NY: Longman.

Fairweather, J. S. (2005). Beyond the rhetoric: Trends in the relative value of teaching and research in faculty salaries. *Journal of Higher Education, 76*, 401–422.

Glassick, C., Huber, M. T.,& Maeroff, G. I. (1997). *Scholarship assessed: A special report on faculty evaluation*. San Francisco, CA: Jossey-Bass.

Handelsman, J., Ebert-May, D., Beichner, R., Bruns, P., Chang, A., DeHaan, R., et al. (2004). Scientific teaching. *Science, 304*, 521–522.

Hansen, E. J. (1998). Creating teachable moments...and making them last. *Innovative Higher Education, 23*, 7–26.

Harter, S. (2006). The challenge of framing a problem: What is your burning question? In C. F. Conrad & R Serlin (Eds.), *The SAGE handbook on research in education: Engaging ideas and enriching inquiry* (pp. 331–348). Thousand Oaks, CA: SAGE.

Huba, M. E., & Freed, J. E. (2000). *Learner-centered assessment on college campuses*. Needham Heights, MA: Allyn and Bacon.

Huber, M. T. (2005). *Balancing acts: The scholarship of teaching and learning in academic careers*. Washington, DC: The American Association for Higher Education and The Carnegie Foundation for the Advancement of Teaching.

Huber, M., & Hutchings, P. (2005). *The advancement of learning: Building the teaching commons*. San Francisco, CA: Jossey-Bass.

Huber, M. T., & Morreale, S. (2002). *Disciplinary styles in the scholarship of teaching and learning: Exploring common ground*. Washington, DC: The American Association for Higher Education and The Carnegie Foundation for the Advancement of Teaching.

Hutchings, P. (Ed.) (2000). *Opening lines: Approaches to the scholarship of teaching and learning*. Princeton, NJ: Carnegie Foundation for the Advancement of Teaching.

Hutchings, P. (2002). *Ethics of inquiry: Issues in the scholarship of teaching and learning*. Menlo Park, CA: The Carnegie Foundation for the Advancement of Teaching.

Hutchings, P., & Shulman, L. E. (1999). The scholarship of teaching: New elaborations, new developments. *Change, 31(5)*, 10–15.

Jenkins, A., Breen, R., Lindsay, R., & Brew, A. (2002). *Re-shaping higher education: Linking teaching and research*. London, England: Kogan Page.

Johnson, M. C., & Malinowski, J. C. (2001). Navigating the active learning swamp: Creating an inviting environment for learning. *Journal of College Science Teaching, 31*, 172–177.

Jones, E. A. (2002). Myths about assessing the impact of problem-based learning on students. *Journal of General Education, 51*, 326–334.

Justice, C., Rice, J., Warry, W., Inglis, S., Miller, S., & Sammon, S. (2007). Inquiry in higher education: Reflections and directions on course design and teaching methods. *Innovative Higher Education, 31*, 201–214.

Kirk, R. E. (2002, August). *Teaching introductory statistics: Some things I have learned*. Paper presented at the Annual Conference of the American Psychological Association, Chicago, IL.

Krathwohl, D. R. (2002). A revision of Bloom's taxonomy: An overview. *Theory into Practice, 41*, 212–218.

Lattuca, L. R., Voigt, L. J., & Fath, K. Q. (2004). Does interdisciplinarity promote learning? Theoretical support and researchable questions. *Review of Higher Education, 28*, 23–48.

Lewthwaite, B. J., & Dunham, H. P. (1999, February). *Enriching teaching scholarship through learning styles*. Paper presented at the Annual Meeting of the American Association of Colleges for Teacher Education, Washington, DC.

Marion, R., & Zeichner, K. (2001). *Practitioner resource guide for action research*. Oxford, OH: National Staff Development Council. (ERIC Document Reproduction Service no. ED472207)

McCann, L. I., Perlman, B., & De Both, T. L. (2001). Instructor evaluations of introductory psychology teaching techniques. *Teaching of Psychology, 28*, 274–276.

McDaniel, E. A., & Colarulli, G. C. (1997). Collaborative teaching in the face of productivity concerns: The dispersed team model. *Innovative Higher Education, 22*, 19–36.

Myers, C. B., & Myers, S. M. (2007). Assessing assessment: The effects of two exam formats on course achievement and evaluation. *Innovative Higher Education, 31*, 227–236.

Nilson, L. B. (2003). *Teaching at its best: A research-based resource for college instructors*. Boston, MA: Anker.

Palaskas, T. A. (2002). Model for selecting technology mediated teaching strategies. *Educational Technology, 42(6)*, 49–54

Palmer, P. J. (1990). Good teaching: A matter of living the mystery. *Change, 22(1)*, 11–16. January.

Palmer, P. J. (1998). *The courage to teach: Exploring the inner landscape of a teacher's life*. San Francisco, CA: Jossey-Bass.

Quarstein, V. A., & Peterson, P. A. (2001). Assessment of cooperative learning: A goal-criterion approach. *Innovative Higher Education, 26*, 59–77.

Rogers, G., Finley, D., & Kline, T. (2001). Understanding individual differences in university undergraduates: A learner needs segmentation approach. *Innovative Higher Education, 25*, 183–196.

Savin-Baden, M. (2000). *Problem-based learning in higher education: Untold stories*. London, England: Society for Research into Higher Education.

Scovic, S. P. (1983, April). *What are "alternative learning approaches" and do they work*? Paper presented at the National School Boards Association Convention, San Francisco, CA.

Shulman, L. S. (1998). Course anatomy: The dissection and analysis of knowledge through teaching. In P. Hutchings (Ed.), *The course portfolio: How instructors can examine their teaching to advance practice and improve student learning* (pp. 5–12). Washington, DC: American Association for Higher Education.

Smith, R. A. (2001). Formative evaluation and the scholarship of teaching and learning. In C. Knapper & P. Cranton (Eds.), *Fresh approaches to the evaluation of teaching* (pp. 51–62). *New directions for teaching and learning*, vol. 88. San Francisco, CA: Jossey Bass.

Wright, M. (2005). Always at odds? Congruence in faculty beliefs about teaching at a research university. *Journal of Higher Education, 76*, 331–353.

TEACHING EXCELLENCE, TEACHING EXPERTISE, AND THE SCHOLARSHIP OF TEACHING

CAROLIN KREBER

ABSTRACT: The previous decade witnessed significant advancements in the scholarship of teaching at the levels of both theory building and program development. Notwithstanding these achievements, there remains considerable ambiguity regarding the meaning of the concept. This ambiguity has implications for faculty evaluation. Excellence in teaching, expertise in teaching, and the scholarship of teaching are analyzed according to the nature and sources of knowledge construction underlying each. Practical examples are included to illustrate differences. It is argued that excellence in teaching and the scholarship of teaching are both important but should be recognized and rewarded in their own right.

My purpose in this conceptual article is to distinguish between three different ways in which higher education instructors can engage with teaching. These three forms of engagement are teaching excellence, teaching expertise, and the scholarship of teaching. Discussing differences and similarities in both the nature and the sources of knowledge construction underlying each, I suggest that scholars of teaching are *excellent teachers* as well as *expert teachers*; but they differ from either one in that scholars of teaching share their knowledge and advance the knowledge of teaching and learning in the discipline in a way that can be peer-reviewed. I conclude by raising some challenges this taxonomy poses for policy and practice.

Background

Teaching continues to be undervalued at research-intensive universities despite numerous initiatives to provoke change (e.g., Knapper & Rogers, 1994; Martin & Ramsden, 2000; Smith, 1991). The classic attempt to address this disparity in the rewards allocated to teaching and research was to suggest that scholarship means more than the discovery of new knowledge in the discipline. It extends to the integration, application, and transmission of knowledge, which has been referred to as the "scholarship of teaching" (Boyer, 1990; Rice, 1992). Though coining the term is typically attributed to Boyer and his colleagues at the Carnegie Foundation for the Advancement of Teaching (Glassick, Huber, & Maeroff, 1997), it has become evident over the past several years that the scholarship of teaching is not exclusively a North American idea but one of international scope. Not only did the previous decade witness a surge of publications on the topic nationally as well as internationally (e.g., Diamond, 1993; Edgerton, Hutchings, & Quinlan, 1991; Glassick, Huber, & Maeroff, 1997; Healey, 2000; Kreber & Cranton, 2000; Menges & Weimer, 1996; Morehead & Shedd, 1996; Paulsen & Feldman, 1995; Richlin, 1993; Shulman, 1998; Taylor, 1993; Trigwell, Martin, Benjamin, & Prosser, 2000; Weimer, 1992), but new programs aimed at promoting the scholarship of teaching were initiated not just in the United States (Cambridge, 2000; Hutchings, 1999), but also most notably in Britain (Baume & Baume, 1996; ILT, 2001) and Australia (Martin & Ramsden, 2000). There is a tendency in both Britain and Australia to conceive of the scholarship of teaching as a campus activity, in other words, as an

Reprinted from *Innovative Higher Education* 27, no. 1 (fall 2002).

endeavor aimed at promoting an institutional environment that is supportive of teaching and learning. In the United States the scholarship of teaching has been conceived of as both a campus activity as well as an activity or career path individual faculty may wish to pursue (Cambridge, 2001).

As a result of these recent initiatives and publications the higher education literature now also offers models on the scholarship of teaching, some of which are empirically derived (e.g., Trigwell et al., 2000; Weston & McAlpine, 2001) while others are deduced from existing theory (e.g., Kreber & Cranton, 2000; Paulsen & Feldman, 1995). The purpose of these models ranges from explaining the attainment, development, and conceptualizations of the scholarship of teaching (Kreber & Cranton, 2000; Trigwell, et al. 2000; Weston & McAlpine, 2001) to showing how it differs and overlaps with other facets of scholarship (Paulsen & Feldman, 1995).

Despite these significant advancements in the domain of "teaching scholarship" over the past decade at both the level of theory or model building as well as the level of program development, the results of a recent survey suggest that the majority of faculty still perceive considerable ambiguity in the meaning of the concept (Franklin & Theall 2001). No less than six years ago Menges and Weimer (1996) had already observed that the "The *scholarship of teaching* has become an amorphous term, equated more with commitment to teaching than with any concrete, substantive sense of definition or consensus as to how this scholarship can be recognized" (p. xii). Likewise, Andresen (2000) cautioned us more recently that "If the notions of *scholarship, scholar* and *scholarly* are to avoid emptiness and become useable as descriptors of teaching, as Ernest Boyer hoped, the concept behind these terms needs clarifying" (p. 137).

In response to this dilemma, attempts were made to define the scholarship of teaching. Based on a philosophical analysis, Andresen (2000) proposed that scholarship, including the scholarship of teaching, should involve critical reflection as well as scrutiny by peers and that it should be driven by an inquiry ethic. Using the research tradition of phenomenography (Marton, 1981), Trigwell et al. (2000) interviewed academics at an Australian university to identify how they construe the concept. The outcome of the study was a model distinguishing five different conceptions that are conceived as hierarchical in nature. The authors argued that conceptions of the scholarship of teaching differ along four dimensions: (1) the sources of information individuals draw upon, (2) the focus of their reflection, (3) the extent and nature of their communication of insights, and (4) their conceptions of teaching and learning (Kember, 1997; Prosser, Trigwell, & Taylor, 1994). Likewise, Kreber (2001, 2002), in a recent survey using the Delphi method, identified conceptualizations of the scholarship of teaching on which academics could reach consensus. In that study, the eleven participants[1] were also asked to identify issues surrounding the scholarship of teaching which they consider to be unresolved to date. Participants in the Delphi study contended that clearer definitions are needed to distinguish the meaning of concepts such as teaching expertise, teaching excellence, and the scholarship of teaching. Perhaps most importantly, panelists agreed that not everybody should be expected to practice the scholarship of teaching but that teaching excellence should be valued in its own right. Despite significant advances in higher education in the area of the scholarship of teaching these studies suggest that a unified definition of the concept continues to be lacking, let alone a clearer understanding of how it differs and overlaps with related phenomena.

A much needed contribution to present discourse on the scholarship of teaching, therefore, would be to provide faculty and academic administrators with a language and an understanding that permits them to distinguish the various ways of practicing post-secondary teaching: excellence in teaching, expertise in teaching, and the scholarship of teaching. Furthermore, in view of panelists' contention that the recognition and assessment of the scholarship of teaching remain important unresolved issues (Kreber, 2002; Theall & Centra, 2001), more precise definitions of teaching excellence, teaching expertise, and the scholarship of teaching could clearly enhance present faculty evaluation practices.

Recent faculty evaluation literature (e.g., Centra, 1993; Glassick et al., 1997; Braskamp & Ory, 1994) has not ignored suggestions to conceptualize scholarship more broadly. However, this literature does not address the question as to whether, and if so how, teaching excellence and the scholarship of teaching should be rewarded differently. I propose that a first step towards achieving a clearer understanding of what is being evaluated is to explore specifically the sources and nature of knowledge construction for teaching excellence, teaching expertise, and the scholarship of teaching. My purpose, therefore, in this article is to discuss three questions:

- What are the sources and nature of knowledge construction in teaching excellence?
- What are the sources and nature of knowledge construction in teaching expertise?
- What are the sources and nature of knowledge construction in the scholarship of teaching?

Teaching Excellence

As already discussed, one of Boyer's (1990) considerations in proposing a more comprehensive conceptualization of scholarship was the widely shared view that, at research-intensive institutions specifically, teaching is given far less weight in tenure and promotion decisions than is research. For some of his followers, the scholarship of teaching then was seen as an appropriate way of "upping the ante with respect to teaching" (Menges & Weimer, 1996) at research-intensive institutions; and the scholarship of teaching was interpreted essentially as teaching excellence (see, for example, Morehead & Shedd, 1996). There might be a difference, however, between *wanting teaching to count* in higher education and *wanting it to count as scholarship* (Smith, 1997).

Based on my previous work as a faculty developer, knowledge of the literature, and research with university teachers, I have observed that the majority of faculty would agree to the following observations about teaching. It is seen as a very time-consuming but also scholarly activity in that it requires sound knowledge of one's discipline as well as a good understanding of how to help students grow within, and perhaps even beyond, the discipline. Also, excellent teachers are seen as those who know how to motivate their students, how to convey concepts, and how to help students overcome difficulty in their learning.

Perhaps there is less commonality in how faculty think teaching excellence comes about. How do excellent teachers know what to do? Mentkowski and associates (2000) discuss four ways in which knowledge about learning and teaching can be constructed: through formal research, collaborative inquiry, the literature, and practice or experience. Granted, excellent teachers may derive their knowledge of how to teach from all of these sources; yet, they may derive it from active experimentation and reflection on personal experience alone. This latter point is crucial to the argument developed here and will be revisited below. First, however, it will be helpful to examine how teaching excellence is typically identified.

Excellence in teaching is usually identified on the basis of a judgement made about *performance*. Students, peers, and in some cases faculty members themselves describe how they perceive the performance. Awards for teaching excellence, for example, are ordinarily not adjudicated on the basis of how much someone *knows* about teaching. Indeed, for the effective practice of teaching and, by implication, the quality of student learning, an assessment of how much someone knows about teaching may even be perceived as irrelevant. In identifying teaching excellence, it is deemed far more pertinent that the *performance* was perceived as successful or effective by those who had the experience (i.e., present and former students, peers, and the instructors themselves).

We now widely accept that it is possible for everyone to become a good teacher who exerts the effort, and we recognize the belief that *good teachers are born not made* as a myth (Weimer, 1990). An experience most faculty share is that preparing courses, offering interesting and motivating lectures and seminars, and supervising and consulting with students require extensive energy and time. In sum, being or becoming a good teacher is hard work; and many colleagues would agree that excellence in teaching performance should be rewarded more highly than is presently the case. An important question that needs to be posed, however, is whether it is this form of teaching excellence that should count as scholarship or whether excellence in teaching and the scholarship of teaching are perhaps different and require different evaluation criteria and rewards. The significant point here is that teaching excellence could be based exclusively on knowledge that teachers construct as a result of their personal teaching experience. Schön (1983) and others argued that this knowledge is generated through "reflection in action" and "reflection on action." Clearly, this is one important and valid form of knowing about teaching. Note also that there is room for this kind of a scholarship of teaching in the model proposed by Trigwell et al. (2000). However, these authors emphasize that the five conceptions they identified are hierarchical in nature with higher-order forms of the scholarships of teaching encompassing the lower-order ones.

An example may illustrate what we usually mean by teaching excellence:

> Chris is an Associate Professor in the Physical Sciences. For the past five years Chris's teaching evaluations have been in the top 5% of his university. At a small ceremony held in recognition of his reception of a well-deserved university teaching award he comments on his teaching this way: "People often ask me how I manage to receive such good evaluations. I tell them 'the secret is you have to love the classroom! You have to find enjoyment in engaging with students. And you have to be attentive to what's happening.' In my view, there is nothing more motivating and gratifying than seeing the light come on in students' eyes. I have not always been a good teacher. When I first started teaching I had no idea about how to teach. I made many mistakes, such as overloading students with readings, filling my lectures with far too much content, and not showing any flexibility in my teaching. I deliberately filled my lectures as I was afraid that students could ask me questions that I would not know the answer to. Over time I realized what worked in my classes and what didn't. I also became more comfortable with not knowing everything. I kept the approaches that worked and threw out the bad stuff. The students like it, and this shows in the excellent work they are doing. I feel I have some valuable advice to share, and that's why I agreed when invited to participate in our peer consultation program.

Analyzing this example in terms of the four dimensions of the scholarship of teaching proposed by Trigwell et al. (2000)—conceptions of teaching, sources of information, focus of the reflection, and communication of insights—Chris has already begun to move towards a conception of teaching that is learning-oriented. At the same time, however, he still operates at the lower end of the information dimension as there is no evidence that he has consulted the literature on teaching and learning, let alone literature that is specific to his discipline. Reflection is evident but unfocused, or directed at the class as a whole, rather than at a particular problem that he seeks to examine in greater depth. Finally, communication of insights does take place but not through peer-reviewed media.

The scholarship of teaching, or higher forms thereof, on the other hand, while not negating the value of the practitioner's personal experience, needs to go beyond this. Thus, we ask if there is value in knowledge about teaching that goes beyond the practitioner's personal experience.

How reasonable is it to assume that knowledge resulting from educational research enhances practice? Norris (2000) criticizes the view that teachers' personal knowledge, constructed on the basis of teaching experience, is superior to theoretical knowledge on teaching as suggested, for example, in the work of Carr (1992), Cochran-Smith and Lytle (1990), Munby and Russell (1994), and Schön (1983). These authors argued that theoretical knowledge has no real relevance to teachers as it cannot be *directly applied to practice*. Norris presents a strong rationale for the consideration of educational theory by teachers, suggesting that it enhances teaching. According to Norris, it is essential that teachers understand the value of theories as "general models" which need to be adapted to educators' specific context, rather than misconstrue them as situational or context-specific problem-solving strategies. Using theory to inform practice then cannot, and should not, occur in the form of a direct application of a recipe to a given problem. It rather implies a series of decision-making processes on the part of the teacher. Norris contended that "How and whether research-based knowledge applies to a given situation is one that is answerable only by those who know the particulars of the situation. When the situation is the classroom, teachers know the most about them." It is here that both the teachers' experience-based knowledge about teaching as well as their formal or research-based knowledge about teaching coincide as equally valid sources of information. As post-secondary teaching is highly contextual, the most effective teachers may likely be those who constantly reflect not only on their personal teaching experience but on the extent to which educational theory explains their experience. This idea will be taken up below.

Teaching Expertise

It is indeed a well-accepted notion within the higher education literature that faculty learn about teaching largely as a result of their personal teaching experience (Boice, 1992; Weimer, 1990). Typically it is a trial and error approach whereby strategies that work well are kept and those that do not work well are dismissed. Though empirical evidence is scarce, it is generally agreed that faculty arrive at their decisions as to which approaches to keep and which to dismiss based on certain reasons. In the language used in the educational literature this kind of reasoning is referred to as "reflection." While reasoning and reflection are at times associated with a conscious sequential problem-solving procedure, for most teachers this decision-making process will be rather intuitive and subconscious. Over time, most faculty develop a repertoire of approaches and strategies that tend to work well. Nonetheless, some teachers continue to engage in reflective thinking about what works and what does not and ask themselves why it worked or did not work. Their attention is focused on specific problems in their teaching practice, and their goal is to solve them. When this reflective process is also self-monitored and self-evaluated, we call it self-regulated learning.

Self-regulation theorists view learning as a process that occurs in three major phases identified as (1) forethought, (2) performance and volitional control, and (3) self-reflection (e.g., Pintrich, 1995; Zimmerman, 1998). Each phase is characterized by various beliefs and processes that have a direct influence on learning. Skillful self-regulators are described as:

- setting specific hierarchical learning goals rather than non-specific goals,
- holding a learning goal orientation rather than a performance goal orientation,
- having high self-efficacy and being intrinsically interested,
- managing to focus on their performance,
- using self-instructional techniques,
- self-monitoring the learning process rather than only the outcome,
- seeking self-evaluation,
- attributing success or failure to the strategies used rather than their ability,
- having positive self-reactions,
- and showing a high level of adaptivity.

The expertise literature (Bereiter & Scardamalia, 1993) suggests that faculty who continuously engage in self-regulating their learning about teaching develop expertise in teaching. In contrast, teachers who at one point engaged in reflection and as a consequence developed a repertoire of effective algorithms, strategies, or routines they rely on exclusively, would, according to this literature, most likely not be considered experts though some may indeed be "effective teachers" or "excellent teachers."

What then is the difference between expert teachers and excellent teachers? The difference is *not* that non-experts are not effective. The difference is that experts are excellent teachers, but excellent teachers are *not necessarily* experts. A closer look at this literature clarifies this distinction. Bereiter and Scardamalia (1993) showed that people pursuing "expert careers" (p. 11) continually reinvest the mental resources set free by the process of pattern learning and automatization in problems they encounter in their work. Thereby they approach these problems at increasingly higher levels of complexity, which, in turn, leads them to develop more sophisticated skills and knowledge. Experienced individuals that carry out only practiced routines, no matter how effective these are, reduce the dimensions of the job to what they are used to doing. This means that experts continuously seek out new opportunities to further their understanding of problems. It is precisely by identifying, analyzing, and solving problems that experts, over time, develop problem solving strategies that are *even more effective*. This desire to be *even more effective* underlies the motivation of experts. Does the present reward structure in higher education support the development of expertise in teaching?

It follows that if being effective is seen as sufficient and being "even more effective" is not externally rewarded, then the internal motivation to become "more effective" needs to be very high.

We usually understand motivation as a force that leads individuals to put effort into behaviors or strategies leading to accomplishing a goal. Reviewing various models of motivation to explain what drives faculty at work, Blackburn and Lawrence (1995) concluded that "Cognitive theories of motivation assume that people make decisions about how to behave by evaluating their capacity to respond to situations and estimating their possible losses" (p. 21). While both Weiner (1985) and Atkinson (1977) emphasize achievement disposition as an important factor in determining the degree of motivation an individual may experience for a given task, Vroom's (1964) expectancy theory stresses the motivational value of the task itself. According to Vroom's expectancy theory, the force guiding the decision-making process can be understood as a combination of the perceived expectancy of a person that goals can be reached and the value the person attributes to the task. While expectancy theory is only one of many lenses that can be applied to explain what motivates faculty at work (for a thorough discussion of non-cognitive as well as cognitive theories of motivation see Blackburn and Lawrence, 1995), it was shown to be helpful in identifying factors that may either foster or hinder faculty's development of teaching expertise (Kreber, 2000b).

Examined through the lens of expectancy theory (Vroom, 1964), we then witness an interesting situation in the academy. Take the two main functions of the professoriate: research and teaching. On the research side, faculty members are rewarded for their excellence by their own institution. These rewards operate on various levels. "Effective researchers" will be granted tenure and promotion. There is a minimal level of performance that is expected and needs to be met, and the bar as to what constitutes this minimal standard has been raised at most research-intensive institutions in recent years. In addition, however, there are institutional incentives that promote performance that goes beyond "effectiveness," put differently, beyond meeting the minimal standard. For example, more articles and more grants mean more money (at those institutions where merit pay still exists!). Apart from institutional incentives there are external rewards such as the prestige that comes along with being acknowledged at international conferences and journals or being invited to share one's special knowledge with the community or industry. Furthermore, at research universities, most faculty find the pursuit of research to be rewarding in a different sense. They like doing it. It provides them with a sense of enjoyment and accomplishment. For some their research is so enjoyable that it approximates optimal experience, or "Flow" (Csikzentmihalyi, 1990). We observe then that this intrinsic motivation to pursue research is further supported by external rewards. This combination of internal and external rewards for varying levels of research activity facilitates the development of expertise in research.

On the teaching side, external rewards for teaching are also present, but there are fewer than for research. Furthermore, effective teaching is generally considered good enough. It would follow that expertise in teaching, going beyond what is necessary, or "becoming even more effective," is not something that is externally rewarded. It matters little whether you receive a teaching award once, or twice, or ten times; but it matters a lot whether you publish one article or two or ten, and it matters a lot whether you receive one external research grant or two or ten. In line with this analysis, for faculty members to develop expertise in teaching this process would rely strongly on an inner or intrinsic motivation with few external rewards. This intrinsic motivation would result from the degree to which they value the satisfaction gained from learning about teaching and the degree to which they believe that their efforts to learn about teaching will be successful (Kreber, 2000b). Clearly, the presence of external rewards would further support this process. Identifying appropriate evaluation criteria would then become important. As will be shown later, expertise in teaching and the scholarship of teaching share important features. First however, let us explore the sources of knowledge leading to the development of teaching expertise.

In order to reach expertise three kinds of knowledge are particularly relevant: declarative knowledge, procedural knowledge, and implicit knowledge (Bereiter & Scardamalia, 1993). An important part of the declarative knowledge of expert teachers is knowledge found in books and articles about teaching and learning. This is precisely the knowledge of educational theory (Norris, 2000) discussed earlier. Expert teachers then would not exclusively rely on experience but would continuously construct new knowledge as they combine their declarative knowledge of educational theory with their procedural knowledge of how to teach. They rely upon their implicit knowledge of how to self-regulate their learning. In this way they advance theory and at the same time perform effectively.

It might be rather naïve to discuss the knowledge of the expert teacher without making reference to the discipline knowledge in the subject matter being taught. Clearly, the very same knowledge domains that are relevant for the development of expertise in teaching—declarative knowledge, procedural knowledge, and implicit or tacit knowledge—underlie the development of expertise in the discipline. When teachers develop expertise, they not only mediate theoretical knowledge about education with their knowledge derived from personal teaching experience, they also develop increasingly better ways of helping students understand the subject matter. When expertise in the discipline is effectively combined with knowledge of how to teach, the latter being derived from both educational theory as well as experience, we witness the construction of *pedagogical content knowledge* (Paulsen, 2001a, b; Shulman, 1987). It is then the construction of pedagogical content knowledge that is characteristic of expert teachers.

The example below illustrates expertise in teaching.

Sally, is a Professor in Chemical Engineering with 12 years of experience. Like Chris, she is recognized as an excellent teacher by her peers. Apart from teaching well, which is reflected in good evaluations, Sally is known for her fairly extensive knowledge of what makes good teaching. Pedagogical journals and newsletters in her field, as well as other general materials such as "To improve the academy," "New directions in teaching and learning," or "The teaching professor," each viciously attacked by numerous, little yellow post-it notes, fill a good part of her office book shelves. Not all of her knowledge is bookish though. She has actively applied the concepts introduced in the literature to specific problems in her own classroom where she uses her personal or experience-based knowledge of working with students in engineering classes, her extensive knowledge of chemical engineering, as well as the knowledge gained from the teaching and learning literature. In doing so she draws on formal and personal sources of knowledge construction about teaching and effectively combines these with her knowledge of the discipline to construct pedagogical content knowledge. Sally has a reputation not just as a good teacher; her peers observe that she continuously furthers her knowledge and that the insights of one week will soon be replaced by new ones.

Analyzing this example in terms of the four dimensions of the scholarship of teaching proposed by Trigwell et al. (2000), we observe that Sally, too, holds a conception of teaching that is learning-oriented. At the same time, however, she operates at the higher end of the information dimension as there is plenty of evidence that she regularly consults literature on teaching and learning within and beyond her specific discipline. Reflection is focused or directed at particular problems that are examined in greater depth. Finally, communication of insights does take place but not through peer-reviewed media.

The scholarship of teaching, or higher forms thereof, on the other hand, while encompassing what is described here, needs to go beyond this.

The Scholarship of Teaching

Would we expect scholars of teaching to be expert teachers? As already discussed, the term *scholarship of teaching* has been construed in many different ways. Kreber and Cranton (2000) as well as Trigwell et al. (2000) described it as a continuum, on which the scholarship of teaching is equated with teaching excellence (for example, Morehead & Shedd, 1996) on the one hand and with publications in peer-reviewed media on the other (for example, Richlin, 2001). Perhaps the most relevant educational knowledge is created, however, neither through experience nor publications alone but through the struggle with the mediation of theory and practice. What needs to be considered are both existing theoretical constructs as well as insights drawn from experience. Interpreted thus, scholars of teaching should be expert teachers; yet, our expectations of such scholars might have to go beyond this. Shulman (1998) suggested that the scholarship of teaching entails a public account of some or all of the following aspects of teaching—vision, design, interaction, outcomes, and analysis—in a manner that can be peer reviewed and used by members of one's community. These descriptors certainly apply to a traditional notion of scholarship, as we find in the case of refereed articles, public presentations, and books on teaching and learning. As we saw earlier, the development of expertise in teaching would then rely heavily on this kind of formal educational theory or "scholarship" in teaching (see also Smith, 2001).

However, the scholarship of teaching can also be public, shared, and peer-reviewed in a less traditional sense. Some have argued that the scholarship of teaching could be documented and shared through teaching portfolios (e.g., Edgerton, Hutchings, & Quinlan, 1991; Kreber, 2001). Others have suggested that the scholarship of teaching is shared also through mentoring colleagues (Weston & McAlpine, 2001) in addition to presentations, research, and publications. In a similar vein and drawing on the work of Pat Hutchings (1999), Cambridge (2000) writes "The scholarship of teaching is not aimed exclusively at publication. Scholars of teaching and learning are exploring multiple ways of making their work public, including the internet, faculty development activities, and public presentations" (p. 57). An example illustrates what practicing the scholarship of teaching could look like:

> Denis is an Assistant Professor of Earth and Atmospheric Sciences. Like Sally, Denis also continuously adapts his teaching to new contexts. In doing so he, too, draws on formal and personal sources of knowledge construction about teaching and effectively combines these with his knowledge of the discipline to construct pedagogical content knowledge. But in addition to what Sally does, he participates in conferences on teaching in his discipline, documents his knowledge through manuscripts that he submits for peer-review, and shares his special knowledge within department or faculty wide discussion groups and mentoring programs. By doing so he validates his knowledge.

Again using Trigwell et al.'s (2000) model to analyze this example, we observe that Denis, too, holds a conception of teaching that is learning-oriented. He also operates at the higher end of the information dimension as he consults the literature on teaching and learning within and beyond his specific discipline. Reflection is focused or directed at particular problems that are examined in greater depth. Finally, communication of insights takes place through peer-reviewed media.

Conclusion

The idea of the scholarship of teaching may only appeal to a small fraction of our faculty. In line with Boyer's initial intent, Hutchings (cited in Cambridge, 2000) suggested "The scholarship of teaching is not for everyone for all time. Faculty members do different kinds of scholarly inquiry and pose different questions at different times in their professional lives. Some scholars will choose to focus on teaching and learning; others will not" (p. 57). However, if only a few colleagues choose this focus in their careers, this does not suggest that the concept has failed. To the contrary, if a small number of faculty in disciplines other than education begin to build a career around exploring the teaching and learning dimension of their discipline, even if perhaps just for a few years as originally suggested by Boyer (1990), we witness a true change in what counts as scholarship. For too long we have conceived of relevant knowledge in the discipline exclusively as that which relates to the content of the field, paying little attention to how knowledge is constructed and transmitted. Many have discussed the relationship between research and teaching with some arguing that there is little to no relationship (e.g., Braxton, 1996; Feldman, 1987; Hattie & Marsh, 1996) and some arguing that there is a strong relationship (Clark, 1997; Colbeck, 1998; Kreber, 2000a; Rae & Frost, 1997; Rowland, 1996). Those who argue that there is a relationship perceive an integration of teaching and research. The greatest integration of research and teaching will occur if faculty are given the opportunity to not only advance the knowledge of their field, but to integrate this with existing knowledge, apply it, and explore the best ways of teaching it.

According to the analysis presented here, *scholars of teaching* are *excellent teachers*, but they differ from both *excellent* and *expert* teachers in that they share their knowledge and advance the knowledge of teaching and learning in the discipline in a way that can be peer-reviewed. They differ from excellent teachers in the nature and sources of their knowledge construction, with personal teaching experience being only one of various valid sources. *Scholars of teaching* are also *expert* teachers in that they engage in focussed reflection on or self-regulated learning about teaching, relying on and building on their declarative knowledge, procedural knowledge, and implicit knowledge of teaching and learning and the discipline. However, they go further so as to make their knowledge public.

Scholars of teaching not only teach well and can demonstrate or share effective practices with colleagues, they also *know more* about teaching. In doing so they draw on formal and personal sources of knowledge construction about teaching, effectively combine this with their knowledge of the discipline to construct *pedagogical content knowledge*, continuously further this knowledge through self-regulated learning processes, and validate their knowledge through peer-review.

Excellence in teaching and the scholarship of teaching are indeed different and should be recognized and rewarded in their own right. By equating the one with the other to "make teaching count" in academe, we may inadvertently downplay the important work done by those of our colleagues who have taken the risk of pursuing the scholarship in teaching within their discipline. However, the opposite scenario—to play down teaching excellence by recognizing scholarship—is also possible. For this reason this article should not conclude without raising some of the challenges the proposed taxonomy poses.

Now that we have fairly clear parameters as to what constitutes the scholarship of teaching (see also the work done by the Carnegie Foundation as well as Kreber & Associates, 2001), what might be the consequences? To what extent can we expect the faculty at large to accept the definitions offered? How inclusive is the notion of the scholarship of teaching as espoused at present? Criticized at one time as being too inclusive and elusive a concept to be helpful to guide faculty work and evaluation, we now may need to ask whether the concept has become too exclusive? I suggested recently that the scholarship of teaching might have become too narrowly defined, too much concerned with inquiry into teaching and learning in one's discipline, the development of pedagogical content knowledge, and peer reviewed publications and presentations, thereby excluding a large proportion of the professoriate who wish to practice the scholarship of teaching from the recognition that the term carries (Kreber, in press b). Is it possible to reconceptualize the scholarship of teaching in such a way that it regains some, yet not all, of its initial inclusiveness? The taxonomy discussed in this article makes sense in logical terms but what we need to explore next is whether it makes sense in practical terms as well. How reasonable is it to assume that we can maintain an egalitarian system of higher education teachers if some teachers are considered to be more scholarly about their teaching than others? Is having different evaluation criteria really the answer? Scholarship is a prestigious concept after all, and universities are known to recognize scholarship. But if scholarship of teaching is considered more prestigious than teaching excellence, would teaching excellence not be undervalued? And wasn't one reason behind efforts to institutionalize the scholarship of teaching in our universities to make teaching count? Clearly, this should not be the only reason behind the scholarship of teaching. Furthermore, not all teaching is scholarly, and differentiating between that which is and that which is not is a meaningful endeavor therefore.

Nevertheless, we need to be careful not to advocate a model of the scholarship of teaching which leads to an undervaluing of teaching excellence in our universities. In practice, therefore, distinguishing between the two makes sense only if each is eventually considered in its own right and valued in its own right, and not by comparing the two to each other. Whether or not such an egalitarian view can be maintained within institutions known to have a reward system in place that recognizes and rewards only the best but takes for granted the good remains to be seen. My purpose in this article has not been to provide criteria to guide faculty evaluations, which has been done elsewhere (e.g., Glassick et al. 1997; Kreber & Cranton, 2000). Rather I hope to engender, and deepen, discussion on the nature of teaching excellence versus the scholarship of teaching.

Note

1. For information regarding panel membership see Kreber (2002) and Kreber (2001)

References

Andresen, L. W. (2000). A useable, trans-disciplinary conception of scholarship. *Higher Education Research and Development, 19*, 137–153.

Atkinson, J. W. (1977). Motivation for achievement. In T. Blass (Ed.), *Personality variables* (pp. 25–108). Hillsdale, NJ: Erlbaum.

Baume, C., & Baume, D. (1996). A national scheme to develop and accredit university teachers. *The International Journal for Academic Development, 1*, 51–58.

Bereiter, C., & Scardamalia, M. (1993). *Surpassing ourselves*. Chicago and La Salle: Open Court.

Blackburn, R. T., & Lawrence, J. H. (1995). *Faculty at work*. San Francisco: Jossey-Bass.

Boice, R. (1992). *The new faculty member*. San Francisco: Jossey-Bass.

Boyer, E. (1990). *Scholarship reconsidered*. Washington, DC: The Carnegie Foundation.

Braskamp, L. A., & Ory, J. C. (1994). *Assessing faculty work: Enhancing individual and institutional performance*. San Francisco: Jossey-Bass Publisers.

Braxton, J. M. (1996). Contrasting perspectives on the relationships between teaching and research. In J. M. Braxton (Ed.), *Faculty teaching and research: Is there a conflict? New Directions for Institutional Research*, no. 90 (pp. 5–14). San Francisco: Jossey-Bass.

Cambridge, B. L. (2000). The scholarship of teaching and learning: A national initiative. In M. Kaplan & D. Lieberman (Eds.), *To improve the academy*, 18, (pp. 55–68). Bolton, MA: Anker.

Cambridge, B. L. (2001, April). *Campus conversations on the scholarship of teaching*. Paper presented as part of the Symposium "More on the scholarship of teaching: Follow-up studies, reactions, and the possible future". American Educational Research Association, Division J, Post-Secondary Education, Seattle, WA.

Carr, D. (1992). Practical enquiry, values, and the problem of educational theory. *Oxford Review of Education, 18*, 241–251.

Centra, J. A. (1993). *Reflective faculty evaluation: Enhancing teaching and determining faculty effectiveness*. San Francisco: Jossey-Bass.

Clark, B. (1997). The modern integration of research activities with teaching and learning. *Journal of Higher Education, 68*, 241–256.

Cochran-Smith, M., & Lytle, S.L. (1990). Research on teaching and teacher research: The issues that divide. *Educational Researcher, 19*(2), 2–11.

Colbeck, C. (1998). Merging in a seamless blend: How faculty integrate research and teaching. *Journal of Higher Education, 96*, 647–672.

Csikzentmihalyi, M. (1990). *Flow. The psychology of optimal experience*. New York: Harper Perennial.

Diamond, R. M. (1993). Changing priorities and the faculty reward system. In R. M. Diamond and B. E. Adam (Eds.), *Recognizing faculty work: Reward systems for the year 2000* (pp. 5–23). *New Directions for Higher Education*, no. 81. San Francisco: Jossey-Bass.

Edgerton, R., Hutchings, P., & Quinlan, K. (1991). *The teaching portfolio: Capturing the scholarship of teaching*. Washington, DC: American Association for Higher Education.

Feldman, K. A. (1987). Research productivity and scholarly accomplishments of college teachers as related to their instructional effectiveness: A review and exploration. *Research in Higher Education, 26*, 227–298.

Franklin, J., & Theall, M. (2001, April). *Faculty opinions about the value and interest of the scholarship of teaching. After a decade, have Boyer's goals been achieved?*. Paper presented as part of the Symposium "More on the scholarship of teaching: Follow-up studies, reactions, and the possible future". American Educational Research Association, Division J, Post-Secondary Education, Seattle, WA.

Glassick, C. E., Huber, M. T., & Maeroff, G.I. (1997). *Scholarship assessed. Evaluation of the professoriate*. San Francisco: Jossey-Bass.

Hattie, J., & Marsh, H.M. (1996). The relationship between research and teaching: A meta-analysis. *Review of Educational Research, 66*, 507–542.

Healey, M. (2000). Developing the scholarship of teaching in higher-education: A discipline-based approach. *Higher Education Research and Development, 19*, 169–189.

Hutchings, P. (1999). *1999 Pew Scholars Institute.* Menlo Park, CA.

ILT (2001). (The Institute for Learning and Teaching in Higher Education). http://www.ilt.ac.uk/about.html

Kember, D. (1997). A reconceptualization of the research into university academics' conceptions of teaching. *Learning and Instruction, 7*, 255–272.

Knapper, C., & Rogers, P. (1994). *Increasing the emphasis on teaching in Ontario universities. Contributed paper.* Task Force on Resource Allocation, Ontario Council on University Affairs: Toronto, Ontario.

Kreber, C. (2000a). How teaching award winners conceptualize academic work: Further thoughts on the meaning of scholarship, *Teaching in Higher Education, 5*, 61–78.

Kreber, C. (2000b). Becoming an expert university teacher: A self-directed process. In H. Long (Ed.), *Practice and theory in self-directed learning* (pp. 131–143). Schaumburg, IL: Motorola University Press.

Kreber, C., & Associates (2001). *Revisiting scholarship: Perspectives on the scholarship of teaching. New Directions for Teaching and Learning*, no 86. San Francisco: Jossey-Bass.

Kreber, C. (2001). Conceptualizing the scholarship of teaching and identifying unresolved issues: The framework for this volume. In C. Kreber (Ed.), *Revisiting Scholarship: Perspectives on the scholarship of teaching (pp. 1–19). New Directions for Teaching and Learning*, no 86.San Francisco: Jossey-Bass.

Kreber, C. (2001). Designing a teaching portfolio based on a formal model of the scholarship of teaching. In D. Lieberman & C. Wehlburg (Eds.), *To improve the academy, 19*, (pp. 268–285). Bolton, MA: Anker.

Kreber, C. (2002). Controversy and consensus on the scholarship of teaching. *Studies in Higher Education, 27*, 151–167.

Kreber, C. (in press). Challenging the dogma: Towards a more inclusive view of the scholarship of teaching. *Journal of Excellence in College Teaching.*

Kreber, C., & Cranton, P. A. (2000). Exploring the scholarship of teaching. *Journal of Higher Education, 71*, 476–495.

Martin, E., & Ramsden, P. (2000). Introduction. *Higher Education Research and Development, 19*, 133–135.

Marton, F. (1981). Phenomenography-describing conceptions of the world around us. *International Science, 10*, 177–200.

Menges, R. J., & Weimer, M. (1996). *Teaching on solid ground: Using scholarship to improve practice.* San Francisco: Jossey-Bass.

Mentkowski, M., & Associates (2000). *Learning that lasts.* San Francisco: Jossey-Bass.

Morehead, J. W., & Shedd, P. J. (1996). Student interviews: A vital role in the scholarship of teaching. *Innovative Higher Education, 20*, 261–269.

Munby, H., & Russell, T. (1994). The authority of experience in learning to teach: Messages from a physics methods class. *Journal of Teacher Education, 45*(2), 86–95.

Norris, S. P. (2000). The pale of consideration when seeking sources of teaching expertise. *American Journal of Education, 108*, 167–195.

Paulsen, M. B. (2001a). After twelve years of teaching the college teaching course. In D. Lieberman & C. Wehlburg (Eds.), *To improve the academy, 19*, (pp. 169–192). Bolton, MA: Anker.

Paulsen, M. B. (2001b). The relation between research and the scholarship of teaching. In C. Kreber (Ed.), *Revisiting scholarship: Perspectives on the scholarship of teaching* (pp. 19–31). *New Directions for Teaching and Learning*, no. 86. San Francisco: Jossey-Bass.

Paulsen, M. B., & Feldman, K. A.(1995). Toward a reconceptualization of scholarship: A human action system with functional imperatives. *Journal of Higher Education, 66*, 615–641.

Pintrich, P. R. (Ed.). (1995). *Understanding self-regulated learning.* San Francisco: Jossey-Bass.

Prosser, M., Trigwell, K., & Taylor, P. (1994). A phenomenographic study of academics' conceptions of science learning and teaching. *Learning and Instruction, 4*, 217–231.

Rae, A., & Frost, P. (Eds) (1997). *Researchers hooked on teaching: Noted scholars discuss the synergies of teaching and research.* Thousand Oaks, CA: Sage Publications.

Rice, R. E. (1992) Toward a broader conception of scholarship: The American context. In T. Whiston and R. Geiger (Eds.), *Research and higher education: The United Kingdom and the United States* (pp. 117–129). Buckingham: SRHE/Open University Press.

Richlin, L. (Ed.) (1993). *Preparing faculty for the new conceptions of scholarship. New Directions for Teaching and Learning*, no. 54. San Francisco: Jossey-Bass.

Richlin, L. (2001). Scholarly teaching and the scholarship of teaching. In C. Kreber (Ed), *Revisiting scholarship: Perspectives on the scholarship of teaching* (pp. 57–69). *New Directions for Teaching and Learning*, No 86. San Francisco: Jossey-Bass.

Rowland, S. (1996). Relationships between teaching and research. *Teaching in Higher Education, 1,* 7–21.

Schön, D. (1983). *The reflective practitioner.* San Francisco: Jossey-Bass.

Shulman, L. S. (1987). Knowledge and teaching. *Harvard Educational Review, 57,* 1–22.

Shulman, L. S. (1998). Course anatomy: The dissection and analysis of knowledge through teaching. In P. Hutchings (Ed.), *The Course Portfolio.* Washington, DC: American Association for Higher Education.

Smith, R. (1997, June). Making teaching count in Canadian higher education: Developing a national agenda. *Teaching and Learning in Higher Education, Newsletter of the Society for Teaching and Learning in Higher Education (STLHE),* pp. 1–10.

Smith, R. (2001). Expertise in teaching and in the scholarship of teaching. In C. Kreber (Ed.), *Revisiting scholarship: Perspectives on the scholarship of teaching* (pp. 69–79). *New Directions for Teaching and Learning,* no. 86. San Francisco: Jossey-Bass.

Smith, S. L. (1991). *Report: Commission of inquiry on Canadian university education.* Ottawa, Ontario: Association of Universities and Colleges of Canada.

Taylor, K. L. (1993). The role of scholarship in unversity teaching. *The Canadian Journal of Higher Education, 23*(3), 64–79.

Theall, M., & Centra, J. (2001). Assessing the scholarship of teaching: Valid decisions from valid evidence. In C. Kreber (Ed.), *Revisiting scholarship: Perspectives on the scholarship of teaching* (pp. 31–45). *New Directions for Teaching and Learning,* no 86. San Francisco: Jossey-Bass.

Trigwell, K., Martin, E., Benjamin, J, & Prosser, M. (2000). Scholarship of teaching: A model. *Higher Education Research and Development, 19,* 155–168.

Vroom, V. (1964). *Work and motivation.* New York: John Wiley.

Weimer, M. (1990). *Improving university teaching.* San Francisco: Jossey-Bass.

Weimer, M. (1992). Scholarship of teaching. *Journal of the Freshman Year Experience, 4*(1), 41–58.

Weiner, B. (1985). An attributional theory of achievement motivation and emotion. *Psychological Review, 92,* 548–573.

Weston, C., & McAlpine, L. (2001). Making explicit the development towards the scholarship of teaching. In C. Kreber (Ed.), *Revisiting scholarship: Perspectives on the scholarship of teaching* (pp. 89–99). *New Directions for Teaching and Learning,* no. 86. San Francisco: Jossey-Bass.

Zimmerman, B. J. (1998). Developing self-fulfilling cycles of academic regulation: An analysis of exemplary models. In D. H. Schunk, & B. J. Zimmerman (Ed.), *Self-regulated learning. From teaching to self-reflective practice* (pp. 1–10). London: The Guilford Press.

EDUCATING LONE WOLVES: PEDAGOGICAL IMPLICATIONS OF HUMAN CAPITAL THEORY

IAN BAPTISTE

There may be adult educators who wish to alleviate social inequalities but whose practices are wedded to human capital theory. In this article, it is argued that educational practices based wholly or partly on human capital theory are unlikely to alleviate social inequities because the theory spawns pedagogical practices that are apolitical, adaptive, and individualistic. By alerting adult educators of the ominous pedagogical implications of human capital theory, it is hoped that they will distance themselves from it and embrace more socially responsible alternatives.

People who choose adult education as a vocation (Collins, 1991) do so in part because they want to alleviate social maladies such as poverty, income inequality, poor health, environmental pollution, and unsafe habitats. Their commitments are expressed in different ways and in various arenas. Some focus their energies on formal education, others in the workplace. Some channel their resources and expertise to individuals and families, others to communities and the broader society. Regardless of the arena, I believe that every educational practice is profoundly influenced by theories of human and social behavior, whether such influence is witting or unwitting. Furthermore, I assume that some theories are better able to explain and address social maladies than others. In fact, I believe that some theories are so flawed that they are likely to exacerbate rather than alleviate social ills. In this article, I examine one such theory: human capital theory. I hope to alert its unwitting loyalists of the theory's malignant force and point the way to more civically responsible practices.

The article is organized as follows: I begin with an overview of human capital theory, tracing its origins, early development, and chronological applications in national educational policies. Next, I analyze some of the theory's assumptions regarding human and social behavior. Then, after summarizing the theory, I use my previous analysis to draw out some of its ominous pedagogical implications. I conclude with suggestions on how adult educators might work to discredit the theory and concomitantly help promote more socially responsible alternatives.

Overview of Human Capital Theory

Definition and Origins

The term *human capital* refers to knowledge, attitudes, and skills that are developed and valued primarily for their economically productive potential. It "refers to the productive capacities of human beings as income-producing agents in an economy" (Hornbeck & Salamon, 1991, p. 3) and to "the present value of past investments in the skills of people" (Blaug, 1970, p. 19). *Human capital formation* is the name given to the process by which such capital is deliberately developed, and the expenditure (in time, money, etc.) is called *human capital investment* (Becker, 1962, p. 9).

The 18th-century economist Adam Smith introduced the notion of humans as capital in his classic *Wealth of Nations* (Smith, 1776/1937). Others, such as Alfred Marshall (1890/1930) and

Reprinted from *Adult Education Quarterly* 51, no. 3 (May 2001), Sage Publications, Inc.

Irvin Fisher (1906), kept the idea alive (Walsh, 1935). Notwithstanding its long history, the theory of humans as capital remained relatively undeveloped well into the 20th century.

> For much of the ensuing two hundred years [after the publication of *Wealth of Nations*], economic thought largely ignored Smith's insights, and focused instead on the role of land, capital stock, and hours of labor as the crucial ingredients in economic growth. (Hornbeck & Salamon, 1991, p. 3)

Walsh (1935) noted that prior to the mid-1900s, discussions about humans as capital were carried on "chiefly in general terms; references being made to *all* men [*sic*] as capital, and to *all* kinds of expenses in rearing and training as [investment]" (p. 255).

There are several reasons given for the delay in formulating a theory of humans as capital. One is the differences of opinion among early theorists regarding the relationship between humans, labor, capital, and earnings. Three camps seem to have emerged. The first (represented by John Stuart Mill and Alfred Marshall) distinguished between the acquired capacities (skills and knowledge) of human beings, which are classed as capital, and human beings themselves. Having a deep-seated moral and philosophical commitment to human freedom and dignity, this group found the mere thought of humans as capital rather offensive. To them, humans were the purpose for which wealth and capital existed: the end to be served by economic endeavor. Marshall, for instance, argued that although it is quite possible and ethical for people to sell their labor, there ought not to be a market in human beings. It should be noted, however, that despite this objection, Marshall's (1890/1930) *Principles of Economics* includes in an appendix a methodology for calculating the private returns on investment in education that, according to Marginson (1993, pp. 33–34), would later become the core of the theory (Schultz, 1961).

A second camp (represented by Adam Smith, Irving Fisher, and the Chicago School) argued that human beings are themselves capital, that the notion of humans as capital is not incompatible with freedom and dignity, and that to the contrary, by investing in themselves, people enlarge the range of choices available to them and so enhance rather than limit their freedom (Schultz, 1961). This group tied earnings to educational expense (capital investment), not just to productivity. Adam Smith (1776/1937), for instance, argued that "a man educated at the expense of much labor . . . may be compared to one . . . expensive machine . . . .The work which he learns to perform . . . over and above the wages of common labor will replace the whole expense of his education" (p. 101). To Smith, then, variations in educational investments (human capital) explained and justified variations in earnings.

Karl Marx represents the third camp. Like Adam Smith (1776/1937), he agreed that greater productivity alone does not account for the higher earnings of educated workers but that the cost of education (investment) also enters into the equation (Marx, 1867/1976). And, like Mill (1859/1956), Marx concurred that workers sell their capacities to labor (their "labor power") rather than themselves. However, Marx argued that the capacity to labor itself is not a form of capital but that a worker's labor power becomes capital only when it is used in the process of production (Marx, 1867/1976, 1894/1981). Thus, contended Marginson (1993, p. 34), Marxist economics diverged from what was to become human capital theory.

A second reason given for the delay in formulating a theory of humans as capital is the widespread use of the Keynesian definition of consumption and investment. According to Blaug (1970), Keynes viewed consumption and investment as mutually exclusive categories: expenditures of two different sectors of the economy, households and businesses, respectively. Keynes regarded education as largely a household expenditure and therefore treated it as pure consumption with no investment component. Consequently, as long as Keynesian economics reigned, the investment component of education remained hidden from view (Blaug, 1970, pp. 16–22).

A third reason given for the delay is the nature of economic production prior to World War II. Briggs (1987) contended that prior to World War II, agricultural and industrial economies did not require large numbers of highly skilled workers, and as such, there was little need for a theory of human capital. But, Briggs argued, the high-technology economies that emerged in the post-World War II era required massive doses of highly skilled workers. And this technological advancement, he believed, provided the grounds for building a theory of human capital (Briggs, 1987, pp. 1201–1210).

Inauguration of the Human Capital Revolution

The articulation of a formal theory of human capital began in the mid-20th century with what has been dubbed the Chicago School (Ali, 1985; Psacharopoulos, 1988; Sobel, 1978; Walters & Rubinson, 1983). Milton Friedman (1962) "signaled the interest of the Chicago school economists in a human capital theory approach" (Marginson, 1993, p. 36). What Friedman (1962) planted, Theodore Schultz watered. In his presidential address at the Seventy-Third Annual Meeting of the American Economic Association on December 28, 1960, Schultz (1961) delivered what is generally considered the inauguration of "the human investment revolution in economic thought" (Sobel, 1978, p. 268, Footnote 2). In that address, Schultz (1961) argued that much of what is commonly labeled *consumption* is really human capital investment. This investment, he stated, includes direct expenditure on education, health, and internal migration; earnings foregone by mature students attending school and by workers acquiring on-the-job training; the use of leisure to improve skills and knowledge; and so on—all of which constitute measures aimed at improving the quality of human effort and, ultimately, workers' productivity. Schultz (1961) wrote, "Although it is obvious that people acquire useful skills and knowledge, it is not so obvious that these skills and knowledge are a form of capital, [or] that this capital is in substantial part a product of deliberate investment" (p. 1). He called the body of knowledge that sought to describe, explain, and validate this phenomenon "human capital theory" (Schultz, 1989, p. 219).

Application of Human Capital Theory to National Educational Policy

Since its ascendancy in the 1960s, there have been three discernable phases of human capital theory's application in national educational policy (Marginson, 1993, p. 40). The first stressed public investment in human capital and was dominated by ambitious claims about the positive and vital link between education and economic growth (Denison, 1962; Schultz, 1959, 1960, 1961). For most developing countries, however, the promised economic boom did not materialize. The failure of the public investment approach to deliver the goods led to a period of eclipse during which alternative theories such as the screening hypothesis took center stage (Arrow, 1973; Marginson, 1993, pp. 43–44; Thurow, 1974). According to Marginson (1993),

> the screening hypothesis focuses on the exchange value of educational qualifications (credentials), rather than the cognitive attributes of the educated worker. The screening theorists see education's fundamental role as that of a selection system for employers. The content of education has little relevance to worker performance or wage levels. Rather, educational credentials act as a surrogate for qualities that employers want, such as willingness and the capacity to learn. (p.44)

By the mid-1980s, human capital theorists began to flex their muscles once more, this time riding on the wave of structural adjustment policies (Organization for Economic Co-operation and Development [OECD], 1987). But, the 1980s incarnation was different from its 1960s precursor in several important ways, one being the mediating effect of technology. Anticipating this mediating effect, Schultz (1975) wrote,

> Very rapid modernization of U.S. agriculture following World War II has more than halved the number of farms; in the ensuing competition to survive and remain in agriculture, the effects of education on the ability to cope with changes in agricultural production are strongly positive in determining who has been able to survive. (p. 836)

Wozniak (1984) agreed with Schultz (1975), arguing that education renders productive services by providing the opportunity to improve allocation decision making and by augmenting individuals' capacities to think systematically and creatively about techniques. This augmentation, Wozniak (1984) believed, enables individuals to use their rational faculties in the process to consciously modify their environment: "By augmenting the ability to learn and the capacity to adjust to disequilibria, education helps workers meet the creativity and flexibility of an advancing technology" (p. 71). To such views the powerful OECD (1987) affixed its stamp of approval: "The development of contemporary economies depends crucially on the knowledge, skills, and attitudes of their workers—in short on human capital. In many respects, human capital has become even more important in recent years" (p. 69).

The human capital theory that the OECD endorsed, however, is markedly different from the 1960s version. The OECD found the earlier version too general, too quantitative, and based on too simplistic theories of education and the economy. Like Schultz (1975) and Wozniak (1984), the OECD argued that education is not the only factor in determining income, as the earlier variant implied, but that the relationship is especially mediated by available technology. Furthermore, the OECD incorporated elements of the screening hypothesis into its revised model. Unlike its earlier framers, the OECD contended that education and training perform important screening functions that are likely to positively affect worker productivity regardless of whether or not the training provides specific, job-related skills. The key, according to the OECD, appears to be the ability of workers to cope with technological changes and to turn them into advantages in the future. The OECD believed that education, through its screening function, streamlines the available pool of flexible and adaptable workers and consequently enhances the efficiency of both the recruitment and production processes (Marginson, 1993; Organization for Economic Co-operation and Development, 1985, 1986a, 1986b, 1986c).

Who should bear the cost of this education? Each individual. According to the OECD (1990), those who make higher investment will be rewarded with "higher earnings, and therefore there is no obvious reason why the rest of the community should be expected to meet their study costs" (Marginson, 1993 p. 49). This, insisted the OECD, is one reason why students should pay for their own studies and why support for them should be in the form of loans rather than grants or scholarships.

To summarize, the contemporary version of human capital theory differs from its predecessors in three important respects: (a) it incorporates technology as a factor that mediates the relationship between human capital and productivity, (b) it integrates elements of the screening hypothesis, and (c) it advocates private over public investment in education.

Outcome, Process, and Human Assumptions of Human Capital Theory

An examination of the basic assumptions of human capital theory is crucial to elucidating those practices it might promote. Let us therefore scrutinize some of those assumptions. I begin with the more obvious outcome assumptions: those concerning the relationship between human capital (education) and economic performance. Then, I move deeper into process assumptions: those concerning the nature of economic behavior. Finally, I examine assumptions about the nature of persons who are supposed to promote those economic behaviors.

On Human Capital and Economic Performance

I wish to focus on two outcome assumptions of human capital theory: first, that there is an unqualified, causal effect of human capital on economic productivity, and second, that differences in workers' earnings are due entirely to differences in their human capital investments. The first assumption asserts that for any given economic enterprise, regardless of what is being produced and of where, how, and under what conditions it is being produced, more educated workers will always be more productive than their less educated counterparts. On this matter, Schultz (1989) made the unqualified declaration that "human capital enhances the productivity of both labor and physical capital. People at each skill level are more productive in a high human capital environment than in one that is low in human capital" (p. 220; cf. Schultz, 1961, pp. 4–7). Ali (1985) agreed, making the unconditional claim that adult literacy

> raises output per worker or labor productivity by providing necessary skills to manpower, facilitating innovations and enhancing geographic and occupational mobility of labor. Viewed in this perspective, expenditure on education [adult literacy] amounts in effect to investment in human resources that raises the quality of people as productive agents. (p. 42)

The production function Ali (1985, pp. 44–47) used to estimate the rate of returns on adult literacy includes measures of physical capital, marginal productivity of labor, level of adult literacy, a scalar for technological know-how, and dummy variables representing a country's overall level of economic development.

Schultz (1989) and Ali (1985) were not merely claiming that more education is the cause of higher productivity. They were also asserting that this relationship is unqualified. Neither author discussed or construed situations in which education might decrease (or at least not increase) productivity. As Ali's (1985) production function reveals, human capital theorists acknowledge mediating factors. But, this acknowledgment does not seem to change their utopian view of education. For instance, regarding the mediating effects of technology, human capital theorists assume that more educated workers are always more technologically savvy than their less educated counterparts and that their superior technological savvy renders them always more productive than their less educated peers. In short, human capital theorists do not envisage situations in which less educated workers might enjoy a productive advantage over their more educated peers.

A second outcome assumption of human capital theory is that differences in workers' earnings are due entirely to differences in their human capital investments. This assumption flows directly from Adam Smith, who, as was pointed out earlier, believed that variations in human capital investment explain and justify variations in earnings (Psacharopoulos, 1988, p. 99; Smith, 1776/1937, p. 101). To human capital theorists, then, all income differences are based on merit not favor.

Gary Becker, a member of the Chicago School and a recipient of a Nobel Prize in Economics for his work on human capital theory, exemplifies this belief in educational meritocracy. He attributed observed income disparities between ethnic groups in the United States solely to disparities in human capital investment:

> Differences [in human capital investment] among ethnic groups in the United States are fascinating. Groups with small families generally spend a lot on each child's education and training, while those with big families spend much less. Japanese, Chinese, Jews and Cuban families have less children who become well educated, while Mexicans, Puerto Ricans, and blacks have big families and the education of their children suffers. (Becker, 1992, p. 11)

Becker (1992) went on to argue that this differential investment alone explains the income disparities that exist between ethnic groups in the United States. Cubans, he asserted, place greater value on economic mobility than Blacks. and because of that, they invest more in human capital than Blacks. He contended that this differential investment alone (generated, presumably, by differential preferences[1]) explains the differential earnings of the two ethnic groups. He drew basically the same conclusion when he examined income disparities existing along lines of gender and social class (see Becker, 1985; Becker & Tomes, 1986). To human capital theorists, then, educational investment is a surefire route to socioeconomic mobility. With adequate educational investment, nothing can hinder one's socioeconomic progress. Those who invest bountifully in education will always reap bountiful socioeconomic rewards; those who invest stingily will reap sparingly. Why is educational investment able to deliver such a utopia? Ostensibly, the answer lies in the nature of human beings themselves, and in the nature of economic behavior they foster. Let us look first at the nature of economic behavior.

On the Nature of Economic Behavior

In terms of giving direction to economic pursuit, Becker (1976) argued that definitions are futile. To distinguish and provide direction to economic enterprise, what is needed, he insisted, is an economic approach (Becker, 1976, pp. 3–4). To him, that approach rests on three pillars: maximizing behavior, market equilibrium, and stable preferences. These three pillars, "used relentlessly and unflinchingly, form the heart of the economic approach" (Becker, 1976, p. 5). The first pillar, maximizing behavior (also referred to as utility maximization), is a subset of rational choice theory, which, according to Jerome Bruner (1990), has its origin in the works of Adam Smith. The theory assumes that human beings only engage in behaviors from which they derive the maximum benefit (Bruner, 1990, p. 28). As utility-maximizing individuals, humans are incapable of engaging in activities other than those that maximize their benefits. The utility maximization argument goes like this: Why does Mary behave in such and such a way? Because she wishes to maximize her benefits. Why would Mary always act to maximize her benefits? Because her human nature compels her to do so. Becker (1976) treated utility maximization as an axiom. Matter-of-factly, he decreed that "everyone recognizes that the economic approach assumes maximizing behavior . . . be it the utility or wealth function of household, firm, union, or government bureau that is maximized" (Becker, 1976, p. 5). To him, nothing more needed to be said on the matter.

Human capital theory recognizes only two legitimate social entities: the utility-maximizing individual and the free market. I discuss the individual in the next section; here, I focus on the free market. Market equilibrium, the second pillar of Becker's (1976) economic approach, rests on the assumption of perfectly competitive, free markets. Markets are arenas in which goods and services are produced and distributed entirely on the basis of supply, demand, and price. The market is ubiquitous and all pervasive, determining, legitimizing, and regulating every aspect of human life and social behavior. All social institutions and phenomena, including governments, families, schools, divorce, marriage, discrimination[2], crime, and so on, are interpreted as markets because, ostensibly and ultimately, they all surrender to market forces and obey the law of utility maximization (Becker, 1976, pp. 9–11, chaps. 2–4). The regulatory forces of the market, operating in concert with people's utility-maximizing nature, ensure that everyone receives mutual and just recompense for their efforts and investments. In support of this view, Becker (1976) argued that

> the economic approach assumes the existence of markets that . . . coordinate the actions of different participants—individuals, firms, even nations—so that their behavior becomes mutually consistent. . . . Prices and other market instruments allocate the scarce resources within a society and thereby constrain the desires of participants and coordinate their actions. In the economic approach these instruments perform most, if not all, of the functions assigned to "structure" in sociological theories. (p. 5)

According to Becker (1976), cost-benefit analysis is the invisible mechanism by which the market coordinates social behavior. Although market information is incomplete and unevenly distributed, that fact does not weaken its regulatory power. This is a very crucial point. Applying this cost-benefit analysis to smoking habits, for instance, Becker argued that people continue to smoke even in the face of lethal health risks, not "because they are ignorant of the consequences or 'incapable' of using the information they possess, but because the life-span forfeited is not worth the cost to them of quitting smoking" (p. 10). To Becker, then, rational economic choice, not ignorance or incapacity, explains nicotine addiction; people remain addicts because they want to, and they want to because addiction constitutes a net benefit to them.

The third pillar of the economic approach is the assumption of stable preferences: that people's desires do not "change substantially over time, nor are they very different between wealthy and poor persons, or even between persons in different societies and cultures" (Becker, 1976, p.5). Preferences do not refer to actual "market goods and services, like oranges, automobiles, or medical care, but to underlying objects of choice that are produced by each household using market goods and services, their own time, and other inputs" (Becker, 1976, p. 5). The underlying objects of choice of which Becker spoke are the "fundamental aspects of life, such as health, prestige, sensual pleasure, benevolence or envy" (p. 5). Becker's assertion of stable preferences assumes, then, that the desire for health, prestige, pleasure, and so on is present and equally potent in all human beings. What differs are the ways they choose to fulfill those desires. This assumption of stable preferences, Becker argued, "provides a stable foundation for generating predictions" about social behavior "and prevents the analyst from succumbing to the temptation of simply postulating the required shift in preferences to 'explain' all apparent contradictions to his predictions" (p. 5).

On Human Nature

The educational utopia described above has its origin in 17th-century English liberalism (Hobbes, 1651/1968; Locke, 1947; Maglen, 1990; Marginson, 1993). The 17th-century English liberal was a radically isolated, pleasure-seeking materialist. Commenting on the material nature of humans, Hobbes (1651/1968) quipped rhetorically,

> Why may we not say that all *Automata* (Engines that move themselves by springs and wheels as does a watch) have an artificial life? For what is the *Heart*, but a *Spring*; and the *Nerves*, but so many *Strings*; and the *Joynts*, but so many *Wheeles*, giving motion to the whole Body? (p. 81)

To Hobbes (1651/1968), then, just as the movement of an engine does not confer on it any special kind of existence beyond ordinary matter, so too the motions of humans (however intricate) do not confer on us any unique, metaphysical characteristics. Robert Dahl (1965), one of America's most celebrated political theorists, echoed well this materialistic sentiment:

> Man is not by instinct a reasonable, reasoning civic-minded being. Many of his most impervious desires and the source of many of his most powerful gratifications can be traced to ancient and persistent biological and physiological drives, needs and wants. Organized political life arrived late in man's evolution; man [had to learn] how to behave as political man. (p. 60)

As far as Dahl (1965) was concerned, humans live primarily to satisfy their biological urges. Social and political organizations are merely means toward those ends. Humans' materiality sentences them to a mere sensory existence so that their every action is governed, ultimately, by their biological drives. Accordingly, they engage in relationships (economic and otherwise) only because of the material happiness and bodily security such relationships promise.

The 17th-century liberal was also by nature a solitary atom, born free of social restraints or responsibility. On this matter, Locke (1947) proclaimed that "men are . . . by nature, all free, equal and independent" (p. 123). He elaborated,

> To understand political power aright . . . we must consider what estate all men are naturally in, and that is, a state of perfect freedom to order their actions, and to dispose of their possessions and persons as they think fit, within the bounds of the law of Nature, without asking leave or depending upon the will of any other man. (p. 76)

This radical isolation (also known as absolutely autonomy) is indispensable to a stable civil society, Locke (1947) contended, for without it, real consent is not possible. And, without real consent, civil society could only be sustained by coercion, making it very fragile and impermanent (Locke, 1947, chap. 8). Radically isolated, materialists are *homo economica*: solitary seekers of material happiness and bodily security. Hobbes (1651/1968) summed up the ascetic, hedonistic condition of humans this way: "The life of man [is] solitary, poore, nasty, brutish"[3] (p. 186). But, although less brutish, Lockean individuals are no less selfish. Like Hobbesian individuals, what propels Lockean men and women into society is not any intrinsic sociability but rather their need to secure and optimize their property (Locke, 1947, p. 139; cf. pp. 71–74). So, whereas in Hobbes's (1651/1968) state of nature, men and women are viewed as avaricious, wild beasts, constantly fighting and devouring one another over limited booty, in Locke's (1947) state of nature, they are conceived as rational animals who, although no less selfish, are able to temper their avarice with economic rationality.

Self-preservation is, logically and naturally, the most fundamental right and deepest desire of brute beasts. Hobbes (1651/1968) reminded us that "the right of nature . . . is the liberty each man has, to use his own power, as he will himself, for the preservation of his own nature; that is to say his own life" (p. 189). Locke (1947) agreed:

> Man being born . . . to perfect freedom and an uncontrolled enjoyment of all the rights and privileges of the law of Nature . . . has by nature a [fundamental right] to preserve his property— that is, his life, liberty, and estate against the injuries and attempts of other men. (p. 117)

Given their solitary, hedonistic nature, what prevents people from devouring one another and civil society from degenerating into a perpetual state of war? Economic rationality: those human behaviors that are fueled by fear of death and the desire for material safety and happiness (which accounts for all human behaviors). Hobbes (1651/1968) explained, "The Passions that incline men to Peace, are Feare of Death; Desire of such things as are necessary to commodious living; and a Hope by their industry to obtain them" (p. 188). Locke (1947) agreed:

> If man in the state of Nature is so free . . . if he be absolute lord of his own person and posses-sions, equal to the greatest and subject to nobody, why will he part with his freedom . . . and subject himself to the dominion and control of any other power? (p. 138)

To this question, Locke (1947) replied,

> though in the state of Nature he has such a right, yet the enjoyment of it is very uncertain and constantly exposed to the invasion of others; for all being kings as much as he, every man his equal, and the greater part no strict observers of equity and justice, the enjoyment of the prop-erty he has in this state is very unsafe, very insecure. This makes him willing to quit this condi-tion which, however free, is full of fear and continual dangers; and it is not without reason that he seeks out and is willing to join with others . . . for the mutual preservation of their lives, lib-erty and estate which I call by the general name—property. (p. 139)

Becker (1976) echoed this 17th-century economic rationality in his opposition to all nonmaterial explanations of human behavior. "Obviously," he contended, "the laws of mathematics, chemistry, physics, and biology have a tremendous influence on [human] behavior" (Becker, 1976, p. 13). But, Becker (1976, pp. 12–13) accorded no explanatory potential to such nonmaterial notions as social responsibility, ignorance, irrationality, values, customs, traditions, social norms, ego, or id. Remi-niscent of Skinnerian Behaviorism (Skinner, 1971), Becker (1976) considered these notions relics of a prescientific era that must be expunged from the lexicon if people are to make economic progress.

There are substantial critiques of human capital theory. Some expose its empirical and theoret-ical flaws. For instance, critics have cited the theory's overly mechanistic, one-dimensional view of human beings; its narrow understanding of labor; its use of correlational data to establish cause; the inconclusiveness of its empirical evidence; and the insurmountable methodological hurdles asso-ciated with calculating returns on educational investment. Among these hurdles are the difficulties of separating educational consumption from investment, of determining the stock of educational capital, and of ascertaining the marginal productivity of education (Barber, 1984; Beckford, 1972; Blaug, 1972, 1976; Bowles & Gintis, 1975; Gintis, 1971; Maglen, 1990; Shaffer, 1961; Thurow, 1982). Other critics have examined the theory's ominous societal impact, for instance, its exacerbation of social inequalities, its development of underdevelopment, "scholarization," and its blaming of the victims (Berg, 1970; Blaug, 1970; Bluestone, 1977; Carnoy, 1977; Frank, 1984, 1989; Marginson, 1993; Paci, 1977; Samoff, 1994; Thurow, 1977, 1983). To these criticisms I add some insights on possible neg-ative impacts the theory might have on day-to-day pedagogical practices. I do so by drawing infer-ences from my interpretation of the theory. Readers are encouraged to test those inferences on the basis of their own experiences. To help me draw out those inferences, I now provide a summary of the theory.

Human Capital Theory: A Summary and Pedagogical Implications

Human capital theorists treat people as *homo economica*: radically isolated, pleasure-seeking materialists who are born free of social constraints or responsibility, who possess no intrinsic socia-bility, and who are driven, ultimately, by the desire for material happiness and bodily security. They assume that these desires are fundamentally the same for all people across space and time (stable preferences), and they believe that each individual will at all times attempt to maximally fulfill those hedonistic desires (maximizing behavior).

Proponents of human capital theory assume that our world is an educational meritocracy in which a person's socioeconomic status is limited, presumably, only by his or her educational investment: More educated people are always more productive than less educated people, and this differential productivity is sufficient to explain all social inequities. Furthermore, human capital theorists construe social inequalities not as injustices, the result of exploitation and oppression, but rather as the natural and inevitable outcomes of a competitive, free market. To them, the free market is the most (if not the only) legitimate social institution; that is, it is the only institution that can adequately and justly govern, regulate, and explain human behaviors and achievements. Like Gary Becker (1976, pp. 7, 12–13), human capital theorists believe that there is no need to appeal to nonmarket forces such as unequal power or structural barriers to explain human and social behavior. They are certain that the invisible hand of the free market—the coordinated forces of price, supply, and demand—is well able to account for "most, if not all, of the functions assigned to 'structure' in sociological theories" (Becker, 1976, p. 5).

Educating Lone Wolves: Pedagogical Implications of Human Capital Theory

The individuals described in human capital theory bear a striking resemblance to lone wolves. In North American mythology, the lone ranger is depicted as the quintessential rugged individual. He is self-sufficient and totally free, requiring nothing of anyone and indebted to no one. He is industrious and shrewd, a law unto himself. But, he is not greedy or selfish. He embodies benevolence and fairness. The lone wolf is also depicted as a rugged individual: self-sufficient, totally free, shrewd, and industrious. But, unlike the lone ranger, the lone wolf is portrayed as a selfish, avaricious beast. Like Hobbesian individuals, lone wolves seek only to maximize their material happiness and bodily security. And, like Lockean individuals, lone wolves enter into packs (market relations) not because of any intrinsic sociability but to secure and preserve their property. Lone wolves are different from lone rangers in another important respect: Their actions are instinctual and adaptive, not intentional or creative. Lone rangers are depicted as intentional and creative beings possessing foresight and the ability to plan and transform their environments. Lone wolves, on the other hand, are portrayed as mere creatures of habit who, operating solely on instincts and biological urges, can only react and adapt to their environs.

What kind of education would best suit lone wolves? In what type of pedagogical environment are they likely to thrive? First, the proper education of lone wolves would be apolitical in its orientation. Educational objectives and activities would be determined by "market analysis" and by technical considerations commonly referred to as "needs assessments" rather than by any ethical or moral philosophy of the educator or program. Consensus would be assumed a priori, not sought through political struggle. All of the needs of all learners would be considered worthwhile and complementary. Little or no attempt would be made to interrogate learners' needs, to question their appropriateness, to ascertain how they are formulated, or to determine whose interests are best and least served. The fulfillment of each learner's needs would be assumed to have no negative bearing on the fulfillment of the needs of other learners. This technical, apolitical practice flows directly from Becker's (1976, p. 5) notions of mutual consistency and stable preferences: People's absolute materiality begets mutual consistency and stable preferences, and stable preferences beget entirely commensurable and complementary desires. When educational programs justify their goals and activities by simply appealing to the "needs of learners," when they treat learners' desires as entirely complementary, and when they ignore or discount serious conflicts of interest between learners and other stakeholders, one can be fairly sure that they are operating (wittingly or unwittingly) under assumptions of human capital theory.

Second, the proper education of lone wolves must be adaptive. However industrious, lone wolves are still mechanical beings, and as such they can be only spectators in the universe. Their existence is foreordained, predestined—fated! Given their fated existence, it would be superfluous and wishful to treat lone wolves as transforming agents. Prudent educational change must therefore be adaptive, focused on accustoming wolves to their new environs, be they physical, social, or technological,

For example, an adaptive adult education program might try to alleviate poverty by attempting to change the behavior of the poor while ignoring the social, political, and economic conditions that help to maintain poverty, or an adaptive program might tackle welfare dependency by attempting to change the behavior of women on welfare while ignoring the social impediments that help to create and sustain that dependency. With adaptive pedagogical practices, then, learners are expected to inculcate behaviors considered essential to the proper functioning of their environs. One might say that learners are educational consumers. And, as customers, they do not—indeed, cannot—produce or create knowledge. Their educational options are either "take what is being offered, or leave it." When educational programs justify their goals and activities by appealing to inexorable forces such as economic cycles, demographic changes, global competition, knowledge economy, or skills employers need and when they treat learners as fated beings whose only options are to consume and adapt, chances are they are wedded to human capital theory.

Third, education suitable for lone wolves would be individualistic. Each learner would be treated as a rugged individual, self-sufficient and totally free. Learners would neither be tied nor indebted to one another. They would come together or interact not to forge some common good or collective purpose but rather to secure and optimize their private property. When sharks and barracudas appear, there will be no need for learners to band together in a collective struggle because each individual learner will be able to effectively neutralize these social parasites simply by enticing them with bags of educational goodies. Like the invincible, indomitable lone wolf, each learner would simply stock up enough ammunition and face the world as an educational Rambo.[4] When educational programs treat learners as rugged, indomitable individuals in need of no other but themselves, it is a fairly accurate guess that they are wedded to human capital theory.

Conclusion

In this article, I have provided an overview of human capital theory, analyzed its basic assumptions, and discussed its pedagogical implications. The theory, I have concluded, treats humans as lone wolves: radically isolated hedonists, creatures of habit (not intentions) who temper their avarice with economic rationality. I have suggested that educational programs that flow from such anthropology would be apolitical, adaptive, and individualistic. They would justify their goals and activities by simply appealing to the needs of learners, and they would treat learners' desires as entirely harmonious, discounting serious conflicts of interest. Such programs would justify their decisions and actions by appealing to inexorable forces such as technological advancement, demographic changes, the knowledge economy, and market cycles, and they would treat learners as fated beings whose only desires and options are to consume and adapt. And, finally, I have argued that educational programs that are wedded to human capital theory would treat learners as rugged individualists indebted to no one and requiring nothing of anyone.

But, maybe human capital theorists have it all wrong. Maybe humans are more than fated adapters. Maybe they are capable of becoming creative transformers. Perhaps it is possible for humans to transcend their lone wolf-like tendencies and become interdependent, social beings as Aristotle and Judeo-Christianity suggest. Perhaps it is not true that people's deepest desires and preferences are, ultimately, material and stable. Perhaps it is possible for human beings to possess a wide range of competing, opposing, and ever-changing desires. Perhaps there are genuine and even irreconcilable conflicts of interest between people such that political struggles (not just market relations) are necessary to attain justice. If it turns out that people do not live in a perfectly competitive, free market; that unequal power always structures their relations; and that structural inequalities exist that confer unfair advantages on some and undue hardships on others, then it is very unlikely that educational programs that are wedded to human capital theory—those that are apolitical, adaptive, and individualistic—will ever be able to redress social inequalities.

So, the next time you hear someone claim (or assume) that education or training is a cure-all; the next time someone offers technical training as the sole solution to poverty, unemployment, or underemployment; or the next time you hear someone explain and justify differences in earnings simply on the basis of differences in educational attainment, beware! You are probably in the company of a lone wolf, also known as a human capital theorist.

In writing this article, I hoped to accomplish two things. First, I wanted to demonstrate that pedagogical practices have deep anthropological and cultural roots and that an understanding of those roots might greatly illumine and aid our educational practices. I hope that I have convinced some readers to take a closer look at theories of human and social behavior, especially those theories attempting to explain the relationship between education and socioeconomic status. In search of such explanations, U.S. educators have tended to privilege psychology. I urge my readers to branch out into the domain broadly labeled *Political economy*: It brings together such disciplines as social and political philosophy, history, sociology, social psychology, economics, and anthropology.

Second, I have tried to alert educators to the social bankruptcy of human capital theory. Admittedly, this attempt is quite preliminary. I trust that others will build on my efforts through pointed critical reviews and empirical studies. For instance, readers may wish to investigate the following questions: What are the specific manifestations of human capital theory in adult education theory and practice? In what ways are pedagogical practices apolitical, adaptive and individualistic? What impact do adult education programs that are wedded to human capital theory have on social inequities? Do they exacerbate or alleviates inequalities? In addition, there is an urgent need to develop and showcase education programs that are exemplary in their alleviation of social inequality. Their contributions must be clearly and unambiguously demonstrated, and their salient features must be identified and described. I invite my readers to join me in these efforts.

Notes

1. Becker (1976) claimed that stable preferences—the belief that human desires are essentially the same across space and time—is a fundamental pillar of his economic theory (see the next section of this article). He seems to be contradicting that claim here (Becker, 1992).
2. Becker (1976, p. 24) acknowledged that discrimination occurs but assumed that the principle of utility maximization will ultimately force people to submit their discriminatory practices to the control of free market forces. Discrimination is therefore treated as a market "distortion" or "imperfection" that will eventually be righted by the "invisible hand of the market" (Becker, 1962, 1975, 1976, p. 24; Friedman, 1953; Smith, 1776/1937).
3. Locke's (1947) notion of men and women was less brutish and nasty than that of Hobbes (1651/1968). Their differences emerge in their views concerning the state of nature. Hobbes (1651/1968) compared the state of nature with a state of war, a state of perpetual aggression "of every one against every one" (p.189). He contended that outside civil society, everyone has a right to absolute power because there can be no legitimate limits to the amount of power one can garner, for power is needed to secure one's inalienable rights: life, liberty, and estate. Only absolute power can secure one's rights absolutely, limited power begets limited security (Hobbes, 1651/1968, pp. 189–201).

   Locke (1947) did not identify a state of nature with a state of war. To him, the former was a condition in which men and women "live together according to reason without a common superior" (p. 84). In this state, each individuals is his or her judge, juror, and executioner. In the state of nature, people's right to power is limited by the law of nature, namely, that "one ought not to harm another in his life, health, liberty or possession" except when one's property is seriously threatened (p. 78). Men and women degenerate into a state of war only when (through ignorance and/or greed) they use their liberty and power illegitimately, that is, in violation of the laws of nature (pp. 76–83).
4. In the movie *Rambo*, American actor Sylvester Stallone plays the part of a one-man army that takes on the world and wins.

References

Ali, S. M. (1985). Contribution of education towards labor productivity. *Pakistan Economic and Social Review, 23*(1), 41–54.

Arrow, K. (1973). Higher education as a filter. *Journal of Public Economics, 2*(3), 193–216.

Barber, B. (1984). *Strong democracy: Participatory politics for a new age.* Berkeley: University of California Press.

Becker, G. (1962). Investment in human capital: A theoretical analysis. *Journal of Political Economy, 70*(Suppl. 5), 9–49.

Becker, G. (1975) *Human capital: A theoretical and empirical analysis, with reference to education* (2nd ed.). New York: National Bureau of Economic Research.

Becker, G. (1976). *The economic approach to human behavior*. Chicago: University of Chicago.

Becker, G. (1985). Human capital, effort, and the sexual division of labor. *Journal of Labor Economics*, 3(1), S33–S58.

Becker, G. (1992). The Adam Smith address: Education, labor force quality, and the economy. *Business Economics*, 27(1), 7–12.

Becker., G. & Tomes, N. (1986). Human capital and the rise and fall of families. *Journal of Labor Economics*, 4(3), S1–S39.

Beckford, G. (1972). *Persistent poverty: Underdevelopment in plantation economies of the third world*. New York: Oxford University Press.

Berg, I. (1970). *Education and job: The great training robbery*. New York: Praeger.

Blaug, M. (1970). A*n introduction to the economics of education*. London: Penguin.

Blaug, M. (1972). The correlation between education and earnings: What does it signify? *Higher Education*, 1(1), 53–76.

Blaug, M. (1976). The empirical status of human capital theory: A slightly jaundiced survey. *Journal of Economic Literature*, 24(3), 827–855.

Bluestone, B. (1977). Economic theory and the fate of the poor. In J. Karabel & A. H. Halsey (Eds.), *Power and ideology in education* (pp. 335–340). New York: Oxford University Press.

Bowles, S., & Gintis, H. (1975). The problem with human capital theory: A Marxian critique. Th*e American Educational* Review, 65(2), 74–82.

Briggs, V. M., Jr. (1987). Human resource development and the formulation of national economic policy. *Journal of Economic* Issues, 21(3), 1207–1240.

Bruner, J. (1990). *Acts of meaning*. Cambridge, MA: Harvard University Press.

Carnoy, M. (1977, January). Education and economic development: The first generation. *Economic Development and Cultural Change*, 25(Suppl.), S428–S448.

Collins, M. (1991). *Adult education as vocation: A critical role for adult educators*. New York: Routledge.

Dahl, R. (1965). *Modern political analysis*. Englewood Cliffs, NJ: Prentice Hall.

Denison, E. (1962). *The sources of economic growth in the United States*. New York: Committee for Economic Development.

Fisher, I. (1906). *The nature of capital and income*. New York: Macmillan.

Frank, A. G. (1984). The unequal and uneven historical development of the world economy. *Contemporary Marxism*, 9, 71–95

Frank, A. G. (1989). The development of underdevelopment. *Monthly Review*, 41(2), 37–51.

Friedman, M. (1953). *Essays in positive economics*. Chicago: University of Chicago.

Friedman, M. (1962). The role of government in education. In M. Friedman (Ed.), *Capitalism and freedom* (pp. 3–43). Chicago: University of Chicago.

Gintis, H. (1971). Educational production relationships: Education, technology, and the characteristics of worker productivity. *The American Educational Review*, 61(2), 266–279.

Hobbes, T. (1968). *Leviathan*. New York: Penguin. (Original work published 1651)

Hornbeck, D. W., & Salamon, L. M. (Eds.). (1991). *Human capital and America's future: An economic strategy for the nineties*. Baltimore: Johns Hopkins University.

Locke, J. (1947). *On politics and education*. Roslyn, NY: Black.

Maglen, L. R. (1990). Challenging the human capital orthodoxy: The education-productivity link re-examined. *The Economic Record*, 66(195), 281–294.

Marginson, S. (1993). *Education and public policy in Australia*. New York: University of Cambridge Press.

Marshall, A. (1930). *Principles of economics* (8th ed.). London: Macmillan. (Original work published 1890).

Marx, K. (1976). *Capital* (Vol. 1, E. Mandel, Ed.). Harmondsworth, UK: Penguin. (Original work published 1867).

Marx, K. (1981). *Capital* (Vol. 3, E. Mandel, Ed.). Harmondsworth, UK: Penguin. (Original work published 1894).

Mill, J. S. (1956). *On liberty* (C. Shields, Ed.). New York: Macmillan. (Original work published 1859).

Organization for Economic Co-operation and Development. (1985). *Education in modern society*. Paris: Author.

Organization for Economic Co-operation and Development. (1986a). *Education and effective economic performance: A preliminary analysis of the issues*. Paris: Author.

Organization for Economic Co-operation and Development. (1986b). *Productivity in industry*. Paris: Author.

Organization for Economic Co-operation and Development. (1986c). *OECD science and technology indicators, no. 2: R&D, inventions and competitiveness*. Paris: Author.

Organization for Economic Co-operation and Development. (1987). *Structural adjustment and economic performance*. Paris: Author.

Organization for Economic Co-operation and Development. (1990). *OECD in figures*. Paris: Author.

Paci, M. (1977). Education and the capitalist labor market. In J. Karabel & A. H. Halsey (Eds.), *Power and ideology in education* (pp. 340–355). New York: Oxford University Press.

Psacharopoulos, G. (1988). Education and development: *A review. Research Observer, 3*, 99–116.

Samoff, J. (1994). (Ed.). *Coping with crisis: Austerity, adjustment and human resources*. New York: UNESCO/ILO.

Schultz, T. W. (1959). Investment in man: An economist view. *The Social Service Review, 33*(2), 109–117.

Schultz, T. W. (1960). Capital formation by education. *Journal of Political Economy, 68*(6), 571–583.

Schultz, T. W. (1961). Investment in human capital. *American Economic Review, 51*(1), 1–17.

Schultz, T. W. (1975). The value of the ability to deal with disequilibrium. *Journal of Economic Literature, 13*(3), 827–846.

Schultz, T. W. (1989). Investment in people: Schooling in low income countries. *Economics of Education Review, 8*(3), 219–223.

Shaffer, H. G.(1961). Investment in human capital: Comment. *The American Economic Review, 51*(5), 1026–1035.

Skinner, B. F. (1971). *Beyond freedom and dignity*. New York: Bantam.

Smith, A. (1937). *Wealth of nations*. New York: Random House. (Original work Published 1776)

Sobel, I. (1978). The human capital revolution in economic development: Its current history and status. *Comparative Educational Review, 22*(2), 279–308.

Thurow, L. C. (1974). Measuring the economic benefits of education. In M.S. Gordon, *Higher education and the labor market* (pp. 373–418). New York: McGraw-Hill.

Thurow, L. C.(1977). Education and economic equality. In J. Karabel & A. H. Halsey (Eds.), *Power and ideology in education* (pp. 325–335). New York: Oxford University Press.

Thurow, L. C. (1982). The failure of education as an economic strategy. *The American Economic Review, 72*(2), 72–76.

Thurow, L. C. (1983). *Dangerous currents*: The state of economics. Oxford, UK: Oxford University Press.

Walsh, J. R. (1935). Capital concept applied to man. *Quarterly Journal of Economics, 49*, 255–285.

Walters, P. B., & Rubinson, R. (1983). Educational expansion and economic output in the United States, 1890–1969: A production function analysis. *American Sociological Review, 48*, 480–493.

Wozniak, G. (1984). The adoption of interrelated innovations: A human capital approach. *Review of Economics and Statistics, 66*(1), 70–79.

EMBRACING CHANGE

TEACHING IN A MULTICULTURAL WORLD

b hooks

Despite the contemporary focus on multiculturalism in our society, particularly in education, there is not nearly enough practical discussion of ways classroom settings can be transformed so that the learning experience is inclusive. If the effort to respect and honor the social reality and experiences of groups in this society who are nonwhite is to be reflected in a pedagogical process, then as teachers—on all levels, from elementary to university settings—we must acknowledge that our styles of teaching may need to change. Let's face it: most of us were taught in classrooms where styles of teachings reflected the notion of a single norm of thought and experience, which we were encouraged to believe was universal. This has been just as true for nonwhite teachers as for white teachers. Most of us learned to teach emulating this model. As a consequence, many teachers are disturbed by the political implications of a multicultural education because they fear losing control in a classroom where there is no one way to approach a subject—only multiple ways and multiple references.

Among educators there has to be an acknowledgment that any effort to transform institutions so that they reflect a multicultural standpoint must take into consideration the fears teachers have when asked to shift their paradigms. There must be training sites where teachers have the opportunity to express those concerns while also learning to create ways to approach the multicultural classroom and curriculum. When I first went to Oberlin College, I was disturbed by what I felt was a lack of understanding on the apart of many professors as to what the multicultural classroom might be like. Chandra Mohanty, my colleague in Women's Studies, shared these concerns. Though we were both untenured, our strong belief that the Oberlin campus was not fully facing the issue of changing curriculum and teaching practices in ways that were progressive and promoting of inclusion led us to consider how we might intervene in this process. We proceeded from the standpoint that the vast majority of Oberlin professors, who are overwhelmingly white, were basically well-meaning, concerned about the quality of education students receive on our campus, and therefore likely to be supportive of any effort at education for critical consciousness. Together, we decided to have a group of seminars focusing on transformative pedagogy that would be open to all professors. Initially, students were also welcome, but we found that their presence inhibited honest discussion. On the first night, for example, several white professors made comments that could be viewed as horribly racist and the students left the group to share what was said around the college. Since our intent was to educate for critical consciousness, we did not want the seminar setting to be a space where anyone would feel attacked or their reputation as a teacher sullied. We did, however, want it to be a space for constructive confrontation and critical interrogation. To ensure that this could happen, we had to exclude students.

At the first meeting, Chandra (whose background is in education) and I talked about the factors that had influenced our pedagogical practices. I emphasized the impact of Freire's work on my thinking. Since my formative education took place in racially segregated schools, I spoke about the experience of learning when one's experience is recognized as central and significant and then how that changed with desegregation, when black children were forced to attend schools where we were regarded as

Reprinted from *Teaching to Transgress: Education as the Practice of Freedom,* by bell hooks (1994), Routledge.

objects and not subjects. Many of the professors present at the first meeting were disturbed by our overt discussion of political standpoints. Again and again, it was necessary to remind everyone that no education is politically neutral. Emphasizing that a white male professor in an English department who teaches only work by "great white men" is making a political decision, we had to work consistently against and through the overwhelming will on the part of folks to deny the politics of racism, sexism, heterosexism, and so forth that inform how and what we teach. We found again and again that almost everyone, especially the old guard, were more disturbed by the overt recognition of the role our political perspectives play in shaping pedagogy than by their passive acceptance of ways of teaching and learning that reflect biases, particularly a white supremacist standpoint.

To share in our efforts at intervention we invited professors from universities around the country to come and talk—both formally and informally—about the kind of work they were doing aimed at transforming teaching and learning so that a multicultural education would be possible. We invited then-Princeton professor of religion and philosophy Cornel West to give a talk on "decentering Western civilization." It was our hope that his very traditional training and his progressive practice as a scholar would give everyone a sense of optimism about our ability to change. In the informal session, a few white male professors were courageously outspoken in their efforts to say that they could accept the need for change, but were uncertain about the implications of the changes. This reminded us that it is difficult for individuals to shift paradigms and that there must be a setting for folks to voice fears, to talk about what they are doing, how they are doing it, and why. One of our most useful meetings was one in which we asked professors from different disciplines (including math and science) to talk informally about how their teaching had been changed by a desire to be more inclusive. Hearing individuals describe concrete strategies was an approach that helped dispel fears. It was crucial that more traditional or conservative professors who had been willing to make changes talk about motivations and strategies.

When the meetings concluded, Chandra and I initially felt a tremendous sense of disappointment. We had not realized how much faculty would need to unlearn racism to learn about colonization and decolonization and to fully appreciate the necessity for creating a democratic liberal arts learning experience.

All too often we found a will to include those considered "marginal" without a willingness to accord their work the same respect and consideration given other work. In Women's Studies, for example, individuals will often focus on women of color at the very end of the semester or lump everything about race and difference together in one section. This kind of tokenism is not multicultural transformation, but it is familiar to us as the change individuals are most likely to make. Let me give another example. What does it mean when a white female English professor is eager to include a work by Toni Morrison on the syllabus of her course but then teaches that work without ever making reference to race or ethnicity? I have heard individual white women "boast" about how they have shown students that black writers are "as good" as the white male canon when they do not call attention to race. Clearly, such pedagogy is not an interrogation of the biases conventional canons (if not all canons) establish, but yet another form of tokenism.

The unwillingness to approach teaching from a standpoint that includes awareness of race, sex, and class is often rooted in the fear that classrooms will be uncontrollable, that emotions and passions will not be contained. To some extent, we all know that whenever we address in the classroom subjects that students are passionate about there is always a possibility of confrontation, forceful expression of ideas, or even conflict. In much of my writing about pedagogy, particularly in classroom settings with great diversity, I have talked about the need to examine critically the way we as teachers conceptualize what the space for learning should be like. Many professors have conveyed to me their feeling that the classroom should be a "safe" place; that usually translates to mean that the professor lectures to a group of quiet students who respond only when they are called on. The experience of professors who educate for critical consciousness indicates that many students, especially students of color, may not feel at all "safe" in what appears to be a neutral setting. It is the absence of a feeling of safety that often promotes prolonged silence or lack of student engagement.

Making the classroom a democratic setting where everyone feels a responsibility to contribute is a central goal of transformative pedagogy. Throughout my teaching career, white professors have often voiced concern to me about nonwhite students who do not talk. As the classroom becomes more diverse, teachers are faced with the way the politics of domination are often reproduced in the educational setting. For example, white male students continue to be the most vocal in our classes. Students of color and some white women express fear that they will be judged as intellectually inadequate by these peers. I have taught brilliant students of color, many of them seniors, who have skillfully managed never to speak in classroom settings. Some express the feeling that they are less likely to suffer any kind of assault if they simply do not assert their subjectivity. They have told me that many professors never showed any interest in hearing their voices. Accepting the decentering of the West globally, embracing multiculturalism, compels educators to focus attention on the issue of voice. Who speaks? Who listens? And why? Caring about whether all students fulfill their responsibility to contribute to learning in the classroom is not a common approach in what Freire has called the "banking system of education" where students are regarded merely as passive consumers. Since so many professors teach from that standpoint, it is difficult to create the kind of learning community that can fully embrace multiculturalism. Students are much more willing to surrender their dependency on the banking system of education than are their teachers. They are also much more willing to face the challenge of multiculturalism:

It has been as a teacher in the classroom setting that I have witnessed the power of a transformative pedagogy rooted in a respect for multiculturalism. Working with a critical pedagogy based on my understanding of Freire's teaching, I enter the classroom with the assumption that we must build "community" in order to create a climate of openness and intellectual rigor. Rather than focusing on issues of safety, I think that a feeling of community creates a sense that there is shared commitment and a common good that binds us. What we all ideally share is the desire to learn—to receive actively knowledge that enhances our intellectual development and our capacity to live more fully in the world. It has been my experience that one way to build community in the classroom is to recognize the value of each individual voice. In my classes, students keep journals and often write paragraphs during class which they read to one another. This happens at least once irrespective of class size. Most of the classes I teach are not small. They range anywhere from thirty to sixty students, and at times I have taught more than one hundred. To hear each other (the sound of different voices), to listen to one another, is an exercise in recognition. It also ensures that no student remains invisible in the classroom. Some students resent having to make a verbal contribution, and so I have had to make it clear from the outset that this is a requirement in my classes. Even if there is a student present whose voice cannot be heard in spoken words, by "signing" (even if we cannot read the signs) they make their presence felt.

When I first entered the multicultural, multiethnic classroom setting I was unprepared. I did not know how to cope effectively with so much "difference." Despite progressive politics, and my deep engagement with the feminist movement, I had never before been compelled to work within a truly diverse setting and I lacked the necessary skills. This is the case with most educators. It is difficult for many educators in the United States to conceptualize how the classroom will look when they are confronted with the demographics which indicate that "whiteness" may cease to be the norm ethnicity in classroom settings on all levels. Hence, educators are poorly prepared when we actually confront diversity. This is why so many of us stubbornly cling to old patterns. As I worked to create teaching strategies that would make a space for multicultural learning, I found it necessary to recognize what I have called in other writing on pedagogy different "cultural codes." To teach effectively a diverse student body, I have to learn these codes. And so do students. This act alone transforms the classroom. The sharing of ideas and information does not always progress as quickly as it may in more homogeneous settings. Often, professors and students have to learn to accept different ways of knowing, new epistemologies, in the multicultural setting.

Just as it may be difficult for professors to shift their paradigms, it is equally difficult for students. I have always believed that students should enjoy learning. Yet I found that there was much more tension in the diverse classroom setting where the philosophy of teaching is rooted in critical pedagogy and (in my case) in feminist critical pedagogy. The presence of tension—and at times even conflict—often meant that students did not enjoy my classes or love me, their professor, as I secretly wanted them to do. Teaching in a traditional discipline from the perspective of critical pedagogy means that I often encounter students who make complaints like, "I thought this was supposed to be an

English class, why are we talking so much about feminism?" (Or, they might add, race or class.) In the transformed classroom there is often a much greater need to explain philosophy, strategy, intent than in the "norm" setting. I have found through the years that many of my students who bitch endlessly while they are taking my classes contact me at a later date to talk about how much that experience meant to them, how much they learned. In my professorial role I had to surrender my need for immediate affirmation of successful teaching (even though some reward is immediate) and accept that students may not appreciate the value of a certain standpoint or process straightaway. The exciting aspect of creating a classroom community where there is respect for individual voices is that there is infinitely more feedback because students do feel free to talk—and talk back. And, yes, often this feedback is critical. Moving away from the need for immediate affirmation was crucial to my growth as a teacher. I learned to respect that shifting paradigms or sharing knowledge in new ways challenges; it takes time for students to experience that challenge as positive.

Students taught me, too, that it is necessary to practice compassion in these new learning settings. I have not forgotten the day a student came to class and told me: "We take your class. We learn to look at the world from a critical standpoint, one that considers race, sex, and class. And we can't enjoy life anymore." Looking out over the class, across race, sexual preference, and ethnicity, I saw students nodding their heads. And I saw for the first time that there can be, and usually is, some degree of pain involved in giving up old ways of thinking and knowing and learning new approaches. I respect that pain. And I include recognition of it now when I teach, that is to say, I teach about shifting paradigms and talk about the discomfort it can cause. White students learning to think more critically about questions of race and racism may go home for the holidays and suddenly see their parents in a different light. They may recognize nonprogressive thinking, racism, and so on, and it may hurt them that new ways of knowing may create estrangement where there was none. Often when students return from breaks I ask them to share with us how ideas that they have learned or worked on in the classroom impacted on their experience outside. This gives them both the opportunity to know that difficult experiences may be common and practice at integrating theory and practice: ways of knowing with habits of being. We practice interrogating habits of being as well as ideas. Through this process we build community.

Despite the focus on diversity, our desires for inclusion, many professors still teach in classrooms that are predominantly white. Often a spirit of tokenism prevails in those settings. This is why it is so crucial that "whiteness" be studied, understood, discussed—so that everyone learns that affirmation of multiculturalism, and an unbiased inclusive perspective, can and should be present whether or not people of color are present. Transforming these classrooms is as great a challenge as learning how to teach well in the setting of diversity. Often, if there is one lone person of color in the classroom she or he is objectified by others and forced to assume the role of "native informant." For example, a novel is read by a Korean American author. White students turn to the one student from a Korean background to explain what they do not understand. This places an unfair responsibility onto that student. Professors can intervene in this process by making it clear from the outset that experience does not make one an expert, and perhaps even by explaining what it means to place someone in the role of "native informant." It must be stated that professors cannot intervene if they also see students as "native informants." Often, students have come to my office complaining about the lack of inclusion in another professor's class. For example, a course on social and political thought in the United States includes no work by women. When students complain to the teacher about this lack of inclusion, they are told to make suggestions of material that can be used. This often places an unfair burden on a student. It also makes it seem that it is only important to address a bias if there is someone complaining. Increasingly, students are making complaints because they want a democratic unbiased liberal arts education.

Multiculturalism compels educators to recognize the narrow boundaries that have shaped the way knowledge is shared in the classroom. It forces us all to recognize our complicity in accepting and perpetuating biases of any kind. Students are eager to break through barriers to knowing. They are willing to surrender to the wonder of re-learning and learning ways of knowing that go against the grain. When we, as educators, allow our pedagogy to be radically changed by our recognition of a multicultural world, we can give students the education they desire and deserve. We can teach in ways that transform consciousness, creating a climate of free expression that is the essence of a truly liberatory liberal arts education.

ADVOCACY EDUCATION

TEACHING, RESEARCH, AND DIFFERENCE IN HIGHER EDUCATION

BECKY ROPERS-HUILMAN AND DENISE TALIAFERRO

Recently, scholars and practitioners have generated urgent questions about how institutions of higher learning should encompass the diversity of participants and paradigms in academic settings. These questions have focused broadly on desired changes in institutional culture or climate (Chang, 2002; Hurtado, Milem, Clayton-Pederson, & Allen, 1998; Kezar & Eckel, 2002; Kolodny, 1996; Minnich, O'Barr, & Rosenfeld, 1988), the implications of reconfiguring disciplinary content and boundaries (Gumport & Snydman, 2002; Stanton & Stewart, 1995), and relationships among and between students, faculty, and administration (De La Luz Reyes & Halcon, 1988; Kraemer, 1997; Turner, Myers, & Creswell, 1997). Most scholarship insists, albeit in varying ways, that those in higher education need to embrace diversity and make teaching and learning environments both welcoming and educationally useful for all participants.

Although this literature has encompassed a broad range of perspectives, we continue to seek literature that both provides and questions strategies and rationales for those of us who are interested in serving as advocates to persons who have typically been marginalized as "diverse others" in our day-to-day academic environments. In this chapter, we want to add to literature on higher education theory and practice related to diversity by exploring the complexities of what we are calling "advocacy education." As faculty members in the field of education, we find that our research, teaching, and advocacy are inextricably linked. When we set out to do any of the three, the other two are implicated in various ways. As such, we use the term "advocacy education" throughout this chapter to convey that understanding. Our purpose in this work is to explore the ways scholars' positions in the academy influence their abilities to effectively act as advocates, teachers, and researchers in multicultural environments. We do this through close examination of our participation in a seminar entitled "Women of Color in College" on a predominantly White southern campus.

Setting the Stage

During the fall semester of 1996, Becky Ropers-Huilman and Stefanie Costner, a graduate student who had been assigned to work with Becky, initiated the development of a group to focus on women of color in college. As scholars of higher education and as persons who were interested in making educational environments more accepting of all participants, they decided that this project would mesh well with their convictions. Becky and Stefanie held an initial organizational meeting a few months before they intended to officially start meeting and decided to hold future discussions in the African American Cultural Center on campus. During the spring semester of 1997, those who chose to participate met about every other week for approximately three hours in the afternoon. This

Reprinted from *Gendered Futures in Higher Education: Critical Perspectives for Change* (2003), State University of New York Press.

group originally consisted of Becky (a White assistant professor in Higher Education Leadership), ten graduate women (one Asian American and nine African American) in English, Higher Education Leadership, and Curriculum and Instruction, and two African American undergraduate women in English and General Sciences. Our ages spanned three decades, with our youngest member only eighteen years old. Denise Taliaferro was one of the graduate students who elected to participate.

We chose to ground our analysis of these experiences using various assumptions embedded in feminist, womanist, critical, and poststructural approaches to knowledge. These assumptions contradict and overlap each other in various ways, yet are united by their assertions that knowledge is partial, political, and related to the identities of its constructors and interpreters. Further assumptions assert the value of:

1. finding differences and sites of conflict rather than themes that can be generalized (Tierney, 1994);

2. telling previously silenced stories (Collins, 1991; Lorde, 1984; Reinharz, 1992);

3. recognizing that there is more than one way to measure the usefulness of research (Fine, 1994; Lather, 1986, 1991, 1994; Reinharz, 1992; Wolf, 1992);

4. suggesting that there is always more than one story that can be told of a given situation (Pagano, 1991; Tierney, 1994; Wolf, 1992).

Guided by these approaches, this section presents the context of the research, examines the theoretical (dis)junctures that informed this work, and considers the ways our positions influenced the questions that we were able to address and the understandings we were able to create.

Using this particular combination of theoretical tenets, we chose not to write this chapter as if we were telling one story. Although we agree on the importance of advocacy education, we often see and thus negotiate the emergent tensions differently. We believe that it is in between our differences that the potential for learning is greatest. In this vein, we attempt to offer a dialogic analysis of advocacy education from at least two perspectives. Becky writes from a White feminist paradigm while Denise writes from a Black womanist one. We are both guided by poststructural understandings that insist on the instability and fluidity of meanings and identities as well. What emerges are points of agreement and points of contention that do not allow us or our readers to come to a final answer about how to participate in advocacy education.

Situated Beings

> The way things are for our life and body allows us only a partial view of things, not the kind of total view we might gain if we were godlike, looking down from the sky. But we can only know as situated beings. (Greene, 1995, p. 26)

Womanist, Scholar, Student

I, Denise, approached this collaborative work from my own peculiar disposition. I am an African American female who grew up in the predominately African American city of Detroit, where I was raised in a family committed to Black nationalist politics. During my freshman year of high school, I made the controversial decision to begin my sophomore year at a predominately White high school located in a middle-class suburb of Detroit. After graduating, I attended UCLA for my undergraduate studies and eventually went to Louisiana State University to complete my masters and doctorate degrees in secondary teaching and curriculum theory.

I say all of this to emphasize that the interaction I have had with White people in my lifetime has almost always been initiated in and mediated through educational settings, where White people—White women in particular—held positions of authority with respect to my education. Stretched between my nationalist background and my commitments to social justice for all, my feelings about the role White people have played in Black education are complicated and contradictory. How can I not respect the efforts of such women as Prudence Crandall and Margaret Walker, who defied the law and risked their lives to educate Black children prior to emancipation? Yet how can I not also be angry because the education they offered often reflected the unworthiness of Black history, culture, and experience? Yet they did not know any better. Did they? These were the tensions that most influenced my interest and participation in the group project and discussions organized by Becky and her graduate assistant, Stefanie.

At the time, I joined the group (as a student) for several reasons. First, I was simply intrigued by the idea of a group of intellectual women mostly of color coming together to share their knowledge and testimonials, laughing, talking, thinking and theorizing about who we are and where we are. I expected that our intellectual forays would be just as full of energy, contradiction, and contestation as they are in the kitchen, the beauty salon, or the front porch. There are few "safe" places, especially within the academy, where women of color engage in rigorous intellectual discussions on our own terms. Second, I wanted to contemplate this feminist–womanist relationship. Like Becky, I believe that it is imperative to engage and disrupt contradictions, instabilities and silences. Yet I did not come to the project with feminist eyes, so to speak. I came with womanist eyes, ones that cannot deny the salience of race in the construction of a gendered self. In fact, when I came to the group, I was grappling with the "other" side of Becky's dilemmas. I wanted to understand why many Black women, including myself, often downplayed the significance of gender in our processes of identifying as marginalized people. Finally, I thought a lot about this White feminist professor's attempt to position herself within a women-of-color student context. Who is she to advocate for us? How will this struggle for recognition and validation of identities play out of and into our conversations? What are the implications of race, gender and power in advocacy work?

Researcher, Teacher, Feminist

Previous study about and involvement in research, teaching and reading about education, and personal experiences had been insufficient to prepare me for my involvement in this group. What I mean by this is that I, Becky, committed to this project before I felt comfortable with the structure of my participation. Unlike what I had been taught in other research and teaching endeavors, I did not have a "problem statement" or a detailed syllabus dictating the terms of my relationships with other participants. Nor did I have a specific question I was trying to answer. I did not consciously know what I wanted or expected to happen. I did not know what my role was to be. I knew only that I wanted to help carve a space in the academy where a group of women of color could speak and have their speaking and experiences validated. I did not know what I wanted to hear or the precise methods through which this validation would take place.

This work was undoubtedly influenced by my move from Madison, Wisconsin to Baton Rouge, Louisiana to take my first assistant professor position at Louisiana State University. LSU has a rich history of serving some populations well while excluding others. Women were not admitted to LSU until 1906; African Americans (currently comprising roughly one-third of the state's population) were not admitted until 1953. Until recently, African American students were assessed a charge for the maintenance of the African American Cultural Center, regardless of their use, while Whites who attend programming at the Center did so free of charge.[1] Fraternities and sororities are largely segregated by race.

I expected to find, and was consciously seeking out, cultural differences in this move from the Midwest to the South. I had a fascination with, and a deep sense of ignorance about, the intense and historic racial tensions that I heard occurred in the "Deep South." I had learned about this region of the United States primarily through history books (that largely focused on war, in my recollection). My understandings of racial tensions came predominantly from educational theorists whose work drew attention to disparities in educational opportunity and experience between various groups of people.

My fascination with racial dynamics is articulated well in Steven Linstead's (1993) description of the motivation fueling any attempts to "know" others:

> The very existence of *another* is information which tells us that we are not *complete,* and the fundamental, intractable compulsion in social life is to reconcile this difference, to complete what is missing to being, to fill our own lack. (p. 61)

I admit that my need to see and understand individuals who have traditionally been characterized as "Others" in relation to me made my involvement in a project focusing on women of color very intriguing. I hoped to hear from these Others, perhaps in an effort to better understand myself and this new situation that I was living within.

My recognition of "incompleteness" developed poignantly during the first semester at LSU. I often heard stories of discrimination and disrespect that occurred in various places on campus—in classrooms, in the union, and at football games. Through my conversations and questionings with students, I began to learn that while parts of our backgrounds were similar, our life experiences were, in some ways, drastically, paradigmatically different. Christine Sleeter (1993) explains, "Spending most of their time with other white people, whites do not see much of the realities of the lives of Americans of color nor encounter their viewpoints in any depth. Nor do they really want to, since those viewpoints would challenge practices and beliefs that benefit white people" (p. 168). I knew I was missing a large part of the world.

I wanted, then, to use my newly acquired "strategic location" as a professor to learn about the experiences of women of color in college and university settings. Further, I wanted to provide a forum through which the students with whom I was working could be validated in an academic setting for forming and articulating theories based on their own experiences. Using my interpretations of feminism and poststructuralism, I wanted to focus on the "local" as a way to generate broader understandings and draw attention to the ways the personal is political. By offering course credit for this experience, I hoped to lend the academy's support to this type of intellectual engagement. My motives, I believed, were clearly set in my understandings of feminism, poststructuralism, and critical theory. Yet, as illustrated throughout the dialogue presented in this chapter, these motives were not simply defined or enacted.

Worldviews

With Womanist Eyes

> Black feminist thought consists of specialized knowledge created by African American women that clarifies a standpoint of and for Black women. In other words, Black feminist thought encompasses theoretical interpretations of Black women's reality by those who live it. (Collins, 1990, p. 581)

When I, Denise, use the expression "womanist eyes," I mean to acknowledge the reality that, because of my cultural and racial positioning, I do not, in fact cannot, interpret our project from a (White) feminist standpoint. In my view, I always understood the project to be a racially charged one, burdened by historical oppressions while struggling toward transcendence. Womanist eyes implicate both a way of thinking and a way of doing. In *Defining Black Feminist Thought*, Patricia Hill Collins (1990) contends that the interdependent relationship between experience and consciousness supports the idea of a Black feminist consciousness that is distinct from that of a White feminist one. She writes:

> Black women's work and family experiences and grounding in traditional African-American culture suggest that African-American women as a group experience a world different from that of those who are not Black and female. Moreover, these concrete experiences can stimulate a distinctive Black feminist consciousness concerning that material reality. Being Black and female may expose African-American women to certain common experiences, which in turn may predispose us to a distinctive group consciousness, but it in no way guarantees that such a consciousness will develop among all women or that it will be articulated as such by the group. (p. 584)

Collins goes on to argue that a Black feminist standpoint has several discernable characteristics. Some of the core themes include a legacy of struggle which has required a sense of independence and self-reliance, a tradition of activism, and attention to the interconnectedness of race, class, and gender oppression. Yet "womanist eyes" do not only recognize the racial and patriarchal roots of power relations; they also act from a cultural standpoint that has emerged from the downside of those relations. Specifically, Alice Walker (1983) coined the term "womanist," and defined it in this way:

> A black feminist, a feminist of color. From the black folk expression of mothers to female children, "You acting womanish," i.e., like a woman. Usually referring to outrageous, audacious, courageous or willful behavior. Wanting to know more and in greater depth than is considered "good" for one. Interested in grown-up doings. Acting grown up. Being grown up. Interchangeable with another black folk expression: "You trying to be grown." Responsible. In charge. - Serious. (p. xi)

The vision Walker calls up is undeniably important to the way Black women have typically had to live their lives. This definition rejects the subservient image that has historically represented White womanhood. Granted, Black women have been physically subdued, yet we have always resisted for the sake of our own lives, cultivating a "grown up" attitude. Both Collins' and Walker's theories are relevant to my interpretations of advocacy education particularly in a multiracial context, and more specifically within the context of the collaborative efforts of Becky, the other group participants, and me. It is important that my use of the expression "womanist eyes" does not lie outside of, or in direct opposition to, the feminist purview. Womanism is in accordance with the primary goal of the feminist movement—"to end sexism, sexist exploitation and oppression" (hooks, 2000). Yet it engages this goal from a collective consciousness that is ontologically and epistemologically distinct from the mainstream White feminist perspective. Womanist eyes cannot but consider how sexism and sexist exploitation are informed by racial ideology. They see the different histories, cultures, and experiences of women of color, and they recognize the nonsynchronous nature of oppression (McCarthy, 1990).

Before I discuss the organization of my response, I want to acknowledge the participation of Luoluo Hong in our project. Luoluo as an Asian American woman was the only other non-African American woman involved in the group. Although I recognize Luoluo as a woman of color and a part of the womanist "vibe" I am constructing, I also want to point out that her experiences as an Asian American woman may at times fall outside of my analysis. Although the Asian female–White female relationship shares similarities with the Black female—White female relationship, I am sure it has its own historical distinctiveness as well.

Unpacking Assumptions of White Feminist Praxis

Based on my emerging aspirations to participate in advocacy, teaching, and research for and with women of color, I, Becky, reflected on the theoretical bases that I commonly rely on in my living and thinking. The stage for this experience was partially set on the confluence of various theories. I am primarily compelled by approaches that label themselves critical, poststructural, or feminist. To my understanding, critical approaches suggest that power relations are uneven and, in part, based on our identity characteristics (Tierney & Rhoads, 1993). Further, power relations have the potential to be changed at local levels. Poststructural approaches suggest that power is fluid and shifting. Power is not an entity, but rather a strategic position (Foucault, 1978). As educators, we operate as the "throughput of discourses" (Hassard, 1993) and, as such, embody both power and resistance in the discourses in which we operate. Feminist approaches suggest that our identities affect our access to power in our society, and that women of all types are negatively affected, albeit differently, by the patriarchy that exists in Western society (Hurtado, 1989; Lerner, 1986). Feminism generally suggests that disrupting patriarchal institutions has the potential to change those negative relations.

I found that my understandings of these frameworks and their potential uses were shaken by this research. For example, why did many women of color resist the strategies and strengths that I thought feminism (through theory and political action) could offer them? Why did they often focus a skeptical eye on poststructuralism, wondering about its usefulness and the effects of its exclusive language? And why were several hesitant to embrace educators who attempted to act "critically" in teaching and learning environments?

While engaging with a book entitled *Critical Race Feminism* (Wing, 1997b), I began to piece together possible responses to several of my questions. Some of the authors of this collection recalled the failures of feminist and poststructural or postmodern approaches to address their needs. Angela Harris (1997) writes of how White feminist scholars broke their promises to the Black women whom the women's movement was courting when they chose to insult Black women by assuming that the experiences of White women would represent their concerns and identities. History indicates that this is a longstanding tension. For example, early in the twentieth century the White members of the National American Women's Suffrage Association (NAWSA) alienated Black women from their efforts to attain the right to vote (Rosenberg, 1992). Early and recent feminist actions have—either purposely or inadvertently—failed to take into consideration the interests of all women.

Postmodernism poses special challenges to interracial understandings as well. Celina Romany (1997) suggests that although postmodern approaches may decenter the essentialized concept of woman, thereby opening up rooms for difference in all of its forms, "This new entrance leads us into a meeting of discourses rather than to an encounter of those differences at the very concrete level of power differentials and unequal distribution of privileges" (p. 22). In a volume entitled *Learning From Our Lives: Women, Research, and Autobiography in Education*, Gloria Ladson-Billings (1997) contributes that Black feminist perspectives, research, and educational approaches need to be based on concrete experiences to be legitimized in various communities. Those experience, in conjunction with theories, provide the context for rich and reliable work.

As I moved through my time with this group, I realized that advocacy education involves participants who are creating new theory together while testing, manipulating, and hearing challenges to our own "tried and true" perspectives. I needed to be open to the possibilities of re-creating a localized theory that worked for this specific group of people involved in this specific project. I also believed what we were creating might be useful in future experiences involving advocacy education.

Reflections

Motivations and Contradictions in Advocacy Education

I consider in this section what I, Becky, have learned about the motivations and contradictions involved in advocacy education, continually thinking about how to be an advocate, teacher, and researcher for and with persons who occupy an identity that is in some ways different from my own. Granted, the contradictions I present are no doubt included in this work because of what I have learned—how I am different from who I was when I started this project. Consequently, what I have chosen to present here—what stood out for me as I moved through this experience—tells as much about me as it does about the complexities within advocacy education. Yet, my identity is not unitary, and although racial dynamics undoubtedly influenced the thoughts I present here and group interactions throughout the semester, I am not sure how my "whiteness" shaped these dynamics. The varying parts of my identity are interwoven. Certainly my feminism, femaleness, northern upbringing, heterosexuality, and age (to name a few) shaped our interactions and my interpretations as well. Still, I offer my thoughts on advocacy education by interrogating the concepts of advocacy and difference, with the hope that they might be useful for others as they rethink the possibilities for advocacy in their own teaching, learning, and research.

Interrogating Advocacy

I believe that advocacy does not need to be limited to others with whom we readily identify based on apparent or assumed identity characteristics. Instead:

> The idea of difference provides an important reminder of the limitations of emancipatory political theory. Emancipation is not a likely prospect unless our political theories and practices stay open to other perspectives, take account of the diverse forms oppression can take, and remain consciously provisional and revisable. (Sypnowich, 1996, p. 288)

Buoyed by the cautious possibilities that Christine Sypnowich offers, one of my primary motivations in fostering this educational experience was to learn how to be an advocate for women of color in collegiate contexts, and then, in some sense, to enact that advocacy. Growing up in a small, White, rural, Mid-western community, my personal experiences with women of color throughout the majority of my life had been minimal. I had read about and engaged in heated dialogues about the importance of examining gendered and racialized relations in educational settings. Still, my knowledge was limited by my infrequent experience with women of color. I wanted to hear about personal experiences that would help me to grapple with and improve my understandings of the educational theory with which I regularly engaged. As Patricia Hill Collins (1991) suggests, "individuals who have lived through the experiences about which they claim to be experts are more believable and credible than those who have merely read or thought about such experiences" (p. 209). Perhaps because I am inclined to agree with Collins' statement, I hesitated to grant myself credibility to engage in this dialogue without first listening to those who were positioned both as subjects and objects therein.

I am well aware of one ironic twist to this belief—in trying to learn how to "do" advocacy, I needed to learn from, even use, members of the group for whom I wanted to serve as an advocate. Although I regularly worked to promote discussions about equity in my family and friend circles prior to this experience, I had consciously done so much less frequently in professional settings. I hoped to use my newly found power as a professor to push the boundaries of my localized experiences, to invoke change that would result in "better" education for, and understandings of, women of color. In moving from theory to practice, I wanted this group to inform my efforts.

As I looked around me in higher education settings, I was reminded of the dearth of women of color in the professorial ranks. Although literature would suggest such absences (Carter, Pearson, & Shavlik, 1996), my experiences at both the University of Wisconsin and Louisiana State University brought the related implications home. At the time, in neither place was there a woman of color at any rank of the professoriate in my department. What was worse was when I realized that it did not feel abnormal for this to be the case. Something was wrong when the absence of a certain identity group was normalized and no longer noticed by others. Seldom did the women in this group see anyone whom they might identify with as a person who shared similar race and gender backgrounds as well as occupational aspirations. The identities of those in various positions of higher education communities demonstrate the valuing of certain persons and the devaluing of others. I hoped the members of our group would learn from and teach each other how to crack the often normalized complacency of racism by preparing themselves for leadership positions in educational institutions or elsewhere.

Within this complicated terrain, I wanted to be an advocate for those who had often told me that their voices were not sought or even heard in most educational environments. Yet, putting myself in the role of advocating for or empowering traditionally marginalized persons was problematic. Empowerment implied that I had a power that I could share with them—something of which I was not yet certain (Ropers-Huilman, 1997; Ropers-Huilman, 1998). Further, it continued to focus the need for change on students, rather than looking to the ways that institutions could change to better accept, accommodate, and use their skills, abilities, and perspectives. As I perceived it, these women seemed quite "empowered"—indeed, they were intelligent and articulate—but they still were not being heard in the ways that they wanted to be within various academic settings. When understood in this context, empowerment again recasts women of color as those who need to change both themselves and the institution. They are the ones who are perceived to be in need of "fixing" and are simultaneously given the assignment to "fix" the institution of which they are a part.

When should we turn attention away from students, and instead focus on the institutional structures that preclude anyone from hearing their empowered speech or responding to their empowered actions? Does empowerment focus on personal agency at the expense of institutional change, and unwittingly perpetuate institutional racism and sexism? What does empowerment mean? Who gets to define it and act on those definitions? While several others and I have discussed some of these complexities elsewhere (Ellsworth, 1992; Lewis, 1993; Orner, 1992; Ropers-Huilman, 1998), the struggles with empowerment relate closely to my understandings about advocacy in teaching and research. Advocacy education must focus on self, students, institutions, and society. If empowerment is to be conceptualized as useful within this framework, it must be reframed to fit these terms. Clearly, though, each engagement demands different strategies to address the unique conditions of each setting.

Interrogating Difference

As another step in learning to advocate, I believed I needed to get to know those persons for whom I wanted to advocate. In my view, the negotiation of group members' wishes and aspirations with my own would eventually set the agenda for my advocacy. As is common with sentiments that seem too tidy and certain, my attempts to learn about difference in this setting were complicated by the realities of our engagements. In this section, I discuss the intersections of advocacy and difference through analysis of the concept of unitary difference, the implications of inclusive and exclusive practices, and the negotiation of voice and speech in advocacy education.

(De)constructing Unitary Difference

In some ways, my curiosity or longing to "know" led me dangerously close to wanting to conceptualize women of color as a unitary group, rather than as a group of individuals who sometimes share common experiences. That sense of "unitary difference" quickly dissipated, though, as our conversations drew out multiple standpoints, beliefs, and experiences. For example, one group member had started college at 15; another had been the only Black student in her school as she was growing up; another had worked as a certified public accountant in the Midwest before returning to do graduate work. Group members' perspectives represented a wide range of views on interracial dating, gender roles, and occupational aspirations. We were certainly a mixed group in many ways.

My understandings of unity were reinforced, though, by what I perceived as a strong feeling of skepticism among the group members for anyone who was not a person of color, and a resulting desire to present what might be called a "facade of unity." As Denise wrote in her reflections, "As a marginalized group of people, we have our own codes for what is to be discussed in public and what is to be kept private. We often feel the pressure to present a united front, despite our disagreements." This facade serves to perpetuate a false unity among certain groups and establish, therefore, that any member of a racial group could be a "representative for the race." In other words, if all members agree, then any member can represent the whole. The rationales for protecting this perceived unity were constructed and deconstructed repeatedly during our group's time together.

In her discussion of black feminist thought, Patricia Hill Collins (1996) establishes that although Black women have certain commonalties, they also are enmeshed in a diversity of experiences and, therefore, in different expressions of their commonalties. Essentialism is especially dangerous for Black women because, "In an essentialist world, black women's experience will always be forcibly fragmented before being subjected to analysis, as those who are 'only interested in race' and those who are 'only interested in gender' take their separate slices of our lives" (Harris, 1997, p. 11). Although perhaps at times useful politically, unity often (dangerously) suggests an essentialism that is potentially harmful to women of color.

So how can we use our own and others' sometimes unitary, sometimes distinct voices to be advocates to change policies, practices, and experiences of and for those whom we perceive to be marginalized? How can we reclaim the usefulness of our own and others' voices within this quagmire of legitimation, essentialism, and difference? In one sense, group members, as well as scholars such as Lisa Delpit (1993) and Michelle Foster (1997), insist that people who are seeking to be allies with—or at least understand—others really listen to them. On the other hand, I have heard group members express their frustration that they are constantly seen as the source for enlightenment about the experiences of African American women or other groups with whom they are perceived to be affiliated (Yamato, 1990). The quandary of trying to learn to be an advocate without assuming unitary difference or, in this case, that group members could be "representatives for their race," limited my interactions with group members and resulted in an ongoing struggle about the processes involved in learning to participate in advocacy education. I struggled with taking up (or wasting?) group time to ask the question, "How can I frame my participation in this group and in higher education settings in a way that is useful to women of color?" I wonder, who should I be listening to if I want to learn to be an advocate? Does advocacy education truly have to be relearned at an intimately local level each time? If so, what implications does that have for those who would like to advocate for institutional and educational change at the policy and practice levels?

I learned from these interactions that while tempting to do so, difference is limiting if it is perceived as all-encompassing, stable or permanent. As several group members reiterated to me, the way one defines "difference" is (re)constructed in relation to others' identities and fluctuating positions, and in constantly changing situations. We pay attention to and emphasize certain aspects of our identities depending on context. As such:

> Ultimately there are as many differences as selves, and thus our invocations of difference always risk essentialism, wherein we reify a certain identity and proclaim its immutable nature, without attention to the differences within the identity itself, or the damage done to the new "other" the reclaimed identity leaves in its wake. (Sypnowich, 1996, p. 285)

Through the stories I heard from the women in this group, I came to believe that because of their precarious positioning at the intersections of race and gender, many women of color are constantly renegotiating their identities and figuring out what strategic positions they should choose from among their various allegiances. As Luoluo Hong, a group member, reminded me in a personal communication, "Perhaps that is the essence of women of color's identities in a predominantly White culture. Non-Whites may necessarily do this negotiation in order to survive, to generate a cohesive self and a connection to community." I wonder about the pain and strength that emerges from these reconstructed identities, and consider how women of color have so often embodied the existence of multiple selves to which postmodernism has relatively recently drawn educators' attention.

When we no longer think of identity as stable or unitary, it is more difficult to engage within advocacy education because a fascination of and desire for difference becomes much more complex. Leslie Roman (1993) expressed her concerns about unequal "others" ever being able to know oppressed persons. But, in some sense, as much as this may not be reasonable or realistic, I want to try to know others. From that location, I think that I can be the best possible advocate for and with them. I want to know those I am trying to support and enact advocacy education with. Audre Lorde's (1984) words suggest the necessity of engaging within this dilemma of difference:

> Where the words of women are crying to be heard, we must each of us recognize our responsibility to seek those words out, to read them and share them and examine them in their pertinence to our lives. That we not hide behind the mockeries of separations that have been imposed upon us and which so often we accept as our own. . . . It is not difference which immobilizes us, but silence. (p. 44)

The positioning of scholars in higher education enables them to hear the calls of women of color in their classrooms and on their campuses if they choose to listen. Through conversation and communication, our differences can become sources of strength, rather than only areas of concern.

(De)constructing Inclusion/Exclusion

Throughout the semester, I better understood another motive for my participation. I wanted to be included in the struggle to value women of color in academe. Much of my learning came through Luoluo, an Asian American woman who had requested that we broaden our focus from "Black women in college" to "Women of color in college." In trying to be inclusive, a Black woman in our group said that Luoluo could certainly participate—after all, she was an "honorary sister girl." In other words, she could participate because she was, perhaps, "Black enough" in her actions and attitudes. As Luoluo later pointed out to me, in the South, "women of color" often seems, by default, to mean "Black women." Her identity as an Asian American woman was obscured by this "honorary" membership into a "Black" group. Yet she wanted to assert that as an Asian American woman, she was a woman of color—with or without anyone else's blessing or permission.

When we discussed the problematics involved in this labeling during a subsequent meeting, I wondered how I would have felt had that honorary title been bestowed on me. In some senses, I desired to be an honorary member of a group that my whiteness prohibited me from ever truly entering. In another sense, I shared with Luoluo a concern about the process or practice of honorary inclusion because it seemed like racial gatekeeping to me. I was afraid that I would be left out of related struggles and consequently wondered: How is this gatekeeping related to oppression?

Is it a necessary political strategy? Where do those people who are not the "norm" within any group fit in? Must they always (ironically) strive to attain and uphold an honorary status in the struggle against oppression?

Another instance provided me with uncertainties about inclusive and exclusive practices in advocacy education. During a conversation about another Black person who was not part of our group, I was told by a group member that they (group members) generally did not say challenging things about other African American people to others who are not African American. They said I was "different," though, and continued their dialogue. In a later conversation, I was told that group members sometimes felt that they did not need to change their manner of speaking around me as they did around most White people (sometimes referred to as "code switching"). I wondered what types of behavior on my part would allow me to know or hear more than others. Why was I different than other White people? I feared that I might do or say something that would make me "the same" as all other "Whites." An additional undercurrent came to the surface reluctantly in my thinking on this topic. Perhaps I was able to act as an advocate precisely because of the structures that I was trying to deconstruct (those that fostered the development of White and middle-class persons while ignoring others). The irony of this positioning implies both a sharp responsibility and an unnerving feeling of being caught up in wrongful desires. I wanted so much to avoid having my "whiteness"— my "difference"—found out. Why was I at least minimally accepted into this group? And where were the boundaries of my acceptance? How are these boundaries harmful, useful, and malleable, to and by whom?

(De)constructing Speech and Difference

I learned from this experience that what I understood to be "respectful communication" was not uniformly accepted or enacted as such by other group members. Instead, we operated within another system of communication that redefined, for me, understandings of respect. When one member of the group was designated formally or informally as the "speaker" for that part of the session, others rarely interrupted. During discussions, though, several group members often spoke loudly over each other, seemingly to suggest that the volume of their voice would assure them the right and space to speak. I had been taught that respectful speech dictated that I wait until there was a brief pause before I spoke. I had learned that one values others by trying to provide them with the comfort, space, and time to speak. Consequently, during the first several meetings of this group, I did not speak much, even though my presence as a professor lent support for my voice. I learned that communication and, relatedly, conceptualizations of respect for others must be negotiated when attempting to engage in advocacy education. Many times, I was negotiated—by the interactions between and among group participants and myself—right out of verbal participation.

Perhaps my silence is good, I tried to tell myself to smother my discomfort. After all, I was concerned about the establishment of a communication style that privileged my thinking. More specifically, I did not want to impose my version of communication as the norm. As Christine Sleeter (1993) points out, whiteness can often inadvertently be established as the norm, even in multicultural interaction. As the only professor and White person involved in the group, I was quite hesitant to express my views because I was afraid that they would either shut down discussion, be followed with over-attendance to my ideas, or be met with a "how could you possibly understand what we're talking about?" look. While not necessarily more "true" or "valid," the experience of talking about myself is different from the experience of talking or asking about others. I wondered about the boundaries of both my "right" to speak with and about others and the usefulness of such attempts. Even when group members encouraged me to participate more verbally in our group discussion, I hesitated. As I reflect now, I understand that my lack of participation had little to do with the actual discussion. Instead, it portrayed somewhat accurately my own concerns about interrole communication. I found myself circling back to the dilemmas related to difference.

Although my silence greatly shaped my participation, I rationalized these actions in many ways. I wanted to be sensitive to those who have suggested that in others' efforts to empower or advocate for them, they have not been listened to. I knew that I was sorely lacking in my understandings of the lived experiences of women of color in college and wanted to listen to enhance that understanding. I wanted to be sensitive to the question that Leslie Roman (1993) poses when she writes:

> The question for scholars working within [First World European and North American contexts] . . . who now confront the crisis of representation, is *not* whether the subaltern can speak. Instead, it is whether privileged (European and North American) white groups are willing to listen when the subaltern speaks and how whites can know the difference between occasions for responsive listening and listening as an excuse for silent collusion with the status quo of racial and neo-colonial inequalities. (p. 79)

Thinking back, I wonder how my silence affected group members and if my lack of verbal participation, lack of exposure of myself, was responsive or merely collusive with the very inequalities I was trying to work against. Had I become the "unknowable other" to them?

In a response to many of the questions I have posed here, I found Adrien Wing's (1997a) assertion that identities are multiplicative, rather than additive, both useful and complicated. For example, she asserts that Black women are assumed to be both "Black" and "woman," although neither of those categories fully includes the unique nature of the interaction between their "blackness" and their "womanness." In her thinking, then, each person is a product, rather than a sum, of the identities that comprise them. As such, our relationships can be both grounded in common factors and shaped by the various elements that our differences infuse into our interactions. Still, how can any of us know the various "multipliers," the identities, at play in the students and teachers we encounter? Without this knowledge, the benefits and detriments of concepts such as "unitary difference," "exclusivity and inclusivity," and "useful speech" quickly become foggy and intertwined. And advocacy education becomes that much more complex.

Splitting the Difference: A Womanist Response

My (Denise's) response to Becky's analysis is a "bottom-up" analysis of our group effort. Essentially, it is my side of the story, which is unavoidably colored by my experiences as an African American female student at LSU between 1994 and 1998. This response is also shaped by my recent experiences as an African American female faculty member who is constantly redefining my own sense of teacher, researcher, and advocate. I have organized my response into three parts. The first deals with the historical legacy that imposes on our group work as well as substantiates the need for it. In the second part, I review inter- and intracultural conflicts that emerge around the notion of "advocacy." And in the third part, I attempt to rethink "advocacy education."

Feminist Disjunctures, Womanist Conjectures

> Black women must have been affected by their experiences during slavery. Some, no doubt, were broken and destroyed, yet the majority survived and, in the process, acquired qualities considered taboo by the nineteenth-century ideology of womanhood. (Davis, 1983, p. 11)

Before I joined the group, I knew there would be tensions, contradictions, and silences. I knew there were many differences in backgrounds, goals, and experiences among other aspects that would set us apart while, at the same time, bringing us—strangely enough—close together. I anticipated the uneasiness that would result, no matter what, from the way raced and gendered legacies would impinge on the present. Yet, I looked forward to breaking through "pc" codes and confronting many things, especially the troubled relationships between White women and women of color. The racial tensions that have shaped even the earliest of feminist movements (Davis, 1983; hooks, 2000) were certainly lurking just below the surface of our initial conversations. Chats that took place on the margins of our collective forays revealed that some of us were indeed suspicious of Becky's relationship to the group. "Suspicious" does not mean we believed that her intentions were unworthy; it does mean, however, that our perceptions were veiled by the remnants of historical circumstance—an age-old distrust of whiteness and authority.

This distrust was not always spoken or explicit or based on personal experience. It was sometimes critically conscious and other times dysconscious; it was sometimes rooted in personal experiences and other times in historical collective experiences. However, whether covert or overt, this distrust was always paradoxical. Our suspicions of Becky had little to do with anything she did or did not do. It was mainly about what she represented historically—a White woman in a position of power, offering her help to us unfortunate women of color. Thus, what was creeping just below the surface of our work was a suspicious air of paternalism.

Historically and in terms of race relations, paternalism has been used to describe the relation between White folk and Black folk as one indicative of a parent–child relationship. In the education of Black people, the notion of paternalism has been significant. Many nineteenth-century advocates of slavery advanced philosophies of paternalism that suggested that slavery was good for Africans because it (slavery by Europeans) taught them how to be "civilized." Also, the missionary efforts of many White organizations in the late nineteenth and early twentieth centuries to educate Black people in the ways of the Bible and other European values, beliefs, and traditions were often rooted in the understanding that Black folk were childlike and needed to be taught the ways of the parent. Paternalism continues to shape the education of Black people in this country. Paternalistic attitudes have supported compensatory programs for, and low expectations of, African American and other children of color. Furthermore, many scholars of color continue to struggle to free themselves from "intellectual paternalism," from the hegemony of Eurocentric paradigms.

It is reasonable, then, to argue that educational advocacy on behalf of African Americans has traditionally been grounded as paternalistic endeavor. Has the White feminist paradigm of advocacy been any different? Although the "parent" now seeks information from the "child," some would argue that paternalism still haunts the mainstream White feminist paradigm. In her essay entitled "Holding My Sister's Hand," bell hooks (1994) attests to how traditional tropes of power manifest in White feminist paradigms:

> [W]ith the increasing institutionalization and problematization of feminist work focused on the construction of feminist theory and the dissemination of feminist knowledge, white women have assumed positions of power that enable them to reproduce the servant–served paradigm in a radically different context. Now black women are put in the position of serving white female desire to know more about race and racism, to "master" the subject. (p. 103)

In the context of our multiracial and multicultural endeavor, I could not help but wonder what Becky meant by "advocacy." What could she do for us? Some of us gave her the benefit of the historical doubt, yet at least one member of the group remained adamantly suspicious, because she was unnerved by the idea that we were being "used" for the benefit of Becky's research.

Inter- and Intracultural Differences in Advocacy Work

> "We are what we know." We are, however, also what we do not know. If what we know about ourselves—our history, our culture, our national identity—is deformed by absences, denials, and incompleteness, then our identity—both as individuals and as Americans—is fragmented. (Pinar, 1993, p. 16)

There is a beautiful irony here. While Becky spent a lot of time reflecting on the challenges she faced in her role as "advocate," I was reflecting on how Becky's style of advocacy was really working for this group of very vibrant, determined, intellectual women of color. Whereas some of Becky's choices contradicted her initial understandings of "advocacy," they were decisions that allowed this diverse group of women to name themselves for themselves. This is an absolutely critical idea, because it displaces anachronistic meanings of advocacy education that have tended to fit nicely into what Freire (1970) has called "banking education." Traditionally, the advocate "helps" her subjects by showing them how to, what to, or when to. Advocacy, in this sense, reinforces hierarchy, domination, and objectification.

Is this kind of advocacy even possible when the advocate is a White feminist trying to "help" a group of women of color who have a historical legacy of self-reliance, independence, and activism on bchalf of themselves and others? Whether we were sitting around Becky's kitchen table, a seminar table in Peabody Hall, a folding table in the African American Cultural Center, or the coffee table in Stefanie's apartment, our multiracial and multicultural interactions refused the order of traditional advocacy. As we discussed interracial relationships, racist and sexist professors, relationships with men of color, code switching, and the salience of race and/or gender, we were also problematizing and redefining advocacy.

While Becky worked on debunking the assumption of unitary difference, I was enthralled by the way we managed to hold onto a collective sense of Black womanhood while at the same time being very different from one another. At times we disagreed adamantly with one another. For instance, when we discussed interracial relationships, at least one of us had dated a White man before and did not see much wrong with it. Others (including myself) simply said, "I have nothing against it, but I have never done it." Someone else tied it back to White slave masters' rape of enslaved Black women. And Becky wondered why it would be racist of her to say she would not date Black men, but not racist of us to say we would not date White men. In this conversation as in many others, none of us seemed to change our positions; nevertheless we did have the opportunity to better understand the reasoning behind other folks' choices. In other instances, we agreed more with one another, taking supportive stances and tones. In this sense, advocacy in action suggests that there is no one advocate who can fully understand the group for whom she advocates. We were all advocates. As Becky was learning to advocate for us, we were, indeed, learning to advocate for Becky as well as for each other and for ourselves.

Another implicit assumption of traditional advocacy work is that there is a "right" way for it to unfold. Although Becky admits that she did not have a certain expectation when we began the project, she, as well as we all, had some vision of what this project might look like. For instance, as Becky has already mentioned, her vision of what our talks would be like was quite different, most of the time, from what actually transpired. We were often "womanish" as we sometimes talked loud, strayed from the topic, and interrupted one another. Although Becky notes her reservations about her silence, it was often appropriate. Does it make sense to bring together a group for the purpose of "getting to know" us or advocating with us and insist or expect that we communicate in a style that is not culturally our own and that can be identified with the very structure that defines our oppression? From a cultural standpoint, because of the ways in which we have been denied, we have had to be audacious to even be heard. Essentially, advocacy education in a multiracial or multicultural context that is "liberatory" must be open to difference and differences that will, at times, bring about contradiction, contestation, and conflict within individual selves as well as between selves. Our group dynamics were unfolding because of, and in spite of, raced and gendered selves.

Another underlying assumption driving Becky's vision was that she could "get to know us." However, Becky's attempt to advocate for us depended far less on her getting to know us than it did on her getting to know herself in relationship to us. Although who we were not was challenging for Becky, I found that Becky's efforts to come to terms with who she was encouraged a trust and an openness among the other women. At one night session, we were grappling with the race–gender issue as Erikah Badu sang, "Who gave you permission to rearrange me?" in the background. At an intense moment, Becky asked a question that, for me, became the most significant question of our project: Who am I to question the salience of race to you as women of color without questioning the salience of gender to me as a White woman? It marked the moment when Becky publicly acknowledged what many White feminists resist. Recognizing the salience of race in the lives of women of color is no substitute for interrogating the way it structures White feminist thinking and discourse. As hooks (1994) goes on to point out, White feminist epistemologies often leave whiteness unproblematized:

> Curiously, most white women writing feminist theory that looks at "difference" and "diversity" do not make white women's lives, works, and experiences the subject of their analysis of "race," but rather focus on black women or women of color. (pp. 103–104)

hooks' point here is imperative because it foreshadows the impossibility of White women advocating, in a traditional sense, for women of color. In a society in which whiteness represents a set of "unmarked and unnamed" cultural practices that often deny difference, race and racism mark off that which is not White as untouchable, sinfully desirable, and/or in need of help (Frankenburg, 1993). As Ruth Frankenburg notes, when race and racism are seen as the "other's" problems, it profoundly affects the possibility of who can help whom. She writes:

> For when white people . . . look at racism, we tend to view it as an issue that people of color face and have to struggle with, but not as an issue that generally involves or implicates us. Viewing racism in this way has serious consequences for how white women look at racism and for how anti-racist work might be framed. With this view, white women can see anti-racist work as an act of compassion for an "other," an optional, extra project, but not one intimately, and organically linked to our own lives. (p. 7)

By posing such a self-reflective inquiry, Becky reconstructed her efforts at advocacy. Advocacy no longer meant her "getting to know us" as raced women, but her getting to know herself as a raced woman in ways that subsequently became mutually beneficial, to her and to us.

Becky's willingness to openly think about the significance of her whiteness opened avenues for us to openly discuss the significance of our femaleness. I emphasize "openly" because I believe that, because we are raced and gendered, we always engage the realities of both, even if we do so dysconsciously (King, 1991).

Advocacy in between Feminist Disjunctures and Womanist Conjectures

> As a [classroom] community, our capacity to generate excitement is deeply affected by our interest in one another, in hearing one another's voices, in recognizing one another's presence. (hooks, 1994, p. 8)

As a Black woman I know that the Black women who have loved and taught me both literally and metaphorically what it means, in some sense, to be Black and a woman, have often warned me not to "talk" too much to those White women: "You can't trust 'em. They think they know it all." So I learned to be nice, but not to say too much. What I have come to realize is that folks talk more when they believe they are being listened to. And folks who are good listeners are folks who realize that they do not know everything, no matter who they are or are not. Thus, listening in dynamic ways is vital.

This idea was reinforced for me as I worked with Becky and the other women in the group. It allowed me to clarify my understanding of how we as advocates and teachers let our co-subjects know that we hear them. Today as an African American woman committed to teaching for social justice, I am inevitably always advocating, teaching, and researching with my students. As I reflect on the time I spent with Becky and the other group members, I keep in mind the tensions, the ongoing struggles, and the successful moments, taking away important lessons. First, it has recently occurred to me that our group project was not simply about advocacy education but also about advocacy through education. Although Becky was clearly working through some notion of how to advocate within a multiracial and multicultural group of women, other group members were not thinking about advocacy at all. We were simply doing it by educating ourselves and each other, by engaging in consciousness raising. Second, advocacy education and advocacy through education that happens across racial–cultural lines cannot successfully function absolutely within an assimilationist paradigm. If it is to be multiracial and multicultural, then it must engage and respect the differences that will unavoidably exist, whether they are different communication styles or different values. Third, advocacy education and advocacy through education in a multiracial and multicultural context requires self-reflection by each and every participant. All must be willing to challenge and be challenged by the differences. Fourth, advocacy education and advocacy through education does not "solve" problems; it helps us work through them as we grapple with truly unanswerable questions. The success of our project is difficult to measure because it lingers in the space in between where definite answers were not and are not possible. Our work together was, nevertheless, valuable not because, at last, we defined what race means to gender or vice versa, not because it testifies to the "real" experiences of women of color or a white feminist ally, and not because it makes any more relevant claims about what it means to be a woman. Rather, our work was and is valuable because it is a demonstration of working through difficulties within and between ourselves, without any absolute claims to having worked them out. In this sense, Becky's most important act of advocacy was simply bringing the group together and allowing it to emerge and to evolve on its own terms.

Ultimately, understanding advocacy education and advocacy through education and its benefits arise out of what Sandra Hollingsworth (1994) calls "relational knowing":

> The concept of knowing through relationship, or relational knowing, involves both the recall of prior knowledge and the reflection on what knowledge is perceived or present in social and political settings . . . we find that relational knowing does not rest in contemplation but becomes clarified in action. (p. 77–78)

It is in this indefinite space in between differences that learning in multicultural and multiracial contexts has its greatest potential.

Final Thoughts on Advocacy Education in Higher Education

> Higher education remains resistant to change, even though there is insurmountable evidence that something is wrong and continues to be wrong despite present efforts to make things right. Glimmers of hope appear, but thus far academia has failed to reach to the heart of the problem. (Turner, Myers, & Creswell, 1997, p. 49)

At least superficially, most higher education institutions today have committed to supporting many forms of diversity. Yet, those who occupy positions that have traditionally been excluded from higher education discourse are still asserting that their voices are not heard, that they are not well represented in leadership positions, and that their working environments are often hostile and unwelcoming (Clark, Garner, Higonnet, & Katrak, 1996; de Castell & Bryson, 1997; Neumann & Peterson, 1997; Tierney & Bensimon, 1996). These testimonies suggest that the "inclusive university" that Turner, Myers, and Creswell (1997) describe as "hospitable, engaging, and supportive providing opportunities for all historically disadvantaged groups" (p. 45) is not yet a reality. We operate in both gendered and raced space that shapes the participation of current and potential participants. It is in everyone's best interests to foster dialogic communities in which we can see, hear, and feel (at least partially) the material effects of each other's life experiences. In this historical moment, higher education needs teachers, researchers, and advocates if we are truly to understand and benefit from the diverse participants and paradigms of which we are a part.

Note

1. According to the Coordinator of Minority Student Services, African American students voted to impose a fee upon themselves for the building and maintenance of the Center. This fee was supported after other attempts to generate support for the funding had failed. It is no longer in place.

References

Carter, D., Pearson C., & Shavlik, D. (1996). Double jeopardy: Women of color in higher education. In C. Turner, M. Garcia, A. Nora, & L. I. Rendon (Eds.) *Racial and ethnic diversity in higher education* (pp. 460–464). Needham Heights, MA: Simon & Schuster. Originally published in 1987.

Chang, M. (2002). Preservation or transformation: Where's the real educational discourse on diversity? *Review of Higher Education*, 25(2), 125–140.

Clark, V. A., Garner, S. N., Higonnet, M. R. Katrak, K. (1996). *Antifeminism in the academy*. New York: Routledge.

Collins, P. H. (1990). Defining black feminist thought. In S. Madison (Ed.) *The woman that I am* (pp. 578–600). New York: St. Martin's Griffin.

Collins, P. H. (1991). *Black feminist thought: Knowledge, consciousness, and the politics of empowerment*. New York: Routledge.

Collins, P. H. (1996). The social construction of Black feminist thought. In C. Turner, M. Garcia, A. Nora, & L. I. Rendon (Eds.) *Racial and ethnic diversity in higher education* (pp. 115–133). Needham Heights, MA: Simon & Schuster.

Davis, A. (1983). *Women, race, and class*. New York: Vintage Books.

De Castell, S., & Bryson, M. (1997). *Radical in(ter)ventions: Identity, politics, and difference/s in educational praxis*. Albany: State University of New York.

De La Luz Reyes, M., & Hamlcon, J. J. (1998). Racism in academia: The old wolf revisited. *Harvard Educational Review*, 58(3), 299–314.

Delpit, L. (1993). The silenced dialogue: Power and pedagogy in educating other people's children. In L. Weis & M. Fine (Eds.) *Beyond silenced voices: Class, race, and gender in United States schools* (pp. 119–139). Albany: State University of New York.

Ellsworth, E. (1992). Why doesn't this feel empowering? Working through the repressive myths of critical pedagogy. In C. Luke & J. Gore (Eds.) *Feminism and critical pedagogy* (pp. 90–119). New York: Routledge.

Fine, M. (1994). Dis-stance and other stances: Negotiations of power inside feminist research. In A. Gitlin (Ed.) *Power and method: Political activism and educational research* (pp. 13–35). New York: Routledge.

Foster, M. (1997, June). *Insider research: What counts as critical*. Keynote address at the Reclaiming voice: Ethnographic Inquiry and Qualitative Research in a Postmodern Age conference, Los Angeles, CA.

Foucault, M. (1978). *The history of sexuality: An introduction*. (Vol. 1). New York: Random House.

Frankenberg, R. (1993). *White women, race matters: The social construction of whiteness*. Minneapolis: University of Minnesota Press.

Freire, P. (1970). *Pedagogy of the oppressed*. New York: Continuum.

Greene, M. (1995). *Releasing the imagination: Essays on education, the arts, and social change*. San Francisco: Jossey-Bass.

Gumport, P. J., & Snydman, S. K. (2002). The formal organization of knowledge: An analysis of academic structure. *Journal of Higher Education*, 73(3), 375–408.

Harris, A. P. (1997). Race and essentialism in feminist legal theory. In A. K. Wing (Ed.) *Critical race feminism: A reader* (pp. 11–18). New York: New York University.

Hassard, J. (1993). Postmodernism and organizational analysis: An overview. In J. Hassard & M. Parker (Eds.) *Postmodernism and organizations* (pp. 1–24). Newbury Park, CA: Sage.

Hollingsworth, S. (1994). *Teacher research and urban literacy education*. New York: Teachers College Press.

hooks, b. (1994). *Teaching to transgress: Education as the practice of freedom*. New York: Routledge.

hooks, b. (2000). *Feminism is for everybody*. Cambridge, MA: South End Press.

Hurtado, A. (1989). Relating to privilege: Seduction and rejection in the subordination of white women and women of color. *Signs*, 14(4), 833–855.

Hurtado, S., Milem, J., Clayton-Pederson, A., & Allen, W. (1998). Enhancing campus climates for racial/ethnic diversity: Educational policy and practice. *Review of Higher Education*, 21(3), 279–302.

Kezar, A., & Eckel, P. (2002). The effect of institutional culture on change strategies in higher education: University principles or culturally responsive concepts? *Journal of Higher Education*, 73(4), 435–460.

King, J. (1991). Dysconscious racism, ideology, identity and the miseducation of teachers. *Journal of Negro Education*, 60, 135–145.

Kolodny, A. (1996). Paying the price of antifeminist intellectual harassment. In V. Clark, S. N. Garner, M. Higonnet, & K. H. Katrak (Eds.) *Antifeminism in the academy* (pp. 3–33). New York: Routledge.

Kraemer, B. A. (1997). The academic and social integration of Hispanic students into college. *Review of Higher Education*, 20(2), 163–180.

Ladson-Billings, G. (1997). For colored girls who have considered suicide when the academy's not enough: Reflections of an African American woman scholar. In A. Neumann & P. Peterson (Eds.) *Learning from our lives: Women, research, and autobiography in education* (pp. 52–70). New York: Teachers College.

Lather, P. (1986). Issues of validity in openly ideological research: Between a rock and a soft place. *Interchange*, 17(4), 63–84.

Lather, P. (1991). *Getting smart: Feminist research and pedagogy with/in the postmodern*. New York: Routledge.

Lather, P. (1994). Fertile obsession: Validity after poststructuralism. In A. Gitlin (Ed.) *Power and method: Political activism and educational research* (pp. 36–60). New York: Routledge.

Lerner, G. (1986). *The creation of patriarchy*. New York: Oxford University Press.

Lewis, M. G. (1993). *Without a word: Teaching beyond women's silence*. New York: Routledge.

Linstead, S. (1993). Deconstruction in the study of organizations. In J. Hassard & M. Parker (Eds.) *Postmodernism and organizations* (pp. 49–70). Newbury Park, CA: Sage.

Lorde, A. (1984). *Sister outsider: Essays and speeches*. Trumansburg, NY: Crossing.

Markie, P. J. (1994). *Professor's duties: Ethical issues in college teaching*. Lanham, MD: Rowman & Littlefield.

McCarthy, C. (1990). *Race and curriculum*. New York: Falmer Press.

Minnich, E., Rosenfeld, R. A., & O'Barr, J. F. (1988). *Reconstructing the academy: Women's education and women's studies*. Chicago: University of Chicago.

Neumann, A., & Peterson, P. (1997). *Learning from our lives: Women, research, and autobiography in education*. New York: Teachers College.

Orner, M. (1992). Interrupting the calls for student voice in "liberatory" education: A feminist poststructuralist perspective. In C. Luke & J. Gore (Eds.) *Feminism and critical pedagogy* (pp. 74–89). New York: Routledge.

Pagano, J. (1991). Moral fictions: The dilemma of theory and practice. In C. Witherell & N. Noddings (Eds.) *Stories lives tell: Narrative and dialogue in education* (pp. 193–206). New York: Teachers College.

Pinar, W. F. (1993). Notes on understanding curriculum as a racial text. In C. McCarthy & W. Crichlow (Eds.) *Race, identity, and representation in education* (pp. 60–70). New York: Routledge.

Reinharz, S. (1992). *Feminist methods in social research*. New York: Oxford University.

Roman, L. (1993). White is a color! White defensiveness, postmodernism, and antiracist pedagogy. In C. McCarthy & W. Crichlow (Eds.) *Race, identity, and representation in education* (pp. 71–88). New York: Routledge.

Romany, C. (1997). Ain't I a feminist? In A. K. Wing (Ed.) *Critical race feminism: A reader* (pp. 19–26). New York: New York University.

Ropers-Huilman, B. (1997). Constructing feminist teachers: Complexities of identity. *Gender and Education*, 9(3), 327–343.

Ropers-Huilman, B. (1998). *Feminist teaching in theory and practice: Situating power and knowledge in poststructural classrooms*. New York: Teachers College.

Rosenberg, R. (1992). *Divided lives: American women in the twentieth century*. New York: Hill & Wang.

Sleeter, C. (1993). How white teachers construct race. In C. McCarthy & W. Crichlow (Eds.) *Race, identity, and representation in education* (pp. 157–171). New York: Routledge.

Stanton, D. C., & Stewart, A. J. (1995). *Feminisms in the academy*. Ann Arbor: University of Michigan.

Sypnowich, C. (1996). Some disquiet about "difference." In M. F. Rogers (Ed.) *Multicultural experiences, multicultural theories* (pp. 278–291). New York: McGraw-Hill.

Tierney, W. G. (1994). On method and hope. In A. Gitlin (Ed.) *Power and method: Political activism and educational research* (pp. 97–115). New York: Routledge.

Tierney, W. G., & Bensimon, E. M. (1996). *Promotion and tenure: Community and socialization in academe*. Albany: State University of New York.

Tierney, W. G., & Rhoads, R. A. (1993). Postmodernism and critical theory in higher education: Implications for research and practice. In J. C. Smart (Ed.) *Higher education: Handbook of theory and research* (pp. 308–343). New York: Agathon.

Turner, C. S. V., Myers, S. L., & Creswell, J. W. (1997). Bittersweet success: Faculty of color in academe. Paper presented at the Annual Meeting of the Association for the Study of Higher Education, Albuquerque, NM.

Walker, A. (1983). *In search of our mother's gardens: Womanist prose*. San Diego: Harcourt Brace Jovanovich.

Wing, A. K. (1997a). Brief reflections toward a multiplicative theory and practice of being. In A. K. Wing (Ed.) *Critical race feminism: A reader* (pp. 27–34). New York: New York University.

Wing, A. K. (1997b). *Critical race feminism: A reader*. New York: New York University.

Wolf, M. (1992). *A thrice told tale: Feminism, postmodernism and ethnographic responsibility*. Stanford, CA: Stanford University.

Yamato, G. (1990). Something about the subject makes it hard to name. In G. Anzaldua (Ed.) *Making face, making soul: Haciendo caras: Creative and critical perspectives by feminists of color* (pp. 20–24). San Francisco: Aunt Lute.

SEEKING SELF-AUTHORSHIP

THE WORLD OF EDUCATORS

M.B. MAGOLDA

I want them [students in winter biology] to appreciate the breadth of zoology and its connections to other disciplines. How do we put together disparate ideas? I'll use my research as examples of how one approaches problems. I want them to understand how information is gained. I want them to appreciate what facts really mean. Tentative facts. That's what all of science is. Subject to change and revision.

—Chris Snowden, Professor, Zoology

I take sociology as my minor. It is all opinions, not hard-core facts where you are wrong [like winter biology]. I know he tried to play it off like there is still a lot of research, that it is a really new concept I guess, but still there is some stuff that is [fact]—like freezing cells. I understand what he was trying to do. He was trying to give examples to show what happened. But if he had just said cryoprotectants whatever, just said the point, I would believe him because he is the teacher. I don't need the proof. It's not like I'm going to argue with him about it.

—Ann, Student, Zoology

Ann is a college senior taking Chris Snowden's winter biology course, an upper division course offered through the zoology department. It is clear that she and Chris come from different perspectives about the nature of science. Ann views it as "hard-core facts" and interpreted Chris's examples as attempts to prove to her what happened. She did not believe his portrayal of cryobiology (the study of life at cold temperatures) as an evolving field; she preferred for him to just tell her the facts that she is sure exist. Chris, in contrast, views science as tentative facts, subject to revision. As he attempts to get Ann and her peers to appreciate how information is gained, she is busy trying to get the right answers. Most likely, he is unaware of the view Ann holds about science versus sociology and how it affects her learning in his course. Simultaneously, although Ann hears Chris describe cryobiology as an evolving field, her meaning-making system has no room for the idea the way Chris means it. So Ann interprets it within the framework of her current understanding about knowledge and how it is acquired. This gap between instructor and student repeats itself daily across classrooms, disciplines, and institutions, making engaging students effectively in learning a major challenge.

The challenge is complicated by diversity in students' views of knowledge. For example, Erica, who sits two seats away at the same lab table from Ann, offered this perspective on winter biology:

He has done a very good job at identifying controversial issues and not only with his lectures but also with our experience, with our individual topics. I think that we have all learned that it is an evolving field and there is always more knowledge that is needed to explain exactly what is going on. Overall with the topics he has introduced we got an overall feel for the scientific processes involved. Now writing the grant proposal, I think that is the other part of his goal is to demonstrate that there is a lot more that needs to be known about whatever particular topic that we are doing. To me that is the point of the grant proposal—to get a feel for what else needs to be known.

Reprinted from *Creating Contexts for Learning and Self-Authorship: Constructive-Developmental Pedagogy*, by Marcia B. Baxter Magolda (1999), by permission of Vanderbilt University Press.

Erica, also a senior, accepted the uncertainty Chris demonstrated through introducing controversy and focused on learning the scientific processes involved. For reasons probably unbeknown to Chris, Erica was more amenable to his approach than was Ann. One reason is that she holds different assumptions about knowledge from those Ann holds. The comments of a third student in the course illuminate these dynamics.

Lynn, a graduate student in the course, explained having held both sets of assumptions in her experience in science:

> You read it in black and white, and that is just the way it is. That carries over when you start reading scientific literature because you read a scientific paper and you do an experiment. It is in writing and in black and white, and that is the way it is. You see a little bit more of the process in how they came to conclusions, but it is still—it takes a while to start reading literature critically. If somebody did the experiment and they published it, it has to be right, it is true. And then when you pick one part and start reading all of the literature, all the publications on that narrow focus, you start realizing there are a lot of people out there who disagree and then will come up with contradicting results. That is a really strange thing! If this person's right because they got it published and this person is right because they got it published, that doesn't work because they both can't be right all of the time. . . . That is a really neat shift to start reading that literature and realizing that these people, it kind of goes hand in hand that the names on these papers are human beings and reading the literature, and realizing because they are human beings their research is not always perfect either and they can come to misleading conclusions, or their data could be skewed or whatever, which could lead to different conclusions. To some extent you can become critical of the research and you can also realize that the people are human. So that can make you more critical of the research but it really makes you put it together more. . . . I think it is tough because people always tell you it is just one of those assumptions you have. I am not sure what actually it is that knocks your assumptions off and makes you realize that "big deal, this person published." It is in black and white; that doesn't mean it is put upon a pedestal and it is right and it is truth and that is the end, that is it period. There is always dot, dot, dot at the end. I think that everyone is going to reach that stage at different points. I reached that stage toward the end of undergrad, probably not until my senior year.

The progression Lynn recounts is the shift from viewing knowledge as certain to viewing it as uncertain. Along with the shift, authorities become human and subsequently fallible. As Lynn eloquently points out, this shift is necessary for students to meet Chris's goal for them to appreciate science as tentative facts. If Chris is to reach his goal and prepare his students to function effectively in their future work, he must try to create the conditions for this shift to occur. As a teacher, Chris Snowden faces a substantive challenge as he tries to reach Ann and Erica, as well as the rest of the class, in his course.

Chris Snowden's experience is typical of many college faculty struggling with engaging learners meaningfully. Most believe that contemporary society demands citizens who are lifelong learners. The information age, the fast-changing nature of work, and the increasing diversity of people and cultures mean that simply taking a body of knowledge from college to adult life is insufficient. Productive citizens, no matter what their role in adult life, must know how to learn as conditions change. College faculties want students to think critically, to know how to inquire, to think for themselves, and to be capable of using relevant information to make informed decisions. Educational reformers tell us that our traditional style of teaching—giving students information—does not yield that outcome. Yet when many of us genuinely try to engage students differently, we become the source of their dissatisfaction. Although Parker Palmer wrote that "dissatisfaction may be a sign that real education has happened" (1998, 94), many faculty fear it. Some faculty react by retreating into the "good old ways," despite evidence that those ways are ineffective. Some faculty blame the students: they are not like they used to be, they are not motivated, they care only about themselves, and they are underprepared due to ill-conceived innovations in secondary schools. Nevertheless, many faculty continue to search for new ways to reach students, for new ways to help students construct knowledge effectively for themselves. How people learn, and how to translate that to educational practice, is one of the most important questions in reforming undergraduate education today (George 1996). This book is intended to help college faculty create the conditions in which students learn to construct knowledge.

I advance constructive-developmentalism as the theoretical foundation of creating such conditions. A constructive-developmental view of learning incorporates two major concepts: (1) that students construct knowledge by organizing and making meaning of their experiences, and (2) that this construction takes place in the context of their evolving assumptions about knowledge itself and students' role in creating it. Piaget's (1932) notion that people construct their reality by virtue of organizing their experiences stands at the foundation of this view. Perry (1970) pointed out that human beings organize meaning, and he laid the groundwork for theories of how assumptions about the nature, limits, and certainty of knowledge evolve during adult life. Numerous frameworks are now available to describe evolving assumptions about knowledge and how they mediate learning; they are described in chapter 2. The goal of learning from this view is what Kegan (1994) calls self-authorship, or the ability to reflect upon one's beliefs, organize one's thoughts and feelings in the context of, but separate from, the thoughts and feelings of others, and literally make up one's own mind.

A constructive-developmental view of teaching takes these two major concepts as central to the teaching-learning interaction. Kegan (1994) points out that knowing *what* our students understand is insufficient; rather, we must know the *way* they understand it. By this he means knowing their organizing principles or assumptions for making meaning of their experience. Teaching, then, becomes a matter of understanding and welcoming students' ways of making meaning and simultaneously engaging them in a journey toward more complex ways of making meaning. Numerous authors (summarized later in this chapter) have advanced conceptualizations of constructive-developmental teaching. These conceptualizations revolve around using students' ways of organizing their experience as a foundation for exploring more complex ways of organizing experience.

Three characteristics of this book distinguish it from contemporary books on teaching. First, the book's overarching purpose is to articulate a form of pedagogy that promotes *self-authorship* in addition to subject mastery. Self-authorship extends beyond critical thinking or making informed judgments because it is not a skill; it is, rather, a way a making meaning of the world and oneself. This concept is inextricably linked to the second characteristic of this book—students' epistemological development.

Contemporary literature advocates connecting with students' experience as a foundation for engaging them in meaningful learning. A dimension of students' experience that is often overlooked, however, is their *intellectual or epistemological development*. Ann, Erica, and Lynn respond differently to Chris Snowden's pedagogy because they hold different epistemic assumptions about the nature, limits, and certainty of knowledge. Research shows that college students' epistemic assumptions range from believing that knowledge is certain and possessed by authorities (Ann's view) to knowledge is uncertain and knowledge claims are possible after exploring the relevant information (Lynn's view). Generally, students move from the certain toward the uncertain sets of assumptions during college (Baxter Magolda 1992; Belenky, Clinchy, Goldberger, and Tarule 1986; King and Kitchener 1994; Perry 1970). Self-authorship is possible only from the latter set of assumptions and is often not achieved during college. Students like Ann who expect authorities to give the answers cannot immediately change their assumptions to self-author their own views. After all, these assumptions are the result of years of schooling in which students are socialized to accept authority and memorize knowledge. Thus, they need experiences like the ones Lynn described to help them reorganize their epistemic assumptions. Pedagogy that fails to take students' current epistemic assumptions into account often fails to engage them meaningfully. A central component of this book is articulating a form of pedagogy that hinges on students' epistemic development to help them move toward self-authorship.

The third unique characteristic of this book is its specific purpose: to identify the *structure* and *process* of implementing constructive-developmental pedagogy in the context of students' epistemological development. Many writers have advanced pedagogies based on student experience, self-authorship, or epistemological development; their work is explored further in this chapter. The description of pedagogy in this book is consistent with and indebted to those writers. My intention, however, is to push our understanding of constructive-developmental pedagogy farther. A previous longitudinal study (Baxter Magolda 1992) using extensive interviews with college students identified the underlying structure of such a pedagogy, or the basic principles that make pedagogy constructive-developmental. A second study involving extensive course observations (including Chris Snowden's winter biology course) and interviews with instructors and students is the source of my descriptions of various processes through which college faculty used constructive-developmental pedagogy to promote self-authorship. Constructive-developmental pedagogy, as it is described in this book, is more than letting students talk and generate their own ideas. It is a matter of creating the developmental conditions that allow them to generate their own ideas effectively, in essence to develop their minds, their voices, and themselves.

Before proceeding, let me clarify what constructive-developmental pedagogy is *not*. Often educators hear the notion of students developing their own minds as students constructing knowledge without regard to existing knowledge. An example from a recent issue of the *Chronicle of Higher Education* illustrates this reaction. Reacting to calls for students to take a more active role in teaching and learning, Kenneth Stunkel wrote that "the best of all worlds for interactive pedagogy is to eliminate the professor altogether, to let students 'take control of their own learning'" (1998, A52). Stunkel interprets calls for student involvement as calls for student control and what he refers to as "self-instruction." This is not what I mean by constructive-developmental pedagogy. Inherent in developing one's mind is learning complex processes for constructing knowledge in order to become capable of joining knowledge communities in doing so.

Chris Snowden's pedagogy clarifies what students learning to construct knowledge means in constructive-developmental pedagogy. Chris views science as subject to revision through ongoing scholarly research and discussion among scientists. His course objectives, included helping students learn the scholarly process through which the scientific community arrives at agreed-upon tentative facts—facts that may be altered by future research and alternate interpretations. Through his teaching, Chris demonstrated the process through which scientific knowledge is socially constructed. He created opportunities for students to learn and practice this process. He did not encourage students to construct knowledge without regard for existing research.

Ira Shor (1992) speaks eloquently to this issue in his discussion of pedagogy that empowers students to think for themselves. He notes that "mutual dialogue is not a know-nothing learning process" (247). Elaborating, he writes,

> [It] does not mean that students have nothing to learn from biology or mathematics or engineering as they now exist. Neither does it mean that students reinvent subject matter each time they study it or that academic expertise of the teacher has no role in the classroom. Formal bodies of knowledge, standard usage, and the teacher's academic background all belong in critical classrooms. As long as existing knowledge is not presented as facts and doctrines to be absorbed without question, as long as existing bodies of knowledge are critiqued and balanced from a multicultural perspective, and as long as the students' own themes and idioms are valued along with standard usage, existing canons are part of critical education. What students and teachers reinvent in problem posing is their relationship to learning and authority. They redefine their relationships to each other, to education, and to expertise. They re-perceive knowledge and power.(35)

Thus, constructive-developmental pedagogy as I describe it in this book is not a know-nothing process. It requires that teachers model the process of constructing knowledge in their disciplines, teach that process to students, and give students opportunities to practice and become proficient at it. As all educators bring their experience, values, and assumptions to this knowledge construction process, so do students; constructive-developmental pedagogy offers opportunities to examine these as they relate to the subject matter and knowledge construction process. Throughout the examples, you will hear educators invite students into the knowledge construction processes of their disciplines, modeling Shor's reinvented relationship to learning and authority rather than an abandonment of existing knowledge.

Much of this book stems from students' thoughts and insights about their learning and the courses that I observed (described later in this chapter). Despite the attention given to connecting to students' experience, writing about teaching is often based on teachers' observations rather than those of students. Understanding students' development and how to promote it requires talking with and listening to students like Ann, Erica, and Lynn. Their stories become the context through which I invite you to explore using constructive-developmental pedagogy to promote self-authorship.

Self-Authorship

Life in contemporary America is complicated. Because the general purpose of education in this country has been to prepare students for productive adult lives, the increasing complexity of adult life in our society requires a complex kind of education. The capacity for lifelong learning is necessary to keep pace with changes in technology, science, the economy, and cultural norms. In every aspect of adult life—both private and public—society demands that people be able to take on responsibility, manage their affairs effectively, and make informed decisions for themselves and their fellow citizens. Robert Kegan (1994) notes that these demands are not merely demands for particular behaviors or skills; rather, they are demands for the way we organize our experience. Referring to ways of organizing experience as "the evolution of consciousness," Kegan describes it as "the personal unfolding of ways of organizing experience that are not simply replaced as we grow but subsumed into more complex systems of mind" (9). This unfolding of ways of organizing experience is what Lynn described at the outset of this chapter. The more complex ways of organizing experience, or of making meaning, are necessary to meet the demands of contemporary adult life. In essence, adult life requires the capacity for self-authorship.

For example, Kegan notes that as workers, adults are expected to "invent or own our work . . . to be self-initiating, self-correcting, self-evaluating . . . to be guided by our own visions . . . to take responsibility for what happens to us . . . to be accomplished masters of our particular work roles, jobs, or careers" (153). These expectations require self-authorship because they require the ability to construct our own visions, make informed decisions in conjunction with coworkers, act appropriately, and take responsibility for those actions. Similarly in the private life domains of parenting and partnering, Kegan sketches demands such as "establish rules and roles; institute a vision of family purpose . . . manage boundaries (inside and outside the family) . . . be psychologically independent from, but closely connected to, our spouses . . . set limits on children, in-laws, oneself, and extrafamily involvements" (86). These expectations, like those in public work life, call for understanding these relationships in a complex way that allows adults to assess and contrast individual and family needs, determine a course of action in connection with but not subsumed by other family members, and take responsibility for those actions. These are not simply skills or behaviors; they emerge from the adults' organization of their experiences and their world.

Self-authorship is simultaneously a cognitive (how one makes meaning of knowledge), interpersonal (how one views oneself in relationship to others), and intrapersonal (how one perceives one's sense of identity) matter. Educators often highlight the cognitive dimension of self-authorship. Learned societies participating in the Association of American Colleges' Liberal Learning, Study-in-Depth, and the Arts and Sciences Major project routinely called for cognitive self-authorship in their reports. The authors of the economics report wrote, "In the economics major we share with other disciplines a desire to empower students with a self-sustaining capacity to think and learn. They should know how to pose questions, collect information, identify and use an appropriate framework to analyze that information, and come to some conclusion" (Association of American Colleges 1990b, 27). The mathematics authors noted that "dealing with complex, open-ended problem situations should be one of the highest priorities of undergraduate mathematics" (85). The interdisciplinary studies report advanced this position:

> We prefer to argue that the ideal IDS graduate will demonstrate intellectual facility having depth, breadth, and synthesis. By depth we mean students must have the necessary technical information about and the methodologies necessary for analysis of a given problem. Students should know how to master the complexities involved in obtaining germane research findings and be aware of the methodologies of the disciplinary contexts in which such information is generated. By breadth we mean students should be exposed to a wide knowledge base and trained to organize information in order to make generalizations from particular cases. By synthesis we mean students should be able to apply integrative skills in order to differentiate and compare different disciplinary perspectives, to clarify how those perspectives relate to the core problem or question, and to devise a resolution based upon the holistic interaction of the various factors and forces involved. (65)

This position articulates the cognitive components of self-authorship advanced by numerous educators and authors of educational reform reports.

Many contemporary educators recognize that the cognitive dimension of self-authorship is intertwined with the interpersonal dimension. Kenneth Bruffee offers an example in the context of the medical profession. He notes that there is a

> perception by many in the medical profession itself that although traditional medical education stuffs young physicians full of facts, it leaves their diagnostic judgment rudimentary and does not develop their ability to interact socially, with either colleagues or patients, over complex, demanding, perhaps life-and-death issues. (1993, 2)

Bruffee's observation indicates that one issue is whether physicians exhibit cognitive self-authorship in making a wise diagnosis on the basis of their knowledge. A second issue, however, is their ability to work effectively with others in interpersonal relationships that play a role in making medical decisions. Bruffee believes that this interpersonal dimension is crucial. He writes, "In any college or university today, mature, effective interdependence—that is, social maturity integrated with intellectual maturity—may be the most important lesson college students should be asked to learn" (1993, 2). Many areas of knowledge blur the lines between cognitive and interpersonal. For example, "most of the critical problems society faces have a biological component. These problems also challenge human values and belief systems. Such subjects as world population, abortion, birth control, acid rain, and biodiversity are central to biology but also reach into the family, economics, and religion" (Association of American Colleges 1990b, 19). These issues require a self-authorship that involves both cognitive and interpersonal dimensions, as do other social issues such as poverty, appreciating diversity, and crime.

These social issues also illustrate Kegan's argument that the intrapersonal dimension is centrally interwoven into self-authorship. Students can learn cognitive inquiry skills, yet not be able to use them to decide what to believe because they have no internal sense of identity or belief system. Adults are aware that they are responsible for making decisions that benefit themselves and their families, yet are unable to take a position different from what important others believe because they have no internally generated belief system. This intrapersonal, internally generated belief system allows for "a construction of the self-as author, maker, critiquer, and remaker of its experience, the self as a system or complex, regulative of its parts" (Kegan 1994, 133). Kegan argues that this sense of self distinguishes persons who are in control of their issues from persons whose issues are in control of them.

Self-authorship, then, is a complicated phenomenon. It is simultaneously an ability to construct knowledge in a contextual world, an ability to construct an internal identity separate from external influences, and an ability to engage in relationships without losing one's internal identity. And higher education has had difficulty enough achieving even the cognitive dimension of self-authorship. The plethora of reports on educational reform in the last decade have charged that undergraduate education is delivered ineffectively, requires passive rather than active learning, does not meaningfully engage students in learning, and does not produce graduates who exhibit self-authorship. After their review of more than 2,600 books and articles on how college affects students, Patrick Terenzini and Ernest Pascarella (1994) posit that the notion that traditional instructional methods provide effective means to teach undergraduates is a myth. They also note,

> Despite the fact that the research evidence, personal experience, and common sense all suggest these assumptions are untenable, most faculty members persist in teaching (and academic administrators encourage it) as if they were true. Individualized and collaborative approaches to instruction are more effective because they respond better to differences in students' levels of preparation, learning styles, and rates. (30)

The Association of American Colleges report (1990a) offers a similar critique:

> The problem is that it [the major] often delivers too much knowledge with too little attention to how that knowledge is being created, what methods and modes of inquiry are employed in its creation, what presuppositions inform it, and what entailments flow from its particular way of knowing. The problem is further compounded when the major ignores questions about relationships between various ways of knowing, and between what students have learned and their lives beyond the academy. (6)

These critiques do not stop at recommending pedagogy that acknowledges the methods and modes of inquiry used in knowledge creation. Connecting what students have learned with their lives beyond the classroom has also become a central component of educational reform prescriptions. This is more complex than applying classroom learning to life outside the classroom. Connecting to students' lived experience means using it as a foundation from which they can explore knowledge and determine what to believe. *Powerful Partnerships: A Shared Responsibility for Learning* (American Association for Higher Education, American College Personnel Association, National Association of Student Personnel Administrators 1998) stresses,

> Rich learning experiences and environments require and enable students to make connections . . . through opportunities to relate their own experience and knowledge to materials being learned; . . . and through pedagogies emphasizing critical analysis of conflicting views and demanding that students make defensible judgments about and demonstrate linkages among bodies of knowledge. (3)

Self-authorship is impossible unless students are able to connect learning with their lived experiences; self-authorship requires making meaning of one's own experience. Parker Palmer asserts that teaching that transforms people occurs only when it "connects with the inward, living core of our students' lives" (1998, 31)—a core he describes as the inner voice of identity and integrity.

The National Science Foundation's recent report *Shaping the Future: New Expectations for Undergraduate Education in Science, Mathematics, Engineering, and Technology* recommends that science, mathematics, engineering, and technology faculty

> believe and affirm that every student can learn, and model good practices that increase learning; start with the student's experience, but have high expectations within a supportive climate; and build inquiry, a sense of wonder and the excitement of discovery, plus communication and teamwork, critical thinking, and life-long learning skills into learning experiences. (1996, 4)

Similarly, the Association of American Colleges report captures the integration of student experience in learning:

> Every student should experience the intellectual excitement that comes from the capacity to extend the known to the unknown and to discern previously unsuspected relationships. Developing these capacities requires acceptance of specific imperatives. Students must be willing to revise what they have held previously as certain by shifting perspectives and they must engage in the kind of collaborative work in which they become open to criticism. This implies an academic community that sees as an important value of liberal learning bringing private precept into public discourse. It implies equally an academic community that insists that difference be negotiated with civility. Public civil discourse depends, among other conditions, on an ethos of corrigibility. Faculty members must take seriously what students believe about a given subject and engage their prior knowledge so that new learning restructures the old, complicating and correcting it rather than merely living side by side with it. (1990a, 12–13)

This vision of learning recognizes that asking students to shift their epistemic assumptions and reevaluate knowledge claims hinges on acknowledging what they currently believe. Starting with student experience and encouraging reevaluation of how to interpret what one believes lead to restructuring one's views. When faculty ignore student experience, students gather information that lives alongside their own views—a form of education that does not promote self-authorship. Self-authorship requires evaluating one's own views in light of existing evidence and constructing a reasonable perspective as a result.

Learning Centered Educational Practice

Wide-ranging critiques including those mentioned here have prompted serious reflection on and reconceptualization of education and teaching in the last decade. Among the outcomes are contemporary views of pedagogy that take a learning-centered approach rather than the traditional teaching-centered approach. The teaching-centered approach focused on knowledge acquisition and control whereas the learning-centered approach focuses on student experience as a context for introducing, working with, and constructing knowledge. Robert Barr and John Tagg (1995) offer a detailed account of this paradigm shift and its implications for educational practice. They describe the instruction paradigm's mission as delivering instruction and transferring knowledge from faculty to students; the learning paradigm's mission is instead producing learning and eliciting student discovery and construction of knowledge. Many contemporary visions of pedagogy place student experience in the foreground, and many build on the experience-based learning notions advanced by John Dewey and Jean Piaget. Highlighting a few of these perspectives is useful here to illustrate advances in thinking about pedagogy as well as to show the missing dimensions in developing pedagogy to promote self-authorship. It is not my intention to offer a comprehensive review of this literature, a task that would require numerous volumes, but to identify major strands of thinking that enlighten the learning-centered approach.

The perspectives I have chosen to highlight here are not all in agreement; these writers may not see themselves as endorsing common perspectives about pedagogy. I use them here to note the dimensions of student experience, self-authorship, and student development. Using these dimensions, advocates of basing teaching on student experience can be organized into three broad categories. The first includes proponents of constructivist teaching, collaborative learning, use of narrative, and incorporating care in education who endorse students' experience and support the notion of self-authorship without placing it clearly as the end goal. A second category includes liberatory, empowering, and critical educators who advance self-authorship as a central goal. What distinguishes the third category from these two is the inclusion of student development. This category, comprised primarily of educators with developmental psychology backgrounds, emphasizes student experience as the foundation for learning, directly advocates promoting self-authorship, and incorporates student development as a central component in the process. A brief overview of these perspectives serves as the context for the view of constructive-developmental pedagogy presented in this book. This overview is not intended to be a comprehensive review of these approaches; rather, it gives prominence to work that speaks to the dimensions of interest here.

An Emphasis on Student Experience

A discussion of student experience inevitably begins with educator and philosopher John Dewey's (1916) conceptualization of education as the reorganization and reconstruction of experience. Knowledge, for Dewey, meant "the working capital, the indispensable resources, of further inquiry; of finding out, or learning, more things" (1916, 158). He viewed thinking as discovering connections between actions and their consequences. Dewey argued accordingly that thinking must start with experience, that thinking could not be cultivated separately from experience. This line of thinking led Dewey to remark "the first approach to any subject in school, if thought is to be aroused and not words acquired, should be as unscholastic as possible" (1916, 154). He meant that experience from students' everyday lives should be used as the starting point, and that course work causing reflection in everyday life would arouse thinking. Problems for reflection must be situated in students' experience rather than imposed by teachers for the purpose of teaching a specific school topic. In Dewey's view the latter did not elicit pursuit of the connections between experiences and their consequences. Dewey believed that learning should be an active process in which students relied on their own experiences and available data from others to work through a problem, to generate inferences and tentative explanations or, in his words, "ideas." Students then should be given opportunities to further develop their ideas and test them to determine their value. Thinking requires experience, activity, and reflection, thus requiring joint effort of the teacher and students rather than the teacher providing students with information.

The joint effort of teacher and students also characterizes collaborative approaches. Kenneth Bruffee takes the position that knowledge is socially constructed, noting that "collaborative learning assumes . . . that knowledge is a consensus among the members of a community of knowledgeable peers—something people construct by talking together and reaching agreement" (1993, 3). Teachers are members of a knowledge community that students want to join, but students need to become fluent in the knowledge community's language to do so. The teacher, in order to help them make this transition, needs not only to be knowledgeable in her or his community, but also to be able to converse in the students' community. The skill to converse in both communities helps the teacher facilitate the students' increasing fluency in the new knowledge community. Students' experience is the source of the teacher learning to converse in their community. As students become members of the new knowledge community, their participation in "talking together and reaching agreement" implies the need for self-authorship—constructing their own perspectives in the context of the knowledge community.

The central nature of the students' role in this joint teacher-student work is evident in the current use of constructivism theory in teaching. Constructivism "describes knowledge as temporary, developmental, non-objective, internally constructed, and socially and culturally mediated" (Twomey Fosnot 1996, ix). Piaget's explanation of meaning-making stands at the foundation of this view. His concept of equilibration (1970, 1977) involved encountering discrepancies between one's way of structuring the world and experience that prompted the person to bring the two back into balance. When rebalancing takes the form of altering one's structure to accommodate the new experience, growth and change occur. Thus, learning begins with the students' understanding of their experience and engages them in remaking meaning of their experiences. Applying constructivist theory to educational practice, von Glasersfeld notes, "The teacher must listen to the student, interpret what the student does and says, and try to build up a 'model' of the student's conceptual structures" (1995, 14). Without understanding the student's conceptual structures, Von Glasersfeld argues that changing the student "can be no more than a hit or miss affair" (1995, 15). Linda Lambert and her colleagues (1995) advocate learning activities that help learners access their experiences, knowledge, and beliefs; that allow for sharing ideas with others; and that offer opportunities for reflection and metacognition. Helping students make meaning of their experience and reshaping conceptual structures is advocating the development of self-authorship. By virtue of its reliance on Piaget, this literature also acknowledges the role of development in learning, albeit in a relatively abstract way.

Feminist scholarship has contributed substantially to the centrality of student experience, and to some degree student development, in learning. Nancy Schniedewind's (1987) discussion of feminist values for teaching emphasizes developing mutual respect, trust, and community in the classroom; shared leadership (or participatory decision making); cooperative structure; integration of cognitive and affective learning; and action to transform values. Schniedewind characterizes feminist education in this way: "We enter into a dialogue with our students, meeting them as human beings, and learning with them in community" (179). The concepts of empowering students to find their own voices, learning from the base of their own experience, and learning in connection with others are central features of feminist pedagogy (Shrewsbury 1987). Yet feminist scholarship moves beyond the role of student experience to the relational nature of the teaching/learning enterprise.

Becky Ropers-Huilman's study of feminist teachers revealed that they responded to student experience by shifting the content and its expression to respond to students' learning positions, and they also "cared about students' experiences both in and out of the classroom" (1998, 46). bell hooks writes that the learning process comes easiest to those who believe teachers' work "is not merely to share information but to share in the intellectual and spiritual growth of our students" (1994, 13). She advocates teaching in a way that "respects and cares for the souls of our students" (13). The value of caring in the teaching relationship stems from the belief that learning is a relational process in which connections to others and to one's own experience make learning more meaningful (Gilligan 1982; Lyons 1993). Gloria Ladson-Billings (1994) advocates a connectedness with students as a key characteristic of effective social relations in teaching. Nel Noddings (1984), using the terms *receptivity*, *relatedness*, and *responsiveness* to characterize caring, advocates maintenance and enhancement of caring as "the primary aim of every educational institution and of every educational effort" (172). Translating caring to teaching practice, Noddings wrote,

> The teacher receives and accepts the student's feeling toward the subject matter; she looks at it and listens to it through his eyes and ears. How else can she interpret the subject matter for him? As she exercises this inclusion, she accepts *his* motives, reaches toward what *he* intends, so long as these motives and intentions do not force an abandonment of her own ethic. (177)

This relationship gives the teacher access to students' perspectives, which she then uses as context to convey her subject matter. Working from the students' motives enhances learning, yet the teacher's motives must be included as well. Self-authorship is implied in helping students pursue their own intentions while learning to understand and interpret the subject matter.

Parker Palmer, acknowledging the value of the feminists' notion of hearing people into speech, advocates a similar stance. He emphasizes "making space for the other, being aware of the other, paying attention to the other, honoring the other" (1998, 46). Palmer notes that teachers who enter empathically into their students' worlds have the potential to be perceived by students as persons able to hear the students' truth. This potential is crucial if student and teacher are to jointly engage in constructing knowledge and if the student is to see herself as a potential author of her own knowledge. bell hooks states that empowering students to author their knowledge also requires teachers committed to their own self-actualization, ones willing to take risks, express vulnerability, and share their own experience in learning settings.

Proponents of narrative in teaching most clearly make the link between student experience and self-authorship. Richard Hopkins (1994) offers narrative as the new root metaphor for education:

> The idea of narrative might provide a cohesive, even protogenic, operating principle for tying lived experience to subject matter in schools. Narrative is a deeply human, linguistic process, a kind of primal developmental impulse. We are storytelling creatures. We do not just tell stories; we live them, create them, define ourselves through them. Our narratives are the expressive, temporal medium through which we construct our functioning personae and give meaning to our experience. (xvi)

Arguing for the primacy of experience in education, Hopkins describes learning as reconstructive query involving "periods of exploration, data gathering, and seeking . . . alternating with periods of reflection, analysis, synthesis, and expressive judgment" (152). When students construct their own stories, incorporating their own lived experience, they are able to open their minds to new challenges and experiences that prompt reconstruction. As a result, narrative education calls for critical thinking and highlights the importance of choice and agency in living one's life.

This reconstruction through narrative is not limited to learning subject matter. Although Hopkins does not use the term *self-authorship*, he links narrative with self-growth and subsequently links education with self-growth, thus using a conceptualization of learning that encompasses multiple dimensions. Other advocates of narrative agree that it is a process through which we envision who we will become (e.g., Bruner 1990; Kerby 1991; Polkinghorne 1988; Witherell and Noddings 1991). The notion of constructing oneself is a part of the process of achieving self-authorship.

An Emphasis on Self-Authorship

A second body of literature on educational reform and pedagogy focuses on liberatory, empowering, and critical education. The primary goal of these visions of education is to empower people to overcome domination. Self-authorship as I have defined it in this chapter is not discussed in these works; however, it is inherent in both the process and the intended outcome of this type of education. Because it teaches students to challenge all authorized knowledge claims, it encourages complex assumptions about knowledge. Paulo Freire's work stands at the core of liberatory education. Freire argued that banking education (or depositing knowledge into students' heads) reproduced culture in its current form, thereby maintaining the oppression of those whose experience was not the basis of the knowledge deposited. Freire's alternative, liberating education, focused instead on a mutual search for knowledge in which learning is jointly owned by students and teachers. The search begins in the students' experience from which teachers and students pose problems for pursuit. Academic subjects become lenses through which they reflect on problems related to their own lives. Freire believed that students became increasingly interested in the problems posed because they could see connections to their own experience and world, and became therefore more critical in their thinking as they reflected on these problems. Freire's goal was to help students recognize their power to reorganize knowledge and society, to think critically to discover meaning in the world and experience, to see and challenge domination in society, and to act to transform society based on that critique (1988; first published in 1970). These achievements necessitate self-authorship, and the joint pursuit of problems relevant to students' lives offers a mechanism for its development.

Ira Shor's account of empowering education adds specificity to Freire's liberatory approach. He suggests that learning starts from the lived experience that students bring to the learning situation, a condition that enhances their participation and their affect toward academic work. It proceeds forward as the teacher and students engage in dialogue or "reflect together on the meaning of their experience and their knowledge" (1992, 86). This democratic process involves shared authority in developing class plans and discussions, selecting themes to address, and summarizing progress. Shor proposed listening to students first, in essence to gain exposure to their language, feelings, and knowledge, in order to establish a base from which to structure the subject matter. Once this foundation is established, the teacher can structure a learning environment in which the students and teacher become coinvestigators of the subject matter. The dialogue that ensues at this point involves students' experience and the teacher's experience, as each explores and exchanges views in learning together. Shor emphasizes that "mutual dialogue is not a know-nothing learning process" (247). The teacher brings her knowledge to the dialogue, but rather than imposing it unilaterally, she introduces it in the context of the students' perspectives and themes. Dewey made the same point regarding the roles of student and teacher:

> This does not mean that the teacher is to stand off and look on; the alternative to furnishing ready-made subject matter and listening to the accuracy with which it is reproduced is not quiescence, but participation, sharing, in an activity. In such shared activity, the teacher is a learner, and the learner is, without knowing it, a teacher—and upon the whole, the less consciousness there is, on either side, of either giving or receiving instruction, the better. (1916, 160)

Shor argues that mutual inquiry involving the teacher's academic talk and the students' everyday talk transforms both. This transformation in students' "talk" undoubtedly involves a transformation in their meaning-making—the dimension I am calling self-authorship. Shor notes, "By sharing authority and assuming teacherly roles, students take greater responsibility for their educations, which can translate into a more intense relationship between them and the learning process" (1996, 199). Shor's extensive stories of shared authority in his own class (1996) illustrate the complexity and possibility of this approach.

Critical theorists adopted Freire's liberation education in addressing the purpose and nature of education in American society, arguing that education should be aimed at democracy and elimination of oppression and marginalization of various groups. Henry Giroux (1988a) called both radical and conservative educators to task for their indifference to "the politics of voice and representation—the forms of narrative and dialogue—around which students make sense of their lives and schools" (114). He argued that educators must pay attention to "the ways in which students, from different class, gender, and ethnic locations, mediate and express their sense of place, time, and history, and their contradictory, uncertain, and incomplete interactions with each other and with the dynamics of schooling" (114).

Giroux argues that student experience, which he defines as "a historical construction and lived practice that is produced and legitimated within particular social forms" (197), should be the object of inquiry in teaching. Starting with students' knowledge offers the opportunity for the teacher to legitimate that knowledge, but Giroux does not argue for unqualified endorsement of that knowledge. Instead he views critical pedagogy as encouraging

> a critique of dominant forms of knowledge and social practices that semantically and emotionally organize meanings and experiences that give students a sense of voice and identity; similarly, it attempts to provide students with the critical knowledge and skills necessary for them to examine their own particular lived experiences and cultural resources. (197)

Giroux argues for using the way students read the world, or their experience, to make school knowledge meaningful for them. Once it is connected, or made meaningful, it is possible to engage students in critical analysis of their experience and intellectual content.

Peter McLaren (1989) also speaks to education for emancipation with students' experience as a centerpiece of learning. McLaren believes that student experience "is intimately related to identity formation" (1989, 226). How students define themselves stems from their experience of culture and society, an understanding of themselves and the world that they bring to the learning setting. He emphasizes the need for teachers to connect with students' experience and self-definitions in order to engage them in critical learning.

Like Dewey and Freire, critical theorists view education as a means to democracy. They believe that empowering students to critically analyze their experience and dominant knowledge will enable them to change social inequities (Giroux 1988b). Critical pedagogy involves respecting and valuing differences among students while simultaneously engaging in dialogue about practices that structure domination; reclaiming histories of marginalized students in an effort to alter social relations; recognizing the role of popular culture in legitimating various versions of history; and attending to identity as an increasingly complex phenomenon (Carlson and Apple 1998). Critical theorists recognize the role of students' unique experience in learning and advocate helping students develop their own voices.

Feminist scholars in the critical tradition also endorse self-authorship in their emphasis on student empowerment, albeit focused on students' "identity and subjective positionality within and among gender, ethnic, class, sexual and other markers of difference" (Carlson and Apple 1998). Feminist pedagogy explores the authority of the teacher, personal experience as a source of knowledge, and different perspectives based on race, class, and culture (Weiler 1998). Many themes of feminist scholarship are inherent in Frances Maher and Mary Kay Tetreault's explorations of feminist classrooms. They identify four central themes in feminist pedagogy: mastery, voice, authority, and positionality.

Mastery takes the form of interpretation rather than definitive conclusions so that students "seek knowledge on their own terms" (17), an idea akin to self-authorship. On the subject of voice, Maher and Tetrault argue that students shape their voices as they "bring their own questions and perspectives to the material, they use relevant personal experiences to shape a narrative of an emerging self" (18). Opening the classroom to students' explorations and voices necessitated new visions of authority on the part of both students and teachers, visions similar to the shared authority Shor advocates. Finally, Maher and Tetrault note that one's position (e.g., gender, race, class), "perhaps more than any other single factor, influences the construction of knowledge, and that positional factors reflect relationships of power both within and outside the classroom itself" (22). Thus, students' position, as women or members of class or racial groups, is a major component of the "experience" from which they make meaning. The notion of position, the same idea Giroux emphasized, is central to Gloria Ladson-Billings's "culturally relevant pedagogy" (1998, 297)—a pedagogy that builds curriculum and learning experiences around students' cultural backgrounds, yet engages them in a critique of social and political systems that marginalize their culture. These perspectives join the centrality of student experience with the intended outcome of self-authorship.

An Emphasis on Student Development and Self-Authorship

The story of Ann, Erica, and Lynn—students in Chris Snowden's winter biology course—at the outset of this chapter illustrated how each woman's assumptions about knowledge mediated her response to the pedagogy used in the course. Proponents of using students' experience (highlighted in the previous sections) emphasize knowing what students understand as a foundation for teaching. Robert Kegan, a leading constructive-developmental theorist and educator, points out, "It is not enough for us to know what our students understand . . . we must also know 'the way he understands it'" (1994, 278). The *way* students understand reflects the organizing principles they use to make meaning of their experience. In the case of Ann, Erica, and Lynn, these are epistemological principles. A body of literature characterized as constructive-developmental illuminates the epistemological, interpersonal, intrapersonal, and moral ways of making meaning evident in adult life. Constructive-developmentalists regard the aim of education as promoting growth in ways of making meaning. Thus, this body of literature emphasizes use of student experience, promotion of self-authorship (an integral component of complex ways of making meaning in all dimensions), and educational practice developed on the basis of students' ways of making meaning of their experience.

Numerous writers who are both developmental psychologists and educators have advocated using the Piagetian foundation of constructive-developmentalism in higher education for the past forty years. Piaget believed that people constructed their reality by virtue of organizing their experiences. Encountering experiences inconsistent with one's current organization (called dissonance) prompted a need for resolving the discrepancy. Piaget advanced that this resolution took place either through incorporating the new experience into the original organization somehow or, if that failed, through reorganizing to accommodate the new experience. The latter process meant growth to a more complex way of making meaning. Constructive-developmentalists believe (and have research evidence to support it) that growth in meaning-making evolves through eras according to regular principles of stability and change (Kegan 1982). These researchers argue for connecting teaching to students' ways of making meaning in order to create the conditions to promote growth to more complex meaning-making. This requires an understanding of ways of making meaning.

Several factors affect adults' response to dissonance, and these factors form the basis of constructive-developmental pedagogy. Obviously, adults must experience dissonance and be challenged to determine its relationship to their way of making meaning. This often happens by virtue of a teacher's expectations in higher education, as was the case in Chris Snowden's course. Patricia King and Karen Kitchener advocate specific ways to introduce this challenge, including "create multiple opportunities for students to examine different points of view on a topic reflectively" (1994, 237) and "create opportunities and provide encouragement for students to make judgments and to explain what they believe" (238). They also suggest targeting expectations and goals to the development range within which students operate, and they offer several examples of assignments that target various ways of making meaning (1994). This matching of expectations to ways of making meaning entails both challenge to address dissonance and support to do so.

Support for students' current ways of making meaning is central to promoting complex meaning-making. William Perry, the pioneer of understanding adults' ways of making meaning, emphasized the importance of listening to students and respecting their current perspectives (1970). Using his work, Laurent Daloz articulated how to mentor adult students to promote their meaning-making. He suggested, among other things, offering adults a structure for learning based on listening to their ways of making meaning, sharing ourselves in the learning relationship, and recognizing the difficult nature of changing one's way of viewing the world (1986). Daloz painted the developmental picture as a journey through which adults needed companionship and guidance to move successfully.

Robert Kegan extended the concept of providing challenge and support simultaneously, using a bridge metaphor. Placing students on one side of a bridge and the educational goal on the other, he argued that educators must create conditions that simultaneously respect and welcome students' ways of making meaning on their side of the bridge yet facilitate their journey toward the other end (1994). Similarly, Mary Belenky, Blythe Clinchy, Nancy Goldberger, and Jill Tarule offered a midwife metaphor for what they called "connected teaching" (1986). They described a connected teacher as one who shares the process of knowing and serves as midwife to "assist the students in giving birth to their own ideas, in making their own tacit knowledge explicit and elaborating it" (217). The midwife metaphor communicates helping students bring their own ideas forth, helping to preserve them while they are fragile at the beginning, and helping students to develop and share their thoughts. This metaphor illustrates that students' ways of knowing are at the center of the interaction; the teacher's action hinges on staying with that development. The connected teacher emphasizes that learning and the development of knowledge take place in, and are the property of, the student. Although the teacher is connected to the student in this process, she is also objective. She attempts to view the situation through the students' eyes and does not allow her own perspective to disregard the students' thoughts on the matter. The trust inherent in this connected teaching approach helps students develop positive affect toward developing their own thoughts. Self-authorship is the eventual goal, but the teaching process focuses on the students' current ability (or lack thereof) to think for themselves.

Developing Pedagogy to Promote Self-Authorship

Collectively, these perspectives provide a rich foundation from which to construct effective pedagogy that promotes self-authorship. They offer compelling arguments for the incorporation of student experience into learning, provide strong evidence for the importance of self-authorship as a goal of education, and emphasize that attention to the ways students make meaning is warranted. Yet they have been used minimally in higher education, even though many of these ideas have existed for years. The lack of their use stems from numerous sources including perceptions of authority, assumptions about knowledge, organizational models in higher education, and the degree of specificity of these conceptualizations.

Our perspectives on our authority as teachers stem from our own experience. Shor (1992) noted that most teachers experienced passive, competitive, and authoritarian methods in school, learning as a result that "to be a teacher means talking a lot and being in charge" (26). Parker Palmer (1993) argued that teachers' diagnosis of students today is one of the major barriers to good teaching. He captures it like this:

> Briefly stated, this diagnosis holds that the classroom behaviors of many students (e.g., their silence, distraction, and embarrassment) reveal them to be essentially brain-dead (due to poor preparation, the dissolution of decent society, MTV, etc.), and that they therefore require pedagogies that function like life-support systems, dripping information into the veins of comatose patients who are unable to feed themselves. If that is a caricature, it is nevertheless instructive: nothing is easier than to slip into a low opinion of students, and that opinion creates teaching practices guaranteed to induce vegetative states even in students who arrive for class alive and well. (11)

Thus, we hesitate to implement new approaches that entail joint teacher-student authority because we are unsure that this amounts to meeting our responsibilities or that students are capable of participating. Palmer warns that "the way we diagnose our students' condition will determine the kind of remedy we offer" (1998, 41).

Views of knowledge are closely intertwined with these notions of authority. Bruffee explains that traditional education operates from a foundational point of view that assumes "knowledge is a kind of substance contained in and given form by the vessel we call the mind. Teachers transfer knowledge from their own fuller vessels to the less full vessels of their students. Teachers impart knowledge that was imparted to them, as it was imparted to them" (1993, 66). This view of knowledge as something to be transferred places the teacher in the position of authority that Shor described. These assumptions about authority and knowledge are inherent in the organizational models prevalent in both secondary and higher education. Hopkins charges that secondary schools display a complete disregard for student experience because they operate from a machine model. He writes, "This model assumes that adults know what children need to know and that the task of teachers is to get what is known somehow into the consciousness and awareness of students and to create conditions in which they take interest and expend effort" (1994, 12). Numerous reports offer evidence that this machine model is alive and well in higher education. Parker Palmer argues that this kind of education has made spectators of students, and he pleads with educators to draw "students into the process, the community, of knowing" (1990, 12). Articulating the link between views of knowledge and classroom practice, he wrote,

> If we regard truth as something handed down from authorities on high, the classroom will look like a dictatorship. If we regard truth as a fiction determined by personal whim, the classroom will look like anarchy. If we regard truth as emerging from a complex process of mutual inquiry, the classroom will look like a resourceful and interdependent community. (1998, 51)

Finally, the visions of new forms of pedagogy recounted here offer more by way of conceptualization than they do specific processes for implementation. Whereas some of these visions offer foundational principles and examples for implementation, determining how to connect to diverse students' ways of making meaning and how to specifically organize teaching to create conditions conducive to growth of the mind remains illusive. Despite growing dissatisfaction with the perceptions of authority and knowledge noted here, educators often stay with those models because they lack specific alternatives. The current book attempts to move pedagogical reform forward by identifying the structure and process for creating conditions to promote self-authorship as well as evidence to support the effectiveness of such pedagogy.

Structure of Constructive-Developmental Pedagogy

One of the specific purposes of this book is to describe the structure underlying constructive-developmental pedagogy. Structure differs from a collection of techniques because it remains constant and useful across contexts. Structure here refers to the principles underlying constructive-developmental pedagogy that guide educational practice across disciplines, student populations, and learning contexts. These principles—validating students as knowers, situating learning in students' experience, and defining learning as mutually constructing meaning—by their definition connect with students' experience and meaning-making as educators and students interact. The origin of these principles is detailed later in this chapter.

Processes of Constructive-Developmental Pedagogy

Because the structure forms a foundation from which to adapt to diverse students and contexts, multiple possibilities exist for the actual processes for implementing constructive-developmental pedagogy. This book describes specific processes of constructive-developmental pedagogy evident in four higher education courses. Each process is conveyed through accounts of class sessions and analyzed for its relationship to the underlying structure. Students' and faculty's response to these processes are also explored in depth to judge effectiveness of these processes for promoting self-authorship and subject mastery.

Origin of the Structure of Constructive-Developmental Pedagogy

The structure I identify for constructive-developmental pedagogy emerged from a previous longitudinal study of students' epistemological development, or their assumptions about the nature, limits, and certainty of knowledge (Baxter Magolda 1992). I initiated that study with 101 students entering college in 1986. Its purpose was to trace epistemological development over the course of college and adulthood with particular attention to the role of gender in that development. In annual interviews I pursued domains that had been shown to illuminate epistemic assumptions. Thus, I invited students to talk freely about their role as learners, the role of instructors and peers in learning, their perception of evaluation of their work, the nature of knowledge, and educational decision making. Qualitative open-ended interviews were used because cognitive development research supported their utility in accessing students' core epistemic assumptions.

The primary outcome of the college phase of the longitudinal study was a description of four ways of knowing, each characterized by a qualitatively different set of epistemic assumptions, and two gender-related patterns within the first three ways of knowing (Baxter Magolda 1992). An overview of these outcomes is presented in chapter 2 to describe students' intellectual development as a foundation for exploring constructive-developmental pedagogy. However, in the course of open discussions of students' learning experiences, they reported experiences that in their view prompted them to alter their epistemic assumptions. Reviewing the transcripts of their audio-recorded interviews surfaced themes that captured the structure of teaching that promoted their epistemological development. I translated those themes to three principles for promoting students' epistemological development (Baxter Magolda 1992). Hearing their stories sparked my interest in pursuing this kind of teaching and led me to the current study of constructive-developmental pedagogy.

The three principles emerging from the longitudinal study are validating students as knowers, situating learning in students' own experience, and defining learning as mutually constructing meaning. *Validating students as knowers* means acknowledging their capacity to hold a point of view, recognizing their current understandings, and supporting them in explaining their current views. Validation as a knower helps students view themselves as capable of learning and knowing, heightening their engagement in learning. *Situating learning in students' own experience* means using students' experience, lives, and current knowledge as a starting point for learning. This places learning in a context students can readily understand. Situating learning in students' experience can draw existing experiences into the learning context or create experiences within the learning context from which students can work. It also means connecting to students' ways of making meaning. *Defining learning as mutually constructing meaning* makes both teacher and student active players in learning. It suggests that the teacher and students put their understandings together by exploring students' experiences and views in the context of knowledge the teacher introduces. Together they construct knowledge that takes experience and evidence into account. Through this mutual construction, misunderstandings in previous knowledge are resolved; thus, validating students as knowers does not mean endorsing misunderstanding.

Together these three principles thus form the structure of constructive-developmental pedagogy—a structure that continuously incorporates students' lived experience and the meaning they have made of it into teaching. This structure is crucial in both connecting to the range of students' development and connecting to a wide range of student experience. Because the principles involve listening to students' thinking and dialogue among learners, students' epistemic assumptions can be surfaced in the learning environment. Understanding and connecting to these assumptions help educators assist students in evaluating and altering their assumptions toward increasing complexity. The principles by their very nature encourage the complex epistemic assumptions that are inherent in self-authorship.

This structure also facilitates developing effective learning opportunities for students with diverse backgrounds and experiences. Because constructive-developmental pedagogy hinges on students' own experience, their particular experiences are surfaced in the learning environment. Understanding and connecting to those experiences help educators gain an appreciation for diverse students; welcoming students' experiences simultaneously makes students feel that they have a place in the learning environment. Validating students as knowers and defining learning as mutually constructing meaning let students know that they are an integral part of the learning process and that their experiences count. Given the increasing diversity of student populations, using a structure that accesses and welcomes all students is crucial to effective pedagogy.

Identifying the Process of Constructive-Developmental Pedagogy

The possibilities of constructive-developmental pedagogy and using the above structure to promote students' epistemological development led to a second study focused on identifying processes through which to implement constructive-developmental pedagogy. Reflections on my teaching during the course of the longitudinal study led to my attempts to promote self-authorship in my courses via constructive-developmental pedagogy. I had only the stories of my longitudinal participants from which to work and hoped to find other instructors who were engaging in promoting self-authorship. I chose to observe courses in hopes of seeing versions of constructive-developmental pedagogy firsthand because my principles had emerged from students reporting to me what they had experienced. My advocacy of constructive-developmental pedagogy resulted in various dialogues with colleagues who viewed the structure as consistent with their values as educators. They were for the most part constructivist and largely unaware of the developmental dimension of constructive-developmental pedagogy. The colleagues who questioned constructive-developmental pedagogy raised issues about its utility in large classes, in content areas such as mathematics and science where subject mastery is vital, and for students with less advanced epistemological development. These issues, in combination with finding colleagues whose values were consistent with constructive-developmental pedagogy, framed my observational study.

I began observing courses in the fall of 1993. I looked particularly for teachers who desired to promote their students' self-authorship, believed that students had something to offer, and were passionate about teaching. My colleague Jo Fischer was coordinating a 200 level educational foundations course that would enroll 286 students. The goal was critical thinking about educational practice. She and another colleague who had conceptualized the course were familiar with my longitudinal study and focused on connecting their course to students' experience. I attended the large weekly course meeting for the semester, attended the instructor seminars (graduate students taught multiple seminar sections), attended the meetings of two seminar sections throughout the semester, and interviewed students in those sections who agreed to participate in the study.

During the 1994 spring semester, a research partner and I gained permission to observe Sam Rivers's Mathematics by Inquiry course taken primarily by juniors and seniors. Sam's course focused on discovery learning, and he was a constructivist teacher at heart who wanted his students to develop their own construction of mathematics. We attended both weekly meetings all semester and interviewed the majority of students in the course.

In the spring semester of 1995, we observed Chris Snowden's winter biology course because Chris thought his values matched the structure of constructive-developmental pedagogy, his course focused on teaching students to think like scientists, and the enrollment was primarily seniors. We attended both weekly meetings of his course and interviewed approximately half of the students enrolled.

All student interviews were conducted at the end of the term to assess students' epistemological development, which was assessed via a written measure at the outset of each course, and to solicit their perceptions of the course and pedagogy. We interviewed instructors at the outset and conclusion of the courses to understand their teaching philosophy and assessment of the course respectively.

Context of the Observational Study

Inherent in the social-constructivist approach to knowledge construction is the notion that knowers decide what to believe based on a thorough understanding of the context. Thus, in order for readers to judge whether the picture of constructive-developmental pedagogy painted here is useful for teaching in other contexts, a full description of the context from which this description emerged is necessary. Both my longitudinal study and the observational study took place at Miami University (Ohio). The following description of the institution and the courses I observed serve as the readers' introduction to the context of the observational study. The courses are described in the order in which they appear in the book.

Miami University

Miami University is a state-assisted, liberal arts institution with an enrollment of approximately sixteen thousand. Admission is competitive; most students rank in the top 20 percent of their high school class. The campus is residential, and involvement in cocurricular life is high.

Approximately 130 majors are offered in six divisions, including arts and sciences, education and allied professions, business administration, fine arts, applied sciences, and interdisciplinary studies. Nearly nine hundred students participate in the honors program.

All students are required to participate in the Miami Plan for Liberal Education to complement specialized work in their major. The liberal education plan emphasizes four goals: "thinking critically, understanding contexts, engaging with other learners, and reflecting and acting" (Miami University 1994, 20). These goals are carried out in the context of thirty-six semester hours of foundational courses in five areas (English composition; fine arts, humanities; social science, world cultures; natural science; mathematics, formal reasoning, technology), nine semester hours in a thematic sequence of advanced work outside the major, and a three-hour senior capstone experience. EDU 200 and Math by Inquiry both serve as foundations courses for the Miami Plan.

The ratio of students to faculty is twenty-to-one. Twenty-seven percent of the full-time faculty are women. The mission of the institution rests heavily on undergraduate teaching, a focus that is evident in students' reports that faculty are available, friendly, and helpful. The promotion and tenure process seriously considers teaching as the most important function of the faculty. Programs such as the Alumni Teaching Scholars program for both junior and senior faculty are aimed at enhancing faculty teaching, as is the annual Lilly Teaching Conference held at Miami. Graduation rates are 68 percent in four years and 80 percent in five years.

Zoo 400/500: Winter Biology

Chris Snowden's conceptualization of science, as well as the nature of winter biology, was evident on his syllabus. He believed that science was an evolving field made up of facts that were subject to revision. He wanted his students to understand how to evaluate scientific knowledge, identify questions, and conduct research that led to such revision. ZOO 400/500 included three juniors, fifteen seniors, and one graduate student who were officially enrolled in the course. Of those students only three were male (a major disappointment to me because the course was also chosen due to its typical high male enrollment). All were zoology majors, and one woman was a double major with zoology and math. Most of the students planned to continue their studies after graduation. Eight were planning to attend medical, dental, optometry, or law school the following year. Others were pursuing physical therapy, environmental science, ecology, or oceanography graduate programs. One planned to work in research and development, and the graduate student planned to pursue her doctorate in the near future. One or two additional people were usually present. One of Chris's graduate assistants audited the course, and others who worked in his lab from graduate students to postdoctoral students sat in routinely. Ten students participated in interviews at the end of the term; all three men enrolled and seven women, including the graduate student and nine seniors.

Chris's love was anything related to the cold. As he said in our first interview, "Some like it hot—in our lab we like it cold!" Thus, the course was his opportunity to engage students with a wide range of subjects, all hinging on life in the cold. His enthusiasm for the topic was ever present in the course, heightened on days when snow was falling outside. Chris's extensive research program, now twenty years in the making, was often used as an example in the course, and he invited students to join him in various endeavors. Some Tuesdays he would share research activities in which he and his lab colleagues had engaged over the weekend. His thirteen years of university teaching made him as comfortable in the classroom as in the lab. He liked his time in the classroom, saying that he could succeed in a purely research environment but preferred the combination of teaching and research, which he viewed as closely linked. His main interest was teaching students "how to do science." Chris's enthusiasm for teaching was as evident in his classroom as was his interest in insects evident in the ladybug collection that occupied his office.

Math 400/500: Math by Inquiry

The syllabus for Math by Inquiry outlined the content and format of the course, both emphasizing discovery learning. Sam Rivers wanted his students to leave with a personal construction of how mathematics worked. This course could be used as a requirement in the mathematics area of the liberal education plan. Most students reported taking it because of the instructor's reputation. Of the sixteen students enrolled, all of whom were women, two were graduate students, eleven were seniors, two were juniors, and one was a sophomore. One was a math major; the rest were education majors with concentrations or minors in math. All were preparing to be teachers with the exception of the two graduate students who were already teaching. The undergraduate students ranged in age from 19 to 22, with four age 21 and four age 22. The two graduate students were 24 and 37 years old. One student was African-American. Four of the students reported that their mothers were teachers; one student's father was a teacher. Five of the students' mothers were homemakers. Twelve students participated in our interviews at the end of the term. This group included the two graduate students, the sophomore, one of the juniors, and eight seniors. The African-American student participated in the interviews.

Sam Rivers had been an elementary and secondary teacher early in his career and could use his experience to relate to the students' goals. His long-standing involvement in teacher education, the institution's reform effort in liberal education, and Project Discovery[1] all culminated in Sam's social-constructivist bent. Sam's personality matched the nature of the course. He had an easy rapport with students, was serious about their learning, and was modest about his extensive expertise. His more than twenty years of teaching at the college level made the college classroom a comfortable place for him. The respect he showed for students as thinkers was a central feature of the course.

EDU 200: Sociocultural Foundations of Education

The nature of EDU 200, as described in the syllabus, was to help students think critically about schooling and education in contemporary America. Goals included learning to recognize, evaluate, and defend positions in educational discourse and learning to interpret, critique, and judge educational practices in various contexts. Sophomores made up the majority (54 percent) of the 286 students enrolled. Seventeen percent were first-year students, 22 percent were juniors, and 7 percent were seniors. Women dominated the group, making up 75 percent of the enrollment. All six university divisions were represented, although 74 percent were in education. The next largest group was from arts and sciences (13 percent) followed by fine arts (7 percent), business (4.5 percent), applied science (1 percent), and interdisciplinary studies (one person). Based on research on students' epistemological development, it is likely that most of the students came to EDU 200 expecting the instructor to play a primary role in dispensing knowledge. The thirteen students I interviewed said that they had never had a class like EDU 200 before except first-year English.

EDU 200 was a required course for all undergraduate teacher education majors and also could be used to meet a foundations requirement in the liberal education plan. Jo Fischer, the large group instructor and coordinator of the course, was trained in the social foundations of education and taught in secondary education prior to coming to the university. Her youth and East Coast-upbringing impacted her teaching style. She used her sharp wit regularly, and her command of popular culture helped her resonate with students' experience. She was fearless in trying unusual techniques (such as yelling "sex" at the outset of one session to get their attention) that most instructors would only joke about. Despite her connection to and compassion for students, Jo was also straightforward and confronted students directly about ideas and their academic efforts. She was comfortable with the subject matter and at ease on the stage in front of three hundred students. She preferred to yell instead of using the microphone.

I purposely selected Jan Nichols's and Kim Conlin's sections to observe based on my observations of all the EDU 200 instructors at an all-day retreat before the start of classes. The retreat focused on discussion of the purpose, plan, and implementation of the course. Jan's and Kim's contributions during the discussion led me to believe that they fully understood the conceptualization of the course Elliot Gardner, the faculty member who conceptualized the course, had articulated and that their teaching experience led them to interact relationally with students. Both were doctoral students at the time they taught EDU 200, but both had full-time teaching experience prior to their doctoral programs in educational administration. Jan taught special education at the secondary level for a number of years; her teaching philosophy hinged on honoring students where they are. Kim taught art, music, and humanities previously in a magnet school setting, and she had master's degrees in guidance and counseling and aesthetic education. Her teaching philosophy focused on collaborative work with students. Both women had teenage children of their own as well. Jan is an outgoing, jovial person who seems comfortable with any audience. Kim is a quiet personality, whose flashes of humor are seen regularly when she gets settled in a group. Both women were confident of their teaching skill and excited about the nature of EDU 200.

Kim's section enrolled twenty students, of whom five were first-year, thirteen were sophomores, and two were juniors. Seven students in Kim's section participated in the project. Of the seven, two were juniors, three were sophomores, and two were first-year students. One of the seven was male. The other five males in that section declined participation. Five of the seven students were education majors; one was in communications; and one was in chemistry. Jan's section enrolled nineteen students, including four first-year students, eleven sophomores, three juniors, and one senior. Six of Jan's nineteen students participated in the project. All six were women; the four men in the class declined our invitation to participate. Four were sophomores, one was a first-year student, and one was a junior. Four were education majors, one a math major, and one a business major.

Context Limitations

The three courses observed involve different disciplines, a range of class ranks, distinct implementations of constructive-developmental pedagogy, and multiple teaching styles. However, discussion of the processes of constructive-developmental pedagogy stemming from these courses is not intended to be generalized across contexts in line with my social-constructivist views. These processes serve as possibilities through which the structure of constructive-developmental pedagogy can be implemented. As you judge transferability to your teaching context, I caution you to consider limitations of the context described here. First, women greatly outnumbered men in all three courses observed. In addition, men were not interested in participating in our study even after we explained the need for more male participants. Second, students of color were minimally represented in these courses and subsequently in our project. This is largely a function of the small number of students of color at the institution. Third, the institution maintains a strong teaching focus despite its enrollment. Thus, the campus climate may be more supportive than some climates of innovative teaching. These dynamics vary across higher educational institutions and may affect transferability of the processes and outcomes of constructive-developmental pedagogy. I firmly believe, however, that the structure—the three principles—offers sufficient flexibility to make its successful use possible in multiple contexts.

Overview of the Book

Because self-authorship is a primary focus of the book, an in-depth exploration of the developmental nature of self-authorship. The epistemological dimension of self-authorship is placed in the foreground; the interpersonal and intrapersonal dimensions are woven around the epistemological to help the reader attain a full understanding of students' development of self-authorship. Pursues the structure of constructive-developmental pedagogy in more detail, illustrating the effects of the three principles on students' development of self-authorship. Also includes my attempts to use this structure in one of my graduate courses. I include these activities and my reflection on them for two reasons. First, I advocate modeling risks that I encourage others to take; thus, sharing my foray into constructive-developmental pedagogy seems appropriate before I ask readers to entertain it in their teaching. My involvement in my graduate course simultaneously allows for an insider perspective and limits my objectivity. Second, sharing excerpts from my graduate course illustrates constructive-developmental pedagogy possibilities with students who hold complex ways of knowing.

Part 2 illustrates three processes for implementing constructive-developmental pedagogy in three different contexts. The variety of processes used in the three courses observed emphasizes the multiple possibilities through which the underlying structure of constructive-developmental pedagogy can be implemented to connect with teacher style, students' development, and disciplinary objectives. Recounts the *interactive lecture* process Chris Snowden used in his senior/graduate biology course. The nature of the interactive lecture is described, illustrated by examples of its use in class sessions. Students' reflections on their learning demonstrate the outcomes of the interactive lecture for helping students learn scientific inquiry. Describes Sam Rivers's *investigating together* approach to teaching and learning mathematics with junior and senior students. Accounts of class sessions show Sam's reliance on constructivist pedagogy and the particular processes he used. His students' reactions demonstrate the effects of learning mathematics in this manner. Illustrates *narrative* processes to teaching social foundations of education to first- and second-year students. Class sessions from two seminar sections as well as the large group session reveal various ways of using storytelling in promoting self-authorship with students whose epistemological development makes self-authorship difficult. Students' reactions highlight how these processes affected their development. The detailed accounts of course sessions in part 2 are intended to offer readers specific details about ways in which constructive-developmental pedagogy can be implemented.

Note

1. Project Discovery is a statewide initiative, funded by the National Science Foundation and the state of Ohio, to improve science and mathematics education. The project advocates discovery, or inquiry, learning.

Generative Paradox in Learner-Centered College Teaching

Douglas Reimondo Robertson

ABSTRACT: The discussion identifies six contradictions that characterize the emergent learner-centered teaching role: (a) control/flow, (b) facilitator/evaluator, (c) teacher learning/student learning, (d) subject expert/teaching expert, (e) caring for students/caring for self, and (f) individual mentor/group leader. Key concepts are presented (conflict, compartmentalized paradox, and generative paradox) which represent points on a continuum of the degree to which college teachers have successfully integrated these fundamental contradictions in the learner-centered teaching role. This article extends an ongoing discussion of integrity in learner-centered teaching by providing a conceptual paradigm and examples for developing consistently productive responses to these six fundamental contradictions in learner-centered teaching.

College teaching means different things to different people. The literature on college teaching yields an assortment of typologies that collect and organize the various approaches of professors to their teaching role (Adelson, 1962; Axelrod, 1973; Baker, Roueche, & Gillett-Karan, 1990; Mann et al., 1970; Pratt, 1989; Pratt & Associates, 1998; Ralph, 1978; Robertson, 1999b, 2000b, 2001, 2002; Sherman, Armistead, Fowler, Barksdale, & Reif, 1987). When I use the term college teaching in this article, I mean learner-centered teaching where teachers construe themselves to be facilitators of student learning as opposed to teacher-centered teaching where teachers see themselves as disseminators or imparters of knowledge. This discussion intends to further conceptualize and develop the learner-centered teaching role.

As the quip has it, "Life is full of obstacle illusions." And so is college teaching. In this article, I focus on one particular set of apparent obstacles to effective and satisfying college teaching—viz., contradictions inherent in the learner-centered teacher role. At least six contradictions in learner-centered college teaching have occurred to me (Robertson, 2003b).

- *Control/flow*: teachers must be disciplined and in control of course content and process but also must be able to go with flow regarding both.

- *Facilitator/evaluator*: teachers must develop trusting relationships with students but also serve as proxy judges for external constituents because they must grade their students.

- *Loving the subject (teacher learning)/loving the students (student learning)*: teachers must be devoted to their own learning of the subject as master learners but also committed to their students' learning of the subject.

- *Subject expert/teaching and learning expert*: teachers must know their disciplines but also must know the learning process for a diverse array of students and how to facilitate that diverse array of learners, which usually is not their discipline.

- *Caring for students/caring for self*: teachers must be able to love both self and others (students) at the same time.

Reprinted from *Innovative Higher Education* 29, no. 3 (spring 2005).

- *Individual mentor/group learning leader*: teachers must sensitively serve both the group as a whole and the individual, idiosyncratic learners within the group.

These contradictions become most evident when the two sides of the opposition compete for teachers' attention, time, and passion.

Contradictions that are fundamental to learner-centered teaching can be experienced by the college teacher as frustrating, debilitating, even paralyzing conflicts. However, these enduring, deep-seated contradictions in the learner-centered teaching role have the potential to be transformed into *generative paradoxes*, or contradictions in which both sides of the opposition are true and both sides feed rather than fight each other. Ideas such as harmony, synergy, and integration describe the dynamics between the oppositions as the contradiction is transformed from a conflict into a generative paradox.

In this article, I develop this concept of generative paradox in college teaching and contrast it with two other possible but less desirable forms which teaching contradictions may take—viz., *conflict* and *compartmentalized paradox*. Conflicts, compartmentalized paradoxes, and generative paradoxes are shown to represent points on a continuum of teacher integrity, i.e., the degree to which a college teacher has productively integrated fundamental contradictions in the teacher role (Robertson, 2003b). This discussion further develops the key concept of generative paradox by illustrating what the six teaching contradictions identified above could look like if they were to be transformed into generative paradoxes.

Conflict and Paradox

A student of mine once wrote in a paper that his future was "fraught with opportunities." I immediately thought of Pogo's alert, "We are confronted with insurmountable opportunities." "Opportunity" is usually something good. When a situation is said to be fraught with something, that something is usually bad, as in "fraught with difficulty" or "fraught with peril." "Fraught with opportunities," the phrase caught my ear and delighted me. The "opportunities" in the phrase are good, but the "fraught" adds the connotation that good outcomes are far from guaranteed and that things could easily get hosed up and yield bad outcomes.

I think that the phrase applies well to learner-centered college teaching, an activity with inherent contradictions. The college teacher experiences these fundamental contradictions as exhausting conflicts or as generative paradoxes depending on the degree to which the teacher is able to integrate the two sides of the contradictions and have these two sides relate productively with each other. Integrating the oppositions in contradictions has a tremendous pay-off but is no small feat. Truly, college teaching is "fraught with opportunities."

Conflict

Previously in my writing about college teaching, I have called learner-centered college teaching a "*conflicted* educational helping relationship" (Robertson, 2001–2002, 2003b). I called it an "educational helping relationship" because learner-centered college teaching focuses on facilitating student learning or helping students to learn (Robertson, 1996, 1997, 1999a, 2000a, 2001–2002, 2003b). I called it "conflicted" because I thought conflicts were inherent to this particular helping role (Robertson, 2001–2002, 2003b). My thinking was similar to Parker Palmer's (1998, pp. 61–87), who also focused on inherent paradoxes in good teaching and their necessary tensions (also see Tiberius, Sinai, & Flak, 2002, who extend Palmer's thinking usefully although they prefer to speak of "dilemmas" rather than "paradoxes"). Palmer evoked the concept of "suffering" as a necessary capacity of good teachers who must hold "in the teacher's heart" paradox's tension and endure until a "larger love" arrives (Palmer, pp. 83–87). Following a similar line of thought regarding pedagogy and paradox, Palmer used the language of tension and suffering, and I spoke of conflict and coping. *Coping* with inherent conflicts seemed to me at the time to be a requirement of the helping profession called learner-centered college teaching (Robertson 2001–2002, 2003b).

My language was wrong, however. More profoundly, my thinking was wrong. The word "conflict" comes from the Latin word *confligere*, to strike together or fight, and is defined as a "clash, competition, or mutual interference of opposing or incompatible forces or qualities (as ideas, interests, wills): . . . an emotional state characterized by indecision, restlessness, uncertainty, and tension resulting from incompatible inner needs or drives of comparable intensity" (s.v., Webster, 1966). The word "cope" derives from the Latin word *colaphus*, blow with the fist, which in turn comes from the Greek word *kolaphos*, buffet, and means "to maintain a contest or combat . . . on even terms or with success . . . to face or encounter and to find necessary expedients to overcome problems and difficulties" (s.v., Webster, 1966). Although learner-centered teaching is not always a serene endeavor, it is not inherently about beating into submission incompatible antagonisms within the role of teacher. This language and thinking did not capture my experience of learner-centered teaching when it functions well. College teaching is an *educational helping relationship*. However, it is not necessarily a *conflicted* relationship; and we can do much better than merely to *cope* with, or suffer and endure (Palmer, 1998), its contradictions.

Paradox

When the college teacher experiences contradictions that are fundamental to the teaching role as conflicts, it generally indicates that the teacher has not integrated well the two sides of those contradictions (Robertson, 2003b). I say "integrated *well*" because integration exists in degrees and can be thought of as a continuum ranging from no integration at all to complete integration to form a new whole from two parts (Robertson, 1988, 2003b). The teacher's lack of integration is experienced as tension or, on a grander scale, an inner war. I came to see that the degree to which the opposing sides of these deep-seated contradictions were brought into synergistic relationship became a way of defining learner-centered teaching integrity, or put more simply, the degree to which the learner-centered teacher "has it together" (Robertson, 2003b).

I believe that we can still speak of a dominant American cultural perspective, notwithstanding the complex, cultural pluralism evident in postmodern American culture. Conflict is probably the typical default mode for experiencing these teaching contradictions in part because the dominant American cultural perspective has an imbedded preference for logical thought. When immersed in this dominant cultural perspective, one usually struggles with thinking in paradoxes, that is, thinking with both sides of a contradiction being true.

Paradoxes are irrational. The roots of the word "paradox" mean beside or beyond thought (s.v., Webster, 1966). Within a worldview dominated by rationality, being irrational should end all claim to legitimacy. Admitted irrationality . . . why then, the discussion is over. End of story. Paradoxes and those who think in them are seen as inscrutable, or beyond examination and understanding. Aristotle taught us that things have to be p or not p, the only two logical options. However, paradox teaches us that p *and* not p are both true. Rationally, we struggle with this proposition.

Intuitively (intuition being paradox's most likely conduit to human understanding), we know that going forward holding both sides of a contradiction as valid is not merely a proposition but what feels like a living truth, something that our lived experience compels us to do. Chemist turned philosopher Michael Polanyi called the kind of knowledge that we can put in words and think about in verbal symbols "articulate knowledge" and the kind of knowledge that we know but cannot say "tacit knowledge" (Polanyi, 1962). Tacitly, we know that apparent antagonisms can both be true and do, in fact, coexist.

In cultures dominated by rationality, articulate knowledge and reason tend to have the upper hand over tacit knowledge and intuition. For example, American writer F. Scott Fitzgerald (1945, p.69) wrote, "The test of a first-rate intelligence is the ability to hold two opposed ideas in the mind at the same time, and still retain the ability to function." This statement is telling in at least two ways. First, the need to be able "to hold two opposed ideas in the mind" is implied to be a necessity, a fact of life, a challenge that is out there to be faced: both sides of a contradiction are in fact sometimes true and need to be held by the mind simultaneously. Second, the fact that Fitzgerald asserts that you have to be a "first-rate intelligence" to avoid becoming paralyzed by thinking in paradoxes indicates how difficult and rare he thinks it is to overcome logic and rationality and do so.

Wedded oppositions, such as those that characterize learner-centered teaching, probably tend to be experienced as irony rather than paradox in a rationality-dominated culture (e.g., Roberts, 2002). With paradox, two opposing propositions are true, simultaneously. With irony, one proposition (not both) is implied to be true (or more true) in contrast to the other proposition, or one proposition is of greater importance than the other proposition and therefore more worthy. Furthermore, with irony, this favored proposition is the one that appearance favors least. With irony, one proposition should prevail over the other, but with the ironical twist, the facade favors the less worthy proposition. With paradox, both propositions win; with irony, a winner and a loser exist. For example, it is ironical that students value teachers whom they can trust with their psychological comfort, yet they learn most deeply from teachers who disrupt that psychological comfort by challenging the students' worldview. In contrast, it is paradoxical that students trust their psychological comfort with certain teachers who premeditatively deconstruct the students' worldviews. In the case of irony, deep learning comes at the expense of teacher trust; in the case of paradox, deep learning and teacher trust can go hand in hand. American culture may be passing through an "age of irony" where irony as a way of thinking and of expressing thought constitutes an informing force of the American Zeitgeist. Being a rationality-dominated culture, an "age of paradox" is unlikely but not out of the question should the American population develop a critical mass of Fitzgerald's "first-rate intelligences."

"There is nothing certain, but the uncertain," an old saw advises us. If the proposition is true, then it is also false. It is true and false at the same time. Logically, we think that we have a problem. Intuitively, we understand that we do not. In an intuitive mode of knowing, a statement being simultaneously true and false causes no problem but instead may express wisdom.

The most productive response to the fundamental contradictions in the learner-centered teaching role is to transform them into paradoxes—things that appear to be incompatible but in fact are not. In order to do this regularly, we need to have a positive attitude toward paradox (for specific strategies regarding self-directed growth, see Robertson, 1988, 2003a, 2003c). Here are a few suggestions which may help to develop such an attitude.

- We need to appreciate or value paradox; facility with paradox is the sign of a "first-rate intelligence."
- We need to resist the impulse to try to resolve paradoxes; they just are, and we should get over it.
- We need to look beyond Aristotle's dualistic logical premise; p or not p is just part of the story.
- We need to listen and give credence to things that we know but cannot say; paradoxes are usually known best intuitively.
- We need to tolerate, even enjoy, ambiguity which often accompanies paradoxes; they are not neat and precise.

In contrast to experiencing oppositions as conflicts, the teacher can transform contradictions that accompany the learner-centered teaching role into at least two kinds of paradoxes: (a) compartmentalized paradoxes, or (b) generative paradoxes. Actually, these two categories of paradox complete a continuum of integration regarding teaching contradictions.

Conflicts

With conflicts, the integration is low or nonexistent; and the two sides of the contradiction fight each other. For example, in the control/flow contradiction, my need to do both may be at war with each other; and I may simply pick one to stick with at the expense of the other. I may decide not to attempt to go with the flow and instead to maintain tight classroom control and adherence to a schedule no matter what.

Compartmentalized paradoxes

With compartmentalized paradoxes, the two sides of a teaching contradiction are not bellicose to each other within the teacher's head, but instead, they co-exist by taking turns. They do not feed each other, but at least they do not fight each other. The teacher engages in "hat talk," as in, "Now I am putting on my control hat, and now, I am putting on my go-with-the-flow hat." Different kinds of teaching and learning activities require different things from the teacher: for instance, a good lecture often requires a different kind of teacher persona (in charge, in control, providing structure and direction for the topic and the session) than the teacher persona required to facilitate an effective experiential exercise (sensitive, empathic, and devoted to the participants' individual and group processes). In compartmentalized paradoxes, the teacher goes from one persona to the next, but the two do not seem well connected—more like changing channels than watching one integrated program.

Generative paradoxes

With generative paradoxes, the two sides of the contradiction feed each other. They are related in a mutually beneficial way. The teacher achieves a win/win relationship among them. Also, rather than existing in a discrete fashion, as in "hat" changing where I operate from one persona or another but not both simultaneously (or in close temporal proximity), with generative paradox the two sides of the contradiction may operate simultaneously, or nearly so. For example, when giving a lecture, teachers may be presenting a topic in an orderly fashion. Nonetheless, when a fertile discussion develops among participants during the course of the lecture, the teachers may go with that particular flow as long as it is producing valuable student learning that relates to the topic even if that learning is not on the teachers' lecture outline or perhaps even in the syllabus, say for instance, a valuable attitudinal development regarding the larger professional field of the course. Often, the lecture is enhanced by this combination of structure and spontaneity, each feeding the other. The demands to be disciplined and to go with the flow are integrated within the teacher allowing the two sides of the contradiction to interact in a mutually productive, synergizing way.

Transforming Teaching Contradictions into Generative Paradoxes

As a way of developing the concept of generative paradox further, I continue with examples for each of the other five common teacher contradictions.

Facilitator/Evaluator

Recall that in the facilitator/evaluator contradiction the teacher must try to develop the specific learner within that learner's idiosyncratic context while also judging that learner according to external frames of reference that are not necessarily the learner's. An example of transforming this contradiction into a generative paradox might involve inviting the students into the teachers' paradox. Teachers could bring to light the two roles and the tension between them as a part of their introduction to the course. I always include an explanation of my teaching philosophy at the beginning of each course so that the students do not have to guess about it. Also, I hope that doing so will stimulate students to develop their own philosophies of teaching and learning. As the teacher, I have a lot of authority in the course like it or not, which sometimes I do, and sometimes I don't, and the students deserve to know my frame of reference for the exercise of that authority. Besides that, from a practical point of view, students behave much more constructively in class if I end the suspense early about my basic approach. An ever-present learning objective in all of my courses is to encourage students to become more proficient as self-directed, lifelong learners, something which benefits from students becoming teachers in the course. Also, regardless of course topic, I am interested in promoting the students' critical thinking and cognitive development. I want them to be able to identify and evaluate deep perspectives, including their own, which is something that William Perry would call achieving the developmental positions of "commitment in relativism" (Perry, 1970). I can invite students into the paradox by asking them what they think of my solutions to the problem of evaluating their learning on behalf of external agencies (i.e., my grading system) and how they would solve the evaluation problem if they were I (by what criteria, based on what performance, and according to what rationale). Asking students to enter into my evaluator role serves the agenda of my facilitator role, which is the other side of this particular teaching contradiction. The outcome is a generative paradox—each side of the opposition relating to the other in a harmonious and productive way.

Loving the Subject (Teacher Learning)/Loving the Students (Student Learning)

Another teaching contradiction involves the fact that most college and university teachers go into this profession at least partly because of a deep love of their subject. For many college teachers getting paid to continue learning a particular subject is a dream come true. Teachers' love of subject and of their own learning of that subject exists simultaneously with a professional responsibility (and we hope, an authentic desire) to love the students and their learning of the subject. As with sibling rivalry, the two loves compete for the teacher's attention, time, and passion. In the interest of achieving harmony, I can take the obvious step of carefully examining my scholarship for ways to incorporate it into my courses so that my learning is feeding the students' learning. This scholarly yield might involve content, but also it might involve the process of knowing itself. I may be able to work into my courses not only findings from my scholarship but also learning about the process of doing scholarship that benefits the students as they learn to do scholarship themselves. The proverb advises us, "Give someone a fish, and you feed them for a day; teach someone to fish, and you feed them for a lifetime." Teaching students the discipline of scholarship is the equivalent of teaching them to fish. Also, I can come to see that helping students to learn a subject actually feeds my learning of that subject. "To teach is to learn twice," the saying instructs us. When I teach something, even something that I think that I know inside and out, I almost always deepen my understanding of it. Having to explain old familiar ideas and patterns in new ways and creating new phrases, metaphors, and examples often illuminates for me a nuance to the idea, a hole in my understanding of it, or a new element to that idea's relationship to another idea. I believe that in most cases if I cannot explain something to both my 9-year-old daughter and a colleague, then I probably do not understand that idea very well. Also, I learn about my scholarship (my own learning of the subject) by seeing it through the eyes of my students, visions that are naive to the assumptive world of my discipline. These lines of thought help me to see how teacher learning and student learning can contribute to each other's development. In so doing, their contradiction becomes a generative paradox.

Subject Expert/Teaching and Learning Expert

Related to the previous teaching contradiction is the one related to the pressure on learner-centered teachers to add to their subject specialty a familiarity with the scholarship on teaching and learning (what learning is and how to help it to happen more effectively). These two subject interests (the teachers' home disciplines and the scholarship of teaching and learning) compete for whatever time teachers carve out for their own scholarship. A possible win/win solution is to become involved in contributing to the scholarship of teaching and learning within one's discipline (Robertson, 2002). Teachers are still connected to their subjects, but they focus their scholarship on the teaching and learning of those subjects. They might even bring these teaching and learning questions to their students and enlist their participation in designing and conducting scholarly projects regarding teaching and learning in their courses. This particular approach would not only create synergies within a contradiction but also across contradictions, as the previous contradiction (teacher learning/student learning) would also be served.

Caring for Students/Caring for Self

Over the years, I have observed in myself and in some of my colleagues the use of learner-centered rhetoric, such as "caring for students," as a way to feel better about ourselves. Ultimately, however, it was all about us. Self absorption is sneaky sometimes. Also, I have observed myself and colleagues going well beyond any reasonable call of duty to respond to the needs and wants of students (no matter how whacky) with behavior which could only be called selfless and which contributed to professionally-related depression or "burnout" as it is commonly known. Selflessness is unhealthy sometimes. I have come to the conclusion that I need to care for myself and for my students simultaneously. These three positions—focusing on the welfare of self while neglecting attention to the other, focusing on the welfare of the other while neglecting attention to self, and focusing on self and other simultaneously—are precisely the three positions that Carol Gilligan discerned in her study of abortion decisions among pregnant women, which then became the positions in her developmental model of the ethic of caring in women (Gilligan, 1982). Achieving generative paradox for the caring for students/caring for self contradiction suggests the need for the teacher to have achieved this third developmental position. To move toward generative paradox, I am helped by remembering my larger, ever-present objective to encourage students to learn to develop themselves holistically (not just intellectually). To a large extent, what we teach is who we are, as Parker Palmer has so eloquently and compellingly pointed out (Palmer, 1998). Therefore, if I want students to learn to develop holistically and to live a healthy, balanced life, I need to model it. If I want students to learn to love themselves while also loving others, I need to model it. Caring for my students at the expense of my health, my family, and my general welfare, is not the kind of teaching that I want to provide. Neither is caring for myself at the expense of my students. I need to model doing both together. Also, from a practical perspective, I need to keep myself fresh in order to serve my students, just as in an airline emergency, the parent needs to put on the oxygen mask before the children in order to optimize the chances that the children will be cared for. Setting appropriate boundaries with student demands helps them learn to take necessary responsibility. Doing scholarship that rejuvenates me, in addition to my teaching, may contribute to the course content as well as model healthy balance. These kinds of measures are just a few ways to achieve generative paradox regarding the caring for students/caring for self contradiction.

Individual Mentor/Group Learning Leader

Finally, learner-centered teaching requires teachers to facilitate individual students who learn at different rates and in different ways while also serving as the learning leader for the group. Teachers need to be able to move on even though not every one "has got it," without leaving anyone behind permanently. One way of achieving a win/win solution to this contradictory demand relates to my previous comments regarding the ways in which helping students to learn the teacher's subject can actually promote the teacher's further learning of that subject. The same dynamic can be true among students. In fulfillment of their group learning leader responsibility, teachers can design group projects in which meaningful incentives exist for students to teach each other and to learn from each other as the groups move along accomplishing the overall agenda and objectives stated on the syllabus. In this way, we have, metaphorically speaking, majority rule along with the individual protections from majority rule that the Bill of Rights provides, a kind of generative paradox that accommodates the individual and the community simultaneously.

Conclusion

Through a character in his story, "Inside and Outside," Hermann Hesse (1972) perceptively observed,

> [T]he distinction between inside and outside is habitual to our thinking, but not necessary. Our mind is capable of passing beyond the dividing line we have drawn for it. Beyond the pairs of opposites of which the world consists, other, new insights begin (p. 263).

Similarly, beyond the apparent contradictions of learner-centered teaching, in the domain of generative paradox, "other, new insights begin." These insights are powerful, almost magical in their ability to create energy and learning among teachers and students alike. With practice, reflection, and in dialog with our colleagues, we become more adept at paradoxical thinking in our teaching and reap the benefits of these insights from "beyond the pairs of opposites," as Hesse phrased it. Most of us have received, not chosen, the limiting habit of thinking in logical dualisms. Often, thinking paradoxically requires a choice on our parts. For many of us, it goes against our grain. I believe that paradoxical thinking is a habit worth choosing. I hope that this essay has contributed to you feeling the same. As William Blake put it in *The Marriage of Heaven and Hell* (1790/1963), "Without Contraries there is no progression" (p. 3).

References

Adelson, J. (1962). The teacher as model. In N. Sanford (Ed.), *The American college: A psychological and social interpretation of the higher learning* (pp. 396–417). New York, NY: Wiley.

Axelrod, J. (1973). *The university teacher as artist: Toward an aesthetic of teaching with emphasis on the humanities.* New York, NY: Free Press.

Baker, G. A., III, Roueche, J. E., & Gillett-Karam, R. (1990). *Teaching as leading: Profiles of excellence in the open-door college.* Washington, DC: The Community College Press/American Association of Community and Junior Colleges.

Blake, W. (1790/1963). *The marriage of heaven and hell.* Coral Gable, FL: University of Miami Press.

Fitzgerald, F. S. (1945). *The crack-up.* New York, NY: New Directions.

Gilligan, C. (1982). *In a different voice: Psychological theory and women's development.* Cambridge, MA: Harvard University Press.

Hesse, H. (1972). Inside and outside. In R. Manhein (Ed. and Trans.), *Stories of Five decades* (pp. 258–270). New York, NY: Farrar, Straus and Giroux.

Mann, R. D., Arnold, S. M., Binder, J. L., Cytrynbaum, S., Newman, B. M., Ringwald, B. E., et al. (1970). *The college classroom: Conflict, change, and learning.* New York, NY: Wiley.

Palmer, P. J. (1998). *The courage to teach: Exploring the inner landscape of a teacher's life.* San Francisco, CA: Jossey-Bass.

Perry, W. G., Jr. (1970). *Forms of intellectual and ethical development in the college years: A scheme.* New York, NY: Holt, Rinehart, and Winston.

Polanyi, M. (1962). *Personal knowledge: Towards a post-critical philosophy.* Chicago, IL: University of Chicago Press.

Pratt, D. D. (1989). Three stages of teacher competence: A developmental perspective. In E. Hayes (Ed.), *Effective teaching styles* (pp. 77–88). *New Directions for Continuing Education* (Vol. 43). San Francisco, CA: Jossey-Bass.

Pratt, D. D., & Associates (1998). *Five perspectives on teaching in adult and higher education.* Malabar, FL: Krieger.

Ralph, N. B. (1978). Faculty development: A stage conception. *Improving College and University Teaching, 26,* 61–63, 66.

Roberts, K. A. (2002). Ironies of effective teaching: Deep structure learning and constructions of the classroom. *Teaching Sociology, 30,* 1–25.

Robertson, D. L. (1988). *Self-directed growth.* Muncie, IN: Accelerated Development.

Robertson, D. L. (1996). Facilitating transformative learning: Attending to the dynamics of the educational helping relationship. *Adult Education Quarterly, 47,* 41–53.

Robertson, D. L. (1997). Transformative learning and transition theory: Toward developing the ability to facilitate insight. *Journal on Excellence in College Teaching, 8,* 105–125.

Robertson, D. L. (1999a). Unconscious displacements in college teacher and student relationships: Conceptualizing, identifying, and managing transference. *Innovative Higher Education, 23,* 151–169.

Robertson, D. L. (1999b). Professors' perspectives on their teaching: A new construct and developmental model. *Innovative Higher Education, 23,* 271–294.

Robertson, D. L. (2000a). Enriching the scholarship of teaching: Determining appropriate cross-professional applications among teaching, counseling, and psychotherapy. *Innovative Higher Education, 25,* 111–125.

Robertson, D. R. (2000b). Professors in space and time: Four utilities of a new metaphor and developmental model for professors-as-teachers. *Journal on Excellence in College Teaching, 11,* 117–132.

Robertson, D. R. (2001). Beyond learner-centeredness: Close encounters of the systemocentric kind. *Journal of Faculty Development, 18,* 7–13.

Robertson, D. R. (2001–2002). College teaching as an educational helping relationship. *Essays on Teaching Excellence* (Vol. 13, p.1). Ft. Collins, CO: The POD Network.

Robertson, D. R. (2002). Creating and supporting an inclusive scholarship of teaching. *The Eastern Scholar, 1,* 46–58.

Robertson, D. R. (2003a). Getting personal about professional development: Why we don't innovate (even when we want to). *Kentucky Journal of Excellence in College Teaching and Learning, 1.* Retrieved from http://www.uky.edu/TLC/MAINPOSTER/galleyproof/Robertson.pdf, pp. 1–23. January 5, 2005.

Robertson, D. R. (2003b). Integrity in learner-centered teaching. In C. M. Wehlburg & S. Chadwick-Blossey (Eds.), *To improve the academy, 21*(pp. 196–211). Bolton, MA: Anker.

Robertson, D. R. (2003c). *Making time, making change: Avoiding overload in college teaching.* Stillwater, OK: New Forums.

Sherman, T. M., Armistead, L. P., Fowler, F., Barksdale, M. A., & Reif, G. (1987). The quest for excellence in university teaching. *Journal of Higher Education, 48,* 66–84.

Tiberius, R. G., Sinai, J., & Flak, E. A. (2002). The role of teacher-learner relationships in medical education. In G. R. Norman, C. P. M. Van der Vleuten, & D. I. Newble (Eds.), *International handbook of research in medical education* (pp. 463–497). Dordrecht, The Netherlands: Kluwer.

Webster's third new international dictionary of the English language, Unabridged (1966). Springfield, IL: G. & C. Merriam.

Maximizing What Students Get Out of College: Testing a Learning Productivity Model

Shouping Hu and George D. Kuh

This study tests a learning productivity model for undergraduates at four-year colleges and universities using hierarchical linear modeling. Data were from 44,238 full-time enrolled undergraduates from 120 four-year colleges and universities who completed the College Student Experiences Questionnaire (CSEQ) between 1990 and 1997. Perceptions of the campus environment influenced student learning productivity by affecting institution-level student effort, learning efficiency, and student gains. Student affairs professionals and other educators can promote higher levels of student learning by helping to create environments that enhance learning efficiency and engage students in educationally purposeful activities.

Student learning is one of the central functions of undergraduate education. Despite considerable evidence that college attendance is associated with numerous desirable short- and long-term effects (Astin, 1993b; Bowen, 1977; Pascarella & Terenzini, 1991), various groups from inside and outside the academy continue to press for improvement in the quality of the baccalaureate experience (Education Commission of the States, 1995; Johnson & Cheatham, 1999; Kellogg Commission, 1997; National Survey of Student Engagement, 2001; Wingspread Group on Higher Education, 1993). Such expectations are understandable, given that more students than ever are participating in higher education and the knowledge, skills, and competencies acquired during college are essential for the postcollege success of individuals, preparation of an informed citizenry, and continued expansion of an information-based economy (Kuh, 2001a).

Unfortunately, much of the current national conversation about college quality tends to center on such things as institutional resources and reputations, variables that are only weakly linked to learning (Astin, 1993b; Pascarella & Terenzini, 1991; National Survey of Student Engagement, 2001). Though states are experimenting with ways to tie funding to aspects of institutional performance (Kuh, 2001b), infrequently considered are the key factors that enhance student-learning—the investments that institutions make to engage students in proven educationally effective practices, inside and outside the classroom (Chickering & Gamson, 1987; National Survey of Student Engagement, 2000, 2001). The weight of the evidence in the higher education literature points to student engagement as a key factor in student learning and personal development (Astin, 1993b; Pascarella & Terenzini, 1991). Student engagement represents the quality of effort students expend on using the institution's resources and facilities, such as the amount of time they spend studying or using the library. Therefore, a challenge common to all colleges and universities is arranging their resources for learning so that students spend more of their time on the activities that matter to their education. In order to do this the higher education community needs to learn more about student engagement as an untapped dimension of collegiate quality including the characteristics of institutions that are more or less effective in engaging their students at high levels and promoting student learning.

Reprinted by permission from *Journal of College Student Development* 44, no. 2 (March/April 2003).

One conception of educationally effective colleges and universities is that they organize their resources, curriculum, and related programs so that students engage at a high level in appropriate activities (Education Commission of the States, 1996; Kuh, 2001b; Kuh, Schuh, Whitt, & Associates, 1991; The Study Group, 1984). As important as it is to engage students in educationally purposeful activities, there are other ways to conceive of improving student learning. One potentially useful idea comes from the economic principle of efficiency; that is, if student effort is a critical input factor in terms of student learning, we could enhance learning output by producing greater gains per unit of student effort (Groccia & Miller, 2000; Imai, 2000). Up to now this feature of learning productivity has not been systematically employed in studies of how college affects students, though Johnstone (1993) inferred its potential utility for increasing institutional productivity. Testing a model of learning efficiency such as the one proposed in this article will provide insight into whether such an approach could add value to college experience and perhaps point student affairs professionals and other educators toward strategies that will maximize student learning during college.

This study delineates and tests a learning productivity model for colleges and universities. The guiding research question is: How do selected institutional characteristics, including students' perceptions of campus environments, contribute to undergraduate learning productivity?

At the core of learning productivity is the concept of learning efficiency, a concept borrowed from the field of economics (Groccia & Miller, 2000; Imai, 2000). Consistent with this economic principle of efficiency, learning efficiency is the institution-level average yield in gains reported by students in 23 important areas of learning and personal development in relation to the sum of effort students expend in educationally purposeful activities (those empirically linked to desired outcomes of college). In addition to learning efficiency, institutions could also promote learning productivity by engaging students in educationally purposeful activities more effectively and by producing higher level of net gains in learning, as we will discuss in the learning productivity model.

Perspectives

Two models are frequently used in the higher education literature to explain undergraduate learning and personal development in college: Astin's (1993a) Input-Environment-Output (I-E-O) model and Pascarella's (1985) causal model. In the I-E-O model, student learning (outcomes) is presumed to be a function of the interactions of inputs and the environment, which encompass student perceptions and behavior as well as an institution's human, financial, and physical resources. As Kim (2001) pointed out, Astin's I-E-O model does not distinguish the environment variables concerning student's individual experiences from the overall institutional "environmental" climate, even though various institutional environmental characteristics could affect individual experiences differently. In the causal model, student learning is presumed to be a function of the interaction of student background characteristics (inputs), institutional characteristics (size, affluence, student-faculty ratio), student interactions with agents of socialization (faculty, peers), student perceptions of the environment, and student quality of effort.

The conceptual approach used in this study separates the environment component of the I-E-O model into two sets of variables to make it more consistent with the causal model. One set of variables represents quality of effort (Pace, 1984), defined as the frequency and scope of student engagement in various educationally purposeful activities that are empirically linked with desired outcomes of college. The environment variables include such measures as institutional type, control, selectivity, and three measures from the College Student Experiences Questionnaire that represent student perceptions of the degree to which their institution emphasizes (a) scholarly and intellectual activity, (b) emphasis on vocational and practical application, and (c) quality of personal relations among different groups (student-student, student-faculty, student-administration). This approach allows for a comprehensive view of how learning is influenced by what students do, what institutions provide, and what students think about their institutions.

The learning productivity model tested in this research assumes that institutions affect student learning in at least three ways as illustrated in Figure 1. First, a college or university can arrange its intellectual resources and design policies and practices to engage students at higher average levels in educational purposeful activities (Astin, 1993b; Hu & Kuh, 2002; Kuh, 2001b; National Survey of Student Engagement, 2000, 2001). Examples of some of these successful approaches are learning communities, small classes for first-year students, capstone courses for seniors, and intrusive developmental advising (Kuh).

Second, student learning can be improved by increasing the learning efficiency or the yield in gains from student effort (Groccia & Miller, 2000; Imai, 2000). In other words, at educationally effective colleges and universities students benefit more in desired ways per unit of effort expended (i.e., the yield in the units of gains from one unit of student effort is greater compared with other institutions); this is because, simply put, learning is accomplished more efficiently. In this study we are primarily interested in examining this path—the learning efficiency approach—and the institutional characteristics that are related to learning efficiency.

The third approach is to increase the average "net" amount that students gain from their college attendance (Ethington, 2000), independent of their engagement in college activities or learning efficiency; however, it is possible that students attending different types of institutions use different baselines when they report gains associated with attending college (Pascarella, 2001). From this standpoint, the differences in the net effects of institutions on student gains in this model could represent the combination of net institutional effects plus the differences in the baseline students used to report their gain.

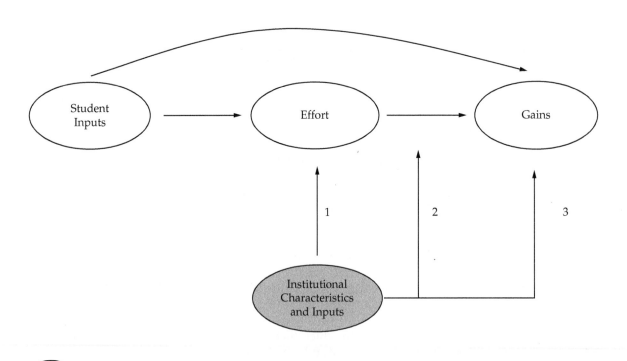

Figure 1 The Learning Productivity Model

Methods

Data Source and Instrument

The sample is composed of 44,238 full-time enrolled undergraduates at 120 four-year colleges and universities who completed the third edition of the College Student Experiences Questionnaire (CSEQ) (Pace, 1990a) between 1990 and 1997. No transfer students are included in the sample; that is, all the students started college and attended only the institution at which they were enrolled when they filled out the CSEQ. This is because the purpose of the study was to examine the impact of institutional characteristics on students and including part-time and transfer students would have confounded the findings, making the results very difficult to interpret.

The institutions included 20 research universities (RUs), 14 doctoral universities (DUs), 41 comprehensive colleges and universities (CCUs), 15 selective liberal arts colleges (SLAs), and 30 general liberal arts colleges (GLAs) (Carnegie Foundation for the Advancement of Teaching, 1994). Table 1 shows the background characteristics of the sample. Women (61%) and first-year students (41%) were somewhat overrepresented compared with the national profile of undergraduates attending four-year colleges and universities before 1998 (Kuh, Vesper, Connolly, & Pace, 1997). Also, about half of the students (44%) were majoring in a preprofessional area.

The College Student Experiences Questionnaire is well suited to address the purposes of this study in that it is based on a simple, but powerful, premise related to student learning: the more students put into using the resources and opportunities an institution provides for their learning and development, the more they benefit (Pace, 1990b; Kuh et al., 1997). Also, the CSEQ has excellent psychometric properties and high-to-moderate potential for assessing student behavior associated with college outcomes (Ewell & Jones, 1996). The items are well constructed, and responding to the questionnaire requires that students reflect on what they are putting into and getting out of their college experience.

As with all college student surveys, the CSEQ relies on self-reports from students. Self-reports are generally valid if they meet three conditions: (a) when the information requested is known to respondents, (b) if the questions are phrased clearly and unambiguously, and (c) if respondents think the questions merit a serious and thoughtful response (see Baird, 1976; Lowman & Williams, 1987; Pace, 1984; Pike, 1989, 1995; Pohlman & Beggs, 1974; Turner & Martin, 1984). CSEQ items satisfy all these conditions. The distributions of responses on the Activities and Gains scales are approximately normal and the psychometric properties of the instrument indicate it is reliable (Kuh et al., 1997). The Gains items ask students how much they think their college or university experience contributed to their own growth and development, and Gain scores are generally consistent with other evidence, such as results from achievement tests (Pace; Pike). Pike found that student reports of their experiences using the CSEQ were positively correlated with relevant achievement test scores.

Variable Specifications

Kuh et al. (1997) describe in detail the psychometric properties of the CSEQ and the scales used in this study. The CSEQ-based variables are defined as follows, while the descriptions and coding of other variables are presented in Table 1.

- Sum of Effort: EFFORTSUM, the sum of student responses to the 14 CSEQ quality of effort scales covering 128 items that ask students how often they engaged in certain college activities. Response options for the effort items are 1 = *never*, 2 = *occasionally*, 3 = *often*, and 4 = *very often*.

- Sum of Gain: GAINSUM, the sum of student responses to the 23 CSEQ gains items which ask students how much their college or university experience contributed to their growth and development during college. Response options for the gains items are 1 = *very little*, 2 = *some*, 3 = *quite a bit*, and 4 = *very much*.

- Five measures of learning outcomes distilled from a factor analysis of the 23 Estimate of Gains items. They are Intellectual Skills, General Education, Personal/Social Development,

TABLE 1
Sample Means, Standard Deviations, and Variable Description on Original Variables

Variable	M(%)	SD	Description
Student-Level Variables (N = 44,238)			
Men	39.00		A dummy variable (1 = Yes, 0 = No)
Women	61.00		Reference group
American Indian and Other	3.00		A dummy variable (1 = *Yes*, 0 = *No*)
Asian or Pacific Islander	7.00		A dummy variable (1 = *Yes*, 0 = *No*)
African American	6.00		A dummy variable (1 = *Yes*, 0 = *No*)
Hispanic	3.00		A dummy variable (1 = *Yes*, 0 = *No*)
White	81.00		Reference group
SES	4.76	1.66	Sum of measures of who pays for college and parents' education, ranging from 2 to 7
Academic Preparation	6.88	1.40	Sum of college grades and educational aspirations, ranging from 2 to 11
Time on Schoolwork	2.85	1.06	Hours per week on academic work, ranging from 1 (*less than 20 hours*) to 5 (*about 50 hours*)
Humanities	15.00		A dummy variable (1 = *Yes*, 0 = *No*)
Math and sciences	24.00		A dummy variable (1 = *Yes*, 0 = *No*)
Social sciences	18.00		A dummy variable (1 = *Yes*, 0 = *No*)
Pre-professional	44.00		Reference group
Sophomore	21.00		A dummy variable (1 = *Yes*, 0 = *No*)
Junior	14.00		A dummy variable (1 = *Yes*, 0 = *No*)
Senior	24.00		A dummy variable (1 = *Yes*, 0 = *No*)
First-year student	41.00		Reference group
Sum of Effort	278.04	45.96	Sum of student responses to quality of effort items, ranging from 128 to 512
Sum of Gain	58.88	11.26	Sum of student responses to gain items, ranging from 23 to 92
General Education	14.38	3.70	Responses to general education gain item, ranging from 6 to 24
Personal Development	13.94	3.24	Responses to personal development gain items, ranging from 5 to 20
Science and Technology	6.38	2.57	Responses to science and technology gain items, ranging from 3 to 12
Vocational Preparation	7.87	2.11	Responses to vocational preparation gain items, ranging from 3 to 12
Intellectual Development	16.33	3.59	Responses to intellectual development gain items, ranging from 6 to 24
School-Level Variables (N = 120)			
RU	17.00		A dummy variable (1 = Yes, 0 = No)
DU	12.00		A dummy variable (1 = Yes, 0 = No)
SLA	12.00		A dummy variable (1 = Yes, 0 = No)
GLA	25.00		A dummy variable (1 = Yes, 0 = No)

(continued)

TABLE 1 *(Continued)*

Variable	M(%)	SD	Description
CCU	34.00		Reference group
Public	44.00		A dummy variable (1 = *Yes*, 0 = *No*)
Private	56.00		Reference group
Institutional selectivity	3.33	1.18	Selectivity measure from *Barron's Profiles of American Colleges* (1996), ranging from 1 (*not competitive*) to 6 (*most competitive*)
Scholarly and Intellectual Environment	15.69	1.04	Scholarly and intellectual emphasis, aggregated to institutional level, ranging from 13.66 to 18.75
Personal Relations Environment	15.33	0.95	Emphasis on quality of personal relations, aggregated to institutional level, ranging from 12.64 to 18.36
Vocational and Practical Environment	9.60	0.67	Vocational and practical emphasis, aggregated to institutional level, ranging from 6.76 to 11.71

NOTE: Descriptive statistics were reported on original measurement scale.

Science/Technology, and Practical/Vocational Preparation (Kuh et al., 1997). Pace (1990b) recommended using the Estimate of Gains factors when the number of respondents is large and the sample is from multiple institutions, as is the case in this study (Kuh et al., 1997). The measures of the 5 gain factors were the sums of the response to the gain items clustered within each gain factor. The response options for the gains items are 1 = *very little*, 2 = *some*, 3 = *quite a bit*, and 4 = *very much*.

- Institutional environment measures: 8 environment scales that assess students' perceptions of aspects of the college environment were clustered into three institutional environment measures to reduce the risk of multicolinearity among variables and reduce the dimensions of institutional environment measures (Kuh et al., 1997). They represent the degree to which students perceive their institution emphasizes scholarly and intellectual activities, vocational preparation, or practical issues in courses; and students' perceptions of the quality of relations that exists among different groups (student-student, student-faculty, student-administration).

Data Analysis

The seven dependent variables specified for this study are Sum of Effort (EFFORTSUM), Sum of Gain (GAINSUM), and the five gain factors made up of the 23 individual gains items. The five gains factors are: Intellectual Skills, General Education, Personal/Social Development, Science/Technology, and Practical/Vocational Preparation (Kuh et al., 1997).

The learning productivity model was tested using Hierarchical Linear Modeling (HLM) (Bryk & Raudenbush, 1992; Ethington, 1997, 2000; Kim, 2001; Raudenbush & Bryk, 2002), an approach especially well-suited to examining questions that require data about student experiences and institutional characteristics. All student-level continuous variables were standardized as z scores ($M = 0$, $SD = 1$), centered on the grand mean of the sample of students. Institution-level continuous variables were also standardized as z scores ($M = 0$, $SD = 1$), centered on the grand mean of the sample of institutions. Centering level-1 variables around grand means permits to interpret the coefficients in level-1 model as adjusted mean outcomes at institution-level to be modeled in level 2 (Bryk & Raudenbush; Raudenbush & Bryk). Because the variables are either dummy-coded categorical variables or z-scored continuous variables, the results are presented in the metric of student-level standard deviation units of outcome variables as standardized coefficients in the conventional regression analysis (Lee & Smith, 1999).

Learning productivity models were estimated in the following steps. More detail about the statistical models is presented in the Appendix. First, we estimated a two-level model by treating Sum of Effort (EFFORTSUM, engagement in educationally purposeful activities) as the dependent variable (Equations 1 and 2 in Appendix). In this step, institutional characteristics are assumed to have a direct effect on the average value of Sum of Effort at the institutional level after controlling for individual student characteristics. Secondly, we estimated a two-level model in which Sum of Gain (GAINSUM) was the dependent variable and Sum of Effort was the independent variable (Equations 3, 4, and 5 in Appendix). In this step, institutional characteristics are assumed to have a direct effect on the average value of Sum of Gain at the institutional level and the institution-level average yield in gains from a unit of Sum of Effort (the learning efficiency indicator), after controlling for individual student characteristics. Then, the five gain factors were introduced separately as dependent variables using the same analytical model as when Sum of Gain was the dependent variable.

In the student-level model (level 1), we controlled for such student background characteristics as gender, race and ethnicity, major field, class level, parental education, time spent on schoolwork per week, and educational aspirations, which are variables that previous research suggested may affect student engagement in college and gain from college (Astin, 1993b; Pascarella & Terenzini, 1991). When Sum of Gain and five gain factors were the dependent variables, Sum of Effort was treated as the independent variable and was grand mean centered. As mentioned earlier, all the student-level variables were centered on the grand mean for the sample, which allowed us to interpret the intercept as the mean outcome for each institution, adjusted for student characteristics in each institution (Bryk & Raudenbush, 1992; Raudenbush & Bryk, 2002).

In the institution-level model (level 2), two sets of variables were analyzed. The first set was the five types of four-year colleges and universities—RUs, DUs, CCUs, SLAs, and GLAs (Carnegie Foundation for the Advancement of Teaching, 1994). The second set of variables was composed of three aggregate measures of the environment mentioned earlier: scholarly and intellectual emphasis, vocational and practical emphasis, and quality of personal relations (Kuh et al., 1997). In addition, institutional selectivity and institutional control were also included when estimating how well the two sets of institutional characteristics predicted learning productivity.

Results

The Unconditional Hierarchical Models

Unconditional hierarchical models were tested to determine the psychometric properties of variables and to partition the total variances in the dependent variables into their with-institution and between-institution components (Table 2). When Sum of Effort is the dependent variable, the within-institution variance was estimated as 0.917 and the between-institution variance as 0.085, resulting in an intraclass

TABLE 2
Results from Unconditional HLM Models

	Sum of Effort	Sum of Gain	General Education	Personal Development	Science & Technology	Vocational Prep	Intellectual Development
Within-Institution variance (sigma squared)	0.917	0.941	0.915	0.971	0.953	0.935	0.947
Between-Institution variance (tau)	0.085	0.074	0.095	0.033	0.060	0.077	0.069
Between-Institution standard deviation	0.291	0.272	0.309	0.181	0.245	0.277	0.263
Reliability (lambda)	0.934	0.924	0.941	0.848	0.909	0.927	0.919
Intraclass correlation	0.085	0.073	0.094	0.033	0.059	0.076	0.068

NOTES: The intraclass correlation indicates the proportion of total variances in the outcome variables lies between institutions; it was computed as follows: intraclass correlation = tau / (tau + sigma squared).

correlation coefficient at 8.5%. The intraclass correlation represents the proportion of variance in the outcomes of interest that lies among groups (Raudenbush & Bryk, 2002). Thus, 8.5% of the total variance in Sum of Effort is due to differences between institutions.

When Sum of Gain was the dependent variable, the within-institution variance was estimated as 0.941 and the between-institution as 0.073. Thus, the intraclass correlation coefficient was 7.3%. Therefore, 7.3% of the total variance in Sum of Gain exists between institutions. These small intraclass correlation coefficients indicate institutional characteristics have relatively little influence on either how students spend the time and energy (Sum of Effort 8.5%) or how much they gain from attending college (Sum of Gain 7.3%). The intraclass correlation coefficients for the five gain factors as dependent variables ranged from 3.3% (Personal Development) to 9.4% (General Education), suggesting that, again, institutional characteristics relative to student characteristics and individual effort do not affect student gains very much (Pascarella & Terenzini, 1991). At the same time, the proportions of variances between institutions still warrant examination and understanding in order to determine ways to more effectively promote student learning and institutional improvement.

The Within-Institution Models

Estimating within-institution models provides information on whether a two-level model (representing student variables and institutional variables) is needed to explain influences on student learning as well as which of the level-1 coefficients could be modeled in level 2. Also, information from the within-institution models is essential to assess the adequacy of the level-2 model.

To test the within-institution (random coefficient) model, the dependent variables were regressed on student-level variables and the coefficients of level-1 variables were specified as random in the level-2 models (no level-2 independent variables included). Because this study seeks to estimate the effect of institution-level variables on student learning, the influence of student-level variables is only briefly summarized. The results from the random coefficient model indicated that Sum of Effort, Sum of Gain, and the five gain factors differed by student characteristics such as gender, race and ethnicity, major field, and class level, consistent with other studies using student as the unit of analysis in conventional regression analyses (Kuh & Hu, 2001). However, although most of the variance in Sum of Effort (91.5%) was associated with student-level characteristics, these characteristics accounted for less than 7.0% for Sum of Effort. This suggested that student Sum of Effort depends less on who the students are (their background characteristics), and more on what students do (their activities) in college. Student background characteristics and Sum of Effort explained about 37.0% for Sum of Gain of the total variance existing at student level. The variance in the five gain factors associated with student characteristics and Sum of Effort ranged from 12.3% (vocational preparation) to 32.0% (science and technology).

The chi-square tests (not tabled) indicated that institution-level mean Sum of Effort, Sum of Gain, and the slope of Sum of Effort vary significantly across institutions. Therefore, it is appropriate to model institution-level mean Sum of Effort, Sum of Gain, and slope of Sum of Effort at level 2 on institutional characteristics.

The Full HLM Model

Table 3 presents the results from the full HLM analysis where the two level models were estimated simultaneously. Institutional sector, selectivity, institutional type, and institutional environment measures were included in the level-2 model, while all variables concerning student characteristics were represented in the level-1 model.

With Sum of Gain and the five gain factors as dependent variables, the slopes of Sum of Effort represent the average baseline yield of Sum of Effort on the respective gains (the learning efficiency indicator), adjusted for student characteristics in each institution. The slope of Sum of Effort line in Table 3 shows that the average yield in Sum of Gain is statistically significant (intercept = 0.563), consistent with the long-standing argument that student engagement in college activities is the key factor in student learning (Astin, 1993b; Kuh, 2001b; Pascarella & Terenzini, 1991). The average yields in the five gain factors from Sum of Effort as reflected by the intercepts were also statistically

TABLE 3
Results from the Full HLM Models

	Sum of Effort Beta	Sig.	Sum of Gain Beta	Sig.	General Education Beta	Sig.	Personal Development Beta	Sig.	Science and Technology Beta	Sig.	Vocational Preparation Beta	Sig.	Intellectual Development Beta	Sig.
Institution–Level Mean	Path 1								Path 3					
Public	-0.098	**	0.048		0.055		0.047		0.060	*	-0.038		0.049	
Selectivity	0.006		-0.033	**	-0.016		0.003		-0.019		-0.014		-0.062	***
RU	0.011		0.014		-0.052		0.004		-0.006		0.049		0.060	
DU	0.048		-0.022		-0.039		0.014		-0.107	***	0.004		0.022	
SLA	0.115	*	-0.074	**	0.042		-0.064	*	-0.125	***	-0.026		-0.114	**
GLA	0.114	**	-0.027		0.015		-0.019		-0.047		-0.004		-0.046	
Scholarly and Intellectual	0.034		0.087	***	0.101	***	-0.003		0.070	***	-0.018		0.137	***
Personal Relations	0.070	**	-0.038	***	-0.046	*	0.006		-0.048	*	0.007		-0.049	**
Vocational and Practical	-0.038	**	0.024	**	-0.014		0.051	***	0.002		0.092	***	-0.012	
Slope of Sum of Effort							Path 2							
Intercept			0.563	***	0.453	***	0.466	***	0.331	***	0.264	***	0.432	***
Public			-0.002		0.002		0.001		-0.009		0.001		-0.007	
Selectivity			0.003		-0.003		-0.015	*	0.004		0.003		0.012	
RU			0.016		0.026		0.016		0.004		0.010		0.009	
DU			0.010		0.014		0.025		0.001		0.007		0.012	
SLA			0.029		0.038	**	0.014		-0.017		0.024		0.037	
GLA			0.005		0.002		0.005		-0.013		0.030		0.009	
Scholarly and Intellectual			0.010		0.016	*	-0.001		0.015	*	0.011		0.002	
Personal Relations			-0.007		-0.007		-0.002		-0.013		-0.017	*	-0.002	
Vocational and Practical			0.004		0.005		-0.008		0.005		0.017	*	0.002	

NOTES: Total number of institutions = 120.
$*p < 0.1, **p < .05, ***p < .01.$

significant, with magnitudes ranging from 0.264 (Vocational Preparation) to 0.466 (Personal Development). These results indicate that student effort is a strong predictor of gains, though the relative contribution of student effort (Sum of Effort) varies depending on the gain dimension.

Institutional influence on the slopes of Sum of Effort (Path 2: the learning efficiency indicator or the learning yield on student Sum of Effort) varied when Sum of Gain and the five gain factors were dependent variables. Although students at public institutions overall were not as engaged (Path 1), there were no statistically significant differences among private and public institutions in the contribution of engagement to the yields in Sum of Gain or the five gain factors. In addition, institutional selectivity had no bearing on Sum of Effort or the yield for Sum of Gain and the five gain factors. The lone exception was Personal Development where selectivity had a negative influence on student learning efficiency. That is, the more selective the institution was, the less efficient it was in converting student effort into personal development gains.

Although students at SLAs and GLAs were more engaged overall (Path 1), the yields for various gains from Sum of Effort did not differ substantially by institutional type with the exception of SLAs (Path 2). Students at SLAs had higher yields on Sum of Gain as well as gains in General Education and Intellectual Development, though the yield coefficient for the Science and Technology gain was negative (but not statistically significant).

The influence of institutional environment on student Sum of Effort (Path 1) and yields in Sum of Gain and five gains factors (Path 2) also varied. Emphasizing scholarly and intellectual activities did not significantly contribute to Sum of Effort, while emphasizing vocational preparation and practical matters had a negative influence. However, high quality personal relations positively affected Sum of Effort. All things being equal, the yields of Sum of Gain and Personal Development and Intellectual Development were not affected by institutional environment measures. However, colleges that emphasize scholarly and intellectual activities had positive effect on yields in General Education and Science and Technology. Institutions with high quality personal relations had a slight negative effect while emphasizing vocational and practical matters positively affected the yield for Vocational Preparation.

Table 3 also shows the coefficient estimates for the effects of institutional type and environments on Sum of Gain and the five gain factors (Path 3), after controlling for Sum of Effort and the yields in respective gains from Sum of Effort. The remaining direct influences shown in Table 3 (Path 3) reflect the combination of influences of the institution on student gains plus the possibility that students at different institutions use different baselines when reporting their gains (Pascarella, 2001). For instance, results in Table 3 suggest attending a SLA appears to have a direct negative influence on Sum of Gain and several other gain factors. These findings should be interpreted with caution, because without further analysis it cannot be said for sure whether SLAs really have negative direct effects on Sum of Gain and other gains, or whether SLA students use a baseline for estimating their gains that is appreciably different from that of their counterparts at other types of colleges and universities (Pascarella). This is also applicable to the interpretation on the direct effects of institutional selectivity on Sum of Gain and gains in Intellectual Development (Path 3 in Table 3), where negative effects of institutional selectivity were found. Clearly this is an area that warrants additional research.

Institutional characteristics such as Carnegie type, selectivity, sector, and the three environment measures in this study appear to account for a relatively small portion of the total variance at the institution level for average Sum of Effort, Sum of Gain, and the slopes of Sum of Effort. The chi-square tests of the respective random components were statistically significant, suggesting other institution-level variables could be added that might explain what accounts for the institutional differences in average Sum of Effort, Sum of Gain, and the slopes of Sum of Effort. The chi-square results also suggest that institutional characteristics are affecting student learning productivity in multiple ways, as reflected in institution-level Sum of Effort, learning efficiency, and Sum of Gain.

Limitations

Though the CSEQ research program is one of the few available databases with information from multiple institutions about the undergraduate experience, the study is limited in several ways.

First, the data are from colleges and universities that voluntarily administered the CSEQ. If results from other institutions were included the findings might change in unknown ways. Also there may be unknown effects on the results due to differences in sampling and administration procedures across institutions. There is also the possibility that as previously mentioned students from different institutions use different baselines when reporting gains (Pascarella, 2001). In addition, even though selectivity was controlled in this study, other factors may affect students' experiences and their openness and receptivity to the impact of college (Pascarella).

Discussion

Keeping these limitations in mind, five findings from this study stand out. First, similar students expending similar amounts of effort engaging in similar kinds of activities while attending different institutions report making different amounts of progress toward many desired outcomes of college. This is in part because some institutions are more learning efficient. Thus, though somewhat controversial, the economic model metaphor for learning productivity may be a potentially instructive way to think about what happens to students in college and how to focus institutional improvement efforts.

Second, since what students gain from college is a product of their total effort in college activities and the yield in gains from their efforts, features of institutional environments can have nontrivial effects both on what and how efficiently students learn. Campus environments that emphasized scholarly and intellectual activities positively affected learning efficiency in General Education and Science and Technology. Schools that emphasized personal relations had positive effects on Sum of Effort and negative effects on learning efficiency in Vocational Preparation. Conversely, institutions that emphasize vocational preparation and practical matters have negative effects on Sum of Effort but predictably positive effects on learning efficiency in Vocational Preparation.

Third, student engagement in educationally purposeful activities has a strong positive effect on student self-reported gains. This finding corroborates many other studies about the impact of college on students (Astin, 1993b; National Survey of Student Engagement, 2000, 2001; Pascarella & Terenzini, 1991). Thus, even though recent cohorts of undergraduate students may differ in many ways from previous groups, the amount of time they devote to their studies and other educationally purposeful activities remains important to valued outcomes of college.

Fourth, this study indicates that several analytical paths are viable for determining the factors that influence student learning during college. The most commonly used approach is measuring what students do in college as represented by the institutional net effect from Sum of Effort. The second path, which merits additional exploration, is the degree to which student effort is efficiently converted into gains. This is reflected by the institutional net effect on the yields in all types of gains from Sum of Effort. The third path tested in this study requires additional validation because of legitimate concerns about the baseline effect on student self-reported gains. This study also empirically confirmed that the conception of three paths of promoting student learning productivity and institutional performance is valid.

Finally, some of the results of this study are seemingly at odds with the results from other studies that incorporate multilevel data, use the student as the unit of analysis, and treat student perceptions of institutional environments as independent variables. For example, Kuh and Hu (2001) reported that individual student perceptions positively affected individual effort and gains at different types of institutions; the current study, however, discovered complex effects of aggregated student perceptions of campus environments on institution-level average student effort and gains. These seemingly contradictory results may be a function of within-institution and between-institution effects, especially when most of the variance is a function of individual students and only a small amount of the variance can be attributed to institutional characteristics (Glisson, 1986; Hu & Kuh, 2001; Pascarella & Terenzini, 1991). Pascarella and Terenzini (1991) explained that the results from different methods often produce different findings, which can also then point to different implications. The findings from this study and previous studies (Kuh & Hu, 2001) are consistent with their observation.

Implications

The results of this study suggest some colleges are more efficient than others in promoting student learning. What can be learned from these "learning-efficient" institutions? That is, what policies and practices are common, and can they be transported and adapted to other institutions? Case studies of different types of learning efficient colleges and universities would be welcome.

At the same time it is important to recognize that institutional characteristics have different and occasionally competing effects on institutional-level average gains and learning efficiency. For instance, emphasizing vocational and practical matters does not appear to promote greater levels of student engagement overall, though it improves the yield of effort in vocational preparation gains. Institutions vary in terms of mission and educational goals; students themselves differ in terms of what they want from college. Varying curricular emphases will also have differential effects on student gains (Pace, 1990b). Colleges and universities should examine the ways in which various dimensions of their environments promote or hinder student learning and take steps to develop these positive learning-centered attributes and minimize those dimensions that inhibit student learning.

As others have observed (Blimling, Whitt, & Associates, 1999; Kuh et al., 1991), student affairs has an important role to play in creating campus environments that affirm and support students to put forth effort in educationally purposeful activities and attain their educational objectives at the highest possible levels (Kuh et al., 1991). The findings from this study indicate that high quality relations among different groups positively affect the amount of effort students put forth. That is, students tend to expend more effort when they perceive that their relations with other students are friendly and supportive, faculty members are approachable and encouraging, and administrators are helpful and considerate (Kuh et al.). Because students spend the majority of their time outside of class, strategies and partnerships between student affairs and academic affairs that tie together in-class and out-of-class experiences have great promise to increase student learning. The challenge to student affairs professionals is to become expert in interpreting and communicating student engagement results to colleagues throughout the institution, taking into account the institutional mission, culture, and other relevant information. For example, does communicating high expectations by faculty members and others have an effect on student perceptions of a scholarly and critical environment? Or is the peer culture and the perceived environment created by being in the presence of other highly motivated, high-ability students a factor? Something akin to the campus audit described by Kuh et al. (1991) may be helpful.

Also, because selective institutions tended to be less efficient in converting student effort into personal development gains, student affairs professionals at these kinds of schools would do well to examine policies, programs, and student experiences in order to determine if intentional interventions are warranted to address this important domain of college outcomes. Instruments such as the CSEQ and the National Survey of Student Engagement (Kuh, 2001b), among others, can be used for this purpose. It is not necessarily the case that students at selective colleges, who tend to be bright, achievement-oriented, and self-directed, cannot benefit from programs and other experiences that foster personal development.

The findings also are consistent with Freeland's (1999) endorsement of using a practice-oriented approach in undergraduate education to help students cultivate the skills needed to succeed vocationally and socially after college. Although institutions that emphasize vocational and practical matters positively influenced effort on the part of individual students and enhanced vocational gains, placing too much emphasis on vocational and practical matters tended to dampen overall levels of engagement. Thus, while student affairs professionals can make valuable contributions by working with students in internships and other activities through which students gain practical competencies, they should also periodically assess whether their substantive programming and individual interactions with students might emphasize career-related goals and activities over other desired outcomes of college.

It may be possible for institutions to have even greater net influences on student gains from college, independent of learning efficiency and the effort students put forth in college activities. But making such claims is risky, especially when self-reported gains are used as the evidence of college impact; this is because of the aforementioned baseline effect–that students attending different institutions may not use the same starting point when estimating the progress they have made since starting college (Pascarella, 2001). Perhaps the most student affairs professionals can glean from such studies is that the results reflect a combination of both the real net impact of college plus the possible influence of students using different baselines for reporting their gains. One of the strategies to further clarify the impact of college on students in this situation is to carefully control the confounding impact of the recruitment function as Pascarella (2001) suggested with more robust measures of precollege student background variables including student openness or receptivity to college experiences.

Conclusion

Taken together, the different findings from this study suggest that institutions, in an effort to improve the quality of undergraduate education, should consider ways to promote student learning both by encouraging higher levels of engagement and seeking ways to increase learning efficiency by improving the gains to effort ratio. Attempts to improve learning productivity must take into account the in-class and out-of-class activities and experiences that contribute directly and indirectly to student learning (Astin, 1993b; Kuh et al., 1991; Pascarella & Terenzini, 1991) as well as students' perceptions of the college environment. Thus, educational leaders, administrators, faculty members, and others committed to enhancing student learning should focus on strategies for engaging students more in educationally purposeful activities and for discovering ways to increase learning efficiency. Student affairs professionals in particular can promote higher levels of student effort and improved learning efficiency by (a) making certain their programs and services are consistent with the educational mission of their institution and appropriate for their students, and (b) concentrating their energies on making campus environments supportive and congenial to student needs and educational goals.

Appendix
Further Explanation of Statistical Models Used in the Study

A two-level model was estimated when Sum of Effort (EFFORTSUM) was the dependent variable.

The student-level model was estimated by:

1. EFFORTSUM $= \beta_0 + \beta_1 X_1 + \beta_2 X_2 + \ldots + \beta_p X_p + \varepsilon$ where X represents student characteristics such as gender, race or ethnicity, academic preparation, and so on, and the coefficients of X represent how student characteristics affect Sum of Effort. This equation suggested that individual student Sum of Effort was a combination of adjusted institutional average sum of effort (β_0) plus influence of student individual characteristics.

Only the intercept (β_0) in Equation (1) was estimated at the institutional level. The institution-level model was specified as:

2. $\beta_0 = \gamma_{00} + \gamma_{01} Z_1 + \gamma_{02} Z_2 + \ldots + \gamma_{0q} Z_q + \nu_0$ where Z represents institutional characteristics such as institutional type, selectivity, environment, and so forth, and the coefficients of Z represent how institutional characteristics affect student effort. This equation suggested that adjusted institutional average sum of effort (β_0) can be influenced by institutional characteristics.

A two-level model was also estimated when Sum of Gain (GAINSUM) was the dependent variable while Sum of Effort (EFFORTSUM) was an independent variable.

The student-level model was estimated by:

3. GAINSUM $= \beta'_0 + \beta'_1 \text{ EFFORTSUM} + \beta'_2 X_2 + \ldots + \beta'_p X_p + \varepsilon'$ where X had the same representation as in equation (1). β' represents how student characteristics affect student Sum of Gain. This equation sets forth individual student Sum of Gain as a combination of adjusted institutional average sum of gain (β'_0) plus influence of student individual

characteristics and student Sum of Effort. The slope of EFFORTSUM (β'_1) can be considered as the yield of learning from student Sum of Effort and represents the learning efficiency.

Both the intercept (β'_0) and the coefficient of EFFORTSUM (β'_1) in Equation (3) were estimated at the institutional level. The institution-level model was specified as:

4. $\beta'_0 = \gamma_{00} + \gamma_{01}Z_1 + \gamma_{02}Z_2 + \ldots + \gamma_{0q}Z_q + v'_0$ and

5. $\beta'_1 = \gamma'_{00} + \gamma'_{01}Z_1 + \gamma'_{02}Z_2 + \ldots + \gamma'_{0q}Z_q + v''_0$ where Z had the same representations as in equation (2). γ' and γ'' represent how institutional characteristics affect institution-level average Sum of Effort and the conversion rate of Sum of Effort to Sum of Gain. Equation (4) suggested that adjusted institutional average baseline Sum of Gain (β'_0) can be influenced by institutional characteristics (plus possible measurement problem associated with student self-report on gains in different institutions), Equation (5) suggested that adjusted institution-level learning efficiency (β'_1) can be influenced by institutional characteristics.

References

Astin, A. W. (1993a). *Assessment for excellence: The philosophy and practice of assessment and evaluation in higher education.* Phoenix, AZ: American Council for Education and Oryx Press.

Astin, A. W. (1993b). *What matters in college: Four critical years revisited.* San Francisco: Jossey-Bass.

Baird, L. L. (1976). *Using self-reports to predict student performance.* New York: The College Board.

Barron's *Profiles of American Colleges.* (1996). Hauppage, NY: Barron's Educational Series.

Blimling, G. S., Whitt, E. J., & Associates (1999). *Good practice in student affairs: Principles to foster student learning.* San Francisco: Jossey-Bass.

Bowen, H. R. (1977). *Investment in learning: The individual and social value of American higher education.* San Francisco: Jossey-Bass.

Bryk, A. S., & Raudenbush, S. W. (1992). *Hierarchical linear models: Applications and data analysis methods.* Newbury Park: Sage.

Carnegie Foundation for the Advancement of Teaching. (1994). *A classification of institutions of higher education.* Princeton, NJ: Carnegie Foundation for the Advancement of Teaching.

Chickering, A. W., & Gamson, Z. F. (1987). Seven principles for good practice in undergraduate education. *AAHE Bulletin, 39*(7), 3–7.

Education Commission of the States. (1995). *Making quality count in undergraduate education.* Denver, CO: Education Commission of the States.

Ethington, C. A. (1997). A hierarchical linear modeling approach to studying college effects. In J. C. Smart (Ed.), *Higher education: Handbook of theory and research* (Vol. 12) (pp. 165–194). New York: Agathon.

Ethington, C. A. (2000). Influences of the normative environment of peer groups on community college students' perceptions of growth and development. *Research in Higher Education, 41*, 703–722.

Ewell, P. T., & Jones, D. P. (1996). *Indicators of "good practice" in undergraduate education: A handbook for development and implementation.* Boulder, CO: National Center for Higher Education Management Systems.

Freeland, R. M. (1999, February 19). How practical experience can help revitalize our tired model of undergraduate education. *Chronicle of Higher Education*, B6.

Glisson, C. (1986). The group versus the individual as the unit of analysis in small-group research. *Research in Social Group Work, 9*, 15–30.

Groccia, J. E., & Miller, J. E. (Eds.). (2000). *Enhancing productivity: Administrative, instructional, and technological strategies.* San Francisco: Jossey-Bass.

Hu, S., & Kuh, G. D. (2001, November). *The institution-student level conundrum: How different methods produce different research findings.* Paper presented in the annual meeting of the Association for the Study of Higher Education, Richmond, VA.

Hu, S., & Kuh, G. D. (2002). Being (dis)engaged in educationally purposeful activities: The influence of student and institutional characteristics. *Research in Higher Education, 43*, 555–575.

Imai, H. (2000). *Student satisfaction, time allocation, and the learning amount at Lingnan University: A microeconomic approach.* Unpublished manuscript. Tuen Mun, Hong Kong: Department of Economics, Lingnan University.

Johnson, C. S., & Cheatham, H. E. (Eds.). (1999). *Higher education trends for the next century: A research agenda for student affairs.* Washington, DC: American College Personnel Association.

Johnstone, D. B. (1993). Enhancing the productivity of learning. *AAHE Bulletin, 46*(4), 4–8.

Kellogg Commission on the Future of State and Land Grant Universities. (1997). *Returning to our roots: The student experience.* Washington, DC: National Association of State Universities and Land Grant Colleges.

Kim, M. M. (2001). Institutional effectiveness of women-only colleges: Cultivating students' desire to influence social conditions. *Journal of Higher Education, 72,* 287–321.

Kuh, G. D. (2001a). College students today: Why we can't leave serendipity to chance. In P. Altbach, P. Gumport, & B. Johnstone (Eds.), *In defense of the American university.* Baltimore: The Johns Hopkins University Press.

Kuh, G. D. (2001b). Assessing what really matters to student learning: Inside the National Survey of Student Engagement. *Change, 33*(3), 10–17, 66.

Kuh, G. D., & Hu, S. (2001). The effects of student-faculty interaction in the 1990s. *Review of Higher Education, 24,* 309–332.

Kuh, G. D., Schuh, J. H., Whitt, E. J., & Associates. (1991). *Involving colleges: Successful approaches to fostering student learning and development outside the classroom.* San Francisco: Jossey-Bass.

Kuh, G. D., Vesper, N., Connolly, M. R., & Pace, C. R. (1997). *College Student Experiences Questionnaire: Revised norms for the third edition.* Bloomington, IN: Center for Postsecondary Research and Planning, School of Education, Indiana University.

Lee, V. E., & Smith, J. B. (1999). Social support and achievement for young adolescents in Chicago: The role of school academic press. *American Educational Research Journal, 36,* 907–945.

Lowman, R. L., & Williams, R. E. (1987). Validity of self-ratings of abilities and competencies. *Journal of Vocational Behavior, 31,* 1–13.

National Survey of Student Engagement. (2000). *NSSE 2000: National benchmarks of effective educational practice.* Bloomington, IN: Indiana Postsecondary Research and Planning.

National Survey of Student Engagement. (2001). *Improving the college experience: National benchmarks for effective educational practice.* Bloomington, IN: Indiana University Center for Postsecondary Research and Planning.

Pace, C. R. (1984). *Measuring the quality of college student experiences.* Los Angeles: University of California, Los Angeles, Center for the Study of Evaluation.

Pace, C. R. (1990a). *College Student Experiences Questionnaire* (3rd ed.). Los Angeles: University of California, Los Angeles, Center for the Study of Evaluation. (Available from the Center for Postsecondary Research and Planning, Indiana University).

Pace, C. R. (1990b). *The undergraduates: A report of their activities and progress in college in the 1980s.* Los Angeles: University of California, Los Angeles, Center for the Study of Evaluation.

Pascarella, E. T. (1985). College environmental influences on learning and cognitive development: A critical review and synthesis. In J. C. Smart (Ed.), *Higher education: Handbook of theory and research, vol. 1* (pp. 1–62). New York: Agathon.

Pascarella, E. T. (2001). Using student self-reported gains to estimate college impact: A cautionary tale. *Journal of College Student Development, 42,* 488–492.

Pascarella, E. T., & Terenzini, P. T. (1991). *How college affects students: Findings and insights from twenty years of research.* San Francisco: Jossey-Bass.

Pike, G. R. (1989). Background, college experiences, and the ACT-COMP exam: Using construct validity to evaluate assessment instruments. *Review of Higher Education, 13,* 91–117.

Pike, G. R. (1995). The relationships between self-reports of college experiences and achievement test scores. *Research in Higher Education, 36,* 1–22.

Pohlman, J. T., & Beggs, D. L. (1974). A study of the validity of self-reported measures of academic growth. *Journal of Educational Measurement, 11,* 115–119.

Raudenbush, S. W., & Bryk, A. S. (2002). *Hierarchical linear models: Applications and data analysis methods* (2nd ed.). Newbury Park: Sage.

The Study Group on the Conditions of Excellence in American Higher Education. (1984). *Involvement in learning: Realizing the potential of American higher education.* Washington, DC: U.S. Department of Education.

Turner, C. F., & Martin, E. (Eds.) (1984). *Surveying subjective phenomena* (Vol. 1). New York: Russell Sage Foundation.

Wingspread Group on Higher Education. (1993). *An American imperative: Higher expectations for higher education.* Racine, WI: Johnson Foundation.

PART VI

*EVALUATION,
ASSESSMENT, AND THE
CURRICULUM*

Part VI: Evaluation, Assessment, and the Curriculum

Every reading in this volume thus far has implications for learning that are ultimately mediated by evaluation and assessment of the curriculum. What do we know about the educational experiences of students in courses, programs, and institutions, how do we know it, and how can we know even better? The readings in this final section each address this line of inquiry in their own way.

As elaborated in several readings thus far, undergraduate education has been undergoing a shift from being teacher-/instruction-/knowledge-centered to being student-/learning-centered in recent years. In "Experiencing a Paradigm Shift through Assessment," Mary Huba and Jann Freed contend that assessment has been and needs to continue being an integral part of this change. After providing a definition of assessment, they describe its "four fundamental elements:" "formulating statements of intended learning outcomes," "developing or selecting assessment measures," "creating experiences leading to outcomes," and "discussing and using assessment results to improve learning." Huba and Freed then offer a historical account of the higher education assessment movement from institutions' financial troubles in the 1970s to state-level calls for accountability to the quality/improvement movements of the 1980s and 1990s. They conclude by enumerating a series of characteristics of learner-centered assessment and discussing how employing such assessment does require an increase of time and energy, but only at the outset of the paradigm shift.

As this shift has been underway for quite some time—and as scholars in the field of higher education have pushed it along with nearly countless studies—it is arguable that the returns on newer and newer research findings are diminishing. This is the position taken by K. Patricia Cross in the next reading, "What Do We Know about Students' Learning, and How Do We Know It?" More specifically, she suggests that "we, as an educational community, are becoming too dependent on what the authorities in research tell us about learning." All of the research on teaching and learning—"gold nuggets" that have been "mined" and turned into "gold bullion"—can be summarized in one "meta-principle," according to Cross: " . . . students who are actively engaged in learning for deeper understanding are likely to learn more than students not so engaged." She concludes by reviewing several principles embraced and advanced in the research community and urges that they be considered not as conclusions, per se, but as the beginnings of conversations about learning at the campus level.

The challenge of not only acquiring valuable information about student learning and other factors related to educational quality but organizing and communicating that information in a meaningful way is taken up by Rachelle Brooks in the next reading, "Measuring University Quality." In this article Brooks builds on the robust literature concerned with quality assessments by focusing on the research methodologies and related critiques of such assessments. To establish a context for her analysis, she states that its "purpose is not to wage additional critiques of quality assessments, but rather to offer a way of better understanding the critiques by bringing them together in a single methodological discussion." Brooks tends to document reputational studies first, illuminating that their roots may be traced to a point in history much earlier than 1983, the inaugural year of the infamous *U.S. News & World Report* rankings. She then details the methodologies and criticisms of assessments based on measures of faculty research productivity and assessments based on measures of students' experiences and learning outcomes. Brooks concludes by making observations of how the strengths and weaknesses of each of the three types of assessments will factor into their use in the future. Specifically, she argues that reputational studies need to be more credible and less costly, faculty productivity assessments need to include better interpretations of inquiry in non-science fields, and more studies of student experience and student learning need to be longitudinal in design.

Sharon Hamilton's "A Principle-Based Approach to Assessing General Education through the Major"—a thorough description of a multi-year initiative at Indiana University—Purdue University

677

Indianapolis (IUPUI) to establish common learning outcomes for all undergraduates—corroborates Brooks' contention that increased complexity in campus-based assessments makes for especially difficulty cross-institutional comparisons. Moreover, Hamilton's article provides a concrete example of how general and specialized education may be conjoined by a concise set of learning goals (e.g., IUPUI's Six "Principles of Undergraduate Learning") operationalized and assessed through the use of an electronic portfolio tool (i.e., "ePort"). Hamilton describes how the IUPUI ePort "captures the entire undergraduate learning experience on one screen" and argues that such developments in technological infrastructure "may well become higher education's best investment in our shared future" because they provide a means to both document and assess "authentic evidence" of learning.

Facilitating students' reflection on their own learning is often a core component of pedagogies that incorporate tools like electronic portfolios; yet, as Sarah Ash and Patti Clayton argue in the next reading, engaging students in meaningful self-reflection can be exceedingly difficult. In their article entitled "The Articulated Learning: An Approach to Guided Reflection and Assessment," they argue that students "need help with connecting their experiences to course material, with challenging their beliefs and assumptions, and with deepening their learning" and that it is "not enough to rely on students' testimonials and self-reports to assess the quality of their learning and the meeting of learning objectives." To address these challenges, Ash and Clayton report on their work with a service-learning program in which student reflection is a keystone of pedagogical and assessment practices. Specifically, they outline what the benefits of "rigorous reflection" can be as well as what they say are the "risks of poor quality reflection" as they explicate what they call a "process of articulating learning (AL)" that can be applied in service-learning programs and other curricular models. Following a description of the questions that guide AL, Ash and Clayton provide actual examples of students' reflective writing and a discussion of how instructor feedback may be incorporated into guiding and assessing students' reflections. To conclude, they suggest how AL may be used in different ways, including as a tool for research and as an instrument in faculty development work.

The value of using student reflections in a research project is evident in the next reading, "General Learning," by Cathy Beyer, Jerry Gillmore, and Andrew Fisher. They open with first-person accounts from nine students, a tiny fraction of such reflections collected in the University of Washington Study of Undergraduate Learning (UW SOUL), to set the context for their presentation of "students' perceptions about how much they learned," "what students said helped their learning," and "what students said hindered their learning." Interspersing excerpts from student interviews and email responses with survey data, Beyer, Gillmore, and Fisher advance two key arguments. First, based on a confirmation that the quantity and quality of learning varies among individual students, they argue that disciplines/majors mediate these differences and, in turn, assessment efforts ought to be concentrated in these areas. And second, they contend that teachers' contributions to student learning must not be underestimated—a notion that "seems obvious on its surface" yet "many projects and programs in higher education are dedicated to reducing faculty time with undergraduates in the classroom," including initiatives that aim to engage students in active learning.

This disconnect between assumptions about the benefits of innovation and its actual outcomes hinted at by Beyer, Gillmore, and Fisher is brought front-and-center in the subsequent reading by Elizabeth Jones, "Myths about Assessing the Impact of Problem-Based Learning on Students." Observing that problem-based learning (PBL) has been embraced enthusiastically by many despite a lack of empirical evidence that links it with improved student learning, Jones details "five myths about the assessment of PBL" in order to ameliorate their counterproductive contributions to PBL assessment and development of research findings. For example, the idea that "problem-solving abilities of undergraduates are the main outcomes to assess within PBL experiences" maintains widespread belief despite the fact that it conceals many other types of learning that can be advanced through PBL (e.g., responding to change, teamwork, self-reflection).

In the next reading, "Qualitative Program Assessment: From Tests to Portfolios" by Patrick Courts and Kathleen McInerney, our attention returns to the use of (non-electronic) portfolios in college and university assessment practices. Among other contributions, this reading provides insight into the process by which those involved in curricular assessment projects may sift and winnow through various instruments to evaluate students' problem-solving skills as well as other reasoning and language skills. Courts and McInerney describe their experience with a multi-year, multi-campus project that began with creating and experimenting with tests of student learning and concluded with the development of a portfolio for assessing student learning. They explain all stages of the process in helpful detail, including how their initial dissatisfaction with students' performance on the tests compelled them to become dissatisfied with the tests themselves, and conclude by offering suggestions for how others can engage such a portfolio project, how they might handle matters like whether or not to construct control groups, and where they ought to direct their attention if students are to be expected to take portfolios seriously.

As a bird's eye view of the readings in this section thus far demonstrates, considerations of evaluation, assessment, and the curriculum oscillate back and forth between defining learning goals and determining how to best ascertain whether and how those goals are being met. What keeps these two concerns in continuous interaction with one another is an overarching view of program quality, a matter addressed by Jennifer Grant Haworth and Clifton Conrad (co-editor of this ASHE Reader) in their chapter entitled "Engaged Teaching and Learning: Staking a Claim for a New Perspective on Program Quality." Here they advance their own grounded theory of program quality—more specifically, an "engagement theory" of program quality—by reviewing literature in the field of higher education and related areas of study and arguing how these other perspectives support the engagement theory and how the engagement theory "extends and re-envisions" these other perspectives.

Janet Macdonald's "Developing Competent e-Learners: The Role of Assessment" reminds us of the ways in which changes in modes of teaching and learning can intervene when configuring goals and assessment practices. She begins her inquiry by observing that " . . . the use of online media for study, and the ready availability of information rich resources on the web, means that students may need to develop competence and self direction at an earlier stage in their undergraduate career." Given the increased demands placed on students in e-learning environments, course goals, instructional methods, and assessments clearly must be revisited. What is particularly unclear, she notes, is whether or how assessments of the formative variety—those communications between teachers and students that guide students' learning mid-course—must be adjusted. Among her findings from a study of two e-learning courses at the Open University in the United Kingdom is the likelihood that formative assessment must be more incremental in order to help students build the increased self-direction needed in digital learning environments.

The pedagogical implications of mediating communications between teachers and learners are the subject of the final reading of this volume, "What is a Rubric?" by Dannelle Stevens and Antonia Levi. Based on their experiences as professors at Portland State University, they explain what rubrics are and how they can contribute to teaching, learning, and assessment. They begin by describing "four basic parts" of a rubric: the description of the assignment, grades or "levels of achievement" applicable to the assignment, the assignment's requisite skills or knowledge, and indications of "what constitutes each level of performance." Stevens and Levi provide examples from actual courses and urge the use of rubrics by extolling their benefits: "Rubrics not only save time in the long run, but they are also valuable pedagogical tools because they make us more aware of our individual teaching styles and methods, allow us to impart more clearly our intentions and expectations, and provide timely, informative feedback to our students."

What do we know about the educational experiences of students in courses, programs, and institutions, how do we know it, and how can we know even better? As the readings in this section demonstrate, these remain open questions. Other important questions arise from the readings as well. Who is served by evaluation and assessment? When will we have learned enough about student learning? Can we engage in a singular concept of evaluation and assessment that satisfies both internal and external constituents? How can we make the best use of technologies, for example, portfolios and rubrics, electronic or otherwise, in our evaluation and assessment practices? How can evaluation and assessment help us place learning at the epicenter of courses, programs, and institutions, and how can evaluation and assessment help us see when and how we fail to do so?

Experiencing a Paradigm Shift Through Assessment

M.E. Huba and J.E. Freed

Definition of insanity: Doing the same thing, the same way, all the time—but expecting different results (Anonymous).

It is tradition. It was a part of my training, and seems like what I should be doing. I feel somehow guilty when I am not lecturing (Creed, 1986, p. 25).

Suddenly I *saw* things differently, and because I *saw* differently, I *thought* differently, I *felt* differently, and I *behaved* differently (Covey, 1989, p. 31).

Making Connections

As you begin to read the chapter, think about ideas and experiences you've already had that are related to experiencing a paradigm shift . . .

- What are your assumptions about how learners learn?
- What are your assumptions about the best way to teach?
- How do you know if your teaching has been successful?
- How have your ideas about teaching and learning changed over the years?
- How can you help your students improve what they learn and how they learn?
- What are your students learning that will help them be successful in the information age?
- In your role as a teacher, what is your relationship to the rest of your institution?
- What do you know about the assessment movement in higher education?
- How do assessment results help you understand what your students know and don't know, what they can do and can't do?

What else do you know about experiencing a paradigm shift?
What questions do you have about experiencing a paradigm shift?

Tomorrow's citizens, tomorrow's leaders, tomorrow's experts are sitting in today's college classrooms. Are they learning what they need to know? Are faculty using teaching methods that prepare them for future roles?

Struggling to answer these questions, those of us who teach in higher education are looking at how we teach and trying to evaluate what we do. This is not an easy task. The many years we spent as students shaped our notions of what teaching is all about. These notions may be so deeply embedded in our world views that they are virtually invisible to us, eluding objective examination. On top of that, many of us have spent additional years teaching as we were taught—practicing the "old ways." Few of us have had opportunities to study teaching the way we study topics in our

Reprinted from *Learner-Centered Assessment on College Campuses: Shifting the Focus from Teaching to Learning*, by Mary E. Huba and Jann E. Freed (1999), Allyn and Bacon, a Pearson Education Company.

own disciplines. It is difficult to step back, analyze current approaches critically, make revisions, and move ahead, confident that the new direction is the right one.

Teacher-Centered and Learner-Centered Paradigms of Instruction

Most of us learned to teach using the lecture method, and research has shown that traditional, teacher-centered methods are "not *in*effective . . . but the evidence is equally clear that these conventional methods are *not* as effective as some other, far less frequently used methods" (Terenzini & Pascarella, 1994, p. 29). In fact, the lecture method is clearly *less effective* than other methods in changing thoughts and attitudes (Bligh, 1972; Eison & Bonwell, 1988). These findings suggest that a change in the traditional method of college teaching is needed in order to enhance student learning (Kellogg Commission on the future of State and Land-Grant Universities, 1997, 1999).

> The primary learning environment for undergraduate students, the fairly passive lecture—discussion format where faculty talk and most students listen, is contrary to almost every principle of an optimal student learning setting . . . Intimate faculty-student contact that encourages feedback, that motivates students, that allows students to perform is the exception and not the norm (Guskin, 1997, pp. 6–7).

The current view in higher education is that we should focus on student learning rather than teaching in order to improve students' college experiences (e.g., Cross, 1998). The reason is not so much that our current approach is "broken" and in need of "fixing," but rather that we are underperforming (Engelkemeyer & Brown, 1998). We are failing to use existing knowledge about learning and our own institutional resources to produce graduates who leave the institution ready to succeed in the information age. "We have failed to realize the synergistic effect of designing, developing, and delivering curricula, programs, and services that collaboratively and collectively deepen, enhance, and enable higher levels of learning" (p. 10).

As shown in Figure 1, the shift from teaching to learning has been endorsed by many prominent leaders and theorists in higher education since the mid-1980s. In addition, in 1998, the Joint Task Force on Student Learning appointed by the American Association for Higher Education (AAHE), the American

---

Students learn by becoming involved . . . Student involvement refers to the amount of physical and psychological energy that the student devotes to the academic experience (Astin, 1985, pp. 133–134).

The routine is always the same: Begin the unit, teach the unit, give the students a test, correct the test, return the test, review the "right" answers with the class, collect the test, and record the grades. Then move on to the next unit. If we continue this practice, how will students learn to use experiences from past units to improve the work they do on future units? (Bonstingl, 1996, p. 30)

Learning is not a spectator sport. Students do not learn much just by sitting in class listening to teachers, memorizing prepackaged assignments, and spitting out answers. They must talk about what they are learning, write about it, relate it to past experiences, apply it to their daily lives. They must make what they learn part of themselves (Chickering & Gamson, 1987, p. 3).

The ultimate criterion of good teaching is effective learning (Cross, 1993, p. 20).

We also know, from research on cognition, that students who reflect on their learning are better learners than those who do not (Cross, 1996, p. 6).

Learning is, after all, the goal of *all* education, and it is through a lens that focuses on learning that we must ultimately examine and judge our effectiveness as educators (Cross, 1996, p. 9).

Students learn what they care about and remember what they understand (Erickson, 1984, p. 51).

Our entire educational system is designed to teach people to do things the one right way as defined by the authority figure. We are taught to recite what we hear or read without critically interacting with the information as it moves in and out of short-term memory. In this exchange, the information leaves no tracks, and independent thinking skills are not developed (Lynch, 1991, p. 64).

Classes in which students are expected to receive information passively rather than to participate actively will probably not be effective in encouraging students to think reflectively. Similarly, tests and assignments that emphasize only others' definitions of the issues or others' conclusions will not help students learn to define and conclude for themselves (King & Kitchener, 1994, p. 239).

Figure 1 Importance of Learner-Centered Teaching from the Viewpoint of Prominent Leaders in Higher Education

College Personnel Association (ACPA), and the National Association of Student Personnel Administrators (Joint Task Force, 1998a, 1998b) alerted us to the need for all segments of a college campus to work together to enhance and deepen student learning. The Task Force developed a set of propositions about learning that can be used by both faculty and student affairs professionals to guide future practice.

The idea of focusing on learning rather than teaching requires that we rethink our role and the role of students in the learning process. To focus on learning rather than teaching, we must challenge our basic assumptions about how people learn and what the roles of a teacher should be. We must unlearn previously acquired teaching habits. We must grapple with fundamental questions about the roles of assessment and feedback in learning. We must change the culture we create in the courses we teach. In other words, we must experience a paradigm shift.

What is a paradigm? Paradigm means model, pattern, or example. A paradigm establishes rules, defines boundaries, and describes how things behave within those boundaries (Barker, 1992). A paradigm is like the rules of a game that define the playing field and the domain of possibilities on that field. A new paradigm changes the playing field by making it larger or smaller, or even moving it somewhere else, which in turn affects the domain of possibilities. Those of us who shift our paradigm regarding teaching and learning have new rules, new boundaries, and new ways of behaving.

To develop new conceptualizations, we must analyze our old ways of thinking and make continuous changes. If our ways of thinking are not analyzed, they remain unchanged, existing patterns continue, and "structures of which we are unaware hold us prisoner" (Senge, 1990, p. 60). When people challenge present paradigms, paradigm structures loosen their hold and individuals begin to alter their behaviors to improve processes and systems. As expressed by Covey (1989) in the quote at the beginning of this chapter, to shift the paradigm, we must experience a personal change. To focus on student learning, we must shift from a traditional teaching paradigm to a learner-centered paradigm.

> Changing the question from *How will I teach this?* to *How will students learn this?* lays bare tacit assumptions about what should be learned and how it should be taught. Specifying what "this" is turns out to be a difficult problem. All too often what is learned turns out not to be what was intended, which often is different also from what was actually taught (Hakel, 1997, p. 19).

Figure 2 is a comparison of the traditional teaching paradigm and the emerging learner-centered paradigm. Similar comparisons can be found in Barr and Tagg (1995); Bonstingl (1992); Boyatzis, Cowen, Kolb and Associates (1995); and Duffy and Jones (1995). When we examine this figure, we see that our thinking about teaching is based on assumptions about the role of students in learning, about our roles as teachers, and about the role of assessment. Our paradigm also includes assumptions about how people learn and about the type of environment or culture that supports learning.

Reflections

As you create your own meaning from the ideas in this section, begin to think about . . .

- Which characteristics in Figure 2 best describe my beliefs and practice as a teacher?
- In what ways does my practice seem to fall within the traditional paradigm?
- In what ways does my practice seem to fall within the learner-centered paradigm?

A Systems Perspective on Learner-Centered Teaching

In addition to examining our own teaching practices as we shift to a learner-centered approach, we must also consider our relationship to the institution in which we teach. This is because we and our students are part of an entire educational system that has developed at our institution from its teaching mission. In a system, each part affects the behaviors and properties of the whole system (Ackoff, 1995). Whenever there is a need for improvement, efforts should be targeted at the system as a whole as well as at the parts individually.

Thus, efforts to promote student-centered teaching and assessing should be made at the academic program and institutional levels, as well as at the level of the individual professor or course. According

Teacher-Centered Paradigm	Learner-Centered Paradigm
Knowledge is transmitted from professor to students.	Students construct knowledge through gathering and synthesizing information and integrating it with the general skills of inquiry, communication, critical thinking, problem solving, and so on.
Students passively receive information.	Students are actively involved.
Emphasis is on acquisition of knowledge outside the context in which it will be used.	Emphasis is on using and communicating knowledge effectively to address enduring and emerging issues and problems in real-life contexts.
Professor's role is to be primary information giver and primary evaluator.	Professor's role is to coach and facilitate. Professor and students evaluate learning together.
Teaching and assessing are separate.	Teaching and assessing are intertwined.
Assessment is used to monitor learning.	Assessment is used to promote and diagnose learning.
Emphasis is on right answers.	Emphasis is on generating better questions and learning from errors.
Desired learning is assessed indirectly through the use of objectively scored tests.	Desired learning is assessed directly through papers, projects, performances, portfolios, and the like.
Focus is on a single discipline.	Approach is compatible with interdisciplinary investigation.
Culture is competitive and individualistic.	Culture is cooperative, collaborative, and supportive.
Only students are viewed as learners.	Professor and students learn together.

Figure 2 Comparison of Teacher-Centered and Learner-Centered Paradigms

See also Barr and Tagg (1995); Bonstingl (1992); Boyatzis, Cowen, Kolb and Associates (1995); Duffy and Jones (1995); and Kleinsasser (1995).

to Senge (1990), systems thinking is a conceptual "framework for seeing interrelationships rather than things, for seeing patterns of change rather than static snapshots" (p. 68). The outcome of a system is based on how each part is interacting with the rest of the parts, not on how each part is doing (Kofman & Senge, 1993).

Conceptualizing higher education as a system may make more sense to students than it does to professors. As professors, we tend to focus on preparing and delivering our own courses, whereas students enroll in and experience a program as a whole. It is stated that students are driven to make sense of their experiences and to actively construct their knowledge by integrating new information with current understanding. This means that, throughout their academic programs, students are developing their general skills and disciplinary expertise by making sense of the curriculum as they experience it. The knowledge, skills, and abilities that students achieve at the end of their programs are affected by how well courses and other experiences in the curriculum fit together and build on each other throughout the undergraduate years.

In this systems view of the curriculum, we must examine how the system fosters student learning. When and where are skills and content knowledge introduced? In which courses are they developed and reinforced? Is there unnecessary duplication of emphasis for some topics, but incomplete coverage for others? Are courses designed to be taken in an order that supports learning? Are the teaching styles and approaches of the faculty who deliver the curriculum compatible with each other and with the principles of student-centered learning? Are they effective?

When we begin to view our programs as systems, we think about our own courses differently. For example, we become aware that prerequisite courses are important inputs into our own courses and that our courses are the inputs for subsequent courses that students will take. The following story illustrates one professor's understanding that students' efforts to make sense of new information will be more effective when courses in a curriculum build on one another.

> I taught the first-level theory course and I was asked to teach the second level. Since I did not know what the third level required, I enrolled in the third level course so that I would know how to teach the second level (Freed & Klugman, 1997, p. 35).

In a systems framework, we work together to design and deliver a curriculum that is coherent to students rather than work separately to design individual courses that we find personally satisfying. We also seek partners in other academic departments, student affairs, the library, the computer center, and other segments of the institution that provide services to enhance learning. Systems thinking continually reminds us that our courses are components of an entire system to support learning.

This type of systems thinking has been encouraged by the assessment movement in higher education. Assessment is a learner-centered movement which encourages us to focus on the student learning component of our teaching as it takes place within the entire system of our institution and within the smaller systems of our academic programs and courses.

Reflections

As you create your own meaning from the ideas in this section, begin to think about . . .

- What kind of "system" am I a part of? How do my courses fit into the curriculum of my academic program?
- How can my faculty colleagues and I dialogue about the interrelationship of courses and experiences in our program?
- How can we involve appropriate colleagues from other parts of the institution?

Definition of Assessment

Learning is the focus and ultimate goal of the learner-centered paradigm. Because of this, assessment plays a key role in shifting to a learner-centered approach. When we assess our students' learning, we force the questions, "What have our students learned and how well have they learned it?" "How successful have we been at what we are trying to accomplish?" Because of this focus on learning, assessment in higher education is sometimes referred to as outcomes assessment or student outcomes assessment.

As shown in Figure 2, assessment in a learner-centered paradigm is also an integral part of teaching. In other words, through assessment, we not only monitor learning, but we also promote learning. As will be explained throughout this book, we can both encourage and shape the type of learning we desire through the types of assessment we use.

We define assessment as follows:

> Assessment is the process of gathering and discussing information from multiple and diverse sources in order to develop a deep understanding of what students know, understand, and can do with their knowledge as a result of their educational experiences; the process culminates when assessment results are used to improve subsequent learning.

In a college or university at which the faculty take a learner-centered approach, the assessment process takes place at all levels—institutional, program, and course. The process is fundamentally the same at all levels, although the focus, methods, and interested parties may change somewhat from level to level.

Furthermore, the process at one level is related to the process at another. For example, the quality of student learning at the end of a program—the focus of program or institutional assessment—depends in part on how and how well we are assessing student learning in our courses. As individuals, are we focusing on developing the knowledge, skills, and abilities that the faculty as a whole have agreed are important? Are we using appropriate teaching and assessing strategies?

In turn, the quality of student learning in courses depends in part on the type of information yielded by program assessment data. Do the programmatic data reveal that we should focus more on student writing? Do they indicate that a particular concept is poorly understood by graduates and needs greater coverage? Do students report that some courses seem outdated or that a prerequisite is misplaced? Program assessment and classroom assessment interact to provide data to enhance student learning.

A practical sense of the many ways in which faculty have approached assessment at their institutions can be found in the 82 case examples provided by Banta, Lund, Black, and Oblander (1996). Illustrations of assessment in general education and various major disciplines are provided from a number of different institutions.

Reflections

As you create your own meaning from the ideas in this section, begin to think about . . .

- How is the definition of assessment presented in this section similar to my own view of assessment?
- How is it different?
- What do I know about assessment at my institution?
- What do I know about assessment in my academic program?
- How do I assess student learning in my courses?
- How does my approach to assessment support learning in my academic program?
- What changes have I made in my courses based on assessment results gathered in my academic program?

Elements of the Assessment Process

There are four fundamental elements of learner-centered assessment. These are shown in Figure 3.

Formulating Statements of Intended Learning Outcomes

The first element of the assessment process is that, as faculty, we develop a set of intended learning outcomes, statements describing our intentions about what students should know, understand, and be able to do with their knowledge when they graduate. Faculty at many institutions have formulated common learning outcomes for all students at the institution. Intended learning outcomes reflecting the discipline should also be developed for each academic program and for each course in the program.

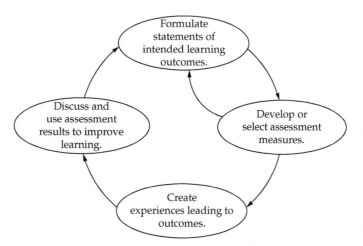

Figure 3 The Assessment Process

These statements typically begin with the phrase, "Students will be able to . . ." The statements are obviously learner-centered, and developing them reflects a systems approach to teaching in the program. When we collectively decide what graduates of an institution or program should know, understand, and be able to do, we are working as a team, rather than as individuals. We are collectively confronting perhaps the most fundamental question in higher education, "What does the degree or certificate that we award mean and how can we prove it?" (Plater, 1998, p. 12)

When assessment takes place at the institutional or academic program level rather than the course level, only the most important goals of the institution or program are addressed in assessment. Learning goals at the institutional level are likely to be more broadly stated than those at the program level, and those at the program level are likely to be more broadly stated than those at the course level. However, achieving the more specific learning goals that we develop for a course or even for a specific class period should help students make progress toward achieving program and/or institutional goals.

Reflections

As you create your own meaning from the ideas in this section, begin to think about . . .

- How successfully have faculty in my program worked together to formulate intended learning outcomes for our program?
- How could we work together to do this?
- What intended outcomes would I develop for my courses that would support program/institutional outcomes?

Developing or Selecting Assessment Measures

The second element of the assessment process is designing or selecting data gathering measures to assess whether or not our intended learning outcomes have been achieved. This element not only provides the foundation for data gathering, but it also brings to a culmination the previous step of determining learning outcomes. This is because the process of designing assessment measures forces us to come to a thorough understanding of what we really mean by our intended learning outcomes (Wiggins & McTighe, 1998). As we develop our assessment measures, we may find ourselves fine-tuning our learning outcomes.

Our assessment measures should include both direct and indirect assessments of student learning (Palomba & Banta, 1999). Direct assessments may take a variety of forms—projects, products, papers/theses, exhibitions, performances, case studies, clinical evaluations, portfolios, interviews, and oral exams. In all of these assessments, we ask students to demonstrate what they know or can do with their knowledge. Most, if not all, of these forms of assessment can be incorporated into typical college courses, although a few (e.g., clinical evaluations) are likely to be used more in some disciplines than in others. At the program level, we can gather assessment data from assessments embedded in courses or design additional assessments that we administer outside of courses.

Indirect assessments of learning include self-report measures such as surveys distributed to students which can be used both in courses and at the program and institutional levels. Other indirect measures used in program or institutional assessment, although not a focus of this book, include surveys of graduates or employers in which respondents share their perceptions about what graduates know or can do with their knowledge.

Both direct and indirect assessment measures should be chosen to provide accurate and useful information for making decisions about learning. In order to do so, they must evaluate the type of learning we desire in our students. For this reason, in this book there will be little discussion of tests comprised of objectively scored paper and pencil test items like multiple-choice and true–false. Many of us use these types of items heavily because they can be easily scored—even by machine—and we rely on the scores that result as the primary contributors to students' final grades. This type of evaluation is appealing because we can collect information efficiently and the results seem easy to interpret.

However, these items typically test only factual knowledge. It is possible to write multiple-choice and true–false items that go beyond checking recall of facts to measure higher-order thinking, and items that do so appear on standardized tests prepared by professional test developers at companies like the Educational Testing Service. However, when objectively scored items are written by individuals without professional training in test development, they tend to focus on factual knowledge.

Another criticism of objectively scored test items is that they assess knowledge bit by bit, item by item, typically with no reference to any eventual real-world application (Resnick & Resnick, 1992). They are only *indirect* indicators of more complex abilities such as reasoning about cutting-edge issues or using information to solve important problems in a particular field. Furthermore, objectively scored tests always have a right answer. For these reasons, when we use them, we send students the message that it is important to master isolated facts and skills and to always know the right answers.

However, the challenges faced by adults in general and by professionals in particular fields tend to be those that require the simultaneous coordination and integration of many aspects of knowledge and skill in situations with few right answers. As Howard Gardner (1991) points out, the ability to take objectively scored tests successfully is a useless skill as soon as one graduates from college. The rest of one's life, he says, is a series of projects.

The perspective of this book is that, in learner-centered teaching, we should design "assessments" to evaluate students' ability to think critically and use their knowledge to address enduring and emerging issues and problems in their disciplines. We define an assessment in the following way:

> An assessment is an activity, assigned by the professor, that yields comprehensive information for analyzing, discussing, and judging a learner's performance of valued abilities and skills.

This book discusses the development and use of assessments like projects, papers, performances, portfolios, or exhibitions that evaluate higher-order thinking and require students to *directly* reveal the very abilities that professors desire. Sometimes these are referred to as authentic assessments because of their intrinsic value (Wiggins, 1989); at other times, they are referred to as performance assessments because they require students to demonstrate their learning. At still other times, they are termed qualitative assessments because they allow us to evaluate the nature and quality of students' work. Further, our scoring is based on subjective judgment using criteria we develop, rather than on an answer key that permits us to objectively sum correct answers. Whatever they are called, these assessments are effective tools for assessing mastery of factual knowledge, but more importantly, for finding out if students can *use* their knowledge effectively to reason and solve problems.

For those of us who would like to continue using objectively scored tests, several excellent resources are available (e.g., Airasian, 1994; Brookhart, 1999; Gronlund & Linn, 1990; Payne, 1997; Stiggins, 1994; Thorndike, Cunningham, Thorndike, & Hagen, 1991). These books include guidelines for writing effective test items, and they give examples of items that measure more than recall of facts.

Reflections

As you create your own meaning from the ideas in this section, begin to think about . . .

- How successfully have faculty in my program worked together to develop and implement a plan for collecting assessment data focused on our learning outcomes? How could we work together to do this?

- Which of our measures are direct assessments of learning?

- Which of our measures are indirect assessments of learning?

- In what ways do I assess factual knowledge?

- How heavily do I use objectively scored test items that I select from publishers' testbanks or that I write myself?

- In what ways do I assess students' ability to use their knowledge as they reason and solve problems?

Creating Experiences Leading to Outcomes

The third element in the assessment process is ensuring that students have experiences both in and outside their courses that help them achieve the intended learning outcomes. If we expect students to achieve our intended outcomes, we must provide them with opportunities to learn what they need to learn. We should design the curriculum as a set of interrelated courses and experiences that will help students achieve the intended learning outcomes.

Students' learning will be affected by the way courses and other required experiences like independent studies, practica, and internships are organized in the curriculum and the order in which they are taken. The appropriateness of the prerequisite courses we designate will also influence how well students learn. Designing the curriculum by working backward from learning outcomes helps make the curriculum a coherent "story of learning" (Plater, 1998, p. 11).

Orchestrating stages in the skill development of students is also part of curriculum development. Where in the curriculum will students learn and practice skills like writing, speaking, teamwork, and problem solving? What teaching strategies will faculty use to help students develop these skills, and how will professors give feedback to students on their progress? Will all professors be responsible for these skills? Will the skills be addressed only in the general education component of the curriculum? Will some courses throughout the course of study be targeted as "intensives" (e.g., writing intensive, problem solving intensive, etc.)? All of these questions are curriculum questions that are central to an assessment program.

As we develop or revise the curriculum, we should include activities and experiences that will help students acquire the knowledge, skills, and understanding that *each* of our learning outcomes requires. Conversely, we should scrutinize each of the activities and experiences that we create in our courses and programs and ask ourselves, "How will this help students achieve the intended learning outcomes of the institution, program, or course?"

Reflections

As you create your own meaning from the ideas in this section, begin to think about . . .

- To what extent do my faculty colleagues and I design and revise curriculum with learning outcomes in mind?
- How could we change our approach to curricular design and revision so that we focus more on helping students achieve intended learning outcomes?
- How could we help students develop more effective skills?

Discussing and Using Assessment Results to Improve Learning

The fourth element is a process for discussing and using the assessment results to improve learning. Within courses, these discussions take place between us and our students, and the focus is on using the results to improve individual student performance. At the program or institutional level, discussions take place among the faculty as a whole.

Through our discussions of assessment results, we gain insights into the type of learning occurring in the program, and we are better able to make informed decisions about needed program changes. We understand what students can do well and in what areas they have not succeeded. We raise questions about the design of the curriculum or about the teaching strategies we use (Walvoord, Bardes, & Denton, 1998). We also develop a better understanding of how to assess learning in a useful manner.

In order to seek additional perspectives, we should share summaries of the process with key stakeholder groups (e.g., students, alumni, advisory groups) who may also provide insights about whether changes are needed in the program's intended learning outcomes, in the curriculum, in teaching strategies used by faculty, or in assessment techniques used. In this stage of the process, we reveal the nature and process of a college education to a broad audience, and we help build trust for institutions of higher education.

With information from the assessment itself as well as the perspectives of students, alumni, advisory groups and others, we can proceed to recommend and implement changes that will improve both the curriculum and the teaching taking place in the program. As discussed assessment data should also be used to inform processes like planning and resource allocation, catalog revision, and program review.

Reflections

As you create your own meaning from the ideas in this section, begin to think about . . .

- When and with whom have I discussed assessment findings and their implications for learning?
- What stakeholder groups would be interested in knowing about learning in my courses and program?

A Brief History of the Assessment Movement in Higher Education

Our role as faculty in assuming primary ownership for assessing academic programs is critical. We are responsible for developing the intended learning outcomes of our academic programs, for developing the curricula on which the programs are based, and for delivering the curricula through our teaching. It naturally follows that we should be responsible for building quality into the programs through evaluating the learning that takes place within them.

Assuming the responsibility for assessment provides us with several opportunities. One is the opportunity to ask important questions about the value and effectiveness of our instructional programs. Another is the opportunity to engage in conversations about student learning with each other. The final opportunity is to use data about student learning to strengthen the way decisions are made, leading to improvement in the curriculum and in instruction.

However, many faculty have been reluctant to engage in assessment because, in some states or regions of the country, assessment has been introduced as a requirement by external agencies such as legislatures or regional or specialized accreditation associations. The reasons for this can be traced historically.

Changing Resources and the Seeds of Reform

The post-war period of the 1950s and 1960s was a time of expansion in higher education (Brubacher & Rudy, 1976). "The enrollment [sic] of World War II veterans created the most rapid growth of colleges and universities in the history of higher education" (Henry, 1975, p. 55). Between 1955 and 1970, the number of students pursuing academic degrees tripled (Henry, 1975, p. 101). Generous support from federal and state governments helped institutions keep pace, culminating in the Johnson years, "golden ones for all of education and not the least for higher education" (Pusey, 1978, p. 109). During this time, the value of a college education was assumed, and universities functioned in a relatively autonomous fashion. There was little need to reveal to external audiences what was happening in college classrooms.

However, by the 1970s, higher education was in a grave financial crisis. Resources available to higher education could not keep pace with rising costs and inflation. Large private donations to institutions, common in the first half of the century, had declined sharply; inflation had reduced institutional income, and it had become increasingly difficult to raise tuition to offset costs and still maintain access to a college education (Brubacher & Rudy, 1976). Politicians were faced with the increasing need to fund welfare, hospitals, prisons (Erwin, 1991), schools, highways, and public utilities (Henry, 1975).

In addition, by the 1970s, the population of students attending college had become more diverse. As the goal of a college education for all became more widespread, college faculties were faced with challenges they had never experienced before. Concerns that college graduates did not have the skills and abilities needed in the workplace surfaced. The public and the politicians who represented them began to question the value of higher education. A movement to bring about reform in higher education—and education at all levels—began (Ewell, 1991).

As a result, in 1984 and 1985 alone, four reports were issued addressing the need for reform on the college campus (Ewell, 1991): *Access to Quality Undergraduate Education* (Southern Regional Education Board, 1985), *Integrity in the College Curriculum* (Association of American Colleges, 1985), *Involvement in Learning* (National Institute of Education, 1984), and *To Reclaim a Legacy* (Bennett, 1984). These reports received less attention than *A Nation at Risk*, the report that triggered the reform movement in elementary and secondary schools. However, according to Ewell, their messages were clear and strong: instruction in higher education must become learner-centered, and learners, faculty, and institutions all need feedback in order to improve.

Calls for Accountability

In some states, politicians assumed the responsibility for initiating reform. A number of legislatures (e.g., Arkansas, Colorado, Florida, Kentucky, Missouri, Ohio, Tennessee) have implemented performance funding programs, and although many such programs have floundered, additional states continue to consider this approach (Ewell, 1998; Serban, 1998). In performance funding, some portion of the public monies earmarked for higher education are allocated to institutions based on institutional ability to meet performance targets like retention rates, graduation rates, or demonstrations of student learning.

For example, the Tennessee legislature mandated that institutions pre-and post-test students, with incentive funding following, based on improvements (Astin, 1993). Florida instituted a "rising junior" test at its public institutions in order to ensure that students were prepared to enter the upper division or receive an associate in arts degree. However, the test was not sensitive to institutional differences and needs, but rather was a common instrument for use at all state-funded institutions and was developed by faculty members from across the state (Astin, 1993; McCabe, 1988).

In part to curtail the direct involvement of state legislatures in higher education, regional accreditation agencies—organizations comprised of institutions of higher education themselves—became involved. Accreditation agencies declared that they would require member institutions to conduct outcomes assessment in order to maintain their status as accredited institutions.

For example, in 1989, the Commission on Institutions of Higher Education of the North Central Association of Colleges and Schools introduced the requirement that every affiliated institution conduct outcomes assessment (Commission on Institutions of Higher Education, 1996). This was one of the few times in its 100-year history that the organization established a program and required every affiliated institution to give evidence within a limited period of time of making a good faith effort to implement it (S. Crow, personal communication, October 29, 1998). As time passed, specialized accrediting bodies—those that accredit professional programs rather than institutions (e.g., business, veterinary medicine, engineering, counseling, architecture)—also began to adopt an outcomes approach to program evaluation.

The Continuous Improvement Movement

Another factor influencing the assessment movement was the continuous improvement movement. Just as higher education was influenced by the business processes of long-range planning in the late 1970s and strategic planning in the mid-1980s, it was influenced in the late 1980s by the use of quality principles and practices. American businesses become involved in quality improvement because of the intense competition resulting from the introduction of better products from foreign countries. Likewise, colleges and universities pursued continuous improvement because of competition or students, the need to reduce costs and improve quality of services, and he desire to enhance learning. The introduction of quality improvement in higher education paralleled the development of the assessment movement, and the two initiatives have much in common.

W. E. Deming is recognized as one of the founders of the quality improvement movement. He believed that continuous improvement is the path to improved quality, greater productivity (less rework and more efficiency), and reduced cost (Deming, 1986). Deming's Fourteen Points (1986), the most cited set of principles for continuous improvement, have been reframed for other settings, one of which is education (Cornesky, 1993, 1994; Greenwood & Gaunt, 1994). Figure 4 outlines the original Fourteen Points according to Deming. Figure 5 presents one example of how Deming's interpretation of quality improvement has been adapted for education.

Gathering data for informed decision making is at the heart of Deming's philosophy of improvement. Deming advocated cross-functional teamwork and partnerships by stressing that barriers must be removed so that people can work together effectively and creatively. Deming believed that people need to have pride in what they do. Therefore, he encouraged education, professional development, and personal self-improvement for everyone Deming, 1986).

---

1. Create constancy of purpose toward improvement of product and service.
2. Adopt the new philosophy and take on leadership for change.
3. Cease dependence on inspection to achieve quality by building quality into the product in the first place.
4. Develop long-term relationships of loyalty and trust with suppliers.
5. Constantly improve systems and processes.
6. Institute training on the job.
7. Institute leadership—the aim of supervision should be to help people do a better job.
8. Drive out fear so that everyone may work effectively.
9. Break down barriers between departments—people must work as a team.
10. Eliminate zero-defect work targets and slogans. Recognize that the causes of low quality and productivity belong to the system, thus lying beyond the power of the workforce.
11. Eliminate numerical quotas and management by objective, substituting leadership instead.
12. Remove barriers to pride of workmanship.
13. Promote education and self-improvement.
14. Involve everyone in accomplishing the transformation.

(Reprinted from *Out of the Crisis* by W. Edwards Deming by permission of MIT and The W. Edwards Deming Institute. Published by MIT, Center for Advanced Educational Services, Cambridge, MA 02139. Copyright 1986 by The W. Edwards Deming Institute.)

Figure 4 Abbreviated Statement of W. Edwards Deming's Fourteen Points for Continuous Improvement

---

1. Pursue continuous improvement of curriculum and learning diligently and constantly.
2. Adopt the system of profound knowledge in your classroom and [institution] as the prime management tool.
3. Build quality into teaching and learning and reduce the inspection of quality into work after the event.
4. Build a partnership relationship with colleagues, students, and . . . employers.
5. Constantly improve the system within which teaching/learning takes place.
6. Take every opportunity to train in new skills and to learn from your pupils.
7. Lead—do not drive or manipulate.
8. Drive out fear of punishment—create joy in learning.
9. Collaborate with colleagues from other departments and functions.
10. Communicate honestly, not through jargon and slogans.
11. So far as possible create a world without grades and rank order.
12. Encourage and celebrate to develop your students' pride in work.
13. Promote the development of the whole person in students and colleagues.
14. Wed your students to learning by the negotiation with them of a quality experience.

[From Greenwood & Gaunt, *Total Quality Management for Schools* (London: Cassell plc). Source: W. E. Deming, `Out of Crisis,' 1982 (adapted to school rather than manufacturing context by L. Richelou and M. S. Greenwood).]

Figure 5 Deming's Fourteen Points Adapted for Education

At the end of the 1980s and the beginning of the 1990s, the quality movement in higher education was relatively new and existed only on the fringes of campus concerns. Research reveals that even though continuous improvement started and has made more progress on the administrative side of most institutions, its principles are becoming increasingly used on the academic side to improve learning and teaching (Freed & Klugman, 1997; Schnell, 1996).

Improvement as Accountability

The preceding discussion illustrates the fact that assessment is a movement that began outside the academy in order to make institutions more accountable to external constituencies. However, it is becoming increasingly clear that the best way for institutions to be accountable to any audience is to incorporate the evaluation of student learning into the way they operate on a regular basis. When faculty collectively take charge of their educational programs, making visible their purpose and intent, and putting in place a databased system of evaluation that focuses on improving student learning, the institution itself is the primary beneficiary while external audiences are satisfied as well.

Reflections

As you create your own meaning from the ideas in this section, begin to think about . . .

- How have the historical factors leading to the assessment movement influenced my environment?
- How have these factors affected faculty *knowledge* about assessment?
- How have these factors affected faculty *attitude* toward assessment?

Assessment and the Improvement of Undergraduate Education

In its report, *Making Quality Count in Undergraduate Education*, the Education Commission of the States proposed twelve quality attributes of good practice in delivering an undergraduate education (1995). "Extensive research on American college students reveals . . . that when colleges and universities systematically engage in these good practices, student performance and satisfaction will improve" (Education Commission of the States, 1996, p. 5). Shown in Figure 6, these attributes address aspects of an institution's organizational culture and values, its curriculum, and the type of instruction that takes place within it (Education Commission of the States, 1996).

One of the attributes is "assessment and prompt feedback," and it is included in the list as an intrinsic element of quality instruction. However, we believe that learner-centered assessment, as discussed in this book, promotes or enhances all the attributes of quality that are listed in Figure 6. Assessment can thus be a powerful tool for improving—even transforming—undergraduate education (Angelo, 1999).

In the following sections, we briefly point out ways in which learner-centered assessment supports the attributes of a quality undergraduate education.

Learner-Centered Assessment Promotes High Expectations

"Students learn more effectively when expectations for learning are placed at high but attainable levels, and when these expectations are communicated clearly from the onset" (Education Commission of the States, 1996, p. 5). Learner-centered assessment clearly supports the principle of high expectations. In a learner-centered assessment environment, students are aware of the faculty's intended learning outcomes before instruction begins. They thus know what we expect them to know, understand, and be able to do with their knowledge. We give them challenging assessment tasks to evaluate their achievement, and using scoring rubrics, we describe for them the characteristics that are present in excellent work. These characteristics derive from the standards to which we hold educated people and practicing professionals in their disciplines.

Quality begins with an organizational culture that values:

1. High expectations
2. Respect for diverse talents and learning styles
3. Emphasis on the early years of study

A quality curriculum requires:

4. Coherence in learning
5. Synthesizing experiences
6. Ongoing practice of learned skills
7. Integrating education and experience

Quality instruction builds in:

8. Active learning
9. Assessment and prompt feedback
10. Collaboration
11. Adequate time on task
12. Out-of-class contact with faculty

(Education Commission of the States, 1995, 1996)

Figure 6 Attributes of Quality Undergraduate Education: What the Research Says

Learner-Centered Assessment Respects Diverse Talents and Learning Styles

In learner-centered assessment, assessment tasks are designed so that students can complete them effectively in many different ways. There is not just one right answer, but rather students have the opportunity to do excellent work that reflects their own unique way of implementing their abilities and skills.

Learner-Centered Assessment Enhances the Early Years of Study

"A consensus is emerging that the first years of undergraduate study—particularly the freshman year—are critical to student success" (Education Commission of the States, 1996, p. 6). Learner-centered assessment enhances the first year of study by engaging students in meaningful intellectual work and helping them discover connections between what they learn in college and the ways in which they will use their knowledge in society or the professions after graduation. This is accomplished by designing assessment tasks that derive from challenging real-world problems and call upon students to use and extend their skills in critical thinking and problem solving.

Learner-Centered Assessment Promotes Coherence in Learning

> Students should be presented with a set of learning experiences that consist of more than merely a required number of courses or credit hours. Instead, the curriculum should be structured in a way that sequences individual courses to reinforce specific outcomes and consciously directs instruction toward meeting those ends (Education Commission of the States, 1996, pp. 6–7).

Learner-centered assessment promotes a coherent curriculum by providing data to guide the curriculum development and revision process. If we want to know whether the curriculum as a whole or the experiences in individual courses are coherent to students, we can ask for their opinions directly. In learner-centered assessment, students give us feedback on their learning in a continual fashion, suggesting ways in which instruction and the curriculum can be improved to help achieve our intended learning outcomes. In addition, through assessment that takes place at the program level, as well as in courses, we can find out what students have learned well and in what areas they need to improve. The resulting information provides direction for curricular improvement.

Learner-Centered Assessment Synthesizes Experiences, Fosters Ongoing Practice of Learned Skills, and Integrates Education and Experience

Learner-centered assessment tasks frequently take the form of projects, papers, exhibitions, and so forth, in which students synthesize the knowledge, abilities, and skills they have learned in the general education curriculum, in their major field, and in their course experiences. These assessments also focus on *using* knowledge to address issues and problems that are important in students' chosen disciplines. Critical thinking, problem solving, and written and oral communication are the vehicles through which students employ their knowledge in the pursuit of important goals in the assessment tasks we give them.

Learner-Centered Assessment Actively Involves Students in Learning and Promotes Adequate Time on Task

All of the forms of learner-centered assessment we have discussed require active learning. Assessment tasks like projects, papers, and so on cannot be completed in a 50-minute time period. They actively involve students in learning over a period of several days or weeks. During this time, we can structure in-class activities to help students acquire the knowledge and skills they need to complete the assessment task. In this way, students are continually focused on achieving the intended learning outcomes of the course and program.

Learner-Centered Assessment Provides Prompt Feedback

When students are completing the assessments we have discussed in this chapter, we can assess their learning as it takes place and provide revelant feedback to guide the process. A major theme of this book is that learners cannot learn anything without feedback. Feedback is part and parcel of learner-centered assessment, whether students are giving feedback to us or we are giving feedback to them. Both types of feedback improve student learning, and this book emphasizes strategies to make feedback both timely and useful.

Learner-Centered Assessment Fosters Collaboration

"Students learn better when engaged in a team effort rather than working on their own . . . it is the way the world outside the academy works" (Education Commission of the States, 1996, p. 8). Unlike conventional tests which students complete silently and alone—and which are often graded on a competitive basis—learner-centered assessments provide opportunities for students to work together and develop their skills in teamwork and cooperation. As students talk about what they know and what they are learning, their knowledge and understanding deepen.

Learner-Centered Assessment Depends on Increased Student-Faculty Contact

In learner-centered assessment, we guide and coach students as they learn to do important things worth doing. We give students feedback on their learning, and we seek feedback from students about how to improve the learning environment. Through the use of portfolios and other self-evaluation activities, we and our students confer together about students' progress toward the intended learning outcomes of the program. This increases contact between us and our students both in and outside the classroom.

Reflections

As you create your own meaning from the ideas in this section, begin to think about . . .

- Which attributes of a quality undergraduate education are present in my courses and my program?
- Which attributes would I most like to enhance?

Learner-Centered Assessment and Time

Using learner-centered assessment may be more time consuming than previous approaches, particularly in the beginning. We will need to take time to confer with our colleagues about fundamental issues like learning outcomes and the coherence of the curriculum. Initially, this will require an extra investment of time and energy as we attempt "to transcend the privacy of our own courses, syllabi, or student programs, let alone our departments, divisions, or schools" (Plater, 1998, p. 13). In our courses, when we try new techniques, we will undoubtedly spend more time analyzing and questioning our past approach to pedagogy and evaluating the new techniques we employ.

We will also discover that our institutions are structured to accommodate the traditional paradigm (Barr, 1998). It takes time and effort to implement a new approach when factors like schedules, room arrangements, reward systems—even the structures of our buildings—have been designed to make the traditional paradigm work efficiently.

Helping students change paradigms will take time as well (Warren, 1997). As we create new learning environments and use new teaching strategies, we will have to guide students to understand new ways of learning.

However, as we, our colleagues, and our students become more familiar and comfortable with learner-centered strategies, the overall time spent on teaching will probably decrease to former levels. We may have to learn to use time more efficiently and effectively at faculty meetings so that we can find the time we need to confer about issues related to learning and assessment on a continuing basis.

In our courses, as Figure 7 shows, we will learn to spend time *differently* than we have in the past. When we prepare to teach, we will continue to keep up-to-date in our disciplines. However, we will spend more time developing materials to facilitate learning and less time organizing presentations of information or constructing objectively scored tests.

	Teacher-Centered Paradigm	Learner-Centered Paradigm
Preparing to teach		
Keeping up-to-date	+++	+++
Developing materials to facilitate learning	—	+++
Preparing a presentation of information	++++	+
Developing objectively scored tests to monitor learning efficiently	+++	—
Teaching		
Facilitating learning	—	+++
Imparting information	++++	+
Giving feedback to improve learning	—	+++
Following up		
Examining grade distributions to monitor learning	+++	—
Using student input to improve the course	—	+++

Figure 7 Allocation of Professor's Time/Effort/Emphasis in Teacher-Centered and Learner-Centered Paradigms

Preparing to facilitate learning rather than lecture about what we know involves designing an approach to teaching that allows students to create their own understanding of the material. We will need to find time to develop materials like statements of intended learning outcomes, questions to guide student discussion of assigned readings, activities that involve students actively in their learning, criteria describing the characteristics of excellent work to use in grading, and assessments that promote enhanced learning.

Facilitating learning rather than imparting information may require the development of new teaching techniques as well. We may have to learn to ask questions that guide student thinking, to facilitate student discussion in ways that lead to increased understanding, to coach students as they work in pairs or groups, and to coordinate in-class student activities. We will have to learn to share our learning outcomes with students and to devote time to periodic discussions of the progress students are making in achieving them. We should seek student input as we develop grading criteria, eliciting students' ideas about the characteristics of excellent work and sharing our ideas as well.

In a learner-centered environment, we will spend more time using these public criteria to discuss students' work with them and evaluate it at various stages of development. The need to monitor how well our students are doing by studying grade distributions will be replaced by more direct involvement in helping students improve their work.

Finally, in each course, we will need to seek and review student feedback about how well the course is helping students to learn and then spend the time to make adjustments that will enhance the learning environment. The payoff of better prepared students justifies the time it takes to make the transformation from teacher-centered to learner-centered practices.

Reflections

As you create your own meaning from the ideas in this section, begin to think about . . .

- On which of the practices in Figure 7 do I spend the most time?
- On which practices would I spend more time if I became more learner-centered?
- On which practices would I spend less time if I became more learner-centered?
- What characteristics of my institution would interfere with a learner-centered approach?

Try Something New

As authors, we have tried to design this book using current principles of learning. One of these principles is that individuals learn best when they have opportunities to examine what they already know about a topic before they encounter new information. This fosters deep learning by helping learners prepare to make connections between current and new knowledge. For this reason, we begin each chapter of this book with a series of questions entitled Making Connections.

We have also referred to the fact that adults learn best when they have opportunities to reflect upon their current knowledge and practice in the light of new information. Throughout this chapter, as well as the others in this book, we have provided opportunities for reflection in the several series of questions entitled Reflections.

A final aspect of the book is the opportunity at the end of each chapter to Try Something New. We suggest that you review your answers to the questions in the Making Connections and Reflections sections in this chapter. Then pursue one or more of the suggested activities below to begin shifting from teaching to learning.

1. Read an article from this chapter and identify three points that have implications for your teaching.
2. Invite a colleague to lunch and bring along a copy of Figure 2. Discuss together those features of your teaching that could be considered elements of the traditional paradigm and those that could be considered learner-centered.

3. Make a list of all the ways that you assess learning in your courses. Discuss your assessment approach with a colleague and seek his/her reactions.

4. Find out what your institution is doing to support the shift from teaching to learning, as well as to establish an assessment culture on campus.

References

Ackoff, R. L. (1995, June). *The challenges of change and the need for systems thinking.* Paper presented at the AAHE Conference on Assessment and Quality, Boston, Massachusetts.

Airasian, P. W. (1994). *Classroom assessment* (2nd ed.). New York: McGraw-Hill, Inc.

Angelo, T. A. (1999, May). Doing assessment as if learning matters most. *AAHE Bulletin*, 3–6.

Association of American Colleges. (1985). *Integrity in the college curriculum: A report to the academic community.* Washington, DC: Association of American Colleges.

Astin, A. W. (1985). *Achieving educational excellence.* San Francisco: Jossey-Bass.

Astin, A. W. (1993). *Assessment for excellence.* Phoenix, AZ: Oryx Press.

Banta, T. W., Lund, J. P., Black, K. E., & Oblander, F. W. (1996). *Assessment in practice: Putting principles to work on college campuses.* San Francisco: Jossey-Bass.

Barker, J. A. (1992). *Paradigms: The business of discovering the future.* New York: Harper Business.

Barr, R. B. (1998, September-October). Obstacles to implementing the learning paradigm—What it takes to overcome them. *About Campus*, 18–25.

Barr, R. B., & Tagg, J. (1995, November/December). From teaching to learning: A new paradigm for undergraduate education. *Change*, 13–25.

Bennett, W. J. (1984). *To reclaim a legacy: A report on the humanities in higher education.* Washington, DC: National Endowment for the Humanities.

Bligh, D. A. (1972). *What's the use of lectures?* Baltimore: Penguin Books.

Bonstingl, J. J. (1992). The total quality classroom. *Educational Leadership, 49* (6) 66–70.

Bonstingl, J. J. (1996). *Schools of quality.* Alexandria, VA: Association for Supervision and Curriculum Development.

Boyatzis, Cowen, Kolb, & Associates, (1995). *Innovation in professional education.* San Francisco: Jossey-Bass.

Brookhart, S. M. (1999). *The art and science of classroom assessment: The missing part of pedagogy.* (ASHE-ERIC Higher Education Report: Vol. 27, No 1). Washington DC: The George Washington University, Graduate School of Education and Human Development.

Brubacher, J. S., & Rudy, W. (1976). *Higher education in transition (3rd ed.).* New York Harper and Row.

Chickering, A. W., & Gamson, Z. F. (1987, March). Seven principles for good practice *AAHE Bulletin*, 3–7.

Commission on Institutions of Higher Education of the North Central Association (1996, February 22). *Commission statement on assessment of student academic achievement.* Chicago: North Central Association.

Cornesky, R. (1993). *The quality professor: Implementing TQM in the classroom.* Madison WI: Magna Publications.

Cornesky, R. (1994). *Quality classroom practices for professors.* Port Orange, FL: Cornesky & Associates.

Covey, S. R. (1989). *The 7 habits of highly effective people.* New York: Simon & Schuster.

Creed, T. (Winter 1986). Why we lecture. *Symposium: A Saint John's Faculty Journal, 5*, 17–32.

Cross, K. P. (1993, February-March). Involving faculty in TQM. *AACC Journal*, 15–20.

Cross, K. P. (1996, March-April). New lenses on learning. *About Campus*, 4–9.

Cross, K. P. (1998, July-August). *Why* learning communities? *Why now? About Campus*, 4–11.

Deming, W. E. (1986). *Out of the crisis.* Cambridge, MA: Massachusetts Institute of Technology Center for Advanced Engineering Study.

Duffy, D. K., & Jones, J. W. (1995). *Teaching within the rhythms of the semester.* San Francisco: Jossey-Bass.

Education Commission of the States. (1995). *Making quality count in undergraduate education.* Denver, CO: Education Commission of the States.

Education Commission of the States. (1996, April). What research says about improving undergraduate education. *AAHE Bulletin*, 5–8.

Eison, J., & Bonwell, C. (1988, March). *Making real the promise of active learning.* Paper presented at the meeting of the American Association for Higher Education, Washington, DC.

Engelkemeyer, S. W., & Brown, S. C. (1998, October). Powerful partnerships: A shared responsibility for learning. *AAHE Bulletin,* 10–12.

Erickson, S. C. (1984). *The essence of good teaching.* San Francisco: Jossey-Bass.

Erwin, T. D. (1991). *Assessing student learning and development.* San Francisco: Jossey-Bass.

Ewell, P. T. (1991). To capture the ineffable: New forms of assessment in higher education. In G. Grant, (Ed.). *Review of Research in Education, 17,* 75–125. Washington, DC: American Educational Research Association.

Ewell, P. T. (1998, May-June). From the states—implementing performance funding in Washington state: Some new takes on an old problem. *Assessment Update, 10* (3), 7–8, 13.

Freed, J. E., & Klugman, M. R. (1997). *Quality principles and practices in higher education: Different questions for different times.* Phoenix, AZ: American Council on Education and The Oryx Press.

Gardner, H. (1991). *The unschooled mind: How children think and how schools should teach.* New York: Basic Books.

Greenwood, M. S., & Gaunt, H. J. (1994). *Total quality management for schools.* London: Cassell.

Gronlund, N. E., & Linn, R. L. (1990). *Measurement and evaluation in teaching* (6th ed.). New York: MacMillan Publishing Company.

Guskin, A. (1997, July-August). Learning more, spending less. *About Campus,* 4–9.

Hakel, M. D. (1997, July-August). What we must learn from Alverno. *About Campus,* 16–21.

Henry, D. D. (1975). *Challenges past, challenges present: An analysis of American higher education since 1930.* San Francisco: Jossey-Bass.

Joint Task Force on Student Learning. (1998a). *Learning principles and collaborative action.* Washington, DC: American Association for Higher Education.

Joint Task Force on Student Learning. (1998b). *Powerful partnerships: A shared responsibility for learning.* Washington, DC: American College Personnel Association. http://www.aahe.org, http://www.acpa.nche.edu, or http://www.naspa.org

Kellogg Commission on the Future of State and Land-Grant Universities. (1997). *Returning to our roots: The student experience.* Washington, DC: National Association of State Universities and Land-Grant Colleges. http://www.nasulgc.org

Kellogg Commission on the Future of State and Land-Grant Universities. (1999). *Returning to our roots: The engaged institution.* Washington, DC: National Association of State Universities and Land-Grant Colleges. http://www.nasulgc.org

King, P. M., & Kitchener, K. S. (1994). *Developing reflective judgment: Understanding and promoting intellectual growth and critical thinking in adolescents and adults.* San Francisco: Jossey-Bass.

Kleinsasser, A. M. (1995, March/April). Assessment culture and national testing. *The Clearing House,* 205–210.

Kofman, F., & Senge, P. M. (1993). Communities of commitment: The heart of learning organizations. *American Management Association,* 5–23.

Lynch, R. F. (1991, April). Shedding the shackles of George Patton, Henry Ford, and first-grade teachers. *Quality Progress,* 64.

McCabe, R. H. (1988). The assessment movement: What next? Who cares? In J. S. Stark & A. Thomas, (Eds.), *Assessment and program evaluation* (pp. 199–203). ASHE Reader Series. Needham Heights, MA: Simon & Schuster Custom Publishing.

National Institute of Education, Study Group on the Conditions of Excellence in American Higher Education. (1984). *Involvement in learning: Realizing the potential of American higher education.* Washington, DC: U. S. Government Printing Office.

Palomba, C. A., & Banta, T. W. (1999). *Assessment essentials.* San Francisco: Jossey-Bass.

Payne, D. A. (1997). *Applied educational assessment.* Belmont, CA: Wadsworth.

Plater, W. M. (1998, November-December). So . . . Why aren't we taking learning seriously? *About Campus,* 9–14.

Pusey, N. M. (1978). *American higher education: 1945–1970.* Cambridge, MA: Harvard University Press.

Resnick, L., & Resnick, D. (1992). Assessing the thinking curriculum: New tools for educational reform. In B. R. Gifford & M. C. O'Connor (Eds.), *Changing assessments: Alternative views of aptitude, achievement and instruction* (pp. 37–75). Boston: Kluwer Academic Publishers.

Schnell, M. S. (1996, April). Could collaboration be on the horizon? *AAHE Bulletin*, 15–17.

Senge, P. M. (1990). *The fifth discipline: The art and practice of the learning organization.* New York: Doubleday/ Currency.

Serban, A. (1998, March-April). The performance funding wave: Views of state policymakers and campus leaders. *Assessment Update, 10* (2), 1–2, 10–11.

Southern Regional Education Board. (1985). *Access to quality undergraduate education: A report to the Southern Regional Education Board by its Commission for Educational Quality.* Atlanta: Southern Regional Education Board.

Stiggins, R. J. (1994). *Student-centered classroom assessment.* New York: Merrill.

Terenzini, P. T., & Pascarella, E. T. (1994, January/February). Living with myths: Undergraduate education in America. *Change*, 28–30.

Thorndike, R. M., Cunningham, G. K., Thorndike, R. L., & Hagen, E.P. (1991). *Measurement and evaluation in psychology and education* (5th ed.). New York: MacMillan.

Walvoord, B. E., Bardes, B., & Denton, J. (1998, September-October). Closing the feed-back loop in classroom-based assessment. *Assessment Update, 10* (5), 1–2, 10–11.

Warren, R. G. (1997, March-April). Engaging students in active learning. *About Campus*, 16–20.

Wiggins, G. (1989, May). A true test: Toward more authentic and equitable assessment. *Phi Delta Kappan*, 703–713.

Wiggins, G., & McTighe, J. (1998). *Understanding by design.* Alexandria, VA: Association for Supervision and Curriculum Development.

WHAT DO WE KNOW ABOUT STUDENTS' LEARNING, AND HOW DO WE KNOW IT?

K. PATRICIA CROSS

Within the past few years, there has been a flood of articles, books, and conference themes entreating colleges and universities to make student learning their top priority. Fortunately, there is more information about learning available to us than ever before in the history of the world; and the amount of research on learning continues to escalate. About 30 years ago, a large book entitled *The Impact of College on Students* by Feldman and Newcomb (1969) appeared, promising to tell us everything we ever wanted to know about student learning in college. The cover blurb assured us that "Everything written of any importance—during the last 40 years—has been thoroughly reviewed, analyzed, and distilled in this definitive compendium of research on higher education and college students. . .". (I doubt that any publisher today would be quite so confident that they had published the definitive book.) Nevertheless, the book lived up to its promise and ran to almost 500 pages, reviewing nearly 1500 research studies.

Almost a quarter of a century later, in 1991, an even larger volume appeared, entitled *How College Affects Students* by Pascarella and Terenzini, running to almost 1000 pages and reviewing nearly 2600 studies. At that rate, I figure that in ten years we should look forward to—if that is the correct terminology—a 2000 page treatise reviewing approximately 5000 studies, telling us perhaps more than we ever wanted to know about what and how students learn in college.

Despite the undeniable value of these books pulling together what we know about student learning in college, I doubt that we will ever see that next volume—either because such a huge compendium of information will no longer be presented via the printed page or because the research will change radically, not just in methodology and customization to more sharply defined issues, but in credibility and usefulness.

Right now we are struggling, as never before, to make research useful—to apply it to the improvement of undergraduate education. The current model for usefulness is to cope with the information explosion by ever-tighter syntheses and distillations. In our times, Pascarella and Terenzini have done the major work of synthesizing thousands of research studies into 1000 pages. Since most administrators and faculty don't have time to read the huge compendiums of information now available, the next step has been to condense 1000 pages into one or two pages of bulleted principles or conclusions.

I have on my desk right now a collection of such distillations of what we know about the learning of college students. The best known, certainly the most widely distributed list, is the "Seven Principles for Good Practice in Undergraduate Education." The Seven Principles were developed by convening a group of scholars of higher education and asking them to derive from their knowledge of the past 50 years of research a set of principles that could be applied to improve learning. Chickering and Gamson (1987) then formulated the conclusions into "seven principles," making them widely available to educators.

In addition to the seven principles, there are the "three critical conditions for excellence" formulated by the Study Group on the Conditions of Excellence in American Higher Education (1984), the nine

Reprinted from *Innovative Higher Education* 23, no. 4 (summer 1999).

strategies for improving student learning set forth by the Oxford Centre for Staff Development (1992) in England, and the twelve attributes of good practice published by the Education Commission of the States (1996). The Task Force on Psychology in Education established by the American Psychological Association has come forth with a dozen learner-centered principles representing psychology's accumulated knowledge about learning and instruction (McCombs, 1992).

We have been using what I call the mining approach to discovering and disseminating information. We are mining tons of ore to come up with a nugget of gold. True, our technology for bringing the ore to the surface is making the mining more feasible than ever before, but are we now faced with the prospect of mining old mines from which most of the gold has already been extracted? Pascarella and Terenzini admitted unabashedly that, "Our conclusions about the changes that occur during college differ in only minor ways from those of Feldman and Newcomb . . ." (p. 563).

I don't want to make light of the contributions of research to knowledge about how college affects students. I think those who have been mining the ore and those who have been extracting the gold have performed valuable services in making the results of research available to a wide audience. But I am going to suggest that we, as an educational community, are becoming too dependent on what the authorities in research tell us about learning.

John Naisbitt said, "We are living in the *time of the parenthesis*, the time between eras . . . a time of change and questioning." (1982, p. 249). Some believe that we are coming to the end of an era that the late Donald Schön, of MIT, called, "technical rationality," and that there is little to be gained by trying to apply rigorous scientific methods to problems that may not lend themselves to easy answers. The professions are in the midst of a crisis of confidence and legitimacy, said Schön, because professional knowledge is mismatched to the conditions of practice. Schön (1983) put the dilemma this way:

> "There is a high, hard ground where practitioners can make effective use of research-based theory and technique, and there is a swampy, lowland where situations are confusing 'messes' incapable of technical solution. The difficulty is that the problems of the high ground, however great their technical interest, are often relatively unimportant to clients or to the larger society, while in the swamp are the problems of greatest human concern. Shall the practitioner stay on the high, hard ground where he can practice rigorously, as he understands rigor, but where he is constrained to deal with problems of relatively little social importance? Or shall he descend into the swamp where he can engage the most important and challenging problems if he is willing to forsake technical rigor?" (1983, p. 42).

The assumption of most researchers is that further refinement of research methods, new statistical controls, more rigorous standards will lead to greater knowledge. Many are now questioning that assumption. It doesn't take much reading of the scholarly literature in education these days to see the huge question marks raised by the philosophical "isms"—constructionism, feminism, modernism, post-modernism. The "isms" are questioning the very nature of knowledge. Until we know what knowledge is, they say, we can't really say how to attain it. In a nutshell—which is perhaps not the way philosophers prefer to present their food for thought—the epistemological question is, do learners discover knowledge that exists "out there" in reality or do they construct it for themselves through a process of language, thought, and social interaction?

Kenneth Bruffee is a professor of English at Brooklyn college and an advocate of "nonfoundational social constructionism," which to my mind, is a rather awkward term for the belief that knowledge is socially constructed rather than discovered. "We construct and maintain knowledge," Bruffee says, "not by examining the world but by negotiating with one another in communities of knowledgeable peers" (1995, p. 9). Knowledge, he says, is "therefore not universal and absolute. It is local and historically changing. We construct it and reconstruct it, time and again, and build it up in layers." (p. 222).

In contrast, the foundational or conventional view of knowledge contends that there is a reality "out there," a foundation upon which all knowledge is built. The task of learners is to discover the world that exists. That means, of course, that there is a right answer and that the experts know what it is or have ways of eventually discovering it though objective scientific research.

The role of teachers and students is quite different in these two epistemologies. The difference is perhaps best illustrated in a series of articles in *Change* that contrasted cooperative and collaborative learning—frankly a topic which, at first blush, seemed to me not something I needed to get excited about. (Bruffee, 1995; Matthews, 1995; Whipple, 1987). But reading more deeply, I discovered that while both pedagogies seemed modern and enlightened in their agreement about the virtues of active learning, students teaching students, learning the skills of teamwork, benefiting from diversity, and most of the other advantages embedded in small group learning, cooperative and collaborative pedagogies had very different ideas about the nature of knowledge and how students should go about achieving knowledge.

Briefly, cooperative learning involves the more conventional notion of cooperation in that students work in small groups on an assigned project or problem under the guidance of the teacher who monitors the groups, making sure that students are staying on task and are coming up with the correct answers. This assumes, of course, that there is a right—or at least a best—answer and that the teacher knows what it is. Cooperative learning is what I think most faculty joining the learning revolution are thinking about.

Collaborative learning is a more radical departure. It involves students working together in small groups to develop their own answer—not necessarily a known answer—through interaction and reaching consensus. Monitoring the groups or correcting "wrong" impressions is not the role of the teacher, since the teacher is not considered the authority on what the answer should be. The teacher would be interacting along with students to arrive at a consensus.

Although the logic of social constructionism seems extreme to conventional education, the challenge it presents is worth serious consideration. Among other things, it lies behind some aspects of multiculturalism, in which the question is: Who says that the truth about the world lies in majority cultures?

Conventional instruction is based on a hierarchical model in which those who know teach those who do not know. Ultimately, there are answers to every question, and scholarship consists of knowing the answer or knowing how to find out. Once that epistemology is accepted, students—and, yes, faculty and administrators, too—can compete for who has the most or best answers. Gene Rice noted that today's colleges and universities are widely viewed as "the place where talented men and women—students, faculty, and administrators—contend for competitive advantage." (Rice, 1996, p. 4). And I can't argue with that. Students are rewarded for their right answers by high grades and selection to the best colleges; faculty are rewarded for their search for right answers by research grants and tenure; and administrators compete for fame for their campus by establishing the greatest storehouses of knowledge with large libraries, computer systems with huge memories, and a prominent research faculty. In sum, the epistemology on which our current educational system is built is that knowledge is accumulated by discovering the "truth" about the reality that exists. It can be discovered through scientific research, stored in libraries and computers, and disseminated via publications and teaching. And, yes, it can be transferred from researchers to practitioners.

The contrasting epistemology that is proposed by many of the "isms" holds that knowledge is constructed by humans through social interaction. Education, therefore, should be based in learning communities where teachers and students act interdependently to construct meaning and understanding. The model is collaborative and egalitarian. According to Bruffee, social constructionism contends that "knowledge is a consensus among the members of a community of knowledgeable peers—something people construct by talking together and reaching agreement" (1995, p. 3).

That is pretty close to what Schön recommended when he suggested that practitioners should engage in a search for knowledge by asking themselves what "kinds of knowing are already embedded in competent practice" (Schön, 1983, p. 29). That would seem to call for communities of practitioners to generate relevant knowledge about the practice of their profession. Teachers would talk with one another about what they have observed in their own learning and the learning of their students.

Another strong sign of a radical shift in our view of how knowledge is generated is found in the work of feminist thinkers about women as learners. Belenky and her colleagues (1986) sparked a strong strain of sympathetic recognition among women teachers and students when they demonstrated that many women display different "ways of knowing" from the male model that has dominated academe for so many years. The male model is characterized by "separate knowing"—a way of learning that is impersonal and objective involving detachment, critical argument, analysis, and other descriptors that we associate with the "scientific method." Many women, however, are "connected learners." "Connected learners" said the authors, "develop procedures for gaining access to other people's knowledge. At the heart of these procedures is the capacity for empathy" (Belenky, 1986, p. 113).

Blythe Clinchy described a connected learner's search for knowledge this way: "She does not ask whether it is right; she asks what it means. When she says, 'Why do you think that?' She doesn't mean, 'What evidence do you have to back that up?' She means, 'What in your experience led you to that position'?" (Clinchy, 1990, p. 122). This student's search for knowledge, argued Clinchy, is best accomplished through connected conversations, "in which each person serves as midwife to each other person's thoughts, and each builds on the other's ideas (p. 123). At heart, a connected conversation is a learning community at its best, and it is also a reflection of changing ideas about the source of knowledge and learning.

The cutting-edge books about the revolution taking place in business are yet another indication of the pervasiveness of a changing perspective about the origins of knowledge. Peter Senge, in his book on the *Fifth Discipline* (1990), goes on at some length about the emergence of new knowledge through dialogue with peers. He calls for "a shift of mind—from seeing ourselves as separate from the world to connected to the world, from seeing problems as caused by someone or something 'out there' to seeing how our own actions create the problems we experience. A learning organization is a place where people are continually discovering how they create their reality. And how they can change it" (pp. 12–13). Once again that sounds like a shift from discovering knowledge that lies in reality "out there," to creating knowledge that lies within human interchange.

If we are entering the 21st century in the parenthesis of philosophical questioning between scientific rigor and other ways of knowing, I cannot help noting the similarities between the developmental stages of personal growth and the developmental stages of society's pursuit of knowledge. Let me explain.

William Perry is perhaps the best known developmentalist to those of us in higher education. He posits nine positions of intellectual development for college students, but the three major positions can be presented briefly. The scheme starts at the low end of intellectual development, with students assuming that there is a right answer to every question and that the answer is known by an authority—namely the professors who are hired to teach them. Students entering college in the early stages of intellectual development have a low tolerance for ambiguity, but they can grant that in some cases we haven't found the answer yet. Their assumption, like ours as a society, is that authorities in research will tell us the answer; and, if they don't know it yet, they will eventually discover it. Like students who want quick and unqualified answers, we prefer that the experts make the answers available to us in brief, clear, unambiguous form, such as the three or seven or twelve principles of learning.

At the mid-level stages of Perry's student development theory, gray areas appear as students begin to discover that authorities often disagree and that the views of their fellow students often differ from their own. In an effort to resolve these inevitable discrepancies, students adopt an "everyone has a right to their own opinion" stance.

This middle stage seems to me to correspond in an eerie way to the developmental stage of society today, as we discover that there are many different views and that authorities often disagree. Certainly we have ample evidence that research authorities disagree on almost everything from the future of the economy to what causes cancer to how children should be raised. Thus we, as a society, have entered the mid-levels of intellectual development by contending that knowledge is a product of one's own experience and each person's experience is democratically and equally valuable. "Everyone has a right to their own opinion" we say. There is a seemingly inexhaustible demand for participatory discussion groups and internet exchanges on what other people think. It is not just television and radio talk shows that display an insatiable curiosity about other people's notions and experiences. Any educational conference that claims to be enlightened must present ample opportunity for discussion groups, workshops, and interactive conversations, and must keep lectures to a minimum—and I am in favor of that. There is a growing impatience and distrust with authoritative knowledge and "experts" in any field, but especially in the messy social sciences such as psychology, sociology, and education. *Time* magazine, in pondering the tendency of the American public to ignore the pronouncements of authorities, observed recently that, "Americans don't listen to pollsters and economists. They listen to neighbors, to friends, to family. . ." (January 5, 1997, p. 91). The questioning philosophical "isms" are controversial right now, but perhaps they are leading society into the mid-level stages of intellectual development by questioning authoritative answers and engaging in discourse, and listening more attentively to experience.

At the highest levels of intellectual development—a stage rarely reached by those who have been studied—there is an affirmation of identity through commitment and self-actualization. Developmental theorists are not very clear about the highest levels of personal development because they haven't seen much of it, and we are not very clear about what a fully-developed intellectual society would look like for the same reason. We haven't yet seen it. But most developmental psychologists are constructivists. They contend that the highest levels of personal development are reached as the person discovers that truth is relative and depends on context. There is not a single right answer, nor is one answer as good as any other. Rather, at the highest levels of development, the individual is able to evaluate truth in terms of the context in which it occurs. In developmental theory, the periods of greatest personal growth are thought to lie in the unnamed and poorly-defined periods *between* stages. It is reasonable to assume that our societal position in the parenthesis offers an especially good opportunity for growth. Is there a societal developmental sequence that progresses from "right answers" to "everyone has a right to their own opinion" to commitment through careful and thoughtful evaluation of truth in context?

Today's theory about human development, it turns out, is not very different from what Socrates was promoting when he defended himself against the charge of corrupting the young by saying that democracy needs citizens who can think for themselves rather than simply defer to authority, who can reason together about choices rather than simply trade claims and counter claims. There are, as we know, charges today that universities are corrupting the young by exposing them to ideas that question the authority of traditional values. But the danger of corrupting the young by requiring them to think for themselves is no greater today than it was in the time of Socrates.

I entitled this essay, "What do we know about student learning, and how do we know it?" The first question, "what do we know about student learning?" is intended to provide me with the opportunity to give a few "right answers;" the second question, How do we know it?" is intended to raise questions about authoritative knowledge.

The most efficient way to answer the first question about what we know about student learning is to collect the gold nuggets already mined from extensive research and melt them down into a gold bullion. In short, I could synthesize the condensed lists or "principles" and develop one or more meta-principles. If I were to do that, I would come up with a grand meta-principle that would say something like this: What we know about student learning is that students who are actively engaged in learning for deeper understanding are likely to learn more than students not so engaged. The disillusioning thing about that conclusion is that we already knew it from our own experience as learners—which is beginning to make the challenging epistemologies of knowledge based in personal and social experience more appealing.

Let us look specifically at the Seven Principles of Good Practice to see what they really tell us: The Seven Principles are stated as follows:

1. Good practice encourages student-faculty contact
2. Good practice encourages cooperation among students
3. Good practice encourages active learning
4. Good practice gives prompt feedback
5. Good practice emphasizes time on task
6. Good practice communicates high expectations
7. Good practice respects diverse talents and ways of knowing. (Chickering & Gamson, 1987)

What the principles really tell us is how to get and keep students actively engaged in learning. Active learning is the grand meta-principle here. What troubles me is that the provision of the list violates its own advice. What we know about learning is that people have to find their own answers by working through the pathways to knowledge. Telling people what the "experts" know is not likely to result in the kind of deeper learning which we want to encourage. Peter Ewell (1997) makes the interesting observation in the *AAHE Bulletin* that our limited success so far in improving learning is due largely to our lack of a deep understanding of what "collegiate learning" really means, and to our implementation of piecemeal reform efforts that don't fit together very well. I wonder if our enthusiasm for bulleted distillations of research findings may not be responsible in part for our failure to understand at some deeper level what constitutes a program of learning.

Let us examine the first principle—good practice encourages student-faculty contact. How do we know that? Mostly through large-scale correlational studies that conclude that students who have frequent contact with faculty members in and out of class are better satisfied with their educational experience, less likely to drop out, and perceive themselves to have learned more than students with less faculty contact (Pascarella & Terenzini, 1991). Now, the experts who pass on that conclusion know the following things at a deeper level than we who receive the conclusion: First, that correlation tells what goes together, but not why. For instance, it is quite possible that the correlation results from successful students being more likely than less successful students to seek contact with faculty. In other words, it is possible that success leads to faculty contact rather than that faculty contact leads to success. It is also possible that faculty who invite frequent student contacts are more likely to be the kind of people who stimulate educational satisfaction than faculty who are not so easily approachable. Thus, it is possible that the more successful we are in bringing about student-faculty contacts—that is spreading this piecemeal practice to include disinterested faculty and less scholarly students—the lower the correlations would become.

The second thing that any researcher working with data on human subjects knows is that there are always exceptions to the finding. In this case, there are students who are very successful and have virtually no contact with faculty; and there are students who have a lot of contact with faculty who drop out of college, dissatisfied and disillusioned.

Does that mean we have mined fool's gold in arriving at the first principle of good practice? Not at all. What it means, I think, is that rather than telling people the right answer, as expert researchers have discovered it, we should mix in a generous dollop of insight derived from our experience as learners and as teachers. What we know from our own experience—sometimes known as common sense—is that, it is not the *amount* of student-faculty contact that is important. Rather it is the quality of the contact. Truth, in this sense, is contextual. Student-faculty contact in one context is growth-enhancing; in another it is not.

What we actually know through combining research with experience is that when faculty show an interest in students, get to know them through informal as well as formal channels, engage in conversations with them, show interest in their intellectual development, then students respond with enthusiasm and engagement. We also know that when faculty take learning seriously, the attitudes of warmth and intellectual engagement are contagious; they are caught by students and colleagues, and the result is a caring campus that is seriously engaged in learning. Measuring the number of student contacts with faculty is at best a surrogate for the quality of interaction. But the kind of research that Schön calls "technical rationality" has a hard time dealing with the infinite variety of contexts that are involved in student/faculty contacts.

Our problem in this awkward time of the parenthesis is that we alternate between searching for "right answers" through research and discounting authoritative answers in favor of our own opinions. We hope that the research provides "right answers" that can be transferred from researcher to practitioner and from teacher to student. Or at the other extreme, we discount research, and insist on personal experience and political expediency—as witness the recent rush to reduce class size, despite conflicting research evidence regarding the efficacy of reduced class size. The question that begs to be answered is not whether small classes result in better learning than large classes, but rather in what teachers could and would do in the context of their own classrooms if class size were reduced. That answer is probably better sought through thoughtful conversations among experienced teachers than it is in the collection of data across large numbers of classrooms categorized only by size.

The challenge for society in the 21st century is to advance beyond the stages of development that result in the authoritarian search for right answers or the egalitarian notion that all ideas are equally valid. Those two stages have dominated our intellectual communities throughout this century.

Researchers—the acknowledged authorities of our times—talk about learning with no reference to the experience of teachers who have spent lifetimes accumulating knowledge about learning. And workshops on faculty development encourage faculty exchange with no reference to what scholars know through study of the matter. My colleague, Mimi Steadman, and I spent several years trying to bring research on learning and experience with teaching together in a book that attempts to integrate teachers' experience and insight with scholarly research on learning (Cross & Steadman, 1996). I am not certain that we have done it, but I am convinced that it can be done.

From our societal position inside the parenthesis as we approach the 21st century, we are questioning how we know what we know, and the developmentalists would say that is good—that offers the potential for growth. Frankly, I find what we know today about students and their learning, and how we know it, troubling because it is so heavily dependent on categorizing students into groups—ironically, just as we are developing the technology for customizing education to individual requirements.

Knowledge about individual differences is lost in much of today's educational research. We purport to know about commuters, part-timers, adult learners, ethnic minorities, women, gays, or any other category that can be represented by checking a box on the measuring instrument. Most of us probably doubt that we could be fairly described by the characteristics of the single or multiple groups to which we belong. Toni Morrison has said "Race is the least reliable information you can have about someone. It's real information, but it tells you next to nothing" (*Time*, Jan. 19, 1998, p. 67).

Bloom (1980) has called the popular demographic descriptors of today "unalterable variables" because, as educators, we can do nothing to change them. Unfortunately, demographic descriptors predominate in the educational research of our times because barriers to equality lie in discrimination based on unalterable variables. Certainly we must continue to investigate the powerful impact of sociological variables on learning—most especially on the *opportunity* for learning—but we must also be constantly aware that there are almost always greater differences within demographic groups than between them. The difference between the height of the shortest and the tallest 14 year olds is far greater than the difference between the average height of 14 year olds and 16 year olds—even though that difference is consistently and statistically significant. Stereotyping 14 year olds as "short" does nothing to advance our knowledge about them.

A heavy dependence on group variables is defensible, I guess, when applied to the old school structures that were designed in times of assembly-line production. The greatest good for the greatest number is a reasonable approach if the task is to march the group through a standard set of learning procedures in a set period of time. But the efficiency of the assembly line approach depends on a normal curve that has a high hump in the middle—that is to say most people cluster in the middle around a fairly small range of difference. With the growing diversity of our student populations, that nice normal curve flattens out, so that there are not very many "average" students anymore—and especially not in open-admission colleges which span the full spectrum of human abilities and human conditions. The problem for us in this time of the parenthesis is that our educational structures are solidly anchored in assembly line procedures while in our future lies the potential for customization and individualization.

A second problem with our heavy dependence on demographic descriptors lies in the growing difficulty of finding that nice neat box on the survey form that places the student firmly and correctly in the appropriate group. The so-called Tiger Woods syndrome[1] applies to racial descriptors, but with participation in lifelong learning related more to life style than to age and with career options being more dependent on personal interest than on gender, group descriptors tell us less and less.

But the third and perhaps most serious barrier to taking learning seriously lies in our failure to take individual differences seriously. Studies of individual differences have almost disappeared from the research scene. It is almost as though there is something a bit unsavory—or at least undemocratic—about individual differences. But learning is about individuals, and improving learning is about understanding what goes on in the mind of the learner. Let me illustrate with a story.

Once upon a time, a young boy was given a beautiful old clock by his grandfather. He was thrilled with the clock, but it quit running after 8 days. Eager to know what was wrong with his clock, he took it to the researchers at the university. The boy thought maybe they would open up the clock to examine the running mechanism, but the researchers said that findings based on study of a single clock would not be generalizable. So they embarked upon a research project.

First they collected a sample of 100 clocks, including clocks of different sizes, colors, and country of manufacture. They then measured very precisely to the minute how long the clocks in each group ran. Upon analyzing their results, they found that while there did not seem to be a statistically significant differences in the running time of clocks of different colors, they did find that small clocks tended to run longer than large clocks; and they found one very exciting relationship. Controlling for color and size, they found that clocks made in Japan tended to run, on average, significantly longer than those made in Switzerland.

Unbeknownst to them—because they didn't open up the clocks to investigate variables, such as quartz mechanisms and pendulums, that were relevant to how clocks ran—Switzerland continued to make some 8-day pendulum clocks whereas clocks from Japan were almost all quartz clocks, supplied with energizer batteries that just kept going on.

The researchers could assure the boy that if he bought a sufficiently large number of clocks from Japan, there was a better chance that he would get a long-running clock than if he bought the same number from Switzerland. Unfortunately, they could neither tell him why clocks from Japan tended to run longer, nor which clocks to buy, nor could they tell him what to do to get his own clock running.

The moral of my story is that if you want to know how students learn, find out what makes them tick. Looking carefully at how even one student learns is often quite revealing, and most of us have an opportunity to observe a wide variety of learners in the act of learning. Moreover, the students that we observe are *our* students in the process of learning *our* discipline; they are the most relevant sample of learners that we could imagine. The problem is that we have not trained ourselves to take learning seriously. Every student who writes a paper, takes a test, asks a question, participates in student activity as leader or follower or who comes to our office hours for conversation or help has a lesson to teach us about how students learn.

Although I may appear to be critical of educational research, I want to assure you that I think research is important to taking learning seriously. In criticizing what I see as our overdependence on correlational and experimental research that leans heavily on group variables, I do not mean to suggest that research on learning is at standstill. Indeed, the new research on neural networks of the brain, meta-cognition, motivation, and the like provides, even at these early stages of development, glimpses of a future rich with promise. That research, however, is going to require of all of us a deeper level of understanding than the research of the past. Research should become the working partner of both our own experience with learning and focused conversations about learning with our colleagues. If we are to take learning seriously, we will need to know what to look for (through research), to observe ourselves in the act of lifelong learning (self-reflection), and to be much more sensitively aware of the learning of the students that we see before us everyday.

At present, I think we are prone to consider research findings as the *conclusion* of our investigations into learning. We might do better to think of them as the *start* of our investigations. For example, rather than assuming that the message of the first principle of the Seven Principles is that we should develop programs to increase student-faculty contact, we might use that research finding as a starting point for discussion about what it is about student-faculty contact that promotes learning. What role has it played in our own experience and why? What, exactly, is it about student-faculty contact that seems to enhance learning? Is it the nature of the individual conversations, or is it the affective feeling of belonging to a learning community? Is it the particular help on a sticking point that shows a student how to learn, or is it the fact that the teacher shows interest—or both? I don't think that researchers know the answers to these questions, and the answers are important if we are to take learning seriously.

But perhaps the most powerful advantage of using research findings to *start* the conversations about learning is that, it is a way to involve faculty and administrators actively in learning about learning. It is one way to push beyond the surface learning that is involved in knowing the slogan, "Good practice encourages student-faculty contact," to the deeper understanding that lies behind the research. People can comply with a new student-faculty contact initiative without fully comprehending that it is their own understanding of why they are engaging in the activity that will determine how well it works. Attending student-faculty get-togethers is one thing; understanding why they work to create a learning community is another; and working actively to assure success is still another.

In conclusion, we know a lot about student learning. We know it through research and scholarship; we know it through our own experience as learners; and we know it through the lessons our students teach us everyday. If we are serious about improving learning, we should use all the resources we can muster.

Note

1. He resents being categorized by race and insists upon recognition of his multiracial heritage.

References

Belenky, M. F., Clinchy, B. M., Goldberger, N. R., & Tarule, J. M. (1986). *Women's ways of knowing: The development of self, voice, and mind.* New York: Basic Books.

Bloom, B. (1980). The new direction in educational research: Alterable variables. *Phi Delta Kappan* (Feb.), 382–385.

Bruffee, K. A. (1995). *Collaborative learning: Higher education, interdependence, and the authority of knowledge.* Baltimore: The Johns Hopkins University Press.

Chickering, A. W., & Gamson, Z. F. (1987). Seven principles for good practice in undergraduate education. *The Wingspread Journal*, 9(2). See also AAHE Bulletin, March, 1987.

Clinchy, B. (1990). Issues of gender in teaching and learning. *Journal on Excellence in College Teaching.*, 1. Reprinted in Feldman, K. A., and Paulsen, M. B. (eds.) (1994) *Teaching and learning in the college classroom.* ASHE Reader Series. Needham Heights, MA: Ginn.

Cross, K. P., & Steadman, M. H. (1996). *Classroom research: Implementing the scholarship of teaching.* San Francisco: Jossey-Bass.

Education Commission of the States (1996). What research says about improving undergraduate education. *AAHE Bulletin*, 48(April), 5–8.

Ewell, P. T. (1997). Organizing for learning. *AAHE Bulletin*, 50(4), 3–6.

Feldman, K. A., & Newcomb, T. M. (1969). *The impact of college on students.* San Francisco: Jossey-Bass.

Matthews, R. S., Cooper, J. L., Davidson, N., & Hawkes, P. (1995). Building bridges between cooperative and collaborative learning. *Change*, 27(July/August), 34–40.

McCombs, B. L. (August, 1992). *Learner-centered psychological principles: Guidelines for school redesign and reform (revised edition).* Washington, DC: American Psychological Association, APA Task Force on Psychology in Education.

Morrison, T. (Jan. 19 1998). *Time Magazine*, p. 8.

Naisbitt, J. (1982). *Megatrends.* New York: Warner Books.

Oxford Centre for Staff Development (1992). *Improving student learning.* Oxford, England: Oxford Brookes University. Reprinted in "Deep Learning, Surface Learning," *AAHE Bulletin*, April 1993, pp. 10–11.

Pascarella, E. T., & Terenzini, P. T. (1991). *How college affects students.* San Francisco: Jossey-Bass.

Schön, D. A. (1983). *The reflective practitioner.* New York: Basic Books.

Study Group on the Conditions of Excellence in American Higher Education (1984). *Involvement in learning: Realizing the potential of American higher education.* Washington, DC: National Institute of Education.

Time Magazine (Jan. 5 1997), p. 91.

Whipple, W. R. (1987). Collaborative learning. *AAHE Bulletin*, 40(2), 3–7.

Acknowledgment

This essay was first presented as a speech at the AAHE National Conference on Higher Education, Atlanta, Georgia, March 24, 1998. It also appears on the AAHE Website: (www.aahe.org).

A PRINCIPLE-BASED APPROACH TO ASSESSING GENERAL EDUCATION THROUGH THE MAJORS

SHARON J. HAMILTON

ABSTRACT: The learning matrix of the IUPUI student electronic portfolio (ePort) will be pilot tested during the fall of 2003. Based on our Principles of Undergraduate Learning, it is intended not only to document and assess both improvement and achievement in these discipline-transcendent skills and ways of knowing, but also to serve as a catalyst for deeper, more insightful, and more connected learning. To students and faculty, both at IUPUI and at other institutions of higher learning across the country, ePort will appear as an attractive and effective product. This article unpacks the processes, dilemmas, and decision-making that went into the development of this ePort learning matrix.

Institutional Context

The Institution and Its Students

IUPUI (Indiana University Purdue University Indianapolis) is an urban public research-extensive institution located in downtown Indianapolis. Combining both Indiana University and Purdue University programs, it houses twenty-two academic and professional schools, with more than 1600 faculty. A majority of its more than 29,000 students come from the city and surrounding counties; several of its professional and graduate programs, however, such as Medicine, Dentistry, and Engineering, attract a high proportion of international students. Since 1996, more than 50% of our undergraduates attend full time. On the other hand, while more of our students attend full time than ever before, they also work, on average, more than 20 hours a week, creating challenges of time management and opportunities for extended intellectual engagement.

Three years ago, the state of Indiana instituted a community college system, a move that enabled IUPUI to redefine its mission, establish higher admission standards, and expand its honors program. It is consequently in the process of transition from a "default choice" for students who could not get into their first choice of college into a first choice for many students in area high schools. As a result, our retention figures have begun to improve over the past two years, although they are still below the norm for our peer institutions.

The Institution and General Education

With so many academic and professional schools, some originally proprietary, some following Purdue traditions, and most with roots in Indiana University, the overall approach to general education was, to say the least, haphazard. In 1991, in preparation for the 1992 NCA accreditation visit, a newly-formed Council on Undergraduate Learning at IUPUI, composed primarily of deans of academic units, and the Academic Affairs Committee of the Faculty Council established a Commission on General Education to oversee development of a centrally coordinated approach to general education for undergraduates at IUPUI. At the time, general education was the responsibility of each school,

Reprinted from the *Journal of General Education* 52, no. 4 (2005), by permission of Pennsylvania State University Press and followed, primarily, a distributive model, wherein each school defined required areas, such as humanities, sciences, and social sciences, and then specified particular requirements within those defined areas. The 1992 NCA Accreditation team noted a need within this distributive approach to identify "desired outcomes for general education . . . amenable to meaningful assessment." Bearing in mind both their initial charge to develop a centrally coordinated approach and the NCA mandate to develop specific learning outcomes for general education, several members of the Commission on General Education attended the 1993 Lilly Endowment Workshop on the Liberal Arts. Out of that workshop, and in conjunction with several other campus committee conversations, the Commission initiated "a process approach" to general education. They set up a series of multi-disciplinary committees, day-long retreats, and town halls to explore fundamental values associated with general education.

This process culminated in the IUPUI Principles of Undergraduate Learning (PULs).

The simplicity of that previous sentence belies the complex, often contentious turf-related negotiations, passionate disagreements, and entrenched attitudes that threatened the process. With twenty-two different academic and professional schools carefully guarding their tuition dollars in a responsibility-centered budgeting system, consensus was not just elusive; it appeared at many times to be downright unattainable. Yet more than 200 faculty persevered in trying first to come to some agreement and second to convince their colleagues that a set of common learning outcomes would provide not only a shared intellectual foundation but also a coherent path for IUPUI students through the morass of school-specific and program-specific requirements.

These PULs are significant not in their uniqueness—they are very similar to the undergraduate learning values in almost any institution of learning—but rather in the fact that they are intended to permeate the undergraduate curriculum instead of being a set of courses or skills concentrated in a student's first two years of college. Students are expected not only to improve their level of competence in each of the PULs during their first and sophomore years, but also to continue to improve their level of competence throughout their undergraduate learning experiences.

Identification of Learning Outcomes to be Assessed

The following outcomes for undergraduate learning were approved by the IUPUI Faculty Council in March of 1998, after considerable discussion, and a winnowing down from a set of first eight and then nine principles originally developed during the 1992 discussions. The six faculty-approved Principles of Undergraduate Learning at IUPUI are:

1. Core Communication and Quantitative Skills, which involve the ability of students to write, read, speak and listen, perform quantitative analysis, and use information resources and technology.

2. Critical Thinking, which involves the ability of students to analyze carefully and logically information and ideas from multiple perspectives.

3. Integration and Application of Knowledge, which involves the ability of students to use information and concepts from studies in multiple disciplines in their intellectual, professional, and community lives.

4. Intellectual Depth, Breadth, and Adaptiveness, which involves the ability of students to examine and organized discipline-specific ways of knowing and apply them to specific issues and problems.

5. Understanding Society and Culture, which involves the ability of students to recognize their own cultural traditions and to understand and appreciate the diversity of the human experience, both within the United States and internationally.

6. Values and Ethics, which involves the ability of students to make judgments with respect to individual conduct, citizenship, and aesthetics.

The Office of Planning and Institutional Improvement (PAII), through its establishment of the Council for Undergraduate Learning and the Commission on General Education, played a significant role in the development and approval process of the PULs, which involved several hundred faculty from all IUPUI academic and professional programs. That same office continued its stewardship of the PULs through another committee, the Program Review and Assessment Committee (PRAC), comprised of two faculty members, one of them generally serving also in some administrative capacity, from each of the twenty-two schools. While the 1998 approval of the PULs resulted in their acceptance both as a significant part of the undergraduate curriculum and as our approach to general education, the approval included no specified mechanism for assessing student growth or achievement in the PULs. Integrating the PULs into the curriculum was implicitly accepted as the responsibility of all faculty, but explicitly stated as the responsibility of no specific faculty. Informal surveys of graduating seniors carried out in some capstone classes between 1998 and 2000 indicated that most students had not encountered the PULs explicitly in any of their courses. Annual assessment reports, submitted to PAII and reported on to PRAC, indicated only sketchy and sporadic integration of the PULs into the curriculum, although professional schools whose accrediting agencies required similar kinds of skills and knowledge were able to integrate the PULs into their curriculum much more readily.

The year 1998 saw not only the approval of the PULs, but also the beginning of the IUPUI Institutional Electronic Portfolio (I-Port), developed as one of the first generation of institutional portfolios as part of the Pew-funded, AAHE-sponsored Urban Universities Portfolio Project. Our portfolio focused on evaluating the processes and evidence related to achieving our mission of providing to our constituents excellence in teaching and learning, research and creative activity, and civic engagement. One of the key challenges of developing the portfolio was how to demonstrate student learning using authentic evidence of learning, not just aggregates of grades and surveys. With so many different academic and professional programs, the obvious point of entry seemed to be the PULs. Additionally, with the impending 2002 NCA accreditation visit, we knew we would need to demonstrate the ways in which the PULs contributed to and interacted with learning in our academic majors, not only as the key component of our general education program but also as principles that permeate the undergraduate learning experience. In other words, if IUPUI defines general education with a set of principles that are intended to permeate the undergraduate learning experience, we need to be able to demonstrate what students know and are able to do in relation to the PULs at both the "general education" level (within the first 56 credit hours) and at the senior level. We need to be able to show both improvement and achievement, and not just in the PULs alone, but as they are integrated into the major and professional programs in ways that enhance student learning and add value to the undergraduate experience.

Concurrent with the approval of the PULs and the development of I-Port was the establishment of the Committee on Liberal Arts and Sciences, charged with exploring the possibility of a common core curriculum. Labelled "The Principled Curriculum," this common core, which took almost three years to develop and become approved, is based upon the PULs, and has played a key role in bringing the PULs to the attention of those faculty who had not been directly involved in the process of their development and approval. One consequence of the Principled Curriculum was a requirement for every course syllabus to include the PULs. Unfortunately, in higher education, such a mandate results more often in perfunctory compliance than in enthusiastic intellectual engagement with the reason behind the mandate, and many course syllabi simply listed the PULs, with no mention of how they were integrated into the course and no further mention during the course. Inclusion of the PULs in course syllabi without further explicit integration in a number of disciplinary areas reinforced the need to determine the extent to which the PULs were playing a significant role in the undergraduate learning experiences of our students.

In 2000, the Dean of the Faculties provided funding for three faculty associates, headed by the Director of Campus Writing, to ascertain the extent to which the PULs were being explicitly integrated into the curriculum. This group met with the academic deans of every academic and professional school, pored through syllabi, and conferred with faculty. The results were, to put the best possible face on it, spotty. Some schools paid no explicit attention at all to the PULs and had no direct evidence to determine whether their students were improving in writing, critical thinking, or understanding of society and culture. Many faculty articulated an assumption that students improved inherently in these areas as a result of their courses in the school, and that passing grades in courses such as freshman writing and oral communication indicated corresponding competence and understanding transferable to other disciplinary areas. Others, particularly the professional schools, had explicitly integrated the PULs into the coursework, and could present a corpus of evidence demonstrating the growth and achievement of their students in these areas. After presenting our findings to PRAC, in a document entitled *Phase 1 of a Study of Student Learning at IUPUI: A working document for the campus*, we decided to present the information on the institutional portfolio in three ways:

a. First we uploaded the narrative discussion of the study, providing an overview of how the PULs were taught, learned, and assessed in each of the schools;

b. Second, we summarized the narrative in the form of a matrix that showed, for each school and PUL, how the PUL was taught and assessed, how it was integrated into student work and learning outcomes, what the school learned from its assessment of the PUL, and how that assessment influenced curricular and pedagogical decisions.

c. Third, we took advantage of the electronic feature of the portfolio to develop an interactive matrix, whereby the visitor to the portfolio could identify which school(s) and which PUL(s) he or she wanted information about. For example, if someone keyed in Liberal Arts and Critical Thinking, they would see how critical thinking was taught and assessed, what forms it took in Liberal Arts, and how Liberal Arts had used its assessment to improve teaching and learning.

This interactive matrix quickly became one of the more demonstrated and visited areas of our institutional portfolio. Whether at national conferences or in campus-level committees, people wanted to see what was occurring in relation to these PULs in certain schools, and any gaps or blanks were blatantly apparent. In particular, the last two columns—What have you learned from your assessment of the PULs? and How have these discoveries influenced curriculum and pedagogy?—were either left blank or barely begun by several schools. The interactive matrix became a powerful catalyst for schools to make the integration of the PULs into their academic work much more explicit, in order to be able to complete their part of the matrix. The most important lesson we learned from this endeavor was that the PULs were not being explicitly or intentionally taught or assessed in any consistent manner across the campus. While it may have been true that students were improving in their ability to think critically or communicate more effectively, we had insufficient evidence to support that claim, or to demonstrate that the PULs were indeed providing a coherent pathway through the undergraduate experience at IUPUI.

I write "insufficient," because we do actually have an accumulating corpus of indirect evidence, through self-reporting on NSSE, on our own first-year and graduating senior surveys, and on reflective writing done concerning the PULs by graduating seniors in the School of Liberal Arts and the School of Science. But we needed to develop a system that would provide direct and authentic evidence of improvement and achievement in learning of these PULs in relation to learning in the major. We needed this system not only for accreditation purposes, in order to demonstrate that our general education program provides an effective foundation for learning, but also for our own purposes, to demonstrate to ourselves and to our constituents that the PULs provide a coherent curricular basis for undergraduate learning at IUPUI, and actually enhance learning in the major. Out of this need grew the impetus for the IUPUI electronic student portfolio (ePort).

Overview of Assessment Process and Method

The Assessment Method

While the mature ePort will have many components, including a resume-building function and a knowledge-mapping function, we are beginning with two features: a learner profile and a learning

Learning Matrix of the IUPUI Student Electronic Portfolio PUL Pre-Survey:

Principle of Undergraduate Learning	Introductory	Intermediate (Intermediate PUL Survey)	Advanced	Experiential (Senior PUL Survey)
1a Core Skills: Written Communication	Add/Edit Help Reflection	Add/Edit Help Reflection	Add/Edit Help Reflection	Add/Edit Help Reflection
1b Core Skills: Analyzing Texts	Add/Edit Help Reflection	Add/Edit Help Reflection	Add/Edit Help Reflection	Add/Edit Help Reflection
1c Core Skills: Oral Communication	Add/Edit Help Reflection	Add/Edit Help Reflection	Add/Edit Help Reflection	Add/Edit Help Reflection
1d Core Skills: Quantitative Problem Solving	Add/Edit Help Reflection	Add/Edit Help Reflection	Add/Edit Help Reflection	Add/Edit Help Reflection
1e Core Skills: Information Literacy	Add/Edit Help Reflection	Add/Edit Help Reflection	Add/Edit Help Reflection	Add/Edit Help Reflection
2. Critical Thinking	Add/Edit Help Reflection	Add/Edit Help Reflection	Add/Edit Help Reflection	Add/Edit Help Reflection
3. Integration and Application of Knowledge	Add/Edit Help Reflection	Add/Edit Help Reflection	Add/Edit Help Reflection	Add/Edit Help Reflection
4. Intellectual Depth, Breadth, and Adaptiveness	Add/Edit Help Reflection	Add/Edit Help Reflection	Add/Edit Help Reflection	Add/Edit Help Reflection
5. Understanding Society and Culture	Add/Edit Help Reflection	Add/Edit Help Reflection	Add/Edit Help Reflection	Add/Edit Help Reflection
6. Values and Ethics	Add/Edit Help Reflection	Add/Edit Help Reflection	Add/Edit Help Reflection	Add/Edit Help Reflection

matrix. The learning matrix is at the heart of the assessment function of ePort, and will, in essence, capture the entire undergraduate learning experience on one screen that will look something like this:

In the matrix, Introductory Level captures evidence of student learning based on campus consensus of what all students should know and be able to do, regardless of major or professional program, after 26 credit hours at IUPUI. Intermediate Level captures evidence after 56 credit hours. The Senior Level captures evidence of student learning of the PULs as they have been integrated into the academic major or professional program. The Experiential Level cuts through all three of the previous levels, and involves evidence of student learning of the PULs in co-curricular and extra-curricular experiences. To date, we are focusing on the Introductory and Intermediate levels.

The development of campus consensus about what all students should know and be able to do in relation to each of the PULs, regardless of academic major or professional program, was a year-long process involving more than a hundred faculty working on multi-disciplinary committees.

Scenario for students uploading documents directly into matrix

1. Student enters PUL Matrix
2. Student clicks on PUL 6: *Values and Ethics:*
3. Student sees:
   a. *Values and Ethics*
   b. *Aesthetics*

4. Student clicks on a. Values and Ethics

5. Student sees:
   a. **Students are able to make judgments with respect to individual conduct and citizenship.**
   b. *Introductory*—Students demonstrate an understanding of how ones *values* influence personal *ethics* and conduct.
   c. *Intermediate*—Students demonstrate an understanding of and respect for the values of others in contrast to their own and are aware of how decisions and conclusions may vary based on different perspectives.

6. If students click on *values*, students see:

   Values provide the foundation for making personal and ethical decisions related to what a person considers to be good or bad, right or wrong. They stem from multiple sources as someone matures (e. g. family, local community, religious affiliations, professional organizations, educational institutions, national forums, etc.). Values are developed through making choices, experiencing challenges, and taking action in accordance with personal beliefs. They are reflected in the judgments people make and the solutions they choose. Values are categorized as moral when they pertain to the human interactions and non-moral when related to inanimate objects. A gun is non-moral but if used by a human, the act may be judged as moral or immoral in regards to the act itself or the motivation for the conduct.

7. **If** students click on *ethics*, students see:

   Ethics refers to the study of moral values held by individuals or groups. A person or an act is considered ethical or moral when it is judged consistent with the values of the group or society (morality). Ethics also establishes the degree of rightness or wrongness for moral conduct or decisions.

8. If students click on *Introductory*, students see:

   To demonstrate your understanding of this PUL at the Introductory level, the documents you upload and your reflection should show the following:
   a. you can explain the relationship between personal values and the choices a person makes.
   b. you can articulate the values that are important to you in making personal choices about conduct and citizenship.
      (May include a situation in which your values influenced your personal ethics and resulting conduct.)

   The documents you choose to illustrate competence at the introductory level may be from 100–200 level courses or from documents you have written related to out of class experiences (campus organizations, religious affiliation, employment, etc.).

   Not every paper needs to show every element, but every element should be represented in the totality of documents you upload in this section or else accounted for in your reflection.

DO YOU WISH TO UPLOAD A DOCUMENT NOW? Y N

9. If student click Y, student sees **a browse/upload screen**
10. IF students click on *Intermediate*, they see:

    To demonstrate your understanding of the PUL at the Intermediate level, the documents you upload and your reflection should show the following:
    a. you can analyze situations and foresee how decisions or conclusions may vary when values, within yourself or between individuals, are conflicting.

    The documents you choose to illustrate competence at the intermediate level may be from 200+ level courses or from documents you have written related to out of class experiences (campus organizations, religious affiliation, employment, etc.).

    Not every paper needs to show every element, but every element should be represented in the totality of documents you upload in this section or else accounted for in your reflection.

DO YOU WISH TO UPLOAD A DOCUMENT NOW? Y N

11. If student click Y, student sees a **browse/upload screen.** For PUL 6b
12. Student enters PUL Matrix
13. Student clicks on PUL 6:
14. Student sees:
    a. *Values and Ethics*
    b. *Aesthetics*

15. Student clicks on PUL 6 (b) Aesthetics
16. Student sees:
    a. **Students are able to make judgments with respect to aesthetics.**
    b. *Introductory*—Students will explain their understanding of *aesthetics* and how it impacts their lives.
    c. *Intermediate*—Students explain the role of aesthetics in society.
       Choose documents that demonstrate your aesthetic awareness.
17. If student clicks on *aesthetics*, student sees:

    Aesthetics is the study of cognition and emotions in relation to beauty and meaning in life. Meaning is attained through intense perceptual, intellectual, and emotional experiences that provide personal insight into the human condition. These aesthetic experiences influence ones personal values and promote active inquiry and reflection.

18. If student clicks on *Introductory*: student sees:

    To demonstrate your understanding of this PUL at the Introductory level, the documents you upload and your reflection should show the following:
    a. you can explain how aesthetics influences decisions you make in your life.
    b. you can evaluate an aesthetic experience and how this strengthened or changed your valuing or understanding of the human condition or culture.

    The documents you choose to illustrate competence at the introductory level may be from 100–200 level courses. OR From documents you have written related to out of class experiences.
    Not every paper needs to show every element, but every element should be represented in the totality of documents you upload in this section or else accounted for in your reflection.

DO YOU WISH TO UPLOAD A DOCUMENT NOW? Y N

19. If student click Y, student sees a **browse/upload screen**
20. If student clicks on *Intermediate*: student sees

    To demonstrate your understanding of this PUL at the Intermediate level, the documents you upload and your reflection should show the following:
    a. you can explain the unique contributions of aesthetic experience to human life and culture.
    b. you can analyze how your aesthetic awareness has been broadened through your studies at IUPUI and the effect of this awareness on your personal development.
    The documents you choose to illustrate competence at the intermediate level may be from 200+ level courses OR from documents you have written related to out of class experiences.
    Not every paper needs to show every element, but every element should be represented in the totality of documents you upload in this section or else accounted for in your reflection.

DO YOU WISH TO UPLOAD A DOCUMENT NOW? Y N

21. If student clicks Y, student sees **a browse/upload screen**

It is currently in its final phases, as faculty work to develop "scenarios" for the portfolio. Here is one, for example, that was just drafted for PUL 6: Values and Ethics:

Students complete the matrix by submitting assignments from their academic and professional classes. These assignments will already have been graded by the professor in each class for content knowledge, and, in some cases but not all, for the particular PUL in the matrix where the student has chosen to upload it. As is evident in the above scenario, students will need to upload several (3–5) documents, generally from different courses or classes, to complete a PUL cell in the matrix at any given level. When students determine that a cell is complete, they click on "Reflection," and will be prompted to write a reflective essay making the case that the uploaded documents do indeed demonstrate the level of competence as specified.

This reflective piece is what takes the portfolio beyond the function of providing authentic evidence of student learning, important as that is in itself. The reflection is intended to catalyze deeper learning, to capture the connections between disparate skills and information from diverse courses, and to move students into an awareness of meaning that transcends discipline-specific knowledge. Simply writing a reflection, however, does not guarantee profound or insightful metacognitive thinking or enhanced understanding. Through workshops offered by national experts, such as Marcia Baxter Magolda, in the development of intellectual understanding, faculty committees are being guided to write prompts for reflective writing for each of the PULs at the Introductory and Intermediate levels. These prompts will be accessible to students through the portfolio infrastructure, in the form of a 'prompt wizard'. The intention is that the "just-in-time" prompts will lead students to the kind of intellectual probing required for connective understanding beneath and beyond course content and will provide the catalyst for deeper, more meaningful learning.

These reflections will then be electronically sent to and read by members of the Senior Academy (retired faculty wanting to remain intellectually connected to IUPUI) and by alumni volunteers who will be trained to read and evaluate the reflections in relation to the campus expectations for learning for each PUL. By drawing upon the expertise of our retired faculty and our alumni, we intend ePort to contribute significantly to a community of learning that extends beyond the immediate campus. These alumni and members of the Senior Academy will send a written response to the students and a 1, 2, or 3 designation, 1 being that the work exceeds expectations; 2 being that it meets expectations; and 3 being that it does not meet expectations. The written response, which can be chosen from a selection of pre-written responses or can be composed by the trained volunteer, will comment on the strengths and weaknesses of the reflection, and the appropriateness of the documents selected by the student to demonstrate the specified PUL,

---

1. How important do you think *written communication* will be in your education at IUPUI?

Not at all important	*Slightly important*	*Moderately important*	*Important*	*Very important*
☐	☐	☐	☐	☐

How would you rate your knowledge level or competence in relation to *written communication*?

Very low	*Somewhat low*	*Moderate*	*Somewhat high*	*Very high*
☐	☐	☐	☐	☐

What does written communication mean to *you* and what role will it play in your education?

Students enter their open-ended response to this question in an expanding word box.

Please limit your response to 300 words.

---

and will include suggestions for writing more effective reflections for the next cell they complete. The 1s, 2s, and 3s will be automatically aggregated according to a wide range of demographic information, so that deans, chairs, and campus administrators will not only have a richer picture of how the PULs are influencing student learning on the campus, but will also be able to pinpoint areas where more attention—and possibly more resources—might be needed to generate improvement. This information will be reinforced by a PUL survey that students will complete during their first month at IUPUI, after they complete 56 credit hours, and during their senior capstone. The survey contains three questions for each PUL, two quantitative in nature, and one qualitative. Example:

Because ePort is being built as part of an enterprise system, these surveys will be emailed to students automatically, according to the number of credit hours they have taken. While information from these surveys provides only indirect evidence of learning, through self-reporting, it will nonetheless enrich the picture of the relationship of the PULs to learning in the major.

The process of design

Who was involved in the design process?

The point person for the conceptual part of the design—given her charge by the Dean of the Faculties—was the Director of Campus Writing and the (then) Director of the Institutional Portfolio. She worked with several different campus committees, including the Faculty Associates, an ePort management committee formed of campus faculty leaders and administrators, the Program Review and Assessment Committee, and ten multidisciplinary PUL committees, each charged with developing consensus about what all students, regardless of academic major or professional program, should know and be able to do in relation to the PULs at 26 credit hours and 56 credit hours.

The point person for research and design (R&D) has changed three times over the past four years of the project, each time stalling the progress of the project while the technological infrastructure was recoded. The first R&D person was a very talented and advanced student working in the IUPUI CyberLab, who cobbled together an infrastructure of the conceptual framework for alpha testing the first year of the pilot. Working from a usability study based on that alpha test, the second point person, the faculty member who directs the CyberLab, began to design an infrastructure that included, but reached far beyond, the conceptual framework envisioned by the faculty committee. After conducting an alpha test of the new structure, that R&D person formed a national consortium for electronic portfolios which currently includes several campuses across the country, such as Penn State, UCLA, Maricopa, Bowling Green, and others. Since the IUPUI portfolio needed to be built as an enterprise system consistent with the language (java) of our course management system, our student information system, and our registrar's office, we began again with a third R&D person, one centrally located in the Indiana University Information Technology Services (UITS) and are now just in the beginning phases of writing the program to realize the conceptual framework we have been working on for more than four years, and have piloted, with the previous technological structures, for two years. Because of financial challenges, the timeline for implementation will depend upon the allocation of resources for programmers, as they incur the major starting-up expense of the project.

Institutional support for the assessment innovation

Administrative support for the conceptual aspect of the project has been outstanding. In fact, in order to facilitate the kind of campus-wide administrative planning required for the project, the Dean of the Faculties promoted the Director of Campus Writing, who had been leading the project, to an Associate Dean of the Faculties position. Support for the financial aspects of the project has been more challenging, primarily because of several concurrent demands on our diminishing resources for technology, not because those making financial decisions about resources doubt the importance of the ePort project. The initial two stages of R&D were funded by soft money from the office of Academic Affairs. Funding the third stage of R&D will be much more extensive, since ePort will be built as part of an enterprise system with one portal into a comprehensive and rich learning environment. Currently, we are working on an internal grant to fund both R&D and assessment of the ePort project, once again with positive support to date from the administration at all levels.

Presenting the Assessment Results

Because we are just entering the (third) pilot, this discussion of assessment results is primarily future-oriented and will address envisioned possibilities.

One major assessment issue we have already addressed is the notion of making faculty grading public. Alverno College has played a leadership role in developing an electronic student portfolio that shows faculty grading and faculty comments, followed by student comments. This kind of approach to assessment, however, is not readily scaleable to a large comprehensive institution with so many different academic schools and professional programs. For several reasons, many IUPUI faculty were resistant to having their grading of and comments on student work made accessible through ePort. Following current tenets of copyright and intellectual property, we determined that, while students "owned" their completed, graded, assignments, faculty "owned" their grading and comments on the students' assignments. Students will decide which assignments they will upload onto their portfolios as evidence of competence in the PULs, but the faculty grades for these assignments will generally not be available (although a process for including grades and/or comments by mutual consent is being built into the technological infrastructure). Either by going through the course management system (Oncourse) or through another secure process, all documents uploaded will be "stamped" or authorized by the appropriate faculty member as having been completed, with a passing grade, in his or her course during that semester. These documents will then become secure, "read-only" documents that cannot be changed by the student (although the student can decide to archive or delete the document).

Since all uploaded documents will already have been assessed for discipline-specific content knowledge, ePort is designed to play a more integrative and comprehensive assessment role. What will be assessed through ePort are the students' selections of documents as evidence of competence in the PULs and their reflective writing making the case that these documents, taken together, really do provide evidence of competence. The people involved in making these assessments are members of the Senior Academy, IUPUI alumni, and faculty, all of whom will be trained in holistic scoring methods, the campus expectations for competence at the Introductory and Intermediate levels, and the reflective writing prompts for each PUL. Checks will be built into the technological infrastructure for inter-rater reliability.

Students will each receive a written response and a 1, 2, or 3 designation for each completed cell on their learning matrix. In our current vision of the project, they will, if they wish, be able to revise and resubmit, but will not be required to, since the comments they will receive will focus on how they might improve subsequent reflections. This initial position, however, is negotiable as students and faculty work through the pilot.

The ePort is intended to use assessment to improve not only the learning of individual students, but also learning throughout the campus community. The 1, 2, and 3 designations will be aggregated according to demographic constructs requested by administrative units. Based on administrative requests, the Office of Information Management and Institutional Research will provide overall reports. At the same time, Deans and Chairs with administrative access to aggregated information will be able to generate specific reports according to their own specific inquiries. For example, the Deans of some academic schools or professional programs may want access to indications of growth and achievement in the PULs according to gender, or to number of credit hours taken that semester, or number of credit hours in relation to number of hours of employment, or direct admits in relation to conditional admits, or any of a wide range of demographic possibilities. We anticipate, for example, if the Chair of the Biology Department learns that 80% of biology majors score either 1(exceeds expectations) or 2 (meets expectations) in critical thinking, but only 40% score either 1 or 2 for values and ethics, that the Chair will explore, with faculty, the curricular and pedagogical implications of those findings. On a broader scale, if the Dean of the Faculties learns that 90% of graduating seniors across the campus score 1 or 2 for oral communication but only 60% of graduating seniors score 1 or 2 for written communication, the Dean may explore allocating resources to a campus-wide emphasis on writing throughout the curriculum. In other words, we anticipate that ePort will provide information to improve learning from the level of each individual student to the level of the entire campus.

Using Assessment Results to Make Changes

Since the project is still in its alpha and beta testing stages, it is too early to report on how ePort has generated assessment results that have led to curricular or pedagogical changes or to reallocation of resources. The strength of the project lies in the potential for ePort to provide the kinds of assessment results that will enable individual students, faculty, chairs, and deans to make evidence-based decisions related to student learning, and to provide these results in ways that safeguard the identities of individual students and individual faculty.

Conclusions

Using student electronic portfolios to assess learning both within majors and across the institution run counter to several traditional feature of our current educational model, which is built primarily on disciplines. As Carol Geary Schneider and Robert Shoenberg of the Association of American Colleges and Universities write:

> Moving forward with a framework for learning that expects broad, deep, and complex accomplishments for every student is a challenge that invites the participation of the entire array of higher education stakeholders. . . . The groundwork for success has already been laid in the form of an emerging consensus about what matters in undergraduate education and some promising educational strategies for getting there. We need to seize the opportunity for building the more purposeful, powerful, and integrative forms of undergraduate education that the consensus now makes possible (1999, p. 35).

The potential of student electronic portfolios to improve learning lies not just in the design, but, even more importantly, in those who will be using them. One major paradox of establishing an institution-wide method of assessment is that, even as it will inevitably change the institution by influencing—possibly even transforming—the culture of teaching and learning, it must at the same time blend into the current institutional culture. Whether the platform is developed in a consortium, purchased from a software developer, or developed on-site, it must be modifiable and customizable in order to suit the educational values of the institution, and of the faculty and students in each department and academic and professional program in the institution. Probably the most significant lesson learned in the development of this approach to assessment is that faculty and students must be involved throughout the process of research and design and the development of the conceptual framework. Additionally, there must be close ties right from the outset between those working on the conceptual development and those working on research and design.

Student electronic portfolios, by providing authentic evidence of student learning, are beginning to play a significant role nationwide in the assessment of teaching and learning. With intentional planning and implementation, they can also play a significant role in catalyzing deeper, more connected learning. Possibly even more important, they can showcase and document the kinds of learning and thinking that transcend specific disciplines and professional programs. The AAC&U Statement on Liberal Learning concludes with the following assertion:

The ability to think, to learn, and to express oneself both rigorously and creatively, the capacity to understand ideas and issues in context, the commitment to live in society, and the yearning for truth are fundamental features of our humanity. In centering education upon these qualities, liberal learning is society's best investment in our shared future.

In centering undergraduate learning upon these qualities, and developing a customizable technological infrastructure to document and assess growth and achievement in these qualities, electronic student portfolios, appropriately designed, may well become higher education's best investment in our shared future.

There are many different models of student electronic portfolios being developed across the country. Most of them are multifunctional, intended for a variety of audiences. The more complex the functions and the more varied the audience, the more expensive the development costs in both time and money. And yet I can imagine no means more powerful for documenting improvement in student learning, presenting authentic evidence of that learning, and for assessing that evidence according to a wide and interactively modifiable set of parameters to meet dynamically changing institutional needs.

Works Cited

AAC&U Statement of Liberal Learning

Hamilton, Sharon J. (2001). Mirror, Mirror to the Mind; What You See(k) is What You Find.

Schneider, Carol Geary and Shoenberg, Robert (1999). Habits Hard to Break: How Persistent Features of Campus Life Frustrate Curricular Reform. *Change*. March/April 1999. 30-35.

Measuring University Quality

Rachelle L. Brooks

Over the last eight decades, numerous assessments have been conducted to measure the quality of research and teaching programs in higher education. This interest in quality originated inside the academy, with studies conducted by and for university leaders; but many contemporary assessments take the form of rankings and ratings designed by commercial media, driven by profit motives, and targeted to prospective students and parents. The earliest assessment research also had a narrow focus due to the lack of quantitative information about many university activities. In recent years, improvements to information technology have moved data collection from a labor-intensive, lengthy endeavor to an activity regularly conducted by and on behalf of universities. But have these innovations in data collection and analysis changed the face of university assessments? Further-more, after decades of assessment research, does the higher education community have a better sense of what university quality is?

At best, the answers are a qualified "somewhat." As additional data are assembled, the measurement of quality can encompass more university activities. In addition, technological advances have improved measurement and analytical techniques. Nonetheless, many assessments continue to falter in dealing with fundamental methodological concepts. They often still make only a weak connection between theoretical definitions of quality and its measures by asserting a single rank or rating system that obscures the methodological and theoretical assumptions built into it. Additionally, many assessments still focus on or privilege one aspect of a university's activities, thereby failing to capture the multidimensional facets of quality.

This article offers both an organizational framework and a methodological discussion of research on assessing institutional quality. It updates prior reviews of assessments to illuminate the advancements in the field and to document the stability which is both an asset and a liability. More than a review of assessments, it also analyzes their critiques to identify underlying methodological issues. Studies conducted during the last two decades receive greater attention to determine whether they have overcome long-standing criticisms.

A methodological analysis of quality assessments and their critiques is relevant to many parties in higher education, including campus officials choosing among alternative assessment strategies, researchers devising new assessment instruments, and scholars or policymakers evaluating assessment results. External accountability demands are increasing in intensity for institutions, as are demands for greater public "transparency" of assessment results (Allen & Bresciani, 2003; Schneider, 2002; Shavelson & Huang, 2003). This climate has created a corresponding need for more and better information about quality assessment practices and alternatives. The institutional investments in assessments are also increasing. They include faculty and administrative time, and resources to develop, administer, and disseminate results. A better understanding of assessment strengths and limitations can help ensure that those investments are made wisely and will serve the intended purposes.

The literature on higher education quality is not lacking on assessment critiques. On the contrary, every assessment of quality generates numerous critiques. However, most critiques are tailored to a single study or type of assessment and do not address a broad range of approaches to measuring

Reprinted by permission from the *Review of Higher Education* 29, no. 1 (fall 2005).

institutional quality. Only rarely have assessments and their critiques been examined as a set and brought into a conversation with one another (Smith & Fiedler, 1971; Webster, 1981). Clifton Conrad and Robert Blackburn (1985) offer among the most comprehensive critiques of research on institutional quality, but many of their conclusions and recommendations for future research have since been addressed in the literature. For example, recent efforts have focused on student learning, an area completely unexplored at the time of Conrad and Blackburn's review. This article updates and expands their work by emphasizing the research methodologies of quality studies.

This study considers the composite set of large-scale multi-institutional assessment initiatives and their critiques in a way that highlights their common weaknesses and strengths. The aim is to strengthen future research on university quality by illuminating the methodological underpinnings of the criticisms across numerous studies. The purpose is not to wage additional critiques of quality assessments, but rather to offer a way of better understanding the critiques by bringing them together in a single methodological discussion. Neither is the purpose to argue for a particular theoretical definition of quality. The merits of a definition will depend on its purpose, audience, and other contextual factors. However, the definition should be explicit, and its methodological execution carefully attended to, because it is oftimes the definition and operationalization of quality that determines a study's strength or weakness.

Organizational and Methodological Frameworks

The assessments are organized around three research areas that represent the expanding definition of quality: reputation, faculty research, and student experiences. The earliest studies were based exclusively on opinion surveys and were vulnerable to critiques about their link to an institution's reputation. The more recent use of faculty research productivity measures are thought to lend greater "objectivity" to assessments. A third approach uses measures of student experiences or their outcomes to assess quality. Most large-scale assessments today do not fit easily into any one of these categories; instead, they use a multi-measure approach that assesses several different aspects of universities. Upon closer inspection, however, one aspect of quality is often still privileged. Therefore, this organizational framework will help to identify the definition of and assumptions about quality underlying the assessments.

Three methodological concepts provide a unifying theme for the assessment critiques: taxonomy, the unit of analysis, and the frame of reference. Each is integrally related to the operationalization of a definition of university quality. The use of a specific taxonomy to designate a universe of cases for comparison determines the institutions to be included in an assessment, which will have an impact on the results. Unfortunately, a taxonomy or classification system for academic units is increasingly difficult to construct cross-institutionally without a consensus about a grouping method for academic programs and divisions. The emphasis on one or another unit of analysis—the university as a whole, individual students, departments, or programs—also presents a variety of measurement and data collection challenges. For example, the unit of analysis dictates a specific level of data that may not be readily available or easily aggregated or disaggregated, and attempts to generalize beyond a specified unit of analysis can lead to faulty conclusions. Finally, an appropriate frame of reference for quality judgments and comparisons influences both the scope of data collection and interpretation. Often the comparative frame of reference may at first seem appropriate, especially when institutions appear to be similarly situated, but differences in program emphasis between institutions can result in irrelevant comparisons.

At the intersection of these methodological issues lies the question of the extent to which a theoretical definition of quality is consistent with its measurement strategy, an additional theme that will guide this article. Lacking sufficient theoretical clarity or methodological precision, many assessments have fallen short of their larger goal of measuring quality. The following three sections of this article will review reputational studies of institutional quality, assessments of faculty scholarly productivity, and research on student experiences and outcomes. The concluding section offers recommendations for improving the study of quality in higher education, from both methodological and theoretical perspectives.

Reputational Studies and Their Critics

The earliest attempts to compare the quality of universities in the United States used a reputational assessment. The most widely cited first study was authored in 1925 by Raymond Hughes, president of Miami University of Ohio. Hughes solicited his faculty for the names of distinguished scholars in 20 fields to create a list of respondents to his reputational survey. From the survey he created a ranking of the 38 top Ph.D.-granting institutions out of the 65 then in existence. In 1934, he prepared a similar ranking of graduate departments at 59 institutions. Each of his studies was based on the opinions of 20 to 60 faculty members, a methodological weakness by today's standards (Cartter, 1966). Twenty-five years later, Hayward Keniston also used a reputational survey to determine how the University of Pennsylvania ranked compared to 25 leading institutions. He queried the chairmen of 24 departments at each of the institutions to develop his ranking of the top departments (Cartter, 1966; Roose & Andersen, 1970).

These early studies were limited in scope, designed to fulfill an administrative purpose with a narrow frame of reference. Only perceptions of the top doctoral-granting universities or fields of study were included in each assessment, and opinions came from small and unrepresentative groups of respondents. Hughes's first study conceived of the university as the unit of analysis, while the reputational assessments following it evaluated departments or programs, a unit more consistent with raters' perspectives given their locations in university departments. Yet despite their limitations, these first assessments were important for establishing the possibility of measuring institutional quality.

In 1964, the American Council on Education began a much more systematic, broadly encompassing assessment of graduate programs (Cartter, 1966). By expanding the number and ranks of faculty members queried for its opinion survey, the assessment aimed to surmount raters' regional or institutional biases. Kenneth Roose and Charles Andersen (1970) followed Cartter's research five years later, replicating his methodology to provide updated results for comparison with his analysis but also expanding the scope of the research considerably by increasing the quantity of fields and programs rated.

These two later studies of university reputation partially met the need for a general taxonomy of programs to expand the scope of cases evaluated. It was no longer satisfactory for assessments to focus only on programs at institutions thought to be the best; rather, the intent became to include all institutions seriously engaged in doctoral training. This effort to create a more comprehensive assessment was coupled with a change in the selection of raters. By soliciting a broader range of faculty, thereby widening the frame of reference, the studies hoped to reduce the inherent selection biases that reportedly plagued the Hughes and Keniston research, which relied on an elite group of faculty as raters. Overall, these changes in methodology did not yield widely differing rankings. The majority of universities in the top 25 in 1925 remained in that tier for most succeeding studies (Conrad & Blackburn, 1985; Kerr, 1991; Webster, 1983).

In 1982, the National Research Council (NRC) produced the next reputational assessment of research-doctorate programs, evaluating 2,699 programs in 32 disciplines (Jones, Lindzey, & Coggeshall, 1982). Many had recognized that these assessments were used by those outside the academy, so the NCR's purpose was broader than providing a tool for internal decision-making. The authors devised a multi-measure approach that combined the reputational survey with a set of "objective," quantitative measures of quality, including program and library size, graduate characteristics, research support, and faculty publication records. However, some critics have charged that these additional measures bore little theoretical relationship to quality, despite their correlation with the reputational scores (Conrad & Blackburn, 1985; Webster, 1983).

In the early 1990s, the NRC began what would become a decennial update to the research-doctorate program rankings, with an expanded scope covering more than 3,600 programs (Goldberger, Maher, & Flattau, 1995). It replicated much of the NCR's 1982 methodology and added several measures of faculty research and student characteristics. The reputational survey received the greatest attention and criticism because it was the basis for rank-ordering programs. This ranking rendered nearly invisible the other program data that were compiled, contrary to the expectations of the study's designers (Roush, 1995). The study also suggested a level of precision in the data that could not be supported. Secondary analyses for a few individual fields found that, when the full distributions of scores were analyzed and compared, instead of only the average score, finer-grained distinctions between programs disappeared (Thursby, 2000; Johnson & Wiley, 1999). Some calculated an overall institutional score by combining the program rankings (Webster & Skinner, 1996), but the varying methodologies for doing so can yield differing results (Orr, 1984).

Shortly after the NRC published its first report, David Webster (1983) observed that undergraduate programs and institutions had yet to be ranked. He called for such an effort to fill the void of information for prospective students about quality at the undergraduate level. That same year *U.S. News & World Report* published its first college ranking of 76 institutions, based exclusively on a reputational survey completed by approximately 1,300 presidents of four-year colleges who listed the top institutions (Machung, 1998). This was the first time that assessment information became easily accessible to prospective undergraduates and their parents, thus creating a dramatic shift in the consumers of quality assessments (Webster, 1992). These rankings were reissued in 1985 and 1987, using the same methodology. After 1987, the pool of respondents was broadened to include other college administrators, and additional "objective" factors were weighted and combined into a composite measure for the ranking. However, the reputational scores still remain the most heavily weighted factor in the index, comprising 25% of the total score (Morse & Flanigan, 2002). *U.S. News & World Report* also ranks doctoral programs and professional schools with reputational surveys the exclusive source of information in many cases. Several other commercial firms have initiated similar and expanded efforts at ranking colleges, universities, and professional schools, since student and parent consumers continue to create a demand for them.

Recent years have seen several secondary analyses of reputational data with the aim of testing the validity of raters' scores against other measures of quality. The total counts of faculty publications and citations, and the number of doctoral degrees awarded, have been found to account together for 90% of the variation in 1995 NRC reputational scores of economics departments (Thursby, 2000). However, other research measures, when examined on a per-faculty basis in economics and other fields, bear a weaker relationship to reputational rankings (Diamond & Graham, 2000; Thursby, 2000). When multivariate regression models are used to predict the 1995 reputational scores, measures of faculty size, faculty research productivity, and doctoral program success are all significantly related to reputation for the majority of fields (Ehrenburg & Hurst, 1996, 1998). Thus, reputational scores demonstrate a high level of overall consistency with other program measures. In addition, the 1995 NRC and *U.S. News & World Report* rankings are highly correlated, lending further credibility to the data (Rogers & Rogers, 1997).

Nonetheless, reputational assessments face numerous criticisms. Critics have contended they are no more than "hearsay," "gossip," or "popularity contests" (Cartter, 1966; Dolan, 1976) because raters may favor the institutions at which they previously studied or those with a similar academic approach. In addition, reputations reportedly have a "staying power" that outlasts changes in the people or the programs (Cartter, 1966; Jones, Lindzey, & Coggeshall, 1982; Webster, 1981).

Criticisms about the "subjectivity" of a reputational methodology grow out of the lack of a common frame of reference for the raters, which varies because individuals provide quality judgments based on what they personally know of an institution or program and how it relates to all others they know. Unfortunately, raters have been found to be largely unfamiliar with as many as one-third of the programs they are asked to rate (Dometrius et al., 1998; Jones et al., 1982); and still assign rankings even when they have a low level of familiarity with the programs (Brooks & Junn, 2002).

A more stable frame of reference yields more reliable data. Therefore, more recent studies have attempted to create a common base of knowledge about programs by providing all raters with information about the number of degrees recently awarded and the program's faculty (Goldberger et al., 1995; Jones et al., 1982). This effort may also combat the time lag associated with reputations because raters receive the most current program information. However, a faculty roster cannot ensure that all raters are comparably informed and may result in raters basing their evaluations on the total number of faculty known at each institution, thus creating a bias in favor of large programs (Graham & Diamond, 1997; Lombardi et al., 2000; Lorden & Martin, 2000). Furthermore, no substantial differences have been found in comparisons of ratings from raters who received such information with those who did not (Jones et al., 1982).

Other critiques of reputational ratings include what has often been called the "halo effect." Programs or departments may receive higher evaluations when they are found within institutions that have, on the whole, a strong reputation (Cartter, 1966; Diamond & Graham, 2000). Thus, the halo effect can be understood as a unit of analysis problem. Although raters are asked to assess the quality of a program or department, this assessment becomes conflated with the quality of the institution as a whole in their minds. The halo effect creates a significant problem for data collection when a university is found to be rated among the top schools for a program of study it does not offer (Webster, 1981), such as when Princeton received a high rating for a law school it does not have, but other disciplines can cite similar examples. Conversely, a strong program at an up-and-coming institution often must overcome the halo effect of other institutions before receiving recognition for its accomplishments (Graham & Diamond, 1997).

Issues of taxonomy are also a major source of weakness for more contemporary reputational studies (Lorden & Martin, 2000). Interdisciplinary fields of research have moved segments of the academy out of well-defined departments and into cross-cutting research cohorts (Graham & Diamond, 1997). The expansion of knowledge and information technology has led to greater research specialization and less adherence to traditional disciplines. As a result, raters may not be as familiar with those working in their own discipline as they are with those in other disciplines engaged in similar research (Diamond & Graham, 2000). However, assessment efforts have difficulty identifying and incorporating these interdisciplinary and highly specified research groupings, primarily because the nomenclature for the research is not standard across institutions. In the absence of a universal classification system for research fields, assessments have been tied to departments, despite acknowledgments of expanded inter-departmental research. The taxonomic decisions made for an assessment also determine who is included and excluded in a ranking, and to whom comparisons will be made, all of which can be very divisive for a field (Frederickson, 2001; Roush, 1995).

Theoretically, reputations should be closely linked to quality, and many contend that surveying a well-informed panel of experts from within the academy is a valid, even desirable, approach to quality assessment (Cartter, 1966). The Cartter and Roose and Andersen studies still serve as models for large-scale assessments of graduate education. To date, the measurement of reputation has changed very little, partly to ensure comparability with earlier studies; but as early as 1980, Judith Lawrence and Kenneth Green began asserting that this lack of innovation was a liability given the changes taking place in higher education. Further institutional transformations have led to calls for the abandonment of reputational ratings (Diamond & Graham, 2000). Nonetheless, a methodological study conducted by the NRC concluded that reputational data are of sufficient value to merit their large-scale collection for its next research-doctorate program assessment (Ostriker & Kuh, 2003). We may hope that this study will motivate many more detailed examinations of prior data collections and careful analyses of the methodological challenges created when using reputational assessments to measure quality.

Faculty Research Productivity

Faculty research is an important component of university quality, but considerable difficulty exists in obtaining data that accurately reflect their accomplishments. Research productivity measures have frequently been developed from data tracking the amount of federal research grants awarded to or expended by universities (Goldberger et al., 1995; Graham & Diamond, 1997; Jones et al., 1982; Lombardi et al., 2000, 2001, 2002). However, this measure does not account for research conducted without extensive funding or funded through private or foundation sources, as are many studies in the social sciences and humanities (F. W. Hoole, personal communication, September 4, 2001; Lombardi et al., 2000). Therefore, the frame of reference for these indicators is primarily science and engineering fields, which require sizable grants for research laboratories. Their link to quality is tenuous, however. While receiving a federal grant indicates that a research *proposal* is distinctive, it does not evaluate the quality of the research *product* (F. W. Hoole, personal communication,

September 4, 2001). In fact, research funding for individual faculty members has not been found to be strongly related to reputational measures of program quality (Beyer & Snipper, 1974).

To better pinpoint the quality of research output, counts of faculty journal publications or citations have been included in many assessments (Jones et. al., 1982; Goldberger et al., 1995; Graham & Diamond, 1997). These data are aggregated and commercially distributed by the Institute for Scientific Information (ISI). Publication and citation data have several methodological weaknesses, some of them mirroring the critiques of federal research funding indicators. ISI limits its indexing primarily to journals, thus reducing its relevance to fields for which journals are the preferred research dissemination method (Webster & Conrad, 1986). Disciplines vary widely with regard to the importance they place on specific scholarly outputs. Journals are favored by scientific disciplines, and books or monographs by some social sciences (Braxton & Bayer, 1986; Braxton & Hargens, 1996; Lorden & Martin, 2000). Citation indices also exclude references to work published in these other non-journal outlets, thereby overlooking citations of work that may be of high quality (Cronin, Snyder, & Atkins, 1997; Reed, 1995). Evidence of the narrow frame of reference for these indicators can also be found in the very high correlation between an institution's total publications (as measured by ISI) and its total federal research expenditures (Toutkoushian et al., 2003).

Some have asserted that journal publication and citation counts would more closely measure program quality if only the most important journals in each field were analyzed (Graham & Diamond, 1997; Lorden & Martin, 2000). Journals have been ranked based upon their "impact factor," which is the ISI's calculation based on the number of times a journal article is cited (Garfield, 1994). Journals with frequently cited articles have higher impact factors. However, a journal cannot be judged entirely by the number of citations its articles receive, because this measure creates a bias toward journals that publish review articles, which are naturally cited with great frequency. Additionally, the extent to which numerous citations reflect the "impact" of a work instead of its "quality" has been hotly debated (Cole, 2000; Lindsey, 1989; Webster, 1981). Critics use the fact of negative citations (which reference a work for its weakness) and self-citations as evidence that quantity and quality are not interchangeable (Lindsey, 1989; MacRoberts & MacRoberts, 1989; Toutkoushian, 1994; Webster, 1981).

Other limitations in these data are related to the unit of analysis. Often, publications and citations for individual faculty members are aggregated up to the program or department. However, the number of publications is related to faculty rank and program size, with large programs and those with more full professors favored (Diamond & Graham, 2000; Tien & Blackburn, 1996; Webster, 1981, 1983). Conceptual difficulties also arise when faculty move between institutions, because choices must be made about whether research done at a previous institution can be justifiably credited to the researcher's current institutional home. The most appropriate unit of analysis for these data is not always clear (i.e., individual vs. department), especially in fields that require institutional investments in research laboratories, for example.

To compensate for the frame of reference limitations of research funding and ISI data, some studies have analyzed the number of awards and honors received by faculty in the arts and humanities (Goldberger et al., 1995; Graham & Diamond, 1997; Lombardi et al., 2000, 2002; & Lombardi, Craig, Capaldi, Gater & Mendonça, 2001). While there is little debate about whether award recipients are the outstanding scholars in their fields, a concern lies in how well this measure enables comparisons. Counts of awards are primarily useful for distinguishing among the highest quality programs, because many institutions have few faculty who have achieved top honors (Webster, 1981). Consequently, this narrow frame of reference results in limited use for this measure beyond distinguishing top-tier institutions from all others. The same can be said of indicators measuring the total number of members for three national academies: the National Academy of Science, the National Academy of Engineering, and the Institute of Medicine (Lombardi et al., 2000, 2001, 2002). This number falls quickly to fewer than 10 for the majority of institutions, offering little help in distinguishing among universities.

Hugh Davis Graham and Nancy Diamond (1997) have raised questions about these measures of faculty productivity, making the case for analyzing quantitative research data in relation to the number of faculty, so as not to overlook those institutions with small but strong programs. When observed on a per capita basis, some indicators reflect very differently on an institution than when analyzed in the aggregate. However, dividing each indicator by the number of faculty is not an unambiguous process. Faculty can be counted in various ways—by the individual department or school or by the institution as a whole, for example—depending on the unit of analysis. Graham and Diamond consistently used the total number of faculty at the university as their divisor, even when the unit of analysis was discipline-based, such as the number of articles published in the sciences. In so doing they created a per capita measure detached from individual faculty activity. In addition, some have found that their rankings lack face-validity because a per capita analysis privileges the efficiency of an enterprise over its quality (F. W. Hoole, personal communication, September 4, 2001).

In sum, attempts to assess the quality of faculty scholarship have been fraught with theoretical and methodological challenges. Because research funding has limited relevance for some disciplines and because all sources of external funding are not observed with existing indicators, these data reveal only a partial picture of university research. Faculty publication and citation data face similar criticisms. While faculty awards and National Academy memberships are a measure of the caliber of the faculty, these indicators create a bar too high for a large majority of institutions by which to identify institutional quality. Nonetheless, these measures provide an important balance to reputational studies and continue to be valued for their purported "objectivity." Unfortunately, these measures provide only a quick glimpse of faculty activity and do not account for the wide range of faculty work undertaken at institutions.

Student Educational Experiences and Outcomes

In addition to academic research, the teaching of graduate and undergraduate students is a primary mission of higher education institutions. Compared to assessing faculty research productivity, the measurement of student experiences and outcomes has been an even more challenging task. The student-related measures most commonly used can be grouped into four main categories: program characteristics, program effectiveness, student satisfaction, and student outcomes.

Program Characteristics

Program characteristics have often been used to gauge the educational experiences of students enrolled in them. The National Science Foundation's Survey of Earned Doctorates is often the data source for graduate measures, including counts of the degrees awarded, and data on student financial support, such as national fellowship grant support and research or teaching assistantships (Goldberger et al., 1995; Jones et al., 1982). These data are usually aggregated up to the program level and analyzed with other characteristics, such as the number of students enrolled.

Although important for tracking trends in doctoral education, these data do not necessarily provide insight into the quality of students' educational experiences. The measures of enrollment and degrees awarded are biased toward larger institutions, as Graham and Diamond (1997) point out, and theoretically conflate quantity with quality. Receipt of a national fellowship to support graduate study is a marker of the quality of a graduate student upon entering a particular program— but not of the program's educational quality. Furthermore, these measures can vary widely by discipline, and consistent differences have been found for women and minority groups (Gilford & Snyder, 1977; Nettles & Millett, in press).

At the undergraduate level, average SAT scores and the proportion of students in the top 10% of their high school graduating class are program characteristics most often examined (Lombardi et al., 2000, 2001, 2002). In addition, most of the commercial rankings, such as *U.S. News & World Report*, *Business Week*, and *Money Magazine* are primarily comprised of program characteristics, including faculty resources, student selectivity, financial resources, and alumni giving. Many of these measures systematically privilege a certain type of institution, creating an inappropriate frame of reference for comparison. For example, institutions that are highly selective, have low student-faculty ratios, and enjoy high rates of annual giving are most often private institutions—not public universities which may be subject to state laws mandating admission for state residents, part-time, and transfer students (Machung, 1998; Gater, 2001). In general, program characteristic data do not provide insight on the impact of these characteristics on individual students. Data on program effectiveness are somewhat more useful in this regard.

Program Effectiveness

The proportion of students completing their intended degree program and the timeliness of completion are often looked to as markers of program effectiveness. The commercial media rankings of undergraduate institutions use six-year graduation rates. Similarly, the National Science Foundation's Survey of Earned Doctorates, which provides data on doctoral level time-to-degree, has been used in several program assessments (Jones et al., 1982; Goldberger et al., 1995). One of the first large-scale, longitudinal efforts to study graduate completion rates was conducted by William Bowen and Neil Rudenstine (1992). They studied students in six fields (English, history, political science, economics, mathematics, and physics), at 10 large research universities, tracking until completion each entering cohort for a 30-year time period—a data collection consisting of 36,000 individual records. Program completion rates and time-to-degree were their primary outcome variables, but they also evaluated the effectiveness of national fellowship programs, examining the relationship between outcomes and various other student financial aid awards. This study is notable in that it was able to build a dataset that examined program-specific factors affecting student outcomes, such as financial aid, teaching, and work in research laboratories. It offered a better conceptualization of the student experiences that led to more effective doctoral education.

More recently, the Survey of Doctoral Student Finances, Experiences, and Achievements also examined the educational and socialization mechanisms of doctoral programs (Nettles & Millett, in press). To determine the factors promoting completion of the Ph.D. degree, they created an 88-item survey to administer in 11 fields of study at 21 universities. Responses from 9,059 doctoral students provided insight into their structures of financial support, levels of scholarly productivity, types of professional socialization, and rate of academic progress. This research emphasized the day-to-day experiences and impressions of doctoral students to identify the combination of events leading to degree completion and career preparation.

These recent studies of enrolled graduate students and their programs' educational and socialization mechanisms help to flesh out the causes of attrition and the circumstances that promote completion. However, program quality cannot be judged exclusively by measures of effectiveness, because satisfaction with one's degree and the usefulness of a program's experiences also contribute to educational quality.

Student Satisfaction

Two recent efforts have emphasized student impressions and their opinions about their educational experiences. Enrolled doctoral students in at least their third year of study were the subjects of the Survey on Doctoral Education and Career Preparation (Golde & Dore, 2001). Begun in 1999, this research aimed to fill the gap in knowledge about doctoral students and their employment preparations and objectives. The sample consisted of students at 27 institutions in 11 fields. The survey queried them about their graduate experiences, career plans, program characteristics, and background information. It focused on the needs of students and the extent to which doctoral programs met those needs in the areas of career development, employment expectations, and knowledge and skill acquisition. This study looked beyond short-term completion rates and defined quality as the ability to meet student expectations about career preparation. By surveying enrolled students, this study investigated the current operation of graduate programs and provided results that could be used to guide reform efforts.

The satisfaction of undergraduate students has been measured with the National Survey of Student Engagement (NSSE), which collects data from enrolled undergraduate students about their classroom and co-curricular activities, and interactions with faculty and peers. These measures of "engagement" have demonstrated a link to educational achievement and learning outcomes and are therefore targeted as a proxy for educational quality. By summarizing students' opinions on and participation in campus-based activities, NSSE data assesses the strengths and weaknesses perceived by students in curriculum, instruction, and campus life (NSSE, 2001). Recent research has found that NSSE data do not bear a strong relationship to *U.S. News* rankings (Pike, 2004), indicating that student impressions of their educational experiences vary irrespective of institutional characteristics.

Overall, information provided by student satisfaction surveys has a limited frame of reference defined by students' experiences and expectations. Unfortunately, students may not have a broad perspective that includes other educational institutions or programs with which to compare their own. In addition, cross-institutional comparisons of these data must be made with attention to any unique or contextual factors that may shape student expectations.

Student Outcomes

A few attempts have been made to assess the concrete learning and career outcomes of educational programs. Employment plans immediately after graduation are reported in the Survey of Earned Doctorates. However, these data are not necessarily a good indication of an individual's career potential. The most diligent effort to collect post-graduate outcome measures was undertaken in the "Ph.D.'s—Ten Years Later" study (Nerad & Cerny, 1999, 2002). Surveys of nearly 6,000 graduates from 61 institutions, administered a decade after they achieved their degrees, provided information about career goals upon graduation, career paths, and job satisfaction. In addition, the survey asked respondents to assess how well their doctoral programs had prepared them for the workforce and to evaluate their feelings about completing the Ph.D. The scope of the study was limited to six disciplines, one in each of the major fields of study: biochemistry, computer science, electrical engineering, English, mathematics, and political science. Their data shed light on the long-term impacts of doctoral degrees and can be used as a model for measuring the career success and employment satisfaction of former students. Despite the disadvantage that this study has limited relevance for current program policymaking, due to the ten-year time lag, many would argue that the long-term career impact of a doctoral degree is a crucial component of program evaluation.

Several recent research projects have begun to focus on undergraduate student outcomes. Taking a track parallel to the doctoral student outcome studies, their aim has been to better understand the educational process by gathering data on current and former student experiences and career paths. The largest such analysis in recent years was headed by William Bowen and Derek Bok (1998), using the Andrew W. Mellon Foundation's College & Beyond database, which combined student data provided by educational institutions with survey data from student respondents. They analyzed data on more than 80,000 undergraduates from 28 colleges and universities who entered in 1951, 1976, or 1989 and made comparisons between students' educational experiences and their civic and employment outcomes. This cohort analysis method yielded interesting evidence about the effectiveness of higher education and could serve as a model for future research, especially if generational differences in the cohorts are addressed or controlled.

The Collegiate Results Instrument (CRI), developed by the Institute for Research on Higher Education and the National Center for Postsecondary Improvement, also studied undergraduate alumni, but with a more recent timeframe of only five to seven years after graduation. Fielded first in 1999, it asked college graduates to report on occupations and incomes, post-baccalaureate educational attainment, skill sets used at their jobs, tasks they felt confident performing, and personal values including community and civic engagement. Eighty institutions participated in the 1999 data collection (Anonymous, 2000), and the instrument is currently being used by Peterson's College Guide to help prospective students compare their own profiles with those of colleges (Greater Expectations National Panel, 2001).

The learning outcomes of undergraduates is the focus of the Collegiate Learning Assessment (CLA, formerly Value Added Assessment Initiative), a recent project of the Council for Aid to Education of the RAND Corporation. Its purpose is to discern the differences in collegiate learning among universities. The project identified three primary outcome variables for analysis: critical thinking, analytic reasoning, and written communication. The explicit unit of analysis is the institution, with the ultimate goal of making comparisons across colleges and universities. Unfortunately, using the institution as the unit of analysis obscures individual and group-specific learning differences and makes the analysis of particular educational contexts or programs impossible.

In general, the more recent graduate and undergraduate student outcomes research addresses important questions of program quality, heretofore uninvestigated by other more long-standing national surveys, such as the Survey of Earned Doctorates. Unfortunately, absent from this research has been a full-scale national sample of students to provide a larger frame of reference for cross-institutional comparisons. In addition, most studies have focused exclusively on either doctoral or baccalaureate training and have left unexamined master's or professional school students. In the future, as the scope of this research expands, debates about the appropriate unit of analysis and dilemmas related to taxonomy and the frame of reference will arise, but these challenges should not outweigh the merits of continuing these investigations.

Overall, the recent emphasis on graduate and undergraduate student outcomes and experiences provides for an encouraging diversity of new methodological approaches that are certain to yield data that will transform current concepts of educational quality. Most likely, a combination of research models that spans throughout and beyond students' educational experiences will serve as the most valuable conduit of information about students. However, student outcomes data cannot exist in a vacuum, and continuing to collect data about program experiences and effectiveness can provide the necessary context for interpreting the results of new studies and directing institutional or program-based policy changes.

Conclusions

Enhancing quality continues to be a uniting force in higher education. Yet self-evident as this ideal may seem, translating that meaning into measurable qualities and quantities is where the greater difficulty lies. Early assessment efforts either assumed a definition of quality without explicitly specifying its boundaries or, more commonly, allowed the data that could be systematically gathered to serve as the operationalization of quality. Today, many challenges must be met to improve quality assessments, perhaps the greatest of which lies in insuring that appropriate measurement strategies and sound methods are employed.

Reputational indicators have been incredibly stable over the years, in part to longitudinally track the status of programs. However, given the cost of surveying large numbers of faculty and administrators, and the high correlation between reputation and other measures of an institution, future reputational studies need a clear rationale for what they offer assessments over and above other, less costly data collections. In addition, reputational studies need innovation to test the utility of various taxonomic decisions and to address comparability among raters with regard to their knowledge and frame of reference when assigning a rating. The organizers of the up-coming National Research Council study of research-doctorate programs are exploring alternatives for conducting their next reputational assessment and have an opportunity to respond to longstanding criticisms with an improved methodology—an opportunity many hope they will seize.

Studies of university research and scholarship have a minimal ability to assess the productivity of faculty in many fields, especially those in the fine arts and humanities, due to the limited frame of reference inherent in the measures. The creation of new measures for research activity in all fields is a first step toward improving quality assessments, so that we may have a better sense of what research looks like in all fields. For example, scholarship in the humanities is in dire need of better measures, as are ways to gauge applied scholarship or research related to teaching and instruction in one's field (Braxton & Del Favero, 2002). Efforts to develop data collections that fill these gaps will greatly improve understandings of faculty work. Then quality frameworks can be imposed on these measures, because many existing indicators do not assess quality as much as they reflect the amount of research being conducted, thereby favoring large programs. Other efforts that account for the number of faculty when analyzing research scholarship leverage only the efficiency of the research enterprise. On their own, neither sheer volume nor efficiency is a good proxy for quality.

The greatest progress in quality assessments has been made in evaluating student experiences and outcomes because the measures offer more than a description of incoming students' talents and abilities. However, further investigations into ways to independently assess the impact of educational programs, outside of how students feel about them, are needed to advance this field. Multiple long-term, longitudinal research efforts will be required to devise reliable measures, which will also need to account for variation in students' incoming abilities. In the meantime, the usefulness of student and alumni opinion data would be greatly enhanced if institutions could tie them to curricular information with samples large enough to examine group differences within educational experiences, such as participation in honors programs, internships, or faculty research projects. In addition, large-scale longitudinal student surveys are needed to connect campus experiences to careers. Such research would be even more valuable if cross-institutional comparisons could be made and if long-term outcomes were traced back to current programs for present-day policymaking.

Institutional and scholarly commitments to the development of new measures in all three areas will yield more and better assessments of quality that permit its multidimensionality to unfold, rather than reducing it to a single rank or rating. While rankings seem destined to remain a part of quality assessment, those that privilege one factor while claiming to be comprehensive result in narrowed perceptions and understandings of quality, both within and outside of higher education. Research that endeavors to address those facets of quality that remain virtually unexplored will have the opposite effect of expanding conceptions about strong educational and research programs. For example, the quality of a university's service to its larger state, local, and national communities, as well as the quality of postdoctoral fellowship experiences, both for advancing a university's research output and for augmenting the training and experience of those serving as postdocs, are areas that can contribute to a multidimensional understanding of quality. Through an exploration of these and other institutional activities, scholars of higher education will be able to assert an important and unique perspective. No single indicator or set of indicators can fully represent the total contribution of higher education to our nation and its communities. However, in an age of increasing expectations for accountability to government entities, institutions need an enhanced ability to demonstrate their capacity as creators and purveyors of knowledge. With stronger and methodologically more rigorous initiatives, colleges and universities will be able to reclaim the agenda of quality assessment and assert for themselves an answer to the question: What is the quality of higher education?

Notes

1. James McKeen Cattell published a reputational survey in *Science* in 1906 that ranked the 1,000 top science scholars. Because it included scientists outside of higher education, working at government bureaus, I do not include it. See Kerr (1991) for a ranking of the top 15 universities in that study.
2. For field-specific discussions of the commercial rankings of graduate and professional schools see, for example, Carter (1998), Frederickson (2001), and Klein and Hamilton (1998).
3. See Beyer and Snipper (1974) for a study of the predictors of the reputational scores in the Cartter (1966) report.

References

Allen, J., & Bresciani, M. J. (2003, January-February). Public institutions, public challenges: On the transparency of assessment results. *Change, 35*(1), 21.

Anonymous. (2000, November/December). Practicing what you preach: Gauging the civic engagement of college graduates. *Change, 32*(6), 53.

Beyer, J. M., & Snipper, R. (1974, Fall). Objective versus subjective indicators of quality in graduate education. *Sociology of Education, 47*, 541–557.

Bowen, W. G., & Bok, D. (1998). *The shape of the river: Long-term consequences of considering race in college and university admissions.* Princeton, NJ: Princeton University Press.

Bowen, W. G., & Rudenstine, N. L. (1992). *In pursuit of the PhD.* Princeton, NJ: Princeton University Press.

Braxton, J. M., & Bayer, A. E. (1986). Assessing faculty scholarly performance. In J. W. Creswell (Ed.), *Measuring faculty research performance*. New Directions for Institutional Research (no. 50, pp. 25–42). San Francisco: Jossey-Bass.

Braxton, J. M., & Del Favero, M. (2002, Summer). Evaluating scholarship performance: Traditional and emergent assessment templates. In C. L., Colbeck (Ed.), *Evaluation faculty performance*. New Directions for Institutional Research (no. 114, pp. 19–31). San Francisco: Jossey-Bass.

Braxton, J. M., & Hargens, L. L. (1996). Variation among academic disciplines: Analytical frameworks and research. In John C. Smart (Ed.), *Handbook of Theory and Research* (Vol. 11, pp. 1–46). New York: Agathon Press.

Brooks, R. L., & Junn, J. (2002). *How well can reputations be measured? Analysis of 1992–93 NRC data*. Unpublished manuscript, Association of American Universities' Assessing Quality of University Education and Research Project.

Carter, T. (1998, March). Rankled by the rankings. *ABA Journal, 84*, 46–52.

Cartter, A. M. (1966). *An assessment of quality in graduate education*. Washington, DC: American Council on Education.

Cole, J. R., (2000). A short history of the use of citations as a measure of the impact of scientific and scholarly work. In B. Cronin & H. B. Atkins (Eds.), *The web of knowledge: A festschrift in honor of Eugene Garfield* (pp. 281–300). Medford, NJ: American Society for Information Science.

Conrad, C. F., & Blackburn, R. T. (1985). Program quality in higher education: A review and critique of literature and research. In J. C. Smart (Ed.), *Higher education: A handbook of theory and research* (Vol. 1, pp. 283–308). New York: Agathon Press.

Cronin, B., Snyder, H., & Atkins, H. (1997). Comparative citation rankings of authors in monographic and journal literature: A study of sociology. *Journal of Documentation, 53*(3), 263–273.

Diamond, N., & Graham, H. D. (2000, July/August). How should we rate research universities? *change, 32*, 20–33.

Dolan, W. P. (1976). *The ranking game: The power of the academic elite*. Lincoln: University of Nebraska Printing and Duplicating Service.

Dometrius, N. C., Hood, M. V., III, Shirkey, K. A., & Kidd, Q. (1998). Bugs in the NRC's doctoral program evaluation data: From mites to hissing cockroaches. *Political Science and Politics, 31*(4), 829–835.

Ehrenberg, R. G., & Hurst, P. J. (1996, May/June). The 1995 NRC ratings of doctoral programs: A hedonic model. *Change, 28*(3), 46–50.

Ehrenberg, R. G., & Hurst, P. J. (1998). The 1995 ratings of doctoral programs: A hedonic model. *Economics of Education Review, 17*(2), 137–148.

Frederickson, H. G. (2001, January/February). Getting ranked. *Change, 33*(1), 49–55.

Garfield, E. (1994). The impact factor. *Current Contents, 25*, 3–7. Retrieved May 10, 2001, from http://www.isinet.com/isi/hot/essays/journalcitationreports/7.html.

Gater, D. S. (2001). *U.S. News & World Report's methodology and rankings of colleges and universities*. Retrieved May 15, 2003, from University of Florida, The Center Web site: http://thecenter.ufl.edu/usnews.html.

Gilford, D. M., & Snyder, J. (1977). *Women and minority Ph.D.'s in the 1970's: A data book*. Washington, DC: National Academy of Sciences.

Goldberger, M. L., Maher, B.A., & Flattau, P.E. (1995). *Research-doctorate programs in the United States: Continuity and change*. Washington, DC: National Academy Press.

Golde, C. M., & Dore, T. M. (2001). At cross purposes: What the experiences of doctoral students reveal about doctoral education. Philadelphia, PA: A report prepared for The Pew Charitable Trusts. Also available at www.phd-survey.org.

Graham, H. D., & Diamond, N. (1997). *The rise of American research universities: Elites and challengers in the postwar era*. Baltimore, MD: Johns Hopkins University Press.

Greater Expectations National Panel. (2001, January). *Beyond U.S. News and World Report: New ways to rate colleges*. Briefing Paper. Retrieved September 5, 2003, from Association of American Colleges & Universities, Greater Expectations Web site: http://www.greaterexpectations.org/briefing_papers/BeyondUSNewsWorldReport.html.

Johnson, K. N., & Wiley, J. D. (1999). *Confidence limits for rank-orderings*. Unpublished manuscript. Available at www.library.wisc.edu/etext/rank/nrelelist.html.

Jones, L. V., Lindzey, G., & Coggeshall, P. E. (1982). *An assessment of research-doctorate programs in the United States*. Washington, DC: National Academy Press.

Kerr, C. (1991, May/June). The new race to be Harvard or Berkeley or Stanford. *Change, 23,* 8–15.

Klein, S. P., & Hamilton, L. (1998, February 18). *The validity of the U.S. News and World Report ranking of ABA law schools.* Retrieved December 12, 2002, from the Association of American Law Schools Web site: http://www.aals.org/validity.html.

Lawrence, J. K., & Green, K. C. (1980). *A question of quality: The higher education ratings game.* AAHE-ERIC/Higher Education Research Report. no. 5. Washington, DC: American Association for Higher Education.

Lindsey, D. (1989). Using citation counts as a measure of quality in science: Measuring what's measurable rather than what's valid. *Scientometrics, 15*(3–4), 189–203.

Lombardi, J. V., Craig, D. D., Capaldi, E. D., & Gater, D. S. (2000, July). *The top American research universities.* An occasional paper from the Lombardi Program on Measuring University Performance, The Center at The University of Florida. Retrieved September 18, 2001, from http://thecenter.ufl.edu/research2000.pdf.

Lombardi, J. V., Craig, D. D., Capaldi, E. D., Gater, D. S., & Mendonça (2001, July). *The top American research universities.* Annual report from The Lombardi Program on Measuring University Performance, The Center at The University of Florida. Retrieved April 14, 2004, from http://thecenter.ufl.edu/research2001.pdf.

Lombardi, J. V., Craig, D. D., Capaldi, E. D., & Gater, D. S. (2002, August). *The top American research universities.* Annual report from The Lombardi Program on Measuring University Performance, The Center at The University of Florida). Retrieved April 14, 2004 from http://thecenter.ufl.edu/research2002.pdf.

Lorden, J., & Martin, L. (2000, February). *Towards a better way to rate research doctoral programs.* A position paper from National Association of State Universities and Land-Grant Colleges' Council on Research Policy and Graduate Education. Retrieved from http://www.nasulgc.org/publications/Towards_A_Better_Way.pdf.

Machung, A. (1998, July/August). Playing the rankings game. *Change, 30,* 12–16.

MacRoberts, M. H., & MacRoberts, B. R. (1989). Problems of citation analysis: A critical review. *Journal of the American Society for Information Science, 40*(5).

Morse, R. J., & Flanigan, S. M. (2002, September 17). America's best colleges 2002: How we rank schools. *U.S. News & World Report,* 104–105. Retrieved September 9, 2002, from http://www.usnews.com/usnews/edu/college/rankings/about/02cbrank.htm.

National Survey of Student Engagement. (2001). *Improving the college experience: National benchmarks of effective educational practice.* NSSE 2001 Report. Bloomington: Indiana University Center for Postsecondary Research and Planning.

Nerad, M., & Cerny, J. (1999, Fall). From rumors to facts: Career outcomes of English Ph.D.s, results from the "Ph.D.s—ten years later" study. Special Issue. *Council of Graduate Schools Communicator, 32,* 1–12.

Nerad, M., & Cerny, J. (2002, August/September). Postdoctoral appointments and employment patterns of science and engineering doctoral recipients ten-plus years after Ph.D. completion: Selected results from the "Ph.D.s—ten years later" study. *Council of Graduate Schools Communicator, 35,* 1–2, 10–11.

Nettles, M. T., & Millett, C. M. (in press). *Demystifying the Ph.D.: The student experience.* Baltimore, MD: Johns Hopkins University Press.

Orr, D. (1984, March). An economist looks at college rankings. *Change, 16,* 45–49.

Ostriker, J. P., & Kuh, C. V. (Eds.). (2003). *Assessing research-doctorate programs: A methodology study.* Washington, DC: National Academies Press.

Pike, G. R. (2004, March). Measuring quality: A comparison of *U.S. News* rankings and NSSE benchmarks. *Research in Higher Education, 45*(2), 193–208.

Reed, K. L. (1995, October). Citation analysis of faculty publication: Beyond Science Citation Index and Social Science Citation Index. *Bulletin of the Medical Library Association, 83*(4), 503–508.

Rogers, E., & Rogers, S. J. (1997, May). High science vs. just selling magazines: How the NRC and *U.S. News* graduate rankings compete. *AAHE Bulletin, 49*(9), 7–10.

Roose, K. D., & Anderson, C. J. (1970). *A rating of graduate programs.* Washington, DC: American Council on Education.

Roush, W. (1995, September 22). Grad school rankings rankle. *Science, 269,* 1660–1662.

Schneider, C. G. (2002, Winter/Spring). Can value-added assessment raise the level of student accomplishment? *Peer Review, 4*(2/3), 4–6.

Shavelson, R. J., & Huang, L. (2003, January-February). Responding responsibly: To the frenzy to assess learning in higher education. *Change, 35*(1), 10–19.

Smith, R., & Fiedler, F. E. (1971). The measurement of scholarly work: A critical review of the literature. *Educational Record, 52,* 225–232.

Thursby, J. G. (2000, June). What do we say about ourselves and what does it mean? Yet another look at economics department research. *Journal of Economic Literature, 38,* 383–404.

Tien, F. F., & Blackburn, R. T. (1996, January-February). Faculty rank system, research motivation, and faculty research productivity: Measure refinement and theory testing. *Journal of Higher Education, 67*(1), 2–22.

Toutkoushian, R. K. (1994). Using citations to measure sex discrimination in faculty salaries. *Review of Higher Education, 18,* 61–82.

Toutkoushian, R. K., Porter, S. R., Danielson, C., & Hollis, P. R. (2003, April). Using publications counts to measure an institution's research productivity. *Research in Higher Education, 44*(2), 121–148.

Webster, D. S. (1981, October). Advantages and disadvantages of methods of assessing quality. *Change, 13,* 20–24.

Webster, D. S. (1983, May/June). America's highest ranked graduate schools, 1925–1982. *Changes, 15,* 20–24.

Webster, D. S. (1992, March/April). Rankings of undergraduate education in the *U.S. News & World Report* and *Money:* Are they any good? *Change, 24,* 18–30.

Webster, D. S., & Conrad, C. F. (1986). Using faculty research performance for academic quality rankings. In J. W. Creswell (Ed.), *Measuring faculty research performance.* New Directions for Institutional Research (no. 50, pp. 25–42). San Francisco: Jossey-Bass.

Webster, D. S., & Skinner, T. (1996, May/June). Rating Ph.D. programs: What the NRC report says . . . and doesn't say. *Change, 28*(3), 22–44.

THE ARTICULATED LEARNING: AN APPROACH TO GUIDED REFLECTION AND ASSESSMENT

SARAH L. ASH AND PATTI H. CLAYTON

ABSTRACT: The value of reflection on experience to enhance learning has been advanced for decades; however, it remains difficult to apply in practice. This paper describes a reflection model that pushes students beyond superficial interpretations of complex issues and facilitates academic mastery, personal growth, civic engagement, critical thinking, and the meaningful demonstration of learning. Although developed in a service-learning program, its general features can support reflection on a range of experiences. It is accessible to both students and instructors, regardless of discipline; and it generates written products that can be used for formative and summative assessment of student learning.

Key Words: service-learning; assessment.

The value of reflection on experience as a way to enhance learning has been advanced for decades. Over seventy years ago, Dewey (1910) described reflective thought as "active, persistent and careful consideration of any belief or supposed form of knowledge in the light of the grounds that support it, and the further conclusions to which it tends" (p. 6). Schön (1983) saw reflection as "a continual interweaving of thinking and doing" (p. 281); and he described the "reflective practitioner" as one who "reflects on the understandings which have been implicit in [one's] action, which [one] surfaces, criticizes, restructures, and embodies in further action" (p. 50). In a review of the reflection models that have been described over the years, Rogers (2001) found the most common definition of reflection as a process that allows the learner to "integrate the understanding gained into one's experience in order to enable better choices or actions in the future as well as enhance one's overall effectiveness" (p. 41). As Rogers pointed out, however, reflection remains a challenging concept for educators to apply in practice in spite of the potential for positive outcomes.

This challenge stems in part from the lack of effective structures to help instructors from diverse disciplines guide students through reflection and meaningful strategies to evaluate the learning outcomes expressed in written products of reflection. Welch (1999) pointed out that it is not enough to tell students to "go and reflect." They need help with connecting their experiences to course material, with challenging their beliefs and assumptions, and with deepening their learning. And it is also not enough to rely on students' testimonials and self-reports to assess the quality of their learning and the meeting of learning objectives. Eyler (2000) suggested that self-reporting leads to a confusion between student satisfaction and student learning, and she called for the development of mechanisms that support students in demonstrating concrete learning outcomes: "What is needed are measures that allow students to show us, rather than tell us, that they have attained greater understanding, ability to apply their knowledge, problem-solving skills and cognitive development" (p. 11).

Faculty and students associated with our service-learning program at North Carolina State University have developed a reflection model that addresses these concerns. In this article we describe first the important, but sometimes unfulfilled, role that reflection plays in service-learning. Next we

Reprinted from *Innovative Higher Education* 29, no. 2, (winter 2004).

outline the framework we have developed to guide reflection, followed by a description of the challenges associated with deepening the students' learning from that process and how we have adjusted our approach accordingly to move them to more critical and higher levels of thinking. Finally we discuss its benefits for faculty professional development and ways in which it might be used as a research tool to investigate the relationships between reflection and learning. Although the model we describe has been used most extensively in the service-learning program, it has the potential to be applied to any pedagogy in which individuals are asked to learn through reflection on experience; and it is based on Bloom's Taxonomy (Bloom, 1956) and standards of critical thinking (Paul, 1993).

Service-Learning as a Model for Reflection

Service-learning, a form of experiential education, is a collaborative teaching and learning strategy designed to promote academic enhancement, personal growth, and civic engagement. Students render meaningful service in community settings that provide experiences related to academic material. Through guided reflection, students examine their experiences critically, thus enhancing the quality of both their learning and their service. Reviewing approaches to service-learning, Eyler, Giles and Schmiede (1996) concluded that reflection is the necessary link that integrates service and learning into a mutually reinforcing relationship. In fact as they point out, "It is critical reflection . . . that provides the transformative link between the action of *serving* and the ideas and understanding of *learning*" (p. 14). Given the centrality of reflection in service-learning, it is an excellent pedagogy with which to model refinements of reflective processes.

Risks of Poor Quality Reflection

The ultimate goal of reflection in service-learning is to help students explore and express what they are learning through their service experiences so that both the learning and the service are enhanced. However, developing ways to achieve and demonstrate high quality reflection has been of concern to educators in the service-learning community for some time (Eyler, 2000; Steinke & Buresh, 2002). As noted by Stanton (1990), when reflection on service is weak, students' learning may be "haphazard, accidental, and superficial" (p. 185). Their learning outcomes are likely to be described vaguely with phrases such as, "I learned a lot," or "I got so much out of my experience." Not only may students learn little or be unable to express articulately the substance of their learning, they may learn the wrong thing. Conrad and Hedin (1990) reminded us of Mark Twain's cat who "learned from sitting on a hot stove lid never to sit again" (p. 87). As with other forms of experiential learning, service-learning frequently puts students in close contact with people or organizations unfamiliar to them but about whom they may have preconceived and unfounded attitudes or beliefs. In theory, such interactions should create precisely the "perplexity, hesitation, doubt" that Dewey (1910, p. 9) saw as key to learning from experience. If students, however, bring their assumptions unchallenged to their reflection on those experiences, they not only close the door to potentially powerful new perspectives, they also allow those experiences to reinforce their stereotypes and prejudices (Hondagneu-Sotelo & Raskoff, 1994). For service-learning in particular, such simplicity in analyzing complex social conditions can result in students supporting the status quo, rather than being the effective agents of change that service-learning proponents hope to help mold (Strand, 1999).

Outcomes of Rigorous Reflection

Eyler and Giles (1999) have found in their research that the more rigorous the reflection in service-learning, the better the learning outcomes. In extensive interviews with students taking service-learning enhanced classes across the country, the investigators found that quantity and quality of reflection were modest but significant predictors of almost all of the outcomes examined except interpersonal development (leadership, communication skills, working well with others). In particular, they were associated with academic learning outcomes, including deeper understanding and better application of subject matter and increased complexity of problem and solution analysis. They were also predictors of openness to new ideas, problem-solving and critical thinking skills. Overall, their research showed that challenging reflection helped to push students to think in new ways and develop alternative explanations for experiences and observations.

Our approach to reflection more clearly demonstrates rather than reports learning; pushes students beyond superficial interpretations of complex issues; and facilitates academic mastery, personal growth, civic engagement and critical thinking. Our experience suggests that this process is valuable in supporting reflection on a range of experiences, including but not limited to service. It is accessible to both students and instructors, regardless of discipline; and it generates written materials that can be used for both formative and summative assessment of student learning. Figure 1 provides a schematic overview of the process that is described in detail in the following section.

1. *Describe service-related experience(s).*

2. *Analyze experience(s) successively from the perspective of each category of service-learning objective:*
   - Personal
   - Civic
   - Academic

3. *Identify the core of an important learning in each category.*

4. *Articulate learning by turning this core idea into a well-developed statement of learning—an articulated learning (AL)—using:*
   - the four guiding questions that structure an AL as an outline.
   - the program-wide service-learning learning objectives to provide guidance/direction in the development of the learning.

5. *Apply standards of critical thinking to the draft ALs through:*
   - Students' self-assessment, and/or
   - Reflection leader feedback, and/or
   - Instructor feedback.

   [Note: Over time, the students improve their ability to apply these standards themselves, before submitting their drafts for review.]

6. *Finalize the ALs, aiming to fulfill all learning objectives in each category and meet standards of critical thinking.*
   [Note: Doing the latter well is generally required for doing the former well.]

7. *Undertake new experience(s).*
   - Including, when feasible, taking action on the goals set/testing the conclusions reached in the ALs.

8. *Continue reflection process outlined here.*
   - Including reflecting on the experience of enacting the goals/testing the conclusions reached in the previous ALs, when this has been done, and articulating additional complexity of learning accordingly.

Figure 1 Overview of the Process of Articulating Learning as Applied to Service-Learning

The Development of a Rigorous Reflection Framework

We have found that structuring reflection mechanisms to include three general phases results in a rigorous reflection framework that maximizes learning and helps to refine reflective skills. These general phases are:

1. *Description* (objectively) of an experience.
2. *Analysis* in accordance with relevant categories of learning.
3. *Articulation* of learning outcomes.

In service-learning, the primary learning objectives can be organized into three categories: academic, personal, and civic. In our reflection framework, based on the work of Kiser (1998), the analysis phase is structured to include consideration of these three areas. When engaged in academic analysis, students examine their experiences in light of specific course concepts, exploring similarities and differences between theory and practice. In analysis from the personal perspective, students consider their feelings, assumptions, strengths, weaknesses, traits, skills, and sense of identity as they are surfaced and sometimes challenged by service-learning experiences. And when examining their service-learning related activities from the civic perspective, students explore decisions made and actions taken in light of consequences for the common good, consider alternative approaches and interpretations, identify elements of power and privilege, and analyze options for short-term versus long-term and sustainable change agency. We are currently developing "diversity" as a fourth category in which students identify and analyze the sources and significance of assumptions or interpretations regarding those different from themselves or others and evaluate strategies for maximizing opportunities and minimizing challenges associated with those differences.

In our most rigorous model of reflection, trained undergraduate reflection leaders guide students through these general phases of reflection in small, out-of-class, reflection sessions. However, this same approach of beginning with objective description and then iteratively examining the experience from each perspective can also happen effectively in the context of journal writing or in-class activities. Whatever the forum for reflection, the *articulating learning* phase brings each reflection activity to a close and establishes a foundation for learners to carry the results of the reflection process forward beyond the immediate experience, improving the quality of future learning and of future experience (related to service or to other aspects of their lives). Therefore, the articulating learning process supports them in recognizing what they have learned through reflection on experience, placing it in context, and expressing it concisely. In other words, it supports them in thinking critically about their own learning.

The Articulated Learning

The product of this entire process is called an *articulated learning* (AL). It is structured in accordance with four guiding questions:

1. What did I learn?

2. How, specifically, did I learn it?

3. Why does this learning matter, or why is it significant?

4. In what ways will I use this learning; or what goals shall I set in accordance with what I have learned in order to improve myself, the quality of my learning, or the quality of my future experiences or service?

A complete AL is a series of paragraphs addressing each of these four prompting questions. It is specific to just one of the categories of learning objectives, such that a single AL articulates an important learning from the academic or the personal or the civic perspective.

The four questions—similar to the "What? So What? Now What?" model developed by the Campus Opportunity Outreach League and based on Kolb's Experiential Learning Cycle of action and reflection (1984)—embody Dewey's theory that reflection leads to better understanding *and* more informed action. To complete the learning cycle as described by Kolb, we are going to begin encouraging faculty to implement service-learning such that students are able to take at least one AL in each category through goal-setting, action on those goals, and reflection on the outcome, resulting in the articulating of new learning.

Analysis of their experiences in accordance with the reflection framework supports students in identifying learning, and the AL process helps them develop and apply or test those learnings in their full complexity. We found, however, that students need more than just the four questions structuring the AL to achieve deep, critical learning. As in the following extreme example, ALs could demonstrate only superficial thinking, such as the learning of a fact:

> I learned that the animal shelter is completely dependent on unpredictable donations for support. I learned this when the shelter coordinator told me that's why she couldn't order dog food in large quantities at one time. This matters because it is important to know how organizations like these are funded. I will use this learning in the future by remembering this fact the next time I'm at the animal shelter and I find that it has had to turn away animals because it lacks the food to feed them.

This "learning" also illustrates a circular or obvious explanation of significance ("It is important because it is important to know this") and only limited thinking about how to use or build on the learnings ("I will remember this next time I am in a similar situation").

We wanted to push students to a better awareness and deeper understanding of the issues that they were confronting in their service-learning experiences. We wanted them to be able to articulate, for example, why the issues are so complex, what factors contribute to or detract from the situation they are experiencing, and the roles that they themselves play as agents of change. In the animal shelter example, we wanted them to compare the approach taken by the coordinator, which was to turn animals away due to insufficient food, to other possible approaches, such as expanding her capacity to take in more animals by finding permanent sources of funding and/or food, identify the reason(s) for her approach, which would require the student seek out this information, and challenges associated with adopting a more sustainable alternative, such as trading off time she would rather spend caring for the animals with time spent soliciting continuous support. We also wanted them to consider more systemic dimensions of this civic issue, considering, for example, the role the coordinator or the student might play in ameliorating the fundamental problem of animal abandonment. With this kind of thinking, students can more fully engage with their experiences, maximizing their learning and their ability to serve.

Just as important, we wanted to create a structure whereby the generation of ALs could serve as the final step of reflection in the wide variety of disciplines in which service-learning is being used at our institution-from animal science to political science to civil engineering. Therefore, it had to be easy to adopt and had to be understood by a diverse population of both instructors and students.

Integration of Program-Wide Learning Objectives

Toward that end, we used questions students address in the second phase (analysis) of our reflection framework as a starting point to create a set of program-level learning objectives (see Appendix A) that can be used in any service-learning-enhanced course in addition to those written by the instructor. They can also serve as a template for more carefully constructing the ALs themselves. In so doing, we were also responding to Eyler's call for "[defined] learning outcomes that would be expected to be enhanced by service participation" (Eyler, 2000, p. 11).

In crafting the specific learning objectives within the academic area, for example, we wanted students to be able to articulate a deepened understanding of the complexities and subtleties of course concepts. However, we realized that prerequisites for such an outcome include recognizing a course concept when they see it at work in their experiences, applying the concept in the context of these experiences, and comparing and contrasting the concept as presented in theory with it as experienced in practice. We also realized that individual students would have differing degrees of achievement in reaching the highest levels of such academic learning, due to differences in their level of cognitive development and in the nature and quality of service-learning implementation in their classes. Accordingly, we decided to present the learning outcomes as a hierarchy within each category (academic, personal, and civic), from the identification of knowledge to a judgment based on critical evaluation. Use of this hierarchical structure supports students in refining their academic learning to the point that they can, for example, make reasoned judgments as to the adequacy of a course-related concept relative to their experience. This approach follows the recommendation by Bradley (1997) that written products from service-learning reflection be structured so that they require students to *observe, analyze,* and *evaluate* their service experience.

Each learning objective also has a set of questions that carry students through the writing of the ALs and that closely mirror those in the reflection framework, helping to tie together the reflection on learning with the articulation of that learning. It is not necessary for students to follow these in a linear fashion. It is more important that they use these questions as a guide by which to focus and check the process and progress of their thinking.

In the following civic AL, the student identified his group's initial use of an "idealistic" rationale to motivate high school students to engage meaningfully in their own community project (learning objective #1); considered motivating them by appealing to their desire for good grades as an alternative approach (learning objective #2); and concluded that that there was value in combining the two approaches in order to achieve both short-term objectives—the students' participation in community service—and a more fundamental change in their attitudes towards such service (learning objective #3). Throughout the AL, the student struggled with the challenges of working toward a collective goal with individuals who have differing motivations, while also trying to change those motivations (learning objective #4).

> *I learned that* developing a careful balance between idealistic and self-serving motives amongst group members is essential in meeting collective objectives. There is a danger associated with trading off "ideal" motives for lesser ones (as acceptance of these motives could lead to less beneficial results), although at the same time unmet objectives will likely result from a leader's unwillingness to work with each individual's motives.

> *I learned this when* the [high school students] have thus far been unreceptive to our group's attempts to persuade them that this project should be about the learning and growth they experience (idealistic motives), rather than the grade they receive in combination with the 6.0 GPA score for an [Advanced Placement] class. I do not want to allow the students to settle for just receiving a grade from their projects (and through settling there is a danger that their personal and community results will be less meaningful), yet at the same time I realized even with these perhaps self-serving motives, the [high school] learning community can still receive tangible benefits that will certainly not be met if our group along with [their instructor] refuses to motivate the students with a grade, what currently matters to them.

> *This learning matters because* individuals working together in a group will always have slightly different (and often self-serving) motives for participation in that group, and although a common vision may be somewhat present, there are still discrepancies in each member's idea of an ideal end-state. In a leadership role, I must be willing to understand that every member may not be involved for the same reasons: in order to have results instead of inaction I need to be uncompromising in my own ideals, while understanding of the non-idealistic motives for action (such as my need for acceptance or their desire for good grades).

> *In light of this learning,* I will recognize the need to harness motives, both idealistic and more self-serving, for the common good, yet at the same time seek to focus mainly on idealistic motivation to the extent that my group members can handle. Specifically, we may have to use grades as a "carrot" for these [high school students], but through reflection and discussion in the classroom I would like to convince as many of them as possible that this project should not be about the grade, or at the very least not reinforce their idea that grades are their only motivation.

Application of Critical Thinking Principles

The process that takes a student from observation to evaluation requires the intellectual discipline of critical thinking. As defined by Paul (1993), "Critical Thinking is a systematic way to form and shape one's thinking. . . . It is thought that is disciplined, comprehensive, based on intellectual standards, and as a result, well-reasoned" (p. 20). Critical thinking serves as a guide to belief and action and, as outlined by Paul, is based on standards that include accuracy, clarity, relevance, depth, breath, logic, and significance.

In order to facilitate the students' critical thinking, we developed a handout with definitions of the standards along with sample AL passages that exemplify each standard, in order to introduce them to the elements of critical thinking and to support them in trying to integrate each element into their thinking process. For example, the preceding AL could be strengthened by the addition of supporting evidence for the claim that the students had been unreceptive to the group's efforts and that they care only about grades. Without this information, the accuracy of the student's evaluation of the alternatives cannot be determined and thus the logic of the conclusion can be challenged. In addition, the student could have provided more clarity with respect to his goals (e.g., identification of specific classroom activities or discussion topics), thus better positioning himself to test the validity of his conclusion through action and further reflection.

The Final Product

Taken together, the learning objectives and critical thinking guide support the reflection process by providing a common language for students and faculty to use to focus and refine the quality of the thinking itself and its articulation. Several rounds of feedback, from the instructor, the reflection leader, and/or others students engaged in the same process, informed by these tools, can produce a civic AL such as the following excerpt:

> *I learned that* my role as a servant-leader should consist of being a "stimulator" (someone who rouses activity in other individuals, which later becomes self-sustaining) rather more so than the "facilitator" role (someone who attempts to make progress easier, but is constantly required to continue progress). . . . Embodying the role of a stimulator can serve to invoke motivation and a sense of empowerment in others whom one stimulates and adds a sustaining component to the progress that is being made with less necessity for continued impulse from the part of the servant leader.
>
> *I learned this when* comparing the consequences of my actions as a reflection leader for the AP Environmental Science students at the beginning of the semester . . . to the role just before and since Spring Break that I have assumed with [a fellow student] in leading them in reflective activities. . . . At first, we offered suggestions of resources for the students to contact for help with their projects and we offered suggestions on their proposals in order to help them increase the likelihood of receiving funding for their efforts. After a while, we began to perceive little to no significant progress, at least per our expectations, on the part of the students and began to reflect on the fact that they might be seeing us as a crutch for the completion of their project objectives, [as evidenced by] their poor level of conversation about proposals and their lack of confidence in the direction of their projects [by] asking us what they [should] do. . . . After leading reflection sessions during class, we have found that our methods—creating provocative activities and framing questions around them—have really invoked deeper thinking in the students [as] gauged by . . . [the] significant amount of breadth, depth, and integration in their responses to the questions and in their articulated learnings. This continued process has really engaged the students in being more self-critical and has caused them to really evaluate their progress . . . more between our visits, as [their teacher] has told us. . . .
>
> *This learning matters because* taking on a role as a "stimulator" . . . can help other individuals to begin holding themselves accountable . . . in completing the tasks that are needed to work toward inducing significant change. . . . While making the project easier through a facilitative role may be necessary given certain circumstances, providing a stimulus to act can be more permanent and multiply the creativity and sense of empowerment, and therefore productivity and progress of members of a group acting to induce change. The challenge arrives when those whom the stimulator is targeting resist the change that is inherent in the power that they are given.
>
> *In light of this learning,* I will work together with other members of my group to develop our methods and integrate new ones for becoming stimulatory agents and determining when a

facilitative or stimulatory role is more necessary during the coming month in which our work with the . . . project will conclude. Preliminarily, we are looking to have another type of reflective session with each class next week for them to evaluate their progress, redefine some of their own goals as necessary, and raise sustainability issues for their projects. . . .

Use of Written Reflection Products for Assessment Purposes

The preceding AL reflects the formative use of the learning objectives and the critical thinking guide to help students organize, frame, and check the quality of their thinking as they write their ALs. However, the ALs can be used for summative assessment as well. First, an AL can be evaluated with respect to the highest level learning objective it meets. Second, the critical thinking standards can be applied to the ALs in the form of a holistic rubric (see Table 1) that we have adapted from Paul's critical thinking standards. The rubric describes four levels of mastery relative to these standards that have been written with specific reference to learning based on a service-related experience. Overall, our approach has some of the same general features as the *ABC* template developed by Welch (1999), which evaluates student journal entries based on the presence of affective, behavioral, and cognitive components. However, the AL process described here provides more support for the writing of the reflection product itself by structuring it around specific learning objectives and explicitly incorporating the standards of critical thinking. This process also allows for the assessment of the quality of the thinking.

Instructors can use the information provided by the learning objective and critical thinking assessment strategies in a variety of ways. For example, the level of student mastery relative to the learning objectives and critical thinking rubric for a particular course concept provides valuable feedback on their teaching by identifying those concepts that appear harder for students to grasp. Possible sources of confusion may become particularly apparent when reading students' attempts to apply the concept to their experiences. Although articulated learnings are not meant to replace all other student learning products in a course, instructors may also find these tools useful for quantifying the reflective or service-learning component of the students' final grades. This helps to fulfill the principle

TABLE 1
Example of Level 4 (of 4) of the Critical Thinking Rubric for Assessing Articulating Learnings

Level 4 does most or all of the following:

- Consistently avoids typographical, spelling and grammatical errors.
- Makes clear the connection(s) between the service-related experience and the dimension being discussed.
- Makes statements of fact that are accurate, supported with evidence. *(Accuracy)*
  - For Academic ALs: Accurately identifies, describes, applies appropriate academic principle.
- Consistently expands on, expresses ideas in another way, provides examples/illustrations. *(Clarity)*
- Describes learning that is relevant to AL category and keeps the discussion specific to the learning being articulated. *(Relevance)*
- Addresses the complexity of the problem; answers important question(s) that are raised; avoids over-simplifying when making connections. *(Depth)*
- Gives meaningful consideration to alternative points of view, interpretations. *(Breadth)*
- Demonstrates a line of reasoning that is logical, with conclusions or goals that follow clearly from it. *(Logic)*
- Draws conclusions, sets goals that address a (the) major issue(s) raised by the experience. *(Significance)*

of experiential education, often challenging, that credit be given not for the experience itself but for learning achieved through reflection on that experience (Walker, 1990).

More generally, because the articulated learning process provides evidence of student learning outcomes, it can help meet the growing demand for accountability in higher education, which requires instructors, departments, programs, and institutions to identify and demonstrate the knowledge, skills, and competencies they want students to have as a result of their educational experience. It allows for assessment that grows out of and is customized to the particular learning objectives in question. Because the articulated learning is a course-embedded process, it is less time-consuming for both students and instructors than interview, focus group, or portfolio methods used or recommended by others (Eyler & Giles, 1999; Gelmon, S.B., Holland, B.A., Driscoll, A., Spring, A., & Kerrigan, S., 2001; Serow, R.C., 1997); and it provides more substantive information than surveys and inventories alone (Gelmon, S.B., Holland, B.A., Driscoll, A., Spring, A, & Kerrigan, S., 2001; Payne, 1993).

Additional Applications

As a Research Tool

We are currently using the ALs and their associated assessment strategy to answer a variety of research questions. For example, how much improvement can students make over the course of the semester in articulating their learning in each of the categories of learning objectives? Are they more likely to make progress in writing in one category as compared to another, and what might be the reasons for such differences? How might attainment of learning outcomes vary with type of service (e.g., one-time versus multiple experiences), reflection process (e.g., reflection sessions versus journal writing only), students' educational level (e.g., freshman versus senior), and discipline (e.g., technical versus humanities)?

We are also looking at the relationship between the learning objectives and the critical thinking rubric to help us better understand and refine both. For example, how can we use the standards of critical thinking to help improve students' ability to master each level of the learning objectives? And are there ways to improve the wording of the learning objectives to provide better support for the students' critical thinking? Finally, we are interested in comparing this model to other assessment strategies such as King and Kitchener's (1994) Reflective Judgment Model, which evaluates student writing relative to levels of intellectual development.

As a Faculty Development Tool

Supporting student reflection both requires and nurtures reflective practice on the part of faculty. Our service-learning program offers workshops on the approach to reflection and assessment described here, and beginning next year we will provide a virtual tutorial on articulating learning for faculty as well as students. Beyond learning to use these tools in support of student reflection, however, we also encourage service-learning faculty to use this process to support their own reflection and subsequent personal and professional development. Our goal is to have them regularly reflect on their teaching experiences, articulate specific "lessons learned" in the process, and share that learning with their students and each other—an outcome that we believe will substantially improve the function of this group of instructors as a learning community. Articulating learning clearly supports our attempts to grow as the "reflective practitioners," of whom Schön speaks, by helping us to understand better the choices we make in the classroom and the assumptions we hold about our students. It also increases our ability to integrate critical thinking principles throughout our teaching as we craft assignments, explain objectives, and consult with students. Finally, it better positions us to support them in the challenge of learning to learn through reflection. As we share our own ALs, we model disciplined reflection, appropriately full of ambiguity and internal tensions. We find that students come to take the process more seriously and to respect and reciprocate our willingness to be vulnerable and receptive to feedback from other perspectives that such sharing implies. Thus, our professional development as faculty is intimately linked with the development of our students.

Future Directions

Eyler, Giles, and Schmiede (1996) noted that reflection "need not be a difficult process, but it does need to be a purposeful and strategic process" (p. 16). This conviction has been at the heart of our efforts to develop a rigorous, adaptable, learner-centered approach that both challenges and supports students in learning through reflection on experience. Our understanding of how to do this well has clearly evolved and will continue to do so, in large part through our own reflective practice. Refinements of the AL process have been guided primarily by the patterns (both positive and problematic) we have found in the ALs themselves and in student feedback. This iterative process will continue in the future as we support faculty and students in using the articulated learning in an increasing array of curricula and institutional settings. In addition, we will be experimenting with ALs as the culminating step of individual guided journal-writing and in-class reflection activities, and we will be using the learning objectives themselves as a stand-alone tool for guiding reflection in the absence of instructor or reflection leader facilitation.

Our experience suggests that positioning articulating learning at the heart of guided reflection—in virtually any learning situation—minimizes the risk, identified by T.S. Eliot (1943), that one might have "had the experience but missed the meaning" (p. 24). And, indeed, it maximizes the unique potential of experiential education to nurture learning in its full richness and complexity.

References

Bloom, B. S. (Ed.). (1956). *Taxonomy of educational objectives, handbook I: Cognitive domain*. New York, NY: David McKay Company.

Bradley, L. R. (1997). Evaluating service-learning: Toward a new paradigm. In A. S. Waterman (Ed.), *Service-Learning: Applications from the research* (pp. 151–171). Mahwah, NJ: Erlbaum.

Conrad, D., & Hedin, D. (1990). Learning from service: Experience is the best teacher—Or is it? In Jane Kendall and Associates (Eds.), *Combining service and learning. I* (pp. 87–98). Raleigh, NC: National Society for Internships and Experiential Education.

Dewey, J. (1910). *How we think*. Boston, MA: D.C. Heath and Company.

Eliot, T. S. (1943). *The four quartets*. New York, NY: Harcourt, Brace, and Company.

Eyler, J. (2000). What do we most need to know about the impact of service-learning on student learning? *Michigan Journal of Community Service Learning*, Special Issue Fall, 11–17.

Eyler, J., & Giles, D. E. (1999). *Where's the learning in service-learning?* San Francisco, CA: Jossey-Bass.

Eyler, J., Giles, D. E., & Schmiede, A. (1996). *A practitioner's guide to reflection in service-learning*. Nashville, TN: Vanderbilt University.

Gelmon, S. B., Holland, B. A., Driscoll, A., Spring, A., & Kerrigan, S. (2001). *Assessing service-learning and civic engagement*. Providence, RI: Campus Compact.

Hondagneu-Sotelo, P., & Raskoff, S. (1994). Community service-learning: Promises and problems. *Teaching Sociology, 22*, 248–254.

Kiser, P. M. (1998). The Integrative Processing Model: A framework for learning in the field experience. *Human Service Education, 18*, 3–13.

King, P. M., & Kitchener, K. S. (1994). *Developing reflective judgment: Understanding and promoting intellectual growth and critical thinking in adolescents and adults*. San Francisco, CA: Jossey-Bass.

Kolb, D. (1984). *Experiential learning*. Englewood Cliffs, NJ: Prentice Hall.

Payne, C. A. (1993). Construction of an instrument to assess the service learning model: Establishing concurrent validity and internal reliability. (Doctoral dissertation, University of Northern Colorado, 1992). *Dissertation Abstracts International, 53/07A*.

Paul, R. (1993). *Critical thinking: What every person needs to survive in a rapidly changing world*. Santa Rosa, CA: Foundation for Critical Thinking.

Rogers, R. (2001). Reflection in higher education: A concept analysis. *Innovative Higher Education, 26*, 37–57.

Schön, D. (1983). *The reflective practitioner: How professionals think in action*. New York, NY: Basic Books.

Serow, R. C. (1997). Research and evaluation on service-learning. In A. S. Waterman (Ed.), *Service-Learning: Applications from the research* (pp. 13–24). Mahwah, NJ: Erlbaum.

Stanton, T.K. (1990). Liberal arts, experiential learning and public service: Necessary ingredients for socially responsible undergraduate education. In Jane Kendall and Associates (Eds.), *Combining service and learning I* (pp. 175–189). Raleigh, NC: National Society for Internships and Experiential Education.

Steinke, P., & Buresh, S. (2002). Cognitive outcomes of service-learning: Reviewing the past and glimpsing the future. *Michigan Journal of Community Service Learning, 8,* 5–14.

Strand, K. J. (1999). Sociology and service-learning: A critical look. In J. Ostrow, G. Hesser, & S. Enos (Eds.), *Cultivating the Sociological Imagination.* (pp. 29–37). New York, NY: American Association for Higher Education.

Walker, U. (1990). Assessing Learning. In Jane Kendall and Associates (Eds.), *Combining service and learning II* (pp. 206–207). Raleigh, NC: National Society for Internships and Experiential Education.

Welch, M. (1999). The ABCs of reflection: A template for students and instructors to implement written reflection in service-learning. *NSEE Quarterly, 25,* 22–25.

Acknowledgment

The reflection framework was originally developed by undergraduates Nick Haltom and Gretchen Lindner, along with Patti Clayton. The four-part structure for articulating learning was developed by undergraduate Jason Grissom. The authors wish to acknowledge Barbi Honeycutt, Virginia Lee, Mary Catherine Brake, Julie David and Myra Day for their assistance in developing the assessment portion of this process.

Appendix A: Service-Learning Program-Wide Learning Objectives
Academic Dimension

1. *Identify and describe course concepts in the context of your service-learning related activities.*
   - Describe the course concept that relates to your service-learning experience.
     -AND-
   - Describe what happened in the experience that relates to that course concept.

2. *Apply course concepts in the context of these activities.*
   - How does the concept help you to better understand, or deal with, issues related to your service-learning experience?
     -AND/OR-
   - How does the service-learning related experience help you to better understand the course concept?

3. *Analyze course concepts in light of what you have experienced in these activities.*
   - In what specific ways are the concept (or your prior understanding of it) and the experience the same and/or different?
     -AND-
   - What complexities do you see now in the concept that you had not been aware of before?
     -AND/OR-
   - What additional questions need to be answered or evidence gathered in order to judge the adequacy/accuracy/appropriateness of the concept when applied to the experience?

4. *Synthesize and evaluate course concepts in light of what you have experienced in your service-learning related activities.*
   - Based on the analysis above, does the concept (or your prior understanding of it) need to be revised and if so, in what specific ways? Provide evidence for your conclusion.
     -AND-

- If revision is necessary, what factors do you think have contributed to the inadequacy in the concept as presented or in your prior understanding of it? (E.g., bias/assumptions/agendas/lack of information on the part of the author/scientist or on your part.)
  -AND-

- Based on the analysis above, what will/might you do differently in your service-learning or other academic-related activities in the future?
  -OR-

- Based on the analysis above, what should/might your service organization do differently in the future and what are the challenges that it night face as it does so?

Personal Dimension[1]

1. Identify and describe an awareness about a personal characteristic that has been enhanced by reflection on your service-learning related activities.

2. Apply this awareness in the context of your service-learning related activities and to other areas of your life now or in the future.

3. Analyze the sources of this characteristic and the steps necessary to use or improve on it in your service-learning related activities and other areas of your life.

4. Develop and evaluate your strategies for personal growth.

Civic Dimension

1. Identify and describe an approach (e.g., decision or action) you or others took or, looking back on it, could have taken.

2. Apply your understanding of your (others') approach in processes of collective action to the relationship between social action and social change.

3. Analyze the appropriateness of the approach taken and the steps necessary to make any needed improvements in the approach.

4. Evaluate your (others') role as an agent(s) of systemic change.

Note

1. The complete list for the Personal and Civic categories are available by contacting the authors at sarah_ash@ncsu.edu.

GENERAL LEARNING

C.H. BEYER, G.M. GILLMORE
AND A.T. FISHER

What helps your learning? "A really good professor—someone who can communicate and knows his subject well, and when you are in the presence of that, you can't NOT learn. You go to class."

What hinders your learning? "The first day you realize the world is not going to fall apart because you do not attend a class is a very dangerous day."

At its beginning, the UW SOUL focused on six areas of learning: personal growth, understanding and appreciating diversity, critical thinking and problem solving, writing, quantitative reasoning, and information literacy. However, we also gathered information on areas of students' learning that fell outside these six areas. This more general information is the subject of this chapter. In addition, this chapter presents comparisons of learning across the six areas.

The chapter makes two major arguments, both of which seem ridiculously obvious. First, we argue that students learn and develop skills in their four years in college—that is to say, they leave knowing more and being able to do more than when they arrived. To those who know the research on learning, this assertion may seem to be an already well-established fact that requires little further support. However some groups continue to raise questions about whether students actually learn anything in college. Others, most recently and eloquently Derek Bok (2006), acknowledge that research shows that students do make learning gains in college (Astin, 1993a; Pascarelli & Terenzini, 1991) but argue that students should be learning more. Bok (2006) argues that faculty need to focus on what students learn, integrating active learning strategies into their classroom teaching, assessing their goals for student learning, and engaging in a continuous improvement process that can foster key institutional purposes (or outcomes) for learning. While these arguments are not entirely new (see Barr & Tagg, 1995), Bok's call for reform, with its emphasis on each institution assessing the learning of its own undergraduates, is welcomed. Indeed, that was our purpose in the UW SOUL. However, as results in this chapter and elsewhere in this book demonstrate, we can show that students are learning, but we cannot determine if they are learning all they could be or whether they had learned "enough." That judgment must be guided by standards and practices in the disciplines.

While all students knew more when they graduated than they had when they entered the university, students' knowledge gains were uneven. Some students improved their abilities to write computer programs but learned little about who they were and what they valued. Some students learned a great deal about power and oppression but little about how to see the empty spaces in a landscape and imagine what might fill them. Still others learned how to talk with ease with people different from themselves at the same time they learned a great deal about globalization and life on the ground in Argentina.

Reprinted from *Inside the Undergraduate Experience: The University of Washington's Study of Undergraduate Learning*, by Catherine Hoffman Beyer, Gerald M. Gillmore, Andrew T. Fisher, and Peter T. Ewell (2007), Jossey-Bass Publishers, Inc.

This chapter demonstrates the unevenness that we believe characterizes undergraduate learning. The chapter shows that learning comes from many directions, and that learning in one arena often inspires learning in others in ways that are hard to predict and track. This complexity lends support to Arnett's (2000) theory of the role of exploration in emerging adulthood.

A second argument in this chapter is that faculty are the key to how much students learn. Again, this point seems obvious on its surface; however, many projects and programs in higher education are dedicated to reducing faculty time with undergraduates in the classroom as both a cost and energy saving approach to learning. Many of these efforts are laudable as approaches to actively engaging students in the learning process, but when they remove faculty from students, institutions also remove possibilities. While we also note the importance of peers to learning, as well as the significance of the mindset and motivation of the students themselves, students told us again and again that, more than any other source, faculty inspired and delivered learning. This learning was not only academic. Sometimes faculty inspired self-awareness. Sometimes they showed students how to understand their neighbors. Perhaps because of the transformations faculty can inspire, students want more interaction with faculty, not less (see also Kvavik & Caruso, 2005).

In contrast, when asked about what hindered learning, students told us that hindrances most often come at their own hands.

Rather than beginning with case studies, as we have in other chapters, we move from this introduction to nine students' comments near the end of their college careers about their learning. The kinds of learning these students describe were nonlinear and messy, demonstrating processes that are difficult to track. Next, we focus on findings related to general learning and on what helped and what hindered students' learning. Finally, we draw conclusions and discuss their implications for teaching and assessment.

Nine Paths

American ethnic studies major: I am more confident in myself and my abilities to talk to people and in my ability to communicate my ideas. I have learned a lot about myself and what I must do to be heard in this society and how as a minority I am often overlooked, so I must make myself unforgettable.

Art major: Every class and every professor has given me something new and valuable, but if I had to pick out one class, it would be the Global Classroom project that I was fortunate to participate in during the 2002 school year. It was unlike any other project. The concept was to create learning opportunities for faculty and students across international boundaries by collaborating with the School of Arts and Design at Tsinghua University on creating posters on a central theme, water awareness. From this project, I really learned what learning through exploration meant. The students had to make a lot of the decisions along the way. From that point on, I began to learn to see many things within context rather than just accepting them on a surface understanding. The global project was also the first time that I really worked in groups. I learned to appreciate others' thoughts and working together. Overall, it was a project that really changed my perception of learning and school.

Business major: There was an astronomy professor who really inspired me with his enthusiasm and his desire to make his students feel the same way he did about astronomy. As a result of his opening lecture, where he posted a chart of the dates and viewing locations of the next full solar eclipses, I decided to go to Madagascar for two weeks this summer to view a full solar eclipse. I told him about this and my plans for the trip, and he was very excited for me. He asked me to let him know of my progress and to send him photographs. This has made me feel like I can contribute to his classroom and to his teaching, because he has not yet been able to see a solar eclipse himself, and I know that he will be excited enough by [my experience] that he will show his future classes some of my photographs. In some small way, I feel like a pioneer for the astronomy department on his behalf, as much as this trip is also a personal journey.

Biology major: Academically speaking, I have learned how to manage my time better, how to hold down classes, homework, a job, and social aspects without having to sacrifice one or the other. I think

I have become better prepared for work loads, am better at approaching staff for questions, and am more focused (finally) on what I want to do in the future. Personal growth has also occurred in the form of maturing, being more open minded and accepting of other views and people. The classes I have taken have been especially helpful in giving me a more diversified outlook, and granted me the ability to be more accepting and open to others' ideas. With some 40,000 students on campus, I have met many with entirely opposite views and backgrounds than my own. The opportunities that are available through the UW and the surrounding area have also participated in my growth and change.

Dance major: I had a mystical experience in my ballet class. I felt comfortable with the movement enough to play with the music. I let go of all my fears of falling, messing up a step, and being watched. Then, I just felt the music of the cello through my entire body.

Engineering major: [In my senior year] I learned that I couldn't take my classes as I had done the past three years. I learned that I wasn't studying to the best of my ability. In the past, I thought studying meant staying up really late and doing a lot of homework problems. But last quarter I learned that going in and having a one-on-one conversation with the professor really helps you learn. I don't know what changed me. I think it was the people I was doing my homework with. It was that we felt really comfortable with the way the professors were teaching the class, and that inspired us to go in and ask questions. And they really encouraged us to go to office hours.

Geography major: I just watched the 2003 commencement two days ago at Husky Stadium. It was the third consecutive time I had seen it, but this one had a profound effect on me. Unlike the previous commencements, I was supposed to be a part of this one. The class of 2003 would have been my graduating class. Constant changes in my major [i.e., I applied to and was turned down by majors four times before I ended up in geography], the specific classes I have chosen to take, and other reasons contributed to the fact that I will be graduating in five years instead of four. . . . Surprisingly enough, I don't regret it. Honestly, graduation is a small objective to strive for while you are at college. As discussed in the UW SOUL focus group this year, going to college dramatically changes one's life. For some, the UW may be the first and only diverse place they have seen or will see. Learning about other cultures makes you grow as a human being. By living and experiencing college life, you are learning about the differences and similarities that each of us possesses—not only culture and ethnicity, but personality as well. In contrast, lingering in a small town is almost like limiting the amount of air you were allowed to breathe. Going to a university and living the experience helps you breathe easier by offering an infinite amount of opportunity. It seldom happens, but sometimes these opportunities beg you to jump at them. Most other times, however, the opportunities are there and one just has to search for them. This is probably the most important thing to learn while at the university.

Scandinavian studies and Norwegian major: After the events of September 11, I am no longer secure in my own ignorance. I knew that Americans weren't liked by some, but had no idea that some people actually hate our very being. The United States is not as safe as I thought it was. Now I know that we are just as susceptible to attacks as other countries. I had to fly two weeks after the attacks happened, and I don't think that I've ever thought about my own mortality as much as I did on that flight. [Also,] two weeks ago my host sister and friend were aboard a plane that crashed outside Milan, Italy. My host sister was just two months younger than me, and now she is dead. I have heard it said many times that the death of young people is meaningless. I have never come to grips with that saying until now. I didn't know about the immense hole loved ones leave behind when they die unexpectedly. I know now.

Women studies major: At the beginning of this year, I realized I needed to get my butt in shape and start being self-motivated in regards to school. It hit me at the beginning of the quarter that I am going to be the first person to graduate from college in my family. I feel that a lot of weight is on my shoulders for me to do good. I think I have taken my classes or my time here for granted, and that is recognizing that I have put in some time but not as much effort as I could have. This year, I manage my time better. I actually manage it; I don't let it go to the wind, even though that is how my personality is. I guess I realized that this really does matter to me. I've realized how much my mom has sacrificed for me to be in this place.

General Findings About Students' Learning

This section of the chapter reports our findings on the following:

- Students' perceptions about how much they learned
- What students said helped their learning
- What students said hindered their learning

Students' Perceptions About How Much They Learned

Each quarter, we asked students to indicate on the quarterly surveys how much they had learned in 26 areas, using a 4-point scale.[1] In analyzing their responses, we averaged quarterly ratings to arrive at a yearly average and averaged over years to arrive at a total average. This approach allowed us to view change over four years. In the few cases where a student did not take all three surveys in a given year, because she took a quarter off or was studying abroad, we averaged across those she did take.

Learned the Most/Learned the Least

Previously, we presented the results of the learning items that were relevant to each chapter. However, we have included those items again in Table 1 to provide a comparative view. The table presents responses to each item averaged over the four years, as well as the ranking of these average ratings. It is important to keep in mind that the means for these items do not represent the cumulative amount that students learned in that area; rather, they represent the average amount students reported learning *each quarter*. For example, the mean for "learning about writing papers that make and support an argument" indicates that each quarter, on average, students learned 2.29 out of 4 in this area.

As Table 1 shows, the five areas where students indicated that they learned most, on average, were:

- Information, theories, and perspectives from their classes
- Understanding more about who they were and what they valued
- Thinking critically about issues
- Working and/or learning independently
- Exploring questions such as "What does this mean?", "Why is this important?", "Why did this happen?", or "What are the implications and outcomes of these results or choices?"

These five items represent a wide range of learning, from course content ("information, theories, and perspectives") to self-knowledge ("who they were and what they valued"), and they reflect goals students had for their own learning when they arrived. Furthermore, they echo students' definitions of what it means to be educated.

The five areas where students reported that they learned the least, on average, were:

- Designing something
- Doing well on multiple-choice exams
- Creating something original
- Writing drafts of papers and using feedback to revise them effectively
- Writing papers whose main purpose was to present information

Again, these results were not surprising when seen in the context of results reported elsewhere in this book. The acts of designing and creating, as we reported earlier, occurred primarily in engineering and arts disciplines and seldom elsewhere. Also, students reported that most of their challenging writing focused on argumentation rather than informative writing. Students' opportunities to draft papers and receive feedback from faculty or TAs on those drafts decreased dramatically after their

TABLE 1
How Much Did You Learn This Quarter About . . . ?

Mean	Rank	Item
		Writing
2.29	15	Writing papers that make and support an argument
2.11	21	Writing answers to essay questions on exams
2.09	22	Writing papers whose main purpose is to present information
2.04	23	Writing drafts of papers and using feedback to revise them effectively
		Critical Thinking
2.86	3	Thinking critically about issues
2.78	5	Exploring questions such as "What does this mean?", "Why is this important?", "Why did this happen?", or "What are the implications and outcomes of these results or choices?"
2.76	6	Critically examining my own thinking, arguments, or opinions.
2.59	8	Revising my attitudes and opinions in light of new information
2.49	10	Constructing arguments to support my own ideas
2.19	18	Challenging a theory, conclusions, arguments, or results of an authority in a discipline
		Information Literacy
2.55	9	Finding and using information
2.43	12	Evaluating the validity and accuracy of information
2.29	16	Using a variety of sources to define and solve problems
		Quantitative Reasoning
2.21	17	Using quantitative analysis or reasoning to understand issues, make arguments, or solve problems in courses other than math
2.16	19	Understanding and solving mathematical problems
		Diversity
2.46	11	Understanding and appreciating diverse philosophies, people, and cultures.
		Personal Growth
2.92	2	Understanding more about who I am and what I value
2.81	4	Working and/or learning independently
2.67	7	Making new friends; being more socially confident
2.34	14	How to work/study with others
		Other
3.24	1	Information, theories, and perspectives from your classes
2.42	13	Understanding the interaction of society and the environment
2.13	20	Speaking effectively
2.04	24	Creating something original
1.94	25	Doing well on multiple-choice exams
1.93	26	Designing something

first year in college, so it is little wonder that they did not learn as much about revision as they did about other aspects of learning.

Finally, the item ranks within our six categories of learning show that the areas with the greatest learning were critical thinking and personal growth, while the areas of least learning were writing and quantitative reasoning (QR). As we will see, the former categories tended to be present in all disciplinary areas, while the least learned categories tended to be more unevenly distributed across the disciplines (e.g., writing in humanities, QR in engineering). Furthermore, writing and QR are more easily defined, tangible activities than are personal growth and critical thinking, which are broader and more fuzzy.

The Effect of the Major on Learning

To better understand the results shown in Table 1, we compared students' responses to all 26 items by the disciplinary area of students' majors, looking at averages for each year and for all four years.[2] In broad-brush terms, we obtained two results: first, that students' assessment of their learning on various items tended to be influenced by their major, which was expected, and second, that this differentiation by major began in the freshmen year, which we did not expect.

The influence of major. There was a significant effect for disciplinary areas for more than one of the years and total across years for 14 of the 26 items.[3] The 12 items for which area of students' major appeared to make little or no significant difference, ordered from the smallest overall eta-squared value (1.6%) to the largest (7.9%), were:

- Evaluating the validity and accuracy of information
- Information, theories, and perspectives from their classes
- Exploring questions such as "What does this mean?", "Why is this important?", "Why did this happen?", or "What are the implications of these results, outcomes, or choices?"
- How to work/study with others
- Revising one's attitudes and opinions in light of new information
- Finding and using information
- Understanding more about who they were and what they valued
- Thinking critically about issues
- Writing papers whose main purpose was to present information
- Working and/or learning independently
- Constructing arguments to support their own ideas
- Making new friends; being more socially confident

It is tempting to suggest that these items, especially those toward the top of the list, may be true goals of a general education, because students perceived that they learned these things at a certain level regardless of discipline. However, it is important to remember that students can place very different meanings on these terms, and those meanings often depend upon their majors, as we noted in previous chapters. For example, we see that students from various disciplines were reasonably equivalent, on average, in their perception of what they learned about "thinking critically about issues." But how students thought critically about issues, what those issues were, and how they expressed that thinking varied greatly as a function of their chosen discipline.

In contrast with these 12 items, 14 of the 26 items showed consistent significant differences by disciplinary area. These items, ordered from highest eta-squared value (55.1%) to lowest (10.4%) were as follows:

- Understanding and solving mathematical problems
- Designing something
- Creating something original

- Using quantitative analysis or reasoning to understand issues, make arguments, or solve problems in courses other than math
- Writing papers that make and support an argument
- Writing answers to essay questions on exams
- Understanding and appreciating diverse philosophies, people, and cultures
- Writing drafts of papers and using feedback to revise them effectively
- Doing well on multiple-choice exams
- Understanding the interaction of society and the environment
- Using a variety of sources to define and solve problems
- Speaking effectively
- Critically examining one's own thinking, arguments, or opinions
- Challenging a theory, conclusions, arguments, or results of an authority in a discipline

Table 2 shows the seven items for which the disciplinary area was the most influential (23.6% or more of the variance explained). The two highest rated areas and the two lowest showed large differences among means for majors. These results largely confirm those reported in previous chapters. Majors in the arts and humanities, for example, reported learning less about solving mathematical problems than did business and engineering majors art and engineering majors learned more about design than majors in the humanities and social sciences reported.

Early differentiation. The result that surprised us was that differences in learning by major began in the freshmen year, before many UW SOUL students were in majors. At the UW, essentially all students enter as premajors. Freshman entrants are expected to declare a major at the end of the

TABLE 2
Survey Items Exhibiting the Greatest Effect of the Major

Item	Eta Squared	Areas With Highest Means	Areas With Lowest Means
Understanding and solving mathematical problems	55.1%	Engineering (2.97) Business (2.66)	Art (1.34) Humanities (1.51)
Designing something	46.9%	Art (3.19) Engineering (2.67)	Humanities (1.53) Social Sci. (1.55)
Creating something original	44.2%	Art (3.54) Engineering (2.42)	Social Sci. (1.74) Business (1.81)
Using quantitative analysis or reasoning to understand issues, make arguments, or solve problems in courses other than math	37.1%	Business (2.69) Engineering (2.65)	Art (1.59) Humanities (1.67)
Writing papers that make and support an argument	31.9%	Humanities (2.62) Social Sci. (2.55)	Engineering (1.76) Science (2.04)
Writing answers to essay questions on exams	24.1%	Social Sci. (2.34) Business (2.35)	Engineering (1.59) Art (1.93)
Understanding and appreciating diverse philosophies, people, and cultures	23.6%	Humanities (2.88) Art (2.74)	Engineering (1.87) Science (2.25)

second year. Thus, during the first and second years of college, few entering freshmen have been admitted to a major. In spite of this, analysis of the first-year surveys showed that 14 of 25[4] items exhibited statistically significant differences among students' *eventual* majors. This proportion of statistically significant items actually decreased slightly for the successive years of data—13 of 26 items for the second and third years and 10 of 26 items for the fourth year. We can also see the near equivalence in average of the eta-squared values across all items for each year, which were 11.4%, 13.1%, 12.3%, and 11.2% for the four years, respectively. If these results were retrospective ratings taken at the end of four years, there would be room for skepticism, but they were not. These were questions students answered at the end of each quarter.

We believe that these results show that students began specializing in their majors early. In the years when faculty and administrators may think that students are engaged in "general education"—broad-based learning about a variety of disciplinary content and methods—students have already oriented themselves toward a specific area, such as humanities or science, if not toward a specific major or department within that area. The distributive model of general education makes this practice particularly easy, and we know that much of this specialization comes about through course selection. For example, students hoping to major in engineering must lock into the engineering curriculum early in order to graduate in a reasonable amount of time. However, our results suggest that early specialization occurs in other disciplines, as well. We also speculate that even students who take the same classes may emphasize different learning outcomes, given their ways of thinking and nascent disciplinary orientation. An eventual psychology major may have learned different things in a sociology class than an eventual English major, for example.

Fall and spring interview responses conducted in students' first year support the survey results that suggest early specialization. In these interviews, we asked 84 freshmen and 47 transfer students what they thought they would major in. Then we compared those responses to their actual majors. By the end of their first year at the UW, 50% of the freshman population and 98% of the transfer students had correctly identified their eventual majors, even though they had not necessarily been admitted to them.

While the university's distributive model of general education makes it easier for students to specialize early than a set of core requirements might, Smart, Feldman, and Ethington (2000) suggest that students come to college *predisposed* by their temperaments to major in certain areas. This is an interesting field of study that needs further investigation. However, whether predisposed by temperament or influenced by classes that captured them, our results show that students specialize early.

What Helped Learning

Information on what helped learning came from a variety of sources—quarterly survey, annual focus groups, interviews, and email questions. The picture drawn by these separate sources of information is coherent: Faculty play the most important role in advancing student learning. It is important that we note here that we are not saying that faculty are solely responsible for learning. Students as early as their second quarter in college note that they are responsible for their academic choices and behaviors. However, faculty have profound influence even on this awareness.

Survey Results on What Helped Learning

The web-based surveys asked students to identify the extent to which 36 items helped them learn. Students were asked to respond on a 4-point scale,[5] or they could indicate that they "did not do" that which was described by the item. Overall, students' responses demonstrated that they believed that faculty, their own efforts, and their peers played key roles in helping them learn.

Table 3 shows the average ratings for all the survey items over all years on what helped students learn. As before, we averaged quarterly responses for the four years of the study, so the mean is the average amount students felt they learned *each quarter*. The table is organized by the average percentage of students who said they had done or experienced the item during each year. Therefore,

TABLE 3
What Helped Your Learning?

Mean	% Didn't Do	Item
		Items that 90%–100% of Students Reported Doing and How Much Each Helped Learning
3.46	0.0	Liking the subject before I take the class
3.45	2.0	Having professor(s)/instructor(s) who seemed to care about my learning
3.43	8.5	My own efforts—reading, studying, doing my homework, going to classes, staying focused
3.40	0.0	Having professor(s)/instructor(s) who were experts in their fields
3.21	9.2	Talking one-on-one with the professor/TA
3.11	3.3	Feeling as though my instructors think I am intelligent and capable
3.09	2.6	Feeling as though my peers think I am intelligent and capable
3.06	5.9	Talking with friends and peers about ideas and values not directly related to class work
3.03	3.3	Thinking for myself rather than being told what is "truth"
3.03	8.5	Emailing the professor/TA
2.77	7.8	Writing papers
2.77	9.8	Learning multiple ways of looking at ideas, events, or experiences from lectures/readings
2.57	9.2	Reading that was challenging
		Items that 66%–89% of Students Reported Doing and How Much Each Helped Learning
3.58	13.1	Having course readings, assignments, lecture notes, or other content materials on the web
3.37	15.7	Having a professor's syllabus on the web
2.98	28.8	Using the Internet to find additional information on a topic, though I was not required to
2.95	23.5	Using the Internet to do required research
2.88	17.0	Asking questions during class
2.78	11.1	Learning about multiple ways of looking at ideas, events, or experiences from discussions with students in class
2.69	33.3	Working with groups on class projects and papers
2.62	31.4	Taking essay exams
		Items that 46%–65% of Students Reported Doing and How Much Each Helped Learning
3.09	40.5	Working with a study group
2.97	35.9	Using the library to do research
2.88	51.6	Doing math problems
2.84	34.6	Being asked to review and assess my own work
2.63	42.5	Taking frequent quizzes
2.52	53.6	Giving an oral presentation
2.26	41.8	Learning about one consistent way to view ideas, events, or experiences
2.05	43.8	Taking multiple-choice exams

(Continued)

TABLE 3 *(Continued)*

Mean	% Didn't Do	Item
		Items that 1%–23% of Students Reported Doing and How Much Each Helped Learning
3.38	99.3	Visiting the math study center
3.17	76.5	Finding a faculty member whom I regard as a mentor
2.98	88.9	Getting one-on-one help from a librarian when doing research in the UW library system
2.98	96.1	Visiting a writing center
2.95	81.0	Joining a club or organization
2.89	92.8	Having instruction in class from a librarian on how to do library/Internet research

the first section of the table reports how much the 90%–100% of the participants who reported doing that item said they had learned from it; the second section reports how much the 66–89% of the students who reported doing those items said that the items had helped their learning; and so on.

As Table 3 shows, students found faculty expertise nearly as helpful as they found faculty concern about their learning. This result is interesting because students and the public often emphasize faculty teaching ability over their level of expertise about a subject, but these results suggest that the two may go hand-in-hand for students, or that at least one is as important as the other. In addition, students got a good deal of help by speaking with faculty one on one, and it is interesting to note that about 90% of them reported they had done so, regardless of the size of classes or of the institution. In addition to help that faculty gave students, survey respondents reported that peers' opinions of their intellect were about as helpful to learning as faculty opinions. In addition, as the table shows, students found that thinking for themselves and being presented with multiple perspectives in class helped their learning, as did email interactions with faculty. Writing papers, learning about multiple ways of looking at ideas, and doing challenging reading were the least helpful, on average, in this group of items.

Table 3 also shows what 66%–89% of the students reported had helped their learning. This group found having course materials on websites very helpful. In fact, overall, the average rating for "having course readings, assignments, lecture notes, or other content materials on the web" was the highest of all the items that students said were helpful to their learning. The table shows that most students found using the Internet on their own to find information was helpful.

Students reported that asking questions in class was helpful. Asking questions and speaking in class were aspects of learning that came up elsewhere in the study. While students knew that asking questions was important to learning, students, particularly in science, math, and engineering reported in interviews and email responses that they were often afraid to speak even in classes of 40 students or fewer. This fear was related to students' concerns about what their peers and faculty members might think of them. Two students' comments on this concern illustrate this issue:

My greatest challenge was learning to communicate with professors, especially in settings of 30 or more students. This is an obstacle which I have to try to overcome with each new professor, each new personality.

In really big lecture halls, sometimes the professor almost doesn't seem like a real person, and they seem unapproachable. It is like the feeling you get when you meet a celebrity—like you shouldn't be talking to them because they are in one space and you are in another.

In addition to identifying question asking as helpful to learning, this 66%–89% identified two items related to peers as helpful—learning that came from discussions with students in class and learning that came from working in groups on projects. These are aspects of class that faculty can orchestrate, but whether or not they help learning often depends on the students themselves.

Table 3 further shows that working in study groups contributed to learning for the 45%–65% of UW SOUL students who had the opportunity to do so. Using the libraries, doing math problems, and being asked to self-assess were also helpful to the students who did those things. This group of students felt that taking frequent quizzes and giving oral presentations did not offer much help to their learning, on average; neither did they find learning about one consistent way to view ideas, events, or experiences helpful. Finally, students reported that taking multiple-choice exams contributed little to their learning. In fact, this item received the lowest average rating of all the items provided to students, suggesting that while multiple-choice exams may help faculty assess what students have learned, students did not believe that taking them contributed to learning.

The last section of Table 3 shows the items that the fewest students reported doing. Interestingly, all of the items that the fewest number of students experienced were ranked at about 2.9 or above. These results show the value of one-to-one type experiences, such as getting individualized help in math, writing, and research, that only a few of our students—one out of four, at best—were able to access. Students in this group also reported that finding a faculty member whom they regarded as a mentor was helpful.

It could be a matter of concern that fewer than 24% of the UW SOUL students said that they had experienced faculty mentoring. However, students' responses to an interview question we asked at the end of their third year indicated that a mentoring relationship is only one kind of faculty connection that students consider meaningful. In spring 2002, we asked all the UW SOUL interviewees if they had made a meaningful connection with a faculty member while at the UW. About 63% said yes and 37% said no. Even if they had reported no meaningful connection with faculty, we followed up by asking all students what they meant by a "meaningful connection:" What would/does such a connection look like?

The two groups—those who had formed a meaningful connection to a faculty member and those who had not—defined "meaningful connection" identically. In addition, we analyzed responses by gender and ethnicity and detected no differences across groups. About 43% defined a meaningful connection with a faculty member as a "personal" relationship, in which the faculty member showed an interest in the student's personal life, as well as in her academic life, and remembered the student's name over time. About 19% of the interviewees described "a mentor relationship," similar to a "personal" relationship, but one where faculty members served as guides or counselors, and had a sustained learning relationship with students. About 12% described the connection as a "recommender" relationship, where the faculty member knew the student well enough (and was willing) to write letters of recommendation on his behalf. A few students—4%—described the faculty connection simply as one that encouraged learning. Finally, about 22% provided definitions that were impossible to categorize.

Students' majors and eventual majors were much less of a factor in their ratings of what helped them learn than they were in how much students said they had learned in the areas studied. Only three of the items exhibited significant differences across majors, and, for the most part, these were no surprise, as Table 4 shows. Data on quantitative reasoning and information literacy have prepared

TABLE 4
Significant Differences by Area of Major in Survey Responses to "What Helped Your Learning?"

Item	Years	Highest Rating	Lowest Rating
Doing math problems	Overall and years 1, 2, and 3	Engineering Sciences	Arts Humanities
Using the library to do research	Overall and years 3 and 4	Social Sciences Arts	Engineering Business
Learning about one consistent way to view ideas, events, or experiences	Overall and years 2, 3, and 4	Art Business	Social Sciences Science

us for the first two of the results. Regarding the third, we can only speculate that majors in the arts and business learn to view phenomena through very particular lenses.

Focus Group Results on What Helped Learning

Students' focus group responses on what helped their learning were very similar to their survey responses across the years of the UW SOUL. Over all four years, students in the focus groups said that professors who were passionate about their subject areas and who demonstrated that they cared about students' learning were the most helpful to their learning. As the survey results also indicated, students reported that their peers, especially when working together in study groups, were very helpful to their learning. Finally, students in several groups mentioned their own roles in learning.

Interview Responses to How Faculty Communicate They Care About Students' Learning

In both survey and focus group responses, students said that their learning was helped by faculty who cared about it. The course evaluation system used at UW asks students to rate the "instructor's interest in whether the student learned,"[6] and after hearing a presentation for faculty on UW SOUL, a faculty member in the psychology department asked if we could determine what things professors did that led students to think faculty members cared about student learning. We put that question on our spring 2002 interviews, and 11 clear themes emerged from students' responses, as follows.

Faculty interact with students in class, engaging them in substantive ways. A total of 87% of the students talked about interaction between the professor and the students in class. Their responses could be placed into three closely related subcategories. About 34% said they felt that professors cared about learning when they asked for questions in class, answered them respectfully and completely, and checked to make sure answers and explanations were clear. Two students' quotations illustrate this large group of responses:

> Every time the professor goes over one main point, they have to ask [if we have questions]—not after they go over five. You really don't think they care if their back is to you and they are writing on the board and they never ask. Even if the students never ask any questions when the professor asks if there are questions, his asking makes us think he cares about our learning.

> Also the way they answer questions in class—their attitude about it. There are times when there are stupid questions, but even then, a teacher who cares about your learning will be nice about it.

A second way that faculty interacted with students in class was to monitor whether students were learning through observation or requests for feedback. About 34% of the interviewees mentioned this way of engaging students, as the following quotation illustrates:

> In class, it registers with them more easily if the student is not catching on to the concepts. They have a tendency to say, "I feel that everyone is not completely getting this, so let's go ahead and break this down a little further." They are monitoring in some way.

Finally, about 19% of the students who spoke about substantive interaction in class said that when professors encouraged students to share opinions or contribute to discussion, students knew that faculty cared about their learning. For example:

> In class, they engage us in discussion and not just lecture at us. It's not just, "Here's a bunch of information; test next week." We are called upon to voice our thoughts and perspectives. We are treated more like human beings. We learn to put into words things that we think. Testing is not just based on "Can you remember this concept?" but "Can you think, can you write, can you formulate ideas?" That brings out the better part of students. I feel more acknowledged as an intellectual mind when I get to express myself.

Faculty design lectures/courses that anticipate and reduce barriers to students' learning. UW SOUL interviewees—about 47%—also talked about the ways that a course's structure and the daily lectures communicated faculty concern for their learning. We were surprised at how carefully students paid attention to faculty use of course structure as a guide through the material. One student said this:

> When it's clear they have put a lot of effort in creating a lesson plan that is geared to our needs. By that I mean, I guess, when it's not coming from the perspective of someone who understands all the bases of the logic for that class, especially when you are talking about a technical difficulty. We need to understand the bases—what are your primary assumptions, things like that, so they start out explaining that first off—kind of a sequential presentation of the material, and coming back to earlier concepts, things like that.

Faculty are accessible in a variety of ways. About 36% of the students interviewed mentioned the importance of encouraging students to come to office hours, of being willing to meet them by appointment and before/after class, and of using email and web sites. This point was also raised in survey results about what helped student learning. In their interviews, some students said that even if they never took advantage of office hours, they were encouraged to learn simply by the professor welcoming them to come speak with him. The following quotation illustrates this group of responses:

> When a professor has a good web site and is accessible by email. When they respond to your emails and are really open to having office hours. When they respond to your needs and are willing to go with your schedule. And when they tell you that in class.

Faculty demonstrate a passion for the subject and are enthusiastic about teaching it. In earlier interviews and in all the focus groups, students spoke of the importance of instructors' enthusiasm for their subjects. The general feeling was that if the faculty member was not passionately interested in her subject, students did not understand why they should care about it. About 26% of the UW SOUL students interviewed spoke about the importance of professors' deep interest in their subjects. The following student's comment serves as an example:

> Their passion about what they are teaching is what makes me want to learn. They don't particularly say that they want us to learn, but their interest in what they are teaching makes you feel that you want to learn more from them. It makes you think that there are things to be learned from them.

The faculty member knows something about students' personal experience or interests and knows some students in the class by name. The importance of personal knowledge was mentioned by 19% of the UW SOUL interviewees. Many of these students said that it did not matter if the professor knew *their* names, but that it was important to know she knew *some* of the students' names. One student's comment illustrates this group:

> When professors learn my name, that really means a lot to me. I want to do better in their class then. I try to introduce myself to the profs, too. When you raise your hand in class, they call on you by name, or if they write a personal message on your midterm or a paper you get back—it could be either criticism or praise—that communicates they care.

Faculty have high expectations for students' learning; they challenge and stretch students' thinking. About 16% of the students who were interviewed explicitly mentioned the value of taking challenging courses and doing challenging coursework. They saw high standards as a sign of caring. One student in this group put it this way:

> They challenge you. They might ask you to retry or redo something, because they don't think it worked. You don't always get the easy way out—that's a sign they care about my learning.

Faculty provide critical feedback that guides students' learning on assignments. Feedback communicated caring to 14% of the UW SOUL interviewees. As one student said:

> Constant feedback. I've had classes where you turn in a homework assignment and they just check it off and others where they dissect it, like yours was the only one. When they do that, you know that they are not just giving you a grade on it, but they are helping you learn it, learn the information.

Faculty are experts in their fields of study. Eight percent of the UW SOUL interviewees mentioned that their instructors' level of expertise communicated caring about learning. As one student said:

> It's really those aspects of being a credible source, someone who gets up there and knows what they are talking about, someone who presents both sides.

Faculty help students do well on tests. About 7% of the students we interviewed said that faculty help in preparing for or understanding the results of exams communicated that professors cared about their learning. When students spoke about this aspect, they often spoke of heroic faculty efforts to ensure that students understood course material. For example:

> In biology last quarter, a couple of my professors had extra review sessions for us to go to. They would schedule them around the time students could take them, even doing some on Sunday night. That was really nice to know—that they were willing to spend their extra time, even on the weekends, to help us.

Faculty treat students with respect and understanding. This theme overlaps with others. For example, when professors ask students for their opinions, students interpret that as respectful treatment. Therefore, we counted comments in this group only when students specifically described how they were treated, and about 7% did so. One example:

> I like teachers who treat the students like scholars, who don't talk down to us and ask us stupid questions—stupid questions meaning that they have the answers and we are trying to guess what they are.

Faculty connect course material to real-world applications and events. Several students (5%) believed that linking course content to the world outside academia demonstrated that faculty cared about students' learning.

These 11 themes generated by the responses of the 85 students we interviewed serve as an interesting guide for faculty. In these responses, students not only outlined the ways that faculty members communicated they cared about students' learning, but, according to research on learning (Bransford, Brown, & Cocking, 2000), students' responses also outlined how to *improve* student learning. In other words, if faculty put these methods in place to communicate they cared about students' learning, they would actually increase it. As Light's (2001) research on student engagement at Harvard has shown, students learn more when they are actively engaged in their courses, and they are more engaged when they are asked to respond, write papers, and discuss what they think about course material. Furthermore, in detailing the roles faculty can play, these 11 themes are consistent with our own UW SOUL survey and email responses to what helped students' learning.

Email Responses to "What Advances Your Education?"

In winter 2002 a former dean and faculty member asked us another question about the meaning of an item on our course evaluations, which speaks to the question of what helps students learn. He wondered how students defined a course as "valuable in advancing my education." To answer his question, we sent an email message to 182 UW SOUL participants that quarter, asking them to tell us what the phrase "valuable in advancing my education" meant to them when they filled out course evaluations. It also asked them to describe briefly what they considered valuable and not valuable about two courses they had taken. Seven major categories emerged from their responses.

Assignments. The majority of students who responded (69%) said that the existence and nature of assignments was critical to feeling that their learning had been advanced. About a third of these students specified that assignments that were challenging and designed to teach them something were valuable, and about 29% spoke of the value of assignments that asked them to apply course material to problems, cases, or real-world examples. Students in this group also spoke of the value of certain kinds of assignments, including

- Reading that was well integrated into the course (23%)
- Hands-on work, such as labs, fieldwork, and field trips (18%)

- Writing assignments (18%)
- Homework that helped them learn something and was not repetitious (15%)
- Research (12%)

Many students specifically stated that assignments should not be merely "busy-work," which they defined as work that required little thinking on their part, asked them to regurgitate information rather than use it, and/or asked them to repeat the same set of tasks in order to memorize information. Several students spoke about the critical importance of feedback on assignments—from papers to problem sets—to their learning. Two students' quotations illustrate this group of responses:

> I think "hands-on" or applied learning is the most influential in advancing my education. This can be learning an equation and practicing how to put it to use in a real-life problem or reading a book and demonstrating how it applies to the world around us.
>
> I do believe that research assignments have contributed greatly to my ability to articulate ideas.

The importance of assignment in advancing student learning suggests that, in general, students do not consider courses that one student described as "lecture-test, lecture-test" as doing much to advance their learning.

Learning that could be applied to majors, careers, or life. About 55% of the email responses focused on applied learning. Of the students who focused on application, the majority (70%) spoke of learning that had a bearing on their majors and/or on their intended careers. Two students' quotations illustrate students' sense of the value of applied learning:

> When I think of the value of classes in terms of advancing my education, I usually think of it in terms of whether or not it's in my major. If the content of the course directly pertains to my planned major, I consider it valuable.
>
> "Valuable in advancing my education" would be that I learned something that makes me a better person or a more well-rounded person and I learned something that I could use or want to know later in life—where I actually take something from the class, [rather than] forget everything after the quarter's over.

Aspects of course design. Closely echoing responses to the question about how faculty communicated that they cared about students' learning, nearly half of the UW SOUL participants—47%—spoke about the importance of course design. These students said that interaction, class discussion, and/or working in groups in class advanced their educations. One out of every three said that when the class challenged them to think, rather than focusing solely on memorization of material, they felt it advanced their educations. Finally, about 14% of those students focusing on course design pointed to well-organized courses, describing these as classes where the pieces—such as labs, reading, and other assignments—were clearly integrated. Two students' comments serve as examples:

> My experiences with his class are not soon forgotten, because, since it is a class he teaches WITH the students, there is always a heightened sense of accountability to do the work and share what you are learning. He understands that education is a journey to be traveled together, rather than something we as students are herded into like dumb cattle.
>
> Active participation is also very valuable because it draws on the wide variety and diversity of student experiences and knowledge in addition to the instructor's.

Professors. About 42% of the respondents said that faculty were the key to advancing their educations. Students focused on three ways professors accomplished this. First, about four out of five of the students who spoke about professors pointed to how they conducted class, including:

- Providing clear, concise, and interesting lectures
- Adding to the required texts (as opposed to just repeating them)
- Using examples, especially those from "real life," to illustrate ideas and concepts

Second, students said that professors advanced their educations when they demonstrated that they cared about students' learning. This group—about a third of those who talked about professors—said that offering help in and outside class, monitoring students' understanding in class, and being accessible before/after class, in office hours, and through email were ways that advanced student learning. Finally, many students said that when a professor was passionate and enthusiastic about her subject area, they were inspired to learn more, and, thus, the professor's own interest advanced students' educations. These responses echoed students' interview comments, reported in the previous section of this chapter, on how faculty communicated they cared about students learning. The following quotation illustrates this set of responses:

> An instructor who shares his/her excitement and knowledge about the class topic(s) is always valuable because s/he can pique students' interest in topics that were of no original interest to them just by being enthusiastic and passionate about the subject, rather than just reading off lecture notes.

Any learning. About 40% of the students said that a course advanced learning when they learned *anything* that they had not known before, including information, methods, and ideas that they believed they would retain, perspectives that changed their thinking or thinking processes, methods or practice in how to be a better critical thinker, or just something new. For example:

> My interpretation is related to how much new insight I gain from a class. I ask myself—did I gain a new perspective on a certain subject? A valuable understanding of it? Was I introduced to a value/conceptual system, which I didn't know before taking this class? Was I given new insights into the subject? But most importantly . . . will this new insight/conceptual system/perspective stay with me one, two, ten years from now? In other words, did I gain a true understanding of something which is valuable [that will] stay with me forever, or was it just a static accumulation of facts/information/disconnected knowledge, which will disappear in a few months?

Students' own actions. About 11% of the respondents mentioned going to class, putting in effort, doing the required work, and taking their coursework seriously as valuable in advancing their educations. As one student said:

> A lot of the work I do is self-driven, and I've found that the many hours (outside of class time) that I dedicate to designing studio projects have been beneficial. Other activities I've also done that have been valuable include library and/or Internet research, as well as going to lectures offered by the College of Architecture.

Interest level. Several students, about 7%, said that classes that were interesting or fun advanced their educations, as this student's response illustrates:

> But there's also those classes that are just plain interesting, even though they aren't in your major.

Responses to the UW SOUL email question on what advanced students' learning confirmed survey, focus group, and interview responses to questions about what helped students learn. Contrary to what some might have predicted, only a few students said that courses that gave them high grades or low grades advanced their learning.

Challenging Courses

Challenging courses helped students' learning. While this result was confirmed repeatedly by our various data sources, specific information about the level of challenge students experienced in the early part of their undergraduate programs came from 230 UW SOUL participants' responses to email questions in 2001. The first of those questions asked students to comment on and provide two examples of the level of academic expectations they were experiencing. The second asked them to note what barriers they had to overcome, if any, to meet academic expectations. In responding to these questions, students indicated that they were experiencing high levels of academic challenge and that several aspects of their courses made them challenging. A list of those we could categorize, as well as the percentage of the students who mentioned them (with students sometimes mentioning more than one), were:

- Level of thinking required to do well (39%)
- Challenging/hard writing assignments (28%)
- Amount and difficulty of reading (12%)
- Time it takes to complete schoolwork (11%)
- The need to learn/work on one's own (10%)
- The focus on learning (8%)
- Good/enthusiastic/clear professors and TAs (5%)
- Level of material presented (5%)
- Unclear, unhelpful professors and TAs (4%)
- Application of course material to real-life contexts (3%)
- The kind of testing (3%)
- A pace that is too fast (2%)
- A large class size (2%)

In the following section we discuss the barriers that students noted as hindrances to their learning.

Similar ideas about the importance of challenging courses can be found throughout the book, particularly in our chapters on critical thinking, writing, and quantitative reasoning. Furthermore, when students were asked in which of their courses they had learned the most and in which the least, they repeatedly said that the courses that presented them with the greatest challenge were the courses they enjoyed the most' and learned the most in. Clearly, challenging courses helped students learn, not only because they asked students to stretch, but because challenge, particularly the "tightrope with a net and a spotter" type of challenge, communicates to students that faculty care about their learning.

Conclusions About What Students Said Helped Their Learning

Through all our methods of asking, students told us that what helped their learning the most were faculty. In surveys, focus groups, interviews, and email responses, students described the ways faculty did and could continue to help them learn, and nearly every point that students made is supported by research on learning. Faculty helped students learn when they asked them to think deeply, engaged them in meaningful ways in class, and gave them assignments that were challenging—assignments designed to teach them something; assignments asking students to apply rather than merely repeat knowledge. Faculty helped students learn when they were accessible and respectful, when they were both knowledgeable and passionate about their fields. It also helped students when faculty structured their courses in ways that anticipated what students would need to know next, and when faculty could name at least some students, even in their largest classes.

In addition to the importance of faculty to students' learning, students noted the importance of peers, particularly in the surveys. Students cared about peers' good opinions of them, learned from working in study groups, and got help from each other formally and informally. Finally, students also mentioned some of the things they did to help themselves learn. But those efforts seemed less important to students than the efforts of inspiring faculty and interactions' with peers.

What Hindered Learning

We did not want to assume that the opposite of what helped students' learning would hinder it, so we asked students what hindered their learning on the quarterly web-based surveys and in focus groups. As with what helped learning, the picture students drew about what hindered their learning was coherent. However, while faculty received the most credit for helping students learn, the students gave themselves the most credit (or should we say, *blame?*) for hindering their learning. And students had many ways of getting in their own way.

Survey Data on What Hindered Learning

We asked students on quarterly surveys to rate 36 factors that might hinder their learning on a 4-point scale.[7] As we did with students' responses to what helped their learning, we averaged responses for each year, and to help us better understand students' responses, we divided the 36 items as indicating obstacles presented by the following:

- Self/procrastination
- Concerns about personal issues
- Faculty
- Self/feelings of inadequacy/fears
- Course practices
- Institutional structure

As Table 5 shows, students believed that what they chose to do and not do presented the most significant barriers to their learning. Four of the six most highly ranked items centered on student

TABLE 5
What Hindered Your Learning?

Item	Mean	Rank
Self/procrastination		
Wanting to play instead of study	2.84	1
My own procrastination	2.64	2
Poor study habits	2.29	4
Too many fun things to do at the UW and in Seattle besides study	2.12	6
Concerns about personal issues		
Relationship worries—parents, girl/boyfriends, friends	2.30	3
Money worries	2.09	8
The amount of time I had to work for wages	1.91	11
Missing my family and friends	1.67	16
Having English as my second language	1.12	33
Concerns over child-care	1.02	35
Faculty		
Professor(s) or TA(s) who were disorganized, confusing, or unclear	2.25	5
A professor or TA who didn't know me	1.65	18
Having a TA/professor whom I could not understand because of bad handwriting/language skills	1.63	19
A professor or TA who seemed to dislike me	1.44	26
Being singled out by the professor/TA or my fellow students because of my race, ethnic background, gender, or sexual orientation.	1.12	32
Self/feelings of inadequacy/fears		
Feeling less well prepared than my peers seemed to be	2.11	7
Not feeling comfortable asking questions or making a point during class	2.04	9
Not knowing anything about the subject before I took the class	1.73	15
Not asking questions during office hours	1.66	17
Feeling underprepared in my writing ability	1.59	21
Feeling as though the level of work demanded was significantly higher than that demanded at my previous educational institution	1.52	22

(Continued)

TABLE 5 *(Continued)*

Item	Mean	Rank
Feeling unprepared in my math ability	1.47	23
Feeling unprepared to do research	1.46	24
Feeling unprepared in my computer skills	1.30	31
Course practices		
Not being able to take the time to review and assess my own work	1.97	10
Getting a low grade early in the quarter	1.88	12
Frequent homework with no feedback	1.86	13
Homework assigned daily or close to daily	1.74	14
Teachers who gave me theories rather than facts	1.62	20
Only getting one point of view in class	1.52	22
Not being challenged in my classes	1.36	28
Getting a high grade early in the quarter	1.36	28
Getting many points of view in class	1.33	30
Institutional structure		
Not getting the courses I wanted or needed	1.45	25
Lack of community at the UW	1.36	28
Difficulty navigating campus or course requirements because of a disability/limited access	1.06	34

procrastination and the attraction of recreational opportunities, and one of the six related to relationship worries. The items, "wanting to play instead of study" and "my own procrastination," were the two most highly rated items by quite a margin. As the table shows, students did not consider the most serious of those obstacles as very significant; only ten hindrances were considered more than "a minor obstacle." Students clearly placed more blame on themselves for failure to learn than they placed on the faculty or university.

The quarterly averages for the item students identified as the most significant obstacle to their learning—"wanting to play instead of study"—revealed a significant eighth order interaction, which is rare in any data set. Figure 1 shows a plot of the averages for each academic term, illustrating the effect and revealing an interesting trend. As the figure shows, the temptation to play rather than study increased from fall to winter to spring each year. It is hardly surprising that the urge to play was the least strong, on average, in the fall quarter of each year, a time when many students have resolved to buckle down. The figure shows why students might so resolve, for their desire to play hindered them most significantly *each spring quarter*. The obstacle of wanting to play instead of study was greatest in the last quarter of their fourth year, for which we even have a term—*senioritis*—which sets in after many students have secured jobs and realized that their GPAs will not be affected greatly by final quarter grades.

In addition to information about how students can distract themselves from their studies with procrastination and entertainment, Table 5 shows, once again, the significant impact that personal relationships had on students' experience in college. There was no significant trend in students' identification of this item as a hindrance, suggesting that relationship worries remained a salient hindrance to learning throughout students' four years. Another item, which ranked in the top six obstacles students selected, was professors and TAs who were unclear and disorganized. This item was clearly the other side of the coin to students' comments about what helped their learning.

The last four items in the top 10 on this list are also important. Two "comfort-level" questions appear in this group. One identified how well prepared students felt in relation to peers, and illustrated, once again, the importance of peers to students' learning. The other pointed to students'

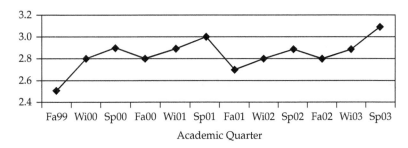

Figure 1 "Wanting to Play Instead of Study" by Quarter
SOURCE: Graphic presented in the *California Master Plan for Higher Education,* 1960

discomfort with speaking in class, a topic we discussed in the previous section of this chapter. Finally, the tenth most frequently chosen obstacle speaks to the importance to students of the need to reflect on and review their work as an aid to their learning. This result indicates that students sense the value of metacognition to their scholarly work, a point discussed in Bransford et al. (2000).

Two other interesting results shown in Table 5 include:

- "Getting a low grade early in the quarter" hindered students' learning more than "getting a high grade early in the quarter"—a result that runs contrary to many faculty assumptions and practices.
- Structural issues, such as "not getting the courses I wanted or needed" and "lack of community at the UW"—both of them major concerns among administrators at most large institutions— had considerably lower overall means than other categories of responses.

As noted earlier, students' choice of major had a large effect on what they felt they learned, but little effect on what helped their learning. Similarly, students' areas of major had little impact on what hindered their learning. Only two items were significant for three of the analyses: "homework assigned daily or nearly daily" and "the amount of time I had to work for wages." The areas for which daily homework was rated the greatest hindrance were business and humanities; majors that rated "daily homework" the least hindrance were engineering and sciences. Regarding time needed to work at a job, art and humanities majors determined this need to be a greater hindrance than science and engineering majors.

Focus Group Results on What Hindered Learning

We asked focus groups what hindered their learning in each of the four years of the study. Students' focus group responses were quite similar to their survey responses, with students each year identifying the obstacles they placed in front of their own learning as the most significant hindrances. As they had in the surveys, students noted that faculty could hinder their learning in a variety of ways—for example, by conducting unclear classes, delivering lectures in a monotone, or actually saying they did not care about teaching.

In addition to asking students what hindered their learning in the focus groups, we asked them to identify the one change that the UW could make that would most improve their learning. Table 6 shows students' responses over the four years of the study. As the table shows, in all four years, improving the quality of teaching was among students' top three recommendations. In addition, students felt their learning could be improved with smaller classes and greater class availability. It is noteworthy that students recommended reducing class size even in their junior and senior years, the years when most students' classes are the smallest.

Challenging Courses: Barriers

When responding to the second question in the winter 2001 email questions, which concerned barriers to meeting academic expectations, students tended to hold themselves responsible, as they had in

TABLE 6
Focus Group Recommendations for the Institution

2000 10 Groups	2001 9 Groups	2002 9 Groups	2003 10 Groups
Smaller classes (7)	Improve faculty teaching (5)	Invest in professors who care and can teach (5)	Hire, train, and retain professors who are excellent teachers (6)
More student-teacher interaction (6)		Smaller classes (4)	Smaller classes (3)
Better professors/TAs (5)		Add more classes to improve availability (3)	Greater class availability (2)

their survey reports. Furthermore, while they mentioned a wide range of barriers, none said that the barriers were insurmountable. The most frequently mentioned barriers to meeting academic expectations were as follows:

- Time issues: balancing life/school needs and demands, time management (26%)
- Procrastination (12%)
- Personal problems (such as depression) or financial issues (12%)
- Feeling uncomfortable asking professors and TAs questions in and outside class (10%)
- No barriers (9%)
- Learning how to study (8%)
- Size of the UW and of classes (4%)
- Unclear or unhelpful professors and TAs (3%)
- No letdown time—every assignment and every class counts (2%)
- Had to get serious, put out effort (2%)
- Feeling isolated by age or because of transferring from a community college (2%)
- Difficulty finding and using resources (2%)

Conclusions About What Students Said Hindered Learning

The most important message we received from students' responses about hindrances to their learning was that they felt their own behavior and choices were the primary obstacles to their learning, as shown in Table 7, which gives a sample of responses from 20 students. We must note, however, that sometimes barriers to students' academic learning can open paths to other kinds of learning that students valued. Friends, for example, were noted as distractions to learning, but students cared a great deal about learning about others and about nurturing their relationships. In addition, peers were considered an important asset to learning, as well as well a potential hindrance. Students considered having wide-ranging experiences while in college part of their definitions of academic success. That meant that their interests in competitive kite flying, biking, movies, and volunteer work may have presented obstacles to academic leaning but, at the same time, met their goal of gaining other kinds of knowledge. Also, while it may seem obvious to faculty and administrators that hours of watching TV and playing video games may be unhealthy for academic performance, there may be ways that some of the activities students cited as obstacles benefited classroom learning. Our point, here, is that the ways and reasons students put up barriers to their own academic learning are complex, as are the outcomes of those barriers.

TABLE 7
20 Barriers to Meeting Academic Expectations

1. "My computer. Computer games."
2. "Napster."
3. "Living with a person who is not in school."
4. "The HUB. Socializing there."
5. "My boyfriend."
6. "I like TV."
7. "I miss one class and that makes it easier to miss the next one."
8. "Time budgeting. I have to shackle myself down to do what I need to do."
9. "A class so boring it would be less painful to stab a pencil into your leg."
10. "If you are going to do well, don't make any friends."
11. "Five hours of commuting a day."
12. "Personal and family stuff."
13. "Just getting over the hump of getting started."
14. "Going shopping on the internet."
15. "Parties don't help either."
16. "The rain."
17. "Napping at inappropriate times."
18. "I got sick this quarter. I took my finals with strep throat."
19. "In some of my really big classes, people talk during the lecture, and it is really frustrating."
20. "I have to work 40 hours per week to put myself through school."

Less complex seemed to be students' sense that faculty members who appeared unconcerned about students' learning or about their own teaching presented obstacles to student learning. While in a secondary position to students' own choices, the ways faculty members could prevent students from learning were important, and students spoke eloquently of its reverse in the previous section.

Conclusions and Implications

We draw six conclusions from the findings in this chapter, which we discuss here, including assessment and teaching implications.

Learning Comes From Multiple Sources and Is Both Individualized and Uneven

That students know more when they leave college than they knew when they entered has been supported by studies reported elsewhere (Bok, 2006; Pascarella & Terenzini, 1991). Our findings on learning suggest that while all students learned, their advances were individualized as well as heavily influence by their majors, confirming findings discussed in previous chapters. Without further belaboring this point about the mediating effects of the disciplines on learning, we note that the strength of this finding across all methods and nearly all measures over time argues for more explicit explanations for what we are doing and why in our classes, whatever the discipline. In addition, it argues for assessment of learning that occurs in academic departments, rather than centrally.

Furthermore, our findings on general learning raise questions about what we mean by general education, particularly in institutions with distributive models. It is clear from the results in previous chapters, as well as in this one, that history, chemistry, and sociology courses at the 100-level require that students know how to read and write in those fields, just as they do at more advanced levels. None of the faculty modifies disciplinary content or methods to make their courses generic for the beginning student's consumption. In addition, it is clear from information on general learning that students begin to differentiate into majors very early, adjusting their course choices according to their majors and their eventual majors. For these reasons, in terms of assessment, we agree with Bok (2006) that it is time to get over our "fixation on general education" (p. 46). If we improve learning in the disciplines, we will have improved general education.

In addition to raising questions about general education, our findings on learning in this chapter show that the shape and content of learning is contingent upon many aspects of students' lives while they are in college. All students learn, but our study shows that learning is uneven, with some students making greater strides in certain areas than others. The directions of growth depend in part on students' own inclinations and attachments, in part on the smorgasbord of possibilities that an institution can offer, and in part on the ways that students' majors defined themselves and conveyed themselves to undergraduates. Further complicating the unevenness of students' learning, these aspects of learning interact in individualized ways that we observed but did not directly study.

Regarding teaching implications, faculty should remember the key roles that their disciplines play in students' overall learning and lives and thus make explicit what students are expected to learn in their courses and disciplines. But we should also remember that our students' learning takes place all over campus, as in well as in places far away from it. This makes assessment of student learning daunting, if we are interested in assessing real learning in all its complexity, rather than in overly simplified, compartmentalized bits of learning. How can we assess Jeremy Nolan's learning against Fiona O'Sullivan's, or Trevor McClintock's against Julianne Guest's for example? Even when looking at a single aspect of learning, how can we meaningfully compare what Carl Swenson and Jennifer Oswald learned about diversity? Given the complexity of the learning that we observed in the UW SOUL, we believe that assessment of student learning must be departmental. However, centrally located assessment can be a powerful partner to departmental assessment, if it is designed to gather information about how students experience college, if it makes room for student definitions of learning, and if it recognizes differences across students and disciplinary practice.

Faculty Are the Key to Students' Learning

No technology, no study group, no pedagogical technique can replace the effect of faculty members who care intensely that students learn about a subject that is dear to their hearts and minds. Again and again, students reported developing a sudden interest in topics they had never cared about before—rocks, the gastric system, Duke Ellington, quadratic equations, Tony Morrison, the Kung!, juvenile delinquency, operant conditioning, the history of science—and nearly always they attributed these sudden fascinations to faculty. Sometimes students attached themselves to majors because of these experiences, and sometimes they did not. But every time students experienced something unexpected that commanded their intellectual attention, their minds were opened to the next experience. With regard to the importance of faculty, we must note that students also pointed to graduate teaching assistants as central to their learning. Their TAs often walked them through learning step by step. One example is Fiona O'Sullivan's history TA, who taught Fiona how to write in her major.

Institutions need to hire, reward, and train excellent teachers and find ways to enhance faculty-student interaction. Institutions need to focus attention on helping graduate students become excellent teachers, even though these investments will not be fully returned to the institutions that make them. Innovation in educational technology should be viewed as an aid to foster meaningful interaction, rather than a substitute for it. Institutions also need to foster and reward multiple approaches to teaching and learning assessment. These assessments must include the learning outcomes that faculty and departments care about, rather than learning outcomes that others think they should care about.

Students Take Responsibility for Hindering Their Own Learning

Faculty are often surprised to learn that students most often blame themselves for failure to learn. While students also point to faculty who are difficult to understand, who do not seem to care about their learning, or whose courses are disorganized or unclear as hindrances to learning, they most frequently cite their own behavior as barriers. However, it is important to note that some of the "personal behaviors" that students described as obstacles actually represent nonacademic goals that students have for their own learning. This conclusion leads us to be gentle in our judgments of student behavior. Even in their political science classes, even as they evaluate each other's short stories or poems, even as they complete an environmental science lab, they are working on the development of their whole selves.

Students Want to Be Intellectually Challenged

Students valued courses that required them to think and asked them to demonstrate that thinking in more than one way. They did not value courses that were easy or that made few intellectual demands on them. Students also wanted to be *taught* to do the thinking required, rather than merely being *required* to do that thinking. They often described ineffective teaching as "teaching by assigning"—an approach in which students were asked to take intellectual leaps or stretch their abilities in assignments and on exams in ways that they had no instruction for doing.

The implications this finding has for teaching are simple in principle though more difficult in practice: we need to ask students to do intellectual work that is challenging, and we need to provide them with instruction for doing it. In addition, we need to help students practice making inferences before we ask them to take such leaps on exams. Furthermore, asking students to demonstrate their thinking in several ways provides classroom faculty and TAs with information about how well we have stepped into the gap with instruction and where we need to do more. In other words, we can assess how well students understand our teaching by including large and small opportunities for them to demonstrate learning in our courses. This kind of classroom-based assessment is the work of faculty members and TAs, rather than departments. There are many good books available on classroom-based assessment, starting with Angelo and Cross's (1993) important book, *Classroom Assessment Technique*.

Demonstrating Caring for Students' Learning Will Improve Their Learning

Students preferred courses that stretched them over courses that did not. In addition, nearly every student we asked said that engaging them in substantive ways in class—asking what they thought, responding to their answers, monitoring their understanding, making room in class for their questions—indicated that faculty cared about their learning. Even though welcoming the opportunity to participate meaningfully in their classes, many students reported that they were embarrassed to ask questions in class, and many also hesitated to ask questions outside class. Even classes that we consider "small"—30–50 students—presented problems for some students who had questions. Faculty who are seen to care about students' learning make questions and responses a normal part of class time and respond respectfully and appreciatively to student questions. They show that higher education is in the question-asking business and that the classroom—however large—is a place where students' questions are not only welcomed but part of an enterprise that requires them to ask questions.

These findings challenge the arguments that students only like "easy" instructors and that course evaluations are "just a popularity contest." UW SOUL students showed little respect for easy classes or easily earned grades, and popular faculty members were those who demonstrated that they cared about students' thinking and learning in ways that appear to guarantee their learning (as also indicated by Bransford et al., 2000).

The teaching implications of this conclusion take us back to the section in this chapter where students described what faculty did to demonstrate that they care about students' learning and what advanced their learning. These two sets of results present a teaching blueprint for faculty members who want to improve student learning.

Students Learn From Each Other

Next to faculty, students name peers, either separately or in the form of study groups, as most helpful to their learning. Regarding teaching, this conclusion suggests that faculty need to build study groups, peer review, small group work, and shared projects into courses whenever possible. Not only is it true that students learn from each other; it is also true that nearly all people work in collaboration with others after school is over. Therefore, faculty provide a service to students by putting them in meaningful relationships with each other over shared needs. In addition, asking students to work together can enhance the social side of a diverse education and address a nonacademic goal that students have for their own learning—the development of social skills.

However, students must be taught about effective collaboration directly and through modeling. A student in a focus group pointed out an interesting fact. He said that students in today's classrooms are being asked to practice teamwork skills by faculty who have never been taught how to be effective team members themselves. He was right; as college students, many of us were rarely asked to work on projects with peers, especially in the arts and humanities. That lack of knowledge and experience causes many of us to "teach" students about working in groups by assigning them to do so—the "teaching by assignment" approach mentioned earlier. However, the power of peers in helping each other learn and the importance of giving students experience in collaboration as a preparation for life after college demand that we make efforts to learn how to teach students to work effectively in groups.

Notes

1. $1 = zero$, $2 = a$ *little*, $3 = a$ *moderate amount*, $4 = a$ *lot*.
2. We used one way analyses of variance and the Eta Squared statistic, which indicates the proportion of total variance accounted for by differences among levels of the independent variable.
3. $P < 0.05$.
4. One item, "Challenging a theory, conclusions, arguments, or results of an authority in a discipline," was added after the first-year surveys.
5. *Didn't do*, $1 = wasn't\ helpful$, $2 = a\ little\ helpful$, $3 = somewhat\ helpful$, $4 = very\ helpful$.
6. *See* www.washington.edu/oea/services/course_eval/index.html
7. $1 = not\ an\ obstacle$, $2 = minor\ obstacle$, $3 = moderate\ obstacle$, $4 = major\ obstacle$.

MYTHS ABOUT ASSESSING THE IMPACT OF PROBLEM-BASED LEARNING ON STUDENTS

ELIZABETH A. JONES

Although problem-based learning (PBL) is increasingly adopted by faculty who teach undergraduate courses, there is little evidence that PBL makes a significant difference in student learning and development over time. Some faculty, who have reviewed the limited assessment evidence, are calling for more assessments to better understand how, when, and if PBL fosters the development of certain types of learning outcomes (Blumberg, 2000). Ideally, PBL should help undergraduates improve their abilities to think critically, analyze and solve complex, real-world problems; find, evaluate, and use appropriate learning resources; work effectively in teams; demonstrate strong written and verbal communication skills; and use content knowledge and intellectual skills to become life-long learners (Duch, Groh, & Allen, 2001). However, there is a dearth of evidence regarding whether PBL helps undergraduates develop these types of outcomes over time.

Although faculty often state specific goals for student learning within their own individual courses, it is challenging to determine if students actually gain more advanced skills and knowledge as they complete series of courses within General Education and their majors. The extent of students' cumulative learning is critical to assess. As faculty devote considerable time and energy to implementing widespread change, it is critical to determine whether the integration of PBL across the undergraduate curriculum has a significant impact upon student learning and development.

Numerous scholars have articulated their beliefs and their own experiences with students. For example, Astin (1985) notes that "students learn by becoming involved . . . Student involvement refers to the amount of physical and psychological energy that the student devotes to the academic experience" (pp. 133–134). Chickering and Gamson (1987) stress that "students do not learn much just by sitting in class listening to teachers . . . They must talk about what they are learning, write about it, relate it to past experiences, apply it to their daily lives. They must make what they learn part of themselves" (p. 3). Finally, Cross (1996) states that "students who reflect on their learning are better learners than those who do not" (p. 9). PBL has the potential to make a difference in terms of student learning and development.

The purpose of this article is to explore five myths about the assessment of PBL. Some faculty and administrators believe these myths reflect reality, but this discussion will reveal selected strategies to build strong assessment processes that can lead to determining whether PBL does make a difference. These myths are not derived from a group of faculty at a particular college or university rather they reflect the collective beliefs of some individuals who attempt to assess PBL. Individuals who believe in these myths are constrained in the decisions they make regarding the assessment of PBL. These myths interfere with the development of assessment plans and contribute to the lack of evidence that is gathered and analyzed. As Terenzini and Pascarella (1994) note, when myths continue to guide thought and action, they can become counterproductive.

The assessment of student learning, especially in these new PBL environments, is complex and challenging. Typically undergraduates are working on projects focused on real-world problems. Often

Reprinted from the *Journal of General Education* 51, no. 4 (2002), by permission of Pennsylvania State University Press.

these problems are embedded within ambiguous conditions and have no single right answer. Their structure is not always apparent (Huba & Freed, 2000) and they reflect the realities of complications found in real life. Students are often asked to work in teams to examine these ill-structured problems. Ideally, faculty expect students to use their knowledge and skills to effectively solve these problems. PBL is a means of developing learning for capability rather than learning for the sake of acquiring only knowledge (Engel, 1991).

Faculty may feel comfortable and have more experience focusing on content or knowledge outcomes that are concerned with the mastery of material specific to a particular course or discipline. The challenge is getting students to develop stronger reasoning or higher-order thinking skills to critically evaluate numerous sources of evidence and derive informed conclusions or solutions in open-ended problems. In PBL, knowledge is used and applied to real world contexts. This means that traditional tests or assessments of pure knowledge do not necessarily tap into the types of skills and abilities that PBL is intended to strengthen over time.

Huba and Freed (2000) define assessment as "the process of gathering and discussing information from multiple and diverse sources in order to develop a deep understanding of what students know, understand, and can do with their knowledge as a result of their educational experiences; the process culminates when assessment results are used to improve subsequent learning" (p. 8). Assessment is an on-going process that is continually open to change and revisions over time.

Myth #1: The Problem-solving Abilities of Undergraduates Are the Main Outcomes to Assess Within PBL Experiences

Some faculty believe that the most important outcome that should be assessed is the problem-solving abilities of undergraduates. Expertise in problem-solving is critical and requires knowledge in order to resolve problems (Kelson, 2000). However, learning is multidimensional, integrated, and revealed in performance over time (Mentkowski & Associates, 2000; American Association of Higher Education, 1992). In a PBL environment, essential learning outcomes might focus on problem-solving, teamwork, written and oral communication skills, as well as dispositions or attitudes. Engel (1991) notes that PBL is a method that can help students achieve the following types of learning:

- adapting to and participating in change;
- dealing with problems, making reasoned decisions in unfamiliar situations;
- reasoning critically and creatively;
- collaborating productively in teams or groups;
- appreciating another person's point of view; and
- identifying one's own strengths and weaknesses and undertaking appropriate remediation such as self-directed learning. (p. 25)

Given the complexity of student learning and multiple essential outcomes, it is critical to define the intended learning outcomes for individual courses and then explicitly demonstrate linkages with the entire General Education program. Since the design of strong PBL experiences can lead to the development of multiple learning outcomes, it is vital to define the intentions and expectations for student learning that not only focus on problem-solving but also incorporate other essential abilities.

Myth #2: There Are No Instruments that Assess Skills, Attitudes, and Knowledge Associated with PBL

Some individuals believe that there are no instruments available to assess the abilities, skills, knowledge, and attitudes associated with PBL. Part of this difficulty arises since faculty may search for the "perfect" instrument to assess student learning and development. Individuals who search for this perfect method are also trying to find a way to assess one particular skill, ability, or very isolated set of knowledge. As one begins to realize that learning is multidimensional, then it is vital to review and use multiple assessment methods. It is unrealistic to find a single method that will fully assess an important student outcome. Faculty can request sample copies of commercially-developed instruments that are available in order to see if any of the instruments meet their needs. Erwin (1999) developed an assessment sourcebook that closely scrutinizes instruments intended to assess writing, critical thinking, and problem-solving. The advantage of using commercially developed instruments (if they assess certain outcomes deemed important by the faculty) is that there is typically evidence about reliability and validity. Another advantage is that national norms for comparison purposes have been developed (Palumbo & Banta, 1999).

It is likely that certain instruments will assess only a limited range of skills or attitudes. Given these gaps, it is critical to supplement instruments with other measures. Faculty may decide to develop their own approaches or methods to assess student learning. The advantages of locally developed instruments are the opportunities they provide for engaging faculty in the assessment process and the likelihood that these methods will closely align with the local curriculum as well as intended learning outcomes (Palumbo & Banta, 1999).

Myth #3: We Can Only Assess What Students Learn Within Individual Courses

Some faculty adopt a course-embedded assessment strategy to determine if students are mastering important knowledge and skills. Individual faculty decide which skills and knowledge are critical and then create their own assessment methods that are ideally linked with their expectations for student performance. While this is a useful beginning point, it can neglect the cumulative effect of student learning over time. A course-embedded approach is limited or constrained by faculty who create their own assessments divorced from other courses in the curriculum. Course-embedded assessments provide a snapshot of student learning often gained within one particular semester. These types of assessments can be more useful if they address overall program outcomes rather than focusing solely on those for a specific course (Huba & Freed, 2000). For example, faculty who teach General Education courses can examine samples of student work to determine if undergraduates in the core curriculum are achieving the desired levels of performance.

In the future, longitudinal designs for assessing student learning would be meaningful. For example, faculty could assess their newly admitted students before they take any college-level course work and thus get indicators of students' prior knowledge and skill levels. Then subsequent assessments could examine the same types of skills and abilities by examining student learning at subsequent points in time such as at the end of the freshmen year or sophomore year and the end of the senior year. Such a longitudinal design gives faculty an opportunity to learn more about how their students are developing with opportunities to make refinements or changes before they graduate.

Assessment works best when it is ongoing rather than episodic (American Association of Higher Education, 1992). Some faculty may expect significant student learning gains during one semester or during the first time that PBL is initially designed and implemented into the General Education curriculum. Since student learning is cumulative over time, undergraduates should gain exposure to PBL through a series of courses that become progressively more complex and more challenging (Engle, 1992). A comprehensive assessment system is needed that provides continuous, seamless tracking of the student's learning and development across the curriculum (Kelson, 2000).

Myth #4: Only Direct Assessments of Student Learning Are Desirable

Some instructors may believe that direct assessments of student learning are the only vehicle to determine the impact of PBL upon undergraduates. These types of assessments focus on learning that is examined within projects, products, papers, exhibitions, performances, case studies, oral exams, presentations, and tests. While these direct measures of student learning are valuable, it is also useful to include indirect measures such as student self-report surveys or interviews, alumni surveys, or employer surveys (Huba & Freed, 2000). Although these methods do not measure student learning directly, they do provide useful information and a greater understanding about stakeholders' perceptions of the learning process and strengths or limitations of their learning experiences.

Mentkowski and Associates (2001) note the challenges associated with promoting "learning that lasts" and stress the importance of integrating learning, development, and performance over time. To determine if learning endures, it is especially useful to gain feedback from college graduates. Once students complete their undergraduate programs and enter the workplace, it is likely that they may see connections between their PBL experiences and their performance in the real world. Asking students about their perceptions of their learning and its application to their current roles can provide meaningful insights. A combination of both direct and indirect assessment methods can provide a fuller portrait of student learning and important perceptions about the process.

Myth #5: Students Will Naturally Learn How to Work Well in a Group. Therefore, Only Group Products Need to Be Assessed Rather than Group Processes

Some faculty have not had substantial experiences working with students in teams. These professors may believe that students will naturally learn how to work together during the semester. Consequently, they may focus primarily on assessing the products generated by student teams. However, one of the missing links is the instructors' role in guiding students and coaching them about how to work effectively within their groups. In addition, it is essential to actually assess the processes of the groups and how individuals contribute to teamwork. As the American Association of Higher Education (AAHE, 1992) notes, assessment requires attention to outcomes, but also and equally, assessment requires attention to the experiences that lead to those outcomes.

Meyers and Jones (1993) delineate five criteria for successful teamwork. These features include the following:

- a sense of interdependence among team member;
- accountability of individual students to both team and instructor;
- frequent face-to-face interaction to promote team goals;
- development of social skills needed for collaboration; and
- critical analyses of group processes.

Research that examines the relationship between learning in groups and student achievement has demonstrated that discussions of group processes and how they might be improved is a critical dimension of group learning activity, and these discussions contribute to improved achievement (Yager, Johnson, Johnson, & Snider, 1986). Without formal assessments of group processes, individual teams may falter and become less successful in mastering important outcomes.

Johnson et al. (1991) suggest that individual students should be rewarded for their own performance as well as the success of the team. Self- and peer-assessments can encourage students to take more responsibility for their own learning so that they can critically determine their own individual contributions along with their peers' productivity. Faculty can encourage students to reflect upon the results of the assessment and use them to improve group processes. Reflection about group processes is critical as students share information, learn how to interpret it, and use it to inform their actions.

Stein and Hurd (2000) provide examples of locally-developed assessment instruments that can be used to gauge the teamwork process. For example, one instrument asks students to assess how their team works and to also reflect upon the roles that an individual adopts for the project, the roles they have taken in the past, and the roles that they are most comfortable with. Students are asked to reflect upon 14 possible roles. These authors provide additional examples that examine the contributions of the individual team member as well as the team's accomplishments.

A range of commercially-developed instruments are also available to assess team work and group processes. The majority of these instruments take only 10 to 15 minutes to complete. In addition, individuals can easily analyze the results and use them to shape meaningful improvements. Jones and RiCharde (in press) examine a variety of aspects related to each teamwork instrument including the purpose, key definitions, cost, time, scores, reliability, and validity. Faculty who want to assess teamwork can consult this sourcebook to determine if there are potential instruments that may meet their needs.

In this brief discussion, five different myths have been highlighted that can limit the scope and degree of assessments undertaken to determine if PBL is making a difference. Although planning and implementing multiple assessments seems time-consuming and complex, it is critical to formally examine whether undergraduates who participate and complete PBL experiences within their General Education curriculum are indeed achieving significant gains in their learning and related abilities. Without rigorous assessments over time, it is difficult to know with confidence that PBL is having a major impact upon student learning and development.

References

American Association of Higher Education (1992). *Principles of Good Practice for Assessing Student Learning*. Washington, D. C.: AAHE Assessment Forum.

Astin, A. W. (1985). *Achieving Educational Excellence*. San Francisco: Jossey-Bass.

Blumberg, P. (2000). Evaluating the evidence that problem-based learners are self-directed learners: A review of the literature. In Evenson and Hmelo, (Eds.), *Problem-Based Learning: A Research Perspective on Learning Interactions*. Mahwah, NJ: Lawrence Erlbaum.

Cross, K. P. (1996). New lenses on learning. *About Campus*, pp. 4–9.

Duch, B. J., Groh, S. E., & Allen, D. E. (2001) (Eds.). *The Power of Problem-Based Learning*. Sterling, VA: Stylus.

Engle, C. E. (1991): Not just a method but a way of learning. In Boud, D. & Feletti, G. (Eds.), *The Challenge of Problem-Based Learning*. New York: St. Martin's Press.

Erwin, D. (1999). *Assessment Sourcebook: A Review of Instruments Designed to Assess Critical Thinking, Problem-Solving, and Writing*. Washington, D. C.: National Center for Education Statistics and the National Postsecondary Education Cooperative.

Huba, M. E. & Freed, J. E. (2000). *Learner-Centered Assessment on College Campuses: Shifting the Focus from Teaching to Learning*. Needham Heights, MA: Allyn and Bacon.

Jones, E. A. and RiCharde, S. (in press). *Assessment Sourcebook: A Review of Instruments to Assess Communication, Teamwork, Leadership, Quantitative, and Information Literacy Skills*. Washington, D.C.: National Postsecondary Education Cooperative and the National Center for Education Statistics.

Kelson, A. C. (2000). Assessment of Students for Proactive Lifelong Learning. In Evenson & Hmelo, (Eds.), *Problem-Based Learning: A Research Perspective on Learning Interactions*. Mahwah, NJ: Lawrence Erlbaum Associates, Publishers.

Mentkowski, M. & Associates (2000). *Learning that Lasts: Integrating Learning, Development, and Performance in College and Beyond*. San Francisco, CA: Jossey-Bass.

Meyers, C. and Jones, T. B. (1993). *Promoting Active Learning Strategies for the College Classroom*. San Francisco, CA: Jossey-Bass.

Palumbo, C. A. & Banta, T. W. (1999). *Assessment Essentials: Planning, Implementing, and Improving Assessment in Higher Education*. San Francisco, CA: Jossey-Bass.

Stein, R. F. & Hurd, S. (2000). *Using Student Teams in the Classroom: A Faculty Guide*. Bolton, MA: Anker Publishing Company, Inc.

Terenzini, P. T. and Pascarella, E.T. (1994). Living with Myths: Undergraduate Education in America. *Change, 26* (1), pp. 28–32.

Yager, R. T., Johnson, R. T., Johnson, D. W. and Snider, B. (1986). The impact of group processing on achievement in cooperative learning groups. *Journal of Social Psychology, 126*, pp. 389–397.

QUALITATIVE PROGRAM ASSESSMENT: FROM TESTS TO PORTFOLIOS

P.L. COURTS AND K.H. MCINERNEY

For several years now, [with support from the Fund for the Improvement of Postsecondary Education], Fredonia has been assessing a new general education program, and they've chosen to go the local route in all cases, with faculty-designed exams to cover a variety of cross-cutting general-education outcomes. I think that's a right idea. . . . In [the final] report they set forth what they learned—and equally interesting, what they didn't learn.

They didn't, for instance, ever learn the "Truth" about their students. In fact, much of their work at the outset entailed discussion—and, I dare say, heated debate—about the soundness of this and that instrument, pilot testing, whether the results could be compared with this way or that, what was valid, what not . . . with the result, as I say, that no truth was learned. What the faculty *did* learn was that . . . students were taking and passing individual courses alright, but they weren't seeing connections; they couldn't put the pieces together.

The solution? No doubt there were (and should be) several. . . . [Fredonia faculty] are now working to develop a portfolio approach to assessment that will give them more in-depth information about each student's ability to put the pieces together, but also—and here's the beauty of the thing—help the student *develop* that ability. (Hutchings 1990, 4)

Indeed, the use of portfolios throws light on the very process of measurement or evaluation. For portfolio assessment occupies an interesting in-between area between the clean, artificial world of carefully controlled assessment ("Take out your pencils. Don't turn over your books till I say 'go'.") and the swampy real world of offices and living rooms where people actually write things for a purpose and where we as actual readers look at texts and cannot agree for the life of us (sometimes for the tenure of us) about what they mean and how good they are. Or to put it differently, use of portfolios highlights the tension between *validity* and *reliability*. (Elbow 1991, xii)

Stories from the Front: The Fredonia Experience

As a teacher of English, I became involved with Fredonia's assessment project primarily because I believed then, and continue to believe, that program assessment and outcomes-based educational systems have potential for tremendous damage unless they are created, implemented, and controlled by *teachers* who understand what actually goes on in classrooms and who also understand how genuinely complex it is to quantify human cognition, cognitive growth, or "learning" in any but the most primitive terms. Everyone involved must resist the temptation to return to simplistic "competency-based" models of education that emphasize discrete, fragmented, and often irrelevant skills.

But regardless of my opinions about the issue, I feared that the State of New York was moving toward a demand for programmatic assessment at the college level and outcomes-based individual assessment in the public school system. Given that fact, I agreed to be a part of a group composed

Reprinted from *Assessment in Higher Education: Politics, Pedagogy, and Portfolios*, by Patrick L. Courts and Kathleen H. McInerney (1993), Greenwood Publishing Group, Inc.

almost entirely of faculty, who would create a series of instruments designed to assess our General College Program. And lately, as I find the public media filled with calls for a national assessment, I am all the more committed to trying to short-circuit the foolishness that is sometimes associated with assessment. And I reiterate that, from my point of view, assessment of any kind that is not clearly and primarily directed at improving what we do in classrooms is a waste of money and time.

So let me begin at my beginning. I do not believe a detailed description of Fredonia's General College Program (hereafter GCP) is either necessary or particularly interesting for the general reader. Let it suffice for me to say that the program is not "competency-" or "skills-based" in any of the traditional senses of those terms. Students have a broad degree of choice among courses across disciplines that have been specially designed or redesigned to emphasize print literacy, metacognitive or reflexive thinking, problem solving, scientific reasoning, a sense of history, and an understanding of foreign cultures and the degrees to which ethnocentrism can inhibit an understanding of other cultures. The major point here is that we were not trying to find out if our students could write business letters, answer multiple-choice questions about a reading passage, fill in a chart of elements and their atomic weights, find India on a blank map, explain the importance of the year 1492, or itemize the basic tenets of Buddhism. Rather, we wanted to find out how much they had grown or improved as writers and readers, how much their mathematical and scientific thinking had matured, and how their ideas about human history and cultural diversity had been affected between their first and third years of college.

A committee was created of twelve faculty members representing a broad variety of disciplines, and we set about the task of boldly going where none of us had ever gone before; I use this Star Trek allusion purposely because for many of us, myself included, the whole endeavor smacked of science fiction involving uncharted space voyages into an investigation of dimensions we were not at all sure we could investigate.

Like typically good scholars, we began by reading everything we could find that had been written about assessment in the years immediately prior to our project. I would like to say that this reading solved our problems, but for the most part it did not provide us with a test or series of tests we might simply implement. Nor had we really expected it to. Instead, the research confirmed what most of us had expected in the first place: Standardized tests manufactured and sold by Educational Testing Service (ETS) or American College Testing (ACT) were of almost no use for several reasons, not the least of which being that they do not really test much of anything other than how well one does on a standardized test. The best assessment instruments are those created by the individuals intimately involved with students, the institution and the programs that are to be assessed (Aper, Cuver, Hinkle 1990, 476).

Consequently, it became immediately and painfully clear that we would have to create our own instruments, test our tests, so to speak, to find out if they provided the information we were searching for, teach ourselves to evaluate student performance on the tests, find a control group at another college, give the tests, score them, evaluate our findings, and make whatever follow-up recommendations we might wish. It was not so much a problem of realizing that we were "in over our heads" that frightened us, as much as it was the realization that this was going to be a long swim up river against a formidable current.

The Process

The full committee began by considering brief presentations from selected members of the group intended to highlight some of the key issues and potential problems we might encounter as we attempted to create assessment instruments for given areas. Immediately following this series of relatively wide-ranging discussions, we split into temporary subgroups in order to create itemized lists of specific skills, abilities, or processes that should be tested in a given area. The subgroup working with reading, writing, and reflexive thinking, for example, had not decided at this point that reflexive thinking would even be a part of the assessment. The importance of these initial discussions cannot be overemphasized: it was only through these initial discussions, as the group articulated relatively obvious items—things like "the ability to create a central focus in an essay," and "the ability to identify an author's central focus in an article," that we began to articulate more complex items (the ability to infer, or to identify underlying assumptions). And this investigation eventually led the group to items involving metacomprehension and metacognition (meaning the ability to recognize relationships between one's own experience and the experience represented in work produced by another author and consciousness of one's own learning style and ways of approaching learning something or learning how to do something).

The point here is that these subgroups were intensely involved in a discovery process that would lead to an articulation of the kinds of things the assessment would eventually assess. These lists were then reviewed and refined by the entire committee. This review was a particularly important step because it would eventually lead to a fully articulated set of "grids" on which all the skills or abilities to be assessed would be listed and, eventually, matched with the test question or exercise that would allow us to assess student performance (See Appendix A: Grid for Reading for an example). Although this grid would evolve as we more fully articulated the various assessment instruments, this beginning was of central importance as it helped us to engage in the process of creating the tests themselves.

Having established the grid and having agreed that we would create instruments that actively engaged students in "doing" whatever kind of thinking, reasoning, or languaging that we wanted to evaluate, we split into three subgroups: one focusing on reading, writing, and reflexive thinking: one focusing on mathematical and scientific reasoning; and one on historicism and ethnocentrism. Each subgroup then (1) created instruments that might assess growth in these areas (as specified on the grid); (2) identified which specific outcomes listed under the General Education Outcomes (See Appendix B) a given instrument might assess; and (3) submitted the "test" to the whole committee for discussion, refinement, and, occasionally, ridicule.

I say *ridicule* with good humor because anyone identified with such a process must become aware that the assessors (a much privileged class) might have tremendous difficulty succeeding on many of the instruments that a given assessment group is using. It was important for all concerned to see me and my sociologist friend laugh in embarrassment when faced with blank maps and told to fill in the names of countries (an instrument later rejected). At another meeting, of course, we had the fun of watching some of our prestigious colleagues fail at some of the problem-solving tasks that had been suggested for use.

As we worked together to examine the tests each subgroup was creating, we also continued to refer to the original grid, making sure that our tests were directly related to our defined purpose. Through this interactive process of examining potential test instruments, referring to the initial grid, trying the tests ourselves, and continual discussion, we eventually arrived at a set of instruments we felt we might use in the assessment. I emphasize these early steps because, without them, without giving them the time and energy they demanded, the project would never have been completed. Throughout the next two years, but especially as we worked together to refine and revise various test instruments, the grid operated as our stable center against which we might consider the value of a given test: (1) matters of efficiency (Does one kind of test allow us to assess more items on the grid than another?); (2) matters of relevance to the task (Does a given instrument assess something that is on the grid?); and (3) matters focusing on the quality of the instrument (Does it address the complexity of the item on the grid, or simply appear to do so?).

An absolutely key point, here is this: anyone engaging in programmatic assessment must be thoroughly familiar with the program that is being assessed and its stated objectives (Aper, Cuver, Hinkle 1990, 476). It was not unusual in our early discussions (and even some later ones) when were were designing the instruments, for one or more individuals to make strong arguments for inclusion of an instrument that would test geographical knowledge, foreign language competency, and so forth. The only problem was that these were not objectives of the program we were assessing. It is all too easy to get caught in the trap of trying to assess everything that some idealized program *should* do or that some group *should* know, regardless of whether or not the program being assessed happens to address all the everythings. It is important to remember that it is rather easy to identify what all educated people *should be able to do*, but we may want to ask whether or not we can do all the things we think that others should do.

At any rate, everyone on the committee tried to do the tests, critiqued them, offered suggestions for change and revision, and sometimes simply decided that a given test was either irrelevant or useless. Once the test were approved by the larger committee, each group set about articulating the criteria by which degrees of success or failure would be measured for each instrument. Creating clearly articulated criteria and hierarchies of criteria ("outcomes," if you will) that might allow us to clearly differentiate one level of performance from another was much more difficult than creating the tests themselves. And this process, along with training ourselves to score the tests, took the most time and energy, aside from actually scoring the final tests. The first part of the process took place over the period of about one year. When it was over, we had nine tests and we were finally ready to "test the tests" by administering them to small groups of students so that we could find out if the tests gave us the information we wanted and so that we could begin to train ourselves to score the tests.

Once we began to examine the first set of student responses to the tests, we found that things were not going as well as we had hoped. Directions on one test had to be carefully refined so that students could not simply define historical events in terms of the last two years of their lives. Problem-solving tests had to be changed because some of them were so difficult that no one could do them at all: if a test is so difficult that no one can do it, one has no basis for examining change or growth; one simply finds out that no one can do it. On the reading test, some of the follow-up questions showed themselves to be either redundant or unnecessary, and the essay we had chosen for them to read proved to be a little too long for the time period we had allotted. In all cases, as we began to try to score the tests, we found ourselves refining scoring criteria in an attempt to make this subjective process of evaluation reliable and valid.

In a sense we began again. We revised the tests, discussed revisions, gave them again, scored them again, and only then felt that we might finally go ahead with the test itself. I will not even go into the problems we had finding another institution with a profile similar to our own that would agree to give the tests, but by the end of two years, we had found an institution to cooperate, we had given the tests, and spent the final year scoring them, evaluating our results, and writing final reports and recommendations.

The following discussion provides a brief description of the tests themselves so that they can be seen in a little better context. But it is important to note that this is simply intended to provide a perspective. If we learned nothing else (and I believe we learned quite a bit) through our involvement with assessment, it is this: qualitative assessment of the kind we are discussing here and the kind that is involved in a portfolio system demands that those doing the assessing create their own instruments, criteria, and scoring system. While a reader may borrow freely from what follows, the first step in assessment is to be sure that you are assessing your program and not someone else's or some fictional program that you have created in your own minds.

All of the following test descriptions are paraphrased and/or quoted from *The GCP and Student Learning: A Report to the Campus*, written by Minda Rae Amiran with The General College Program Assessment Committee, August 1989, and referred to as the GCP Report in the following discussion. (For a complementary discussion of the Fredonia assessment and related assessment projects at Western College at Miami University of Ohio, see Amiran, Schilling, and Schilling).

The Instruments

Writing Test. To test our students' writing ability, we asked entering first-year students, entering transfer students, and upperclass students who had not been transfer students to describe and analyze what they had found to be a major problem with the educational system in their high schools. We chose the subject because we wanted to be sure to present the writers with a topic about which all would have adequate background experience and knowledge to allow them to write concretely and, hopefully, with some engagement. The essays were first scored holistically, and then on the basis of separate criteria like the ability to create a clear central point, offer supporting evidence, analyze reasons, and write Standard English.

Reading Test. Because we desired to avoid the artificiality inherent in most comprehension tests and the multiple-choice questions that characterize such tests, we chose to give the students a twelve-page article from an introductory anthology in sociology. We chose the particular article because it focused on a community's response to two groups of young people, one of which was comprised of "good" kids, and the other of which was composed of rowdier kids. Our primary concern was that the students would have enough background knowledge to bring to the text to allow them to transact with it constructively and with some interest. The students were then asked to provide several sentences of response to a series of questions based on the reading. These questions asked them to identify the author's main point, his supporting evidence, the implications of his essay, his underlying assumptions, and the organizing principle used by the author. Further, in hopes of seeing to what extent students could place the reading in their own context and experience, measuring its sense or nonsense against their own experiences, we also asked them to explain why they agreed or disagreed with the author's main point, illustrating their opinion through a relevant personal experience. Students had ninety minutes in which to complete the test.

Reflexive Thinking. Before describing this particular test, a brief digression may help here. Initially, we had intended to call this test Metacognitive Thinking, but early in the design stages we knew that we could not begin to examine the complexities involved in metacognition through a single test. At the same time, we believe that metacognition is central and essential for the most proficient degrees of learning to occur. Since *metacognition* is a relatively new concept in education, easily oversimplified, some defining should help her. By *metacognition*, we do not simply mean the ability to structure one's own approaches to learning a concept or solving a problem (though this could be a part of the broader definition). Metacognition involves more than the self-knowledge that "I always approach a long writing assignment by making an outline (or by free writing, or whatever)." Metacognition suggests a *meta*-level of consciousness of one's own thought processes. As such, it involves an almost simultaneous, conscious degree of self-awareness:. "This is how I approach or think about a situation (problem, issue, concept)"; "this is how I might best approach this particular concept in order to more fully understand it"; "this is how I am thinking about this issue, and it is or is not effective"; "these are the other possible approaches I might take instead."

At its most basic level, a lack of metacognition (or *metacomprehension*) characterizes the learner who has "studied" the chapter for the test, believes that s/he "knows" the material, but is then completely baffled when faced with the test itself. Not only did this learner not know that s/he did not know, she does not understand how to go about knowing (Weaver 1988, 24).

Of course, at its most advanced levels, some kind of full consciousness of self and self's interaction with others, one might reasonably argue that no one is ever genuinely metacognitive. We certainly find it difficult to imagine this degree of metacognition. One is tempted to say that "it takes one to know one," adding that only a self-deceptive egocentric would claim to be fully metacognitive. Anything that involves thinking about one's own thinking presents us with the most serious complexities (and, some might argue, impossibilities). And yet, as difficult as it is to describe, some learners pretty clearly enjoy a higher degree of self-conscious awareness of their own learning processes than others. And it also appears clear to us that the most powerful learners are those who are best able to monitor their own learning processes: These are the learners who "know when they know" and are able to structure their own learning so that they can productively move on from that self-knowledge toward more and fuller knowing. Furthermore, these learners "know when they do not know," which puts them in the position of using a different approach to the problem or seeking help.

While our reflexive thinking test only scratches that surface of assessing students' metacognitive abilities in this more complex sense, it does, at least, approach the issue. But given the obvious importance of developing higher degrees of metacognition, we believe that portfolios most directly suggest ways both to develop and to assess this essential ability.

Likewise, our sense of the importance of metacognition is directly related to the importance we place on actively engaging students in the writing process, across the curriculum, in order that they might consistently attempt to use language to articulate and examine what it is they think: As a linguistic process, writing uniquely allows learners to be surprised by what they know, discover what they do not know, and use what they know to know more (Murray 1985, 7). More directly, writing is first and foremost a self-reflective process that is both regressive and progressive in the same moment. As writers use writing to discover what it is they are trying to say, they also discover more that needs to be said. In the moment of writing, the writer moves between the roles of writer, producing the text, and reader, reading what has been written:

> In the moment of author(iz)ing, the moment of writing, the writer is reading (using language to make sense of) that which is in there (inside the writer) in order to externalize it through the surface structures of language. . . . In the moment of externalizing the meaning, . . . the writer engages in the recursive process of reading what he is writing and writing what he is reading. The two processes are inextricably bound together. (Courts 1991, 110)

In the Fredonia assessment, hoping to find the extent to which our students are conscious of their own learning processes, we asked them to write a brief description of something they learned outside of school and then to answer follow-up questions examining what they had written. These follow-up questions asked them to identify the major factors influencing the learning event they described, to identify any pattern that characterized the learning experience, and to contrast that with any patterns they observed in school learning situations, to draw any conclusions they might about learning in general, and to comment on the ways schools structure the learning experience. They had one hour for the entire task.

Quantitative Problem Solving. We created two similar tests of four questions each

to assess student problem solving. One question on each test could be solved through very simple algebra, once the equations had been properly set up. Another was an open-ended estimation problem, under realistic conditions of uncertainty. Problems three and four were identical on the two tests, though their order was reversed: the first of the pair was supplied with prompts, the second was not; though the setting of each problem was different, the algebraic solutions were very similar (Amiran 1989, 13–14).

In addition to being asked to solve the problem, students were asked to state their assumptions and explain their reasoning process. For example, one question was as follows: John has a pail with 40 washers in it and finds the total weight to be 175 ounces. Sue weighs the same pail with 20 washers in it and finds the total to be 95 ounces. (a) how much does each washer weigh? (b) how much does the pail weight? (c) no matter how trivial they may seem, what assumptions did you make in solving the problem? (Throughout the assessment, it was questions like this last one, *c*, that were particularly important to us because we were trying to assess students' *thinking processes* rather than their knowledge of unrelated bits of information.)

Scientific Reasoning. Students had to do two tasks for this exam: First, they had "to design an experiment to show the relationship between hours of exposure to sunlight and rate of growth in spider plants," and second, they had "to critique the report of a study on the correlation between amount of brown rice consumed and incidence of gout among older men" (Amiran 1989, 17).

Socioethical Understanding. There were three parts to this section of the exam:

1. " 'History' asks student to list ten of the most important events in human record, and choosing one of those events, to name three other events that would not have occurred or would have been very different if the chosen even had not taken place."

2. " 'Exchange Student' has students answer some uncomplimentary questions about the United States asked by an otherwise friendly Western European exchange student."

3. " 'Malbavia' posits a third world kingdom undergoing modernization as a result of newly discovered mineral wealth, and asks the students, as part of a UN team, to infer societal effects and make recommendations, some of which have to do with prevailing practices of hospitality and human sacrifice" (Amiran 1989, 19–20).

What Happened Next: Results

For the sake of brevity, I will only report some of the most interesting generalizations that are supported by the assessment project. Though none of us would agree that what the students wrote in the composition test was particularly well-written, it was in this area that we saw the most obvious and greatest growth. Students clearly had improved as writers. But the results on the reading test were disturbing for several reasons: First, instead of finding improvement in their reading abilities, we found little significant growth in many important areas related to reading. Second, while this might not be reason for alarm if the first-year students had shown strong reading abilities, such was not the case. Third, while most of the students accurately identified the main point of the essay they read, and many did well in identifying the author's supporting evidence, few did well in identifying the implications of the essay, in articulating the author's assumptions, or in seeing relationships between the article, their own lives, and the society in which they live. In short, after achieving success at a literal level, these readers were unable to do much more.

Unfortunately, this inability to move beyond the literal, to generalize and abstract, characterized our findings on all the other tests. Finally, the results on the reading test caused us to question the results on the writing test: if students had improved significantly as writers, one might reasonably expect similar improvement in their reading abilities. If such results did not occur, then one had to question what it was we had tested on the writing test. This confusion further increased our interest in implementing a portfolio system of some sort.

As for the other tests, let me simply present some findings quoted from the GCP Report: "In absolute terms, few students proved very adept at reflexive thinking" (Amiran 1989, 12). Most of the students "lack the problem-solving or reasoning skills that would help them think the [algebraic] problem through in an orderly way [often complaining] that they don't like math or never have been good at it." (Amiran 1979, 16). Likewise, they were very weak in recognizing the assumptions they had to make in order to solve the problems they had been given.

On the scientific reasoning, students' performance "leaves much to be desired" (Amiran 1989, 18). Their comments suggested a student belief that unless one had a course in which a specific body of information had been studied, one could not conceivably begin to solve the problem. But since the problems were not based on specific knowledge of a given area of science, this indicated to us that the students knew little about scientific reasoning, empirical scientific methodology, complexity of identifying cause-effect relationships without a clearly established control, or researcher bias.

In the area of historical understanding and presentism, students were weak both in terms of establishing a chronology of events and in terms of seeing causal relationships between or among events. And results on socioethical reasoning left us with increasing cause for concern.

The problem is not that there is no growth, but the growth is generally minimal and the level of performance is seldom particularly gratifying.

Obviously, none of us was particularly pleased with what we found. On the other hand, we were not generally too surprised. By trying to measure growth in students' thinking and languaging processes, we knew that we were trying to assess ground that is seldom addressed in schools or colleges. Most testing focuses on assessing students' mastery of discrete bits of information and/or isolated fragmented skills. And we had consciously and purposefully avoided those kinds of tests. We know that our students "know something"; we wanted to find out what they could do with what they know and what kinds of growth they might have experienced as a result of their participation in the General College Program.

If the results are dispiriting, however, they also offer rays of light insofar as they suggest several things: (1) while students did not show a high degree of metacognition, they did indicate a considerable degree of awareness of how schools were failing them and offered plenty of suggestions about what needs to be changed; and (2) the results also indicated that, if we care about our students being something more than repositories of information, if we want them to be thinkers and doers, then we need to emphasize thinking and doing across the curriculum. And we need to empower teachers at the same time.

We at Fredonia know, for example, that our faculty have been participating in highly structured workshops in writing across the curriculum over the past seven years, and this is the only area in which we found significant growth. Of course, it is not particularly revolutionary to suggest that if we want something to change, we need to help faculty make the change instead of simply carping and casting blame. But all too often one finds little support for faculty development workshops of any kind at any level. In our case, however, the dean of General Studies has organized additional workshops for faculty to help them address multiculturalism in their own classrooms and disciplines. And small cadres of mathematicians and science faculty have begun to gather to address some of the more disturbing findings. On its own initiative, the Math Department conducted workshops for the faculty members who teach the introductory mathematics courses that most of our students take to fulfill their general program requirements. These workshops focused on examining ways to help students become more proficient as problem solvers. Likewise, small committees of faculty in the sciences, social sciences, and humanities worked to develop classroom activities that would help students become more aware of their own biases and assumptions. Further, as a result of the findings, many of us involved with the assessment and other interested faculty have worked individually to change the ways in which we teach our courses in order to try to address some of the things the assessment reveals. In terms of curriculum, the English Department is in the process of implementing a three-course core in the major that will emphasize multicultural literatures and engage students in the conscious exploration of ethnocentrism as it affects the critical reader's understanding of a work. Faculty in all disciplines are trying to help students become more conscious of the approaches that characterize the reasoning processes that form the basis of a given discipline.

Have many people simply disregarded the study? Yes, of course. These are real human beings, and they act just as you might expect. In short, there has been no miracle here, but there has been some progress. Have the devastating budget cuts SUNY is presently undergoing severely interfered with the changes that the assessment suggests need to be made? Absolutely. And will the past and continuing budget cuts cause administrators to compromise the quality of the General College Program rather than improve it? Probably. It is, then, fair to say that the Fredonia assessment has not yet had the results many of us hoped it might have. In fairness, however, to all involved, small changes are occurring and a core of interested faculty and administrators remain committed to using assessment to improve programs and classroom instruction.

On the other hand, it is not unusual to find administrators who are more interested in the assessment itself than in the actions that need to be taken as a result of assessment findings. And it is even more common to find that there is more money available for assessment than there is to support the faculty and curricular development that should grow out of assessment projects. Obviously, this presents a seriously pessimistic view of the entire endeavor. Why engage in all this work if it is to come to naught because education in the United States is being devastated by a weak economy? Instead of a trickle-down effect, we seem simply to be trickled on. Why fight for local autonomy in assessment and put forth the time and energy involved in creating qualitative assessment instruments when pressures for a system of standardized national assessment surround us? Why continue to work within a superimposed system that often appears to be characterized by teacher and student bashing orchestrated by secretaries of education? Why bother at all when the destructive rhetoric that has surrounded American education over the past decade is equalled only by the continuing decline of economic support for education in this country?

Our first answer is to return to what we said earlier. If for no other reason, teachers need to be involved in order to defend themselves and their students against inappropriate assessment instruments. Second, we are professionals and must refuse to give in to ignorance or political manipulation. But beyond that, honest, well-planned assessment, carefully evaluated by those directly responsible for instruction and curriculum does offer us the possibility to do a better job. I do not think any of us needs assessment projects to tell us that schools are not teaching students as well as we might like. Thus we do not need assessment to tell us that there is a problem. Rather, we need assessment projects that might help us identify specific elements of teaching and learning that need to be changed.

The Fredonia assessment offers some ideas for the kinds of instruments faculty might create to shape their own assessment projects and suggests some very clear directions we might take to improve the quality of our students learning. Furthermore, as we intend to explain in the next few pages, portfolio assessment, carefully created and implemented, can be one of the most constructive instruments in qualitative assessment. More directly, in the face of the negatives implied above, it is essential that faculties take charge of assessment and create their own instruments *before* something is imposed on them.

Additionally, we know now that faculty development workshops can have an observable effect on instruction. We know that students can and will improve as writers if writing across the curriculum is actually implemented instead of simply being talked about. We know that our system of lecturing and testing appears to reinforce the learning of literal facts but apparently does little to help students become more powerful thinkers and doers. We know that science courses stressing large amounts of discrete facts appear to have little effect on a student's understanding of the nature of science, and that mathematics courses that stress formulaic approaches to solving problems do little to improve students' understanding of mathematics as a discipline or to help them become more adept at solving problems. Also, even with respect to the specific contents of a given course or discipline, it appears clear that students retain very few of those facts that seemed to control the courses while they were taking them. Finally, a good assessment project may also reveal, as it did at Fredonia, that we are not nearly as successful in accomplishing some of our goals as we might wish to pretend. Anyone involved with assessment needs to be prepared to hear some news s/he may not wish to hear.

Our own major interest in the project was and is how it will affect our teaching and our students' learning. And it has. But perhaps the most significant change that has occurred so far has been a direct result of the ironic contradiction that occurs when one considers the difference between students' performance on the writing exam versus the reading exam.

Perhaps because my own major interests lie in the areas of metacognition, reading, and writing, it should be little surprise that I disliked our writing exam from the very beginning, even though I chaired the subcommittee responsible for creating it. Asking our students to engage in a significant act of writing in a fifty-minute period, and then judging that as though it represents real writing borders on a kind of lunacy. We knew from the start that the fifty-minute time limitation, the fact that students did not have time to prewrite, write, receive feedback, and revise all combined to put the students in the middle of an artificial writing activity. But even with all these problems, our results indicated that students improved in this kind of writing, suggesting that our Writing-Across-the-Curriculum efforts had some positive effect. Even so, one cannot create such an assessment tool and not also be haunted by a statement like the following. " 'I just don't get it,' said Ruby, a senior at a major state university in the Lower 48. 'In the writing classes, they tell you how important it is to do all this prewriting and revision stuff. Then they give you an exit test where you can't use any of it' " (Wauters 1991, 57).

As has already been mentioned, at the very beginning of the creation of the writing test, we had agreed that portfolios containing student writing over a period of years offered one of the best ways to go about evaluating their writing, but now we became more committed than ever to the idea because we saw that a carefully planned portfolio requirement might not only provide data useful in program assessment (Ewell 1991, 46). More importantly to many of us, such a project might help students become better writers, readers, and thinkers. Consequently, some of us had long ago decided to try to implement a collegewide portfolio requirement consisting of selected pieces of a student's writing over a period of three to four years: these collections of student work might best serve as the instrument for assessing their growth as writers because they would contain writing that students had an opportunity to shape and revise.

Only after the fact, however, did it occur to us that portfolios like this might be shaped in a variety of ways. Students might add critiques of their writing, looking back at what they produced over several years in order to establish a reflective, metacognitive consciousness of their thinking processes and/or the changes in these processes they might constructively undertake. If students had to maintain such portfolios in any given discipline, wherein those portfolios might be shaped in ways most appropriate to the learning demanded in the discipline, the portfolios might serve as instruments for both individual and programmatic assessment. Equally important, the portfolio idea lends itself to helping students examine their own reading, writing, and thinking processes; it gives them an opportunity to examine their own intellectual growth over a period of years; and it gives them an opportunity to see the areas in literacy and thinking in which they need further work. In short, portfolios lend themselves powerfully to outcomes-based assessment.

Having said all that, let me add that designing a portfolio requirement at any level is very complex and needs to be begun with great care. If I have learned nothing else as a teacher and as one interested in assessment and outcomes-based education it is this: never try to do everything at once; keep it simple at first; and make very sure you know what you are trying to achieve before you implement any approach. It is absolutely crucial to be "'clear on a more-or-less campuswide basis about why assessment is being undertaken, who is to be assessed, and what educational outcomes are to be assessed. An inadequate conceptual foundation for an assessment program will produce confusion, anxiety, and more heat than light'" (Apers, et al. quoting Terenzini 1990, 476).

Portfolios and Program Assessment

From the outset, let us be clear about the following. *First*, this discussion of portfolios is not intended to suggest that we were dissatisfied with the instruments used in the GCP assessment—quite the contrary. We are not suggesting that portfolios are the only useful instruments for assessment of student learning. We will, however, make the case that portfolios might form the center of an any ongoing system of either programmatic or individual assessment. *Second*, we are not in favor of gatekeeping devices; improve teaching and the gates will be unnecessary. *Third*, although many portfolio assessment systems presently focus primarily on assessing student improvement as writers, with the portfolios most often tied directly to first-year, required composition courses and, occasionally, some writing-intensive courses, courses in disciplines other than English—we believe their usefulness extends well beyond assessing a single skill or course. *Fourth*, we are much impressed and encouraged by a considerably different approach to portfolio assessment as exemplified by the work done by faculty at the Evergreen State College, Olympia, Washington: This brave, and apparently successful, group wanted to measure cognitive development in their students over the four-year college experience. Using portfolio collections of student self-evaluations, they used a system of ratings based on Perry's developmental scale to score the writing selections (Thompson 1991; Perry 1970).

Our excitement about projects like the one conducted by the Evergreen group is not intended to minimize the importance of the more focused efforts directed at assessing growth in "Freshman Composition, ENG 101." We simply feel that the potential for portfolios goes well beyond a focus on writing, per se: Perhaps the greatest usefulness of portfolios will occur when their contents are directly related to student performance in academic programs and majors across the curriculum and over several years. Experiments like your own (yet to come) and those of institutions like Fredonia and Evergreen should eventually help us all to understand better what, exactly, it is that we and our students are doing.

What follows, then, is a step-by-step series of suggestions that we encourage you to consider as you begin to articulate your own portfolio requirement. Unfortunately, the step-by-step journey that is outlined next bears more similarity to Dorothy's journey through Oz than it does to a clearly drawn line on a map: Lions and tigers and assessors, oh my!

Following The Yellow Brick Road

Getting Started

Discuss the general concept with sympathetic members in your own discipline or department, and do not try to *convert* your colleagues.

Begin small, using your own classes and those of one or two cooperative colleagues to experiment with portfolios. This step should, necessarily, involve you and some colleagues in a discussion of the kinds of writing required in given courses and additional writing activities that might be appropriate in given courses. This will help significantly when you and others begin to shape the portfolios more specifically for programmatic assessment, because it will give you some sense of the kinds of things students might include in a portfolio and the kinds of student work that might most directly contribute to program assessment.

Try to engage a standing committee in your department, a curriculum committee perhaps, to help articulate the specific goals of the major (or program) you wish to assess. In many cases, this will introduce the first major obstacle in the process. It is not at all unusual to find out that while "everyone knows the objectives of the program, and everyone agrees on the skills or proficiencies that should characterize each successful undergraduate chemistry (or sociology, or philosophy) major," no one has articulated the specifics. In many academic majors, the course contents, directions of the major, and objectives have simply grown, somewhat like Topsy. Members of the discipline at large, some anomalous group or professional association, "agree" that x, y, and z are essential to a given major. Consequently, these courses are required of all undergraduates majoring in the discipline. But then, Professor Smith, a much-published and powerful personality convinces the department that his pet courses are at least as important as x, y, and z, so these become part of the major requirements. And of course, the department rebels know that their courses, intended to deconstruct the major itself and everything the establishment believes is necessary, must also be included. Pretty soon, in desperation, the requirements are discontinued and students are encouraged to take thirty credit hours from among a broad array of wonderful courses offered by the department.

Frankly, we are not terribly dismayed by such a system. Clearly some disciplines demand core requirements and a system of sequencing, but given the arguments that often surround such curricular decisions, we wonder just how clear any of this will ever be. The point, here, is this: until the program or major is defined in terms of observable, albeit qualitative, outcomes that are central to most of the courses in the program, there can be no programmatic assessment. Why? Because in fact, there is no program. An accidental or incidental amalgamation of courses all called *psychology courses* can hardly be called a "program." Nor can it be assessed.

Problems enter rather quickly and obviously at this point. In fact, it looks like a good reason to return to standardized multiple-choice exams and focus on discrete bits of information that are emphasized in isolated courses. Even though this is a fraudulent kind of assessment, at least it's possible to do it. But as most of us know, the discrete facts and unrelated pieces of information are the things we all forgot shortly after we graduated. So assessing this kind of learning is rather silly.

Articulating Objectives

All that we've said above pretty clearly suggests that members of the department or program will necessarily have to reflect on their own courses, looking beyond specific information, to identify the kinds of thinking they are trying to teach their students: what are the thought processes, abilities, and skills that underlie the discipline and most of the courses within it? Fortunately, as problematic as this stage is, it is not impossible and may be one of the most beneficial aspects of being involved in assessment. Students already know that relationships between and among courses are not particularly clear, or at least they do not always see the interrelationships. Instructors need to learn this so that they can begin to help make the interrelationships clearer, when they exist, and create them when it is appropriate.

Of course, you may find some of your colleagues ready to explain, with care and patience, that "you can't assess critical thinking or other complex kinds of reasoning because the students don't know enough yet. First you must teach them the basic facts of the discipline, and only later (in graduate school, we guess) will they know enough to do any complex thinking or reasoning." And it should come as no surprise that this kind of statement is reflected in what students apparently believe when they say that they cannot do something because they never took a course in it. But the fact is that most disciplines genuinely share more in common than is often realized and articulated. Most disciplines and academic programs emphasize (or *believe* they emphasize) some intermixture of the following: (1) critical/analytical thinking; (2) clear reasoning (logical, mathematical, scientific, analogic, metaphoric); (3) creative thinking; and (4) the ability to speak, listen, read, and write with "reasonable" proficiency in the discipline.

More specifically, most disciplines expect students to be able to read, comprehend, and comment articulately on literature in the field. In science and mathematics, students are expected to be able to "do" science and math (but so also are they expected to "do" history, sociology, philosophy . . . if they major in one of those disciplines).

The potential difficulties involved in this step of the process are precisely why each group needs to devise its own assessment program. By identifying the objectives and desired outcomes central to a given major or program, the faculty will necessarily gain a greater sense of their own mission. Likewise, once these have been identified, instructors can begin to examine their own courses to see to what extent they try to help students achieve such objectives or be able to produce specific outcomes.

Consequently, professional self-examination must follow the identification of objectives and outcomes that one wishes to assess. After all, if the instructors teaching the courses are not actively and consciously teaching students to achieve the central objectives of the discipline, why would anyone bother to assess whether or not they are learning them? (Unless, of course, it is to find out that they can already "do" whatever it is we want them to be able to "do," which would attest to the irrelevancy of the discipline, we suppose.) But a reminder of the Fredonia experience is in order—or perhaps just a reminder to use common sense: we already know that we are not doing an adequate job of teaching students to be literate, articulate participants in many of the fields they study. Therefore we first need to more clearly identify what it is we want them to learn as a result of our teaching. And then . . .

Instructors need to identify for themselves and for their colleagues, which activities/requirements in their courses contribute to helping students achieve which objectives, and what exactly will comprise the portfolios. While this step sometimes suggests the trammelling of academic freedom, it need not and should not do so. It is absolutely essential that everyone involved keep in mind the fact that the issue is programmatic assessment; it is not an attempt to point accusatory fingers at particular courses or faculty members. In most cases, faculty will find that key courses already require assignments that will fit naturally and usefully into programmatic assessment. And the portfolio entries need not always be directly tied to course requirements. The following questions might assist in such an examination:

1. How do lab reports (or analytical/critical essays) provide evidence that the fledgling scientist (or philosopher and so on) is doing or is learning to do science (or philosophy and so on): what are the specifics that will indicate a successful report versus a weak one; what activities in the course contribute to teaching the students how to do successful reports; what student work derives from the course that might be included in a portfolio?

2. At the time they declare their desire to major in a given field, should students be asked to write "entry papers" for inclusion in the portfolios? If you wish to find out about the nature of student attitudes toward a discipline, their reasons for choosing it (as opposed to our assumptions about why they have chosen it), what they want to learn—such entry papers are essential. Aside from providing valuable information about the students we are teaching in our courses, these entry papers allow teachers to more fully understand and deal with mismatches between student expectations and program objectives. Of course, it should be obvious that the entry papers must be carefully described in terms of how they are to be used within the portfolio and as part of the program assessment. If entry papers are required, will exit papers also be required? What will they help you find out?

3. Will it be helpful for the fledgling mathematicians or scientists to write descriptions of the processes they go through in solving problems or doing experiments (as opposed to simply including a lab report or mathematical solution)? Likewise, might it be helpful to have the sociology or philosophy students write personal narratives of how they approached understanding a major concept or how they approached a research project? Note, here, that these kinds of written assignments can easily be required *in addition* to the requirements and expectations within a given course. Instructors might simply tell students that during the course of the semester they must complete at least one of these kinds of narratives for inclusion in their portfolios; a failure to do so will affect the grade in the course. Again, any decision to include such writing in the portfolios must be driven by a prior decision about how the piece will be assessed and how it contributes to assessing the objectives of the program.

4. Should instructors or students decide which work is included in the portfolios (or should they work together to make such decisions)?

5. How much should be included in the portfolio? While one might think that "more is better," it is well to remember that someone is going to have to assess these portfolios, and that almost certainly means more than simply sitting down and reading quickly through the entries to form some generalized judgment (though holistic scoring will often be a significant part of the overall assessment of portfolios). Since most students take courses in a major over a period of about five to six semesters (using the first year or two to complete general college requirements), would it make sense to require that each portfolio contain six entries: an entry paper, papers written in at least four different courses in the major, and an exit paper?

6. Should the portfolio entries be carefully prescribed and described so that each student's portfolio will essentially contain the same amount and kinds of work that another student's portfolio contains? For programmatic assessment, it seems clear to us that this is probably necessary in order for valid, reliable judgements of portfolios to result. For example, though possibilities are endless, students might be expected to include in their portfolios an entry paper, a description of how they approached solving a problem (mastering a complex concept, developing a skill . . .); a research paper (or critical/analytical paper); an out-of-class essay exam (or, perhaps—dare we say it—a creative paper?); a paper explaining the most significant or complex aspect of the discipline they have been studying; and a self-reflective exit paper. Obviously, the contents of the portfolio will be essentially prescribed by the specific objectives/performances/outcomes that the group has decided to assess.

7. Should portfolio entries be limited to written work, or might it be appropriate in some disciplines to include photographs or videotapes of student's productions or of students actually doing something in a lab or teaching situation?

Scoring Portfolios

Now we come to the sticky question of scoring portfolios: that is, having created a system of qualitative, subjective assessment, how does one go about "objectifying" it in any sense of the term *objective*? Needless to say, it is best to start by being at home with relativism and remaining highly conscious of the purpose of the assessment. In programmatic assessment, you begin by (1) clarifying what it is you want to assess; (2) carefully constructing your instruments (in this case the portfolios and their prescribed contents); (3) defining what you consider to accurately represent weak, adequate, and strong performances for each of the pieces required in the portfolio; and (4) articulating highly specified criteria for scoring the quality of performance. Remember the importance of the grid we created for the Fredonia assessment project (See Appendix A).

Once the system for scoring has been articulated and agreed upon, it is time to teach yourselves how to score the portfolio entries, a process that will take considerable time, commitment, and the ability to compromise. Quite simply, no matter how well you have planned things up to this point, the entire project will fall apart unless this part of the process is carefully and openly addressed, so it is worth examining what is involved rather carefully.

First, remember that you are not going to score all the portfolios of all the students. Ask your local statistician to tell you what percentage of your majors you must score in order to have a statistically reliable sample. Second, do not underestimate the amount of time and energy the scoring will take. Scorers who are forced to do too much at a given sitting or over an extended period of time will score differently when they are tired (or fed up) than when they began the process. Third, create a system of subgroups. Staying with the example we have already created in which the portfolios contain six entries, it would make sense to create five to six subgroups to score each of the separate entries. Given the description we provided above, one subgroup of scorers might be responsible for comparing the entry and exit papers (unless, of course, it was more appropriate to establish criteria for scoring these two pieces separately). Each of the other subgroups would then be responsible for scoring one specific kind of entry.

Once the groups are created, the training begins. Over and over each scorer will have to be reminded that the scoring system is directly related to the criteria that have been established. It is all too easy to believe that one is scoring a piece of writing to examine the individual's expertise in problem solving when, in fact, the scorer is focusing on punctuation or syntax. Before the scoring is even begun, it is wise for each group to reexamine the criteria and discuss them. Following this discussion, each member of the group begins to score an identical set of selected portfolio entries. Next, the scores are charted, and each individual scorer *explains* his/her score.

This is "sticky wicket" time, indeed, or at least it can be. We italicized the word *explains* because the scorers must avoid defensiveness, argument, sarcasm, personal attacks, and homicide. The key element in this process is coming to a mutual understanding of what is *really* intended by the criteria that were previously established. What seemed perfectly clear before the process began suddenly becomes muddy, and it is essential that the mud be eliminated.

Consider what might occur when a group of scorers used the following criteria to score a portfolio entry focusing on problem solving in which the writer was to solve some specified problem and then produce a brief narrative explaining the steps s/he employed in the process of solving it:

A. The writer clearly articulates each step of the problem-solving process in which s/he engaged.

B. The writer articulates most of the important steps in which s/he engaged, but does not present a full explanation of the solution.

C. The writer is unable to articulately explain the problem-solving process in which s/he engaged.

After scoring an entry, using these criteria, one scorer gives the entry a grade of A, another gives it a grade of B, and a third gives it a grade of C. Believe us it happens! And at the beginning of the process it occurs more often than you might expect. But why?

The explanation is relatively simple, and very important. One scorer explains the A as follows: "This entry is exceptionally well-written; in fact the student writes better than most of the students I teach. The explanation is interesting, clear, and the student clearly arrived at the correct answer to the problem." The scorer who assigned the B says, "What you say is true, but the fact is that, even though this is well-written, the writer does not really explain the reasoning process in the step-by-step fashion demanded by the criterion. S/he states many of the steps, but not all of them." And finally the scorer who assigned a C says, "In a sense I agree with both of you, but the criteria clearly say that the student is to *explain* the process. But this writer simply *states* a few important steps and leaves the reader to figure it out." And we have not included the fourth scorer who gave the paper a score of A because "the solution suggests genuine insight into the problem-solving process, considerably more than I generally see in our students, and there is no way you can give this a low score."

What is important to note here is not which of the individuals is right or wrong—remember we began with a commitment to relativism. In a sense, each of them may be right. But in order to score portfolios, in order to assess anything, the scorers must come to full and conscious agreement on what they *really* mean by those criteria they were applying. The trick is to score the entries in direct relationship to an agreed upon definition of the criteria. And this means, at the beginning of this training process, that most of the criteria that had been originally articulated will undergo laborious reexamination. Indeed, it is not unusual, at this stage, for the individuals to find it necessary to define words that they thought were clearly agreed upon prior to the act of scoring: "What is the difference between 'stating' and 'explaining'? Since it is the writer's prerogative to decide what process s/he engaged in, how can you say that s/he did not include steps in which s/he engaged? Are you not explaining the steps in which *you* engaged?" "To what extent does it matter if the solution is right or wrong if the explanation of the steps is well done?"

In some cases, the group may decide to rewrite criteria to make them clearer or more explicit and eliminate as much confusion as possible. For example, referring to the sample criteria presented above, the group would almost certainly want to rewrite criterion C because the split infinitive "to articulately explain" creates a nonparallel structure (and different meaning) from what is probably intended by the use of the word "explain" in criteria A and B. In other cases, certain criteria may simply have to be eliminated because the scorers cannot mutually agree on their application.

While this may seem like an almost impossible morass, it is not. Even in scoring the reflective thinking exam in the Fredonia assessment, the exam that caused us the most difficulty in scoring, we eventually managed to arrive at a sense of mutual agreement about what we "meant" by the criteria. It is important to keep in mind that this kind of assessment is difficult (and even threatening) precisely because it relies on language and subjective, qualitative decisions about the exact meaning of specific words. One can hardly engage in this kind of assessment without coming to grips with the confusion and sometimes deceit that hides beneath statistical results on standardized, "objective" exams. Quite simply, if it can be this difficult for a small group of highly intelligent people to agree on the meaning of a given term as they apply it to a piece of writing, how much more difficult must it be for the students who must decipher the hidden biases and idiosyncratic meanings of the people who create "objective" reading comprehension tests, or worse yet, tests that rely on analogies? And how much harder to believe that a multiple-choice test that gives you a "critical-thinking" score is addressing relevant criteria or criteria relevant to your college's program.

It should be clear from the above that the Scoring System itself must be clearly articulated and mutually understood. For example, if the group decided to use letter grades (A, B, C, D . . .), the letters must eventually be correlated with numbers (A = 5 points . . .). Using this system, scorers must remember that the score of A is related to the stated criteria and *not* to the A that might be given for work in a course in which the criteria might very well be different. Of course, why not simply use numbers instead of letters? And you may find that this works for you. In the Fredonia Assessment, different subgroups used different systems; and by now it should be obvious that the essential element is having all the scorers of a given test understand and be comfortable with whatever system you employ.

Additionally, you must decide how many scoring differentiations you wish to make: one might argue that a scoring system ranging from 1 to 15, clearly related to fifteen carefully differentiated degrees of performance would be better than one ranging from 1 to 6. The finer the differentiations, the more statistically revealing the scores will be. Unfortunately, the finer the distinctions, the more difficult they are for the scorers to make.

And it is important to consider whether or not a *holistic* system of scoring will be helpful, in addition to the itemized scores tied to specific criteria. In the Fredonia assessment, for example, each scorer began by giving each protocol on the writing test a holistic score. In this case, each scorer was directed to read the protocol twice and immediately give it a score ranging from A to E (including pluses and minuses) based on an overall impression of the general success of the piece of writing. We later found such a system quite useful in judging the relative merit of the itemized criteria and settling disputes between scorers.

While itemized criteria can clearly be important for certain kinds of assessment, we do not mean to imply that they are always necessary. At Miami of Ohio, a university conducting a variety of interesting assessment experiments, scorers examined student writing portfolios in a global manner. As they read through the students' portfolios, the participating faculty were asked

> not to assess *how well* we had met the goals, but rather *where* they saw evidence of an assignment that required skills or abilities that the program faculty viewed as important; for example, assignments that gave evidence of emphasis on "critical thinking," or reflected our "quantitative reasoning across the curriculum" effort. In describing "what" we were doing, rather than "how well" we were doing, we fostered discussion that took on a less defensive tone. This permitted a level of sharing that had not occurred in any of our previous discussions of assessment. (Amiran, Schilling, and Schilling forthcoming, 12)

One might clearly apply holistic scoring to find out whether or not the academic program is asking students to write "much" or "enough," whether or not students are encouraged or assisted in any kind of revision process, and whether or not students appear to improve as writer/thinkers over a given period of time. Or scorers might assess portfolios descriptively: What kinds of thinking are evidenced in the portfolio contents? As always, the central problem of how any of this is done depends entirely on *what* it is you are trying to find out.

But we must still address some other issues involved in scoring: How many scorers need to score a given protocol (in the Fredonia project we agreed that two scorers would score each protocol)? And what happens when scores for a given protocol seriously conflict: that is, when one scorer scores an item as an *A* but another gives it a *C–*. Obviously, one solution would be to simply average the scores, but such a system is likely to result in most scores ending up in some sort of midrange. Several approaches to the problem suggest themselves: First, the two scorers might discuss their scores trying to determine whether or not each is genuinely committed to a score and can explain its relationship to the stated criteria. Second, in the event that this does not lead to a relatively immediate change by one of the scorers, a third reader can be used to settle the dispute: whichever of the original scores is closest to that of the third reader is averaged with that of the third reader for the official score.

Clearly, it is important to remember that we agreed to accept a relativistic world: qualitative assessment is not "objectively" perfect, but what is, really? In the Fredonia experience, we found the process of training ourselves to score to be the most gruelling part of the entire process. But once it was finished, we were ready to move beyond our self-training and begin the real scoring.

Additional Considerations

So far so good? Maybe, but not quite. Here are some considerations that have yet to be confronted. For example, what about control groups?

It may appear, at first, that program assessment demands the establishment of some sort of control group against which to measure growth and improvement in a given area. Otherwise, all we will have at the end of this long, laborious process is a group of scores unrelated to a group of randomly selected portfolios. To be able to say that a given portfolio is clearly "better" than another hardly provides the information necessary for the evaluation of a program. In the Fredonia assessment, our design included the use of a control group from another college whose student body was similar to our own (based on entrance requirements) but whose general college program was quite different. And while such a design may significantly increase the kinds of information assessments might reveal, it also creates some significant complexities.

At Fredonia we felt the need for a control group because we were not simply trying to find out if students improved in certain areas. Without a control group, we could not have found out if the General College Program, per se, was affecting student learning (as opposed to the growth one might find just because students happen to be in college). Depending on what one is trying to assess, however, control groups may be unnecessary, as Amiran, Schilling, and Schilling point out in their comparative discussion of assessment projects at Fredonia and Western College (at Miami University of Ohio):

> Fredonia began with a focus on locally constructed assessment for an internal audience but found it needed a comparative study with an external institution. Western College began with an external focus on nationally normed means of assessment, moved through its collaboration with Fredonia and on to a purely local, internally oriented descriptive approach. It is not a matter of finding what is right for each institution, but of understanding that different foci are right for the same institution at different stages in its assessment process. If Western had not begun with normed instruments it would not have appreciated its need for descriptive measures. If Fredonia had not undertaken its comparative study, it would not have been properly cautious in interpreting its local results. Comparative and local, external and internal foci, outcomes and activities, judgements by others and oneself—these alternate as figure and ground in the assessment "picture," and it may be important to retain one's ability to keep reversing them. It is also important to affirm the value of the complexity that baffles us in assessing liberal education: we cannot draw Leviathan with a hook (forthcoming, 18).

Control Groups?

Toward the end of this chapter, we discuss methods of using the portfolios without control groups, but we believe that control groups may, in fact, be necessary to achieve certain ends: that is, especially if the assessment intends to compare one program against another, a demonstrably different one, and probably when the assessment is primarily directed at curriculum revision. To establish such a control group, you must find an institution whose student profile is similar to your own but whose program is significantly different. Second, those who teach in the program must agree to implement portfolio requirements exactly as you have defined them, which is no small task in and of itself. Third, the scorers at your institution must agree to score the portfolios that have been completed by the students at the control institution. To say that the problems of working out all the details involved here are significant is a gross understatement.

A little backtracking will be helpful here. Begin by reconsidering the purpose of the assessment project. As we have stated several times, our purpose for assessment focuses on improving teaching and learning. At present, anyone who has conducted the project as we have thus far described it would be in position of deciding that students are generally performing well, adequately, or inadequately as determined by a variety of measures used for scoring the various kinds of entries within the portfolios. But if your needs demand a control group, must you necessarily go outside your own institution?

Not necessarily. Indeed, a somewhat obvious solution immediately presents itself. For this kind of assessment, you must identify one group of students as the initial group to be assessed and another group of your own students to be the control group. And this system suggests several possible alternatives depending on the make up of your institution. In some larger institutions, for example, a given major or program may offer several distinct "tracks" for students. English Education majors might take a required sequence of courses that significantly differ from those taken by other English majors. In psychology, students heading toward clinical work in the field might take a sequence of courses significantly different from those more interested in research.

More often than not, however, this is unlikely to be the case; students in a given major or program are most likely to take courses that are either distinctly similar or have distinctly similar requirements. In these cases, we suggest that a group of students entering a program or major in a given semester be identified to comprise the control group and that a group of students entering the program or major at least two years later be identified as the experimental group whose progress will be measured against the first group. Still some very significant issues need to be resolved.

At this point, having established a control group and a second group with which to contrast scores, not much has really been accomplished. Consider this hypothetical situation. Group 1 is identified as all those entering the program in September 1994; Group 2 is composed of students entering the program in September 1996. By 1998, the assessors should be in the position of making some powerful judgements about the program, right? Wrong.

By simply establishing two different groups, one must ask what exactly is being compared? In this case, assuming that the program has remained essentially the same over the four-year period, almost no conclusions can be drawn about the program. If the program remains substantially the same, an improvement in student scores would simply indicate that the students had somehow, on their own, done better than their predecessors. If they perform poorly, one might assume that this group of students was simply not as capable as previous groups. In either case, little could be said about the program.

And this returns us to a beginning point. The whole reason for the endeavor, in the first place, is to improve instruction. The idea is to make changes in instruction and to assess whether or not the changes contribute to greater student growth and learning. Consequently, once the portfolio assessment has begun, the faculty should immediately begin the process of redesigning all elements of the program or major or courses that they feel might improve the quality of student learning. By beginning such redesigning immediately, faculty would have a two-year period to prepare to implement changes; thus the second groups of students would be exposed to a program that was significantly different in its attempt to help students improve at the kinds of skills, processes, thinking that the program intends to develop and that the portfolios are designed to measure.

In the short term, what we have described may suggest a kind of madness. The key, here, is to remember the purpose of assessment. First and foremost, it should be aimed at improving instruction rather than simply providing state agencies with "proof" that the program is an effective one through some series of short-term, deceitful assessment instruments. While the system we propose clearly involves long-term involvement and takes a considerable amount of time to complete, these qualities must be recognized as inherent in assessment projects that assess anything of importance. In fact, the system we have just described would be an ongoing one with new groups being identified every two years, or at least as often as the ongoing assessment leads to changes in instruction. We may find out, of course, that nothing changes over time and that all the instructional changes that have been implemented result in no improvements in students' performances. Obviously, this would be disturbing, but important, information. At the very least, it might suggest that the institution needed to look outside itself for help in improving the program or major. More likely, however, the ongoing system of assessment would allow those teaching the program to monitor their continued commitment to good teaching and document needs for changes in what is actually going on in courses or changes resulting from changing student populations.

No Control Groups

While control groups may be essential for certain kinds of assessment, we strongly agree with Minda Rae Amiran who so significantly assisted us in this section of the book. We paraphrase her at length, here, because her comments were so helpful to us. She points out that a portfolio being used to assess a major in a discipline like chemistry would not demand the creation of control groups: it would be clear that "any chemistry the students have learned they have learned through that department (or possibly in related internships or summer jobs). In a department with a defined curriculum, there is no reason why actual portfolios can't be compared to faculty-developed pictures of what a student should know or be able to do as a result of the program." Clearly, she goes on, if students evidence a lack of knowledge or ability deemed essential by the faculty, the department can begin to change its curriculum and/or system of instruction. And while Amiran reiterates that "curricular changes" might be best approached through the use of a control group, she suggests some ways of avoiding the "laborious steps" we itemized in the above section on establishing control groups:

> One could have students collect everything they wrote to answer questions such as [the following]: "How much and what kinds of writing are our students actually doing?" "What kinds of critical thinking are our students engaging in?" "What kinds of problems (texts, theories, authors) can our students address?" One could have students compile selective portfolios with reflections to assess the successes of the program in stimulating the making of connections and metacognition. One could specify the ingredients of portfolios to judge the general level of senior-year seminar papers or projects as compared to sophomore-year research papers. (personal letter, 1992)

Student Commitment

To paraphrase Dorothy, it really does not look much like Kansas, does it? One final qualification must yet be made, however. What good does any of this do if the students do not take it seriously, if the work in the portfolio is viewed by the students as some sort of busy work imposed on them by the institution, as an activity that has nothing to do with their own learning and growth? What if they "borrow" papers from other students in order to fulfill the portfolio requirement? And if they have had the opportunity to work with peer editors to get help from writing tutors, whose work is it that is being evaluated?

Let us take these concerns one at a time. First, we believe that if the portfolios are not directly tied to the students' growth and learning, then there is no reason to expect the students to take them seriously. Portfolio assessment that is divorced from the students' growth invites carelessness and lack of commitment from the students (at best) and plagiarism (at worst). But it has been our experience to find that when students see the contents of a portfolio to be directly tied to their own learning and growth, when the portfolios function as an important part of their discussions with their teachers and advisors, students take them very seriously. And it is for this reason that the next chapter on the role of portfolios in the learning and assessment of the individual student is particularly important to us.

Let us not forget that last question: whose paper is it, really, when the writer has received considerable editorial assistance? The manuscript for this book, for example, has gone through several drafts. We have received feedback from readers and editorial assistance from friends, spouses, and colleagues. Indeed, we quote extensively from Minda Rae Amiran's critical commentary in one of our drafts. Praeger Publishing Company assigned a professional editor to assist in the production of this book. And quite frankly, we appreciated all that help.

Nevertheless, we still think that this is our book. Does it not make more sense for us to try to teach our students to be a part of our professional world instead of locking them outside of it with demands that most of us would find ludicrous? What good is assessment of any kind if it does not contribute to students' learning?

ENGAGED TEACHING AND LEARNING: STAKING A CLAIM FOR A NEW PERSPECTIVE ON PROGRAM QUALITY

J.G. HAWORTH AND C.F. CONRAD

In this chapter we stake a claim that the engagement theory advances a new perspective on program quality—one that not only builds on and brings together disparate literatures but also extends and deepens current understanding of program quality. We do this by first examining various writings and studies in the program quality and other higher education literatures that support the engagement theory. We then discuss the major ways in which the theory extends and re-envisions current understandings of program quality.

The Engagement Theory Builds On, and Brings Together, Current Views of Program Quality

The engagement theory finds some support in the literature on program quality. Other higher education literatures—notably those on teaching and learning, college impact, adult education, leadership, and organizational culture—supply additional support for it as well. Following, we build upon and integrate selected studies and writings to document the broad range of support for the engagement theory. We begin with the literature on program quality and then turn to other relevant higher education literatures.

Support from the Program Quality Literature

Support for some of the attributes in the engagement theory exists in the program quality literature. Regarding the first cluster of attributes—diverse and invested participants—few scholars have emphasized the significance of diverse faculty and diverse students to program quality (Association of American Colleges 1992). Several, however, have stressed the importance of faculty commitment and student involvement and effort, which are clearly encompassed within our concept of engagement. For instance, in their study of more than two hundred chemistry, history, and psychology programs, Mary Jo Clark, Rodney Hartnett, and Leonard Baird (1976) identified faculty concern for students and student commitment (motivation) as two key features of high-quality doctoral programs. In other major national studies, Alexander Astin (1977, 1980, 1993) and George Kuh (1981) found that students who become actively involved in their learning have higher-quality experiences in college, and C. Robert Pace (1980, 1986) found that the quality of student effort significantly enhances students' learning experiences. Moreover, two groups of researchers have identified administrative leadership as an attribute of high-quality academic programs (Clark, Hartnett, and Baird 1976; Young, Blackburn, Conrad, and Cameron 1989).

Two studies in the program quality literature support the importance of participatory cultures, the second cluster of attributes in our theory. George Kuh (1981) lends support to our findings that

Reprinted from *Emblems of Quality in Higher Education: Developing and Sustaining High-Quality Programs*, by Jennifer Grant Haworth and Clifton Conrad (1996), Allyn and Bacon, a Pearson Education Company.

a shared program direction and a community of learners are important features of a high-quality program. In his monograph, *Indices of Quality in the Undergraduate Experience*, Kuh (1981) concluded that both a "clarity of purpose" (at the institutional, rather than the program, level) and a "generative learning community" enrich the quality of students' experiences in undergraduate education. Similarly, in their review of educational quality in the major, the Association of American Colleges (1992) identified clearly stated program goals and a "supportive community" as two key elements of "strong" undergraduate programs. We found no support in the program quality literature concerning the importance of a risk-taking environment.

Support for the third cluster of attributes in the theory—interactive teaching and learning—is likewise thin in the program quality literature. Only out-of-class activities enjoys direct empirical support in the published discourse on program quality in higher education (Kuh 1981). However, critical dialogue and mentoring receive indirect support in various studies and writings that emphasize the importance of informal faculty-student interaction in maintaining high-quality programs (Association of American Colleges 1992; Kuh 1981; Student Task Force on Education at Stanford 1973).

Several reports and scholarly writings provide support for the fourth cluster of attributes in our theory: connected program requirements. C. W. Minkel and Mary P. Richards (1986) identified a core of planned course work and a culminating experience (a thesis, project, or internship) as important attributes of high-quality master's programs. Similarly, the Council of Graduate Schools (1981, 3) stated that "quality" master's programs require students to complete a "pre-planned and coherent sequence" of courses as well as a "component demonstrating creativity" such as a thesis or internship. Other scholars have also argued for the salience of these requirements (Association of American Colleges 1992; Ames 1979; Glazer 1986).

Finally, adequate resources—the fifth cluster of attributes in the engagement theory—has an extensive base of support in the program quality literature. Since the early 1960s, many scholars have conducted studies that have established empirical relationships between institutional and program resources—such as expenditures per student, faculty salaries, research funds, and physical facilities (including institutional library holdings)—and programs considered to be of high quality (Abbott and Barlow 1972; Astin and Solmon 1981; Beyer and Snipper 1974; Cartter 1966; Clark, Hartnett, and Baird 1976; Conrad and Blackburn 1985a, 1986; Janes 1969; Jones, Lindzey, and Coggeshall 1982; Jordan 1963; Lavendar, Mathers, and Pease 1971; Morgan, Kearney, and Regens 1976; Perkins and Snell 1962). Also, many scholars have argued that financial and physical resources are critical to maintaining high-quality programs.

More broadly, the engagement theory builds on all five of the major views of program quality that we derived from the literature. The first cluster of attributes—diverse and invested faculty and students—finds selective support in the Faculty View, the Student Quality-and-Effort View, and the Multi-Dimensional/Multi-Level View. The fourth cluster of attributes—connected program requirements—enjoys support in the Curriculum Requirements View as well as the Multi-Dimensional/Multi-Level View. The fifth cluster of attributes in the theory—adequate program resources—finds strong support in the Resources View of program quality.

Support in Other Literatures

In broad strokes, there is considerable support for our engagement theory in the higher education reform, teaching and learning, college impact, adult education, leadership, and organizational theory literatures. In particular, research and scholarship in these literatures strongly supports several clusters in the theory—notably participatory cultures and interactive teaching and learning—that have not received widespread attention in the literature on program quality.

The first cluster of attributes—diverse and invested participants—finds selective support in the teaching and learning, college impact, and leader ship literatures. These literatures are replete with scholarly writings and empirical studies that emphasize the importance of faculty and students who bring diverse scholarly, educational, and professional experiences to the higher learning (see, for example, Astin 1993; Conrad, Haworth, and Millar 1993; Gamson 1992; Minnich 1990; Pascarella and Terenzini 1991). In particular, authors of several major college impact studies have identified numerous positive effects that accrue to students who interact with faculty and other students from backgrounds different than their own (Astin 1993; Newman and Newman 1978; Pascarella and Terenzini 1991).[1] Moreover, the teaching and learning and college impact literatures provide considerable evidence supporting the importance of faculty and student involvement—and, by implication, engagement—in the teaching and learning process (Astin 1980, 1984, 1993; Chickering and Gamson 1987; Conrad, Haworth, and Millar 1993; Feldman and Newcomb 1969; Pace 1984; Parker and Schmidt 1982; Pascarella and Terenzini 1991).

In the extensive literature on leadership in higher education, we also found support for the critical role that engaged leaders play in developing and sustaining high-quality programs. This literature supports our proposition that engaged leaders not only champion their programs to internal and external audiences, but that they also tend to view leadership as a team effort in which they encourage and support faculty, student, alumni, and employer participation in various informal program leadership roles. Some scholars provide exhortatory as well as empirical support for the effectiveness of a "team-oriented" or "participatory" approach to leadership (Bensimon and Neumann 1993; Chaffee and Tierney 1988; Eisenstat and Cohen 1990; Gabarro 1987; Seymour 1992).

The second cluster of attributes in the theory—participatory cultures—also enjoys a broad base of support in the teaching and learning, college impact, and organizational theory literatures. To begin with, several works buttress our finding that a shared program direction is, in the words of Arthur Chickering and Zelda Gamson (1987), important to "good practice" in academic programs. Moreover, many scholarly publications emphasize the value of learning communities at both the undergraduate and graduate levels (Carnegie Foundation for the Advancement of Teaching 1990; Chickering and Gamson 1987; Conrad, Haworth, and Millar 1993; Gabelnick, MacGregor, Matthews, and Smith 1990; Gaff 1991; Gamson 1984; Hill 1985; Palmer 1983; Spitzberg and Thorndike 1992; Study Group on the Conditions of Excellence in Higher Education 1984). For example, in their monograph on learning communities, Faith Gabelnick and her colleagues identified a number of student outcomes associated with learning communities that dovetail with our findings. These outcomes include higher levels of academic achievement (as measured by college grade point averages), a greater appreciation for collaborative approaches to learning, improved self-confidence and self-esteem, a stronger appreciation for other students' perspectives in the learning process, and an improved ability to make "intellectual connections" across disparate texts and courses (1990, 63–71).

In sifting through these diverse literatures, we identified only a few works that highlighted the importance of a risk-taking environment. To wit Parker Palmer (1983) underscores the need to create "open" and "hospitable" learning spaces in which students feel free to receive each other's "newborn ideas with openness and care" as well as to "make the painful things possible, things without which no learning can occur—things like exposing ignorance, testing tentative hypotheses, challenging false and partial information, and mutual criticism of thought" (74). In their studies of effective teachers, Joseph Lowman (1984) and Ken Macrorie (1984) also provide empirical support for a risk-taking environment. Lowman (1984), for example, identified a number of behaviors that "superb" college professors use to build rapport and encourage risk-taking in the classroom, while Macrorie (1984) found that "exemplary" teachers consistently built classroom climates in which students were enabled "to take chances that sometimes result[ed] in failure" and were encouraged "to use their mistakes productively" (229).

Feminist literature also includes publications that directly or indirectly emphasize the importance of learning communities and a risk-taking environment (Belenky, Clinchy, Goldberger, and Tarule 1986; Katz 1985; Klein 1987; Schneidewind 1987; Shrewsbury 1987). More broadly, there is a considerable quantity of feminist literature that advocates a pedagogy that is anchored in empowerment, collaborative learning, and "creative community" (Shrewsbury 1987, 8).

Many scholarly writings and empirical studies also provide a wide range of support for integrative teaching and learning, the third cluster of attributes in the theory. In the teaching and learning, higher education reform, college impact, and adult education literatures, we identified many publications that supported all five of the attributes in this cluster. Moreover, we identified numerous writings that support the value of an interactive approach to teaching and learning (Boyer 1987; Bruffee

1987, 1993; Chickering and Gamson 1987; Cross 1987; McKeachie 1969; Palmer 1983; Study Group on the Conditions of Excellence in American Higher Education 1984).

Referred to throughout the teaching and learning literature as "critical awareness" (Gamson 1984), "reflective dialogue" (Schön 1987), or "dialogical interaction" (Freire 1970), there are myriad writings and studies that emphasize the importance of critical dialogue among faculty and students (Brookfield 1987; Bruffee 1993; Conrad, Haworth, and Millar 1993; Gabelnick, MacGregor, Matthews, and Smith 1990; Kurfiss 1988; Shor 1980, 1987; Shrewsbury 1987). For the most part, these writings stress the need for faculty and students to engage in ongoing conversations in which they question their own and others' assumptions in order to enhance and expand their awareness of complex issues. For example, in their case studies of "liberatory" undergraduate programs, feminist classrooms, and "exemplary" teachers, Gamson (1984), Belenky et al. (1986), and Macrorie (1984) sketch portraitures of faculty and student engagement in critical dialogue and emphasize the positive effects that such dialogues have on student learning and development.

In reviewing the higher education reform, teaching and learning, and college impact literatures, we also identified many articles and books that underscored the value of integrative learning. For instance, in *Seven Principles for Good Practice in Undergraduate Education*, Arthur Chickering and Zelda Gamson highlight the need for active learning, an integral component of integrative learning: "Learning is not a spectator sport. Students do not learn much just by sitting in class listening to teachers, memorizing prepackaged assignments, and spitting out answers. They must talk about what they are learning, write about it, relate it to past experiences, apply it to their daily lives. They must make what they learn part of themselves" (1987, 3). We also took note of many other authors who share Chickering and Gamson's assessment, most of whom provide empirical support to back up their position (Association of American College's Task Force on General Education 1988; Astin 1993; Bonwell and Eison 1991; Conrad, Haworth, and Millar 1993; Cross 1987; Fisher 1978; Gamson 1984; Light 1990; Macrorie 1984; McKeachie 1969; Meyers and Jones, 1993; Palmer 1983; Pascarella and Terenzini 1991; Sorcinelli 1991; Study Group on the Conditions of Excellence in American Higher Education 1984; Wulff and Nyquist 1988).

We found considerable support for mentoring, the third attribute in this cluster, in the teaching and learning and college impact literatures (Blackwell 1989; Hoyte and Collett 1993; Jacobi 1991; Light 1992; Lipschutz 1993; Lyons, Scroggins, and Rule 1990; Merriam, 1983; Pascarella and Terenzini 1991; Schön 1987; Sorcinelli 1991). Numerous college impact studies, for example, emphasize the positive effects that frequent and informal interactions with at least one faculty member have on student learning and development (Astin 1993; Hoyte and Collett 1993; Pascarella 1980; Snow 1973; Terenzini, Pascarella, and Lorang 1982; Wilson, Gaff, Dienst, Wood, and Bavry 1975). Among others, these effects include greater satisfaction with the college experience (Astin 1993; Pascarella 1980), enhanced certainty of career choice (Astin 1993; Wilson et al. 1975), and increased self-confidence and self-esteem (Astin 1993; Hoyte and Collett 1993). For example, in their longitudinal study of the impact of college professors on students, Robert Wilson and his colleagues accentuated the importance of mentoring and concluded that "the relationships that faculty and students develop outside the classroom may well be the part of teaching which has the greatest impact on students" (107).

There is considerable exhortatory and empirical support for cooperative peer learning in the elementary and secondary as well as the higher education literatures (Astin 1993; Bouton and Garth 1983; Chickering and Gamson 1987; Johnson and Johnson 1989, 1991; Johnson, Johnson, and Smith 1991; Kagan, 1988, Light 1990, McKeachie, Pintrich, Yi-Guang, and Smith 1986; Palmer 1983; Romer 1985; Slavin 1980, 1983, 1990; Sorcinelli 1991). To wit, in their review of 137 studies on cooperative learning methods at the college level, Roger Johnson, David Johnson, and Karl Smith (1991) found that cooperative learning groups enhanced productivity, fostered more committed and positive relationships among students, increased peer social support, and improved students' self-esteem. Along these same lines, Johnson and his colleagues (1981) conducted a series of meta-analyses in which the weight of the evidence confirmed that cooperative learning approaches surpass competitive or individualistic learning methods in promoting achievement among students. Other scholars, including Robert Slavin (1980, 1983 1990) and James Cooper and Randall Mueck (1990), have also documented the effectiveness of cooperative learning.

Moreover, several studies have highlighted the importance of out-of-class activities in students' undergraduate and graduate experiences (Boyen 1987; Kuh 1993; Wilson 1966). In one of the most comprehensive qualitative studies ever conducted on the topic in American higher education, George Kuh, John Schuh, and Elizabeth Whitt (1991) found that participation in out-of-class activities had a number of favorable effects on students' growth and development. Among others, these included enhanced social competence, self-awareness, and self-worth. Other college impact studies have likewise shown that student involvement in out-of-class activities produces similar outcomes (Astin 1977, 1993; Baxter Magolda 1992; Pascarella, Ethington and Smart 1988).

Several publications offer strong support for the fourth cluster of attributes in the engagement theory—connected program requirements. Along side the voluminous literature on undergraduate education that emphasizes the importance of planned breadth and depth course work (American Association of Colleges 1985; Bennett 1984; Carnegie Foundation for the Advancement of Teaching 1977; Conrad 1978), a number of writers have stressed the advantages of experiential learning—such as internships or practica—at both the undergraduate and graduate levels (Jacobs and Allen 1982; Keetor 1976, 1980; Keeton and Tate 1978; Kolb 1984; Maehl 1982; Panel on Alternate Approaches to Graduate Education 1973).

Finally, while support for the last cluster of attributes—adequate resources—is abundant in the program quality literature, it is sparse in other higher education literatures. Indeed, aside from studies on the effects on financial aid on students (Leslie and Brinkman 1988; Pascarella and Terenzini 1991) and various higher education reform reports calling for broadened definitions of faculty scholarship and greater financial investment in faculty development programs (American Association of Colleges 1985; Boyen 1990; Study Group on the Conditions of Excellence in American Higher Education 1984), there seem to be few publications outside the program quality literature that emphasize the importance of monetary and non-monetary resources for students, faculty, and program infrastructures.

While the engagement theory finds considerable support in extant literatures, the theory does more than simply build on current views of program quality and related attributes: It also brings together many attributes of high-quality programs that, in one form of another, have been identified in disparate literatures (at both the undergraduate and graduate levels) but have not been brought to bear directly on program quality. In so doing, the theory at once builds on and connects these literatures in ways that contribute to a more comprehensive and holistic perspective on program quality in higher education than currently exists.

How the Engagement Theory Extends and Re-envisions Current Views of Program Quality

While the engagement theory clearly builds on and integrates current conceptions, it also moves significantly beyond existing studies and writings in ways that invite reexamination of traditional views and assumptions about program quality. From our perspective, the theory extends and re-envisions current understandings of program quality in five major ways.

First, the engagement theory highlights the pivotal role that people—faculty, administrators, and students who engage in mutually supportive teaching and learning—play in fostering enriching learning experiences for students that promote their growth and development. In accenting the commitments of time and energy that program participants make to their own and others' learning, the engagement theory builds on and moves beyond conventional views of high-quality programs. These views tend to perceive high-quality programs as being more narrowly fueled by students—whether through active student learning (Meyers and Jones 1993), student involvement (Astin 1977 and 1993), or student effort (Pace 1980 and 1986)—or by non-human factors such as curriculum requirements and resources. Of particular note, both Alexander Astin and C. Robert Pace—along with many people who have written on active learning—have emphasized the importance of student involvement and effort in enhancing students' learning. While the engagement theory is anchored in part in this insight, it goes far beyond it to emphasize the importance of students' investments in teaching as well as the dual roles of faculty and administrators.

Second, the theory extends and deepens current understanding of program quality by advancing a number of new attributes, and clusters of attributes, that have not been integrated into the literature on program quality. In particular, two of the five clusters of attributes in the engagement theory (participatory cultures and interactive teaching and learning) identify attributes that are not currently included in the program quality literature—such as critical dialogue, integrative learning, and a risk-taking environment. In short, the engagement theory provides people with new insights into those characteristics that are most important to the quality of their programs.

Third, by defining high-quality programs as those which provide enriching learning experiences for students that have positive effects on their development, the theory provides people throughout higher education with a new vantage point for understanding program quality. Not only does this vantage point recognize student learning and development as the primary purpose of the higher learning (Astin, 1985), but it also embraces a complementary conceptual template that is organized around understanding and exploring relationships among program attributes, learning experiences, and student outcomes.[2]

Fourth, through connecting and extending current conceptions, the engagement theory provides a comprehensive and integrated theory of program quality. Anchored in a large body of empirical research along with supporting explanations as to how and why specific program attributes enhance students' learning, our work systematically identifies and integrates program attributes into a unified theory of program quality. Indeed, the engagement theory represents the only formal theory of program quality in the literature. For the first time, practitioners and scholars alike are invited to consider an inclusive and integrated theory of program quality.

Fifth, as a comprehensive new perspective for enriching our understanding of quality, the engagement theory provides a new framework for assessing and improving academic program quality. As elaborated on in the previous chapter, this theory can help stakeholders throughout higher education in their efforts to assess and improve the quality of students' learning in undergraduate and graduate programs.

A Final Note

We stake a claim that the engagement perspective can appreciably enhance the way that people think about program quality in higher education: not only does the theory build on and bring together current views, but it extends and re-envisions them as well. Thus, the theory offers new insight into program quality—in essence, a new perspective—that may be as applicable to undergraduate and doctoral education as they are to master's education.

In closing, it is our hope that the engagement theory will contribute to the ongoing discourse about program quality in higher education and serve as an impetus for strengthening program quality within colleges and universities. To that end, we invite stakeholders to reexamine traditional assumptions and beliefs about academic program quality in higher education in light of our findings and conclusions.

Notes

1. In his national study of more than 45,000 faculty and students, for instance, Alexander Astin (1993) found that undergraduate students who socialized with someone from another racial or ethnic group reported gains in cognitive and affective development (especially increased cultural awareness) and were more satisfied with their college experiences.

2. For the most part, individuals writing on program quality have identified and studied attributes of program quality without systematically examining their consequences for students' learning experiences, much less the effects of these learning experiences on students' growth and development. The program quality literature, for example, is replete with studies that identify faculty research productivity as a key attribute of program quality. Yet none of these studies provide empirical evidence to establish that faculty research productivity contributes to enriching learning experiences for students that positively affect their growth and development.

Developing Competent E-learners: The Role of Assessment

Janet Macdonald

We know assessment plays a major formative role in driving student learning appropriately; but what implications does this have for online courses? Is it more important than in a face to face context, or less so? Should we reconceptualize the ways in which we assess students, or are existing methods, tried and tested in conventional teaching and learning situations, appropriate? This paper discusses the practical implications of implementing these online pedagogies and illustrates the powerful formative effects, both intended and unintentional, of assessment on student learning and behaviour. It draws on examples from recent research on two e-learning courses at UK Open University.

Introduction

The use of electronic media for flexible course delivery provides new opportunities for teaching and learning. The emphasis on asynchronicity brought by email and online conferencing brings with it an increased scope for flexibility in study routines, and meets a growing demand for part time study, continuous professional development and lifelong learning. Indeed, e-learning has achieved prominence as the 'Philosopher's Stone' for future development in higher and further education, and yet there is little common understanding as to its meaning, and the implications for its effective use.

Mason (2002) outlines a wide spectrum of interests and understandings attached to the term e-learning, and concludes that many continue to see it as a convenient medium for content delivery and testing students. However, electronic media offer a variety of ways of presenting or structuring learning opportunities which were not previously available on distance courses. They offer new ways to access and combine information, and the possibility to keep in touch on a more regular and continuous basis, so that students need no longer work in isolation, but belong to an electronic `community of learners' (Collis, 1998).

In fact, the communicative potential of e-learning has given rise to a generation of courses which employ a social constructivist approach, by using online media to support distributed collaborative interaction and dialogue, and access to information rich resources. Such courses place importance on understanding, rather than on memorizing and reproducing facts, and on the contribution of social interaction and collaboration to learning.

Constructivist philosophy accommodates a family of closely related pedagogies, which optimize the potential of e-learning environments. The family includes collaborative learning (McConnell, 2001), activity-based learning (Macdonald & Twining, 2002), resource-based learning (Macdonald et al., 2001) and problem-based learning (Ronteltap & Eurelings, 2002). These four pedagogies lay different emphases on particular facets of constructivist philosophy, as their names suggest. They all operate by providing opportunities for students to learn by engaging in activities, which might involve collaborative work, or problem solving, or open access to electronic resources. In practice, many e-learning courses adopt all four approaches to varying degrees, alongside more conventional modes of delivery.

Reprinted from *Assessment & Evaluation in Higher Education* 29, no. 2 (April 2004), Taylor & Francis, Ltd.

The pioneers in e-learning research and course development have tended to concentrate their studies on postgraduate courses, often having small numbers of students, where e-learning has been the subject of study, as well as being the medium used for interaction. Many useful lessons have been learnt from these courses. However, e-learning is rapidly being mainstreamed at all levels of study, for a wide variety of courses, and therefore it is increasingly important to identify the conditions for success, in terms of expectations on the students, and the implications for course design and presentation.

What Is a Competent E-learner?

E-learning courses make certain demands on the students who study them. Inevitably, using a computer as a study tool involves basic ICT skills which need to be mastered, and this eventually leads to a familiarity with the relevant hardware and software tools. We know that this familiarity with the environment is a critical factor for student online participation (Mason & Bacsich, 1998). There is a strong argument for maintaining a common interface across e-learning courses, so that students benefit from this continuity. Beyond this, students need to learn how to use the computer as a study tool. They may need to accommodate screen based study, with its limitations on flexibility, and the implications for time management; in addition to learning how to manage files effectively. Word processing offers new approaches to writing, and enhanced possibilities for the re-drafting of scripts.

E-learning courses with constructivist approaches will by definition demand the development of a self-directed approach to study. Of course, under traditional university models of teaching and learning, encouraging students to develop any independence and self-direction in learning is a lengthy and gradual process (Perry, 1970), which develops throughout a graduate course of study. E-learning courses have been introduced at all levels of the undergraduate curriculum, and so students may be exposed to these relatively unfamiliar demands at an early stage in their academic career.

Since e-learning offers students access to the opinions of peers and the resources of the web, such self-directed study requires competence in two major areas: information literacy and online collaborative learning. The term information literacy has been in use particularly in the USA and Australia, in connection with self-directed lifelong learning (see Bruce & Candy, 2000). Its characteristics include recognizing the need for information, being able to identify and locate it, gaining access to it, then evaluating, organizing it and using it effectively (American Association of College and Research Libraries, 1999). Students need to recognize the gaps in their knowledge, in order to establish what they need to find out, and Hill (1999) underlines the significance of subject knowledge, in providing the framework for further exploration and research, in addition to confidence and metacognition. It is clearly not enough to teach students searching techniques, and then to assume that they will be competent investigators. In addition, the use of information from a variety of sources presupposes some understanding of plagiarism, and the role of academic evidence in developing an argument. Indeed the support of students in this area is highly problematic, and McDowell (2002) describes a wide spectrum of approaches to the use of electronic resources within courses.

There is similar complexity in online collaborative learning. Salmon (2000) proposes a number of progressive stages of development, which include access and motivation, socialization, information exchange, knowledge construction and development. These stages illustrate the interplay between competence, and affective factors such as growing confidence, motivation and group dynamics. And of course if students are to communicate effectively within an academic discipline, then they need to become familiar with the language of a discipline and the academic genre. Lea and Street (1998) maintain that this familiarity with the discourse is a defining factor in students' abilities to read and write appropriately within a discipline. In fact, this familiarity grows as they practice writing conference messages on course topics, and reading, or eventually responding to messages from others.

Finally, if students are required to collaborate to undertake a common task, as opposed to making optional contributions to a conference, then they need to practise team working and negotiation skills, group decision making and task management (see Schrage, 1990). Again, affective issues may be significant here, for example group cohesion, and the evolution of mutual trust. It follows that the whole process of competence in online collaboration certainly requires practice, and will take some time to develop.

In short, I have argued that the competent e-learner will have developed communicative and interpretive ability using electronic media. This involves the use of computers as an effective study tool, but it also implies the development of the critical and analytical abilities to work as a self-directed learner, together with the communicative abilities to work with, and learn from peers. In other words, competence in e-learning has many parallels with competence in learning, and is probably acquired as a developmental progression, alongside developing confidence and metacognition, and a growing understanding of a discipline. However, the use of online media for study, and the ready availability of information rich resources on the web, means that students may need to develop competence and self direction at an earlier stage in their undergraduate career than they would in more conventional distance courses. Course design and outcomes will need to reflect and support these needs.

A significant body of research supports the view that the design of assessment is critical in determining the direction of student effort, and that assessment is vital in providing a channel of communication between students and their mentors (see Black & William, 1998). This role for assessment is increasingly important for campus-based universities, as well as in a traditional distance learning context (Higgins et al., 2002). But to what extent can the formative power of assessment be deployed to develop competent e-learners, and does it differ in any way from assessment to develop competent learners?

E-learning at the UK Open University

Course materials, activities and assessment at the UK Open University are designed, tested and produced by a central course team, and distributed at scale to a large student population. At local level, the University employs part-time tutors, who act as the human interface between the university and its students. They support their students primarily through detailed correspondence tuition on summative assignments, which are commonly spaced at intervals throughout the course. The courses in general attract mature students, who study part-time. Undergraduate students are accepted with no previous qualification, and may study courses at any level, in any order, although the expectation is that those students studying a second level course will have previously followed an entry-level course.

The University is actively encouraging the use of online media on its courses, indeed there are now 284 courses involving 100,000 students, in which online media are used to varying extent. The e-learning courses referred to in this paper were both 60 point second level undergraduate courses from the Technology and Education Faculties. Both courses adopted a constructivist approach and employed an electronic environment to engage students in a variety of activities.

The Technology course THD204, 'IT and Society' explored social and technological issues associated with IT developments. It was presented from 1995 until 2001, to approximately 1500 undergraduates each year. The course adopted a resource based and collaborative approach, delivered through a combination of printed course books, a CD-ROM indexed library of academic articles, and an Internet Home Page which gave access to resources for further reading.

The Education course E211, 'Learning matters: challenges of the information age', was presented in 2001 to 200 students. The course aimed to empower students to deepen their understanding of learning, and offered a variety of perspectives on learning, with particular reference to the growing influence of ICTs. It placed an overt emphasis on experiential learning and reflective analysis, whilst being relatively low in print delivered content, in comparison with conventionally produced distance courses. Course activities represented an integration of three types of task, in addition to course readings and videos:

- Participation in online conferencing and internet searching with fellow students;
- Hands-on experience of ICT as a tool for structuring reflection on learning;
- Maintenance of a portfolio in which students recorded personal learning experiences and made notes on course readings and various other activities.

In this paper I discuss the lessons learnt on assessment design for developing competent e-learners, by drawing on examples from two qualitative studies of these two e-learning courses; both studies are reported in detail elsewhere (Macdonald et al., 2001; Macdonald & Twining, 2002). Although both courses engaged students in learning overtly about e-learning, I believe that the lessons learnt here will be applicable to any e-learning course which makes use of activities such as those described above, because it is likely to make similar demands on its learners.

Assessment to Create E-learning Opportunities at Critical Points

If a course is based on active learning and experiential approaches, then it is critical that students actually do the activities they are set, so that they engage with the learning process and derive benefit from the course. In a classroom situation there is some expectation that students, once in the room, will participate, at least to some extent, in the activities set for them. Distance learners are not the same.

Intuitively one might expect little guarantee that students will undertake any element of a course in the prescribed manner, unless there is sufficient motivation to do so, and Lockwood (1992) describes the balance of 'costs and benefits' undertaken by distance learners when considering whether to undertake in-text activities. Whether e-learners are any less likely to participate than other distance learners is difficult to say. Some students might be attracted to the 'fun' element in activities, others might be motivated by online interaction, whilst others might see online activities as intrinsically 'lightweight' in comparison with traditional course content. Obviously, this issue of participation is of critical importance where activities form a central part of the course. It is even more critical where activities involve online collaboration, because non-participation by one student impacts on other students.

Our own experiences illustrate this point. Throughout the course E211, students were expected to engage in online discussion in groups of 15–20, which were moderated by their tutor. The course materials provided them with discussion points to follow through in their tutor groups. Mid-way through the course, students were given an online collaborative activity, on which they were expected to work in sub-groups of four to six students. They were required to search for resources on the Internet and to reflect on their experiences of online collaborative working.

We discovered that for about half the tutor groups, participation had waned since the start of the course, and the sub-groups achieved limited success in the collaborative task. Arguably the extent of success was related to a variety of factors, and the skills and moderation tactics of the various tutors undoubtedly played a significant part in this (Mason & Bacsich, 1998). However, the greatest hurdle to successful participation was the lack of integration of assessment with the collaborative task. At the same time, an impending assignment, which was not related to the activity, materially detracted from student efforts.

> . . . timing and incentive are both important—a number of my students commented that they would have completed this activity (and taken a more active part) but stopped when they felt they had to give priority to work on assignments. (Tutor)

There will always be students who recognize the value of online participation for their learning, and appreciate the benefits of belonging to an online community. But the only time when most students will undertake activities is when they are linked to assessment. The assignment will always take priority, and may detract from non-assessed activities. Of course, there are always exceptions, and some students will ignore activities even when they are linked to assessment (Thomas & Carswell, 2000).

An assignment which requires reflection on a topic of online debate, or on the application of a particular skill in operating course software, helps to ensure participation by most students, if it is timed to coincide with the relevant activity. The following example (Figure 1) illustrates how an assignment can cover course content while also encouraging students to undertake an online collaborative activity.

Assessment of collaboration may not necessarily be effective in *measuring* the learning which takes place, and the practice of awarding marks for participation, or the nature and form of

Summarize an article on a course topic
Post summary to online conference
Discuss the issues arising in the conference
Marks given for:

• Summary of article

• Reflection on key points of online debate

• Two messages contributed, each supported by another message to illustrate an ability to interact and
  build on peer contributions.

Figure 1 Assignment 1

• Write an essay on a relevant course issue, using material from the CD-ROM library
• Compare the use of three different search methods used to collect material for your essay, describing outcomes, and offer an assessment of the various methods

Figure 2 Assignment 2

contributions can be problematic, because of the need for reliability if several markers are involved. For example, Goodfellow (2001) describes how online assessment practices can be considerably more subjective and difficult to monitor than conventional marking, because of uneven levels of participation and a requirement for flexibility in the assessment of those who were readers rather than contributors. In fact, Knight (2002) points out that summative assessment of `uncontroversial' course content will always be easier to achieve than any assignment which sets out to measure the process of learning. Nevertheless, assessment is invaluable as a way of *affording students the opportunity to learn* at critical points in the course, and a few marks can be very effective in providing that opportunity. In this respect it is certainly more significant for online courses than it is for conventional campus based courses.

Assessment to Support the Developing E-learner

I have argued that the road to competence in e-learning is a complex one, in which the student must acquire competence in basic transferable skills before they are equipped to undertake tasks demanding of higher order literacies. Because of this complexity, and the degree to which much competence in e-learning is embedded within an understanding and familiarity with a discipline, it becomes important that the process of study be overtly supported in course outcomes, whatever the course. Further, the development of the more complex competences such as information literacy in electronic environments builds upon a familiarity with basic skills, therefore students may need incremental support throughout the course, to develop these skills gradually.

Our studies have illustrated how the assessment strategy can be designed to provide this support. Of course, the extent to which this is important will depend on the competence of the students at the start of the course. And perhaps five years into the future this will be less significant that it is at present. For example, we found that many students on THD204 experienced serious problems with information overload when working on some resource-based project work, in spite of the provision of a computer based tutorial designed to help them learn how to use software. The project work was too complex for many students to handle, because not only did they need to be competent in negotiating the environment, they also had to formulate queries effectively and to assess the relevance of the material retrieved. We had devised an exercise in an early assignment which required students to practise the basic skills and become competent with the environment (see Figure 2).

However, this strategy was only partially effective. Although the students were marginally better prepared for coping with resource-based study in subsequent project work, many remained unconfident with the resource-based approach and still felt that they were lacking in information literacy. This probably reflects the longer timescale needed to develop such competence, and also the relationship of information literacy to an understanding of the discipline, which for second level students was as yet poorly developed.

My second example is taken from E211, where an assignment required students to construct a hypertext essay using a hypermedia authoring tool called Hypernote.

In this essay, they discussed course concepts, using hypertext to illustrate the relationships between them, and links to video clips as illustrative examples. We found that the majority of students felt confident with the software, although many had really only got to grips with it during completion of the assignment. Their tutors commented that many students put all their effort into mastering the software, at the expense of content and analysis in their written work.

> The middle of the road students . . . lost some of the content, value and relevance, while `tinkering' with the tool. (Tutor)

Although the course had included a series of activities which were designed to build students' confidence in using the software, students received no marks or feedback on these activities, which were not integrated with the assessment strategy. Not surprisingly, many students had either missed out the activities altogether, or otherwise assigned a low priority to them.

Such tasks as learning to use search tools, or conferencing software, or getting to know your fellow students online, take time and practice. There are two important aspects to the formative role played by assessment in these examples. The first was a motivational force, derived from the summative aspects of the assessment, which drove student learning so that they undertook the activities set at an appropriate time, and in a conscientious way. The second was the feedback, which helped students to check that they were `on the right track'. Feedback which is designed to give students a running commentary on their progress must be delivered in a timely manner if it is to be effective and usable before the next assignment, and this is a case where web based assessment can offer a solution to this progress and achievement testing (see Charman, 1999).

Assessment in Which E-learners Participate

If we are to develop self-direction in e-learners, and a more independent approach to learning, then it makes sense to allow them to participate more in the assessment process. It is after all a better reflection of the more open, student-centred courses which we are designing for them. This must be an important direction for assessing e-learners, and networking offers a number of opportunities, many of which are familiar to face-to-face teaching, with additional enhancements provided by the options to archive resources, and the advantage afforded by asynchronous discussion in providing time for reflection.

There are a variety of ways in which networking can be used to encourage student participation in assessment, and one direction is to provide enhanced formative feedback. There are certain times when this is particularly appropriate. For example, we found that students on both courses described here valued comments on assignments, in particular at the start of the course. It appeared that they needed all the help they could get in these initial stages, in order to write appropriately, in an unfamiliar genre, for an unfamiliar course.

> At least now I have a feel for what to expect when it comes to writing these essays and so I hope that the experience of this first assignment may hold me in better stead for the future. (Student)

Using networking, feedback can be given to a whole tutorial group, forming the basis for online discussion and dialogue on interpretations of assignment wording or criteria, while at the same time offering some relief to the marker's workload. In this context, model answers have been used in order to give examples of effective writing or well-structured assignments (see Barrett & Paradis, 1988; Macdonald, 2001). Building on this principle we have experimented with an `electronic scrapbook' of writing samples drawn from assignments written by students, as a way of using student resources to illustrate a number of teaching points and a range of writing styles (see Figure 3). Such a scrapbook

[...]

Every course has its own particular approach to writing, and this course is no exception. I have put together a few examples from your scripts to illustrate some approaches to writing. You can learn from each other!

Introduction

Remember that you need to set the scene. *Why* is this question important? Why is a good question to ask yourself when you are planning an introduction. Then 'what' definitions. . . And the 'how': how you are going to discuss it. These three don't have to come in a particular order. Have a look at the following examples:

1. I am going to look at the situated view of learning as explained in the E211 course and give examples of personal experiences which show the connections between the theory and the practice of this view of learning . . .

2. What is 'learning situation'? Although in this analysis I use terms such as 'my personal learning situation' in order to situate my argument within the context of the course, the truth is my 'situation' interacting with another student in First Class is not the same as my 'situation' reading a course text or authoring hypermedia . . .

3. The screenshot above, taken from a First Class conference, shows some of the participants in this year's E211. Traditional approaches to learning might see us a uniform group of learners, all ready and waiting to be filled with the same information in exactly the same way. A 'situated' view of learning would on the other hand, acknowledge us as individuals, each encountering a different learning situation as a result of our prior experiences and the unique personal context within which we are studying . . .

Figure 3 An Electronic Scrapbook

can be archived and used in subsequent presentations, although of course it tends to lose some of its 'today relevance' if the scripts are not from recognizable students.

However, by definition such formative feedback is received retrospectively, and many students often feel that they would like more help *before* assignment submission. Often tutors will provide this kind of proactive support in traditional face-to-face tutorials held prior to an assignment, but there are other options for online media. At an informal level some students have used computer conferencing for peer support in assignment preparation.

> One aspect of conferencing which I find useful . . . is the exchange of actual pieces of work. With modern technology it is simple to attach a file of work to a conference message for people to look at and comment on . . . It has proved very interesting and useful to be able to look at how other people have approached activities. (Student)

A natural progression is the concept of iterative assignment development, where assignments are submitted for formative review by the tutor, so that constructive comments can be used to develop the written work (Davis & Berrow, 1998; McConnell, 1999). This is after all the way in which academics operate when writing academic papers, and the process becomes very simple using networking. There are institutional constraints in operating such an exercise at scale, and it is not widely in use at the UK Open University.

At a more advanced level, students might participate in assessment through peer review. Students can learn to comment on each other's work as an integral part of summative assessment, and this has been shown to be an effective approach when helping them to develop a critical approach to their written work (see, for example, Boud & Falchikov, 1989). The use of networking means that this is now feasible for distance learners (Macdonald, 2001), and gains the added advantage that scripts can be submitted anonymously, if that is appropriate. Peer review is a demanding task for undergraduates, because they need the confidence firstly to judge fellow students' work, and secondly to be able to give a critique without giving offence. However, with appropriate scaffolding to guide students, it is feasible, and has been demonstrated successfully with 200 students on a second level course at the UK Open University.

Assessment Which Is Appropriately Aligned

I make no claim here that assessing e-learning is really radically different from assessing learning: the same principles apply. Basically, the key to supporting e-learning development will lie in an understanding of the complexity of the processes which we are asking our students to undertake. E-learning courses which adopt a constructivist philosophy may impose new and unfamiliar demands on the students who study them. E-learning involves a complex mix of basic transferable skills and literacies, many of which are embedded within an understanding of a discipline. E-learning courses may expose students to a more demanding approach to study, requiring greater self-direction and a critical approach to study than has been the norm in the early undergraduate years. All this means that it is important to support e-learning development, whatever the subject of the course.

The following comments summarize some suggestions on assessment design for e-learning, while recognizing that considerations of validity and authentic assessment always need to be balanced against feasibility and marking reliability.

- The assessment of e-learning courses has a variety of roles to play in supporting course outcomes, and ensuring that students are equipped to benefit from the rich learning environment. The assessment of e-learning need not necessarily be online, although there are times when that is appropriate, for example when rapid feedback is required on progress and achievement testing.

- Constructivist approaches to study require students to learn by engaging in a variety of activities, which may involve collaborative work, problem solving or resource based learning. If such activities are central to course outcomes, then it is important that students undertake them conscientiously. Assessment strategy can afford students an opportunity for learning at critical points in the course.

- Since e-learning is such a complex process, students will benefit from incremental support through assignments which encourage them to build their skills gradually, and provide feedback on their efforts. Assessment strategy can support e-learning development, whatever the subject or level of the course.

- If e-learners are to be offered greater autonomy, then they need to develop a self directed approach. Networks can be employed to deliver enhanced versions of innovative assignments familiar to face to face situations. For example, model answers, electronic scrapbooks, online peer review and iterative assignment development. In this way, assessment strategy can be designed to engage student participation.

References

American Association of College and Research Libraries (1999) *Information literacy competency standards for Higher Education.* Available online at: www.csusm.edu/acrl/il/index.html

Barrett, E. & Paradis, J. (1988) Teaching writing in an online classroom, *Harvard Educational Review, 58(2)*, 154–171.

Black, P. & William, D. (1998) Assessment and classroom learning, *Assessment in Education, 5*, 7–75.

Boud, D. & Falchikov, N. (1989) Quantitative studies of student self-assessment in higher education: a critical analysis of findings, *Higher Education, 18(5)*, 529–549.

Bruce, C. & Candy, P. (Eds) (2000) *Information literacy around the world. Advances in programs and research* (Wagga Wagga, Centre for Information Studies, Charles Sturt University).

Charman, D. (1999) Issues and impacts of using computer based assessments for formative assessment, in: S. Brown, P. Race & J. Bull (Eds) *Computer assisted assessment in higher Education* (SEDA/Kogan Page), 85–93.

Collis, B. (1998) New didactics for university instruction: why and how? *Computers and Education, 31*, 373–393.

Davis, R. & Berrow, T. (1998) An evaluation of the use of computer supported peer review for developing higher level skills, *Computers and Education, 30(1/2)*, 111–115.

Goodfellow, R. (2001) Credit where it is due: assessing students' contributions to collaborative online learning, in: D. Murphy, R. Walker & G. Webb (Eds) *Online learning and teaching with technology* (London, Kogan Page), 73–80.

Higgins, R., Hartley, P. & Skelton, A. (2002) The conscientious consumer: reconsidering the role of assessment feedback in student learning, *Studies in Higher Education*, 27(1), 52–64.

Hill, J. (1999) A conceptual framework for understanding information seeking in Open Ended Information Systems, *Educational Technology Research and Development*, 47(1), 5–27.

Knight, P. (2002) Summative assessment in higher education: practices in disarray, *Studies in Higher Education*, 27(3), 275–286.

Lea, M. & Street, B. (1998) Student writing in higher education: an academic literacies approach, *Studies in Higher Education*, 23(2), 157–172.

Lockwood, F. (1992) *Activities in self instructional texts* (London, Kogan Page).

Macdonald, J. (1999) *Appropriate assessment for resource based learning in networked environments*. Unpublished Ph.D. thesis, Open University, UK.

Macdonald, J. (2001) Exploiting online interactivity to enhance assignment development and feedback on an ODL course, *Open Learning*, 16(2), 179–189.

Macdonald, J., Heap, N. & Mason, R. (2001) `Have I learnt it?' Evaluating skills for resource based study using electronic resources, *British Journal of Educational Technology*, 32(4), 419–434.

Macdonald, J. & Twining, P. (2002) Assessing activity based learning for a networked course, *British Journal of Educational Technology*, 33(5), 605–620.

Mason, R. (2002) *E-learning: what have we learnt? Improving Student Learning using Learning Technologies*, Proceedings, 9th Improving Student Learning Symposium, 2001, 27–34.

Mason, R. & Bacsich, P. (1998) Embedding computer conferencing into University teaching, *Computers in Education*, 30(3/4), 249–258.

McConnell, D. (1999) Examining a collaborative assessment process in networked lifelong learning, *Journal of Computer Assisted Learning*, 15, 232–243.

McConnell, D. (2001) *Implementing computer supported co-operative learning* (London, Kogan).

McDowell, L. (2002) Electronic information resources in undergraduate education: an exploratory study of opportunities for student learning and independence, *British Journal of Educational Technology*, 33(3), 255–266.

Perry, W. G. (1970) *Forms of intellectual and ethical development in the college years* (New York, Holt, Rinchart & Winston).

Ronteltap, F. & Eurelings, A. (2002) Activity and interaction of students in an electronic learning environment for problem based learning, *Distance Education*, 23(1), 11–22.

Salmon, G. (2000) *E moderating. The key to teaching and learning online* (London, Kogan Page).

Schrage, M. (1990) *Shared minds: the new technologies of collaboration* (New York, Random House).

Thomas, P. & Carswell, L. (2000) Learning through collaboration in a distributed education environment, *Educational Technology and Society*, 3(3), 1–15.

Acknowledgment

My grateful thanks to my colleague Dr. Pete Cannell for his thoughtful contributions and critical comments on this script.

WHAT IS A RUBRIC?

D.D. STEVENS AND A.J. LEVI

\Ru"bric\, n. [OE. rubriche, OF. rubriche, F. rubrique (cf. it. rubrica), fr. L. rubrica red earth for coloring, red chalk, the title of a law (because written in red), fr. ruber red. See red.] That part of any work in the early manuscripts and typography which was colored red, to distinguish it from other portions. Hence, specifically: (a) A titlepage, or part of it, especially that giving the date and place of printing; also, the initial letters, etc., when printed in red. (b) (Law books) The title of a statute;—so called as being anciently written in red letters.—Bell. (c) (Liturgies) The directions and rules for the conduct of service, formerly written or printed in red; hence, also, an ecclesiastical or episcopal injunction;—usually in the plural.

—Webster's Unabridged Dictionary, 1913

Rubric: n 1: an authoritative rule 2: an explanation or definition of an obscure word in a text [syn: gloss] 3: a heading that is printed in red or in a special type v : adorn with ruby red color.

—WordNet, 1997

Today, a rubric retains its connection to authoritative rule and particularly to "redness." In fact, professors like us who use rubrics often consider them the most effective grading devices since the invention of red ink.

At its most basic, a rubric is a scoring tool that lays out the specific expectations for an assignment. Rubrics divide an assignment into its component parts and provide a detailed description of what constitutes acceptable or unacceptable levels of performance for each of those parts. Rubrics can be used for grading a large variety of assignments and tasks: research papers, book critiques, discussion participation, laboratory reports, portfolios, group work, oral presentations, and more.

Dr. Dannelle Stevens and Dr. Antonia Levi teach at Portland State University in the Graduate School of Education and the University Studies Program, respectively. Rubrics are used quite extensively for grading at Portland State University, especially in the core University Studies program. One reason for this is that the University Studies Program uses rubrics annually to assess its experimental, interdisciplinary, yearlong Freshman Inquiry core. Because that assessment is carried out by, among others, the faculty who teach Freshman Inquiry, and because most faculty from all departments eventually do teach Freshman Inquiry, this means that the faculty at Portland State are given a chance to see close up what rubrics can do in terms of assessment. Many quickly see the benefits of using rubrics for their own forms of classroom assessment, including grading.

In this book, we will show you what a rubric is, why so many professors at Portland State University are so enthusiastic about rubrics, and how you can construct and use your own rubrics. Based on our own experiences and those of our colleagues, we will also show you how to share the construction or expand the use of rubrics to become an effective part of the teaching process. We will describe the various models of rubric construction and show how different professors have used rubrics in different ways in different classroom contexts and disciplines. All the rubrics used in this book derive from actual use in real classrooms.

Reprinted from *Introduction To Rubrics: An Assessment Tool To Save Grading Time, Convey Effective Feedback and Promote Student Learning*, by Dannelle D. Stevens and Antonia J. Levi (2004), by permission of Stylus Publishing.

Do You Need a Rubric?

How do you know if you need a rubric? One sure sign is if you check off more than three items from the following list:

❑ You are getting carpal tunnel syndrome from writing the same comments on almost every student paper.

❑ It's 3 A.M. The stack of papers on your desk is fast approaching the ceiling. You're already 4 weeks behind in your grading, and it's clear that you won't be finishing it tonight either.

❑ Students often complain that they cannot read the notes you labored so long to produce.

❑ You have graded all your papers and worry that the last ones were graded slightly differently from the first ones.

❑ You want students to complete a complex assignment that integrates all the work over the term and are not sure how to communicate all the varied expectations easily and clearly.

❑ You want students to develop the ability to reflect on ill-structured problems but you aren't sure how to clearly communicate that to them.

❑ You give a carefully planned assignment that you never used before and to your surprise, it takes the whole class period to explain it to students.

❑ You give a long narrative description of the assignment in the syllabus, but the students continually ask two to three questions per class about your expectations.

❑ You are spending long periods of time on the phone with the Writing Center or other tutorial services because the students you sent there are unable to explain the assignments or expectations clearly.

❑ You work with your colleagues and collaborate on designing the same assignments for program courses, yet you wonder if your grading scales are different.

❑ You've sometimes been disappointed by whole assignments because all or most of your class turned out to be unaware of academic expectations so basic that you neglected to mention them (e.g., the need for citations or page numbers).

❑ You have worked very hard to explain the complex end-of-term paper; yet students are starting to regard you as an enemy out to trick them with incomprehensible assignments.

❑ You're starting to wonder if they're right.

Rubrics set you on the path to addressing these concerns.

What Are the Parts of a Rubric?

Rubrics are composed of four basic parts in which the professor sets out the parameters of the assignment. The parties and processes involved in making a rubric can and should vary tremendously, but the basic format remains the same. In its simplest form, the rubric includes a task description (the assignment), a scale of some sort (levels of achievement, possibly in the form of grades), the dimensions of the assignment (a breakdown of the skills/knowledge involved in the assignment), and descriptions of what constitutes each level of performance (specific feedback) all set out on a grid, as shown in Figure 1.

We usually use a simple Microsoft Word table to create our grids using the "elegant" format found in the "auto format" section. Our sample grid shows three scales and four dimensions. This is the most common, but sometimes we use more. Rarely, however, do we go over our maximum of five scale levels and six to seven dimensions.

In this chapter, we will look at the four component parts of the rubric and, using an oral presentation assignment as an example, develop the above grid *part-by-part* until it is a useful grading tool (a usable rubric) for the professor and a clear indication of expectations and actual performance for the student.

TITLE
Task Description

	Scale level 1	Scale level 2	Scale level 3
Dimension 1			
Dimension 2			
Dimension 3			
Dimension 4			

Figure 1 Basic Rubric Grid Format

Part-by-Part Development of a Rubric

Part 1: Task Description

The task description is almost always originally framed by the instructor and involves a "performance" of some sort by the student. The task can take the form of a specific assignment, such as a paper, a poster, or a presentation. The task can also apply to overall behavior, such as participation, use of proper lab protocols, and behavioral expectations in the classroom.

We place the task description, usually cut and pasted from the syllabus, at the top of the grading rubric, partly to remind ourselves how the assignment was written as we grade, and to have a handy reference later on when we may decide to reuse the same rubric.

More important, however, we find that the task assignment grabs the students' attention in a way nothing else can, when placed at the top of what they know will be a grading tool. With the added reference to their grades, the task assignment and the rubric criteria become more immediate to students and are more carefully read. Students focus on grades. Sad, but true. We might as well take advantage of it to communicate our expectations as clearly as possible.

If the assignment is too long to be included in its entirety on the rubric, or if there is some other reason for not including it there, we put the title of the full assignment at the top of the rubric: for example, "Rubric for Oral Presentation." This will at least remind the students that there is a full description elsewhere, and it will facilitate later reference and analysis for the professor. Sometimes we go further and add the words "see syllabus" or "see handout." Another possibility is to put the larger task description along the side of the rubric. For reading and grading ease, rubrics should seldom, if ever, be more than one page long.

Most rubrics will contain both a descriptive title and a task description. Figure 2 illustrates Part 1 of our sample rubric with the title and task description highlighted.

Part 2: Scale

The scale describes how well or poorly any given task has been performed and occupies yet another side of the grid to complete the rubric's evaluative goal. Terms used to describe the level of performance should be tactful but clear. In the generic rubric, words such as "mastery," "partial mastery," "progressing," and "emerging" provide a more positive, active, verb description of what is expected next from the student and also mitigate the potential shock of low marks in the lowest levels of the scale. Some professors may prefer to use nonjudgmental, noncompetitive language, such as "high level," "middle level," and "beginning level," whereas others prefer numbers or even grades.

Here are some commonly used labels compiled by Huba and Freed (2000):

- Sophisticated, competent, partly competent, not yet competent (NSF Synthesis Engineering Education Coalition, 1997)

- Exemplary, proficient, marginal, unacceptable

- Advanced, intermediate high, intermediate, novice (American Council of Teachers of Foreign Languages, 1986, p. 278)

Changing Communities in Our City

Task Description: Each student will make a 5-minute presentation on the changes in one Portland community over the past thirty years. The student may focus the presentation in any way he or she wishes, but there needs to be a thesis of some sort, not just a chronological exposition. The presentation should include appropriate photographs, maps, graphs, and other visual aids for the audience.

	Scale level 1	Scale level 2	Scale level 3
Dimension 1			
Dimension 2			
Dimension 3			
Dimension 4			

Figure 2 Part 1: Task Description

Changing Communities in Our City

Task Description: Each student will make a 5-minute presentation on the changes in one Portland community over the past thirty years. The student may focus the presentation in any way he or she wishes, but there needs to be a thesis of some sort, not just a chronological exposition. The presentation should include appropriate photographs, maps, graphs, and other visual aids for the audience.

	Excellent	Competent	Needs work
Dimension 1			
Dimension 2			
Dimension 3			
Dimension 4			

Figure 3 Part 2: Scales

- distinguished, proficient, intermediate, novice (Gotcher, 1997):
- accomplished, average, developing, beginning (College of Education, 1997)

(Huba & Freed, 2000, p. 180)

We almost always confine ourselves to three levels of performance when we first construct a rubric. After the rubric has been used on a real assignment, we often expand that to five. It is much easier to refine the descriptions of the assignment and create more levels after seeing what our students actually do.

Figure 3 presents the Part 2 version of our rubric where the scale has been highlighted.

There is no set formula for the number of levels a rubric scale should have. Most professors prefer to clearly describe the performances at three or even five levels using a scale. But five levels is enough. The more levels there are, the more difficult it becomes to differentiate between them and to articulate precisely why one student's work falls into the scale level it does. On the other hand, more specific levels make the task clearer for the student and they reduce the professor's time needed to furnish detailed grading notes. Most professors consider three to be the optimum number of levels on a rubric scale.

If a professor chooses to describe only one level, the rubric is called a holistic rubric or a scoring guide rubric. It usually contains a description of the highest level of performance expected for each dimension, followed by room for scoring and describing in a "Comments" column just how far the student has come toward achieving or not achieving that level. Scoring guide rubrics, however, usually require considerable additional explanation in the form of written notes and so are more time-consuming than grading with a three-to-five-level rubric.

Part 3: Dimensions

The dimensions of a rubric lay out the parts of the task simply and completely. A rubric can also clarify for students how their task can be broken down into components and which of those components are most important. Is it the grammar? The analysis? The factual content? The research techniques? And how much weight is given to each of these aspects of the assignment? Although it is not necessary to weight the different dimensions differently, adding points or percentages to each dimension further emphasizes the relative importance of each aspect of the task.

Dimensions should actually represent the type of component skills students must combine in a successful scholarly work, such as the need for a firm grasp of content, technique, citation, examples, analysis, and a use of language appropriate to the occasion. When well done, the dimensions of a rubric (usually listed along one side of the rubric) will not only outline these component skills, but after the work is graded, should provide a quick overview of the student's strengths and weaknesses in each dimension.

Dimension need not and should not include any description of the quality of the performance. "Organization," for example, is a common dimension, but not "Good Organization." We leave the question of the quality of student work within that dimension to the scale and the description of the dimension, as illustrated in Part 4 of the rubric development.

Breaking up the assignment into its distinct dimensions leads to a kind of task analysis with the components of the task clearly identified. Both students and professors find this useful. It tells the

Changing Communities in Our City

Task Description: Each student will make a 5-minute presentation on the changes in one Portland community over the past thirty years. The student may focus the presentation in any way he or she wishes, but there needs to be a thesis of some sort, not just a chronological exposition. The presentation should include appropriate photographs, maps, graphs, and other visual aids for the audience.

	Excellent	Competent	Needs work
Knowledge/understanding 20%/20 points			
Thinking/inquiry 30%/30 points			
Communication 20%/20 points			
Use of visual aids 20%/20 points			
Presentation skills 10%/10 points			

Figure 4 Part 3: Dimensions

student much more than a mere task assignment or a grade reflecting only the finished product. Together with good descriptions, the dimensions of a rubric provide detailed feedback on specific parts of the assignment and how well or poorly those were carried out. This is especially useful in assignments such as our oral presentation example in which many different dimensions come into play, as shown in Figure 4, where the dimensions, Part 3 of the rubric, are highlighted on page 11.

Part 4: Description of the Dimensions

Dimensions alone are all-encompassing categories, so for each of the dimensions, a rubric should also contain at the very least a description of the highest level of performance in that dimension. A rubric that contains only the description of the highest level of performance is called a scoring guide rubric and is shown in Figure 5.

Scoring guide rubrics allow for greater flexibility and the personal touch, but the need to explain in writing where the student has failed to meet the highest levels of performance does increase the time it takes to grade using scoring guide rubrics.

Changing Communities in Our City

Task Description: Each student will make a 5-minute presentation on the changes in one Portland community over the past thirty years. The student may focus the presentation in any way he or she wishes, but there needs to be a thesis of some sort, not just a chronological exposition. The presentation should include appropriate photographs, maps, graphs, and other visual aids for the audience.

	Criteria	Comments	Points

Knowledge/understanding
 	
20%
	The presentation demonstrates
	   a depth of historical understanding
	   by using relevant and accurate
	   detail to support the student's thesis.
	Research is thorough and goes
	   beyond what was presented
	   in class or in the assigned texts.		

Thinking/inquiry
30%
	The presentation is centered around
	   a thesis, which shows a highly
	   developed awareness of
	   historiographic or social issues and
	   a high level of conceptual ability.		

Communication
 	
20%
	The presentation is imaginative
	   and effective in conveying
	   ideas to the audience.
	The presenter responds effectively
	   to audience reactions
	   and questions.		

Use of visual aids
20%
	The presentation includes appropriate
	   and easily understood visual aids,
	   which the presenter refers to and
	   explains at appropriate moments in
	   the presentation.		

Presentation skills
10%
	The presenter speaks clearly and loudly
	   enough to be heard, using eye contact,
	   a lively tone, gestures, and body
	   language to engage the audience.		

Figure 5 Part 4: Scoring Guide Rubric: Description of Dimensions at Highest Level of Performance

Changing Communities in Our City

Task Description: Each student will make a 5-minute presentation on the changes in one Portland community over the past thirty years. The student may focus the presentation in any way he or she wishes, but there needs to be a thesis of some sort, not just a chronological exposition. The presentation should include appropriate photographs, maps, graphs, and other visual aids for the audience.

	Excellent	Competent	Needs work
Knowledge/ understanding 20%	The presentation demonstrates a depth of historical understanding by using relevant and accurate detail to support the student's thesis. Research is thorough and goes beyond what was presented in class or in the assigned texts.	The presentation uses knowledge that is generally accurate with only minor inaccuracies and that is generally relevant to the student's thesis. Research is adequate but does not go much beyond what was presented in class or in the assigned text.	The presentation uses little relevant or accurate information, not even that which was presented in class or in the assigned texts. Little or no research is apparent
Thinking/inquiry 30%	The presentation is centered around a thesis, which shows a highly developed awareness of historiographic or social issues and a high level of conceptual ability.	The presentation shows an analytical structure and a central thesis, but the analysis is not always fully developed or linked to the thesis.	The presentation shows no analytical structure and no central thesis.
Communication 20%	The presentation is imaginative and effective in conveying ideas to the audience. The presenter responds effectively to audience reactions and questions.	Presentation techniques used are effective in conveying main ideas, but they are a bit unimaginative. Some questions from the audience remain unanswered.	The presentation fails to capture the interest of the audience and/or is confusing in what is to be communicated.
Use of visual aids 20%	The presentation includes appropriate and easily understood visual aids, which the presenter refers to and explains at appropriate moments in the presentation.	The presentation includes appropriate visual aids, but these are too few, are in a format that makes them difficult to use or understand, or the presenter does not refer to or explain them in the presentation.	The presentation includes no visual aids or includes visual aids that are inappropriate or too small or messy to be understood. The presenter makes no mention of them in the presentation
Presentation skills 10%	The presenter speaks clearly and loudly enough to be heard, using eye contact, a lively tone, gestures, and body language to engage the audience.	The presenter speaks clearly and loudly enough to be heard but tends to drone or fails to use eye contact, gestures, and body language consistently or effectively at times.	The presenter cannot be heard or speaks so unclearly that she or he cannot be understood. There is no attempt to engage the audience through eye contact, gestures, or body language.

Figure 6 Part 4: Three-Level Rubric: Description of Dimensions with all Levels of Performance Described

For most tasks, we prefer to use a rubric that contains at least three scales and a description of the most common ways in which students fail to meet the highest level of expectations. Figure 6 illustrates the rubric with three levels on the scale that was actually used for grading the "Changing Communities in Our City" assignment. Note how the next level down on the scale indicates the difference between that level of performance and the ideal, whereas the last level places the emphasis on what might have been accomplished but was not. This puts the emphasis not on the failure alone, but also on the possibilities. This final rubric emphasizes Part 4 of rubric development for an oral presentation with the descriptions of the dimensions highlighted.

In this sample rubric, the descriptions are limited enough that when a student does not fit neatly into one column or the other, we can convey that fact by circling elements of two or more columns. Under "Presentation skills," for example, we might easily find ourselves circling a "using eye contact and a lively tone" in the "excellent" column, but circling "fails to use" and "gestures and body language consistently or effectively at times" in the "Competent" column. When the descriptions are more comprehensive and include more options, we often use boxes that can be checked off beside each element of the description to make conveying this mixed response easier and tidier.

Seen in its entirety, the rubric for this oral presentation may seem more of a task than simply grading students the old-fashioned way. Stripped down to its four components, however, and developed step by step, it becomes a template on which to place the expectations most professors have in the backs of their minds anyway.

Creating Your First Rubric: Is It Worth the Time and Effort?

Professors who regularly construct and use rubrics can create a rubric like the oral presentation rubric we used as an example in less than an hour, less if they are simply modifying an existing rubric designed for a similar assignment. For beginners, however, the first few rubrics may take more time than they save.

This time is not wasted, however. When we first began constructing and using rubrics, we quickly found that they not only cut down on grading time and provided fuller feedback to our students, but they affected our classroom preparation and instruction as well.

The first step in constructing or adapting any rubric is quite simply a time of reflection, of putting into words basic assumptions and beliefs about teaching, assessment, and scholarship. We put ourselves in the place of our students by recalling our own student days and focusing not only *what* we learned but *how* we learned it best—that is, what expectations were clear, what assignments were significant, and what feedback was helpful. That reflection translated into classroom practices as we became more adept at imparting not only our knowledge and expectations for each assignment, but what we hoped our students would accomplish through fulfilling the assignments we gave. Further down the road, we realized our students were not like us and out assignments should acknowledge different student learning styles.

We even began to involve our students in developing the rubrics. In so doing, we found that, as Cafferalla and Clark (1999) concluded in their analysis of studies of adult learners, making the process of learning as collaborative as possible for our students resulted in better teaching.

Moreover, although the first few rubrics may take considerable time to construct, they do save time in grading, right from the very beginning. When the sample rubric used in this chapter was used in a class of more than thirty students, for example, the time taken to grade the presentations was reduced to the actual class time in which the presentations were given, plus an extra hour or so devoted to adding a few individualized notes to each rubric. We simply circled whatever categories applied during or immediately after the student presented. Aside from saving time, this meant that the grades and comments were handed back to the students the very next class period, while the memory of the assignment was fresh in their minds. Timely feedback means more student learning.

Rubrics not only save time in the long run, but they are also a valuable pedagogical tools because they make us more aware of our individual teaching styles and methods, allow us to impart more clearly our intentions and expectations, and provide timely, informative feedback to our students.